iGAAP 2017

A guide to IFRS reporting

iGAAP 2017

A guide to IFRS reporting

VOLUME A
PART 2

Published by Wolters Kluwer (UK) Ltd
145 London Road
Kingston upon Thames KT2 6SR
United Kingdom
Telephone +44 (0)844 561 8166
Facsimile +44 (0)208 247 2638
E-mail: cch@wolterskluwer.com
Website: www.cch.co.uk

ISBN 978-1-78540-368-2

British Library Cataloguing-in-Publication Data

A catalogue record for this book is available from the British Library

Typeset by Innodata Inc., India.

Printed and bound by CPI Group (UK) Ltd, Croydon, CR0 4YY

Table of Contents

Volume A, Part 1

Volume A, Part 2

Table of Contents

A17   Leases

Contents

1   Introduction

1.1   Overview of IFRS 16

IFRS 16 *Leases* provides a comprehensive model for the identification of lease arrangements and their treatment in the financial statements of both lessees and lessors.

IFRS 16 was issued in January 2016 and is required to be applied for annual periods beginning on or after 1 January 2019. Prior to the effective date, entities may continue to apply the predecessor Standard and related Interpretations (see below). Alternatively, an entity may choose to apply IFRS 16 in advance of the effective date provided that it discloses that fact and that it also applies IFRS 15 *Revenue from Contracts from Customers* (see **section 14** for detailed transition provisions).

IFRS 16 supersedes the following:

* IAS 17 *Leases* (see **appendix A4**);

* IFRIC 4 *Determining whether an Arrangement contains a Lease* (see **2.7** in **appendix A4**);

* SIC-15 *Operating Leases – Incentives* (see **7.2.3** and **8.4.8** in **appendix A4**); and

* SIC-27 *Evaluating the Substance of Transactions Involving the Legal Form of a Lease* (see **3.2** in **appendix A4**).

1.2   Comparison of IFRS 16 with predecessor IFRSs

1.2.1   Comparison with predecessor IFRSs – definition of a lease

1.2.1.1   Control model for the identification of leases

IFRS 16 introduces a control model for the identification of leases, in contrast to the focus on 'risks and rewards' in IAS 17 and IFRIC 4. It distinguishes between leases and service contracts on the basis of whether a customer controls the use of an identified asset for a period of time. Guidance is provided regarding the meaning of control (comprising both a 'benefits' element and a 'power' element) and the identification of a specific asset, including assessment of substitution rights (see **section 4**).

1.2.1.2   Removal of pricing from criteria for identification of a lease

Under IFRIC 4, leases include arrangements where the likelihood of parties other than the customer taking more than an insignificant amount of the output is remote, and the price that the customer would pay for the output is neither contractually fixed per unit of output nor equal to the current market price per unit of output as of the time of delivery of the output. In contrast, the definition of a lease in IFRS 16 requires, among other things, a customer to receive substantially all of the economic benefits from using the asset during the arrangement, but there are no provisions regarding the pricing of the arrangement (see **4.4.2**).

1.2.2   Comparison with predecessor IFRSs – lessees

1.2.2.1   Distinction between operating and finance leases removed

For lessee accounting, the distinction between operating and finance leases in IAS 17 has been removed. All leases are brought 'on balance sheet' (subject to limited exemptions for short-term leases and leases of low-value assets – see **1.2.2.3**).

1.2.2.2   Recognition of 'right-of-use' assets

Under IFRS 16, a lessee recognises a 'right-of-use' asset for all leases (subject to specified exemptions – see **1.2.2.3**), which represents its right to use the underlying leased asset for the period of the lease. Therefore, there has been a shift from the approach in IAS 17 under which, for finance leases, the accounting is designed to portray the nature of the arrangement as financing the acquisition of the underlying asset.

> The Basis of Conclusions for IFRS 16 also refers to the possibility of an 'in-substance purchase' – where the effect of a contract is to transfer control of the underlying asset itself (as opposed to conveying the right to control the use of the underlying asset for a period of time) (see **4.2.2**). In such circumstances, the transaction is a sale or purchase within the scope of other Standards (e.g. IFRS 15 *Revenue from Contracts with Customers* or IAS 16 *Property, Plant and Equipment*).

1.2.2.3   Recognition exemptions available for short-term leases and leases of low-value assets

In response to concerns raised over the cost of applying the requirements of IFRS 16, the IASB decided to provide optional recognition exemptions for lessees in respect of short-term leases (lease term 12 months or less) and leases of low-value assets ('low-value' is not specifically defined but the Basis of Conclusions on IFRS 16 indicates that the IASB had in mind assets with a value, when new, in the order of magnitude of US$5,000 or less). Leases to which these exemptions are applied are accounted for by simply recognising an expense, typically straight-line, over the lease term (so, in a manner consistent with the accounting for operating leases under IAS 17 or a service contract) (see **8.2**).

1.2.2.4   Measurement of right-of-use assets

Right-of-use assets are initially measured at estimated cost – based on the aggregate of lease payments already paid (reduced by any lease incentives), the lease liability (see **1.2.2.5**), incremental costs of obtaining the lease, and an estimate of restoration costs to be incurred at the end of the lease. The restriction under IAS 17, specifying that the initial measurement of an asset recognised under a finance lease could not exceed the fair value of that asset, is no longer relevant.

Subsequently to initial recognition, if a lessee applies the fair value model in IAS 40 *Investment Property* to its investment property, it is also required to apply that fair value model to right-of-use assets that meet the definition of investment property in IAS 40.

The new Standard sets out specific requirements regarding when and how the carrying amount of the right-of-use asset is subsequently adjusted to reflect changes in the lease liability.

See **8.4.1** and **8.5.1** for the detailed requirements regarding the measurement of right-of-use assets.

1.2.2.5 Measurement of lease liability

The lease liability is measured initially at the present value of lease payments discounted using the discount rate implicit in the lease (or, if that rate cannot be readily determined, the lessee's incremental borrowing rate). As for the measurement of the right-of-use asset (see **1.2.2.4**), the restriction based on the fair value of the leased asset has been removed.

Subsequent measurement of the lease liability under IFRS 16 is similar to that for finance lease liabilities under IAS 17.

See **8.4.2** and **8.5.2** for the detailed requirements regarding the measurement of lease liabilities.

1.2.2.6 Determination of the lease term

The principles in IFRS 16 regarding the determination of the lease term (see **section 6**) are in line with those in IAS 17, but clarify the factors to consider in assessing whether extension options are likely to be exercised and that the assessment of break clauses is consistent with the assessment of extension options.

1.2.2.7 Components of 'lease payments'

The lease payments to be included in the lease liability under IFRS 16 (see **section 7**) are largely in line with those recognised for finance leases under IAS 17. The new Standard provides guidance on 'in-substance' fixed payments (see **7.3**) and specifies different treatments for variable lease payments depending on their nature (see **7.5**).

1.2.2.8 Effect on profit or loss

The recognition of expenses associated with right-of-use assets (depreciation typically recognised on a straight-line basis) and lease liabilities (interest calculated using a constant rate of return method) represents probably the most significant impact of IFRS 16 on a lessee's net profit. The expectation for lessees will be:

- more lease expenses recognised in the early periods of a lease, and less in the later periods ('front-loaded' finance charge on lease liability versus straight-line expense under IAS 17's operating lease approach); and

- a shift in lease expense classification from operating expenses to financing costs and amortisation (i.e. moving below metrics such as operating profit, EBITDA or EBIT). There are some exceptions: any variable lease payments not included in the initial measurement of the lease liability are classified as operating expenses, as are the expenses associated with short-term and low-value asset leases for which recognition exemptions are applied.

1.2.2.9 Effect on statement of cash flows

Lessees' statements of cash flows will be affected to the extent that operating lease payments (previously classified as operating cash flows) are split between repayment of the lease liability (financing cash flow) and interest paid (classification dependent on the entity's accounting policy – see **5.5.2** in **chapter A21**).

Payments for leases of low-value assets and short-term leases not recognised in the statement of financial position (see **8.2**) and variable lease payments linked to future performance or use of an underlying asset (see **7.5.3**) will continue to be classified as operating cash flows.

1.2.2.10 Lessees' disclosures

IFRS 16 introduces significantly expanded disclosure requirements as compared to IAS 17 by defining specific disclosures regarding right-of-use assets as well as lease liabilities.

1.2.3 Comparison with predecessor IFRSs – lessors

For lessors, the requirements of IAS 17 have been carried forward largely intact, with the distinction between a finance lease and an operating lease being retained. Changes have been made in relation to the definition of a lease (see **section 4**), and lessor disclosures (see **section 12**). IFRS 16 also includes requirements and examples on subleases (see **10.6**) in the light of the new lessee accounting requirements, and requirements on lease modifications (see **11.1.4** and **11.2.8**).

Note that the Standard does not include any recognition exemptions for lessors equivalent to those available to lessees (see **1.2.2.3**).

1.2.4 Comparison with predecessor IFRSs – sale and leaseback transactions

Under IFRS 16, in a sale and leaseback transaction the seller must first assess whether the criteria in IFRS 15 for a sale to be recognised have been met – IAS 17 contains no equivalent requirement. If, under

IFRS 15, a sale is to be recognised then the right-of-use asset leased back is measured as a proportion of the underlying asset's previous carrying amount, based on the liability for lease payments divided by the fair value of the underlying asset (see **section 13**). This has the effect of restricting any profit recognised on disposal of the asset compared to the amount that would be recognised under IAS 17 in a sale and operating leaseback.

2 General principles

2.1 Objective of IFRS 16 and general application

The objective of IFRS 16 is to ensure that lessees and lessors provide relevant information in a manner that faithfully represents their lease transactions in their financial statements. This information provides a basis for users of financial statements to assess the effect that leases have on the financial position, financial performance and cash flows of an entity. [IFRS 16:1]

When applying IFRS 16, an entity is required to consider:

- all relevant facts and circumstances; and
- the terms and conditions of contracts.

A contract is defined as "[a]n agreement between two or more parties that creates enforceable rights and obligations". [IFRS 16:Appendix A]

Note that the application of IFRS 16 is not restricted to contracts, or portions of contracts, that are specifically described or labelled as leases (see **section 4**).

2.2 Requirement to apply IFRS 16 consistently

IFRS 16 should be applied consistently to contracts with similar characteristics and in similar circumstances. [IFRS 16:2]

2.3 Practical expedient – application to a portfolio of leases

Although IFRS 16 specifies the accounting for an individual lease, as a practical expedient the Standard can be applied to a portfolio of leases with similar characteristics provided that it is reasonably expected that the effects on the financial statements of applying a portfolio approach will not differ materially from applying IFRS 16 to the individual leases within that portfolio. When accounting for a portfolio, estimates and assumptions that reflect the size and composition of the portfolio should be used. [IFRS 16:B1]

Falling within the scope of this practical expedient are circumstances when an entity enters into a single contract to lease a number of identical assets. Take, for example, a contract to lease 20 printers (assumed for the purposes of this example to be high-volume commercial printers that do not qualify as low-value assets (see **8.2.3**)). As discussed at **5.1**, if the printers can be operated on a stand-alone basis, the right to use each printer is required to be accounted for as a separate lease component. The practical expedient helps to reduce that complexity by permitting the entity to account for the leases as one portfolio, rather than recognising and accounting for 20 leases separately.

The following example, which is reproduced from the illustrative examples accompanying IFRS 16, illustrates how an entity might identify portfolios of leases for the purpose of applying this practical expedient. It also illustrates the accounting for leases of low-value assets (see **8.2** for explanation and detailed requirements).

Example 2.3

Portfolio application

[IFRS 16:IE3, Example 11]

A lessee in the pharmaceutical manufacturing and distribution industry (Lessee) has the following leases:

(a)   *leases of real estate (both office buildings and warehouses).*

(b)   *leases of manufacturing equipment.*

(c)   *leases of company cars, both for sales personnel and senior management and of varying quality, specification and value.*

(d)   *leases of trucks and vans used for delivery purposes, of varying size and value.*

(e)   *leases of IT equipment for use by individual employees (such as laptop computers, desktop computers, hand held computer devices, desktop printers and mobile phones).*

(f)   *leases of servers, including many individual modules that increase the storage capacity of those servers. The modules have been added to the mainframe servers over time as Lessee has needed to increase the storage capacity of the servers.*

(g)   *leases of office equipment:*

  (i)   *office furniture (such as chairs, desks and office partitions);*

  (ii)   *water dispensers; and*

  (iii)   *high-capacity multifunction photocopier devices.*

Leases of low-value assets [see **8.2** for explanation and detailed requirements]

Lessee determines that the following leases qualify as leases of low-value assets on the basis that the underlying assets, when new, are individually of low value:

(a)   leases of IT equipment for use by individual employees; and

(b)   leases of office furniture and water dispensers.

Lessee elects to apply the requirements in [IFRS 16:6] in accounting for all of those leases.

Although each module within the servers, if considered individually, might be an asset of low value, the leases of modules within the servers do not qualify as leases of low-value assets. This is because each module is highly interrelated with other parts of the servers. Lessee would not lease the modules without also leasing the servers [(see **8.2.3.5** for further discussion)].

Portfolio application

As a result, Lessee applies the recognition and measurement requirements in IFRS 16 to its leases of real estate, manufacturing equipment, company cars, trucks and vans, servers and high-capacity multifunction photocopier devices. In doing so, Lessee groups its company cars, trucks and vans into portfolios.

Lessee's company cars are leased under a series of master lease agreements. Lessee uses eight different types of company car, which vary by price and are assigned to staff on the basis of seniority and territory. Lessee has a master lease agreement for each different type of company car. The individual leases within each master lease agreement are all similar (including similar start and end dates), but the terms and conditions generally vary from one master lease agreement to another. Because the individual leases within each master lease agreement are similar to each other, Lessee reasonably expects that applying the requirements of IFRS 16 to each master lease agreement would not result in a materially different effect than applying the requirements of IFRS 16 to each individual lease within the master lease agreement. Consequently, Lessee concludes that it can apply the requirements of IFRS 16 to each master lease agreement as a portfolio. In addition, Lessee concludes that two of the eight master lease agreements are similar and cover substantially similar types of company cars in similar territories. Lessee reasonably expects that the effect of applying IFRS 16 to the combined portfolio of leases within the two master lease agreements would not differ materially from applying IFRS 16 to each lease within that combined portfolio. Lessee, therefore, concludes that it can further combine those two master lease agreements into a single lease portfolio.

Lessee's trucks and vans are leased under individual lease agreements. There are 6,500 leases in total. All of the truck leases have similar terms, as do all of the van leases. The truck leases are generally for four years and involve similar models of truck. The van leases are generally for five years and involve similar models of van. Lessee reasonably expects that applying the requirements of IFRS 16 to portfolios of truck leases and van leases, grouped by type of underlying asset, territory and the quarter of the year within which the lease was entered into, would not result in a materially different effect from applying those requirements to each individual truck or van lease. Consequently, Lessee applies the requirements of IFRS 16 to different portfolios of truck and van leases, rather than to 6,500 individual leases.

2.4   Combining contracts

Two or more contracts that are interdependent should be combined and accounted for as a single contract. This requirement applies when:

[IFRS 16:B2]

- the contracts are entered into at or near the same time; and

- the contracts are with the same counterparty (or related parties of the counterparty); and

- one or more of the following criteria are met:

  - the contracts are negotiated as a package with an overall commercial objective that cannot be understood without considering the contracts together; or

  - the amount of consideration to be paid in one contract depends on the price or performance of the other contract; or

  - the rights to use underlying assets conveyed in the contracts (or some rights to use underlying assets conveyed in each of the contracts) form a single lease component as described in IFRS 16:B32 (see **5.1.2**).

The requirements of IFRS 16:B2 are intended to capture circumstances in which an entity enters into a number of contracts in contemplation of one another such that the transactions, in substance, form a single arrangement that achieves an overall commercial objective that cannot be understood without considering the contracts together.

For example, assume that a lessee enters into a one-year lease of an asset with particular characteristics. The lessee also enters into a one-year lease for an asset with those same characteristics starting in one year's time and a similar forward contract starting in two years' time and in three years' time. The terms and conditions of all four contracts are negotiated in contemplation of each other such that the overall economic effect cannot be understood without reference to the series of transactions as a whole. In effect, the lessee has entered into a four-year lease. In such situations, accounting for the contracts independently of each other might not result in a faithful representation of the combined transaction. [IFRS 16:BC130]

3 Scope

3.1 Scope – general

IFRS 16 should be applied to all leases except the following:

[IFRS 16:3]

(a) leases to explore for or use minerals, oil, natural gas and similar non-regenerative resources;

> IFRS 6 *Exploration for and Evaluation of Mineral Resources* specifies the accounting for rights to explore for and evaluate mineral resources (see **chapter A40**).

(b) leases of biological assets within the scope of IAS 41 *Agriculture* held by a lessee (see **chapter A38**);

> For entities that have adopted *Agriculture: Bearer Plants (Amendments to IAS 16 and IAS 41)* (issued in June 2014 and effective for annual periods beginning on or after 1 January 2016, with earlier application permitted), biological assets that are bearer plants are within the scope of IAS 16 *Property, Plant and Equipment* rather than IAS 41 (see **2.6** in **chapter A7**) and, consequently, are within the scope of IFRS 16. Therefore, for example, leases of bearer plants such as orchards and vineyards held by a lessee are within the scope of IFRS 16. [IFRS 16:BC68(b)]

(c) service concession arrangements within the scope of IFRIC 12 *Service Concession Arrangements* (see **chapter A35**);

(d) licences of intellectual property granted by a lessor within the scope of IFRS 15 *Revenue from Contracts with Customers* (see **section 11** of **chapter A14**); and

(e) rights held by a lessee under licensing agreements within the scope of IAS 38 *Intangible Assets* (see **chapter A9**) for such items as motion picture films, video recordings, plays, manuscripts, patents and copyrights.

A lessee is permitted, but not required, to apply IFRS 16 to leases of intangible assets other than those described in IFRS 16:3(e). [IFRS 16:4]

> Leases of 'other' intangible assets in the context of IFRS 16:4 might include, for example, exclusive licences for brands or trademarks held by a lessee. Such leases were previously considered to fall within the scope of IAS 17. The IASB decided to permit, but not require, entities to account for these leases in accordance with IFRS 16. Although there is no conceptual basis for excluding them from the scope of IFRS 16, the Board considered that a more comprehensive review of the accounting

for intangible assets is required before requiring leases of intangible assets to be accounted for under the new Standard. [IFRS 16:BC71]

3.2 Long-term leases of land

The IASB considered, but decided against, a scope exclusion for long-term leases of land (see IFRS 16:BC78). Therefore, such leases should be accounted for in accordance with IFRS 16.

3.3 Leases of investment property

Unlike IAS 17, IFRS 16 contains no scope exclusions in relation to investment property. Therefore, all aspects of leases of investment property are accounted for under IFRS 16.

Consequential amendments arising from IFRS 16 have amended the definition of investment property in IAS 40 *Investment Property* to include both owned investment property and investment property held by a lessee as a right-of-use asset. Under IFRS 16:34 (see **8.5.1.5**), if a lessee applies IAS 40's fair value model to its owned investment property, it is also required to apply that fair value model to right-of-use assets that meet the definition of investment property.

3.4 Subleases

Leases of right-of-use assets in a sublease are within the scope of IFRS 16, subject to the exclusions set out at **3.1**. [IFRS 16:3]

Subleases are required to be accounted for in the same way as other leases (see **10.6**) and, accordingly, are within the scope of IFRS 16. [IFRS 16:BC73]

3.5 Leases of inventories

IFRS 16 does not specifically exclude leases of inventories from its scope. However, the IASB believes that few such transactions would meet the definition of a lease under IFRS 16 because a lessee is unlikely to be able to hold an asset that it leases (and that is owned by another party) for sale in the ordinary course of business, or for consumption in the process of production for sale in the ordinary course of business. [IFRS 16:BC74]

3.6 Derivatives embedded in a lease

IFRS 16 includes specific requirements for features of a lease such as options and residual value guarantees that may meet the definition of a derivative. Any other derivatives embedded in a lease should be accounted for in accordance with IFRS 9 *Financial Instruments* (or, for entities that have not yet adopted IFRS 9, IAS 39 *Financial Instruments: Recognition and Measurement*). [IFRS 16:BC81]

3.7 Short-term leases and leases of low-value items

IFRS 16 applies to all leases except those specifically excluded under IFRS 16:3 (see **3.1**). However, the Standard includes recognition exemptions available to lessees for short-term leases and leases of low-value items and specifies alternative requirements (see **8.2**).

4 Identifying a lease

4.1 Definition of a lease

A lease is defined as "[a] contract, or part of a contract, that conveys the right to use an asset (the underlying asset) for a period of time in exchange for consideration". [IFRS 16:Appendix A]

IFRS 16 supersedes IFRIC 4 *Determining whether an Arrangement contains a Lease* and SIC-27 *Evaluating the Substance of Transactions Involving the Legal Form of a Lease*. Although the detailed requirements regarding the identification of a lease are amended by IFRS 16, the key principles of IFRIC 4 and SIC-27 are carried forward, i.e. that:

- some arrangements that do not take the legal form of a lease may nevertheless meet the definition of a lease under the Standard; and

- not all transactions that involve the legal form of a lease will fall within the definition of a lease under the Standard.

4.2 Determination as to whether a contract is, or contains, a lease

4.2.1 Requirement to assess whether a contract is, or contains, a lease

At inception of a contract, an entity is required to assess whether the contract is, or contains, a lease. A contract is, or contains, a lease if the contract conveys the right to control the use of an identified asset for a period of time in exchange for consideration. [IFRS 16:9]

Key aspects of this definition are that:

- the asset that is the subject of a lease must be specifically identified (see **4.3**); and

- a lease must convey the right to control the use (see **4.4**) of that identified asset for a period of time.

For the purposes of IFRS 16:9, a 'period of time' may be described in terms of the amount of use of an identified asset (e.g. the number of production units that an item of equipment will be used to produce). [IFRS 16:10]

An entity is required to assess whether a contract contains a lease at inception of the contract, rather than at commencement of the lease term (see **6.3** for an explanation of these terms).

This is necessary because a lessor is required to classify a lease as either a finance lease or an operating lease at the inception date (see **10.1.2**). In addition, a lessee is required to disclose information about leases not yet commenced to which the lessee is committed if that information is relevant to users of financial statements (see **9.2.9.1**). [IFRS 16:BC110]

Examples 1 to 10 of the illustrative examples accompanying IFRS 16 (summarised at **4.6**) illustrate how an entity determines whether a contract is or contains a lease. Although the IASB believes that, in most cases, the assessment as to whether a contract is or contains a lease should be straightforward, it acknowledges that significant judgement will be required to make this assessment in some cases. [IFRS 16:BC109]

See **4.5** for a flowchart, reproduced from IFRS 16, which summarises the steps involved in the assessment as to whether a contract is, or contains, a lease. These steps are discussed in detail in **4.3** and **4.4**.

4.2.2 Lease vs 'in-substance' sale or purchase

When assessing the nature of a contract, an entity should consider whether the contract transfers control of the underlying asset itself (as opposed to conveying the right to control the use of the underlying asset for a period of time). If so, the transaction is a sale or purchase within the scope of other Standards (e.g. IFRS 15 *Revenue from Contracts with Customers* or IAS 16 *Property, Plant and Equipment*). [IFRS 16:BC140]

4.2.3 Leases vs service contracts

IAS 16 aims to distinguish a lease from a service contract on the basis of whether a customer is able to control the use of the asset being leased. If the customer controls the use of an identified asset (see **4.3**) for a period of time, then the contract contains a lease. This will be the case if the customer can make the important decisions about the use of the asset in a similar way to that in which it makes decisions about owned assets that it uses (see **4.4**). In contrast, in a service contract, the supplier controls the use of any assets used to deliver the service. [IFRS 16:BC105]

4.2.4 Customer has control for only a portion of the term of a contract

If the customer has the right to control the use of an identified asset for only a portion of the term of a contract, the contract contains a lease for that portion of the lease term. [IFRS 16:B10]

4.2.5 Assessment required for each potential separate lease component

The assessment as to whether a contract contains a lease should be made for each potential separate lease component (see **section 5**). [IFRS 16:B12]

4.2.6 Assessing whether a contract contains a lease when the customer is a joint arrangement

When a contract to receive goods or services is entered into by, or on behalf of, a joint arrangement (as defined in IFRS 11 *Joint Arrangements* – see **chapter A27**), the joint arrangement is considered to be the customer in the contract. Accordingly, when assessing whether such a contract contains a lease, an entity should assess whether the joint arrangement has the right to control the use of an identified asset throughout the period of use. [IFRS 16:B11]

IFRS 16:B11 clarifies that this is the case, irrespective of which entity signed the contract. Accordingly, if the parties to the joint arrangement collectively have the right to control the use of an identified asset throughout the period of use through their joint control of the arrangement, the contract contains a lease. It is not appropriate to conclude that a contract does not contain a lease on the grounds that each of the parties to the joint arrangement either obtains only a portion of the economic benefits from use of the underlying asset or does not unilaterally direct the use of the underlying asset. [IFRS 16:BC126]

This guidance is particularly relevant for joint operations where each of the parties has direct rights and obligations for the lease and for which, in the absence of this guidance, it might not have been clear whether control should be viewed from the perspective of the joint operation.

4.2.7   Reassessment as to whether a contract is, or contains, a lease

An entity should reassess whether a contract is, or contains, a lease only if the terms and conditions of the contract are changed. [IFRS 16:11]

4.3   Identified asset

4.3.1   Identification of an asset – general

The asset that is the subject of a lease must be specifically identified. This will be the case if either of the following applies:

[IFRS 16:B13]

- the asset is explicitly specified in the contract (e.g. a specific serial number); or

- the asset is implicitly specified at the time that it is made available for use by the customer (e.g. when there is only one asset that is capable of being used to meet the contract terms).

4.3.2   Substantive substitution rights

4.3.2.1   Right to use an identified asset is undermined by substantive substitution right

Even if an asset is specified as discussed in **4.3.1**, a customer is not considered to have the right to use an identified asset (and, therefore, the contract is not a lease) if the supplier has a substantive right to substitute the asset throughout the period of use. [IFRS 16:B14]

The 'period of use' is "[t]he total period of time that an asset is used to fulfil a contract with a customer (including any non-consecutive periods of time)". [IFRS 16:Appendix A]

If a supplier has a substantive right to substitute the asset throughout the period of use, there is no identified asset and the contract does not contain a lease. This is because the supplier, and not the customer, controls the use of the asset in such circumstances. [IFRS 16:BC112]

If a substitution clause is not substantive because it does not change the substance of the contract (i.e. the conditions set out in **4.3.2.2** are not met), that substitution clause does not affect an entity's assessment as to whether a contract contains a lease. [IFRS 16:BC113]

The illustrative examples accompanying IFRS 16 (as summarised at **4.6**) include a number of scenarios in which substitution rights are considered.

4.3.2.2   Substantive substitution right – definition

A supplier's right to substitute an asset is substantive only if both of the following conditions are met:

[IFRS 16:B14]

- the supplier has the practical ability to substitute alternative assets throughout the period of use (e.g. the customer cannot prevent the supplier from substituting the asset and alternative assets are readily available to the supplier or could be sourced by the supplier within a reasonable period of time); and

- the supplier would benefit economically from exercising its right to substitute the asset (i.e. the economic benefits associated with substituting the asset are expected to exceed the costs associated with substituting the asset).

Substitution rights are not substantive if it is not likely, or practically or economically feasible, for the supplier to exercise those rights. The IASB believes that, in many cases, it will be clear that the supplier would not benefit from the exercise of a substitution right because of the costs associated with substituting the asset. [IFRS 16:BC113]

4.3.2.3   Substitution on or after a specified future date or dependent on the occurrence of a specified event

If the supplier has a right or an obligation to substitute the asset only on or after either a particular date or the occurrence of a specified event, the supplier's substitution right is not substantive because the supplier does not have the practical ability to substitute alternative assets throughout the period of use. [IFRS 16:B15]

4.3.2.4   Evaluation to be based on circumstances at inception and to exclude consideration of future events not considered likely to occur

An entity's evaluation of whether a supplier's substitution right is substantive should be based on facts and circumstances at inception of the contract. [IFRS 16:B16]

Future events that, at inception of the contract, are not considered likely to occur should be excluded from the evaluation. Examples of such future events include:

[IFRS 16:B16]

- an agreement by a future customer to pay an above market rate for use of the asset;

- the introduction of new technology that is not substantially developed at inception of the contract;

- a substantial difference between the customer's use of the asset, or the performance of the asset, and the use or performance considered likely at inception of the contract; and

- a substantial difference between the market price of the asset during the period of use, and the market price considered likely at inception of the contract.

> If a supplier would benefit from substitution only in circumstances that are not likely to occur, such as those listed in IFRS 16:B16, those substitution rights are not substantive, regardless of whether the circumstances are specified in the contract. [IFRS 16:BC114]

4.3.2.5   Substitution costs generally higher when the asset is located at the customer's premises or elsewhere

If the asset is located at the customer's premises or elsewhere, the costs associated with substitution are generally higher than when located at the supplier's premises and, therefore, are more likely to exceed the benefits associated with substituting the asset. [IFRS 16:B17]

4.3.2.6   Substitution for repairs or technical upgrade

A supplier's right or obligation to substitute the asset for repairs and maintenance, if the asset is not operating properly or if a technical upgrade becomes available, does not preclude the customer from having the right to use an identified asset. [IFRS 16:B18]

4.3.2.7   Customer cannot readily determine whether the supplier has substantive substitution rights

If the customer cannot readily determine whether the supplier has a substantive substitution right, the customer should presume that any substitution right is not substantive. [IFRS 16:B19]

> The IASB believes that it should generally be relatively clear from the facts and circumstances whether substitution rights are substantive, and the Board intends that customers should assess whether substitution rights are substantive if they are reasonably able to do so. However, the requirement in IFRS 16:B19 is intended to clarify that a customer is not expected to exert undue effort in order to provide evidence that a substitution right is not substantive. [IFRS 16:BC115]

4.3.3 Portions of assets

A capacity portion of an asset is an identified asset if it is physically distinct (e.g. a floor of a building). [IFRS 16:B20]

A capacity or other portion of an asset that is not physically distinct (e.g. a capacity portion of a fibre optic cable or a pipeline) is not an identified asset, unless it represents substantially all of the capacity of the asset and thereby provides the customer with the right to obtain substantially all of the economic benefits from use of the asset. [IFRS 16:B20]

> The IASB concluded that a customer is unlikely to have the right to control the use of a capacity portion of a larger asset if that portion is not physically distinct because decisions about the use of the asset are typically made at the larger asset level. [IFRS 16:BC116]

4.4 The right to control the use of an identified asset

4.4.1 Elements of 'control'

To assess whether a contract conveys the right to control the use of an identified asset for a period of time (as required under IFRS 16:9 – see **4.2.1**), an entity is required to assess whether, throughout the period of use, the customer has both of the following:

- the right to obtain substantially all of the economic benefits from use of the identified asset (see **4.4.2**); and

- the right to direct the use of the identified asset (see **4.4.3**).

The 'period of use' is "[t]he total period of time that an asset is used to fulfil a contract with a customer (including any non-consecutive periods of time)". [IFRS 16:Appendix A]

> As discussed in the following sections, the IASB decided that to control the use of an asset, a customer is required to have not only the right to obtain substantially all of the economic benefits from use of an asset throughout the period of use (a 'benefits' element) but also the ability to direct the use of that asset (a 'power' element). The shift in focus from 'risks and rewards' to 'control' is consistent with other recent Standards (e.g. IFRS 10 *Consolidated Financial Statements* (see **chapter A24**) and IFRS 15 *Revenue from Contracts with Customers* (see **chapter A14**)) and with the IASB's proposals regarding control in the Conceptual Framework exposure draft (see **section 9** of **chapter A2**).

4.4.2 Right to economic benefits from use

4.4.2.1 Customer must have the right to obtain substantially all of the economic benefits from use of the asset

To control the use of an identified asset, a customer must have the right to obtain substantially all of the economic benefits from use of the asset throughout the period of use (e.g. by having exclusive use of the asset throughout that period). [IFRS 16:B21]

> Therefore, in circumstances when an asset might be considered to be implicitly identified (e.g. the supplier has only one machine capable of delivering the customer's requirements), if the supplier can regularly use the machine for other purposes during the course of the contract (e.g. to supply other customers), the customer does not have the right to obtain substantially all of the economic benefits from the use of that asset and there is no lease.

4.4.2.2 Nature of economic benefits from use of the asset

Economic benefits from use of an asset can be obtained by the customer in many ways (e.g. by using, holding or sub-leasing the asset); they include the primary output and by-products generated from use of the asset, and other economic benefits from using the asset that could be realised from a commercial transaction with a third party. [IFRS 16:B21] All of these benefits should be considered in the assessment of whether the contract conveys the right to substantially all the economic benefits from the use of the asset.

> The assessment as to whether a contract contains a lease should not consider economic benefits relating to ownership of an asset (e.g. tax benefits as a result of owning an asset). This is because a lease does not convey ownership of the underlying asset. [IFRS 16:BC118]

4.4.2.3 Restrictions on economic benefits available to the customer

The economic benefits to be considered are those that are available within the defined scope of the customer's right to use the asset. For example:

[IFRS 16:B22]

- if a contract limits the use of a motor vehicle to only one particular territory during the period of use, only the economic benefits from use of the motor vehicle within that territory should be considered; and

- if a contract specifies that a customer can drive a motor vehicle only up to a particular number of miles during the period of use, only the economic benefits from use of the motor vehicle for the permitted mileage should be considered.

Therefore, potential additional economic benefits outside the scope of the customer's rights (e.g. in the second bullet point above, beyond the specified mileage for the motor vehicle) are not relevant to the determination as to whether the customer has the right to obtain substantially all of the economic benefits from use of the asset throughout the period of use.

4.4.2.4 Customer required to pay a portion of the cash flows derived from use of the asset as consideration

If a contract requires a customer to pay the supplier or another party a portion of the cash flows derived from use of an asset as consideration, those cash flows paid as consideration should be considered to be part of the economic benefits that the customer obtains from use of the asset. [IFRS 16:B23]

For example, if the customer is required to pay the supplier a percentage of sales from use of retail space as consideration for that use, that requirement does not prevent the customer from having the right to obtain substantially all of the economic benefits from use of the retail space. This is because the total cash flows arising from those sales are considered to be economic benefits that the customer obtains from use of the retail space, a portion of which it then pays to the supplier as consideration for the right to use that space. [IFRS 16:B23]

4.4.3 Right to direct the use

4.4.3.1 Circumstances when the customer has the right to direct the use of an identified asset

A customer has the right to direct the use of an identified asset throughout the period of use only if either:

[IFRS 16:B24]

(a) the customer has the right to direct how and for what purpose the asset is used throughout the period of use (see **4.4.3.2**); or

(b) the relevant decisions about how and for what purpose the asset is used are predetermined and specified conditions are met (see **4.4.3.3**).

If neither of the conditions in IFRS 16:B24 is met, the supplier directs how and for what purpose the asset is used and, consequently, the contract does not contain a lease.

4.4.3.2   How and for what purpose the asset is used

Note that, as explained in IFRS 16:BC120, 'how and for what purpose' an asset is used is a single concept (i.e. 'how' an asset is used is not assessed separately from 'for what purpose' an asset is used).

A customer has the right to direct how and for what purpose the asset is used if it can change how and for what purpose the asset is used throughout the period of use. In making this assessment, the focus is on whether the customer has decision-making rights that affect the economic benefits to be derived from use of the asset. [IFRS 16:B25]

The decision-making rights that are most relevant for this purpose are likely to be different for different contracts, depending on the nature of the asset and the terms and conditions of the contract. Depending on the circumstances, these could include rights to change:

[IFRS 16:B25 & B26]

- the type of output that is produced by the asset (e.g. to decide whether to use a shipping container to transport goods or for storage, or to decide upon the mix of products sold from retail space);

- when the output is produced (e.g. to decide when an item of machinery or a power plant will be used);

- where the output is produced (e.g. to decide upon the destination of a truck or a ship, or to decide where an item of equipment is used); and

- whether the output is produced, and the quantity of that output (e.g. to decide whether to produce energy from a power plant and how much energy to produce from that power plant).

Rights that are limited to operating or maintaining the asset are examples of rights that *do not* grant the right to change how and for what purpose the asset is used. Although such rights are often essential to the efficient use of an asset, they are not rights to direct how and for what purpose the asset is used and are often dependent on the decisions about how and for what purpose the asset is used. [IFRS 16:B27]

Therefore, for example, if the contract covers the use of a fleet of trucks for an agreed period and the customer has the right to decide how and when the trucks are used, the fact that the supplier continues to operate and maintain the trucks does not undermine the customer's ability to direct the use of the trucks.

In the IASB's view, the decisions about how and for what purpose an asset is used are more important in determining control of the use of an asset than other decisions to be made about use, including decisions about operating and maintaining the asset. This is because decisions about how and for what purpose an asset is used determine how, and what, economic benefits are derived from use. [IFRS 16:BC120]

However, rights to operate an asset may grant the customer the right to direct the use of the asset if the relevant decisions about how and for what purpose the asset is used are predetermined as contemplated in IFRS 16:B24(b)(i) (see **4.4.3.3**).

4.4.3.3 *Relevant decisions are predetermined*

The relevant decisions about how and for what purpose the asset is used can be predetermined in a number of ways. For example, the relevant decisions can be predetermined by the design of the asset or by contractual restrictions on the use of the asset. [IFRS 16:B28]

When decisions about how and for what purpose an asset is used are predetermined, they cannot be changed by either the customer or the supplier during the period of use. The IASB noted that it would expect these circumstances to arise in relatively few cases. [IFRS 16:BC121]

When the relevant decisions about how and for what purpose the asset is used are predetermined, a customer has the right to direct the use of an identified asset throughout the period of use only if either:

[IFRS 16:B24(b)]

(i) the customer has the right to operate the asset (or to direct others to operate the asset in a manner that it determines) throughout the period of use, without the supplier having the right to change those operating instructions; or

(ii) the customer designed the asset (or specific aspects of the asset) in a way that predetermines how and for what purpose the asset will be used throughout the period of use.

The approach to determining whether a customer has the right to direct the use of an identified asset changes if the decisions about how and for what purpose an asset is used are predetermined. IFRS 16 clarifies that, in such circumstances, a customer can still direct the use of an asset if it has the right to operate the asset, or if it designed the asset in a way that predetermines how and for what purpose the asset will be used. In either of these cases, the customer controls rights of use that extend beyond the rights of a customer in a typical supply or service contract (i.e. the customer has rights that extend beyond solely ordering and receiving output from the asset). In these cases, the customer has the right to make (or, in the case of design, has already made) decisions that affect the economic benefits to be derived from use of the asset throughout the period of use. [IFRS 16:BC122]

For example, consider a contract for the use of a fleet of trucks for an agreed period where the contract specifies how and for what purpose the trucks are to be used (e.g. to carry rock from a specified quarry site to crushing facilities); these matters have been agreed between the parties prior to the commencement date and they cannot be changed. In such circumstances, if the customer has the right to operate the trucks throughout the period of use, under IFRS 16:B24(b)(i) it has the right to direct the use of the trucks, notwithstanding its inability to change how and for what purpose the trucks are used. In contrast, if the supplier is the operator, then the customer does not have the right to direct the use of the trucks, and there is no lease.

The concept of directing use through design (as contemplated in IFRS 16:B24(b)(ii)) is explored in Example 9A of the illustrative examples accompanying IFRS 16 (see table at **4.6** for summary). In the situation described, the customer purchases all of the output of a solar farm with predetermined activities. Although the customer makes no decisions during the life of the farm, it has the right to direct the use of the farm as a result of having designed the asset before it was constructed.

4.4.3.4 Decisions determined during and before the period of use

In assessing whether a customer has the right to direct the use of an asset, an entity should consider only rights to make decisions about the use of the asset during the period of use, unless the customer designed the asset (or specific aspects of the asset) as described in IFRS 16:B24(b)(ii) (see **4.4.3.3**). Consequently, unless the conditions in IFRS 16:B24(b)(ii) exist, an entity should not consider decisions that are predetermined before the period of use. [IFRS 16:B29]

For example, if a customer is able only to specify the output of an asset before the period of use, the customer does not have the right to direct the use of that asset. The ability to specify the output in a contract before the period of use, without any other decision-making rights relating to the use of the asset, gives a customer the same rights as any customer that purchases goods or services. [IFRS 16:B29]

It will not be unusual for a customer to specify its requirements prior to the commencement of a contract and to reach an agreement with the supplier as to how those requirements will be met. For example, a customer requires a supply of iron over an extended period. It agrees with the supplier prior to the commencement of supply that this requirement will be met by utilising all of the capacity of a specifically identified smelting plant operating for an agreed number of hours over that period. Assuming that the customer was not involved in the design of the smelting plant, the fact that it is able to specify the output of the smelting plant before the period of use does not mean that it has the right to direct the use of the plant. In this scenario:

- if the customer has the right to change how and for what purpose the smelting plant is used during the period of use, the customer has the right to direct the use of the smelting plant and, subject to other conditions, there may be a lease;

- if the supplier has the right to change how and for what purpose the smelting plant is used during the period of use, the supplier has the right to direct the use of the smelting plant and there is no lease; and

- if neither party has the right to change how and for what purpose the smelting plant is used, its activities are predetermined, and the right to direct its use will be determined by which entity is operating the smelting plant during the period of use (see **4.4.3.3**).

4.4.3.5 Protective rights

A contract may include terms and conditions designed to protect the supplier's interest in the asset or other assets, to protect its personnel, or to ensure the supplier's compliance with laws or regulations. These are examples of protective rights. For example, a contract may:

[IFRS 16:B30]

- specify the maximum amount of use of an asset or limit where or when the customer can use the asset; or

- require a customer to follow particular operating practices; or

- require a customer to inform the supplier of changes in how an asset will be used.

Rights of this nature typically define the scope of the customer's right of use but do not, in isolation, prevent the customer from having the right to direct the use of an asset. [IFRS 16:B30]

The illustrative examples accompanying IFRS 16 cite examples of protective rights, including the following

- Example 1A describes a situation in which the customer generally determines when, where and how rail cars are used, but subject to restrictions on the types of cargo (e.g. explosives) that can be carried. These restrictions are considered to be protective rights of the supplier and to define the scope of the customer's right to use the rail cars, but not to limit the customer's right to direct the use of the rail cars within that defined scope.

- Example 6B describes a situation in which the customer generally determines whether, where and when a ship sails, as well as the cargo it will carry, but contractual restrictions prevent the customer from sailing the ship into waters at a high risk of piracy or carrying hazardous material as cargo. Again, these restrictions are considered to be protective rights that protect the supplier's investment in the ship and the supplier's personnel. They define the scope of the customer's right to use the ship but they do not limit the customer's right to direct the use of the ship within that defined scope.

4.5 Summary flowchart

The following flowchart, which is reproduced from IFRS 16, summarises the steps involved in the assessment as to whether a contract is, or contains, a lease. [IFRS 16:B31]

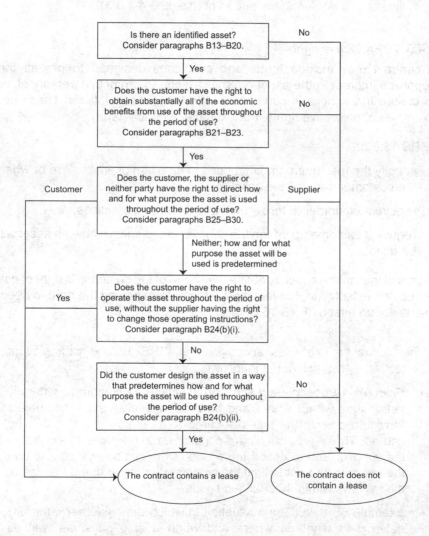

4.6 Illustrative examples

The illustrative examples accompanying IFRS 16 include 10 examples of how an entity determines whether a contract is, or contains, a lease.

These examples are summarised in a tabular format below, in each case highlighting the key determinants as to whether the contract is, or contains, a lease. Please refer to the full text of the illustrative examples accompanying IFRS 16 for complete details in each case.

Example	Identified asset?	Substantive substitution rights?	Customer has a right to control the use of the identified asset?	Lease?
1A – Contract between Customer and a freight carrier (Supplier) provides Customer with the use of 10 rail cars of a particular type for five years. Supplier also provides engines and drivers when requested by Customer.	Yes. Specific rail cars identified in contract.	No. Can only be substituted for repairs or maintenance.	Yes. Customer has exclusive use of rail cars during the contract period so that it has the right to substantially all of the economic benefits from use of the rail cars. Customer has the right to change how and for what purpose the cars are used – it directs when and where the cars are used, and which goods are transported. Supplier's rights (restrictions on specified types of cargo) are protective only. Supplier's control of engines required to transport the rail cars does not give it the right to control the use of the cars.	Yes – lease of rail cars (not engines).
1B – Contract between Customer and Supplier requires Supplier to transport a specified quantity of goods by using a specified type of rail car in accordance with a stated timetable for five years.	No. Supplier has large pool of similar items and none are specified in the contract.	Yes. Alternatives are readily available at minimal cost. Supplier benefits economically by using its pool of available rolling stock in the most efficient manner.	No. Supplier selects which are used for each delivery and obtains substantially all of the economic benefits from use of the rail cars.	No. Customer is purchasing freight capacity (service).

Example	Identified asset?	Substantive substitution rights?	Customer has a right to control the use of the identified asset?	Lease?
2 – Coffee company (Customer) enters into a contract with an airport operator (Supplier) to use an agreed amount of space in the airport (precise location not specified) to sell its goods for a three-year period.	No. Many areas available for Customer to locate its kiosk and none specified in the contract.	Yes. Alternatives are readily available at minimal cost. Supplier benefits economically by using its retail space in the most efficient manner.	No. Supplier selects which space is allocated to Customer and obtains substantially all of the economic benefits from use of the concession space.	No. Customer is purchasing space, which can be changed at the discretion of the supplier, and is a service.
3A – Customer enters into a 15-year contract with a utilities company (Supplier) for the right to use three specified, physically distinct dark fibres within a larger cable connecting Hong Kong to Tokyo.	Yes. Fibres are specifically identified in the contract and are physically distinct from other fibres within the cable.	No. Can only be substituted for repairs or maintenance.	Yes. Customer has exclusive use of fibres during the contract period so that it has the right to substantially all of the economic benefits from use. Customer has the right to change how and for what purpose the fibres are used – it decides when and whether the fibres are connected and the type and volume of data transported.	Yes – lease of specified fibres.
3B – Customer enters into a 15-year contract with Supplier for the right to use a specified amount of capacity within a cable connecting Hong Kong to Tokyo.	No. Customer is purchasing capacity, equivalent to it having the use of three fibres, but specific fibres are not identified. Capacity purchased is not physically distinct and does not represent substantially all the capacity of the cable.	Yes. Alternatives are readily available. Supplier benefits economically by using fibres in the most efficient manner.	No. Supplier makes all of the relevant decisions and has the right to substantially all of the economic benefits from use of the fibres.	No. Customer is purchasing transmission capacity (service).

Example	Identified asset?	Substantive substitution rights?	Customer has a right to control the use of the identified asset?	Lease?
4 – Customer enters into a contract with a property owner (Supplier) to use Retail Unit A for a five-year period. Retail Unit A is part of a larger retail space with many retail units.	Yes. Specific retail unit identified in the contract.	No. Although Supplier has the practical ability to substitute another retail unit, it would be required to pay relocation expenses and the circumstances in which it would benefit economically (major new tenant) are, at the inception date, not considered likely to arise.	Yes. Customer has exclusive use and has the right to obtain all of the economic benefits from use of the retail unit during the contract period (notwithstanding the requirement to make variable payments based on retail sales to the Supplier). Customer makes all of the relevant decisions regarding what to sell and at what price. Supplier's inputs (cleaning, security, advertising) do not give it the right to decide how and for what purpose the retail space is used.	Yes – lease of specific retail unit.
5 – Customer enters into a contract with Supplier for the use of a truck for one week to transport cargo from New York to San Francisco.	Yes. Specific truck identified in the contract.	No.	Yes. Customer has exclusive use and has the right to obtain all of the economic benefits from use of the truck during the contract period. Although how and for what purpose the truck is used is predetermined, Customer operates the truck and, therefore, has the right to direct the use of the truck (see **4.4.3.3**).	Yes – lease of truck. Because the duration of the lease is one week, it is a short-term lease (see **8.2.2**).

Example	Identified asset?	Substantive substitution rights?	Customer has a right to control the use of the identified asset?	Lease?
6A – Customer enters into a contract with a ship owner (Supplier) for the transportation of cargo from Rotterdam to Sydney on a specified ship.	Yes. Specific ship identified in the contract.	No.	No. Customer occupies substantially all of the capacity of the ship and therefore has the right to substantially all of the economic benefits from use of the ship during the contract period. However, how and for what purpose the ship is used is predetermined and Supplier operates the ship. Therefore, Customer does not have the right to direct the use of the ship (see **4.4.3.3**).	No. Customer is purchasing transport service.
6B – Customer enters into a contract with Supplier for the use of a specified ship for a five-year period.	Yes. Specific ship identified in the contract.	No.	Yes. Customer occupies substantially all of the capacity of the ship and therefore has the right to substantially all of the economic benefits from use of the ship during the contract period. Customer makes the relevant decisions about whether, where and when the ship sails (subject to contractual restrictions designed to protect Supplier's investment and personnel). Although Supplier operates the ship, it is in accordance with Customer's decisions regarding how and for what purpose the ship is used.	Yes – lease of ship for the contract period.

Example	Identified asset?	Substantive substitution rights?	Customer has a right to control the use of the identified asset?	Lease?
7 – Customer enters into a contract with an aircraft owner (Supplier) for the use of an explicitly specified aircraft for a two-year period. The contract details the interior and exterior specifications for the aircraft.	Yes. Specific aircraft identified in the contract.	No. Although Supplier has the right to substitute another aircraft, the costs of outfitting any substitute to the standard specified in the contract mean that Supplier would not be expected to benefit economically from substitution.	Yes. Customer has exclusive use and has the right to obtain all of the economic benefits from use of the aircraft during the contract period. Contractual and legal restrictions define the scope of the Customer's right of use. Within that defined scope, Customer makes the relevant decisions about how and for what purpose the aircraft is used. Although Supplier operates the aircraft, it is in accordance with Customer's decisions regarding whether, where and when the aircraft travels.	Yes – lease of aircraft for the contract period.
8 – Customer enters into a contract with a manufacturer (Supplier) to purchase a particular type, quality and quantity of shirts for a three-year period.	Yes. Factory implicitly specified because Supplier can fulfil the contract only through the use of its one factory.	No. No alternative factory available.	No. Customer does not have the right to obtain all of the economic benefits from use of the factory during the contract period because its output does not represent substantially all of the output of the factory and Supplier can use spare capacity to supply other customers. Also, Supplier directs the use of the factory (Customer has the same rights as other customers).	No. Customer is purchasing shirts (goods).

Example	Identified asset?	Substantive substitution rights?	Customer has a right to control the use of the identified asset?	Lease?
9A – A utility company (Customer) enters into a contract with a power company (Supplier) to purchase all of the electricity produced by a new solar farm for 20 years. Customer designed the solar farm.	Yes. Specific solar farm identified in the contract.	No.	Yes. Customer has exclusive use and has the right to obtain all of the economic benefits from use of the solar farm during the contract period (Supplier's benefits in the form of tax credits are economic benefits from ownership rather than use). Although how and for what purpose the solar farm is used is predetermined, Customer's design of the farm has given it the right to direct the use of the farm (see **4.4.3.3**).	Yes – lease of solar farm for the contract period.
9B – Customer enters into a contract with Supplier to purchase all of the power produced by an explicitly specified power plant for three years. Supplier designed the power plant and operates it.	Yes. Specific power plant identified in the contract.	No.	No. Customer has exclusive use and has the right to obtain all of the economic benefits from use of the power plant during the contract period. However, how and for what purpose the plant is used is predetermined and Customer did not design the plant and Supplier operates the plant. Therefore, Customer does not have the right to direct the use of the plant (see **4.4.3.3**).	No. Customer is purchasing a power supply (service).

Example	Identified asset?	Substantive substitution rights?	Customer has a right to control the use of the identified asset?	Lease?
9C – Customer enters into a contract with Supplier to purchase all of the power produced by an explicitly specified power plant for 10 years. Customer determines timing and quantity of power produced.	Yes. Specific power plant identified in the contract.	No.	Yes. Customer has exclusive use and has the right to obtain all of the economic benefits from use of the power plant during the contract period. Customer makes the relevant decisions about how and for what purpose the plant is used. Although Supplier operates the plant, it is in accordance with Customer's decisions regarding the timing and quantity of power produced.	Yes – lease of power plant for the contract period.
10A – Customer enters into a contract with a telecommunications company (Supplier) for network services for two years.	Not considered.	Not considered.	No. Customer does not control the use of the servers. Supplier is the only party that can make relevant decisions about the servers during the period of use – it decides how data is transported using the services, whether to reconfigure the servers and whether to use the servers for another purpose.	No. Customer is purchasing network services.

Example	Identified asset?	Substantive substitution rights?	Customer has a right to control the use of the identified asset?	Lease?
10B – Customer enters into a contract with an information technology company (Supplier) for the use of an identified server for three years.	Yes. Specific server identified in the contract.	No. Server can only be substituted if it malfunctions.	Yes. Customer has exclusive use and has the right to obtain all of the economic benefits from use of the server during the contract period. Customer makes the relevant decisions about how and for what purpose the server is used.	Yes – lease of the server for the contract period.

5   Separating components of a contract

5.1   Separating components of a contract – requirements applicable for both lessees and lessors

5.1.1   Requirement to separate components of a contract

If a contract is, or contains, a lease, an entity is required to account for each lease component within the contract as a lease separately from non-lease components of the contract, unless the entity applies the practical expedient in IFRS 16:15 (see **5.2.3**).

Some contracts contain both lease and non-lease (service) components. For example, a contract for a car may combine a lease with maintenance services. Other contracts contain two or more lease components. For example, a single contract may include leases of land, buildings and equipment. [IFRS 16:BC133]

The IASB considers that the identification of separate lease components in a lease contract is similar to the identification of performance obligations in a revenue contract – in both circumstances, an entity is trying to identify whether a customer or a lessee is contracting for a number of separate deliverables or contracting for one deliverable that may incorporate a number of different assets. Accordingly, rather than developing new requirements addressing how to identify separate lease components, the IASB decided to include in IFRS 16 requirements similar to those in IFRS 15 *Revenue from Contracts with Customers* on the identification of performance obligations. The IASB intends that those requirements in IFRS 16 are applied in a similar way to their application within the context of a revenue contract in IFRS 15. [IFRS 16:BC134]

Note that the effect of the practical expedient described in **5.2.3** is that lessees have a choice as to whether to separate the non-lease components of a contract.

5.1.2 Identification of separate lease components

The right to use an underlying asset is a separate lease component if both:

[IFRS 16:B32]

- the lessee can benefit from use of the underlying asset either on its own or together with other resources that are readily available to the lessee. Readily available resources are goods or services that are sold or leased separately (by the lessor or other suppliers) or resources that the lessee has already obtained (from the lessor or from other transactions or events); and

- the underlying asset is neither highly dependent on, nor highly interrelated with, the other underlying assets in the contract. For example, the fact that a lessee could decide not to lease the underlying asset without significantly affecting its rights to use other underlying assets in the contract might indicate that the underlying asset is not highly dependent on, or highly interrelated with, those other underlying assets.

Take, for example, a contract for the hire of a pneumatic hammer and an air-compressor for breaking up concrete (assume that the contract meets the definition of a lease). The hammer only works with an air-compressor. However, the hammer is not linked to the specific air-compressor and could be used with a different compressor purchased or hired elsewhere. In this example, having regard to the conditions in IFRS 16:B32, the contract is considered to have two separate lease components.

In contrast, consider a contract for the hire of two interdependent items of equipment that have been specifically configured to work in unison so that neither item can be readily substituted. In this case, the contract is likely to be considered to consist of only one lease.

Note that, even when separate lease components are identified, if the lease components have similar characteristics, it may be possible to account for them as a single portfolio under IFRS 16:B1 (see **2.3**).

The following example, which is reproduced from the illustrative examples accompanying IFRS 16, illustrates the application of IFRS 16:B32.

Example 5.1.2

Identification of lease components

[IFRS 16:IE4, Example 12 (part)]

Lessor leases a bulldozer, a truck and a long-reach excavator to Lessee to be used in Lessee's mining operations for four years. Lessor also agrees to maintain each item of equipment throughout the lease term. The total consideration in the contract is CU600,000, payable in annual instalments of CU150,000, and a variable amount that depends on the hours of work performed in maintaining the long-reach excavator. The variable payment is capped at 2 per cent of the replacement cost of the long-reach excavator. The consideration includes the cost of maintenance services for each item of equipment.

Lessee accounts for the non-lease components (maintenance services) separately from each lease of equipment applying [IFRS 16:12]. Lessee does not elect the practical expedient in [IFRS 16:15 – see **5.2.3**]. Lessee considers the requirements in [IFRS 16:B32] and concludes that the lease of the bulldozer, the lease of the truck and the lease of the long-reach excavator are each separate lease components. This is because:

(a) Lessee can benefit from use of each of the three items of equipment on its own or together with other readily available resources (for example, Lessee could readily lease or purchase an alternative truck or excavator to use in its operations); and

(b) although Lessee is leasing all three items of equipment for one purpose (ie to engage in mining operations), the machines are neither highly dependent on, nor highly interrelated with, each other. Lessee's ability to derive benefit from the lease of each item of equipment is not significantly affected by its decision to lease, or not lease, the other equipment from Lessor.

Consequently, Lessee concludes that there are three lease components and three non-lease components (maintenance services) in the contract.

continued at example 5.2.1 ......

5.1.3   Activities and costs that do not transfer a good or service to the lessee

A contract may include an amount payable by the lessee for activities and costs that do not transfer a good or service to the lessee. For example, a lessor may include in the total amount payable a charge for administrative tasks, or other costs it incurs associated with the lease, that do not transfer a good or service to the lessee. Such amounts payable do not give rise to a separate component of the contract, but are considered to be part of the total consideration that is allocated to the separately identified components of the contract. [IFRS 16:B33]

For example, a contract includes a lease component (hire of a machine) and a non-lease component (maintenance of the machine over the lease term). The contract also provides for an additional charge for administrative tasks of 2 per cent of the amounts otherwise payable under the contract. Because these administrative tasks do not transfer a good or service to the lessee, the additional charge is not considered to be a separate component of the contract. Rather, assuming that the lessee does not elect to use the practical expedient in IFRS 16:15 (see **5.2.3**), both the lessee and the lessor account for the hire and maintenance components separately and the administration charge is included in the total consideration to be allocated between those components.

5.2 Separating components of a contract – lessees

5.2.1 Consideration to be allocated based on relative stand-alone prices

For lessees, the consideration in a contract should be allocated between lease and non-lease components (if any) on the basis of the relative stand-alone price of each lease component and the aggregate stand-alone price of the non-lease components. [IFRS 16:13]

The relative stand-alone price of lease and non-lease components should be determined on the basis of the price the lessor, or a similar supplier, would charge an entity for that component, or a similar component, separately. If an observable stand-alone price is not readily available, the lessee should estimate the stand-alone price, maximising the use of observable information. [IFRS 16:14]

IFRS 16:14 permits a lessee to estimate the stand-alone prices of lease components because it may not have the necessary information to determine the lessor's stand-alone prices. The Standard requires the lessee to maximise the use of observable information – for example, the price charged by other suppliers or the price charged by the supplier to other customers.

In addition, having regard to the likelihood that a lessee may not have complete information on the lessor's pricing model, the IASB has granted relief from the requirement to separate non-lease components (see **5.2.3**).

The following example, which is reproduced from the illustrative examples accompanying IFRS 16, illustrates the application of IFRS 16:13 and 14.

Example 5.2.1

Allocation of consideration between lease and non-lease components

[IFRS 16:IE4, Example 12 (part 2)]

... continued from example 5.1.2

Lessee applies the guidance in [IFRS 16:13 and 14] to allocate the consideration in the contract to the three lease components and the non-lease components.

Several suppliers provide maintenance services for a similar bulldozer and a similar truck. Accordingly, there are observable stand-alone prices for the maintenance services for those two items of leased equipment. Lessee is able to establish observable stand-alone prices for the maintenance of the bulldozer and the truck of CU32,000 and CU16,000, respectively, assuming similar payment terms to those in the contract with Lessor. The long-reach excavator is highly specialised and, accordingly, other suppliers do not lease or provide maintenance services for similar excavators. Nonetheless, Lessor provides four-year maintenance service contracts to customers that purchase similar long-reach excavators from Lessor. The observable consideration for those four-year maintenance service contracts is a fixed amount of CU56,000, payable over four years, and a variable amount that depends on the hours of work performed in maintaining the long-reach excavator. That variable payment is capped at 2 per cent of the replacement cost of the long-reach excavator. Consequently, Lessee estimates the stand-alone price of the maintenance services for the long-reach excavator to be CU56,000 plus any variable amounts. Lessee is able to establish observable stand-alone prices for the leases of the bulldozer, the truck and the long-reach excavator of CU170,000, CU102,000 and CU224,000, respectively.

Lessee allocates the fixed consideration in the contract (CU600,000) to the lease and non-lease components as follows:

CU	Bulldozer	Truck	Long-reach excavator	Total
Lease	170,000	102,000	224,000	496,000
Non-lease				104,000
Total fixed consideration				600,000

Lessee allocates all of the variable consideration to the maintenance of the long-reach excavator, and, thus, to the non-lease components of the contract. Lessee then accounts for each lease component applying the guidance in IFRS 16, treating the allocated consideration as the lease payments for each lease component.

5.2.2 Accounting for non-lease components

Unless the practical expedient in IFRS 16:15 (see **5.2.3**) is applied, a lessee should account for non-lease components in a contract in accordance with other applicable Standards. [IFRS 16:16]

IFRS 16 only deals with the accounting for lease components of a contract – not the accounting for services. The IASB considers that the accounting for services (or the service components of a contract) should not be affected, regardless of whether the contract is only for services or includes the purchase, or lease, of an asset as well as services. [IFRS 16:BC135]

Consequently, although IFRS 16 requires entities to separate non-lease components (unless the practical expedient in IFRS 16:15 is used) and to allocate consideration to those non-lease components in aggregate, it does not specify how the aggregate allocation should be apportioned between separate non-lease components nor the subsequent accounting for such consideration. These matters will be determined under other applicable Standards.

5.2.3 Relief from requirement to separate non-lease components from lease components – practical expedient

As a practical expedient, a lessee may elect not to separate non-lease components from lease components, and instead account for each lease component and any associated non-lease components as a single lease component. This election should be made by class of underlying asset. [IFRS 16:15]

Note that, if the practical expedient is adopted, an entity accounts for the combined lease and non-lease component as a single lease component – it is not permitted to account for the combined lease and non-lease component as a service. Note also that IFRS 16:15 does not provide any relief from the requirement to account separately for individual lease components if the conditions in IFRS 16:B32 (see **5.1.2**) are met; however, in some circumstances, an entity may be able to apply a portfolio approach (see **2.3**).

5.2.4 No relief from requirement to separate embedded derivatives

The relief from the requirement to separate non-lease components described in **5.2.3** is not available in respect of embedded derivatives that meet the criteria for separation from a host contract as set out in paragraph 4.3.3 of IFRS 9 *Financial Instruments* (or, for entities that have not yet adopted IFRS 9, paragraph 11 of IAS 39 *Financial Instruments: Recognition and Measurement*) (see also **3.6**). [IFRS 16:15]

5.3 Separating components of a contract – lessors

If a contract contains a lease component and one or more additional lease or non-lease components, a lessor should allocate the consideration in the contract by applying paragraphs 73 to 90 of IFRS 15 *Revenue from Contracts with Customers* (see **section 8** in **chapter A14**).

> Lessors are therefore required to allocate the consideration in a contract between lease and non-lease components using the requirements in IFRS 15 regarding the allocation of the transaction price to performance obligations. This approach is designed to ensure consistency for entities that are both a lessor and a seller of goods or services in the same contract. [IFRS 16:BC136]
>
> Although IFRS 16 includes a practical expedient permitting lessees not to separate non-lease components from lease components (see **5.2.3**), there is no equivalent practical expedient for lessors. The IASB believes that a lessor should be able to separate payments made for lease and non-lease components. This is because the lessor would need to have information about the value of each component, or a reasonable estimate of it, when pricing the contract. [IFRS 16:BC135(a)]

6 Lease term

6.1 Definition of lease term

The lease term is defined as "the non-cancellable period for which a lessee has the right to use an underlying asset, together with both:

[IFRS 16:18]

- periods covered by an option to extend the lease if the lessee is reasonably certain to exercise that option; and

- periods covered by an option to terminate the lease if the lessee is reasonably certain not to exercise that option".

> See **6.5** to **6.7** for a discussion of lessor and lessee termination and extension options.

6.2 Consideration of enforceability

As part of its assessment of the lease term and the length of the non-cancellable period of a lease, an entity should consider the definition of a contract ("[a]n agreement between two or more parties that creates enforceable right and obligations") and determine the period for which the contract is enforceable. [IFRS 16:B34]

For the purposes of IFRS 16, a contract is considered to exist only when it creates rights and obligations that are enforceable. Any non-cancellable period or notice period in a lease meets the definition of a contract and, therefore, should be included as part of the lease term. Any options to extend or terminate the lease that are included in the lease term must also be enforceable.

In assessing the enforceability of a contract, an entity should consider whether the lessor can refuse a request from the lessee to extend the lease. If optional periods are not enforceable (e.g. if the lessee cannot enforce the extension of the lease without the agreement of the lessor), the lessee does not have the right to use the asset beyond the non-cancellable period. By definition, there is no contract beyond the non-cancellable period (plus any notice period) if there are no enforceable rights and obligations existing between the lessee and lessor beyond that term. [IFRS 16:BC127]

A lease is no longer enforceable when the lessee and the lessor each has the right to terminate the lease without permission from the other party with no more than an insignificant penalty. [IFRS 16:B34]

6.3   Beginning of lease term

The lease term begins on the 'commencement date' of the lease. [IFRS 16:B36] This is defined as the date on which the lessor makes an underlying asset available for use by a lessee. [IFRS 16:Appendix A] It is the date on which the lessee initially recognises and measures right-of-use assets and lease liabilities (see **section 8**). It is also the date on which the lessor recognises assets held under a finance lease in its statement of financial position (see **11.1.1**).

IFRS 16 makes an important distinction between the 'inception date' and the 'commencement date' of a lease. The inception date of the lease is defined as the earlier of the date of the lease agreement and the date of commitment by the parties to the principal provisions of the lease. [IFRS 16:Appendix A] This is the date on which an entity evaluates a contract to determine whether it is, or contains, a lease (see **section 4**). For lessors, it is also the date at which the classification of a lease is determined (see **section 10**).

Therefore, although important assessments are made at the inception date, the assets, liabilities, income and expenses resulting from a lease are not recognised in the financial statements or measured until the commencement date (see IFRS 16:BC142 to BC144 for further discussion).

A lessee does not obtain and control its right to use the underlying asset until the commencement date. Before that date, the lessor has not yet performed under the contract. Although a lessee may have a right and an obligation to exchange lease payments for a right-of-use asset from the date of inception, the lessee is unlikely to have an obligation to make lease payments before the asset is made available for its use. [IFRS 16:BC142]. If such circumstances do arise (i.e. if the entity is required to make payments for the right to use the underlying asset before the commencement date), IFRS 16:B44 explicitly requires that they be included in lease payments (see **8.3.2**).

Example 6.3

Lease payments on assets not in use

Company X is planning a major expansion of its oil production capacity beginning in 20X2. In order to ensure sufficient shipping capacity is available when production increases, Company X enters into a lease contract on 1 January 20X1 for rail cars to ship the oil. The rail cars will be made available to Company X from 1 July 20X1. Company X does not expect to use the rail cars for its own shipping purposes until 20X2, but it may consider other options (e.g. to rent out the cars to other producers) in the second half of 20X1. The sole reason for entering into the lease contract in 20X1 is to ensure that the rail cars will be available to Company X in 20X2.

The inception date of the lease is 1 January 20X1 (or any earlier date on which the parties committed to the principal provisions of the lease). This is the date on which Company X evaluates the contract to determine whether it is, or contains, a lease. Assume that, having regard to the requirements set out in **4.3** (identified assets, no substantive substitution rights and, from 1 July 20X1, the right to control the use of the rail cars), Company X determines that the contract is a lease. (In fact, each of the rail cars may be considered a separate lease component – see **section 5**. However, it is assumed that Company X applies the practical expedient in IFRS 16:B1 (see **2.3**) and accounts for the portfolio of leases together.)

The lessor makes the rail cars available for use by Company X on 1 July 20X1. Company X has the right to control the use of the rail cars from that date. Although Company X does not intend to use the rail cars until 20X2, it has the right to determine how and for what purpose the rail cars are used from 1 July 20X1. If Company X chooses to store the rail cars rather than use them for a period of time, this is a demonstration of its control over those cars. Therefore, 1 July 20X1 is the commencement date of the lease and the assets, liabilities, income and expenses resulting from the lease are recognised and measured from that date.

The depreciation of the right-of-use asset should commence from 1 July 20X1 (i.e. the commencement date – see **8.5.1.3**) even if the rail cars are not used until 20X2.

6.4 Rent-free periods

The lease term includes any rent-free periods provided to the lessee by the lessor. [IFRS 16:B36]

6.5 Lessor termination options

If only a lessor has the right to terminate a lease, the non-cancellable period of the lease includes the period covered by the option to terminate the lease. [IFRS 16:B35]

A lessor's right to terminate a lease is ignored when determining the lease term because, in that case, the lessee has an unconditional obligation to pay for the right to use the asset for the period of the lease, unless and until the lessor decides to terminate the lease. [IFRS 16:BC128]

This principle applies for the determination of the lease term for the lessor as well as for the lessee – there is no assessment regarding whether the lessor is reasonably certain not to terminate, as is the case with lessee termination options (see **6.6**).

6.6 Assessment of lessee extension and termination options

In contrast to lessor termination options, if the lessee has the right to extend or terminate the lease, there are enforceable rights and obligations beyond the initial non-cancellable period and the parties to the lease are required to consider those optional periods in their assessment of the lease term. [IFRS 16:BC128]

In accordance with IFRS 16:18 (see **6.1**), the lease term will be considered to extend beyond the non-cancellable period if the lessee has an extension option that it is considered to be reasonable certain to exercise, or a termination option that it is considered to be reasonably certain not to exercise.

At the commencement date, the entity should assess whether the lessee is reasonably certain:

[IFRS 16:B37]

- to exercise an option to extend the lease; or
- to exercise an option to purchase the underlying asset; or
- not to exercise an option to terminate the lease.

In making these assessments, the entity considers all relevant facts and circumstances that create an economic incentive for the lessee to exercise, or not to exercise, the option, including any expected changes in facts and circumstances from the commencement date until the exercise date of the option. [IFRS 16:19 & B37]

Examples of factors to consider when making these assessments include, but are not limited to:

[IFRS 16:B37]

- contractual terms and conditions for the optional periods compared with market rates, such as:

  - the amount of payments for the lease in any optional period;

  - the amount of any variable payments for the lease or other contingent payments, such as payments resulting from termination penalties and residual value guarantees; and

  - the terms and conditions of any options that are exercisable after initial optional periods (e.g. a purchase option that is exercisable at the end of an extension period at a rate that is currently below market rates);

- significant leasehold improvements undertaken (or expected to be undertaken) over the term of the contract that are expected to have significant economic benefit for the lessee when the option to extend or terminate the lease, or to purchase the underlying asset, becomes exercisable;

- costs relating to the termination of the lease, such as:

  - negotiation costs;

  - relocation costs;

  - costs of identifying another underlying asset suitable for the lessee's needs;

  - costs of integrating a new asset into the lessee's operations; and

  - termination penalties and similar costs, including costs associated with returning the underlying asset in a contractually specified condition or to a contractually specified location;

- the importance of that underlying asset to the lessee's operations (considering, for example, whether the underlying asset is a specialised asset, the location of the underlying asset and the availability of suitable alternatives); and

- conditionality associated with exercising the option (i.e. when the option can be exercised only if one or more conditions are met), and the likelihood that those conditions will exist.

An option to extend or terminate a lease may be combined with one or more other contractual features (e.g. a residual value guarantee) such that the lessee guarantees the lessor a minimum or fixed cash return that is substantially the same regardless of whether the option is exercised. In such cases, and notwithstanding the guidance on in-substance fixed payments in IFRS 16:B42 (see **7.3.2**), an entity should assume that the lessee is reasonably certain to exercise the option to extend the lease, or not to exercise the option to terminate the lease. [IFRS 16:B38]

The shorter the non-cancellable period of a lease, the more likely a lessee is to exercise an option to extend the lease or not to exercise an option to terminate the lease. This is because the costs associated with obtaining a replacement asset are likely to be proportionately higher the shorter the non-cancellable period. [IFRS 16:B39]

A lessee's past practice regarding the period over which it has typically used particular types of assets (whether leased or owned), and its economic reasons for doing so, may provide information that is helpful in assessing whether the lessee is reasonably certain to exercise, or not to exercise, an option. For example, if a lessee has typically used particular types of assets for a particular period of time, or if the lessee has a practice of frequently exercising options on leases of particular types of underlying assets, the lessee should consider the economic reasons for that past practice in assessing whether it is reasonably certain to exercise an option on leases of those assets. [IFRS 16:B40]

6.7　Reassessment of extension and termination options

A lessee should reassess whether it is reasonably certain to exercise an extension option, or not to exercise a termination option, upon the occurrence of either a significant event or a significant change in circumstances that:

[IFRS 16:20]

- is within the control of the lessee; and

- affects whether the lessee is reasonably certain to exercise an option not previously included in its determination of the lease term, or not to exercise an option previously included in its determination of the lease term.

In principle, the IASB is of the view that users of financial statements receive more relevant information if lessees reassess extension, termination and purchase options on a regular basis. However, requiring reassessment at each reporting date would be costly for an entity with many leases that include options. In order to address that concern, while still providing useful information to users of financial statements, the Board decided that an appropriate balance would be achieved by requiring reassessment only if both of the criteria in IFRS 16:20 are met. Consequently, reassessment is required only upon the occurrence of a significant event or a significant change in circumstances that is within the control of the lessee and that affects whether the lessee is reasonably certain to exercise, or not to exercise, an option to extend a lease, to terminate a lease or to purchase an underlying asset. Limiting the reassessment requirement to events within the control of the lessee means that a lessee is not required to reassess options in response to purely market-based events or changes in circumstances. To assist lessees, IFRS 16:B41 (see below) includes some examples of possible triggering events to help entities apply judgement in identifying significant events or significant changes in circumstances that trigger reassessment. [IFRS 16:BC184 - BC186]

Examples of significant events or changes in circumstances as contemplated in IFRS 16:20 include:

[IFRS 16:B41]

- significant leasehold improvements not anticipated at the commencement date that are expected to have significant economic benefit for the lessee when the option to extend or terminate the lease, or to purchase the underlying asset, becomes exercisable;

- a significant modification to, or customisation of, the underlying asset that was not anticipated at the commencement date;

- the inception of a sublease of the underlying asset for a period beyond the end of the previously determined lease term; and

- a business decision of the lessee that is directly relevant to exercising, or not exercising, an option (e.g. a decision to extend the lease of a complementary asset, to dispose of an alternative asset or to dispose of a business unit within which the right-of-use asset is employed).

6.8   Revision of lease term

An entity should revise the lease term if there is a change in the non-cancellable period of a lease. For example, the non-cancellable period of a lease will change if one of the following occurs:

[IFRS 16:21]

- the lessee exercises an option not previously included in the entity's determination of the lease term;

- the lessee does not exercise an option previously included in the entity's determination of the lease term;

- an event occurs that contractually obliges the lessee to exercise an option not previously included in the entity's determination of the lease term; or

- an event occurs that contractually prohibits the lessee from exercising an option previously included in the entity's determination of the lease term.

The lease term may also be revised following a reassessment as to whether an extension option is reasonably certain to be exercised, or a termination option is reasonably certain not to be exercised (see **6.7**). Although such a reassessment does not affect the non-cancellable period, it affects the total lease term comprised of the non-cancellable period and reasonably certain extension periods (see **6.1**).

7 Lease payments

7.1 Lease payments – definition

A number of the measurement requirements in IFRS 16 are determined by reference to the 'lease payments'. Lease payments are defined as payments made by a lessee to a lessor relating to the right to use an underlying asset during the lease term, comprising the following:

[IFRS 16:Appendix A]

- fixed payments (including in-substance fixed payments – see **7.3**), less any lease incentives (see **7.4**);

- variable lease payments that depend on an index or a rate (see **7.5.2**);

- the exercise price of a purchase option if the lessee is reasonably certain to exercise that option (see **7.6**);

- payments of penalties for terminating the lease, if the lease term reflects the lessee exercising an option to terminate the lease; and

- residual value guarantees as set out in **7.7**.

In accordance with IFRS 16:18 (see **6.1**), the lease term will be considered to extend beyond the non-cancellable period if the lessee has an extension option that it is considered to be reasonably certain to exercise, or a termination option that it is considered to be reasonably certain not to exercise. Therefore, lease payments include optional payments payable after the non-cancellable period if it is considered reasonably certain that the lease will extend beyond that period.

Lease payments exclude (1) variable lease payments linked to sale or use (see **7.5.3**), and (2) optional payments payable after the non-cancellable period if it is *not* considered reasonably certain that the lessee will extend the lease beyond that period.

7.2 Exclusion of payments allocated to non-lease components

Entities are generally required to separate lease and non-lease components of a contract (see **section 5**).

For a lessee, lease payments do not include payments allocated to non-lease components of a contract, unless the lessee has elected to combine lease and non-lease components under the practical expedient permitted under IFRS 16:15 (see **5.2.3**). [IFRS 16:Appendix A]

For a lessor, lease payments do not include payments allocated to non-lease components. [IFRS 16:Appendix A]

> For a lessor, there is no practical expedient permitting lease and non-lease components to be combined (see **5.3**).

7.3 Fixed payments

7.3.1 Fixed payments – definition

Fixed payments are defined as "[p]ayments made by a lessee to a lessor for the right to use an underlying asset during the lease term, excluding variable lease payments". [IFRS 16:Appendix A]

> See **7.5** for a discussion of variable lease payments.

7.3.2 'In-substance' fixed lease payments

'In-substance' fixed lease payments, which are specifically required to be included in lease payments (see **7.1**), are payments that may, in form, contain variability but that, in substance, are unavoidable. [IFRS 16:B42]

In-substance fixed lease payments exist, for example, if:

[IFRS 16:B42]

- payments are structured as variable lease payments, but there is no genuine variability in those payments. Those payments contain variable clauses that do not have real economic substance. Examples of those types of payments include:

  - payments that must be made only if an asset is proven to be capable of operating during the lease, or only if an event occurs that has no genuine possibility of not occurring; or

  - payments that are initially structured as variable lease payments linked to the use of the underlying asset but for which the variability will be resolved at some point after the commencement date so that the payments become fixed for the remainder of the lease term. Those payments become in-substance fixed payments when the variability is resolved;

- there is more than one set of payments that a lessee could make, but only one of those sets of payments is realistic. In this case, an entity should include within lease payments the realistic set of payments; and

- there is more than one realistic set of payments that a lessee could make, but it must make at least one of those sets of payments. In this case, an entity should include within lease payments the set of payments that aggregates to the lowest amount (on a discounted basis).

IFRS 16 requires a lessee to include in-substance fixed lease payments in the measurement of lease liabilities because those payments are unavoidable and, thus, are economically indistinguishable from fixed lease payments. [IFRS 16:BC164]

7.4   Lease incentives

Lease incentives are defined as "[p]ayments made by a lessor to a lessee associated with a lease, or the reimbursement or assumption by a lessor of costs of a lessee". [IFRS 16:Appendix A]

Such incentives may take the form, for example, of an up-front cash payment to the lessee or a reimbursement or assumption by the lessor of costs of the lessee (e.g. relocation costs and costs associated with a pre-existing lease commitment of the lessee).

Such payments are offset against lease payments made by the lessee to the lessor (see **7.1**). When any incentives are paid to the lessee, even if they are not part of the formal lease agreement, they should be offset against lease payments.

7.5   Variable lease payments

7.5.1   *Variable lease payments – definition*

Variable lease payments are defined as "[t]he portion of payments made by a lessee to a lessor for the right to use an underlying asset during the lease term that varies because of changes in facts or circumstances occurring after the commencement date, other than the passage of time". [IFRS 16:Appendix A]

Variability arises if lease payments are linked to:

[IFRS 16:BC163]

- price changes due to changes in a market rate or the value of an index. For example, lease payments might be adjusted for changes in a benchmark interest rate or a consumer price index (see **7.5.2**);

- the lessee's performance derived from the underlying asset. For example, a lease of retail property may specify that lease payments are based on a specified percentage of sales made from that property (see **7.5.3**); or

- the use of the underlying asset. For example, a vehicle lease may require the lessee to make additional lease payments if the lessee exceeds a specified mileage (see **7.5.3**).

7.5.2 Variable lease payments that depend on an index or a rate

7.5.2.1 Lease liability initially measured using the index or rate as at the commencement date

Variable lease payments that depend on an index or a rate (which, as indicated in **7.1**, should be included within lease payments) include, for example, payments linked to a consumer price index, payments linked to a benchmark interest rate (such as LIBOR) or payments that vary to reflect changes in market rental rates. [IFRS 16:28]

When measuring a lessee's lease liability (see **8.4.2.1**) or a lessor's net investment in a lease (see **11.1.1**), such payments should initially be measured using the index or rate as at the commencement date (see **6.3**).

Variable lease payments that depend on an index or a rate are included in lease payments. They meet the definition of liabilities for the lessee because they are unavoidable and do not depend on any future activity of the lessee. Any uncertainty, therefore, relates to the measurement of the liability that arises from those payments and not to the existence of that liability. [IFRS 16:BC165]

At initial recognition, such payments are measured using the index or rate at the commencement date (without estimating changes in the index or rate over the remainder of the lease term). The IASB considered that using forecasting techniques or forward rates to estimate changes in the index or rate would be costly, and might introduce measurement uncertainty and reduce comparability between entities. [IFRS 16:BC166]

7.5.2.2 Variable lease payments that depend on an index – example

The following example, which is reproduced from the illustrative examples accompanying IFRS 16, illustrates how a lessee accounts for variable lease payments that depend on an index.

Example 7.5.2.2

Variable lease payments that depend on an index

[IFRS 16:IE6, Example 14A]

Lessee enters into a 10-year lease of property with annual lease payments of CU50,000, payable at the beginning of each year. The contract specifies that lease payments will increase every two years on the basis of the increase in the Consumer Price Index for the preceding 24 months. The Consumer Price Index at the commencement date is 125. This example ignores any initial direct costs. The rate implicit in the lease is not readily determinable. Lessee's incremental borrowing rate is 5 per cent per annum, which reflects the fixed rate at which Lessee could borrow an amount similar to the value of the right-of-use asset, in the same currency, for a 10-year term, and with similar collateral.

At the commencement date, Lessee makes the lease payment for the first year and measures the lease liability at the present value of the remaining nine payments of CU50,000, discounted at the interest rate of 5 per cent per annum, which is CU355,391.

Lessee initially recognises assets and liabilities in relation to the lease as follows.

Right-of-use asset	CU405,391	
Lease liability		CU355,391
Cash (lease payment for the first year)		CU50,000

Lessee expects to consume the right-of-use asset's future economic benefits evenly over the lease term and, thus, depreciates the right-of-use asset on a straight-line basis.

During the first two years of the lease, Lessee recognises in aggregate the following related to the lease.

Interest expense	CU33,928	
Lease liability		CU33,928
Depreciation charge (CU405,391 ÷ 10 × 2 years)	CU81,078	
Right-of-use asset		CU81,078

At the beginning of the second year, Lessee makes the lease payment for the second year and recognises the following.

Lease liability	CU50,000	
Cash		CU50,000

At the beginning of the third year, before accounting for the change in future lease payments resulting from a change in the Consumer Price Index and making the lease payment for the third year, the lease liability is CU339,319 (the present value of eight payments of CU50,000 discounted at the interest rate of 5 per cent per annum = CU355,391 + CU33,928 – CU50,000).

At the beginning of the third year of the lease the Consumer Price Index is 135.

The payment for the third year, adjusted for the Consumer Price Index, is CU54,000 (CU50,000 × 135 ÷ 125). Because there is a change in the future lease payments resulting from a change in the Consumer Price Index used to determine those payments, Lessee remeasures the lease liability to reflect those revised lease payments, ie the lease liability now reflects eight annual lease payments of CU54,000.

At the beginning of the third year, Lessee remeasures the lease liability at the present value of eight payments of CU54,000 discounted at an unchanged discount rate of 5 per cent per annum, which is CU366,464. Lessee increases the lease liability by CU27,145, which represents the difference between the remeasured liability of CU366,464 and its previous carrying amount of CU339,319. The corresponding adjustment is made to the right-of-use asset, recognised as follows.

Right-of-use asset	CU27,145	
Lease liability		CU27,145

At the beginning of the third year, Lessee makes the lease payment for the third year and recognises the following.

Lease liability	CU54,000	
Cash		CU54,000

7.5.2.3 Variable lease payments that depend on a rate – example

When variable payments depend on a rate, the accounting is a little different, as illustrated in the following example.

Example 7.5.2.3

Variable lease payment that depend on a rate

Entity B enters into a lease for 10 years, with a single lease payment payable at the beginning of each year. The initial lease payment is CU1,000. Lease payments will increase by the rate of LIBOR each year. At the date of commencement of the lease, LIBOR is 2 per cent. Assume that the interest rate implicit in the lease is 5 per cent.

In accordance with IFRS 16:27(b), the lease payments should initially be measured using the rate (i.e. LIBOR) as at the commencement date. LIBOR at that date is 2 per cent; therefore, in measuring the lease liability, it is assumed that each year the payments will increase by 2 per cent, as follows.

Year	Lease payment	Discount factor	Present value of lease payment
	CU		CU
1	1,000	1	1,000
2	1,020	0.952	971
3	1,040	0.907	943
4	1,061	0.863	916
5	1,082	0.822	889
6	1,104	0.784	866
7	1,126	0.746	840
8	1,149	0.711	817
9	1,172	0.677	793
10	1,195	0.645	771
			8,806

Therefore, the lease liability is initially measured at CU8,806.

7.5.2.4 Rent reviews to market rates or upward-only

When a lease contract includes the potential for rent reviews (whether to market rates or upwards only), the lease payments included in the measurement of the lessee's lease liability and the lessor's net investment in the lease at the commencement date will be the payments agreed at inception, without consideration of future rent reviews.

Whether a lease specifies a rent of CU100 annually plus market increases, or CU100 annually resetting up or down to market every five years, the lease payments recognised at the commencement date are CU100 annually. Any increase or decrease as a result of subsequent rent reviews will be recognised when the adjustment to the lease payments takes effect (see **8.5.2.7**).

The basis of any rent review under a lease should be evaluated carefully to determine whether the rent review resets the lease payments to market at the date of the review or whether, in substance, the amount of change in the lease payments at the date of the review was fixed at inception. In the latter case, the changes in rent would represent 'in-substance' fixed payments (see **7.3**) and would therefore be included in lease payments from the commencement date.

7.5.3   Variable lease payments linked to future performance or use of an underlying asset

Variable lease payments linked to future performance or use of an underlying asset are excluded from the measurement of lease liabilities (see IFRS 16:BC168 and BC169 for a discussion of the IASB's considerations in this regard).

Such payments are required to be recognised in profit or loss in the period in which the event or condition that triggers those payments occurs (see **8.5.2.3**).

The following example, which is reproduced from the illustrative examples accompanying IFRS 16, illustrates how a lessee accounts for variable lease payments not included in the measurement of the lease liability.

Example 7.5.3

Variable lease payments linked to sales

[IFRS 16:IE6, Example 14B]

*Assume the same facts as [**Example 7.5.2.2**] except that Lessee is also required to make variable lease payments for each year of the lease, which are determined as 1 per cent of Lessee's sales generated from the leased property.*

At the commencement date, Lessee measures the right-of-use asset and the lease liability recognised at the same amounts as in [**Example 7.5.2.2**]. This is because the additional variable lease payments are linked to future sales and, thus, do not meet the definition of lease payments. Consequently, those payments are not included in the measurement of the asset and liability.

Right-of-use asset		CU405,391
Lease liability		CU355,391
Cash (lease payment for the first year)		CU50,000

Lessee prepares financial statements on an annual basis. During the first year of the lease, Lessee generates sales of CU800,000 from the leased property.

Lessee incurs an additional expense related to the lease of CU8,000 (CU800,000 × 1 per cent), which Lessee recognises in profit or loss in the first year of the lease [see **8.5.2.3**].

7.6   Options to purchase the underlying asset

Purchase options are required to be included in the measurement of a lessee's lease liability and a lessor's lease receivable in the same way as options to extend the term of a lease (i.e. the exercise price of a purchase option is included in the measurement of a lease liability/

receivable if the lessee is reasonably certain to exercise that option). The IASB views a purchase option as effectively the ultimate option to extend the lease term. A lessee that has an option to extend a lease for all of the remaining economic life of the underlying asset is, economically, in a similar position to a lessee that has an option to purchase the underlying asset. [IFRS 16:BC173]

7.7 Residual value guarantees

A residual value guarantee is defined as "[a] guarantee made to a lessor by a party unrelated to the lessor that the value (or part of the value) of an underlying asset at the end of a lease will be at least a specified amount". [IFRS 16:Appendix A]

For a lessee, lease payments include amounts expected to be payable by the lessee under residual value guarantees. [IFRS 16:Appendix A]

A lessee should estimate the amount that it expects to pay to the lessor under a residual value guarantee and include that amount in the measurement of its lease liability. This treatment reflects the fact that payments resulting from a residual value guarantee cannot be avoided by the lessee – the lessee has an unconditional obligation to pay the lessor if the value of the underlying asset moves in a particular way. Accordingly, any uncertainty relating to the payment of a residual value guarantee does not relate to whether the lessee has an obligation. Instead, it relates to the amount that the lessee may have to pay, which can vary in response to movements in the value of the underlying asset. In that respect, residual value guarantees are similar to variable lease payments that depend on an index or a rate for the lessee (see **7.5.2**). [IFRS 16:BC170 & BC171]

For a lessor, lease payments include any residual value guarantees provided to the lessor by the lessee, a party related to the lessee or a third party unrelated to the lessor that is financially capable of discharging the obligations under the guarantee. [IFRS 16:Appendix A]

8 Accounting by lessees

8.1 Recognition – general

At the commencement date of a lease, a lessee is required to recognise both:

[IFRS 16:22]

- a right-of-use asset; and
- a lease liability.

8.2 Recognition exemptions

8.2.1 Recognition exemptions – general

A lessee may elect not to apply the requirements in IFRS 16:22 to 49 (recognition requirements as described at **8.1**, measurement requirements described at **8.4**, and presentation requirements described at **9.1**) to:

[IFRS 16:5]

- short-term leases (see **8.2.2**); and

- leases for which the underlying asset is of low value (see **8.2.3** and subject to the exception in **8.2.3.5**).

For short-term leases or leases of low-value items to which this exemption is applied, lease payments are recognised as an expense over the lease term (see **8.2.4**).

8.2.2 Short-term leases

8.2.2.1 Short-term lease – definition

A short-term lease is defined as "[a] lease that, at the commencement date, has a lease term of 12 months or less". [IFRS 16:Appendix A]

A lease that contains a purchase option cannot be classified as a short-term lease. [IFRS 16:Appendix A]

> For the purposes of the definition of a short-term lease, the lease term should be determined under the general requirements of IFRS 16 (see **section 6**). Consequently, lessees will need to assess the effect of extension and termination options.
>
> Note that the prohibition on a lease containing a purchase option being classified as a short-term lease applies for any lease containing a purchase option, irrespective of the probability that the option will be exercised.
>
> Note that there is no restriction on qualification as a short-term lease based on the value of the underlying asset or the amount of the consideration paid. This exemption is available for high-value items that are leased for the short-term.

8.2.2.2 Election to be made on a class-by-class basis

The election to take the recognition exemption for short-term leases is required to be made by class of underlying asset to which the right of use relates. A class of underlying asset is a grouping of underlying assets of a similar nature and use in an entity's operations. [IFRS 16:8]

For example, consider an entity that has leased several items of office equipment – some for less than 12 months and some for longer than 12 months, with none containing purchase options. Assuming that the items of office equipment are all considered to be of the same class, if the entity wishes to use the short-term lease exemption it must apply that exemption for all of the leases with terms of 12 months or less. The leases with terms longer than 12 months will be accounted for in accordance with the general recognition and measurement requirements for lessees.

8.2.2.3   Impact of lease modifications

If a lessee accounts for short-term leases applying IFRS 16:6 (see **8.2.4**), it should consider the lease to be a new lease for the purposes of IFRS 16 if:

[IFRS 16:7]

- there is a lease modification; or

- there is any change in the lease term (e.g. the lessee exercises an option not previously included in its determination of the lease term).

See **8.7** for the definition of lease modifications and the accounting treatment generally required. In the context of a short-term lease, any lease modification (and, specifically, any change in the lease term) will be considered a new lease which will need to be reassessed to determine if it qualifies for the short-term lease exemption.

See **2.4** for IFRS 16's requirements regarding circumstances when two or more contracts that are interdependent should be combined and accounted for as a single contract. One specific example cited in this regard is when a lessee enters into a number of one-year leases at the same time and with the same counterparty, to follow sequentially such that the overall economic effect is a lease for the entire term. In that situation, if the conditions in IFRS 16:B2 are met, the leases would be combined and accounted for as a single lease (which would not qualify for the short-term lease exemption).

8.2.3   Leases of low-value assets

8.2.3.1   Low-value assets – definition and examples

IFRS 16 does not provide an explicit definition for what is meant by 'low-value' assets. However, the Basis of Conclusions states that "[a]t the time of reaching decisions about the exemption in 2015, the IASB had in mind leases of underlying assets with a value, when new, in the order of magnitude of US$5,000 or less". [IFRS 16:BC100]

Examples of low-value underlying assets can include tablet and personal computers, small items of office furniture and telephones. [IFRS 16:B8]

8.2.3.2 Assessment independent of the size or nature of the lessee

The assessment as to whether an underlying asset is of low value is performed on an absolute basis. Subject to the exception in IFRS 16:B7 regarding head leases (see **8.2.3.6**), and the exclusion of assets that are highly dependent on, or interrelated with, other assets (see **8.2.3.5**), leases of low-value assets qualify for the accounting treatment in IFRS 16:6 (see **8.2.4**) regardless of whether those leases are material to the lessee. The assessment is not affected by the size, nature or circumstances of the lessee. Accordingly, different lessees are expected to reach the same conclusions about whether a particular underlying asset is of low value. [IFRS 16:B4]

8.2.3.3 Assessment to be based on the value of the asset when new

The value of an underlying asset should be assessed based on the value of the asset when it is new, regardless of the age of the asset being leased. [IFRS 16:B3]

A lease of an underlying asset does not qualify as a lease of a low-value asset if the nature of the asset is such that, when new, the asset is typically not of low value. For example, leases of cars would not qualify as leases of low-value assets because a new car would typically not be of low value. [IFRS 16:B6]

8.2.3.4 Election available on lease-by-lease basis

The exemption for leases of low-value assets is available on a lease-by-lease basis. [IFRS 16:8]

In particular, an entity is not required to consider the aggregate of the leases identified as relating to low-value assets to determine if the overall effect is material (see also **8.2.3.2**).

Subject to IFRS 16's general requirements regarding the combination of interdependent contracts (see **2.4**), and the specific requirements in IFRS 16:B5 regarding assets that are highly interdependent or highly interrelated (see **8.2.3.5**), each lease is assessed separately.

For example, a hospital enters into a rental contract for a large number of hospital beds. Each bed within the contract constitutes an identified underlying asset and the other conditions for identification of a lease are met. The value of an individual hospital bed would be considered to be 'low', even though the contract for all of the beds is not. The conditions of IFRS 16:B5 are met (the hospital can benefit from the use of an individual bed together with other resources that are already available, and each individual bed does not need other assets to make it functional for patients). Consequently each bed qualifies as a low-value asset and the entity can elect to apply the low-value asset exemption to all of the beds under the contract.

8.2.3.5 Assets that are highly dependent on, or highly interrelated with, other assets do not qualify as low-value assets

A lease will qualify for this exemption only if:

[IFRS 16:B5]

- the lessee can benefit from use of the underlying asset on its own or together with other resources that are readily available to the lessee; and

- the underlying asset is not highly dependent on, or highly interrelated with, other assets.

Therefore, if either (1) the lessee cannot benefit from the underlying asset on its own or together with other readily available resources, or (2) the underlying asset is highly dependent on, or highly interrelated with, other underlying assets, the recognition exemption for low-value assets cannot be applied to that individual asset (unless the overall asset, combining the highly dependent or highly interrelated assets, is itself low value). In this context, the IASB had in mind large assets made up of a number of individual leases of low-value assets (such as IT equipment made up of individually low-value component parts).

See **example 2.3** which sets out a scenario in which some items of IT equipment (laptop computers, desktop computers, hand held computer devices, desktop printers and mobile phones) qualify for the low-value asset exemption but others (individual modules that increase the storage capacity of mainframe servers) do not. Although each module within the servers, if considered individually, might be an asset of low value, the leases of modules within the servers do not qualify as leases of low-value assets. This is because each module is highly interrelated with other parts of the servers.

8.2.3.6 Head leases do not qualify as low-value assets

If a lessee subleases an asset, or expects to sublease an asset, the head lease does not qualify as a lease of a low-value asset. [IFRS 16:B7]

8.2.4 Recognition of lease payments for short-term leases and leases of low-value assets

If a lessee elects to apply the exemption in IFRS 16:5 to either short-term leases or leases of low-value assets, it should recognise the lease payments associated with those leases as an expense on either a straight-line basis over the lease term, or on another systematic basis if that basis is more representative of the pattern of the lessee's benefit. [IFRS 16:6]

> For example, if the lease payments for an asset are based on the actual usage of that asset, or are revised periodically to reflect the efficiency of the asset or current market rates, the amounts actually payable may be an appropriate measure.
>
> The lease payments to be spread on a straight-line (or other systematic) basis are after deduction of any lease incentives (see **7.4**). The lease term includes any rent-free periods (see **6.4**). The following examples illustrate the recognition of lease payments under IFRS 16:6 when such features are present.

Example 8.2.4A

Recognition of lease payments (including lease incentives) for low-value assets

Entity A leases office equipment for five years. The total value of the equipment when new is CU5,000 (determined by Entity A to be 'low value'). Entity A elects to apply the low-value asset exemption.

Lease payments are payable as follows.

Year 1:	CUnil (rent-free period)
Years 2 and 3:	CU1,750 per year
Years 4 and 5:	CU1,500 per year

In addition, the lessor provides a lease incentive with a value of CU500. The lessee's benefit under the lease arises on a straight-line basis over the full lease term.

Applying IFRS 16:6 to the lease payments:

Total payments: (CU1,750 × 2) + (CU1,500 × 2) − CU500 = CU6,000

Length of lease: 5 years

Lease expense recognised each year: CU1,200 (CU6,000/5)

Example 8.2.4B

Period over which lease incentives should be recognised

Entity B leases office equipment for five years. The total value of the equipment when new is CU5,000 (determined by Entity B to be 'low value'). Entity B elects to apply the low-value asset exemption.

The lease includes a clause requiring lease payments to be repriced to market rates part-way through the lease term. The lessor grants an incentive to Entity B to enter into the lease arrangement.

Over what period should the lease incentive be recognised (i.e. over the whole of the lease term or over the period up to the repricing of lease payments to market rates)?

The lease incentive should be recognised over the lease term. It should be recognised on a straight-line basis, unless another systematic basis is more representative of the time pattern of Entity B's benefit from use of the leased asset.

The IFRIC (now the IFRS Interpretations Committee) was asked to consider this issue in 2005 (in the context of SIC-15 *Operating Leases – Incentives*, but equally applicable for entities applying the low-value asset exemption under IFRS 16). Specifically, the IFRIC was asked to consider whether the lease incentive should be recognised over the shorter period ending when the lease payments are adjusted to market rates on the basis that the lease expense of a lessee after a lease is repriced to market ought to be comparable with the lease expense of an entity entering into a new lease at that same time at market rates. The IFRIC did not accept this argument and confirmed that the general requirements for spreading lease incentives over the entire lease term should apply.

8.3 Lessee involvement with the underlying asset before the commencement date

8.3.1 Costs of the lessee relating to the construction or design of the underlying asset

Parties may negotiate a lease before the underlying asset is available for use by the lessee. For some leases, the underlying asset may need to be constructed or redesigned for use by the lessee. Depending on the terms and conditions of the contract, a lessee may be required to make payments relating to the construction or design of the asset. If a lessee incurs costs relating to the construction or design of an underlying asset, the lessee should account for those costs applying other applicable Standards (e.g. IAS 16 *Property, Plant and Equipment*). [IFRS 16:B43 & B44]

Such costs (e.g. amounts payable by an entity to construct a bespoke property that it will ultimately lease from another entity – sometimes referred to as 'build-to-suit' leases) do not qualify as initial direct costs (as discussed at **8.4.1.2**); they are not included within the carrying amount of the right-of-use asset under IFRS 16, but rather are accounted for as a separate asset (assuming the recognition criteria of the relevant Standard are met).

8.3.2 Payments for the right to use the underlying asset made before the commencement date

Costs relating to the construction or design of an underlying asset (as described in **8.3.1**) do not include payments made by the lessee for the right to use the underlying asset. Payments for the right to use an underlying asset are payments for a lease, regardless of the timing of those payments. [IFRS 16:B44] They are included within the initial measurement of the right-of-use asset (see **8.4.1**).

8.3.3 Legal title to the underlying asset

A lessee may obtain legal title to an underlying asset before that legal title is transferred to the lessor and the asset is leased to the lessee. Obtaining legal title does not in itself determine how to account for the transaction. [IFRS 16:B45]

If the lessee controls (or obtains control of) the underlying asset before that asset is transferred to the lessor, the transaction is a sale and leaseback transaction accounted for by applying IFRS 16:98 to 103 (see **section 13**). [IFRS 16:B46]

However, if the lessee does not obtain control of the underlying asset before the asset is transferred to the lessor, the transaction is not a sale and leaseback transaction. For example, this may be the case if a manufacturer, a lessor and a lessee negotiate a transaction for the purchase of an asset from the manufacturer by the lessor, which is in turn leased to the lessee. The lessee may obtain legal title to the underlying asset before legal title transfers to the lessor. In this case, if the lessee obtains legal title to the underlying asset but does not obtain control of the asset before it is transferred to the lessor, the transaction is not accounted for as a sale and leaseback transaction, but as a lease. [IFRS 16:B47]

8.4 Initial measurement

8.4.1 Initial measurement of the right-of-use asset

8.4.1.1 Right-of-use asset to be measured initially at cost
At the commencement date, the right-of-use asset should be measured at cost. [IFRS 16:23]

For this purpose, cost comprises:

[IFRS 16:24]

(a) the amount of the initial measurement of the lease liability, as described in IFRS 16:26 (see **8.4.2**);

(b) any lease payments made at or before the commencement date (see **8.3.2**), less any lease incentives received (see **7.4** for a definition of lease incentives);

(c) any initial direct costs incurred by the lessee (see **8.4.1.2**); and

(d) an estimate of costs to be incurred by the lessee in dismantling and removing the underlying asset, restoring the site on which it is located or restoring the underlying asset to the condition required by the terms and conditions of the lease, unless those costs are incurred to produce inventories. The lessee incurs the obligation for those costs either at the commencement date or as a consequence of having used the asset during a particular period (see **8.4.1.3**).

See **example 8.6** for an illustration of the initial and subsequent measurement of a lessee's right-of-use asset and lease liability.

8.4.1.2   Initial direct costs

Initial direct costs are the "[i]ncremental costs of obtaining a lease that would not have been incurred if the lease had not been obtained, except for such costs incurred by a manufacturer or dealer lessor in connection with a finance lease". [IFRS 16:Appendix A]

Initial direct costs are, typically, costs incurred in negotiating and securing lease arrangements. They exclude costs incurred by a lessee relating to the construction or design of an underlying asset (see **8.3.1**). See **11.1.1.3** for further discussion on the nature of initial direct costs.

8.4.1.3   Restoration costs

Under IFRS 16:24(d), the initial cost of a right-of-use asset includes an estimate of costs to be incurred by the lessee in dismantling and removing the underlying asset, restoring the site on which it is located or restoring the underlying asset to the condition required by the terms and conditions of the lease, unless those costs are incurred to produce inventories.

The lessee incurs the obligation for those costs either at the commencement date or as a consequence of having used the underlying asset during a particular period. [IFRS 16:24(d)]

The costs described in IFRS 16:24(d) should be recognised as part of the cost of the right-of-use asset when the lessee incurs an obligation for those costs. The lessee should apply IAS 2 *Inventories* to costs that are incurred during a particular period as a consequence of having used the right-of-use asset to produce inventories during that period. The obligations for such costs accounted for applying IFRS 16 or IAS 2 are recognised and measured applying IAS 37 *Provisions, Contingent Liabilities and Contingent Assets*. [IFRS 16:25]

At initial recognition, the estimated liability for such restoration costs is recognised as a provision under IAS 37 *Provisions, Contingent Liabilities and Contingent Assets* if an obligating event has already occurred. It is not included as part of the lease liability.

As a consequential amendment arising from IFRS 16, the scope of IFRIC 1 *Changes in Existing Decommissioning, Restoration and Similar Liabilities* has been amended to include restoration costs of this nature that are recognised as part of the cost of a right-of-use asset under IFRS 16:24(d). Therefore, any change in the entity's estimate of such costs after initial recognition should be accounted for in accordance with that Interpretation which, for right-of-use assets measured subsequent to initial recognition using a cost model, will result in such changes being added to, or deducted from, the cost of the right-of-use asset.

Sometimes lease contracts stipulate that the underlying asset must be returned to the lessor in the same condition as when originally leased. The appropriate accounting in such circumstances depends on the particular lease clause. For example, the underlying asset may suffer general wear and tear that is merely a result of being used. In such circumstances, it may be necessary gradually to build up a provision to repair or maintain the asset over the lease term, so that it can be returned to the lessor in its original condition. Generally, in these circumstances, it would be inappropriate to recognise a provision for all of the estimated maintenance costs at the outset of the lease. Conversely, other contracts may require specific work to be performed; for example, the contract may stipulate that the asset must be painted at the end of the lease before being returned to the lessor. In such circumstances, it may be appropriate to recognise a provision at the outset of the lease because, by signing the lease contract, the entity has committed itself to painting the asset, irrespective of any wear and tear suffered.

Repairs and maintenance obligations under leases are discussed further at **8.1** in **chapter A12**.

8.4.2 Initial measurement of the lease liability

8.4.2.1 Lease liability to be measured initially at the present value of unpaid lease payments

At the commencement date, the lease liability should be measured at the present value of the lease payments that are not paid at that date. [IFRS 16:26]

See **section 7** for a discussion of the components of 'lease payments' for the purposes of this measurement.

8.4.2.2 Discount rate

The lease payments should be discounted using:

[IFRS 16:26]

- the interest rate implicit in the lease; or

- if the interest rate implicit in the lease cannot be readily determined, the lessee's incremental borrowing rate.

The interest rate implicit in the lease is defined as "[t]he rate of interest that causes the present value of (a) the lease payments and (b) the unguaranteed residual value to equal the sum of (i) the fair value of the underlying asset and (ii) any initial direct costs of the lessor". [IFRS 16:Appendix A] The unguaranteed residual value is defined as "[t]hat portion of the residual value of the underlying asset, the realisation of which by a lessor is not assured or is guaranteed solely by a party related to the lessor". [IFRS 16:Appendix A]

The lessee's incremental borrowing rate is defined as "[t]he rate of interest that a lessee would have to pay to borrow over a similar term, and with a similar security, the funds necessary to obtain an asset of a similar value to the right-of-use asset in a similar economic environment". [IFRS 16:Appendix A]

When the lease is denominated in a foreign currency, the lessee's incremental borrowing rate should be the rate at which the lessee could obtain funding for the asset in the foreign currency.

The IASB's objective in specifying the discount rate to apply to a lease is to specify a rate that reflects how the contract is priced. With this in mind, the IASB decided that, if readily determinable by the lessee, a lessee should use the interest rate implicit in the lease. [IFRS 16:BC160]

The interest rate implicit in the lease is likely to be similar to the lessee's incremental borrowing rate in many cases. This is because both rates, as they have been defined in IFRS 16, take into account the credit standing of the lessee, the length of the lease, the nature and quality of the collateral provided and the economic environment in which the transaction occurs. However, the interest rate implicit in the lease is generally also affected by a lessor's estimate of the residual value of the underlying asset at the end of the lease, and may be affected by taxes and other factors known only to the lessor, such as any initial direct costs of the lessor. Consequently, the IASB noted that it is likely to be difficult for lessees to determine the interest rate implicit in the lease for many leases, particularly those for which the underlying asset has a significant residual value at the end of the lease. [IFRS 16:BC161]

The IASB noted that, depending on the nature of the underlying asset and the terms and conditions of the lease, a lessee may be able to refer to a rate that is readily observable as a starting point when determining its incremental borrowing rate for a lease (e.g. the rate that a lessee has paid, or would pay, to borrow money to purchase the type of asset being leased, or the property yield when determining the discount rate to apply to property leases). Nonetheless, because the lessee's incremental borrowing rate is defined to take into account the terms and conditions of the lease, a lessee should adjust such observable rates as needed to determine its incremental borrowing rate. [IFRS 16:BC162]

8.5 Subsequent measurement

8.5.1 Subsequent measurement of the right-of-use asset

8.5.1.1 Subsequent measurement of the right-of-use asset – general
After the commencement date, the right-of-use asset should be measured using a cost model (see **8.5.1.2**), unless it applies either of the measurement models described in IFRS 16:34 and 35 (see **8.5.1.5** and **8.5.1.6**, respectively). [IFRS 16:29]

8.5.1.2 Cost model for right-of-use assets
Under the cost model, the right-of-use asset is measured at cost:

[IFRS 16:30]

- less any accumulated depreciation and any accumulated impairment losses (see **8.5.1.3** and **8.5.1.4**, respectively); and

- adjusted for any remeasurement of the lease liability specified in IFRS 16:36(c) (see **8.5.2.1**).

8.5.1.3 Depreciation for right-of-use assets
Right-of-use assets measured under the cost model should be depreciated in accordance with the depreciation requirements in IAS 16 (see **section 7** in **chapter A7**), subject to the following:

[IFRS 16:31 & 32]

- if the lease transfers ownership of the underlying asset to the lessee by the end of the lease term, or if the cost of the right-of-use asset reflects that the lessee will exercise a purchase option, the right-of-use asset should be depreciated from the commencement date to the end of the useful life of the underlying asset;

- otherwise, the right-of-use asset should be depreciated from the commencement date to the earlier of the end of the useful life of the right-of-use asset and the end of the lease term.

The useful life of an asset is defined as "[t]he period over which an asset is expected to be available for use by an entity; or the number of production or similar units expected to be obtained from an asset by an entity". [IFRS 16:Appendix A]

> Therefore, if the ownership of the underlying asset transfers to the lessee at the end of the lease term, or it is reasonably certain that the lessee will exercise a purchase option, depreciation is based on the useful life of the *underlying* asset. Otherwise, depreciation is determined by reference to the useful life of the right-of-use asset (provided that is not longer than the lease term).

8.5.1.4 Impairment for right-of-use assets

A lessee should apply IAS 36 *Impairment of Assets* to determine whether the right-of-use asset is impaired and to account for any impairment loss identified. [IFRS 16:33]

8.5.1.5 Right-of-use assets that meet the definition of investment property

If a lessee applies the fair value model in IAS 40 *Investment Property* to its investment property, it is also required to apply that fair value model to right-of-use assets that meet the definition of investment property in IAS 40. [IFRS 16:34]

> IFRS 16 has amended the scope of IAS 40 by defining investment property to include both owned investment property and investment property held by a lessee as a right-of-use asset. A lessee is required to account for right-of-use assets that meet the definition of investment property in a manner consistent with its policy for owned investment property – i.e. using either the cost model and disclosing fair value, or using the fair value model. [IFRS 16:BC178]

8.5.1.6   *Right-of-use assets that relate to a class of revalued property, plant and equipment*

If right-of-use assets relate to a class of property, plant and equipment to which the lessee applies the revaluation model in IAS 16 (see **section 6** in **chapter A7**), a lessee may elect to apply that revaluation model to all of the right-of-use assets that relate to that class of property, plant and equipment. [IFRS 16:35]

> Therefore, for property, plant and equipment:
>
> * if the class of owned assets to which right-of-assets relate is measured using the cost model, the right-of-use assets should also be accounted for using the cost model; but
>
> * if the class of assets to which right-of-use assets relate is measured using IAS 16's revaluation model, a lessee can choose whether to measure right-of-use assets at fair value. This choice is made on a class-by-class basis. This is in contrast to right-of-use assets that meet the definition of investment property for which the accounting model to be followed is determined by the lessee's accounting policy for owned investment property (see **8.5.1.5**).

8.5.2   Subsequent measurement of the right-of-use liability

8.5.2.1   *Subsequent measurement of the lease liability – general*

After the commencement date, the lease liability should be measured by:

[IFRS 16:36]

(a) increasing the carrying amount to reflect interest on the lease liability;

(b) reducing the carrying amount to reflect the lease payments made; and

(c) remeasuring the carrying amount to reflect any reassessment or lease modifications specified in IFRS 16:39 to 46 (see **8.5.2.4**), or to reflect revised in-substance fixed lease payments (see **7.3**).

> Lease liabilities are measured on an ongoing basis similarly to other financial liabilities, using an effective interest method, so that the carrying amount of the lease liability is measured on an amortised cost basis and the interest expense is allocated over the lease term. IFRS 16 does not require or permit a lessee to measure lease liabilities at fair value after initial measurement. [IFRS 16:BC182 & BC183]

8.5.2.2   *Recognising interest on the lease liability*

Interest on the lease liability in each period during the lease term should be the amount that produces a constant periodic rate of interest on the remaining balance of the lease liability. For these purposes, the periodic rate of interest is the discount rate used in the initial measurement of the lease liability (see **8.4.2.2**) or, if applicable, the revised discount rate described in IFRS 16:41 or 43 (see **8.5.2.5** to **8.5.2.7**) or IFRS 16:45(c) (see **8.7.3**). [IFRS 16:37]

8.5.2.3 Amounts to be recognised in profit or loss

After the commencement date, a lessee should recognise in profit or loss (unless the costs are included in the carrying amount of another asset applying other applicable IFRSs), both:

[IFRS 16:38]

- interest on the lease liability; and

- variable lease payments not included in the measurement of the lease liability in the period in which the event or condition that triggers those payments occurs (see also **7.5.3**).

8.5.2.4 Remeasurement of the lease liability – general

After the commencement date, if changes to the lease payments occur, the lease liability should be remeasured in accordance with IFRS 16:40 to 43 (see **8.5.2.5** to **8.5.2.7**). The amount of the remeasurement of the lease liability should generally be recognised as an adjustment to the right-of-use asset (see **8.5.1.2**). However, if the carrying amount of the right-of-use asset is reduced to zero and there is a further reduction in the measurement of the lease liability, the remaining remeasurement should be recognised in profit or loss. [IFRS 16:39]

8.5.2.5 Remeasurements arising from a change in the lease term or reassessment of purchase option

The lease liability should be remeasured by discounting the revised lease payments *using a revised discount rate*, if either:

[IFRS 16:40]

- there is a change in the lease term (see **6.7** and **6.8**), in which case the revised lease payments should be determined on the basis of the revised lease term; or

- there is a change in the assessment of an option to purchase the underlying asset, assessed considering the events and circumstances described in IFRS 16:20 and 21 (see **6.7** and **6.8**) in the context of a purchase option, in which case the revised lease payments should be determined to reflect the change in amounts payable under the purchase option.

In most cases, an entity should not reassess the discount rate during the lease term. However, IFRS 16 requires a lessee to remeasure the lease liability using revised payments and a revised discount rate when there is a change in the lease term or a change in the assessment of whether the lessee is reasonably certain to exercise an option to purchase the underlying asset. In the IASB's view, in those circumstances, the economics of the lease have changed and it is appropriate to reassess the discount rate to be consistent with the change in the lease payments included in the measurement of the lease liability (and right-of-use asset). [IFRS 16:BC193 & BC194]

In applying IFRS 16:40, the revised discount rate used should be:

[IFRS 16:41]

- the interest rate implicit in the lease for the remainder of the lease term; or

- if the interest rate implicit in the lease cannot be readily determined, the lessee's incremental borrowing rate at the date of reassessment.

8.5.2.6 Remeasurements arising from a change in the amounts expected to be payable under a residual value guarantee

The lease liability should be remeasured by discounting the revised lease payments (i.e. reflecting the change in the residual value guarantee) using an *unchanged* discount rate, unless the change in the residual value guarantee results from a change in floating interest rates, in which case the lessee should use a revised discount rate that reflects changes in the interest rate. [IFRS 16:42(a) & 43]

8.5.2.7 Remeasurements arising from a change in future lease payments resulting from a change in an index or a rate

These requirements apply when there is a change in future lease payments resulting from a change in an index or a rate used to determine those payments (including, for example, a change to reflect changes in market rental rates following a market rent review). In such circumstances, the lease liability should be remeasured to reflect those revised lease payments only when there is a change in the cash flows (i.e. when the adjustment to the lease payments takes effect – see **example 8.5.2.7**). [IFRS 16:42(b)]

The IASB decided that a lessee should reassess variable lease payments that are determined by reference to an index or a rate only when there is a change in the cash flows resulting from a change in the reference index or rate. This approach is considered to be less complex and costly to apply than requiring a lessee to reassess variable lease payments at each reporting date. [IFRS 16:BC190]

The revised lease payments for the remainder of the lease term should be determined based on the revised contractual payments. They should be discounted using an *unchanged* discount rate, unless the change in the lease payments results from a change in floating interest rates, in which case the lessee should use a revised discount rate that reflects changes in the interest rate. [IFRS 16:42(b) & 43]

IFRS 16 generally does not permit an entity to reassess the discount rate during the lease term. An exception is made when there is a change in the lease term or a change in the assessment regarding a purchase option (see **8.5.2.5**). The IASB also decided that, in a floating interest rate lease, a lessee should use a revised discount rate to remeasure the lease liability when there is a change in lease payments resulting from changes in the floating interest rate. This approach is consistent with the requirements in IFRS 9 *Financial Instruments* (or, for entities that have not yet adopted IFRS 9, IAS 39 *Financial Instruments: Recognition and Measurement*) for the measurement of floating-rate financial liabilities subsequently measured at amortised cost. [IFRS 16:BC195]

Example 8.5.2.7

Remeasurements arising from a change in future lease payments resulting from a change in an index

On 1 January 20X1, Entity A leases a property for a lease term of eight years. The lease payments for the first three years have been agreed at CU100 per year. The lease payments will be reset on 1 January 20X4 (and, subsequently, on 1 January 20X7) on the basis of the increase in the Retail Price Index (RPI) for the preceding three years. All lease payments are made at the end of the relevant year.

At 1 January 20X1 (the commencement date), the RPI is 100 and Entity A measures its lease liability at CU646 (eight payments of CU100 payable in arrears, discounted at the interest rate implicit in the lease of 5 per cent).

The RPI increases each year; it is 108 on 1 January 20X4 and 113 on 1 January 20X7.

In its financial statements for the years ended 31 December 20X1, 31 December 20X2 and 31 December 20X3, Entity A makes no adjustment for increases in RPI because there is no change in cash flows in those years. In its financial statements for year ended 31 December 20X4 (and subsequently 20X7), Entity A recalculates its liability based on the increased RPI. These adjustments are added to the carrying amount of the lease liability and the related right-of-use asset, subject to the requirements of IFRS 16:39 (see **8.5.2.4**).

Year	Opening lease liability	Adjustment	Interest	Repayment	Closing lease liability
	CU	CU	CU	CU	CU
20X1	646	–	32	-100	578
20X2	578	–	29	-100	507
20X3	507	–	25	-100	432
20X4	432	35[a]	22	-108	381
20X5	381	–	19	-108	292
20X6	292	–	16	-108	200
20X7	200	9[b]	11	-113	107
20X8	107	–	6	-113	0

[a] Difference between five remaining payments of CU100 discounted at 5 per cent and five remaining payments of CU108 discounted at 5 per cent.

[b] Difference between two remaining payments of CU108 discounted at 5 per cent and two remaining payments of CU113 discounted at 5 per cent.

8.5.2.8 Foreign currency exchange

IFRS 16 does not provide specific requirements as to how a lessee should account for the effects of foreign currency exchange differences relating to lease liabilities that are denominated in a foreign currency. In line with other financial liabilities, a lessee's lease liability is a monetary item and consequently, if denominated in a foreign currency, is required to be remeasured using closing rates at the end of each reporting period applying IAS 21 *The Effects of Changes in Foreign Exchange Rates* (see **chapter A19**). Such foreign exchange differences are recognised in profit or loss and not as an adjustment to the carrying amount of the right-of-use asset. [IFRS 16:BC196 - BC198]

8.6 Illustrative example – lessee measurement

The following example, reproduced from the illustrative examples accompanying IFRS 16, illustrates how a lessee measures right-of-use assets and lease liabilities. It also illustrates how a lessee accounts for a change in the lease term.

Example 8.6

Measurement by a lessee and accounting for a change in the lease term

[IFRS 16:IE5, Example 13]

Part 1 – Initial measurement of the right-of-use asset and the lease liability

Lessee enters into a 10-year lease of a floor of a building, with an option to extend for five years. Lease payments are CU50,000 per year during the initial term and CU55,000 per year during the optional period, all payable at the beginning of each year. To obtain the lease, Lessee incurs initial direct costs of CU20,000, of which CU15,000 relates to a payment to a former tenant occupying that floor of the building and CU5,000 relates to a commission paid to the real estate agent that arranged the lease. As an incentive to Lessee for entering into the lease, Lessor agrees to reimburse to Lessee the real estate commission of CU5,000 and Lessee's leasehold improvements of CU7,000.

At the commencement date, Lessee concludes that it is not reasonably certain to exercise the option to extend the lease and, therefore, determines that the lease term is 10 years.

The interest rate implicit in the lease is not readily determinable. Lessee's incremental borrowing rate is 5 per cent per annum, which reflects the fixed rate at which Lessee could borrow an amount similar to the value of the right-of-use asset, in the same currency, for a 10-year term, and with similar collateral.

At the commencement date, Lessee makes the lease payment for the first year, incurs initial direct costs, receives lease incentives from Lessor and measures the lease liability at the present value of the remaining nine payments of CU50,000, discounted at the interest rate of 5 per cent per annum, which is CU355,391.

Lessee initially recognises assets and liabilities in relation to the lease as follows.

Right-of-use asset	CU405,391	
Lease liability		CU355,391
Cash (lease payment for the first year)		CU50,000
Right-of-use asset	CU20,000	
Cash (initial direct costs)		CU20,000
Cash (lease incentive)	CU5,000	
Right-of-use asset		CU5,000

Lessee accounts for the reimbursement of leasehold improvements from Lessor applying other relevant Standards and not as a lease incentive applying IFRS 16. This is because costs incurred on leasehold improvements by Lessee are not included within the cost of the right-of-use asset.

Part 2 – Subsequent measurement and accounting for a change in the lease term

In the sixth year of the lease, Lessee acquires Entity A. Entity A has been leasing a floor in another building. The lease entered into by Entity A contains a termination option that is exercisable by Entity A. Following the acquisition of Entity A, Lessee needs two floors in a building suitable for the increased workforce. To minimise costs, Lessee (a) enters into a separate eight-year lease of another floor in the building leased that will be available for use at the end of Year 7 and (b) terminates early the lease entered into by Entity A with effect from the beginning of Year 8.

Moving Entity A's staff to the same building occupied by Lessee creates an economic incentive for Lessee to extend its original lease at the end of the non-cancellable period of 10 years. The acquisition of Entity A and the relocation of Entity A's staff is a significant event that is within the control of Lessee and affects whether Lessee is reasonably certain to exercise the extension option not previously included in its determination of the lease term. This is because the original floor has greater utility (and thus provides greater benefits) to Lessee than alternative assets that could be leased for a similar amount to the lease payments for the optional period – Lessee would incur additional costs if it were to lease a similar floor in a different building because the workforce would be located in different buildings. Consequently, at the end of Year 6, Lessee concludes that it is now reasonably certain to exercise the option to extend its original lease as a result of its acquisition and planned relocation of Entity A.

Lessee's incremental borrowing rate at the end of Year 6 is 6 per cent per annum, which reflects the fixed rate at which Lessee could borrow an amount similar to the value of the right-of-use asset, in the same currency, for a nine-year term, and with similar collateral. Lessee expects to consume the right-of-use asset's future economic benefits evenly over the lease term and, thus, depreciates the right-of-use asset on a straight-line basis.

The right-of-use asset and the lease liability from Year 1 to Year 6 are as follows.

| | Lease liability | | | | Right-of-use asset | | |
| | Beginning balance | Lease payment | 5% interest expense | Ending balance | Beginning balance | Depreciation charge | Ending balance |
Year	CU	CU	CU	CU	CU	CU	CU
1	355,391	–	17,770	373,161	420,391	(42,039)	378,352
2	373,161	(50,000)	16,158	339,319	378,352	(42,039)	336,313
3	339,319	(50,000)	14,466	303,785	336,313	(42,039)	294,274
4	303,785	(50,000)	12,689	266,474	294,274	(42,039)	252,235
5	266,474	(50,000)	10,823	227,297	252,235	(42,039)	210,196
6	227,297	(50,000)	8,865	186,162	210,196	(42,039)	168,157

At the end of the sixth year, before accounting for the change in the lease term, the lease liability is CU186,162 (the present value of four remaining payments of CU50,000, discounted at the original interest rate of 5 per cent per annum). Interest expense of CU8,865 is recognised in Year 6. Lessee's right-of-use asset is CU168,157.

Lessee remeasures the lease liability at the present value of four payments of CU50,000 followed by five payments of CU55,000, all discounted at the revised discount rate of 6 per cent per annum, which is CU378,174. Lessee increases the lease liability by CU192,012, which represents the difference between the remeasured liability of CU378,174 and its previous carrying amount of CU186,162. The corresponding adjustment is made to the right-of-use asset to reflect the cost of the additional right of use, recognised as follows.

Right-of-use asset	CU192,012	
Lease liability		CU192,012

Following the remeasurement, the carrying amount of Lessee's right-of-use asset is CU360,169 (ie CU168,157 + CU192,012). From the beginning of Year 7 Lessee calculates the interest expense on the lease liability at the revised discount rate of 6 per cent per annum.

The right-of-use asset and the lease liability from Year 7 to Year 15 are as follows.

	Lease liability				Right-of-use asset		
			6%				
	Beginning balance	Lease payment	interest expense	Ending balance	Beginning balance	Depreciation charge	Ending balance
Year	CU	CU	CU	CU	CU	CU	CU
7	378,174	(50,000)	19,690	347,864	360,169	(40,019)	320,150
8	347,864	(50,000)	17,872	315,736	320,150	(40,019)	280,131
9	315,736	(50,000)	15,944	281,680	280,131	(40,019)	240,112
10	281,680	(50,000)	13,901	245,581	240,112	(40,019)	200,093
11	245,581	(55,000)	11,435	202,016	200,093	(40,019)	160,074
12	202,016	(55,000)	8,821	155,837	160,074	(40,019)	120,055
13	155,837	(55,000)	6,050	106,887	120,055	(40,019)	80,036
14	106,887	(55,000)	3,113	55,000	80,036	(40,018)	40,018
15	55,000	(55,000)	–	–	40,018	(40,018)	–

8.7   Lease modifications

8.7.1   Lease modification – definition

A 'lease modification' is defined as "[a] change in the scope of a lease, or the consideration for a lease, that was not part of the original terms and conditions of the lease (for example, adding or terminating the right to use one or more underlying assets, or extending or shortening the contractual lease term)". [IFRS 16:Appendix A]

The 'effective date of the modification' is "[t]he date when both parties agree to a lease modification". [IFRS 16:Appendix A]

8.7.2   Conditions for treating a lease modification as a separate lease

A lease modification should be accounted for as a separate lease if both of the following apply:

[IFRS 16:44]

- the modification increases the scope of the lease by adding the right to use one or more underlying assets; and

- the consideration for the lease increases by an amount commensurate with the stand-alone price for the increase in scope and any appropriate adjustments to that stand-alone price to reflect the circumstances of the particular contract.

When the conditions in IFRS 16:44 are met, the modification is considered to result in the creation of a new lease that is separate from the original lease. [IFRS 16:BC202] The agreement for the right to use one or more additional assets is accounted for as a separate lease (or leases) to which the requirements of IFRS 16 are applied independently of the original lease.

The following example, reproduced from the illustrative examples accompanying IFRS 16, illustrates a modification that should be accounted for as a separate lease.

Example 8.7.2

Modification that is a separate lease

[IFRS 16:IE7, Example 15]

Lessee enters into a 10-year lease for 2,000 square metres of office space. At the beginning of Year 6, Lessee and Lessor agree to amend the original lease for the remaining five years to include an additional 3,000 square metres of office space in the same building. The additional space is made available for use by Lessee at the end of the second quarter of Year 6. The increase in total consideration for the lease is commensurate with the current market rate for the new 3,000 square metres of office space, adjusted for the discount that Lessee receives reflecting that Lessor does not incur costs that it would otherwise have incurred if leasing the same space to a new tenant (for example, marketing costs).

Lessee accounts for the modification as a separate lease, separate from the original 10-year lease. This is because the modification grants Lessee an additional right to use an underlying asset, and the increase in consideration for the lease is commensurate with the stand-alone price of the additional right-of-use adjusted to reflect the circumstances of the contract. In this example, the additional underlying asset is the new 3,000 square metres of office space. Accordingly, at the commencement date of the new lease (at the end of the second quarter of Year 6), Lessee recognises a right-of-use asset and a lease liability relating to the lease of the additional 3,000 square metres of office space. Lessee does not make any adjustments to the accounting for the original lease of 2,000 square metres of office space as a result of this modification.

8.7.3 Lease modifications that are not accounted for as a separate lease

For a lease modification that is *not* accounted for as a separate lease, at the effective date of the lease modification, the lessee should:

[IFRS 16:45]

(a) allocate the consideration in the modified contract applying the requirements of IFRS 16:13 to 16 (see **5.2**);

(b) determine the lease term of the modified lease applying the requirements of IFRS 16:18 and 19 (see **section 6**); and

(c) remeasure the lease liability by discounting the revised lease payments using a revised discount rate. The revised discount rate is determined as:

   (i) the interest rate implicit in the lease for the remainder of the lease term; or

   (ii) if the interest rate implicit in the lease cannot be readily determined, the lessee's incremental borrowing rate at the effective date of the modification.

The lessee should account for the remeasurement of the lease liability as follows:

[IFRS 16:46]

(a) for lease modifications that decrease the scope of the lease, by decreasing the carrying amount of the right-of-use asset to reflect the partial or full termination of the lease. Any gain or loss relating to the partial or full termination of the lease should be recognised in profit or loss; and

(b) for all other lease modifications, making a corresponding adjustment to the right-of-use asset.

For the lease modifications dealt with under IFRS 16:46(b), the original lease is not terminated because there is no decrease in scope. The lessee continues to have the right to use the underlying asset identified in the original lease. For lease modifications that increase the scope of a lease, the adjustment to the carrying amount of the right-of-use asset effectively represents the cost of the additional right of use acquired as a result of the modification. For lease modifications that change the consideration paid for a lease, the adjustment to the carrying amount of the right-of-use asset effectively represents a change in the cost of the right-of-use asset as a result of the modification. The use of a revised discount rate in remeasuring the lease liability reflects that, in modifying the lease, there is a change in the interest rate implicit in the lease (which the discount rate is intended to approximate). [IFRS 16:BC203(b)]

Example 8.7.3A

Modification that increases the scope of the lease by extending the contractual lease term

[IFRS 16:IE7, Example 16]

Lessee enters into a 10-year lease for 5,000 square metres of office space. The annual lease payments are CU100,000 payable at the end of each year. The interest rate implicit in the lease cannot be readily determined. Lessee's incremental borrowing rate at the commencement date is 6 per cent per annum. At the beginning of Year 7, Lessee and Lessor agree to amend the original lease by extending the contractual lease term by four years. The annual lease payments are unchanged (ie CU100,000 payable at the end of each year from Year 7 to Year 14). Lessee's incremental borrowing rate at the beginning of Year 7 is 7 per cent per annum.

At the effective date of the modification (at the beginning of Year 7), Lessee remeasures the lease liability based on: (a) an eight-year remaining lease term, (b) annual payments of CU100,000 and (c) Lessee's incremental borrowing rate of 7 per cent per annum. The modified lease liability equals CU597,130. The lease liability immediately before the modification (including the recognition of the interest expense until the end of Year 6) is CU346,511. Lessee recognises the difference between the carrying amount of the modified lease liability and the carrying amount of the lease liability immediately before the modification (CU250,619) as an adjustment to the right-of-use asset.

Example 8.7.3B

Modification that decreases the scope of the lease

[IFRS 16:IE7, Example 17]

Lessee enters into a 10-year lease for 5,000 square metres of office space. The annual lease payments are CU50,000 payable at the end of each year. The interest rate implicit in the lease cannot be readily determined. Lessee's incremental borrowing rate at the commencement date is 6 per cent per annum. At the beginning of Year 6, Lessee and Lessor agree to amend the original lease to reduce the space to only 2,500 square metres of the original space starting from the end of the first quarter of Year 6. The annual fixed lease payments (from Year 6 to Year 10) are CU30,000. Lessee's incremental borrowing rate at the beginning of Year 6 is 5 per cent per annum.

At the effective date of the modification (at the beginning of Year 6), Lessee remeasures the lease liability based on: (a) a five-year remaining lease term, (b) annual payments of CU30,000 and (c) Lessee's incremental borrowing rate of 5 per cent per annum. This equals CU129,884. Lessee determines the proportionate decrease in the carrying amount of the right-of-use asset on the basis of the remaining right-of-use asset (ie 2,500 square metres corresponding to 50 per cent of the original right-of-use asset).

50 per cent of the pre-modification right-of-use asset (CU184,002) is CU92,001. Fifty per cent of the pre-modification lease liability (CU210,618) is CU105,309.

Consequently, Lessee reduces the carrying amount of the right-of-use asset by CU92,001 and the carrying amount of the lease liability by CU105,309.

Lessee recognises the difference between the decrease in the lease liability and the decrease in the right-of-use asset (CU105,309 – CU92,001 = CU13,308) as a gain in profit or loss at the effective date of the modification (at the beginning of Year 6).

Lessee recognises the difference between the remaining lease liability of CU105,309 and the modified lease liability of CU129,884 (which equals CU24,575) as an adjustment to the right-of-use asset reflecting the change in the consideration paid for the lease and the revised discount rate.

Example 8.7.3C

Modification that both increases and decreases the scope of the lease

[IFRS 16:IE7, Example 18]

Lessee enters into a 10-year lease for 2,000 square metres of office space. The annual lease payments are CU100,000 payable at the end of each year. The interest rate implicit in the lease cannot be readily determined. Lessee's incremental borrowing rate at the commencement date is 6 per cent per annum. At the beginning of Year 6, Lessee and Lessor agree to amend the original lease to (a) include an additional 1,500 square metres of space in the same building starting from the beginning of Year 6 and (b) reduce the lease term from 10 years to eight years. The annual fixed payment for the 3,500 square metres is CU150,000 payable at the end of each year (from Year 6 to Year 8). Lessee's incremental borrowing rate at the beginning of Year 6 is 7 per cent per annum.

The consideration for the increase in scope of 1,500 square metres of space is not commensurate with the stand-alone price for that increase adjusted to reflect the circumstances of the contract. Consequently, Lessee does not account for the increase in scope that adds the right to use an additional 1,500 square metres of space as a separate lease.

The pre-modification right-of-use asset and the pre-modification lease liability in relation to the lease are as follows.

	Lease liability				Right-of-use asset		
	Beginning balance	6% interest expense	Lease payment	Ending balance	Beginning balance	Depreciation charge	Ending balance
Year	CU	CU	CU	CU	CU	CU	CU
1	736,009	44,160	(100,000)	680,169	736,009	(73,601)	662,408
2	680,169	40,810	(100,000)	620,979	662,408	(73,601)	588,807
3	620,979	37,259	(100,000)	558,238	588,807	(73,601)	515,206
4	558,238	33,494	(100,000)	491,732	515,206	(73,601)	441,605
5	491,732	29,504	(100,000)	421,236	441,605	(73,601)	368,004
6	421,236		(100,000)		368,004		

At the effective date of the modification (at the beginning of Year 6), Lessee remeasures the lease liability on the basis of: (a) a three-year remaining lease term, (b) annual payments of CU150,000 and (c) Lessee's incremental borrowing rate of 7 per cent per annum. The modified liability equals CU393,647, of which (a) CU131,216 relates to the increase of CU50,000 in the annual lease payments from Year 6 to Year 8 and (b) CU262,431 relates to the remaining three annual lease payments of CU100,000 from Year 6 to Year 8.

Decrease in the lease term

At the effective date of the modification (at the beginning of Year 6), the pre-modification right-of-use asset is CU368,004. Lessee determines the proportionate decrease in the carrying amount of the right-of-use asset based on the remaining right-of-use asset for the original 2,000 square metres of office space (ie a remaining three-year lease term rather than the original five-year lease term). The remaining right-of-use asset for the original 2,000 square metres of office space is CU220,802 (ie CU368,004 ÷ 5 × 3 years).

At the effective date of the modification (at the beginning of Year 6), the pre-modification lease liability is CU421,236. The remaining lease liability for the original 2,000 square metres of office space is CU267,301 (ie present value of three annual lease payments of CU100,000, discounted at the original discount rate of 6 per cent per annum).

Consequently, Lessee reduces the carrying amount of the right-of-use asset by CU147,202 (CU368,004 − CU220,802), and the carrying amount of the lease liability by CU153,935 (CU421,236 − CU267,301). Lessee recognises the difference between the decrease in the lease liability and the decrease in the right-of-use asset (CU153,935 − CU147,202 = CU6,733) as a gain in profit or loss at the effective date of the modification (at the beginning of Year 6).

Lease liability	*CU153,935*	
Right-of-use asset		*CU147,202*
Gain		*CU6,733*

At the effective date of the modification (at the beginning of Year 6), Lessee recognises the effect of the remeasurement of the remaining lease liability reflecting the revised discount rate of 7 per cent per annum, which is CU4,870 (CU267,301 − CU262,431), as an adjustment to the right-of-use asset.

Lease liability	*CU4,870*	
Right-of-use asset		*CU4,870*

Increase in the leased space

At the commencement date of the lease for the additional 1,500 square metres of space (at the beginning of Year 6), Lessee recognises the increase in the lease liability related to the increase in scope of CU131,216 (ie present value of three annual lease payments of CU50,000, discounted at the revised interest rate of 7 per cent per annum) as an adjustment to the right-of-use asset.

Right-of-use asset	*CU131,216*	
Lease liability		*CU131,216*

The modified right-of-use asset and the modified lease liability in relation to the modified lease are as follows.

	Lease liability				Right-of-use asset		
	Beginning balance	7% interest expense	Lease payment	Ending balance	Beginning balance	Depreciation charge	Ending balance
Year	CU	CU	CU	CU	CU	CU	CU
6	393,647	27,556	(150,000)	271,203	347,148	(115,716)	231,432
7	271,203	18,984	(150,000)	140,187	231,432	(115,716)	115,716
8	140,187	9,813	(150,000)	–	115,716	(115,716)	–

Example 8.7.3D

Modification that is a change in consideration only

[IFRS 16:IE7, Example 19]

Lessee enters into a 10-year lease for 5,000 square metres of office space. At the beginning of Year 6, Lessee and Lessor agree to amend the original lease for the remaining five years to reduce the lease payments from CU100,000 per year to CU95,000 per year. The interest rate implicit in the lease cannot be readily determined. Lessee's incremental borrowing rate at the commencement date is 6 per cent per annum. Lessee's incremental borrowing rate at the beginning of Year 6 is 7 per cent per annum. The annual lease payments are payable at the end of each year.

At the effective date of the modification (at the beginning of Year 6), Lessee remeasures the lease liability based on: (a) a five-year remaining lease term, (b) annual payments of CU95,000 and (c) Lessee's incremental borrowing rate of 7 per cent per annum. Lessee recognises the difference between the carrying amount of the modified liability (CU389,519) and the lease liability immediately before the modification (CU421,236) of CU31,717 as an adjustment to the right-of-use asset.

9 Presentation and disclosure – lessees

9.1 Presentation

9.1.1 Presentation – statement of financial position

A lessee should either present in the statement of financial position, or disclose in the notes:

[IFRS 16:47]

- right-of-use assets separately from other assets; and

- lease liabilities separately from other liabilities.

If right-of-use assets are not presented separately in the statement of financial position, the lessee should:

[IFRS 16:47]

- include right-of-use assets within the same line item as that within which the corresponding underlying assets would be presented if they were owned; and

- disclose which line items in the statement of financial position include those right-of-use assets.

If lease liabilities are not presented separately in the statement of financial position, the lessee should disclose which line items in the statement of financial position include those liabilities. [IFRS 16:47]

The requirement for separate presentation of right-of-use assets does not apply to right-of-use assets that meet the definition of investment property, which should be presented in the statement of financial position as investment property. [IFRS 16:48]

9.1.2 Presentation – statement of profit or loss and other comprehensive income

In the statement of profit or loss and other comprehensive income:

[IFRS 16:49]

- the interest expense on the lease liability should be presented separately from the depreciation charge for the right-of-use asset; and

- the interest expense on the lease liability is a component of finance costs which, in accordance with paragraph 82(b) of IAS 1 *Presentation of Financial Statements* (see **5.2.1** in **chapter A4**), is required to be presented separately in the statement of profit or loss and other comprehensive income.

9.1.3 Presentation – statement of cash flows

In the statement of cash flows, a lessee should classify:

[IFRS 16:50]

- cash payments for the principal portion of the lease liability within cash flows from financing activities;

- cash payments for the interest portion of the lease liability applying the requirements in IAS 7 *Statement of Cash Flows* for interest paid (see **5.5.2** in **chapter A21** for a discussion of the choices available); and

- short-term lease payments, payments for leases of low-value assets and variable lease payments not included in the measurement of the lease liability within cash flows from operating activities.

See **5.4.3** in **chapter A21** for a discussion of the appropriate presentation of cash flows in the context of sale and leaseback transactions.

9.2   Disclosure

9.2.1   Disclosure – general objective

The objective of the disclosure requirements for lessees is that sufficient information is disclosed in the notes, taken together with the information provided in the statement of financial position, statement of profit or loss and statement of cash flows, to provide a basis for users of financial statements to assess the effect that leases have on the financial position, financial performance and cash flows of the lessee. IFRS 16:52 to 60 (see **9.2.2** to **9.2.9**) specify requirements designed to meet this objective. [IFRS 16:51]

9.2.2   Information to be disclosed in a single note or separate section

A lessee should disclose information about its leases for which it is a lessee in a single note or separate section in its financial statements. However, a lessee need not duplicate information that is already presented elsewhere in the financial statements, provided that the information is incorporated by cross-reference in the single note or separate section about leases. [IFRS 16:52]

9.2.3   Short-term leases or leases of low-value assets

A lessee that accounts for short-term leases or leases of low-value assets in accordance with IFRS 16:6 (see **8.2**) is required to disclose that fact. [IFRS 16:60]

9.2.4   Disclosure of amounts reflected in financial statements

The following amounts are required to be disclosed for the reporting period:

[IFRS 16:53]

(a)   depreciation charge for right-of-use assets by class of underlying asset;

(b)   interest expense on lease liabilities;

(c)   the expense relating to short-term leases accounted for under IFRS 16:6 (see **8.2**). This expense need not include the expense relating to leases with a lease term of one month or less;

(d)   the expense relating to leases of low-value assets accounted for applying IFRS 16:6 (see **8.2**). This expense should not include the expense relating to short-term leases of low-value assets reported under (c) above;

(e) the expense relating to variable lease payments not included in the measurement of lease liabilities (see **8.5.2.3**);

(f)   income from subleasing right-of-use assets;

(g) total cash outflow for leases;

(h) additions to right-of-use assets;

(i)   gains or losses arising from sale and leaseback transactions; and

(j)   the carrying amount of right-of-use assets at the end of the reporting period by class of underlying asset.

The disclosures specified in IFRS 16:53 should be reported in a tabular format, unless another format is more appropriate. [IFRS 16:54]

The amounts disclosed under IFRS 16:53 should include costs that a lessee has included in the carrying amount of another asset during the reporting period. [IFRS 16:54]

9.2.5   Disclosure of lease commitments for short-term leases

Disclosure is required of the amount of a lessee's lease commitments for short-term leases accounted for applying IFRS 16:6 (see **8.2**) if the portfolio of short-term leases to which the lessee is committed at the end of the reporting period is dissimilar to the portfolio of short-term leases to which the short-term lease expense disclosed under IFRS 16:53(c) (see **9.2.4**) relates. [IFRS 16:55]

> This disclosure requirement may be triggered in the year in which IFRS 16 is applied if an entity applies the practical expedient allowed for lease terms expected to end within 12 months of the date of initial application (see **14.6.3.2**).

9.2.6   Right-of-use assets meeting the definition of investment property

If right-of-use assets meet the definition of investment property, the disclosure requirements of IAS 40 *Investment Property* (see **9.2** of **chapter A8**) should be applied. In that case, a lessee is not required to provide the disclosures in IFRS 16:53(a), (f), (h) or (j) (see **9.2.4**) for those right-of-use assets. [IFRS 16:56]

9.2.7 Right-of-use assets measured at revalued amounts under IAS 16

If a lessee measures right-of-use assets at revalued amounts applying IAS 16 *Property, Plant and Equipment*, it should disclose the information required by IAS 16:77 (see **11.2.2** in **chapter A7**) for those right-of-use assets. [IFRS 16:57]

9.2.8 Maturity analysis for lease liabilities

Lessees are required to present a maturity analysis of lease liabilities applying paragraphs 39 and B11 of IFRS 7 *Financial Instruments: Disclosures* (see **5.2.2.2** in **chapter B11** or, for entities that have not yet adopted IFRS 9 *Financial Instruments*, **5.2.2.2** in **chapter C12**). This analysis should be presented separately from the maturity analyses of other financial liabilities. [IFRS 16:58]

> The IASB is of the view that it is appropriate to apply the same maturity analysis disclosure requirements to lease liabilities as those applied to other financial liabilities. This is because the lessee accounting model in IFRS 16 is based on the premise that a lease liability is a financial liability. [IFRS 16:BC222]
>
> Applying IFRS 7 to lease liabilities requires lessees to apply judgement in selecting time bands for the maturity analysis that provide the most useful information to users of the financial statements. In some circumstances, a maturity analysis presenting cash flows for each of the first five years and a total for the periods thereafter (as required under IAS 17) may be appropriate; in other circumstances presentation of other time bands (possibly more detailed) may be more relevant. For example, for a portfolio of 15- to 20-year leases, the requirements of IFRS 7 should lead a lessee to provide a more detailed maturity analysis than a single amount for the years beyond the fifth year. [IFRS 16:BC221]

9.2.9 Additional information regarding the scope of lease activities

9.2.9.1 General requirement to disclose additional information

In addition to the disclosures required under IFRS 16:53 to 58 (see **9.2.4** to **9.2.8**), a lessee is required to disclose additional qualitative and quantitative information about its leasing activities necessary to meet the disclosure objective in IFRS 16:51 (see **9.2.1**). This additional information may include, but is not limited to, information that helps users of financial statements to assess:

[IFRS 16:59]

- the nature of the lessee's leasing activities;

- future cash outflows to which the lessee is potentially exposed that are not reflected in the measurement of lease liabilities. This includes exposure arising from:

  - variable lease payments (see **9.2.9.2**);

  - extension options and termination options (see **9.2.9.3**);

  - residual value guarantees (see **9.2.9.4**); and

  - leases not yet commenced to which the lessee is committed;

- restrictions or covenants imposed by leases; and

- sale and leaseback transactions (**9.2.9.5**).

In determining whether additional information about leasing activities is necessary to meet the disclosure objective in IFRS 16:51 (see **9.2.1**), a lessee should consider:

[IFRS 16:B48]

- whether that information is relevant to users of financial statements. A lessee should provide additional information as specified in IFRS 16:59 (see above) only if that information is expected to be relevant to users of financial statements. In this context, this is likely to be the case if it helps those users to understand:

  - the flexibility provided by leases (e.g. if a lessee can reduce its exposure by exercising termination options or renewing leases with favourable terms and conditions);

  - restrictions imposed by leases (e.g. if the entity is required to maintain particular financial ratios);

  - sensitivity of reported information to key variables (e.g. to future variable lease payments);

  - exposure to other risks arising from leases; and

  - deviations from industry practice (e.g. unusual or unique lease terms and conditions that affect a lessee's lease portfolio); and

- whether that information is apparent from information either presented in the primary financial statements or disclosed in the notes. A lessee need not duplicate information that is already presented elsewhere in the financial statements.

IFRS 16 therefore requires a lessee to disclose any material entity-specific information that is necessary in order to meet the disclosure objective and is not covered elsewhere in the financial statements. IFRS 16 supplements this requirement with a list of user information needs that additional disclosures should address (see **9.2.9.2** to **9.2.9.5**), and with illustrative examples of disclosures (see example **9.2.9.2** and example **9.2.9.3**) that a lessee might provide in complying with the additional disclosure requirements. These examples are not exhaustive. Nonetheless, the IASB thinks that the illustrative examples are useful in demonstrating that judgement should be applied in determining the most useful and relevant disclosures, which will depend on a lessee's individual circumstances. In the IASB's view, this approach facilitates the provision of more relevant and useful disclosures by:

[IFRS 16:BC225]

- discouraging the use of generic or 'boilerplate' statements; and

- enabling a lessee to apply judgement to identify the information that is relevant to users of financial statements and focus its efforts on providing that information.

9.2.9.2 Additional information relating to variable lease payments

Additional information relating to variable lease payments that, depending on the circumstances, may be needed to satisfy the disclosure objective in IFRS 16:51 (see **9.2.1**) could include information that helps users of financial statements to assess, for example:

[IFRS 16:B49]

- the lessee's reasons for using variable lease payments and the prevalence of those payments;

- the relative magnitude of variable lease payments to fixed payments;

- key variables upon which variable lease payments depend and how payments are expected to vary in response to changes in those key variables; and

- other operational and financial effects of variable lease payments.

The following example, which is reproduced from the illustrative examples accompanying IFRS 16, illustrates how a lessee with different types of lease portfolios might comply with these disclosure requirements regarding variable lease payments.

Example 9.2.9.2

Example disclosures – variable payment terms

[IFRS 16:IE9, Example 22]

Note: This example shows only current period information. IAS 1 *Presentation of Financial Statements* requires an entity to present comparative information.

Lessee with a high volume of leases with some consistent payment terms

Example 22A: a retailer (Lessee) operates a number of different branded retail stores – A, B, C and D. Lessee has a high volume of property leases. Lessee's group policy is to negotiate variable payment terms for newly established stores. Lessee concludes that information about variable lease payments is relevant to users of its financial statements and is not available elsewhere in its financial statements. In particular, Lessee concludes that information about the proportion of total lease payments that arise from variable payments, and the sensitivity of those variable lease payments to changes in sales, is the information that is relevant to users of its financial statements. This information is similar to that reported to Lessee's senior management about variable lease payments.

Some of the property leases within the group contain variable payment terms that are linked to sales generated from the store. Variable payment terms are used, when possible, in newly established stores in order to link rental payments to store cash flows and minimise fixed costs. Fixed and variable rental payments by store brand for the period ended 31 December 20X0 are summarised below.

	Stores	Fixed payments	Variable payments	Total payments	Estimated annual impact on total brand rent of a 1% increase in sales
	No.	CU	CU	CU	%
Brand A	4,522	3,854	120	3,974	0.03%
Brand B	965	865	105	970	0.11%
Brand C	124	26	163	189	0.86%
Brand D	652	152	444	596	0.74%
	6,263	4,897	832	5,729	0.15%

Refer to the management commentary for store information presented on a like-for-like basis and to Note X for segmental information applying IFRS 8 *Operating Segments* relating to Brands A - D.

Example 22B: a retailer (Lessee) has a high volume of property leases of retail stores. Many of these leases contain variable payment terms linked to sales from the store. Lessee's group policy sets out the circumstances in which variable payment terms are used and all lease negotiations must be approved centrally. Lease payments are monitored centrally. Lessee concludes that information about variable lease payments is relevant to users of its financial statements and is not available elsewhere in its financial statements. In particular, Lessee concludes that information about the different types of contractual terms it uses with respect to variable lease payments, the effect of those terms on its financial performance and the sensitivity of variable lease payments to changes in sales is the information that is relevant to users of its financial statements. This is similar to the information that is reported to Lessee's senior management about variable lease payments.

Many of the property leases within the group contain variable payment terms that are linked to the volume of sales made from leased stores. These terms are used, when possible, in order to match lease payments with stores generating higher cash flows. For individual stores, up to 100 per cent of lease payments are on the basis of variable payment terms and there is a wide range of sales percentages applied. In some cases, variable payment terms also contain minimum annual payments and caps. Lease payments and terms for the period ended 31 December 20X0 are summarised below.

	Stores	Fixed payments	Variable payments	Total payments
	No.	CU	CU	CU
Fixed rent only	1,490	1,153	–	1,153
Variable rent with no minimum	986	–	562	562
Variable rent with minimum	3,089	1,091	1,435	2,526
	5,565	**2,244**	**1,997**	**4,241**

A 1 per cent increase in sales across all stores in the group would be expected to increase total lease payments by approximately 0.6 - 0.7 per cent. A 5 per cent increase in sales across all stores in the group would be expected to increase total lease payments by approximately 2.6 - 2.8 per cent.

Lessee with a high volume of leases with a wide range of different payment terms

Example 22C: a retailer (Lessee) has a high volume of property leases of retail stores. These leases contain a wide range of different variable payment terms. Lease terms are negotiated and monitored by local management. Lessee concludes that information about variable lease payments is relevant to users of its financial statements and is not available elsewhere in its financial statements. Lessee concludes that information about how its property lease portfolio is managed is the information that is relevant to users of its financial statements. Lessee also concludes that information about the expected level of variable lease payments in the coming year (similar to that reported internally to senior management) is also relevant to users of its financial statements.

Many of the property leases within the group contain variable payment terms. Local management are responsible for store margins. Accordingly, lease terms are negotiated by local management and contain a wide range of payment terms. Variable payment terms are used for a variety of reasons, including minimising the fixed cost base for newly established stores or for reasons of margin control and operational flexibility. Variable lease payment terms vary widely across the group:

(a)   the majority of variable payment terms are based on a range of percentages of store sales;

(b)   lease payments based on variable terms range from 0 - 20 per cent of total lease payments on an individual property; and

(c)   some variable payment terms include minimum or cap clauses.

The overall financial effect of using variable payment terms is that higher rental costs are incurred by stores with higher sales. This facilitates the management of margins across the group.

Variable rent expenses are expected to continue to represent a similar proportion of store sales in future years.

9.2.9.3   Additional information relating to extension options or termination options

Additional information relating to extension options or termination options that, depending on the circumstances, may be needed to satisfy the disclosure objective in IFRS 16:51 (see **9.2.1**) could include information that helps users of financial statements to assess, for example:

[IFRS 16:B50]

*   the lessee's reasons for using extension options or termination options and the prevalence of those options;

*   the relative magnitude of optional lease payments to lease payments;

*   the prevalence of the exercise of options that were not included in the measurement of lease liabilities; and

*   other operational and financial effects of those options.

The following example, which is reproduced from the illustrative examples accompanying IFRS 16, illustrates how a lessee with different types of lease portfolios might comply with these disclosure requirements regarding extension options and termination options.

Example 9.2.9.3

Example disclosures – extension options and termination options

[IFRS 16:IE10, Example 23]

Note: This example shows only current period information. IAS 1 *Presentation of Financial Statements* requires an entity to present comparative information.

Lessee with a high volume of leases, that have a wide range of different terms and conditions, which are not managed centrally

Example 23A: Lessee has a high volume of equipment leases with a wide range of different terms and conditions. Lease terms are negotiated and monitored by local management. Lessee concludes that information about how it manages the use of termination and extension options is the information that is relevant to users of its financial statements and is not available elsewhere in its financial statements. Lessee also concludes that information about (a) the financial effect of reassessing options and (b) the proportion of its short-term lease portfolio resulting from leases with annual break clauses is also relevant to users of its financial statements.

Extension and termination options are included in a number of equipment leases across the group. Local teams are responsible for managing their leases and, accordingly, lease terms are negotiated on an individual basis and contain a wide range of different terms and conditions. Extension and termination options are included, when possible, to provide local management with greater flexibility to align its need for access to equipment with the fulfilment of customer contracts. The individual terms and conditions used vary across the group.

The majority of extension and termination options held are exercisable only by Lessee and not by the respective lessors. In cases in which Lessee is not reasonably certain to use an optional extended lease term, payments associated with the optional period are not included within lease liabilities.

During 20X0, the financial effect of revising lease terms to reflect the effect of exercising extension and termination options was an increase in recognised lease liabilities of CU489.

In addition, Lessee has a number of lease arrangements containing annual break clauses at no penalty. These leases are classified as short-term leases and are not included within lease liabilities. The short-term lease expense of CU30 recognised during 20X0 included CU27 relating to leases with an annual break clause.

Lessee with a high volume of leases with some consistent terms and options

Example 23B: a restaurateur (Lessee) has a high volume of property leases containing penalty-free termination options that are exercisable at the option of Lessee. Lessee's group policy is to have termination options in leases of more than five years, whenever possible. Lessee has a central property team that negotiates leases. Lessee concludes that information about termination options is relevant to users of its financial statements and is not available elsewhere in its financial statements. In particular, Lessee concludes that information about

(a) the potential exposure to future lease payments that are not included in the measurement of lease liabilities and (b) the proportion of termination options that have been exercised historically is the information that is relevant to users of its financial statements. Lessee also notes that presenting this information on the basis of the same restaurant brands for which segment information is disclosed applying IFRS 8 is relevant to users of its financial statements. This is similar to the information that is reported to Lessee's senior management about termination options.

Many of the property leases across the group contain termination options. These options are used to limit the period to which the group is committed to individual lease contracts and to maximise operational flexibility in terms of opening and closing individual restaurants. For most leases of restaurants, recognised lease liabilities do not include potential future rental payments after the exercise date of termination options because Lessee is not reasonably certain to extend the lease beyond that date. This is the case for most leases for which a longer lease period can be enforced only by Lessee and not by the landlord, and for which there is no penalty associated with the option.

Potential future rental payments relating to periods following the exercise date of termination options are summarised below.

Business segment	Lease liabilities recognised (discounted)	Potential future lease payments not included in lease liabilities (undiscounted)		
		Payable during 20X1 - 20X5	Payable during 20X6 - 20Y0	Total
	CU	CU	CU	CU
Brand A	569	71	94	165
Brand B	2,455	968	594	1,562
Brand C	269	99	55	154
Brand D	1,002	230	180	410
Brand E	914	181	231	502
	5,209	1,549	1,244	2,793

The table below summarises the rate of exercise of termination options during 20X0.

Business segment	Termination option exercisable during 20X0	Termination option not exercised	Termination option exercised
	No. of leases	No. of leases	No. of leases
Brand A	33	30	3
Brand B	86	69	17
Brand C	19	18	1
Brand D	30	5	25
Brand E	66	40	26
	234	162	72

Example 23C: Lessee has a high volume of large equipment leases containing extension options that are exercisable by Lessee during the lease. Lessee's group policy is to use extension options to align, when possible, committed lease terms for large equipment with the initial contractual term of associated customer contracts, whilst retaining flexibility to manage its large equipment and reallocate assets across contracts. Lessee concludes that information about extension options is relevant to users of its financial statements and is not available elsewhere in its financial statements. In particular, Lessee concludes that (a) information about the potential exposure to future lease payments that are not included in the measurement of lease liabilities and (b) information about the historical rate of exercise of extension options is the information that is relevant to users of its financial statements. This is similar to the information that is reported to Lessee's senior management about extension options.

Many of the large equipment leases across the group contain extension options. These terms are used to maximise operational flexibility in terms of managing contracts. These terms are not reflected in measuring lease liabilities in many cases because the options are not reasonably certain to be exercised. This is generally the case when the underlying large equipment has not been allocated for use on a particular customer contract after the exercise date of an extension option. The table below summarises potential future rental payments relating to periods following the exercise dates of extension options.

Business segment	Lease liabilities recognised (discounted)	Potential future lease payments not included in lease liabilities (discounted)	Historical rate of extension options
	CU	CU	%
Brand A	569	799	52%
Brand B	2,455	269	69%
Brand C	269	99	75%
Brand D	1,002	111	41%
Brand E	914	312	76%
	5,209	1,590	67%

9.2.9.4 Additional information relating to residual value guarantees

Additional information relating to residual value guarantees that, depending on the circumstances, may be needed to satisfy the disclosure objective in IFRS 16:51 (see **9.2.1**) could include information that helps users of financial statements to assess, for example:

[IFRS 16:B51]

- the lessee's reasons for providing residual value guarantees and the prevalence of those guarantees;
- the magnitude of a lessee's exposure to residual value risk;
- the nature of underlying assets for which those guarantees are provided; and
- other operational and financial effects of those guarantees.

9.2.9.5   Additional information relating to sale and leaseback transactions

Additional information relating to sale and leaseback transactions that, depending on the circumstances, may be needed to satisfy the disclosure objective in IFRS 16:51 (see **9.2.1**) could include information that helps users of financial statements to assess, for example:

[IFRS 16:B52]

- the lessee's reasons for sale and leaseback transactions and the prevalence of those transactions;

- key terms and conditions of individual sale and leaseback transactions;

- payments not included in the measurement of lease liabilities; and

- the cash flow effect of sale and leaseback transactions in the reporting period.

10   Classification of leases by lessors

10.1   Classification of leases – general

10.1.1   Each lease to be classified as either an operating lease or a finance lease

A lessor is required to classify each of its leases as either an operating lease or a finance lease. [IFRS 16:61]

The key distinction to be made by lessors in accounting for leases under IFRS 16 is whether the lease in question is either:

- a simple short-term hire arrangement (an operating lease), whereby rentals are dealt with in profit or loss with the only impact on the statement of financial position relating to the timing of payments; or

- in the nature of an arrangement for financing the acquisition of an asset (a finance lease), when the presentation in the financial statements will depart from the legal form of the transaction and be based on the economic substance (i.e. as if the underlying asset had been sold to the lessee).

10.1.2   Lease classification determined at the inception date

Lease classification is determined at the inception date and is reassessed only if there is a lease modification. [IFRS 16:66]

A lease modification is defined as "[a] change in the scope of a lease, or the consideration for a lease, that was not part of the original terms and conditions of the lease (for example, adding or terminating the right to use one or more underlying assets, or extending or shortening the contractual lease term)". [IFRS 16:Appendix A]

Changes in estimates (e.g. changes in estimates of the economic life or of the residual value of the underlying asset), or changes in circumstances (e.g. default by the lessee), do not give rise to a new lease classification. [IFRS 16:66]

> See **11.1.4** for the appropriate treatment for modifications to finance leases and **11.2.8** for the appropriate treatment for modifications to operating leases.

If a lease contract includes terms and conditions to adjust the lease payments for particular changes that occur between the inception date and the commencement date (e.g. a change in the lessor's cost of the underlying asset or a change in the lessor's cost of financing the lease), for the purposes of classifying the lease, the effect of any such changes is deemed to have taken place at inception. [IFRS 16:B54]

> There may be a time lag between the inception date and the commencement date (see **6.3** for an explanation of both terms), and the amounts involved in the lease arrangement may change between the two – most commonly when the asset is being constructed and the final cost is not known at inception.

10.1.3   *Classification of leases acquired in a business combination*

> When a group acquires a new subsidiary in a business combination, the classification of the subsidiary's leases in which it is the lessor is not reassessed at the date of the business combination for the purposes of the consolidated financial statements. The subsidiary's leases will be classified in the consolidated financial statements on the basis of their terms at original inception, and without regard to the remaining lease term from the acquisition date. Thus, in particular, if the acquiree has appropriately treated a lease as a finance lease, that lease will also be treated as a finance lease in the consolidated financial statements, even if the majority of the lease term has expired before the acquisition date.
>
> This treatment is required under paragraph 17 of IFRS 3 *Business Combinations* as an exception to that Standard's general principle that an acquirer should classify the assets acquired and liabilities assumed in a business combination on the basis of conditions as they exist at the acquisition date. IFRS 3:17 requires the acquiree's lease contracts in which it is the lessor to be classified on the basis of the contractual terms and other factors at the inception of the contract (or, if the terms of the contract have been modified in a manner that would change its classification, at the date of that modification, which might be the acquisition date). See also **7.1.2.2** in **chapter A25**.

10.2   Distinction between a finance lease and an operating lease

10.2.1   Finance lease – definition

A finance lease is a lease that transfers substantially all the risks and rewards incidental to ownership of an underlying asset to the lessee. [IFRS 16:62]

10.2.2   Operating lease – definition

An operating lease is a lease that does not transfer substantially all the risks and rewards incidental to ownership of an underlying asset. [IFRS 16:62]

10.2.3   Nature of risks and rewards incidental to ownership

Based on the definitions in **10.2.1** and **10.2.2**, the classification of leases for lessors under IFRS 16 is determined according to the extent to which the risks and rewards incidental to ownership of the underlying asset lie with the lessor or the lessee.

[IFRS 16:B53]

- The risks incidental to ownership include, but are not limited to, the possibility of losses from idle capacity or technological obsolescence, and of variations in the future economic benefits expected to flow to the entity due to changing economic conditions.

- The rewards incidental to ownership include, but are not limited to, an expectation of profitable operation over the underlying asset's economic life and of gain from appreciation in value or realisation of a residual value.

10.2.4   Classification to be determined based on the substance of the transaction

Whether a lease is a finance lease or an operating lease depends on the substance of the transaction rather than the form of the contract. [IFRS 16:63]

10.3   Situations that will generally lead to finance lease classification

IFRS 16 gives examples of situations that, individually or in combination, would normally lead to a lease being classified as a finance lease. The indicators in IFRS 16:63 relate to transfer of title and other factors in the primary period of the lease and should be regarded as the primary indicators. IFRS 16:64 sets out additional indicators, which will sometimes be relevant. Primary indicators of a finance lease are:

[IFRS 16:63]

* the lease transfers ownership of the underlying asset to the lessee by the end of the lease term;

> A lease can be considered to transfer ownership of the underlying asset when transfer of legal title, and thus continued ownership of risks and rewards, is automatic either under the lease agreement or under a side agreement that forms part of the overall lease arrangement (e.g. when the lessor has entered into a separate forward sale agreement with the lessee). This condition will also be met, in substance, when the lessor has a put option requiring the lessee to acquire legal title, and the option is structured in such a manner that it is reasonably certain to be exercised by the lessor.

* the lessee has the option to purchase the underlying asset at a price that is expected to be sufficiently lower than the fair value at the date the option becomes exercisable such that, at the inception date, it is reasonably certain that the option will be exercised;

> This condition extends that referred to in the previous bullet point to a lessee call option at a price that makes its exercise commercially likely to occur. An option to purchase at a low or nominal amount is a typical example of this type of arrangement.
>
> In some lease arrangements, rather than the lessee having a bargain purchase option, its parent (perhaps with no operations other than to act as an investment holding company) has the option to acquire the underlying asset at a low or nominal value at the end of the lease term. In these circumstances, it is reasonably certain that the parent will exercise the option to acquire the underlying asset. Although the option to acquire the underlying asset is not held by the lessee, the substance of the arrangement is that only the lessee will have use of the underlying asset. As a result, such arrangements will normally lead to classification of the lease as a finance lease.
>
> When a lease involves identical put and call options (at the end of the lease term, the lessee has a call option to acquire the underlying asset at a specified price and the lessor has a corresponding put option for the same value), the substance is that of a forward contract. At the end of the lease term, the lessee will exercise the call option if the market value of the underlying asset exceeds the exercise price of the option; the lessor will exercise the put option if the market price is less than the exercise price of the option. Therefore, either the put option or the call option is reasonably certain to be exercised at the end of the lease term, and the lessee will acquire the underlying asset at the end of the lease term. Consequently, the lease should normally be classified as a finance lease.

- the lease term is for the major part of the economic life of the underlying asset, even if title is not transferred;

> This condition covers the circumstances when substantially all the economic benefits of the underlying asset are consumed over the lease term during which the lessee controls the underlying asset. There is no specific threshold in IFRS 16 delineating the 'major part' of an asset's economic life and thresholds established by other GAAPs should not be considered definitive. Instead, it is necessary to consider the substance of a lease and to classify it according to whether the agreement transfers substantially all of the risks and rewards of ownership as discussed at **10.2.3**.

Example 10.3

Evaluating the economic life of a building

Company A constructs a building and, on completion of construction, leases it to Company B for 25 years. At the end of the lease term, the title to the land and building is retained by Company A. If the economic life of the building is 50 years, this lease apparently is not for the major part of the economic life of the building; therefore, in the absence of other indicators that the lease is a finance lease, it is likely that Company A would classify it as an operating lease. To determine the economic life of the building, Company A should consider a number of factors:

- if all important maintenance and refurbishment costs are paid by the lessee and this obligation forms part of the lease, this requirement should be taken into account because it may extend the economic life;

- if the lease requires Company B to maintain the building in the same condition as at the inception of the lease ('making good dilapidations'), this requirement could extend the economic life;

- if the building is unlikely to be leased for any additional period in its present condition because of an aspect of its design, operation or location (i.e. it is 'functionally obsolete'), the economic life may be shorter; and

- if the building is considered to be functionally obsolete, but a tenant still wants to rent it, the building will retain a degree of economic life.

This list is not exhaustive and each building should be considered separately based on the specific facts and circumstances.

Consideration of the economic life of a building will often reveal a difference between the life of the shell of the building and the life of the interior of the building. In many scenarios, the shell of the building will be key to the overall economic life of that asset. For example, in the case of shops or offices, the interior of the building is usually regularly refurbished by the lessee (often as required under the lease) in order for it to continue to be an economically viable property for the lessee. If refurbishment of the interior is carried out at regular (e.g. 10-year) intervals, consideration of the economic life of the building based on the expected life of the shell of the property may be appropriate. Regular repair and refurbishment would extend the expected economic life of the asset and, when this is contractually required under the lease, should be taken into account in the assessment of economic life at the inception of the lease.

Note that when renewal or purchase options exist, these should be assessed at the inception date (see **6.3**) to determine whether it is reasonably certain that the option will be exercised. The lease term will include the further term when, at the inception date, exercise of the option is assessed to be reasonably certain.

- at the inception date, the present value of the lease payments amounts to at least substantially all of the fair value of the underlying asset;

This condition tests whether the lessor receives a full return of its initial investment. As with economic life, there is no specific threshold in IFRS 16 delineating what constitutes 'substantially all' of the fair value of an underlying asset and thresholds established by other GAAPs should not be considered definitive. Instead, as discussed above, it is necessary to consider the substance of a lease and determine its classification based on whether the agreement transfers substantially all of the risks and rewards of ownership.

When the lease term has been extended by renewal or purchase options (as discussed in the previous point), the lease payments will include payments due with respect to this further term.

- the underlying asset is of such a specialised nature that only the lessee can use it without major modifications.

When this condition is met, it is likely that the underlying asset will have been constructed to the lessee's specifications such that its market value is limited. It follows that the lessor will seek to recover its investment from the primary lease term.

Other indicators that, individually or in combination, could also lead to a lease being classified as a finance lease are:

[IFRS 16:64]

- if the lessee can cancel the lease, the lessor's losses associated with the cancellation are borne by the lessee;
- gains or losses from fluctuations in the fair value of the residual accrue to the lessee (e.g. in the form of a rent rebate equalling most of the sales proceeds at the end of the lease);

If the lessee does not acquire legal title by the end of the lease, it may nevertheless bear the risk of variation in the residual value of the underlying asset; leases will commonly provide for a substantial fixed final rental (a 'balloon rental') followed by a repayment equal to all or substantially all of the sales proceeds from disposal of the underlying asset.

When the risk of variation in the residual value of the underlying asset is shared between the lessor and the lessee, it is necessary to consider the specific facts and circumstances in order to assess whether the risk retained by the lessor is significant. A risk of variation in the residual value of the asset retained by the lessor that may be significant only in circumstances considered to be remote may suggest that the lease is appropriately classified as a finance lease.

- the lessee has the ability to continue the lease for a secondary period at a rent that is substantially lower than market rent.

A bargain renewal option exists when a lessee has the ability to continue the lease for a secondary period at a rent that is substantially lower than market rent. The rent for a secondary period would be considered substantially lower than market rent if it would be economically rational for the lessee to continue the lease at that lower rent.

Rental for a secondary period either at a nominal amount or substantially below market rates suggests both that (1) the lessor has received the required return from its initial investment, and (2) that the lessee is likely to choose to enter into such a secondary period.

Factors to consider in determining whether a renewal option represents a bargain include:

- the nature of the underlying asset;

- the possibility of technological obsolescence;

- the possibility of higher operating and maintenance costs over the secondary rent period; and

- costs to be incurred by the lessor to find a new lessee and to prepare the underlying asset for a new lessee.

Assume that the rental payments in the renewal period are equal to a specified percentage of the original monthly payments. One approach to assessing whether this represents a bargain would be to compare the implicit interest rates determined by assuming that (1) the lease is terminated at the end of the original lease term, and (2) that the lease is renewed at the reduced rental payments. Appropriate estimates of the residual value of the underlying asset at the end of the original term and at the end of the renewal period should be included in the computations. If the implicit interest rate increases or remains substantially the same when the renewal option is assumed to be exercised, it is appropriate to conclude that the renewal option is not a bargain. The assessment of whether the interest rate differential is a bargain is made at the inception date and will depend on both the economic conditions prevailing in the relevant jurisdiction and the circumstances of the parties to the lease agreement.

Although the factors set out above are intended to identify the key characteristics of a finance lease, they are not always conclusive. IFRS 16 underlines the requirement to consider the whole of the arrangement, and the extent to which the risks and rewards incidental to ownership are transferred. Although a lease may appear to fall within the definition of a finance lease, having regard to the characteristics referred to above, there may be other features that demonstrate that the lease does not transfer substantially all of the risks and rewards incidental to ownership of the underlying asset. By way of example, the Standard cites circumstances in which ownership of the asset transfers at the end of the lease, but in exchange for a variable payment equal to its then fair value. Similarly, if there are variable lease payments, as a result of which the lessee does not have substantially all of the risks and rewards incidental to ownership of the underlying asset, the lease will not be classified as a finance lease. [IFRS 16:65]

The evaluation of a lease will require an examination of the lease agreement, including any supporting schedules and side letters (particularly when these include the monetary amounts of rental payments), and arrangements for the return and disposal of the underlying asset. The most relevant evidence will be found in clauses dealing with:

- rental payments and rebates (normally contained in a schedule to the lease agreement) to be used to consider whether the lease payments amount to at least substantially all of the fair value of the underlying asset; and

- arrangements that apply once the lease has run its normal full term (e.g. the existence of options, balloon payments, guarantees, process for disposal of the underlying asset).

Clauses dealing with the following issues will be of less relevance:

- maintenance and insurance (not normally a significant element of overall cost); and

- arrangements for termination that are unlikely to be applicable in practice (e.g. following insolvency of the lessee or failure to pay rentals when due).

10.4 Effect of exercise of options on lease classification

The following examples illustrate how the exercise of an option will not affect the classification of a lease, which is only reassessed if there is a lease modification (see **10.1.2**).

Example 10.4A

Exercise of a renewal option in an operating lease arrangement

Company A leases a property to Company B for 10 years. The lease includes a renewal option under which Company B may extend the lease contract at the end of the lease. At the inception of the lease, exercise of the renewal option is not considered to be reasonably certain, and the lease is classified as an operating lease.

Company B must give notice no later than two years before the end of the lease term if it intends to exercise the renewal option. The commercial rationale for this deadline is to allow Company A to market the leased asset for sale or lease to another party if Company B chooses not to exercise the renewal option. Towards the end of the eighth year of the lease, Company B serves notice that it will renew the lease contract, thereby extending the lease.

The notification that a renewal option will be exercised does not require reassessment of the classification of the lease because it does not represent a lease modification as defined in IFRS 16:Appendix A as follows.

> "A change in the scope of a lease, or the consideration for a lease, that was not part of the original terms and conditions of the lease (for example, adding or terminating the right to use one or more underlying assets, or extending or shortening the contractual lease term)." [IFRS 16:Appendix A]

In the circumstances described, the lease contains a renewal option but, at the inception date, exercise of the option is not considered to be reasonably certain. Subsequent notification by Company B represents a change in circumstance indicating the intention to renew, but this option was part of the original terms and conditions of the lease; consequently, the lease is not reassessed. When the lease is renewed at the end of the lease term, Company A effectively enters into a new lease that is classified in accordance with the general requirements of IFRS 16 (see **10.3**). The inception of the new lease will occur on the date of exercise of the option, but the commencement date will be two years later, at the end of the original lease.

However, if (1) the original lease did not include a renewal option and the lease is renegotiated in Year 8 to include one, or (2) the terms of an existing renewal option in a lease are changed, such an adjustment constitutes a modification in accordance with IFRS 16. In such circumstances, classification of the lease should be reassessed at the date of modification (i.e. in Year 8).

Example 10.4B

Exercise of a renewal option in a finance lease arrangement

An asset is leased under a finance lease under which the lease term is shorter than the useful life of the leased asset. Subsequent to initial recognition, an option to renew the lease is exercised. At the inception of the lease, it was not reasonably certain that the option would be exercised and, consequently, the renewal option was not taken into account in assessing the lease term.

In substance, the renewal of the lease is a separate lease agreement; therefore, the existing lease should continue to be accounted for as a finance lease to the end of its original term. Subsequently, the renewed lease should be classified as a finance lease or an operating lease according to the facts and circumstances and accounted for in accordance with the requirements in IFRS 16 for finance or operating leases, as appropriate.

Example 10.4C

Exercise of a purchase option in a lease arrangement

Company A leases a property to Company B for 10 years. The lease includes an option under which Company B may purchase the asset at the market price of the asset at the end of the lease. Company B may exercise the option no later than two years before the lease expires. The commercial rationale for this is to allow Company A to market the leased asset for sale or lease to a third party if Company B chooses not to exercise the purchase option. At the inception date, Company A assesses that it is not reasonably certain that the purchase option will be exercised and the lease is classified as an operating lease.

Towards the end of Year 8, Company B serves notice that it will purchase the property, thereby creating a binding purchase commitment. Company B will not acquire legal title to the property until exercise of the option at the end of Year 10.

Notification that the purchase option will be exercised does not lead to reassessment of the classification of the lease because it does not represent a lease modification as defined in IFRS 16:Appendix A (see example **10.4A**). In the circumstances described, the purchase price for the asset will be determined at the end of the original 10-year lease term, and paid for on exercise of the option at the end of Year 10. The original terms of the operating lease agreement have not been modified. Company A continues to account for the operating lease until the purchase option is exercised at the end of Year 10, when Company A will account for a sale of the property.

However if, at the date of notification, the option price is renegotiated to be the market price for the asset at the date of notification and the original lease term is shortened to eight years, this would constitute a lease modification (see **11.1.4**), and would be accounted for accordingly.

10.5 Leases of land and buildings

10.5.1 Requirement to assess the classification of land and buildings elements separately

When a lease includes both land and buildings elements, a lessor should assess the classification of each element as a finance or an operating lease separately in accordance with IFRS 16:62 to 66, B53 and B54 (see **10.2**). In determining whether the land element is an operating lease or a finance lease, an important consideration is that land normally has an indefinite economic life. [IFRS 16:B55]

Leases of land are assessed in the same way as all other leases. Land normally has an indefinite economic life, so it is unlikely that the lease term will be for the major part of the economic life of the asset. Nevertheless, some of the other characteristics described at **10.2** may be met, in which case a lease of land may be a finance lease. In particular, if, at the inception date, the present value of the lease payments amounts to at least substantially all of the fair value of the underlying asset, it is possible that a lease of land will be a finance lease. Note, however, that leases of land (and buildings) for long periods will often be subject to rent reviews, which may mean that the lessor has not transferred substantially all the risks and rewards incidental to ownership.

10.5.2 Splitting leases of land and buildings

Whenever necessary in order to classify and account for a lease of land and buildings, a lessor should allocate the lease payments (including any lump-sum up-front payments) between the land and the buildings elements in proportion to the relative fair values of the leasehold interests in the land element and buildings element of the lease at the inception date. [IFRS 16:B56]

Note that this split is *not* on the basis of the relative fair values of the land and buildings. The IASB concluded that the allocation of the minimum lease payments should reflect the extent to which they are intended to compensate the lessor for the use of the separate elements. The future economic benefits of a building are likely to be consumed to some extent over the term of a lease. Therefore, the lease payments allocated to the buildings should reflect not only the lessor's return on its investment in the buildings, but also the recovery of the value of the buildings consumed over the lease term. In contrast, land with an indefinite useful life should maintain its value beyond the lease term and, therefore, the lessor does not normally need compensation for any consumption of the economic benefits inherent in the land. [IFRS 16:BCZ246 & BCZ247]

If the lease payments cannot be allocated reliably between the land and buildings elements, the entire lease is classified as a finance lease, unless it is clear that both elements are operating leases, in which case the entire lease is classified as an operating lease. [IFRS 16:B56]

One of the most common applications of the previous paragraphs is likely to be in legal jurisdictions where the ownership of property is held only via leasehold interests. Typically, the government retains ownership of all land, and leasehold interests in land and buildings are the only means of purchasing such assets. In these circumstances, because similar land and buildings are not sold or leased separately, it may not be possible to arrive at a meaningful allocation of the lease payments.

For a lease of land and buildings under which the amount for the land element is immaterial to the lease, IFRS 16 allows that the land and buildings may be treated as a single unit for the purpose of lease classification. The IASB considers that, in such circumstances, the benefits of separating the two elements and accounting for each separately may not outweigh the costs.

The lease is classified in accordance with the general criteria discussed in **10.2**. In such cases, the economic life of the buildings is regarded as the economic life of the entire underlying asset. [IFRS 16:B57 & BCZ249]

10.6 Subleases

10.6.1 Subleases – classification

IFRS 16 requires an intermediate lessor to account for a head lease and a sublease as two separate contracts, applying both the lessee and lessor accounting requirements. This approach is considered to be appropriate because, in general each contract is negotiated separately, with the counterparty to the sublease being a different entity from the counterparty to the head lease. Accordingly, for an intermediate lessor, the obligations that arise from the head lease are generally not extinguished by the terms and conditions of the sublease. [IFRS 16:BC232]

In classifying a sublease, an intermediate lessor should classify the sublease as a finance lease or an operating lease as follows:

[IFRS 16:B58]

- if the head lease is a short-term lease that the entity, as a lessee, has accounted for applying IFRS 16:6 (see **8.2**), the sublease should be classified as an operating lease;

- otherwise, the sublease should be classified by reference to the right-of-use asset arising from the head lease, rather than by reference to the underlying asset (e.g. the item of property, plant or equipment that is the subject of the lease).

In classifying a sublease by reference to the right-of-use asset arising from the head lease, an intermediate lessor will classify more subleases as finance leases than it would have done if those same subleases were classified by reference to the underlying asset. The intermediate lessor only has a right to use the underlying asset for a period of time. If the sublease is for all of the remaining term of the head lease, the intermediate lessor has in effect transferred that right to another party. [IFRS 16:BC234]

The following examples, reproduced from the illustrative examples accompanying IFRS 16, illustrate the application of the requirements in IFRS 16 for an intermediate lessor that enters into a head lease and a sublease of the same underlying asset.

Example 10.6.1A

Sublease classified as a finance lease

[IFRS 16:IE8, Example 20]

Head lease – An intermediate lessor enters into a five-year lease for 5,000 square metres of office space (the head lease) with Entity A (the head lessor).

Sublease – At the beginning of Year 3, the intermediate lessor subleases the 5,000 square metres of office space for the remaining three years of the head lease to a sublessee.

The intermediate lessor classifies the sublease by reference to the right-of-use asset arising from the head lease. The intermediate lessor classifies the sublease as a finance lease, having considered the requirements in [IFRS 16:61 to 66].

When the intermediate lessor enters into the sublease, the intermediate lessor:

(a) derecognises the right-of-use asset relating to the head lease that it transfers to the sublessee and recognises the net investment in the sublease;

(b) recognises any difference between the right-of-use asset and the net investment in the sublease in profit or loss; and

(c) retains the lease liability relating to the head lease in its statement of financial position, which represents the lease payments owed to the head lessor.

During the term of the sublease, the intermediate lessor recognises both finance income on the sublease and interest expense on the head lease.

Example 10.6.1B

Sublease classified as an operating lease

[IFRS 16:IE8, Example 21]

Head lease – An intermediate lessor enters into a five-year lease for 5,000 square metres of office space (the head lease) with Entity A (the head lessor).

Sublease – At commencement of the head lease, the intermediate lessor subleases the 5,000 square metres of office space for two years to a sublessee.

The intermediate lessor classifies the sublease by reference to the right-of-use asset arising from the head lease. The intermediate lessor classifies the sublease as an operating lease, having considered the requirements in [IFRS 16:61 to 66].

When the intermediate lessor enters into the sublease, the intermediate lessor retains the lease liability and the right-of-use asset relating to the head lease in its statement of financial position.

During the term of the sublease, the intermediate lessor:

(a) recognises a depreciation charge for the right-of-use asset and interest on the lease liability; and

(b) recognises lease income from the sublease.

10.6.2   Subleases – presentation

IFRS 16 does not include requirements relating to the presentation of subleases. The IASB decided that specific requirements were not warranted because there is sufficient guidance in other Standards. In particular, applying the requirements for offsetting in IAS 1 *Presentation of Financial Statements* (see **2.8** in **chapter A4**), an intermediate lessor should not offset assets and liabilities arising from a head lease and a sublease of the same underlying asset, unless the financial instruments requirements for offsetting are met. The IASB considered whether to create an exception that would permit or require an intermediate lessor to offset assets and liabilities arising from a head lease and a sublease of the same underlying asset. However, the IASB noted that the exposures arising from those assets and liabilities are different from the exposures arising from a single net lease receivable or lease liability, and concluded that presenting these on a net basis could provide misleading information about an intermediate lessor's financial position, because it could obscure the existence of some transactions. [IFRS 16:BC235]

For the same reasons, the IASB also decided that an intermediate lessor should not offset lease income and lease expenses relating to a head lease and a sublease of the same underlying asset, unless the requirements for offsetting in IAS 1 are met. [IFRS 16:BC236]

11   Accounting by lessors

11.1   Accounting for finance leases by lessors

11.1.1   *Recognition and measurement at the commencement date – general*

11.1.1.1   *Recognition and measurement – general*

At the commencement date, a lessor should recognise assets held under a finance lease in its statement of financial position and present them as a receivable at an amount equal to the net investment in the lease. [IFRS 16:67]

Initially, the lessor will recognise a finance lease receivable under IFRS 16:67, at the amount equal to the net investment in the lease. Subsequently, finance income will be recognised at a constant rate on the net investment under IFRS 16:75 (see **11.1.3**). During any 'rent-free' period, this will result in the accrued finance income increasing the finance lease receivable.

11.1.1.2   *Net investment in the lease – definition*

The net investment in the lease is the gross investment in the lease discounted at the interest rate implicit in the lease. [IFRS 16:Appendix A] The gross investment in the lease is the sum of (1) lease payments receivable by the lessor under a finance lease, and (2) any unguaranteed residual value accruing to the lessor. [IFRS 16:Appendix A]

The interest rate implicit in the lease is the rate of interest that causes the present value of (a) the lease payments, and (b) the unguaranteed residual to equal to the sum of (i) the fair value of the underlying asset, and (ii) any initial direct costs of the lessor. [IFRS 16:Appendix A]

If the lessor grants any incentives to the lessee, such as an initial rent-free period, then, at the inception of the lease, the calculation of the lease payments and determination of the interest rate implicit in the lease will factor in nil payments by the lessee during such a rent-free period.

11.1.1.3 Initial direct costs

For lessors (other than a manufacturer or dealer lessor), initial direct costs are required to be included in the initial measurement of the net investment in the lease, and reduce the amount of income recognised over the lease term. The definition of the interest rate implicit in the lease set out at **11.1.1.2** results in such costs being included automatically in the finance lease receivable; there is no need to add them separately. [IFRS 16:69]

Initial direct costs are defined as the "[i]ncremental costs of obtaining a lease that would not have been incurred if the lease had not been obtained, except for such costs incurred by a manufacturer or dealer lessor in connection with a finance lease". [IFRS 16:Appendix A]

Under IAS 17, the definition of initial direct costs is "incremental costs that are directly attributable to negotiating and arranging a lease, except for such costs incurred by manufacturer or dealer lessors". The reason for changing the definition for initial direct costs in IFRS 16 is to be consistent with the definition of 'incremental costs of obtaining a contract' in IFRS 15 *Revenue from Contracts with Customers*, to ensure that costs incurred by a lessor to obtain a lease are accounted for consistently with costs incurred to obtain other contracts with customers. [IFRS 16:BC237] See **12.2** in **chapter A14** for further guidance drawn from IFRS 15, including an example illustrating the distinction between costs that are incremental and those that are not.

In the context of identifying initial direct costs, the key question is whether the costs under consideration would have been incurred irrespective of whether the lease was obtained. If the answer is 'yes', then the costs are not initial direct costs. Therefore, for example, the salaries of permanent staff employed to negotiate and arrange new leases are not initial direct costs because they will be incurred irrespective of whether the lease is obtained. In contrast, 'signing commissions' paid to employees when a specific lease is finalised, or commissions paid to agents for the introduction of interested parties who subsequently sign up as tenants, will qualify as initial direct costs and should be included in the initial measurement of the net investment in the lease. Other costs frequently identified as initial direct costs are legal and other professional fees associated with the arrangement and negotiation of a lease, although these should be carefully scrutinised to ensure that they are genuinely incremental (i.e. that they do not include, for example, any 'retainer' element or fees of a more general nature).

This interpretation of 'incremental' in this context has been considered and affirmed by the IFRS Interpretations Committee (see March 2014 *IFRIC Update*). Although the Committee were dealing with IAS 17 at that time, the same principles apply under IFRS 16. Although IFRS 16:BC65 identifies the definition of initial direct costs as an aspect in respect of which lessor accounting has changed under the new Standard, the change does not appear to be substantive.

Note that although the IFRS Interpretations Committee considered this issue specifically in the context of finance leases under IAS 17, the guidance applies equally to operating leases under that Standard and to both finance and operating leases under IFRS 16.

11.1.1.4 Initial measurement of the lease payments included in the net investment in the lease

At the commencement date, the lease payments included in the measurement of the net investment in the lease comprise the following payments for the right to use the underlying asset during the lease term that are not received at the commencement date:

[IFRS 16:70]

- fixed payments (including in-substance fixed payments as described in IFRS 16:B42 – see **7.3.2**), less any lease incentives payable;

- variable lease payments that depend on an index or a rate, initially measured using the index or rate as at the commencement date (see **7.5.2**);

- any residual value guarantees provided to the lessor by the lessee, a party related to the lessee or a third party unrelated to the lessor that is financially capable of discharging the obligations under the guarantee;

- the exercise price of a purchase option if the lessee is reasonably certain to exercise that option (assessed considering the factors described in IFRS 16:B37 – see **6.6**); and

- payments of penalties for terminating the lease, if the lease term reflects the lessee exercising an option to terminate the lease.

11.1.2 Recognition and measurement at the commencement date – manufacturer and dealer lessors

At the commencement date, a manufacturer or dealer lessor should recognise the following for each of its finance leases:

[IFRS 16:71]

- revenue, which is the fair value of the underlying asset, or, if lower, the present value of the lease payments accruing to the lessor, discounted using a market rate of interest;

- the cost of sale, which is the cost (or carrying amount if different) of the underlying asset less the present value of the unguaranteed residual value; and

- selling profit or loss (which is the difference between revenue and the cost of sale) in accordance with its policy for outright sales to which IFRS 15 *Revenue from Contracts with Customers* applies. The selling profit or loss on a finance lease should be recognised at the commencement date, regardless of whether the lessor transfers the underlying asset as described in IFRS 15.

Manufacturers or dealers often offer to customers the choice of either buying or leasing an asset. A finance lease of an asset by a manufacturer or dealer lessor gives rise to profit or loss equivalent to the profit or loss resulting from an outright sale of the underlying asset, at normal selling prices, reflecting any applicable volume or trade discounts. [IFRS 16:72]

Manufacturer or dealer lessors sometimes quote artificially low rates of interest in order to attract customers. The use of such a rate would result in a lessor recognising an excessive portion of the total income from the transaction at the commencement date. If artificially low rates of interest are quoted, the selling profit should be restricted to that which would apply if a market rate of interest were charged. [IFRS 16:73]

Costs incurred by a manufacturer or dealer lessor in connection with obtaining a finance lease should be recognised as an expense at the commencement date because they are mainly related to earning the manufacturer or dealer's selling profit. Such costs are excluded from the definition of initial direct costs (see **11.1.1.3**) and, accordingly, are excluded from the net investment in the lease. [IFRS 16:74]

11.1.3 Subsequent measurement

11.1.3.1 Finance lease income recognised at a constant periodic rate of return on the net investment

The lessor recognises finance income over the lease term so as to reflect a constant periodic rate of return on its net investment in the finance lease. [IFRS 16:75] This is achieved by allocating the rentals (net of any charges for services etc.) received by the lessor between finance income to the lessor and repayment of the debtor balance.

11.1.3.2 Derecognition and impairment

The derecognition and impairment requirements of IFRS 9 *Financial Instruments* (or, for entities that have not yet adopted IFRS 9, IAS 39 *Financial Instruments: Recognition and Measurement*) apply to a lessor's net investment in a lease. [IFRS 16:77]

11.1.3.3 Changes in unguaranteed residual values

IFRS 16 emphasises that estimated unguaranteed residual values used in computing the lessor's gross investment in a lease should be reviewed regularly. When there has been a reduction in the estimated unguaranteed residual value, the income allocation over the lease term is revised and any reduction in respect of amounts already accrued is recognised immediately. [IFRS 16:77]

Changes in the unguaranteed residual value of the underlying asset will only affect the finance lease receivable if the changes indicate impairment of the receivable and, subsequently, reversal of impairment.

IFRS 16:67 requires the lessor's net investment in the finance lease to be shown as a finance lease receivable. The net investment in the finance lease is equal to the unguaranteed residual value accruing to the lessor plus the lease payments receivable, discounted at the interest rate implicit in the lease. The subsequent measurement of the lease receivable is specified by IFRS 16 and by the derecognition and impairment requirements of IFRS 9 *Financial Instruments* (or, for entities that have not yet adopted IFRS 9, IAS 39 *Financial Instruments: Recognition and Measurement*). The recognition of finance income is based on a constant rate of return on the net investment. Finance income is recognised at the rate implicit in the lease on the total net investment including the unguaranteed residual value.

11.1.3.4 Asset under a finance lease classified as held for sale

When an asset under a finance lease is classified as held for sale (or included in a disposal group that is classified as held for sale) in accordance with IFRS 5 *Non-current Assets Held for Sale and Discontinued Operations*, it is accounted for in accordance with that Standard (see **chapter A20**). [IFRS 16:78]

11.1.4 Lease modifications

11.1.4.1 Modifications to finance leases accounted for as separate leases

A lessor should account for a modification to a finance lease as a separate lease if both:

[IFRS 16:79]

- the modification increases the scope of the lease by adding the right to use one or more underlying assets; and

- the consideration for the lease increases by an amount commensurate with the stand-alone price for the increase in scope and any appropriate adjustments to that stand-alone price to reflect the circumstances of the particular contract.

The IASB considers that a modification meeting both of the conditions in IFRS 16:79 in substance represents the creation of a new lease that is separate from the original lease. This requirement is substantially aligned with equivalent requirements in IFRS 15 *Revenue from Contracts with Customers* that require a seller to account for modifications that add distinct goods or services as separate contracts if those additional goods or services are priced commensurately with their stand-alone selling price (see **10.2** in **chapter A14**). [IFRS 16:BC238]

11.1.4.2 Modifications to finance leases not accounted for as separate leases

For a modification to a finance lease that is not accounted for as a separate lease, a lessor should account for the modification as follows:

[IFRS 16:80]

- if the lease would have been classified as an operating lease had the modification been in effect at the inception date, the lessor should:

  - account for the lease modification as a new lease from the effective date of the modification; and

  - measure the carrying amount of the underlying asset as the net investment in the lease immediately before the effective date of the lease modification;

- otherwise, the lessor should apply the requirements of IFRS 9 *Financial Instruments* (or, for entities that have not yet adopted IFRS 9, IAS 39 *Financial Instruments: Recognition and Measurement*).

For modifications to a finance lease that are *not* accounted for as a separate lease (i.e. modifications that do not meet both of the conditions set out in IFRS 16:79 (see **11.1.4.1**), IFRS 16 requires a lessor to account for the modification applying IFRS 9 (or, for entities that have not yet adopted IFRS 9, IAS 39) unless the lease would have been classified as an operating lease if the modification had been in effect at the inception date. The IASB expects that this approach will not result in any substantive change to previous lessor accounting for modifications of finance leases. This is because, although IAS 17 does not include requirements relating to lease modifications, the IASB understands that a lessor generally applies an approach that is consistent with the requirements in IFRS 9 (or the equivalent requirements in IAS 39) to the net investment in a finance lease. [IFRS 16:BC239]

11.2 Accounting for operating leases by lessors

11.2.1 Recognition of lease income

Lease payments from operating leases should be recognised as income on a straight-line basis unless another systematic basis is more representative of the pattern in which benefit from the use of the underlying asset is diminished. [IFRS 16:81]

IFRS 16:81 requires lease payments under an operating lease to be recognised as income on a straight-line basis over the lease term, unless another systematic basis is more representative of the pattern in which benefit from the use of the underlying asset is diminished. The question arises as to whether variable lease payments in an operating lease should be estimated at the inception date and recognised on a straight-line basis over the lease term.

IFRS 16:70 specifies that, for finance leases, the lease payments included in the measurement of the net investment in a lease at commencement date include variable lease payments that depend on an index or a rate; other variable payments (e.g. those linked to future performance or use of an underlying asset) are excluded from the measurement of the net investment and are instead recognised as income when they arise. The treatment adopted for variable lease payments under operating leases should be consistent with these requirements.

Therefore, variable lease payments under operating leases, other than those that are dependent on an index or a rate, should not be estimated and included in the total lease payments to be recognised on a straight-line basis over the lease term; instead, they should be recognised as income in the period in which they are earned.

In July 2006, in the context of IAS 17 *Leases*, the IFRIC (now the IFRS Interpretations Committee) considered whether an estimate of contingent rents payable (receivable) under an operating lease should be included in the total lease payments (lease income) to be recognised on a straight-line basis over the lease term. The IFRIC noted that, although the Standard is unclear on this issue, this has not, in general, led to contingent rents being included in the amount to be recognised on a straight-line basis over the lease term. Accordingly, the IFRIC decided not to add this issue to its agenda. This conclusion is equally valid under IFRS 16.

Some contracts provide for annual payments in an operating lease to increase by a fixed annual percentage over the life of the lease. It is sometimes suggested that, if such increases are intended to compensate for expected annual inflation over the lease period, it may be acceptable to recognise them in each accounting period as they arise.

Such a treatment is not appropriate. The lease payments should be recognised on a straight-line basis over the lease term unless another systematic basis is more representative of the time pattern of the user's benefit.

This was confirmed by the IFRIC (now the IFRS Interpretations Committee) in the November 2005 *IFRIC Update* in the context of IAS 17; the conclusion is equally valid under IFRS 16.

11.2.2   Costs incurred in earning lease income

Costs incurred in earning the lease income, including depreciation, are recognised as an expense. [IFRS 16:82]

11.2.3   Initial direct costs

When initial direct costs are incurred by lessors in obtaining an operating lease, these should be added to the carrying amount of the underlying asset and recognised as an expense over the lease term on the same basis as the lease income. [IFRS 16:83]

See **11.1.1.3** for further discussion on the nature of initial direct costs.

11.2.4   Depreciation of assets subject to operating leases

The depreciation of leased assets should be on a basis consistent with the lessor's normal depreciation policy for similar assets, and the depreciation expense should be calculated on the basis set out in IAS 16 *Property, Plant and Equipment* or IAS 38 *Intangible Assets*, as appropriate (see **chapters A7** and **A9**, respectively). [IFRS 16:84]

A problem of income and cost matching may arise when a lessor arranges specific finance for the purchase of an asset that is leased under an operating lease. When the finance is repaid from cash generated by rental receipts, the application of the previous paragraphs will result in:

- rental income recognised on a straight-line basis;

- depreciation expense recognised, say, on a straight-line basis; and

- finance costs front-end loaded because they will be charged as a constant percentage of capital outstanding.

The effect may be that the three items taken together show a loss in earlier years, and a profit in later years. It is sometimes argued that one way to address this issue is to view the leased asset as having some of the attributes of a financial asset. A method of depreciation that would be consistent with viewing the asset as having attributes of a financial asset is one which reflects the time value of money, for example the annuity method. This would result in a lower depreciation charge in earlier years and a more constant net profit after interest.

However, use of the annuity method of depreciation is not permitted. IFRS 16:84 states that the lessor should apply its normal depreciation policy for similar assets and the depreciation expense should be calculated on the basis set out in IAS 16. IAS 16:60 states that the depreciation method used should reflect the pattern in which the asset's future economic benefits are expected to be consumed. The method should be based on the economic depreciation of the asset, not on the return from the asset. Therefore, the consideration of the time value of money in the depreciation calculation is not permitted.

11.2.5   Impairment of assets subject to operating leases

IAS 36 *Impairment of Assets* should be applied to determine whether an underlying asset subject to an operating lease is impaired and to account for any impairment loss identified (see **chapter A10**). [IFRS 16:85]

11.2.6   Accounting by manufacturer and dealer lessors

A manufacturer or dealer lessor should not recognise any selling profit on entering into an operating lease because it is not the equivalent of a sale. [IFRS 16:86]

11.2.7   Assets cease to be rented and become held for sale

Entities that, in the course of their ordinary activities, routinely sell items that they have held for rental to others are required to transfer those assets to inventories at their carrying amount when they cease to be rented and become held for sale. This is discussed further at **9.3** in **chapter A7**.

11.2.8   Modifications to operating leases

A lessor should account for a modification to an operating lease as a new lease from the effective date of the modification, considering any prepaid or accrued lease payments relating to the original lease as part of the lease payments for the new lease. [IFRS 16:87]

The approach set out in IFRS 16:87 is consistent with the approach required by IFRS 15 if, at the time of a contract modification (that is accounted for as a separate contract), the remaining goods or services to be transferred are distinct from the goods or services already transferred. It is also expected that this approach will not result in any substantive change to previous lessor accounting. [IFRS 16:BC240]

11.2.9   Presentation of assets subject to operating leases

Lessors should present assets subject to operating leases in their statements of financial position according to the nature of the underlying asset. [IFRS 16:88]

12 Disclosure – lessors

12.1 Disclosure – general objective

The objective of the disclosure requirements for lessors is for lessors to disclose information in the notes that, together with the information provided in the statement of financial position, statement of profit or loss and statement of cash flows, gives a basis for users of financial statements to assess the effect that leases have on the financial position, financial performance and cash flows of the lessor. IFRS 16:90 to 97 (see **12.2** to **12.4**) specify requirements designed to meet this objective. [IFRS 16:89]

> The lessor disclosure requirements in IFRS 16 are more extensive than those in IAS 17 to enable users of financial statements to better evaluate the amount, timing and uncertainty of cash flows arising from a lessor's leasing activities. The disclosure requirements have been expanded to address the perception that the lessor accounting model in IAS 17 does not provide sufficient information relating to all elements of a lessor's leasing activities. [IFRS 16:BC251] See IFRS 16:BC252 to BC259 for an explanation of the rationale behind the most significant additional requirements.

12.2 Disclosures – finance leases

The following amounts should be disclosed for the reporting period for finance leases:

[IFRS 16:90(a)]

- selling profit or loss;

- finance income on the net investment in the lease; and

- income relating to variable lease payments not included in the measurement of the net investment in the lease.

These disclosures should be presented in a tabular format, unless another format is more appropriate. [IFRS 16:91]

A lessor should also:

[IFRS 16:93 & 94]

- provide a qualitative and quantitative explanation of the significant changes in the carrying amount of the net investment in finance leases;

- disclose a maturity analysis of the lease payments receivable, showing the undiscounted lease payments to be received on an annual basis for a minimum of each of the first five years and a total of the amounts for the remaining years; and

- reconcile the undiscounted lease payments to the net investment in the lease. This reconciliation should identify the unearned finance income relating to the lease payments receivable and any discounted unguaranteed residual value.

12.3   Disclosures – operating leases

For operating leases, a lessor should disclose its lease income for the reporting period, separately disclosing income relating to variable lease payments that do not depend on an index or a rate. [IFRS 16:90(b)]

These disclosures should be presented in a tabular format, unless another format is more appropriate. [IFRS 16:91]

For items of property, plant and equipment subject to an operating lease, a lessor should apply the disclosure requirements of IAS 16 *Property, Plant and Equipment*. For this purpose, each class of property, plant and equipment should be segregated into assets subject to operating leases and assets not subject to operating leases (i.e. the disclosures required by IAS 16 should be provided separately for assets subject to an operating lease (by class of underlying asset) and owned assets held and used by the lessor. [IFRS 16:95]

The disclosure requirements in IAS 36 *Impairment of Assets*, IAS 38 *Intangible Assets*, IAS 40 *Investment Property* and IAS 41 *Agriculture* should be applied for assets subject to operating leases. [IFRS 16:96]

A lessor should disclose a maturity analysis of lease payments, showing the undiscounted lease payments to be received on an annual basis for a minimum of each of the first five years and a total of the amounts for the remaining years. [IFRS 16:97]

12.4   Additional qualitative and quantitative information

A lessor should disclose additional qualitative and quantitative information about its leasing activities necessary to meet the disclosure objective in IFRS 16:89 (see **12.1**). This additional information includes, but is not limited to, information that helps users of financial statements to assess:

[IFRS 16:92]

- the nature of the lessor's leasing activities; and
- how the lessor manages the risk associated with any rights it retains in underlying assets. In particular, a lessor should disclose its risk management strategy for the rights it retains in underlying assets, including any means by which the lessor reduces that risk. Such means may include, for example, buy-back agreements, residual value guarantees or variable lease payments for use in excess of specified limits.

13   Sale and leaseback transactions

13.1   Sale and leaseback transactions – general

If an entity (the seller-lessee) transfers an asset to another entity (the buyer-lessor) and leases that asset back from the buyer-lessor, both the seller-lessee and the buyer-lessor are required to account for the transfer contract and the lease by applying IFRS 16:99 to 103 (see **13.2** to **13.4**). [IFRS 16:98]

> In considering whether a transaction should be accounted for as a sale and leaseback transaction, an entity should consider not only those transactions structured in the form of a legal sale and leaseback, but should also consider other forms of transactions for which the economic effect is the same as a legal sale and leaseback (e.g. a sale and leaseback transaction may be structured in the form of a lease and leaseback). [IFRS 16:BC261]

13.2   Assessing whether the transfer of the asset is a sale

An entity should apply the requirements for determining when a performance obligation is satisfied in IFRS 15 *Revenue from Contracts with Customers* (see **9.1** in **chapter A14**) to determine whether the transfer of an asset is accounted for as a sale of that asset. [IFRS 16:99]

> IFRS 16 provides no additional application guidance regarding the determination as to whether there is a sale in a sale and leaseback transaction (i.e. regarding how to apply the IFRS 15 requirements relating to the satisfaction of performance obligations to sale and leaseback transactions). This is because the IASB considers that the principles in IFRS 15 can be applied appropriately and consistently to sale and leaseback transactions without any further guidance. [IFRS 16:BC264]
>
> Applying the guidance in IFRS 15, the transfer of an asset is accounted for as a sale when the buyer-lessor obtains control of the asset. In the context of sale and leaseback transactions, it can generally be assumed that the relevant requirements are IFRS 15's requirements regarding satisfaction of a performance obligation 'at a point in time' (as opposed to 'over time') (see guidance in IFRS 15:31 to 34 (**9.1** in **chapter A14**) and indicators of the transfer of control in IFRS 15.38 (**9.4** in **chapter A14**)).

13.3   Transfer of the asset is a sale

13.3.1   Transfer of the asset is a sale at fair value – general requirements

If the transfer of an asset by the seller-lessee satisfies the requirements of IFRS 15 to be accounted for as a sale of the asset:

[IFRS 16:100]

- the seller-lessee should measure the right-of-use asset arising from the leaseback at the proportion of the previous carrying amount of the asset that relates to the right of use retained by the seller-lessee. Accordingly, the seller-lessee should recognise only the amount of any gain or loss that relates to the rights transferred to the buyer-lessor; and

- the buyer-lessor should account for the purchase of the asset applying applicable IFRSs, and for the lease applying the lessor accounting requirements in IFRS 16.

Example 13.3.1

Sale and leaseback – transfer is a sale at fair value and leaseback is a finance lease from lessor's perspective

Entity A holds a ship in its statement of financial position at a carrying amount of CU8,000. Entity A enters into a contract to dispose of the ship to Entity B for its fair value of CU13,000. At the same time, Entity A enters into a contract to lease the ship back from Entity B for 20 years, with annual payments of CU900 payable in advance each year. The interest rate implicit in the lease is 5 per cent, resulting in a net present value for the annual lease payments of CU11,777. The lease payments are considered to be at market terms. The transfer of the ship to Entity B is determined to satisfy the requirements in IFRS 15 to be accounted for as a sale.

Accounting by Entity A (seller-lessee)

Entity A recognises the disposal of the underlying asset (the ship) and the acquisition of a right-of-use asset (the right to use the ship for the lease term).

The right-of-use asset recognised by Entity A is the proportion of the previous carrying amount that relates to the right-of-use retained. This proportion is calculated as follows.

$$\frac{\text{CU11,777 (the discounted lease payments for the 20-year right-of-use asset)}}{\text{CU13,000 (the fair value of the ship)}} = 0.906$$

Therefore, the right-of-use asset is calculated as CU7,248 (CU8,000 (the previous carrying amount of the ship) × 0.906).

The total gain on sale of the ship to Entity B is CU5,000 (sale price of CU13,000 – carrying amount of CU8,000), of which:

- CU4,529 (0.906 × CU5,000) relates to the right-of-use asset retained by the seller-lessee; and
- CU471 (the balance) relates to the rights transferred to the buyer-lessor. The gain recognised by Entity A is restricted to this amount.

Therefore, the journal entry recorded by Entity A for the sale of the ship and the subsequent leaseback is as follows.

		CU	CU
Dr	Cash	13,000	
Cr	Ship		8,000
Dr	Right-of-use asset (ship)	7,248	
Cr	Lease liability		11,777
Cr	Gain on disposal (profit or loss)		471

The right-of-use asset and lease liability are accounted for subsequent to initial recognition in accordance with the requirements set out in **section 8**.

Accounting by Entity B (buyer-lessor)

Assuming that the leaseback is classified as a finance lease from the lessor's perspective, Entity B recognises the lease receivable at an amount equal to its net investment in the lease.

Therefore, the journal entries recorded by Entity B are as follows.

		CU	CU
Dr	Ship	13,000	
Cr	Cash		13,000

To recognise the purchase of the ship.

		CU	CU
Dr	Finance lease receivable*	13,000	
Cr	Ship		13,000

To derecognise the ship under the finance lease recognise the lease receivable.

* The finance lease receivable represents Entity B's net investment in the lease, being the present value of the lease payments of CU11,777 and an assumed estimated residual value (unguaranteed) of CU1,223.

Entity B's net investment in the lease is accounted for subsequent to initial recognition in accordance with the requirements set out in **11.1**.

Example 13.3.1 illustrates that the gain recognised by the seller-lessee in a sale and leaseback transaction is restricted by reference to the proportion of the asset that has been transferred to the buyer-lessor.

It is worth contrasting the accounting outcome for the seller-lessee with the previous requirements under IAS 17.

- If the transaction gave rise to a finance leaseback, no gain or loss would have been recognised. Under IAS 17, the substance of the transaction was considered to be that no disposal of the asset had taken place – both before and after the transaction, the underlying asset (i.e. the ship) was recognised in the statement of financial position of the seller-lessee. In contrast, under IFRS 16, the accounting recognises the sale of the underlying asset and its replacement by a 'right-of-use' asset (i.e. the right to use the underlying asset for the period of the lease), and any gain or loss arising is recognised to the extent that there has been a substantive transfer of economic benefits to the buyer-lessor.

- If the transaction gave rise to an operating leaseback, and the sale price was considered to represent fair value, the gain or loss arising would have been recognised in full. Under IAS 17, the substance of the transaction was considered to be that the seller-lessee had disposed of its entire interest in the underlying asset. In contrast, under IFRS 16, most leases will be considered to give rise to a right-of-use asset for the seller-lessee. As a result, any gain or loss will be restricted due to the fact that the seller-lessee retains an interest in the asset.

13.3.2 Transactions other than at market terms

If either (1) the fair value of the consideration for the sale of an asset does not equal the fair value of the asset, or (2) the payments for the lease are not at market rates, the following adjustments are required to measure the sale proceeds at fair value:

[IFRS 16:101]

- any below-market terms should be accounted for as a prepayment of lease payments; and

- any above-market terms should be accounted for as additional financing provided by the buyer-lessor to the seller-lessee.

The entity should measure any potential adjustment required by IFRS 16:101 (see above) on the basis of the more readily determinable of:

[IFRS 16:102]

- the difference between the fair value of the consideration for the sale and the fair value of the asset; and

- the difference between the present value of the contractual payments for the lease and the present value of payments for the lease at market rates.

The following example, reproduced from the illustrative examples accompanying IFRS 16, illustrates the application for the requirements in IFRS 16:99 to 102 for a seller-lessee and a buyer-lessor when the sales proceeds exceed the fair value of the underlying asset.

Example 13.3.2

Sale and leaseback transaction

[IFRS 16:IE11, Example 24]

An entity (Seller-lessee) sells a building to another entity (Buyer-lessor) for cash of CU2,000,000. Immediately before the transaction, the building is carried at a cost of CU1,000,000. At the same time, Seller-lessee enters into a contract with Buyer-lessor for the right to use the building for 18 years, with annual payments of CU120,000 payable at the end of each year. The terms and conditions of the transaction are such that the transfer of the building by Seller-lessee satisfies the requirements for determining when a performance obligation is satisfied in IFRS 15 Revenue from Contracts with Customers. *Accordingly, Seller-lessee and Buyer-lessor account for the transaction as a sale and leaseback. This example ignores any initial direct costs.*

The fair value of the building at the date of sale is CU1,800,000. Because the consideration for the sale of the building is not at fair value, Seller-lessee and Buyer-lessor make adjustments to measure the sale proceeds at fair value. The amount of the excess sale price of CU200,000 (CU2,000,000 – CU1,800,000) is recognised as additional financing provided by Buyer-lessor to Seller-lessee.

The interest rate implicit in the lease is 4.5 per cent per annum, which is readily determinable by Seller-lessee. The present value of the annual payments (18 payments of CU120,000, discounted at 4.5 per cent per annum) amounts to CU1,459,200, of which CU200,000 relates to the additional financing and CU1,259,200 relates to the lease – corresponding to 18 annual payments of CU16,447 and CU103,553, respectively.

Buyer-lessor classifies the lease of the building as an operating lease.

Seller-lessee

At the commencement date, Seller-lessee measures the right-of-use asset arising from the leaseback of the building at the proportion of the previous carrying amount of the building that relates to the right of use retained by Seller-lessee, which is CU699,555. This is calculated as: CU1,000,000 (the carrying amount of the building) ÷ CU1,800,000 (the fair value of the building) × CU1,259,200 (the discounted lease payments for the 18-year right-of-use asset).

Seller-lessee recognises only the amount of the gain that relates to the rights transferred to Buyer-lessor of CU240,355 calculated as follows. The gain on sale of building amounts to CU800,000 (CU1,800,000 – CU1,000,000), of which:

(a) CU559,645 (CU800,000 ÷ CU1,800,000 × CU1,259,200) relates to the right to use the building retained by Seller-lessee; and

(b) CU240,355 (CU800,000 ÷ CU1,800,000 × (CU1,800,000 – CU1,259,200)) relates to the rights transferred to Buyer-lessor.

At the commencement date, Seller-lessee accounts for the transaction as follows.

Cash	CU2,000,000	
Right-of-use asset	CU699,555	
Building		CU1,000,000
Financial liability		CU1,459,200
Gain on rights transferred		CU240,355

Buyer-lessor

At the commencement date, Buyer-lessor accounts for the transaction as follows.

Building	CU1,800,000	
Financial asset (18 payments of CU16,447, discounted at 4.5 per cent per annum)	CU200,000	
Cash		CU2,000,000

After the commencement date, Buyer-lessor accounts for the lease by treating CU103,553 of the annual payments of CU120,000 as lease payments. The remaining CU16,447 of annual payments received from Seller-lessee are accounted for as (a) payments received to settle the financial asset of CU200,000 and (b) interest revenue.

13.4   Transfer of the asset is not a sale

If the transfer of an asset by the seller-lessee does not satisfy the requirements of IFRS 15 to be accounted for as a sale of the asset:

[IFRS 16:103]

- the seller-lessee should continue to recognise the transferred asset and should recognise a financial liability equal to the transfer proceeds. It should account for the financial liability applying IFRS 9 *Financial Instruments* (or, for entities that have not yet adopted IFRS 9, IAS 39 *Financial Instruments: Recognition and Measurement*); and

- the buyer-lessor should not recognise the transferred asset and should recognise a financial asset equal to the transfer proceeds. It should account for the financial asset applying IFRS 9 (or, for entities that have not yet adopted IFRS 9, IAS 39).

A sale may not have occurred, for example, if the seller-lessee has a substantive repurchase option with respect to the underlying asset. IFRS 16:BC262(c) refers to the fact that, under IFRS 15, if an entity has a right to repurchase an asset, the customer does not obtain control of the asset, because the customer is limited in its ability to direct the use of, and obtain substantially all of the remaining benefits from the asset, even though the customer may have physical possession of the asset.

In such circumstances, no sale is recognised by the seller-lessee and no purchase is recognised by the buyer-lessor. Instead, the seller-lessee and buyer-lessor are required to account for any amounts received or paid relating to the leaseback as a financial asset or a financial liability applying IFRS 9 (or IAS 39). This is because such a transaction represents, in substance, a financing arrangement. [IFRS 16:BC265]

14   Effective date and transition

14.1   Effective date

IFRS 16 is required to be adopted for annual reporting periods beginning on or after 1 January 2019. An entity is permitted to apply IFRS 16 in advance of that date provided that it also:

[IFRS 16:C1]

- discloses that fact; and

- applies IFRS 15 *Revenue from Contracts with Customers* at or before the date of initial application of IFRS 16.

The 'date of initial application' is the beginning of the annual reporting period in which an entity first applies IFRS 16. [IFRS 16:C2]

Therefore, for example, for an entity adopting IFRS 16 for the first time in the year beginning 1 January 2019, the date of initial application is 1 January 2019 irrespective of whether the Standard is applied with full retrospective effect (see **14.5**).

14.2   Transition – overview

The IASB is conscious of the significant costs that entities could incur on transition to IFRS 16. The Standard includes a number of transition reliefs and practical expedients designed to allow an entity to minimise those costs without significantly compromising the quality of the financial information reported.

Both lessees and lessors are permitted to grandfather assessments regarding whether a contract existing at the date of initial application contains a lease (see **14.3**). If an entity decides not to use this practical expedient, it may incur significant costs in re-examining all of its contracts to determine if they contain a lease.

For lessors, apart from one specific exception in respect of subleases, no adjustments are required on transition from IAS 17 to IFRS 16 because lessor accounting under IFRS 16 is largely consistent with the requirements of IAS 17 (see **14.4**).

The situation is more complex for lessees, who need to focus on a number of key decisions. The most significant choices available to a lessee on transition (i.e. in addition to the choice regarding whether it will reassess its contracts, as discussed at **14.3**) are set out below.

| 1. | Whether to apply IFRS 16 to all of its leases retrospectively in accordance with IAS 8 *Accounting Policies, Changes in Accounting Estimates and Errors* or using the cumulative catch-up approach. | • If the lessee opts for full retrospective application, all of its leases (both finance and operating under IAS 17) will be required to be restated in accordance with IFRS 16. No further reliefs are available. See **14.5** for further discussion.

• If the lessee opts for the cumulative catch-up approach, it does not restate amounts previously reported and it applies specific rules for measuring right-of-use assets and lease liabilities (see **14.6.2** for leases previously identified as finance leases and **14.6.3** for leases previously identified as operating leases). It also has the option to apply specific transition reliefs and practical expedients in respect of leases previously identified as operating leases (see following points and illustration at **14.7**). |
| 2. | Under the cumulative catch-up approach, whether to apply the practical expedient for leases previously classified as operating leases and ending within 12 months of the date of initial application. | On a lease-by-lease basis, the practical expedient permits such leases to be accounted for as short-term leases, irrespective of whether the original lease term was for more than 12 months (see **14.6.3.2**). |

3.	Under the cumulative catch-up approach, whether (on initial recognition) to apply the practical expedients permitted in respect of the measurement of lease liabilities arising from leases previously classified as operating leases.	On a lease-by-lease basis, an entity can choose to: • apply a single discount rate to a portfolio of leases with reasonably similar characteristics; and/or • use hindsight, such as in determining the lease term if the contract contains options to extend or terminate the lease. See **14.6.3.4** for details.
4.	Under the cumulative catch-up approach, whether (on initial recognition) to apply the practical expedients permitted in respect of the measurement of right-of-use assets arising from leases previously classified as operating leases.	On a lease-by-lease basis, an entity can choose to: • adjust the right-of-use asset by the amount of any provision for onerous leases recognised under IAS 37 so as to approximate impairment; and/or • exclude initial direct costs from the measurement of the right-of-use asset. See **14.6.3.7** for details.

IFRS 16 also specifies disclosure requirements for lessees applying the cumulative catch-up approach (see **14.6.3.8**), requirements for sale and leaseback transactions (see **14.8**) and requirements for assets or liabilities previously recognised by a lessee in a business combination relating to favourable or unfavourable terms of an operating lease (see **14.9**).

14.3 Transition – definition of a lease (both lessees and lessors)

As a practical expedient, an entity is not required to reassess whether a contract is, or contains, a lease at the date of initial application. Instead, the entity is permitted:

[IFRS 16:C3]

• to apply IFRS 16 to contracts that were previously identified as leases applying IAS 17 *Leases* and IFRIC 4 *Determining whether an Arrangement contains a Lease*. The entity should apply the transition requirements in IFRS 16:C5 to C18 (see **14.4** to **14.8**) to those leases; and

• not to apply IFRS 16 to contracts that were not previously identified as containing a lease applying IAS 17 and IFRIC 4.

If an entity chooses to apply this practical expedient, it is required to:

[IFRS 16:C4]

- disclose that fact;

- apply the practical expedient to all of its contracts; and

- consequently, apply IFRS 16's requirements regarding the identification of leases (see **section 4**) only to contracts entered into (or modified) on or after the date of initial application.

This relief applies for both lessees and lessors. It permits an entity to retain its existing assessment as to whether a contract contains a lease for all ongoing contracts entered into before the date of transition. The entity assumes that existing leases continue to be leases under IFRS 16 and existing service contracts continue to be service contracts – it is only required to apply the IFRS 16 definition of a lease to contracts entered into on or after the date of transition. The IASB has allowed this practical expedient so that entities are not required to incur the costs of detailed reassessments when it is expected that the determination will not change for the vast majority of contracts.

If the practical expedient is applied, it is required to be applied to all of the entity's contracts – no 'cherry-picking' is permitted.

If an entity does not apply this expedient, it is required to examine all of its contracts in the context of IFRS 16 to determine whether they contain a lease. This may be a costly exercise and entities will need to consider whether the benefits of identifying potential differences in assessment under IFRS 16 justify the cost. The IASB's view is that, although IFRS 16 contains more detailed guidance on the identification of a lease, there are not many contracts where the lease *versus* service contract assessment will differ under the new Standard (but see **1.2.1.1**).

Whether this practical expedient is applied or not does not restrict a lessee's ability to choose between retrospective application of IFRS 16 or the cumulative catch-up approach (see **14.5**).

14.4 Transition for lessors

Except as described in IFRS 16:C15 (see below), a lessor is not required to make any adjustments on transition for leases in which it is a lessor and should account for those leases applying IFRS 16 from the date of initial application. [IFRS 16:C14]

As described in **section 11**, the accounting requirements for lessors under IFRS 16 are substantially unchanged from those in IAS 17.

Consequently, a lessor is not generally required to make any adjustments on transition to IFRS 16.

An intermediate lessor should:

[IFRS 16:C15]

- reassess subleases that were previously classified as operating leases and are ongoing at the date of initial application, to determine whether each sublease should be classified as an operating lease or a finance lease applying IFRS 16. The intermediate lessor should perform this assessment at the date of initial application on the basis of the remaining contractual terms and conditions of the head lease and sublease at that date; and

- for subleases that are classified as operating leases under IAS 17, but finance leases under IFRS 16, account for the sublease as a new finance lease entered into at the date of initial application.

IFRS 16 requires an intermediate lessor to evaluate the classification of a sublease by reference to the right-of-use asset arising from the head lease and not by reference to the underlying asset as is required under IAS 17. As a result, in some cases, subleases that are classified by an intermediate lessor as operating leases applying IAS 17 may be classified as finance leases applying IFRS 16. If an intermediate lessor were to continue to apply previous operating lease accounting to such subleases, it would recognise the right-of-use asset arising from the head lease, despite the fact that, in effect, it no longer has a right to use the underlying asset. To avoid this misleading outcome, IFRS 16:C15 requires an intermediate lessor to reassess a sublease that is classified as an operating lease applying IAS 17 at the date of initial application to determine whether the sublease should be classified as an operating lease or a finance lease applying IFRS 16, and to account for it accordingly. [IFRS 16:BC289 - BC291]

14.5 Transition for lessees – choice between full retrospective application and 'cumulative catch-up approach'

A lessee can choose to apply IFRS 16 to its leases either:

[IFRS 16:C5]

(a) retrospectively to each prior reporting period presented, applying IAS 8 *Accounting Policies, Changes in Accounting Estimates and Errors* (see below); or

(b) using the cumulative catch-up approach – under which the Standard is applied retrospectively with the cumulative effect recognised at the date of initial application in accordance with IFRS 16:C7 to C13 (see **14.6**).

Whichever option is selected under IFRS 16:C5 should be applied consistently to all leases in which the entity is a lessee. [IFRS 16:C6]

If a lessee chooses under IFRS 16:C5 to apply IFRS 16 retrospectively in accordance with IAS 8, it is required to apply the requirements of that Standard in full to all of its leases. This means that it is required to:

- prepare its financial statements as if IFRS 16 had always been applied;

- restate comparative information for all periods presented, potentially requiring a third statement of financial position; and

- disclose the effect of applying IFRS 16 on a line-by-line basis.

Under the general requirements for retrospective application in IAS 8, an entity is required to adjust the opening balances in the earliest period presented for the cumulative effect of applying IFRS 16 up to that date. Therefore, if an entity applies IFRS 16 for the first time in an annual period beginning 1 January 2019, and it presents one year of comparative information, it is required to determine and recognise the cumulative effect of applying the new Standard at 1 January 2018 and also to restate the amounts reported for the year ended 31 December 2018, which will originally have been reported under IAS 17. In accordance with the requirements of IAS 1 *Presentation of Financial Statements* (see **2.10.4** in **chapter A4**), this will potentially require inclusion of a third statement of financial position. This means that the entity will need to run parallel systems for 2018 in order to capture the required information, which is likely to be very costly. It is for this reason that the IASB decided to permit the cumulative catch-up approach (see **14.6**).

Lessees opting for full retrospective application are not permitted to take advantage of any of the reliefs described in **14.6** (so, for example, right-of-use assets and lease liabilities must be measured in accordance with the general requirements described in **8.4** and **8.5**). However, such entities are permitted to 'grandfather' assessments made under IAS 17 and IFRIC 4 regarding whether a contract contains a lease (i.e. they are permitted to apply the practical expedient described in **14.3**).

14.6   Transition for lessees – the cumulative catch-up approach

14.6.1   Cumulative catch-up approach – general

Rather than apply IFRS 16 retrospectively in accordance with IAS 8, lessees are permitted to apply IFRS 16:C5(b) under which comparative information is not restated. If this approach is selected, the lessee recognises the cumulative effect of initially applying IFRS 16 as an adjustment to the opening balance of retained earnings (or other component of equity, as appropriate) at the date of initial application. [IFRS 16:C7]

If a lessee opts to use the cumulative catch-up approach:

- it recognises the cumulative effect of initial application at the date of initial application (i.e. if an entity applies IFRS 16 for the first time in an accounting period beginning 1 January 2019, it recognises the cumulative effect of application by adjusting balances at 1 January 2019);

- it does not restate comparative information – if there is a difference between the assets and liabilities introduced then an adjustment is made to opening retained earnings;

- it carries forward amounts previously recognised in respect of leases classified as finance leases (see **14.6.2**);

- it is permitted to apply a number of additional transition reliefs and practical expedients for leases previously classified as operating leases (see **14.6.3**); and

- it is required to disclose the effect of applying the cumulative catch-up approach (see **14.6.3.8**).

Importantly, the lessee is not required to run parallel systems at any point; information in comparative periods is reported on an IAS 17 basis and reporting moves to the IFRS 16 basis on the first day of the first accounting period in which the new Standard is applied.

14.6.2   *Cumulative catch-up approach – leases previously classified as finance leases*

For lessees applying the cumulative catch-up approach, for leases that were previously classified as finance leases, the carrying amounts of the right-of-use asset and the lease liability at the date of initial application are the carrying amounts of the lease asset and lease liability immediately before that date measured applying IAS 17. IFRS 16 is applied to such right-of-use assets and lease liabilities from the date of initial application. [IFRS 16:C11]

Note that the treatment set out in IFRS 16:C11 for finance lease assets and liabilities is mandatory – unless a lessee has opted for full retrospective application of IFRS 16 (see **14.5**), it is not permitted to restate such assets and liabilities on transition to IFRS 16.

The lessee accounting model in IFRS 16 is similar to the accounting requirements for finance leases in IAS 17. The availability of the practical expedient in IFRS 16:C3 to avoid reassessing whether a contract contains a lease (see **14.3**) and the requirement to carry forward balances previously recognised under IAS 17 as set out in IFRS 16:C11 mean that lessees in finance leases are unlikely to encounter significant issues on transition.

14.6.3 Cumulative catch-up approach – leases previously classified as operating leases

14.6.3.1 Leases of low-value assets

The recognition exemption available to lessees under IFRS 16 in respect of leases of low-value assets is discussed in detail at **8.2**. In making its assessment regarding the effect of transition, a lessee will need to determine the extent to which it will use this exemption (the choice is available on a lease-by-lease basis). To the extent that the recognition exemption is selected, no adjustments are required on transition for leases previously classified as operating leases. The requirements of IFRS 16 should be applied from the date of initial application. [IFRS 16:C9(a)]

14.6.3.2 Leases ending within 12 months of the date of initial application – practical expedient

As a practical expedient, available on a lease-by-lease basis, lessees applying the cumulative catch-up approach are permitted not to recognise right-of-use assets or lease liabilities in respect of leases previously classified as operating leases for which the lease term ends within 12 months of the date of initial application. When this option is taken, the lessee:

[IFRS 16:C10(c)]

- accounts for such leases in the same way as short-term leases as described in IFRS 16:6 (see **8.2**); and

- includes the cost associated with those leases within the disclosure of short-term lease expense (see **9.2.4**) in the annual reporting period that includes the date of initial application.

This additional relief is a pragmatic measure introduced to allow lessees to avoid incurring costs for little benefit. The relief effectively extends the short-term recognition exemption generally available for lease terms of 12 months or less to lease terms expected to end within 12 months of the date of initial application irrespective of when the lease term commenced. On a lease-by-lease basis, a lessee can choose to continue to account for such leases as it does under IAS 17.

Note that, if this relief is taken, so that the expense in relation to such leases is included in the amount disclosed for the short-term lease expense under IFRS 16:53(c) (see **9.2.4**), this may trigger the disclosure requirement in IFRS 16:55 (see **9.2.5**).

14.6.3.3 Recognition and measurement of lease liabilities

Lessees applying the cumulative catch-up approach are required to recognise a lease liability at the date of initial application in respect of leases previously classified as operating leases. The lease liability should be measured at the present value of the remaining lease payments, discounted using the lessee's incremental borrowing rate at the date of initial application. [IFRS 16:C8(a)]

When applying the cumulative catch-up approach for leases previously classified as operating leases, therefore, the lessee:

- ignores lease payments already made. The lease liability is measured by reference to the lease payments for the remainder of the lease term; and

- Ignores any information it has regarding the interest rate implicit in individual leases or the lessee's incremental borrowing rate at the commencement of individual leases. The lessee's incremental borrowing rate at the date of initial application is not necessarily a single discount rate; it will vary among leases according to the term of the lease and the nature of the security held (see **8.4.2.2**). However, lessees are permitted to use a single rate for a portfolio of leases with reasonably similar characteristics (see **14.6.3.4**).

14.6.3.4 Lease liabilities for leases previously classified as operating leases – practical expedients

On a lease-by-lease basis, an entity can choose to use one or both of the following practical expedients in respect of the measurement of lease liabilities relating to leases previously classified as operating leases:

- apply a single discount rate to a portfolio of leases with reasonably similar characteristics (such as leases with a similar remaining lease term for a similar class of underlying asset in a similar economic environment); [IFRS 16:C10(a)] and/or

- use hindsight, such as in determining the lease term if the contract contains options to extend or terminate the lease. [IFRS 16:C10(e)]

For example, consider an entity that entered into a lease a number of years before the date of initial application of IFRS 16 and that determined at the commencement of the lease that it was not reasonably certain to exercise an extension option. If, at the date of initial application, the entity has become reasonably certain to exercise the extension option, under IFRS 16:C10(e) it is permitted to measure the lease liability based on its assessment at the date of initial application (i.e. it is not required to reconstruct the accounting on the basis of its original assessment).

14.6.3.5 Recognition and measurement of right-of-use assets

Lessees applying the cumulative catch-up approach are required to recognise a right-of-use asset at the date of initial application in respect of leases previously classified as operating leases. Such assets should be measured either:

[IFRS 16:C8(b)]

(i) retrospectively, as if IFRS 16 had been applied since the commencement date, but discounted using the lessee's incremental borrowing rate at the date of initial application; or

(ii) at an amount equal to the lease liability, adjusted by the amount of any prepaid or accrued lease payments relating to that lease recognised in the statement of financial position immediately before the date of initial application.

The selection of measurement basis for right-of-use assets under IFRS 16:8(b) is made on a lease-by-lease basis.

Entities are free to determine which measurement basis to apply to which leases. If a lessee elects retrospective measurement of a right-of-use asset under IFRS 16:C8(b)(i), it needs to have the necessary historical information to arrive at the carrying amount of the asset at the commencement of the lease and to calculate depreciation from that date, although it will use the incremental borrowing rate at the date of initial application. It may be costly to reconstruct such information. However, it is anticipated that entities will be willing to incur such costs for high-value items so as to avoid the recognition of higher lease-related costs in profit or loss in the years after transition (normally, because the lease liability falls more slowly under amortised cost accounting than the right-of-use asset, setting the asset equal to the liability part-way through the lease will mean that the carrying amount of the asset is higher than it would otherwise be, thus producing a higher depreciation expense post-transition). It is expected that lessees will generally apply IFRS 16:C8(b)(ii)) for high-volume low-value leases for which the costs of applying a more accurate transition approach outweigh the benefit of achieving a 'correct' post-transition income statement. [IFRS 16:BC283 - BC286]

IAS 36 *Impairment of Assets* should also be applied to right-of-use assets at the date of initial application, unless the lessee applies the practical expedient in IFRS 16:C10(b) (see **14.6.3.7**). [IFRS 16:C8(c)]

14.6.3.6 Specific requirements regarding investment property leases

Notwithstanding the requirements in IFRS 16:C8, as set out in **14.6.3.3** and **14.6.3.5**, for leases previously classified as operating leases, a lessee:

[IFRS 16:C9(b) & (c)]

- is not required to make any adjustments on transition for leases previously accounted for as investment property using the fair value model in IAS 40 *Investment Property*. The right-of-use asset and the lease liability arising from those leases should be accounted for under IAS 40 and IFRS 16 from the date of initial application; and

- is required to measure the right-of-use asset at fair value at the date of initial application for leases previously accounted for as operating leases and that will be accounted for as investment property using the fair value model in IAS 40 from the date of initial application. The lessee's right-of-use asset and the lease liability arising from those leases are required to be accounted for under IAS 40 and IFRS 16 from the date of initial application.

14.6.3.7 Right-of-use assets – practical expedients

On a lease-by-lease basis, an entity can choose to use one or both of the following practical expedients in respect of the measurement of right-of-use assets arising from leases previously classified as operating leases:

[IFRS 16:C10]

- rely on its assessment as to whether leases are onerous applying IAS 37 *Provisions, Contingent Liabilities and Contingent Assets* immediately before the date of initial application as an alternative to performing an impairment review. If a lessee chooses this practical expedient, it should adjust the right-of-use asset at the date of initial application by the amount of any provision for onerous leases recognised in the statement of financial position immediately before the date of initial application; and

> In accordance with IFRS 16:C8(c) (see **14.6.3.5**), lessees are required to consider whether right-of-use assets are impaired at the date of initial recognition. This practical expedient offers lessees a simplified approach based on the fact that if a right-of-use asset is impaired at the date of initial application, the equivalent operating lease will have been an onerous lease under IAS 37. IFRS 16 therefore permits a lessee to adjust the right-of-use asset on transition by the amount of any previously recognised onerous lease provision; this expedient is not expected to have a significant effect on reported information. [IFRS 16:BC287]

- exclude initial direct costs from the measurement of the right-of-use asset at the date of initial application.

> As discussed in **8.4.1.2**, initial direct costs are incremental costs that a lessee would not have incurred if it had not entered the lease contract. Such costs are generally included in the initial measurement of a right-of-use asset. This practical expedient permits a lessee to exclude such costs from right-of-use assets recognised for the first time when IFRS 16 is first applied; the choice is available on a lease-by-lease basis. It allows an entity to avoid the costs of identifying initial direct costs which may have been incurred several years previously.

14.6.3.8 Disclosure requirements for lessee's applying the cumulative catch-up approach

Lessees applying the cumulative catch-up approach are required to disclose information about initial application required by paragraph 28 of IAS 8 *Accounting Policies, Changes in Accounting Estimates and Errors* (see **3.4.1** in **chapter A5**) except for the information specified in paragraph 28(f) of IAS 8. Instead of the information specified in IAS 8:28(f), the lessee is required to disclose:

[IFRS 16:C12]

- the weighted average lessee's incremental borrowing rate applied to lease liabilities recognised in the statement of financial position at the date of initial application; and

- an explanation of any difference between:

  - operating lease commitments disclosed applying IAS 17 at the end of the annual reporting period immediately preceding the date of initial application, discounted using the incremental borrowing rate at the date of initial application as described in IFRS 16:C8(a) (see **14.6.3.3**); and

  - lease liabilities recognised in the statement of financial position at the date of initial application.

If a lessee uses one or more of the specified practical expedients in IFRS 16:C10 (see **14.6.3.2**, **14.6.3.4** and **14.6.3.7**), it is required to disclose that fact. [IFRS 16:C13]

14.7 Illustration of application of lessee transition options

The main choices available to lessees regarding how to transition to IFRS 16 and bring assets and liabilities on-balance sheet (as described in detail in **14.5** and **14.6**) are summarised in the following decision tree.

Options for lessees transitioning to IFRS 16

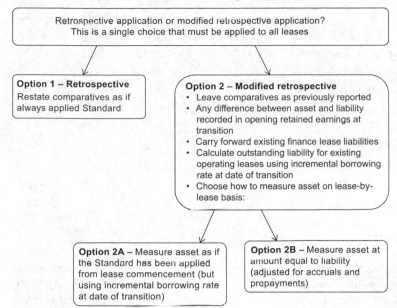

Applying these options to a simple example reveals the potential for differing impacts on the statement of financial position at transition and the subsequent expense recognised in the income statement.

Example facts:

- five-year lease, entered into on 1 January 2017;

- CU100 payable on second day of each year;

- 8 per cent discount rate on lease commencement;

- 12 per cent incremental borrowing rate at date of initial application (1 January 2019); and

- straight-line depreciation of the right- of-use asset is appropriate

Option 1

The liability and asset are both calculated as if IFRS 16 had always been applied, with comparative amounts restated. The liability on the commencement date of the lease is calculated as the present value of the future rentals, discounted using a rate of 8 per cent.

The impact on the statement of financial position as at the date of transition is a reduction in net assets of CU19 (asset of CU259 and liability of CU278), with an expense of CU281 recognised in profit or loss post-transition.

Date	Asset	Liability	Total expense
	CU	CU	CU
Lease commencement – 1 Jan 2017	431	431	
Year ended 31 Dec 2017	345	358	113
Year ended 31 Dec 2018	259	278	106
Amounts recognised at transition on 1 Jan 2019	259	278	
Year ended 31 Dec 2019	172	193	102
Year ended 31 Dec 2020	86	100	93
Year ended 31 Dec 2021	0	0	86
Total expense post-transition			281

Option 2A

Comparative amounts are not restated and the liability is calculated as the present value of the three outstanding rentals of CU100, discounted using the incremental borrowing rate at the date of transition of 12 per cent.

The asset is calculated as if IFRS 16 had always been applied, but using the incremental borrowing rate at the date of transition of 12 per cent.

Date	Asset	Liability	Total expense
	CU	CU	CU
Lease commencement – 1 Jan 2017	404		
Year ended 31 Dec 2017	323		
Year ended 31 Dec 2018	242		
Amounts recognised at transition on 1 Jan 2019	242	269	
Year ended 31 Dec 2019	161	189	101
Year ended 31 Dec 2020	81	100	92
Year ended 31 Dec 2021	0	0	81
Total expense post-transition			274

The impact on the statement of financial position as at the date of transition is a reduction in net assets of CU27 (asset of CU242 and liability of CU269), with an expense of CU274 recognised in profit or loss post-transition.

Option 2B

Comparative amounts are not restated and the liability is calculated as the present value of the three outstanding rentals of CU100, discounted using the incremental borrowing rate at the date of transition of 12 per cent. The asset is then set equal to the liability.

Date	Asset	Liability	Total expense
	CU	CU	CU
Amounts recognised at transition on 1 Jan 2019	269	269	
Year ended 31 Dec 2019	179	189	110
Year ended 31 Dec 2020	90	100	100
Year ended 31 Dec 2021	0	0	90
Total expense post-transition			300

The net impact on the statement of financial position as at the date of transition is nil (asset = liability) but the expense post-transition is CU300.

Comparison of transition options

Overall, it can be seen that in straightforward scenarios, Options 1 and 2A both reduce net assets on transition, although if the incremental borrowing rate at the date of transition is different to the discount rate the amount of the reduction will likely differ.

Option 2B leads to nil impact on net assets at transition but, because the asset is set higher than it otherwise would have been, the expense post-transition is higher than under Options 1 and 2A.

An advantage of Options 2A and 2B is that they don't require an entity to go back and determine what the discount rate would have been at lease commencement. For longer-term leases that began several years ago, this may result in significant time savings, albeit determining an incremental borrowing rate can still present its own challenges.

14.8 Sale and leaseback transactions before the date of initial application

An entity should not reassess sale and leaseback transactions entered into before the date of initial application to determine whether the transfer of the underlying asset satisfies the requirements in IFRS 15 *Revenue from Contracts with Customers* to be accounted for as a sale. [IFRS 16:C16]

If a sale and leaseback transaction was previously accounted for as a sale and a finance lease, the seller-lessee should:

[IFRS 16:C17]

- account for the leaseback in the same way as it accounts for any other finance lease that exists at the date of initial application; and

- continue to amortise any gain on sale over the lease term.

If a sale and leaseback transaction was accounted for as a sale and an operating lease under IAS 17, the seller-lessee should:

[IFRS 16:C18]

- account for the leaseback in the same way as it accounts for any other operating lease that exists at the date of initial application; and

- adjust the leaseback right-of-use asset for any deferred gains or losses that relate to off-market terms recognised in the statement of financial position immediately before the date of initial application.

The transition provisions for sale and leaseback transactions are consistent with the general transition requirements for all leases. A seller-lessee should not perform any retrospective accounting specific to the sale element of a sale and leaseback transaction on transition to IFRS 16. A seller-lessee is required to account for the leaseback on transition to IFRS 16 in the same way as it accounts for any other lease that is in existence at the date of initial application.

A seller-lessee should apply the approach to gain or loss recognition on sale and leaseback transactions in IFRS 16 (see **section 13**) only to sale and leaseback transactions entered into after the date of initial application of IFRS 16. The IASB concluded that the costs of applying a retrospective approach would outweigh the benefits in terms of reported information. [IFRS 16:BC292 - BC294]

14.9 Assets or liabilities previously recognised by a lessee relating to favourable or unfavourable terms of an operating lease

If a lessee previously recognised an asset or a liability applying IFRS 3 *Business Combinations* relating to favourable or unfavourable terms of an operating lease acquired as part of a business combination, the lessee should derecognise that asset or liability and adjust the carrying amount of the right-of-use asset by a corresponding amount at the date of initial application. [IFRS 16:C1]

A18 Borrowing costs

Contents

1   Introduction

1.1   Overview of IAS 23

IAS 23 *Borrowing Costs* requires that borrowing costs directly attributable to the acquisition, construction or production of a 'qualifying asset' (one that necessarily takes a substantial period of time to get ready for its intended use or sale) are included in the cost of the asset. Other borrowing costs are recognised as an expense.

1.2   Amendments to IAS 23 since the last edition of this manual

IAS 23 was most recently amended in January 2016 by consequential amendments arising from IFRS 16 *Leases* (effective for annual periods beginning on or after 1 January 2019, with earlier application permitted). The amendments update the definition of borrowing costs to reflect the requirements of IFRS 16 (see **2.2**).

2   Core principle and scope

2.1   Core principle

The core principle of IAS 23 is that borrowing costs directly attributable to the acquisition, construction or production of a qualifying asset form part of the cost of that asset. Other borrowing costs are recognised as an expense. [IAS 23:1]

2.2   Borrowing costs – definition

Borrowing costs are defined as interest and other costs that an entity incurs in connection with the borrowing of funds. [IAS 23:5]

Borrowing costs may include:

[IAS 23:6]

- interest expense calculated using the effective interest method as described in IFRS 9 *Financial Instruments* (or, for entities that have not yet adopted IFRS 9, IAS 39 *Financial Instruments: Recognition and Measurement*). See **4.1** in **chapter B6** (or, for entities that have not yet adopted IFRS 9, **4.1** in **chapter C6**) for further discussion;

- for entities that have adopted IFRS 16 *Leases*, interest in respect of liabilities recognised in accordance with that Standard;

- for entities that have not yet adopted IFRS 16, finance charges in respect of finance leases recognised in accordance with IAS 17 *Leases*; and

- exchange differences arising from foreign currency borrowings to the extent that they are regarded as an adjustment to interest costs (see **2.4**).

2.3 Scope – exemptions

An entity is not required to apply IAS 23 to borrowing costs directly attributable to the acquisition, construction or production of:

[IAS 23:4]

(a) a qualifying asset (as defined in **3.2.1**) measured at fair value (e.g. a biological asset within the scope of IAS 41 *Agriculture* or an investment property under construction measured at fair value); or

(b) inventories that are manufactured, or otherwise produced, in large quantities on a repetitive basis.

IAS 23:4 was amended in June 2014 by *Agriculture: Bearer Plants (Amendments to IAS 16 and IAS 41)* to clarify that the biological assets referred to in that paragraph are those that fall within the scope of IAS 41 *Agriculture*. Also as part of the June 2014 consequential amendments to IAS 23, a specific reference to 'bearer plants' has been added to the list of assets that, depending on the circumstances, may be qualifying assets (see **3.2.1**).

The exemption for assets measured at fair value in IAS 23:4 recognises that the measurement of such assets is not affected by the amount of borrowing costs incurred during their construction or production period. The exemption for inventories manufactured in large quantities on a repetitive basis acknowledges the difficulty both in allocating borrowing costs to such inventories and monitoring those borrowing costs until the inventories are sold. The IASB concluded that it should not require entities to capitalise borrowing costs on such inventories because the costs of capitalisation were likely to exceed the potential benefits.

These exemptions are optional rather than mandatory. Accordingly, an entity can choose, as a matter of accounting policy, whether to apply the requirements of IAS 23 to borrowing costs that relate to assets measured at fair value and/or inventories produced in large quantities on a repetitive basis.

2.4 Exchange differences to be included in borrowing costs

2.4.1 Exchange differences to be included in borrowing costs – general

IAS 23 includes no further clarification as to what is meant by the inclusion of exchange differences 'to the extent that they are regarded as an adjustment to interest costs'. The question has been addressed by the IFRIC (now the IFRS Interpretations Committee) – see January 2008 *IFRIC Update*. The IFRIC reaffirmed that how an entity applies IAS 23 to foreign currency borrowings is a matter of accounting policy requiring the exercise of judgement. When the accounting policy adopted is relevant to an understanding of the financial statements, it should be disclosed as required by IAS 1 *Presentation of Financial Statements*.

It is clear that not all exchange differences arising from foreign currency borrowings can be regarded as an adjustment to interest costs; otherwise, there would be no requirement for the qualifying terminology used in IAS 23:6(e). The extent to which exchange differences can be so considered depends on the terms and conditions of the foreign currency borrowing.

Qualifying interest costs denominated in the foreign currency, translated at the actual exchange rate on the date on which the expense is incurred, should be classified as borrowing costs. Although exchange rate fluctuations may mean that this amount is substantially higher or lower than the interest costs contemplated when the original financing decision was made, the full amount is appropriately treated as borrowing costs.

Some exchange differences relating to the principal may be regarded as an adjustment to interest costs (and, therefore, taken into account in determining the amount of borrowing costs capitalised) but only to the extent that the adjustment does not decrease or increase the interest costs to an amount below or above a notional borrowing cost based on commercial interest rates prevailing in the functional currency at the date of initial recognition of the borrowing. In other words, the amount of borrowing costs that may be capitalised should lie between the following two amounts:

(1) actual interest costs denominated in the foreign currency, translated at the actual exchange rate on the date on which the expense is incurred; and

(2) notional borrowing costs based on commercial interest rates prevailing in the functional currency at the date of initial recognition of the borrowing.

Whether any adjustments for exchange differences are made to the amount determined under (1) above is an accounting policy choice and should be applied consistently.

The extent to which foreign exchange differences can be regarded as borrowing costs is illustrated in **example 2.4.2** and **example 2.4.3**.

2.4.2   Exchange differences that increase borrowing costs

Example 2.4.2

Exchange differences that increase borrowing costs

Entity X, which prepares its financial statements in its functional currency of Thailand Baht (THB), enters into a borrowing arrangement with terms and conditions as set out below.

Amount borrowed (in the foreign currency)	US$100 million
Date of initial recognition of the borrowing	1 January 20X1
Exchange rate at the date of initial recognition of the borrowing	THB25:US$1
Interest rate on foreign borrowings (in US$)	6% per annum (fixed)
Interest rate on similar borrowing in THB at the date of initial recognition of the borrowing	12% per annum (fixed)
Average exchange rate for 20X1	THB36:US$1
Closing exchange rate for 20X1	THB47:US$1

The following interest payments were made in 20X1.

Interest payments (6% × US$100 million)	US$6 million
Translated at average rate	THB216 million

Entity X should capitalise THB216 million, being the qualifying interest costs denominated in the foreign currency, translated at the actual exchange rate on the date on which the expense is incurred.

In addition, Entity X may choose as its accounting policy to regard exchange differences as an adjustment to interest costs. If it does so, in order to determine the maximum potential adjustment to interest costs for exchange differences, Entity X should determine the borrowing costs that would have been incurred in the 20X1 reporting period if the funds had been borrowed in THB. The calculation is set out below.

THB equivalent of US$100 million at 1 January 20X1	THB2,500 million
Annual interest expense based on THB interest rates (12%)	THB300 million

---

In the above scenario, the notional borrowing cost in the entity's functional currency of THB300 million is the 'cap' on the amount to be classified as borrowing costs. Consequently, when it has made the relevant accounting policy choice, Entity X should capitalise an amount of borrowing costs between THB216 million and THB300 million.

The foreign exchange loss incurred on the retranslation of the principal amount of the US$100 million borrowings at the end of the 20X1 reporting period is calculated as follows.

THB equivalent at opening rate of THB25:US$1	THB2,500 million
THB equivalent at closing rate of THB47:US$1	THB4,700 million
Foreign exchange loss	THB2,200 million

As calculated above, the cap on the amount to be classified as borrowing costs in the 20X1 accounting period is THB300 million. The difference of THB84 million between this amount and THB216 million (being the qualifying interest costs denominated in the foreign currency, translated at the actual exchange rate on the date on which the expense is incurred) is the amount of foreign exchange losses on the principal eligible for capitalisation. The remaining exchange loss on the principal (THB2,116 million) is recognised in profit or loss in the year.

If the retranslation of the US$100 million at the end of the 20X1 reporting period gave rise to a foreign exchange gain, the entire gain should be recognised in profit or loss. The amount of capitalised borrowing costs would be THB216 million (interest costs denominated in the foreign currency, translated at the actual exchange rate on the date on which the expense is incurred). No adjustment to interest costs for exchange differences should be made, because any such adjustment would result in an amount of borrowing costs outside the acceptable range.

2.4.3   Exchange differences that decrease borrowing costs

Example 2.4.3

Exchange differences that decrease borrowing costs

Entity Y, which prepares its financial statements in its functional currency of Thailand Baht (THB), enters into a borrowing arrangement with terms and conditions as set out below.

Amount borrowed (in the foreign currency)	US$100 million
Date of initial recognition of the borrowing	1 January 20X1
Exchange rate at the date of initial recognition of the borrowing	THB25:US$1
Interest rate on foreign borrowings (in US$)	6% per annum (fixed)
Interest rate on similar borrowing in THB as at the date of initial recognition of the borrowing	8% per annum (fixed)

Average exchange rate for 20X1	THB36:US$1
Closing exchange rate for 20X1	THB22:US$1

The following interest payments were made in 20X1.

Interest payments (6% × US$100 million)	US$6 million
Translated at average rate	THB216 million

Entity Y should capitalise THB216 million, being the qualifying interest costs denominated in the foreign currency, translated at the actual exchange rate on the date on which the expense is incurred.

In addition, Entity Y may choose as its accounting policy to regard exchange differences as an adjustment to interest costs. If it does so, in order to determine the maximum potential adjustment to interest costs for exchange differences, Entity Y should determine the borrowing costs that would have been incurred in the 20X1 reporting period if the funds had been borrowed in THB. The calculation is set out below.

THB equivalent of US$100 million at 1 January 20X1	THB2,500 million
Annual interest expense based on THB interest rates (8%)	THB200 million

In the circumstances described, the notional borrowing cost in the entity's functional currency of THB200 million is the 'floor' on the amount to be classified as borrowing costs. Consequently, when it has made the relevant accounting policy choice, Entity Y should capitalise an amount of borrowing costs between THB200 million and THB216 million.

The foreign exchange gain incurred on the retranslation of the principal amount of the US$100 million borrowings at the end of the 20X1 reporting period is calculated as follows.

THB equivalent at opening rate of THB25:US$1	THB2,500 million
THB equivalent at closing rate of THB22:US$1	THB2,200 million
Foreign exchange gain	THB300 million

As calculated above, the floor on the amount to be classified as borrowing costs in the 20X1 accounting period is THB200 million. The difference of THB16 million between this amount and THB216 million (being the qualifying interest costs denominated in the foreign currency, translated at the actual exchange rate on the date on which the expense is incurred) is the amount of the foreign exchange gain on the principal to be offset in borrowing costs. The remaining exchange gain on the principal (THB284 million) is recognised in profit or loss in the year.

If the retranslation of the US$100 million at the end of the 20X1 reporting period gave rise to a foreign exchange loss, the entire loss should be recognised in profit or loss. The amount of capitalised borrowing costs would be THB216 million (interest costs denominated in the foreign currency, translated at the actual exchange rate on the date on which the expense is incurred). No adjustment to interest costs for exchange differences should be made, as any such adjustment would result in an amount of borrowing costs outside the acceptable range of amounts.

2.5 Costs associated with shares and similar instruments classified as financial liabilities

IAS 23 does not deal with the actual or imputed cost of equity, including preferred capital not classified as a liability. [IAS 23:3]

By implication, IAS 23 *does* apply to costs associated with shares and similar financial instruments that are classified as liabilities, in accordance with the requirements of IAS 32 *Financial Instruments: Presentation*. Under IAS 32:35, the dividends paid on such instruments are recognised in profit or loss as an expense. IAS 32:36 states that "dividend payments on shares wholly recognised as liabilities are recognised as expenses in the same way as interest on a bond".

Although the definition of borrowing costs in IAS 23:5 (see **2.2**) does not define what is meant by 'the borrowing of funds', the classification of shares and similar instruments as liabilities means that they should be considered to represent such borrowings. As a result, the costs of servicing those shares (e.g. dividends) fall within the definition of borrowing costs.

2.6 Imputed interest on convertible debt instruments

In accordance with IAS 32, the liability component of a convertible debt instrument is presented on an amortised cost basis using the coupon rate for an equivalent non-convertible debt. The imputed interest is recognised in profit or loss using the effective interest method. Therefore, it is appropriate for the imputed interest expense in relation to the liability component of the convertible debt instrument to be included in borrowing costs eligible for capitalisation.

2.7 Refinancing gains and losses

An entity may be required to recognise 'refinancing' gains or losses relating to borrowings for a number of reasons; for example, such gains or losses might arise in the context of:

- a substantial modification of the terms of borrowings (see **4.1** in **chapter B8** or, for entities that have not yet adopted IFRS 9 *Financial Instruments*, **4.1** in **chapter C8**); or

- early repayment (i.e. extinguishment) of borrowings (see **section 4**
  of **chapter B8** or, for entities that have not yet adopted IFRS 9,
  section 4 of **chapter C8**).

Such gains and losses do not qualify as part of borrowing costs that are
eligible for capitalisation under IAS 23. IFRS 9 (or, prior to the adoption
of IFRS 9, IAS 39) is clear that 'refinancing' gains and losses should be
recognised in profit or loss when they arise.

3   Recognition of borrowing costs

3.1   Recognition of borrowing costs – general

Borrowing costs that are directly attributable to the acquisition, construction
or production of a qualifying asset are capitalised as part of the cost of the
qualifying asset. Other borrowing costs are recognised as an expense in
the period in which they are incurred. [IAS 23:8 & 9]

Note that IAS 23 does not permit an accounting policy of expensing all
borrowing costs.

When an entity applies IAS 29 *Financial Reporting in Hyperinflationary
Economies*, it recognises as an expense the part of borrowing costs that
compensates for inflation during the same period in accordance with
IAS 29:21 (see **5.1.5** in **chapter A37**). [IAS 23:9]

3.2   Qualifying assets

3.2.1   *Qualifying assets – definition*

A qualifying asset is defined as an asset that necessarily takes a substantial
period of time to get ready for its intended use or sale. [IAS 23:5]

IAS 23 does not provide any guidance on what constitutes a
'substantial period of time'. The specific facts and circumstances should
be considered in each case. For example, it is likely that a period of
twelve months or more might be considered 'substantial'.

Depending on the circumstances, any of the following may be qualifying
assets:

[IAS 23:7]

- inventories;
- manufacturing plants;

- power generation facilities;
- intangible assets;
- investment properties; and
- bearer plants.

IAS 23:7 was amended in June 2014 by *Agriculture: Bearer Plants (Amendments to IAS 16 and IAS 41)* to clarify that, depending on the circumstances, bearer plants (accounted for under IAS 16 *Property, Plant and Equipment* following the June 2014 amendments) may be qualifying assets.

The following are *not* qualifying assets:

[IAS 23:7]

- assets that are ready for their intended use or sale when acquired;
- financial assets; and
- inventories that are manufactured, or otherwise produced, over a short period of time.

3.2.2 Assets with an extended delivery period

IAS 16 *Property, Plant and Equipment* identifies delivery and handling costs as part of the cost of an item of property, plant and equipment. It includes such activities as part of the process of preparing the asset for its intended use. The shipping of an asset is therefore part of its acquisition and, consequently, borrowing costs attributable to the shipping period can be considered to be borrowing costs directly attributable to the acquisition of the asset as required by IAS 23.

For example, an entity orders and pays for a large piece of equipment from overseas that will take six months (in this example judged to be a 'substantial' period of time for the purposes of IAS 23) to arrive. A loan is raised to finance the acquisition. The equipment is already manufactured and available for shipment. Therefore, the period between payment for the equipment and its installation is only caused by shipping time. The asset is recognised by the entity on the date of shipping by the supplier because (in this example) that is the date on which control passes to the entity. Borrowing costs incurred on the loan raised to finance the acquisition will be capitalised as part of the cost of the equipment up to the date that the asset arrives at its destination, is installed and is ready for its intended use.

3.2.3   *Investments accounted for using the equity method*

Investments accounted for using the equity method are not qualifying assets because they are financial assets, and IAS 23:7 states that financial assets are not qualifying assets.

It is sometimes argued, when a vehicle is established for the purpose of constructing a qualifying asset, that the substance of the arrangement is that the investment is itself a qualifying asset for the investor. The logic is most appealing in the case of projects organised by a limited number of investors to pool resources in developing production facilities or properties. It is argued that, from the investor's perspective, the amount of borrowing costs capitalised should not be different simply because construction of the qualifying asset is through a separate investee vehicle, rather than by the investing entity itself.

However, the accounting for the investor's interest in the vehicle will determine whether or not there is a qualifying asset. If the vehicle is an associate or a joint venture accounted for using the equity method under IAS 28 *Investments in Associates and Joint Ventures*, the interest is a financial asset, and capitalisation of borrowing costs is not permitted by IAS 23.

Example 3.2.3

Investments accounted for using the equity method

Company X invests in construction contracts via participating interests in single-purpose entities. The entities are associates, and are accounted for using the equity method of accounting.

If Company X borrows funds for the purpose of funding the construction activities in these vehicles, should it capitalise borrowing costs as part of the carrying amount of the investments?

No. Borrowing costs should not be capitalised in these circumstances. Investments in associates are financial assets. IAS 23:7 states that financial assets are not qualifying assets.

3.2.4   *Joint operations*

In contrast to the prohibition on capitalisation of borrowing costs in respect of investments accounted for using the equity method (as described in **3.2.3**), when a joint arrangement meets the definition of a joint operation under IFRS 11 *Joint Arrangements*, the entity will instead recognise its share of the assets and liabilities of the joint operation, and capitalisation of borrowing costs will be required to the extent that any of the assets are qualifying assets (see **3.2.1**).

The investor's share of the qualifying assets of a joint operation are accounted for as qualifying assets of the investor and, therefore, capitalisation of borrowing costs incurred to fund the construction of those qualifying assets is required, provided that all of the conditions of IAS 23 are met.

3.3 Borrowing costs

3.3.1 Borrowing costs eligible for capitalisation – general

See **2.2** for IAS 23's definition of borrowing costs.

The borrowing costs that are eligible for capitalisation are those borrowing costs that would have been avoided if the expenditure on the qualifying asset had not been made. [IAS 23:10]

Paragraph 8 of IFRIC 1 *Changes in Existing Decommissioning, Restoration and Similar Liabilities* makes clear that capitalisation is not permitted for the periodic unwinding of the discount in relation to changes in obligations to dismantle, remove and restore items of property, plant and equipment. Instead, the periodic unwinding of the discount is recognised in profit or loss as a finance cost as it occurs.

3.3.2 Specific borrowing costs

When funds are borrowed specifically for the purpose of acquiring or constructing a qualifying asset, the amount of borrowing costs eligible for capitalisation is the actual borrowing costs incurred on those funds during the period. [IAS 23:12]

The financing arrangements may result in the specific borrowings being drawn down prior to some or all of the funds being utilised to finance the qualifying asset. In such circumstances, any investment income earned on the temporary investment of the funds, pending their expenditure on the qualifying asset, should be deducted from the actual borrowing costs incurred to arrive at the borrowing costs eligible for capitalisation. [IAS 23:13]

Example 3.3.2

Specific borrowing costs offset by investment income on excess funds

An entity borrows CU20 million to finance the construction of a factory. The funds are to be drawn down on a monthly basis in four equal amounts. Payment of construction costs occurs throughout each month, rather than coinciding with the draw-downs. During each month, the entity invests any excess funds drawn down in accordance with the financing arrangements in short-term bank deposits.

In its financial statements for the year, the entity should capitalise, as part of the cost of construction of the factory, the actual borrowing costs on the CU20 million borrowing (incurred during the period of construction), less the interest income derived from the temporary investments in bank deposits.

3.3.3 General borrowing costs

3.3.3.1 Issues arising when a qualifying asset is funded from general borrowings

When a qualifying asset is funded from a pool of general borrowings, the amount of the borrowing costs eligible for capitalisation is not so obvious. While the basic principle in IAS 23:10 (see **3.3.1**) still applies, there may be practical difficulties in identifying a direct relationship between the particular borrowings utilised and the qualifying assets.

3.3.3.2 Calculation of capitalisation rate

When a qualifying asset is funded from a pool of general borrowings, IAS 23:14 requires that the amount of the borrowing costs to be capitalised should be determined by applying an appropriate capitalisation rate to the expenditure on the qualifying asset.

The capitalisation rate is calculated as follows:

[IAS 23:14]

$$\frac{\text{Total general borrowing costs for the period (i.e. excluding specific borrowings)}}{\text{Weighted average total general borrowings (i.e. excluding specific borrowings)}}$$

Example 3.3.3.2

Qualifying asset funded from a general borrowing pool

An entity centrally co-ordinates its financing activities through a treasury function, with borrowings being raised to finance general requirements, including the acquisition and development of qualifying assets.

During the year ended 31 December 20X1, the entity commenced a property development project and incurred the following expenditure.

	CU'000
1 June	5,000
1 October	10,000
1 November	10,000

The entity had total borrowings outstanding during the period, and incurred interest on those borrowings, as follows.

	Balance outstanding CU'000	Interest CU'000
Long-term loans*		
10 years at 10%	35,000	3,500
5 years at 8%	10,000	800
Short-term loans**	12,000	1,600
Bank overdraft**	5,000	500
	62,000	6,400

*   There was no movement on long-term loans in the period.

**   The amounts disclosed for short-term loans and the bank overdraft represent the average amounts outstanding during the period and the interest incurred at variable rates.

The appropriate capitalisation rate to be applied to the expenditure on the qualifying asset is calculated as follows:

$$\frac{\text{Total borrowing costs for the period}}{\text{Weighted average total borrowings}} = \frac{6,400}{62,000} = 10.32\%$$

Interest capitalised is therefore calculated as follows:

	CU'000
CU5 million × 7/12 × 10.32%	301
CU10 million × 3/12 × 10.32%	258
CU10 million × 2/12 × 10.32%	172
Interest capitalised for the period	731

3.3.3.3   Expenditure to which the capitalisation rate is applied

In the calculation of borrowing costs to be capitalised, the amount of expenditure on a qualifying asset should consist only of payments of cash, transfers of other assets or the assumption of interest-bearing liabilities, and should be reduced by any pre-sale deposits, progress payments or grants received in connection with the qualifying asset. The average carrying amount of the asset during a period, including borrowing costs previously capitalised, is normally a reasonable approximation of the expenditures to which the capitalisation rate is applied in that period. [IAS 23:18]

3.3.3.4   Borrowing costs capitalised limited to the borrowing costs incurred

The capitalisation of general borrowing costs calculated using the capitalisation rate is subject to the condition that the amount of borrowing costs capitalised should not exceed the actual borrowing costs incurred during that same period. [IAS 23:14]

Because the amount of borrowing costs capitalised may not exceed the amount of borrowing costs actually incurred, 'notional' interest expenses may not be capitalised. This point has particular relevance for groups with centralised banking arrangements whereby the 'banking' entity charges or credits interest to the other group entities in respect of its balances with those entities. Interest charged by one member of a group to another cannot be capitalised in the consolidated financial statements except to the extent that it represents an interest expense actually borne by the group on external borrowings. Intragroup interest is eliminated on consolidation.

Example 3.3.3.4

Borrowing costs capitalised limited to the borrowing costs incurred in a group context

A group consists of a parent, P, and two subsidiaries, S1 and S2. S1 is engaged in the construction of a power plant that is wholly financed by fellow subsidiary S2, which obtains the necessary funds through general bank borrowings. No intragroup interest is charged by S2 to S1. The terms of the loan from S2 to S1 specify that it is repayable on demand.

In the circumstances described, no interest should be capitalised in either of the individual financial statements of S1 or S2. S1 has incurred no borrowing costs, and S2 has no qualifying asset.

However, it will be appropriate to capitalise interest in the consolidated financial statements of P, provided that the amount capitalised fairly reflects the interest cost to the group of borrowings from third parties which could have been avoided if the expenditure on the qualifying asset had not been made.

3.3.3.5   *Investment income on excess funds borrowed generally*

When funds are borrowed generally, interest income earned on excess funds should not be offset against the interest cost in determining the appropriate capitalisation rate, nor in determining the limit on capitalisation by reference to the amount of borrowing costs incurred during the period.

3.3.3.6   *Assets funded from specified cash balances*

When an entity has a general borrowing pool, it may nevertheless consider that expenditure on certain assets is met out of specified cash balances. In such circumstances, the question arises as to whether the entity is required under IAS 23:14 to capitalise 'deemed' borrowing costs in respect of the expenditure on such assets.

This question is not specifically dealt with in IAS 23. IAS 23:14 refers to "the extent that an entity borrows funds generally and uses them for the purpose of obtaining a qualifying asset". Therefore, it appears that to the extent that the asset is demonstrably not paid for out of borrowings (e.g. it is paid for out of the cash proceeds of an equity issue), there is no requirement to capitalise a deemed interest cost.

To understand this position, contrast the IAS 23 requirements with those of US GAAP, which state that the interest cost required to be capitalised is that which would theoretically have been avoided by using the funds expended to repay existing borrowings. Therefore, whenever an entity has a general borrowing pool, it is required to capitalise the borrowing costs that would have been avoided if the cash balances had been used to repay those borrowings.

Under IAS 23:14, there is no requirement to capitalise a 'deemed' interest cost, although it appears that adopting the approach required by US GAAP is also acceptable.

3.3.3.7 Use of insurance proceeds to fund the reconstruction of an asset

Example 3.3.3.7

Use of insurance proceeds to fund the reconstruction of an asset

Company A had a factory that was destroyed by fire. Insurance proceeds have been received and are being used to reconstruct the factory. Company A has a general borrowing pool.

Because costs are incurred on the general borrowing pool, is Company A required to capitalise a deemed interest cost in respect of the reconstruction, even though the construction is funded from the insurance proceeds which are lodged in a separate bank account?

The capitalisation of borrowing costs is not necessarily required in these circumstances. The construction of the replacement asset is a distinct event and should be assessed separately for the purpose of determining the appropriateness of capitalisation of borrowing costs.

The general question as to whether an entity is required to capitalise borrowing costs, even when it has identified the source of the funding for the qualifying asset as cash balances, is dealt with at **3.3.3.6**. The only distinction in the case of insurance proceeds is that the entity may be legally required to use the insurance proceeds for the purposes of the reconstruction. When this is the case, the option of repayment of the borrowings is not available, and the borrowing costs are not avoidable. Therefore, the option of capitalising a 'deemed' interest cost is not available in such circumstances.

3.3.3.8 General borrowings for a financial institution

For a financial institution, customer deposits should be included within general borrowings for the purpose of calculating a capitalisation rate if the deposits are considered to be a borrowing as contemplated in IAS 23. The term 'borrowing' is not specifically defined in IAS 23 or elsewhere in IFRSs, and the determination as to what constitutes a borrowing for a financial institution will require the exercise of judgement.

An acceptable approach to determining whether an obligation of a financial institution represents a borrowing would be to consider the classification of the associated cash flows in the statement of cash flows. Paragraph 6 of IAS 7 *Statement of Cash Flows* states that "[f]inancing activities are activities that result in changes in the size and composition of the contributed equity and borrowings of the entity". Following this approach, therefore, for the purpose of calculating the general capitalisation rate, an entity would include within general borrowings any liabilities for which the associated cash flows are presented as financing cash flows (unless that borrowing is directly attributable to a qualifying asset as described in IAS 23:10).

3.3.4 Impact of tax on capitalised borrowing costs

Although IAS 23 does not specifically mention tax, it is clear from the way that borrowing costs are defined that the amount to be capitalised is not affected by whether tax relief will be obtained in respect of borrowing costs (i.e. borrowing costs will be capitalised on a gross basis, and not net of any relevant tax relief). In some jurisdictions, tax relief may be received on borrowing costs when they are incurred, irrespective of whether those costs are capitalised. When this is the case, a temporary difference will arise and the entity should apply the requirements of IAS 12 *Income Taxes* (see **chapter A13** for further guidance).

3.4 Interaction of capitalisation of borrowing costs and hedge accounting

The interaction between the capitalisation of borrowing costs and hedge accounting is discussed at **3.13** in **chapter B9** (or, for entities that have not yet adopted IFRS 9 *Financial Instruments*, **2.6** in **chapter C10**).

3.5   Period of capitalisation

3.5.1   *Commencement of capitalisation*

3.5.1.1   *Commencement of capitalisation – general*

IAS 23:17 states that borrowing costs should be capitalised from the commencement date. The commencement date for capitalisation is the date when the following three conditions are first met:

- expenditures for the asset are being incurred;

- borrowing costs are being incurred; and

- activities that are necessary to prepare the asset for its intended use or sale are being undertaken.

Example 3.5.1.1

Deposit paid for the acquisition of an asset

Company A places an order with a supplier for the acquisition of an asset. The asset will not be received for a substantial period of time. At the time of placing the order, Company A pays a substantial deposit. The remainder of the cost of the asset is paid on delivery.

If Company A incurs borrowing costs in respect of the deposit paid, are those borrowing costs eligible for capitalisation?

In determining whether any borrowing costs incurred are eligible for capitalisation, an assessment is required of all the facts and circumstances and the nature of the deposit paid by Company A. Some common examples are described below.

Deposit represents payment on account for an asset built to Company A's specifications

An asset that is manufactured for Company A in accordance with Company A's specification, is a qualifying asset. The deposit represents a payment on account for the supplier's services.

For example, Company A contracts a supplier to construct a property on Company A's land to Company A's specification based on architects' plans provided by Company A. Any payments made by Company A to the supplier are for the construction services provided by the supplier and, therefore, are directly related to the manufacture or construction of the property. Consequently, borrowing costs incurred by Company A during the construction period are eligible for capitalisation and should be capitalised as part of the cost of the asset.

Deposit secures place in a waiting list to acquire standard goods

IAS 23:7 states that "[a]ssets that are ready for their intended use or sale when acquired are not qualifying assets". In such cases, a deposit may primarily serve to secure Company A's place in a waiting list.

A common example is the manufacture of top-end cars when the customer may select from standard customisation options (e.g. paint colour, air conditioning, parking sensors). There is generally a waiting list for such cars. In order to secure its place in the waiting list and guarantee delivery of the new car, Company A may pay a substantial deposit when the order is placed. However, if it is clear that the deposit does not affect the total amount payable to the supplier for the car, any borrowing costs Company A incurs on the deposit do not qualify for capitalisation because they do not arise in relation to the manufacture of the car.

Note that if the payment of the deposit for an asset reduces the overall price that would otherwise have been payable for the asset, it is appropriate to recognise the implicit financing as part of the cost of the asset (see **example 4.3.2C** in **chapter A7** for discussion and illustration).

The term 'activities' in this context is interpreted as having a broad meaning and should include all steps necessary to prepare the asset for its intended use. Such activities include initial technical and administrative work, such as activities associated with obtaining permits, prior to the commencement of the physical construction of the asset. [IAS 23:19]

The mere holding of an asset, however, without any associated development activities, does not entitle an entity to capitalise related borrowing costs. [IAS 23:19] A typical example is the holding of land banks that are not undergoing activities necessary to prepare them for their intended use. Capitalisation of borrowing costs should only commence when such activities are being undertaken as part of a specific development plan to change an asset's condition.

3.5.1.2 Commencement date of capitalisation prior to the date of application of IAS 23 (as revised in 2007)

The requirements of IAS 23 (as revised in 2007) apply only to borrowing costs relating to qualifying assets for which the commencement date for capitalisation is on or after the date when an entity first applied that Standard (effective date 1 January 2009 or an earlier date designated by the entity). [IAS 23:27 & 28]

Therefore, when IAS 23(2007) was first adopted, qualifying assets for which the commencement date had already occurred (referred to below as 'pre-existing' qualifying assets) were not restated. In addition, any borrowing costs relating to such assets continue to be accounted for in accordance with the entity's previous accounting policy for borrowing costs until the end of the capitalisation period (see **3.5.3**), as follows.

- When an entity's previous accounting policy was to expense all borrowing costs when incurred, the entity should continue to expense all borrowing costs relating to pre-existing qualifying assets, including any borrowing costs incurred after the date when IAS 23(2007) is first applied.

- When an entity's accounting policy had always been to capitalise borrowing costs relating to qualifying assets, there was generally no change on application of the revised Standard. One exception may be if the entity took one of the scope exemptions discussed in **2.3**, having previously capitalised borrowing costs for such assets. In such cases, the new policy (of expensing borrowing costs for such exempt assets) is not applied to pre-existing qualifying assets, and borrowing costs relating to such assets, including any borrowing costs incurred after the date when IAS 23(2007) is first applied, continue to be capitalised in accordance with the previous version of the Standard.

Example 3.5.1.2

Commencement date of capitalisation prior to the date of application of IAS 23(2007)

Prior to adopting IAS 23(2007), Entity A followed the benchmark treatment under the previous version of the Standard and expensed all borrowing costs when incurred.

Entity A engaged in the following construction projects prior to and during the 2009 reporting period:

- Asset 1 – construction commenced 1 January 2006, construction completed 30 June 2007 (still held by Entity A as property, plant and equipment);

- Asset 2 – construction commenced 1 January 2006, construction completed 30 June 2009 (still held by Entity A as property, plant and equipment);

- Asset 3 – construction commenced 1 July 2005, expected completion date 31 December 2017; and

- Asset 4 – construction commenced 1 July 2009, expected completion date 31 December 2017.

All of these assets meet the definition of 'qualifying assets' under IAS 23. Assume that the 'construction commenced' noted in each case is the appropriate date for commencement of capitalisation of borrowing costs under IAS 23.

If Entity A chose to apply the revised Standard from 1 January 2009 (i.e. the effective date), it should continue to expense borrowing costs incurred on Assets 2 and 3 (even after 1 January 2009) because the date for commencement of capitalisation of borrowing costs for those assets was before 1 January 2009. Similarly, Asset 1 would not be restated. Entity A should only apply the new policy of capitalising borrowing costs to Asset 4.

If Entity A designated 1 January 2006 as its date for application of the revised Standard, it would not have restated Asset 3 and should continue to expense borrowing costs incurred on Asset 3 because the date for commencement of capitalisation of borrowing costs for Asset 3 was before 1 January 2006. However, Entity A should apply the new policy of capitalising borrowing costs to Assets 1, 2 and 4 from the date of commencement to the date of completion. (A prior period adjustment would have been required to restate any borrowing costs incurred in relation to those assets previously recognised as an expense and, in the case of Asset 1, to adjust the depreciation charged on the asset before 1 January 2009.)

3.5.2   Suspension of capitalisation

Capitalisation of borrowing costs should generally continue as long as the three conditions listed at **3.5.1.1** are met. If, however, the entity suspends activities related to development for an extended period, capitalisation of borrowing costs should also cease until such time as activities are resumed. [IAS 23:20] Such interruptions in development may occur, for example, due to cash flow difficulties or a desire to hold back development while the market is in depression, in which case the borrowing costs incurred during the period of suspension are not considered to be a necessary cost of development and therefore cannot be capitalised. On the other hand, temporary delays that are necessary or expected in the process of getting an asset ready for its intended use, or which result from a natural delay such as adverse weather conditions that are common to the location, do not require the suspension of capitalisation. [IAS 23:21]

3.5.3   Cessation of capitalisation

3.5.3.1   Cessation of capitalisation – general

Borrowing costs should only be capitalised to the extent that they accrue during the period of production. In accordance with IAS 23:22, capitalisation should cease when substantially all of the activities necessary to prepare the qualifying asset for its intended use or sale are complete.

An asset is normally ready for its intended use or sale when the physical construction of the asset is complete, even when routine administrative work is continuing. If minor modifications, such as the decoration of a property to the purchaser's specification, are all that are still outstanding, this indicates that substantially all the activities are complete. [IAS 23:23]

Capitalisation will therefore generally cease when the physical construction of an asset is complete, because at that stage the asset will be substantially ready for its intended use, notwithstanding that further time might be necessary to complete routine administrative work, market the asset or, in the case of an investment property, find a tenant.

3.5.3.2   Delay between completion of construction and obtaining regulatory consents

Regulatory consents (e.g. health and safety clearance) are sometimes required before an asset is permitted to be brought into use. Management will normally seek to ensure that such consents are in place very close to the time frame for physical completion and testing, so that the consents do not slow down the commencement of operations. When a delay in obtaining consents, which prevents the start of operations, could have been avoided by the entity, this should be seen as abnormal and similar in effect to a suspension of development, so that capitalisation of borrowing costs should cease (see **3.5.2**). However, when it is not possible to avoid a delay between physical completion and obtaining such consents (e.g. when it is not possible to apply for consents until after physical completion), capitalisation of borrowing costs will continue to be appropriate until the consents are obtained, i.e. until the asset is ready for its intended use. (See also **example 4.2.9** in **chapter A7** relating to approval for occupation for a self-constructed property.)

3.5.3.3   Completion of an asset is intentionally delayed

When the completion of an asset is intentionally delayed, continued capitalisation of borrowing costs is not permitted. For example, in the case of property development, it is customary for the developer to defer installation of certain fixtures and fittings and the decoration work until units are sold, so that purchasers may choose their own specifications. Such delays relate more to the marketing of units than to the asset construction process.

3.5.3.4   Cessation of capitalisation for maturing inventories

For maturing inventories, it is sometimes difficult to determine when the 'period of production' ends, i.e. when inventories are being held for sale as opposed to being held to mature. For example, whisky is 'mature' after three years, but goes on improving with age for many more years. Provided that it is consistent with the entity's business model to hold such items so that they mature further, it would seem acceptable to continue to add borrowing costs to the value of such maturing inventories for as long as it can be demonstrated that the particular item of inventory continues to increase in value solely on account of increasing age, rather than because of market fluctuations or inflation. If this cannot be demonstrated, then the inventories should be regarded as held for sale and no further borrowing costs should be capitalised. (Note that, in some cases, items such as whisky may qualify for the exemption described in **2.3** for inventories that are manufactured, or otherwise produced, in large quantities on a repetitive basis.)

3.5.3.5   Investment property subject to lessee fit-out

Example 3.5.3.5

Investment property subject to lessee fit-out

When a lessor completes a property subject to fit-out, and transfers it to the lessee, who then carries out further work to bring the property to the condition necessary for its intended use, from the perspective of the lessor the property is available for its intended use at the time the lessee takes possession. This is the commencement date of the lease (as defined in IFRS 16 *Leases* (see **6.3** in **chapter A17**) or, for entities that have not yet adopted IFRS 16, in IAS 17 *Leases* (see **4.3.3** in **appendix A4**)); it is also the date at which the lessor ceases capitalisation of borrowing costs (unless there is a delay between the lessor completing work and the lessee taking possession, in which case capitalisation will cease at the earlier date).

3.5.3.6   Qualifying asset constructed in stages

When a qualifying asset is constructed in stages, and each stage or part can be used or sold individually while construction of the remaining development continues, capitalisation of the borrowing costs related to that part should cease when substantially all of the activities necessary to prepare that part for its intended use or sale are completed. [IAS 23:24] A development comprising several buildings or units, each of which can be used or sold individually, is an example of this type of qualifying asset. For an asset that must be completed in its entirety before any part of the asset can be used as intended, however, the borrowing costs should be capitalised until all of the activities necessary to prepare the entire asset for its intended use or sale are substantially complete. An example of this might be a manufacturing facility involving a sequence of processes, where production cannot begin until all the processes are in place.

Example 3.5.3.6

Cessation of capitalisation when construction completed in stages

A cable service supplier is building a cable network covering many franchise areas. The construction is carried out sequentially for each franchise area. Once the construction in each franchise area is completed, the network is available for use in that area. The expenditure is being funded from a general borrowing pool.

Should capitalisation of borrowing costs cease at the end of the entire project, or at the completion of each individual franchise area?

Capitalisation related to each stage ceases on the completion of the individual stage of the project, rather than when the project as a whole is completed. Under IAS 23:24, when the construction of a qualifying asset is completed in parts, and each part is capable of being used while construction continues on other parts, capitalisation of borrowing costs should cease when substantially all the activities necessary to prepare that part for its intended use or sale are completed. In this example, therefore, capitalisation of borrowing costs for each franchise area ceases as and when substantially all of the activities necessary to prepare the cable network in the particular franchise area for use are completed. Note that capitalisation of borrowing costs in other franchise areas still under construction should continue.

3.6 Recognition of an impairment loss or write-down

When the carrying amount or the expected ultimate cost of the qualifying asset exceeds its recoverable amount or net realisable value, the carrying amount is written down or written off in accordance with the requirements of other IFRSs. In certain circumstances, the amount of the write-down or write-off is written back in accordance with those other IFRSs. [IAS 23:16]

Therefore, once borrowing costs have been identified as appropriate for capitalisation, they should be capitalised as part of the cost of the qualifying asset. This is so even in those circumstances when the expected ultimate cost of the qualifying asset exceeds its recoverable amount (or net realisable value for inventories). In such cases, the appropriate treatment is to capitalise the borrowing costs as part of the gross carrying amount of the asset, and then recognise an impairment loss for any excess over the estimated recoverable amount or net realisable value in accordance with the requirements of IAS 36 *Impairment of Assets* or IAS 2 *Inventories*, as appropriate.

4 Disclosure

Entities are required to disclose:

[IAS 23:26]

- the amount of borrowing costs capitalised during the period; and
- the capitalisation rate used to determine the amount of borrowing costs eligible for capitalisation.

A19 The effects of changes in foreign exchange rates

Contents

1 Introduction

1.1 Overview of IAS 21

IAS 21 *The Effects of Changes in Foreign Exchange Rates* outlines how to account for foreign currency transactions and operations in financial statements, and also how to translate financial statements into a presentation currency. An entity is required to determine a functional currency (for each of its operations, if necessary) based on the primary economic environment in which it operates and generally records foreign currency transactions using the spot conversion rate to that functional currency on the date of the transaction.

1.2 Amendments to IAS 21 since the last edition of this manual

IAS 21 was most recently amended in January 2016 by minor consequential amendments arising from IFRS 16 *Leases* (effective for annual periods beginning on or after 1 January 2019, with earlier application permitted). The amendments clarify items related to leases that should be classified as monetary and non-monetary (see **3.4.1**).

2 Foreign currency transactions and scope of IAS 21

2.1 Foreign currency items within the scope of IAS 21

An entity may enter into foreign currency transactions in two principal ways:

- it may enter directly into transactions denominated in a foreign currency; and

- it may have foreign operations.

In addition, an entity may present its financial statements in a foreign currency.

IAS 21 prescribes how to account for transactions in a foreign currency and how to translate foreign operations for inclusion in the financial statements of an entity, whether by consolidation or the equity method. The Standard also addresses how to translate financial statements into a presentation currency. [IAS 21:3]

2.2 Foreign currency items excluded from the scope of IAS 21

IAS 21 excludes from its scope those foreign currency derivatives to which IFRS 9 *Financial Instruments* (or, for entities that have not yet adopted IFRS 9, IAS 39 *Financial Instruments: Recognition and Measurement*) applies (see **chapters B4** and **B5** or, for entities that have not yet adopted IFRS 9, **chapters C4** and **C5**). Foreign currency derivatives that are not within the scope of IFRS 9 (or, for entities that have not yet adopted

IFRS 9, IAS 39) (e.g. some foreign currency derivatives that are embedded in other contracts) are within the scope of IAS 21. In addition, IAS 21 applies when an entity translates amounts relating to derivatives from its functional currency to its presentation currency. [IAS 21:3 & 4]

Although IAS 21 defines a net investment in a foreign operation (see **section 3**), the accounting treatment for a hedge of a net investment of a foreign operation is dealt with in IFRS 9 (or, for entities that have not yet adopted IFRS 9, IAS 39). Similarly, IFRS 9 (IAS 39) applies to hedge accounting for a designated item hedged for foreign exchange risk. IAS 21 specifically excludes from its scope the measurement of foreign currency items that are subject to hedge accounting. [IAS 21:5] These items are discussed in **chapter B9** (or, for entities that have not yet adopted IFRS 9, **chapter C9**) on hedge accounting.

Example 2.2

Hedging a net investment in a foreign operation

Company S, a Swedish entity with the Swedish krona as its functional currency, has a subsidiary with the US dollar as its functional currency. Company S has a third-party long-term debt agreement in the amount of US$4,000,000. Company S designates US$2,000,000 of the debt at the beginning of the year as a hedge of its net investment in the foreign subsidiary.

The part of the debt qualifying as a hedging instrument is outside the scope of IAS 21 and is instead accounted for under IFRS 9 (or, for entities that have not yet adopted IFRS 9, IAS 39). The portion of the debt instrument that is not designated in the hedging relationship is, however, still within the scope of IAS 21.

See **chapter B9** (or, for entities that have not yet adopted IFRS 9, **chapter C9**) for guidance on hedges of net investments in a foreign operation and on hedge effectiveness.

IAS 21 does not address the presentation of cash flows arising from transactions in a foreign currency in a statement of cash flows, nor the translation of cash flows of a foreign operation; these issues are addressed in IAS 7 *Statement of Cash Flows* (see **chapter A21**). [IAS 21:7]

3 Reporting foreign currency transactions in the functional currency

3.1 Foreign currency transaction – definition

A foreign currency transaction is a transaction that is denominated or requires settlement in a foreign currency. [IAS 21:20] A foreign currency is a currency other than the functional currency of the entity. [IAS 21:8] For example, an entity may:

- buy or sell goods or services at a price denominated in a foreign currency;

- borrow or lend funds such that the amounts payable or receivable are denominated in a foreign currency; and/or

- acquire or dispose of assets, or incur or settle liabilities, denominated in a foreign currency.

When an entity directly enters into such transactions, it is exposed to the cash flow effects of changes in value of the foreign currency. An entity must convert foreign currency items into its functional currency in order to recognise those items in its accounting records. Once recognised, exchange differences will arise when changes in exchange rates affect the carrying amounts.

3.2 Functional currency

3.2.1 Functional currency – general

The functional currency of an entity is the currency of the primary economic environment in which the entity operates. [IAS 21:8]

In preparing financial statements, each entity is required to determine its functional currency in accordance with IAS 21:9 to 14. This applies whether the entity is a stand-alone entity, an entity with foreign operations (such as a parent) or a foreign operation (such as a subsidiary or branch). There is no concept of a 'group functional currency' in IFRSs.

An entity's functional currency is a matter of fact, not of choice. In practice, judgement is required in assessing which currency is the functional currency. Because this is a question of fact, an entity's functional currency will change only if there is a change in the primary economic environment in which the entity operates (see **3.2.8.1**).

3.2.2 Primary indicators of a functional currency

IAS 21:9 explains that the primary economic environment in which an entity operates is normally the one in which it primarily generates and expends cash. When determining its functional currency, an entity considers:

[IAS 21:9]

(a) the currency that mainly influences sales prices for goods and services (which is often the currency in which those sales prices are denominated and settled) and the currency of the country whose competitive forces and regulations mainly determine the sales prices of its goods and services; and

(b)   the currency that mainly influences labour, material and other costs of providing goods or services (which will often be the currency in which such costs are denominated and settled).

It is widely accepted, for example, that prices for oil are determined in US dollars. Therefore, the sales prices of an entity whose primary activity is to sell oil are influenced by the US dollar. This is true regardless of the currency that appears on its sales invoices because, when that currency is a local currency, the local currency price will nevertheless have been determined by reference to the US dollar. As a consequence, such entities often have the US dollar as their functional currency, subject to the other primary indicators in IAS 21:9 (i.e. labour, material and other costs of providing the goods or services).

3.2.3   Further indicators of a functional currency

When determining its functional currency, an entity may also need to consider:

[IAS 21:10]

(a)   the currency in which funds from financing activities (i.e. issuing debt and equity instruments) are generated; and

(b)   the currency in which receipts from operating activities are usually retained.

3.2.4   Assessing whether the functional currency of a foreign operation is the same as that of a reporting entity to which it is related

If an entity is a foreign operation, additional factors may also need to be considered in determining whether its functional currency is the same as that of the reporting entity of which it is a subsidiary, branch, associate or joint arrangement:

[IAS 21:11]

(a)   whether the activities of the foreign operation are carried out as an extension of that reporting entity, rather than being carried out with a significant degree of autonomy. If the foreign operation only sells goods imported from that reporting entity and remits the proceeds to it, this will be an example of the former. An example of the latter is when the foreign operation accumulates cash and other monetary items, incurs expenses, generates income and arranges borrowings, all substantially in its local currency;

(b)   whether transactions with that reporting entity are a high or a low proportion of the foreign operation's activities;

(c)   whether cash flows from the activities of the foreign operation directly affect the cash flows of that reporting entity and are readily available for remittance to it; and

(d)   whether cash flows from the activities of the foreign operation are sufficient to service existing and normally expected debt obligations without funds being made available by that reporting entity.

> If a foreign operation carries on business as if it were an extension of the reporting entity of which it is a subsidiary, branch, associate or joint arrangement, the functional currency of the foreign operation is the same as that of the reporting entity; it would be contradictory to assert that such a foreign operation (sometimes referred to as an 'integral foreign operation') operates in a primary economic environment different from the reporting entity of which it is a subsidiary, branch, associate or joint arrangement. [IAS 21:BC6]

3.2.5   *Identifying the functional currency when the indicators are mixed*

When indicators are mixed and the functional currency is not obvious, management should use judgement to determine the functional currency that most faithfully represents the economic effects of transactions, events and conditions. As part of this approach, management should give priority to the primary indicators in **3.2.2** before considering the indicators in **3.2.3** and **3.2.4**. [IAS 21:12]

> Consideration of the following additional factors, based on the nature of the foreign operation, may assist in the determination of functional currency.
>
> * If an intermediate parent carries out duties related to the sub-group in which it holds investments (e.g. if the intermediate parent has different directors/employees from the ultimate parent entity, has its own reporting responsibilities, produces consolidated financial statements including the sub-group, actively manages a series of operations in a geographical area and, therefore, incurs costs in a local currency), this would indicate that the functional currency of the entity is not necessarily the same as that of its parent entity. If the intermediate parent exists solely in order for the ultimate parent to obtain a tax, regulatory, jurisdictional or legal type of benefit it would not otherwise receive, this indicates that it is an extension of its parent entity.
>
> * If the foreign operation is clearly set up as a structured or special purpose entity, its activities are being conducted on behalf of the parent entity (e.g. employee benefit trusts, leasing vehicles etc.) and the structured or special purpose entity is an extension of the parent

entity, this indicates that it should have the same functional currency as that of the parent entity.

- For a treasury entity, it is necessary to assess whether it exists (1) to serve the funding and cash management needs of the group as a whole (i.e. it constitutes an extension of the parent entity), or (2) solely to service a specific sub-group. In the latter case, the functional currency of the treasury entity may be different from that of the parent entity.

- A 'money-box' entity is an entity that holds cash only. In accordance with the factors in IAS 21:9 to 12, it is not the currency of the cash that the entity holds that is the deciding factor in determining functional currency. Consistent with the bullet points above, it is necessary to consider for whose benefit the money-box entity exists, which will determine its functional currency.

Example 3.2.5

Identifying the functional currency

Company M has identified the Euro as its functional currency. Company M establishes two entities, Company P and Company Q. Company P is incorporated in the US and Company Q is incorporated in the UK. The following transactions occurred:

- Company M loaned £2 million each to Company P and Company Q, and both recognised the advance as an intragroup payable;

- Company Q borrowed an additional £3 million from an unrelated third party. Company P guaranteed this third party loan;

- Company Q invested its entire £5 million in building a manufacturing facility to serve the domestic UK market. Company Q intends to repay the loan to the third party from the profit generated through its manufacturing operations (which generate cash flows in Sterling); and

- Company P used its £2 million loan from Company M to invest in marketable securities in international markets. Its investing strategies are determined by Company M. Company P does not have any other activities or purposes.

What are the functional currencies of Company P and Company Q?

In general, the functional currency identified for an entity should provide information about the entity that is useful and reflects the economic substance of the underlying events and circumstances relevant to that entity. If a particular currency is used to a significant extent in, or has a significant impact on, the entity, that currency may be an appropriate currency to be used as the functional currency.

In the circumstances described, it is likely that Sterling would be identified as Company Q's functional currency because that is the currency of the country that influences the sale prices and costs of its goods, as well as the regulations and competitive forces under which it operates.

On the other hand, even though Company P is domiciled in the US, it does not appear to have a significant degree of autonomy and its activities (investing in marketable securities) appear to be carried out as an extension of Company M. Consequently, in accordance with IAS 21:11(a), it is likely that the Euro would be identified as Company P's functional currency.

3.2.6 Identifying the functional currency of an investment fund

Some features common to investment funds include the following (the list is not exhaustive).

- Investors in the fund subscribe and redeem their investments in a specific currency. It may not be permitted, depending on the fund's policies or regulatory requirements, to subscribe or redeem such investments in any other currency.

- The fund may conduct its investment activities through subsidiaries set up in various jurisdictions to take advantage of tax treaties, double taxation agreements and concessions.

- The investment fund's policies may allow it to invest in various securities regardless of jurisdiction, industry or currency. Consequently, investment transactions and the related income and expenses may be denominated in several currencies.

- Investment management fees may be invoiced and received in a specific currency.

- Other costs of operating the fund may be denominated in the local currency of the jurisdiction in which the fund physically operates.

Given these complexities, how should the functional currency of an investment fund be identified?

IAS 21:12 clarifies that, in determining the functional currency of an entity, management should consider the guidance in IAS 21:9 to 11 (see **3.2.2** to **3.2.4**) – giving IAS 21:9 priority before considering IAS 21:10 and 11.

IAS 21:12 also states that, when the indicators in IAS 21:9 to 11 are mixed and the functional currency is not obvious "management uses its judgement to determine the functional currency that most faithfully represents the economic effects of the underlying transactions, events and conditions".

In the context of an investment fund, IAS 21:9 does not seem immediately relevant and is difficult to apply because its factors are directed towards entities that provide goods and services. However, the same underlying principle can be applied to a fund with a mandate to buy and sell securities to generate a return for investors. Hence, the currency of the country whose competitive forces and regulations mainly determine the fund's revenue should be considered when determining the functional currency. In addition, the currencies in which the fund's labour costs and operating expenses are sourced and incurred should also be considered.

However, when a fund's functional currency is not obvious from the analysis above, consideration of the secondary indicators in IAS 21:10 (see **3.2.3**) may provide additional evidence. The currency in which the fund raises finance from investors (i.e. the investor's participation in a fund) and makes distributions to investors (e.g. on redemption) should be considered. The currency in which dividends on investments or interest inflows are received and retained will provide additional evidence of the functional currency.

The indicators in IAS 21:11 (see **3.2.4**) should also be considered if they are relevant to an investment fund (in a foreign operation).

3.2.7   Functional currency is the currency of a hyperinflationary economy

When the functional currency is the currency of a hyperinflationary economy, the entity's financial statements are restated in accordance with IAS 29 *Financial Reporting in Hyperinflationary Economies* (see **chapter A37**). An entity cannot avoid restatement in accordance with IAS 29 by, for example, adopting as its functional currency a currency other than the functional currency determined in accordance with IAS 21 (such as the functional currency of its parent). [IAS 21:14]

3.2.8   Change in functional currency

3.2.8.1   Circumstances in which an entity's functional currency can be changed

As noted at **3.2.1**, the functional currency of an entity reflects the underlying transactions, events and conditions that are relevant to the entity. Accordingly, once determined, the functional currency can be changed only if there is a change to those underlying transactions, events and conditions. [IAS 21:13] For example, a change in the currency that mainly influences the sales prices of goods and services may lead to a change in an entity's functional currency. [IAS 21:36]

Example 3.2.8.1A

Impact of foreign currency borrowings on functional currency

Company K's functional currency is the Euro. Company K accounts for its 43 per cent investment in Company M, a Mexican entity, using the equity method of accounting. Company M's functional currency is the Mexican peso. During the current year, Company M entered into a 200 million Euro third-party borrowing denominated in Euro. Most of Company M's operations, labour costs and purchases are denominated in the peso and incurred in the domestic market.

Is it appropriate for Company M to change its functional currency from the peso to the Euro?

Because the majority of Company M's operations, sales, purchases, labour costs etc. are denominated in the Mexican peso, and Mexico is the country that drives the competitive forces and regulations of that entity, Company M should continue using the Mexican peso as its functional currency. Although, in accordance with IAS 21:10, a large third-party financing in a different currency may in some circumstances provide evidence to support a change in functional currency, greater weight must be given to the factors discussed in IAS 21:9 (sales, purchases, labour costs etc.). Accordingly, in the circumstances described, the new financing is not sufficient, in and of itself, to justify a change in the functional currency from the peso to the Euro.

Example 3.2.8.1B

Change in functional currency

KI, located in Ireland, is a wholly-owned subsidiary of Company K. The US dollar is Company K's functional currency and KI has previously identified the Euro as its functional currency. The functional currency was identified because KI's sales and purchases were denominated primarily in Euro, as were all of KI's labour costs.

During the fourth quarter, KI's operations began to change. KI's sales decreased due to a loss of some sizable contracts while Company K's sales increased due to new significant contracts. Company K began using KI's manufacturing facilities in order to meet its sales orders. KI closed down its sales department because KI will no longer need to generate its own sales as more than 80 per cent will originate from Company K's operations. In addition, Company K has built a new facility to produce the materials needed in KI's manufacturing processes. As at the end of the reporting period, KI began receiving all materials from Company K instead of from outside suppliers.

Based on the changes in KI's business, KI expects cash inflows and outflows, except for wages, primarily to be denominated in US dollars.

IAS 21:36 states that a change in the currency that influences mainly the sales prices of goods and services may lead to a change in functional currency. In addition, the changes in KI's activities may be such that they are now primarily an extension of the reporting entity, Company K, as discussed in IAS 21:11(a).

There is evidence to suggest that KI's functional currency may have changed. Firstly, the currency of revenues has changed from the Euro to primarily the US dollar. This change does not appear to be temporary because the sales department has been closed down. Secondly, the currency of cash outflows for materials has also changed to the US dollar. Company K has built a new facility that will make these materials, so this change does not appear to be temporary either. Lastly, the position of KI's operations within Company K's overall operating strategy has changed, from a self-supporting, stand-alone operating entity to what is primarily a manufacturing facility of Company K.

3.2.8.2   Date at which change in functional currency is recognised

A change in functional currency should be reported as of the date it is determined that there has been a change in the underlying events and circumstances relevant to the reporting entity that justifies a change in the functional currency. This could occur on any date during the year. For convenience, and as a practical matter, there is a practice of using a date at the beginning of the most recent period (annual or interim, as the case might be).

In accordance with IAS 21:35, when there is a change in an entity's functional currency, the entity applies the translation procedures applicable to the new functional currency prospectively from the date of the change.

In other words, all items are translated into the new functional currency using the exchange rate at the date of the change. The resulting translated amounts for non-monetary items are treated as their historical cost. Exchange differences arising from the translation of a foreign operation previously recognised in other comprehensive income are not reclassified from equity to profit or loss until the disposal of the operation (see **section 6**). [IAS 21:37]

See **5.8** for an example of a change in both the functional and the presentation currencies.

An entity should disclose when there has been a change in functional currency, and the reasons for the change (see **9.2**).

3.2.8.3   Change in functional currency – reassessment of liability/equity classification

A change in functional currency may lead to a reassessment of the liability/equity classification of a financial instrument (see **section 8** of **chapter B3** or, for entities that have not yet adopted IFRS 9, **section 8** of **chapter C3** for further discussion).

3.3 Initial recognition of foreign currency transactions

3.3.1 *Transactions to be recognised at spot rate at the date of the transaction*

The functional currency amount at which transactions denominated in foreign currencies should initially be recognised will be determined by using the exchange rate appropriate to the transaction. This is the spot rate between the functional currency and the foreign currency at the date of the transaction. [IAS 21:21] The date of the transaction is the date on which the transaction first qualifies for recognition in accordance with IFRSs. [IAS 21:22]

Example 3.3.1

Initial recognition of purchase of inventories

An entity with a functional currency of Sterling buys inventories for US$15,000. The spot rate is £1 = US$1.50. The inventories are measured at initial recognition at £10,000 (US$15,000/1.50).

3.3.2 *Use of average rate that approximates the actual rate*

For practical reasons, a rate that approximates the actual rate at the date of the transaction is often used. For example, an average rate for a week or a month might be used for all transactions in each foreign currency occurring during that period. If exchange rates fluctuate significantly, however, the use of the average rate for a period is inappropriate. [IAS 21:22]

It is common practice for entities that engage in a large number of foreign currency transactions to fix, for a period, the rate of exchange used to measure those transactions in their accounting records and to disregard day-to-day fluctuations in exchange rates. When this approach is used, care must be taken to ensure that the carrying amount of non-monetary assets (e.g. inventories or property, plant and equipment) is not materially different from what it would have been if actual rates had been used for translation. The actual rates should be used if a material difference would arise compared to average rates (e.g. to measure large one-off transactions such as the acquisition of property, plant and equipment or if there is a significant and unexpected movement in exchange rates).

IAS 21 clearly acknowledges that some degree of approximation is acceptable. It will be a matter of judgement, on the basis of an entity's specific facts and circumstances, whether it is appropriate to derive an average rate for the entire year or whether the year should be analysed into shorter periods (e.g. quarterly periods, months or weeks) with an average rate determined for each.

3.4   Reporting foreign currency items at the end of subsequent reporting periods – monetary items

3.4.1   Monetary items – definition

Monetary items are defined as units of currency held and assets and liabilities to be received or paid in a fixed or determinable number of units of currency. [IAS 21:8]

Under IAS 21, foreign currency monetary items are treated differently from foreign currency non-monetary items. The essential feature of a monetary item is the right to receive (or the obligation to deliver) a fixed or determinable number of units of currency. [IAS 21:16] Conversely, a non-monetary item does not carry this right or obligation.

The following table lists a number of the most common monetary and non-monetary items.

Monetary items	Non-monetary items
Cash	Property, plant and equipment
Bank balances and loans	Intangible assets
Deposits*	For entities that have adopted IFRS 16, right-of-use assets
Employee benefit liability**	
Accrued expenses	Goodwill
Trade payables	Shareholders' equity
Taxation payable / refundable	For entities that have not yet adopted IFRS 16, prepaid rent
Debt securities	
Trade receivables	Investments in associates
Allowance for doubtful debts (because trade receivables are monetary)	Advances received on sales or paid on purchases provided that they are linked to specific sales or purchases
Notes and other receivables	Inventories
Notes and other payables	Allowance for inventory obsolescence (because inventories are non-monetary)
Accrued income	
Holiday pay provision	Deferred income
Deferred tax assets/liabilities	Equity securities
Lease liabilities (or, for entities that have not yet adopted IFRS 16, payables under finance leases)	Provisions to be settled by the delivery of a non-monetary asset

*   When an entity has made a prepayment it is necessary to consider whether it is refundable. When it is refundable, it is similar in nature to a deposit and, therefore, is a monetary item (i.e. it is a right to receive a fixed or determinable number of units of currency). Conversely, when it is not refundable, it is non-monetary (see IAS 21:16).

** In practice, it is usually appropriate to regard a defined benefit asset or obligation as a monetary item. But it is possible to argue that some components, particularly relating to equity securities, should be regarded as non-monetary. However, for most entities,

---

this would lead to a level of complexity that is unwarranted. It is relatively uncommon for a defined benefit arrangement to be denominated in a currency other than the functional currency of the entity.

A contract to receive (or deliver) a variable number of the entity's own equity instruments or a variable amount of assets in which the fair value to be received (or delivered) equals a fixed or determinable number of currency units is also a monetary item. [IAS 21:16]

For example, an issued US$100,000 loan note repayable in ordinary shares to the value of US$100,000 meets the definition of a monetary item.

When preference shares are classified as debt by the issuer, they are typically a monetary liability for the issuer and a monetary asset for the holder. When preference shares are classified as equity by the issuer, they are recognised in equity by the issuer, typically using the rate on the date that they were issued. They are a non-monetary asset for the holder and, on initial recognition, are typically recognised using the rate on the date that they were acquired. Such assets may often subsequently be measured at fair value and the fair value should reflect the rate at the date of the valuation.

3.4.2   Reporting monetary items at the end of subsequent reporting periods

At the end of each reporting period, foreign currency monetary items are translated using the closing rate, i.e. the spot exchange rate at the end of the reporting period. [IAS 21:23(a)]

Example 3.4.2

Translation of foreign-currency denominated revenue with refundable cash-advance receipt

Entity A, whose functional currency is Japanese yen (JPY), is a 31 December year-end entity.

On 31 August 20X1, Entity A enters into an agreement to sell goods to a third-party customer in the United States for US$1,000. On 30 September 20X1, Entity A receives a cash advance of US$100 from the US customer. The customer has the right to demand repayment of the advance at any time up to delivery of the goods on 28 February 20X2.

Key events and foreign exchange rates prevailing on each date are summarised below. Note that, for simplicity, the effect of the time value of money is ignored.

Dates	Events	FX Rates
31 August 20X1	Agreement	US$1 = JPY70
30 September 20X1	Receipt of cash advance	US$1 = JPY80
31 December 20X1	Reporting year end	US$1 = JPY90
28 February 20X2	Revenue recognition	US$1 = JPY100
31 March 20X2	Receipt of final payment	US$1 = JPY105

In these circumstances, the advance received represents a continuing exposure to exchange rate fluctuations for Entity A, and it meets the definition of a monetary item under IAS 21:8 (see **3.4.1**). Consequently, the advance received should be retranslated at the end of Entity A's reporting period and until it becomes non-refundable (in this example, 28 February 20X2). The following entries are recorded.

On 30 September 20X1, the receipt of the cash advance is recorded as follows.

		JPY	JPY
Dr	Cash (US$100 × 80)	8,000	
Cr	Advance received (deferred revenue)		8,000

Retranslation of the refundable cash advance at 31 December 20X1 is recorded as follows.

		JPY	JPY
Dr	Foreign exchange loss (profit or loss)	1,000	
Cr	Advance received (US$100 × (90 – 80))		1,000

Retranslation of the refundable advance and revenue recognition on 28 February 20X2 are recorded in the following entries.

		JPY	JPY
Dr	Foreign exchange loss (profit or loss)	1,000	
Cr	Advance received (US$100 × (100 – 90))		1,000
Dr	Advance received	10,000	
Dr	Trade receivables (US$900 × 100)	90,000	
Cr	Revenue (US$1,000 × 100)		100,000

When the final settlement is received on 31 March 20X2, the following entry is recorded.

		JPY	JPY
Dr	Cash (US$900 × 105)	94,500	
Cr	Trade receivables		90,000
Cr	Foreign exchange gain (profit or loss)		4,500

3.4.3   Recognition of exchange differences arising on monetary items – general

Exchange differences arise on:

- settlement of monetary items at a date subsequent to initial recognition; and

- remeasurement of an entity's monetary items at rates different from those at which they were either initially recognised (if in the period) or previously measured (at the end of the previous reporting period).

Such exchange differences must be recognised in profit or loss in the period in which they arise, except as described in **3.4.4**. [IAS 21:28]

As noted in **2.2**, however, if an item is within the scope of IFRS 9 *Financial Instruments* (or, for entities that have not yet adopted IFRS 9, IAS 39 *Financial Instruments: Recognition and Measurement*) (e.g. it is a foreign currency derivative within the scope of IFRS 9 or IAS 39 or a debt instrument that qualifies as a hedging instrument), IAS 21 does not apply and IFRS 9 (or IAS 39) should be applied instead.

An exchange difference on a foreign currency monetary item occurs when there is a change in the exchange rate between the transaction date and the date of settlement. When the transaction is settled within the same accounting period as that in which it occurred, the entire exchange difference is recognised in that period. When the transaction is settled in a different accounting period to that in which it occurred, the exchange difference to be recognised in each period is determined by the change in exchange rates during that period. [IAS 21:29]

Example 3.4.3A

Exchange differences arising on borrowings denominated in a foreign currency

Exchange gains or losses are the result of movements in the exchange rate between the functional currency of an entity and the foreign currency in which receivables or payables are denominated. For example, an entity has the US dollar as its functional currency and it has borrowed Japanese yen resulting in a yen-denominated payable. Exchange gains or losses should be recognised in profit or loss on the outstanding yen-denominated debt for changes in the spot rate of exchange between the Japanese yen and the US dollar at the end of the reporting period.

Example 3.4.3B

Foreign currency defined benefit post-employment benefit plan

Entity A has a defined benefit post-employment benefit plan that invests in UK securities under which the benefits to employees are denominated in Sterling. The functional currency of Entity A, determined in accordance with IAS 21, is the US dollar.

Entity A classifies pensions and other employee benefits to be paid in cash as monetary items in accordance with IAS 21:16 (see **3.4.1**). Therefore, at the end of each reporting period, the post-employment benefit asset or liability should be translated using the closing rate. The foreign exchange exposure arises as a result of the functional currency of Entity A (i.e. the post-employment benefit plan itself is not affected by the US dollar). Consequently, any exchange difference arising from the translation of the post-employment benefit asset or liability at the end of the reporting period represents a foreign currency exposure for Entity A, and should be recognised in profit or loss in accordance with IAS 21:28. Amounts recognised in profit or loss in accordance with paragraph 120 of IAS 19 *Employee Benefits* (see **7.5.1** in **chapter A15**) are generally translated using the average rate as an approximation of the exchange rates at the dates of the transactions.

Example 3.4.3C

Remeasurement of a decommissioning obligation expected to be paid in a foreign currency

The appropriate treatment for the remeasurement of a decommissioning obligation expected to be paid in a foreign currency depends on whether the decommissioning obligation is a financial liability in the scope of IAS 32 *Financial Instruments: Presentation*, or a provision in the scope of IAS 37 *Provisions, Contingent Liabilities and Contingent Assets*.

A decommissioning obligation qualifies as a financial liability under IAS 32:11 only if there is a contractual obligation to deliver cash or another financial asset to settle the obligation. Financial liabilities are monetary items for the purposes of IAS 21:23(a) (see **3.4.1**) and 28 and, therefore, a foreign currency denominated decommissioning obligation that meets the definition of a financial liability is translated at the closing rate at the end of each reporting period and any exchange differences arising are recognised in profit or loss in the period in which they arise.

A decommissioning obligation that does not meet the definition of a financial liability is accounted for as a provision within the scope of IAS 37 (see **chapter A12**). IAS 37:14 requires that a provision be recognised when (1) the entity has a present obligation (legal or constructive) as a result of a past event, (2) it is probable that an outflow of resources will be required to settle the obligation, and (3) a reliable estimate can be made of the amount of the obligation. A provision is subject to subsequent adjustments reflecting revisions to the original estimate or timing of undiscounted cash flows to settle the obligation.

A provision, therefore, is not a contractual obligation to deliver a fixed or determinable foreign currency denominated amount. An entity may estimate the expected outflow in a foreign currency (discounting these cash flows with the appropriate interest rate relevant to the foreign currency) and then convert the provision into functional currency using the spot rate at the date the provision is recognised. This is all part of the estimation process which should be accounted for in accordance with IFRIC Interpretation 1 *Changes in Existing Decommissioning, Restoration and Similar Liabilities*. The required accounting treatment for changes in the estimated outflow of resources required to settle the obligation (including any exchange differences) depends on whether the related asset is measured using the cost model or using the revaluation model, and is outlined in IFRIC 1:5 to 7 (see **4.4** in **chapter A7**).

3.4.4 Recognition of exchange differences arising on monetary items that form part of the net investment in a foreign operation

3.4.4.1 Monetary items that form part of the net investment in a foreign operation

The net investment in a foreign operation is the amount of the reporting entity's interest in the net assets of that operation. [IAS 21:8]

An entity may have a monetary item that is receivable from, or payable to, a foreign operation. An item for which settlement is neither planned nor likely to occur in the foreseeable future is, in substance, part of the entity's net investment in that foreign operation. An example is a long-term financing loan to the foreign operation with no fixed repayment terms, for which management confirms that repayment is neither planned nor likely to occur in the future. Such monetary items may include long-term receivables or loans. They do not include trade receivables or trade payables. [IAS 21:15]

Exchange gains or losses on monetary items that form part of the net investment in a foreign operation are recognised in accordance with IAS 21:32 and 33 (see **3.4.4.2**).

IAS 21 does not specify a time period that might qualify as the 'foreseeable future'. Therefore, the term 'foreseeable future' does not imply a specific time period, but is an intent-based indicator, i.e. an intragroup receivable or payable may qualify as part of the net investment in the foreign operation when:

- the parent does not intend to require repayment of the intragroup account (which cannot be represented if the debt has a maturity date that is not waived); and

- the parent's management views the intragroup account as part of its investment in the foreign operation.

A history of repayments is likely to be indicative that an advance or loan does not form part of the investment in a foreign operation.

Example 3.4.4.1A

Rolling or minimum intragroup balances viewed as long-term investments

Company A, with the Singapore dollar as its functional currency, advances Euro to its foreign subsidiary, Company B. Company B has identified the Euro as its functional currency. Company B may repay some of the advances but, generally, they are replaced with new advances within a very short time frame (e.g. three to five days). In total, Company B generally has 50 million Euro advances outstanding at all times.

It is not appropriate for Company A to treat the Euro advances as part of its net investment in Company B because rolling balance and minimum balance intragroup accounts generally do not form part of the net investment in a foreign operation under IAS 21. IAS 21:15 specifically excludes trade receivables and trade payables as qualifying assets and liabilities. Intragroup transactions must be evaluated on an individual basis, not on an aggregate or net basis.

Example 3.4.4.1B

Parent guarantee of foreign subsidiary's debt

A Swiss entity, Company R, has a Mexican subsidiary, Company S, with the Mexican peso as its functional currency. Company S borrows Swiss francs from a Swiss bank and Company R guarantees repayment of the loan. Company R has the ability to provide an intragroup loan to Company S, but decided not to do so for tax reasons. Interest payments are made by Company S, and not Company R. It is not anticipated that the subsidiary itself will repay the loan in the foreseeable future.

Although Company R has guaranteed its subsidiary's foreign-currency denominated debt to a third party, that guarantee will not bring the third-party loan within the scope of its net investment in the subsidiary as set out in IAS 21:15. Consequently, the translation gains or losses on the Swiss franc-denominated bank debt are recognised in profit or loss, both in Company S's financial statements and in Company R's consolidated financial statements.

Example 3.4.4.1C

Foreign-currency denominated intragroup payables arising in the normal course of business

Company J, a Japanese parent, has a wholly-owned Mexican subsidiary, Company M. Company M's management has previously identified the Mexican peso as the entity's functional currency because Company M's sales to third parties are denominated in Mexican pesos, as are its labour costs. Raw material purchases from Company J are denominated in Japanese yen and have resulted in intragroup payables to Company J that are also denominated in Japanese yen. In previous reporting periods, Company M has made cash repayments to Company J relating to these payables. However, no fixed repayment terms have been agreed for the intragroup payables. Although no specific amount has been formally designated as such, the management of Company M believes that a portion of the amounts due to Company J are of a long-term nature.

It is not appropriate for the portion of the amounts due that are of a long-term nature to be considered part of Company J's net investment in Company M because IAS 21:15 specifically excludes trade receivables and payables from forming part of an entity's net investment in a foreign operation. Therefore, such balances do not qualify for the exception in IAS 21:15. Moreover, the fact that Company M has made previous cash repayments to Company J leads to a presumption that Company M has the intent to repay the intragroup payables.

However, if Company M negotiates a separate financing long-term advance with its parent, Company J, such that repayment of the advance is not planned or anticipated in the foreseeable future, gains or losses resulting from future foreign currency fluctuations may be accounted for as part of Company J's net investment prospectively from the date of the advance or note payable.

Example 3.4.4.1D

Short-term intragroup debt

Company C is a wholly-owned US subsidiary of Company D, a Dutch-based parent. Company C has notes due to Company D that are denominated in Euro. The notes have stated maturities ranging from six months to one year. Although the notes are short-term by contract, the parent provides a representation each year that it will not demand repayment in that year. Historically, the notes have been renewed each year.

The short-term notes do not qualify for the exception in IAS 21:15.

In order to qualify as long-term investment, settlement must neither be planned nor likely to occur in the foreseeable future. Rolling intragroup balances generally do not form part of the net investment in a foreign operation under IAS 21:15. In the circumstances described, the parent has only represented that it will not require repayment in that year on the rolled-over short-term notes. It has not represented that it will not demand repayment of the notes in the foreseeable future.

Example 3.4.4.1E

Replacement of foreign-currency denominated debt with a long-term advance

Company L is a Lesotho subsidiary of Company S, a South African parent. Company L has the loti as its functional currency and Company S has the

South African rand as its functional currency. Company L has taken out third-party rand-denominated debt which gives rise to exchange losses. In a restructuring of finances, Company S will repay Company L's foreign currency (rand) denominated debt and Company S will advance replacement funds to Company L denominated in the loti.

It would not be appropriate in this transaction for Company S to consider the exchange differences arising on settlement of the third-party rand-denominated debt as relating to its net investment in Company L. The intragroup borrowing and settlement of third-party debt should be accounted for separately.

Although IAS 21:15 discusses the accounting for an intragroup foreign currency advance that is of a long-term nature, the transactions should be accounted for as they occur. Therefore, any foreign currency adjustments related to settlement of the third-party debt should be recognised in profit or loss in the period in which the exchange rate changes. However, if the advance from Company S to Company L is of a long-term nature for which settlement is not planned or anticipated in the foreseeable future, it may be treated as part of Company S's net investment in Company L pursuant to IAS 21:15.

Example 3.4.4.1F

Foreign currency perpetual loan

Entity A, whose functional currency is Sterling, has a foreign operation in the form of a wholly-owned subsidiary, Entity B, with a Euro functional currency. Entity B issues to Entity A perpetual debt (i.e. the debt has no maturity) denominated in Euro with an annual interest rate of 6 per cent. The perpetual debt has no issuer call option or holder put option. Thus, contractually, it is just an infinite stream of interest payments in Euro.

In Entity A's consolidated financial statements, the perpetual debt is appropriately considered a monetary item "for which settlement is neither planned nor likely to occur in the foreseeable future", i.e. the perpetual debt can be considered part of Entity A's net investment in Entity B. Through the origination of the perpetual debt, Entity A has made a permanent investment in Entity B. The interest payments are treated as interest receivable by Entity A and interest payable by Entity B, not as repayment of the debt principal. Therefore, the fact that the interest payments are perpetual does not mean that settlement is planned or likely to occur.

Example 3.4.4.1G

Transaction gains or losses on dividends

If a foreign subsidiary with a functional currency different from that of its parent declares a dividend to the parent (the legal effect being such that the parent's right to the dividend is established), and there is a significant time lag between the date of recognition of the dividend revenue and the date when cash is received, a translation gain or loss will arise on the parent's dividend receivable account.

IAS 21 does not address the accounting for such gains and losses specifically. However, the receivable is a monetary item and does not meet the criteria to be treated as part of the net investment in the subsidiary (on the basis that payment is expected in the foreseeable future). Accordingly, gains and losses on retranslating the monetary item should be taken to profit or loss by the parent, and should not be reclassified on consolidation of the subsidiary.

This may be contrasted with the exchange gains and losses arising when an interest in a subsidiary is retranslated on consolidation, which are recognised in other comprehensive income (see **4.3.1**). IAS 21:41 states that the reason for not recognising such translation adjustments in profit or loss for the period is that the changes in the exchange rates have little or no direct effect on the present and future cash flows from operations of either the foreign entity or the reporting entity. When a dividend has already given rise to an asset in the parent, however, changes in exchange rates have a direct effect on the parent's future cash inflows (see also the discussion in **5.4**).

3.4.4.2 Exchange differences on monetary items to be recognised outside profit or loss

Certain monetary items are outside the scope of IAS 21 because they are instead dealt with by IFRS 9 or, for entities that have not yet adopted IFRS 9, IAS 39 (e.g. an item designated as a hedging instrument). For monetary items within the scope of IAS 21, however, there is only one exception to the requirement that exchange differences are recognised in profit or loss. When a monetary item forms part of a reporting entity's net investment in a foreign operation (see **3.4.4.1**):

[IAS 21:32]

- exchange differences are recognised in profit or loss in the separate financial statements of the reporting entity and of the foreign operation, as appropriate; but

- in any financial statements that include both the reporting entity and the foreign operation (e.g. consolidated financial statements if the foreign operation is a subsidiary), such exchange differences are recognised initially in other comprehensive income and reclassified from equity to profit or loss on disposal of the net investment in accordance with IAS 21:48 (see **section 6**).

The effect of this in the 'consolidated' financial statements (i.e. those that combine the reporting entity and the foreign operation) is as follows:

[IAS 21:33]

- a monetary item denominated in the functional currency of the reporting entity gives rise to an exchange difference in the foreign operation, and this is recognised in other comprehensive income as above;

- a monetary item denominated in the functional currency of the foreign operation gives rise to an exchange difference in the reporting entity, and this is recognised in other comprehensive income as above; and

- a monetary item denominated in a currency other than the functional currency of either the reporting entity or the foreign operation gives rise to an exchange difference in the separate financial statements of both the foreign operation and the reporting entity, and these are recognised in other comprehensive income as above.

3.4.4.3 Changing the form of a long-term investment which forms part of the net investment in a foreign operation

Example 3.4.4.3

Changing the form of a long-term investment which forms part of the net investment in a foreign operation

A UK entity, Company A, has a Canadian subsidiary to which it has made advances that are denominated in Canadian dollars. Company A has previously represented its intention that the advances are a long-term investment. Consequently, exchange gains and losses on the advances have been recognised in other comprehensive income in the consolidated financial statements in accordance with IAS 21:32. There have been no previous repayments of these advances.

As a result of a decline in the Canadian dollar compared to Sterling, the value of the advances has declined. In order to receive a tax deduction in the UK for the decrease, Company A would like to require the Canadian subsidiary to repay the advances. However, Company A does not want to realise a loss on the transaction for accounting purposes. Company A proposes to contribute cash to the Canadian subsidiary in the form of a capital contribution and the Canadian subsidiary will immediately use the cash received to repay the advances.

Does the proposed transaction require Company A to recognise a loss for the elimination of the amount of the cumulative translation adjustment pertaining to the advances?

No. In the proposed transaction, Company A is replacing one form of long-term investment (long-term advances) with another form of long-term investment (capital contribution). The translation adjustment attributable to the long-term intragroup advances should remain as a component of equity until the disposal or partial disposal of the Canadian subsidiary, at which time it should be reclassified from equity to profit or loss as a reclassification adjustment.

3.4.4.4 Change in circumstances so that a monetary item becomes part of the net investment in a foreign operation

An entity may not initially regard an intragroup loan as being part of the net investment in a subsidiary, but circumstances may later change such that it is so regarded. From the date at which the criteria for regarding the loan as part of the parent's net investment in the subsidiary are met, the changed nature of the loan should be accounted for prospectively, with exchange differences arising after that date taken to a separate component of equity on consolidation, together with those exchange differences arising on retranslation of the net assets and income and expenses of the subsidiary.

In some circumstances, it is necessary to exercise a degree of judgement as to the date from which the criteria are met. Therefore, it is necessary to consider carefully all of the available evidence in arriving at this judgement.

3.4.4.5 Loans or advances from other group entities

The entity that has a monetary item receivable from, or payable to, the foreign operation may be the parent entity or any subsidiary in the group, including another foreign operation. [IAS 21:15A]

For example, an entity has two subsidiaries, A and B. Subsidiary B is a foreign operation. Subsidiary A grants a loan to Subsidiary B. Subsidiary A's loan receivable from Subsidiary B would be part of the entity's net investment in Subsidiary B if settlement of the loan is neither planned nor likely to occur in the foreseeable future. [IAS 21:15A]

Therefore, a monetary item for which settlement is neither planned nor likely to occur in the foreseeable future forms part of a reporting entity's net investment in a foreign operation regardless of whether the monetary item results from a transaction with the reporting entity or any of its subsidiaries (see IAS 21:BC25E).

3.4.4.6 Loans or advances denominated in another currency

Most frequently, a monetary item that forms part of a reporting entity's net investment in a foreign operation under IAS 21:15 and 15A is denominated in the functional currency of the foreign operation or alternatively in the functional currency of the reporting entity. However, it may be denominated in a currency other than the functional currency of either entity. For example, the monetary item may be denominated in a currency that is more readily convertible than the local domestic currency of the foreign operation.

IAS 21:33 is clear that foreign exchange differences on a monetary item denominated in a currency other than the functional currency of either the reporting entity or the foreign operation also qualify for initial recognition in other comprehensive income in the consolidated financial statements, provided that the criteria in IAS 21:15 and 15A are met.

IAS 21:BC25E also confirms that a monetary item for which settlement is neither planned nor likely to occur in the foreseeable future forms part of a reporting entity's net investment in a foreign operation regardless of the currency of the monetary item.

3.5   Reporting foreign currency items at the end of subsequent reporting periods – non-monetary items

3.5.1   Non-monetary items measured in terms of historical cost

The carrying amount of non-monetary items at the end of subsequent reporting periods is determined in conjunction with other relevant IFRSs.

Non-monetary items that are measured in terms of historical cost in a foreign currency are translated using the spot exchange rate at the date of the transaction, i.e. they remain at the initial recognised amount and are not retranslated. [IAS 21:23(b)] These balances reflect the historical cost in the functional currency of acquiring the items.

Example 3.5.1

Non-monetary item measured at historical cost

Company T, whose functional currency is the Euro, has not yet adopted IFRS 9 *Financial Instruments*. It holds an investment in a Japanese entity. The investment is accounted for appropriately under IAS 39:46(c) at cost because it does not have a quoted market price in an active market and its fair value cannot be reliably measured. Company T's initial investment was made in Japanese yen and represented 4.3 million Euro at the date of acquisition of the investment. At the end of the reporting period, the historical cost in Japanese yen, if translated at the closing rate, would correspond to 6 million Euro.

It would not be appropriate to recognise the 1.7 million Euro increase as a translation gain. IAS 21:23 states that non-monetary items denominated in a foreign currency measured in terms of historical cost should be reported using the exchange rate at the date of the transaction. Accordingly, the investment should continue to be measured at 4.3 million Euro.

3.5.2   Non-monetary items measured at fair value

Non-monetary items that are measured at fair value in a foreign currency are translated using the spot exchange rates at the date when the value was measured. [IAS 21:23(c)]

3.5.3 Carrying amount of non-monetary item determined by comparing two or more amounts

Sometimes the carrying amount of an item is determined by comparing two or more amounts, for example:

- the lower of cost and net realisable value for inventories (IAS 2 *Inventories*); or

- the lower of an asset's previous carrying amount and its recoverable amount to determine the amount of an impairment loss (IAS 36 *Impairment of Assets*).

When the asset is non-monetary and is measured in a foreign currency, the carrying amount is determined as the lower of:

[IAS 21:25]

- the cost or carrying amount translated at the exchange rate at the date that amount was determined (the rate at the transaction date for items carried at historical cost); and

- the net realisable value or recoverable amount, as appropriate, translated at the exchange rate at the date that value was determined. This will be the closing rate if the value was determined at the end of the reporting period.

The effect of this may be that an impairment loss is recognised in the functional currency but would not be recognised in the foreign currency, or *vice versa*.

Example 3.5.3

Determining net realisable value for inventories

Company A is a UK entity, and has Sterling as its functional currency.

Company A purchases inventories for €150 when the exchange rate is £1:€1.50. Company A plans to sell the inventories in Euro.

At the end of the reporting period, the exchange rate is £1:€1.20. The inventories are slightly damaged and Company A determines the net realisable value (NRV) to be €120.

How should Company A determine the Sterling carrying amount of the inventories at the end of the reporting period?

The carrying amount at the end of the reporting period (i.e. the lower of cost and NRV) is determined by comparing:

- cost of €150 translated at the transaction date rate of £1:€1.50; with
- NRV of €120 translated at the closing rate of £1:€1.20.

> These are both £100, so there is no write-down of inventories in the financial statements at the end of the reporting period.
>
> When measuring NRV, the currency in which the inventories will be sold is used. For Company A, this is Euro. In the circumstances described, at the end of the reporting period, the inventories are impaired in Euro (by €30) but not in Sterling, because the exchange rate has moved. Consequently, no impairment is recognised in Company A's financial statements.

3.5.4   Recognition of exchange differences on non-monetary items

3.5.4.1   Recognition of exchange differences on non-monetary items – general

When a gain or loss on a non-monetary item is recognised in profit or loss, any exchange component of that gain or loss is also recognised in profit or loss. When a gain or loss on a non-monetary item is recognised in other comprehensive income, any exchange component of that gain or loss is also recognised in other comprehensive income. [IAS 21:30]

For example, IAS 16 *Property, Plant and Equipment* requires some gains and losses arising on a revaluation of property, plant and equipment to be recognised in other comprehensive income. When such an asset is measured in a foreign currency, IAS 21:23(c) requires the revalued amount to be translated using the rate at the date the value is determined, resulting in an exchange difference that is also recognised in other comprehensive income. [IAS 21:31]

Example 3.5.4.1

Non-monetary asset measured at fair value in a foreign currency

On 1 November 20X1, Company A (Sterling functional currency) buys a building to be used as its new head office for US$50,000,000, with full payment being made on that date. The exchange rate is US$1.68:£1. At the end of Company A's reporting period, 31 December 20X1, the building is not depreciated because it is not yet available for use. The exchange rate is US$1.71:£1 and the fair value of the building is US$60,000,000 at that date.

The journal entries are as follows.

1 November 20X1

		£	£
Dr	Property, plant and equipment	29,761,905	
Cr	Cash		29,761,905

To recognise the US$ transaction in the functional currency at the exchange rate at the time of the transaction of US$1.68:£1.

Depending on whether Company A accounts for its owner-occupied buildings at cost (less accumulated depreciation and impairment losses), or at a revalued amount, subsequent accounting entries are as follows.

At cost (less accumulated depreciation and impairment losses)

31 December 20X1

The building is a non-monetary item and held at historical cost. It continues to be measured at £29,761,905 (i.e. at the transaction rate).

At revalued amount

31 December 20X1

The building is a non-monetary item and held at fair value. It is retranslated at the rate of exchange at the date of valuation.

		£	£
Dr	Property, plant and equipment	5,325,814	
Cr	Revaluation gain (other comprehensive income)		5,325,814

To recognise a gain in fair value of £5,325,814 (£35,087,719 – £29,761,905), which includes the exchange component.

Note that when an asset's revalued amount is less than its carrying amount, and no credit balance exists in the revaluation surplus in respect of the asset, an expense is recognised in profit or loss.

3.5.4.2   Foreign-currency denominated available-for-sale financial assets (for entities that have not yet adopted IFRS 9)

In accordance with IAS 39, available-for-sale financial assets are measured at fair value with fair value gains or losses recognised in other comprehensive income and reclassified from equity to profit or loss when the asset is derecognised or impaired (see **3.1.4** in **chapter C6**).

For the purpose of recognising foreign exchange gains and losses in respect of available-for-sale financial assets that are monetary items, IAS 39:AG83 requires that such items be treated as if they are carried at amortised cost in the foreign currency. Therefore, exchange differences resulting from changes in amortised cost are recognised in profit or loss, with other changes in the carrying amount recognised in other comprehensive income in accordance with IAS 39:55(b).

This treatment results in the cumulative gain or loss recognised in other comprehensive income being the difference between the amortised cost (adjusted for impairment, if any) and the fair value of the instrument in the functional currency of the reporting entity. The approach is illustrated in a numerical example (IAS 39:IG.E.3.2) – which is reproduced as **example 3.3.4** in **chapter C6**.

For non-monetary available-for-sale financial assets (e.g. equity investments), the gain or loss that is recognised in other comprehensive income includes any related foreign currency component.

3.6   Exchange rates – other considerations

3.6.1   Several exchange rates available

In some circumstances, there may be several exchange rates available (e.g. when a country is experiencing turmoil and its government has imposed an exchange rate that is different from the spot exchange rate in order to discourage the outflow of capital from that country).

When several exchange rates are available, the rate to be used is that at which the future cash flows represented by the transaction or balance could have been settled if those cash flows had occurred at the measurement date. [IAS 21:26]

3.6.2   Unofficial exchange rate for translation and remeasurement

When there is both an official exchange rate *and* an unofficial exchange rate, and the unofficial exchange rate is used both widely and legally for the purposes of currency conversions, a parallel or dual exchange rate situation exists.

In such circumstances, if it can be demonstrated reasonably that transactions have been or will be settled at the unofficial rate (including currency exchanges for dividend or profit repatriations), it is appropriate to use the unofficial rate for translation and remeasurement purposes.

Example 3.6.2

Dividend remittance rate specified by government

A country is experiencing economic turmoil, and the government has imposed an exchange rate different from the spot market exchange rate in order to discourage capital from leaving the country. The new rate is the dividend remittance rate. This specific exchange rate applies to all remittances of earnings or dividends distributed outside the country.

Which rate should be used by a parent in translating a subsidiary operating in such a foreign country?

IAS 21:8 defines the closing rate as "the spot exchange rate at the end of the reporting period". The closing rate should be the rate the entity currently would

---

pay or receive in the market. Therefore, in the circumstances described, the dividend remittance rate would be appropriate for translation purposes because cash flows to the reporting entity can only occur at this rate, and the realisation of a net investment is dependent upon cash flows from that foreign entity.

Unusual circumstances that may permit an entity to use the market exchange rate in translating a foreign subsidiary in the circumstances described above would include (1) a history of obtaining the market exchange rate for such transactions, and (2) the ability to source funds at the market exchange rate. Otherwise, the dividend remittance rate should be used.

Careful judgement should be applied to determine whether circumstances such as those described result in loss of control of the foreign subsidiary (see **section 12** in **chapter A24**).

3.6.3 Lack of exchangeability between two currencies

When exchangeability between two currencies is temporarily lacking, the rate used is the first subsequent rate at which exchanges could be made. [IAS 21:26]

3.6.4 Exchange rate movements after the end of the reporting period

Example 3.6.4

Exchange rate movements after the end of the reporting period

Company G is a German entity with a Russian subsidiary. The subsidiary's functional currency is the Russian ruble. The subsidiary has Euro-denominated debt. The Russian ruble exchange rate against the Euro has fluctuated significantly in the two months before and after the end of the reporting period.

IAS 21:23(a) states that foreign currency monetary items should be reported at the end of each reporting period using the closing rate, with no exceptions specified. It would not be appropriate to use an exchange rate subsequent to the end of the reporting period, even though exchange rates are volatile.

Due to the significant volatility in exchange rates, however, the effect on foreign currency monetary items of a change in exchange rates occurring after the end of the reporting period should be disclosed in accordance with IAS 10 *Events after the Reporting Period* if the change is of such significance that non-disclosure would affect the ability of users of the financial statements to make proper evaluations and decisions (see **7.1** in **chapter A22**).

3.7 Accounting records in a currency other than the functional currency

When an entity keeps its accounting records in a currency other than its functional currency, at the time the entity prepares its financial statements all amounts are translated into the functional currency in accordance with IAS 21:20 to 26, so as to produce the same amounts in the functional currency as would have occurred had the items been recognised initially in the functional currency. [IAS 21:34]

4   Presentation currency

4.1   Presentation currency – definition

The presentation currency is defined as the currency in which the financial statements are presented. [IAS 21:8] Unlike an entity's functional currency, the presentation currency can be any currency of choice. This choice is available both in the entity's 'main' financial statements and, if prepared, any separate financial statements. [IAS 21:19]

An entity normally presents its financial statements in the same currency as its functional currency; however, an entity may choose to present its financial statements in a different currency. Presenting the financial statements in a currency other than the functional currency does not change the way in which the underlying items are measured. It merely expresses the underlying amounts, which are measured in the functional currency, in a different currency.

4.2   Choice of presentation currency

The most common use of a presentation currency is in the context of a consolidated group. When a group contains entities with different functional currencies, the results and financial position of each entity must be expressed in a common currency in order to produce the consolidated financial statements. The presentation currency of the consolidated financial statements of the group is often, but not always, the functional currency of the parent.

A corporate group may have extensive operations in many countries and conduct its business largely in international markets. It may be difficult to identify the most appropriate presentation currency. An international currency such as Sterling, the US dollar or the Euro might be used. For example, for entities that raise capital in international markets, the use of an international currency may be of benefit to the users of the financial statements.

Individual entities, or groups where all of the entities have the same functional currency, may also choose to present their financial statements in a currency other than their functional currency. This option may be selected, for example:

- to provide information to overseas shareholders; or
- for the purpose of preparing statutory financial statements in some jurisdictions where entities are required to present their financial statements in the local currency even if this is not their functional currency; or
- by a subsidiary that wishes to present its financial statements in the functional currency of its parent when that is different from its own functional currency.

4.3 Translation to a presentation currency

4.3.1 Translation to a presentation currency – general

Except when the functional currency is the currency of a hyperinflationary economy (see **4.4**), an entity's results and financial position are translated from its functional currency into a different presentation currency using the following procedures:

[IAS 21:39]

(a) assets and liabilities for each statement of financial position presented (i.e. including comparative amounts) are translated at the closing rate at the date of that statement of financial position;

(b) for each period presented (i.e. including comparative periods), income and expenses recognised in the period are translated at the exchange rates at the dates of the transactions; and

(c) all resulting exchange differences are recognised in other comprehensive income.

Cash flows are translated on a basis similar to that required for income and expenses, i.e. using the exchange rates at the transaction dates (see paragraphs 25 and 26 of IAS 7 *Statement of Cash Flows*).

Equity transactions (e.g. contributions to equity share capital, distributions to owners of equity) are also translated at the exchange rates at the transaction dates.

For practical reasons, a rate that approximates the exchange rates at the dates of the transactions (e.g. an average rate for the period) is often used to translate income and expense items in step (b) above. If exchange rates fluctuate significantly, however, the use of the average rate for a period is inappropriate. [IAS 21:40]

4.3.2   Recognition of exchange differences arising on translation to a presentation currency

IAS 21:41 explains that exchange differences resulting from translation into a presentation currency are not recognised in profit or loss because those changes in exchange rates have little or no direct effect on the present and future cash flows from operations.

The exchange differences arising on translation to the presentation currency result from:

[IAS 21:41]

- translating income and expenses at the exchange rates at the dates of the transactions and assets and liabilities at the closing rate; and

- translating the opening net assets at an exchange rate (closing rate) different from that at which they were previously reported.

The cumulative amount of the exchange differences is presented in a separate component of equity until disposal of the foreign operation (see **section 6**). [IAS 21:41]

As set out in **4.3.1**, IAS 21:39 provides rules for the translation of income, expenses, assets and liabilities; however, it does not refer to the translation, or retranslation, of share capital or other equity reserves. IAS 21:39(c) requires that exchange differences arising from translation should be recognised in other comprehensive income and later reclassified to profit or loss on disposal or partial disposal; those amounts do not reflect any retranslation of share capital or other equity reserves. Accordingly, the 'foreign currency translation reserve' should not include any amounts for the retranslation of share capital or other equity reserves.

Although IAS 21 does not specifically prohibit the retranslation of share capital and other equity reserves, such a retranslation would have no meaning for financial reporting purposes, because any 'differences' arising would never be reclassified to profit or loss.

Accordingly, it is generally considered most meaningful to translate share capital and other components of equity using the historical rate, i.e. the exchange rate at the date of issue of share capital, or at the date of the associated transaction for other equity reserves. In particular, if this approach is adopted:

- when translating share capital into the presentation currency, the rate at the date of issue would be used. Thus, more than one historical rate will apply when share capital is issued at different times; and

- when translating a revaluation reserve (e.g. when an item of property is revalued in accordance with IAS 16 *Property, Plant and Equipment*) into the presentation currency, the rate at the date of each revaluation would be used. Thus, more than one historical rate will apply when a revaluation reserve relates to assets that have been revalued at different times.

4.4   Translation to the presentation currency from the currency of a hyperinflationary economy

When an entity's functional currency is the currency of a hyperinflationary economy, the entity must first restate its financial statements in accordance with IAS 29 *Financial Reporting in Hyperinflationary Economies* before translating its results into its chosen presentation currency (see **chapter A37**). Note, however, that the treatment of comparative amounts translated into the currency of a non-hyperinflationary economy is different, as discussed below. [IAS 21:43]

Once the entity's financial statements have been restated in accordance with IAS 29, if the entity chooses to present them in a different presentation currency, the results and financial position of that entity are translated into a different presentation currency as follows:

[IAS 21:42]

- all amounts (i.e. assets, liabilities, equity items, income and expenses, including comparative amounts) are translated at the closing rate at the date of the statement of financial position; except that

- when comparative amounts are translated into the currency of a non-hyperinflationary economy, all amounts are those presented in the prior financial statements (i.e. they are not adjusted for subsequent changes in the price level or subsequent changes in exchange rates).

Note that the different treatment of comparative amounts described above does not apply when the presentation currency is that of a (different) hyperinflationary economy. In those circumstances, all amounts are translated at the closing rate of the most recent statement of financial position presented (i.e. last year's comparative amounts, as adjusted for subsequent changes in the price level, are translated at this year's closing rate).

When the economy ceases to be hyperinflationary and the entity no longer restates its financial statements in accordance with IAS 29, it uses as the historical costs for translation into the presentation currency the amounts restated to the price level at the date the entity ceased restating its financial statements. [IAS 21:43]

Example 4.4

Comparative amounts in the consolidated financial statements of a parent when the economy of the functional currency of a subsidiary becomes hyperinflationary in the current reporting period

In 20X9, Subsidiary A's functional currency is determined to be that of a hyperinflationary currency. As required by IFRIC 7 *Applying the Restatement Approach under IAS 29 Financial Reporting in Hyperinflationary Economies*, the comparative amounts in Subsidiary A's financial statements are retrospectively restated as if the subsidiary's functional currency had always been that of a hyperinflationary currency. The presentation currency of the consolidated financial statements in which Subsidiary A is included is not that of a hyperinflationary economy.

Should the comparative amounts relating to Subsidiary A in the 20X9 consolidated financial statements of its parent be restated?

No. IAS 21:42 (see above) describes the procedures for the translation of a foreign operation whose functional currency is the currency of a hyperinflationary economy. IAS 21:42(b) specifies that "when amounts are translated into the currency of a non-hyperinflationary economy, comparative amounts shall be those that were presented as current year amounts in the relevant prior year financial statements (i.e. not adjusted for subsequent changes in the price level or subsequent changes in exchange rates)".

Therefore, in the circumstances described, the comparative amounts relating to Subsidiary A in the 20X9 consolidated financial statements should not be restated. Only the current period amounts reported in the consolidated financial statements will be affected by Subsidiary A's accounting under IAS 29.

4.5   Translation from a non-hyperinflationary functional currency into a hyperinflationary presentation currency

Example 4.5

Translation from a non-hyperinflationary functional currency into a hyperinflationary presentation currency

Entity A is located in a jurisdiction with a hyperinflationary economy. Entity A has determined that its functional currency is the currency of a non-hyperinflationary economy. However, due to local regulations, Entity A must present its financial statements in its local currency (i.e. in the currency of a hyperinflationary economy).

How should Entity A's financial statements be translated into its hyperinflationary presentation currency?

Because Entity A's functional currency is not the currency of a hyperinflationary economy, Entity A is outside the scope of IAS 29 *Financial Reporting in Hyperinflationary Economies* (see IAS 29:1).

Accordingly, in order to translate its financial statements to the hyperinflationary presentation currency, Entity A must use the following method described in IAS 21:39:

- assets and liabilities for each statement of financial position should be translated at the closing rate of the date of that statement of financial position;

- income and expenses should be translated at the exchange rates at the dates of the relevant transactions; and

- all resulting exchange differences should be recognised in other comprehensive income.

5 Translation of a foreign operation

5.1 Foreign operation – definition

A foreign operation is an entity that is a subsidiary, associate, joint arrangement or branch of a reporting entity, the activities of which are based or conducted in a country or currency other than those of the reporting entity. [IAS 21:8]

The definition of a foreign operation includes a branch of a reporting entity and it is clear from IAS 21 that it is possible for such a branch to have a different functional currency from that of the entity itself. It follows, therefore, that a single legal entity may consist of several operations with different functional currencies. But, in practice, this will not be common and will arise primarily when branches are largely autonomous and have been combined as a single legal entity for tax or similar reasons.

5.2 General requirements for the translation of a foreign operation

In addition to the procedures discussed in **section 4**, there are other rules in IAS 21 that apply when the results and financial position of a foreign operation are translated into a presentation currency for inclusion in the financial statements of a reporting entity, whether by consolidation or the equity method. [IAS 21:44] These rules deal with:

- exchange differences attributable to non-controlling interests (see **5.3**);

- exchange differences on intragroup transactions (see **5.4**);

- financial statements of foreign operations prepared to a different date (see **5.5**); and

- goodwill and fair value adjustments (see **5.6**).

The incorporation of the results and financial position of a foreign operation in the financial statements of a reporting entity follows normal consolidation procedures as set out in IFRS 10 *Consolidated Financial Statements*, IAS 28 *Investments in Associates and Joint Ventures* and IFRS 11 *Joint Arrangements*. [IAS 21:45] These Standards are discussed in **chapters A24**, **A26** and **A27**, respectively.

5.3   Exchange differences attributable to non-controlling interests

When a foreign operation is consolidated but is not wholly owned, accumulated exchange differences arising from translation and attributable to non-controlling interests are allocated to, and recognised as part of, non-controlling interests in the consolidated statement of financial position. [IAS 21:41]

5.4   Exchange differences on intragroup transactions

An intragroup monetary asset (or liability), whether short-term or long-term, cannot be eliminated against the corresponding intragroup liability (or asset) without showing exchange differences in the consolidated financial statements.

The monetary item represents a commitment to convert one currency into another and, consequently, the entity is exposed to an exchange gain or loss.

Accordingly, in the consolidated financial statements of the reporting entity, such an exchange difference is recognised in profit or loss unless it is a monetary item that forms part of the reporting entity's net investment in the foreign operation – see **3.4.4**. [IAS 21:45]

Example 5.4

Exchange gain or loss on intragroup loan

A UK parent, Company X, has a wholly-owned subsidiary in the US, Company Y. Company X's functional currency is Sterling and Company Y's is US dollars. Company X has provided a loan in Sterling to Company Y. The loan is not regarded as part of Company X's net investment in Company Y.

No exchange difference arises in the separate financial statements of the UK parent because the loan receivable is denominated in Company X's functional currency. In the subsidiary's separate financial statements, the loan payable is a monetary item and exchange differences arising on retranslation into Company Y's functional currency of US dollars are recognised in profit or loss in accordance with IAS 21:32.

On consolidation, although the intragroup loan is eliminated from the statement of financial position, the related exchange gain or loss recognised in Company Y's separate financial statements in respect of the Sterling loan payable survives the consolidation process, so that the gain or loss is also recognised in consolidated profit or loss.

Similar logic will apply when Company X has an unsettled balance with Company Y in respect of a recognised dividend receivable. The dividend receivable is a monetary item and must be retranslated into Sterling with foreign exchange gains or losses recognised in profit or loss.

See **3.4.4.4** for a discussion of the accounting implications when changes in circumstances result in an entity regarding a pre-existing intragroup loan as becoming part of the net investment in a subsidiary.

5.5 Financial statements of a foreign operation prepared to a different date

A foreign operation may prepare financial statements to a date different from that of the reporting entity, e.g. for tax reasons or if legislation in its country requires financial statements to be prepared to a specific date. Often the foreign operation will prepare additional statements to the same date as those of the reporting entity (investor) for inclusion in the consolidated financial statements.

When it is impracticable to prepare additional statements, IFRS 10 *Consolidated Financial Statements* allows the use of a different date, provided that the difference is no greater than three months and adjustments are made for the effects of any significant transactions or other events that occur between the different dates.

If the foreign operation's financial statements are prepared to a different date, the assets and liabilities of the foreign operation are translated at the exchange rate at that date (i.e. at the end of the reporting period of the foreign operation). In accordance with IFRS 10, adjustments are made for significant changes in exchange rates up to the end of the reporting period of the reporting entity. For example, significant movements may arise between the two dates if the functional currency of the foreign operation devalues significantly against that of the reporting entity. [IAS 21:46]

Example 5.5

Financial statements of a foreign operation prepared to a different date

A parent includes a foreign subsidiary's financial statements for the year ended 30 November in the parent's consolidated financial statements for the year ended 31 December. Between 30 November and 31 December, the functional currency of the subsidiary devalues significantly against the parent's functional currency (which is also the presentation currency of the group).

When the financial statements of a subsidiary used in the consolidated financial statements are prepared to a date different from that of the parent, IFRS 10 requires adjustments to be made for the effects of significant events or transactions that occur between that date and the date of the parent's financial

---

statements. The rate used for the translation of the foreign subsidiary's financial statements should be the spot rate at 30 November, as required by IAS 21:46, but, separately, it is necessary to consider which assets and liabilities might be affected significantly by the devaluation. Different items may be affected in different ways. For example:

- a further adjustment may be required for significant non-monetary assets of the subsidiary to retranslate them using the rate at 31 December, with a corresponding adjustment to the exchange differences recognised in other comprehensive income;

- conversely, for any significant monetary assets of the subsidiary that are denominated in the functional currency of the parent, there may be little impact on the consolidated statement of financial position. However, a further adjustment may be required to recognise in profit or loss the exchange gains that arose on those items in the subsidiary during December, with a corresponding adjustment to the exchange differences recognised in other comprehensive income.

The same approach is used in applying the equity method to associates and joint ventures in accordance with IAS 28 *Investments in Associates and Joint Ventures*. [IAS 21:46]

5.6   Goodwill and fair value adjustments

5.6.1   Goodwill and fair value adjustments – general

Any goodwill arising on the acquisition of a foreign operation and any fair value adjustments to the carrying amounts of assets and liabilities arising on the acquisition of that foreign operation are:

[IAS 21:47]

- treated as assets and liabilities of the foreign operation, and therefore expressed in the functional currency of the foreign operation; and

- translated at the closing rate in accordance with IAS 21:39 and IAS 21:42.

The level at which goodwill is allocated for functional currency purposes (see **5.6.2**) may differ from the level at which goodwill is tested for impairment in accordance with IAS 36 *Impairment of Assets* (see **8.2.8** in **chapter A10**).

5.6.2 Interaction between IAS 21 and IAS 36

Example 5.6.2A

Allocation of goodwill arising from the acquisition of a foreign operation

Company A, a French entity with the Euro as its functional currency, acquires Company S, a Swiss entity. Following the acquisition, the functional currency of Company S continues to be the Swiss franc (CHF).

One of Company A's other subsidiaries, Company D (also located in France with the Euro (€) as its functional currency) is expected to benefit from the synergies of the acquisition. Company D represents a cash-generating unit (CGU) as defined in IAS 36:6. Consequently, in accordance with IAS 36:80, part of the goodwill arising on the acquisition of Company S is allocated to Company D's CGU for the purposes of impairment testing.

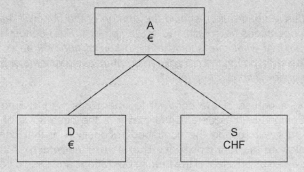

Should the goodwill allocated to Company D be considered a Swiss franc or a Euro-denominated asset going forward? At what rate should the goodwill allocated to Company D be converted for the purposes of preparing the consolidated financial statements of Entity A and performing goodwill impairment tests?

The goodwill allocated to Company D is a Euro-denominated asset.

IAS 21:BC31 states that "goodwill arises only because of the investment in the foreign entity and has no existence apart from that entity. ... [W]hen the acquired entity comprises a number of businesses with different functional currencies, the cash flows that support the continued recognition of goodwill are generated in those different functional currencies".

While one would generally expect that the 'foreign' operation supporting the continued recognition of goodwill is part of the foreign operation acquired, this is not always the case. In allocating a portion of the goodwill to Company D, Company A has determined that it is the cash flows of a CGU with a Euro functional currency (Company D), rather than those of the Swiss entity, that will support the continued recognition of the goodwill. Therefore, goodwill should be treated as an asset of Company D for the purposes of IAS 21:47.

The goodwill allocated to Company D should be translated at the rate in effect on the date of its allocation to Company D (i.e. the date of acquisition).

Example 5.6.2B

Reallocation of goodwill to a foreign operation

Company A, a French entity with the Euro as its functional currency, acquires Company B, a UK entity (functional currency Sterling). In accordance with IAS 36:80, the goodwill arising on the acquisition is allocated to Company A's various UK operations (including Company B) that are expected to primarily benefit from the synergies of the combination. In accordance with IAS 21:47, the goodwill is considered a Sterling asset and is translated at the closing rate.

Several years later, Company A undertakes an internal reorganisation and some of the UK operations are transferred to France. In accordance with IAS 36:87, Company A reallocates a portion of the goodwill originally generated on the acquisition of Company B to its French operations using a relative value approach.

Following this reorganisation, should the portion of the goodwill reallocated to the French operations be considered a Sterling or a Euro-denominated asset going forward? At what rate should that portion of goodwill be converted for the purposes of preparing the consolidated financial statements of Entity A and performing goodwill impairment tests?

In allocating a portion of the goodwill to operations with a Euro functional currency, Company A has determined that it is the cash flows of its French operations that will support the continued recognition of that portion of the goodwill following the reorganisation. Therefore, that portion of the goodwill should be treated as an asset of the French operations and should be converted from Sterling at the rate in effect on the date of the reallocation (in this case on the date of the internal reorganisation) to determine the Euro carrying amount going forward.

5.7   Multi-level consolidations

Example 5.7

Multi-level consolidation

A Swiss parent wholly owns a second-tier German subsidiary. The German subsidiary wholly owns a third-tier British subsidiary. The local currency is the functional currency for all entities, and the presentation currency of the consolidated entity is the Swiss franc. Each entity has third-party foreign-currency-denominated debt.

Under IAS 21, what is the appropriate accounting for the foreign-currency transactions and the foreign-currency financial statements in the consolidation of the subsidiaries with the Swiss parent?

The British and German subsidiaries recognise translation gains and losses on their respective third-party foreign-currency-denominated debt in their individual or separate financial statements using the closing rate at the end of the reporting period in accordance with IAS 21:23. The translation gains and losses are recognised in profit or loss and are not reversed out of profit or loss on consolidation.

In its separate financial statements, the Swiss parent recognises translation gains and losses on its third-party foreign-currency-denominated debt in profit or loss, just as its subsidiaries do for their foreign-currency-denominated debt.

If an intermediate consolidation exercise is performed, the German subsidiary translates the British subsidiary's Sterling-denominated financial statements into Euro-denominated financial statements. The Sterling-to-Euro exchange differences are recognised in other comprehensive income in the intermediate consolidated financial statements. The Swiss parent then translates the Euro-denominated, consolidated financial statements of the German subsidiary into Swiss francs and recognises the resulting exchange differences in other comprehensive income in the ultimate consolidated financial statements.

If an intermediate consolidation exercise is not performed, the Swiss parent translates the Sterling-denominated financial statements of the British subsidiary and the Euro-denominated financial statements of the German subsidiary into Swiss francs. The exchange differences arising are recognised in other comprehensive income.

IFRIC 16 *Hedges of a Net Investment in a Foreign Operation* notes that the aggregate net amount recognised in the foreign currency translation reserve in respect of all foreign operations is not affected by whether the ultimate parent uses the direct or the step-by-step method of consolidation. IFRIC 16 is discussed at **6.6** in **chapter B9** (or, for entities that have not yet adopted IFRS 9 *Financial Instruments*, **2.3** in **chapter C9**).

5.8 Change in both presentation and functional currencies

Example 5.8

Change in both presentation and functional currencies

Company A is preparing its financial statements for the year ended 31 December 20X8. In the previous reporting period ended 31 December 20X7, the Euro was both the functional currency and the presentation currency of Company A.

With effect from 1 January 20X8, because of changes in trading arrangements that meet the requirements of IAS 21:36, the functional currency of Company A is changed to the US dollar (US$). In accordance with IAS 21:37 (see **3.2.8.2**), Company A applies the new functional currency prospectively from 1 January 20X8.

In addition, Company A chooses to change its presentation currency from the Euro to US$ for the period ended 31 December 20X8.

Should the change in presentation currency be viewed as a change in accounting policy to be applied retrospectively?

If so, which Euro/US$ exchange rate should be applied to:

- *the assets and liabilities of Company A at 31 December 20X7;*
- *the statement of comprehensive income of Company A for the reporting period ended 31 December 20X7; and*
- *the opening equity of Company A at 1 January 20X7?*

Unlike its functional currency, an entity's presentation currency can be any currency of choice. Therefore, the change in the presentation currency is a change in accounting policy and, as a consequence, should be applied retrospectively in accordance with IAS 8 *Accounting Policies, Changes in Accounting Estimates and Errors*. This contrasts with the change in functional currency that, in accordance with IAS 21:37, is accounted for prospectively from the date of the change.

Therefore, in the financial statements of Company A for the year ended 31 December 20X8:

- for the 20X8 (current) period, US$ is both the functional and the presentation currency; whereas
- for the 20X7 (comparative) period, the functional currency remains the Euro and the presentation currency is restated to US$.

A retrospective change in presentation currency to US$ gives the same result as if the presentation currency had always been US$. This is achieved by applying the following rates of exchange:

- for the assets and liabilities of Company A at 31 December 20X7, the closing exchange rate at that date;
- for the statement of comprehensive income of Company A for the reporting period ended 31 December 20X7, the exchange rates at the dates of the transactions or, if it offers a reasonable approximation, the average rate for the period; and
- for the opening equity of Company A at 1 January 20X7, the historical rate (i.e. the rate at the date of issue of each equity instrument and average rate for each period in which retained earnings arose).

The 20X8 financial statements will therefore include an exchange reserve in the comparative period, to reflect the fact that the presentation currency (US$) differs from the functional currency (Euro) in that period. This exchange reserve is retained in the 20X8 period and in subsequent periods, regardless of the fact that from 1 January 20X8 the presentation currency is the same as the functional currency.

The following detailed workings illustrate these principles.

In its 20X7 financial statements, when the Euro was both the functional and the presentation currency, Company A reported the following amounts.

20X7 Statement of financial position (€)			20X7 Income statement (€)		
Assets	1,000	180 Share capital	Revenue	100	80 Expenses
		20 Retained earnings[a]			20 Profit
		800 Liabilities			
	1,000	1,000		100	100

[a] For simplicity, this example assumes that the only movement in retained earnings since the inception of Company A is the profit for the year 20X7; in practice, historical retained earnings for each period would have to be translated at the average exchange rate for that period.

The relevant exchange rates are as follows.

	31/12/20X6	Average 20X7	31/12/20X7
€/US$	1.40	1.37	1.47

At the date of issue of the share capital of Company A (in 20X0), the Euro/US dollar (US$) exchange rate was 1.60.

Company A is required to perform the following steps to reflect the changes in functional and presentation currencies in its 20X8 financial statements.

1. Restate comparative reporting period (20X7) to US$ presentation currency

The statement of financial position and statement of profit or loss (income statement) for the comparative period (20X7) are restated as follows.

20X7 Statement of financial position (US$)			20X7 Income statement (US$)[b]		
Assets[a]	1,470	288 Share capital[c]	Revenue	137	110 Expenses
		(21) Exchange reserve[d]			27 Profit
		27 Retained earnings[e]			
		1,176 Liabilities[a]			
	1,470	1,470		137	137

[a] Figures translated from Euro to US$ using the closing exchange rate at 31/12/20X7 of 1.47.

[b] Figures translated from Euro to US$ using the average 20X7 exchange rate of 1.37.

[c] Equity (share capital in this scenario) translated from Euro to US$ using the historical exchange rate at the date of issue of 1.60.

[d] The exchange reserve represents the sum of (1) the difference between the net assets at the end of 20X6 (Euro180) translated at the historical exchange rate, in this case at the date of issue of the share capital, (US$288) and the closing 20X6 exchange rate (US$252), and (2) the difference between the opening net assets at opening exchange rate (US$252) plus profit for the year at average exchange rate (US$27) and the closing net assets at closing exchange rate (US$294). The total in (2) (a credit of US$15) is recognised as an item of other comprehensive income.

[e] Retained earnings will be each year's profit at the average exchange rate for the year.

2. Change to US$ functional currency in current reporting period (20X8)

Assume that Company A earns revenue of US$130 and incurs expenses of US$70 during 20X8 and that assets increase to US$1,654 and liabilities to US$1,300. The statement of financial position and the statement of profit or loss (income statement) for the current reporting period (20X8) are as follows.

20X8 Statement of financial position (US$)				20X8 Income statement (US$)			
Assets	1,654	288	Share capital[a]	Revenue	130	70	Expenses
		87	Retained earnings[b]			60	Profit
		(21)	Exchange reserve[c]				
		1,300	Liabilities				
	1,654	1,654			130	130	

[a] Equity (share capital in this scenario) translated from Euro to US$ using the historical exchange rate at the date of issue.

[b] Retained earnings made up of profit of US$60 for the current period plus profit from each of the previous periods of US$27.

[c] The exchange reserve reported in 20X7 is retained in 20X8 (and in future accounting periods), regardless of the fact that from 1 January 20X8 the functional currency of Company A is the same as its presentation currency.

6   Disposal or partial disposal of a foreign operation

6.1   Transactions or events giving rise to a disposal or a partial disposal

An entity may dispose or partially dispose of its interest in a foreign operation through sale, liquidation, repayment of share capital or abandonment of all, or part, of that entity. [IAS 21:49]

Disposals and partial disposals can arise directly or indirectly. For example, an entity's ownership interest could be reduced by the entity selling shares to a third party, through the entity choosing not to participate in a rights issue by the investee, or by the investee repurchasing equity shares from the entity but not from other investors.

6.2   Transactions or events accounted for as a 'disposal'

In addition to the disposal of an entity's entire interest in a foreign operation, the following partial disposals are accounted for as disposals:

[IAS 21:48A]

- when the partial disposal involves the loss of control of a subsidiary that includes a foreign operation, regardless of whether the entity retains a non-controlling interest in its former subsidiary after the partial disposal; and

- when the retained interest after the partial disposal of an interest in a joint arrangement or a partial disposal of an interest in an associate that includes a foreign operation is a financial asset that includes a foreign operation.

IAS 21 specifies different accounting for exchange differences accumulated in equity for 'disposals' and 'partial disposals'. A disposal of a foreign operation can occur either when the foreign operation is disposed of in its entirety or in one of the additional circumstances set out in IAS 21:48A when the disposal of a partial interest is accounted for as a 'full' disposal.

The following events are accounted for as partial disposals rather than disposals:

- the loss of joint control over a joint arrangement that includes a foreign operation, but the retention of an ongoing interest in that entity that is accounted for as an associate; and

- the less common scenario in which the disposal of part of an associate that includes a foreign operation results in the loss of significant influence but the retention of an ongoing interest in that entity that is accounted for as a joint arrangement.

Example 6.2 illustrates the accounting for a disposal of a partial interest that is accounted for as a full disposal.

Example 6.2

Loss of control of a wholly-owned foreign operation

A parent, Company P, has held a 100 per cent interest in a subsidiary, Company S, for a number of years. Company S is a foreign operation and, in accordance with IAS 21:39, exchange differences of CU2.5 million relating to Company S have been recognised in other comprehensive income and accumulated in a separate component of equity.

Company P disposes of 51 per cent of its interest in Company S, resulting in loss of control. Its retained interest of 49 per cent ensures that it retains significant influence over Company S.

When an entity loses control of a subsidiary that includes a foreign operation, this is accounted for as a full disposal under IAS 21 irrespective of (1) the nature of the event, transaction or change in circumstances leading to the loss of control, and (2) whether the entity retains an interest in the former subsidiary.

Consequently, the cumulative amount of the exchange differences relating to that operation, previously recognised in other comprehensive income and accumulated in equity, is reclassified from equity to profit or loss when the gain or loss on disposal is recognised.

In line with the requirements discussed in **6.3.1**, in the circumstances described, notwithstanding Company P's continuing influence over Company S, all of the exchange differences of CU2.5 million are reclassified from equity to profit or loss and are included in the calculation of the profit or loss on disposal of Company S.

6.3   Treatment required for exchange differences when a disposal occurs

6.3.1   *Exchange differences attributable to the parent*

On disposal of a foreign operation, the cumulative amount of the exchange differences relating to that operation, previously recognised in other comprehensive income and accumulated in a separate component of equity, is reclassified from equity to profit or loss (as a reclassification adjustment) when the gain or loss on disposal is recognised. [IAS 21:48]

When a transaction or event is accounted for as a full disposal, all of the relevant exchanges differences previously accumulated in equity by the parent are reclassified to profit or loss, even when the entity retains a continuing interest in the investee (see **example 6.2**).

6.3.2   *Exchange differences attributable to non-controlling interests*

When an entity disposes of a partially-owned subsidiary, the cumulative amount of the exchange differences relating to that foreign operation that have previously been attributed to the non-controlling interests is derecognised, but is not reclassified to profit or loss. [IAS 21:48B]

The cumulative amount of the exchange differences attributable to the non-controlling interests will have been allocated to, and recognised as part of, non-controlling interests in the consolidated statement of financial position, in accordance with IAS 21:41 (see **5.3**) and IAS 21:48C (see **6.4.2**). The gain or loss recognised in profit or loss on the disposal of a partially-owned subsidiary includes the amount of non-controlling interests derecognised – thus it will already reflect those cumulative exchange differences.

Example 6.3.2

Loss of control of a partially-owned foreign operation – exchange differences attributable to non-controlling interests

A parent, Company P, has held an 80 per cent interest in a subsidiary, Company S, for a number of years. Company S is a foreign operation and, in accordance with IAS 21:39, exchange differences of CU2.5 million relating to Company S have been recognised in other comprehensive income. 80 per cent of the exchange differences (i.e. CU2 million) have been accumulated in Company P's foreign currency translation reserve in equity, and the remainder has been attributed to non-controlling interests.

Company P disposes of a 31 per cent interest in Company S, resulting in loss of control. Its retained interest of 49 per cent ensures that it retains significant influence over Company S. As illustrated in **example 6.2**, notwithstanding this continuing influence, all of the exchange differences of CU2.5 million are required to be derecognised.

In accordance with IAS 21:48, the exchange differences attributable to Company P (CU2 million) are reclassified to profit or loss from the foreign currency translation reserve in equity and included in the calculation of the profit or loss on disposal of Company S.

In accordance with IAS 21:48B, the exchange differences attributable to the non-controlling interests (CU0.5 million) are derecognised, but they are not separately reclassified to profit or loss. Those exchange differences were already reflected as part of non-controlling interests in the consolidated statement of financial position and are (as described in paragraph B98 of IFRS 10 *Consolidated Financial Statements* – see **12.3.1** in **chapter A24**) included in the calculation of the profit or loss on disposal of Company S as part of the carrying amount of the non-controlling interests derecognised.

6.4 Treatment required for exchange differences when a partial disposal occurs

6.4.1 Partial disposal – definition

A partial disposal of an entity's interest in a foreign operation is "any reduction in an entity's ownership interest in a foreign operation, except those reductions in paragraph 48A [see **6.2**] that are accounted for as disposals". [IAS 21:48D] For partial disposals as defined, the Standard distinguishes between:

[IAS 21:48C]

- the partial disposal of a subsidiary that includes a foreign operation (i.e. reduction in ownership interest but control is retained); and

- all other partial disposals.

6.4.2   Partial disposal of a subsidiary that includes a foreign operation

When there is a partial disposal of a subsidiary that includes a foreign operation, entities are required to re-attribute the proportionate share of the cumulative amount of the exchange differences recognised in other comprehensive income to the non-controlling interests in that foreign operation. [IAS 21:48C]

> The transfer, or re-attribution, required in respect of the partial disposal of a subsidiary should be recognised in equity. Therefore, the exchange differences relating to the portion of the investment disposed of are not recognised in profit or loss as a reclassification adjustment at the date of the transaction. Nor are they reclassified to profit or loss at the date of ultimate disposal of the partially-owned subsidiary (see **6.3.2**). This treatment, illustrated in **example 6.4.2**, reflects the general approach adopted under IFRS 10 *Consolidated Financial Statements* that changes in a parent's ownership interest in a subsidiary that do not result in a loss of control are accounted for as equity transactions.

Example 6.4.2

Reduction in proportionate interest in a subsidiary that includes a foreign operation

A parent, Company P, has held a 100 per cent interest in a subsidiary, Company S, for a number of years. Company S is a foreign operation and, in accordance with IAS 21:39, exchange differences of CU2.5 million relating to Company S have been recognised in other comprehensive income and accumulated in a separate component of equity.

Entity P disposes of 20 per cent of its interest in Company S, but retains control over the subsidiary. This transaction is classified as a partial disposal of Company S because there has been a reduction in Entity P's ownership interest but no loss of control

When a parent disposes of part of its interest in a subsidiary that includes a foreign operation, but it retains control of that subsidiary, IAS 21:48C requires that the parent should re-attribute the proportionate share of the cumulative amount of the exchange differences recognised in other comprehensive income to the non-controlling interests in that foreign operation.

Consequently, in the circumstances described, at the date of the transaction, 20 per cent of the cumulative exchange differences (i.e. CU0.5 million) are transferred within equity from the foreign currency translation reserve to non-controlling interests. No amounts are reclassified to profit or loss.

6.4.3 Partial disposals other than the partial disposal of a subsidiary

For any partial disposal of a foreign operation other than the partial disposal of a subsidiary, entities are required to reclassify to profit or loss only the proportionate share of the cumulative amount of the exchange differences recognised in other comprehensive income. [IAS 21:48C]

Example 6.4.3 illustrates the application of IAS 21:48C to the partial disposal of an associate.

Example 6.4.3

Reduction in proportionate interest in an associate with no loss of significant influence

An investor, Company I, has held a 40 per cent interest in an associate, Company B, for a number of years. Company B is a foreign operation and, in accordance with IAS 21:39, exchange differences of CU50,000 relating to Company B have been recognised in other comprehensive income and accumulated in the foreign currency translation reserve.

Company I disposes of a 10 per cent interest in Company B, but retains significant influence over the associate through its remaining 30 per cent shareholding. This transaction is classified as a partial disposal of Company B because there has been a reduction in Entity P's ownership interest but no loss of significant influence.

When an investor disposes of part of its interest in an associate that includes a foreign operation but retains significant influence over that associate, IAS 21:48C requires that the investor reclassify to profit or loss the proportionate share of the cumulative amount of the exchange differences previously recognised in other comprehensive income.

Consequently, in the circumstances described, at the date of the transaction one quarter of the cumulative exchange differences (i.e. CU12,500) are reclassified from equity to profit or loss.

6.4.4 Meaning of the term partial disposal – reductions in an entity's absolute interest with no change in proportionate interest

IAS 21:48D defines a partial disposal of an entity's interest in a foreign operation as "any reduction in an entity's ownership interest in a foreign operation, except those reductions in paragraph 48A [of IAS 21] that are accounted for as disposals". IAS 21 does not provide any further guidance on what is meant by "any reduction in an entity's ownership interest in a foreign operation".

When there has been a reduction in the percentage equity ownership of a foreign operation (such as described in **example 6.4.2** and **example 6.4.3**), it is clear that the entity's ownership interest has been reduced and that, therefore, a partial disposal has occurred. However, there are other transactions that do not affect an investor's percentage equity ownership but that could be argued to reduce its ownership interest in the foreign operation; for example:

- a pro rata repayment of capital by the foreign operation to all investors;

- repayment of a loan or redemption of non-equity shares that form part of the net investment in the foreign operation; or

- the payment by the foreign operation of a dividend to all shareholders in proportion to their shareholdings.

The question arises as to whether a partial disposal occurs only when there is a reduction in the proportionate (relative) equity ownership interest in a foreign operation or whether a partial disposal can also occur when there is a reduction in the entity's absolute interest in the foreign operation but no reduction in the proportionate equity ownership interest.

This question was considered by the IFRS Interpretations Committee in September 2010. The Committee considered a proposal to amend the wording of IAS 21:48D to 'clarify' that reclassification of exchange differences is appropriate when any absolute reduction in the net investment occurred. This proposal was rejected by the Committee and no consensus emerged. The September 2010 *IFRIC Update* reported the Committee's decision as follows.

> "The Committee considers that different interpretations could lead to diversity in practice in the application of IAS 21 on the reclassification of the FCTR [foreign currency translation reserve] when repayment of investment in a foreign operation occurs. However, the Committee decided neither to add this issue to its agenda nor to recommend the Board to address this issue through Annual Improvements because it did not think that it would be able to reach a consensus on the issue on a timely basis."

The view expressed by the IFRS Interpretations Committee indicates that the Committee regards both interpretations of the requirements of IAS 21:48D as acceptable.

The 'proportionate' approach is straightforward and easily understood and might, therefore, be seen as preferable. Under this method, a transaction that does not reduce the investor's percentage equity ownership of a foreign operation will not result in the reclassification or re-attribution of cumulative exchange differences previously recognised in other comprehensive income.

Application of the 'absolute' approach, on the other hand, involves many challenges – particularly in the context of partial disposals of subsidiaries. Under this method, reclassification or re-attribution of amounts held in the foreign currency translation reserve may arise in circumstances when the investor's percentage equity ownership does not change. However, a number of issues arise in applying such an approach that were not addressed by the IFRS Interpretations Committee and that are not explained by IAS 21. These include the following in respect of the mechanics of such an approach:

- the amount that should be re-attributed from the foreign currency translation reserve to non-controlling interests on a pro rata repayment of capital to all equity holders by a partially-owned subsidiary. It is unclear how in these circumstances exchange differences have been 'transferred' from the parent to the non-controlling interests; and

- the calculation of the 'proportionate share' of exchange differences to reclassify or re-attribute on repayment of a loan that forms part of the net investment in a foreign operation (i.e. the exchange differences relating to the repaid loan or a proportionate amount of the total exchange differences recognised on the investment).

In addition, there are circumstances in which application of an absolute approach does not appear to result in an outcome that is a relevant or representationally faithful depiction of the 'partial disposal' transaction:

- it does not appear appropriate to re-attribute amounts from the foreign currency translation reserve to non-controlling interests when a subsidiary that includes a foreign operation is wholly owned before and after the partial disposal transaction; and

- it could be argued that payment of a dividend reduces the absolute interest in an investee. However, IAS 21:BC35 expresses an intention that dividends recognised in profit or loss in accordance with paragraph 12 of IAS 27 *Separate Financial Statements* cannot be considered a disposal or partial disposal of a net investment in IAS 21.

Entities need to make accounting policy choices between the proportionate and absolute reduction approaches and, if applicable, how the absolute reduction approach is applied. An entity's accounting policies should be disclosed when material.

6.5 Write-downs

A write-down of the carrying amount of a foreign operation, either because of its own losses or because of an impairment loss recognised by the investor, does not constitute a partial disposal. Accordingly, no part of the foreign exchange gain or loss recognised in other comprehensive income is reclassified to profit or loss at the time of a write-down. [IAS 21:49]

7   Tax effects of exchange differences

Gains and losses on foreign currency transactions and exchange differences arising on translating the results and financial position of an entity (including a foreign operation) into a different currency may have tax effects. IAS 12 *Income Taxes* applies to these tax effects (see **chapter A13**). [IAS 21:50] IAS 12:61A requires current and deferred tax to be recognised outside profit or loss if the tax relates to items that are recognised, in the same or a different period, outside profit or loss.

Example 7

Deferred taxes on translation adjustments

Entity N is a Norwegian corporation (functional currency Norwegian krone) with a wholly-owned subsidiary, Entity S, operating in the Swedish tax jurisdiction. The functional currency of Entity S is the Swedish krona. Historically, no earnings have been repatriated to Entity N because the parent considers its investment to be permanent.

Should deferred income tax assets and liabilities be recognised on the adjustments resulting from translation of Entity S's financial statements into Norwegian krone?

It depends.

IAS 21:50 provides that any tax effects associated with gains and losses on foreign currency transactions and exchange differences arising from the translation of the financial statements of an entity (including foreign operations) should be accounted for in accordance with IAS 12.

Under IAS 12:39, deferred income tax liabilities may not be accrued by Entity N if both of the following conditions are satisfied:

- Entity N is able to control the timing of the reversal of the temporary difference; and
- it is probable that the temporary difference will not reverse in the foreseeable future.

Recognition of deferred tax assets, in general, would not be appropriate if Entity N's intention is to maintain the investment in the long term, such that it is not probable that the deferred tax asset would be recovered.

---

8 SIC-7 *Introduction of the Euro*

SIC-7 *Introduction of the Euro* explains that the requirements of IAS 21 regarding the translation of foreign currency transactions and financial statements of foreign operations should be applied to the fixing of exchange rates when countries join the Economic and Monetary Union (EMU) and change over to the Euro, as follows:

[SIC-7:4]

(a) foreign currency monetary assets and liabilities resulting from transactions continue to be translated into the functional currency at the closing rate. Any resulting exchange differences are recognised as income or expense immediately, except that an entity continues to apply its existing accounting policy for exchange gains and losses relating to hedges of the currency risk of a forecast transaction;

(b) cumulative exchange differences relating to the translation of financial statements of foreign operations, recognised in other comprehensive income, are accumulated in equity and are reclassified from equity to profit or loss only on the disposal or partial disposal of the net investment in the foreign operation; and

(c) exchange differences resulting from the translation of liabilities denominated in participating currencies should not be included in the carrying amount of related assets.

Example 8

Introduction of the Euro – comparative amounts

The functional currency of Entity A, based in Slovakia, was previously the Slovak Crown. Entity A presented its 31 December 2008 financial statements in that currency. Slovakia adopts the Euro as its national currency on 1 January 2009. Consequently, Entity A needs to recognise a change in functional currency as at 1 January 2009. It will present its financial statements at 31 December 2009 in its new functional currency of the Euro.

The conversion rate from the Slovak Crown to the Euro (also referred to as the 'parity' rate) was fixed in July 2008.

How should Entity A translate the comparative information at 31 December 2008 from Slovak Crowns to Euro when preparing its 31 December 2009 financial statements in Euro?

Neither SIC-7 nor IAS 21 directly addresses how comparative amounts should be converted when a change in functional currency arises not from a change in entity-specific circumstances, but because the original functional currency has ceased to exist and is officially converted into another currency at a fixed rate. Paragraph 11 of IAS 8 *Accounting Policies, Changes in Accounting Estimates and Errors* indicates that, in the absence of a specific Standard that applies to the transaction, the requirements in IFRSs dealing with similar and related issues should be considered.

Therefore, Entity A has an accounting policy choice. There are two acceptable alternatives:

- it can choose to treat the changeover to the Euro as similar to any other change in presentation currency for the comparative period – in which case it would translate the comparative amounts using rates applicable at the dates of the transactions consistent with IAS 21:38 to 41 (see also **5.7**); or

- in the absence of guidance specific to these circumstances, when the change in functional/presentation currency is not due to entity-specific circumstances, Entity A can choose to maintain the relationship between balances by applying the parity rate established on the changeover to the Euro to all the comparative amounts.

9   Presentation and disclosure

9.1   General requirements

The following should be disclosed:

[IAS 21:52]

(a) the amount of exchange differences recognised in profit or loss except for those arising on financial instruments measured at fair value through profit or loss in accordance with IFRS 9 *Financial Instruments* (or, for entities that have not yet adopted IFRS 9, IAS 39 *Financial Instruments: Recognition and Measurement*); and

(b) net exchange differences recognised in other comprehensive income and accumulated in a separate component of equity, and a reconciliation of the amount of such exchange differences at the beginning and end of the period.

IAS 21 is silent regarding where in profit or loss foreign currency exchange gains and losses should be presented. The presentation should follow the nature of the transactions to which the foreign currency gains and losses are linked. As such, recognising foreign currency gains and losses relating to operational activities (e.g. on trade receivables/ trade payables etc.) within income from operations, and recognising foreign currency exchange gains and losses related to debt in finance costs, would be appropriate. When relevant to an understanding of the entity's financial performance, presentation as a separate line item will be appropriate.

9.2 Change in functional currency

If there has been a change in the functional currency of either

- the reporting entity, or
- a significant foreign operation,

that fact should be stated, and the reason for the change in functional currency disclosed. [IAS 21:54]

> As explained in **3.2.8.1**, the functional currency of an operation is a matter of fact, not a choice, and it will only change when there is a change in the primary economic environment of the operation. Consequently, it will be appropriate when describing the reason for the change in functional currency to focus on explaining that change in the primary economic environment.

9.3 Presentation currency different from functional currency

If the presentation currency is not the same as the functional currency (or, for a group, the functional currency of the parent), that fact should be stated. The functional currency should be disclosed, together with the reason for using a different presentation currency. [IAS 21:53]

When an entity presents its financial statements in a currency other than its functional currency (or, for a group, in a currency other than the functional currency of the parent), the financial statements may be described as complying with IFRSs only if they comply with all the requirements of each applicable Standard and each applicable Interpretation of those Standards including the translation method set out in IAS 21:39 and 42 (see **4.3** and **4.4**). [IAS 21:55]

9.4 Supplementary information in other currencies

When an entity displays its financial statements or other financial information in a currency that is different from either its functional currency or its presentation currency and the requirements of IAS 21:55 are not met (see **9.3**), it is required to:

[IAS 21:57]

(a) clearly identify the information as supplementary information, to distinguish it from the information that complies with IFRSs;

(b) disclose the currency in which the supplementary information is displayed; and

(c) disclose the entity's functional currency and the method of translation used to determine the supplementary information.

Entities sometimes present their financial statements or other financial information in a currency that is not the functional currency without meeting the requirements of IAS 21:55. For example, an entity may convert into another currency only selected items from its financial statements; alternatively, an entity whose functional currency is not that of a hyperinflationary economy may convert the financial statements into another currency by translating all items at the most recent closing rate. Such conversions are not in accordance with International Financial Reporting Standards and the disclosures set out above are required. [IAS 21:56]

10   Future developments

In October 2015, the IFRS Interpretations Committee issued a draft Interpretation, DI/2015/2 *Foreign Currency Transactions and Advance Consideration*. The proposals were developed to provide guidance on how an entity should determine the date of a transaction and, therefore, the spot exchange rate to be used when reporting foreign currency transactions in situations where payment is made or received in advance.

The comment period for the draft Interpretation ended on 19 January 2016. At the time of writing, the final Interpretation is expected to be issued early in 2017.

A20 Non-current assets held for sale and discontinued operations

Contents

1 Introduction

1.1 Overview of IFRS 5

IFRS 5 *Non-current Assets Held for Sale and Discontinued Operations* outlines how to account for non-current assets held for sale (or for distribution to owners). In general terms, assets (or disposal groups) held for sale are not depreciated, are measured at the lower of carrying amount and fair value less costs to sell, and are presented separately in the statement of financial position. Specific disclosures are also required for discontinued operations and disposals of non-current assets.

1.2 Amendments to IFRS 5 since the last edition of this manual

None. IFRS 5 was most recently amended in September 2014.

2 Scope

2.1 Scope – general

The classification and presentation requirements of IFRS 5 apply to all recognised non-current assets and disposal groups of an entity, but specified classes of assets are not subject to its measurement requirements and instead continue to be measured in accordance with other Standards (see **2.4**). [IFRS 5:2]

The requirements of IFRS 5 also extend to non-current assets (or disposal groups) classified as held for distribution to owners acting in their capacity as owners in accordance with IFRIC 17 *Distributions of Non-cash Assets to Owners* (see **6.3.2** in **chapter A4**). The application of IFRS 5's requirements to such non-current assets (or disposal groups) is discussed in **3.5** and **4.9**.

Although IFRS 5 deals with the measurement and presentation of non-current assets (and disposal groups) held for sale and held for distribution, it does *not* cover liability recognition for costs associated with the disposal of non-current assets (or disposal groups) such as one-time termination benefits, lease termination costs, facility-closing costs and employee-relocation costs. Liability recognition for such costs is covered by other Standards, such as IAS 19 *Employee Benefits* and IAS 37 *Provisions, Contingent Liabilities and Contingent Assets* (see **chapters A15** and **A12**, respectively).

2.2 Non-current assets – definition

Non-current assets are assets that do not meet the definition of a current asset. An entity classifies an asset as current when:

[IFRS 5:Appendix A]

(a) it expects to realise the asset, or intends to sell or consume it, in its normal operating cycle;

(b) it holds the asset primarily for the purpose of trading;

(c) it expects to realise the asset within twelve months after the reporting period; or

(d) the asset is cash or a cash equivalent (as defined in IAS 7 *Statement of Cash Flows)*, unless the asset is restricted from being exchanged or used to settle a liability for at least twelve months after the reporting period.

The definition of a current asset in Appendix A to IFRS 5 is identical to the definition in paragraph 66 of IAS 1 *Presentation of Financial Statements* (see **4.2.1** in **chapter A4**).

2.3   Disposal group – definition

A disposal group is a group of assets to be disposed of, by sale or otherwise, together as a group in a single transaction and liabilities directly associated with those assets that will be transferred in the transaction. [IFRS 5:Appendix A] A disposal group may be a group of cash-generating units, a single cash-generating unit or part of a cash-generating unit.

If the group includes a cash-generating unit to which goodwill has been allocated under IAS 36 *Impairment of Assets* (see **8.2.8** in **chapter A10**), or includes an operation within such a cash-generating unit, the associated goodwill is included within the disposal group.

When an asset is being sold individually, IFRS 5 applies only if it is a non-current asset. When a group of assets is being disposed of in a single transaction, the classification and presentation requirements of IFRS 5 apply to the disposal group as a whole.

Therefore, when a business is being sold, IFRS 5 applies to all recognised assets and liabilities of that business, including goodwill. The definition of a disposal group is, however, much wider than this. It requires neither that the disposal involve a 'business', nor that the group include any non-current assets. At an extreme, therefore, it is apparently possible for a group of inventories intended to be sold in a single transaction to constitute a disposal group. In practice, it is doubtful whether it would be helpful to users for such items to be removed from inventories and classified separately as assets held for sale. Accordingly, some care and judgement may be necessary when interpreting and applying the definition of a disposal group.

See also **2.4.2** for a discussion of the application of the measurement requirements of IFRS 5 to disposal groups that do not include any scoped-in non-current assets.

A liability should be included in a disposal group only if it will be transferred with the assets in the transaction. It is possible for some liabilities of a business not to be transferred. For example, an entity may sell the trade and assets of a business but retain warranty obligations relating to past sales. Similarly, an entity may retain borrowings with the intention of repaying them from the proceeds of disposal. In both of these examples, the liabilities to be retained should be excluded from the disposal group.

2.4 Non-current assets excluded from the scope of measurement requirements

2.4.1 'Scoped-out' non-current assets

The measurement requirements of IFRS 5 do not apply to the following assets (which are covered by the Standards listed):

[IFRS 5:5]

(a) deferred tax assets (IAS 12 *Income Taxes* – see **chapter A13**);

(b) assets arising from employee benefits (IAS 19 *Employee Benefits* – see **chapter A15**);

(c) financial assets within the scope of IFRS 9 *Financial Instruments* (see **chapter B2**) or, for entities that have not yet adopted IFRS 9, IAS 39 *Financial Instruments: Recognition and Measurement* (see **chapter C2**);

(d) non-current assets that are accounted for in accordance with the fair value model in IAS 40 *Investment Property* (see **chapter A8**, or for entities that have not yet adopted IFRS 16, **appendix A5**);

   Note that when investment property is accounted for in accordance with the cost model in IAS 40, it falls within the scope of the measurement requirements of IFRS 5.

(e) non-current assets that are measured at fair value less costs to sell in accordance with IAS 41 *Agriculture* (see **chapter A38**); and

(f) contractual rights under insurance contracts as defined in IFRS 4 *Insurance Contracts* (see **chapter A39**).

The non-current assets listed above are excluded from the measurement requirements of IFRS 5 when they are held for sale (or held for distribution) either as individual assets or when they form part of a disposal group.

The exclusions relate only to the measurement requirements of IFRS 5 – the classification and presentation requirements of IFRS 5 apply to all non-current assets.

> For convenience, the term 'scoped-out' non-current assets is used elsewhere in this chapter to refer to the assets listed at (a) to (f) above. Non-current assets other than those listed are referred to as 'scoped-in' non-current assets.

Disposal groups may include both scoped-in and scoped-out non-current assets. If a disposal group includes any scoped-in non-current asset(s), the measurement requirements of IFRS 5 apply to the group as a whole, so that the group is measured at the lower of its carrying amount and fair value less costs to sell. [IFRS 5:4]

> When scoped-out non-current assets form part of a disposal group, the measurement requirements of IFRS 5 can be more complex than they may at first appear. Those requirements are discussed at **4.4**.

2.4.2   Disposal groups that do not include any scoped-in non-current assets

> Some entities, such as financial institutions, may identify disposal groups that do not contain any IFRS 5 scoped-in non-current assets. For example, consider Entity A (a bank) that is about to finalise the disposal of 100 per cent of its subsidiary, Entity B, which is a legal entity and which meets the definition of a business under IFRS 3 *Business Combinations*. Entity B is a disposal group but does not contain any IFRS 5 scoped-in non-current assets. The business is made up of current and non-current financial assets and liabilities only (all of the support for the activities, which are of a financial nature, has been outsourced). The disposal group is being sold at a loss (i.e. the proceeds of disposal are lower than the net of the carrying amounts of the individual assets and liabilities under IFRS 9 or, for entities that have not yet adopted IFRS 9, under IAS 39).
>
> The question arises as to whether the disposal group is subject to the measurement principles of IFRS 5, given that it does not contain any IFRS 5 scoped-in non-current assets. The Standard does not provide clear guidance in this regard.
>
> The relevant requirements in the Standard are as follows.
>
> - IFRS 5:2 (see **2.1**) states that "[t]he measurement requirements of this IFRS apply to all recognised non-current assets and disposal groups (as set out in [IFRS 5:4]), except for those assets listed in

[IFRS 5:5] which shall continue to be measured in accordance with the Standard noted".

- IFRS 5:4 (see **2.4.1**) states that "[i]f a non-current asset within the scope of the measurement requirements of this IFRS is part of a disposal group, the measurement requirements of this IFRS apply to the group as a whole".

It is not clear whether a disposal group that contains no IFRS 5 scoped-in non-current assets is subject to the measurement principles of IFRS 5. In particular, it is not clear whether the bracketed reference in IFRS 5:2 to 4 is intended to limit the measurement requirements to those disposal groups described in IFRS 5:4.

One could read IFRS 5:2 and 4 to indicate that if a disposal group does not contain any IFRS 5 scoped-in non-current assets, the measurement principles in IFRS 5 do not apply to the disposal group. If this view is taken, the financial assets and liabilities of Entity B will be measured in accordance with IFRS 9 (or, for entities that have not yet adopted IFRS 9, IAS 39) and the loss on disposal will be recognised only when those assets and liabilities are disposed of.

Equally, one could take the view that the measurement requirements of IFRS 5 may be applied even if a disposal group contains no scoped-in non-current assets, on the basis of the following arguments:

- the Standard does not state explicitly that its measurement principles should not be applied to such a disposal group; and

- it is most relevant to measure any disposal group at the amount that will ultimately be realised upon disposal.

This view is also consistent with one of the underlying principles of IFRS 5 – i.e. that losses on disposals of businesses should be recognised when the IFRS 5 criteria for qualification as held for sale are met. If this latter view is taken, the disposal group will be remeasured in accordance with IFRS 5 when the held for sale criteria are met.

In the absence of clear guidance in the Standard, one of the two approaches described above should be applied consistently as an accounting policy choice.

The allocation of impairment losses that exceed the carrying amount of scoped-in non-current assets is discussed at **4.4.3**.

This issue has been discussed by the IFRS Interpretations Committee; the January 2016 *IFRIC Update* included the question as to whether the measurement requirements of IFRS 5 apply to a disposal group that consists mainly, or entirely, of financial instruments as one of a list of IFRS 5 issues discussed by the Committee but upon which the Committee did not reach a conclusion.

2.5   Current assets

It follows from the discussion at **2.4** that current assets can be affected by the requirements of IFRS 5, but only when they are part of a disposal group. In particular:

- if a current asset is part of a disposal group that also contains scoped-in non-current assets, the disposal group as a whole is subject to both the measurement requirements and the classification and presentation requirements of IFRS 5 (so that the disposal group as a whole is measured at the lower of its carrying amount and fair value less costs to sell);

- if a current asset is part of a disposal group that does not contain any scoped-in non-current assets, the entity should determine as a matter of accounting policy whether the disposal group as a whole is subject only to the classification and presentation requirements of IFRS 5, or whether it is also subject to the Standard's measurement requirements (see **2.4.2**); and

- a current asset being sold as an individual asset (i.e. not as part of a disposal group) is never classified as held for sale under IFRS 5.

3   Classification of non-current assets (or disposal groups) as held for sale

3.1   Assets that are to be sold

3.1.1   *Assets that are to be sold – general requirements*

The overall principle of IFRS 5 is that a non-current asset (or disposal group) should be classified as held for sale if its carrying amount will be recovered principally through a sale transaction rather than through continuing use. [IFRS 5:6] The Standard specifies certain requirements and conditions that must be met for this to be the case.

The two general requirements for a non-current asset (or disposal group) to be classified as held for sale are that:

[IFRS 5:7]

- the asset (or disposal group) must be available for immediate sale in its present condition subject only to terms that are usual and customary for sales of such assets (or disposal groups); and

- its sale must be highly probable.

These requirements are discussed further at **3.1.5** to **3.1.8**.

Unless and until they meet the held for sale criteria, the following should not be reclassified as current assets:

[IFRS 5:3]

- assets of a class that an entity would normally regard as non-current that are acquired exclusively with a view to resale; and

- assets classified as non-current in accordance with IAS 1 *Presentation of Financial Statements*.

The treatment of assets acquired exclusively with a view to resale is discussed in **section 5**.

3.1.2 Held for sale criteria met after the reporting period

If the held for sale criteria are not met until after the reporting period, non-current assets (or disposal groups) should not be classified as held for sale. Instead, the disclosures required by IFRS 5:41(a), (b) and (d) (discussed at **7.4**) should be provided. [IFRS 5:12]

3.1.3 Comparative amounts not restated on classification as held for sale

The separate presentation of non-current assets and disposal groups in the statement of financial position under IFRS 5 is not applied retrospectively. Assets held for sale are presented as such if they meet IFRS 5's conditions at the end of the reporting period; comparative amounts are not restated. For example, if an asset qualifies as held for sale during 20X2, it should be classified as such in the statement of financial position at the end of 20X2, but not in the 20X1 comparative amounts.

This differs from IFRS 5's requirements regarding the presentation of discontinued operations in the statement of comprehensive income (see **6.3.1**); IFRS 5's requirements regarding the presentation of discontinued operations do require reclassification of the results of those operations for comparative periods. Thus, if an operation qualifies as discontinued during 20X2, it should be classified as discontinued in the statement of comprehensive income for the whole of 20X2 and also in the 20X1 comparative amounts.

3.1.4 Negative 'sales proceeds' expected on disposal of a disposal group

IFRS 5:6 states that "[a]n entity shall classify a non-current asset (or disposal group) as held for sale if its carrying amount will be recovered principally through a sale transaction rather than through continuing use". IFRS 5:13 clarifies (see **3.2**) that "[a]n entity shall not classify as held for sale a non-current asset (or disposal group) that is to be abandoned". IFRS 5 is silent, however, regarding whether it is acceptable to classify a disposal group as held for sale when an entity will have to pay a third party to accept that disposal group. This scenario can arise when the liabilities of the disposal group exceed its assets.

It is appropriate for such a disposal group to be classified as held for sale in some circumstances, but it is necessary to assess the substance of the transaction.

Neither 'sale' nor 'abandonment' is defined in IFRSs. If the transaction under consideration involves a third party and does not result in the disposal group being dissolved or liquidated, the disposal group is unlikely to be considered as 'abandoned'. Accordingly, the disposal group will be classified as held for sale if it meets the criteria in IFRS 5.

However, when an entity has to pay a third party to accept a disposal group that will subsequently be dissolved or liquidated, classification as held for sale may not be appropriate. An entity cannot 'convert' an asset or a group of assets that is to be abandoned to one that qualifies as held for sale simply by paying a third party to take over the entity's decommissioning, rehabilitation or similar obligations. It is necessary to look at the substance of the transaction and, rather than examining the buyer's future intentions regarding the use of the asset(s) (which might not be known to the seller), the focus should be on an evaluation from the seller's viewpoint.

The seller should consider whether there has been a transfer of all risks and rewards (including decommissioning and rehabilitation obligations), or whether the substance of the transaction is that the seller has effectively contracted a third party to scrap the asset (or assets). The 'sale' of a very limited number of assets plus a decommissioning liability with negative net proceeds from the transaction could indicate that the latter is the case, but careful judgement is required of the relevant facts and circumstances.

3.1.5   Available for immediate sale

3.1.5.1   Available for immediate sale – general

IFRS 5:7 requires that "the asset (or disposal group) must be available for immediate sale in its present condition subject only to terms that are usual and customary for sales of such assets (or disposal groups)". No further guidance on what this might mean is included within the Standard itself, but the implementation guidance accompanying IFRS 5 states that a non-current asset (or disposal group) is available for immediate sale if an entity currently has the intention and ability to transfer the asset (or disposal group) to a buyer in its present condition. The implementation guidance also sets out various examples illustrating this point, which are reproduced below.

Example 3.1.5.1A

Availability for immediate sale (1)

[Guidance on implementing IFRS 5:Example 1]

An entity is committed to a plan to sell its headquarters building and has initiated actions to locate a buyer.

(a)   The entity intends to transfer the building to a buyer after it vacates the building. The time necessary to vacate the building is usual and customary for sales of such assets. The criterion in IFRS 5:7 would be met at the plan commitment date.

(b)   The entity will continue to use the building until construction of a new headquarters building is completed. The entity does not intend to transfer the existing building to a buyer until after construction of the new building is completed (and it vacates the existing building). The delay in the timing of the transfer of the existing building imposed by the entity (seller) demonstrates that the building is not available for immediate sale. The criterion in IFRS 5:7 would not be met until construction of the new building is completed, even if a firm purchase commitment for the future transfer of the existing building is obtained earlier.

Example 3.1.5.1B

Availability for immediate sale (2)

[Guidance on implementing IFRS 5:Example 2]

An entity is committed to a plan to sell a manufacturing facility and has initiated actions to locate a buyer. At the plan commitment date, there is a backlog of uncompleted customer orders.

(a)   The entity intends to sell the manufacturing facility with its operations. Any uncompleted customer orders at the sale date will be transferred to the buyer. The transfer of uncompleted customer orders at the sale date will not affect the timing of the transfer of the facility. The criterion in IFRS 5:7 would be met at the plan commitment date.

(b)   The entity intends to sell the manufacturing facility, but without its operations. The entity does not intend to transfer the facility to a buyer until after it ceases all operations of the facility and eliminates the backlog of uncompleted customer orders. The delay in the timing of the transfer of the facility imposed by the entity (seller) demonstrates that the facility is not available for immediate sale. The criterion in IFRS 5:7 would not be met until the operations of the facility cease, even if a firm purchase commitment for the future transfer of the facility were obtained earlier.

Example 3.1.5.1C

Availability for immediate sale (3)

[Guidance on implementing IFRS 5:Example 3]

An entity acquires through foreclosure a property comprising land and buildings that it intends to sell.

(a)   The entity does not intend to transfer the property to a buyer until after it completes renovations to increase the property's sales value. The delay in the timing of the transfer of the property imposed by the entity (seller) demonstrates that the property is not available for immediate sale. The criterion in IFRS 5:7 would not be met until the renovations are completed.

(b)   After the renovations are completed and the property is classified as held for sale but before a firm purchase commitment is obtained, the entity becomes aware of environmental damage requiring remediation. The entity still intends to sell the property. However, the entity does not have the ability to transfer the property to a buyer until after the remediation is completed. The delay in the timing of the transfer of the property imposed by others before a firm purchase commitment is obtained demonstrates that the property is not available for immediate sale. The criterion in IFRS 5:7 would not continue to be met. The property would be reclassified as held and used in accordance with IFRS 5:26.

The fact that an asset is likely to be sold in the next twelve months, possibly for scrap, is not sufficient for it to be classified as held for sale. Among the criteria for classification as held for sale are that the asset is available for immediate sale and that an active programme to locate a buyer has been initiated. If an entity needs to carry on using an asset for a period of time before selling it for scrap, it is clear that the criteria for classification as held for sale have not been met because the asset is not available for immediate sale.

3.1.5.2   Activities required to be carried out before sale

When relatively minor pre-selling activities are outstanding, and those activities are usually performed immediately before an asset is transferred, the asset could nevertheless be appropriately treated as available for immediate sale.

Conversely, when an asset is still in the course of construction, and significant activities will need to be performed before it can be transferred, it is unlikely that it could be regarded as available for immediate sale.

In the Basis for Conclusions on IFRS 5, the IASB has confirmed that assets that are being used are not precluded from classification as held for sale if they meet the criteria set out in IFRS 5:7. This will be the case, for example, when an entity continues to operate an asset while actively marketing it. This is because, if a non-current asset is available for immediate sale, the remaining use of the asset is incidental to its recovery through sale and the carrying amount of the asset will be recovered principally through sale. [IFRS 5:BC23]

The following additional examples illustrate further circumstances in which assets (or disposal groups) may or may not be regarded as available for immediate sale.

Example 3.1.5.2A

Operational requirement to operate a non-current asset group to be disposed of by sale

Company D is a joint venture between two multi-national diversified manufacturers. On 28 December 20X2, management having the appropriate level of authority approved and committed Company D to a restructuring plan that included both employee terminations and plant disposals. The plan specifically identified all significant actions to be taken to complete the plan, activities that will not be continued, including the location of those activities and the method of disposal, and the expected date of completion (within one year). As part of the restructuring plan, Company D will continue to operate Plant B until June 20X3, at which time an alternative plant (Plant L) will be able to absorb Plant B's capacity.

It is not appropriate to classify Plant B as held for sale at 31 December 20X2. Company D has an operational requirement to continue to operate Plant B until June 20X3 and, as such, Plant B has not met the requirement of IFRS 5:7 because it is not available for immediate sale. Additionally, Company D should reconsider the period over which Plant B is being depreciated and perform a detailed impairment review of Plant B in accordance with IAS 36 *Impairment of Assets*.

Example 3.1.5.2B

Completion of planned overhauls prior to disposal by sale

On 1 March 20X2, an entity announces plans to close and sell one of its manufacturing facilities. The entity is required to perform major building and equipment overhauls to be able to market the facility effectively. The facility is closed from 30 April 20X2, and the overhauls are completed on 31 May 20X2. Immediately after the completion of the overhauls, the entity begins to market the facility and the facility is sold on 15 July 20X2.

It is not appropriate to classify the manufacturing facility as held for sale in the entity's statement of financial position at 31 March 20X2. At that date, the entity has not met the conditions of IFRS 5:7 which require that the asset "must be available for immediate sale in its present condition...". Assuming all the other conditions of IFRS 5:7 are met, the entity should classify the asset as held for sale on 31 May 20X2, the date that the overhauls are completed and the entity begins to market the facility.

Example 3.1.5.2C

Capital expenditures in the normal course of business of a held for sale component

Company G owns and operates cable television franchises throughout Europe. In June 20X2, Company G commits to a plan and enters into an agreement to sell its franchises in France and Germany to Company J, subject to approval by regulators. During the time that Company G waits for regulatory approval, it is required by the sales agreement to continue to expand the cable networks of the franchises to be sold, as subscribers demand service. Such capital expenditures are common to all cable franchises and Company G would have had to make the expenditures even if it did not sell the franchises. Company G expects to invest significantly in the French and German franchises before their sale to Company J is consummated.

Assuming that regulatory approval is usual and customary for these sales, and all the other conditions of IFRS 5:7 and 8 have been met, Company G should classify the French and German franchises as held for sale in its statement of financial position at 30 June 20X2, because the capital expenditures that it is required to make are usual and customary for the operation of such assets (i.e. the assets are "available for immediate sale in [their] present condition" regardless of the capital expenditures to be incurred). Company G is operating and selling a live cable franchise and there is an expectation that Company G will have to make certain capital expenditures in the normal course of business to accommodate new subscribers.

3.1.5.3 *Plan for sale with a back-up plan to distribute to owners*

Example 3.1.5.3

Plan for sale with a back-up plan to distribute to owners

In 20X1, Entity A's board of directors approves a detailed plan to sell a non-current asset. In addition, as a back-up plan, the directors agree that if the asset is not sold within 9 months, it will be distributed to its owners.

Provided that the directors' plan to sell the non-current asset otherwise meets the criteria in IFRS 5:7 to 9, the non-current asset should be classified as held for sale. Specifically, in accordance with IFRS 5:8, it will be necessary to demonstrate that (1) an active programme to locate a buyer and complete the sale of the asset has been initiated, (2) the asset is being actively marketed for sale at a reasonable price, and (3) the directors have a reasonable expectation that the sale will be completed within 12 months.

The fact that the directors have discussed and agreed to a back-up plan if the sale of the asset is not completed within a specified time period does not mean that it is inappropriate to classify the asset as held for sale. In contrast if, instead of being committed to sell the asset with the distribution alternative seen only as a back-up, the entity planned to dispose of the asset but had not committed to either sale or distribution to the owners as a means of completing that disposal, the asset should not be classified as held for sale or held for distribution to owners. This is because the criteria in IFRS 5:8 (classification as held for sale – see **3.1.6.2**) and IFRS 5:12A (classification as held for distribution – see **3.5**) both refer to a commitment to the specific method of disposal and, consequently, are mutually exclusive.

3.1.6 Sale required to be highly probable

3.1.6.1 Highly probable – definition

IFRS 5 defines 'highly probable' as meaning "[s]ignificantly more likely than probable", where 'probable' means "[m]ore likely than not". [IFRS 5:Appendix A]

3.1.6.2 Highly probable – specific conditions

A number of specific conditions must be satisfied for the sale of a non-current asset (or disposal group) to qualify as highly probable:

[IFRS 5:8]

- the appropriate level of management must be committed to a plan to sell the asset (or disposal group);

- an active programme to locate a buyer and complete the plan must have been initiated;

- the asset (or disposal group) must be actively marketed for sale at a price that is reasonable in relation to its current fair value; and

- except as discussed at **3.1.8**, the sale should be expected to qualify for recognition as a completed sale within one year from the date of classification, and actions required to complete the plan should indicate that it is unlikely that significant changes to the plan will be made or that the plan will be withdrawn.

IFRS 5 is clear that a sale must be expected within one year from the date of classification, so it will not necessarily be sufficient to anticipate that the asset will be sold in the next accounting period. For example, for an entity to conclude that an asset meets the held for sale criteria in March 20X0, it must be expected that it will be sold by March 20X1, irrespective of the date of the entity's financial year end.

The implementation guidance accompanying the Standard includes the following illustration of the application of the criteria in IFRS 5:7 and 8.

Example 3.1.6.2

Completion of sale expected within one year

[Guidance on implementing IFRS 5:Example 4]

To qualify for classification as held for sale, the sale of a non-current asset (or disposal group) must be highly probable (IFRS 5:7), and transfer of the asset (or disposal group) must be expected to qualify for recognition as a completed sale within one year (IFRS 5:8). That criterion would not be met if, for example:

(a)   an entity that is a commercial leasing and finance company is holding for sale or lease equipment that has recently ceased to be leased and the ultimate form of a future transaction (sale or lease) has not yet been determined; or

(b)   an entity is committed to a plan to 'sell' a property that is in use as part of a sale and leaseback transaction, but the transfer does not qualify to be accounted for as a sale in accordance with paragraph 99 of IFRS 16 *Leases* and, instead, will be accounted for in accordance with paragraph 103 of IFRS 16.

Note that the wording in **example 3.1.6.2** has been amended by consequential amendments arising from IFRS 16 *Leases* (issued in January 2016 and effective for annual periods beginning on or after 1 January 2019). The amendments are not substantive from an IFRS 5 perspective. Prior to the amendments, point (b) read as follows: "an entity is committed to a plan to 'sell' a property that is in use, and the transfer of the property will be accounted for as a sale and finance leaseback".

3.1.6.3   *Management commitment to sale*

Careful judgement is needed when a disposal transaction must be brought back to the board of directors for approval before it can proceed, because this may indicate that the entity is not yet committed to a disposal.

Often, the board of directors will authorise a particular individual to dispose of an asset provided that a particular price, judged to be fair value, is achieved. If the board of directors has not delegated the power to sell, this may suggest that the board of directors is not yet committed to a disposal at fair value. For example, the board of directors might still decline a proposed sale at fair value if it believes that the market assessment of fair value currently undervalues the asset.

Example 3.1.6.3

Board approval of plan to dispose of an operating segment to shareholders

Company D is contemplating a disposal of one of its operating segments, Company E. The proposal is that this will be effected by issuing shares in Company E to certain shareholders of Company D in exchange for shares that they currently hold in Company D. Company D anticipates that (1) the disposal will occur prior to the end of its calendar year ending 31 December 20X2, and (2) that it will receive a ruling from the taxing authority that no tax liability will arise as a result of the transaction. Subsequent to issuing the second quarter interim report, the following events occur:

- Company D receives a ruling from the taxing authority indicating that the proposed disposal will be considered a non-taxable transaction; and

- Company D's board of directors appoints a committee to explore the transaction. The committee is charged to explore the following: (1) the precise ratio at which Company E shares will be offered for exchange to the Company D shareholders; (2) the minimum number of shares required for Company D to make the disposal economically feasible; and (3) other criteria that must be met for Company D to complete the transaction. The committee is required to report to the board for approval of the conditions related to the proposed disposal.

Company D has indicated that if the structure, timing and terms of the transaction are not approved by the board, Company D will continue to control and operate Company E. There are currently no alternative disposal plans being contemplated.

At the time that the ruling is received from the taxing authority and the committee of the board is appointed, Company D does not meet the criteria to classify the operating segment as held for sale. IFRS 5:8 clarifies that for a sale to be highly probable, the "appropriate level of management must be committed to a plan to sell the asset". Approval by the board of directors would generally constitute this level of commitment.

3.1.6.4 Plan of sale requiring shareholder approval

The probability of shareholders' approval, if required in the jurisdiction, should be considered as part of the assessment of whether a sale is highly probable. [IFRS 5:8]

Accordingly, it is necessary to consider whether it is highly probable that shareholders' approval will be obtained.

Example 3.1.6.4A

Plan of sale requiring shareholder approval (1)

At the end of the reporting period, an entity's board of directors has approved a plan to sell a non-current asset. The eventual disposal requires approval by a majority of the entity's shareholders through a formal vote which will take place after the reporting period. At the end of the reporting period, a majority of the entity's shareholders have provided the entity with signed irrevocable agreements stating that they will vote their shares in favour of the disposal.

The 'highly probable' test is met because the shareholders have irrevocably committed to approving the transaction and, therefore, the formal vote by the shareholders is merely a formality.

Example 3.1.6.4B

Plan of sale requiring shareholder approval (2)

Company A holds an 80 per cent interest in a subsidiary, Company B. At the year end, the board of directors of Company B has approved a plan to sell a non-current asset to Company A. The eventual disposal requires approval by a majority of Company B's shareholders through a formal vote which will take place after the reporting period. For a transaction with a major shareholder (in this case, the parent), the minority shareholders are given protection in law if the value of the transaction exceeds a specified threshold. The law prevents Company A from participating in the formal vote on such a transaction. Company B has not received any undertakings to vote in a particular manner from any of the shareholders. It is possible that the proposed transaction may be controversial, and the outcome of the shareholder vote is uncertain.

From Company B's perspective, the 'highly probable' test is not met at the end of the reporting period because the outcome of the formal vote by the remaining shareholders is too uncertain.

3.1.6.5   Disposal by means of an initial public offering (IPO) requiring regulatory approval

---

Example 3.1.6.5

Disposal by means of an initial public offering (IPO) requiring regulatory approval

Entity A plans to dispose of its Subsidiary X (a disposal group) by means of an IPO. The planned IPO has been approved by the board of directors. For an IPO to occur in Entity A's jurisdiction, the local securities regulator must approve a prospectus; at the reporting date, regulatory approval for the prospectus has not been received.

The detailed criteria for qualification as held for sale, set out in IFRS 5:7 to 9, require that the asset (or disposal group) must be available for immediate sale

---

in its present condition, subject only to terms that are usual and customary for sales of such assets (or disposal groups), and its sale must be *highly probable*. Entity A will need to ensure that all of these criteria are met.

In particular, in relation to the requirement for regulatory approval of the IPO (assumed to be 'usual and customary' in Entity A's jurisdiction), Entity A's assessment as to whether the disposal is 'highly probable' will require consideration of the following (not an exhaustive list):

- whether, in general, the IPO regulatory process in Entity A's jurisdiction is such that there is more than a remote likelihood of regulatory approval either being denied or delayed (such that the IPO will not be completed successfully within one year, other than in circumstances permitted under IFRS 5:9). This assessment would take into account the historical experience of entities undergoing the same process;

- whether the progress of Entity A's application for approval is following the normal course in Entity A's jurisdiction or whether the progress made to date indicates that there are any issues or concerns that may result in denial or delay of the application; and

- whether there is any indication or experience in the market suggesting that Subsidiary X's nature (e.g. participation in regulated/politically sensitive sector, significant size) will result in Entity A's application being subject to additional scrutiny.

Entity A will also need to have regard to whether the IPO requires shareholder approval (see **3.1.6.4**)

3.1.7   Impairment reviews for assets not qualifying as held for sale

The criteria for classifying an asset (or a disposal group) as held for sale set out in IFRS 5:7 and 8 are very rigorous. Failure to meet these criteria should not, however, result in potentially impaired assets not being written down to their recoverable amounts.

When an entity has indicated its intention to sell an asset (or a disposal group) with a carrying amount that may exceed its fair value less costs of disposal, but the asset does not qualify as held for sale, the entity should consider this to be an impairment loss indicator under IAS 36 *Impairment of Assets* (see **chapter A10**), which would require the entity to perform an impairment review. The useful life used in estimating the future cash flows for the purpose of determining the asset's value in use should reflect the entity's intention to sell the asset.

IAS 36:21 notes that the fair value less costs of disposal of an asset to be disposed of will often approximate its value in use, because the value in use calculation will consist mainly of the net disposal proceeds. This is because the future cash flows from continuing use of the asset until its disposal are likely to be negligible.

3.1.8   Extension of the period required to complete a sale

IFRS 5:9 notes that, on occasion, events or circumstances may extend the period to complete the sale beyond one year. Provided that the delay is caused by events or circumstances beyond the entity's control and there is sufficient evidence that the entity remains committed to its plan to sell the asset (or disposal group), such an extension does not preclude an asset (or a disposal group) from being classified as held for sale.

Appendix B to IFRS 5 specifies that held for sale classification will continue to be available in the following situations:

[IFRS 5:B1]

> "(a) at the date an entity commits itself to a plan to sell a non-current asset (or disposal group) it reasonably expects that others (not a buyer) will impose conditions on the transfer of the asset (or disposal group) that will extend the period required to complete the sale, and:
>
> > (i) actions necessary to respond to those conditions cannot be initiated until after a firm purchase commitment is obtained, and
> >
> > (ii) a firm purchase commitment is highly probable within one year.
>
> (b) an entity obtains a firm purchase commitment and, as a result, a buyer or others unexpectedly impose conditions on the transfer of a non-current asset (or disposal group) previously classified as held for sale that will extend the period required to complete the sale, and:
>
> > (i) timely actions necessary to respond to the conditions have been taken, and
> >
> > (ii) a favourable resolution of the delaying factors is expected.
>
> (c) during the initial one-year period, circumstances arise that were previously considered unlikely and, as a result, a non-current asset (or disposal group) previously classified as held for sale is not sold by the end of that period, and:
>
> > (i) during the initial one-year period the entity took action necessary to respond to the change in circumstances,
> >
> > (ii) the non-current asset (or disposal group) is being actively marketed at a price that is reasonable, given the change in circumstances, and
> >
> > (iii) the criteria in paragraphs 7 and 8 [of the Standard] are met."

A firm purchase commitment is an agreement with an unrelated party, binding on both parties and usually legally enforceable, that (a) specifies all significant terms, including the price and timing of the transactions, and (b) includes a disincentive for non-performance that is sufficiently large to make performance highly probable. [IFRS 5:Appendix A]

> It would appear that this is an exhaustive list and that any particular scenario should be considered against this list to determine whether the necessary criteria are met.

The criteria in IFRS 5:7 and 8, referred to above, are, respectively, the general requirements discussed at **3.1.1** and the specific conditions discussed at **3.1.5.1** and **3.1.6.2**.

However, whenever the circumstances set out at IFRS 5:B1 arise, so that the period expected to complete a sale is extended, an entity should consider carefully whether it is still appropriate to classify the asset as held for sale. Although IFRS 5 allows for the classification to be retained when specific criteria are met, such unanticipated conditions or circumstances may cause the entity to reconsider whether it intends to proceed with its plan to dispose of the asset.

The implementation guidance accompanying IFRS 5 includes the following examples of the limited situations in which the period required to complete a sale may extend beyond one year but not breach the held for sale criteria.

Example 3.1.8A

Completion of sale expected within one year – exceptions (1)

[Guidance on implementing IFRS 5:Example 5]

An entity in the power generating industry is committed to a plan to sell a disposal group that represents a significant portion of its regulated operations. The sale requires regulatory approval, which could extend the period required to complete the sale beyond one year. Actions necessary to obtain that approval cannot be initiated until after a buyer is known and a firm purchase commitment is obtained. However, a firm purchase commitment is highly probable within one year. In that situation, the conditions in IFRS 5:B1(a) for an exception to the one-year requirement in IFRS 5:8 would be met.

Example 3.1.8B

Completion of sale expected within one year – exceptions (2)

[Guidance on implementing IFRS 5:Example 6]

An entity is committed to a plan to sell a manufacturing facility in its present condition and classifies the facility as held for sale at that date. After a firm purchase commitment is obtained, the buyer's inspection of the property identifies environmental damage not previously known to exist. The entity is required by the buyer to make good the damage, which will extend the period required to complete the sale beyond one year. However, the entity has initiated actions to make good the damage, and satisfactory rectification of the damage is highly probable. In that situation, the conditions in IFRS 5:B1(b) for an exception to the one-year requirement in IFRS 5:8 would be met.

Example 3.1.8C

Completion of sale expected within one year – exceptions (3)

[Guidance on implementing IFRS 5:Example 7]

An entity is committed to a plan to sell a non-current asset and classifies the asset as held for sale at that date.

(a) During the initial one-year period, the market conditions that existed at the date the asset was classified initially as held for sale deteriorate and, as a result, the asset is not sold by the end of that period. During that period, the entity actively solicited but did not receive any reasonable offers to purchase the asset and, in response, reduced the price. The asset continues to be actively marketed at a price that is reasonable given the change in market conditions, and the criteria in IFRS 5:7 & 8 are therefore met. In that situation, the conditions in IFRS 5:B1(c) for an exception to the one-year requirement in IFRS 5:8 would be met. At the end of the initial one-year period, the asset would continue to be classified as held for sale.

(b) During the following one-year period, market conditions deteriorate further, and the asset is not sold by the end of that period. The entity believes that the market conditions will improve and has not further reduced the price of the asset. The asset continues to be held for sale, but at a price in excess of its current fair value. In that situation, the absence of a price reduction demonstrates that the asset is not available for immediate sale as required by IFRS 5:7. In addition, IFRS 5:8 also requires an asset to be marketed at a price that is reasonable in relation to its current fair value. Therefore, the conditions in IFRS 5:B1(c) for an exception to the one-year requirement in IFRS 5:8 would not be met. The asset would be reclassified as held and used in accordance with IFRS 5:26.

The following additional example illustrates further circumstances in which assets may qualify as held for sale despite an extension beyond one year.

Example 3.1.8D

Non-current assets to be disposed of by sale requiring approval by bankruptcy court

Company S has filed for reorganisation under a local bankruptcy code, and has entered into an agreement to sell the assets and liabilities of one of its wholly-owned subsidiaries to a third party. The sale has been authorised by the directors and approved by the creditors. However, the sale requires approval from the bankruptcy court. The role of the bankruptcy court in this jurisdiction primarily is to ensure compliance with legal procedures regarding bankruptcy filings. Management considers that it is highly probable that the bankruptcy court will approve the sale, but Company S has not received approval from the bankruptcy court at the period end.

Company S is not precluded from classifying the disposal group as held for sale. In accordance with IFRS 5:8, the appropriate level of management has committed to the plan to dispose of the group of assets and liabilities. The criteria in IFRS 5:7 require that the disposal group be available for immediate sale. Because the sale agreement must be approved by the bankruptcy court prior to finalisation of the sale, circumstances may arise that extend the period to complete the sale beyond one year. Such an extension does not preclude a disposal group from being classified as held for sale if the delay is caused by events or circumstances beyond the entity's control and there is sufficient evidence that the entity remains committed to its plan to sell the disposal group.

Note, however, that bankruptcy courts may have different roles in different jurisdictions and this could affect the above conclusion. Further, in certain situations, the appropriate level of management may not yet have committed to the plan to dispose while it awaits the ruling of the bankruptcy court. If the appropriate level of management is not yet committed to disposal, classification of the assets and liabilities as held for sale would be inappropriate.

3.2   Assets that are to be abandoned

As noted at **3.1.1**, assets held for sale are those whose carrying amounts will be recovered principally through a sale transaction rather than through continuing use. In circumstances when assets or disposal groups are to be abandoned, rather than sold, there will be no sale transaction, so that the carrying amounts of the assets or disposal groups can only be recovered through continuing use. Therefore, assets to be abandoned do not qualify as held for sale under IFRS 5 and should not be classified as such in the statement of financial position. [IFRS 5:13]

When non-current assets have been retired from active use, but they do not meet the criteria for classification as held for sale, they should not be presented separately in the statement of financial position because their carrying amounts may not be recovered principally through sale. [IFRS 5:BC23]

Example 3.2A

Non-current assets to be abandoned as part of corporate restructuring

An entity has committed to a plan of restructuring and expects that some of its assets will be disposed of through abandonment. The assets will continue to be used until their abandonment.

Because no sales proceeds will be received on abandonment, should all of the assets to be abandoned as part of the restructuring be written down to zero carrying amount at the date the entity becomes committed to the restructuring?

No. Non-current assets to be disposed of by abandonment, whether or not as part of a restructuring, do not qualify as held for sale because their carrying amounts will not be recovered principally through sale. Therefore, the requirements of IFRS 5 do not apply.

Instead, the assets should be evaluated for impairment in accordance with IAS 36. Additionally, the entity should revise the estimated useful lives of the assets in accordance with IAS 16 *Property, Plant and Equipment* to reflect the use of the assets over their shortened useful lives, and recognise the depreciation expense in continuing operations until the date of disposal. Only in unusual situations would the recoverable amount of a non-current asset to be abandoned be zero while it is still being used, because the continued use of the non-current asset demonstrates the existence of service potential.

If an impairment loss is recognised relating to assets that are part of a component that has qualified for presentation as a discontinued operation in accordance with IFRS 5:13, the impairment loss should be presented in discontinued operations.

Nevertheless, for the purpose of presentation in the statements of comprehensive income and cash flows, a disposal group to be abandoned could meet the definition of a discontinued operation at the date on which it ceases to be used (see **6.2.1**). The implementation guidance accompanying IFRS 5 illustrates this point as follows.

Example 3.2B

Presenting a discontinued operation that has been abandoned

[Guidance on implementing IFRS 5:Example 9]

In October 20X5 an entity decides to abandon all of its cotton mills, which constitute a major line of business. All work stops at the cotton mills during the year ended 31 December 20X6. In the financial statements for the year ended 31 December 20X5, results and cash flows of the cotton mills are treated as continuing operations. In the financial statements for the year ended 31 December 20X6, the results and cash flows of the cotton mills are treated as discontinued operations and the entity makes the disclosures required by IFRS 5:33 & 34.

Example 3.2C

Classification of non-current assets (or disposal groups) that are to be abandoned

Group A, operating in the construction industry, decides to abandon its property rental interests with effect from 30 June 20X2. The property rental business operates via a number of property leases, including both finance leases and operating leases. Group A has determined that the property rental business represents a component of its entity. Group A plans to allow the leases to run to the end of the lease terms because that is the lowest cost option for exiting the business. No alterations will be made to any of the leases and, effectively, the business will be run on 'autopilot'. This process will take a number of years.

It is not appropriate for Group A to classify its property rental business as a discontinued operation in its 31 December 20X2 financial statements. For an operation to be classified as discontinued, it must either have been disposed of or meet the held for sale criteria. [IFRS 5:32] In addition, IFRS 5:13 states that an operation to be abandoned should only be treated as a discontinued operation if it has actually been abandoned. Although Group A is not seeking new tenants, it continues to provide landlord services and maintain the buildings in a good state of repair etc. Therefore, the operations have not yet been abandoned, have not been disposed of, and do not meet the criteria for classification as held for sale. Consequently, they should not be classified as discontinued operations.

When a non-current asset has been temporarily taken out of use, it should not be accounted for as if it had been abandoned. [IFRS 5:14] The implementation guidance accompanying IFRS 5 includes the following illustration.

Example 3.2D

Determining whether an asset has been abandoned

[Guidance on implementing IFRS 5:Example 8]

An entity ceases to use a manufacturing plant because demand for its product has declined. However, the plant is maintained in workable condition and it is expected that it will be brought back into use if demand picks up. The plant is not regarded as abandoned.

In practice, when an entity is closing an operation, it may intend to sell some assets and to scrap others. Care should be exercised in such circumstances because the former may qualify as held for sale but the latter do not.

3.3   Assets that are to be exchanged

For an asset to qualify as held for sale, it is necessary that the carrying amount will be recovered principally through sale, i.e. that sale proceeds will be received. It is not necessary that the intended sale of a non-current asset should be in exchange for cash; it is, however, necessary that the expected exchange would qualify for recognition as a completed sale (see **3.1.6.2**). Thus, if an entity intends to exchange a non-current asset for another non-current asset, the IFRS 5 conditions for classification as held for sale cannot be met unless the exchange will have commercial substance in accordance with IAS 16. [IFRS 5:10]

IAS 16 states that an entity should determine whether an exchange transaction has commercial substance by considering the extent to which its future cash flows are expected to change as a result of the transaction (see **4.3.3** in **chapter A7**). An exchange transaction has commercial substance if:

[IAS 16:25]

- either:

  - the configuration (risk, timing and amount) of the cash flows of the asset received differs from the configuration of the cash flows of the asset transferred; *or*

  - the entity-specific value of the portion of the entity's operations affected by the transaction changes as a result of the exchange; *and*

- the difference arising in either of the two circumstances outlined above is significant relative to the fair value of the assets exchanged.

3.4   Disposals and partial disposals

3.4.1   Sale plan involving loss of control of a subsidiary

When an entity is committed to a sale plan involving loss of control of a subsidiary, all of the assets and liabilities of that subsidiary are classified as held for sale, regardless of whether the entity will retain a non-controlling interest in its former subsidiary after the sale. [IFRS 5:8A]

IFRS 5:8A reflects the IASB's conclusion that loss of control is a significant economic event that changes the nature of an investment. The parent-subsidiary relationship ceases to exist and an investor-investee relationship begins that differs significantly from the former parent-subsidiary relationship. The new investor-investee relationship is recognised and measured initially at the date when control is lost.

Example 3.4.1A and **example 3.4.1B** illustrate this principle.

Example 3.4.1A

Disposal of subsidiary with retention of associate interest

Entity D, which has a 31 December reporting date, holds a 70 per cent interest in a subsidiary. On 1 July 20X6, Entity D enters into an unconditional, binding agreement to dispose of 30 per cent of its interest. The 30 per cent interest is disposed of in February 20X7, at which point Entity D ceases to have control and instead has significant influence.

The planned disposal of shares results in the subsidiary being classified as a disposal group held for sale that should be accounted for in accordance with IFRS 5 from the date the criteria for classification as held for sale are met.

For the purposes of the 20X6 financial statements, the subsidiary continues to be consolidated (i.e. 100 per cent of the assets and liabilities of the subsidiary are consolidated), but presentation is collapsed into two lines in the statement of financial position (i.e. non-current assets held for sale and associated liabilities). If the disposal group qualifies as a discontinued operation, the presentation in the statement of comprehensive income is collapsed into one single line in accordance with IFRS 5:33 (see **section 6**).

In 20X7, Entity D consolidates the subsidiary for the first two months of the financial year (classifying amounts as arising from discontinued operations, if appropriate). Following the disposal of shares, Entity D accounts for the disposal of the subsidiary, recognising any gain or loss in profit or loss. The gain or loss arising on the disposal is calculated in accordance with paragraph 25 of IFRS 10 *Consolidated Financial Statements*. Thereafter, the 40 per cent interest held on an ongoing basis will be accounted for as an associate, i.e. using the equity method.

Example 3.4.1B

Dilution of interest in a subsidiary through rights offer

Company H has a wholly-owned subsidiary, Company B. Company B makes a rights offer to Company H's shareholders, proposing to issue 10 of its own shares for each share held in Company H. To receive the rights, the shareholders must pay fair value for the shares issued and accept the offer by a specified deadline.

After the issuance of shares under the rights offer, Company H will hold 35 per cent of Company B. As a result, Company H will relinquish control over Company B but will retain significant influence.

Should the rights offer be regarded as a sale transaction under IFRS 5?

The rights offer is effectively Company H's disposal of a portion of its interest in Company B to a preferred group of bidders if the rights are taken up. Because the shares will be issued at fair value, Company H will receive proceeds for the sale of 65 per cent of its investment in Company B to its shareholders.

This disposal will change the nature of the investment in Company B from a subsidiary to that of an associate. Accordingly, the entire investment in Company B will be recognised as a disposal group held for sale if the investment is available for sale in its present condition and the sale is regarded as highly probable (i.e. it is highly probable that the rights will be taken up).

3.4.2 Investment in an associate or a joint venture classified as held for sale

The detailed requirements regarding investments in associates and joint ventures classified as held for sale are discussed at **4.3** in **chapter A26**. **Example 4.3F** in this chapter illustrates the required accounting on reclassification as held for sale.

3.5   Assets that are to be distributed to owners

The requirements of IFRS 5 also extend to a non-current asset (or disposal group) that is classified as held for distribution to owners acting in their capacity as owners in accordance with IFRIC 17 *Distributions of Non-cash Assets to Owners* (see **6.3.2** in **chapter A4**).

A non-current asset (or disposal group) is classified as held for distribution to owners when the entity is committed to distribute the asset (or disposal group) to the owners. For this to be the case, the assets must be available for immediate distribution in their present condition and the distribution must be highly probable. [IFRS 5:12A]

See **3.1.6.1** for IFRS 5's definition of 'highly probable'. For the distribution to be highly probable:

[IFRS 5:12A]

- actions to complete the distribution must have been initiated and should be expected to be completed within one year from the date of classification; and

- actions required to complete the distribution should indicate that it is unlikely that significant changes to the distribution will be made or that the distribution will be withdrawn.

The probability of shareholders' approval (if required in the jurisdiction) should be considered as part of the assessment of whether the distribution is highly probable (see **3.1.6.4**).

The measurement requirements for a non-current asset (or disposal group) classified as held for distribution to owners are discussed at **4.9**.

3.6   Assets ceasing to qualify as held for sale or held for distribution to owners

When an asset (or a disposal group) has been classified as held for sale or as held for distribution to owners, but the requirements and conditions discussed in this section are no longer met, the asset (or disposal group) should be removed from the held for sale or held for distribution to owners category, respectively. [IFRS 5:26] The measurement requirements that apply in such circumstances are discussed at **4.8**.

4 Measuring assets (and disposal groups) held for sale

4.1 Measurement at the lower of carrying amount and fair value less costs to sell

When non-current assets and disposal groups are classified as held for sale, they are required to be measured at the lower of their carrying amount and fair value less costs to sell. [IFRS 5:15]

The comparison of carrying amount and fair value less costs to sell is carried out on the date the non-current asset (or disposal group) is first classified as held for sale, and then again at each subsequent reporting date while it continues to meet the held for sale criteria.

Note that it is necessary to consider the requirements of IFRS 5 in this regard not only for items meeting the criteria as held for sale at the end of the reporting period, but also for 'in-period' disposals, including assets sold during the reporting period that were not classified as held for sale at the previous reporting date (see **9.2** in **chapter A7** for detailed illustration).

4.2 Fair value – definition

Fair value is defined as "[t]he price that would be received to sell an asset or paid to transfer a liability in an orderly transaction between market participants at the measurement date. (See IFRS 13.)" [IFRS 5:Appendix A]

The requirements of IFRS 13 are discussed in **chapter A6**.

4.3 Individual assets held for sale

Certain assets (listed at **2.4.1**) are outside the scope of IFRS 5's measurement requirements. When classified as held for sale, those scoped-out non-current assets continue to be measured in accordance with the Standards that applied before they were classified as held for sale, although the presentation and disclosure requirements of IFRS 5 apply.

All other individual non-current assets held for sale (i.e. scoped-in non-current assets) are measured at the lower of their carrying amount and fair value less costs to sell. [IFRS 5:15] The definition of fair value is set out at **4.2**. Costs to sell are discussed at **4.5**.

If assets are carried at fair value prior to initial classification, the requirement to deduct costs to sell from fair value will result in the immediate recognition of a loss in profit or loss.

The detailed requirements are as follows.

- The carrying amount of the non-current asset is measured in accordance with applicable IFRSs immediately before initial classification as held for sale. [IFRS 5:18]

> IFRS 5:18 applies to assets carried at revalued amounts (e.g. under IAS 16 *Property, Plant and Equipment* or IAS 38 *Intangible Assets*) such that revaluations must be updated in accordance with the appropriate Standard immediately prior to classification as held for sale if the carrying amount is materially different from fair value. Revaluations of assets should be updated immediately prior to classification as held for sale and any change in the value of an asset (whether upward or downward) should be recognised in accordance with the relevant IFRS. (For illustration, see **example 4.2C** and **example 4.2D**, and **example 9.2** in **chapter A7**.)
>
> IAS 16 and IAS 38 require that assets accounted for at revalued amounts should be measured after initial recognition at their fair value at the date of revaluation less any subsequent accumulated depreciation/amortisation and accumulated impairment losses. Revaluations are required to be made with sufficient regularity to ensure that the carrying amount of the asset does not differ materially from its fair value. Therefore, immediately prior to classification as held for sale, an entity should assess whether the carrying amount of a revalued asset is materially different from its fair value and, if so, a revaluation is required.
>
> For assets within the scope of IAS 36 *Impairment of Assets*, if there is any indication of an impairment loss, an impairment review should be carried out prior to reclassification as held for sale (see **example 4.3C**). Although IAS 36 specifically excludes from its scope assets classified as held for sale, that Standard does apply immediately before initial classification as held for sale.

- If the carrying amount determined in accordance with IFRS 5:18 exceeds the asset's fair value less costs to sell, an impairment loss is recognised to reduce the carrying amount to fair value less costs to sell. [IFRS 5:20]

> For example, immediately on classification as held for sale and at each subsequent reporting date, property previously measured under IAS 16 is remeasured in accordance with IFRS 5. In accordance with IFRS 5:20 and 37, any impairment loss arising subsequent to classification as held for sale is recognised in profit or loss.

- Once classified as held for sale, a non-current asset is no longer depreciated or amortised. [IFRS 5:25]

> A non-current asset is no longer depreciated or amortised, even if the entity continues to use it within the business.

- A gain should be recognised for any subsequent increase in fair value less costs to sell of an asset, but not in excess of the cumulative impairment loss recognised in accordance with IFRS 5 or previously in accordance with IAS 36. [IFRS 5:21]

> If an impairment loss was recognised in relation to a non-current asset prior to its classification as held for sale, it is possible that a net remeasurement gain may be recognised while it is classified as held for sale. However, it should be noted that, although earlier impairment losses may in effect be reversed, the same is not true for accumulated depreciation.

Assets acquired exclusively with a view to their subsequent disposal (e.g. as part of a business combination), are discussed in **section 5**.

Example 4.3A

Recognition of impairment losses

A freehold property was originally acquired for CU400,000. Some years later, after cumulative depreciation of CU110,000 has been recognised, the property is classified as held for sale.

At the time of classification as held for sale:

- carrying amount is CU290,000; and
- fair value less costs to sell is assessed at CU300,000.

Accordingly, there is no write-down on classification as held for sale and the property is carried at CU290,000. Following classification as held for sale, no further depreciation is recognised.

At the next reporting date, the property market has declined and fair value less costs to sell is reassessed at CU285,000. Accordingly, a loss of CU5,000 is recognised in profit or loss and the property is carried at CU285,000.

Subsequently, the property is sold for CU288,000, at which time a gain of CU3,000 is recognised.

Example 4.3B

Reversals of impairment losses

A freehold property was originally acquired for CU400,000. Some years later, after cumulative depreciation of CU110,000 has been recognised, an impairment loss of CU35,000 is recognised, taking the carrying amount to CU255,000, which represents the estimated value in use of the property. Shortly thereafter, as a consequence of a proposed move to new premises, the freehold property is classified as held for sale.

At the time of classification as held for sale:

• carrying amount is CU255,000; and
• fair value less costs to sell is assessed at CU250,000.

Accordingly, the initial write-down on classification as held for sale is CU5,000 and the property is carried at CU250,000. Following classification as held for sale, no further depreciation is recognised.

At the next reporting date, the property market has improved and fair value less costs to sell is reassessed at CU265,000. The gain of CU15,000 is less than the cumulative impairment losses recognised to date (CU35,000 + CU5,000 = CU40,000). Accordingly, it is credited in profit or loss and the property is carried at CU265,000.

Six months after that, the property market has continued to improve, and fair value less costs to sell is now assessed at CU300,000. This further gain of CU35,000 is, however, in excess of the cumulative impairment losses recognised to date (CU35,000 + CU5,000 – CU15,000 = CU25,000). Accordingly, a restricted gain of CU25,000 is credited in profit or loss and the property is carried at CU290,000.

Subsequently, the property is sold for CU300,000, at which time a gain of CU10,000 is recognised.

Example 4.3C

Recognition of an impairment loss on an item of property, plant and equipment previously carried at a revalued amount

An entity decides to sell an item of property, plant and equipment and the criteria for classification as held for sale are met. The asset has previously been accounted for under IAS 16's revaluation model. On the date of reclassification, both the fair value and the fair value less costs to sell of the asset are lower than its current carrying amount. The write-down to fair value less costs to sell should be accounted for as follows.

Step 1: update valuation (fair value)

As required by IFRS 5:18 (see above), revaluations of assets should be updated immediately prior to classification as held for sale and any change in the value of the asset (whether upward or downward) should be recognised in accordance with the relevant IFRS.

Therefore, in the circumstances described, the first step is to write down the carrying amount of the asset to its fair value. In accordance with the requirements of IAS 16:40, the revaluation decrease should be recognised in other comprehensive income to the extent that any credit balance exists in the revaluation reserve for that asset, with any excess being recognised in profit or loss.

Step 2: consider recoverable amount (higher of fair value less costs to sell* and value in use)

Next, the entity is required to assess whether there is any indication that the asset is impaired. Therefore, the carrying amount of the asset should be compared to its recoverable amount determined under IAS 36 and, if the recoverable amount is lower, an impairment loss should be recognised.

Given that the revalued asset has already been remeasured to fair value at Step 1, impairment at Step 2 would only arise if the value in use of the asset is lower than its fair value. If this is the case, then the asset will be written down to the higher of fair value less costs to sell* and value in use; that is, the maximum impairment loss to be recognised is the amount of the estimated costs to sell*. If recognition of an impairment loss is required, the impairment loss should be accounted for as a revaluation decrease in accordance with IAS 16 (see Step 1). [IAS 36:60]

Step 3: reclassify the asset as held for sale

Upon reclassification of the asset as held for sale, it should be measured at its fair value less costs to sell. If value in use was higher than fair value less costs to sell* at Step 2, then there will be a write-down at Step 3.

IFRS 5:BC47 and BC48 make it clear that this impairment loss is recognised in profit or loss in the same way as any asset that, before classification as held for sale, had not been revalued.

Any change in the value of the asset subsequent to reclassification as held for sale is accounted for in accordance with IFRS 5. In particular, any impairment loss arising subsequent to reclassification is recognised in profit or loss (see IFRS 5:20 and 37). Once classified as held for sale, the asset is no longer depreciated. [IFRS 5:25]

* IAS 36 uses the term 'fair value less costs of disposal' instead of 'fair value less costs to sell'. However, IAS 36 defines both terms by reference to deducting 'costs of disposal' which has the same meaning as 'costs to sell' in IFRS 5 see **4.5**.

Example 4.3D

Reversal of impairment losses on an asset with a prior revaluation decrease but no prior impairment loss under IAS 36

An entity holds land (original cost CU100,000), previously carried at a revalued amount of CU250,000 in accordance with IAS 16, which is classified as held for sale in accordance with IFRS 5.

- Before its reclassification as held for sale, a revaluation decrease was recognised on the land in accordance with IAS 16. The revaluation decrease of CU50,000 was recognised in other comprehensive income.

- Immediately before its reclassification as held for sale, the land was carried at a revalued amount of CU200,000 in accordance with IAS 16, which was also the appropriate measure on initial classification as held for sale under IFRS 5.
- Since the land's reclassification as held for sale, the entity has recognised an impairment loss of CU20,000 in profit or loss (in accordance with IFRS 5) because the land's fair value less costs to sell fell to CU180,000.
- On the reporting date, the land has not been sold and it still satisfies the criteria for classification as held for sale. Its fair value less costs to sell has increased to CU215,000.

Summary of the land's history	CU
Revalued carrying amount prior to revaluation decrease	250,000
Revaluation decrease recognised in other comprehensive income in accordance with IAS 16	(50,000)
Revalued carrying amount immediately before classification as held for sale	200,000
Impairment loss recognised in profit or loss in accordance with IFRS 5	(20,000)
Fair value less costs to sell under IFRS 5	180,000
Fair value less costs to sell on the reporting date	215,000
Fair value movement	35,000

IFRS 5 only allows the reversal of impairment losses and not revaluation decreases. Consequently, the impairment-loss reversal is limited to CU20,000 (i.e. the amount of the impairment loss recognised under IFRS 5). The additional fair value gain of CU15,000 (CU35,000 − CU20,000) cannot be recognised because it was initially recognised in other comprehensive income as a revaluation decrease and not as an impairment loss.

Example 4.3E

Reversal of impairment losses on an asset previously classified as property, plant and equipment with prior impairment loss

Summary of asset's history	CU
Property purchased on 1 July 20X4 at cost (nil residual value and a useful life of 10 years)	500,000
Depreciation for 2 years [(CU500,000/10) × 2]	(100,000)
Impairment loss recognised in accordance with IAS 36 at 30 June 20X6	(100,000)
Carrying amount at 30 June 20X6	300,000
Depreciation for the year (CU300,000/8)	(37,500)
Carrying amount at 30 June 20X7 immediately before classification as held for sale under IFRS 5	262,500

Summary of asset's history	CU
Write-down to fair value less costs to sell in accordance with IFRS 5 on classification as held for sale at 30 June 20X7	(100,000)
Carrying amount at 30 June 2007 after classification as held for sale	162,500

On 30 June 20X8, the asset is still held for sale and fair value less costs to sell has increased by CU200,000 to CU362,500.

The reversal of prior impairment losses is limited to the carrying amount that would have been determined at the date the property was classified as held for sale under IFRS 5, as if no prior impairment loss had been recognised under IAS 36. The carrying amount cannot be increased beyond CU350,000 because that is the amount that would have been determined at the date the property was classified as held for sale if no previous impairment loss had been recognised under IAS 36 (i.e. the original cost of CU500,000 less accumulated depreciation of CU150,000 over three years). Accordingly, even though the fair value less costs to sell has increased by CU200,000 (i.e. by an amount equivalent to all prior impairment losses and write-downs under IAS 36 and IFRS 5), the reversal is limited to CU187,500 (i.e. CU350,000 – CU162,500).

Example 4.3F

Interest in associate reclassified as held for sale

Company X has a 25 per cent associate, Company A, which it accounts for using the equity method in accordance with IAS 28 *Investments in Associates and Joint Ventures*. Prior to the end of the reporting period, Company X decides to sell its interest in Company A and all the criteria in IFRS 5 for classification as held for sale are met. At the date of classification as held for sale, Company X ceases to apply the equity method for the associate and accounts for its interest in Company A at the lower of carrying amount and fair value less costs to sell. [IFRS 5:15] For IFRS 5 measurement purposes, the carrying amount at the date of classification as held for sale is the 'frozen' equity method carrying amount, i.e. the amount at which the associate was recognised under the equity method immediately prior to reclassification.

When an associate has itself classified assets as held for sale, although this may affect the amount of profit recognised when the investor applies the equity method for the associate, it is not otherwise relevant for the investor. Either the investor will recognise the investment in the associate as a one-line item in accordance with IAS 28 or it will classify the associate itself as held for sale when the IFRS 5 criteria are met.

4.4   Disposal groups

4.4.1   Measurement requirements for disposal groups on initial classification as held for sale

The measurement requirements for disposal groups are for the most part similar to those relating to individual non-current assets. But they are complicated by the treatment of those assets (listed at **2.4.1**) that are outside the scope of IFRS 5's measurement requirements (the scoped-out non-current assets).

The general principle is that a disposal group held for sale is measured at the lower of its carrying amount and fair value less costs to sell. [IFRS 5:15] The detailed requirements on initial classification are as follows.

- Immediately before initial classification as held for sale, the carrying amounts of all the individual assets and liabilities in the disposal group are measured in accordance with applicable IFRSs. [IFRS 5:18]

  > For example, investment property held at fair value will be measured in accordance with IAS 40 *Investment Property,* factory equipment in accordance with IAS 16 *Property, Plant and Equipment,* inventories in accordance with IAS 2 *Inventories* and derivative financial liabilities in accordance with IFRS 9 *Financial Instruments* (or, for entities that have not yet adopted IFRS 9, IAS 39 *Financial Instruments: Recognition and Measurement*). Any changes in the carrying amounts of the assets and liabilities are recognised as usual in accordance with the relevant IFRS.
  >
  > If there is any indication of an impairment loss for assets falling within the scope of IAS 36 *Impairment of Assets*, an impairment review is carried out and, if necessary, an impairment loss is recognised in accordance with IAS 36.

- If fair value less costs to sell for the disposal group is below the aggregate carrying amount of all of the assets and liabilities included in the disposal group, the disposal group is written down. The impairment loss is recognised in profit or loss for the period. [IFRS 5:20 & 37]

  > When a disposal group has been written down to fair value less costs to sell, it does not necessarily follow that there will be no gain or loss presented at the time of the disposal. This is because some of the items that have been recognised in other comprehensive income may be reclassified to profit or loss on disposal, giving rise to a reported gain or loss. Examples include cumulative translation differences and, for entities that have not yet adopted IFRS 9, gains or losses on available- for-sale financial assets recognised in other comprehensive income.

4.4.2 Subsequent remeasurements of disposal groups

On subsequent remeasurement of a disposal group, the detailed requirements are as follows.

- Assets and liabilities that are not within the scope of the measurement requirements of IFRS 5 (i.e. scoped-out non-current assets as listed at **2.4.1**, current assets and all liabilities) are first remeasured in accordance with applicable IFRSs, and the carrying amount of the disposal group is adjusted to reflect these remeasurements. [IFRS 5:19]

> For example, the carrying amounts for inventories will be adjusted to the lower of cost and net realisable value.

- Interest and other expenses attributable to liabilities within the disposal group continue to be recognised. [IFRS 5:25]

- Other non-current assets (i.e. those within the scope of IFRS 5's measurement requirements – the scoped-in non-current assets) are no longer depreciated or amortised. [IFRS 5:25]

- The fair value less costs to sell of the disposal group is calculated.

- If the updated carrying amount of the disposal group exceeds its fair value less costs to sell, the excess is written off as a further impairment loss. [IFRS 5:20]

- A gain is recognised for any subsequent increase in fair value less costs to sell of a disposal group: [IFRS 5:22]

  - to the extent that it has not been recognised in the remeasurement of scoped-out non-current assets, current assets and liabilities; but

  - not in excess of the cumulative impairment loss recognised, either in accordance with IFRS 5 or previously in accordance with IAS 36, on the scoped-in non-current assets (note that the requirements of IFRS 5:22 are discussed in more detail at **4.4.4**).

Example 4.4.2

Impairment losses arising in a disposal group

A disposal group includes an investment property (previously accounted for under the fair value model in IAS 40 and, consequently, excluded from the measurement requirements of IFRS 5) and other assets. None of the other assets has been previously impaired and they are all within the scope of IFRS 5's measurement requirements. Immediately prior to classification as held for sale, the investment property is remeasured under IAS 40 to fair value of CU300,000. The aggregate carrying amount of the other assets under applicable IFRSs is CU250,000, resulting in a total carrying amount for the disposal group of CU550,000.

The fair value less costs to sell of the disposal group as a whole is initially estimated at CU560,000. Accordingly, there is no initial write-down on classification as held for sale, and the disposal group is carried at CU550,000.

At the next reporting date, the fair value of the investment property has fallen to CU280,000, and the fair value less costs to sell of the disposal group as a whole is reassessed at CU515,000. Accordingly:

- the loss of CU20,000 on the investment property is recognised under IAS 40 (as required by IFRS 5:19);

- this brings the carrying amount of the disposal group down to CU530,000, but the fair value less costs to sell of the disposal group is only CU515,000; and

- accordingly, a further loss of CU15,000 is recognised, bringing the carrying amount of the disposal group down to CU515,000.

In accordance with IFRS 5:23 (see **4.4.3**), this further impairment loss is allocated first to reduce any goodwill in the disposal group, and then pro rata between the other scoped-in non-current assets; no further allocation is made to the investment property because it is outside the scope of IFRS 5's measurement requirements.

4.4.3   *Allocation of an impairment loss (or reversal) within a disposal group*

When an impairment loss is recognised (or reversed) for a disposal group, it is allocated between the scoped-in non-current assets using the order of allocation set out in IAS 36:104(a) and (b) and IAS 36:122. [IFRS 5:23] The order of allocation of impairment losses under IFRS 5 is therefore:

- first, to reduce the carrying amount of any goodwill allocated to the disposal group;

- then, to the other scoped-in non-current assets of the group, pro rata on the basis of the carrying amount of each of those assets.

These requirements are illustrated in **example 4.4.3A** and **example 4.4.3B**.

When a disposal group is written down to fair value less costs to sell, the methodology described by IFRS 5 allocates the adjustment against the scoped-in non-current assets in the disposal group – it does not require any allocation to other assets (current assets and non-current assets specifically excluded from the scope of IFRS 15 under IFRS 5:5) or the liabilities of the disposal group. This is true even if the adjustment has arisen because the fair value of liabilities (e.g. fixed-rate borrowings) is higher than their carrying amount. Accordingly, although the net amount included for the disposal group will be the fair value less costs to sell of the disposal group as a whole, the gross amounts presented separately for assets and liabilities may differ significantly from the fair value less costs to sell of those individual assets and liabilities.

The approach required by IFRS 5 of calculating an impairment loss based on the fair value less costs to sell of a disposal group as a whole, and then allocating that loss in accordance with IFRS 15:23, can lead to the carrying amount of some or all of the scoped-in non-current assets being reduced below their recoverable amount (i.e. the higher of fair value less costs to sell and value in use).

This issue has been discussed by the IFRS Interpretations Committee, who stated as follows in the January 2016 *IFRIC Update*.

> "The Interpretations Committee noted that paragraph 23 of IFRS 5 addresses the recognition of impairment losses for a disposal group. It also noted that in determining the order of allocation of impairment losses to non-current assets that are within the scope of the measurement requirements of that Standard, paragraph 23 refers to paragraphs 104 and 122 of IAS 36 *Impairment of Assets*, which set out requirements regarding the order of allocation of impairment losses. However, it does not refer to paragraph 105 of IAS 36, which restricts the impairment losses allocated to individual assets by requiring that an asset is not written down to less than the higher of its fair value less costs of disposal, its value in use and zero. Consequently, the Interpretations Committee observed that the restriction in paragraph 105 of IAS 36 does not apply when allocating an impairment loss for a disposal group to the non-current assets that are within the scope of the measurement requirements of IFRS 5. The Interpretations Committee understood this to mean that the amount of impairment that should be recognised for a disposal group would not be restricted by the fair value less costs of disposal or value in use of those non-current assets that are within the scope of the measurement requirements of IFRS 5."

The impairment loss identified for a disposal group may exceed the carrying amount of the scoped-in non-current assets within that disposal group. This scenario could arise if, for example, the carrying amount of scoped-in non-current assets is small, but there are fixed-rate borrowings (carried at amortised cost) with a fair value significantly in excess of carrying amount. IFRS 5 does not provide any guidance regarding how to account for this excess and a number of approaches might be possible. For example, to the extent that the write-down exceeds the carrying amount of scoped-in non-current assets, that excess:

- might be allocated against other assets (i.e. those outside the scope of the measurement requirements in IFRS 5); or

- might not be recognised at all.

An entity should adopt an acceptable approach, to be applied consistently as an accounting policy choice.

The IFRS Interpretations Committee discussed this issue but, as reported in the January 2016 *IFRIC Update*, did not reach a conclusion on the appropriate treatment to apply in these circumstances.

See also **2.4.2** for a discussion of disposal groups that do not include any scoped-in non-current assets.

The implementation guidance accompanying the Standard includes the following illustration of the allocation of an impairment loss to the assets of a disposal group.

The wording of the example below reflects amendments made by IFRS 9. The amendments have not had any substantive effect.

Example 4.4.3A

Allocation of an impairment loss to a disposal group

[Guidance on implementing IFRS 5:Example 10]

An entity plans to dispose of a group of its assets (as an asset sale). The assets form a disposal group, and are measured as follows:

	Carrying amount at the end of the reporting period before classification as held for sale	Carrying amount as remeasured immediately before classification as held for sale
	CU	CU
Goodwill	1,500	1,500
Property, plant and equipment (carried at revalued amounts)	4,600	4,000
Property, plant and equipment (carried at cost)	5,700	5,700
Inventory	2,400	2,200
Investments in equity instruments	1,800	1,500
Total	**16,000**	**14,900**

The entity recognises the loss of CU1,100 (CU16,000 – CU14,900) immediately before classifying the disposal group as held for sale.

The entity measures the fair value less costs to sell of the disposal group as CU13,000. Because an entity measures a disposal group classified as held for sale at the lower of its carrying amount and fair value less costs to sell, the entity recognises an impairment loss of CU1,900 (CU14,900 – CU13,000) when the group is initially classified as held for sale

The impairment loss is allocated to non-current assets to which the measurement requirements of the IFRS are applicable. Therefore, no impairment loss is allocated to inventory and investments in equity instruments. The loss is allocated to the other assets in the order of allocation set out in paragraphs 104 and 122 of IAS 36 (as revised in 2004).

The allocation can be illustrated as follows:

	Carrying amount as remeasured immediately before classification as held for sale	Allocated impairment loss	Carrying amount after allocation of impairment loss
	CU	CU	CU
Goodwill	1,500	(1,500)	–
Property, plant and equipment (carried at revalued amounts)	4,000	(165)	3,835
Property, plant and equipment (carried at cost)	5,700	(235)	5,465
Inventory	2,200	–	2,200
Investments in equity instruments	1,500	–	1,500
Total	**14,900**	**(1,900)**	**13,000**

First, the impairment loss reduces any amount of goodwill. Then, the residual loss is allocated to other assets pro rata based on the carrying amounts of those assets.

A further example is set out below.

Example 4.4.3B

Allocation of an impairment loss to a disposal group

Company Z intends to sell a division, Division D, which is not a separate legal entity. Division D (the disposal group) meets all the criteria in IFRS 5 to be classified as held for sale. Division D is a service organisation with few non-current assets. The carrying amounts of assets and liabilities held in Division D (measured in accordance with applicable IFRSs immediately prior to classification as held for sale) are as follows.

	Carrying amount
	CU
Property, plant and equipment: Asset A	75
Property, plant and equipment: Asset B	25
Receivables	300
Cash	50
Total assets	450
Post-employment benefits	130
Trade payables	180

	Carrying amount
	CU
Other current liabilities	100
Total liabilities	410
Net assets	40

The fair value of the disposal group is CU30. All financial liabilities are accounted for at amortised cost, and costs to sell are estimated at CU2. The disposal group, therefore, should be written down to CU28 [CU30 – CU2].

IFRS 5:20 requires that the full write-down of CU12 [CU40 – CU28] be recognised against the disposal group. In accordance with IFRS 5:23, the whole CU12 should reduce the non-current assets within the scope of IFRS 5's measurement requirements (in this case property, plant and equipment) to CU88 in total. The write-down is allocated pro rata on the basis of the carrying amount of each asset in the group. This would require the entity to recognise CU9 [(75 ÷ 100) × 12] against Asset A and CU3 [(25 ÷ 100) × 12] against Asset B.

4.4.4   Recognising gains in relation to a disposal group

As discussed at **4.4.2**, although under IFRS 5:19 gains and losses relating to scoped-out non-current assets continue to be recognised in accordance with applicable IFRSs when a disposal group has been reclassified as held for sale, IFRS 5:22 restricts the extent to which gains can separately be recognised in respect of a disposal group.

"An entity shall recognise a gain for any subsequent increase in fair value less costs to sell of a disposal group:

(a)   to the extent that it has not been recognised in accordance with paragraph 19; but

(b)   not in excess of the cumulative impairment loss that has been recognised, either in accordance with this IFRS or previously in accordance with IAS 36, on the non-current assets that are within the scope of the measurement requirements of this IFRS."

Example 4.4.4A

Reversals of impairment losses in a disposal group containing scoped-out non-current assets

A disposal group includes an investment property (previously accounted for under the fair value model in IAS 40 and, consequently, excluded from the measurement requirements of IFRS 5) and other assets. None of the other assets has been previously impaired and they are all within the scope of IFRS 5's measurement requirements. The disposal group does not contain any goodwill.

Immediately prior to classification as held for sale, the investment property is remeasured under IAS 40 to fair value of CU300,000. The aggregate carrying amount of the other assets under applicable IFRSs is CU250,000, resulting in a total carrying amount for the disposal group of CU550,000.

The fair value less costs to sell of the disposal group as a whole is initially estimated at CU520,000. Accordingly, the initial write-down on classification as held for sale is CU30,000 and the disposal group is carried at CU520,000. The CU30,000 impairment loss is allocated first to reduce any goodwill in the disposal group (in this case CUnil), and then pro rata between the other scoped-in non-current assets (without allocation to the investment property because it is outside the scope of IFRS 5's measurement requirements).

At the next reporting date, the fair value of the investment property has increased to CU310,000 and the fair value less costs to sell of the disposal group as a whole is reassessed at CU570,000. Accordingly:

- the gain of CU10,000 on the investment property is recognised under IAS 40 (as required by IFRS 5:19);

- this brings the carrying amount of the disposal group up to CU530,000 (CU310,000 + CU220,000), which is less than the fair value less costs to sell (CU570,000);

- the fair value less costs to sell of the disposal group has increased by CU50,000 (CU570,000 – CU520,000) but, under IFRS 5:22, this must be reduced by the amount already recognised in respect of the scoped-out non-current assets (i.e. the CU10,000 gain on the investment property);

- the remaining CU40,000 is then capped at the amount of cumulative impairment losses, namely CU30,000 (as noted, there were no previous impairment losses under IAS 36); and

- a further gain of CU30,000 is recognised, bringing the carrying amount of the disposal group up to CU560,000 (CU530,000 + CU30,000). The reversal is allocated to the scoped-in non-current assets.

In the circumstances described in **example 4.4.4A**, the disposal group did not include any goodwill. The appropriate accounting for an increase in fair value less costs to sell for a disposal group containing goodwill is not as clear-cut and varying interpretations are applied. This is discussed at **4.4.5**.

At first glance, it might appear that the purpose of IFRS 5:22 is to isolate gains and losses relating to scoped-out non-current assets and then to recognise gains relating to the rest of the disposal group only to the extent that they reverse previous impairment losses. In fact, the drafting of IFRS 5:22 is not as equitable as this. Care is needed when applying it, as illustrated in the following example.

Example 4.4.4B

Recognising subsequent measurement gains on disposal groups containing scoped-out non-current assets

A disposal group held for sale includes a freehold property carried under IAS 16's cost model on which an impairment loss of CU100,000 was recognised prior to the asset being classified as held for sale. No adjustments are necessary when the disposal group is classified as held for sale. Some time after the disposal group has been classified as held for sale, the property increases in value by CU50,000, causing a corresponding increase of CU50,000 in the fair value less costs to sell of the disposal group. The disposal group does not contain any goodwill.

Scenario 1

Assume that scoped-out non-current assets included in the disposal group have increased in value by CU10,000 and the increase in value has been recognised in accordance with the requirements of other Standards (as required by IFRS 5:19), so that the disposal group as a whole has increased in value by CU60,000. Applying the requirements of IFRS 5:22, this total gain of CU60,000 is reduced by CU10,000 (the amount in respect of scoped-out non-current assets), leaving a balance of CU50,000. This is less than the cumulative impairment loss of CU100,000 previously recognised under IAS 36, so a gain of CU50,000 should be recognised (in addition to the gain of CU10,000 recognised in respect of the scoped-out non-current assets).

Scenario 2

Assume instead that the scoped-out non-current assets have decreased in value by CU40,000, so that the disposal group as a whole has increased in value by a net CU10,000. Applying the requirements of IFRS 5:22, only this net increase in the fair value less costs to sell can be considered for recognition. This is not restricted by any amounts recognised in respect of scoped-out non-current assets (which are negative), and is less than the cumulative impairment loss of CU100,000 previously recognised in respect of the property. Consequently, a gain of only CU10,000 should be recognised. Because losses of CU40,000 have been recognised in respect of the scoped-out non-current assets, the net effect is that losses of CU30,000 are recognised.

Scenario 3

Finally, assume instead that the scoped-out non-current assets have decreased in value by CU60,000, so that the disposal group as a whole has decreased in value by a net CU10,000. Applying the requirements of IFRS 5:22, there is no increase in the fair value less costs to sell of the disposal group, so no gain can be recognised. Consequently, only the losses of CU60,000 should be recognised (in respect of the scoped-out non-current assets), even though the disposal group has decreased in value by only CU10,000.

Thus, the recognition of subsequent changes in measurement can be affected by how the scoped-out non-current assets in the disposal group have changed in value.

4.4.5   Reversal of an impairment loss in a disposal group that contains goodwill

The appropriate accounting for an increase in fair value less costs to sell for a disposal group containing goodwill is not always clear-cut and varying interpretations are applied.

Consider the following scenario. A disposal group is classified as held for sale in accordance with IFRS 5. The disposal group contains goodwill and other non-current assets within the scope of the measurement requirements of IFRS 5. The fair value less costs to sell of the disposal group is less than the carrying amount immediately prior to classification as held for sale. The impairment loss is recognised on the date of classification as held for sale and, based on the requirements of IFRS 5:23, is allocated entirely against goodwill. Accordingly, no adjustments are made to the carrying amounts of the other non-current assets as a result of the impairment.

At the next reporting date, but prior to its disposal, the fair value less costs to sell of the disposal group has recovered in value to the extent of the impairment loss previously recognised.

None of the assets within the disposal group had previously been impaired prior to their classification as held for sale under IFRS 5.

The question arises whether a gain should be recognised for the increase in fair value less costs to sell of the disposal group.

IFRS literature is unclear on this subject and two alternative approaches, as discussed below, are considered acceptable. Whichever approach is adopted, it should be applied consistently as an accounting policy choice.

Approach 1 – increase in fair value less costs to sell is not recognised

An entity could determine not to recognise the increase in fair value less costs to sell on the basis that the restrictions in IAS 36 on reversals of impairment for goodwill apply in the circumstances described.

Proponents of this approach note that IFRS 5:23 requires that a reversal of an impairment loss be allocated in the order of allocation set out in IAS 36:122. IAS 36:122 states that "[a] reversal of an impairment loss for a cash-generating unit shall be allocated to the assets of the unit, *except for goodwill*, pro rata with the carrying amounts of those assets" (emphasis added). Accordingly, it is argued that this guidance supports the view that that any impairment loss previously allocated to goodwill cannot subsequently be reversed.

Approach 2 – increase in fair value less costs to sell is recognised

An entity could determine to recognise the increase in fair value less costs to sell on the basis that IFRS 5:22 requires that "[a]n entity shall recognise a gain for any subsequent increase in fair value less costs to sell of a disposal group ... but not in excess of the cumulative impairment loss that has been recognised either in accordance with this IFRS or previously in accordance with IAS 36 on the non-current assets that are within the scope of the measurement requirements of this IFRS".

Because IFRS 5:22 does not exclude goodwill, it is considered to require upwards remeasurement, even for goodwill.

Proponents of this approach argue that this approach is more appropriate because:

- the disposal group can be effectively regarded as a single asset without 'looking through' to underlying assets and goodwill. Therefore, the recognition and measurement requirements of IFRS 5 should be applied to the disposal group as a whole; and

- it would result in a carrying amount for the disposal group that reflects management's best estimate of the fair value less costs to sell of the disposal group, which is considered to be the most relevant measurement basis. If an entity were to follow Approach 1, this would at times result in a measurement basis that deviates from what management ultimately expects to realise on the disposal of the disposal group.

When this approach is adopted, the question arises as to how the increase in fair value should be allocated. In the circumstances described, in accordance with IAS 36:122, it would not be appropriate to allocate any of the increase to the entity's non-current assets other than goodwill because such an allocation would result in those assets having a carrying amount within the disposal group in excess of their original carrying amount (as outlined above, none of the impairment loss was allocated to those assets). It would seem most appropriate to recognise the increase in fair value as an adjustment to goodwill. However, in the absence of any explicit guidance, it could be presented as an unallocated amount within the disposal group unit of account.

See **example 4.4.5** for an illustration of Approaches 1 and 2.

This conflict was discussed by the IFRS Interpretations Committee in 2009 and 2010 and no consensus emerged; the March 2010 *IFRIC Update* stated, in part, as follows.

"The Committee received a request for guidance on whether an impairment loss for a disposal group classified as held for sale can be reversed if it relates to the reversal of an impairment loss recognised for goodwill.

The Committee noted a potential conflict between the guidance in paragraph 22 and paragraph 23 of IFRS 5 relating to the recognition and allocation of the reversal of an impairment loss for a disposal group when it relates to goodwill. However, the Committee also observed that the issue may not be resolved efficiently within the confines of existing IFRSs and the Framework and that it is not probable that the Committee will be able to reach a consensus on a timely basis."

Further discussions in 2015 and 2016 similarly did not result in a conclusion, with the January 2016 *IFRIC Update* including this as one of a list of IFRS 5 issues discussed by the Committee but upon which the Committee did not reach a conclusion.

Example 4.4.5

Reversal of an impairment loss in a disposal group that contains goodwill

A disposal group includes the following assets and liabilities:

- goodwill of CU150,000;
- other scoped-in non-current assets of CU750,000; and
- other scoped-out non-current assets, current assets, and current and non-current liabilities, with a net carrying amount of CU200,000.

No impairment losses have previously been recognised in respect of any of the disposal group's assets.

At the date of classification as held for sale, the fair value less costs to sell of the disposal group is estimated to be CU850,000. Accordingly, the initial write-down on classification as held for sale is CU250,000.

The scoped-out non-current assets, current assets, and current and non-current liabilities are determined to be appropriately measured at CU200,000 in accordance with applicable IFRSs.

Consequently, in accordance with IFRS 5:23, the impairment loss of CU250,000 is allocated to the scoped-in non-current assets as follows:

- the first CU150,000 is allocated against goodwill; and
- the remaining CU100,000 is allocated on a pro rata basis to the other scoped-in non-current assets.

At the next reporting date, the net carrying amount of the scoped-out non-current assets, current assets, and current and non-current liabilities remains at CU200,000 in accordance with applicable IFRSs. The fair value less costs to sell of the disposal group as a whole is estimated to be CU1,000,000 which indicates, prima facie, that a gain of CU150,000 should be recognised.

However, as discussed above, to the extent that the original impairment loss was allocated against goodwill, the requirements of IFRS 5 are subject to varying interpretations and the appropriate treatment depends on the entity's selected accounting policy:

- if the entity's accounting policy is not to recognise the increase in fair value to the extent that the original impairment loss was allocated against goodwill (Approach 1 as discussed above), the gain recognised is restricted to CU100,000 and this is allocated on a pro rata basis to the scoped-in non-current assets excluding goodwill; and

- if the entity's accounting policy is to recognise the entire increase in fair value (Approach 2 as discussed above), the gain of CU150,000 is allocated as follows:

  - the first CU100,000 is allocated on a pro rata basis to the scoped-in non-current assets excluding goodwill; and

  - the remaining CU50,000 is either recognised as an adjustment to goodwill (preferred approach) or is presented as an unallocated amount within the disposal group.

The following tables summarise the effects of Approaches 1 and 2. Note that, if Approach 1 is followed, the resulting carrying amount of the disposal group (CU950,000) is less than its fair value less costs to sell (CU1,000,000).

Approach 1

	Original carrying amount	Impairment loss recognised on classification as held for sale	Reversal of impairment loss	Final carrying amount
	CU'000	CU'000	CU'000	CU'000
Goodwill	150	(150)	–	–
Other scoped-in non-current assets	750	(100)	100	750
Other assets and liabilities	200	–	–	200
Total	1,100	(250)	100	950

Approach 2

	Original carrying amount	Impairment loss recognised on classification as held for sale	Reversal of impairment loss	Final carrying amount
	CU'000	CU'000	CU'000	CU'000
Goodwill	150	(150)	50*	50
Other scoped-in non-current assets	750	(100)	100	750
Other assets and liabilities	200	–	–	200
Total	1,100	(250)	150	1,000

* As discussed above, an alternative may be to present this amount as an unallocated adjustment within the disposal group.

4.4.6   Accumulated translation adjustments relating to a foreign operation held for sale

When a disposal group consists of the assets and liabilities of a foreign operation in respect of which accumulated exchange differences have been recognised in other comprehensive income, the question arises as to whether the classification as held for sale triggers the requirement to reclassify the accumulated exchange differences from equity to profit or loss.

IAS 21 *The Effects of Changes in Foreign Exchange Rates* requires exchange differences to be reclassified from equity to profit or loss at the time of disposal of the operation. IFRS 5:BC37 and BC38 clarify that exchange differences should not be so reclassified at the time when the disposal group is classified as held for sale; they should only be reclassified when the asset or disposal group is sold. These paragraphs also make it clear that the exchange differences are not taken into account when determining whether a disposal group needs to be written down to fair value less costs to sell.

This will be the case even when the requirement in IFRS 5:15 to measure a disposal group at the lower of its carrying amount and fair value less costs to sell results in the recognition of a loss that will be followed by the recognition of a gain when the disposal group is sold and foreign currency translation gains are reclassified to profit or loss.

In accordance with IFRS 5:38, any accumulated exchange differences held in equity relating to a disposal group classified as held for sale are required to be presented separately.

4.5   Measuring costs to sell

4.5.1   Costs to sell – definition

Costs to sell are the incremental costs directly attributable to the disposal of an asset (or a disposal group), excluding finance costs and income tax expense. [IFRS 5:Appendix A]

The definition of 'costs to sell' in IFRS 5 is identical to the definition of 'costs of disposal' in IAS 36 Impairment of Assets. Therefore, although the Standards use different terms, there is no difference between IFRS 5's 'fair value less costs to sell' and IAS 36's 'fair value less costs of disposal'.

4.5.2   Facility-holding and similar costs

Facility-holding costs (e.g. insurance, security services, utility expenses etc.) to be incurred between the date of classifying the asset as held for sale and the date of ultimate disposal should not be recognised as costs to sell. Such costs are not incremental costs directly attributable to the disposal of an asset (or a disposal group) because they would be incurred whether or not the facility was being sold.

Similar logic applies to other internal costs. For example, although particular employees may be involved with the process of disposing of the asset or disposal group, in many cases their remuneration will not be judged to be incremental.

Costs that arise directly as a result of the disposal may not necessarily be costs to sell. For example, when the disposal of a particular subsidiary will result in an obligation to pay restructuring costs (e.g. redundancy costs), although these costs arise as a consequence of the disposal, they are not 'costs to sell'.

4.5.3   Costs to sell measured at present value

If the sale of an asset (or a disposal group) is expected to occur beyond one year, costs to sell are measured at their present value, i.e. discounted for the time value of money. The subsequent unwinding of the discount is presented in profit or loss as a financing cost. [IFRS 5:17]

Only in specified limited circumstances (discussed at **3.1.8**) will an asset or a disposal group that is not expected to be sold within one year be classified as held for sale. Accordingly, the requirement to discount costs to sell should apply only in those limited circumstances.

4.6   Gains and losses on disposal

To the extent that gains or losses arising on the sale of a non-current asset (or disposal group) have not previously been recognised through remeasurement, they are recognised when the asset or disposal group is derecognised. IFRS 5:24 notes that requirements relating to derecognition are set out in:

*   IAS 16:67 to 72 for property, plant and equipment; and
*   IAS 38:112 to 117 for intangible assets.

4.7   Additional evidence obtained subsequent to the end of the reporting period

When additional evidence is obtained subsequent to the end of the reporting period relating to a non-current asset (or disposal group) classified as held for sale, the accounting is determined in accordance with IAS 10 *Events after the Reporting Period* (see **chapter A22**). Therefore:

- if the evidence relates to conditions that existed at the end of the reporting period, it is accounted for as an adjusting event (i.e. the entity adjusts the amounts recognised in its financial statements); and

- if the evidence relates to conditions that arose after the reporting period, it is a non-adjusting event (i.e. the entity does not adjust the amounts recognised in its financial statements). Additional disclosure will be required, however, if the impact is material.

Example 4.7

Additional evidence obtained regarding the fair value of an asset subsequent to the end of the reporting period

Company T has met the requirements for classifying an asset as held for sale at the end of the reporting period. Accordingly, Company T has classified the asset as held for sale in its annual financial statements and has written down the carrying amount of the asset to its estimated fair value less costs to sell. Subsequent to the end of the reporting period, but prior to issuing the financial statements, Company T enters into a final agreement to sell the asset at a value which is less than the estimated fair value less costs to sell.

Should Company T consider the final agreement and adjust the fair value less costs to sell of the asset at the end of the reporting period?

Company T should evaluate the factors that led to the decrease in value of the asset between its classification as held for sale and the determination of the actual sales price. If the value of the asset changed after the end of Company T's reporting period, Company T should not adjust the carrying amount of the asset at the end of the reporting period. However, if facts and circumstances indicate that the value of the asset remained unchanged between the time Company T classified it as held for sale and the determination of the final sales price, and the sales price determined after the end of the reporting period provided additional evidence of conditions that existed at the end of the reporting period, which were indicative of the true estimate of the fair value, then Company T should use the price established in the sales agreement as the basis of its estimate of fair value less costs to sell.

4.8   Changes to a plan for disposal

4.8.1   Reclassification from held for sale or held for distribution

When an asset or a disposal group has previously been classified as held for sale, but the held for sale criteria (see **3.1.1**) are no longer met, the asset or disposal group should be removed from the held for sale category. Similarly, when an asset or a disposal group has previously been classified as held for distribution to owners, but the held for distribution criteria (see **3.5**) are no longer met, the asset or disposal group should be removed from the held for distribution category. [IFRS 5:26]

IFRS 5:26 (and IFRS 5:27 to 29 – see **4.8.3** and **4.8.4**) were amended in September 2014 by *Annual Improvements to IFRSs: 2012-2014 Cycle* to address specific references to the treatment required when the criteria for classification as held for distribution to owners are no longer met. The overall effect of these amendments is to clarify that the requirements of IFRS 5 regarding changes to a plan to sell a non-current asset or a disposal group apply equally to changes to a plan to distribute a non-current asset or a disposal group to the entity's owners.

The September 2014 amendments also added IFRS 5:26A (see **4.8.2**), which sets out guidance for when an asset or a disposal group is reclassified from held for sale to held for distribution, or *vice versa*.

The September 2014 amendments are effective for annual periods beginning on or after 1 January 2016, with earlier application permitted. The amendments are required to be applied prospectively to changes in a method of disposal that occur in annual periods beginning on or after 1 January 2016 (or earlier date of application). If an entity applies the September 2014 amendments in financial statements for a period beginning before 1 January 2016, that fact is required to be disclosed. [IFRS 5:44L]

4.8.2   Reclassification from held for sale to held for distribution, or vice versa

When an asset or a disposal group is reclassified directly from held for sale to held for distribution to owners (or directly from held for distribution to owners to held for sale), the change in classification is considered a continuation of the original plan for the disposal. Specifically:

[IFRS 5:26A]

- the entity should not follow the guidance set out in IFRS 5:27 to 29 (see **4.8.3** and **4.8.4**). Instead, the entity should apply the classification, presentation and measurement requirements in IFRS 5 that are applicable to the new method of disposal;

- the entity should measure the non-current asset or disposal group by following the requirements in IFRS 5:15 (if reclassified as held for sale – see **4.4.1**), or IFRS 5:15A (if reclassified as held for distribution to owners – see **4.9**). Any reduction or increase in the fair value less costs to sell or costs to distribute of the non-current asset or disposal group should be recognised in accordance with IFRS 5:20 to 25 (see **4.4**); and

- the date of classification in accordance with IFRS 5:8 (see **3.1.6.2**) or IFRS 5:12A (see **3.5**) is not changed. However, this does not preclude an extension of the period required to complete a sale or a distribution to owners if the conditions in IFRS 5:9 are met (see **3.1.8**).

> IFRS 5:26A was added as part of the September 2014 amendments to IFRS 5 (see **4.8.1**). It reflects the IASB's view that, when an entity reclassifies an asset or a disposal group directly from held for sale to held for distribution, or *vice versa*, this should not be accounted for as a new plan for the disposal. Rather, it should be treated as a continuation of the original plan. [IFRS 5:BC72G]

4.8.3 Remeasuring a non-current asset or disposal group no longer held for sale or distribution

When a non-current asset or disposal group ceases to be classified as held for sale or as held for distribution to owners (or ceases to be included in a disposal group classified as held for sale or as held for distribution to owners), it should be measured at the lower of:

[IFRS 5:27]

(a) its carrying amount before the asset (or disposal group) was classified as held for sale or as held for distribution to owners, adjusted for any depreciation, amortisation or revaluations that would have been recognised had the asset (or disposal group) not been classified as held for sale or as held for distribution to owners; and

(b) its recoverable amount at the date of the subsequent decision not to sell or distribute.

> This in effect restates the asset or disposal group at the value at which it would have been recognised had it never been classified as held for sale or as held for distribution, taking into account any impairment losses. Part (b) includes an impairment assessment, which seems appropriate because an impairment loss indicator (e.g. a fall in market value) could be driving the decision not to sell the asset.

Recoverable amount is the higher of fair value less costs of disposal and value in use. Value in use is the present value of the estimated future cash flows expected to arise from the continuing use of an asset and from its disposal at the end of its useful life. If a non-current asset is part of a cash-generating unit, its recoverable amount is the carrying amount that would have been recognised after the allocation of any impairment loss arising on that cash-generating unit in accordance with IAS 36.

When IFRS 5:27 triggers an adjustment to the asset's carrying amount, the adjustment is generally included in profit or loss from continuing operations in the period in which the held for sale or held for distribution criteria are no longer met. If the asset is property, plant and equipment or an intangible asset that had been revalued in accordance with IAS 16 or IAS 38 before classification as held for sale or held for distribution to owners, the adjustment is treated as a revaluation increase or decrease. The adjustment should be included in the same caption in the statement of comprehensive income used to present other gains or losses on held for sale or held for distribution items not meeting the definition of discontinued operations (see **7.2**). [IFRS 5:28]

These requirements are illustrated in **example 4.8.3**.

IFRS 5:28 also requires that financial statements for the periods since classification as held for sale or as held for distribution to owners should be amended accordingly if the disposal group or non-current asset that ceases to be classified as held for sale or as held for distribution to owners is a subsidiary, joint operation, joint venture, associate, or a portion of an interest in a joint venture or an associate.

> IFRS 5:27 and 28 have been amended to reflect the September 2014 amendments to IFRS 5 (see **4.8.1**).

Example 4.8.3

Remeasuring non-current assets that are no longer held for sale

Company C has a number of operations including the manufacture and sale of leisure equipment. Company C has a 31 December year end. In January, Company C adopts a plan to sell all of the assets and liabilities of the leisure equipment operations. Having met the requirements of IFRS 5:7 and 8 at the end of the first quarter, Company C appropriately classifies those assets and liabilities as a disposal group held for sale.

In June, Company C decides not to sell certain existing trademarks and licence arrangements associated with the leisure equipment operations. Subsequent to the sale of the other assets and liabilities, Company C will continue to generate revenue (and incur the associated costs) from its trademarks and licences.

How should Company C account for the identified trademarks and licences that are no longer held for sale?

Company C must reclassify the trademarks and licence arrangements out of assets held for sale. Company C should measure the trademarks and licence arrangements at the lower of (1) their carrying amounts before being classified as held for sale less any amortisation expense that would have been recognised if they had not been classified as held for sale, and (2) their recoverable amount at the date of the subsequent decision not to sell.

If this requirement triggers an adjustment to the carrying amounts of the trademarks and licences, assuming that the assets were not revalued in accordance with IAS 38 before classification as held for sale, the adjustment should be included in profit or loss from continuing operations in the period in which the held for sale criteria are no longer met. The adjustment should be included in the same caption in the statement of comprehensive income used to present other gains or losses, if any, on held for sale items not meeting the definition of discontinued operations. [IFRS 5:28]

If the remaining assets and liabilities of the leisure equipment operations continue to meet the conditions in IFRS 5:7 and 8, Company C should continue to classify those remaining assets and liabilities as held for sale.

4.8.4   Assets or liabilities remaining after an asset or a liability is removed from a disposal group

If an individual asset or liability is removed from a disposal group classified as held for sale or as held for distribution to owners, the remaining assets and liabilities of the disposal group will continue to be measured as a group only if the group continues to meet the criteria for classification as held for sale (see **3.1.1**) or held for distribution to owners (see **3.5**), respectively. Otherwise:

[IFRS 5:29]

- any non-current assets of the group that individually meet the criteria to be classified as held for sale or as held for distribution to owners should be measured individually at the lower of their carrying amounts and fair values less costs to sell, or costs to distribute, at that date;

- any non-current assets that do not meet the criteria for held for sale are removed from the held for sale category and measured in accordance with **4.8.3**; and

- any non-current assets that do not meet the criteria for held for distribution to owners are removed from the held for distribution to owners category and measured in accordance with **4.8.3**.

IFRS 5:29 has been amended to reflect the September 2014 amendments to IFRS 5 (see **4.8.1**).

4.9   Non-current assets and disposal groups held for distribution to owners

When a non-current asset (or disposal group) is classified as held for distribution to owners (see **3.5**), it should be measured at the lower of its carrying amount and fair value less costs to distribute. [IFRS 5:15A] Costs to distribute are the incremental costs directly attributable to the distribution, excluding finance costs and income tax expense.

5 Assets acquired exclusively with a view to subsequent disposal

An entity may acquire a non-current asset (or disposal group) exclusively with a view to its subsequent disposal (e.g. as part of a business combination). In such circumstances, the non-current asset (or disposal group) is classified as held for sale at the acquisition date only if:

[IFRS 5:11]

- the requirement that a sale is expected to be completed within one year (see **3.1.6.2**) is met (unless the exceptions discussed in **3.1.8** apply); and

- it is highly probable (i.e. significantly more likely than probable) that any of the other general requirements (see **3.1.1**) and specific conditions (see **3.1.5** and **3.1.6**) that are not met at that date will be met within a short period following the acquisition (usually within three months).

If a newly acquired asset (or disposal group) meets the criteria to be classified as held for sale, it will be measured on initial recognition at the lower of its carrying amount had it not been so classified (e.g. cost) and fair value less costs to sell. Accordingly, if an asset or a disposal group is acquired as part of a business combination exclusively with a view to resale, it will be measured at fair value less costs to sell. [IFRS 5:16]

A subsidiary acquired exclusively with a view to resale is not excluded from consolidation. It is consolidated under IFRS 10 *Consolidated Financial Statements* but may be subject to the presentation and measurement requirements of IFRS 5. The result is that, when the criteria set out in IFRS 5:11 (see above) are met, the subsidiary's assets and liabilities are presented as held for sale in the statement of financial position.

The results of a subsidiary acquired exclusively with a view to resale will be presented within discontinued operations in the statement of comprehensive income when the subsidiary is a component of the reporting entity that either has been disposed of, or is classified as held for sale (see **6.2**).

The estimated costs to sell such a subsidiary will not be recognised as an expense at the time of the acquisition but instead will be reflected indirectly in the amount that is attributable to goodwill from the business combination.

Only limited disclosures are required in respect of subsidiaries acquired exclusively with a view to resale. Specifically:

- IFRS 5:33(b) and (c) allow that the analyses of amounts included in the statement of comprehensive income and the statement of cash flows generally required for discontinued operations are not required for disposal groups that are newly acquired subsidiaries that meet the criteria to be classified as held for sale on acquisition (see **6.3.1** and **6.3.2**); and

- IFRS 5:39 provides that if a disposal group is a newly acquired subsidiary that meets the criteria to be classified as held for sale on acquisition, the general requirement under IFRS 5:38 to disclose major classes of assets and liabilities does not apply (see **7.3.1**).

Because only limited disclosures are required in relation to subsidiaries acquired exclusively with a view to resale, it may be possible to simplify the consolidation process. Nevertheless, it will be important to consider whether consolidation adjustments are required in relation to the subsidiary; these might be necessary, for example, to eliminate intragroup profits on material transactions between the subsidiary and the group.

Example 5

Measuring and presenting subsidiaries acquired with a view to resale and classified as held for sale

[Guidance on implementing IFRS 5:Example 13]

Entity A acquires an entity H, which is a holding company with two subsidiaries, S1 and S2. S2 is acquired exclusively with a view to sale and meets the criteria to be classified as held for sale. In accordance with IFRS 5:32(c), S2 is also a discontinued operation.

The fair value less costs to sell of S2 is CU135. A accounts for S2 as follows:

- initially, A measures the identifiable liabilities of S2 at fair value, say at CU40

- initially, A measures the acquired assets as the fair value less costs to sell of S2 (CU135) plus the fair value of the identifiable liabilities (CU40), ie at CU175

- at the end of the reporting period, A remeasures the disposal group at the lower of its cost and fair value less costs to sell, say at CU130. The liabilities are remeasured in accordance with applicable IFRSs, say at CU35. The total assets are measured at CU130 + CU35, ie at CU165

- at the end of the reporting period, A presents the assets and liabilities separately from other assets and liabilities in its consolidated financial statements as illustrated in [**example 7.3.1**], and

- in the statement of comprehensive income, A presents the total of the post-tax profit or loss of S2 and the post-tax gain or loss recognised on the

> subsequent remeasurement of S2, which equals the remeasurement of the disposal group from CU135 to CU130.
>
> Further analysis of the assets and liabilities or of the change in value of the disposal group is not required.

6 Discontinued operations

6.1 Separate presentation of discontinued operations – general

The overall objective of IFRS 5's presentation and disclosure requirements is to enable users to evaluate the financial effects of discontinued operations and disposals of non-current assets (or disposal groups). [IFRS 5:30] To this end, the Standard distinguishes discontinued operations from other operations and presents them separately.

Some operations that are to be disposed of will be classified as discontinued operations, resulting in gains and losses relating to them (including those for any corresponding disposal group) being presented separately in the statement of comprehensive income. Other operations, disposal groups and assets held for sale will not be classified as discontinued operations and gains and losses relating to them will be presented as part of continuing operations.

It is worth noting that there need be no link between assets (or disposal groups) held for sale and operations classified as discontinued. In particular, it may be the case that:

- a disposal group that is classified as held for sale does not qualify as a discontinued operation (e.g. because it does not represent a separate major line of business or geographical area of operations); or

- an operation is classified as discontinued even though none of its assets has ever qualified as held for sale (e.g. because it has been abandoned).

6.2 Identification of discontinued operations

6.2.1 Discontinued operation – definition

A discontinued operation is a component of an entity that either has been disposed of or is classified as held for sale and:

[IFRS 5:32 and Appendix A]

(a) represents a separate major line of business or geographical area of operations; or

(b) is part of a single co-ordinated plan to dispose of a separate major line of business or geographical area of operations; or

(c) is a subsidiary acquired exclusively with a view to resale.

IFRS 5:31 explains that a component of an entity "comprises operations and cash flows that can be clearly distinguished, operationally and for financial reporting purposes, from the rest of the entity. In other words, a component of an entity will have been a cash-generating unit or a group of cash-generating units while being held for use". Consistent with IAS 36 *Impairment of Assets*, a cash-generating unit is defined as the smallest identifiable group of assets that generates cash inflows that are largely independent of the cash inflows from other assets or groups of assets. [IFRS 5:Appendix A]

6.2.2 Classification of a component that is to be abandoned

As discussed at **3.2**, a disposal group to be abandoned could meet the definition of a discontinued operation at the date on which the assets within it cease to be used. This is illustrated in **example 6.2.2**.

Example 6.2.2

Classification of a component that is to be abandoned

On 15 December 20X2, Company M (which has a 31 December year end) announces a plan to abandon the operations of its subsidiary, Company E. Company M has determined that Company E represents a component of the entity as defined in IFRS 5. Under the plan for abandonment, Company E will cease to accept any new business from 31 December 20X2. Company M anticipates that Company E will be able to wrap up production of all remaining orders, ancillary operations and close both the plant and office facilities by 15 March 20X3.

Should Company M classify the operations of Company E as discontinued operations in its 31 December 20X2 financial statements?

No. IFRS 5:13 states that while assets or disposal groups to be abandoned may not be classified as held for sale, a disposal group may be classified as a discontinued operation if the group represents a component of an entity and meets the criteria in IFRS 5:32. IFRS 5:32 requires a component to be disposed of, or classified as held for sale, prior to being presented as a discontinued operation. Because an item to be abandoned cannot be classified as held for sale (see **3.2**), it cannot meet the IFRS 5:32 criteria until it is actually abandoned. Therefore, in the circumstances described, Company M should not classify the operations of Company E as discontinued operations in its 31 December 20X2 financial statements.

However, at 15 December 20X2, Company M may identify an impairment loss indicator under IAS 36, and may need to test the assets of Company E for recoverability. In addition, Company M may need to revise its depreciation estimates in accordance with IAS 16 *Property, Plant and Equipment* to reflect the use of Company E's assets over their shortened useful lives.

6.2.3   Disposal of a portion of a component

Example 6.2.3

Disposal of a portion of a component

Entity S is a wholly-owned subsidiary of Entity A. Entity S enters into an agreement to dispose of a portion of its operations. In Entity A's consolidated financial statements, Entity S is a single cash-generating unit (CGU) and constitutes a component as defined in IFRS 5. The portion of Entity S to be sold (the Entity S Disposal Group) meets the criteria in IFRS 5:6 to 14 to be classified as a disposal group held for sale.

The Entity S Disposal Group should not be reported as a discontinued operation in Entity A's consolidated financial statements.

To meet the IFRS 5 definition of a discontinued operation, the Entity S Disposal Group must be a component of an entity. A component of an entity is defined in IFRS 5:31 as "operations and cash flows that can be clearly distinguished operationally and for financial reporting purposes, from the rest of the entity. In other words, a component of an entity will have been a CGU or a group of CGUs while being held for use". It follows that a component of an entity cannot be smaller than a CGU.

In the circumstances described, because management has determined that Entity S is a single CGU, the Entity S Disposal Group (being only a portion of Entity S) does not meet the definition of a component of Entity A. Consequently, the Entity S Disposal Group cannot be presented as a discontinued operation; it is considered as the disposal of a portion of Entity S's operations.

In contrast, if the Entity S Disposal Group comprised all of the operations of Entity S but excluded a limited number of its assets, liabilities or both, the Entity S Disposal Group would be presented as a discontinued operation.

6.2.4   Component to be disposed of includes some assets not classified as held for sale

Example 6.2.4

Component to be disposed of includes some assets not classified as held for sale

Entity P intends to discontinue all of its property development activities, which are reported as a separate segment (Segment A) under IFRS 8 *Operating Segments*. The property development activities are carried out principally through Subsidiary X (a wholly-owned subsidiary), but also include two individual property assets of other subsidiaries, which are classified as inventory under IAS 2 *Inventories*. Entity P has a single co-ordinated plan for its exit strategy, under which separate buyers have been identified for Company X and for the other property assets.

At the reporting date, Company X meets the held for sale criteria under IFRS 5 and is classified as a disposal group held for sale. The other property assets that form part of Segment A are not part of the disposal group because they are to be sold to a separate buyer. They do not individually qualify as held for sale because they are current assets outside the scope of IFRS 5. If the two property assets were non-current assets, they would meet IFRS 5's held for sale criteria (i.e. they are available for immediate sale and their sale is highly probable).

Company X represents approximately 50 per cent of the total assets and liabilities and financial results of Segment A.

Should Segment A be presented as a discontinued operation in Entity P's consolidated financial statements?

Yes. Segment A is a component of Entity P that represents a separate major line of business. In addition, even though two separate buyers have been identified, this is part of a single co-ordinated plan to dispose of the segment.

If the individual property assets were non-current assets they would meet IFRS 5's held for sale criteria. The only reason that they do not qualify as held for sale is that they are current assets and, therefore, outside the scope of IFRS 5.

The determination as to whether Segment A meets the definition of a discontinued operation should not be altered solely because some of the segment assets are not included in a disposal group and they are not individually classified as held for sale under IFRS 5 because they are current assets. Because all the assets and liabilities of Segment A are, in substance, held for sale (although they are not all classified as such), the segment should be presented as discontinued.

This is in contrast to the circumstances in which an entity is planning to sell only part of a segment's operations (see **example 6.2.3**). In such circumstances, not all of the operations are, in substance, held for sale and a discontinued operation can only be identified when the component to be disposed of (i.e. the subset of the segment's operations) is in itself a cash-generating unit or a group of cash-generating units.

6.2.5 Combining separate restructuring plans into a single discontinued operation

Example 6.2.5

Combining separate restructuring plans into a single discontinued operation

An entity is completing various separate restructuring plans that will result in the disposal of multiple lines of business as well as the disposal of significant portions of other lines of business. These businesses operate in a number of geographical areas. All of the assets to be disposed of meet the requirements in IFRS 5:6 to 14 to be classified as held for sale.

Each single coordinated plan should be evaluated separately under the guidance in IFRS 5 to determine whether the items disposed of that are part of that plan meet the conditions for reporting as a discontinued operation.

To meet the definition of a discontinued operation under IFRS 5:32, the component of the entity to be disposed of must represent "a separate major line of business or geographical area of operations", be "part of a single co-ordinated plan" for such disposal, or be a subsidiary acquired exclusively with a view to resale.

Because the entity has various separate restructuring plans for multiple businesses in a number of geographical areas, the entity should not combine all assets to be disposed of as a single discontinued operation.

6.2.6   Investments accounted for using the equity method

In some circumstances, the disposal of a stand-alone investment in equity securities accounted for using the equity method may be classified as a discontinued operation in the investor's consolidated financial statements. If the entity's business model includes conducting operations through strategic investments in associates and joint ventures accounted for using the equity method, it may be possible to demonstrate that the investment is a component of the entity as described in IFRS 5:31. In other cases, the operations relating to an investment accounted for using the equity method are not sufficient to establish a component of the investor as described in IFRS 5:31.

If a component of an entity has operations that include, but are not limited to, operations relating to an investment accounted for using the equity method, and the conditions for reporting the component as a discontinued operation are met (as set out in IFRS 5:32), all of the operations of the component should be reported as discontinued operations.

An investor should not present its share of the discontinued operations of an investee accounted for using the equity method as a discontinued operation in its consolidated financial statements. Paragraph 82(c) of IAS 1 *Presentation of Financial Statements* requires a separate line item in the statement of comprehensive income for investments accounted for using the equity method. It would not be appropriate to break out of that line item an amount that relates to the discontinued operations of the associate. In addition, it is unlikely that a component of an investment accounted for using the equity method could be determined to be a component of the investor as described in IFRS 5:31.

6.2.7 Disposal achieved in stages

Example 6.2.7

Disposal achieved in stages

On 15 December 20X1, Company Z decided to sell 65 per cent of its wholly-owned subsidiary, Company X. At that time, it was determined that the subsidiary met the requirements to be classified as a disposal group held for sale and a discontinued operation (because Company X represented a major line of business). On 1 April 20X2, Company Z sold 65 per cent of Company X to Company Y. Subsequent to the disposal, Company Z's investment in Company X was classified as an associate. On 30 June 20X3, Company Z decided to sell its remaining 35 per cent interest in Company X to Company Y. The sale was completed on 31 August 20X3.

When should Company Z classify the results of Company X's operations as a discontinued operation, if at all?

A subsidiary that represents a major line of business should be classified as a discontinued operation at the earlier of its disposal date, or when that subsidiary meets the held for sale criteria in IFRS 5:7. When an entity is committed to a sale plan involving loss of control of a subsidiary, all of the assets and liabilities of that subsidiary are classified as held for sale, regardless of whether the entity will retain a non-controlling interest in its former subsidiary after the sale (IFRS 5:8A – see **3.4.1**). Therefore, provided that the other criteria are met, Company X should be presented as a discontinued operation in Company Z's first consolidated financial statements on or after 15 December 20X1.

6.2.8 Sale of a component to more than one buyer

Example 6.2.8

Sale of a component to more than one buyer

Company C manufactures and markets men's shoes and coats. Company C discloses two operating segments under IFRS 8, the Shoe Group and the Coat Group. Company C also discloses certain trademark and licence agreements within each segment.

The operations and cash flows of the Shoe Group can be clearly distinguished operationally and for financial reporting purposes from the rest of Company C. Therefore, the Shoe Group is a component of Company C. In the fourth quarter of 20X2, Company C completed a transaction to sell the majority of the Shoe Group's manufacturing and distribution operations to Company E. In addition, management, having the appropriate level of authority, has committed to a formal plan of sale for the remaining assets of the Shoe Group.

> *In light of the formal plan to dispose of the remaining Shoe Group assets, should Company C present the Shoe Group as a discontinued operation at 31 December 20X2?*
>
> Yes. While the definition of a disposal group requires a sale in a single transaction, a discontinued operation may comprise several disposal groups. At 31 December 20X2, one disposal group (the majority of the Shoe Group's operations) has already been sold and a second (the remaining assets of the Group) is classified as held for sale (assuming all of the requirements of IFRS 5:7 are met). Therefore, the operating segment qualifies for classification as a discontinued operation.

6.2.9   Allocation of part of an asset's cost to discontinued operations

> **Example 6.2.9**
>
> **Allocation of part of an asset's cost to discontinued operations**
>
> Company T, a public entity, currently reports three operating segments. In the current year, Company T implemented a new centralised computer system to be used by each of the three operating segments. Subsequent to the implementation of the computer system, Company T entered into an agreement to sell one of the operating segments. The disposal of the segment will be accounted for as a discontinued operation.
>
> *Is it appropriate for Company T to allocate a portion of the costs incurred on the new computer system to the disposal group for the operating segment being sold in determining the gain or loss on the disposal of the segment (i.e. to treat the asset as if part of it is being sold)?*
>
> No. In order for an asset to be classified as held for sale, it must be available for immediate sale in its present condition. There are no plans to sell the central computer system, and, thus, it should not be included in the assets to be disposed of. Therefore, Company T may not allocate a portion of the costs incurred on the new computer system to the disposal group for the operating segment being disposed of. Additionally, any impairment loss recognised by Company T in respect of the central computer system should not be included in discontinued operations.

6.2.10   Routine disposals of components

> Certain entities (e.g. real estate investment trusts, retailers and restaurants) routinely dispose of asset groups that meet the definition of a component of an entity in IFRS 5:31. Such routine disposals of components will not generally represent a separate major line of business or geographical area of operations, as required by IFRS 5:32(a). Therefore, many routine disposals of components will not be classified as discontinued operations.

6.3 Presenting discontinued operations

6.3.1 *Presentation in the statement of comprehensive income*

6.3.1.1 *Amounts to be presented in the statement of comprehensive income*

IFRS 5:33(a) requires the presentation of a single amount in the statement of comprehensive income comprising the total of:

(i)   the post-tax profit or loss of discontinued operations; and

(ii) the post-tax gain or loss recognised on the measurement to fair value less costs to sell or on the disposal of the assets or disposal group(s) constituting the discontinued operation.

In addition, this single amount must be analysed, either in the notes or in the statement of comprehensive income, into:

[IFRS 5:33(b)]

(i)   the revenue, expenses and pre-tax profit or loss of discontinued operations;

(ii)   the related income tax expense as required by IAS 12:81(h);

(iii) the gain or loss recognised on the measurement to fair value less costs to sell or on the disposal of the assets or disposal group(s) constituting the discontinued operation; and

(iv)   the related income tax expense as required by paragraph IAS 12:81(h).

If this analysis is included in the statement of comprehensive income, it should be shown separately from continuing operations, in a section identified as relating to discontinued operations. The analysis is not required for disposal groups that are newly acquired subsidiaries that meet the criteria to be classified as held for sale on acquisition (see **section 5**).

Entities are also required to disclose the amount of income from continuing operations and from discontinued operations attributable to owners of the parent. These disclosures (which are illustrated in the implementation guidance accompanying IFRS 5, reproduced as **example 6.3.1.1**) may be presented either in the notes or in the statement of comprehensive income. [IFRS 5:33(d)]

When an entity presents items of profit or loss in a separate statement of profit or loss as described in IAS 1:10A, that statement of profit or loss is also required to present a separate section identified as relating to discontinued operations. [IFRS 5:33A]

When amounts relating to discontinued operations are separately presented, the comparative figures for prior periods are also re-presented, so that the disclosures relate to all operations that have been discontinued by the end of the reporting period for the latest period presented. [IFRS 5:34]

IFRS 5:5B clarifies that disclosures in other IFRSs do not apply to discontinued operations unless those IFRSs require specific disclosures in respect of discontinued operations (see **section 7**).

The implementation guidance accompanying the Standard includes the following illustration of presentation in the statement of comprehensive income.

Example 6.3.1.1

Presenting discontinued operations in the statement of comprehensive income

[Guidance on implementing IFRS 5:Example 11]

XYZ GROUP – STATEMENT OF COMPREHENSIVE INCOME FOR THE YEAR ENDED 31 DECEMBER 20X2

(illustrating the classification of expenses by function)

(in thousands of currency units)	20X2	20X1
Discontinued operations		
Revenue	X	X
Cost of sales	(X)	(X)
Gross profit	X	X
Other income	X	X
Distribution costs	(X)	(X)
Administrative expenses	(X)	(X)
Other expenses	(X)	(X)
Finance costs	(X)	(X)
Share of profit of associates	X	X
Profit before tax	X	X
Income tax expense	(X)	(X)
Profit for the period from continuing operations	X	X
Discontinued operations		
Profit for the period from discontinued operations[a]	X	X
Profit for the period	X	X
Attributable to:		
Owners of the parent		
Profit for the period from continuing operations	X	X
Profit for the period from discontinued operations	X	X
Profit for the period attributable to owners of the parent	X	X

(in thousands of currency units)	20X2	20X1
Discontinued operations		
Profit for the period attributable to owners of the parent	X	X
Non-controlling interests		
Profit for the period from continuing operations	X	X
Profit for the period from discontinued operations	X̲	X̲
Profit for the period attributable to non-controlling interests	X̲	X̲
	X̳	X̳

(a)   The required analysis would be given in the notes.

6.3.1.2   Disclosure of components of income and expense

IFRS 5:5B clarifies that disclosures in other IFRSs do not apply to discontinued operations unless those IFRSs require specific disclosures in respect of discontinued operations (see **section 7**). Accordingly, the amounts disclosed under requirements such as those listed below need relate only to continuing operations:

- disclosure of analysis of expenses under IAS 1 *Presentation of Financial Statements*;

- disclosure of finance costs and finance income under IAS 1 and IFRS 7 *Financial Instruments: Disclosures*; and

- disclosure of the components of income tax under IAS 12 *Income Taxes*.

6.3.1.3   Allocated corporate overhead costs included in discontinued operations

An entity should include in amounts reported for discontinued operations only those costs that are clearly identifiable as costs of the component that is being disposed of and that will not be recognised on an ongoing basis by the entity. The following examples illustrate this principle.

Example 6.3.1.3A

Allocated corporate overhead costs included in discontinued operations (1)

An entity has a general workers' compensation insurance policy for all of its operations, the cost of which is allocated to each operation based on the number of employees in the operation. The entity's insurance costs will be reduced by CU1 million as a result of the disposal of an operation which meets the criteria for classification as discontinued. It is appropriate for the entity to allocate CU1 million insurance costs to the discontinued operation.

Example 6.3.1.3B

Allocated corporate overhead costs included in discontinued operations (2)

An entity allocates the salary costs of its executive committee to all of its operations based on total revenues. No executive has direct responsibility for the operation being disposed of, which meets the criteria for classification as discontinued. However, two of the executives will transfer with the operation. The entity should not allocate the salaries of the transferred executives to discontinued operations because the costs are not clearly identifiable as costs of the component.

6.3.1.4 Earnings per share presentation of discontinued operations

Earnings per share amounts should be shown separately when an entity reports discontinued operations. Paragraph 68 of IAS 33 *Earnings per Share* requires an entity that reports discontinued operations to present basic and diluted per-share amounts for discontinued operations either in the statement of comprehensive income or in the notes to the financial statements. This disclosure is required in addition to the presentation of basic and diluted per-share amounts for profit or loss from continuing operations and profit or loss for the year, both of which should be shown in the statement of comprehensive income with equal prominence.

See **7.1.4** in **chapter A31** for a discussion regarding whether it is necessary to present earnings per share information separately for each discontinued operation.

6.3.1.5 Classification of non-controlling interests in discontinued operations

---

Example 6.3.1.5

Classification of non-controlling interests in discontinued operations

Company T owns 85 per cent of Company V. Company T consolidates Company V and accounts for the remaining 15 per cent ownership in Company V as a non-controlling interest. On 31 August 20X2, Company T commits to a plan to sell its 85 per cent interest in Company V. All of the criteria of IFRS 5:7, 31 and 32 are met at 31 August, and Company T classifies Company V as a discontinued operation at that date.

How should Company T present the 15 per cent non-controlling interest in Company V in Company T's 30 September 20X2 consolidated financial statements?

IAS 1 and the accompanying implementation guidance make clear that in the statement of comprehensive income, amounts reported for non-controlling interests are allocations. Therefore, the amount reported in respect of non-controlling interests is unaffected by whether an operation is continuing or discontinued.

Note that IFRS 5:33(d) requires entities to disclose the amount of income from continuing operations and from discontinued operations attributable to owners of the parent – thereby effectively requiring an analysis of non-controlling interests between continuing and discontinued operations. These disclosures (which are illustrated in **example 6.3.1.1**) may be presented either in the notes or in the statement of comprehensive income.

6.3.1.6 Presentation of gain or loss arising from a sale of a subsidiary being a discontinued operation, with retention of a non-controlling interest

Example 6.3.1.6

Presentation of gain of loss arising from a sale of a subsidiary being a discontinued operation, with retention of a non-controlling interest

Entity R enters into an agreement to sell a partial interest in its subsidiary, Entity S. Following the transaction, Entity R will retain a non-controlling interest in Entity S. The subsidiary meets the definition of a discontinued operation. When Entity R disposes of its controlling interest in Entity S, the gain or loss on disposal is calculated in accordance with IFRS 10:25 (see **12.3.1** in **chapter A24**), and includes the effect of remeasuring Entity R's retained interest in Entity S at fair value.

Should the gain or loss arising on the remeasurement to fair value of Entity R's retained interest in Entity S be included within the gain or loss from discontinued operations presented in accordance with IFRS 5:33?

Yes. IFRS 5:33(a)(ii) requires that the amount presented for the gain or loss from discontinued operations should include the gain or loss recognised on disposal of the assets or disposal group(s) constituting the discontinued operation. IFRS 10:25 (with supporting guidance in IFRS 10:B98) defines the calculation of that gain or loss as including the remeasurement to fair value of any retained interest in the former subsidiary.

6.3.1.7 Elimination of intragroup items

Example 6.3.1.7A

Intragroup sales to a discontinued operation with external sales

Company N is a paper manufacturer with factories around the country. Company N also owns a distribution business, Company X, which buys paper from Company N and then sells the paper to external customers. Company N is planning to sell Company X to another paper manufacturer. In its consolidated financial statements, Company N has appropriately eliminated the intragroup sales between itself and Company X and, therefore, only recognises the sales from Company X to the external customers. Company X will be classified as a discontinued operation in the second quarter financial statements.

Following its disposal, Company X will continue to purchase paper from Company N to sell to external customers. Therefore, Company N will continue to have sales to Company X that will not be eliminated once it is no longer a consolidated subsidiary.

How should sales, cost of sales, and profit be reported in Company N's consolidated financial statements following classification of Company X as a discontinued operation?

The sales from Company N to Company X should continue to be eliminated in the consolidation. Any profit made from sales to external parties by the discontinued operation (Company X) would be presented outside continuing operations. Therefore, the profit on the corresponding sales made by Company N should be shown in the continuing operations of Company N.

For example: Company N sells paper to Company X for CU6 with a cost of CU4. Company N's profit is CU2. Company X sells paper to external customers for CU7 with a cost (Company X's purchase price from Company N) of CU6. Company X's profit is CU1. In the consolidated financial statements of Company N, the intragroup sales of CU6 should be eliminated along with the CU6 cost of sales, leaving a profit of CU3. The CU3 margin will come through as CU2 in continuing operations (representing the sales from Company N to Company X) and CU1 in discontinued operations (representing the sales from Company X to the external customers).

Therefore, Company N's consolidated financial statements should present sales from continuing operations of CU6, cost of sales from continuing operations of CU4, a profit of CU2 from continuing operations, and a profit of CU1 in discontinued operations because the sale was to an external entity. In the following year (assuming the same facts), when Company N sells paper to Company X, it will have sales of CU6, CU4 cost of sales and CU2 profit in its continuing operations (and will not have the additional CU1 profit from sales to external customers).

In accordance with IFRS 5:33(b), the single amount for discontinued operations (CU1 in the above example) should be analysed between its components either in the statement of comprehensive income or in the notes: revenue of CU1, cost of sales of nil, and profit of CU1.

Example 6.3.1.7B

Intragroup purchases held in inventories of a discontinued operation

Company N is a paper manufacturer with factories around the country. Company N owns a distribution business, Company X, which buys paper from Company N and then sells the paper to external customers. Company N is planning to sell Company X to another paper manufacturer. In its consolidated financial statements, Company N has appropriately eliminated the intragroup sales between itself and Company X and, therefore, only recognises the sales from Company X to the external customers. Company X will be classified as a discontinued operation in the second quarter financial statements.

Company X holds paper purchased from Company N as inventories for a period before selling it externally. Accordingly, the group does not recognise any revenue at the time of selling paper to Company X; it only recognises revenue when Company X sells paper externally. Following its disposal, Company X will continue to purchase paper from Company N to sell to external customers. Therefore, Company N will continue to have sales to Company X that will not be eliminated once it is no longer a consolidated subsidiary. But, following the disposal of Company X, the group will recognise revenue at the time paper is sold to Company X.

Should those intragroup sales between Company N and Company X that have not been passed on to external customers (i.e. for which the paper remains in Company X's inventories) remain in continuing operations?

No. While IFRS 5 requires the separate presentation of discontinued operations, the requirement to eliminate intragroup items is not changed from that in IFRS 10 *Consolidated Financial Statements*. Therefore, the sales should be fully eliminated and not reported by the group until an external sale occurs.

Example 6.3.1.7C

Elimination of intragroup interest charged to a discontinued operation

Group P consists of a number of entities, including the parent, Entity P, and a subsidiary, Entity S. During 20X1, Entity P charges interest to Entity S in respect of an intragroup receivable.

At 31 December 20X1, Entity S is sold. It meets the criteria for classification as a discontinued operation. The amount due from Entity S to Entity P is not repaid as part of the disposal transaction. Entity P continues to hold it as a receivable and will charge the same interest as in prior years.

For the purposes of Group P's consolidated financial statements, should the intragroup interest charged to Entity S be eliminated (following normal consolidation procedures) or should it be recognised as income in continuing operations and as an expense in discontinued operations (with a view to presenting the components of profit or loss as they will appear in future periods)?

The intragroup interest should be eliminated on consolidation. While IFRS 5 requires the separate presentation of discontinued operations, the requirement to eliminate intragroup items is not changed from that in IFRS 10.

6.3.1.8   *Presentation of tax income arising on discontinued operations*

Example 6.3.1.8

Presentation of tax income arising on discontinued operations

A group with principal operations in Country A and Country B disposes of part of its operations in Country B in the current year. The component disposed of qualifies as a discontinued operation under IFRS 5.

Operations in Country B had unrecognised tax losses brought forward from previous years. A deferred tax asset was not previously recognised because it was not considered probable that taxable profits would be available against which the deductible temporary difference could be utilised (the future profitability of the business was uncertain and the group had not yet identified the potential disposal of the operations in Country B as a tax planning opportunity to create taxable profits). The disposal of the component generates a taxable gain against which all the unrecognised losses brought forward can be applied.

The fact that the losses brought forward are recoverable against the taxable profit from sale of part of the operations in Country B does not necessarily indicate that the recovery of brought-forward tax losses is directly attributable to the discontinued operations.

It is necessary to consider whether the operating losses arose specifically from the discontinued operations. All factors should be considered, including whether:

- the losses have previously been disclosed as part of a segment being disposed of;

- the factors that gave rise to the previous losses will continue to exist after the disposal; or

- the losses arose partially from operations retained and partially from those sold, in which case an allocation between continuing and discontinuing operations would be appropriate.

When the operating losses are not directly attributable to the discontinued operations but relate to the operations retained in Country B, the income tax effects will be presented as part of continuing operations. While the disposal has created a taxable gain against which the losses can be used, the income tax effects are not directly attributable to the operations being disposed of and, therefore, do not qualify as part of the discontinued operations.

6.3.2   *Disclosures in the statement of cash flows*

The net cash flows attributable to the operating, investing and financing activities of discontinued operations must be shown, either in the notes or in the statement of cash flows. These disclosures are not required for disposal groups that are newly acquired subsidiaries that meet the criteria to be classified as held for sale on acquisition (see **section 5**). [IFRS 5:33(c)]

The comparative figures for prior periods are also re-presented, so that the disclosures relate to all operations that have been discontinued by the end of the reporting period for the latest period presented. [IFRS 5:34]

It is not acceptable to present the cash flows arising from continuing operations and discontinued operations as separate sections in the statement of cash flows. IFRS 5:33(c) adds an additional disclosure requirement in respect of cash flows arising from discontinued operations but it does not amend the requirements of IAS 7 *Statement of Cash Flows*; therefore, the requirement in IAS 7:10 to present cash flows classified by activity applies to the entity's total cash flows (i.e. the aggregate of continuing and discontinued operations). This is in contrast to the impact of IFRS 5 on the structure of the statement of comprehensive income, which results in the statement being divided into separate sections for continuing and discontinued operations, with no presentation of aggregate amounts (other than the total profit for the year).

Similarly, it is not acceptable to present on the face of the statement of cash flows (1) the gross cash flows attributable to continuing activities, and (2) only the net cash flows attributable to each of the operating, investing and financing activities of the discontinued operations (with the gross cash flows presented separately in the notes). IAS 7:21 requires the separate presentation of all major classes of gross cash receipts and gross cash payments. It is therefore inappropriate to exclude the gross cash flows attributable to the discontinued operations from the statement of cash flows and to present only the net cash flows attributable to the operating, investing and financing activities of the discontinued operations.

Possible approaches to presenting the information required by IFRS 5:33(c) while still complying with IAS 7's disclosure requirements include:

- presenting a separate note setting out the specific information required by IFRS 5:33(c), with no split between continuing and discontinued activities on the face of the statement of cash flows;

- presenting additional sub-analyses of the specified totals between continuing and discontinued operations on the face of the statement of cash flows; and

- presenting additional columns in the statement of cash flows showing the amount attributable to discontinued operations and the amount attributable to continuing operations for each IAS 7 line item, together with a column showing the total for each line item.

Note that entities will need to consider whether any proposed presentation will be accepted by local regulators.

Example 6.3.2

Presentation of taxes on sale of discontinued operations in statement of cash flows

Company P sold its international business to Company J for CU12 billion. As a result of the sale, Company P paid taxes related to the gain on the sale of approximately CU3 billion. Company P has appropriately determined to report the sale of the international business as a discontinued operation in its statement of comprehensive income. In its statement of cash flows, Company P has proposed including the taxes on the gain as a component of cash flows from investing activities, below the net proceeds from the sale of the international business.

Is it appropriate to present taxes associated with the proceeds from the sale of a component of an entity as part of investing activities in the statement of cash flows?

Yes. IAS 7:35 states that taxes should be classified as operating activities "unless they can be specifically identified with financing and investing activities". The disposal of non-current assets would be considered investing activities and, therefore, allocation of the tax effect of the sale to investing activities would be appropriate.

6.3.3 Adjustments to prior period disposals

6.3.3.1 Re-estimation of a gain or loss on disposal of a discontinued operation

It may be necessary occasionally to estimate a gain or loss on disposal of a discontinued operation, so that further adjustments arise in a subsequent period. When adjustments are made to amounts previously presented in discontinued operations that are directly related to the disposal of a discontinued operation in a prior period, they are classified separately in discontinued operations, and the nature and amount of such adjustments are disclosed. [IFRS 5:35]

IFRS 5:35 gives the following examples of circumstances that may trigger such adjustments:

- the resolution of uncertainties arising from the terms of the disposal transaction, such as the resolution of purchase price adjustments and indemnification issues with the purchaser;

- the resolution of uncertainties arising from and directly related to the operations of the component before its disposal, such as environmental and warranty obligations retained by the seller; and

- the settlement of employee benefit plan obligations if the settlement is directly related to the disposal transaction.

6.3.3.2 Reporting retained equity interest sold in a subsequent period

Example 6.3.3.2

Reporting retained equity interest sold in a subsequent period

Company D is proposing to sell a subsidiary, Company T, which qualifies as a discontinued operation under IFRS 5. Because this transaction arose from an unexpected offer from Company X, a third party, Company D does not have immediate plans for use of the proceeds from this sale. Accordingly, Company D would like to retain an equity interest (common stock) of up to 10 per cent in Company T for the next four to five years. Company D's retained equity interest in Company T would not be sufficient to enable Company D to exercise significant influence over Company T.

Additionally, Company D will have a put option on the retained equity interest in Company T to sell this interest over a four to five year period to Company X. Company X also will receive a call option to purchase the equity interest retained by D at the end of the four- to five-year period.

How should Company D report gains on the sale of the retained interest in Company T in subsequent periods?

Changes in the carrying amount of assets received as consideration on the disposal, or of residual interests in the business, should be classified within continuing operations. IFRS 5:35 requires adjustments to amounts previously reported in discontinued operations that are directly related to the disposal of a component of an entity in a prior period to be classified separately in the current period in discontinued operations. Developments subsequent to the disposal date that are not directly related to the disposal of the component or the operations of the component prior to disposal will not meet the criteria in IFRS 5:35. Subsequent changes in the carrying amount of assets received upon disposal of a component do not affect the determination of gain or loss at the disposal date, but represent the consequences of management's subsequent decisions to hold or sell those assets. Gains and losses, dividend and interest income, and portfolio management expenses associated with assets received as consideration for discontinued operations should be reported within continuing operations.

The gains resulting from Company D exercising its put option to sell a portion of its retained interest in Company T, or gains resulting from Company X exercising its call option to purchase the remaining interest in Company T, should be reported within continuing operations because they are not related directly to Company D's initial sale of Company T to Company X, and are the result of management's decision to hold and then sell an investment. Furthermore, any increases or decreases that may need to be reflected under IFRS 9 *Financial Instruments* (or, for entities that have not yet adopted IFRS 9, IAS 39 *Financial Instruments: Recognition and Measurement*) should be reported as part of continuing operations.

6.3.3.3 Interest income on note receivable from discontinued operations

---

Example 6.3.3.3

Interest income on note receivable from discontinued operations

In October 20X2, Company P properly accounted for a component of its entity as a discontinued operation in accordance with IFRS 5. As part of the discontinuation, Company P retained a note receivable from the component. Subsequent to October 20X2, Company P received interest income from the note receivable. Interest income recognised totalled CU43,000 in 20X2, and CU250,000 in 20X3.

During the fourth quarter of 20X3, the component previously disposed of defaulted on the note receivable and stopped paying interest. As a result of that default and other factors, Company P believes that the note receivable has been impaired and that the amount should be written off during the fourth quarter of 20X3.

Company P believes that the 20X2 financial statements did not contain an error because there was no indication when the 20X2 financial statements were prepared that the note receivable was impaired.

What is the appropriate classification for the interest income on the note receivable subsequent to the discontinuation?

Income from a financial asset received as part of the proceeds of disposal of discontinued operations should be reported as part of continuing operations. The carrying amount of assets received as consideration in the disposal or of residual interests in the business should be classified within continuing operations. Subsequent changes in the carrying amount of assets received upon disposal of a component do not affect the determination of the gain or loss at the disposal date, but represent the consequences of management's subsequent decisions to hold those assets.

Accordingly, the interest income associated with assets received as consideration for discontinued operations or with residual interests in the business should be reported within continuing operations. Company P should also recognise any impairment loss on the note receivable within continuing operations in the current year.

6.3.3.4 Ongoing pension obligations

Example 6.3.3.4

Ongoing pension obligations

Company B, a publicly held entity, previously closed two of its four chemical plants and retained the obligation for the defined benefit pension plans at the facilities. In the current year, Company B has spun-off its remaining chemical division through a share distribution to its current shareholders. Prior to approving the spin-off, the Pension Governmental Agency (PGA) required Company B to retain the pension obligations for the two chemical plants that were previously

---

closed. This agreement was required because the PGA believed Company B was more financially viable than the spun-off division and, accordingly, was more likely to be in a position to settle the remaining pension obligations.

At the end of Company B's current reporting period, the pension obligations for the two closed plants are underfunded by approximately CU22 million. Because the participants are no longer earning additional pension benefits under the plans, the only component of net periodic pension cost each year is the net interest on the net defined benefit liability. Historically, Company B has recognised the net periodic pension cost for the plans at the two closed plants within continuing operations each year.

Management contends that because the entire division was spun-off in the current year, all future net interest on the net defined benefit liability associated with these plans should be accrued as part of discontinued operations in the current year. Accordingly, management has proposed calculating the total future net interest on the net defined benefit liability associated with the plans (over their remaining payout period) and accruing this amount as part of discontinued operations in the current year.

Is it appropriate for Company B to recognise as an immediate cost in discontinued operations an accrual for the future net interest on the net defined benefit liability associated with the pension obligations that have been retained?

No. Company B made a decision not to settle the pension obligations at the time the two plants were closed and a second decision not to fund the obligations fully. As a result of these decisions, Company B continues to incur net interest on the net defined benefit liability. Therefore, the net interest on the net defined benefit liability is a component of the net periodic pension cost and should be recognised as a period cost and included in the determination of profit from continuing operations.

6.3.5 Changes to a plan of sale

As discussed at **4.8**, sometimes an entity's plans will change so that a component ceases to qualify as held for sale. When this occurs, the results of that operation should be reclassified from discontinued operations to continuing operations, both for the current and prior periods. The amounts for prior periods should be described as having been re-presented. [IFRS 5:36]

7 Other presentation and disclosure requirements

7.1 Disclosure requirements of other IFRSs apply in limited circumstances

IFRS 5 specifies the disclosures required in respect of non-current assets (or disposal groups) classified as held for sale or discontinued operations. IFRS 5:5B states that disclosure requirements in other IFRSs do not apply to such assets (or disposal groups) unless those IFRSs require:

[IFRS 5:5B]

(a) specific disclosures in respect of non-current assets (or disposal groups) classified as held for sale or discontinued operations; or

(b) disclosures about measurement of assets and liabilities within a disposal group that are not within the scope of the measurement requirement of IFRS 5 and such disclosures are not already provided in the other notes to the financial statements.

IFRS 5:5B clarifies that the disclosure requirements of another IFRS do not apply to scoped-in non-current assets classified as held for sale or included in a disposal group held for sale unless explicitly stated in that other IFRS. For other assets and liabilities (i.e. those excluded from the scope of the measurement requirements of IFRS 5) that are included within a disposal group classified as held for sale, IFRS 5:5B means that the disclosure requirements of other IFRSs apply *to the extent that those disclosure requirements relate to measurement*.

For example, the disclosure requirements of IFRS 13 *Fair Value Measurement* apply to scoped-in non-current assets classified as held for sale or included in a disposal group held for sale that are measured at fair value less costs to sell in accordance with IFRS 5 because they are specifically referred to in the scope provisions of IFRS 13 (see **section 2** of **chapter A6**). For assets and liabilities excluded from the scope of the measurement requirements of IFRS 5 that are included within a disposal group classified as held for sale and that are measured at fair value, the disclosure requirements of IFRS 13 apply to the extent that those disclosure requirements relate to measurement. In fact, as discussed in **section 11** of **chapter A6**, given that IFRS 13 as a whole is concerned with the measurement of fair value, and with disclosures regarding the measurement of fair value, all of the disclosure requirements of IFRS 13 relate to 'measurement' and, consequently, should be applied.

Under IFRS 5:5(c) (see **2.4.1**), all financial assets within the scope of IFRS 9 *Financial Instruments* (or, for entities that have not yet adopted IFRS 9, IAS 39 *Financial Instruments: Recognition and Measurement*) are excluded from the scope of the measurement requirements of IFRS 5. Therefore, in the context of IFRS 7 *Financial Instruments: Disclosures*, IFRS 5:5B means that the disclosure requirements of IFRS 7 apply to individual non-current financial assets held for sale and to financial assets and liabilities that form part of a disposal group to the extent that those disclosure requirements relate to measurement.

The specific disclosure requirements of IFRS 7 that apply should be determined as a matter of judgement. In some circumstances, the applicable disclosures about measurement may be limited to:

- the accounting policies and measurement bases for financial assets and liabilities (see IFRS 7:21); and

- the carrying amount of each category of financial asset and liability (see IFRS 7:8).

In some cases it could be argued that, for example, the liquidity risk, credit risk and market risk disclosures, among others, are not relevant to financial assets held for sale and financial assets and liabilities within a disposal group in the scope of IFRS 5's presentation and disclosure requirements.

Additional disclosures about non-current assets (or disposal groups) classified as held for sale or discontinued operations may be necessary to comply with the general requirements of IAS 1 *Presentation of Financial Statements*, in particular IAS 1:15 and 125 (see **3.1** and **7.3** in **chapter A4**). [IFRS 5:5B]

7.2 Gains or losses relating to continuing operations

Gains or losses on the remeasurement of a non-current asset (or disposal group) classified as held for sale that does not meet the definition of a discontinued operation are included in profit or loss from continuing operations. [IFRS 5:37]

When a non-current asset ceases to qualify as held for sale, IFRS 5:28 requires any resulting measurement adjustment (see **4.8.3**) to be presented "in the same caption in the statement of comprehensive income used to present a gain or loss, if any, recognised in accordance with paragraph 37". The intention appears to be that all gains and losses relating to any particular asset (or disposal group) should be presented within the same caption in the statement of comprehensive income – not that gains and losses on all items held for sale should be aggregated within a single caption. Thus, for example, gains and losses relating to properties held for sale might be presented in a different caption in the statement of comprehensive income from those relating to disposals of minor businesses that do not qualify as discontinued operations.

7.3 Non-current assets and disposal groups classified as held for sale

7.3.1 Presentation of non-current assets and disposal groups held for sale

Non-current assets held for sale and the assets of a disposal group held for sale are presented separately from other assets in the statement of financial position. Similarly, the liabilities of a disposal group held for sale are presented separately from other liabilities in the statement of financial position. Those assets and liabilities should not be offset and presented as a single amount. [IFRS 5:38]

There should be separate disclosure, either in the statement of financial position or in the notes, of the major classes of assets and liabilities classified as held for sale (except when the disposal group is a newly acquired subsidiary that meets the criteria to be classified as held for sale on acquisition). Any cumulative income or expense recognised in other comprehensive income relating to a non-current asset (or disposal group) classified as held for sale (e.g. fair value changes on a financial asset measured at fair value through other comprehensive income under IFRS 9, or classified as available for sale under IAS 39) should also be presented separately. [IFRS 5:38]

> Although IFRS 5 states that non-current assets held for sale, and assets of disposal groups held for sale, should be presented separately in the statement of financial position, it does not specifically address the issue as to whether those assets should be presented as current or non-current. The illustrative example issued with IFRS 5 (reproduced as **example 7.3.1**) presents them as current assets – and this will usually be the appropriate presentation because the general condition for classification as held for sale is that disposal is anticipated within one year of the reporting period (see **3.1.6.2**). However, as discussed at **3.1.8**, there are exceptions to this general principle, and the entity may be aware that the disposal will not occur until after one year. In such circumstances, if none of the other criteria for classification as a current asset (see **2.2**) are met, it appears that the assets should be presented as non-current assets.

When the disposal group is a newly acquired subsidiary that meets the criteria to be classified as held for sale on acquisition (see **section 5**), disclosure of the major classes of assets and liabilities is not required. [IFRS 5:39]

Comparative amounts for non-current assets or for the assets and liabilities of disposal groups held for sale in the statements of financial position for prior periods are not reclassified or re-presented to reflect the classification in the statement of financial position for the latest period presented. [IFRS 5:40]

The implementation guidance accompanying IFRS 5 includes the following illustration of presentation in the statement of financial position.

> The wording of the example below reflects amendments made by IFRS 9. The amendments have not had any substantive effect.

Example 7.3.1

Presenting non-current assets or disposal groups classified as held for sale

[Guidance on implementing IFRS 5:Example 12]

At the end of 20X5, an entity decides to dispose of part of its assets (and directly associated liabilities). The disposal, which meets the criteria in IFRS 5:7 & 8 to be classified as held for sale, takes the form of two disposal groups, as follows:

	Carrying amount after classification as held for sale	
	Disposal group I:	Disposal group II:
	CU	CU
Property, plant and equipment	4,900	1,700
Investments in equity instruments	1,400[a]	–
Liabilities	(2,400)	(900)
Net carrying amount of disposal group	**3,900**	**800**

[a] An amount of CU400 relating to these assets has been recognised in other comprehensive income and accumulated in equity.

The presentation in the entity's statement of financial position of the disposal groups classified as held for sale can be shown as follows:

	20X5	20X4
ASSETS		
Non-current assets		
AAA	X	X
BBB	X	X
CCC	X	X
	X	X
Current assets		
DDD	X	X
EEE	X	X
	X	X
Non-current assets classified as held for sale	8,000	–
	X	X
Total assets	X	X
EQUITY AND LIABILITIES		
Equity attributable to equity holders of the parent		
FFF	X	X
GGG	X	X

	20X5	20X4
Amounts recognised in other comprehensive income and accumulated in equity relating to non-current assets held for sale	400	–
	X	X
Non-controlling interest	X	X
Total equity	X	X
Non-current liabilities		
HHH	X	X
III	X	X
JJJ	X	X
	X	X
Current liabilities		
KKK	X	X
LLL	X	X
MMM	X	X
	X	X
Liabilities directly associated with non-current assets classified as held for sale	3,300	–
	X	X
Total liabilities	X	X
Total equity and liabilities	X	X

The presentation requirements for assets (or disposal groups) classified as held for sale at the end of the reporting period do not apply retrospectively. The comparative statements of financial position for any previous periods are therefore not re-presented.

7.3.2 Elimination of intragroup balances between a disposal group held for sale and other group entities

Example 7.3.2

Elimination of intragroup balances between a disposal group held for sale and other group entities

Group P consists of a number of entities, including the parent, Entity P, and a subsidiary, Entity S. At 31 December 20X1, Entity S meets the criteria for classification as a disposal group held for sale and its assets and liabilities are presented separately in accordance with IFRS 5:38.

The net carrying amount of Entity S's assets and liabilities is CU5 million, which is lower than the fair value less costs to sell of the disposal group. Entity S's liabilities include a loan of CU1 million from its parent, Entity P.

In Group P's consolidated financial statements, should the intragroup payable of CU1 million owing to Entity P be eliminated prior to the segregation of the assets and liabilities of Entity S for presentation as a disposal group held for sale?

Yes. IFRS 5 deals with classification and measurement of assets (disposal groups) held for sale and does not override the general consolidation principles in IFRS 10 *Consolidated Financial Statements*. IFRS 10:B86(c) requires that intragroup balances should be eliminated in full. Consequently, intragroup balances between a disposal group classified as held for sale and other entities within the group should be eliminated in full prior to applying the classification and measurement principles of IFRS 5.

In the circumstances described, Group P's consolidated financial statements will present Entity S's assets and liabilities separately in accordance with the requirements of IFRS 5:38, with a net carrying amount of CU6 million (because the CU1 million payable to Entity P is eliminated on consolidation).

7.4 Additional disclosures

In any period in which a non-current asset (or disposal group) has been either classified as held for sale or sold, the following information should be provided in the notes to the financial statements:

[IFRS 5:41]

(a) a description of the non-current asset (or disposal group);

(b) a description of the facts and circumstances of the sale, or leading to the expected disposal, and the expected manner and timing of that disposal;

(c) the gain or loss recognised in accordance with IFRS 5:20 to 22 (see **section 4**) and, if not separately presented in the statement of comprehensive income, the caption in the statement of comprehensive income that includes that gain or loss; and

(d) if applicable, the reportable segment in which the non-current asset (or disposal group) is presented in accordance with IFRS 8 *Operating Segments*.

When the held for sale criteria are not met until after the reporting period, non-current assets (or disposal groups) should not be classified as held for sale. Instead, disclosures (a), (b) and (d) above should be provided. [IFRS 5:12]

IFRS 5:42 requires certain disclosures when there has been a change to a plan of sale, such that either an asset (or a disposal group) previously classified as held for sale no longer meets the criteria, or an individual asset or liability has been removed from a disposal group classified as held for sale. In the period of the decision to change the plan to sell the non-current asset (or disposal group), the financial statements should disclose:

- a description of the facts and circumstances leading to the decision; and

- the effect of the decision on the results of operations for the period and any prior periods presented.

A21 Statement of cash flows

Contents

1   Introduction

1.1   Overview of IAS 7

IAS 7 *Statement of Cash Flows* requires an entity to present a statement of cash flows as an integral part of its primary financial statements. Cash flows are classified and presented as operating activities (using either the 'direct' or the 'indirect' method), investing activities or financing activities, with the latter two categories generally presented on a gross basis.

Although the title of IAS 7 is *Statement of Cash Flows*, entities are not required to use that title for the statement itself. [IAS 1:10]

For example, some entities instead use the title 'Cash flow statement'.

1.2   Amendments to IAS 7 since the last edition of this manual

The following amendments have been made to IAS 7 since the last edition of this manual.

- January 2016 – consequential amendments arising from IFRS 16 *Leases* to reflect the fact that, for lessees, the distinction between finance and operating leases has been removed and that all leases are now 'on-balance sheet' (subject to exemptions for short-term leases and leases of low-value assets). Examples of non-cash transactions and financing cash flows in IAS 7 (see **3.3** and **5.4.2**, respectively) have been amended to refer to leases in general, rather than specifically to finance leases. These amendments should be applied when an entity adopts IFRS 16.

- January 2016 – amendments arising from *Disclosure Initiative – Amendments to IAS 7*. The amendments require an entity to provide additional disclosures regarding its financing activities and information relevant to understanding the entity's liquidity (see **9.2**). These amendments are effective for annual periods beginning on or after 1 January 2017, with earlier application permitted.

2   Scope

IAS 7 requires all reporting entities to present a statement of cash flows prepared in accordance with that Standard. The statement of cash flows should be presented as an integral part of the financial statements. [IAS 7:1]

3   Presentation of a statement of cash flows

3.1   General requirements for presentation of a statement of cash flows

The basic requirement of IAS 7 is that an entity should prepare and present a statement of cash flows that reports the cash flows of the entity during the period classified into operating, investing and financing activities. [IAS 7:10]

Under the general requirements of IAS 1 *Presentation of Financial Statements*, comparative information in respect of the preceding period should be presented for all amounts reported in the current period's statement of cash flows and the supporting notes. Consequently, an entity should present, as a minimum, two statements of cash flows. [IAS 1:38 & 38A]

When an entity prepares only individual or separate financial statements, the statement of cash flows will be for the individual entity. When consolidated financial statements are prepared, a consolidated statement of cash flows will be presented. When an entity produces both separate financial statements and consolidated financial statements, a statement of cash flows will be required for each.

3.2   Cash flows permitted to be reported on a net basis

Cash inflows should generally be reported separately from outflows. However, IAS 7 does permit the following cash flows to be reported on a net basis:

[IAS 7:22]

- receipts and payments on behalf of customers when the cash flows reflect the activities of the customer rather than those of the entity (such as the collection of rent on behalf of the owner of a property, funds held for customers by an investment entity, or the acceptance and repayment of demand deposits by a bank); and

- receipts and payments for items in which the turnover is quick, the amounts are large and the maturities are short (such as advances and repayments of principal amounts relating to credit card customers, purchases and sales of investments, and commercial paper or other short-term borrowings with a maturity period of three months or less).

For financial institutions, the following additional cash flows may be reported on a net basis:

[IAS 7:24]

- cash receipts and payments for the acceptance and repayment of deposits with a fixed maturity date;

- the placement of deposits with and withdrawal of deposits from other financial institutions; and

- cash advances and loans made to customers and the repayment of those advances and loans.

3.3 Exclusion of non-cash transactions

Cash flows are defined as inflows and outflows of cash and cash equivalents (see **section 4**). [IAS 7:6]

As a general principle, only transactions that require the use of cash or cash equivalents should be included in a statement of cash flows. Note, however, that when the indirect method of presenting cash flows from operating activities is used (as discussed at **5.2.4**), this will result in some non-cash items appearing in the statement of cash flows as adjustments to profit or loss for the period. Investing and financing activities that do not require the use of cash or cash equivalents are always excluded from the statement of cash flows. [IAS 7:43]

Examples of investing and financing transactions that do not result in cash flows and, consequently, are excluded from the statement of cash flows, include:

- acquisitions of assets by way of a lease (or, for entities that have not yet adopted IFRS 16, a finance lease) (but the payments for lease rentals are cash flows);

- acquisitions or disposals of assets (other than cash) in return for equity securities;

- exchanges of non-monetary assets such as property, plant and equipment, and inventories;

- the issue of bonus shares to holders of the entity's equity;

- the receipt of bonus shares from another entity in which the reporting entity holds an investment; and

- the conversion of debt securities into equity securities.

The inception of a lease contract (or, for entities that have not yet adopted IFRS 16, a finance lease contract) is one of the most commonly encountered non-cash transactions. Such a transaction, although reflected in the statement of financial position by recognising an asset and a matching liability, should not be reflected in the statement of cash flows because the reporting entity neither pays nor receives cash. It is not appropriate to show a cash outflow in respect of an asset purchase and the drawdown of a loan.

When transactions of a non-cash nature occur, IAS 7 requires that they be disclosed elsewhere in the financial statements in a way that provides all of the relevant information about those investing and financing activities. [IAS 7:43] This disclosure will normally be in narrative form in the notes.

3.4 Exclusion of movements between items that constitute cash or cash equivalents

Movements between items that constitute cash or cash equivalents are excluded from cash flows, because these components are part of the cash management of an entity rather than part of its operating, investing and financing activities. Cash management includes the investment of excess cash in cash equivalents. [IAS 7:9]

> For example, when an entity uses cash to purchase a short-term investment meeting the definition of a cash equivalent, the purchase is not shown in the statement of cash flows.

4 Cash and cash equivalents

4.1 Cash

4.1.1 Cash – definition

Cash comprises cash on hand and demand deposits. [IAS 7:6]

4.1.2 Demand deposits

> The term 'demand deposits' is not defined in IAS 7, but the term may be taken to refer to deposits where the reporting entity can withdraw cash without giving any notice and without suffering any penalty. A seven-day call deposit would therefore not qualify as cash, because seven days notice of withdrawal is required. The deposit could, however, be reported as a cash equivalent (see **4.2**).
>
> Similarly, if an entity has an account with its bank under which the entity is required to give 90 days' notice to the bank before it can withdraw money, the account does not meet the definition of cash because it is not a demand deposit. However, only 90 days' notice is required and, therefore, it may meet the definition of a cash equivalent.
>
> The term 'demand deposits' is not restricted to deposits with banks or financial institutions.

4.1.3   Minimum average cash balances

Some entities have banking arrangements that require them to maintain a minimum average cash balance over a specified period instead of a constant minimum balance at the end of each day. It is therefore possible to have balances below the threshold for certain days as long as the average balance over the period is in excess of the minimum requirement. For such arrangements, it is necessary to consider whether the balance can be withdrawn on demand, in a way similar to demand deposits; i.e. whether the entity can withdraw the cash without giving any notice and without suffering any penalty. If these criteria are met, the cash balances will meet the definition of cash in IAS 7.

4.2   Cash equivalents

4.2.1   Cash equivalents – definition

Cash equivalents are defined as short-term, highly liquid investments that are readily convertible to known amounts of cash and which are subject to an insignificant risk of changes in value. [IAS 7:6]

4.2.2   Cash equivalents – held to meet short-term cash commitments

IAS 7 explains that cash equivalents are held for the purpose of meeting short-term cash commitments rather than for investment or other purposes. [IAS 7:7] Therefore, in order to determine whether a particular investment qualifies for classification as a cash equivalent, it is necessary to look at the purpose for which it is held. Even though the investment may meet the definition set out in **4.2.1**, unless it is held for the purpose of meeting short-term cash commitments, it will not be classified as a cash equivalent.

For example, an entity purchases a two-year bond in the market when the bond only has two months remaining before its redemption date. The purchase is made for investment purposes. The bond does not qualify as a cash equivalent because, even though it meets the definition in IAS 7:6, it is not held for the purpose of meeting short-term cash commitments.

4.2.3   Cash equivalents – presumption of maturity of three months or less

The definition of cash equivalents includes the requirement that they be held for the 'short-term'. In order to qualify as such, IAS 7 states that the investment will *normally* have a maturity of three months or less from the date of acquisition. [IAS 7:7] Therefore, the requirement for a three-month maturity is not part of the definition, but will nevertheless be a presumption except in very exceptional circumstances.

IAS 7 implicitly suggests that only in unusual cases will investments with more than three months to maturity nevertheless be free from significant risk of changes in value (arising, for example, from changes in interest rates). An entity purchasing a two-year bond in the market when the bond only has three months remaining before its redemption date could therefore classify the bond as a cash equivalent (assuming that there are no other factors causing it to be subject to a significant risk of change in value, and that the underlying purpose of holding the bond is to meet short-term cash commitments – see **4.2.2**). However, the reference to three months or less 'from the date of acquisition' means that, if the entity instead purchased the same two-year bond when it had four months remaining before maturity, the entity could not classify the bond as a cash equivalent either at the date of purchase or once it has less than three months remaining to maturity (unless it could justify a departure from the three-month guideline, in which case the instrument would be classified as a cash equivalent throughout the entire four months).

The three-month limit may appear somewhat arbitrary, but the intention is to promote consistency between entities.

Example 4.2.3

Repurchase agreements as cash equivalents

An entity invests excess funds in short-term repurchase agreements with a term of two months. The underlying debt securities involved in the transaction have maturities in excess of three months. These repurchase agreements will be classified as cash equivalents provided that (1) there are no other factors that would subject the instruments to a significant risk of change in value, and (2) the underlying purpose for holding the repurchase agreements is to meet short-term cash commitments. The critical factor is the maturity of the repurchase agreements themselves, not the underlying debt securities.

4.2.4 Classification of foreign currency investments as cash equivalents

Provided that the definition of a cash equivalent is met, there is no reason why an investment acquired in a foreign currency could not be classified as a cash equivalent. Indeed, IAS 7 refers specifically to cash and cash equivalents held or due in a foreign currency. [IAS 7:28]

4.2.5 Classification of equity investments as cash equivalents

Equity investments will not normally meet the definition of a cash equivalent because, even when they are readily convertible to cash, the amount of that cash is generally not known and the risk of changes in value is generally not insignificant, although there are exceptions. The example of an exception given in IAS 7 is that of preferred shares with a specific redemption date which, when acquired, are close to maturity. The majority of equity investments will not meet the definition, however, and therefore cannot be classified as cash equivalents. [IAS 7:7]

4.2.6 Classification of gold bullion as cash equivalents

Gold (and similar traded commodities) will not qualify as cash equivalents for the same reason as equity investments (see **4.2.5**). In addition, the guidance on implementing IFRS 9 *Financial Instruments* confirms that gold bullion "is a commodity. Although bullion is highly liquid, there is no contractual right to receive cash or another financial asset inherent in bullion". [IFRS 9:IG.B.1] For entities that have not yet adopted IFRS 9, this text is also reflected in the guidance on implementing IAS 39 *Financial Instruments: Recognition and Measurement.*

4.2.7 Bank overdrafts presented as a component of cash equivalents

The definition of cash equivalents makes no reference to the inclusion of bank borrowings. Bank borrowings are generally considered to be financing cash flows. However, IAS 7 acknowledges that bank overdrafts repayable on demand may form an integral part of an entity's cash management, in which case they should be included as a component of cash and cash equivalents. A characteristic of such banking arrangements is that the bank balance often fluctuates from being positive to being overdrawn. [IAS 7:8]

IAS 7 does not therefore mandate the inclusion of bank overdrafts in cash equivalents in all circumstances. But it does require their inclusion when the bank overdraft forms an integral part of the entity's cash management. IAS 7:8 also emphasises that bank borrowings are generally considered to be financing activities. Therefore, the Standard does not allow for other short-term loans (e.g. short-term bank loans, advances from factors or similar credit arrangements, credit import loans, trust receipt loans) to be classified as cash equivalents, because they are financing in nature.

4.2.8 Money market funds generally excluded from cash equivalents

Money market funds are open-ended mutual funds that invest in short-term debt instruments such as treasury bills, certificates of deposit and commercial paper. Because the main purpose of the investment is the preservation of principal, with modest dividends, the net asset value of such an investment remains fairly constant.

IAS 7:7 specifies that equity investments (such as shares in investment funds) are excluded from cash equivalents unless they are, in substance, cash equivalents (e.g. preferred shares acquired within a short period of their maturity and with a specified redemption date).

IAS 7:7 states that "[c]ash equivalents are held for the purpose of meeting short-term cash commitments". In this context, the critical criteria in the definition of cash equivalents set out in IAS 7:6 are the requirements that cash equivalents be "readily convertible to known amounts of cash" and "subject to insignificant risk of changes in value".

The first criterion means that the investment must be readily convertible to cash (e.g. through redemption with the fund). The amount of cash that will be received must be known at the time of the initial investment (e.g. on the basis of a constant CU1 net asset value per unit); the units of money market funds cannot be considered cash equivalents simply because they can be converted to cash at any time at the then prevailing market price in an active market.

The second criterion means that an entity needs to assess the risk of future changes in value at the time of initial investment, and must be satisfied that the risk is insignificant. This can be determined through consideration of the fund's investment rules or by establishing the nature of the underlying investments.

This is consistent with the agenda decision published by the IFRIC (now the IFRS Interpretations Committee) in the July 2009 *IFRIC Update*.

4.2.9   Change in policy for components of cash equivalents

IAS 7:47 states that the effect of any change in the policy for determining components of cash and cash equivalents (e.g. a change in the classification of financial instruments previously considered to be part of an entity's investment portfolio) is reported in accordance with IAS 8 *Accounting Policies, Changes in Accounting Estimates and Errors*. IAS 8 requires that comparative amounts are restated and additional disclosures (e.g. the reasons for the change) are made.

These disclosures are not triggered, however, simply because an entity presents an instrument as a cash equivalent in a particular year that was not there in the previous year. For example, in the current year an entity has, for the first time, classified an investment in a 90-day notice account as a cash equivalent. If the 90-day account is included in cash equivalents for the first time because the account was only opened during the current year, then this does not represent a change in accounting policy. If the entity held equivalent balances in the prior year, but classified them as investing, and during the current year decided that they were more appropriately classified as cash equivalents (even though its reasons for holding them have not changed), then this is a change in accounting policy (provided that there has been no change of substance in the accounts and the level of funds kept in them) and the requirements of IAS 8 are triggered.

Because IAS 7 focuses on the reason for holding a particular balance, the same types of investments may be classified differently from year to year, without this constituting a change in accounting policy. For example, in a particular year an entity may hold short-term bonds for the purpose of generating investment returns, and they are therefore not classified as cash equivalents. In the following year, perhaps because of a change in the cash flow profile of the entity, the same type of investments may be held, but this time they may be held for the purpose of meeting short-term cash commitments, and they are therefore classified as cash equivalents. In such circumstances, the bonds will be classified in a different manner in the two years, but this will not constitute a change in accounting policy and, therefore, comparative amounts should not be restated.

5 Classification of cash flows

5.1 Classification of cash flows – general

Cash flows should be classified by operating, investing or financing activities. [IAS 7:10]

Unlike IFRS requirements for other financial statements (e.g. statement of comprehensive income and statement of financial position), the headings for the statement of cash flows are standard, and should not be altered to suit individual circumstances (unless, very exceptionally, the use of the standard wording is likely to mislead readers of the financial statements). There are no requirements, however, that would prevent further sub-classifications or analyses appropriate to the entity's business being shown within these three headings in the statement of cash flows.

Cash flows should be classified under the standard headings in the most appropriate manner for the entity's business. [IAS 7:11] Thus, for example, the purchase of an investment might be an investing activity for a manufacturing entity but might be part of the operating activities of a financial institution.

Example 5.1A

Classification of decommissioning payments

Entity K is a mobile telecommunications company. To maintain its nation-wide mobile phone network, Entity K owns thousands of wireless base station facilities (i.e. antennae) at multiple locations.

For some of its base station facilities, Entity K is under a legal obligation to dismantle and remove the antennae at the end of their useful lives. In such circumstances, Entity K recognises its initial estimate of the relevant decommissioning costs as part of the cost of the antennae when they are first acquired or constructed, and recognises an equivalent provision. Changes in the measurement of the decommissioning liabilities are accounted for under IFRIC 1 *Changes in Existing Decommissioning, Restoration and Similar Liabilities*. Payments made to dismantle and remove the antennae at the end of their useful lives are offset against the appropriate provision.

For other facilities, Entity K has no obligation to dismantle and remove the antennae. In such circumstances, any decommissioning costs are recognised when incurred.

How should Entity K classify payments made to dismantle and remove antennae in its statement of cash flows? In particular, is the cash flow classification affected by whether a decommissioning obligation was recognised when the antenna was first purchased or constructed?

Cash flows should be classified in accordance with the nature of the activity to which they relate, following the definitions of operating, investing and financing activities in IAS 7:6. IAS 7:11 states that an entity presents its cash flows from operating, investing and financing activities in a manner which is most appropriate to its business.

Focusing on the nature of the activity in the circumstances under consideration, a cash outflow to remove or dismantle one of its facilities is a central part of Entity K's principal revenue-producing activities (i.e. to maintain its wireless network) as contemplated in IAS 7:14. Consequently, such payments should be classified as operating cash outflows (see **5.2.1**), irrespective of whether a decommissioning obligation was recognised when the asset was first purchased or constructed.

One scenario in which the classification of the payment might vary is if, when a base station facility is acquired or constructed, Entity K were to make an up-front payment to a third party to cover the dismantling and removal costs when they arise. This up-front payment would result in a recognised asset in Entity K's statement of financial position and it could be argued, by reference to IAS 7:16 (see **5.3.3**), that the nature of the up-front cash outflow is investing.

When a single payment or receipt of cash represents a number of smaller payments or receipts, each should be classified according to its nature. [IAS 7:12] For example, when the settlement of a financial liability involves the repayment of principal and interest, the cash flows will be dealt with separately (see **5.5.4**). Similarly, lease payments (or, for entities that have not yet adopted IFRS 16, finance lease payments) will be segregated between their capital and interest components.

Example 5.1B

Classification of lease payments (or, for entities that have not yet adopted IFRS 16, finance lease payments)

An entity makes a payment of CU100,000 under a lease (or, for entities that have not yet adopted IFRS 16, a finance lease). In its financial statements, it allocates CU20,000 to interest and CU80,000 as a repayment of loan capital.

In its statement of cash flows, CU80,000 will be classified as a financing cash flow and CU20,000 will be classified according to the entity's general classification for interest (see **5.5.2**).

5.2 Operating activities

5.2.1 Operating activities – definition

Operating activities are defined as the principal revenue-producing activities of the entity and other activities that are not investing or financing activities. [IAS 7:6]

Therefore, 'operating' is the residual category for the purpose of presenting cash flows. If a cash flow does not fall within the scope of investing or financing activities (see **5.3** and **5.4**, respectively) then it will be classified as operating.

5.2.2 Cash flows from operating activities – examples

Examples of cash flows from operating activities are:

- cash received in the year from customers (in respect of sales of goods or services rendered either in the year, or in an earlier year, or received in advance in respect of the sale of goods or services to be rendered in a later year);
- cash payments in the year to suppliers (for raw materials or goods for resale whether supplied in the current year, or an earlier year, or to be supplied in a later year);
- the payment of wages and salaries to employees;
- tax and other payments on behalf of employees;
- the payment of rent on property used in the business operations;
- royalties received in the year;

- cash receipts and cash payments of an insurance entity for premiums and claims, annuities and other policy benefits;

- the payment of insurance premiums;

- cash payments or refunds of income taxes that cannot be specifically identified with financing or investing activities (see **5.6**);

- cash flows arising from futures contracts, forward contracts, option contracts or swap contracts hedging a transaction that is itself classified as operating; and

- cash flows arising from the purchase and sale of securities and loans held for dealing or trading purposes.

Cash flows from operating activities should be reported using either the direct method or the indirect method (see **5.2.3** and **5.2.4**, respectively). [IAS 7:18] IAS 7 encourages the use of the direct method.

5.2.3   Presentation of operating cash flows using the direct method

Under the direct method, each major class of gross cash receipts and gross cash payments is disclosed separately. [IAS 7:18(a)] **Example 5.2.3** illustrates the operating cash flows section of a statement of cash flows using the direct method.

Example 5.2.3

Direct method of presenting operating cash flows

	Year ended 31 Dec 20X1	Year ended 31 Dec 20X1
	CU'000	CU'000
Cash flows from operating activities		
Cash receipts from customers	252,376	
Cash paid to suppliers	(127,045)	
Cash paid to and on behalf of employees	(78,014)	
Other cash payments	(12,038)	
Cash generated from operations	35,279	
Interest paid	(5,933)	
Income taxes paid	(13,447)	
Net cash from operating activities		15,899

5.2.4 Presentation of operating cash flows using the indirect method

5.2.4.1 Indirect method for presenting operating cash flows – general

The indirect method starts with the profit or loss and adjusts it for:

[IAS 7:18(b)]

- any non-cash items included in its calculation (such as depreciation or movements in provisions);

- any cash flows in the period that were reported in the profit or loss of an earlier period or will be reported in profit or loss of a future period (e.g. operating accruals and prepayments, settlement of a liability for restructuring costs accrued in the prior period); and

- any items of income and expense that are related to investing or financing cash flows.

5.2.4.2 Alternatives for presenting operating cash flows using the indirect method

IAS 7 describes two ways of presenting operating cash flows using the indirect method. The first (and the most commonly used) starts with profit or loss and then adjusts it for:

[IAS 7:20]

- changes during the period in inventories and operating receivables and payables;

- non-cash items such as depreciation, provisions, deferred taxes, unrealised foreign currency gains and losses, undistributed profits of associates, and non-controlling interests; and

- all other items for which the cash effects are investing or financing cash flows.

The presentation for operating cash flows using the indirect method is illustrated in **example 5.2.4.2A**.

IAS 7 is not explicit as to whether these adjustments should be presented in the statement of cash flows or in a supporting note. The illustrative example in Appendix A to IAS 7 shows them in the statement of cash flows and, therefore, this is the preferred presentation. It is the most common presentation used by entities applying IAS 7, and is also the presentation used in the IFRS illustrative financial statements published by the IASB. However, presentation of the adjustments in the notes is generally acceptable.

Example 5.2.4.2A

Indirect method of presenting operating cash flows (1)

	Year ended 31 Dec 20X1	Year ended 31 Dec 20X1
	CU'000	CU'000
Cash flows from operating activities		
Profit before taxation	19,696	
Adjustments for:		
Depreciation	6,174	
Foreign exchange loss	829	
Interest expense*	7,305	
Profit before working capital changes	34,004	
Increase in trade and other receivables	(7,601)	
Increase in trade payables	5,224	
Decrease in inventories	3,652	
Cash generated from operations	35,279	
Interest paid*	(5,933)	
Income taxes paid	(13,447)	
Net cash from operating activities		15,899

*   'Interest expense' is included above as an 'adjustment' to profit before tax. If interest
       is considered an operating activity, the adjustment from profit to cash flow is the
       difference between the interest expense in profit or loss and the interest actually paid
       during the period, i.e. CU1,372,000. However, in order that the amount of interest
       paid can be disclosed separately as required by IAS 7:31 (see **5.5.1**), this example
       adds back the interest expense in full and then deducts the full amount of interest
       paid.

The alternative indirect method of presentation shows the revenues and
expenses that are disclosed in the statement of comprehensive income and
adjusts these for the changes during the period in operating receivables
and payables and in inventories. [IAS 7:20] This alternative is rarely used
in practice. The alternative presentation is illustrated in **example 5.2.4.2B**.

Example 5.2.4.2B

Indirect method of presenting operating cash flows (2)

	Year ended 31 Dec 20X1	Year ended 31 Dec 20X1
	CU'000	CU'000
Cash flows from operating activities		
Revenue	259,376	
Operating expenses excluding depreciation	(225,372)	
Profit before working capital changes	34,004	
Increase in trade and other receivables	(7,601)	
Increase in trade payables	5,224	
Decrease in inventories	3,652	
Cash generated from operations	35,279	
Interest paid	(5,933)	
Income taxes paid	(13,447)	
Net cash from operating activities		15,899

5.2.4.3 Indirect method: which profit or loss?

When using the indirect method of presentation for operating cash flows, IAS 7:18(b) requires that 'profit or loss' be adjusted for (1) the effects of transactions of a non-cash nature, (2) any deferrals or accruals of past or future operating cash receipts or payments, and (3) items of income or expense associated with investing or financing cash flows. But which 'profit or loss' is the appropriate starting point for the presentation of these adjustments?

The illustrative example in Appendix A to IAS 7 starts with 'profit before taxation'; therefore, this is the preferred presentation.

Entities that choose to present an operating result in the statement of comprehensive income (or separate statement of profit or loss) (see **5.2.4.4** in **chapter A4**) may, however, wish to use that operating result as the starting point for the presentation of adjustments. Unless the entity has a discontinued operation (see below), the items presented between operating result and profit/loss before taxation are generally non-operating cash flows (share of results of associates, interest paid etc.). When this is the case, rather than using profit/loss before taxation as the starting point, and subsequently adjusting for all of the items between that amount and the operating result, it appears generally acceptable to use the operating result as the starting point. However, entities should take into consideration any specific requirements by local regulators.

When an entity has a discontinued operation, the results of which are presented under IFRS 5 *Non-current Assets Held for Sale and Discontinued Operations*, the 'profit before tax' presented in the statement of comprehensive income (or separate statement of profit or loss) relates only to continuing operations. In these circumstances, there is more than one way in which the requirements of IAS 7:18(b) can be met.

The first approach, which is the preferred approach, is to start with the total presented for profit or loss under paragraph 81A of IAS 1 *Presentation of Financial Statements*; this includes both continuing and discontinued operations. The amount can then be adjusted for the items required under IAS 7:18(b). The advantage of this approach is that it results in a very clear link between the amounts presented in the statement of comprehensive income (or separate statement of profit or loss) and the amounts presented in the statement of cash flows. The disadvantage is that it can result in a long list of adjustments being presented in the statement of cash flows. This approach is illustrated in **example 5.2.4.3A**.

Another solution, for entities presenting an operating result, would be to start with the operating profit from continuing operations and to add to this the operating profit from discontinued operations, to arrive at an operating profit for the reporting entity as a whole. As discussed above, this would reduce the number of adjustments presented in the statement of cash flows, and may provide a clearer presentation for the user of the statement of cash flows. The disadvantage is that it is not so easily linked to the amounts presented in the statement of comprehensive income (or separate statement of profit or loss). This approach is illustrated in **example 5.2.4.3B**.

Note, however, that it is not considered acceptable to use a non-GAAP measure, such as EBITDA, as a starting point for the presentation of adjustments.

Example 5.2.4.3A

Presentation of adjustments from profit to operating cash flows – profit or loss as starting point

	Year ended 31 Dec 20X1 CU'000	Year ended 31 Dec 20X0 CU'000
Operating activities		
Profit for the year	100,366	19,626
Adjustments for:		
Share of profit of associates	(12,763)	(983)

	Year ended 31 Dec 20X1	Year ended 31 Dec 20X0
	CU'000	CU'000
Investment revenues	(3,501)	(717)
Other gains and losses	563	44
Finance costs	36,680	32,995
Income tax expense	17,983	4,199
Gain on disposal of discontinued operation	(8,493)	–
Depreciation of property, plant and equipment	29,517	19,042
Impairment loss on fixtures and equipment	4,130	247
......		

Example 5.2.4.3B

Presentation of adjustments from profit to operating cash flows – operating profit as starting point

	Year ended 31 Dec 20X1	Year ended 31 Dec 20X0
	CU'000	CU'000
Operating activities		
Operating profit from continuing operations	126,342	49,774
Operating profit from discontinued operations	4,493	5,390
Total operating profit	130,835	55,164
Adjustments for:		
Depreciation of property, plant and equipment	29,517	19,042
Impairment loss on fixtures and equipment	4,130	247
......		

5.2.5 Sales taxes

IAS 7 does not explicitly address whether cash flows reported in accordance with IAS 7 should be measured as inclusive or exclusive of sales taxes.

The IFRIC (now the IFRS Interpretations Committee) was asked to consider this issue in 2005, specifically in connection with value added tax (VAT) (see August 2005 *IFRIC Update*). Different practices were expected to emerge, the differences being most marked for entities that adopt the direct method of reporting operating cash flows (see **5.2.3**). The Committee did not add the project to its agenda, but recommended that the treatment of VAT should be considered by the IASB as part of a future financial statement presentation project.

In the absence of any explicit guidance, the issue should be considered in the context of IAS 7:50 which encourages disclosure of additional information when it may be relevant to users in understanding the financial information and liquidity of an entity. Therefore, an entity should disclose whether gross cash flows are presented inclusive or exclusive of sales taxes. In addition, such disclosure would be considered necessary to comply with IAS 1 *Presentation of Financial Statements.* In particular, IAS 1:112(c) requires that the notes provide additional information that is not presented in the statement of comprehensive income, statement of financial position, statement of changes in equity or statement of cash flows, but is relevant to an understanding of any of them.

5.2.6   Cash flows associated with assets held for rental to others

For entities that are in the business of renting out assets to others, the cash inflows arising from renting out the assets and the associated operating costs are classified as operating cash flows.

Cash payments to manufacture or acquire assets held for rental to others and subsequently held for sale as described in paragraph 68A of IAS 16 *Property, Plant and Equipment* (see **9.3** in **chapter A7**) are cash flows from operating activities. The cash receipts from rents and subsequent sales of such assets are also cash flows from operating activities. [IAS 7:14]

5.3   Investing activities

5.3.1   Investing activities – definition

Investing activities are defined as the acquisition and disposal of long-term assets and other investments not included in cash equivalents. [IAS 7:6] Major classes of gross cash receipts and gross cash payments arising from investing activities should be reported separately, except to the extent that cash flows described in IAS 7:22 and 24 are reported on a net basis (see **3.2**). [IAS 7:21]

5.3.2   Cash flows from investing activities – examples

Examples of cash flows arising from investing activities include:

[IAS 7:16]

- payments to acquire property, plant and equipment (including self-constructed property, plant and equipment – but see **5.5.3** in respect of interest capitalised), intangible assets and other long-term assets;

- payments in respect of development costs that have been capitalised (but see **5.5.3** in respect of interest capitalised);

- cash received from the sale of property, plant and equipment, intangible assets and other long-term assets;

- payments to acquire equity or debt instruments of other entities or interests in joint ventures (although, in some circumstances, these may need to be classified either as cash equivalents or, if they are held for dealing purposes, as operating cash flows);

- cash receipts from the sale of equity or debt instruments of other entities or interests in joint ventures (although, again, these may instead need to be classified either as cash equivalents or, if the assets were held for dealing purposes, as operating cash flows);

- cash advances and loans made to other parties (other than loans made by a financial institution);

- cash received following the repayment of advances and loans made to other parties (other than loans made by a financial institution); and

- payments for and receipts from futures contracts, forward contracts, option contracts and swap contracts provided that the contracts:

  - are not held for dealing or trading purposes;

  - are not financing in nature; and

  - are not hedging a transaction that itself is classified as operating or financing.

As noted above, cash flows associated with the acquisition and disposal of property, plant and equipment, intangible and other long-term assets will generally be classified as investing activities. However, for entities that routinely sell items of property, plant and equipment that they have previously held for rental to others, the resulting cash flows are cash flows from operating activities (see **5.2.6**).

5.3.3 Classification of expenditure as operating or investing

Only expenditures resulting in a recognised asset in the statement of financial position are eligible for classification as investing activities. [IAS 7:16]

Consequently, expenditure for exploration and evaluation activities would be classed as investing activities only if the entity's accounting policy is to capitalise such costs.

5.4   Financing activities

5.4.1   Financing activities – definition

Financing activities are defined as activities that result in changes in the size and composition of the contributed equity and borrowings of the entity. [IAS 7:6] Major classes of gross cash receipts and gross cash payments arising from financing activities should be reported separately, except to the extent that cash flows described in IAS 7:22 and 24 are reported on a net basis (see **3.2**). [IAS 7:21]

5.4.2   Cash flows from financing activities – examples

Examples of cash flows arising from financing activities are:

[IAS 7:17]

- cash receipts from issuing shares or other equity instruments;

- payments to owners to purchase or redeem shares in the entity;

- cash flows arising from futures contracts, forward contracts, option contracts or swap contracts hedging a transaction that is itself classified as financing;

- cash receipts from issuing debentures, loans, notes, bonds, mortgages and other borrowings, whether short-term or long-term;

- repayments of borrowings; and

- when the reporting entity is a lessee, that part of the payments under a lease (or, for entities that have not yet adopted IFRS 16, a finance lease) that will be treated in the statement of financial position as a repayment of the loan from the lessor (i.e. the capital element).

5.4.3   Sale and leaseback transactions

5.4.3.1   Sale and leaseback transactions – entities that have adopted IFRS 16

The appropriate classification of cash flows arising from a sale and leaseback transaction will depend on the accounting for the transaction under IFRS 16. In accordance with IFRS 16:99, the seller-lessee in a sale and leaseback transaction is required to determine whether the transfer of the underlying asset to the lessor qualifies as a sale, applying the requirements for determining when a performance obligation is satisfied in IFRS 15 *Revenue from Contracts with Customers*.

If the lessee determines that the transaction *does not* qualify as a sale, it continues to recognise the underlying asset and recognises a financial liability equal to the transfer proceeds. [IFRS 16:103] This accounting reflects that, in substance, the transaction is a financing arrangement.

The cash inflow arising from the transfer to the lessor should, therefore, be classified as a financing cash flow. In accordance with IFRS 9 *Financial Instruments* (or, for entities that have not yet adopted IFRS 9, IAS 39 *Financial Instruments: Recognition and Measurement*), repayments of the lease obligation will be split between principal and interest, with the principal element classified as a financing cash flow, and the interest classified in accordance with the entity's general policy for classification of interest paid.

If the transfer of the underlying asset by the seller-lessee satisfies the requirements of IFRS 15 and as a result the transaction *does* qualify as a sale, in accordance with IFRS 16:100 the sale and leaseback transaction is accounted for as a disposal of the underlying asset with a right-of-use asset recognised in respect of the leaseback (subject to exemptions for short-term leases and leases of low-value assets – see below). The receipt of cash from the disposal should be presented in the statement of cash flows as an investing cash flow. The leaseback is treated in the same way as other lease transactions; the acquisition of the right-of-use asset is a non-cash transaction (see **3.3**) and lease payments are split between principal and interest and presented in the statement of cash flows according to their nature (see **example 5.1B**).

If the recognition exemption in IFRS 16:5 for either short-term leases or leases of low value assets is applied to the leaseback, lease payments made will be classified as operating cash flows.

5.4.3.2   *Sale and leaseback transactions – entities that have not adopted IFRS 16*

Under IAS 17, the treatment of cash flows arising from a sale and leaseback transaction depends on whether the leaseback is a finance lease or an operating lease.

In a sale and finance-leaseback transaction, the substance of the arrangement is considered to be that the asset is not 'sold' but that the lessor makes a loan to the lessee with the asset as security. From an accounting perspective, the entity has not disposed of the asset. In this case, the receipt from the 'sale' of the asset should be included as a financing cash flow rather than an investing cash flow. Subsequent lease payments are split between principal and interest and presented in the statement of cash flows according to their nature (see **example 5.1B**).

In contrast, when the substance of the transaction is that the asset is sold and then an operating lease is put in place, the receipt from the disposal of the asset should be included as an investing cash flow. Lease payments, which are presented as operating expenses in the statement of comprehensive income, will be presented as operating cash flows.

5.4.4   Factoring

IAS 7 does not provide guidance on the treatment of factored receivables in a statement of cash flows. When receivables are factored in circumstances qualifying for derecognition of the receivables, no particular problems arise. The receipt of the proceeds from the factor will simply be treated as an operating cash flow, just as if it had been received directly from the customer. However, when receivables are factored in circumstances that do not qualify for derecognition of the receivables, and the advances from factors are treated as financing creditors in the statement of financial position, the appropriate treatment is less clear.

IAS 7 requires cash flows to be analysed under the standard headings according to the substance of the underlying transactions. When factoring is viewed as being, in substance, a financing transaction, it might be argued that all of the cash flows received from the factor should be viewed as financing cash inflows. This would be consistent with the treatment of leases (or, for entities that have not yet adopted IFRS 16, finance leases) prescribed by IAS 7, when entering into the lease is viewed as a non-cash transaction and so does not appear in the statement of cash flows. The capital elements of the lease payments then appear as a financing outflow. This could be argued as leading to an overstatement of the financing outflows, and an understatement of the investing outflows. But the treatment for leases (or, for entities that have not yet adopted IFRS 16, finance leases) is specifically required by IAS 7 and is well established.

It could be argued that a similar principle should be applied to factored receivables. The distortion would be more significant, however, and potentially the entity would have no operating cash inflows at all if all of its receivables were factored in circumstances that do not qualify for derecognition. It appears questionable whether showing all of an entity's sales revenue as cash flows from financing could be said to give a true and fair view of its cash flows. Also, importantly, the treatment of factored receivables is not referred to in IAS 7, whereas the treatment of leases is specifically addressed.

If it is concluded that the receipts from the factor should be viewed as operating cash flows rather than financing cash flows (because they are, in substance, the receipts from trade customers), there is a second question to be addressed. This is whether all of the cash flows should be shown as operating or whether the movement on the financing creditor should be treated as a financing cash flow. The preferable treatment is to show this movement as a financing cash flow because this results in operating cash flows including the cash flows from the customers as if the factoring had not been entered into. It also results in financing cash flows as if the customers had been financed by a loan. Finally, it also reflects the IAS 7 definition of financing activities as those "that result in changes in the size and composition of … borrowings".

Due to lack of clarity in IAS 7 as to the appropriate treatment of such transactions, it is important that the policy adopted is clearly explained.

5.5 Interest and dividends

5.5.1 Presentation of cash flows from interest and dividends – general

IAS 7:31 states that cash flows from interest and dividends paid and received:

- should each be disclosed separately; and
- should be classified in a consistent manner from period to period as either operating, investing or financing activities.

5.5.2 Classification of interest and dividends paid and received

IAS 7 permits each entity to choose how it wishes to classify its interest and dividends, provided that the classification is consistently applied from period to period.

The Standard suggests that dividends paid should be reported in either financing or operating activities. The argument for the classification of dividends paid as financing outflows is that the dividends represent a cost of obtaining financial resources. The argument in favour of classification within operating activities is that such classification will assist users to determine the ability of an entity to pay dividends out of operating cash flows. [IAS 7:34]

Interest paid, and interest and dividends received, should generally be classified as operating cash flows by a financial institution. For other entities, IAS 7 suggests that these items might similarly be classified as operating activities because they are included in arriving at profit or loss for the period. Interest paid could be classified as a financing cash flow, however, and interest and dividends received could be classified as investing cash flows, because the first is a cost of obtaining financial resources, and the last two are returns on investments. [IAS 7:33]

5.5.3 Presentation of interest capitalised

The total amount of interest paid during a period is disclosed in the statement of cash flows whether it has been recognised as an expense in profit or loss or capitalised in accordance with IAS 23 (see **chapter A18**). [IAS 7:32]

5.5.4 Debt securities issued at a discount or premium

For more complex financial instruments, it is important not to confuse principal amounts of finance with the nominal amounts of the instruments concerned. The principal amount of a financing arrangement is the amount borrowed at the beginning of the arrangement. It is not necessarily the same as any amount shown as the nominal amount of the financial instrument. This distinction is necessary to ensure that cash flows relating to finance costs are appropriately classified.

If an entity issues debt securities at a discount or a premium (e.g. zero-coupon debt securities), the proceeds received from issuing the debt securities should be classified as a financing cash inflow. The excess of the amounts paid out (during the life of the instrument and at maturity) over the amount received when the debt securities were issued should be reported as a cash outflow, classified in the same way as interest paid.

Example 5.5.4

Zero-coupon bond issued at a discount

An entity receives CU100,000 on 1 January 20X1, when it issues a zero-coupon bond. On 31 December 20X5, it redeems the bond by paying cash of CU140,255 to the bondholder. In its statements of comprehensive income for the five years ended 31 December 20X5, the entity classifies the CU40,255 as interest expense.

In its statement of cash flows for the year ended 31 December 20X5, CU100,000 is classified as a financing cash flow and CU40,255 is classified according to the entity's general classification for interest (see **5.5.2**).

5.5.5 Investments in debt securities acquired at a discount or a premium

If an entity invests in debt securities at a discount or a premium (e.g. zero-coupon bonds), the cash paid at acquisition is classified as an investing cash flow.

The excess of the amounts received (during the life of the instrument and on maturity) over the amount of the original investment should be reported as a cash inflow, classified in the same way as interest received (see **5.5.2**).

5.5.6 Shares classified as liabilities

When instruments that are legally shares are classified as financial liabilities in accordance with IAS 32 *Financial Instruments: Presentation* (e.g. certain preference shares), the question arises as to how the cash flows relating to the dividends paid on those instruments should be classified in the statement of cash flows.

IAS 7:31 to 34 (see **5.5.1** to **5.5.3**) set out considerations for the classification of interest and dividends and allow entities a number of alternatives. The only absolute requirements are that interest and dividends received and paid should each be disclosed separately, and that each should be classified in a consistent manner from period to period as either operating, investing or financing activities.

When instruments that are legally shares are classified as financial liabilities under IAS 32, the dividends paid on those shares will be presented as part of the interest expense in the statement of comprehensive income. It follows that, in the statement of cash flows, the dividends paid on such shares should similarly be presented as interest paid and not as dividends and, therefore, should be classified consistently with other interest payable.

5.5.7 Treasury shares

The acquisition by an entity of its own equity instruments represents a transaction with owners (who have given up their equity interest) rather than a gain or loss to the entity and, accordingly, any consideration paid is recognised as a deduction in equity (see IAS 32:33). When consideration paid is in the form of cash, the associated cash flows should be classified as cash flows from financing activities.

5.6 Taxes

Unless they can be specifically identified with financing or investing activities, cash flows arising from taxes on income should be classified as operating cash flows. Cash flows arising from taxes are required to be separately disclosed. [IAS 7:35]

Clearly, transactions of all types may have tax consequences. Identifying whether each amount of income or expense included in the tax computation derives from operating, investing or financing activities is a relatively simple task. Identifying the *cash flows*, however, is not always so easy. IAS 7 points out that, because it is often impracticable to identify tax cash flows in respect of investing and financing activities, and because such cash flows often arise in a different period from the cash flows of the underlying transaction, taxes paid should generally be classified as cash flows from operating activities. [IAS 7:36]

When it is practicable to identify a tax cash flow with an individual transaction that is classified as investing or financing, the tax cash flow will be classified as investing or financing in accordance with the underlying transaction. In these circumstances, the total amount of taxes paid is also disclosed.

Example 5.6

Classification of tax cash flows relating to share-based payment arrangements

Entity A has an equity-settled share-based payment arrangement. The tax deduction available under local tax laws in respect of the arrangement is greater than the cumulative expense recognised under IFRS 2 *Share-based Payment*.

Paragraph 68C of IAS 12 *Income Taxes* states that "[i]f the amount of the tax deduction (or estimated future tax deduction) [relating to remuneration paid in shares, share options, or other equity instruments of the entity] exceeds the amount of the related cumulative remuneration expense, this indicates that the tax deduction relates not only to remuneration expense but also to an equity item. In this situation, the excess of the associated current or deferred tax should be recognised directly in equity".

Should the tax cash flow representing the 'excess tax deduction' recognised in equity be classified as an operating or a financing cash flow?

In the circumstances described, when tax cash flows are paid net, there will generally not be a separate cash inflow relating to the tax deduction for the share-based payment arrangement; rather, the deduction will be reflected in a reduced cash outflow for taxes payable. IAS 7:36 points out that, because it is often impracticable to identify tax cash flows in respect of investing and financing activities, and because such cash flows often arise in a different period from the cash flows of the underlying transaction, taxes paid should generally be classified as cash flows from operating activities.

In the majority of cases, there will not be a specific cash flow identified with the tax deduction for the share-based payment arrangement and, therefore, the taxes paid will be classified as cash flows from operating activities. In the rare circumstances when a specific cash flow can be identified, following the logic in IAS 12:68C, the cash flow relating to the excess tax deduction may be considered to relate to the issue of equity (i.e. it may be classified as a financing cash flow), or it may be considered to relate to employee services (i.e. it may be classified as an operating cash flow). An entity should determine the appropriate classification as a matter of accounting policy and apply the policy consistently.

---

6 Investments in subsidiaries, associates and joint ventures

When an entity prepares a consolidated statement of cash flows, that statement of cash flows includes the cash flows of consolidated subsidiaries, but excludes any that are intragroup.

> When a consolidated subsidiary is only partly owned by the group, the dividends paid to the non-controlling interests (but not the dividends paid to group entities) are classified as either financing or operating cash outflows, consistently with the classification of dividends paid by the parent (see **5.5.2**).

When an interest in an associate, a joint venture or a subsidiary is accounted for using the equity or the cost method, the investor's statement of cash flows reports only the cash flows between itself and the investee, such as dividends and advances. [IAS 7:37 & 38]

7 Changes in ownership interests in subsidiaries and other businesses

7.1 Separate presentation of cash flows relating to changes in ownership interests

7.1.1 Changes in ownership interests involving a change in control

When an entity has obtained or lost control of subsidiaries or other businesses during the reporting period, the aggregate cash flows arising should be presented separately and classified as investing activities. [IAS 7:39] The single-line entry in the statement of cash flows comprises the amount of cash paid or received as consideration for obtaining or losing control, net of the cash and cash equivalents in the subsidiaries or businesses at the date of the transaction, event or change in circumstance. [IAS 7:42] The cash flow effects of losing control are not to be deducted from those of obtaining control. Rather, each is to be shown separately. [IAS 7:41]

> These requirements apply to all transactions, events or other circumstances that result in a parent obtaining or losing control of a subsidiary. This can occur without the parent receiving or paying out cash (e.g. in the circumstances of a rights issue by the subsidiary – see **7.2**) and also when there is a change in circumstances but no change in absolute or relative ownership interests. The focus of the requirements is on whether control has been obtained or lost; if so, associated cash flows will always be classified as investing.

When the parent obtains or loses control without paying or receiving cash, investing cash flows still arise if there are cash balances in the subsidiary at the time of acquisition or disposal, as illustrated in **example 7.2**. This is because the amount reported in the statement of cash flows for consideration is net of cash and cash equivalents in the subsidiary.

Example 7.1.1

Cash flows arising on sale of a subsidiary

On 30 June 20X1, an entity sells its 100 per cent holding in a subsidiary for CU900,000. At that date, the net assets of the subsidiary included in the consolidated statement of financial position are as follows.

	CU'000
Property, plant and equipment	500
Inventories	150
Accounts receivable	230
Cash	80
Cash equivalents	100
Trade payables	(110)
Long-term debt	(300)
	650

The consideration is received during the year ended 31 December 20X1 and comprises cash of CU300,000 and equity shares of CU600,000.

In the investing activities section of the statement of cash flows for the year ended 31 December 20X1, the entry in respect of the sale of the subsidiary will be an inflow of CU120,000 (being CU300,000 cash received less cash and cash equivalents of CU180,000 in the subsidiary at the date of sale). The cash and cash equivalents of CU180,000 in the subsidiary at the date of sale are deducted from the cash received because the cash and cash equivalents of the group are reduced by this amount as a result of the sale of the subsidiary.

If the cash consideration of CU300,000 were instead received over two years with CU150,000 being received in 20X1 and CU150,000 being received in 20X2, the investing activities section of the statement of cash flows would present an outflow in 20X1 of CU30,000 (being CU150,000 less the cash and cash equivalents of CU180,000) and an inflow in 20X2 of CU150,000.

The group's property, plant and equipment is reduced by CU500,000 as a result of the sale. However, this is not presented in the statement of cash flows as a sale of property, plant and equipment for cash.

When the indirect method is used to present the operating activities section of the statement of cash flows, the increase or decrease in inventories and accounts receivable and payable will need to be adjusted for the sale of the subsidiary. Taking inventories as an example, assume that on 31 December 20X1 the inventories in the consolidated statement of financial position total CU950,000 and at 31 December 20X0 total CU1,000,000. In the adjustments from profit before taxation to the operating cash flow, the movement in inventories is an increase of CU100,000 (being the decrease in the year of CU50,000 offset by the subsidiary's inventories in the consolidated statement of financial position at the date of sale of CU150,000).

Each of the following should be disclosed, in aggregate, in respect of both obtaining and losing control of subsidiaries or other businesses during the period:

[IAS 7:40]

- the total consideration paid or received;

- the portion of the consideration consisting of cash and cash equivalents;

- the amount of cash and cash equivalents in the subsidiaries or other businesses over which control is obtained or lost; and

- the amount of the assets and liabilities other than cash or cash equivalents in the subsidiaries or other businesses over which control is obtained or lost, summarised by each major category.

An investment entity (as defined in IFRS 10 – see **section 13** of **chapter A24**) need not provide the disclosures required under the third and fourth bullets above in relation to a subsidiary that is required to be measured at fair value through profit or loss. [IAS 7:40A]

7.1.2 Changes in ownership interests in a subsidiary not resulting in a loss of control

When there has been a change in ownership interests in a subsidiary, but the transaction, event or circumstance has not resulted in a loss of control, the associated cash flows are classified as financing activities, unless the subsidiary is held by an investment entity (as defined in IFRS 10 – see **section 13** of **chapter A24**) and is required to be measured at fair value through profit or loss. The treatment can be contrasted with that required for cash flows associated with a loss of control, as discussed at **7.1.1**, which are classified as investing activities. [IAS 7:42A]

Such changes will arise from transactions such as the purchase or sale by a parent of a subsidiary's equity instruments. Transactions of this nature are accounted for as equity transactions – i.e. as transactions with owners in their capacity as owners, unless the subsidiary is held by an investment entity (as defined in IFRS 10 – see **section 13** of **chapter A24**) and is required to be measured at fair value through profit or loss. The requirements of IAS 7:42A ensure that the cash flows are classified in the same way as other transactions with owners described in IAS 7:17 (see **5.3**). [IAS 7:42B]

7.2   Cash flows arising from shares issued by a subsidiary

IAS 7:17(a) states that cash proceeds from issuing shares should be classified as financing activities. IAS 7:39 states that cash flows arising as a result of a transaction, event or change in circumstance when control of a subsidiary is lost should be classified as investing activities. The question arises as to how the cash flows from a rights issue by a partly-owned subsidiary should be reflected in the statement of cash flows.

Take, for example, a rights issue when the shares of the subsidiary are issued on a pro rata basis to its parent and to the other shareholders (i.e. the non-controlling interests). In the subsidiary's own statement of cash flows, the entire proceeds from the rights issue should be shown under financing activities because they clearly represent a cash inflow from issuing shares. In the consolidated statement of cash flows, when shares are issued to the parent and to the other shareholders on a pro rata basis such that the percentage interest held by the group is not changed, the cash received from issuing shares to the parent will be eliminated on consolidation, leaving the receipt from the other shareholders as a cash inflow to the group. Because there is no change in the group's interest in the subsidiary, this cash flow is also financing in nature, and should be classified as such in the consolidated statement of cash flows.

When shares are issued only to the other shareholders (i.e. the non-controlling interests), the treatment in the subsidiary's own statement of cash flows is the same as that described above. From the group perspective, although the other shareholders have injected new funds into the subsidiary, the issue of shares outside the group gives rise to a reduction in the group's interest in the subsidiary. The presentation in the consolidated statement of cash flows will depend on whether control has been lost as a result of that reduction. Following the principles outlined at **7.1.1**, when the transaction has resulted in a loss of control, the associated cash flows should be classified as investing activities in accordance with IAS 7:39. When control remains with the parent, the transaction is considered an equity transaction and the associated cash flows are classified as financing in accordance with IAS 7:42A (see **7.1.2**). This is illustrated in the following example.

Example 7.2

Loss of control as a result of shares issued by a subsidiary

Company P enters into a joint arrangement with Company Q under which Company Q acquires a 50 per cent interest in Company R, formerly a wholly-owned subsidiary of Company P. Company R, which issues new shares to Company Q for cash, has a bank overdraft of CU250,000 at the date that it ceases to be a subsidiary of Company P. The bank overdraft is included as a component of cash and cash equivalents for the purposes of preparing the statement of cash flows.

Following the disposal transaction, Company P's investment in Company R is classified as a joint venture under IFRS 11 *Joint Arrangements* (and, consequently, accounted for using the equity method).

How should the change in status from a subsidiary to a joint venture be reflected in the consolidated statement of cash flows?

Although Company P retains a 50 per cent interest, Company R is no longer part of the group, and its cash flows will no longer be consolidated. Under IAS 7:39 (see **7.1.1**), when a transaction results in the loss of control of a subsidiary, the amount to be shown under investing activities comprises cash and cash equivalents received as consideration net of any cash or cash equivalents transferred. In this case, because the shares were issued directly to Company Q by Company R, Company P receives no disposal proceeds. Therefore, the only amount to be presented in the consolidated statement of cash flows is an investing cash inflow of CU250,000, representing the balance on the subsidiary's overdraft at the date it ceases to be a subsidiary.

7.3 Cash flows arising subsequent to an acquisition

Cash flows relating to an acquisition may arise subsequent to the acquisition. Examples of cash outflows include the payment of deferred and contingent consideration. Examples of cash inflows include the receipt of proceeds of a warranty claim or in respect of an indemnification asset. IAS 7 provides no explicit guidance on the treatment of such items.

Consideration payable shortly after the acquisition date

When consideration is payable shortly after the acquisition date, so that no adjustment is necessary for the effects of discounting, the cash outflow will be classified as investing. This is because there is no significant financing element and the payment clearly represents the cost of making the acquisition.

Deferred consideration

In the case of deferred consideration, both the principal and any interest element could be presented as financing cash flows (assuming that the entity's policy is to classify interest as a financing cash flow) on the basis that the payments represent the servicing and settlement of a financing liability recognised on the acquisition. This approach is consistent with IFRS 3 *Business Combinations* which requires the discounting of deferred consideration. It is also consistent with the treatment of leases under IFRS 16 (or, for entities that have not yet adopted IFRS 16, finance leases under IAS 17), when the inception of the lease is treated as a non-cash transaction so that the cash cost of acquiring the asset is recognised in financing cash flows over the lease term.

Contingent consideration

In the case of contingent consideration, under IFRS 3 it is only the acquisition-date fair value of contingent consideration that is recognised as part of the consideration transferred in exchange for the acquiree (and, consequently, affects goodwill). Changes in the fair value of contingent consideration that do not relate to facts and circumstances that existed at the acquisition date, but result from events after that date, do not adjust goodwill. When contingent consideration is not equity, changes in its fair value will be recognised in profit or loss, consistent with changes in measurement for any financial liability or any liability under IAS 37 *Provisions, Contingent Liabilities and Contingent Assets*. Because these changes are not treated as a cost of the acquisition, and do not adjust goodwill, the payment of contingent consideration could be presented as a financing cash flow.

Warranties

Warranties may be received from the seller regarding the value and condition of the assets of the acquiree and its business, and are often short term in nature. For example, the seller may warrant that, at the acquisition date, there will be at least a specified level of working capital within the business, with a warranty payment becoming due to the extent that the actual level of working capital turns out to be lower. When a warranty payment is determined based on the facts and circumstances that existed at the acquisition date, any receipt by the acquirer is, in substance, an adjustment to the consideration paid for the acquisition (and, consequently, gives rise to a reduction in goodwill). Generally, such a payment will be made shortly after the acquisition date and will not include any significant financing element, in which case it should be shown as an investing cash flow in the statement of cash flows. When such a payment is deferred and includes a significant financing element, it should be classified as a financing cash flow, following the logic outlined above in respect of deferred consideration.

Indemnification asset

When a seller provides an indemnity, giving rise to an indemnification asset, it is agreeing to reimburse the buyer for specific outflows it may incur. Because receipts under indemnities are a direct reimbursement of an outflow incurred, the receipt should be classified in accordance with the nature of the cash outflow. This matching of inflows and outflows is consistent with the treatment of reimbursement assets under IAS 37.

8 Foreign currency cash flows

Foreign currency cash flows arise in two instances – when the reporting entity enters into an external transaction involving inflows or outflows in a foreign currency, and when the consolidated cash flow statement includes the cash flows of an overseas subsidiary.

When the reporting entity enters into an external transaction involving inflows or outflows in a foreign currency, the cash flows should be presented in the statement of cash flows in the entity's functional currency by translating the foreign currency cash flow at the rate of exchange applying on the date of the cash flow. [IAS 7:25]

Example 8

Foreign currency cash flows

An entity, whose functional currency is Sterling, buys an item of equipment for US$100,000. It recognises the purchase in its accounting records on the date of delivery of the equipment. The rate of exchange on that date ($2 to £1) results in the equipment being recognised at £50,000. The invoice for the equipment is settled by bank transfer 30 days later, at which date £55,000 is needed to settle the liability. The exchange difference of £5,000 is recognised in profit or loss.

The purchase of the equipment should be presented in the statement of cash flows as an investing cash outflow of £55,000. Therefore, if the operating cash flows are shown using the indirect method, one of the adjustments to net profit will be to adjust for the exchange difference of £5,000.

If the item purchased had been goods for resale, then the cash flow for the purchase would have been reported in operating (not investing) cash flows. Under the requirements of IAS 7, a cash outflow of £55,000 would have been included in the operating cash flows section of the statement of cash flows in respect of the purchase. In the statement of comprehensive income, the cost of the goods, recognised at £50,000, would have been included in purchases and the exchange difference of £5,000 would have been recognised in arriving at profit for the year. Therefore, the full £55,000 would have been recognised in the statement of comprehensive income in arriving at the net profit for the year. Consequently, if the operating cash flows are shown using the indirect method, there will be no need to adjust for the exchange difference of £5,000.

The cash flows of a foreign subsidiary should be included in the group statement of cash flows translated at the exchange rate between the functional currency and the foreign currency ruling on the dates of the cash flows. [IAS 7:26]

IAS 7:27 states that cash flows denominated in a foreign currency are to be reported in a manner consistent with IAS 21 *The Effects of Changes in Foreign Exchange Rates*. IAS 21 permits the use of an average exchange rate that approximates to the actual rate. For example, a weighted average exchange rate for the period may be used for the translation of foreign currency transactions or the translation of the cash flows of a foreign subsidiary. IAS 21 does not permit the cash flows of a foreign subsidiary to be translated using the rate of exchange ruling at the end of the reporting period.

> For individually significant transactions, however, it may be necessary to use the actual exchange rate. This would particularly be the case when a significant level of additional cash funding is passed from a parent to an overseas subsidiary, because otherwise it will not be possible to eliminate the intragroup cash flows.

Unrealised gains and losses arising from movements in exchange rates do not represent cash flows. However, the effect of exchange rate changes on cash and cash equivalents held or due in a foreign currency is reported in the statement of cash flows in order to reconcile the balance of cash and cash equivalents at the start and end of the period. This amount is to be presented separately from cash flows from operating, investing and financing activities. The amount includes the differences, if any, had those cash flows been reported using the rate of exchange ruling at the end of period. [IAS 7:28]

9   Additional disclosure requirements

9.1   Non-cash transactions

When an entity enters into an investing or financing transaction that does not involve the use of cash or cash equivalents, the transaction is excluded from the statement of cash flows (see **3.3**). The entity should, however, disclose sufficient information in the financial statements to give a user all the relevant information about the transaction. [IAS 7:43]

9.2   Changes in liabilities arising from financing activities

An entity should provide disclosures to enable users of the financial statements to evaluate changes in liabilities arising from financing activities, including both changes arising from cash flows and non-cash changes. Liabilities arising from financing activities are those for which cash flows were, or future cash flows will be, classified in the statement of cash flows within financing activities. [IAS 7:44A & 44C]

An entity is also required to provide disclosures to enable users of the financial statements to evaluate changes in financial assets (e.g. assets that hedge liabilities arising from financing activities) if cash flows from those financial assets were, or future cash flows will be, included within financing activities. [IAS 7:44A & 44C]

The disclosures should include:

[IAS 7:44B]

- changes from financing cash flows;

- changes arising as a result of obtaining or losing control of subsidiaries or other businesses;

- the effect of changes in foreign exchange rates;

- changes in fair values; and

- other changes.

An entity may present these disclosures as a reconciliation between the opening and closing balances in the statement of financial position for liabilities arising from financing activities. When a reconciliation is presented, sufficient information should be provided to link items in the reconciliation to the statement of financial position and the statement of cash flows. [IAS 7:44D]

If the disclosures are combined with disclosures of changes in other assets and liabilities, the changes in liabilities from financing activities should be disclosed separately from the changes in other assets and liabilities. [IAS 7:44E]

> **Example 9.2**, which is reproduced from the illustrative examples accompanying IAS 7, illustrates one possible way of providing the disclosures required by IFRS 15:44A to 44E. The example shows only current periods. Other than in the first year of application of the January 2016 amendments (see below), corresponding amounts for the preceding period are required to be presented in accordance with IAS 1 *Presentation of Financial Statements*.

Example 9.2

Reconciliation of liabilities arising from financing activities

[IAS 7: Illustrative Example C (extract)]

	20X1	Cash flows	Acquisition	Foreign exchange movement	Fair value changes	20X2
				Non-cash changes		
Long-term borrowings	22,000	(1,000)	–	–	–	21,000
Short-term borrowings	10,000	(500)	–	200	–	9,700
Lease liabilities	4,000	(800)	300	–	–	3,500
Assets held to hedge long-term borrowings	(675)	150	–	–	(25)	(550)
Total liabilities from financing activities	35,325	(2,150)	300	200	(25)	33,650

Paragraphs 44A to 44E of IAS 7 were added by *Disclosure Initiative – Amendments to IAS 7* in January 2016 as part of the IASB's wider Disclosure Initiative project. The amendments are effective for periods beginning on or after 1 January 2017, with earlier application permitted. Comparative information for preceding periods is not required in the first year of application of these requirements. [IAS 7:60]

9.3 Components of cash and cash equivalents

The components of cash and cash equivalents should be disclosed, and a reconciliation presented between the amounts in the statement of cash flows and the equivalent items reported in the statement of financial position. [IAS 7:45] As required by IAS 1 *Presentation of Financial Statements*, the policy adopted in determining the composition of cash and cash equivalents should also be disclosed. [IAS 7:46]

9.4 Balances not available for use by the group

The amount of significant cash and cash equivalent balances that are not available for use by the group should be disclosed, together with a commentary by management. [IAS 7:48] This disclosure requirement might be triggered by a subsidiary operating in a country where exchange controls or other legal restrictions apply and, thus, the cash and cash equivalents in that subsidiary are not available for general use by other members of the group. Another example might be when substantial amounts of cash are held in escrow accounts and are only available for use on a particular project.

Restrictions on the use of cash or cash equivalents do not alter the classification of the restricted amounts in the statement of financial position or statement of cash flows. For example, when there are restrictions on the transfer of amounts from a foreign subsidiary, the amounts are treated as part of group cash and cash equivalents in the consolidated statement of cash flows presented by the group if they meet the definition of cash and cash equivalents in the foreign subsidiary; disclosure is made in accordance with IAS 7:48.

9.5 Additional recommended disclosures

IAS 7:50 suggests that additional information may be relevant to users in understanding the financial position and liquidity of an entity. Disclosure of this information, together with a commentary by management, is encouraged and may include:

- the amount of undrawn borrowing facilities that may be available for future operating activities and to settle capital commitments, indicating any restrictions on the use of these facilities;

- the aggregate amount of cash flows that represent increases in operating capacity separately from those cash flows that are required to maintain operating capacity; and

- the amount of the cash flows arising from the operating, investing and financing activities of each reportable segment under IFRS 8 *Operating Segments*.

A22 Events after the reporting period

Contents

1 Introduction

1.1 Overview of IAS 10

IAS 10 *Events after the Reporting Period* prescribes when an entity should adjust its financial statements for events after the reporting period, and the disclosures that an entity should make about the date when the financial statements were authorised for issue and about events after the reporting period.

1.2 Amendments to IAS 10 since the last edition of this manual

None. IAS 10 was most recently amended in July 2014.

2 Events after the reporting period – definition

IAS 10 defines events after the reporting period as those events, both favourable and unfavourable, that occur between the end of the reporting period and the date on which the financial statements are authorised for issue. [IAS 10:3]

Events after the reporting period include all events up to the date when the financial statements are authorised for issue. The Standard states explicitly that events occurring after the publication of a profit announcement or of other selected financial information but before the financial statements are authorised for issue fall within the scope of the Standard (see **3.2**). [IAS 10:7]

A distinction is drawn between two types of events after the reporting period:

[IAS 10:3]

- adjusting events – being those that provide evidence of conditions that existed at the end of the reporting period (see **section 4**); and

- non-adjusting events – being those that are indicative of conditions that arose after the reporting period (see **section 5**).

3 Date when financial statements are authorised for issue

3.1 Date when financial statements are authorised for issue – general

Although the date when financial statements are authorised for issue is not defined, IAS 10 gives some guidance on how the phrase should be interpreted.

IAS 10 provides specific guidance about two common arrangements for approval of financial statements. These are considered in **3.2** and **3.3**. Circumstances which differ from those described (e.g. when there is a supervisory board but it is not made up solely of non-executives) will require careful consideration based on the particular facts. However, the common theme of the examples given in IAS 10 is that it is approval by management that is relevant rather than approval by shareholders or a high supervisory level body appointed to oversee management.

3.2 Approval by shareholders

When an entity is required to submit its financial statements to its shareholders for approval after the financial statements have been issued, the financial statements are nevertheless authorised for issue on the date of issue, not the date when shareholders approve the financial statements. [IAS 10:5]

This is illustrated in the following example which is reproduced from IAS 10:5.

Example 3.2

Approval by shareholders

[IAS 10:5]

The management of an entity completes draft financial statements for the year to 31 December 20X1 on 28 February 20X2. On 18 March 20X2, the board of directors reviews the financial statements and authorises them for issue. The entity announces its profit and selected other financial information on 19 March 20X2. The financial statements are made available to shareholders and others on 1 April 20X2. The shareholders approve the financial statements at their annual meeting on 15 May 20X2 and the approved financial statements are then filed with a regulatory body on 17 May 20X2.

The financial statements are authorised for issue on 18 March 20X2 (date of board authorisation for issue).

In this example, the public announcement is after the financial statements have been authorised for issue. In some jurisdictions, an entity may be permitted or required to make a 'preliminary announcement' of selected financial information before the full financial statements are authorised for issue. For example, this may be necessary because the information is regarded as 'price sensitive' and must be announced without delay. In such circumstances, events after the public announcement must be taken into account when the board approves the full financial statements. It is, therefore, possible that the information in the full financial statements may differ from that in the earlier public announcement.

3.3 Approval by supervisory board

When the management of an entity is required to issue its financial statements to a supervisory board (made up solely of non-executives) for approval, the financial statements are authorised for issue when the management authorises them for issue to the supervisory board. [IAS 10:6]

This is illustrated in the following example which is reproduced from IAS 10:6.

Example 3.3

Approval by supervisory board

[IAS 10:6]

On 18 March 20X2, the management of an entity authorises financial statements for issue to its supervisory board. The supervisory board is made up solely of non-executives and may include representatives of employees and other outside interests. The supervisory board approves the financial statements on 26 March 20X2. The financial statements are made available to shareholders and others on 1 April 20X2. The shareholders approve the financial statements at their annual meeting on 15 May 20X2 and the financial statements are then filed with a regulatory body on 17 May 20X2.

The financial statements are authorised for issue on 18 March 20X2 (date of management authorisation for issue to the supervisory board).

3.4 'Dual dating' of financial statements

The question of dual dating of financial statements has been considered by the IFRS Interpretations Committee and is discussed in the May 2013 *IFRIC Update*. Specifically, the Interpretations Committee was asked to clarify the accounting implications of applying IAS 10 when previously issued financial statements are reissued in connection with an offering document. The question arises in jurisdictions in which securities laws and regulatory practices require an entity to reissue its previously issued annual financial statements in connection with an offering document, when the most recently filed interim financial statements reflect matters that are accounted for retrospectively under the applicable accounting standards. In these jurisdictions, securities laws and regulatory practices do not require or permit the entity, in its reissued financial statements, to recognise events or transactions that occur between the time the financial statements were first authorised for issue and the time the financial statements are reissued, unless the adjustment is required by national regulation; instead, securities laws and regulatory practices require the entity to recognise in its reissued financial statements only those adjustments that would ordinarily be made to the comparatives in the following year's financial statements. These adjustments would include, for example, adjustments for changes in accounting policy that are applied retrospectively, but would not include changes in accounting estimates. The submitter asked the Interpretations Committee to clarify whether IAS 10 permits only one date of authorisation for issue (i.e. 'dual dating' is not permitted) when considered within the context of reissuing previously issued financial statements in connection with an offering document.

The Interpretations Committee noted the following:

- that the scope of IAS 10 is the accounting for, and disclosure of, events after the reporting period and that the objective of this Standard is to prescribe (1) when an entity should adjust its financial statements for events after the reporting period, and (2) the disclosures that an entity should give about the date when the financial statements were authorised for issue and about events after the reporting period;

- that financial statements prepared in accordance with IAS 10 should reflect all adjusting and non-adjusting events up to the date that the financial statements are authorised for issue; and

- that IAS 10 does not address the presentation of reissued financial statements in an offering document when the originally issued financial statements have not been withdrawn, but the reissued financial statements are provided either as supplementary information or a re-presentation of the original financial statements in an offering document in accordance with regulatory requirements.

On the basis of the above, and because the question arises in multiple jurisdictions, each with particular securities laws and regulations which may dictate the form for re-presentations of financial statements, the Interpretations Committee decided not to add this issue to its agenda.

Example 3.4

'Dual dating' of financial statements

On 1 August 20X0, the directors of Entity R authorise its financial statements for the year ended 30 June 20X0 to be issued to its shareholders. The financial statements are due to be filed with a regulator on 1 September 20X0.

On 20 August 20X0, an event occurs that would have been classified as a non-adjusting event after the reporting period in accordance with IAS 10:3 (see **section 5**) if the event had occurred before the financial statements were authorised for issue. The directors of Entity R would like to amend (via disclosure) the financial statements that are to be filed with the regulator. They would like to use a 'dual dating' procedure whereby the authorisation date for the financial statements in general would be disclosed as 1 August 20X0, but the specific note containing the updated disclosures would be described as authorised at 20 August 20X0.

> Is Entity R permitted to dual date its financial statements as described for the purpose of incorporating a subsequent event at a date later than the original date of authorisation of the financial statements?
>
> No. The date of authorisation for financial statements in IAS 10:17 and 18 refers to the financial statements as a whole. There is no provision for different components of the financial statements to be authorised for issue at different dates.

The question as to whether and how an entity is entitled to amend its financial statements after they have been authorised for issue is not addressed in IFRSs. Such matters will generally be dealt with in local laws or regulations. However, if under local laws or regulations an entity is entitled and wishes to amend its financial statements in such circumstances, the 'date of authorisation for issue' under IAS 10 would be amended to the later date and it would apply to the financial statements as a whole. As a result, the directors would be required to consider the impact of all material events occurring on or before the new date of authorisation for issue in accordance with IAS 10.

4 Adjusting events

4.1 Adjusting events – definition

Adjusting events are defined as those events after the reporting period that provide evidence of conditions that existed at the end of the reporting period. [IAS 10:3]

The amounts recognised in the financial statements are adjusted to reflect adjusting events after the reporting period. [IAS 10:8]

> The general principle established by IAS 10 is that financial statements should be prepared so as to reflect events occurring up to the end of the reporting period and conditions existing at the end of the reporting period. Because adjusting events provide additional evidence of conditions existing at the end of the reporting period, the amounts recognised in the financial statements are adjusted for their effect.

4.2 Adjusting events – examples

The following are examples of adjusting events:

[IAS 10:9]

- a court case may be resolved after the reporting period which, because it confirms that the entity already had a present obligation at the end of the reporting period, requires the entity to adjust a provision already recognised, or to recognise a provision instead of merely disclosing a contingent liability;

- information may be received after the reporting period indicating that an asset was impaired at the end of the reporting period, or that the amount of a previously recognised impairment loss for that asset needs to be adjusted. For example:

  - if a customer's bankruptcy occurs after the reporting period, this usually confirms that the customer was credit-impaired at the end of the reporting period (but see **example 5.2B** regarding bankruptcy as a result of events occurring after the reporting period); and

  For entities that have not yet adopted IFRS 9 *Financial Instruments*, IAS 10:9 refers to a customer's bankruptcy after the year end confirming that "a loss existed at the end of the reporting period on a trade receivable and that the entity needs to adjust the carrying amount of the trade receivable". The principle is unchanged – the wording of IAS 10 has been updated to reflect IFRS 9's revised requirements regarding recognition of impairment of financial instruments.

  - the sale price achieved for inventories sold after the reporting period may provide evidence about their net realisable value at the end of the reporting period;

  IAS 10 states that the sale of inventories after the reporting period may provide evidence about their net realisable value at the end of the reporting period. Prices for inventories may fall for a variety of reasons, including specific factors such as the introduction of competing products and more general factors such as economic conditions in target markets. However, such changes generally happen over a period of time. The sale of inventories at a loss after the end of the reporting period as a result of competitive pressures will usually indicate that those competitive pressures existed at the end of the reporting period.

  Nevertheless, there will be some circumstances in which there is clear evidence of a fall in value after the end of the reporting period. For example, this could be true for commodities with a market price. It could also be true when the inventories have suffered physical damage after the end of the reporting period. Such circumstances should be accounted for as non-adjusting events.

- the cost of assets purchased, or the proceeds from assets sold, before the end of the reporting period may be determined after the reporting period;

- the amount of profit-sharing or bonus-payment provisions may be determined after the reporting period, if the entity had a present legal or constructive obligation at the end of the reporting period to make such payments as a result of events before that date; and

- fraud or errors may be discovered that show that the financial statements were incorrect.

5 Non-adjusting events

5.1 Non-adjusting events – definition

Non-adjusting events are defined as events after the reporting period that are indicative of conditions that arose after the reporting period. [IAS 10:3]

Non-adjusting events do not give rise to a need for changes in the amounts recognised in the financial statements, but should be disclosed (see **7.1**) if they are material, such that non-disclosure could affect the economic decisions that users make on the basis of the financial statements. [IAS 10:10 & 21]

5.2 Non-adjusting events – examples

An example of a non-adjusting event, given in IAS 10, is a decline in the fair value of investments between the end of the reporting period and the date when the financial statements are authorised for issue. The decline in fair value does not normally relate to the condition of the investments at the end of the reporting period. Instead, it reflects circumstances that have arisen subsequently. The entity does not, therefore, adjust the amounts recognised in its financial statements for the investments. Similarly, amounts disclosed for the investments at the end of the reporting period are not updated but additional disclosure may be required under IAS 10:21 (see **7.1**). [IAS 10:11]

> For quoted investments with a readily ascertainable market price, it will be straightforward to distinguish between the fair value at the end of the reporting period and any subsequent change in that value. However, for unquoted investments, the position will not usually be so clear. Proceeds of disposal after the end of the reporting period will sometimes provide the best available source of evidence of the value of the investment at the end of the reporting period. In other cases, it will be clear that there are circumstances which affected the value after the end of the reporting period. All of the evidence should be carefully considered in such cases.

As discussed at **5.3**, dividends to holders of equity instruments that are declared after the reporting period should not be recognised as a liability at the end of the reporting period. The declaration of such a dividend is therefore a non-adjusting event.

As explained at **4.3.8** in **chapter A4**, the agreement of a lender to waive or vary loan covenants after the end of the reporting period is treated as a non-adjusting event.

The following are other examples of non-adjusting events mentioned in IAS 10 and generally requiring disclosure:

[IAS 10:22]

- a major business combination after the reporting period (IFRS 3 *Business Combinations* requires specific disclosures in such cases – see **13.1** in **chapter A25**) or disposing of a major subsidiary;

- announcing a plan to discontinue an operation;

- major purchases of assets, classification of assets as held for sale in accordance with IFRS 5 *Non-current Assets Held for Sale and Discontinued Operations* (see **chapter A20**), other disposals of assets, or expropriation of major assets by government;

> A non-current asset or disposal group may be classified as held for sale only if it meets the relevant criteria at the end of the reporting period. However, if the relevant criteria are met after the end of the reporting period but before the financial statements are authorised for issue, IFRS 5 requires specified disclosures to be made (see **chapter A20**).

- the destruction of a major production plant by a fire after the reporting period;

- announcing, or commencing the implementation of, a major restructuring (dealt with in IAS 37 *Provisions, Contingent Liabilities and Contingent Assets* – see **chapter A12**);

- major ordinary share transactions and potential ordinary share transactions after the reporting period (IAS 33 *Earnings per Share* requires an entity to disclose a description of such transactions, other than when such transactions involve capitalisation or bonus issues, share splits or reverse share splits, all of which are required to be adjusted under IAS 33);

- abnormally large changes after the reporting period in asset prices or foreign exchange rates (see **example 5.2C**);

- changes in tax rates or tax laws enacted or announced after the reporting period that have a significant effect on current and deferred tax assets and liabilities (see **5.6**);

- entering into significant commitments or contingent liabilities (e.g. by issuing significant guarantees); and

- commencing major litigation arising solely out of events that occurred after the reporting period.

However, some of the items listed above, such as disposals of subsidiaries or assets after the end of the reporting period, may nevertheless be indicators of impairment.

The following examples provide some illustrations of how to distinguish between adjusting and non-adjusting events after the end of the reporting period.

Example 5.2A

Decline in value of share portfolio after the reporting period

An entity has a portfolio of shares. After the end of the reporting period, there has been a substantial fall in the value of the stock market. The entity's accounting policy is to measure the shares at fair value. The entity is not permitted to adjust the fair value of the shares for the decline in value subsequent to the end of the reporting period (i.e. the event is a non-adjusting event after the reporting period). If the impact is significant, however, the entity may be required to disclose the decline in fair value between the end of the reporting period and the date when the financial statements are authorised for issue (see **7.1**).

Example 5.2B

Default by customer after the reporting period

An entity sells goods on credit to a third party. At the end of the reporting period, there was no doubt about the customer's ability to pay. In the process of the finalisation of the financial statements, the entity is informed that the customer is going into liquidation as a result of events that occurred after the reporting period. No impairment of the trade receivable should be recognised in the financial statements, because the statement of financial position appropriately reflects the circumstances as at the end of the reporting period. If the impact is significant, however, the entity may be required to disclose the impact of the customer's default after the reporting period (see **7.1**).

Most often, a customer's bankruptcy after the end of the reporting period is the culmination of a sequence of events that started before the reporting date, so that the impairment of the trade receivables will need to be recognised in the financial statements. It is, nevertheless, not impossible for such bankruptcy to be triggered entirely after the reporting period (e.g. through mismanagement of large derivative contracts).

Example 5.2C

Significant movements in exchange rates after the reporting period

An entity translates foreign currency items at spot rate at the end of each reporting period. In 20X1, due to significant economic upheaval in Country A, that country's currency was devalued after the end of the reporting period. Nevertheless, for the purposes of the year-end financial statements, items should be translated using the closing rate at the end of the reporting period. If the effect of the exchange rate movements after the reporting period is significant, disclosure may be required (see **7.1**).

5.3   Discretionary dividends proposed after the reporting period

Dividends to holders of equity instruments (as defined in IAS 32 *Financial Instruments: Presentation*) that are declared after the reporting period should not be recognised as a liability at the end of the reporting period. [IAS 10:12] If dividends are declared after the reporting period but before the financial statements are authorised for issue, the dividends are not recognised as a liability at the end of the reporting period because no obligation exists at that time. [IAS 10:13]

Before it was amended by IFRIC 17 *Distributions of Non-cash Assets to Owners*, IAS 10:13 included a clarification of the meaning of 'declared' in this context. It stated that dividends are declared when they "are appropriately authorised and no longer at the discretion of the entity". This expression was removed from IAS 10:13 as a consequential amendment and now appears in IFRIC 17:10. The reasons for this are set out in IFRIC 17:BC18 to BC20 which explain that the Interpretation did not change the principle regarding the appropriate timing for the recognition of dividends payable. The 'declaration' of dividends by management does not, therefore, result in a liability when that decision is subject to further approval or when management retains discretion to reverse its decision.

Disclosure is required if such dividends are declared after the reporting period, but before the financial statements are authorised for issue (see **7.1**). [IAS 10:13]

5.4 Recognition of a liability for mandatory dividends based on annual profits

Example 5.4

Recognition of a liability for mandatory dividends based on annual profits

Entity A operates in a jurisdiction where all entities are required to distribute a proportion of annual profits to their equity shareholders. When an entity is first established, it is required by corporate law to specify a minimum percentage of annual profits to be distributed to its shareholders. A shareholders' meeting is held subsequent to the year end at which final dividends are approved based on the entity's annual financial statements. Subject to the approval of shareholders, the proportion of profits distributed may exceed the minimum specified by law; however, the shareholders may not avoid payment of the specified minimum percentage.

If an entity has losses in the current year or net accumulated losses after considering prior year results, then it is not required to distribute dividends.

Entity A is required to distribute at least 25 per cent of its annual profits. For the year ended 31 December 20X1, annual profits amount to CU150,000 and Entity A has no accumulated losses brought forward from previous accounting periods. The directors propose to distribute CU50,000, subject to approval by shareholders; shareholder approval had not been obtained at 31 December 20X1.

It is assumed that Entity A is not required to recognise a liability under IAS 32 *Financial Instruments: Presentation* because the statutory obligation does not give rise to a financial liability.

In Entity A's financial statements for the year ended 31 December 20X1, a liability of CU37,500 (i.e. 25 per cent of CU150,000) should be recognised for dividends.

IAS 10's general requirement that dividends proposed after the reporting period should not be recognised as a liability is discussed in **5.3**. In the circumstances under consideration, however, Entity A has a legal obligation to distribute 25 per cent of its annual profits. This obligation exists at 31 December 20X1 and, consequently, should be recognised in the financial statements for the year then ended.

In respect of the 'excess' dividend of CU12,500 (i.e. CU50,000 – CU37,500), no obligation exists at the end of the reporting period because shareholder approval remains outstanding and the payment of the excess dividend remains at the discretion of Entity A. Consequently, the requirements of IAS 10:12 apply and no liability is recognised. In accordance with paragraph 137(a) of IAS 1 *Presentation of Financial Statements*, the amount of the unrecognised dividends and the related amount per share should be disclosed in the notes to the financial statements.

See **example 5.6.19** in **chapter A32** for a discussion of the requirement to recognise a liability in such circumstances at interim reporting dates.

5.5 Rescinding of dividends

As discussed in **5.3**, IAS 10 is clear regarding the treatment of dividends declared after the reporting period. Other situations may arise that are more complex – and the appropriate treatments will be affected by the legal requirements in the jurisdiction concerned. The following examples illustrate three such circumstances.

Example 5.5A

Rescinding of illegal dividends paid before the end of the reporting period

Company A distributes dividends to its shareholders at the end of each quarterly interim reporting period. Therefore, at the end of the annual reporting period, Company A has paid out all of the dividends allocated for the period. After the end of the annual reporting period, but before the financial statements are authorised for issue, Company A discovers an error in its final interim financial report relating to conditions that existed at the end of the reporting period. The financial statements are adjusted accordingly, as required by IAS 10. The adjustment reduces profits available for dividend distribution below the level at which dividends were paid (i.e. a portion of the dividends distributed during the period should not have been paid out). In the jurisdiction in which Company A operates, there is a legally binding requirement that dividends distributed in excess of available profits be repaid. Therefore, Company A issues demands to its shareholders for return of the appropriate portion of the dividends.

The rescinding of the dividends is an adjusting event. The need to rescind the dividends arises as a result of the discovery of an error that has been accounted for as an adjusting event. Moreover, the rescinding of the dividends itself meets the definition of an adjusting event because it provides evidence of conditions that existed at the end of the reporting period (i.e. at the end of the reporting period, the dividends were illegal).

Therefore, a receivable should be recognised in the statement of financial position for the dividends to the extent that they are repayable.

Example 5.5B

Rescinding of dividends paid before the end of the reporting period due to cash flow shortage

At the end of the annual reporting period, Company A has paid out all of the dividends allocated for the period. After the end of the reporting period, Company A has a cash flow shortage and requests shareholders to return a portion of the dividends paid during the reporting period.

This is not an adjusting event. This request for the dividends to be returned arises as a result of circumstances that arose after the end of the reporting period. If the dividends are returned, they should be accounted for as a capital contribution in the subsequent period, not a reduction of the dividends paid.

Example 5.5C

Legal right to rescind interim dividend declared but not paid

An entity declares an interim dividend during the reporting period; it remains unpaid at the end of the reporting period. Under local law, the directors have the right subsequently to vary or rescind this dividend.

The dividends should not be recognised as an obligation in the financial statements. IAS 10:13 confirms that dividends should not be recognised unless an obligation to pay exists at the end of the reporting period. Such an obligation does not arise until the dividends are no longer at the discretion of the entity.

5.6 Changes in tax rates after the reporting period

For current and deferred tax balances, the amounts recognised in the financial statements are based on tax rates and laws enacted or substantively enacted at the end of the reporting period. In certain circumstances, they may reflect the impact of changes to tax rates and laws that have been announced at the end of the reporting period, if such announcement has the substantive effect of actual enactment. To the extent that changes have not been substantively enacted at the end of the reporting period, however, they should not be reflected in the amounts recognised in the financial statements (see **4.5.2** in **chapter A13**).

5.7 Dividends receivable

In accordance with IFRS 9 *Financial Instruments*, dividends receivable should be recognised in profit or loss only when:

[IFRS 9:5.7.1A]

- the entity's right to receive payment of the dividend is established;

- it is probable that the economic benefits associated with the dividend will flow to the entity; and

- the amount of the dividend can be measured reliably.

For entities that have not yet adopted IFRS 9, equivalent requirements are included in paragraph 55A of IAS 39 *Financial Instruments: Recognition and Measurement*.

Therefore, dividends receivable (including those receivable from subsidiaries and associates) should not be recognised until the shareholder's right to receive payment is established. When dividends are declared by an investee after the reporting period such that, at the end of the reporting period, the investor had no right to receive payment, then neither the investor nor the investee should adjust its financial statements.

6   Going concern

An entity's financial statements should not be prepared on a going concern basis if management determines after the reporting period either that it intends to liquidate the entity or to cease trading, or that it has no realistic alternative but to do so. [IAS 10:14]

As illustrated in the following example, this requirement of IAS 10:14 is a rare exception to the general rule that decisions taken after the end of the reporting period should not be regarded as adjusting events.

Example 6

Voluntary liquidation after the reporting period

An owner-managed entity's reporting date is 31 December 20X1. At the reporting date, the entity is trading profitably and the owner-managers expect that it will continue to do so; they have no intention to liquidate the entity or to cease trading. But in March 20X2, before the financial statements are authorised for issue, the owner-managers experience an unexpected change in personal circumstances and decide to put the entity into voluntary liquidation.

The entity's 20X1 financial statements should be prepared on a basis other than that of a going concern.

If operating results and financial position deteriorate after the reporting period, this may indicate a need to consider whether the going concern assumption is still appropriate. If the going concern assumption is no longer appropriate, the effect is so pervasive that IAS 10 requires a fundamental change in the basis of accounting, rather than an adjustment to the amounts recognised within the original basis of accounting. [IAS 10:15]

Although IAS 10:15 refers to the need for a fundamental change in the basis of accounting, IFRSs provide no guidance about what the alternative basis may involve. The going concern basis is considered more fully in **2.5** in **chapter A4**. As explained at **2.5.5** in **chapter A4**, the basis of accounting may not be 'fundamentally' different when the financial statements are prepared on a basis other than going concern. In particular, even if an entity has ceased trading, the financial statements should generally be prepared on a basis that is consistent with IFRSs but amended to reflect the fact that the going concern assumption is not appropriate. Such a basis accommodates writing down assets to their net realisable value and providing for contractual commitments which may have become onerous as a consequence of the decision to cease trading.

7 Disclosure

7.1 Non-adjusting events

When non-adjusting events after the reporting period are material, non-disclosure could influence the economic decisions of users taken on the basis of the financial statements. Accordingly, the entity should disclose the following information for each material category of non-adjusting event after the reporting period:

[IAS 10:21]

- the nature of the event; and

- an estimate of its financial effect, or a statement that such an estimate cannot be made.

Examples of non-adjusting events which may require disclosure in the financial statements are described in **section 5**.

7.2 Date of authorisation for Issue

It is important for users of financial statements to know when the financial statements were authorised for issue (see **section 3**) because they do not reflect events after that date. [IAS 10:18]

The entity is required to disclose the date when the financial statements were authorised for issue and who gave that authorisation. [IAS 10:17]

IAS 10 does not specify the location of these disclosures. Subject to local legal and regulatory requirements, they might, for example, be made on the face of the statement of financial position or another primary statement, or in the notes. They might also be included in a statement of directors' responsibilities but only if that statement forms part of the financial statements. Inclusion of these disclosures in a separate statement outside of the financial statements, but which refers to the financial statements, would not be acceptable.

If the entity's owners or others have the power to amend the financial statements after issue, that fact should be disclosed. [IAS 10:17]

7.3   Updating disclosures about conditions at the end of the reporting period

IAS 10 also requires that, if an entity receives information after the reporting period about conditions that existed at the end of the reporting period, it should update disclosures that relate to those conditions in the light of the new information. [IAS 10:19] For example, when new evidence becomes available after the reporting period about a contingent liability that existed at the end of the reporting period, the disclosures about the contingent liability in the financial statements, made in accordance with IAS 37 *Provisions, Contingent Liabilities and Contingent Assets*, will be updated based on the new information. [IAS 10:20]

7.4   Dividends proposed or declared after the reporting period

When dividends are proposed or declared after the reporting period, but before the financial statements are authorised for issue, the entity is required to disclose in the notes to the financial statements the amount of such dividends and the related amount per share (see also **7.4.2** in **chapter A4**). [IAS 1:137(a)]

7.5   Going concern

Disclosures are required by IAS 1 *Presentation of Financial Statements* when:

* the financial statements are not prepared on a going concern basis; or

* management is aware of material uncertainties related to events or conditions that may cast significant doubt upon the entity's ability to continue as a going concern. The events or conditions requiring disclosure may arise after the reporting period.

These disclosures are discussed at **2.5** in **chapter A4**.

A23 Related party disclosures

Contents

1   Introduction

1.1   Overview of IAS 24

IAS 24 *Related Party Disclosures* requires disclosures about related party relationships as well as transactions and outstanding balances with an entity's related parties. The Standard defines various classes of entities and people as related parties and sets out the disclosures required in respect of those parties, including the compensation of key management personnel.

1.2   Amendments to IAS 24 since the last edition of this manual

None. IAS 24 was most recently amended in December 2013.

2   Purpose of related party disclosures

The objective of IAS 24 is to ensure that financial statements contain the disclosures necessary to draw attention to the possibility that the reported financial position and results may have been affected by the existence of related parties and by transactions and outstanding balances with related parties. [IAS 24:1] The Standard clarifies that 'outstanding balances' include commitments.

IAS 24 notes that related party relationships are a normal feature of business and commerce. It is common, for example, for entities to operate separate parts of their activities through subsidiaries, associates or joint ventures. Such relationships can have an effect on the operating results and financial position of the reporting entity. They may lead to transactions being entered into between the related parties that would not be entered into between unrelated parties, or to transactions being effected at different amounts from those that would prevail between unrelated parties.

The Standard also considers the implications of the existence of related party relationships – even if there are no transactions between the parties concerned. It acknowledges that the mere existence of the relationship may be sufficient to affect the transactions of the reporting entity with other parties. For example, a subsidiary might terminate relations with a trading partner following the acquisition by its parent of a fellow subsidiary engaged in the same trade as the former partner. Alternatively, one party might refrain from acting because of the significant influence of another – for example, a subsidiary might be instructed by its parent not to engage in research and development.

For these reasons, IAS 24 concludes that knowledge of an entity's transactions, outstanding balances (including commitments), and relationships with related parties may affect assessments of its operations by users of financial statements, including assessments of the risks and opportunities facing the entity.

3 Scope and exemptions

3.1 Scope – general

IAS 24 should be applied in:

[IAS 24:2]

- identifying related party relationships and transactions;

- identifying outstanding balances (including commitments) between an entity and its related parties;

- identifying the circumstances in which disclosure of such relationships, transactions and balances is required; and

- determining the disclosures to be made about those items.

IAS 24 does not apply to the measurement of related party transactions.

3.2 Consolidated financial statements

Related party transactions and outstanding balances with other entities in a group are required to be disclosed. Such intragroup transactions and outstanding balances are, however, eliminated on consolidation, except for those between an investment entity and its subsidiaries measured at fair value through profit or loss. [IAS 24:4]

IAS 24 contains no specific exemptions for intragroup transactions in consolidated financial statements. When intragroup transactions and outstanding balances are eliminated, they do not form part of the consolidated financial statements; consequently, such related party transactions and outstanding balances between group members are not disclosed under IAS 24.

Intragroup related party transactions between an investment entity and its subsidiaries measured at fair value through profit or loss are not eliminated in the preparation of the consolidated financial statements of the group. Accordingly, transactions and outstanding balances between an investment entity and its unconsolidated subsidiaries are required to be disclosed under IAS 24.

3.3 Separate and individual financial statements

When a parent or investor presents separate financial statements in accordance with IAS 27 *Separate Financial Statements*, IAS 24 applies equally to those separate financial statements. IAS 24 also applies to individual financial statements. [IAS 24:3]

There are no exemptions available to subsidiaries in respect of transactions and balances with other group entities. Related party transactions and outstanding balances with other entities in a group are disclosed in an entity's separate or individual financial statements. [IAS 24:4]

3.4 Relationships that change during the period

A related party relationship might have commenced or ceased during the reporting period. The question arises as to what impact this has on the related party disclosures required under IAS 24:13 (disclosure of related party relationships when control exists and identification of the parent and ultimate controlling party) and IAS 24:18 (disclosure of transactions between related parties) – see **5.1** and **5.3.1**, respectively.

The disclosure requirements of IAS 24:13 and 18 do not specify whether the related party relationship should exist at the reporting date in order for the two parties to be considered related. Consequently, it is unclear whether related party relationships or transactions between parties should be disclosed if the parties were related during the reporting period, but have ceased to be related at the end of the reporting period. The IASB amended IAS 24:18 to confirm that only related party transactions during the periods covered by the financial statements should be disclosed but the amendments did not address the above issues.

Equally, the Standard is unclear regarding the appropriate disclosures when a transaction between parties occurred during the period at a time when they were not related but they have become related parties before the end of the reporting period.

In respect of related party relationships when control exists and the identification of the parent and ultimate controlling party, the disclosures should include all entities that were the parent or ultimate controlling party of the reporting entity for any part of the reporting period or at the time of issue of the financial statements. When there has been a change in the parent or ultimate controlling party during the reporting period, disclosure of the identity of both enables external users to access relevant publicly available information for both (e.g. consolidated financial statements for each parent/ultimate controlling party in which the reporting entity has been consolidated for part of the reporting period).

In respect of the disclosures regarding transactions between related parties under IAS 24:18, the amounts of such transactions and details regarding terms and conditions etc. should be disclosed for those transactions if the parties were related at the time of the transaction.

Outstanding balances, including related allowances for doubtful debts, should be disclosed in respect of parties that were related parties either at the end of the reporting period or at the time of the transaction that gave rise to the outstanding balance. If the parties were related at the time of a transaction, disclosure of any outstanding balances provides useful information to external users regarding the settlement of related party transactions, even if the parties are no longer related at the end of the reporting period. Similarly, the disclosure of outstanding balances with parties that are related at the end of the reporting period, but were not related at the time of the transaction, enables users of the financial statements to assess the potential impact of the related party relationship on the future financial position and performance of the reporting entity.

If parties become related after the reporting date, but before the financial statements are authorised for issue, disclosures regarding the new related party may be required in accordance with paragraph 21 of IAS 10 *Events After the Reporting Period*. If the new related party relationship is considered to be a material non-adjusting event after the reporting period, IAS 10:21 requires disclosure of the nature of the event and an estimate of its financial effect (or a statement that such an estimate cannot be made). In disclosing the estimate of the financial effect of a material new related party relationship, the disclosures required by IAS 24 may be relevant.

3.5   Parties related to a group

IAS 24 does not specifically address the use of the term 'related party' in the context of consolidated financial statements. The most appropriate approach, however, appears to be to disclose only those transactions with parties who are related parties of the group as a whole. This approach, by implication, means considering the group in its role as reporting entity and considering which parties are related to it under IAS 24. Thus, for example, the Chief Financial Officer of a subsidiary may be a member of the key management personnel of the subsidiary, but may not be viewed as a member of the key management personnel for the group unless he or she has authority and responsibility for planning, directing and controlling activities at a group level. This degree of influence at a group level may arise as a consequence of the individual having a management role at the parent entity level or, if the subsidiary is significant, directly as a result of his or her authority over and responsibility for a significant component of the group.

3.6   Government-related entities

A reporting entity is exempt from the disclosure requirements set out in IAS 24:18 (see **5.3.1**) in relation to related party transactions and outstanding balances (including commitments) with:

[IAS 24:25]

- a government that has control or joint control of, or significant influence over, the reporting entity; and

- another entity that is a related party because the same government has control or joint control of, or significant influence over, both the reporting entity and the other entity.

When a reporting entity applies the exemption in IAS 24:25, some disclosures are still required to meet the objective of IAS 24 (see **5.4**).

The following example, taken from the illustrative examples accompanying IAS 24, illustrates the application of the partial exemption.

Example 3.6

Partial exemption for government-related entities

[IAS 24:IE1 - IE2, Example 1(part)]

Government G directly or indirectly controls Entities 1 and 2 and Entities A, B, C and D. Person X is a member of the key personnel of Entity 1.

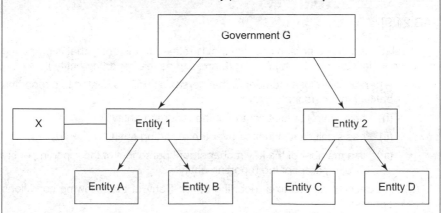

For Entity A's financial statements, the exemption in paragraph 25 [of IAS 24] applies to:

- transactions with Government G; and
- transactions with Entities 1 and 2 and Entities B, C and D.

However, that exemption does not apply to transactions with Person X.

---

4 Definitions

4.1 Related party

4.1.1 Overall requirement to consider the substance of potential related party relationships

IAS 24 requires the substance of each potential related party relationship to be considered, and not merely the legal form. [IAS 24:10]

> The list of related party relationships falling within the scope of IAS 24 set out in IAS 24:9 is exhaustive. Types of relationships not contained within that list are outside the scope of the Standard. However, the determination as to whether a relationship falls within one of the categories listed can involve considerable judgement, with focus on the substance of a relationship and not merely its legal form.

4.1.2 Related party – definition

IAS 24 provides the following definition of a related party.

[IAS 24:9]

"A related party is a person or entity that is related to the entity that is preparing its financial statements (in [IAS 24] referred to as the 'reporting entity').

(a) A person or a close member of that person's family is related to a reporting entity if that person:

    (i) has control or joint control of the reporting entity;

    (ii) has significant influence over the reporting entity; or

    (iii) is a member of the key management personnel of the reporting entity or of a parent of the reporting entity.

(b) An entity is related to a reporting entity if any of the following conditions applies:

    (i) The entity and the reporting entity are members of the same group (which means that each parent, subsidiary and fellow subsidiary is related to the others).

    (ii) One entity is an associate or joint venture of the other entity (or an associate or joint venture of a member of a group of which the other entity is a member).

    (iii) Both entities are joint ventures of the same third party.

    (iv) One entity is a joint venture of a third entity and the other entity is an associate of the third entity.

    (v) The entity is a post-employment benefit plan for the benefit of employees of either the reporting entity or an entity related to the reporting entity. If the reporting entity is itself such a plan, the sponsoring employers are also related to the reporting entity.

    (vi) The entity is controlled or jointly controlled by a person identified in (a).

(vii) A person identified in (a)(i) has significant influence over the entity or is a member of the key management personnel of the entity (or of a parent of the entity).

(viii) The entity, or any member of a group of which it is a part, provides key management personnel services to the reporting entity or to the parent of the reporting entity."

IAS 24:12 clarifies that, for the purposes of the definition of a related party, an associate includes subsidiaries of the associate and a joint venture includes subsidiaries of the joint venture. This means that an associate's subsidiary and the investor that has significant influence over the associate are related to each other in accordance with IAS 24:9(b)(ii).

4.1.3   Joint operations as defined in IFRS 11

The definition of a related party under IAS 24:9(b) (see **4.1.2**) encompasses 'joint ventures' but not 'joint operations'. The term 'joint venture' is clearly defined in IFRS 11:Appendix A and it does not include joint operations. As discussed at **4.1.1**, the list of related party relationships falling within the scope of the Standard as set out in IAS 24:9 is exhaustive and types of relationships not contained within that list are outside the scope of IAS 24.

It is not wholly clear whether this exclusion of joint operations from the scope of IAS 24 was intended by the IASB. The exclusion is not specifically discussed in the Standard or in the Basis for Conclusions on IAS 24. However, it is consistent with the position taken by the Board on a number of related issues, i.e. that a joint operation is viewed as being part of the entity itself. For example, paragraph 52 of the Basis for Conclusions on IFRS 12 *Disclosure of Interests in Other Entities* discusses the fact that IFRS 12 does not require summarised financial information for joint operations as follows.

"Assets and liabilities arising from joint operations are an entity's assets and liabilities and consequently are recognised in the entity's financial statements. Those assets and liabilities would be accounted for in accordance with the requirements of applicable IFRSs, and would be subject to the relevant disclosure requirements of those IFRSs. Therefore the Board concluded that entities should not be required to provide summarised financial information separately for joint operations."

Although the wording of IAS 24:9 means that entities are not required to provide related party disclosures in respect of transactions with joint operations, entities may wish to consider making disclosure on a voluntary basis if the information is material.

4.1.4 Examples illustrating the application of the definition of related party

The Standard includes a number of examples which illustrate the application of the definition of a related party to five scenarios. These examples are reproduced below.

Example 4.1.4A

Associates and subsidiaries

[IAS 24:IE4 - IE8, Example 2]

Parent entity has a controlling interest in Subsidiaries A, B and C and has significant influence over Associates 1 and 2. Subsidiary C has significant influence over Associate 3.

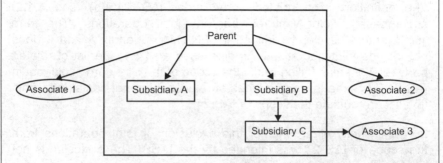

For Parent's separate financial statements, Subsidiaries A, B and C and Associates 1, 2 and 3 are related parties. [*IAS 24:9(b)(i) & (ii)*]

For Subsidiary A's financial statements, Parent, Subsidiaries B and C and Associates 1, 2 and 3 are related parties. For Subsidiary B's separate financial statements, Parent, Subsidiaries A and C and Associates 1, 2 and 3 are related parties. For Subsidiary C's financial statements, Parent, Subsidiaries A and B and Associates 1, 2 and 3 are related parties. [*IAS 24:9(b)(i) & (ii)*]

For the financial statements of Associates 1, 2 and 3, Parent and Subsidiaries A, B and C are related parties. Associates 1, 2 and 3 are not related to each other. [*IAS 24:9(b)(ii)*]

For Parent's consolidated financial statements, Associates 1, 2 and 3 are related to the Group. [*IAS 24:9(b)(ii)*]

Example 4.1.4B

Key management personnel

[IAS 24:IE9 - IE15, Example 3]

A person, X, has a 100 per cent investment in Entity A and is a member of the key management personnel of Entity C. Entity B has a 100 per cent investment in Entity C.

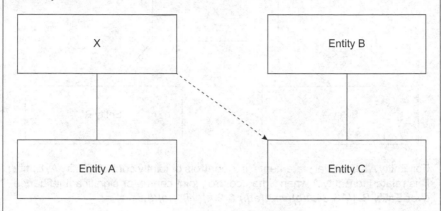

For Entity C's financial statements, Entity A is related to Entity C because X controls Entity A and is a member of the key management personnel of Entity C. [*IAS 24:9(b)(vi) - (a)(iii)*]

For Entity C's financial statements, Entity A is also related to Entity C if X is a member of the key management personnel of Entity B and not of Entity C. [*IAS 24:9(b)(vi) - (a)(iii)*]

Furthermore, the outcome described in [*the previous two paragraphs*] will be the same if X has joint control over Entity A. [*IAS 24:9(b)(vi) - (a)(iii)*] (If X had only significant influence over Entity A and not control or joint control, then Entities A and C would not be related to each other.)

For Entity A's financial statements, Entity C is related to Entity A because X controls A and is a member of Entity C's key management personnel. [*IAS 24:9(b)(vii) - (a)(i)*]

Furthermore, the outcome described in [*the preceding paragraph*] will be the same if X has joint control over Entity A. The outcome will also be the same if X is a member of key management personnel of Entity B and not of Entity C. [*IAS 24:9(b)(vii) - (a)(i)*]

For Entity B's consolidated financial statements, Entity A is a related party of the Group if X is a member of key management personnel of the Group. [*IAS 24:9(b)(vi) - (a)(iii)*]

Example 4.1.4C

Person as investor

[IAS 24:IE16 - IE19, Example 4]

A person, X, has an investment in Entity A and Entity B.

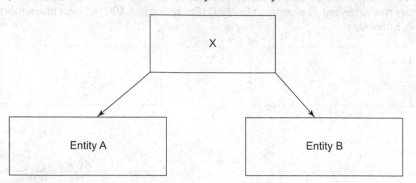

For Entity A's financial statements, if X controls or jointly controls Entity A, Entity B is related to Entity A when X has control, joint control or significant influence over Entity B. [*IAS 24:9(b)(vi) - (a)(i) & 9(b)(vii) - (a)(i)*]

For Entity B's financial statements, if X controls or jointly controls Entity A, Entity A is related to Entity B when X has control, joint control or significant influence over Entity B. [*IAS 24:9(b)(vi) - (a)(i) & 9(b)(vi) - (a)(ii)*]

If X has significant influence over both Entity A and Entity B, Entities A and B are not related to each other.

Example 4.1.4D

Close members of the family holding investments

[IAS 24:IE20 - IE23, Example 5]

A person, X, is the domestic partner of Y. X has an investment in Entity A and Y has an investment in Entity B.

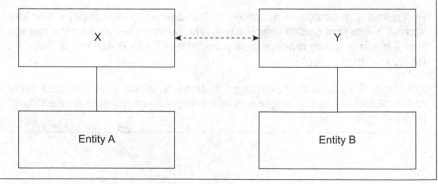

For Entity A's financial statements, if X controls or jointly controls Entity A, Entity B is related to Entity A when Y has control, joint control or significant influence over Entity B. [*IAS 24:9(b)(vi) - (a)(i) & 9(b)(vii) - (a)(l)*]

For Entity B's financial statements, if X controls or jointly controls Entity A, Entity A is related to Entity B when Y has control, joint control or significant influence over Entity B. [*IAS 24:9(b)(vi) - (a)(i) & 9(b)(vi) - (a)(ii)*]

If X has significant influence over Entity A and Y has significant influence over Entity B, Entities A and B are not related to each other.

Example 4.1.4E

Entity with joint control

[IAS 24:IE24 - IE26, Example 6]

Entity A has both (i) joint control over Entity B and (ii) joint control or significant influence over Entity C.

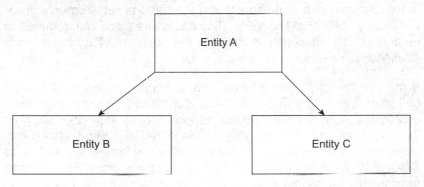

For Entity B's financial statements, Entity C is related to Entity B. [*IAS 24:9(b)(iii) & (iv)*]

Similarly, for Entity C's financial statements, Entity B is related to Entity C. [*IAS 24:9(b)(iii) & (iv)*]

4.1.5 Parties that are not related

The following are not related parties:

[IAS 24:11]

(a) two entities simply because they have a director or other member of key management personnel in common or because a member of key management personnel of one entity has significant influence over the other entity;

(b) two venturers simply because they share joint control of a joint venture;

(c) (i) providers of finance,

    (ii) trade unions,

    (iii) public utilities, and

    (iv) departments and agencies of a government that does not control, jointly control or significantly influence the reporting entity,

simply by virtue of their normal dealings with an entity (even though they may affect the freedom of action of an entity or participate in its decision-making process); and

(d) a customer, supplier, franchisor, distributor or general agent with whom an entity transacts a significant volume of business, simply by virtue of the resulting economic dependence.

It is important to understand that IAS 24:11 does not provide a blanket exemption from the requirements of the Standard for the relationships listed. If the reporting entity has a related party relationship, as defined in IAS 24, with one of these entities, the general requirements apply. Essentially, IAS 24:11 clarifies that disclosures are not required in respect of the relationships listed in the absence of a related party relationship for some other reason.

It may be the case, for example, that a supplier operates a system of inducements (e.g. loans or bank guarantees) in exchange for a customer's agreement to source supplies solely from that supplier. This, of itself, will not normally create a related party relationship. However, it is necessary to consider whether the agreement allows the supplier to direct the relevant activities of the customer. For example, provided that it is not economically prohibitive for the customer to terminate the relationship with the supplier if more favourable terms are available elsewhere, such an agreement does not create a related party relationship.

A bank may provide loan finance to an entity and charge it a fee for doing so. IAS 24:11 does not require disclosure of the relationship and transactions between the entity and its providers of finance simply as a result of those dealings; disclosure is not required unless the bank and the entity are otherwise related. This may be contrasted with the situation in which a venture capitalist, with an equity stake giving it significant influence over an entity, procures external loan finance for that entity and charges a fee for doing so. In the latter case, the investee and the venture capitalist are already related (because the venture capitalist has significant influence over the entity). Therefore, the exemption does not apply and all transactions (including the fees) should be disclosed.

4.1.6 Arrangements involving more than two parties

Careful judgement should be exercised in determining whether contracts are in substance between related parties. For example, in a series of transactions involving three or more parties in which two of the parties are related, it may be that in substance all the transactions should be seen as one overall arrangement between related parties.

Example 4.1.6

Arrangements involving more than two parties

Mr X owns 100 per cent of Company A and Company B. Mr Y owns 100 per cent of Company C. Mr X and Mr Y have no family relationship; Mr X has no investment in or other involvement with Company C; Mr Y has no investment in or other involvement with Company A or Company B.

Company A owns a building, with a carrying amount of CU100 and a fair value of CU150. Company A sells the building to Company C for CU100, and Company C immediately sells it on to Company B for CU100.

On the basis of the information provided, and assuming no other relevant relationships, Company C is not a related party of Company A or Company B for the purposes of IAS 24.

However, careful judgement is required to determine whether the arrangement is in substance between related parties. In the circumstances described, it is likely that the transfers of the building from Company A to Company C, and from Company C to Company B will be considered as linked transactions, in which case the arrangement as a whole should be disclosed as a related party transaction because the substance of the arrangement would appear to be that of an overall agreement whereby Company A sells the building for CU100 (i.e. carrying amount) to its related party, Company B.

4.1.7 Post-employment benefit plans

IAS 24:9(b)(v) states that a post-employment benefit plan for the benefit of the employees of the reporting entity (or of any entity that is a related party of the reporting entity) is a related party of the reporting entity. If the reporting entity is itself such a post-employment plan, the sponsoring employers are also related to the reporting entity.

However, if an entity's employees are members of an industry-wide pension scheme, which is open to all employees of entities that operate in that industry and participate in that industry-wide scheme, it is unlikely that the pension scheme is a related party of the entity. This is because it is unlikely that any one entity controls, jointly controls or exercises significant influence over the industry-wide pension scheme. An industry-wide scheme is not "for the benefit of employees of either the reporting entity or an entity related to the reporting entity" – rather, it is for the benefit of all employees in that industry.

4.2   Definitions taken from other Standards

The terms 'control' and 'investment entity', 'joint control' and 'significant influence' are defined in IFRS 10 *Consolidated Financial Statements*, IFRS 11 *Joint Arrangements* and IAS 28 *Investments in Associates and Joint Ventures*, respectively, and are used in IAS 24 with the meanings specified in those Standards (see **chapters A24**, **A27** and **A26**, respectively). [IAS 24:9]

4.3   Close members of the family of a person

Close members of the family of a person are those family members who may be expected to influence, or be influenced by, that person in their dealings with the entity and include:

[IAS 24:9]

- that person's children and spouse or domestic partner;

- children of that person's spouse or domestic partner; and

- dependants of that person or that person's spouse or domestic partner.

In its agenda decision published in May 2015 *IFRIC Update*, the IFRS Interpretations Committee confirmed that the family members listed in IAS 24:9 should always be classified as close members of the family of a person.

The list of examples of close family members in IAS 24:9 is not intended to be exhaustive, and it is necessary to examine a much wider range of relationships under IAS 24. The IFRS Interpretations Committee also confirmed this principle in its agenda decision issued in May 2015. Depending on the assessment of specific facts and circumstances, other family members (e.g. brothers, sisters, parents or grandparents) could qualify as close family members.

The Standard refers to those family members who may be *expected* to influence, or be influenced by, the person. The test is not, therefore, one of whether influence exists in practice, but whether users of the financial statements would expect such influence to exist.

4.4   Key management personnel

Key management personnel are those persons having authority and responsibility for planning, directing and controlling the activities of an entity, directly or indirectly, including any director (whether executive or otherwise) of that entity. [IAS 24:9]

IAS 24:9(a)(iii) states that a person is related to the reporting entity if that person "is a member of the key management personnel of the reporting entity or of *a* parent of the reporting entity" (emphasis added). Therefore, a party is related to an entity if the party is a member of the key management personnel of *any* of the entity's parents, i.e. its immediate, intermediate and ultimate parents.

Individuals other than directors may fall to be classified as key management personnel, according to the degree of their authority and responsibility. Therefore, the explicit requirement to disclose the remuneration of key management personnel (see **5.2**) may result in the disclosure of remuneration of individuals other than directors.

It is usually the case that those with authority and responsibility for planning, directing and controlling the activities of the group are the board of directors of the parent. However, key management personnel might in some instances include directors of subsidiaries who are not directors of the parent and senior managers who are not directors; for example, if an entity's board is entirely comprised of non-executive directors, it is possible that the most senior executives would also be regarded as key management personnel.

Similarly, in the case of an overseas subsidiary with no directors based in the overseas location, a 'general manager' might be regarded as key management personnel of the subsidiary.

When an entity has a major trading subsidiary which represents a substantial proportion of the group, the management of that subsidiary might be regarded as key management personnel of the group, but it would be necessary to have regard to the autonomy of the management team and whether all major decisions were subject to the approval of the parent's board.

Key management personnel are usually permanent members of staff. However, this is not a requirement of the Standard; consequently, key management personnel could also include seconded staff, or people engaged under management or outsourcing contracts.

See **5.2.8** for a discussion of the requirements of IAS 24 for disclosure of compensation when a management entity is involved.

4.5   Related party transactions

A related party transaction is defined as a transfer of resources, services or obligations between a reporting entity and a related party, regardless of whether a price is charged. [IAS 24:9]

The last phrase in this definition ('regardless of whether a price is charged') means that it is not possible to rely only on an entity's normal accounting records (general ledger, cash book, sales ledger etc.) to identify related party transactions. In addition, there will need to be a process for tracking any goods or services received or provided free of charge (see **5.3.4**).

It is not uncommon for directors to give guarantees in respect of the borrowings of an entity, often without making a charge to the entity. The provision of such a guarantee will be a related party transaction.

4.6   Government

IAS 24 includes a definition of 'government' for the purposes of the partial exemption from the disclosure requirements of IAS 24 for government-related entities (see **3.6**). Government refers to government, government agencies and similar bodies whether local, national or international. [IAS 24:9] This definition is identical to the one used in IAS 20 *Accounting for Government Grants and Disclosure of Government Assistance* (see **chapter A36**).

4.7   Government-related entity

A government-related entity is an entity that is controlled, jointly controlled or significantly influenced by a government. [IAS 24:9]

5   Disclosure requirements

5.1   Relationships

Regardless of whether there have been transactions with related parties, an entity is required to disclose:

[IAS 24:13]

- the name of its parent and, if different, the ultimate controlling party; and

- if neither the entity's parent nor the ultimate controlling party produces consolidated financial statements available for public use, the name of the next most senior parent that does so. The next most senior parent is the first parent in the group, above the immediate parent, that produces consolidated financial statements available for public use.

See **3.4** for a discussion regarding when there have been changes in the parent or ultimate controlling party during or after the end of the reporting period.

IAS 24 indicates that relationships involving control should be disclosed, even when there have been no transactions between the parties, to enable users of financial statements to form a view about the effects of related party relationships on the entity. [IAS 24:14]

The requirements of IAS 24:13 are in addition to the disclosure requirements of IAS 27 *Separate Financial Statements* and IFRS 12 *Disclosure of Interests in Other Entities*. [IAS 24:15]

The ultimate controlling party may or may not be a corporate entity. The requirement to disclose the entity's ultimate controlling *party* means that, if such control is exercised by an individual, or by a group of individuals acting in concert, their identity must be disclosed.

5.2 Compensation of key management personnel

5.2.1 Disclosures required regarding compensation of key management personnel

The total compensation of key management personnel is required to be disclosed, and analysed between:

[IAS 24:17]

- short-term employee benefits;
- post-employment benefits;
- other long-term benefits;
- termination benefits; and
- share-based payment.

5.2.2 Compensation – definition

Compensation includes all employee benefits, as defined in IAS 19 *Employee Benefits* (see **chapter A15**). It includes those benefits to which IFRS 2 *Share-based Payment* applies. Compensation includes:

[IAS 24:9]

- short-term employee benefits, such as wages, salaries, and social security contributions, paid annual leave and paid sick leave, profit-sharing and bonuses (if payable within twelve months of the end of the period) and non-monetary benefits (such as medical care, housing, cars, and free or subsidised goods or services) for current employees;

- post-employment benefits such as pensions, other retirement benefits, post-employment life insurance and post-employment medical care;

- other long-term employee benefits, including long-service leave or sabbatical leave, jubilee or other long-service benefits, long-term disability benefits and, if they are not payable wholly within twelve months after the end of the period, profit-sharing, bonuses and deferred compensation;

- termination benefits; and

- share-based payment.

Employee benefits are all forms of consideration paid, payable or provided by the entity, or on behalf of the entity, in exchange for services rendered to the entity. They also include such consideration paid on behalf of a parent of the entity in respect of the entity. [IAS 24:9]

5.2.3   Payments for services to more than one entity

The disclosure required is in respect of services provided to the entity. Therefore, when key management personnel are paid a single salary in respect of services to more than one entity within the group, the amounts paid should be allocated between the services provided to the different group entities for the purposes of the separate or individual financial statements of each group entity.

5.2.4   Negative compensation amount for key management personnel

Example 5.2.4

Negative compensation amount for key management personnel

Members of key management personnel have been granted options under an entity's executive share option plan. The options vest over a three-year period and include a non-market vesting condition. In 20X1 and 20X2, it is estimated that the non-market vesting condition will be satisfied and, accordingly, under IFRS 2, the entity recognises an expense for these options on this basis. In 20X3 (the current reporting period), the non-market vesting condition is not satisfied and, therefore, the entity reverses the cumulative expense recognised in 20X1 and 20X2 in accordance with the requirements of IFRS 2:20.

Should this 'negative expense' be included in the amounts disclosed for the compensation of key management personnel when the non-market vesting condition is not satisfied and the entity 'trues up' its recognised IFRS 2 expense in 20X3?

Yes. IAS 24 requires disclosure of key management personnel compensation, which is defined to include all employee benefits (as defined in IAS 19 and including those employee benefits to which IFRS 2 applies).

IAS 24 does not provide guidance on the measurement of the amounts to be disclosed for such compensation. Reference should therefore be made to the measurement guidance contained in other Standards (such as IAS 19 and IFRS 2) in order to determine amounts to be disclosed. Accordingly, it is appropriate to 'true up' the amount disclosed as share-based payment compensation when options do not vest as a consequence of non-market vesting conditions not being satisfied in a manner that is consistent with the treatment adopted in the measurement of the expense recognised under IFRS 2.

In such circumstances, entities should consider whether they ought to provide additional disclosure to explain this negative amount included in the measurement of the amounts disclosed for the compensation of key management personnel, particularly in the light of any comparative amount provided.

5.2.5 Compensation of key management personnel who are members of an entity's defined benefit retirement benefit plan

IAS 24 does not provide guidance as to the measurement of amounts to be disclosed with respect to members of key management personnel who are also members of an entity's defined benefit retirement benefit plan. Reference should therefore be made to the measurement guidance contained in other Standards, such as IAS 19, in order to determine the measurement of the compensation to be disclosed. The entity should include in the amounts disclosed the cost of an employee benefit, attributable to the services rendered by the employee to the entity, with respect to the employee's participation in the defined benefit plan. The entity should establish its own accounting policy regarding how the amount is determined. The entity should disclose the method adopted and as much information as possible given the information available. The policy adopted should be applied on a consistent basis.

IAS 19 does not prescribe whether an entity should present service cost and net interest on the net defined benefit liability (asset) as components of a single item of income or expense in profit or loss. The following accounting policies might be considered acceptable, depending on an entity's circumstances:

- disclosure of the amount of the total IAS 19 expense recognised in profit or loss that is attributable to the key management personnel; or

- disclosure of the amount of the IAS 19 service cost that is attributable to the key management personnel.

The following accounting policies would be considered unacceptable:

- no disclosure of key management personnel employee benefits because of the complexity of calculation;

- disclosure of the IAS 19 service cost as reduced by interest income on plan assets but without including interest cost on the defined benefit obligation that is attributable to the key management personnel; or

- disclosure of the contribution by the entity to the employee defined benefit plan with respect to the key management personnel only.

In determining the amount to be disclosed as compensation, entities should consider all of the relevant facts, circumstances and complexities associated with IAS 19 including, among others, whether the employee defined benefit plan is for key management personnel only, or whether it also includes other employees.

5.2.6   Non-monetary benefits to key management

Example 5.2.6

Non-monetary benefits to key management

A member of key management personnel is given, as part of his employment package, the benefit of staying in a residential property owned by the entity. The property was bought by the entity 50 years ago. The value of the property has increased significantly compared to its cost. The market rental of a similar property is CU100,000 per annum. The depreciation recognised on the property is CU5,000 per annum.

How should the non-monetary benefit to the member of key management personnel be disclosed?

IAS 24:18 (see **5.3.1**) states that if an entity has had related party transactions during the periods covered by the financial statements, it should disclose the nature of the related party relationship as well as information about those transactions and outstanding balances, including commitments, necessary for users to understand the potential effect of the relationship on the financial statements. These disclosure requirements are in addition to the requirements in IAS 24:17.

For the purposes of IAS 24:18, it would be appropriate to disclose the depreciation recognised in the period, because that is the amount the entity has recognised in profit or loss in respect of the benefits.

IAS 24 does not require disclosure of the fair value of the benefit provided. The entity should consider whether the amount recognised reflects the nature of the benefit provided. If the fair value of the benefit can be measured reliably, disclosure of additional information that is relevant to users, including a description of the terms and conditions of the compensation, is to be encouraged.

5.2.7 Payments to trusts controlled by key management personnel

Example 5.2.7

Payments to trusts controlled by key management personnel

Mr. X, who is a member of the key management personnel of Entity A, has set up a trust to receive a proportion of his remuneration from Entity A; his close family members are the sole beneficiaries of the trust.

Are the amounts paid to the trust disclosable under IAS 24:17?

Yes. IAS 24:17 requires the disclosure of key management personnel compensation in total and for specified categories. IAS 24:9 defines compensation to include "all forms of consideration paid, payable or provided by the entity ... in exchange for services rendered to the entity". Therefore, any amounts paid by the entity in respect of the services of Mr. X are disclosable, irrespective of the payee.

It is also very likely that the trust will be a related party of Entity A in its own right in accordance with IAS 24:9(b)(vi).

5.2.8 Compensation to key management personnel paid through a management entity

If the reporting entity obtains key management personnel services from another entity (the management entity), the reporting entity is not required to apply the requirements of IAS 24:17 (see **5.2.1**) to the compensation paid or payable by the management entity to the management entity's employees or directors. [IAS 24:17A]

It is often impracticable for a reporting entity to access the detailed information that is required by IAS 24:17 (see **5.2.1**) when compensation is paid to a separate entity as fees. Consequently, IAS 24:17A provides relief so that the reporting entity is not required to disclose components of key compensation to key management personnel that is paid through another entity. However, the reporting entity is required to disclose other related party transactions with the management entity (e.g. loans) under the general requirements of IAS 24:18 (see **5.3.1**) and, specifically, the service fee paid or payable to the management entity (see **5.3.3**).

5.3 Other related party transactions

5.3.1 Requirement to disclose details of other transactions with related parties – general

In addition to the compensation of key management personnel (as discussed in **5.2**), an entity is required to disclose details of any other transactions with its related parties during the periods covered by the financial statements. If such transactions have occurred, IAS 24 requires disclosure of:

[IAS 24:18]

- the nature of the related party relationship; and

- information about the transactions and outstanding balances, including commitments, necessary for an understanding of the potential effect of the relationship on the financial statements.

The following examples are cited in the Standard of related party transactions that require disclosure:

[IAS 24:21]

- purchases or sales of goods (finished or unfinished);

- purchases or sales of properties or other assets;

- rendering or receiving of services;

- leases;

- transfers of research and development;

- transfers under licence agreements;

- transfers under finance arrangements (including loans and equity contributions in cash or in kind);

- provision of guarantees or collateral;

- settlement of liabilities on behalf of the entity or by the entity on behalf of that related party; and

- commitments to do something if a particular event occurs or does not occur in the future, including executory contracts (recognised and unrecognised).

Participation by a parent or subsidiary in a defined benefit plan that shares risks between group entities is a transaction between related parties (see IAS 19:42, as discussed at **5.2.4** in **chapter A15**). [IAS 24:22]

The list of examples in IAS 24:21 is not intended to be exhaustive, and any event meeting the definition of a related party transaction (see **4.5**) should be disclosed if it is material.

The payment of a dividend to a related party constitutes a related party transaction. However, in some cases, the information may already be disclosed and it may not be necessary to provide additional disclosures to meet the requirements of IAS 24. For example, if disclosure is made of (1) the fact that the reporting entity is wholly owned, (2) the fact that the ownership has not changed in the reporting period, and (3) details of dividends paid and proposed, it is not necessary to state explicitly that the dividend has been paid to the owner.

5.3.2 Details to be disclosed

The following *minimum* disclosures are required:

[IAS 24:18]

* the amount of the transactions;
* the amount of outstanding balances, including commitments, and:
  * their terms and conditions, including whether they are secured, and the nature of the consideration to be provided in settlement; and
  * details of any guarantees given or received;
* provisions for doubtful debts related to the amount of the outstanding balances; and
* the expense recognised during the period in respect of bad or doubtful debts due from related parties.

The details listed in IAS 24:18 are not exhaustive, and other significant aspects of the transactions will be required to be disclosed, if such disclosure is necessary for an understanding of the financial statements.

An entity cannot avoid disclosure simply because the transaction is on normal market terms.

5.3.3 Amounts incurred for the provision of key management personnel services by a separate management entity

An entity is required to disclose amounts incurred for the provision of key management personnel services that are provided by a separate management entity. [IAS 24:18A]

5.3.4 Aggregation

IAS 24 states that items of a similar nature may be disclosed in aggregate, except when separate disclosure is necessary for an understanding of the effects of related party transactions on the financial statements. [IAS 24:24]

Related parties may include a number of parties who have the same or similar relationships with the entity, such as a group of owners, members of key management personnel etc. IAS 24 is not specific as to whether transactions with such related parties with similar relationships to the entity can be disclosed in aggregate, nor as to the circumstances that might lead to separate disclosure of items of a similar nature.

The principal objective of IAS 24 is to provide useful information to the users of financial statements while avoiding excessive disclosure when the related party transactions comprise many items of a routine nature, such as in a normal trading relationship between group entities. Therefore, transactions with related parties with similar relationships may be disclosed in aggregate unless a transaction is individually significant. A significant transaction with a specific related party should not be concealed within an aggregated disclosure.

5.3.5 Analysis of transactions and balances

The disclosures set out in IAS 24:18 (see **5.3.2**) are required to be made separately for each of the following categories:

[IAS 24:19]

- the parent;

- entities with joint control of or significant influence over the entity;

- subsidiaries;

- associates;

- joint ventures in which the entity is a joint venturer;

- key management personnel of the entity or its parent; and

- other related parties.

The classification of amounts payable to, and receivable from, related parties in the different categories set out above is an extension of the disclosure requirements in IAS 1 *Presentation of Financial Statements* for information to be presented either in the statement of financial position or in the notes. The categories are intended to provide a more comprehensive analysis of related party balances and apply to related party transactions. [IAS 24:20]

5.3.6 Reference to transactions carried out at arm's length

IAS 24 specifically states that it is inappropriate to indicate that transactions were carried out at arm's length unless such an assertion can be substantiated. [IAS 24:23]

If no price is charged for a transaction that would have given rise to a cost if the transaction had been entered into with an unrelated party, then this fact should be disclosed. In a group context, it is particularly important to consider services that are provided by the parent free of charge. For example, administrative services provided free of charge or group banking arrangements that result in lower finance costs may be disclosable if their effect is material (i.e. if the financial effect of such arrangements has a material impact on the results disclosed in the financial statements).

In addition to the related party disclosures required under IAS 24, when goods and services are provided by a parent or owner to its subsidiary free of charge, it will be appropriate to consider whether a capital contribution should be recognised. Similarly, when goods and services are provided by a subsidiary to a parent free of charge, it will be appropriate to consider whether a distribution should be recognised.

5.3.7 Comparative information

The general requirement to present comparative information under IAS 1 means it is necessary to present comparative information for related party transactions. There are various areas of uncertainty, however, as to which amounts are appropriately disclosed as comparative information for related party disclosures. For example:

- a party is a related party in the current year, but was not in the prior year. Should transactions with that party in the prior year be disclosed as comparative information, even though it was not a related party in that prior year?

- a party was a related party in the prior year, but is not in the current year. Should transactions with that party in the prior year (which were disclosed in that year's financial statements) be disclosed again?

IAS 24 does not address these issues specifically. It is necessary to look at the underlying objective of the Standard. The purpose of the disclosures required by IAS 24 is to draw attention to the possibility that the financial statements have been affected by related party transactions. The transactions that may have affected the current period's results are those with parties that were related in the current period. The appropriate comparative information (i.e. transactions that may have affected the comparative period's results), would therefore be transactions with parties that were related in the comparative period. Under this approach, the financial statements should disclose:

- the impact on amounts reported in the current year of transactions with parties who are related during the current year; and

- as comparative information, the impact on amounts reported in the prior year of transactions with parties who were related during the prior year.

When this is deemed to give insufficient explanation, additional disclosures may be provided.

Examples 5.3.7A and **5.3.7B** illustrate this approach.

Example 5.3.7A

Transactions with party related in the current period but not in the prior period

Sales were made to A Limited in both the current and prior periods.

If A Limited is a related party in the current period, but was not a related party in the prior period, should comparative amounts be disclosed for sales made to A Limited?

Comparative amounts should not be disclosed for sales made to A Limited, because there was no related party relationship that may have affected the comparative period's results. If the absence of comparative information may lead to confusion, an additional explanation might be provided, stating that, while similar transactions were entered into in the prior period, they were not related party transactions, because the related party relationship did not exist in that period.

Example 5.3.7B

Transactions with party related in the prior period but not in the current period

Sales were made to B Limited in both the current and prior periods.

If B Limited was a related party in the prior period, but is not a related party in the current period, should the prior period's sales be disclosed as related party transactions again in the current period's financial statements? If so, should the current period's sales also be disclosed even though B Limited is no longer a related party?

The prior period's sales should be disclosed again, because the related party transactions may have had an impact on the comparative figures in the financial statements. The current period's sales to B Limited should not be disclosed, because B Limited is no longer a related party. When the inclusion of comparative amounts but no current period figures may lead to confusion, an additional explanation might be provided, stating that, while similar transactions occurred in the current period, they are not related party transactions, because the related party relationship did not exist in that period.

5.4 Government-related entities

When the exemption for government-related entities is applied (see **3.6**), IAS 24 requires the reporting entity to disclose certain information in the spirit of the objective of IAS 24 to provide "disclosures necessary to draw attention to the possibility that its financial position and profit or loss may have been affected by the existence of related parties and by transactions and outstanding balances, including commitments, with such parties". [IAS 24:1]

The requirements of IAS 24:26 aim to meet this objective. An entity applying the exemption is required to disclose:

[IAS 24:26]

(a) the name of the government and the nature of its relationship with the reporting entity (i.e. control, joint control or significant influence);

(b) the following information in sufficient detail to enable users of the entity's financial statements to understand the effect of the related party transactions on its financial statements:

   (i) the nature and amount of each individually significant transaction; and

   (ii) for other transactions that are collectively, but not individually, significant, a qualitative or quantitative indication of their extent. Types of transactions include those listed in IAS 24:21 (see **5.3.1**).

IAS 24 requires judgement to be used in determining the level of detail to be disclosed in accordance with the requirement of IAS 24:26(b). It states that the closeness of the related party relationship and other factors relevant in establishing the level of significance of the transaction should be considered such as whether the transaction is:

[IAS 24:27]

- significant in terms of size;

- carried out on non-market terms;

- outside normal day-to-day business operations, such as the purchase and sale of businesses;

- disclosed to regulatory or supervisory authorities;

- reported to senior management; or

- subject to shareholder approval.

The Standard includes illustrative disclosure requirements that could be made when a reporting entity takes advantage of the partial exemption provided in the Standard. These are reproduced below. **Examples 5.4A** and **5.4B** set out example disclosure in Entity A's financial statements (refer to **example 3.6**) to comply with IAS 24:26(b)(i) for individually significant transactions.

Example 5.4A

Example of disclosure for individually significant transaction carried out on non-market terms

[IAS 24:IE3]

On 15 January 20X1 Entity A, a utility company in which Government G indirectly owns 75 per cent of outstanding shares, sold a 10 hectare piece

---

of land to another government-related utility company for CU5 million. On 31 December 20X0 a plot of land in a similar location, of a similar size and with similar characteristics, was sold for CU3 million. There had not been any appreciation or depreciation of the land in the intervening period. See note X [of the financial statements] for disclosure of government assistance as required by IAS 20 *Accounting for Government Grants and Disclosure of Government Assistance* and notes Y and Z [of the financial statements] for compliance with other relevant IFRSs.

Example 5.4B

Example of disclosure for individually significant transaction because of size of transaction

[IAS 24:IE3]

In the year ended December 20X1 Government G provided Entity A, a utility company in which Government G indirectly owns 75 per cent of outstanding shares, with a loan equivalent to 50 per cent of its funding requirement, repayable in quarterly instalments over the next five years. Interest is charged on the loan at a rate of 3 per cent, which is comparable to that charged on Entity A's bank loans.* See notes Y and Z [of the financial statements] for compliance with other relevant IFRSs.

* *If the reporting entity had concluded that this transaction constituted government assistance it would have needed to consider the disclosure requirements in IAS 20.*

Example 5.4C is an example of disclosure to comply with IAS 24:26(b)(ii) for Entity A (refer to **example 3.6**) when transactions are collectively significant.

Example 5.4C

Example of disclosure of collectively significant transactions

[IAS 24:IE3]

Government G, indirectly, owns 75 per cent of Entity A's outstanding shares. Entity A's significant transactions with Government G and other entities controlled, jointly controlled or significantly influenced by Government G are [a large portion of its sales of goods and purchases of raw materials] or [about 50 per cent of its sales of goods and about 35 per cent of its purchases of raw materials].

The company also benefits from guarantees by Government G of the company's bank borrowing. See note X [of the financial statements] for disclosure of government assistance as required by IAS 20 *Accounting for Government Grants and Disclosure of Government Assistance* and notes Y and Z [of the financial statements] for compliance with other relevant IFRSs.

A24 Consolidated financial statements

Contents

1 Introduction

1.1 Overview of IFRS 10

IFRS 10 *Consolidated Financial Statements* outlines the requirements for the preparation and presentation of consolidated financial statements, generally requiring entities to consolidate investees that it controls. Control requires exposure or rights to variable returns and the ability to affect those returns through power over an investee.

1.2 Application of the IFRS 10 framework

IFRS 10 is a complex Standard and requires the application of significant judgement in a number of respects. The summary below is intended to provide a guide for users to navigate the key concepts running through the Standard. The summary does not address all of the requirements of the Standard – users should refer to the more detailed discussions later in this chapter and to the text of the Standard for a complete understanding.

Requirement of the Standard	Detailed discussion
IFRS 10 first establishes a general principle that **parent entities** are required to prepare consolidated financial statements. A parent is only exempt from this requirement if it is a non-listed parent that is itself a wholly-owned subsidiary of a parent that prepares financial statements under IFRSs that are publicly available (or a partially-owned subsidiary of such a parent, and none of its other owners have objected). To qualify for exemption, the financial statements of the entity's ultimate or immediate parent should include the subsidiaries of that parent either by consolidation or by measurement at fair value through profit or loss in accordance with IFRS 10.	**Section 3**
A parent that is an investment entity is required to measure its subsidiaries at fair value through profit or loss, except for subsidiaries that are required to be consolidated (i.e. those that are not themselves investment entities and whose main purpose and activities are providing services that relate to the investment entity's investment activities). If the investment entity parent is required to measure all of its subsidiaries at fair value through profit or loss, it is not permitted to present consolidated financial statements.	**Section 13**

Requirement of the Standard	Detailed discussion
A **subsidiary** is defined as an entity that is controlled by another entity. When a parent (other than an investment entity) prepares consolidated financial statements, it is required to consolidate all of its subsidiaries – there are no exceptions. Specific rules apply for subsidiaries that are classified as held for sale in accordance with IFRS 5 *Non-current Assets Held for Sale and Discontinued Operations*.	Section 4
IFRS 10 uses the concept of **'control'** as the determining factor in assessing whether an investee is a subsidiary. Sometimes, the determination as to who controls an entity will be very straightforward; it may be clear that control over the investee is exercised by means of equity instruments (e.g. ordinary shares) that give the holder proportionate voting rights. In many scenarios, an investor that holds a majority of those voting rights, in the absence of any other factors, controls the investee. For more complex scenarios, more judgement may be required.	Section 5
IFRS 10's definition of control involves three elements: (1) **power** over the investee, (2) exposure, or rights, to **variable returns** from involvement with the investee, and (3) the ability to **use power** over the investee **to affect the amount of the investor's returns**. An investor must possess all three elements to conclude that it controls an investee. The assessment of control is based on all relevant facts and circumstances, and the conclusion is required to be reassessed if there is an indication that there are changes to any of the three elements of control.	Sections 5 - 8
The assessment requires an investor to determine whether it is exposed, or has rights, to **variable returns** (the second element of control). The term 'returns' should be interpreted broadly to include both positive and negative returns and can encompass synergistic returns as well as more direct returns. For this purpose, variable returns may include fixed interest payable to a bondholder, because such interest payments are subject to default risk and they expose the bondholder to the credit risk of the issuer.	Section 7
The assessment requires an investor to determine whether it has the ability to **use its power to affect** the amount of its returns (the third element of control). Careful judgement is required in making this assessment, particularly in circumstances in which it is not immediately clear whether the investor should be regarded as a principal or as an agent (e.g. some fund managers and similar entities). IFRS 10 provides detailed guidance and several examples to illustrate the factors to be considered.	Section 8

Requirement of the Standard	Detailed discussion
The most complex analysis in IFRS 10 relates to the first element of control – whether the investor has **power** over the investee (i.e. whether the investor has existing rights that give it the current ability to direct the 'relevant activities' of the investee). Extensive application guidance is provided to assist in the determination as to whether an investor has power over an investee in complex scenarios, including:	
• identification of the **relevant activities** (i.e. the activities that significantly affect the investee's returns);	6.2
• consideration of how **decisions** regarding the relevant activities are made; and	6.3
• whether the investor's rights give it the **current ability** to direct the relevant activities.	6.4
The determination as to whether the investor's rights give it the current ability to direct the relevant activities focuses on:	
• the investor's current **ability to direct** the relevant activities, rather than the actual exercise of power;	6.4.1
• **indicators/evidence** that should be considered in determining whether the investor's rights are sufficient to give it power;	6.4.2/6.4.3
• the nature of **'substantive' rights** (the rights that will determine whether an entity has power) and **'protective' rights** (in themselves not sufficient to result in power over an investee);	6.4.4/6.4.5
• whether the relevant activities are directed through **voting rights**, including (1) consideration of circumstances when majority voting rights are not necessary to direct the relevant activities, and (2) the existence of potential voting rights; and	
• whether voting or similar rights do not have a significant effect on the investee's returns.	6.4.6

Requirement of the Standard	Detailed discussion
Situations that merit particular attention include:	
• **'de facto'** *control* – when an investor with less than 50 per cent of the voting rights of an investee has control of the investee for reasons other than contractual arrangements and potential voting rights. (Note that IFRS 10 does not use the term '*de facto*' control.) In assessing whether control exists in such scenarios, IFRS 10 requires entities to take into account all facts and circumstances, including the size of the investor's holding of voting rights relative to the size and dispersion of other vote holders, and voting patterns of the other vote holders at previous shareholders' meetings;	6.4.6.7
• *potential voting rights* – IFRS 10 requires potential voting rights, such as those arising from convertible instruments or options, to be taken into account in the assessment of control; the Standard does not limit potential voting rights to those that are currently exercisable or convertible. (All relevant facts and circumstances need to be considered when assessing whether control exists as a result of potential voting rights);	6.4.6.8
• *structured entities* – when an entity is designed so that voting or similar rights are not the dominant factor in deciding who controls the entity (e.g. when any voting rights relate to administrative tasks only and the relevant activities are directed by means of contractual arrangements);	6.4.7
• *agency relationships* – when a decision maker is acting as an agent for another party. A decision maker that has decision-making authority over the relevant activities of an investee does not have control of the investee when it is merely an agent acting on behalf of another party. Conversely, an investor that has delegated decision-making rights to its agent should treat the delegated decision-making rights as if they were held by the investor directly when assessing whether the investor has control of the investee; and	8.2.1

Requirement of the Standard	Detailed discussion
• **when a portion of an investee should be deemed to be a separate entity** – when a particular set of assets and liabilities of an investee (i.e. a portion of an investee) should be deemed to be a separate entity for the purposes of determining whether that portion of the investee is a subsidiary of the investor. IFRS 10 states that a portion of an investee (often called a 'silo') is treated as a separate entity for consolidation purposes when, in substance, that portion is 'ring-fenced' from the rest of the investee.	4.3
The detailed requirements for the preparation of consolidated financial statements include requirements regarding (1) the use of uniform accounting policies, (2) the elimination of intragroup balances and transactions, (3) the presentation of non-controlling interests, and (4) accounting for disposals and partial disposals.	Section 10

1.3 Amendments to IFRS 10 since the last edition of this manual

IFRS 10 was most recently amended in December 2015. The effect of the December 2015 amendments is to defer indefinitely the effective date of earlier amendments to IFRS 10 issued in September 2014 arising from *Sale or Contribution of Assets between an Investor and its Associate or Joint Venture (Amendments to IFRS 10 and IAS 28)* (see **12.3.1** and **12.4**).

2 Objective of IFRS 10

The objective of IFRS 10 is to establish principles for the presentation and preparation of consolidated financial statements when an entity controls one or more other entities. [IFRS 10:1]

To meet this objective, IFRS 10:

[IFRS 10:2]

- requires an entity (the parent) that controls one or more other entities (subsidiaries) to present consolidated financial statements;

- defines the principle of control, and establishes control as the basis for consolidation;

- sets out how to apply the principle of control to identify whether an investor controls an investee and, consequently, is required to consolidate the investee;

- sets out the accounting requirements for the preparation of consolidated financial statements; and

- defines an investment entity and sets out an exception to consolidating particular subsidiaries of an investment entity.

3 Scope of IFRS 10

3.1 General requirement to present consolidated financial statements

IFRS 10 requires that a parent (i.e. an entity that controls one or more entities) should present consolidated financial statements. [IFRS 10:4] Consolidated financial statements are defined as "[t]he financial statements of a group in which the assets, liabilities, equity, income, expenses and cash flows of the parent and its subsidiaries are presented as those of a single economic entity". [IFRS 10:Appendix A]

IFRS 10 does not deal with the accounting requirements for business combinations and their effect on consolidation, including goodwill arising from business combinations. [IFRS 10:3] The accounting requirements for business combinations are discussed in **chapter A25**.

3.2 Employee benefit plans excluded from the scope of IFRS 10

IFRS 10 does not apply to post-employment benefit plans or other long-term employee benefit plans to which IAS 19 *Employee Benefits* applies. [IFRS 10:4A]

The wording of the scope exclusion in IFRS 10:4A is confusing. At first glance, it appears to say that IFRS 10 does not apply to financial statements presented by post-employment benefit plans or other long-term employee benefit plans. But IFRS 10 does not apply to the financial statements of such plans; rather, they are within the scope of IAS 26 *Accounting and Reporting by Retirement Benefit Plans* (see **chapter A41**).

Instead, employers are required to apply IAS 19 in accounting for employee benefit plans, and it appears that the exclusion in IFRS 10:4A is intended to apply to such employers and to exempt them from having to consider whether benefit plans of the nature described meet the definition of a subsidiary (which would result in a requirement to consolidate them). Without this exemption, it seems possible that some benefit plans might have been required to be consolidated as structured entities.

3.3 Exemption from presenting consolidated financial statements for a parent that is itself a subsidiary

An entity that has subsidiaries need not present consolidated financial statements if it meets all of the following conditions:

[IFRS 10:4(a)]

- the entity is itself either (1) a wholly-owned subsidiary, or (2) a partially-owned subsidiary and all its other owners (including those not otherwise entitled to vote) have been informed about, and do not object to, the entity not presenting consolidated financial statements;

- the entity's debt or equity instruments are not traded in a public market (i.e. a domestic or foreign stock exchange or an over-the-counter market, including local and regional markets);

- the entity did not file, nor is it in the process of filing, its financial statements with a securities commission or other regulatory organisation for the purpose of issuing any class of instruments in a public market; and

- the ultimate or any intermediate parent of the entity produces financial statements available for public use that comply with IFRSs, in which subsidiaries are consolidated or are measured at fair value through profit or loss in accordance with IFRS 10.

The criteria in IFRS 10:4(a) were amended by *Investment Entities: Applying the Consolidation Exemption (Amendments to IFRS 10, IFRS 12 and IAS 28)*, issued in December 2014 and effective for annual periods beginning on or after 1 January 2016, with earlier application permitted. If an entity applies the December 2014 amendments for a period beginning before 1 January 2016, it is required to disclose that fact. [IFRS 10:C1D]

The December 2014 amendments have clarified that the exemption under IFRS 10:4(a) is available to a parent entity that is a subsidiary of an investment entity, even if the investment entity measures all of its subsidiaries at fair value.

The criteria in IFRS 10:4(a) are only met if the ultimate or any intermediate parent produces financial statements available for public use that comply with IFRSs *as issued by the IASB* in which its subsidiaries are included either by consolidation or by measurement at fair value through profit or loss in accordance with IFRS 10.

Similarly, if the parent complies with the *International Financial Reporting Standard for Small and Medium-sized Entities* (see **appendix A6**), but not full IFRSs, the above criteria are not met.

If the parent complies instead with a modified version of IFRSs (e.g. IFRSs as endorsed for use in a particular jurisdiction), but does not comply with IFRSs as issued by the IASB (because it applies some accounting treatment that is allowed under the modified version of IFRSs but not under IFRSs as issued by the IASB), the above criteria are not met.

3.4   Parent has no subsidiary at the end of the reporting period

IFRS 10:20 (see **10.3**) requires that the income and expenses of a subsidiary should be included in the consolidated financial statements until the date on which the parent loses control of the subsidiary. Accordingly, when a parent has had subsidiaries at any time during a reporting period, IFRS 10 requires consolidated financial statements to be presented (unless any of the exemptions in IFRS 10 is available).

3.5   No bases for exclusion of subsidiaries from consolidation (other than for investment entities)

Other than for investment entities (see **section 13**), when consolidated financial statements are presented, IFRS 10 does not allow any bases for exclusion of subsidiaries from consolidation. Notably:

- a subsidiary is not excluded from consolidation on the basis that control is temporary. If, on acquisition, a subsidiary meets the criteria to be classified as held for sale in accordance with IFRS 5 *Non-current Assets Held for Sale and Discontinued Operations*, it is included in the consolidation but is accounted for under that Standard (see **chapter A20**);

- a subsidiary is not excluded from consolidation on the basis that there are severe long-term restrictions that impair its ability to transfer funds to the parent. The IASB has concluded that a parent, when assessing its ability to control a subsidiary, should consider restrictions on the transfer of funds from the subsidiary to the parent but that, in themselves, such restrictions do not preclude control; and

- a subsidiary is not excluded from consolidation on the grounds that its activities are substantially different from those of the parent and/or the rest of the group. Information regarding the different nature of the activities of a subsidiary can be appropriately disclosed in accordance with IFRS 8 *Operating Segments*.

4   Identification of parents and subsidiaries

4.1   Definitions – parent and subsidiary

A parent is "[a]n entity that controls one or more entities". [IFRS 10:Appendix A]

A subsidiary is "[a]n entity that is controlled by another entity" (which will be its parent). [IFRS 10:Appendix A]

A group consists of a parent and its subsidiaries. [IFRS 10:Appendix A]

There are two key aspects to the definition of a subsidiary:

- the concept of 'control' (which is discussed in detail in **section 5**); and

- what constitutes an entity (see **4.2**).

4.2   Meaning of an 'entity'

IFRS 10 does not define what is meant by an 'entity'. The definition of a subsidiary previously included in IAS 27(2008) *Consolidated and Separate Financial Statements* stated explicitly that the term encompassed an unincorporated entity. Although this clarification has not been carried forward to IFRS 10, it seems clear that a subsidiary need not be a corporate entity (e.g. it can be a partnership or a trust).

In addition, IFRS 10 allows that, in specified circumstances, a portion of an investee (often called a 'silo' or 'cell') may be accounted for as a 'deemed separate entity' (see **4.3**).

4.3   Determining whether a portion of an investee is a deemed separate entity

In some situations, an investor may have interests in a particular set of assets and liabilities of an investee (a portion of an investee) by virtue of legal or contractual arrangements, rather than in the entire legal entity. In addition, in some jurisdictions, legal entities are divided into separate parts (often referred to as 'silos' or 'cells').

In such circumstances, the question arises as to whether it is possible to consider only an individual silo or a portion of an investee (rather than the entire legal entity) as a separate entity for the purposes of the consolidation assessment.

IFRS 10 requires an investor to treat a portion of an investee as a deemed separate entity if, and only if, the following conditions are met:

[IFRS 10:B77]

- specified assets of the investee (and related credit enhancements, if any) are the only source of payment for specified liabilities of, or specified other interests in, the investee;

- parties other than those with the specified liability do not have rights or obligations related to the specified assets or to residual cash flows from those assets; and

- in substance, none of the returns from the specified assets can be used by the remaining investee and none of the liabilities of the deemed separate entity are payable from the assets of the remaining investee.

Therefore, the key to determining whether a portion of an entity is a deemed separate entity under IFRS 10 is whether the portion of the investee is, in substance, 'ring-fenced' from the overall investee.

When the conditions in IFRS 10:B77 are met, the investor should determine whether it has control of the deemed separate entity using IFRS 10's general definition of control (see **section 5**). In particular, the investor should:

[IFRS 10:B78]

- identify the activities that significantly affect the returns of the deemed separate entity and how those activities are directed in order to assess whether it has power over that portion of the investee;

- consider whether it has exposure or rights to variable returns from its involvement with the deemed separate entity; and

- consider whether it has the ability to use its power over that portion of the investee to affect the amount of the investor's returns.

If an investor controls a deemed separate entity, the investor should consolidate that deemed separate entity. In such circumstances, other parties should exclude that portion of the investee when assessing control of, and in consolidating, the investee. [IFRS 10:B79]

4.4   Horizontal groups

Consolidated financial statements are not required for a 'horizontal group', i.e. when two or more reporting entities are controlled by a common shareholding, such as that held by a private individual. IFRS 10 requires the presentation of consolidated financial statements when an *entity* controls one or more other entities. To the extent that entities are controlled by the same *individual*, there is no requirement in IFRSs that consolidated financial statements be presented.

The existence of a controlling individual, and transactions between entities that are under common control and other related parties, are required to be disclosed under IAS 24 *Related Party Disclosures* (see **chapter A23**).

5 Assessment of control

5.1 Control – definition

An investor controls an investee when the investor "is exposed, or has rights, to variable returns from its involvement with the investee and has the ability to affect those returns through its power over the investee". [IFRS 10:6 & Appendix A]

Specifically, an investor controls an investee if and only if the investor has all of the following elements:

[IFRS 10:7 & B2]

- power over the investee;
- exposure, or rights, to variable returns from its involvement with the investee; and
- the ability to use its power over the investee to affect the amount of the investor's returns.

Power is defined as "existing rights that give the current ability to direct the relevant activities" (see **section 6**). [IFRS 10:Appendix A]

An investor must possess all three elements to conclude that it controls an investee.

The diagram below depicts the three elements of control and the relationship between them.

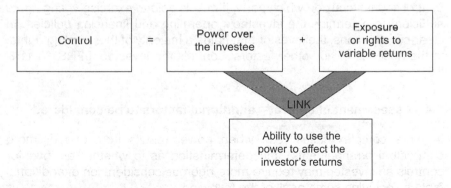

An investor is required to consider all facts and circumstances in assessing whether it controls an investee. [IFRS 10:8] In practice, the determination as to who controls an investee can be complex.

5.2 Requirement for an investor to assess whether it has control

An investor, regardless of the nature of its involvement with an entity (the investee), is required to determine whether it is a parent by assessing whether it controls the investee. [IFRS 10:5]

Although IFRS 10 refers to an 'investor' having control, it does not define the term 'investor'. IFRS 10:5 states that an investor may have control of an investee "regardless of the nature of its involvement". As a specific example, IFRS 10:B15 states that control may be achieved through a management contract if the contract gives the holder the ability to direct the relevant activities (see **8.2**). Therefore, there is no requirement for the investor's interest in the investee to be in the form of debt or equity instruments.

An investor is required to reassess whether it controls an investee if facts and circumstances indicate that there are changes to one or more of the three elements of control listed in **5.1** (see **section 9**). [IFRS 10:8]

5.3   Assessment of control – purpose and design of the investee

When assessing control, the investor should first consider the purpose and design of the investee in order to identify (1) the relevant activities (i.e. the activities of the investee that significantly affect the investee's returns), (2) how decisions about the relevant activities are made, (3) who has the current ability to direct those activities, and (4) who receives returns from those activities. [IFRS 10:B5]

Sometimes, this assessment will be very straightforward; it may be clear that control over the investee is exercised directly and solely by means of equity instruments (e.g. ordinary shares) that give the holder proportionate voting rights. In such circumstances, unless more complex arrangements have been put in place that alter decision-making, the assessment of control should focus on which party, if any, is able to exercise voting rights sufficient to determine the investee's operating and financing policies. In clear-cut situations, the investor that holds a majority of those voting rights, in the absence of any other factors, controls the investee. [IFRS 10:11 & B6]

5.4   Assessment of control – additional factors to be considered

In more complex cases (e.g. when power results from one or more contractual arrangements), the determination as to whether an investor controls an investee may require more rigorous consideration of additional factors, including some or all of the following:

[IFRS 10:11, B3 & B7]

- whether the investor has power over the investee, i.e.:
  - what the relevant activities are (see **6.2**);
  - how decisions about those activities are made (see **6.3**); and

- whether the rights of the investor give it the current ability to direct the relevant activities (see **6.4**);

- whether the investor is exposed, or has rights, to variable returns from its involvement with the investee (see **section 7**); and

- whether the investor has the ability to use its power over the investee to affect the amount of the investor's returns (see **section 8**).

5.5 Only one party can control an investee

The Basis for Conclusions on IFRS 10 states that:

[IFRS 10:BC69 & BC70]

- only one party (if any) can control an investee; and

- the fact that other entities have protective rights relating to the activities of an investee (see **6.4.5**) does not prevent an investor from having control of an investee.

Therefore, when two or more investors collectively control an investee (i.e. the investors must act together to direct the relevant activities of the investee), no investor can direct the activities without the co-operation of the others and, consequently, no investor individually controls the investee. In such cases, each investor should account for its interest in the investee in accordance with the applicable IFRSs, as appropriate (e.g. IFRS 11 *Joint Arrangements*, IAS 28 *Investments in Associates and Joint Ventures*, IFRS 9 *Financial Instruments* or, for entities that have not yet adopted IFRS 9, IAS 39 *Financial Instruments: Recognition and Measurement*). [IFRS 10:9]

5.6 Limited partnerships

A limited partnership is typically a form of partnership that offers the protection of limited liability to some of its partners (the 'limited partners'). Structures for limited partnerships and the functions of a general partner of a limited partnership vary widely between jurisdictions and from partnership to partnership. A limited partnership generally must meet specified legal and tax criteria to qualify as a limited partnership; therefore, the structure is often form-driven. The rights and obligations of general partners in limited partnerships are usually different from those of limited partners. Often, the limited partners are not permitted to take part in the management of the limited partnership, which is solely the responsibility of the general partner(s). Some general partners perform a function designed solely to satisfy the criteria to qualify the entity as a limited partnership.

The determination as to whether an investor has control of a limited partnership will always need to take account of the specific partnership structure and any relevant jurisdictional factors. In general, in applying the three elements of the definition of control in IFRS 10 (i.e. having power over the investee, exposure or rights to variable returns from the investee, and the ability to use power to affect returns):

- a partnership in which the general partner has no beneficial interest in the partnership net assets or net income is unlikely to meet the definition of a subsidiary of the general partner (but it is important to ensure that all returns to the general partner have been identified and considered);

- it is possible for a limited partner to have a majority economic interest in a partnership without having power over the relevant activities; this might occur when it can be demonstrated that another partner has control and does not act as agent for the limited partner; but

- a limited partner who is also the sole general partner, or who has power to remove the sole general partner, may exercise control such that the partnership meets the definition of a subsidiary of the limited partner.

The determination as to whether any of the partners controls the partnership is a matter requiring careful judgement based on the relevant facts and circumstances.

5.7   Employee share trusts

Employee share trusts (sometimes established in conjunction with employee share ownership plans (ESOPs) or employee share plans) are designed to acquire an entity's shares and distribute the shares to employees under remuneration schemes. The detailed structure of such trusts varies, but often includes the following:

- the trust holds shares in the sponsoring entity (or another group entity) to be sold or transferred to employees under the terms of a share-based payment plan;

- the trust acquires shares either directly from the sponsoring entity or by purchasing them in the market. These acquisitions may be financed by a cash contribution or loan from the sponsoring entity or by a third-party loan (often guaranteed by the sponsoring entity); and

- the activities of the trust are narrowly defined, typically in a trust deed.

See **section 9** of **chapter A16** for a discussion of the factors that should be considered when determining whether a sponsoring entity applying IFRS 10 controls a trust established as part of an employee remuneration scheme.

6 Power over an investee

6.1 Power over an investee – definition

An investor has power over an investee when the investor has existing rights that give it the current ability to direct the relevant activities. [IFRS 10:10]

Key steps in the determination as to whether an entity has power over an investee are:

- identifying the relevant activities (see **6.2**);

- understanding how decisions about relevant activities are made (see **6.3**); and

- determining whether the investor's rights give it the current ability to direct the relevant activities (see **6.4**).

6.2 Identifying the relevant activities

6.2.1 Relevant activities – general

Relevant activities are defined as "activities of the investee that significantly affect the investee's returns". [IFRS 10:Appendix A]

It could be difficult to determine the relevant activities of an investee in certain scenarios. In these situations, it is important for an investor to understand the purpose and design of an investee (see **5.3**).

IFRS 10 requires an investor to focus on the activities that significantly affect the returns of an investee.

- When the investee is directed through voting or similar rights (see **6.4.6**), power often relates to governing the strategic operating and financing policies of an investee. However, as explained in the Basis for Conclusions on IFRS 10, that is only one of the ways in which power to direct the activities of an investee can be achieved. In the IASB's view, referring to the power to govern the financial and operating policies of an investee is not necessarily appropriate for investees that are not directed through voting or similar rights. [IFRS 10:BC42]

- It is important to focus on activities that have a *significant* effect on the investee's returns rather than on administrative activities that have little or no effect on the investee's returns. This focus

> is particularly important when assessing control of investees that are not directed through voting or similar rights and for which there may be multiple parties with decision-making rights over different activities. [IFRS 10:BC57 & BC58]

IFRS 10 does not provide a definitive list of which activities should be considered to be relevant activities but rather observes that, for many investees, various operating and financing activities significantly affect their returns. Examples of activities that, depending on the circumstances, can be relevant activities include, but are not limited to:

[IFRS 10:B11]

- selling and purchasing of goods or services;
- managing financial assets during their life (including upon default);
- selecting, acquiring or disposing of assets;
- researching and developing new products or processes; and
- determining a funding structure or obtaining funding.

> In practice, the variety of purposes and designs of investees means that 'relevant activities' will also vary. Ultimately, it is necessary to exercise judgement, taking into account all relevant facts and circumstances.

6.2.2   Relevant activities – structured entities with predetermined activities

It is common for a structured entity to operate in a largely predetermined way so that few or seemingly no decisions are made in conducting the entity's ongoing activities after its formation. At inception, most rights, obligations and activities that could be directed are predefined and limited by contractual provisions. However, the fact that a structured entity operates in a largely predetermined way does not necessarily mean that the entity has no relevant activities.

In practice, virtually all structured entities that operate in a predetermined way have relevant activities. Relevant activities are not necessarily activities that require decisions to be made in the normal course of the entity's activities; such decisions may be required only when particular circumstances arise or events occur. In such cases, the decisions about the entity's activities when the specified circumstances or events occur may be the relevant activities of the structured entity, especially if those decisions can significantly affect the returns of the structured entity. The fact that the right to make decisions is contingent on particular circumstances arising or an event occurring does not in itself affect the assessment as to whether an investor has power over the structured entity. The particular circumstances or events need not have occurred for an investor with the ability to make those decisions to have power over the structured entity (see IFRS 10:B53).

A structured entity operating in a largely predetermined way will most commonly be established to invest in assets that are expected to provide a predictable level of return with little or no ongoing input from investors. However, decisions outside the predetermined parameters may need to be taken when that return fails to materialise. Examples of those decisions may include:

- for a portfolio of high quality receivables, the decision on how to pursue recovery in the event of default;

- for a portfolio of debt securities, the decision to change the criteria for investment to permit investment in, say, AA-rated securities in the event that the population of AAA-rated issuers diminishes;

- for a portfolio of equity investments, the decision to sell or hold an investment in the event of a significant, unexpected fall in value; or

- for a portfolio of property interests, the course of action to take in the event of default by a blue-chip tenant or significant physical damage to a property.

Such decisions significantly affect the returns of the structured entity and, therefore, they are the relevant activities of the structured entity. Consequently, the analysis of who has power over the structured entity should focus on the ability to make those decisions.

This principle is also illustrated in the following example from the Basis for Conclusions on IFRS 10.

Example 6.2.2

[IFRS 10:BC80]

Assume that the purpose of a securitisation vehicle is to allocate risks (mainly credit risk) and benefits (cash flows received) of a portfolio of receivables to the parties involved with the vehicle. The vehicle is designed in such a way that the only activity that can be directed, and can significantly affect the returns from the transaction, is managing those receivables when they default. An investor might have the current ability to direct those activities that significantly affect the returns of the transaction by, for example, writing a put option on the receivables that is triggered when the receivables default. The design of the vehicle ensures that the investor has decision-making authority over the relevant activities at the only time that such decision-making authority is required. In this situation, the terms of the put agreement are integral to the overall transaction and the establishment of the investee. Therefore, the terms of the put agreement would be considered together with the founding documents of the investee to conclude whether the investor has the current ability to direct the activities of the securitisation vehicle that significantly affect the returns of the transaction (even before the default of the receivables).

Note that it is expected to be extremely rare for a structured entity to have no relevant activities (i.e. it operates on full 'autopilot' and the only decisions to be made after formation of the structured entity relate to administrative activities that will not significantly affect the investee's returns). Such a determination should be made only after a thorough analysis of both the expected activities of the structured entity and decisions to be taken in response to contingent events (see **6.2.3** for additional guidance for those rare circumstances when such a determination is made).

6.2.3 Relevant activities – involvement in the design of a structured entity operating on autopilot

It is common for a structured entity to operate in a way so that seemingly no decisions are made in conducting the entity's ongoing activities after its formation (i.e. the entity effectively operates on 'autopilot'). A thorough understanding of (1) the purpose and design of the structured entity, and (2) any decisions to be made after its formation, is critical in assessing who has power.

As discussed in **6.2.2**, virtually all structured entities that operate in a largely predetermined way have relevant activities. However, there may be extremely rare situations when, after careful assessment of the purpose and design of a structured entity, the only decisions to be made after formation of the entity relate to administrative activities that will not significantly affect the investee's returns. If this is the case, there are no decisions to be made on relevant activities of the structured entity subsequent to its formation and the only decisions that significantly affect the returns of the structured entity are the decisions taken at the formation stage.

In those extremely rare situations when there are no decisions to be made on relevant activities after formation of a structured entity, an investor can have power over the structured entity as a result of the investor's decisions and involvement in the design and creation of the structured entity. Specifically, the initial design of the entity may be the relevant activity that significantly affects the returns of the structured entity. Consequently, in determining whether an investor has power over the structured entity, the activities performed and decisions made as part of the entity's design at formation should be assessed carefully.

Nevertheless, the fact that an investor is involved in the design of an investee does not necessarily mean that the investor has decision-making rights to direct the relevant activities of the investee. Often, several parties are involved in the design of an investee and the final structure of the investee includes whatever is agreed to by all those parties (see IFRS 10:BC77). Consequently, an investor's involvement in establishing an investee would not, in isolation, be sufficient evidence to determine that the investor has power over the entity.

In making this assessment, an investor should consider the significance of its interest in the investee and its involvement in the design of the investee (including an assessment of the scope of its decision-making authority during the design process). The more significant an investor's (1) interest, and (2) involvement in the design of the investee, the more indicative it is that the investor had the ability and incentive to make decisions for its own benefit and, therefore, that it has power over the investee.

6.3 How decisions about relevant activities are made

6.3.1 Decisions about relevant activities

Having identified the relevant activities of an investee, the next key step in understanding who has power over an investee is to understand the mechanisms for making decisions about those relevant activities.

Examples of decisions about relevant activities include, but are not limited to:

[IFRS 10:B12]

- establishing operating and capital decisions of the investee, including budgets; and
- appointing and remunerating an investee's key management personnel or service providers and terminating their services or employment.

Accordingly, it will often be appropriate to focus on the purpose and design of the investee and how decisions are made in relation to, for example:

- changes of strategic direction, including acquisitions and disposals of subsidiaries;
- major capital purchases and disposals;
- appointment and remuneration of directors and other key management personnel;
- approval of the annual plan and budget; and
- dividend policy (see also the discussion in **section 7**).

6.3.2   Identifying how relevant activities are directed in complex scenarios

6.3.2.1   Two or more investors with the ability to direct the relevant activities

If two or more investors each have existing rights that give them the unilateral ability to direct different relevant activities of an investee, the investor that has the current ability to direct the activities that *most* significantly affect the returns of the investee has power over the investee. [IFRS 10:13]

> Note that the IASB has confirmed in the Basis for Conclusions on IFRS 10 that only one party (if any) can control an investee. [IFRS 10:BC69]

6.3.2.2   Two or more investors with the ability to direct relevant activities at different times

In some situations, an entity may have different relevant activities before and after a particular set of circumstances arises or event occurs. When two or more investors have the current ability to direct relevant activities and those activities occur at different times, the investors should determine which investor is able to direct the activities that most significantly affect those returns consistently with the treatment of concurrent decision-making rights. IFRS 10 requires investors to reconsider the assessment over time if relevant facts or circumstances change (see **section 9**). [IFRS 10:B13]

> **Examples 6.3.2.2A** and **6.3.2.2B**, which are examples from the Standard, illustrate the application of IFRS 10:B13. The examples are intended only to illustrate scenarios in which investors each have the unilateral ability to direct different relevant activities; they are not intended to provide a definitive conclusion as to which activities should be considered to be the activities that most significantly affect the investee's returns. Ultimately, it is necessary to exercise judgement, taking into account all relevant facts and circumstances.
>
> In addition, it is important to note that **examples 6.3.2.2A** and **6.3.2.2B** deal only with the first element of control (i.e. who has power over an investee). To determine who has control of the investee, the other two elements of control referred to in **5.1** (i.e. exposure or rights to variable returns, and the ability to use the power to affect the investor's returns) should also be considered.

Example 6.3.2.2A

Investors have unilateral ability to direct different relevant activities that occur at different times

[IFRS 10:Appendix B Example 1]

Two investors form an investee to develop and market a medical product. One investor is responsible for developing and obtaining regulatory approval of the medical product – that responsibility includes having the unilateral ability to make all decisions relating to the development of the product and to obtaining regulatory approval. Once the regulator has approved the product, the other investor will manufacture and market it – this investor has the unilateral ability to make all decisions about the manufacture and marketing of the product. If all the activities – developing and obtaining regulatory approval as well as manufacturing and marketing of the medical product – are relevant activities, each investor needs to determine whether it is able to direct the activities that *most* significantly affect the investee's returns. Accordingly, each investor needs to consider whether developing and obtaining regulatory approval or the manufacturing and marketing of the medical product is the activity that *most* significantly affects the investee's returns and whether it is able to direct that activity. In determining which investor has power, the investors would consider:

(a)   the purpose and design of the investee;

(b)   the factors that determine the profit margin, revenue and value of the investee as well as the value of the medical product;

(c)   the effect on the investee's returns resulting from each investor's decision-making authority with respect to the factors in (b); and

(d)   the investors' exposure to variability of returns.

In this particular example, the investors would also consider:

(e)   the uncertainty of, and effort required in, obtaining regulatory approval (considering the investor's record of successfully developing and obtaining regulatory approval of medical products); and

(f)   which investor controls the medical product once the development phase is successful.

Example 6.3.2.2B

Investor has the ability to direct the relevant activities until certain events occur

[IFRS 10:Appendix B Example 2]

An investment vehicle (the investee) is created and financed with a debt instrument held by an investor (the debt investor) and equity instruments held by a number of other investors. The equity tranche is designed to absorb the first losses and to receive any residual return from the investee. One of the equity investors who holds 30 per cent of the equity is also the asset manager. The investee uses its proceeds to purchase a portfolio of financial assets, exposing the investee to the credit risk associated with the possible default of principal and interest payments of the assets. The transaction is marketed to the debt investor as an investment with minimal exposure to the credit risk associated with the possible default of the assets in the portfolio because of the nature of these assets and because the equity tranche is designed to absorb the first losses of the investee. The returns of the investee are significantly affected by the management of the investee's asset portfolio, which includes decisions about the selection, acquisition and disposal of the assets within portfolio guidelines and the management upon default of any portfolio assets. All those activities are managed by the asset manager until defaults reach a specified proportion of the portfolio value (ie when the value of the portfolio is such that the equity tranche of the investee has been consumed). From that time, a third-party trustee manages the assets according to the instructions of the debt investor. Managing the investee's asset portfolio is the relevant activity of the investee. The asset manager has the ability to direct the relevant activities until defaulted assets reach the specified proportion of the portfolio value; the debt investor has the ability to direct the relevant activities when the value of defaulted assets surpasses that specified proportion of the portfolio value. The asset manager and the debt investor each need to determine whether they are able to direct the activities that *most* significantly affect the investee's returns, including considering the purpose and design of the investee as well as each party's exposure to variability of returns.

6.3.2.3 Entity has more than one governing body

In practice, entities will have a variety of governance structures, frequently determined by the regulatory requirements in relevant jurisdictions and/or agreements between their shareholders. A clear understanding of the governance structure of an investee is essential in order to identify how decisions about relevant activities are made.

In some situations, the direction of the relevant activities of an investee is determined by majority vote at shareholders' meetings. In such cases, an investor that has the ability to cast the majority of votes at shareholders' meetings generally has power over the investee.

When an investee has more than one governing body, it is important to understand the rights and obligations of each governing body. It should not be assumed merely because one body has oversight of another that the former is necessarily the body that makes decisions about the relevant activities of the entity. In all cases, the assessment of control should be based on a careful analysis of all relevant facts and circumstances.

6.3.2.4 Majority of directors are independent

In many jurisdictions, best practice or mandatory corporate governance codes require that an entity appoint directors who are independent. The term 'independent director' has a variety of meanings in different jurisdictions, but it is generally taken to describe a director who does not represent a specific shareholder.

If the majority of an entity's directors are independent, it should not be automatically assumed that none of the shareholders has power over decisions made by the directors.

In assessing whether a particular shareholder controls an entity, all relevant facts and circumstances should be considered. [IFRS 10:8] As discussed at **6.3.2.3**, a clear understanding of the governance structure of an investee is essential in order to identify how decisions about relevant activities are made and, consequently, who has power over the investee. In the circumstances under consideration, this would involve analysing both the process for decision making at a director level and the extent to which decisions over relevant activities are taken by the directors rather than via a shareholder vote.

In the context of an entity with independent directors, it is necessary to consider the role of those directors in making decisions regarding relevant activities. It may be that their role is limited to ensuring that proper governance procedures are followed (through, for example, membership of an audit or nominations committee); this may involve challenging the basis for decisions made by the non-independent directors (in, for example, a committee of which the independent directors are not members) but not active involvement in the decision-making process.

In circumstances such as these, it may be that an investor can exercise power over decisions made by an entity's directors through power over a majority of an entity's non-independent directors. As for other decision makers (see **8.2.6**), powers to appoint and remove independent directors should also be considered.

6.4 Whether the investor's rights give it the current ability to direct the relevant activities

6.4.1 Focus on the 'ability to direct' rather than the actual exercise of power

Power arises from rights. To have power over an investee, an investor must have existing rights that give the investor the current ability to direct the relevant activities. [IFRS 10:11 & B14] Therefore, the assessment of power is based on the investor's *ability* to direct the relevant activities of the investee; specifically, IFRS 10 does not require the investor to have actually exercised its power. An investor with the current ability to direct the relevant activities of an investee has power over the investee even if its rights to direct have yet to be exercised. Conversely, evidence that the investor has been directing the relevant activities of the investee can help determine whether the investor has power, but such evidence is not, in itself, conclusive in determining whether the investor has power over the investee. [IFRS 10:12]

An investor can have power over an investee even if other entities have existing rights that give them the current ability to participate in the direction of the relevant activities (e.g. when another entity has significant influence). [IFRS 10:14]

6.4.2 Rights that give an investor power over an investee

The rights that give an investor power can differ between investees. [IFRS 10:B14] Different types of rights that, either individually or in combination, can give an investor power over an investee include, but are not limited to:

[IFRS 10:B15]

- rights in the form of voting rights (or potential voting rights) of an investee (see **6.4.6**);

- rights to appoint, reassign or remove members of an investee's key management personnel who have the ability to direct the relevant activities;

- rights to appoint or remove another entity that directs the relevant activities;

- rights to direct the investee to enter into, or veto any changes to, transactions for the benefit of the investor; and

- other rights (such as decision-making rights specified in a management contract) that give the holder the ability to direct the relevant activities.

The specific factors that apply when voting or similar rights do not have a significant effect on the investee's returns are considered in **6.4.7**.

6.4.3 Evidence to be considered when it is difficult to determine whether the investor's rights are sufficient to give it power

When it is difficult to determine whether an investor's rights are sufficient to give it power over an investee, to enable the assessment of power to be made, the investor should consider evidence regarding whether it has the practical ability to direct the relevant activities unilaterally. Consideration is given, but is not limited, to whether:

[IFRS 10:B18]

- the investor can, without having the contractual right to do so, appoint or approve the investee's key management personnel who have the ability to direct the relevant activities;

- the investor can, without having the contractual right to do so, direct the investee to enter into, or can veto any changes to, significant transactions for the benefit of the investor;

- the investor can dominate either the nominations process for electing members of the investee's governing body or the obtaining of proxies from other holders of voting rights;

- the investee's key management personnel are related parties of the investor (e.g. the chief executive officer of the investee and the chief executive officer of the investor are the same person); and/or

- the majority of the members of the investee's governing body are related parties of the investor.

When considered together with the investor's rights and the indicators in IFRS 10:B19 and B20 (see below), the factors listed in IFRS 10:B18 may provide evidence that the investor's rights are sufficient to give it power over the investee.

Sometimes there will be indications that the investor has a special relationship with the investee, which suggests that the investor has more than a passive interest in the investee. The existence of any individual indicator, or a particular combination of indicators, does not necessarily mean that the power criterion is met. However, having more than a passive interest in the investee may indicate that the investor has other related rights sufficient to give it power or provide evidence of existing power over an investee. For example, the following suggests that the investor has more than a passive interest in the investee and, in combination with other rights, may indicate that the investor has power over the investee:

[IFRS 10:B19]

- the investee's key management personnel who have the ability to direct the relevant activities are current or previous employees of the investor;

- the investee's operations are dependent on the investor, such as in the following situations:

  - the investee depends on the investor to fund a significant portion of its operations;

  - the investor guarantees a significant portion of the investee's obligations;

  - the investee depends on the investor for critical services, technology, supplies or raw materials;

  - the investor controls assets such as licences or trademarks that are critical to the investee's operations; and/or

  - the investee depends on the investor for key management personnel, such as when the investor's personnel have specialised knowledge of the investee's operations;

- a significant portion of the investee's activities either involve or are conducted on behalf of the investor; and/or

- the investor's exposure, or rights, to returns from its involvement with the investee is disproportionately greater than its voting or other similar rights. For example, there may be a situation in which an investor is entitled, or exposed, to more than half of the returns of the investee but holds less than half of the voting rights of the investee.

The greater an investor's exposure, or rights, to variability of returns from its involvement with an investee, the greater is the incentive for the investor to obtain rights sufficient to give it power. Therefore, having a large exposure to variability of returns is an indicator that the investor may have power. However, the extent of the investor's exposure does not, in itself, determine whether an investor has power over the investee. [IFRS 10:20]

When the factors set out in IFRS 10:B18 and the indicators set out in IFRS 10:B19 and B20 are considered together with an investor's rights, greater weight should be given to the evidence of power described in IFRS 10:B18.

6.4.4 Substantive rights

6.4.4.1 Determining whether rights are substantive

In assessing whether it has power, an investor considers only substantive rights relating to an investee; the substantive rights to be considered are those held by the investor and those held by others. For a right to be substantive, the holder must have the practical ability to exercise that right. [IFRS 10:B9 & B22]

Determining whether or not rights are substantive requires the exercise of judgement, taking into account all facts and circumstances. IFRS 10 sets out a number of factors that an investor should consider in assessing whether rights are substantive (the list is not exhaustive):

[IFRS 10:B23]

- whether there are any barriers (economic or otherwise) that prevent the holder (or holders) from exercising the rights (see **6.4.4.2**);

- when the exercise of rights requires the agreement of more than one party, or when the rights are held by more than one party, whether a mechanism is in place that provides those parties with the practical ability to exercise their rights collectively if they choose to do so (see **6.4.4.3**); and

- whether the party or parties that hold the rights would benefit from the exercise of those rights (see **6.4.4.4**).

In addition, for a right to be substantive, the right needs to be exercisable when decisions about the direction of the relevant activities need to be made (see **6.4.4.5**). [IFRS 10:B24]

Consideration of the factors listed in IFRS 10:B23 (and discussed in more detail in **6.4.4.2** to **6.4.4.4**) will assist in the determination as to whether an investor has a real ability in practice to direct the relevant activities of an investee. Ultimately, the assessment as to whether rights are substantive is a matter requiring the exercise of careful judgement taking into account all available facts and circumstances.

6.4.4.2 Barriers that may prevent the exercise of rights

Examples of barriers that may prevent a holder (or holders) of rights from exercising those rights, which could lead to a conclusion that the rights are not substantive, include but are not limited to:

[IFRS 10:B23(a)]

- financial penalties and incentives that would prevent (or deter) the holder from exercising its rights;

- an exercise or conversion price that creates a financial barrier that would prevent (or deter) the holder from exercising its rights;

- terms and conditions that make it unlikely that the rights would be exercised (e.g. conditions that narrowly limit the timing of their exercise);

- the absence of an explicit, reasonable mechanism in the founding documents of an investee or in applicable laws or regulations that would allow the holder to exercise its rights;

- the inability of the holder of the rights to obtain the information necessary to exercise its rights;

- operational barriers or incentives that would prevent (or deter) the holder from exercising its rights (e.g. the absence of other managers willing or able to provide the specialised services or provide the services and take on other interests held by the incumbent manager); and/or

- legal or regulatory requirements that prevent the holder from exercising its rights (e.g. when a foreign investor is prohibited from exercising its rights).

6.4.4.3 Mechanism in place to allow the exercise of collective rights

When the exercise of rights requires the agreement of more than one party, or when the rights are held by more than one party, it will generally be necessary to have a mechanism in place that provides those parties with the practical ability to exercise their rights collectively if they choose to do so. The lack of such a mechanism is an indicator that the rights may not be substantive. The more parties that are required to agree to exercise the rights, the less likely it is that those rights are substantive. [IFRS 10:B23(b)]

IFRS 10 notes that a board of directors whose members are independent of the decision maker may serve as a mechanism for numerous investors to act collectively in exercising their rights. Therefore, removal rights exercisable by an independent board of directors are more likely to be substantive than if the same rights were exercisable individually by a large number of investors. [IFRS 10:B23(b)]

6.4.4.4   Whether holders would benefit from the exercise of the rights

Rights are more likely to be substantive when the party or parties that hold the rights would benefit from the exercise of those rights.

> Rights that result in an entity having the ability to direct the relevant activities of an investee will generally result in benefits for the entity. Unless the entity is acting as an agent (see **section 8**), it would be unusual for the entity not to receive any benefits when it has the current ability to direct the relevant activities of an investee. Those benefits may be monetary (e.g. cash dividends from ownership of ordinary shares of an investee) or non-monetary (e.g. by realising synergies between the investor and the investee).

When a party holds potential voting rights in an investee (e.g. share options, warrants and convertible instruments), IFRS 10 states that that party should consider the exercise or conversion price of the instrument in determining whether the exercise or conversion of the instruments would benefit the holder. The terms and conditions of potential voting rights are more likely to be substantive when the instrument is 'in the money' or the investor would benefit for other reasons (e.g. by realising synergies between the investor and the investee) from the exercise or conversion of the instrument (see **6.4.6.8** for more detail). [IFRS 10:B23(c)]

> When potential voting rights are out of the money, they are less likely to be substantive – but they may be so. It is necessary to exercise judgement based on a careful analysis of all of the relevant facts and circumstances. For example, even if share options are out of the money and are expected to be out of the money in the future, they may still be substantive taking into account the control premium that the holder would be prepared to pay in exercising the options.
>
> Determining whether a potential voting right is substantive is not based solely on a comparison of the strike or conversion price of the instrument and the current market price of its underlying share. Although the strike or conversion price is one factor to consider, determining whether potential voting rights are substantive requires a holistic approach, considering a variety of factors. This includes assessing the purpose and design of the instrument, considering whether the investor can benefit for other reasons such as by realising synergies between the investor and the investee, and determining whether there are any barriers (financial

or otherwise) that would prevent the holder of potential voting rights from exercising or converting those rights (see IFRS 10:BC124).

Potential voting rights could also arise through a forward contract. In such cases, consideration of the exercise or conversion price of the instrument may not be relevant, because the holder may not have discretion to avoid obtaining the underlying shares or other instruments. IFRS 10:B23(c) does not explicitly state that consideration of the exercise or conversion price of an instrument is not relevant if the exercise or conversion is not at the discretion of either party, as in a forward contract – but this would seem to be the logical interpretation. Take, for example, an investor that holds a forward contract to purchase additional shares in an investee that cannot be settled net. One important feature of such a contract is that the holder does not have a choice as to whether to 'exercise' – the holder is required to make payments under the forward contract when they fall due, and will receive the additional shares. Consequently, it does not seem relevant to consider the potential benefit of the exercise of the rights for the investor when determining whether the potential voting rights are substantive, because the additional shares will be obtained in any case. In such circumstances, the key determinant will be the timing of the forward contract, i.e. whether the additional shares will be obtained before decisions about the direction of the relevant activities need to be made (see **6.4.4.5**).

6.4.4.5 Whether the rights are exercisable when decisions about the relevant activities of an investee need to be made

A further condition that must be met before rights are considered to be substantive is that the rights must be exercisable when decisions about the direction of the relevant activities need to be made. Generally, to be substantive, the rights need to be currently exercisable. However, sometimes rights can be substantive even though the rights are not currently exercisable. [IFRS 10:B24]

This condition is most obviously applicable in the context of potential voting rights (see **6.4.6.8**). In developing IFRS 10, the IASB considered whether potential voting rights before exercise or conversion can give their holder the current ability to direct the activities of an investee. The IASB concluded that potential voting rights could do so when (1) the rights are substantive, and (2) the rights on exercise or conversion (when considered together with other existing rights of the holder, if any) give the holder the current ability to direct the relevant activities of the investee. In the IASB's view, a holder of substantive potential rights is, in effect, in the same position as a passive majority shareholder or a holder of substantive 'kick-out' rights. The control model would provide that, in the absence of other factors, a majority shareholder controls an investee even though it can take time for the shareholder to organise a meeting and exercise its voting rights. In a similar manner, the holder of potential voting rights must also take steps to obtain its voting rights. In each case, the question is whether those steps are so significant that they prevent the investor from having the current ability to direct the relevant activities of the investee (see IFRS 10:BC120 and BC121).

This principle is illustrated in the following examples.

Example 6.4.4.5

Rights can only be exercised at the next shareholders' meeting

[IFRS 10:Appendix B Examples 3 to 3D]

Example 3

The investee has annual shareholder meetings at which decisions to direct the relevant activities are made. The next scheduled shareholders' meeting is in eight months. However, shareholders that individually or collectively hold at least 5 per cent of the voting rights can call a special meeting to change the existing policies over the relevant activities, but a requirement to give notice to the other shareholders means that such a meeting cannot be held for at least 30 days. Policies over the relevant activities can be changed only at special or scheduled shareholders' meetings. This includes the approval of material sales of assets as well as the making or disposing of significant investments.

The above fact pattern applies to examples 3A–3D described below. Each example is considered in isolation.

Example 3A

An investor holds a majority of the voting rights in the investee. The investor's voting rights are substantive because the investor is able to make decisions about the direction of the relevant activities when they need to be made. The fact that it takes 30 days before the investor can exercise its voting rights does not stop the investor from having the current ability to direct the relevant activities from the moment the investor acquires the shareholding.

Example 3B

An investor is party to a forward contract to acquire the majority of shares in the investee. The forward contract's settlement date is in 25 days. The existing shareholders are unable to change the existing policies over the relevant activities because a special meeting cannot be held for at least 30 days, at which point the forward contract will have been settled. Thus, the investor has rights that are essentially equivalent to the majority shareholder in example 3A above (ie the investor holding the forward contract can make decisions about the direction of the relevant activities when they need to be made).

The investor's forward contract is a substantive right that gives the investor the current ability to direct the relevant activities even before the forward contract is settled.

Example 3C

An investor holds a substantive option to acquire the majority of shares in the investee that is exercisable in 25 days and is deeply in the money. The same conclusion would be reached as in example 3B.

Example 3D

An investor is party to a forward contract to acquire the majority of shares in the investee, with no other related rights over the investee. The forward contract's settlement date is in six months. In contrast to the examples above, the investor does not have the current ability to direct the relevant activities. The existing shareholders have the current ability to direct the relevant activities because they can change the existing policies over the relevant activities before the forward contract is settled.

Substantive rights exercisable by other parties can prevent an investor from controlling the investee to which those rights relate. Such substantive rights do not require the holders to have the ability to initiate decisions. As long as the rights are not merely protective (see **6.4.5**), substantive rights held by other parties may prevent the investor from controlling the investee even if the rights give the holders only the current ability to approve or block decisions that relate to the relevant activities. [IFRS 10:B25]

6.4.5 Protective rights

6.4.5.1 Determining whether rights are protective

In evaluating whether rights give an investor power over an investee, an investor is required to assess whether its rights, and rights held by others, are protective rights. [IFRS 10:B26]

Protective rights are defined as "[r]ights designed to protect the interest of the party holding those rights without giving that party power over the entity to which those rights relate". [IFRS 10:Appendix A] Given the nature of protective rights, an investor that has only protective rights cannot have power or prevent another party from having power over an investee. [IFRS 10:14 & B27]

IFRS 10 states that protective rights relate to fundamental changes to the activities of an investee or apply in exceptional circumstances. However, not all rights that apply in exceptional circumstances or are contingent on events are protective. [IFRS 10:B26]

Examples of protective rights include, but are not limited to:

[IFRS 10:B28]

- a lender's right to restrict a borrower from undertaking activities that could significantly change the credit risk of the borrower to the detriment of the lender;

- the right of a party holding a non-controlling interest in an investee to approve capital expenditure greater than that required in the ordinary course of business, or to approve the issue of equity or debt instruments; and

- the right of a lender to seize the assets of a borrower if the borrower fails to meet specified loan repayment conditions.

Sometimes structured entities are created to hold a single asset. The purchase of the asset is financed by a loan for which the asset serves as collateral. In the event of a default on the loan, the lender has the right to seize the asset but does not have recourse to any other assets of the structured entity or to the assets of any other party. When the entity is established, it will contain only the asset and the loan secured against it.

The fact that the structured entity holds a single asset does not change the assessment as to whether the lender's right to seize the asset is a protective right. In isolation, the number of assets held by a structured entity is not a relevant factor in assessing whether a right is protective. If a right is protective in nature, it should be treated as such regardless of whether the right relates to one of many assets held by an entity or whether it relates to the only asset held. The purpose of the lender's rights should be assessed to determine whether they are intended to give the lender power over the entity or only to protect the lender's interests under the loan agreement.

See **9.2** for guidance on reassessing a lender's rights on default or breach of a loan covenant.

Example 6.4.5.1

Supplementary rights prevent a shareholder with majority voting rights from having control

Entity A, Entity B and Entity C own 60 per cent, 20 per cent and 20 per cent, respectively, of the ordinary shares of Entity D. Except when a supplementary right is exercised, decisions on the relevant activities of Entity D are made based on majority votes at shareholders' meetings.

However, the shareholders of Entity D have entered into an agreement whereby Entity B and Entity C have a supplementary right at shareholders' meetings if either disagrees with proposals regarding relevant activities made by Entity A. If Entity B or Entity C exercises its supplementary rights, proposals can only be approved by shareholders holding at least 75 per cent of the voting rights.

In the circumstances described, the supplementary rights held by Entity B and Entity C are not merely protective rights; the supplementary rights not only protect the interests of Entity B and Entity C but also give them the ability to prevent another party (i.e. Entity A) from making unilateral decisions over the relevant activities of Entity D. Taking into account the supplementary rights held by Entity B and Entity C, Entity A does not have control of Entity D.

Note that Entity D does not meet the definition of a joint arrangement, because neither Entity B nor Entity C is able to prevent decisions being made by withholding consent (see **section 4** in **chapter A27**).

6.4.5.2 Assessment of protective rights – franchises

In the context of protective rights, IFRS 10 considers the specific circumstances of a franchise agreement for which the investee is the franchisee. Such a franchise agreement often gives the franchisor rights that are designed to protect the franchise brand. Franchise agreements typically give franchisors some decision-making rights with respect to the operations of the franchisee. [IFRS 10:B29] The following considerations are relevant:

[IFRS 10:B30 - B33]

- generally, franchisors' rights do not restrict the ability of parties other than the franchisor to make decisions that have a significant effect on the franchisee's returns;

- the rights of the franchisor in franchise agreements do not necessarily give the franchisor the current ability to direct the activities that significantly affect the franchisee's returns;

- it is necessary to distinguish between having the current ability to make decisions that significantly affect the franchisee's returns and having the ability to make decisions that protect the franchise brand. The franchisor does not have power over the franchisee if other parties have existing rights that give them the current ability to direct the relevant activities of the franchisee;

- by entering into the franchise agreement, the franchisee has made a unilateral decision to operate its business in accordance with the terms of the franchise agreement, but for its own account; and

- control over such fundamental decisions as the legal form of the franchisee and its funding structure may be determined by parties other than the franchisor and may significantly affect the returns of the franchisee. The lower the level of financial support provided by the franchisor and the lower the franchisor's exposure to variability of returns from the franchisee, the more likely it is that the franchisor has only protective rights.

6.4.6 Relevant activities are directed through voting rights

6.4.6.1 Relevant activities directed through voting rights – general

Frequently, it will be voting or similar rights that give an investor power, either individually or in combination with other arrangements. For example, this will generally be the case when an investee has a range of operating and financing activities that significantly affect the investee's returns and when substantive decision-making with respect to these activities is required continuously. [IFRS 10:B16]

Sections **6.4.6.2** to **6.4.6.4** describe the requirements that should be considered if the relevant activities of an investee are directed through voting rights.

6.4.6.2   Power with a majority of voting rights

An investor that holds a majority of the voting rights of an investee has power in the following situations (subject to the exceptions described in **6.4.6.3**):

[IFRS 10:B35]

- the relevant activities of the investee are directed by a vote of the holder of the majority of the voting rights (see **example 6.4.6.2A**); or

- a majority of the members of the governing body that directs the relevant activities of the investee are appointed by a vote of the holder of the majority of the voting rights (see **example 6.4.6.2B**).

Example 6.4.6.2A

Relevant activities of an investee are directed by a shareholder with a majority of the voting rights in the investee

Entity A and Entity B own 60 per cent and 40 per cent, respectively, of the ordinary shares of Entity C.

The relevant activities of Entity C are directed based on majority votes at shareholders' meetings. Each ordinary share carries one vote at shareholders' meetings.

In the absence of other factors (e.g. a shareholders' agreement between Entity A and Entity B that provides otherwise), the relevant activities of Entity C are directed by the party that has the majority of the voting rights in Entity C.

Therefore, in the absence of other relevant factors, Entity A has power over Entity C because it is the holder of the majority of the voting rights in Entity C.

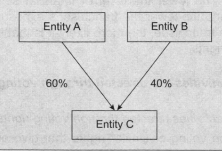

Example 6.4.6.2B

Relevant activities of an investee are directed by a governing body and the majority of the members of the governing body are appointed by a shareholder with a majority of the voting rights in the investee

Entity A and Entity B own 60 per cent and 40 per cent, respectively, of the ordinary shares of Entity C.

The relevant activities of Entity C are directed based on majority votes at meetings of the board of directors.

Entity A and Entity B are entitled to appoint six and four directors, respectively, in proportion to their ownership interests in Entity C.

Therefore, in the absence of other relevant factors, Entity A has power over Entity C because it has the right to appoint the majority of members of the board of directors that direct the relevant activities of Entity C.

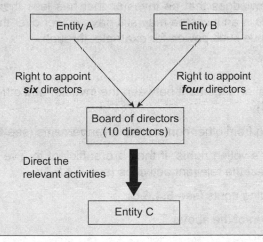

6.4.6.3 Majority of the voting rights but no power

An investor that holds more than half of the voting rights of an investee will only have power over the investee through those voting rights if they are substantive and provide the investor with the current ability to direct the relevant activities, which often will be through determining operating and financing policies. [IFRS 10:B36]

Sometimes, although an investor holds a majority of the voting rights in an investee, it does not have power over the investee. This will arise when the investor's majority voting rights are not substantive. IFRS 10 cites two such situations.

- When another entity has existing rights that provide it with the right to direct the relevant activities of the investee and that entity is not an agent of the investor, the investor does not have power over the investee. [IFRS 10:B36]

- When the relevant activities of the investee are subject to direction by a government, court, administrator, receiver, liquidator or regulator. In such circumstances, the holder of the majority voting rights cannot have power. [IFRS 10:B37]

As noted at **12.1**, it should not be assumed that the appointment of an administrator, receiver or liquidator necessarily prevents a holder of the majority of voting rights from having power. Rather, it is necessary to consider the powers held by the administrator, receiver or liquidator, and whether they are sufficient to prevent the investor from directing the relevant activities of the investee. Although this will often be the case, a liquidation, receivership or administration order may not result in loss of control by a holder of the majority of voting rights.

6.4.6.4 *Power achieved with less than a majority of the voting rights*

IFRS 10 acknowledges that an investor that has less than a majority of the voting rights in an investee may still have power over the investee. An investor may have such power, for example, through:

[IFRS 10:B38]

- a contractual arrangement between the investor and other vote holders (see **6.4.6.5**);

- rights arising from other contractual arrangements (see **6.4.6.6**);

- the investor's voting rights, if they are sufficient to give it the practical ability to direct the relevant activities (see **6.4.6.7**);

- potential voting rights (see **6.4.6.8**); or

- a combination of the above.

6.4.6.5 *Contractual arrangement with other vote holders*

A contractual arrangement entered into between an investor and other vote holders can give the investor the right to exercise voting rights sufficient to give the investor power, even if the investor itself does not have voting rights sufficient to give it power without the contractual arrangement. A contractual arrangement might ensure that the investor can direct enough other vote holders on how to vote to enable the investor to make decisions about the relevant activities. [IFRS 10:B39]

Example 6.4.6.5A

Contractual arrangements with other vote holders (1)

Entity E has four shareholders – Entity A, Entity B, Entity C and Entity D.

Entity A owns 40 per cent of the ordinary shares of Entity E while each of the other shareholders owns 20 per cent.

The relevant activities of Entity E are directed by its board of directors comprised of six directors: three appointed by Entity A, and one each appointed by Entity B, Entity C and Entity D.

Separately, Entities A and B have entered into a contractual arrangement that requires the director appointed by Entity B to vote in the same way as the directors appointed by Entity A.

Absent other factors, the fact that the contractual arrangement effectively gives Entity A a majority of votes at board meetings in relation to the relevant activities provides Entity A with power over Entity E, even though Entity A does not hold a majority of the voting rights in Entity E.

Example 6.4.6.5B

Contractual arrangements with other vote holders (2)

Entity E has four shareholders – Entity A, Entity B, Entity C and Entity D.

Entity A owns 40 per cent of the ordinary shares of Entity E while each of the other shareholders owns 20 per cent.

The relevant activities of Entity E are directed by its board of directors comprised of six directors: three appointed by Entity A, and one each appointed by Entity B, Entity C and Entity D.

In order to avoid deadlock in board deliberations, the shareholders have entered into an agreement to the effect that one of the directors appointed by Entity A acts as the chairman of the board and has an additional casting vote at board meetings.

The shareholders' agreement effectively gives Entity A a majority of votes at board meetings in relation to the relevant activities. Absent other factors, this provides Entity A with power over Entity E, even though Entity A does not hold a majority of the voting rights in Entity E.

6.4.6.6 *Rights from other contractual arrangements*

Other decision-making rights, in combination with voting rights, can give an investor the current ability to direct the relevant activities. For example, the rights specified in a contractual arrangement in combination with voting rights may be sufficient to give an investor the current ability to direct the manufacturing processes of an investee or to direct other operating or financing activities of an investee that significantly affect the investee's returns. [IFRS 10:B40]

IFRS 10 notes that, in the absence of any other rights, the fact that the investee is economically dependent on the investor (e.g. if the investor is the investee's key supplier) does not lead to the investor having power over the investee. [IFRS 10:B40]

6.4.6.7 The practical ability to direct the relevant activities by virtue of the voting rights held ('de facto power')

Even when an investor with less than a majority of voting rights has not entered into additional contractual arrangements (see **6.4.6.5** and **6.4.6.6**), it may still have power over the investee if its voting rights give it "the practical ability to direct the relevant activities unilaterally". [IFRS 10:B41]

> The circumstances addressed in IFRS 10:B41 involve what is commonly referred to as 'de facto control'.

IFRS 10 includes specific guidance on how to determine whether an investor that does not hold a majority of voting rights has de facto power over an investee. In making this determination, the investor is required to consider all facts and circumstances. A two-step approach is adopted.

Step 1

Step 1 requires the investor to focus on three specific factors.

[IFRS 10:B42(a) - (c)]

(a) the size of the investor's holding of voting rights relative to the size and dispersion of holdings of the other vote holders (see below);

(b) potential voting rights held by the investor, other vote holders or other parties (see **6.4.6.8**); and

(c) rights arising from other contractual arrangements (see **6.4.6.6**).

> IFRS 10 does not include any 'bright lines' regarding how to determine whether the absolute and/or relative size of the investor's holding is sufficient to meet the power criterion, or how to determine whether the holdings of other parties are widely dispersed.

When considering the size of the investor's holding relative to the size and dispersion of holdings of the other vote holders, IFRS 10 observes that the likelihood of the investor having the current ability to direct the relevant activities of the investee increases with:

[IFRS 10:B42(a)]

- the number of voting rights an investor holds (i.e. the absolute size of the holding);

- the proportion of voting rights an investor holds relative to other vote holders (i.e. the relative size of the holding); and

- the number of parties that would need to act together to outvote the investor (i.e. the extent of dispersion of other holdings).

The fewer voting rights held by the investor, and the fewer parties that would need to act together to outvote the investor, the more reliance would be placed on additional facts and circumstances to assess whether the investor's rights are sufficient to give it power (see Step 2 below). [IFRS 10:B45]

Ultimately, it is necessary to exercise careful judgement taking into account all facts and circumstances. In performing the analysis, the following factors should be considered (the list is not exhaustive):

*   the nature of decisions that must be referred to a shareholder vote;

*   whether there is any indication that some voters are related parties;

*   whether there are any arrangements (contractual or otherwise) between voters to make decisions collectively. Mechanisms that allow other vote holders to exchange their views should also be considered; and

*   the legal framework, including any practices and restrictions that affect shareholder behaviour (which will often vary between jurisdictions).

The factors listed in IFRS 10:B42(a) to (c) should be considered first to determine whether these factors alone are sufficient to determine conclusively that either (1) the investor has power over the investee, or (2) the investor does not have power over the investee. [IFRS 10:B43 & B44] When the direction of relevant activities is determined by majority vote and an investor holds significantly more voting rights than any other vote holder or organised group of vote holders, and the other shareholdings are widely dispersed, it may be clear, after considering the factors listed in IFRS 10:B42(a) to (c) alone, that the investor has power over the investee. [IFRS 10:B43]

If the analysis in Step 1 is inconclusive, the investor should move on to Step 2.

Step 2

If, having considered the factors listed in IFRS 10:B42(a) to (c), the investor is unable to conclude as to whether it has power over the investee, it considers any additional facts and circumstances that indicate the investor has, or does not have, the current ability to direct the relevant activities at the time that decisions need to be made, such as whether other shareholders are passive in nature as demonstrated by voting patterns at previous shareholders' meetings. This further analysis should include a review of the factors and indicators set out in IFRS 10:B18 to B20 (i.e. evidence to be considered when it is difficult to determine whether the investor's rights are sufficient to give it power – see **6.4.3**). [IFRS 10:B42(d) & B45]

When the facts and circumstances in IFRS 10:B18 to B20 are considered together with the investor's rights, greater weight should be given to the evidence of power in IFRS 10:B18 than to the indicators of power in IFRS 10:B19 and B20. [IFRS 10:B45]

If, having considered these additional facts and circumstances, it is still not clear whether the investor has power over the investee, the investor does not control the investee. [IFRS 10:B46]

Appendix B to IFRS 10 sets out five examples illustrating the assessment for *de facto* power over an investee.

Example 6.4.6.7A

Assessment of *de facto* power – only Step 1 required (1)

[IFRS 10:Appendix B Example 4]

An investor acquires 48 per cent of the voting rights of an investee. The remaining voting rights are held by thousands of shareholders, none individually holding more than 1 per cent of the voting rights. None of the shareholders has any arrangements to consult any of the others or make collective decisions. When assessing the proportion of voting rights to acquire, on the basis of the relative size of the other shareholdings, the investor determined that a 48 per cent interest would be sufficient to give it control. In this case, on the basis of the absolute size of its holding and the relative size of the other shareholdings, the investor concludes that it has a sufficiently dominant voting interest to meet the power criterion without the need to consider any other evidence of power.

Example 6.4.6.7B

Assessment of *de facto* power – only Step 1 required (2)

[IFRS 10:Appendix B Example 5]

Investor A holds 40 per cent of the voting rights of an investee and twelve other investors each hold 5 per cent of the voting rights of the investee. A shareholder agreement grants investor A the right to appoint, remove and set the remuneration of management responsible for directing the relevant activities. To change the agreement, a two-thirds majority vote of the shareholders is required. In this case, investor A concludes that the absolute size of the investor's holding and the relative size of the other shareholdings alone are not conclusive in determining whether the investor has rights sufficient to give it power. However, investor A determines that its contractual right to appoint, remove and set the remuneration of management is sufficient to conclude that it has power over the investee. The fact that investor A might not have exercised this right or the likelihood of investor A exercising its right to select, appoint or remove management shall not be considered when assessing whether investor A has power.

Example 6.4.6.7C

Assessment of *de facto* power – only Step 1 required (3)

[IFRS 10:Appendix B Example 6]

Investor A holds 45 per cent of the voting rights of an investee. Two other investors each hold 26 per cent of the voting rights of the investee. The remaining voting rights are held by three other shareholders, each holding 1 per cent. There are no other arrangements that affect decision-making. In this case, the size of investor A's voting interest and its size relative to the other shareholdings are sufficient to conclude that investor A does not have power. Only two other investors would need to co-operate to be able to prevent investor A from directing the relevant activities of the investee.

Example 6.4.6.7D

Assessment of *de facto* power – Steps 1 and 2 required (1)

[IFRS 10:Appendix B Example 7]

An investor holds 45 per cent of the voting rights of an investee. Eleven other shareholders each hold 5 per cent of the voting rights of the investee. None of the shareholders has contractual arrangements to consult any of the others or make collective decisions. In this case, the absolute size of the investor's holding and the relative size of the other shareholdings alone are not conclusive in determining whether the investor has rights sufficient to give it power over the investee. Additional facts and circumstances that may provide evidence that the investor has, or does not have, power shall be considered.

Example 6.4.6.7E

Assessment of *de facto* power – Steps 1 and 2 required (2)

[IFRS 10:Appendix B Example 8]

An investor holds 35 per cent of the voting rights of an investee. Three other shareholders each hold 5 per cent of the voting rights of the investee. The remaining voting rights are held by numerous other shareholders, none individually holding more than 1 per cent of the voting rights. None of the shareholders has arrangements to consult any of the others or make collective decisions. Decisions about the relevant activities of the investee require the approval of a majority of votes cast at relevant shareholders' meetings – 75 per cent of the voting rights of the investee have been cast at recent relevant shareholders' meetings. In this case, the active participation of the other shareholders at recent shareholders' meetings indicates that the investor would not have the practical ability to direct the relevant activities unilaterally, regardless of whether the investor has directed the relevant activities because a sufficient number of other shareholders voted in the same way as the investor.

6.4.6.8   Potential voting rights

Potential voting rights are rights to obtain voting rights of an investee, such as those arising from convertible instruments or options, including forward contracts. [IFRS 10:B47]

In order to determine whether it has power over an investee, an investor should consider potential voting rights that it holds and potential voting rights held by other parties; however, the investor should only consider voting rights if they are substantive. [IFRS 10:B47] IFRS 10's guidance regarding the identification of rights that are substantive, which applies equally to potential voting rights, is discussed in detail at **6.4.4**.

> As discussed in detail in **6.4.4**, the following factors should be considered in assessing whether rights are substantive (the list is not exhaustive):
>
> - whether there are any barriers (economic or otherwise) that prevent the holder (or holders) from exercising the rights (see **6.4.4.2**);
>
> - when the exercise of rights requires the agreement of more than one party, or when the rights are held by more than one party, whether a mechanism is in place that provides those parties with the practical ability to exercise their rights collectively if they choose to do so (see **6.4.4.3**);
>
> - whether the party or parties that hold the rights would benefit from the exercise of those rights (see **6.4.4.4**); and
>
> - whether the right is exercisable when decisions about the direction of the relevant activities need to be made (see **6.4.4.5**).
>
> If it is determined that the potential voting rights held by an investor are substantive, and that the investor controls the investee, the next step will be to determine the appropriate allocation of profit or loss and changes in equity (see **10.4**).

When considering potential voting rights, the investor should consider the purpose and design of the instrument, as well as the purpose and design of any other involvement the investor has with the investee. This includes an assessment of the various terms and conditions of the instrument as well as the investor's apparent expectations, motives and reasons for agreeing to those terms and conditions. [IFRS 10:B48]

If the investor also has voting or other decision-making rights relating to the investee's activities, the investor should assess whether those rights, in combination with potential voting rights, give the investor power. [IFRS 10:B49]

Substantive potential voting rights alone, or in combination with other rights, can give an investor the current ability to direct the relevant activities. For example, this is likely to be the case when an investor holds 40 per cent of the voting rights of an investee and, in accordance with IFRS 10:B23 (see **6.4.4.1**), holds substantive rights arising from options to acquire a further 20 per cent of the voting rights. [IFRS 10:B50]

The following examples are provided in Appendix B to IFRS 10.

Example 6.4.6.8A

One investor holds the majority of the voting rights while another investor has minority voting rights and an option to acquire further voting rights

[IFRS 10:Appendix B Example 9]

Investor A holds 70 per cent of the voting rights of an investee. Investor B has 30 per cent of the voting rights of the investee as well as an option to acquire half of investor A's voting rights. The option is exercisable for the next two years at a fixed price that is deeply out of the money (and is expected to remain so for that two-year period). Investor A has been exercising its votes and is actively directing the relevant activities of the investee. In such a case, investor A is likely to meet the power criterion because it appears to have the current ability to direct the relevant activities. Although investor B has currently exercisable options to purchase additional voting rights (that, if exercised, would give it a majority of the voting rights in the investee), the terms and conditions associated with those options are such that the options are not considered substantive.

Example 6.4.6.8B

Investors have equal voting rights in an investee but one investor has substantive potential voting rights in addition to the existing voting rights

[IFRS 10:Appendix B Example 10]

Investor A and two other investors each hold a third of the voting rights of an investee. The investee's business activity is closely related to investor A. In addition to its equity instruments, investor A also holds debt instruments that are convertible into ordinary shares of the investee at any time for a fixed price that is out of the money (but not deeply out of the money). If the debt were converted, investor A would hold 60 per cent of the voting rights of the investee. Investor A would benefit from realising synergies if the debt instruments were converted into ordinary shares. Investor A has power over the investee because it holds voting rights of the investee together with substantive potential voting rights that give it the current ability to direct the relevant activities.

6.4.7 Power when voting rights do not have a significant effect on the investee's returns

In contrast to the scenarios discussed in **6.4.6**, in some circumstances voting rights cannot have a significant effect on an investee's returns (e.g. when contractual arrangements determine the direction of the relevant activities and voting rights relate to administrative tasks only). [IFRS 10:B17]

This situation will most commonly arise when a structured entity is created with legal arrangements that impose strict limits on the decision-making powers of its governing body in relation to the relevant activities.

IFRS 10 emphasises that, in complex situations, it is necessary to consider the purpose and design of the investee so as to identify the relevant activities of the investee, the rights of each investor and whether any of the investors has the ability to control the investee. [IFRS 10:B7 & B3]

In such circumstances, the investor needs to assess the contractual arrangements in order to determine whether it has rights sufficient to give it power over the investee. To make this assessment, the investor will need to consider:

[IFRS 10:B17]

- the purpose and design of the investee (see below);
- additional factors specifically required by IFRS 10:B51 to B54 to be considered when voting or similar rights do not have a significant effect on the investee's returns (see below); and
- additional factors specifically required by IFRS 10:B18 to B20 to be considered when it is difficult to determine whether an investor's rights are sufficient to give it power over an investee (see **6.4.3**).

When an investee has been designed so that voting rights are not the dominant factor in determining who controls it, an investor should also focus on the following matters when considering the purpose and design of the investee:

[IFRS 10:B8]

- the risks to which the investee was designed to be exposed;
- the risks it was designed to pass on to the parties involved with the investee; and
- whether the investor is exposed to some or all of those risks.

In such circumstances, consideration of the risks includes not only the downside risk, but also the potential for upside. [IFRS 10:B8]

All risks of an investee do not necessarily have associated relevant activities. Even though a particular risk may be present and may affect the parties involved, the entity may not have been designed to undertake activities that manage that risk. As a result, there may not be a relevant activity in relation to that risk (e.g. the entity's founding documents may preclude any activities to manage the risk exposure).

When a risk does not have an associated relevant activity, an investor will not be able to affect the variability in its returns resulting from that risk. Therefore, the assessment of the first and third elements of control specified by IFRS 10:7 (i.e. the power of an investor over the investee, and the ability of the investor to use that power to affect the amount of the investor's returns – see **section 5**) would focus on other risks present for which there are associated relevant activities.

This possibility is illustrated in **example 6.4.7A**.

However, even when there is no relevant activity in relation to a risk, the variability resulting from that risk would be included in the analysis of whether a decision maker is acting as a principal or as an agent as required by IFRS 10:B60 (see also **8.2.5**). As indicated in IFRS 10:B72 (see **8.2.4**), the greater the magnitude of, and the variability associated with, a decision maker's aggregate economic interests, the more likely it is a principal.

Example 6.4.7A

Risks with no associated relevant activities

An entity is set up to purchase CU100 million of 30-year fixed rate residential mortgages from a financial institution. The entity is financed with CU100 million of 30-year fixed-rate senior and subordinated debt securities.

Each month the holders of the debt securities receive interest payments as interest is received on the mortgages, and any principal payments received by the entity are used to redeem a pro-rata portion of the beneficial interests based on their subordination. The entity's founding documents prohibit the entity from selling the mortgages, purchasing any further investments, or engaging in any derivative transactions.

The entity thus exposes its investors to the following risks.

- Credit risk – the risk that mortgages may default.
- Prepayment risk – the risk that mortgages will be prepaid, resulting in lower subsequent interest receipts.
- Interest rate risk – the risk that the fair value of the fixed-rate mortgages will fluctuate as market interest rates change.

Due to the restrictions placed on the entity by its founding documents, the possible activities to manage prepayment risk (e.g. the purchase of additional collateral) or interest rate risk (e.g. entering into a fixed-to-variable interest rate swap) are not available and, therefore, there are no relevant activities relating to these risks.

The analysis of whether an investor has the ability to use its power over the entity to affect the amount of its returns would, in this case, focus on credit risk. Accordingly, the investors would need to identify the activities that relate to the credit risk and who has the ability to make decisions related to these activities.

However, variability from prepayment risk and interest rate risk would be included in the analysis of whether the decision maker identified is acting as a principal or as an agent (i.e. in evaluating the magnitude of, and the variability associated with, a decision maker's aggregate economic interests in the entity – see **8.2**).

In assessing the purpose and design of an investee, the investor should consider the involvement and decisions made at the investee's inception as part of its design and evaluate whether the transaction terms and features of the involvement provide the investor with rights that are sufficient to give it power. IFRS 10 states explicitly that being involved in the design of an investee alone is not sufficient to give an investor control. However, involvement in the design may indicate that the investor has the opportunity to obtain rights that are sufficient to give it power over the investee. [IFRS 10:B51]

In the IASB's view, being involved in the design of an investee does not necessarily mean that an investor has decision-making rights to direct the relevant activities. This is because, often, several parties are involved in the design of an investee and the final structure of the investee includes whatever is agreed by all those parties (including investors, the sponsor of the investee, the transferor(s) of the assets held by the investee and other parties involved in the transaction). In addition, the benefits from being involved in setting up an investee could cease as soon as the investee is established. Therefore, the Board concluded that, in isolation, being involved in setting up an investee would not be an appropriate basis for consolidation (see IFRS 10:BC77 and BC78).

The investor should also consider contractual arrangements such as call rights, put rights and liquidation rights established at the investee's inception. When these contractual arrangements involve activities that are closely related to the investee, then these activities are, in substance, an integral part of the investee's overall activities, even though they may occur outside the legal boundaries of the investee. Therefore, explicit or implicit decision-making rights embedded in contractual arrangements that are closely related to the investee need to be considered as relevant activities when determining who has power over the investee. [IFRS 10:B52]

For some investees, relevant activities occur only when particular circumstances arise or events occur. The investee may be designed so that the direction of its activities and its returns are predetermined unless and until those particular circumstances arise or events occur. In this case, only the decisions about the investee's activities when those circumstances or events occur can significantly affect its returns and thus be relevant activities. The circumstances or events need not have occurred for an investor with the ability to make those decisions to have power. The fact that the right to make decisions is contingent on circumstances arising or an event occurring does not, in itself, make those rights protective. [IFRS 10:B53]

Moreover, an investor may have an explicit or implicit commitment to ensure that an investee continues to operate as designed. Such a commitment may increase the investor's exposure to the variability of returns and thus increase the incentive for the investor to obtain rights sufficient to give it power. Therefore, a commitment to ensure that an investee operates as designed may be an indicator that the investor has power, but does not, by itself, give an investor power; nor does it prevent another party from having power. [IFRS 10:B54]

Two examples set out in Appendix B to IFRS 10 illustrate how to apply the above requirements.

Example 6.4.7B

Activities of an investee are predetermined until a particular event occurs

[IFRS 10:Appendix B Example 11]

An investee's only business activity, as specified in its founding documents, is to purchase receivables and service them on a day-to-day basis for its investors. The servicing on a day-to-day basis includes the collection and passing on of principal and interest payments as they fall due. Upon default of a receivable the investee automatically puts the receivable to an investor as agreed separately in a put agreement between the investor and the investee. The only relevant activity is managing the receivables upon default because it is the only activity that can significantly affect the investee's returns. Managing the receivables before default is not a relevant activity because it does not require substantive decisions to be made that could significantly affect the investee's returns – the activities before default are predetermined and amount only to collecting cash flows as they fall due and passing them on to investors. Therefore, only the investor's right to manage the assets upon default should be considered when assessing the overall activities of the investee that significantly affect the investee's returns. In this example, the design of the investee ensures that the investor has decision-making authority over the activities that significantly affect the returns at the only time that such decision-making authority is required. The terms of the put agreement are integral to the overall transaction and the establishment of the investee. Therefore, the terms of the put agreement together with the founding documents of the investee lead to the conclusion that the investor has power over the investee even though the investor takes ownership of the receivables only upon default and manages the defaulted receivables outside the legal boundaries of the investee.

> **Example 6.4.7C**
>
> **Only assets of investee are receivables**
>
> [IFRS 10:Appendix B Example 12]
>
> The only assets of an investee are receivables. When the purpose and design of the investee are considered, it is determined that the only relevant activity is managing the receivables upon default. The party that has the ability to manage the defaulting receivables has power over the investee, irrespective of whether any of the borrowers have defaulted.

7   Exposure, or rights, to variable returns from an investee

7.1   Exposure, or rights, to variable returns – general

The second element of control is that an investor is exposed, or has rights, to variable returns from its involvement with the investee. This is the case when the investor's returns from its involvement have the potential to vary as a result of the investee's performance. The investor's returns can be only positive, only negative, or both positive and negative. [IFRS 10:15]

In particular, therefore, an investor with only downside risk, or only upside risk, is still exposed to variable returns.

The IASB has confirmed its intention that the term 'returns' should be interpreted broadly and that it encompasses synergistic returns as well as more direct returns. In practice, an investor can benefit from controlling an investee in a variety of ways. The Board concluded that to narrow the definition of returns would artificially restrict those ways of benefiting (see IFRS 10:BC63).

Only one investor can control an investee, but more than one party can share in the returns of an investee (e.g. holders of non-controlling interests can share in the profits or distributions of an investee). [IFRS 10:16]

Examples of returns include:

[IFRS 10:B57]

- dividends, other distributions of economic benefits from an investee (e.g. interest from debt securities issued by the investee), and changes in the value of the investor's investment in that investee;

- remuneration for servicing an investee's assets or liabilities, fees and exposure to loss from providing credit or liquidity support, residual interests in the investee's assets and liabilities on liquidation of that investee, tax benefits, and access to future liquidity that an investor has from its involvement with an investee; and

- returns that are not available to other interest holders. For example, an investor might use its assets in combination with the assets of the investee, such as combining operating functions to achieve economies of scale, cost savings, sourcing scarce products, gaining access to proprietary knowledge or limiting some operations or assets, to enhance the value of the investor's other assets.

If an investor is exposed to variable returns by holding equity instruments, those returns may take the form of changes in value of the equity instruments as well as dividends. Often the unilateral ability to set dividend policy is a key factor in demonstrating control, but there may be circumstances in which control exists even though the investor does not have the ability to set dividend policy.

Variable returns are returns that are not fixed and have the potential to vary as a result of the performance of an investee. In assessing whether returns from an investee are variable and how variable those returns are, IFRS 10 requires an investor to consider the substance of the arrangement, regardless of the legal form of the returns. [IFRS 10:B56]

IFRS 10 provides the following examples of variable returns.

[IFRS 10:B56]

- An investor holds a bond with fixed interest payments. The fixed interest payments are variable returns for the purposes of IFRS 10 because they are subject to default risk and they expose the investor to the credit risk of the issuer of the bond. The amount of variability (i.e. how variable those returns are) will depend on the credit risk of the bond.

- An investor receives fixed performance fees in return for managing assets of the investee. The fixed performance fees are variable returns because they expose the investor to the performance risk of the investee. The amount of variability will depend on the investee's ability to generate sufficient income to pay the fee.

These examples illustrate the need to focus on the substance of an arrangement, regardless of the legal form of the returns. In the examples, the legal form is that of a fixed return, but the substance of the return is that it is variable because it will be affected by the ability of the investee to pay.

7.2 Determining whether a derivative instrument exposes its holder to variable returns

IFRS 10:BC66 provides the following example.

> "For example, assume an entity (entity A) is established to provide investment opportunities for investors who wish to have exposure to entity Z's credit risk (entity Z is unrelated to any other party involved in the arrangement). Entity A obtains funding by issuing to those investors notes that are linked to entity Z's credit risk (credit-linked notes) and uses the proceeds to invest in a portfolio of risk-free financial assets. Entity A obtains exposure to entity Z's credit risk by entering into a credit default swap (CDS) with a swap counterparty. The CDS passes entity Z's credit risk to entity A, in return for a fee paid by the swap counterparty. The investors in entity A receive a higher return that reflects both entity A's return from its asset portfolio and the CDS fee."

The paragraph concludes that "[t]he swap counterparty does not have involvement with entity A that exposes it to variability of returns from the performance of entity A because the CDS transfers variability to entity A, rather than absorbing variability of returns of entity A".

However, no further explanation is provided regarding the factors to be considered in determining whether an entity is exposed to variable returns as a result of derivative instruments.

When returns from derivative instruments are not affected by the investee's performance, such derivatives do not expose the counterparty to variable returns from the investee. This is consistent with the circumstances described in IFRS10:BC66 (see above) when the conclusion is that the counterparty does not have an interest that exposes it to variability of returns because the returns earned by the counterparty of the CDS are affected primarily by changes in Entity Z's credit risk, rather than changes in Entity A's performance.

In more complicated cases, the determination as to whether a derivative instrument exposes its holder to variable returns of an investee may require a more detailed assessment of all relevant facts, to determine if the holder's return from its involvement has the potential to vary as a result of the investee's performance. To perform this evaluation, an analysis of the purpose and design of the investee is often useful, including:

- how the investee is designed to absorb and transfer various types of risks (such as credit risk, interest rate risk, foreign currency exchange risk, commodity price risk, equity price risk, operational risk etc.); and

- why the investee was created, for example:

  - which parties initiated and participated significantly in setting up the investee;

- the motivation for such parties to be involved in the design of the investee;

- the variability that the entity is designed to create and pass along to its interest holders (i.e. the purpose of the entity); and

- how the investee's interests were negotiated with or marketed to potential investors.

In order to understand whether an investor is exposed to variable returns from its involvement with the entity, it is important to establish a full understanding of the relationship with the investee, including but not limited to, the terms of the derivative contract(s) entered into and the nature of the investee's interests issued.

8 Link between power and returns

8.1 Link between power and returns – general

The third and final element of control is that, in addition to having power over the investee and being exposed, or having rights, to variable returns from its involvement with the investee, the investor must have the ability to use its power to affect the investor's returns from its involvement with the investee. [IFRS 10:17]

In this context, an investor with decision-making rights is required to determine whether it is acting as a principal or as an agent. An investor that is an agent does not control an investee when it exercises decision-making rights delegated to it. [IFRS 10:18]

IFRS 10:B58 to B72, which are discussed in detail in **8.2**, contain extensive guidance for the assessment as to whether a decision maker is acting as a principal or as an agent.

8.2 Determining whether a decision maker is a principal or an agent

8.2.1 Determining whether a decision maker is a principal or an agent – general

When an entity with decision-making rights (a decision maker) is considering whether it controls an investee, it is required to determine whether it is a principal or an agent. Similarly, an investor is required to determine whether another entity with decision-making rights is acting as an agent for the investor. [IFRS 10:Appendix A & B58]

A decision maker is an agent when it is primarily engaged to act on behalf and for the benefit of another party or parties (the principal(s)). Such a decision maker does not control the investee when it exercises its decision-making powers. [IFRS 10:B58]

A decision maker is not an agent simply because other parties can benefit from the decisions that it makes. [IFRS 10:B58]

Sometimes a principal's power may be held and exercisable by an agent, but on behalf of the principal. [IFRS 10:B58] An investor may delegate its decision-making authority to an agent on some specific issues or on all relevant activities. When assessing whether it controls an investee, the investor should treat the decision-making rights delegated to its agent as held by the investor directly. When there is more than one principal, each of the principals should assess whether it has power over the investee by considering the requirements in IFRS 10:B5 to B54 (see earlier sections of this chapter). [IFRS 10:B59]

IFRS 10 states that, when a single party holds a substantive right to remove the decision maker and can remove the decision maker without cause, this, in isolation, is sufficient to conclude that the decision maker is an agent. [IFRS 10:B65]

> Substantive rights are discussed in **6.4.4**. It is necessary to consider the timing of a removal right when assessing whether it is substantive.

In all other circumstances, in determining whether it is an agent, the decision maker is required to consider the overall relationship between itself, the investee being managed, and other parties involved with the investee. In particular, all of the following factors should be considered:

[IFRS 10:B60]

- the scope of the decision maker's decision-making authority over the investee (see **8.2.2**);

- the rights held by other parties (see **8.2.3**);

- the remuneration to which the decision maker is entitled in accordance with the remuneration agreement(s) (see **8.2.4**); and

- the decision maker's exposure to variability of returns from other interests that it holds in the investee (see **8.2.5**).

All available facts and circumstances should be taken into account in making the assessment. Depending on the specific facts and circumstances, a particular factor may be a stronger indicator of an agency relationship than others and, consequently, would receive a greater weighting than other factors in assessing whether a decision maker is a principal or an agent. [IFRS 10:B60 & B61]

8.2.2   Scope of the decision-making authority

The scope of a decision maker's decision-making authority is evaluated by considering:

[IFRS 10:B62]

- the activities that are permitted according to the decision-making agreement(s) and specified by law; and

- the discretion that the decision maker has when making decisions about those activities.

This assessment requires the decision maker to consider the purpose and design of the investee, the risks to which the investee was designed to be exposed, the risks it was designed to pass on to the parties involved, and the level of involvement the decision maker had in the design of the investee. [IFRS 10:B63]

IFRS 10:B63 notes that when a decision maker is significantly involved in the design of the investee (including the determination of the scope of decision-making authority), this may indicate that the decision maker had the opportunity and incentive to obtain rights that result in the decision maker having the ability to direct the relevant activities. [IFRS 10:B63]

8.2.3   Rights held by other parties

8.2.3.1   Consideration of the rights held by other parties – general

Substantive rights held by other parties may affect the decision maker's ability to direct the relevant activities of an investee. Substantive removal or other rights may indicate that the decision maker is an agent. [IFRS 10:B64]

IFRS 10's guidance on how to determine whether rights are substantive is discussed in **6.4.4**.

IFRS 10 includes the following guidance on how substantive rights should affect the evaluation as to whether a decision maker is a principal or an agent.

- As mentioned at **8.2.2**, if a single party holds substantive removal rights (i.e. rights to deprive the decision maker of its decision-making authority) and can remove the decision maker without cause, this feature, in isolation, is sufficient to conclude that the decision maker is an agent. [IFRS 10:Appendix A & B65]

- If more than one party holds such removal rights (and no individual party can remove the decision maker without the agreement of other parties), those rights are not, in isolation, conclusive in determining that a decision maker acts primarily on behalf and for the benefit of others. The greater the number of parties required to act together to exercise rights to remove a decision maker, and the greater the magnitude of, and variability associated with, the decision maker's other economic interests (i.e. remuneration and other interests), the less the weighting that should be placed on this factor. [IFRS 10:B65]

- As part of the analysis, any rights exercisable by an investee's board of directors (or other governing body) and their effect on the decision-making authority should be considered. When the decision-making authority of a decision maker can be removed by an independent governing body, removal rights exercisable by the governing body may be more likely to be substantive than if the same rights were exercisable individually by a large number of investors. [IFRS 10:B67 & B23(b)]

These requirements focus on how difficult it is for other parties to remove the decision maker. The more difficult it is for a decision maker to be removed by other parties via their removal rights, the less likely it is that the decision maker is an agent.

Substantive rights held by other parties that place restrictions on a decision maker's discretion to make decisions should be considered in a similar manner to removal rights to determine whether the decision maker is an agent. For example, when a decision maker is required to obtain approval from a small number of other parties for its actions, the decision maker is generally an agent. [IFRS 10:B66]

8.2.3.2   Liquidation, withdrawal and redemption rights as substantive removal rights

IFRS 10 defines a removal right as the right to deprive the decision maker of its decision-making authority. IFRS 10:BC140 states that "some other rights (such as some liquidation rights) may have the same effect on the decision maker as removal rights. If those other rights meet the definition of removal rights, they should be treated as such regardless of their label".

Other rights are equivalent to a substantive removal right if they place the entity's investors holding those rights in the same position as if they had the right to remove a decision maker without cause. The assessment of other rights should focus on the consequence of those rights and whether the rights, if exercised, give their holders the practical ability to remove the decision maker from directing the relevant activities of the investee.

The following analysis considers 'liquidation' rights, 'withdrawal' rights and 'redemption' rights. The term 'liquidation' may refer to different processes in different jurisdictions but, for the purpose of this discussion, it denotes a process of disposing of the assets and settling the liabilities of an entity and distributing the net proceeds to investors. 'Withdrawal' and 'redemption' refer here to any means by which an investor can extract the value of its investment from an investee.

Liquidation rights

A liquidation right could be equivalent to a substantive removal right if it allows the investors holding the right to liquidate the investee, establish a new entity with the same assets, and hire a new party to manage and direct the relevant activities of the entity. When assessing whether a liquidation right is equivalent to a substantive removal right, the investor should consider all relevant facts and circumstances. For example, the rights are unlikely to be considered substantive removal rights if:

- the assets of the investee are not readily marketable or there is no mechanism in place for the investor to obtain the same assets;

- the assets require specialised management or expertise that parties other than the current decision maker do not have; or

- there is a non-compete agreement that would prohibit parties other than the decision maker from managing the assets.

As stated in IFRS 10:B65, if more than one party holds substantive removal rights and no single party can remove the decision maker without the agreement of other parties, those removal rights are not, in isolation, conclusive in determining that a decision maker acts as an agent on behalf of others. Liquidation rights that are equivalent to removal rights may be held by more than one party and agreement of other parties may be required to exercise the right. In such circumstances, the liquidation rights do not, in isolation, provide conclusive evidence that a decision maker acts as an agent. Rather, the greater the number of parties required to act together to exercise rights to remove a decision maker and the greater the magnitude of, and variability associated with, the decision maker's other economic interests (i.e. remuneration and other interests), the less weighting should be placed on this factor.

Withdrawal and redemption rights

In some circumstances, a withdrawal or redemption right may also be equivalent to a substantive removal right if it would deprive the decision maker of its ability to direct the relevant activities of the entity. Specifically, if the ownership interests in an entity are held by only a few investors, the decision maker may be compelled to liquidate the entity upon redemption by those investors.

For example, if an entity has a single investor and the investor has the right to withdraw its investment, receive the entity's underlying assets and hire a different party to manage those assets, this right would, in the absence of other relevant facts and circumstances as described above in respect of liquidation rights, be equivalent to a substantive removal right. Similarly, the founding documents of an entity may specify that redemption of an investor's investment in the entity would result in liquidation of the entity. In such circumstances, the withdrawal right would also be equivalent to a liquidation right and, potentially, a substantive removal right. However, if the withdrawal right would not result in the liquidation of the entity, the withdrawal right would not be equivalent to a substantive removal right because the decision maker could continue to manage the relevant activities of the (possibly significantly smaller) entity following withdrawal.

8.2.4 Remuneration to which the decision maker is entitled

The greater the magnitude of, and variability associated with, the decision maker's remuneration relative to the returns expected from the activities of the investee, the more likely the decision maker is a principal. [IFRS 10:B68]

In determining whether it is a principal or an agent, the decision maker should also consider whether the following conditions exist:

[IFRS 10:B69]

- the remuneration of the decision maker is commensurate with the services provided; and

- the remuneration agreement includes only terms, conditions or amounts that are customarily present in arrangements for similar services and level of skills negotiated on an arm's length basis.

A decision maker cannot be an agent unless the conditions listed in IFRS 10:B69 are present. However, the presence of these two factors, in isolation, is not sufficient to conclude that the decision maker is an agent. [IFRS 10:B70]

When a single party holds a substantive right to remove the decision maker and can remove the decision maker without cause, this, in isolation, is sufficient to conclude that the decision maker is an agent (see **8.2.1**). When this is the case, IFRS 10:B61 notes that it is not necessary to consider other factors (such as remuneration) – so the conditions above need not be present.

In all other cases, the conditions in IFRS 10:B69 are necessary but not sufficient for classification as an agent. The purpose of the requirement to consider these factors is to determine whether the remuneration for the decision maker is merely compensation for its services as an agent.

8.2.5 Decision maker's exposure to variability of returns from other interests in an investee

8.2.5.1 Decision maker's exposure to variability of returns from other interests – general

A decision maker that holds other interests in an investee (e.g. investments in the investee or provides guarantees with respect to the performance of the investee) should consider its exposure to variability of returns from those interests in assessing whether it is an agent. Holding other interests in an investee indicates that the decision maker may be a principal. [IFRS 10:B71]

In evaluating its exposure to variability of returns from other interests in an investee, the decision maker should consider the following:

[IFRS 10:B72]

- the greater the magnitude of, and variability associated with, its economic interests (considering its remuneration and other interests in aggregate), the more likely the decision maker is a principal; and

- whether its exposure to variability of returns is different from that of the other investors and, if so, whether this might influence its actions. For example, this might be the case when a decision maker holds subordinated interests in, or provides other forms of credit enhancement to, an investee.

The decision maker should evaluate its exposure relative to the total variability of returns of the investee. Such an evaluation is made primarily on the basis of returns expected from the activities of the investee but should not ignore the maximum exposure of the decision maker to variability of returns of the investee through other interests that the decision maker holds. [IFRS 10:B72]

8.2.5.2 Reputational risk and maximum exposure to variability of returns

Exposures to variability of returns may sometimes arise even when there is no legal or contractual arrangement. For example, a financial institution involved in managing a securitisation or investment vehicle of which it was the sponsor may decide to provide funding or other support to the vehicle if the vehicle experiences financial difficulties. The financial institution may provide support even though it is not contractually obliged to do so because allowing the vehicle to fail would damage the institution's wider business interests. This is commonly referred to as 'reputational risk' (see IFRS 10:BC37).

When assessing control, reputational risk is a factor to consider along with other facts and circumstances. It is not an indicator of power in its own right, but may increase an investor's incentive to secure rights that give the investor power over an investee (see IFRS 10:BC39).

Including the exposure to variability arising from reputational risk in evaluating the exposure to variability of returns could have a significant effect on the assessment of whether the decision maker is a principal or an agent.

In assessing whether a decision maker is exercising its decision-making rights as a principal or as an agent, all facts and circumstances should be considered. The weight given to the exposure arising from reputational risk in this assessment depends on the likelihood of the decision maker being economically compelled to step in to support the investee if that investee experiences financial difficulties, despite not being contractually obliged to do so, in order to mitigate the reputational damage that would otherwise occur. The more likely it is that the decision maker will take steps to limit any damage to its reputation, the more weight is given to the exposure from reputational risk because it is more likely that the decision maker is exercising its decision-making rights as a principal.

A relevant factor in this consideration may be whether the vehicle's sponsor has put in place arrangements to address potential difficulties (e.g. by arranging a third-party liquidity facility for the vehicle). The terms of such arrangements should be considered carefully to determine the weight to be given to the arrangement in assessing the likelihood of the sponsor stepping in. For example, if the arrangement contains force majeure or material adverse change clauses, or even if no such financing arrangements are in place, this may indicate that it is more likely that the sponsor will need to step in to protect its reputation in the event of such difficulties occurring.

Another relevant factor to consider may be evidence that the investor has previously stepped in to maintain its reputation. If, historically, the sponsor has supported an investee when the investee has experienced financial difficulty in order to maintain the sponsor's reputation, this may indicate that the sponsor is more likely to do so again. Similarly, if history shows a trend of other sponsors stepping in to mitigate reputational damage in similar scenarios, this may indicate that the sponsor is more likely to do the same in the case of difficulties occurring.

The decision maker should reassess whether it controls the investee if facts and circumstances indicate that there are changes to one or more of the elements of control (see **section 9**). Accordingly, the decision maker should consider whether its assessment that it acts as an agent or a principal has changed.

An investor should disclose sufficient information to enable users of the investor's financial statements to understand the nature and extent of the investor's risks arising from reputational risk and any changes therein (see paragraphs 7, 10 and 24 of IFRS 12 *Disclosure of Interests in Other Entities*).

8.2.6   *Assessing whether a fund manager is a principal or an agent*

The fund manager of an investment fund typically has decision-making authority (power) over relevant activities of the fund because the fund manager can decide which investments the fund should acquire or dispose of. The fund manager is also often exposed to variable returns from the fund through the management fees it receives and, potentially, because it is an investor in the fund. Accordingly, when a fund manager has power, and exposure or rights to variable returns, the fund manager should determine if it controls the fund based on an assessment as to whether it uses its power over the fund for its own benefit (i.e. as a principal) or for the benefit of others (i.e. as an agent).

As required by IFRS 10:B60 (see **8.2.1**), the following factors should be considered in assessing whether a decision maker (i.e. the fund manager in the circumstances under consideration) is acting as a principal or an agent (the list is not exhaustive):

(a) the scope of its decision-making authority;

(b) the rights held by other parties;

(c) the remuneration of the decision maker; and

(d) the decision maker's exposure to variability of returns from other interests that it holds in the entity.

Different weightings should be applied to each of these factors on the basis of the particular facts and circumstances.

The factors in IFRS 10:B60 should be considered together rather than in isolation and might be thought of as a means of answering two key questions.

- How much discretion does the fund manager have to make decisions without intervention by other parties?

- What is the extent and variability of the fund manager's economic interest in the outcome of those decisions?

The *more discretion* a fund manager has to make decisions and the *larger* its economic interest in the outcome of those decisions, the more likely it is that the fund manager is making decisions to affect its own returns from the entity (and is, therefore, acting as a principal rather than as an agent of other investors).

Consideration of the scope of the fund manager's decision-making authority and the rights held by other parties (i.e. the factors set out in IFRS 10:B60(a) and B60(b) above) provides a framework to assess the level of discretion a fund manager has in making decisions, while consideration of the remuneration of the fund manager and the fund manager's exposure to variability of returns from other interests (i.e. the factors set out in IFRS 10:B60(c) and B60(d) above) facilitates an assessment of the extent and variability of the fund manager's economic interest in the outcome of those decisions.

The scope of the fund manager's decision-making authority

IFRS 10:B62 states that the evaluation of the scope of a decision maker's authority should consider the activities that the decision maker is permitted to perform according to the decision-making agreement(s) and specified by law. In addition, the evaluation should consider the discretion that the decision maker has when making decisions about those activities.

As noted in IFRS 10:BC138, the IASB considered whether a decision maker should always be considered an agent if the breadth of its decision-making authority is restricted by contractual arrangements, but it rejected such a conclusion. The Board reached its decision for two reasons:

- its belief that it is rare for a parent to have unrestricted power over a subsidiary because other parties often have protective rights that restrict the decision-making powers of a parent; and

- its concern that such a conclusion would inappropriately lead to many investees, such as securitisation vehicles, not being considered subsidiaries of a decision maker.

Accordingly, the Board decided that a decision maker can have power over an investee if it has discretion in directing the relevant activities, even if those activities are restricted when the investee is established.

This view is illustrated in Examples 14B and 15 in Appendix B to IFRS 10 (see **8.2.7**); these examples illustrate circumstances in which a fund manager is constrained by the founding documents of the fund and/or local laws and regulations, but the decision maker is still determined to be acting as principal, in part because it has decision-making rights within those constraints.

Therefore, the fact that a fund manager is required to abide by a fund's investment policies does not indicate that the fund manager is acting as an agent; although such policies define the fund's relevant activities, the fund manager may still have full discretion to make decisions regarding those relevant activities. The scope of a fund manager's decision-making authority may indicate an agency relationship when there are relevant activities permitted by the fund's founding documents or by law that are not directed by the fund manager.

In evaluating the scope of a fund manager's decision-making authority, it is necessary to consider whether another party (e.g. an investment committee) has substantive rights to veto or overturn decisions made by the fund manager. When there is an investment committee, the composition of that committee (including who appointed the members) and the nature of its rights should be assessed. If the rights of the committee are limited to ensuring that the fund manager complies with the fund's investment policy, those rights should be considered to be protective rights (see **6.4.5**) which would not prevent the fund manager acting as a principal.

IFRS 10:B63 also states that the purpose and design of the investee and the level of involvement of a decision maker in that process should be considered in determining whether the decision maker has the ability to direct the relevant activities. Consideration of design is discussed further at **6.2.3**.

IFRS 10:B74 states that the decision-making rights of a *de facto* agent (being a party acting on the fund manager's behalf) are considered together with the fund manager's own decision-making rights in assessing control.

Rights held by other parties

In the case of a fund manager, consideration of this factor typically requires an assessment of the rights of other investors to remove the fund manager from office with or without cause (often referred to as 'kick-out' rights). As discussed at **8.2.3.2**, there are circumstances in which an investor's liquidation, redemption or withdrawal rights can, in substance, be considered equivalent to kick-out rights.

Examples 14A and 14B in Appendix B to IFRS 10 (see **8.2.7**) state that a right to remove a fund manager only for breach of contract is considered to be a protective right, which would not prevent the fund manager acting as a principal.

Consideration of the significance of kick-out rights requires two further questions to be answered.

Are the kick-out rights substantive?

IFRS 10:BC139 states that the assessment of whether rights held by other parties are substantive is made in the same way in the context of an agent/principal analysis as for any other right held by other parties (i.e. in assessing whether those parties have the practical ability to prevent the decision maker from directing the activities of the investee).

Accordingly, a fund manager should consider the factors in IFRS 10:B23 (see **6.4.4.1**) to determine whether the rights are substantive and whether there are any barriers to exercising the rights. Specifically, the fund manager should consider (1) if any other parties are willing or able to provide the management services (i.e. whether the services performed by the fund manager are specialised and can be provided by another manager), (2) whether there is a mechanism to exercise the kick-out rights, and (3) whether any conditions narrowly limit the timing of exercise of the kick-out rights.

How many investors need to agree to exercise the kick-out rights?

IFRS 10:B65 notes that "when a single party holds substantive removal rights and can remove the decision maker without cause, this, in isolation, is sufficient to conclude that the decision maker is an agent [and thus does not control the investee]". (Note that IFRS 10:BC135 concludes that a governing body such as a board of directors is not generally viewed as a single party in this context.)

Away from this extreme, the terms of kick-out rights and the number of investors required to exercise the rights will need to be considered carefully. IFRS 10:B65 states that, when assessing the effect of kick-out rights, "the greater the number of parties required to act together to exercise rights to remove a decision maker and the greater the magnitude of, and variability associated with, the decision maker's other economic interests (i.e. remuneration and other interests), the less the weighting that shall be placed on this factor".

A kick-out right may be enforceable only following a majority vote of investors; for a fund with hundreds or thousands of investors, each of whom holds only a single vote, such a right would not be a strong indicator that the fund manager is acting as an agent of those investors. Conversely, a kick-out right exercisable by a few investors would be considered to be much more significant.

The remuneration of the fund manager

The remuneration of a fund manager may comprise various components (e.g. a fixed monetary amount, an amount calculated as a fixed percentage of the value of assets being managed and/or a performance-related fee that is earned only if specified targets are met).

Depending on the performance of the fund, a fee calculated as a fixed percentage of the value of assets being managed (e.g. 1 per cent of the fund's assets under management) may represent a very small or a very large proportion of the total income of the fund for a particular year. When evaluating fees of this nature, the entity should consider the purpose and design of the fee and its likely effect over the life of the fund.

IFRS 10:B56 notes that fixed performance fees for managing an investee's assets are variable returns because they expose the fund manager to the performance risk of the fund. The amount of variability depends on the investee's ability to generate sufficient income to pay the fee.

Remuneration commensurate with services provided and terms customarily present in arrangements for similar services

IFRS 10:B69 requires that, in determining whether it is a principal or an agent, a fund manager should consider whether:

- its remuneration is commensurate with the services it provides; and

- the remuneration agreement includes only terms, conditions or amounts that are customarily present in arrangements for similar services and level of skills negotiated on an arm's length basis.

If these two conditions are not present, the fund manager cannot be an agent. However, as clarified in IFRS 10:B70, meeting those conditions in isolation is not sufficient to conclude that a fund manager is an agent. A fund manager that is determined not to be an agent because these two conditions are not present would have to consider other relevant facts and circumstances to determine whether it should consolidate the investee.

IFRS 10 does not provide any guidance on how to assess whether the conditions in IFRS 10:B69 are present. In practice, an evaluation of the following may be useful in making this assessment:

- the terms, conditions and amounts of remuneration of managers of comparable funds; and

- the level of investment in the fund by independent third-party investors (because unrelated investors in the fund may be an indicator that the remuneration of the fund manager was negotiated to reflect market conditions).

The decision maker's exposure to variability of returns

IFRS 10 is clear that, in assessing whether it is acting as a principal or an agent, the fund manager would need to consider the magnitude of, and variability associated with, its remuneration *in aggregate with* any other interests (e.g. a direct investment) in the fund (see IFRS 10:B72).

In respect of this evaluation, IFRS 10:B72 states as follows:

- the evaluation should be made primarily on the basis of returns expected from the activities of the investee, but should not ignore the maximum exposure to variability of returns; and

- the evaluation should include consideration of whether the fund manager's exposure to variability of returns is different from that of the other investors.

Returns expected from the activities of the investee

Remuneration and other interests in a fund may provide a fund manager with returns that differ depending on the level of performance of the fund.

- A fund manager may be remunerated through a performance fee that varies depending on the fund's level of performance (e.g. the fund manager may receive a higher proportion of profits when the fund meets higher performance targets) as a means of aligning the interests of the fund manager with those of the other investors. In this case, a careful assessment is required of all performance levels. The performance fee to be included in the analysis should be based on the level of performance fee expected to be received. Even if a specified minimum level of performance is required for a fund manager to receive *any* performance fee, it is likely that the fund manager expects to achieve that specified level because the target will have been established with the agreement of the other investors at a realistic level to incentivise the fund manager.

- A fund may have various classes of instrument that absorb variability in the fund's performance by different amounts (e.g. tranches of debt with varying levels of seniority plus residual equity shares). The more variability that is absorbed by the instruments held by the fund manager, the more likely it is that the fund manager is acting as a principal (this is illustrated in Example 15 in Appendix B to IFRS 10 – see **8.2.7**).

Maximum exposure to variability of returns

Exposure to reputational risk (see **8.2.5.2**) may be a relevant factor to consider when performing the analysis. In addition, the fund manager should consider the reason for providing any contractual arrangements (e.g. credit insurance for an investee), even when the expectation is that it will not need to act under such arrangements.

Variability of returns different from that of other investors

If a fund manager's economic interests diverge from those of other investors, it is more likely that the fund manager is influenced in its decision-making by its own economic interests and, therefore, is acting as a principal.

This might occur if the fund manager holds a different class of investment from other investors (e.g. the fund manager holds the subordinate tranche of securities in a leveraged fund).

In situations when a fund manager has a different exposure to other interest holders, despite having a contractual obligation to act in the best interest of all investors, the divergence in economic interest is an important factor to consider in determining whether a fund manager is acting as a principal or an agent.

IFRS 10:B74 states that the exposure to variability of returns of a *de facto* agent (being a party acting on the fund manager's behalf) is considered together with the fund manager's own exposure in assessing control.

The combined effect of a decision maker's discretion and its economic interests

The final determination as to whether a fund manager is acting as a principal or as an agent will generally require consideration of the two key questions identified earlier in combination and will, in many cases, require the exercise of judgement based on the relevant facts and circumstances.

A starting point for considering a fund manager's exposure to variability of returns in aggregate could be to calculate the fund manager's aggregate share of a change in the value of the fund. For example, in Example 14B the fund manager receives a fee of 1 per cent of assets under management and a bonus of 20 per cent of profits if a specified profit level is reached (not specified in the example, but taken into account in the analysis so apparently expected to be reached) and holds a 20 per cent investment in the fund.

Thus, if the value of the fund's investments increases by CU100, and the fund's profits are such that the fund manager qualifies for a bonus, the fund manager will be exposed to the variability in the fund's returns in the following ways.

		CU
Management fee	CU100 × 1%	1.00
Bonus	CU99 (after effect of management fee) × 20%	19.80
Increase in value of investment	CU79.2 (after effect of management fee and bonus) × 20%	15.84
		36.64

If a quantitative analysis is performed, it should be used in conjunction with a consideration of the qualitative characteristics of those interests and how they change depending on the performance of the fund. As discussed in IFRS 10:BC142, the IASB decided against prescribing a purely quantitative approach to assessing a decision maker's exposure to variability in returns as that would create a 'bright line' that could lead to inappropriate consolidation conclusions in some situations.

The examples in Appendix B to IFRS 10, which are summarised below and reproduced in **8.2.7**, provide some assistance in determining whether a fund manager is acting as an agent or as a principal based on a number of factors.

Example in Appendix B to IFRS 10						
	13	14A	14B	14C	15	16
Management fee	1% of net asset value	1% of assets under management				Various interests, significantly different from other investors
Bonus (if specified profit achieved)	–	20% of profits			10% of profits	
Investment in fund	10%	2%	20%	20%	35%	
Limits on decision-making powers	According to narrowly-defined parameters in mandate	Must be in accordance with fund's governing documents			Within parameters of prospectus	Must act in best interests of all investors
Kick-out rights	None	For breach of contract only	For breach of contract only	Board can decide each year not to renew contract and other fund managers could provide services	Without cause, but requires majority of large number of investors	None
Conclusion	Agent	Agent	Principal	Agent	Principal	Principal

The following observations are made in respect of the examples in Appendix B to IFRS 10 summarised above and the conclusions reached.

- In line with the discussion in IFRS 10:B65, substantive kick-out rights can (as in Example 14C) lead to a conclusion that a fund manager is acting as an agent, even when it has a high level of economic interest in the fund. Although Example 14C does not provide details regarding the composition of Board or the number of the Board members/investors (but states that all are independent of the fund manager and appointed by investors), in practice these factors may also need to be considered before concluding that a fund manager is acting as an agent.

- In all of the examples, the fund manager's remuneration is deemed to be 'market-based' and 'commensurate with the services provided'. Thus, the restriction on being considered an agent set out in IFRS 10:B69 and B70 does not apply.

- In Example 15, the fund manager's investment represents only 3.5 per cent of the total investment in the fund at formation (because the fund manager holds none of the debt instruments issued by the fund that represent 90 per cent of the fund's total investment). However, because the equity interests in the fund (of which the fund manager holds 35 per cent) are subordinate to, and provide first loss protection for, the debt investors, the fund manager absorbs a high proportion of the variability arising from the fund's performance and the fund manager is determined to be acting as principal.

8.2.7 Examples

Appendix B to IFRS 10 includes a number of examples illustrating how to apply the requirements for determining whether a decision maker (fund manager) is acting as an agent. These examples are reproduced below for convenience.

Example 8.2.7A

Evaluation of whether fund manager is agent or principal (1)

[IFRS 10:Appendix B Example 13]

A decision maker (fund manager) establishes, markets and manages a publicly traded, regulated fund according to narrowly defined parameters set out in the investment mandate as required by its local laws and regulations. The fund was marketed to investors as an investment in a diversified portfolio of equity securities of publicly traded entities. Within the defined parameters, the fund manager has discretion about the assets in which to invest. The fund manager has made a 10 per cent pro rata investment in the fund and receives a market-based fee for its services equal to 1 per cent of the net asset value of the fund. The fees are commensurate with the services provided. The fund manager does not have any obligation to fund losses beyond its 10 per cent investment. The fund is not required to establish, and has not established, an independent board of directors. The investors do not hold any substantive rights that would affect the decision-making authority of the fund manager, but can redeem their interests within particular limits set by the fund.

Although operating within the parameters set out in the investment mandate and in accordance with the regulatory requirements, the fund manager has decision-making rights that give it the current ability to direct the relevant activities of the fund – the investors do not hold substantive rights that could affect the fund manager's decision-making authority. The fund manager receives a market-based fee for its services that is commensurate with the services provided and has also made a pro rata investment in the fund. The remuneration and its investment expose the fund manager to variability of returns from the activities of the fund without creating exposure that is of such significance that it indicates that the fund manager is a principal.

In this example, consideration of the fund manager's exposure to variability of returns from the fund together with its decision-making authority within restricted parameters indicates that the fund manager is an agent. Thus, the fund manager concludes that it does not control the fund.

Example 8.2.7B

Evaluation of whether fund manager is agent or principal (2)

[IFRS 10:Appendix B Examples 14 to 14C]

Example 14

A decision maker establishes, markets and manages a fund that provides investment opportunities to a number of investors. The decision maker (fund manager) must make decisions in the best interests of all investors and in accordance with the fund's governing agreements. Nonetheless, the fund manager has wide decision-making discretion. The fund manager receives a market-based fee for its services equal to 1 per cent of assets under management and 20 per cent of all the fund's profits if a specified profit level is achieved. The fees are commensurate with the services provided.

Although it must make decisions in the best interests of all investors, the fund manager has extensive decision-making authority to direct the relevant activities of the fund. The fund manager is paid fixed and performance-related fees that are commensurate with the services provided. In addition, the remuneration aligns the interests of the fund manager with those of the other investors to increase the value of the fund, without creating exposure to variability of returns from the activities of the fund that is of such significance that the remuneration, when considered in isolation, indicates that the fund manager is a principal.

The above fact pattern and analysis applies to examples 14A–14C described below. Each example is considered in isolation.

Example 14A

The fund manager also has a 2 per cent investment in the fund that aligns its interests with those of the other investors. The fund manager does not have any obligation to fund losses beyond its 2 per cent investment. The investors can remove the fund manager by a simple majority vote, but only for breach of contract.

The fund manager's 2 per cent investment increases its exposure to variability of returns from the activities of the fund without creating exposure that is of such significance that it indicates that the fund manager is a principal. The other investors' rights to remove the fund manager are considered to be protective rights because they are exercisable only for breach of contract. In this example, although the fund manager has extensive decision-making authority and is exposed to variability of returns from its interest and remuneration, the fund manager's exposure indicates that the fund manager is an agent. Thus, the fund manager concludes that it does not control the fund.

Example 14B

The fund manager has a more substantial pro rata investment in the fund, but does not have any obligation to fund losses beyond that investment. The investors can remove the fund manager by a simple majority vote, but only for breach of contract.

In this example, the other investors' rights to remove the fund manager are considered to be protective rights because they are exercisable only for breach of contract. Although the fund manager is paid fixed and performance-related fees that are commensurate with the services provided, the combination of the fund manager's investment together with its remuneration could create exposure to variability of returns from the activities of the fund that is of such significance that it indicates that the fund manager is a principal. The greater the magnitude of, and variability associated with, the fund manager's economic interests (considering its remuneration and other interests in aggregate), the more emphasis the fund manager would place on those economic interests in the analysis, and the more likely the fund manager is a principal.

For example, having considered its remuneration and the other factors, the fund manager might consider a 20 per cent investment to be sufficient to conclude that it controls the fund. However, in different circumstances (ie if the remuneration or other factors are different), control may arise when the level of investment is different.

Example 14C

The fund manager has a 20 per cent pro rata investment in the fund, but does not have any obligation to fund losses beyond its 20 per cent investment. The fund has a board of directors, all of whose members are independent of the fund manager and are appointed by the other investors. The board appoints the fund manager annually. If the board decided not to renew the fund manager's contract, the services performed by the fund manager could be performed by other managers in the industry.

Although the fund manager is paid fixed and performance-related fees that are commensurate with the services provided, the combination of the fund manager's 20 per cent investment together with its remuneration creates exposure to variability of returns from the activities of the fund that is of such significance that it indicates that the fund manager is a principal. However, the investors have substantive rights to remove the fund manager – the board of directors provides a mechanism to ensure that the investors can remove the fund manager if they decide to do so.

In this example, the fund manager places greater emphasis on the substantive removal rights in the analysis. Thus, although the fund manager has extensive decision-making authority and is exposed to variability of returns of the fund from its remuneration and investment, the substantive rights held by the other investors indicate that the fund manager is an agent. Thus, the fund manager concludes that it does not control the fund.

Example 8.2.7C

Evaluation of whether fund manager is agent or principal (3)

[IFRS 10:Appendix B Example 15]

An investee is created to purchase a portfolio of fixed rate asset-backed securities, funded by fixed rate debt instruments and equity instruments. The equity instruments are designed to provide first loss protection to the debt investors and receive any residual returns of the investee. The transaction was marketed to potential debt investors as an investment in a portfolio of asset-backed securities with exposure to the credit risk associated with the possible default of the issuers of the asset-backed securities in the portfolio and to the interest rate risk associated with the management of the portfolio. On formation, the equity instruments represent 10 per cent of the value of the assets purchased. A decision maker (the asset manager) manages the active asset portfolio by making investment decisions within the parameters set out in the investee's prospectus. For those services, the asset manager receives a market-based fixed fee (ie 1 per cent of assets under management) and performance-related fees (ie 10 per cent of profits) if the investee's profits exceed a specified level. The fees are commensurate with the services provided. The asset manager holds 35 per cent of the equity in the investee. The remaining 65 per cent of the equity, and all the debt instruments, are held by a large number of widely dispersed unrelated third party investors. The asset manager can be removed, without cause, by a simple majority decision of the other investors.

The asset manager is paid fixed and performance-related fees that are commensurate with the services provided. The remuneration aligns the interests of the fund manager with those of the other investors to increase the value of the fund. The asset manager has exposure to variability of returns from the activities of the fund because it holds 35 per cent of the equity and from its remuneration.

Although operating within the parameters set out in the investee's prospectus, the asset manager has the current ability to make investment decisions that significantly affect the investee's returns – the removal rights held by the other investors receive little weighting in the analysis because those rights are held by a large number of widely dispersed investors. In this example, the asset manager places greater emphasis on its exposure to variability of returns of the fund from its equity interest, which is subordinate to the debt instruments. Holding 35 per cent of the equity creates subordinated exposure to losses and rights to returns of the investee, which are of such significance that it indicates that the asset manager is a principal. Thus, the asset manager concludes that it controls the investee.

Example 8.2.7D

Evaluation of whether fund manager is agent or principal (4)

[IFRS 10:Appendix B Example 16]

A decision maker (the sponsor) sponsors a multi-seller conduit, which issues short-term debt instruments to unrelated third party investors. The transaction was marketed to potential investors as an investment in a portfolio of highly rated medium-term assets with minimal exposure to the credit risk associated with the possible default by the issuers of the assets in the portfolio. Various transferors sell high quality medium-term asset portfolios to the conduit. Each transferor services the portfolio of assets that it sells to the conduit and manages receivables on default for a market-based servicing fee. Each transferor also provides first loss protection against credit losses from its asset portfolio through over-collateralisation of the assets transferred to the conduit. The sponsor establishes the terms of the conduit and manages the operations of the conduit for a market-based fee. The fee is commensurate with the services provided. The sponsor approves the sellers permitted to sell to the conduit, approves the assets to be purchased by the conduit and makes decisions about the funding of the conduit. The sponsor must act in the best interests of all investors.

The sponsor is entitled to any residual return of the conduit and also provides credit enhancement and liquidity facilities to the conduit. The credit enhancement provided by the sponsor absorbs losses of up to 5 per cent of all of the conduit's assets, after losses are absorbed by the transferors. The liquidity facilities are not advanced against defaulted assets. The investors do not hold substantive rights that could affect the decision-making authority of the sponsor.

Even though the sponsor is paid a market-based fee for its services that is commensurate with the services provided, the sponsor has exposure to variability of returns from the activities of the conduit because of its rights to any residual returns of the conduit and the provision of credit enhancement and liquidity facilities (ie the conduit is exposed to liquidity risk by using short-term debt instruments to fund medium-term assets). Even though each of the transferors has decision-making rights that affect the value of the assets of the conduit, the sponsor has extensive decision-making authority that gives it the current ability to direct the activities that most significantly affect the conduit's returns (ie the sponsor established the terms of the conduit, has the right to make decisions about the assets (approving the assets purchased and the transferors of those assets) and the funding of the conduit (for which new investment must be found on a regular basis)). The right to residual returns of the conduit and the provision of credit enhancement and liquidity facilities expose the sponsor to variability of returns from the activities of the conduit that is different from that of the other investors. Accordingly, that exposure indicates that the sponsor is a principal and thus the sponsor concludes that it controls the conduit. The sponsor's obligation to act in the best interest of all investors does not prevent the sponsor from being a principal.

8.3   *De facto* agents

In addition to considering whether a decision maker is acting as a principal or as an agent for another party (see **8.2**), an investor is also required to consider the nature of its relationships with other parties and whether those other parties are acting on the investor's behalf – i.e. they are acting as *de facto* agents. [IFRS 10:B73] A party is a *de facto* agent when the investor has, or those that direct the activities of the investor have, the ability to direct that party to act on the investor's behalf. [IFRS 10:B74]

Judgement is required in assessing whether a party is acting as a *de facto* agent for another party, taking into account not only the nature of the relationship between the parties involved but also how they interact with each other and the investor. [IFRS 10:B73] Such a relationship need not involve a contractual arrangement. [IFRS 10:B74]

When an investor has a *de facto* agent, the investor should consider its *de facto* agent's decision-making rights and its indirect exposure, or rights, to variable returns through the *de facto* agent together with its own when assessing control of an investee. [IFRS 10:B74]

IFRS 10 gives examples of parties that might act as *de facto* agents for an investor by virtue of their relationships with the investor:

[IFRS 10:B75]

- the investor's related parties as defined in IAS 24 *Related Party Disclosures* (see **chapter A23**);

- a party that received its interest in the investee as a contribution or loan from the investor;

- a party that has agreed not to sell, transfer or encumber its interests in the investee without the investor's prior approval (except for situations in which the investor and the other party have the right of prior approval and the rights are based on mutually agreed terms by willing independent parties);

- a party that cannot finance its operations without subordinated financial support from the investor;

- an investee for which the majority of the members of its governing body or for which its key management personnel are the same as those of the investor; and

- a party that has a close business relationship with the investor, such as the relationship between a professional service provider and one of its significant clients.

9 Continuous assessment of control

9.1 Continuous assessment of control – general

IFRS 10 requires an investor to reassess whether or not it controls an investee when facts and circumstances indicate that there are changes to one or more of the three elements of control, namely:

[IFRS 10:8 & B80]

- power over the investee;

- exposure, or rights, to variable returns from involvement with the investee; and

- the ability to use the power over the investee to affect the amount of the returns.

The IASB has clarified what is meant by the 'continuous assessment' of control as set out above following some concerns expressed by respondents to the exposure draft preceding the Standard. Specifically, the Board has confirmed that (1) the requirement for reassessment of control is not restricted to reporting dates, and (2) it is not automatically necessary to reassess all control or potential control relationships at each reporting date. [IFRS 10:BC151]

An investor's initial assessment of control or its status as a principal or an agent would not change simply because of a change in market conditions (e.g. a change in the investee's returns driven by market conditions), unless the change in market conditions changes one or more of the three elements of control listed above or changes the overall relationship between a principal and an agent. [IFRS 10:B85]

IFRS 10 gives a number of examples of circumstances that may suggest that there has been a change in the elements of control.

- There is a change in how power over an investee can be exercised. For example, changes to decision-making rights can mean that the relevant activities are no longer directed through voting rights, but instead other agreements (e.g. contracts) give another party or parties the current ability to direct the relevant activities of the investee. Such a change can arise from an event in which the investor has no involvement (e.g. if decision-making rights held by another party or parties that previously prevented the investor from controlling an investee have lapsed). [IFRS 10:B81 & B82]

- There is a change affecting the investor's exposure, or rights, to variable returns from its involvement with the investee (e.g. if a contract to receive performance-related fees is terminated and, as a result, the investor ceases to be entitled to receive variable returns from its involvement with the investee). [IFRS 10:B83]

- There are changes in the overall relationship between the investor and other relevant parties that may change the status of the investor as to whether it acts as a principal or an agent. For example, if changes to the rights of the investor, or of other parties, occur, the investor should reconsider its status as a principal or an agent. [IFRS 10:B84]

9.2 Reassessment of a lender's rights on default or breach of a loan covenant

A loan agreement will commonly confer upon the lender rights that can be exercised in the event of the borrower breaching a loan covenant and/or defaulting on payments due under the loan agreement (e.g. the right to seize an asset provided by a borrower as collateral). Frequently, such rights are regarded as 'protective rights' and, consequently, are not considered to give the lender power over (and consequently control of) the borrower (see **6.4.5**). However, in some circumstances, the rights are not merely protective and may give the lender power over the borrower on the occurrence of a breach or default.

When a lender's rights under a loan agreement are enforceable upon default or breach of a loan covenant by the borrower, in some circumstances the lender will have obtained control of the borrower. In determining whether it has obtained power over a borrower defaulting on a loan or breaching a covenant, a lender should consider:

- whether the lender's rights are regarded as protective in nature both before and after the default or breach and hence do not give the lender power over the borrower (Scenario 1 below);

- whether the lender's rights have been amended as a result of the default or breach to give the lender power over the borrower (Scenario 2 below); or

- whether the terms of the loan agreement were originally designed to give power in the event of a default or breach (Scenario 3 below).

When the rights give the lender power over the borrower in the event of a default or breach, if the other two elements of control exist (i.e. the exposure or rights to variable returns and the ability to use the power to affect the investor's returns – see **section 5**), the lender has control over that entity.

The following examples illustrate these considerations.

Scenario 1: right to seize collateral exercised upon breach of covenant

The terms of a loan agreement give a lender the right to take possession of a property which is pledged as collateral for the loan in the event that the borrower breaches a loan covenant by failing to maintain an agreed level of interest cover. This covenant is subsequently breached and, in accordance with the original loan agreement, the lender can take possession of the property.

In these circumstances, the lender's right to seize the property is protective in nature (because it is designed only to protect the lender's rights under the loan agreement). When the covenant is breached, the lender is only entitled to exercise that protective right. Accordingly, the lender has not obtained power over the borrower.

Scenario 2: right to seize collateral renegotiated upon breach of covenant

The facts are as in Scenario 1 but, in this case, the lender has rights over all assets of the borrower up to the value of the loan outstanding. At the point of breach, the borrower has insufficient assets to satisfy the lender's rights and instead negotiates a waiver of the covenant in return for the lender taking power over the relevant activities of the borrower (e.g. approval of the annual budget, capital expenditure, renewal of lease agreements and appointment of key management personnel).

In these circumstances, the lender's rights have been changed from protective rights to rights designed to give power over the borrower. Given that the other two elements of control exist (i.e. the lender has exposure to variable returns from the loan and can use its power to affect those returns), the lender now has taken control of the borrower.

Similarly, control over the borrower could be obtained by the lender agreeing to exchange its rights under the loan for a controlling share of the borrower's equity.

Scenario 3: power over significant management decisions upon breach of covenant

The terms of a loan agreement give a lender power over relevant activities in the event of a breach of covenant (e.g. approval of the annual budget, capital expenditure, renewal of lease agreements and appointment of key management personnel).

In these circumstances, reassessment of the lender's rights upon breach of covenant would result in a conclusion that the lender has obtained power over the borrower as a result of the original terms of the loan agreement. Given that the other two elements of control exist (i.e. the lender has exposure to variable returns from the loan and can use its power to affect those returns), the lender now has control of the borrower.

It should also be noted that the rights of a lender in the event of financial difficulty of, or default by, a borrower may vary by jurisdiction as a result of local insolvency laws. The effect of such laws should be considered in assessing the nature of a lender's rights.

10 Accounting requirements

10.1 Consolidation procedures

10.1.1 Consolidation procedures – general

The discussion in this section is in respect of those subsidiaries that are consolidated by an entity in accordance with IFRS 10. It does not apply to those subsidiaries of an investment entity that are required to be measured at fair value through profit or loss (see **section 13**).

When preparing consolidated financial statements, the entity should:

[IFRS 10:B86]

- combine like items of assets, liabilities, equity, income, expenses and cash flows of the parent with those of its subsidiaries;

  > For example, the cash, trade receivables and prepayments of the parent and each subsidiary are added together to arrive at the cash, trade receivables and prepayments of the group, before consolidation adjustments are made. The objective is that consolidated financial statements should present the information for a parent and its subsidiaries as if they were the financial statements of a single economic entity.

- offset (eliminate) the carrying amount of the parent's investment in each subsidiary and the parent's portion of equity of each subsidiary. Any related goodwill is recognised in accordance with IFRS 3 *Business Combinations* (see **chapter A25**); and

- eliminate in full intragroup assets and liabilities, equity, income, expenses and cash flows relating to transactions between entities of the group, and the profits or losses resulting from intragroup transactions that are recognised in assets such as inventories and fixed assets (see **10.1.3**).

  > Note that exchange differences arising on a loan between group entities with different functional currencies will not be eliminated. They will be recognised in consolidated profit or loss, unless the criteria in paragraph 15 of IAS 21 *The Effects of Changes in Foreign Exchange Rates* are met (see **3.4.4** in **chapter A19**).

10.1.2 Reciprocal interests

> Reciprocal interests represent situations in which two entities hold equity interests in each other. An analogy to paragraph 33 of IAS 32 *Financial Instruments: Presentation* is appropriate (i.e. reciprocal interests should be treated in a similar manner to treasury shares). In its consolidated financial statements, reciprocal interests should be presented by a parent as a reduction of both its investment in the subsidiary and its equity in the earnings of the subsidiary.

10.1.3 Elimination of intragroup transactions

10.1.3.1 Elimination of intragroup transactions – general

In order to present financial statements for the group in a consolidated format, the effects of transactions between group entities should be eliminated. IFRS 10 requires that intragroup transactions and the resulting unrealised profits and losses be eliminated in full. [IFRS 10:B86(c)]

Liabilities due by one group entity to another should be set off against the corresponding asset in the other group entity's financial statements; sales made by one group entity to another should be excluded both from revenue and from cost of sales or the appropriate expense heading in consolidated profit or loss; dividends received from a subsidiary should be excluded from consolidated profit or loss and set off against the corresponding movement in equity.

Adjustments such as those referred to in the previous paragraph are not required to be made for transactions between group entities and investments that are accounted for using the equity method in the consolidated financial statements (e.g. associates) – see **4.4** in **chapter A26**.

To the extent that the buying entity has on-sold the goods in question to a third party, the eliminations of sales and cost of sales are all that is required, and no adjustments to consolidated profit or loss for the period, or to net assets, are needed. However, to the extent that the goods in question are still on hand at the end of the reporting period, and are carried at an amount that is in excess of cost to the group, the amount of the intragroup profit should be eliminated, and the carrying amount of the assets should be reduced to the cost to the group (adjusted, when appropriate, for subsequent depreciation based on that cost figure).

For transactions between group entities, unrealised profits resulting from intragroup transactions that are included in the carrying amount of assets, such as inventories and property, plant and equipment, are eliminated in full. The requirement to eliminate such profits in full applies to the transactions of all subsidiaries that are consolidated – even those in which the group's interest is less than 100 per cent.

For entities that are accounted for using the equity method in the consolidated financial statements (e.g. associates), unrealised profits are generally eliminated to the extent of the investor's interest in the associate (see **4.4.14** in **chapter A26**).

10.1.3.2   *Unrealised profit in inventories*

When one group entity sells goods to another, the selling entity, as a separate legal entity, recognises profits made on those sales. However, if these goods are still held as inventories by the buying entity at the end of the reporting period, the profit recognised by the selling entity (when viewed from the standpoint of the group as a whole) has not yet been earned, and will not be earned until the goods are eventually sold outside the group. On consolidation, the unrealised profit on closing inventories should be eliminated from the group's profit, and the closing inventories of the group should be measured at cost to the group.

When the goods are sold by a parent to a subsidiary, all of the profit on the transaction is eliminated, irrespective of the percentage of the shares held by the parent. In other words, the group is not permitted to take credit for the share of profit that is attributable to any non-controlling interests.

Example 10.1.3.2A

Unrealised profit in inventories (1)

A Limited has an 80 per cent subsidiary, B Limited. During 20X1, A Limited sells goods, which originally cost CU20,000, to B Limited for CU30,000. At 31 December 20X1, B Limited continues to hold half of those goods as inventories.

The inventories held by B Limited include an unrealised profit of CU5,000. On consolidation, this profit must be eliminated in full – irrespective of any non-controlling interests.

Therefore, the required entries on consolidation, to eliminate all of the effects of the transaction, are as follows.

		CU	CU
Dr	Consolidated revenue	30,000	
Cr	Consolidated cost of sales		30,000
Dr	Consolidated cost of sales (closing inventories)	5,000	
Cr	Closing inventories		5,000

To eliminate the effects of the intragroup transaction.

When the goods are sold by a non-wholly-owned subsidiary to another group entity (whether the parent or a fellow subsidiary), all of the unrealised profit should also be eliminated.

In these circumstances (i.e. sales by a non-wholly-owned subsidiary to another group entity), a question arises as to how to calculate the amount of unrealised profit to be allocated to non-controlling interests.

- Method 1: allocate to non-controlling interests their proportionate share of the elimination of the unrealised profit. This approach eliminates the profit in the selling entity.

- Method 2: no part of the elimination of the unrealised profit is allocated to the non-controlling interests, acknowledging that they are still entitled to their full share of profit arising on intragroup sales. Under this approach, the amount attributed to the non-controlling interests reflects their entitlement to the share capital and reserves of the subsidiary.

IFRS 10 does not specify which treatment is more appropriate and, in practice, both alternatives are commonly adopted. Whichever approach is adopted, it should be applied consistently as an accounting policy choice.

Example 10.1.3.2B

Unrealised profit in inventories (2)

C Limited has two subsidiaries: D Limited, in which it has an 80 per cent interest; and E Limited, in which it has a 75 per cent interest. During the reporting period, D Limited sold goods to E Limited for CU100,000. The goods had been manufactured by D Limited at a cost of CU70,000. Of these goods, E Limited had sold one half by the end of the reporting period.

In the preparation of C Limited's consolidated financial statements, the unrealised profit remaining in inventories still held by E Limited will be eliminated. These inventories were transferred from D Limited to E Limited at a value of CU50,000, and their cost to the group was CU35,000. The intragroup profit to be eliminated from inventories, therefore, is CU15,000.

If C Limited's accounting policy is to allocate a proportion of the elimination of the unrealised profit to the non-controlling interests (NCIs) (Method 1 as described above), the proportion attributed to the NCIs is determined by reference to their proportionate interest in the selling subsidiary, D Limited (i.e. 20 per cent). The eliminated unrealised profit attributed to the NCIs is therefore CU15,000 × 20 per cent = CU3,000.

Therefore, under Method 1, the required journal entries in the consolidated financial statements are as follows.

		CU	CU
Dr	Consolidated revenue	100,000	
Cr	Consolidated cost of sales		100,000
Dr	Consolidated cost of sales (closing inventories)	15,000	
Cr	Closing inventories		15,000
Dr	NCIs	3,000	
Cr	Retained earnings		3,000

To eliminate the effects of the intragroup transaction.

If C Limited's accounting policy is not to allocate any of the elimination of the unrealised profit to the NCIs (Method 2 as described above), all of the CU15,000 is attributable to the owners of the parent and the final entry above (transferring a portion of the elimination of the unrealised profit to the NCIs) is not required.

10.1.3.3   Unrealised profit on transfer of a non-current asset

Similar to the treatment described **10.1.3.2** for unrealised profits in inventories, unrealised profits arising from intragroup transfers of non-current assets are also eliminated from the consolidated financial statements.

Example 10.1.3.3

Unrealised profit on transfer of a non-current asset

F Limited holds 80 per cent of the issued share capital of G Limited. G Limited purchased a machine on 1 January 20X1 at a cost of CU4 million. The machine has a life of 10 years.

On 1 January 20X3, G Limited sells the machine to F Limited at a price of CU3.6 million, being its fair value.

In preparing the consolidated financial statements of F Limited at 31 December 20X3, the effects of the sale from G Limited to F Limited should be eliminated.

At 31 December 20X3, the carrying amount of the machine in the books of F Limited will be CU3.15 million, after depreciation of CU450,000 has been recognised (i.e. assuming that the cost to F Limited of CU3.6 million will be written off over the asset's remaining life of eight years).

G Limited will have recognised a profit on transfer of the asset of CU400,000 (disposal proceeds of CU3.6 million less carrying amount, after two years depreciation, of CU3.2 million).

If there had been no transfer, the asset would have been included in the statement of financial position of G Limited at 31 December 20X3 at CU2.8 million and depreciation of CU400,000 would have been recognised in the 20X3 reporting period.

Therefore, the required consolidation entries are as follows.

		CU'000	CU'000
Dr	Consolidated profit or loss (profit on sale)	400	
Cr	Consolidated profit or loss (excess depreciation)		50
Dr	Machine (restore to original cost)	400	
Cr	Accumulated depreciation (based on original date of acquisition)		750

To eliminate the effects of the intragroup transaction.

Because G Limited (the seller) is a non-wholly-owned subsidiary, F Limited will need to apply its accounting policy regarding whether to allocate a proportion of the elimination of the unrealised profit to non-controlling interests (NCIs). If F Limited's accounting policy is to allocate a proportion of the elimination of the unrealised profit to NCIs (Method 1 described at **10.1.3.2**), a further entry is required to allocate a proportion of the profit or loss adjustment to the NCIs.

This ensures that the amount presented for NCIs in the consolidated financial statements appropriately reflects the NCIs' share of the net assets reported in the consolidated financial statements (i.e. after the elimination of the intragroup profit and consequential excess depreciation). The proportion to be attributed to the non-controlling interests is determined as follows.

	CU'000
NCIs' share of profit on sale (20% × CU400,000)	80
NCIs' share of excess depreciation (20% × CU50,000)	(10)
	70

Therefore, under Method 1, the following additional journal entry is required.

	CU'000	CU'000
Dr NCIs	70	
Cr Retained earnings		70

If F Limited's accounting policy is not to allocate any of the elimination of the unrealised profit to the NCIs (Method 2 as described at **10.1.3.2**), all of the profit or loss adjustment of CU350,000 is attributable to the owners of the parent and this final entry is not required.

10.1.3.4 Unrealised losses

Losses arising on an intragroup transaction may indicate an impairment that requires recognition in the consolidated financial statements. [IFRS 10:B86]

Example 10.1.3.4

Unrealised losses

The facts are as in **example 10.1.3.3**, except that the machine was transferred from G Limited to F Limited at CU2.4 million, being its fair value.

At 31 December 20X3, the carrying amount of the machine in the books of F Limited will be CU2.1 million, after depreciation of CU300,000 has been recognised (i.e. assuming that the cost of CU2.4 million will be written off over the asset's remaining life of eight years).

G Limited will have recognised a loss on transfer of the asset of CU800,000 (disposal proceeds of CU2.4 million less carrying amount of CU3.2 million).

If there had been no transfer, the asset would have been included in the statement of financial position of G Limited at 31 December 20X3 at CU2.8 million and depreciation of CU400,000 would have been recognised in the 20X3 reporting period.

Provided that the entity is satisfied that the original carrying amount of the asset can be recovered, the following consolidation entries are required.

		CU'000	CU'000
Dr	Consolidated profit or loss (additional depreciation)	100	
Cr	Consolidated profit or loss (loss on sale)		800
Dr	Machine (restore to original cost)	1,600	
Cr	Accumulated depreciation (based on original date of acquisition)		900

To eliminate the effects of the intragroup transaction.

Because G (the seller) is a non-wholly-owned subsidiary, F Limited will need to apply its accounting policy regarding the allocation of a proportion of the elimination of the unrealised profit/loss to non-controlling interests (NCIs). If F Limited's accounting policy is to allocate a proportion of the elimination of the unrealised profit/loss to NCIs (Method 1 described at **10.1.3.2**), a further entry is required to allocate a proportion of the profit or loss adjustment to the NCIs. This ensures that the amount presented for NCIs in the consolidated financial statements appropriately reflects the NCIs' share of the net assets reported in the consolidated financial statements (i.e. after the elimination of the intragroup loss and consequential additional depreciation). The proportion to be attributed to the NCIs is determined as follows.

	CU'000
NCIs' share of unrealised loss on sale (20 per cent × CU800,000)	160
NCIs' share of additional depreciation (20 per cent × CU100,000)	(20)
	140

Therefore, under Method 1, the following additional journal entry is required.

		CU'000	CU'000
Dr	Retained earnings	140	
Cr	NCIs		140

If F Limited's accounting policy is not to allocate any of the elimination of the unrealised loss to the NCIs (Method 2 described at **10.1.3.2**), this final entry is not required.

Note that when the transfer at the lower amount indicates that the previous carrying amount of the asset cannot be recovered, an impairment loss should be recognised in accordance with IAS 36 *Impairment of Assets*.

10.1.3.5   Deferred tax

Temporary differences may arise from the elimination of profits and losses resulting from intragroup transactions; the related income tax effects should be accounted for in accordance with IAS 12 *Income Taxes* (see **chapter A13** for a detailed discussion of the issues arising). [IFRS 10:B86]

10.1.4 Measurement of income and expenses based on amounts recognised in consolidated financial statements

For consolidation purposes, the income and expenses of an acquired subsidiary are based on the amounts of the assets and liabilities recognised in the consolidated financial statements at the subsidiary's acquisition date. For example, the depreciation expense recognised after the acquisition date is based on the fair values of the related depreciable assets recognised in the consolidated financial statements at the acquisition date. [IFRS 10:B88]

10.2 Uniform accounting policies

Consolidated financial statements should be prepared using uniform accounting policies for like transactions and other events in similar circumstances. [IFRS 10:19]

When such group accounting policies are not adopted in the financial statements of a member of the group, appropriate adjustments should be made in preparing the consolidated financial statements to ensure conformity with the group's accounting policies. [IFRS 10:B87]

10.3 Commencement and cessation of consolidation

Consolidation of a subsidiary should begin from the date the investor obtains control and cease when the investor loses control. Therefore, income and expenses of a subsidiary should be included in the consolidated financial statements from the date the parent gains control of the subsidiary until the date when the parent ceases to have control of the subsidiary. [IFRS 10:20 & B88]

Accordingly, when a parent has had subsidiaries at any time during a reporting period, IFRS 10 requires consolidated financial statements to be presented (unless the exemption in **3.3** is available). Subsidiaries classified as held for sale are discussed at **3.5**.

10.4 Potential voting rights – impact on consolidation

The effect of potential voting interests on the assessment of control is discussed in **6.4.6.8**. This section focuses on the impact of potential voting rights on the 'mechanics' of consolidation once it has been determined that the investee is a subsidiary.

When potential voting rights, or other derivatives containing potential voting rights, exist, the proportion of profit or loss and changes in equity of a subsidiary allocated to the parent and non-controlling interests in preparing consolidated financial statements is determined solely on the basis of existing ownership interests and does not reflect the possible exercise or conversion of potential voting rights and other derivatives, except as described below. [IFRS 10:B89]

An entity sometimes has, in substance, an existing ownership interest as a result of a transaction that currently gives the entity access to the returns associated with an ownership interest. In such circumstances, the proportion allocated to the parent and the non-controlling interests should take into account the eventual exercise of those potential voting rights and other derivatives that currently give the entity access to the returns. [IFRS 10:B90]

In the circumstances described in IFRS 10:B90, the instruments that contain such potential voting rights are not subject to the requirements of IFRS 9 *Financial Instruments* (or, for entities that have not yet adopted IFRS 9, IAS 39 *Financial Instruments: Recognition and Measurement*). In all other cases, instruments containing potential voting rights in a subsidiary are accounted for in accordance with IFRS 9 (or, for entities that have not yet adopted IFRS 9, IAS 39). [IFRS 10:B91]

Example 10.4A

Assessment of in-substance present access to the returns associated with an ownership interest

P Limited holds 60 per cent of the shares in S Limited. It has been determined that this 60 per cent interest results in P Limited controlling S Limited. P Limited also holds an option to acquire an additional 20 per cent of the shares in S Limited.

What factors should P Limited consider in assessing whether its option to acquire an additional 20 per cent interest results, in substance, in P Limited having "an existing ownership interest that currently gives access to the returns associated with an ownership interest" as contemplated in IFRS 10:B90?

The term 'returns associated with an ownership interest' is not defined in IFRSs. However, the economic benefits commonly associated with an ownership interest in an entity may include, for example, access to changes in value of the entity and rights to dividend cash flows.

The determination as to whether a potential voting right corresponds to an in-substance ownership interest will require the exercise of judgement based on the specific terms of the potential voting right. In making that determination, it is helpful to focus on whether the parent is already, in substance, in the same economic position as if it owned the shares that are the subject of the potential voting right (the underlying shares).

One scenario in which this will often be true is when the parent holds a call option with a zero strike price that can be converted into the underlying shares with no notice period. Assuming that it has the practical ability to exercise its option, the parent can ensure that it receives the same return as if it already owned the shares (e.g. by exercising the option prior to any dividend being paid).

When assessing whether its option to acquire an additional 20 per cent interest corresponds to an in-substance ownership interest, other factors that may need to be considered by P Limited include, but are not limited to, the following.

- Is P Limited able to ensure that it receives all or substantially all of the returns to which it would be entitled if it already owned the shares (e.g. by way of dividends and share appreciation)? For example, this might be achieved either through an agreement that any dividends paid to the current holder of the underlying shares will be passed on to P Limited (e.g. in cash or by an adjustment to the exercise price), or by P Limited being in a position to ensure that no dividends are paid until after it has obtained the underlying shares. If P Limited is unable to access some of the returns to which it would be entitled if it already owned the shares, this may suggest that it does not have an in-substance ownership interest.

- What is the basis for the option exercise price? If the transaction price is based on the fair value of the underlying shares at the transaction date (i.e. the date the option is exercised), this will typically indicate that the economic benefits of ownership are retained by the current holder of the underlying shares until the option is exercised.

- Is the option currently exercisable? If the option is not currently exercisable, it should be considered to result in an in-substance ownership interest only if P Limited has the ability to prevent the current holder of the underlying shares from receiving the economic benefits of ownership until such time as the option becomes exercisable.

- Does the option have economic substance? When the terms of the option have no economic substance, such that P Limited could not conceivably be expected to exercise the rights under the option, the economic benefits of ownership have not been transferred to P Limited.

Note that the considerations and factors set out above also apply to potential voting rights held by a third party. For example, X Limited, a third party, has an option to acquire 5 per cent of the shares in S Limited from P Limited. In determining the appropriate proportions of profit or loss and changes in equity of S Limited to be allocated to P Limited and to the non-controlling interests, P Limited needs to determine whether the potential voting rights held by X Limited represent an in-substance ownership interest for X Limited (see also **example 10.4D**).

Example 10.4B describes another scenario in which there is an in-substance ownership interest (involving a forward contract and the parent having the right to dividends prior to exercise).

Example 10.4B

In-substance existing ownership interest

Entity A holds 49 per cent of the ordinary shares of Entity B. The remaining 51 per cent of the ordinary shares of Entity B are owned by three independent parties, each owning 17 per cent of the ordinary shares of Entity B. In addition, Entity A has entered into a forward contract with one of the other shareholders to acquire an additional 5 per cent of the ordinary shares of Entity B. The forward contract will be settled in two years' time. The terms of the forward contract give Entity A the right to receive dividends, if any, relating to the 5 per cent ownership interest during the two-year intervening period. They also oblige the other shareholder to vote in accordance with the instructions of Entity A on the 5 per cent of ordinary shares subject to the forward contract during the two-year intervening period.

It is determined in this example that Entity A controls Entity B (i.e. Entity A is the parent of Entity B). This determination is based on all relevant facts and circumstances, including Entity A's existing 49 per cent ownership interest and the forward contract (which allows Entity A to control the votes attached to the shares subject to the forward contract). The forward contract gives Entity A rights to dividends during the intervening period meaning that it has in-substance current access to the returns associated with the 5 per cent shareholding. When Entity A prepares its consolidated financial statements, the proportions allocated to Entity A and to the non-controlling interests of Entity B are 54 per cent and 46 per cent, respectively.

Note that, under Section 2.1 of IFRS 9 *Financial Instruments* (or, for entities that have not yet adopted IFRS 9, paragraph 2 of IAS 39 *Financial Instruments: Recognition and Measurement*), the forward contract is not subject to the requirements of IFRS 9 (or IAS 39) because it is accounted for as an interest in a subsidiary under IFRS 10.

Example 10.4C examines the appropriate accounting when a potential voting right is determined to result in a parent gaining control of a subsidiary (including the impact of in-substance ownership interests).

Example 10.4C

Potential voting rights result in control

Entity A is granted a call option over 100 per cent of the shares of Entity B (which meets the definition of a business) with an option exercise period of three months. Within this period, the call option is exercisable at any time. The call option has economic substance.

Entity A pays CU50 for the call option. The option exercise price is fixed and amounts to CU60. At the date that the option is purchased, the carrying amount of the net assets of Entity B is CU85 and their fair value is CU95. The fair value of the option is CU50.

The assessment as to whether Entity A can be considered to control Entity B solely as a result of holding the call option will involve the exercise of judgement and consideration of all of the relevant factors (see **6.4.4** and **6.4.6.8**).

(Note that, if the call option does not result in Entity A gaining control of Entity B, Entity B does not meet the definition of a subsidiary of Entity A and, until exercised, the option is accounted for under the requirements of IFRS 9 (or, for entities that have not yet adopted IFRS 9, IAS 39) – see **example 8.1** in **chapter A25**.)

Assuming that the call option results in Entity A controlling Entity B, how should this be reflected in Entity A's consolidated financial statements prepared to a reporting date occurring during the exercise period?

If it is concluded that Entity A controls Entity B, the appropriate accounting will depend on whether the call option is considered to result in an in-substance ownership interest. This assessment will require the exercise of careful judgement (see **example 10.4A**).

Scenario 1 – call option results in an in-substance ownership interest

If it is determined that the call option results in an in-substance ownership interest, the financial statements should reflect Entity A's acquisition of a 100 per cent interest in Entity B at the date of grant of the call option. The consideration transferred is the price paid for the option plus the present value of the fixed exercise price, with any unwinding of the discount being recognised in profit or loss over the option period until exercise. No non-controlling interests (NCIs) are recognised.

The detailed accounting is as follows (note that, for simplicity, the effect of discounting is ignored).

If the call option results in an in-substance ownership interest, the option is in effect accounted for as if it had been exercised already, with the exercise price of CU60 being treated as deferred consideration payable. Therefore, the following entries are recorded in the consolidated financial statements of Entity A.

		CU	CU
Dr	Net assets	95	
Dr	Goodwill	15	
Cr	NCIs		–
Cr	Cash		50
Cr	Liability (exercise price)		60

When the call option is exercised, the transaction is treated as the settlement of deferred consideration. The following entries are recorded on exercise of the call option.

		CU	CU
Dr	Liability (exercise price)	60	
Cr	Cash		60

Scenario 2 – call option does not result in an in-substance ownership interest

If the call option does not result in an in-substance ownership interest, the requirements of IFRS 10:B90 (see above) do not apply and, in accordance with

IFRS 10:B89, the proportion of profit or loss and changes in equity allocated to the parent and NCIs should be determined solely on the basis of existing ownership interests. Consequently, 100 per cent is allocated to NCIs. The option meets the definition of equity in IAS 32 *Financial Instruments: Presentation* because it is for a fixed amount of own equity and a fixed amount of cash. Therefore, any consideration paid for the purchased call option is presented within equity and is not subsequently remeasured.

The detailed accounting is as follows (note that, for simplicity, the effect of discounting is ignored).

If the call option does not result in an in-substance ownership interest, the following entries are recorded in the consolidated financial statements of Entity A.

		CU	CU
Dr	Net assets	95	
Dr	Goodwill	–	
Dr	Consideration paid for option (equity)	50	
Cr	NCIs		95
Cr	Cash		50

This accounting assumes that the NCIs are measured at CU95, being the proportionate share of the fair value of the identifiable net assets acquired. Paragraph 19 of IFRS 3 *Business Combinations* would also allow the NCIs (which represent a present ownership interest) to be measured at fair value, with a corresponding adjustment to goodwill.

The NCIs would be presented as a component of equity in the statement of financial position.

Because the option meets the definition of equity in IAS 32, the consideration paid for the call option of CU50 is presented within equity and is not subsequently remeasured.

When the option is exercised, the transaction represents Entity A's acquisition of the NCIs. Consequently, under IFRS 10:23 (see **11.4**), it is accounted for as an equity transaction. Any difference between the option exercise price paid, the carrying amount of the call option derecognised and the carrying amount of the NCIs at the date of exercise is recognised in equity; no amount is recognised in profit or loss and there is no adjustment to goodwill. The following entries are recorded on exercise of the call option.

		CU	CU
Dr	NCIs	95	
Dr	Equity	15	
Cr	Cash		60
Cr	Carrying value of option (equity)		50

Example 10.4D illustrates the circumstances when potential voting rights are held by NCIs and their impact on consolidated financial statements.

Example 10.4D

Potential voting rights held by non-controlling interests – impact on consolidated financial statements

Entity P acquires 100 per cent of the shares of Entity S from Entity Z. At the date of acquisition, Entity P writes a call option to Entity X, a third party, over 20 per cent of the shares of Entity S with an option exercise period of three months. Within this period, the call option is exercisable at any time. The call option has economic substance, and its exercise price is not deeply out of the money.

It is determined that Entity P controls Entity S.

The appropriate treatment for the call option held by Entity X in Entity P's consolidated financial statements prepared to a reporting date during the exercise period depends on whether the call option is considered to result in an in-substance ownership interest for Entity X. This assessment will require the exercise of careful judgement (see **example 10.4A**).

Scenario 1 – call option results in an in-substance ownership interest

If it is determined that the call option results in an in-substance ownership interest for Entity X, the consolidated financial statements should reflect Entity P's acquisition of a 100 per cent interest in Entity S followed by the immediate disposal of a 20 per cent interest in Entity S to Entity X at the date of grant of the call option. Entity P applies IFRS 3 in accounting for the acquisition of its 100 per cent interest. The disposal of the 20 per cent interest to Entity X is accounted for as an equity transaction in accordance with IFRS 10:23 (see **11.4**). Non-controlling interests (NCIs) of 20 per cent should be recognised. Any difference between the amount recognised as NCIs, the consideration received for the written call option (if any) and the present value of the option exercise price should be recognised in equity.

In these circumstances, the option is in effect accounted for as if it had been exercised by Entity X already, with the exercise price being treated as deferred consideration receivable. Any unwinding of the discount on the deferred consideration receivable is recognised in profit or loss over the option period until exercise of the option.

When the call option is exercised by Entity X, the transaction is treated by Entity P as the settlement of deferred consideration receivable.

Scenario 2 – call option does not result in an in-substance ownership interest

If the call option does not result in an in-substance ownership interest for Entity X, the requirements of IFRS 10:B90 (see above) do not apply and, in accordance with IFRS 10:B89, the proportion of profit or loss and changes in

---

equity allocated to Entity P and the NCIs should be determined solely on the basis of existing ownership interests. Consequently, 100 per cent is allocated to Entity P and no NCIs are recognised.

In these circumstances, the option is accounted for as a financial instrument. If it meets the definition of equity in accordance with IAS 32, the amount received for the call option (if any) is recognised in equity and not subsequently remeasured. If the option does not meet the definition of equity, it is accounted for as a derivative liability in accordance with IFRS 9 (or, for entities that have not yet adopted IFRS 9, IAS 39) and subsequently measured at fair value, with any changes in fair value recognised in profit or loss.

When the option is exercised by Entity X, the transaction represents a disposal by Entity P of 20 per cent in Entity S to NCIs. Consequently, under IFRS 10:23, it is accounted for as an equity transaction. Any difference between the option exercise price received, the carrying amount of the option at the date of exercise and the amount by which the NCIs are adjusted is recognised in equity. (The carrying amount of the option will be its fair value at the date of exercise if it has been accounted for as a derivative liability, or the amount initially recognised in equity if it meets the definition of equity.) There is no adjustment to goodwill and no amount is recognised in profit or loss as a result of exercise of the option.

10.5   Derivatives over own equity

Derivatives over own equity in the consolidated financial statements include those derivatives over the equity instruments of the parent as well as derivatives over the equity instruments of the group's subsidiaries and should be classified as a financial asset, a financial liability or equity in accordance with IAS 32. The classification and measurement requirements for derivatives over own equity are discussed in **chapter B3** (or, for entities that have not yet adopted IFRS 9, in **chapter C3**).

10.6   Reporting dates and periods of subsidiaries

10.6.1   *Parent and subsidiaries to prepare financial statements to the same reporting date when practicable*

The financial statements of the parent and its subsidiaries used for the purposes of preparing consolidated financial statements should, whenever practicable, have the same reporting date. [IFRS 10:B92]

10.6.2 Circumstances when it may be appropriate for a parent and a subsidiary to have different reporting dates

The following are examples of circumstances in which it may be necessary or appropriate for a subsidiary to have a different reporting period from its parent:

- local legislation requiring financial statements to be prepared to a specified date;

- the normal trading cycle in certain activities (e.g. agriculture) may make it desirable for subsidiaries to have financial years which end at a particular time of the year (e.g. when crops have been harvested). In addition, subsidiaries with cyclical trades, such as retail businesses, may wish to avoid a year-end routine during busy pre-Christmas trading when inventory levels are high; or

- a change in reporting date may have seriously adverse tax consequences, or significant tax advantages may arise from having a different reporting date.

Nevertheless, in such circumstances, the subsidiary should prepare additional financial statements corresponding to the group's reporting period for consolidation purposes, unless it is impracticable to do so. Such impracticability may arise, for example, when entities are unable to comply with the parent's timetable for preparing annual financial statements (which will usually be framed with a view to avoiding undue delay in publication). This may result in some subsidiaries closing their books one or two months earlier than the parent in order to allow time to complete and transmit information for consolidation. Even then, a time lag between the ends of the reporting periods of longer than three months is not permitted (see **10.6.4**).

10.6.3 Requirements when a parent and a subsidiary have different reporting dates

When the end of the reporting period of the parent is different from that of a subsidiary, the subsidiary should prepare, for consolidation purposes, additional financial information as of the same date as the financial statements of the parent to enable the parent to consolidate the financial information of the subsidiary, unless it is impracticable to do so. [IFRS 10:B92]

If it is impracticable to do so, the parent should consolidate the financial information of the subsidiary using the most recent financial statements of the subsidiary adjusted for the effects of significant transactions or events that occur between the date of those financial statements and the date of the consolidated financial statements. [IFRS 10:B93]

IFRS 10 does not define 'significant transactions or events', but they may include business combinations, asset impairments, and the crystallisation of contingent liabilities. A potentially significant transaction or event requires a careful analysis of the relevant facts and circumstances to determine if an adjustment is required.

When a subsidiary prepares financial statements for a different reporting period, it is also necessary to review the subsidiary's statement of financial position to ensure that items are still correctly classified as current or non-current at the end of the group's reporting period (see **10.6.5**).

10.6.4   Difference between the date of the consolidated financial statements and the reporting date of a subsidiary not to exceed three months

IFRS 10 includes an additional restriction that, in any case, the difference between the date of the subsidiary's financial statements and that of the parent's financial statements should be no more than three months. In addition, IFRS 10 requires that the length of the reporting periods and any difference between the dates of the financial statements should be the same from period to period. [IFRS 10:B93]

10.6.5   Classification as current or non-current when parent and subsidiary have different reporting dates

Example 10.6.5

Classification as current or non-current when parent and subsidiary have different reporting dates

A subsidiary with an accounting year end of 31 December 20X1 has a loan outstanding that is due for repayment on 1 January 20X3. The debt is appropriately classified as non-current in the subsidiary's statement of financial position.

The subsidiary is consolidated in the financial statements of its parent, which are prepared to 31 March 20X2. Due to the time lag, the subsidiary's loan falls due less than 12 months from the end of the parent's reporting period. The appropriate classification of the loan as current or non-current should be determined by reference to the year end of the parent which, in this case, results in classification of the loan as a current liability because the amount is repayable nine months after the parent's year end.

10.6.6 Change in reporting period of a subsidiary

Example 10.6.6

Change in reporting period of a subsidiary

In prior reporting periods, a subsidiary (Company S) used a 31 December reporting date whereas its parent's reporting date was 31 March. In accordance with IFRS 10:B93 (see **10.6.3**), for consolidation purposes each year the parent adjusted Company S's financial statements for the period ended 31 December for significant transactions or events that took place between 1 January and 31 March.

In 20X2, Company S changes its reporting date to align to that of its parent (31 March). As a result of this change, Company S will prepare financial statements for the 12-month periods ended 31 March 20X1 and 31 March 20X2. The financial statements for the year ended 31 March 20X1 may differ from those used for consolidation in the prior period, because the latter used financial statements as of 31 December 20X0 adjusted for significant events that took place between 1 January 20X1 and 31 March 20X1.

Should the adjustment resulting from Company S's change in reporting date be recognised in the consolidated financial statements as a change in accounting policy or as a change in estimate?

In prior reporting periods, for consolidation purposes, the parent estimated what Company S's financial statements for the period ended 31 March would have been by adjusting the subsidiary's financial statements for the period ended 31 December for significant transactions or events that took place in the intervening period. The change in Company S's reporting date will result in a revision of the parent's previous estimate of Company S's 31 March 20X1 financial statements. Therefore, the adjustments required in preparing the consolidated financial statements should be recognised as a change in estimate.

Because Company S's reporting date was changed in the accounting period ending 31 March 20X2, in accordance with paragraph 36 of IAS 8 *Accounting Policies, Changes in Accounting Estimates and Errors*, the impact of the change in estimate should be recognised prospectively in consolidated profit or loss for the year ended 31 March 20X2.

When there is a change in an entity's reporting date, IFRSs do not specify how any transitional period should be determined. To illustrate, in the scenario described in **example 10.6.6**, when Company S changes its reporting date from December to March, IFRSs do not specify whether Company S should prepare financial statements for a transitional period of three months or 15 months. Often, there will be specific regulatory and jurisdictional requirements that should be considered.

11 Non-controlling interests

11.1 Non-controlling interests – general

IFRS 10 defines a non-controlling interest as "equity in a subsidiary not attributable, directly or indirectly, to a parent". [IFRS 10:Appendix A]

For an investment entity, non-controlling interests are only recognised in respect of those subsidiaries, if any, that are consolidated (see also **13.3.2.3**).

As discussed at **10.1.1**, the basic consolidation process involves the aggregation of the assets, liabilities, income and expenses of the individual group entities. Therefore, when a subsidiary is not wholly owned by the reporting group, an adjustment is required to take account of the interests of the outside shareholders.

Financial instruments should be treated as non-controlling interests in the consolidated financial statements only if issued by a subsidiary and classified as equity under IAS 32 *Financial Instruments: Presentation* in both the subsidiary's financial statements and the parent's consolidated financial statements. A financial instrument classified by a subsidiary as a liability is not a non-controlling interest in the consolidated financial statements. Furthermore, financial instruments classified as liabilities in the parent's consolidated financial statements under IAS 32 are also not considered non-controlling interests, even if classified as equity in the subsidiary's financial statements (for further guidance, see **chapter B3** for entities applying IFRS 9 *Financial Instruments* or **chapter C3** for entities applying IAS 39 *Financial Instruments: Recognition and Measurement*).

11.2 Measurement of non-controlling interests

11.2.1 Profit or loss and items of other comprehensive income attributable to non-controlling interests

When a subsidiary is not wholly owned, the profit or loss and each component of other comprehensive income of the subsidiary are required to be allocated between the owners of the parent and the non-controlling interests. Amounts should be attributed to the non-controlling interests even if this results in the non-controlling interests having a deficit balance. [IFRS 10:B94]

As discussed at **10.4**, IFRS 10 requires the allocation to be on the basis of existing ownership interests, including 'in-substance' existing ownership interests. [IFRS 10:B90]

Generally, profit or loss and items of other comprehensive income will be attributed to the non-controlling interests by reference to the proportion of shares held, because this proportion typically corresponds to the existing ownership interests of the non-controlling interests. But sometimes this will not be the case; for example, when there is a separate agreement between parties that results in profits being allocated on some other basis, it is necessary to consider whether that other basis determines the attribution of earnings to the non-controlling interests. Careful judgement should be exercised in determining whether the effect of such a contractual agreement is to alter the allocation to the non-controlling interests or to create an obligation that needs to be recognised as a liability by the group.

11.2.2 Two classes of shares

IFRS 10 explicitly provides that if a subsidiary has outstanding cumulative preference shares that are classified as equity and held by non-controlling interests, the parent computes its share of profits or losses after adjusting for the dividends on such shares, whether or not the dividends have been declared. [IFRS 10:B95] By comparison, dividends in respect of non-cumulative preference shares classified as equity only affect the allocation of profits or losses when declared.

11.2.3 Part of an interest in a subsidiary held indirectly through an associate

> **Example 11.2.3**
>
> **Part of an interest In a subsidiary held indirectly through an associate**
>
> Parent P owns 70 per cent of Subsidiary S. It also owns 40 per cent of Associate A, over which it has significant influence and which it accounts for using the equity method. Associate A owns the remaining 30 per cent of Subsidiary S.
>
> *How should Parent P determine the non-controlling interests (NCIs) in Subsidiary S for the purposes of its consolidated financial statements?*
>
> It depends on whether Parent P views the equity method of accounting as a one-line consolidation or as a valuation methodology (see **4.4.10** in **chapter A26**).
>
> Whether the equity method is considered a one-line consolidation or a valuation methodology is a matter of accounting policy to be applied consistently to all associates and to all aspects of the application of the equity method.
>
> *Equity method as a one-line consolidation*
>
> Under this view, many of the adjustments and calculations normally performed for consolidation purposes are also performed when applying the equity method.

If Parent P's accounting policy is to apply the equity method as a one-line consolidation, it should include in its percentage of ownership in Subsidiary S the interest held indirectly through Associate A; that is, it should determine the NCIs using the indirect method. Under the indirect method, the proportion of equity and total comprehensive income of Subsidiary S allocated to the NCIs in Parent P's consolidated financial statements is 18 per cent (i.e. 30% × 60%), being the proportion not held by Parent P, its subsidiaries, joint ventures or associates.

Equity method as a valuation methodology

This is often referred to as a 'closed box' approach to the equity method.

If Parent P's accounting policy is to apply the equity method as a valuation methodology, it should not include the interest in Subsidiary S held by Associate A in determining its percentage of ownership in Subsidiary S; that is, it should determine the NCIs using the direct method. Under the direct method, the proportion of equity and total comprehensive income of Subsidiary S allocated to the NCIs in Parent P's consolidated financial statements is 30 per cent, being the proportion not held by Parent P or its subsidiaries.

11.3 Presentation of non-controlling interests

For the presentation of non-controlling interests, the requirements are as follows:

- non-controlling interests should be presented in the consolidated statement of financial position within equity, separately from the equity of the owners of the parent; [IFRS 10:22] and

- the following items should be presented, in addition to the profit or loss and other comprehensive income sections, as allocation of profit or loss and other comprehensive income for the period:

  [IAS 1:81B]

  - profit or loss for the period attributable to (i) non-controlling interests, and (ii) owners of the parent; and

  - comprehensive income for the period attributable to (i) non-controlling interests, and (ii) owners of the parent.

11.4 Changes in the proportion held by non-controlling interests

11.4.1 Change in the parent's ownership interest without loss of control

When there is a change in a parent's ownership interest in a subsidiary, but the parent does not cease to have control, this is accounted for as an equity transaction (i.e. a transaction with owners in their capacity as owners). [IFRS 10:23]

In particular, therefore, when a parent increases or decreases its stake in an existing subsidiary without losing control, no adjustment is made to goodwill or any other assets or liabilities, and no gain or loss is reported.

11.4.2 Change in the proportion of equity held by non-controlling interests

When the proportion of the equity held by non-controlling interests changes, the carrying amounts of the controlling and non-controlling interests are adjusted to reflect the changes in their relative interests in the subsidiary. Any difference between (1) the amount by which the non-controlling interests are adjusted, and (2) the fair value of the consideration paid or received is recognised directly in equity and attributed to the owners of the parent. [IFRS 10:B96]

For transactions between the parent and non-controlling interests, IFRS 10 does not provide any detailed guidance on how to measure the amount to be allocated to the parent and non-controlling interests to reflect a change in their relative interests in the subsidiary. More than one approach may be possible, as discussed in **examples 11.4.5B** and **11.4.5C**.

11.4.3 Non-controlling interest created other than in a business combination

IFRS 10 does not specifically address situations when a non-controlling interest is created through a transaction other than a business combination (e.g. a parent disposes of 25 per cent of a previously wholly-owned subsidiary); in particular, it provides no guidance as to how the non-controlling interest should be measured. One approach would be to recognise any difference between the fair value of the consideration paid and the non-controlling interest's proportionate share of the carrying amount of the identifiable net assets directly in equity attributable to the owners of the parent. There may be other acceptable approaches to reflecting the change in relative interests; these approaches should similarly result in no adjustment to goodwill or to profit or loss.

11.4.4 Costs of buying out a non-controlling interest or selling an interest in a subsidiary without losing control

Under IFRS 10:23, the following transactions are accounted for as equity transactions:

- the buy-out of non-controlling interest (NCIs) by a parent; and
- the sale of an interest in a subsidiary without losing control.

The question arises as to how the costs relating to such transactions should be treated in the consolidated financial statements.

Paragraph 35 of IAS 32 *Financial Instruments: Presentation* requires that the "[t]ransaction costs of an equity transaction shall be accounted for as a deduction from equity". IAS 32:37 clarifies that this treatment should be applied "to the extent [the transaction costs] are incremental costs directly attributable to the equity transaction that otherwise would have been avoided". In addition, IAS 32:33 requires that "[n]o gain or loss shall be recognised in profit or loss on the purchase, sale, issue or cancellation of an entity's own equity instruments".

It follows that the costs of buying out a non-controlling interest should also be accounted for as a deduction from equity in the consolidated financial statements provided that they are incremental costs in accordance with IAS 32:37 (see previous paragraph). Similarly, the costs of selling part of the parent's interest in a subsidiary without losing control should be deducted from equity in the consolidated financial statements, provided that the costs meet the requirements in IAS 32:37.

11.4.5   Implications of the measurement basis of non-controlling interests

The adjustment to the carrying amount of non-controlling interests and the consequential adjustment to the equity attributed to the owners of the parent following a transaction with the parent will be affected by the choice of measurement basis for non-controlling interests that represent present ownership interests at acquisition date (see **7.3.2** in **chapter A25**). The IASB explains the difference as follows.

[IFRS 3(2008):BC218]

"The third difference [due to the choice of measurement basis for non-controlling interests] arises if the acquirer subsequently purchases some (or all) of the shares held by the non-controlling shareholders. If the non-controlling interests are acquired, presumably at fair value, the equity of the group is reduced by the non-controlling interests' share of any unrecognised changes in the fair value of the net assets of the business, including goodwill. If the non-controlling interest is measured initially as a proportionate share of the acquiree's identifiable net assets, rather than at fair value, that reduction in the reported equity attributable to the acquirer is likely to be larger. This matter was considered further in the IASB's deliberations on the proposed amendments to IAS 27."

The difference is highlighted in the following examples.

Example 11.4.5A

Parent acquires all of the non-controlling interests

In 20X1, Entity A acquired a 75 per cent equity interest in Entity B for cash consideration of CU90,000. Entity B's identifiable net assets at fair value were CU100,000. The fair value of the 25 per cent non-controlling interests (NCIs) was CU28,000. Goodwill, on the two alternative bases for measuring NCIs that represent present ownership interests at acquisition, is calculated as follows.

	NCIs @ % of net assets	NCIs @ fair value
	CU	CU
Fair value of consideration	90,000	90,000
NCIs	25,000	28,000
	115,000	118,000
Fair value of net assets	100,000	100,000
Goodwill	15,000	18,000

In the subsequent years, Entity B increased net assets by CU20,000 to CU120,000. This is reflected in the carrying amount within equity attributed to NCIs as follows.

	NCIs @ % of net assets	NCIs @ fair value
	CU	CU
NCIs at acquisition	25,000	28,000
Increase (25% × CU20,000)*	5,000	5,000
Carrying amount	30,000	33,000

*   Cumulative profit attributable to NCIs since acquisition

In 20X6, Entity A acquired the 25 per cent equity interest held by NCIs for cash consideration of CU35,000. The adjustment to equity will be as follows.

	NCIs @ % of net assets	NCIs @ fair value
	CU	CU
Fair value of consideration	35,000	35,000
Carrying amount of NCIs	30,000	33,000
Negative movement in equity attributed to the owners of the parent	5,000	2,000

As indicated in IFRS 3:BC218, the reduction in the equity attributed to the owners of the parent is greater if the option was taken to measure NCIs that represent present ownership interests at acquisition date as a proportionate share of the acquiree's identifiable net assets. The treatment has the effect of including the NCIs' share of goodwill directly in equity, although goodwill itself is unaffected. This outcome will always occur when the fair value basis is greater than the net asset basis at acquisition date.

Example 11.4.5B

Parent acquires some of the non-controlling interests

The facts are as in **example 11.4.5A** except that, rather than acquire all of the non-controlling interests (NCIs), Entity A acquires an additional 15 per cent equity interest held by NCIs for cash consideration of CU21,000. The adjustment to the carrying amount of NCIs will be as follows.

	NCIs @ % of net assets	NCIs @ fair value
	CU	CU
Balance as in **example 11.4.5A**	30,000	33,000
Transfer to parent (15/25ths)*	18,000	19,800
10% interest carried forward	12,000	13,200

*   In this example, it is assumed that NCIs are reduced proportionately. Under the fair value option, the closing balance represents 10/25th of the acquisition date fair value (CU11,200) plus 10 per cent of the change in net assets since acquisition (CU2,000). As discussed at **11.4.2**, other approaches may also be acceptable to determine the amount by which NCIs are adjusted.

The adjustment to equity will be as follows.

	NCIs @ % of net assets	NCIs @ fair value
	CU	CU
Fair value of consideration	21,000	21,000
Change to NCIs (as above)	18,000	19,800
Negative movement in the equity attributed to the owners of the parent	3,000	1,200

Example 11.4.5C

Parent disposes of part of its interest to non-controlling interests

In 20X1, Entity A acquired a 100 per cent equity interest in Entity B for cash consideration of CU125,000. Entity B's identifiable net assets at fair value were CU100,000. Goodwill of CU25,000 was identified and recognised.

In the subsequent years, Entity B increased net assets by CU20,000 to CU120,000. This is reflected in equity attributable to the parent.

Entity A then disposed of 30 per cent of its equity interest to non-controlling interests (NCIs) for CU40,000. The adjustment to equity will be as follows.

	CU
Fair value of consideration received	40,000
Amount recognised as NCIs (30% × 120,000)*	36,000
Positive movement in parent equity	4,000

* In this example, it is assumed that NCIs are measured based on their share of identifiable assets. Other approaches may also be acceptable to determine the amount by which NCIs are adjusted (e.g. NCIs might instead be measured initially at the fair value of consideration received, CU40,000).

Note that there is no adjustment to the carrying amount of goodwill of CU25,000 because control has been retained.

11.4.6   Non-cash acquisition of non-controlling interests

Example 11.4.6

Non-cash acquisition of non-controlling interest

Entity P has an 80 per cent interest in Entity Q. The remaining 20 per cent is owned by Entity R.

In Entity P's consolidated financial statements, the carrying amount of Entity R's non-controlling interest (NCI) in Entity Q is CU30 million. Entity P purchases Entity R's interest for consideration of an intangible asset with a fair value of CU40 million. The carrying amount of the intangible asset in Entity P's financial statements is CU20 million.

When it purchases Entity R's interest in Entity Q, how should Entity P account for the difference of CU20 million between the fair value of the intangible asset (i.e. the consideration for the purchase) and its carrying amount?

Entity P should recognise a gain of CU20 million in profit or loss in respect of the difference between the fair value of the intangible asset and its carrying amount. This is in accordance with paragraph 113 of IAS 38 *Intangible Assets** which requires that "[t]he gain or loss arising from the derecognition of an intangible asset shall be determined as the difference between the net disposal proceeds, if any, and the carrying amount of the asset. It shall be recognised in profit or loss when the asset is derecognised (unless IFRS 16 [*Leases* or, for entities that have not yet adopted IFRS 16, IAS 17 *Leases*] requires otherwise on a sale and leaseback)".

In contrast, the difference of CU10 million between the carrying amount of the NCI (CU30 million) and the fair value of the consideration paid (CU40 million) is recognised in equity in accordance with IFRS 10:B96.

Therefore, the journal entry required to record Entity P's purchase of Entity R's interest is as follows.

		CU'000	CU'000
Dr	NCIs	30,000	
Dr	Equity	10,000	
Cr	Intangible asset		20,000
Cr	Gain (profit or loss)		20,000

*   Similar requirements apply for other categories of assets. For example, if the asset transferred as consideration is an item of property, plant and equipment, the equivalent reference is paragraph 68 of IAS 16 *Property, Plant and Equipment*.

This conclusion was confirmed by the IFRS Interpretations Committee in the January 2013 *IFRIC Update*.

12   Accounting for loss of control of a subsidiary

12.1   Circumstances when a loss of control can occur

When a parent loses control, the investee no longer meets the definition of a subsidiary and, consequently, it is no longer consolidated. A loss of control can occur with or without a change in absolute or relative ownership interests. It could occur, for example, when a subsidiary becomes subject to the control of a government, court, administrator or regulator. It could also occur as a result of a contractual agreement.

A common example of loss of control without any change in absolute or relative ownership interests is when a subsidiary becomes subject to insolvency proceedings involving the appointment of a receiver or liquidator, if the effect is that the shareholders cease to have control. Although this will often be the case in a liquidation, a receivership or administration order may not involve loss of control by the shareholders.

Another example of loss of control without any change in absolute or relative ownership interests would be the seizure of the assets or operations of an overseas subsidiary by the local government.

Short-term restrictions on cash flows from a subsidiary, perhaps because of exchange controls or restrictions on distributions of profits in a foreign jurisdiction, do not generally result in a loss of control. The fact that a parent may not be able to remit dividends from the subsidiary, or use the funds for other parts of the group outside the country of operation, does not by itself indicate that the ability to transfer funds in the longer term has been significantly impaired. Indeed, subsidiaries are often set up in the face of such restrictions and are, presumably, expected to produce economic benefits for the parent.

12.2 Loss of control as a result of multiple arrangements

A parent might lose control of a subsidiary in two or more arrangements (transactions). However, sometimes circumstances indicate that the multiple arrangements should be accounted for as a single transaction. In determining whether to account for the arrangements as a single transaction, a parent should consider all the terms and conditions of the arrangements and their economic effects. IFRS 10 states that one or more of the following may indicate that the parent should account for the multiple arrangements as a single transaction:

[IFRS 10:B97]

- they are entered into at the same time or in contemplation of each other;

- they form a single transaction designed to achieve an overall commercial effect;

- the occurrence of one arrangement is dependent on the occurrence of at least one other arrangement; and/or

- one arrangement considered on its own is not economically justified, but it is economically justified when considered together with other arrangements. An example is when one disposal of shares is priced below market and is compensated for by a subsequent disposal priced above market.

12.3 Accounting implications of a loss of control

12.3.1 Accounting implications of a loss of control – general

The requirements discussed in this section are based on the text of IFRS 10 prior to the September 2014 amendments *Sale or Contribution of Assets between an Investor and its Associate or Joint Venture (Amendments to IFRS 10 and IAS 28)*. Although, when finalised, the September 2014 amendments were stated to be effective for annual periods beginning on or after 1 January 2016, with earlier application permitted, subsequent amendments to IFRS 10 issued in December 2015 have deferred indefinitely the effective date of the September 2014 amendments pending finalisation of a larger research project on the equity method of accounting (scope and timetable yet to be determined). For periods prior to the, as yet unspecified, effective date of the September 2014 amendments, or the effective date of any alternative amendments made following completion of the Board's research project, entities may choose to apply the amendments but they are not required to do so.

See **12.4** for a summary of the impact of the September 2014 amendments and the amended text of the affected paragraphs in IFRS 10.

When a parent loses control of a subsidiary, the steps set out below are followed.

[IFRS 10:25, B98 & B99]

- The assets (including any goodwill) and liabilities of the subsidiary are derecognised at their carrying amounts at the date when control is lost.
- The carrying amount of any non-controlling interests in the former subsidiary at the date when control is lost (including any components of other comprehensive income attributable to them) is derecognised.
- The parent recognises the fair value of the consideration received, if any, from the transaction, event or circumstances that resulted in the loss of control.
- If the transaction, event or circumstances that resulted in the loss of control involves a distribution of shares of the subsidiary to owners in their capacity as owners, that distribution is recognised.
- Any investment retained in the former subsidiary is recognised at its fair value at the date when control is lost.
- The amounts recognised in other comprehensive income in relation to the former subsidiary are reclassified to profit or loss, or transferred directly to retained earnings if required by other IFRSs (see **12.3.2**).
- Any resulting difference is recognised as a gain or loss in profit or loss attributable to the parent.

For the purposes of the calculation of the gain or loss on disposal, the carrying amount of the subsidiary should include any goodwill carried in the statement of financial position in respect of the subsidiary. However, when goodwill has previously been eliminated against reserves prior to transition to IFRSs, IFRS 1 *First-time Adoption of International Financial Reporting Standards* prohibits it from being reclassified to profit or loss on subsequent disposal.

Note that when an entity ceases to have control of a subsidiary as a result of selling its controlling interest to an existing associate or joint venture, or as a result of contributing its controlling interest to an associate or a joint venture, there is a conflict between the requirements of IFRS 10 and IAS 28 *Investments in Associates and Joint Ventures* regarding the appropriate accounting.

According to IFRS 10:25, upon loss of control of a subsidiary, a parent derecognises the assets and liabilities of the subsidiary (including non-controlling interests) in full and measures any investment retained in the former subsidiary at its fair value. A remeasurement gain or loss that forms part of the total gain or loss on the disposal of the subsidiary is recognised in profit or loss. In contrast, IAS 28:28 only permits recognition of the gain or loss "to the extent of unrelated investors' interests in the associate or joint venture".

In the absence of any other relevant guidance, entities have, in effect, an accounting policy choice of applying either the approach in IFRS 10 or the approach in IAS 28 because the two Standards have equal status in the IFRS literature. Both approaches are illustrated in **example 12.3.3C**. Although the IASB issued amendments designed to address this conflict in September 2014 (see **12.4**), the Board subsequently deferred the effective date of the amendments indefinitely so that there continues to be more than one acceptable approach.

12.3.2   Amounts previously recognised in other comprehensive income

When a parent loses control of a subsidiary, all amounts recognised in other comprehensive income in relation to that subsidiary should be accounted for on the same basis as would be required if the parent had directly disposed of the related assets or liabilities. Therefore:

[IFRS 10:B99]

- if a gain or loss previously recognised in other comprehensive income would be reclassified to profit or loss on the disposal of the related assets or liabilities, the parent reclassifies the gain or loss from equity to profit or loss when it loses control of the subsidiary; and

- if a revaluation surplus previously recognised in other comprehensive income would be transferred directly to retained earnings on the disposal of the asset, the revaluation surplus is transferred directly to retained earnings when the parent loses control of the subsidiary.

For example:

- if a subsidiary has debt instruments measured at fair value through other comprehensive income under IFRS 9 *Financial Instruments* (or, for entities that have not yet adopted IFRS 9, financial assets classified as available-for-sale financial assets under IAS 39 *Financial Instruments: Recognition and Measurement*) and the parent loses control of the subsidiary, all of the gain or loss previously recognised in other comprehensive income and accumulated in equity in relation to those assets is reclassified to profit or loss; but

- if a subsidiary has a policy of revaluing property, plant and equipment, all of the gain or loss previously recognised in other comprehensive income and accumulated in equity in relation to the revalued property, plant and equipment is transferred directly to retained earnings.

Paragraph 48 of IAS 21 *The Effects of Changes in Foreign Exchange Rates* sets out specific requirements regarding the treatment of foreign exchange differences accumulated in equity when control is lost on disposal of a subsidiary (see **section 6** of **chapter A19**).

12.3.3   Interest retained in the former subsidiary

The fair value of any investment retained in the former subsidiary at the date when control is lost is regarded as the fair value on initial recognition of a financial asset in accordance with IFRS 9 (or, for entities that have not yet adopted IFRS 9, IAS 39) or, when appropriate, the cost on initial recognition of an investment in an associate or a joint venture. [IFRS 10:25(b)]

Example 12.3.3A

Parent disposes of its controlling interest but retains a financial asset

In 20X1, Entity A acquired a 100 per cent equity interest in Entity B for cash consideration of CU125,000. Entity B's identifiable net assets at fair value were CU100,000. Goodwill of CU25,000 was identified and recognised.

In the subsequent years, Entity B reported net profits of CU20,000. Its net assets (including goodwill) reported in Entity A's consolidated financial statements therefore increased to CU145,000.

Entity A then sold 90 per cent of its equity interest for cash consideration of CU138,000. The residual 10 per cent equity interest is a financial asset within the scope of IFRS 9 (or, for entities that have not yet adopted IFRS 9, IAS 39) and has a fair value of CU15,000.

In accordance with IFRS 10:B98, the gain recognised in profit or loss on disposal of the 90 per cent equity interest is calculated as follows.

	CU
Fair value of consideration received	138,000
Fair value of residual interest	15,000
	153,000
Less: net assets and goodwill derecognised	(145,000)
	8,000

The residual 10 per cent equity interest will be initially measured at fair value in accordance with IFRS 9:5.1.1 (or, for entities that have not yet adopted IFRS 9, IAS 39:43); its subsequent measurement will depend upon its classification under IFRS 9 (IAS 39).

Paragraph 19(a) of IFRS 12 *Disclosure of Interests in Other Entities* requires disclosure of "the portion of that gain or loss attributable to recognising any investment retained in the former subsidiary at its fair value at the date when control is lost". The amount would be determined as follows.

	CU
Fair value of residual interest	15,000
Less: 10 per cent of net assets and goodwill derecognised (10% × CU145,000)	(14,500)
Portion of gain	500

Example 12.3.3B

Parent disposes of its controlling interest but retains an associate interest

In 20X1, Entity F acquired a 100 per cent equity interest in Entity G for cash consideration of CU125,000. Entity G's identifiable net assets at fair value were CU100,000. Goodwill of CU25,000 was identified and recognised.

In the subsequent years, Entity G reported net profits of CU20,000. Its net assets (including goodwill) reported in Entity F's consolidated financial statements therefore increased to CU145,000.

Entity F then disposed of 75 per cent of its equity interest to a third party for cash consideration of CU115,000. The residual 25 per cent equity interest is classified as an associate under IAS 28 and has a fair value of CU38,000.

The gain recognised in profit or loss on disposal of the 75 per cent equity interest is calculated as follows.

	CU
Fair value of consideration received	115,000
Fair value of residual interest	38,000
	153,000
Less: net assets and goodwill derecognised	(145,000)
Gain	8,000

Subsequent accounting under IAS 28 on an equity-accounting basis will require an exercise to assess the fair value of Entity G's identifiable net assets on the date that control is lost. Goodwill will be identified by comparing the initial fair value of the interest of CU38,000 with the residual share (25 per cent) of identifiable net assets at fair value.

Paragraph 19(a) of IFRS 12 *Disclosure of Interests in Other Entities* requires disclosure of "the portion of that gain or loss attributable to measuring any investment retained in the former subsidiary at its fair value at the date when control is lost". The amount would be determined as follows.

	CU
Fair value of residual interest	38,000
Less: 25 per cent of net assets and goodwill derecognised (25% × CU145,000)	(36,250)
Portion of gain	1,750

Example 12.3.3C

Parent disposes of its controlling interest to an existing associate

Note: this example illustrates the application of IFRS 10 for entities that have not yet adopted the September 2014 amendments Sale or Contribution of Assets between an Investor and its Associate or Joint Venture (Amendments to IFRS 10 and IAS 28) *(see 12.3.1).*

In 20X1, Entity A acquired a 100 per cent equity interest in Entity B for cash consideration of CU125,000. Entity B's identifiable net assets at fair value were CU100,000. Goodwill of CU25,000 was identified and recognised.

In the subsequent years, Entity B reported net profits of CU20,000. Its net assets (including goodwill) reported in Entity A's consolidated financial statements therefore increased to CU145,000.

Entity A then sold 100 per cent of its equity interest to an existing associate, Entity C, for cash consideration of CU153,000. Entity A has a 25 per cent interest in Entity C.

As discussed at **12.3.1**, there is a conflict between the requirements of IFRS 10 and those of IAS 28 in these circumstances and Entity A has, in effect, an accounting policy choice of applying the requirements of either Standard.

Approach 1 – Entity A applies the requirements of IFRS 10 and recognises the profit on disposal in full

In accordance with IFRS 10:B98, the gain recognised in profit or loss on disposal of the 100 per cent equity interest is calculated as follows.

	CU
Fair value of consideration received	153,000
Less: net assets and goodwill derecognised	(145,000)
	8,000

Approach 2 – Entity A applies the requirements of IAS 28 and recognises the profit on disposal only to the extent of unrelated investors' interests in the associate

The gain is calculated as above but, in accordance with IAS 28:28, Entity A recognises:

- a gain of CU6,000 (CU8,000 × 75 per cent) in profit or loss (being the gain on disposal relating to unrelated investors' interests in Entity C); and

- a reduction in its investment in Entity C of CU2,000 (CU8,000 × 25 per cent) (being the gain on disposal relating to its interest in Entity C).

Subsequent accounting under IAS 28 on an equity-accounting basis will require an exercise to assess the fair value of Entity B's identifiable net assets on the date that control is lost. Goodwill will be identified by comparing the initial fair value of the interest of CU153,000 with the identifiable net assets at fair value.

Example 12.3.3C illustrates the conflict between IFRS 10:B98 and IAS 28:28 that arises in respect of a 'downstream' transaction in which a subsidiary is sold to an existing associate or joint venture (as described in **12.3.1**). A similar conflict arises when a parent contributes its controlling interest in a subsidiary to an associate or a joint venture in exchange for an equity interest in the associate or joint venture (see discussion at **4.4.15.3** in **chapter A26**).

12.3.4 Disposal of part of an interest in a subsidiary

When part of an investment in a subsidiary is sold during the reporting period, the status of the investment immediately after the disposal should determine the accounting. For example:

- if a parent sells a portion of its investment in a subsidiary, but does not lose control, the consolidated financial statements at the end of the period should include the assets, liabilities, and operations of the subsidiary, and reflect the new non-controlling interest from the date of the transaction. No gain or loss should be reported in comprehensive income because this is an equity transaction (see **11.4.1**);

- if the parent loses control of the subsidiary, but still retains significant influence or joint control over the entity, that remaining investment should be reflected in the statement of financial position at the end of the period as a single line item, using the equity method in accordance with IAS 28. The subsequent results of operations should also be reported using the equity method. If the disposal qualifies as a discontinued operation, presentation of the discontinued operation should follow IFRS 5 *Non-current Assets Held for Sale and Discontinued Operations* from the date that the operation qualifies as held for sale (see **3.4.1** in **chapter A20**); and

- if the parent loses control of the subsidiary and retains an interest that does not allow it to exert significant influence or joint control over the entity, the remaining interest in the entity should be accounted for in accordance with IFRS 9 (or, for entities that have not yet adopted IFRS 9, IAS 39) from the date of the disposal. If the sale of the subsidiary qualifies as a discontinued operation, presentation of the discontinued operation should follow IFRS 5 from the date that the operation qualifies as held for sale (see **3.4.1** in **chapter A20**).

12.3.5 Deemed disposals

A deemed disposal of an interest in a subsidiary, joint venture or associate may arise through the parent not taking up its full entitlement in a rights issue, a payment of scrip dividends not taken up by the parent, the issue of shares to other shareholders, or the exercise of options or warrants granted to another party. As a result, the parent's shareholding is reduced or diluted.

Any gain or loss arising as a result of a deemed disposal (which can occur only when control is lost as a result of the deemed disposal) should be recognised in profit or loss.

12.3.6 Allocation of goodwill on disposal of a subsidiary

An entity may dispose of a subsidiary that forms part of a group of cash-generating units to which goodwill has been allocated. In such circumstances, paragraph 86 of IAS 36 *Impairment of Assets* includes guidance on how the goodwill should be allocated between the operation disposed of and those operations that have been retained (see **8.2.8.4** in **chapter A10**).

12.4 September 2014 amendments *Sale or Contribution of Assets between an Investor and its Associate or Joint Venture*

In September 2014, the IASB issued *Sale or Contribution of Assets between an Investor and its Associate or Joint Venture (Amendments to IFRS 10 and IAS 28)*. The September 2014 amendments were designed to address a conflict between the requirements of IAS 28 *Investments in Associates and Joint Ventures* and IFRS 10 (as described at **12.3.1**) by requiring different treatments for assets that constitute a business and those that do not (see below for amended requirements); this distinction and the required accounting would apply in both IFRS 10 and IAS 28, thus eliminating the inconsistency between the Standards.

The effect of the amendments is to specify as follows.

- In a transaction involving an associate or a joint venture, the extent of gain or loss recognition depends on whether the assets sold or contributed constitute a business.

- When an entity:
  - sells or contributes assets that constitute a business to a joint venture or an associate; or
  - loses control of a subsidiary that contains a business but it retains joint control or significant influence;

  the gain or loss resulting from that transaction is recognised in full.

- Conversely, when an entity:
  - sells or contributes assets that do not constitute a business to a joint venture or an associate; or

- loses control of a subsidiary that does not contain a business but it retains joint control or significant influence in a transaction involving an associate or a joint venture;

the gain or loss resulting from that transaction is recognised only to the extent of the unrelated investors' interests in the joint venture or associate, i.e. the entity's share of the gain or loss is eliminated. A new example added to the Standard (see **example 12.4**) illustrates the appropriate accounting in such circumstances.

Following finalisation of the September 2014 amendments, the IASB identified several practical issues affecting the implementation of the amendments. As a result, in December 2015 the IASB deferred the effective date of the September 2014 amendments indefinitely pending finalisation of a larger research project on equity accounting (scope and timetable yet to be determined).

For periods prior to the, as yet unspecified, effective date of the September 2014 amendments, or the effective date of any alternative amendments made following completion of the IASB's research project, entities may choose between:

- applying the September 2014 amendments (as described below), in which case the appropriate accounting is determined based on whether the assets sold or contributed constitute a business as described above; and

- continuing to apply the requirements of IFRS 10 and IAS 28 prior to the September 2014 amendments (as described in **12.3**). If this alternative is selected, entities continue to have an accounting policy choice of applying either the approach in IFRS 10 or the approach in IAS 28 (as illustrated in example **12.3.3C**).

Entities that cannot formally adopt the September 2014 amendments (e.g. due to a requirement for endorsement of changes to IFRSs in their jurisdiction) may adopt an accounting policy consistent with those amendments (i.e. distinguishing between transactions on the basis of whether the subsidiary being sold or contributed constitutes a business) provided that the requirements of paragraph 14(b) of IAS 8 *Accounting Policies, Changes in Accounting Estimates and Errors* are met (i.e. the change in policy results in the financial statements providing reliable and more relevant information). However, such a 'voluntary' change in policy would have to be applied retrospectively in accordance with IAS 8; the transition provisions of the September 2014 amendments (which allow for prospective application to transactions occurring after a specified date) would not be available.

When a parent loses control of a subsidiary:

[IFRS 10:25 (as amended by the September 2014 amendments) & B98]

- the assets (including any goodwill) and liabilities of the subsidiary are derecognised at their carrying amounts at the date when control is lost;

- the carrying amount of any non-controlling interests in the former subsidiary at the date when control is lost (including any components of other comprehensive income attributable to them) is derecognised;

- the parent recognises the fair value of the consideration received, if any, from the transaction, event or circumstances that resulted in the loss of control; and

- if the transaction, event or circumstances that resulted in the loss of control involves a distribution of shares of the subsidiary to owners in their capacity as owners, that distribution is recognised.

Unless the transaction falls within the scope of IFRS 10:B99A (see below):

[IFRS 10:25 (as amended by the September 2014 amendments), B98 & B99]

- any investment retained is recognised at its fair value at the date when control is lost. That fair value is regarded as the fair value on initial recognition of a financial asset in accordance with IFRS 9 (or, for entities that have not yet adopted IFRS 9, IAS 39) or the cost on initial recognition of an investment in an associate or a joint venture, if applicable. The retained interest and any amounts owed by or to the former subsidiary are accounted for in accordance with relevant IFRSs;

- the amounts recognised in other comprehensive income in relation to the former subsidiary are reclassified to profit or loss, or transferred directly to retained earnings if required by other IFRSs (see **12.3.2**); and

- any resulting difference is recognised as a gain or loss in profit or loss attributable to the parent.

IFRS 10:B99A (see below) applies when a parent loses control of a subsidiary that does not contain a business, as defined in IFRS 3 *Business Combinations*, as a result of a transaction involving an associate or a joint venture that is accounted for using the equity method.

> IFRS 10:B99A therefore applies, for example, when an entity ceases to have control of a subsidiary that does not contain a business, as a result of selling it to an existing associate or joint venture, or as a result of contributing it to a joint venture.

When IFRS 10:B99A applies:

- the gain or loss arising from the transaction is calculated as specified in IFRS 10:B98 and B99 (see above);

- the gain or loss (including the amounts previously recognised in other comprehensive income that would be reclassified to profit or loss in accordance with IFRS 10:B99 – see **12.3.2**) is recognised in the parent's profit or loss only to the extent of the unrelated investors' interest in the associate or joint venture;

- if the parent retains an investment in the former subsidiary and the former subsidiary is now an associate or a joint venture accounted for using the equity method, the parent recognises the part of the gain or loss resulting from the remeasurement at fair value of the investment retained in that former subsidiary in its profit or loss only to the extent of the unrelated investors' interests in the new associate or joint venture;

- the remaining part of the gain is eliminated against the carrying amount of the investment retained in the former subsidiary; and

- if the parent retains an investment in the former subsidiary that is now accounted for in accordance with IFRS 9 (or, for entities that have not yet adopted IFRS 9, IAS 39), the part of the gain or loss resulting from the remeasurement at fair value of the investment retained in the former subsidiary is recognised in full in the parent's profit or loss.

Example 12.4

Sale of a subsidiary to an associate (entities that have adopted the September 2014 amendments)

[IFRS 10:Appendix B Example 17]

A parent has a 100 per cent interest in a subsidiary that does not contain a business. The parent sells 70 per cent of its interest in the subsidiary to an associate in which it has a 20 per cent interest. As a consequence of this transaction the parent loses control of the subsidiary. The carrying amount of the net assets of the subsidiary is CU100 and the carrying amount of the interest sold is CU70 (CU70 = CU100 × 70%). The fair value of the consideration received is CU210, which is also the fair value of the interest sold. The investment retained in the former subsidiary is an associate accounted for using the equity method and its fair value is CU90. The gain determined in accordance with [IFRS 10:B98 and B99], before the elimination required by [IFRS 10:B99A], is CU200 (CU200 = CU210 + CU90 – CU100). This gain comprises two parts:

(a) the gain (CU140) resulting from the sale of the 70 per cent interest in the subsidiary to the associate. This gain is the difference between the fair value of the consideration received (CU210) and the carrying amount of the interest sold (CU70). According to [IFRS 10:B99A], the parent recognises in its profit or loss the amount of the gain attributable to the unrelated investors' interests in the existing associate. This is 80 per cent of this gain, that is CU112 (CU112 = CU140 × 80%). The remaining 20 per cent of the gain (CU28 = CU140 × 20%) is eliminated against the carrying amount of the investment in the existing associate.

(b) the gain (CU60) resulting from the remeasurement at fair value of the investment directly retained in the former subsidiary. This gain is the difference between the fair value of the investment retained in the former subsidiary (CU90) and 30 per cent of the carrying amount of the net assets of the subsidiary (CU30 = CU100 × 30%). According to [IFRS 10:B99A], the parent recognises in its profit or loss the amount of the gain attributable to the unrelated investors' interests in the new associate. This is 56 per cent (70% × 80%) of the gain, that is CU34 (CU34 = CU60 × 56%). The remaining 44 per cent of the gain CU26 (CU26 = CU60 × 44%) is eliminated against the carrying amount of the investment retained in the former subsidiary.

13   Investment entities

13.1   Exception to general consolidation requirements for investment entities

IFRS 10 includes an exception from its general consolidation requirements for 'investment entities' as defined, and requires such entities to measure their investments in subsidiaries at fair value through profit or loss (other than subsidiaries that are required to be consolidated – i.e. those that are not themselves investment entities and whose main purpose and activities are providing services that relate to the investment entity's investment activities).

Notable characteristics of the exception are as follows.

- It is applied at an entity level – i.e. it is focussed on the nature of the entity that holds the investment in a subsidiary (or subsidiaries), not on the nature of the investments. [IFRS 10:BC226]

- It is a mandatory exception to IFRS 10's general consolidation requirements, rather than an optional exemption. If an entity meets the definition of an investment entity, it is required to apply the accounting requirements in IFRS 10:31 to 33 (see **13.3**).

- The exception does *not* carry through to the consolidated financial statements of a non-investment entity parent of an investment entity (see **13.3.4**).

The investment entity requirements in IFRS 10, discussed in detail in the following sections, are principally concerned with establishing whether an entity qualifies as an investment entity. In defining an investment entity, and describing the typical features of an investment entity, the Standard avoids the use of 'bright lines'. Accordingly, it will be necessary to exercise judgement in applying the requirements.

13.2 Determining whether an entity is an investment entity

13.2.1 General requirement for a parent to determine if it is an investment entity

A parent entity is required to determine if it is an investment entity. [IFRS 10:27] It is required to consider all facts and circumstances in making this determination, including its purpose and design. [IFRS 10:B85A]

IFRS 10:27 (see **13.2.2**) sets out three criteria (or 'elements') that differentiate investment entities from other entities and that *must* be met in order for an entity to qualify as an investment entity. Detailed guidance on the application of these criteria is provided in Appendix B to the Standard (see **13.2.3** to **13.2.5**).

In addition, IFRS 10:28 lists four 'typical characteristics' of an investment entity (see **13.2.6**). An entity is not required to display all of these characteristics in order to qualify as an investment entity, but the absence of one or more of these characteristics indicates that additional judgement is needed in determining whether it meets the definition.

The Standard provides a number of examples illustrating how to determine whether an entity is an investment entity (see **13.2.7**).

A change in facts or circumstances that affects whether the entity meets the three criteria making up the definition of an investment entity, or the four typical characteristics of such entities, will lead to a reassessment of an entity's status as an investment entity (see **13.2.8**).

13.2.2 Investment entity – definition

An investment entity is defined as an entity that:

[IFRS 10:27]

- obtains funds from one or more investors for the purpose of providing those investor(s) with investment management services (see **13.2.3**);

- commits to its investor(s) that its business purpose is to invest funds solely for returns from capital appreciation, investment income, or both (see **13.2.4**); and

- measures and evaluates the performance of substantially all of its investments on a fair value basis (see **13.2.5**).

13.2.3 Obtaining funds for the purpose of providing investment management services

The first of the criteria that must be met for an entity to qualify as an investment entity is that the entity obtains funds from one or more investors for the purpose of providing those investor(s) with investment management services. [IFRS 10:27(a)]

The Standard provides no further guidance on this first element of the definition of an investment entity. In the Basis for Conclusions on IFRS 10, the Board notes that the provision of investment management services differentiates investment entities from other entities. [IFRS 10:BC237]

13.2.4 Business purpose to invest funds solely for investment returns

13.2.4.1 Commitment to invest funds solely for investment returns

The second of the criteria to qualify as an investment entity is that the entity has committed to its investor(s) that its business purpose is to invest funds solely for returns from capital appreciation, investment income, or both. [IFRS 10:27(b)]

13.2.4.2 Evidence of an investment entity's business purpose

Evidence of an investment entity's business purpose may be provided by:

[IFRS 10:B85B]

- documents that describe the entity's investment objectives (e.g. the entity's offering memorandum, publications distributed by the entity, and other corporate or partnership documents);

- its investment plans (see **13.2.4.7**); and

- the manner in which the entity presents itself to other parties (e.g. potential investors or potential investees). For example, an investment entity may present its business as providing medium-term investment for capital appreciation. In contrast, if an investor presents its objective as the joint development, production or marketing of products with its investees, this is inconsistent with the business purpose of an investment entity, because the entity will earn returns from the development, production or marketing activity as well as from its investments (see also **13.2.4.8**).

13.2.4.3 Investment entity permitted to provide investment-related services

In addition to its own investing activities, an investment entity may provide investment-related services (e.g. investment advisory services, investment management, investment support and administrative services). These services may be provided to third parties as well as to the investors in the investment entity; services to third parties may be substantial to the entity, subject to the entity continuing to meet the definition of an investment entity. [IFRS 10:B85C]

In the Board's view, the provision of such investment-related services to third parties is simply an extension of the investment entity's investment activities and is within the business model of an investment entity. Although such an entity may earn fee income from the provision of investment-related services, its sole business purpose is still investing for capital appreciation, investment income, or both (whether for itself, for its investors, or for external parties). [IFRS 10:BC239]

The wording of IFRS 10:B85C was amended by December 2014 amendments to IFRS 10 to clarify that investment-related services provided by an investment entity to third parties must be ancillary to its core investing activities. An entity whose main purpose is to provide investment-related services in exchange for consideration from third parties has a business purpose that is different from the business purpose of an investment entity. This is because the entity's main activity is earning fee income in exchange for its services. In contrast, for an entity that qualifies as an investment entity, such fee income (which could be substantial in amount) will be derived from its core investment activities, which are designed for earning capital appreciation, investment income or both. [IFRS 10:BC240F]

The December 2014 amendments to IFRS 10 are effective for annual periods beginning on or after 1 January 2016, with earlier application permitted. If an entity applies the December 2014 amendments for a period beginning before 1 January 2016, it is required to disclose that fact. [IFRS 10:C1D]

13.2.4.4 Investment entity permitted to participate in specified additional investment-related activities in limited circumstances

An investment entity may also participate in the following investment-related activities, either directly or through a subsidiary, in limited circumstances:

[IFRS 10:B85D]

- providing management services and strategic advice to an investee; and

- providing financial support to an investee (e.g. a loan, capital commitment or guarantee).

These additional activities are only permitted when (1) they are undertaken to maximise the investment return (capital appreciation or investment income) from the investment entity's investees, and (2) they do not represent a separate substantial business activity or a separate substantial source of income to the investment entity. [IFRS 10:B85D]

The IASB considered prohibiting investment entities from engaging in activities of the nature described in IFRS 10:B85D. However, the Board understands that an investment entity may engage in these activities in order to maximise the overall value of the investee (i.e. to maximise capital appreciation), rather than to obtain other benefits. Consequently, the Board believes that these activities can be consistent with the overall activities of an investment entity and should not be prohibited as long as they do not represent a separate substantial business activity or source of income other than capital appreciation. [IFRS 10:BC241]

13.2.4.5 Evaluating a parent's involvement in the activities of its subsidiaries

When evaluating an entity's involvement in the activities of its subsidiaries, it is more important to focus on *why* the parent is so involved than the *extent* of its involvement.

A parent that is actively involved in the management of its subsidiaries will therefore need to consider the following.

- How it presents itself to other parties (see **13.2.4.2**). A parent that is heavily involved in its subsidiaries' activities may be more likely, in corporate or partnership documents or other publications, to discuss its aims and performance in terms of those activities rather than in terms of the investment returns generated.

- Whether it is obtaining benefits from its subsidiaries other than capital appreciation and investment income (see **13.2.4.8**). Significant involvement in a subsidiary's activities may, for example, be for the purposes of managing agreements between the subsidiary and other members of the group or to develop technology that will benefit the group as a whole.

In addition, the entity should consider the requirement under IFRS 10:B85K (see **13.2.5**) that, in order to demonstrate that it measures and evaluates the performance of substantially all of its investments on a fair value basis, it should report fair value information internally to its key management personnel, who use fair value as the primary measurement attribute to evaluate the performance of substantially all of its investments and to make investment decisions. When a parent is actively involved in the management of a subsidiary and, as a result, receives operational information on the subsidiary's activities, an assessment should be made as to whether key management personnel are using this information rather than fair value data as the primary basis for evaluating performance.

13.2.4.6 Subsidiary providing investment-related services or activities required to be consolidated

If an investment entity has a subsidiary that is not itself an investment entity and whose main purpose and activities are providing investment-related services or activities that relate to the investment entity's investment activities (such as those described in IFRS 10:B85C and B85D – see **13.2.4.3** and **13.2.4.4**) to the investment entity or other parties, that subsidiary should be consolidated (see **13.3.3**). If the subsidiary that provides the investment-related services or activities is itself an investment entity, the investment entity parent should measure that subsidiary at fair value through profit or loss (see **13.3.2.1**). [IFRS 10:B85E]

Amendments to IFRS 10 in December 2014 clarified that subsidiaries of investment entities that are themselves investment entities are required to be measured at fair value through profit or loss in accordance with IFRS 10:31 (see **13.3.2.1**).

The Board considers services of the nature described in IFRS 10:85E as an extension of the operations of the investment entity and, therefore, concluded that subsidiaries that provide these services should be consolidated. [IFRS 10:BC240]

Although IFRS 10:B85C and B85D provide examples of 'investment-related services' and 'investment-related activities', the terms are not precisely defined; consequently, in some circumstances, it can be difficult to interpret the requirements in order to determine whether a particular subsidiary should be consolidated (see further discussion at **13.3.3.1**).

The December 2014 amendments to IFRS 10 are effective for annual periods beginning on or after 1 January 2016, with earlier application permitted. If an entity applies the December 2014 amendments for a period beginning before 1 January 2016, it is required to disclose that fact. [IFRS 10:C1D]

13.2.4.7   Investment plans (exit strategies)

In satisfying the business purpose element of the definition of an investment entity (see **13.2.4.1**), the notion of an investment time frame is critical. One feature that differentiates an investment entity from other entities is that an investment entity does not plan to hold its investments indefinitely; it holds them for a limited period. [IFRS 10:B85F]

The Standard sets the following requirements in respect of exit strategies.

[IFRS 10:B85F]

- An investment entity is required to document exit strategies for how it plans to realise capital appreciation from substantially all of its equity investments and non-financial asset investments.

- It is also required to have an exit strategy for any debt instruments that have the potential to be held indefinitely (e.g. perpetual debt investments).

- The entity is not required to document specific exit strategies for each individual investment but it is required to identify different potential strategies for different types or portfolios of investments, including a substantive time frame for exiting the investments.

- Exit mechanisms that are only put in place for default events (e.g. a breach of contract or non-performance) are not considered exit strategies for the purpose of this assessment.

Examples of exit strategies include:

[IFRS 10:B85G]

- for investments in private equity securities – an initial public offering, a private placement, a trade sale of a business, distributions (to investors) of ownership interests in investees, and sales of assets (including the sale of an investee's assets followed by a liquidation of the investee);

- for equity investments that are traded in a public market – selling the investment in a private placement or in a public market; and

- for real estate investments – selling the real estate through specialised property dealers or the open market.

Under IFRS 10:B85F, an investment entity is *required* to have documented exit strategies for substantially all of its investments that can be held indefinitely (equity investments, non-financial investments, and debt investments with an indefinite life). An entity may also hold debt investments with fixed maturities (e.g. to manage liquidity risk or to mitigate the risk from holding other types of more volatile investments). The investment entity may plan to hold some of these debt investments to maturity. Although the entity may not have an exit strategy for these debt investments, it does not plan to hold them indefinitely. The Board decided that such an entity should not be prohibited from qualifying as an investment entity provided that, in accordance with IFRS 10:27(c) (see **13.2.5**), substantially all of its investments (including debt investments) are measured at fair value. [IFRS 10:BC245 & BC246]

When an investment entity has an investment in another investment entity that is formed in connection with the entity for legal, regulatory, tax or similar business reasons, the investment entity investor need not have an exit strategy for that investment, provided that the investment entity investee has appropriate exit strategies for its investments. [IFRS 10:B85H]

Example 13.2.4.7

Exit strategy for equity investments holding fixed-term assets

Entity G is listed on a stock exchange and has a wide range of shareholders. Its business model, as set out in its listing prospectus, is to raise capital from investors in order to acquire controlling interests in entities which hold fixed-term assets. Entity G has committed to its investors that its business purpose is to invest funds solely for returns from capital appreciation, investment income, or both.

Entity G expects to hold these investments for the whole of the life of the underlying assets. The investments will then be liquidated. Entity G measures and evaluates the performance of all of its investments on a fair value basis, and reports internally on this basis.

It is clear that an investment entity does not need an exit strategy for assets with a limited life, even if it plans to hold them to maturity (see IFRS 10:BC245). However, in the circumstances under consideration, Entity G holds the fixed-term assets indirectly through equity investments which have the potential to be held indefinitely. Entity G therefore needs to have documented exit strategies for the entities in which it has invested. Although the entities themselves do not have limited lives, because Entity G's business model is that they will be liquidated after a pre-determined period, this is evidence of an exit strategy.

The only exception to this requirement is if the entities in which Entity G invests are themselves investment entities (see IFRS 10:B85H above); if the conditions in that paragraph were met, Entity G would not need to plan to liquidate the investment entity investee entities after the fixed-term investments have matured.

There is no requirement that the exit be achieved in a single transaction, nor that it be achieved within a short period. Therefore, an exit may be achieved gradually through a series of transactions. Any interest retained in the investment during this exit period should continue to be measured and evaluated on a fair value basis.

13.2.4.8 Earnings from investments

The existence of benefits other than capital appreciation and/or investment income may indicate that the business purpose element of the definition of an investment entity is not met.

If the entity, or another member of the group containing the entity (i.e. the group that is controlled by the investment entity's ultimate parent) obtains, or has the objective of obtaining, additional benefits from the entity's investments that are not available to other parties that are not related to the investee, this means that the entity is not investing solely for capital appreciation, investment income, or both, as is required under IFRS 10:B27(b). [IFRS 10:B85I]

Such benefits (which would undermine qualification as an investment entity) include, but are not limited to:

[IFRS 10:B85I]

(a) the acquisition, use, exchange or exploitation of the processes, assets or technology of an investee. This would include the entity or another group member having disproportionate, or exclusive, rights to acquire assets, technology, products or services of any investee (e.g. by holding an option to purchase an asset from an investee if the asset's development is deemed successful);

(b) joint arrangements (as defined in IFRS 11 *Joint Arrangements*) or other agreements between the entity (or another group member) and an investee to develop, produce, market or provide products or services;

(c) financial guarantees or assets provided by an investee to serve as collateral for borrowing arrangements of the entity or another group member (however, an investment entity would still be able to use an investment in an investee as collateral for any of its borrowings);

(d) an option held by a related party of the entity to purchase (from that entity or another group member) an ownership interest in an investee of the entity; and

(e) except as described in IFRS 10:B85J (see below), transactions between the entity or another group member and an investee that:

   (i) are on terms that are unavailable to entities that are not related parties of either the entity, another group member or the investee;

   (ii) are not at fair value; or

   (iii) represent a substantial portion of the investee's or the entity's business activity, including business activities of other group entities.

The specific prohibition on such additional benefits has been included in IFRS 10 in response to a concern that an entity that meets the definition of an investment entity could be inserted into a larger corporate structure to achieve a particular accounting outcome. For example, a parent entity could use an 'internal' subsidiary that is an investment entity to invest in subsidiaries that may be making losses (e.g. research and development activities on behalf of the overall group) and would record its investments at fair value, rather than reflecting the underlying activities of the investee. [IFRS 10:BC242]

An investment entity may have a strategy to invest in more than one investee in the same industry, market or geographical area in order to benefit from synergies that increase the capital appreciation and investment income from those investees. Notwithstanding IFRS 10:B85I(e) (see above), an entity is not disqualified from being classified as an investment entity merely because such investees trade with each other. [IFRS 10:B85J]

Investing in more than one investment in the same industry, market or geographical area in order to benefit from synergies that increase the capital appreciation of those investments is a common investment strategy in the private equity industry. Transactions or synergies between investments in such circumstances may increase the fair value of each investment and, consequently, increase the assets reported by the investment entity. Accordingly, the Board decided that such transactions or synergies that arise between the investments of an investment entity should not be prohibited because their existence does not necessarily mean that the investment entity is receiving any returns beyond solely capital appreciation, investment income, or both. [IFRS 10:BC243]

13.2.5 Investments measured and evaluated on a fair value basis

The third criteria to qualify as an investment entity is that the entity should measure and evaluate substantially all of its investments on a fair value basis. [IFRS 10:27(c)]

In order to demonstrate that it meets this requirement, an investment entity is required to:

[IFRS 10:B85K]

- provide its investors with fair value information and measure substantially all of its investments at fair value in its financial statements whenever fair value is required or permitted in accordance with IFRSs (see below); and

- report fair value information internally to its key management personnel (as defined in IAS 24 *Related Party Disclosures*), who use fair value as the primary measurement attribute to evaluate the performance of substantially all of its investments and to make investment decisions.

Accordingly, in order to meet the definition of an investment entity, an entity will need to:

[IFRS 10:B85L]

- select the fair value model for investment property under IAS 40 *Investment Property*;

- select the exemption from applying the equity method in IAS 28 *Investments in Associates and Joint Ventures*; and

- measure its financial assets at fair value under IFRS 9 *Financial Instruments* (or, for entities that have not yet adopted IFRS 9, IAS 39 *Financial Instruments: Recognition and Measurement*).

Consequently, an entity that would otherwise meet the definition of an investment entity (and, therefore, would not be permitted to consolidate its subsidiaries other than those that fall within the scope of IFRS 10:32 – see **13.3.3**) may fail to qualify as an investment entity if it selects accounting policy alternatives other than those described above.

For interests in investment property, and in associates and joint arrangements, measured at fair value, movements in fair value are always recognised in profit or loss. For financial assets measured at fair value, movements in fair value may, according to the circumstances, be recognised in profit or loss or in other comprehensive income (either under IFRS 9 or in respect of available-for-sale financial assets under IAS 39). If an entity measures some of its financial asset investments at fair value, and movements in fair value are recognised in other comprehensive income, this satisfies the fair value measurement element of the definition of an investment entity. [IFRS 10:BC251]

In respect of financial asset investments:

- for entities applying IFRS 9, under IFRS 9:B4.1.6, an entity that manages its investments and assesses their performance on a fair value basis will fail the business model test for measurement of financial assets at amortised cost (including for those investments that are held to maturity by an investment entity as described in IFRS 10:BC245). Accordingly, all financial asset investments (including debt investments that pass the contractual flow characteristics test at IFRS 9:4.1.2(b)) will be measured at fair value; and

- for entities applying IAS 39, measurement at fair value will always be possible at initial recognition of the asset, whether by determining that the asset is held for trading, by applying the fair value option to financial assets managed on a fair value basis, or by classifying the asset as available for sale [IAS 39.9].

Note that this third element of the investment entity definition applies only in relation to an investment entity's *investments*. An investment entity is not required to measure its non-investment assets (e.g. head office property and related equipment), or its liabilities, at fair value. [IFRS 10.B85M]

Non-investment assets could also include short-term receivables such as amounts due relating to administrative activities, from the disposal of securities or (when the investment entity provides investment-related services to third parties, as permitted under IFRS 10:B85C) for management services provided.

13.2.6   Typical characteristics of an investment entity

13.2.6.1   Features identified as typical characteristics of an investment entity

In assessing whether it meets the definition of an investment entity (as set out in **13.2.2**), an entity is required to consider whether it has the following typical characteristics of an investment entity:

[IFRS 10:28]

(a) it has more than one investment (see **13.2.6.2**);

(b) it has more than one investor (see **13.2.6.3**);

(c) it has investors that are not related parties of the entity (see **13.2.6.4**); and

(d) it has ownership interests in the form of equity or similar interests (see **13.2.6.5**).

The absence of any of these typical characteristics does not necessarily disqualify an entity from being classified as an investment entity. However, when an investment entity does not have all of these typical characteristics, it is required to provide the additional disclosure required by paragraph 9A of IFRS 12 *Disclosure of Interests in Other Entities* (see **5.2** in **chapter A28**). [IFRS 10:28]

The features identified in IFRS 10:28 as 'typical characteristics' of an investment entity have been included in the Standard to help an entity to determine whether it qualifies as an investment entity. An entity is not required to display all of these characteristics in order to qualify as an investment entity, but the absence of one or more of the characteristics may indicate that additional judgement is needed in determining whether it meets the definition. When an entity is determined to be an investment entity, despite not having one or more of the typical characteristics, it is required to disclose why it nevertheless meets the definition of an investment entity. [IFRS 10:28 & IFRS 12:9A]

13.2.6.2 More than one investment

An investment entity typically holds several investments to diversify its risk and maximise its returns. An entity may hold a portfolio of investments directly or indirectly (e.g. holding a single investment in another investment entity that itself holds several investments). [IFRS 10:B85O]

If an entity holds only a single investment, this does not necessarily prevent it from meeting the definition of an investment entity. For example, an investment entity may hold only a single investment when the entity:

[IFRS 10:B85P]

- is in its start-up period and has not yet identified suitable investments and, therefore, has not yet executed its investment plan to acquire several investments;

- has not yet made other investments to replace those it has disposed of;

- is established to pool investors' funds to invest in a single investment when that investment is unobtainable by individual investors (e.g. when the required minimum investment is too high for an individual investor); or

- is in the process of liquidation.

13.2.6.3   More than one investor

Typically, an investment entity has several investors who pool their funds to gain access to investment management services and investment opportunities to which they might not have had access individually. If an entity has several investors, this makes it less likely that the entity, or other members of the group containing the entity, obtains benefits other than capital appreciation or investment income (see **13.2.4.8**). [IFRS 10:B85Q]

Alternatively, an investment entity may be formed by, or for, a single investor that represents or supports the interests of a wider group of investors (e.g. a pension fund, government investment fund or family trust). [IFRS 10:B85R]

There may also be times when the entity temporarily has a single investor. For example, an investment entity may have only a single investor when the entity:

[IFRS 10:B85S]

- is within its initial offering period, which has not expired and the entity is actively identifying suitable investors;

- has not yet identified suitable investors to replace ownership interests that have been redeemed; or

- is in the process of liquidation.

Example 13.2.6.3

Investment entity status determined by considering the structure as a whole

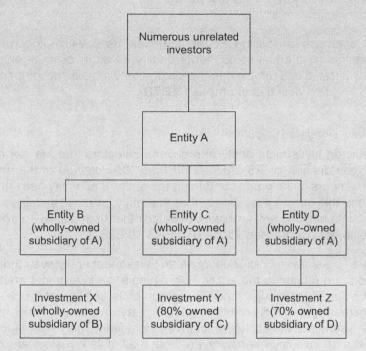

Entities B, C and D are all wholly-owned subsidiaries of Entity A that have been created for regulatory purposes to hold directly Entity A's portfolio of investments. Each of these holds a controlling equity interest in a single investment. No other activities are carried out by these entities.

Entities A, B, C and D each meet the definition of an investment entity in IFRS 10:27:

- they have all obtained funds for the purpose of providing investors with investment management services;

- the business purpose of the structure is to invest funds solely for returns from capital appreciation, investment income, or both;

- potential exit strategies have been identified and documented for investments X, Y and Z. On this basis and, in accordance with IFRS 10:B85H, Entity A is not required to have exit strategies for Entities B, C and D; and

- the investments held are measured and evaluated on a fair value basis.

Note that, when considered individually, each of Entities B, C and D displays only one of the four typical characteristics of an investment entity described in IFRS 10:28 (i.e. ownership interests in the form of equity or similar interests). However, in determining their investment entity status, Entities B, C and D need to be considered in the context of the fund structure as a whole because their purpose and design is solely to enable the fund to meet the regulatory requirements of particular jurisdictions. When Entities B, C and D are considered together with Entity A, they meet the definition and display the typical characteristics of an investment entity. Consequently, Entities B, C and D each meet the definition of an investment entity.

This approach of looking at the structure as a whole in order to determine if individual components qualify as an investment entity is also illustrated in Example 4 in the illustrative examples accompanying IFRS 10 (reproduced at **example 13.2.7D**).

13.2.6.4 Unrelated investors

Typically, an investment entity has several investors that are not related parties (as defined in IAS 24 *Related Party Disclosures*) of the entity or other members of the group containing the entity. If an entity has unrelated investors, this makes it less likely that the entity, or other members of the group containing the entity, obtains benefits other than capital appreciation or investment income (see **13.2.4.8**). [IFRS 10:B85T]

However, an entity may still qualify as an investment entity even though its investors are related to the entity. For example, an investment entity may set up a separate 'parallel' fund for a group of its employees (such as key management personnel) or other related party investor(s), which mirrors the investments of the entity's main investment fund. This parallel fund may qualify as an investment entity even though all of its investors are related parties. [IFRS 10:B85U]

13.2.6.5 Ownership interests in the form of equity or similar interests

An investment entity is typically, but is not required to be, a separate legal entity. Ownership interests in an investment entity are typically in the form of equity or similar interests (e.g. partnership interests), to which proportionate shares of the net assets of the investment entity are attributed. However, having different classes of investors, some of which have rights only to a specific investment or groups of investments or which have different proportionate shares of the net assets, does not preclude an entity from being an investment entity. [IFRS 10:B85V]

In addition, an entity that has significant ownership interests in the form of debt that, in accordance with other applicable IFRSs, does not meet the definition of equity, may still qualify as an investment entity, provided that the debt holders are exposed to variable returns from changes in the fair value of the entity's net assets. [IFRS 10:B85W]

The Board considers that an investment entity would typically have ownership interests in the form of equity or similar (e.g. partnership) interests that entitle investors to a proportionate share of the net assets of the investment entity. This characteristic explains in part why fair value is more relevant to investment entity investors: each unit of ownership in the investment entity entitles an investor to a proportionate share of the net assets of that investment entity. The value of each ownership interest is linked directly to the fair value of the investment entity's investments. [IFRS 10:BC264]

The Basis for Conclusions also explicitly states that "[t]he Board does not believe that an entity that provides its investors only a return of their investment plus interest should qualify as an investment entity". [IFRS 10:BC265]

13.2.6.6 Entity displays none of the typical characteristics of an investment entity

In the Basis for Conclusions on IFRS 10, the IASB considers the possibility that an entity might qualify as an investment entity even though it displays none of the typical characteristics, as follows.

"The Board thinks that it is very unlikely that an entity that displays none of the typical characteristics of an Investment entity would meet the definition of one. However, it may be possible in rare circumstances. For example, a pension fund that has a single investor and does not issue equity ownership interests could qualify as an investment entity even if it only holds a single investment temporarily (eg at commencement or wind-down of the entity)." [IFRS 10:BC234]

13.2.7 Illustrative examples

The following illustrative examples that accompany, but are not part of, IFRS 10 illustrate the considerations involved in determining whether an entity is an investment entity.

Example 13.2.7A

[IFRS 10.IE1 - IE6, Example 1]

An entity, Limited Partnership, is formed in 20X1 as a limited partnership with a 10-year life. The offering memorandum states that Limited Partnership's purpose is to invest in entities with rapid growth potential, with the objective of realising capital appreciation over their life. Entity GP (the general partner of Limited Partnership) provides 1 per cent of the capital to Limited Partnership and has the responsibility of identifying suitable investments for the partnership. Approximately 75 limited partners, who are unrelated to Entity GP, provide 99 per cent of the capital to the partnership.

Limited Partnership begins its investment activities in 20X1. However, no suitable investments are identified by the end of 20X1. In 20X2 Limited Partnership acquires a controlling interest in one entity, ABC Corporation. Limited Partnership is unable to close another Investment transaction until

---

20X3, at which time it acquires equity interests in five additional operating companies. Other than acquiring these equity interests, Limited Partnership conducts no other activities. Limited Partnership measures and evaluates its investments on a fair value basis and this information is provided to Entity GP and the external investors.

Limited Partnership has plans to dispose of its interests in each of its investees during the 10-year stated life of the partnership. Such disposals include the outright sale for cash, the distribution of marketable equity securities to investors following the successful public offering of the investees' securities and the disposal of investments to the public or other unrelated entities.

Conclusion

From the information provided, Limited Partnership meets the definition of an investment entity from formation in 20X1 to 31 December 20X3 because the following conditions exist:

(a) Limited Partnership has obtained funds from the limited partners and is providing those limited partners with investment management services;

(b) Limited Partnership's only activity is acquiring equity interests in operating companies with the purpose of realising capital appreciation over the life of the investments. Limited Partnership has identified and documented exit strategies for its investments, all of which are equity investments; and

(c) Limited Partnership measures and evaluates its investments on a fair value basis and reports this financial information to its investors.

In addition, Limited Partnership displays the following typical characteristics of an investment entity:

(a) Limited Partnership is funded by many investors;

(b) its limited partners are unrelated to Limited Partnership; and

(c) ownership in Limited Partnership is represented by units of partnership interests acquired through a capital contribution.

Limited Partnership does not hold more than one investment throughout the period. However, this is because it was still in its start-up period and had not identified suitable investment opportunities.

Example 13.2.7B

[IFRS 10:IE7 & IE8, Example 2]

High Technology Fund was formed by Technology Corporation to invest in technology start-up companies for capital appreciation. Technology Corporation holds a 70 per cent interest in High Technology Fund and controls High Technology Fund; the other 30 per cent ownership interest in High Technology Fund is owned by 10 unrelated investors. Technology Corporation holds options to acquire investments held by High Technology Fund, at their fair value, which would be exercised if the technology developed by the investees would benefit the operations of Technology Corporation. No plans for exiting the investments have been identified by High Technology Fund. High Technology Fund is managed by an investment adviser that acts as agent for the investors in High Technology Fund.

Conclusion

Even though High Technology Fund's business purpose is investing for capital appreciation and it provides investment management services to its investors, High Technology Fund is not an investment entity because of the following arrangements and circumstances:

(a) Technology Corporation, the parent of High Technology Fund, holds options to acquire investments in investees held by High Technology Fund if the assets developed by the investees would benefit the operations of Technology Corporation. This provides a benefit in addition to capital appreciation or investment income; and

(b) the investment plans of High Technology Fund do not include exit strategies for its investments, which are equity investments. The options held by Technology Corporation are not controlled by High Technology Fund and do not constitute an exit strategy.

Example 13.2.7C

[IFRS 10:IE9 - IE11, Example 3]

Real Estate Entity was formed to develop, own and operate retail, office and other commercial properties. Real Estate Entity typically holds its property in separate wholly-owned subsidiaries, which have no other substantial assets or liabilities other than borrowings used to finance the related investment property. Real Estate Entity and each of its subsidiaries report their investment properties at fair value in accordance with IAS 40 *Investment Property*. Real Estate Entity does not have a set time frame for disposing of its property investments, but uses fair value to help identify the optimal time for disposal. Although fair value is one performance indicator, Real Estate Entity and its investors use other measures, including information about expected cash flows, rental revenues and expenses, to assess performance and to make investment decisions. The key management personnel of Real Estate Entity do not consider fair value information to be the primary measurement attribute to evaluate the performance of its investments but rather a part of a group of equally relevant key performance indicators.

Real Estate Entity undertakes extensive property and asset management activities, including property maintenance, capital expenditure, redevelopment, marketing and tenant selection, some of which it outsources to third parties. This includes the selection of properties for refurbishment, development and the negotiation with suppliers for the design and construction work to be done to develop such properties. This development activity forms a separate substantial part of Real Estate Entity's business activities.

Conclusion

Real Estate Entity does not meet the definition of an investment entity because:

(a) Real Estate Entity has a separate substantial business activity that involves the active management of its property portfolio, including lease negotiations, refurbishments and development activities, and marketing of properties to provide benefits other than capital appreciation, investment income, or both;

(b) the investment plans of Real Estate Entity do not include specified exit strategies for its investments. As a result, Real Estate Entity plans to hold those property investments indefinitely; and

(c) although Real Estate Entity reports its investment properties at fair value in accordance with IAS 40, fair value is not the primary measurement attribute used by management to evaluate the performance of its investments. Other performance indicators are used to evaluate performance and make investment decisions.

Example 13.2.7D

[IFRS 10:IE12 - IE15, Example 4]

An entity, Master Fund, is formed in 20X1 with a 10-year life. The equity of Master Fund is held by two related feeder funds. The feeder funds are established in connection with each other to meet legal, regulatory, tax or similar requirements. The feeder funds are capitalised with a 1 per cent investment from the general partner and 99 per cent from equity investors that are unrelated to the general partner (with no party holding a controlling financial interest).

The purpose of Master Fund is to hold a portfolio of investments in order to generate capital appreciation and investment income (such as dividends, interest or rental income). The investment objective communicated to investors is that the sole purpose of the Master-Feeder structure is to provide investment opportunities for investors in separate market niches to invest in a large pool of assets. Master Fund has identified and documented exit strategies for the equity and non-financial investments that it holds. Master Fund holds a portfolio of short- and medium-term debt investments, some of which will be held until maturity and some of which will be traded but Master Fund has not specifically identified which investments will be held and which will be traded. Master Fund measures and evaluates substantially all of its investments, including its debt investments, on a fair value basis. In addition, investors receive periodic financial information, on a fair value basis, from the feeder funds. Ownership in both Master Fund and the feeder funds is represented through units of equity.

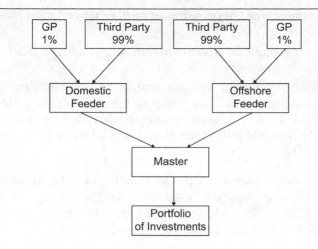

Conclusion

Master Fund and the feeder funds each meet the definition of an investment entity. The following conditions exist:

(a)   both Master Fund and the feeder funds have obtained funds for the purpose of providing investors with investment management services;

(b)   the Master-Feeder structure's business purpose, which was communicated directly to investors of the feeder funds, is investing solely for capital appreciation and investment income and Master Fund has identified and documented potential exit strategies for its equity and non-financial investments;

(c)   although the feeder funds do not have an exit strategy for their interests in Master Fund, the feeder funds can nevertheless be considered to have an exit strategy for their investments because Master Fund was formed in connection with the feeder funds and holds investments on behalf of the feeder funds; and

(d)   the investments held by Master Fund are measured and evaluated on a fair value basis and information about the investments made by Master Fund is provided to investors on a fair value basis through the feeder funds.

Master Fund and the feeder funds were formed in connection with each other for legal, regulatory, tax or similar requirements. When considered together, they display the following typical characteristics of an investment entity:

(a)   the feeder funds indirectly hold more than one investment because Master Fund holds a portfolio of investments;

(b)   although Master Fund is wholly capitalised by the feeder funds, the feeder funds are funded by many investors who are unrelated to the feeder funds (and to the general partner); and

(c)   ownership in the feeder funds is represented by units of equity interests acquired through a capital contribution.

13.2.8   Reassessment of investment entity status

13.2.8.1   Requirement for a parent to reassess whether it is an investment entity

If facts and circumstances indicate that there are changes to one or more of the three elements that make up the definition of an investment entity (see **13.2.2**), or the typical characteristics of an investment entity (see **13.2.6.1**), a parent is required to reassess whether it is an investment entity. [IFRS 10:29]

A parent that either ceases to be an investment entity or becomes an investment entity is required to account for the change in its status prospectively from the date at which the change in status occurs (see **13.2.8.2** and **13.2.8.3**). [IFRS 10:30]

13.2.8.2   Entity ceasing to be an investment entity

When an entity ceases to be an investment entity, the change in status is accounted for as a 'deemed acquisition' of the entity's subsidiaries, as follows:

[IFRS 10:B100]

- the entity applies IFRS 3 *Business Combinations* to any subsidiary that was previously measured at fair value through profit or loss;

- the date of the change of status (i.e. the date the entity ceases to be an investment entity) is the deemed acquisition date for such subsidiaries;

- the fair value of a subsidiary at the date of change in status is the deemed consideration for the purpose of measuring any goodwill or gain from a bargain purchase; and

- all subsidiaries of the entity are consolidated in accordance with the general requirements of IFRS 10 from the date of change of status.

13.2.8.3   Entity becoming an investment entity

When an entity becomes an investment entity, the change in status should be accounted for as a 'deemed disposal' or 'loss of control' of the entity's subsidiaries:

[IFRS 10:B101]

- the entity ceases to consolidate its subsidiaries at the date of the change in status (i.e. from the date it becomes an investment entity), except for any subsidiary that is not itself an investment entity and that provides investment-related services or activities that continues to be consolidated in accordance with IFRS 10:32 (see **13.3.3.1**); and

- it applies the requirements of IFRS 10:25 and 26 (see **section 12**) to those subsidiaries that it ceases to consolidate as though the investment entity had lost control of those subsidiaries at that date.

When applying the requirements of IFRS 10:25 and 26, the fair value of a subsidiary at the date the entity ceases to be an investment entity should be used as the consideration received. Any gain or loss arising on the deemed disposal should be recognised in profit or loss. This treats the change in the business purpose of the investor as a significant economic event and is consistent with the rationale for gains and losses being recognised in profit or loss when control is lost. [IFRS 10:BC271]

13.3   Measurement requirements for investment entities

13.3.1   Requirements for measurement of an investment entity's subsidiaries – general

An investment entity is required to:

- consolidate any of its subsidiaries (other than subsidiaries that are themselves investment entities) that provide investment-related services or activities (see **13.3.3**); and

- measure all other subsidiaries at fair value through profit or loss (see **13.3.2**).

13.3.2   Subsidiaries required to be measured at fair value

13.3.2.1   General requirement to measure subsidiaries at fair value

Except for subsidiaries required to be consolidated under IFRS 10:32 (see **13.3.3.1**), an investment entity should not consolidate its subsidiaries or apply IFRS 3 *Business Combinations* when it obtains control of another entity. [IFRS 10:31]

Instead, an investment entity is required to measure an investment in a subsidiary at fair value through profit or loss in accordance with IFRS 9 *Financial Instruments* (or, for entities that have not yet adopted IFRS 9, in accordance with IAS 39 *Financial Instruments: Recognition and Measurement*). [IFRS 10:31]

13.3.2.2   No consolidated financial statements if all subsidiaries are measured at fair value

A parent that is an investment entity should not present consolidated financial statements if it is required under IFRS 10:31 to measure all of its subsidiaries at fair value through profit or loss. [IFRS 10:4B]. In such circumstances, an investment entity should prepare separate financial statements, and specific additional requirements apply (see **6.3** of **chapter A29**).

Amendments to IFRS 10 in December 2014 restructured the guidance in IFRS 10:4B and clarified that an investment entity that is required to measure all of its subsidiaries at fair value through profit or loss is prohibited from presenting consolidated financial statements.

The December 2014 amendments to IFRS 10 are effective for annual periods beginning on or after 1 January 2016, with earlier application permitted. If an entity applies the December 2014 amendments for a period beginning before 1 January 2016, it is required to disclose that fact. [IFRS 10:C1D]

13.3.2.3 Unit of account for fair value measurement

IFRS 10:31 requires that an investment entity should measure an investment in a subsidiary at fair value through profit or loss in accordance with IFRS 9 (or, for entities that have not yet adopted IFRS 9, IAS 39). The question arises as to whether that reference to IFRS 9 (or IAS 39) (1) refers only to the measurement basis of the investment (and that the unit of account should be determined in accordance with IFRS 10), or (2) also prescribes the unit of account for such investments (which would indicate that the unit of account should be the individual financial instrument).

See **3.2.1** in **chapter A6** for a discussion of recent debates regarding the appropriate unit of account for investments in subsidiaries.

13.3.2.4 Investment entity with both direct and indirect subsidiaries

When an investment entity has both direct and indirect subsidiaries, it recognises the fair value of its investments in direct subsidiaries only; this should reflect the value of its investments in the indirect subsidiaries.

Example 13.3.2.4

Investment entity with both direct and indirect subsidiaries

Entity C (an investment entity) holds all of the shares in Entity D, which in turn holds 90 per cent of the shares in Entity E. Neither Entity D nor Entity E provides investment-related services or activities.

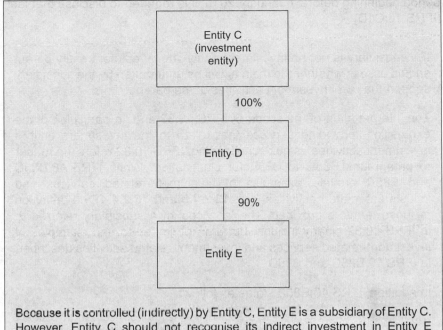

Because it is controlled (indirectly) by Entity C, Entity E is a subsidiary of Entity C. However, Entity C should not recognise its indirect investment in Entity E separately in its financial statements. Rather, it measures and recognises the fair value of its direct investment in Entity D only; the fair value of Entity C's investment in Entity D will reflect the value of Entity D's investment in Entity E.

13.3.3 Subsidiaries required to be consolidated

13.3.3.1 General requirement to consolidate subsidiaries that provide investment-related services or activities

If an investment entity has a subsidiary that is not itself an investment entity and whose main purpose and activities are providing services that relate to the investment entity's investment activities, it is required to consolidate that subsidiary in accordance with the general requirements of IFRS 10:19 to 26 (see **sections 10** to **12**) and to apply the requirements of IFRS 3 to the acquisition of any such subsidiary. [IFRS 10:32]

Amendments to IFRS 10 in December 2014 have clarified that IFRS 10:32 applies only to subsidiaries of investment entities that are not themselves investment entities. Consequently, subsidiaries of investment entities that are themselves investment entities are required to be measured at fair value through profit or loss in accordance with IFRS 10:31 (see **13.3.2.1**).

The December 2014 amendments to IFRS 10 are effective for annual periods beginning on or after 1 January 2016, with earlier application permitted. If an entity applies the December 2014 amendments for a period beginning before 1 January 2016, it is required to disclose that fact. [IFRS 10:C1D]

If a subsidiary is not an investment entity, the investment entity parent should assess whether the main activities undertaken by the subsidiary support the core investment activities of the parent.

The interpretation of the scope of IFRS 10:32 and, in particular, of the expression "providing services that relate to the investment entity's investment activities" is quite challenging. IFRS 10:32 refers the reader to paragraphs B85C to B85E for clarification. While IFRS 10:B85C and B85D provide examples of investment-related services and investment-related activities (see **13.2.4.3** and **13.2.4.4**), no definition of those terms is provided. The 'services' of a subsidiary referred to in IFRS 10:32 clearly include, but are not limited to, the examples of investment-related services and investment-related activities described in IFRS 10:B85C and B85D.

In addition, IFRS 10:B85E states as follows.

"If an investment entity has a subsidiary that is not itself an investment entity and whose main purpose and activities are providing investment-related services or activities that relate to the investment entity's investment activities, such as those described in [IFRS 10:B85C and B85D], to the entity or other parties, it shall consolidate that subsidiary in accordance with [IFRS 10:32]."

This paragraph again makes clear that the services contemplated in IFRS 10:32 are not limited to those services and activities listed in IFRS 10:B85C and B85D. In addition, IFRS 10:B85E clarifies that, although the services contemplated in IFRS 10:32 are required to 'relate to' the investment entity's investment activities, the services can be provided to third parties.

Further clarification is provided in IFRS 10:BC240H, which was added as part of the December 2014 amendments to IFRS 10, as follows.

- If the subsidiary is not an investment entity, the investment entity parent should assess whether the main activities undertaken by the subsidiary support the core investment activities of the parent. If so, the subsidiary's activities are considered to be an extension of the parent's core investing activities and the subsidiary should be consolidated in accordance with IFRS 10:32.

- A subsidiary of an investment entity that provides support services to its parent and other members of the group (e.g. administration, treasury, payroll and accounting services) is considered to be providing those services as an extension of the operations of the parent. Such a non-investment entity subsidiary would be consolidated in accordance with IFRS 10:32.

13.3.3.2 Is tax optimisation an investment-related service?

In order to manage their investments in the most tax efficient way, some investment entities establish one or more subsidiaries (commonly referred to as 'tax blockers') in particular jurisdictions, which own the portfolio of investments in the group structure. The question arises as to whether the tax optimisation effect of a tax-blocker subsidiary should be considered a service relating to the investment entity's activities, resulting in its consolidation by its investment entity parent.

This question has been considered by the IFRS Interpretations Committee. The following extract from the March 2014 *IFRIC Update* explains their view.

"The Interpretations Committee noted that, according to paragraph BC272 of IFRS 10, the IASB thinks that fair value measurement of all of an investment entity's subsidiaries would provide the most useful information, except for subsidiaries providing investment-related services or activities. In addition, the Interpretations Committee noted that the IASB had considered requiring an investment entity to consolidate investment entity subsidiaries that are formed for tax purposes, but had decided against this.

The Interpretations Committee noted that one of the characteristics of [tax-blocker subsidiaries] is that there is no activity within the subsidiary. Accordingly, the Interpretations Committee considers that the parent should not consolidate such subsidiaries, because they do not provide investment-related services or activities, and do not meet the requirements to be consolidated in accordance with paragraph 32 of IFRS 10. The parent should therefore account for such an intermediate subsidiary at fair value."

It should be noted that the IFRS Interpretations Committee only considered tax blocker subsidiaries that have no activities. If the subsidiary does have activities, further considerations apply.

13.3.4 Non-investment entity parent of an investment entity

Unless a parent is itself an investment entity, it is required to consolidate all entities that it controls, including those controlled through a subsidiary that is an investment entity. [IFRS 10:33]

Example 13.3.4

Non-investment entity parent of an investment entity

Entity P is not an investment entity. One of its subsidiaries, Entity I, is an investment entity. Entity I has a subsidiary, Entity A. Entity A does not provide investment-related services or activities and, under IFRS 10:31, is required to be accounted for in Entity I's financial statements at fair value through profit or loss.

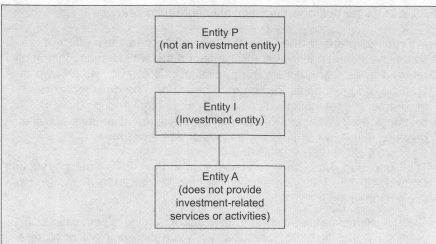

When Entity P prepares its consolidated financial statements, it is required to consolidate Entity A. Because Entity P is not itself an investment entity, it is required to consolidate all entities that it controls, including those controlled through a subsidiary that is an investment entity. In the circumstances described, Entity P is not provided with any relief from consolidation, and must apply the general requirements of IFRS 10 to all of its subsidiaries; this includes Entity A.

For such non-investment entity parents:

- all subsidiaries are required to be consolidated; and
- for investments in associates or joint ventures held through a subsidiary that is an investment entity, the exemption from equity method accounting in IAS 28 *Investments in Associates and Joint Ventures* may be retained at the parent level (see **4.2.2.4** in **chapter A26**).

13.3.5 *Non-investment entity investor in an associate or a joint venture that is an investment entity*

When an entity that is not itself an investment entity has an interest in an associate or a joint venture that is an investment entity, the entity may, when applying the equity method, retain the fair value measurement applied by that investment entity associate's or joint venture's interests in subsidiaries. [IAS 28:36A] See **4.4.13** in **chapter A26** for further discussion.

13.3.6 *Requirements for measurement of other investments held by an investment entity*

For categories of investments other than subsidiaries (e.g. financial assets, investments in associates and investments in joint ventures) held by an investment entity, the appropriate accounting is specified in other applicable IFRSs (e.g. IFRS 9 *Financial Instruments* (or, for entities that have not yet adopted IFRS 9, IAS 39 *Financial Instruments: Recognition and Measurement*) and IAS 28 *Investments in Associates and Joint Ventures*). However, to meet the requirement that an investment entity measures and evaluates substantially all of its investments on a fair value basis (see **13.2.5**), an investment entity must:

- elect to account for its investment property at fair value under IAS 40 (see **5.2** in **chapter A8**, or for entities that have not yet adopted IFRS 16, **5.2** in **appendix A5**);

- elect to account for its associates and joint ventures at fair value in accordance with IAS 28's exemption from equity method accounting (see **4.2.2.4** in **chapter A26**); and

- if eligible, measure its financial assets at fair value (see also **13.2.5**).

These requirements can be summarised as follows.

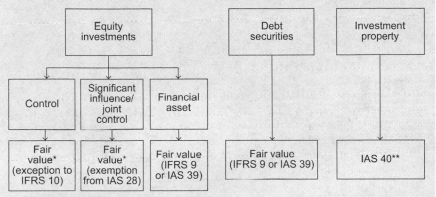

* Fair value is through profit or loss in accordance with IFRS 9 or IAS 39
** Fair value is through profit or loss in accordance with IAS 40

A25 Business combinations

Contents

1 Introduction

1.1 Overview of IFRS 3

IFRS 3 *Business Combinations* outlines the accounting when an acquirer obtains control of a business (e.g. an acquisition or a merger). Business combinations within the scope of IFRS 3 are accounted for using the 'acquisition method', which generally requires assets acquired and liabilities assumed to be measured at their fair values at the acquisition date.

1.2 Amendments to IFRS 3 since the last edition of this manual

IFRS 3 was amended in January 2016 by consequential amendments arising from IFRS 16 *Leases*. The principal effects of the January 2016 amendments to IFRS 3 are as follows:

- to recognise that, for entities that have adopted IFRS 16, the distinction between finance and operating leases is relevant for lessors only (see **7.1.2.2** and **7.4.1**);

- to add a new exception from IFRS 3's general recognition and measurement principles in respect of right-of-use assets and lease liabilities recognised under IFRS 16 (see **7.5.9**); and

- to remove the guidance on measurement of operating leases in which the acquiree is a lessee (and on the recognition of intangible assets associated with such operating leases), which is no longer relevant under IFRS 16 (see **7.4.1**, **7.4.2.3** and **7.4.2.4**).

The consequential amendments to IFRS 3 are required to be applied when an entity applies IFRS 16 (effective for annual periods beginning on or after 1 January 2019, with earlier application permitted – see **section 14** of **chapter A17** for detailed transition requirements).

2 Scope

2.1 Scope – general

IFRS 3 applies to a transaction or other event that meets the definition of a business combination. [IFRS 3:2]

The requirements of IFRS 3 do not apply to the acquisition by an investment entity, as defined in IFRS 10 *Consolidated Financial Statements*, of an investment in a subsidiary that is required to be measured at fair value through profit or loss. [IFRS 3:2A]

2.2 Definitions

Appendix A to IFRS 3 provides the following definitions for terms in the Standard.

- A **business combination** is "[a] transaction or other event in which an acquirer obtains control of one or more businesses. Transactions sometimes referred to as 'true mergers' or 'mergers of equals' are also business combinations as that term is used in this IFRS".

- A **business** is "[a]n integrated set of activities and assets that is capable of being conducted and managed for the purpose of providing a return in the form of dividends, lower costs or other economic benefits directly to investors or other owners, members or participants".

2.3 Transactions outside the scope of IFRS 3

2.3.1 Scope exemptions – general

IFRS 3 does not apply to the following transactions:

[IFRS 3:2]

- the accounting for the formation of a joint arrangement in the financial statements of the joint venture itself;

- the acquisition of an asset or a group of assets that does not constitute a business (discussed in **section 4**); and

- a combination between entities or businesses under common control (see **2.3.2**).

> The scope of IFRS 3 includes business combinations involving mutual entities (see **2.4**) and business combinations achieved by contract alone (see **8.5.2** and **9.2.2**).

2.3.2 Common control transactions

A combination of entities or businesses under common control (commonly referred to as a 'common control transaction') is "… a business combination in which all of the combining entities or businesses are ultimately controlled by the same party or parties both before and after the combination, and that control is not transitory". [IFRS 3:B1]

Examples of ultimate controlling parties include:

- an individual, or a group of individuals who, as a result of contractual arrangements, collectively control an entity (even when those individuals are not subject to financial reporting requirements); [IFRS 3:B2 & B3] and

- a parent entity (even when the controlled entity is excluded from its consolidated financial statements). [IFRS 3:B4]

There is currently no specific guidance on accounting for common control transactions under IFRSs. In the absence of specific guidance, entities involved in common control transactions should select an appropriate accounting policy using the hierarchy described in paragraphs 10 to 12 of IAS 8 *Accounting Policies, Changes in Accounting Estimates and Errors* (see **chapter A5**). Because the hierarchy permits the consideration of pronouncements of other standard-setting bodies, the guidance on group reorganisations in both UK GAAP and US GAAP may be useful in some circumstances – this guidance produces a result that is similar to pooling.

Example 2.3.2A

Example of a common control transaction

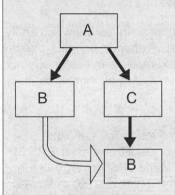

B and C are wholly-owned subsidiaries of A.

A transfers its equity interest in B to C. In exchange, C issues further equity shares to A.

The transaction is a common control transaction because both B and C are under the common control of A.

Example 2.3.2B

Use of a newly formed entity to restructure part of a group before sale

A new entity (Entity A) is formed by a parent (Entity P). Entity A issues equity instruments to acquire one or more subsidiaries that are part of Entity P's existing group. This reorganisation is effected to facilitate the sale of the subsidiaries acquired by Entity A.

Is the reorganisation a business combination within the scope of IFRS 3?

No. This reorganisation is outside the scope of IFRS 3 because it meets the definition of a business combination of entities under common control set out in IFRS 3:B1.

The definition in IFRS 3:B1 requires that "all of the combining entities or businesses are ultimately controlled by the same party or parties both before and after the business combination, and that control is not transitory". In the example set out above it might be argued that, because control of Entity A is transitory, the reorganisation should be within the scope of IFRS 3.

However, IFRS 3:B18 requires that when "a new entity is formed to issue equity [instruments] to effect a business combination, one of the combining entities that existed before the business combination shall be identified as the acquirer" on the basis of the evidence available. To be consistent with this principle, the test under IFRS 3:B1 as to whether the combining entities are under common control should be applied to the combining entities that existed before the combination, excluding the newly formed entity.

Therefore, in the circumstances described, because the combining entities that existed before the reorganisation were entities under common control that was not transitory, the reorganisation is excluded from the scope of IFRS 3.

The conclusion above was confirmed by the IFRIC (now the IFRS Interpretations Committee) in the March 2006 *IFRIC Update*.

2.4   Combinations involving mutual entities

A mutual entity is defined as "[a]n entity, other than an investor-owned entity, that provides dividends, lower costs or other economic benefits directly to its owners, members or participants. For example, a mutual insurance company, a credit union and a co-operative entity are all mutual entities". [IFRS 3:Appendix A]

The inclusion of credit unions and co-operatives in the definition of a mutual entity (and, consequently, within the scope of the revised IFRS 3) caused concern among many constituents, some of whom argued that applying the normal business combination requirements to combinations of credit unions could cause adverse economic consequences for those entities. Other constituents argued that co-operatives do not fit within the definition of a mutual entity and that they were sufficiently different from other entities to justify different methods of combination accounting.

The IASB was not persuaded by these arguments and decided to include all combinations involving such entities within the scope of the revised IFRS 3 without amendment, but with limited additional guidance as to how the relevant requirements should be applied.

Combinations involving mutual entities are considered in two sections:

- identification of the acquirer is considered at **5.3.2**; and
- measurement issues, including goodwill, are considered at **9.2.3**.

3　The acquisition method of accounting

IFRS 3 requires that all business combinations be accounted for by applying the acquisition method. [IFRS 3:4] In addition to determining whether a transaction or other event is a business combination (IFRS 3:3), four stages in the application of the acquisition method are listed:

[IFRS 3:5]

(a)　identifying the acquirer;

(b)　determining the acquisition date;

(c)　recognising and measuring the identifiable assets acquired, the liabilities assumed and any non-controlling interest in the acquiree; and

(d)　recognising and measuring goodwill or a gain from a bargain purchase.

However, taking all the requirements of the Standard into account, there are seven distinct steps to be considered and these are listed in the following chart, with a cross-reference to the relevant section of this chapter.

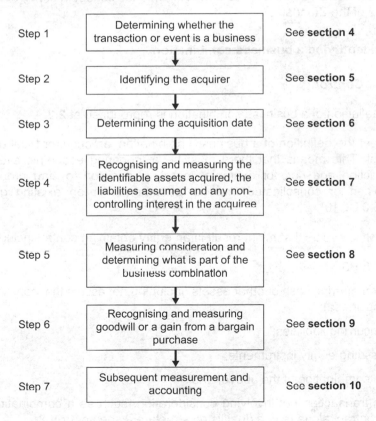

Step 1	Determining whether the transaction or event is a business	See **section 4**
Step 2	Identifying the acquirer	See **section 5**
Step 3	Determining the acquisition date	See **section 6**
Step 4	Recognising and measuring the identifiable assets acquired, the liabilities assumed and any non-controlling interest in the acquiree	See **section 7**
Step 5	Measuring consideration and determining what is part of the business combination	See **section 8**
Step 6	Recognising and measuring goodwill or a gain from a bargain purchase	See **section 9**
Step 7	Subsequent measurement and accounting	See **section 10**

Subsequent sections of this chapter deal with special situations.

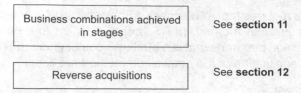

| Business combinations achieved in stages | See **section 11** |

| Reverse acquisitions | See **section 12** |

Finally, **section 13** deals with disclosure.

4   Identifying a business combination

4.1   Scope of IFRS 3

The first stage in accounting for an acquisition is to determine whether a transaction or other event is a business combination, which requires that the assets acquired and liabilities assumed constitute a business. [IFRS 3:3] The transaction or event should be analysed by applying the definition of a business combination, and the detailed guidance set out in paragraphs B5 to B12 of the Standard.

4.2   Identifying a business combination

4.2.1   *Control*

The definition of a business combination is reproduced at **2.2**.

To meet the definition of a business combination, an acquirer must obtain control. This means that there must be a triggering economic event or transaction and not, for example, merely a decision to start preparing combined or consolidated financial statements for an existing group. [IFRS 3:BC10]

Economic events that might result in an entity obtaining control include:

[IFRS 3:B5]

(a)   transferring cash or other assets (including net assets that constitute a business);

(b)   incurring liabilities;

(c)   issuing equity instruments;

(d)   a combination of the above; and

(e)   a transaction not involving consideration, such as a combination by contract alone (e.g. a dual listed structure – see **section 8**).

Other examples of events that might result in an entity obtaining control:

- an investee undertaking a selective buy-back transaction which results in the entity achieving a majority ownership in the investee without changing the number of equity instruments held in the investee;

- the expiry of an agreement with other shareholders when that agreement prevented the entity from controlling the investee (e.g. another shareholder had participative rights (right of veto) over major financing and operating policy decisions); and

- a 'creep acquisition' of equity instruments in an investee through a dividend reinvestment plan or bonus issue that increases the entity's holding to a controlling level.

4.2.2   Possible structures

The structure of a business combination may be determined by a variety of factors, including legal and tax strategies. Other factors might include market considerations and regulatory considerations. Examples of structures include:

[IFRS 3:B6]

(a)   one business becomes a subsidiary of another;

(b)   two entities are legally merged into one entity;

(c)   one entity transfers its net assets to another entity;

(d)   an entity's owners transfer their equity interests to the owners of another entity;

(e)   two or more entities transfer their net assets, or the owners transfer their equity interests, to a newly formed entity (sometimes termed a 'roll-up' or 'put-together' transaction); and

(f)   a group of former owners of one entity obtains control of a combined entity.

Examples of other legal structures that might be used to effect business combinations include:

- transactions that involve a dual listing and equalisation arrangements between two entities (see **8.5.2.1**);

- a contractual arrangement between two entities that has the effect of creating one entity in substance (i.e. a 'stapling' arrangement);

- a contractual arrangement that provides a third party with all economic returns, and responsibility for risks, in relation to an investee, even though the legal ownership of ordinary capital is with another entity (e.g. a 'pass-through' arrangement); and

- arrangements whereby an entity is the beneficial owner of an interest held in trust but the trustee is the legal owner of that interest.

4.3 Identifying a business

4.3.1 Identifying a business – general

The definition of a business is reproduced at **2.2**. This definition of a business encompasses entities with inputs and processes that have not yet begun to produce outputs. An integrated set of, say, research activities and assets might be identified as a business because it is *capable* of being conducted and managed for the purpose of providing a return (see **4.3.4**).

The application guidance in IFRS 3:B7 to B12 (see **4.3.2** to **4.3.4**) is a theoretical description of a business. Although there are some useful clues, it does not provide a practical checklist for what constitutes a business.

In most cases, it will be obvious whether an integrated set of activities and assets should be regarded as a business. But when this is not clear, it will be necessary to apply judgement, taking account of all the relevant facts and circumstances.

The IASB has issued an exposure draft proposing clearer application guidance to help distinguish between a business and a group of assets when applying IFRS 3 (see **14.2**).

4.3.2 Presence of goodwill

Paragraph B12 provides an over-arching test based on the presence of goodwill.

[IFRS 3:B12]

"In the absence of evidence to the contrary, a particular set of assets and activities in which goodwill is present shall be presumed to be a business. However, a business need not have goodwill."

No further guidance on identifying the presence of goodwill is provided in the Standard. Goodwill may be likely to occur when the particular set of assets or activities includes a trade or operating activity that generates revenue. In addition, the requirements in relation to accounting for transactions that are not business combinations (see **4.4**) require an entity to measure the fair values of the acquired assets and liabilities so as to allocate proportionately the cost of the group of assets and liabilities. This analysis may quickly identify that the total consideration paid exceeds the aggregate fair value of the assets acquired and liabilities assumed, potentially indicating the existence of goodwill.

4.3.3   Inputs, processes and outputs

The guidance describes a business as consisting of inputs and processes applied to those inputs that have the ability to create outputs. Although outputs are usually present, they are not required for an integrated set of activities and assets to qualify as a business. [IFRS 3:B7]

The following points are summarised from IFRS 3:B7 to B11:

(a)   inputs are economic resources including employees, materials and non-current assets including rights of use;

(b)   processes are systems, standards, protocols, conventions or rules that, when applied to inputs, create outputs. Examples would include strategic management, operations and resource management. Accounting, billing, payroll and similar administrative systems typically are not used to create outputs;

(c)   outputs provide a return in the form of dividends, lower costs or other economic benefits to stakeholders;

(d)   as a result of an acquisition, an acquirer may combine the acquiree's inputs and processes with its own with the result that it is not necessary that all pre-acquisition inputs and processes remain unchanged;

(e)   a business may not have outputs (e.g. when it is in a development stage);

(f)   a business may or may not have liabilities; and

(g)   the assessment as to whether a particular set of assets and activities is a business is made by reference to whether the integrated set is capable of being conducted and managed as a business by a market participant – it is not relevant whether the seller operated the set as a business or whether the acquirer intends to operate the set as a business.

Example 4.3.3A

Outsourcing arrangements

Entity A decides to outsource its information technology to a third party. Before the outsourcing, this function was operated as a cost centre for the business as a whole, rather than as a business. The staff of the outsourced department (together with all necessary plant and equipment and other working capital) are transferred to the third party, and a contractual arrangement is entered into with the third party for the provision of the service to Entity A on an ongoing basis.

Does this transfer of assets, liabilities and employees from Entity A to a service provider in the context of signing an outsourcing contract constitute a business combination under IFRS 3?

The key question is whether the transferred set of assets and activities is capable of being operated as a business. This assessment is made by reference to whether the integrated set is capable of being conducted and managed as a business by a market participant; it is not relevant whether the seller operated the set as a business or whether the acquirer intends to operate the set as a business.

While they were part of the outsourcing entity, the operations generally would not have been considered a business and would not have been operated as such. However, the third party that acquires the assets and liabilities and takes on the staff could be seen to have acquired a business if the transferred set of assets and activities is capable of being operated as a business.

The assessment may be more difficult in a situation when some, but not all, of the assets are transferred. But the same conclusion is likely to be reached when the transferred assets and employees are used as the 'seed capital' to offer similar services to other parties.

When assessing whether a particular set of assets and activities is a business, it is important to consider the normal nature of the assets and activities in the relevant business sector or industry. In some industries, there may be a relatively low number of assets required as inputs, working capital requirements may be low, or the number of employees used in the process of creating outputs may be low. The acquisition of assets and activities in these types of industries must be assessed by reference to these normal levels.

Example 4.3.3B

Industries in which the required inputs are minimal

Entity A acquires a set of assets and activities that represents the ownership and management of a group of pipelines used for the transport of oil, gas and other hydrocarbons on behalf of a number of customers. The operation has a limited number of employees (mainly engaged in maintenance of the pipelines and billing of customers), a system used for tracking transported hydrocarbons and a minor amount of working capital. The transaction involves the transfer of employees and systems, but not the working capital.

In the circumstances described, the assets and processes acquired are together sufficient to generate the intended output and, therefore, the group of pipelines will meet the definition of a business. As a result, the transaction will be accounted for as a business combination.

4.3.4 Development stage entities

A development stage entity that has no outputs may still be considered a business. The acquirer should consider other factors to determine whether an integrated set of activities and assets in the development stage is a business. Those factors include, but are not limited to, whether the set:

[IFRS 3:B10]

(a) has begun planned principal activities;

(b) has employees, intellectual property and other inputs and processes that could be applied to those inputs;

(c) is pursuing a plan to produce outputs; and

(d) will be able to obtain access to customers that will purchase the outputs.

Not all of those factors need to be present for a particular integrated set of activities and assets in the development stage to qualify as a business. [IFRS 3:B10]

4.4 Accounting for a transaction that is not a business combination

4.4.1 Accounting for an asset acquisition

When a transaction or other event does not meet the definition of a business combination due to the asset or group of assets not meeting the definition of a business, it is termed an 'asset acquisition'. In such circumstances, the acquirer:

[IFRS 3:2(b)]

- identifies and recognises the individual identifiable assets acquired (including those assets that meet the definition of, and recognition criteria for, intangible assets in IAS 38 *Intangible Assets* – see **section 4** of **chapter A9**) and liabilities assumed; and

- allocates the cost of the group of assets and liabilities to the individual identifiable assets and liabilities on the basis of their relative fair values at the date of purchase.

Such a transaction or event does not give rise to goodwill or a gain on a bargain purchase.

The acquisition of a group of financial assets not representing a business is discussed at **4.4.4**.

There are other important differences between accounting for an asset acquisition and a business combination. In particular:

- **transaction costs** in an asset acquisition are generally capitalised as part of the cost of the assets acquired in accordance with applicable Standards (e.g. IAS 16 *Property, Plant and Equipment*). In contrast, acquisition-related costs to effect a business combination do not form part of the consideration transferred and are expensed in the periods in which the costs are incurred and the services received, with the exception of costs to issue debt or equity securities (see **8.4** for further guidance);

- **deferred taxes** are recognised on most temporary differences relating to assets acquired and liabilities assumed in a business combination, whereas IAS 12 *Income Taxes* prohibits the recognition of deferred tax for temporary differences that arise upon the initial recognition of an asset or a liability in a transaction that is not a business combination and that affects neither accounting nor taxable profit (see **chapter A13** for further guidance); and

- **contingent liabilities** acquired in an asset acquisition are not recognised because they do not meet the recognition criteria in IAS 37 *Provisions, Contingent Liabilities and Contingent Assets*. In a business combination, the requirements of IFRS 3 may result in the recognition of contingent liabilities that would not qualify for recognition under IAS 37 (see **7.5.1** for further guidance).

4.4.2   Purchasing a 'shell' company

In corporate groups, it is common for subsidiaries to be used for specific purposes (e.g. to house particular operations, to act as service companies, or for other structuring purposes). Frequently, rather than incorporating a new entity for each purpose, a 'shell' or 'off-the-shelf' company will be purchased.

The purchase of a shell or off-the-shelf company is not a business combination as defined in IFRS 3 because the acquired entity does not constitute a business as defined in IFRS 3.

The purchase of a shell company should be accounted for in the same way as the incorporation of a new subsidiary. In the separate financial statements of the parent, in accordance with paragraph 10 of IAS 27 *Separate Financial Statements*, the investment should initially be measured at cost (i.e. the cost of incorporating or acquiring the shell company), or in accordance with IFRS 9 *Financial Instruments* (or, for entities that have not yet adopted IFRS 9, IAS 39 *Financial Instruments: Recognition and Measurement*), or (for entities that have adopted the August 2014 amendments to IAS 27 – see **5.1** in **chapter A29**) using the equity method in accordance with IAS 28 *Investments in Associates and Joint Ventures*. In the consolidated financial statements, the costs should be accounted for as start-up costs in accordance with IAS 38 and recognised as an expense when incurred.

4.4.3 Exploration and evaluation assets held in corporate shells

In some jurisdictions, it is common for rights to tenure over exploration and evaluation interests to be held in separate corporate entities for each tenement, area of interest, field etc. Management of exploration and evaluation activities is centralised, including any plant and equipment used, employees, service and other contracts, and similar items.

In many cases, the transfer of a particular exploration and evaluation interest involves the legal transfer of the company, rather than the underlying right or title over the interest.

When a corporate entity is acquired in these circumstances, it is likely that the acquisition will not meet the definition of a business combination, because the acquisition is in substance the acquisition of the exploration and evaluation interest rather than the acquisition of a business. In the consolidated financial statements, such a transaction should be accounted for in accordance with the purchaser's accounting policy for exploration and evaluation under IFRS 6 *Exploration for and Evaluation of Mineral Resources* (discussed in **chapter A40**) rather than as a business combination.

4.4.4 Acquiring a group of financial assets not representing a business

IFRS 9:5.1.1 requires that, except for trade receivables that do not have a significant financing component, financial assets and financial liabilities should be initially recognised at fair value (plus, in the case of instruments not held at fair value through profit or loss, transaction costs that are directly attributable). In accordance with IFRS 13 *Fair Value Measurement*, the best evidence of fair value is a quoted price in an active market.

*When an entity acquires a group of financial assets not representing a business that includes financial assets traded in an active market, the question arises as to whether the assets should be recognised based on an allocation of the purchase price (under IFRS 3:2(b) as set out in **4.4.1**) or at fair value (under IFRS 9 or, for entities that have not yet adopted IFRS 9, IAS 39)?*

IFRS 9 (or, for entities that have not yet adopted IFRS 9, IAS 39) is the relevant Standard for the initial recognition of financial assets. Therefore, the individual assets within the group should be recognised at their fair values on the date of acquisition. If there is a difference between the consideration paid for the group of assets and the sum of the fair values of the individual financial assets, the difference should be accounted for under IFRS 9 (or IAS 39).

4.4.5   Acquisition of tax losses at less than fair value

Example 4.4.5

Acquisition of tax losses at less than fair value

Company A acquires Company B, which is a shell entity with valuable unused tax losses. Company B does not meet the definition of a business under IFRS 3 and, therefore, the transaction is not a business combination for the purposes of that Standard.

Company A acquires Company B (and, therefore, the tax losses) for CU100,000. This is significantly lower than the tax asset that would be recognised in respect of the tax losses under IAS 12 (CU1 million). Company A expects to be able to utilise all of the available losses.

How should the transaction be accounted for in the consolidated financial statements of Company A?

On the date of acquisition, Company A should recognise the deferred tax asset acquired at the amount paid (i.e. at CU100,000).

Subsequently, the unused tax losses in Company B are available for use against Company A's taxable profits and should be accounted for in accordance with the requirements of IAS 12.

4.4.6   Increase in stake in entity with single asset from associate to subsidiary – measurement in consolidated financial statements

Example 4.4.6

Increase in stake in entity with single asset from associate to subsidiary – measurement in consolidated financial statements

In 20X1, Entity A was a founding shareholder of Entity X with a 30 per cent stake and was determined to have significant influence over Entity X. All the subscription cash contributed in Entity X was used to purchase a mining licence under which no exploration has yet taken place. The mining licence is Entity X's only asset and Entity X is not considered to meet the definition of a business for the purposes of IFRS 3.

In its 20X1 consolidated financial statements, Entity A accounted for Entity X using the equity method; there was no change in Entity A's share of the net assets of Entity X between the date that Entity X was established and the end of the 20X1 reporting period. During 20X2, Entity A acquires a further 70 per cent of Entity X.

In Entity A's 20X2 consolidated financial statements, what should be the carrying amount of the mining licence owned by Entity X?

The preferred approach is to include the mining licence in the consolidated statement of financial position at its cost, which is the sum of the cost of the original 30 per cent interest in Entity X and the cost of the additional 70 per cent interest. This 'cost' approach reflects the requirements of IFRS 3:2(b); because Entity X does not constitute a business, the transaction is accounted for as the purchase of a single asset and the cost of the transaction should be allocated in its entirety to that asset.

An alternative approach would be to account for the mining licence in Entity A's consolidated financial statements at the sum of (1) the fair value of Entity A's associate stake in Entity X at the date of obtaining control of Entity X, and (2) the cost of the additional 70 per cent interest acquired during 20X2. This approach is supported by analogy to the requirements of IFRS 3:41 and 42 regarding business combinations achieved in stages (see **section 11**). When this approach is adopted, it will result in the recognition of a gain or loss in profit or loss reflecting the difference at the date of obtaining control between the carrying amount and the fair value of Entity A's original 30 per cent interest in Entity X.

Whichever treatment is adopted, it should be applied consistently as an accounting policy choice.

5 Identifying the acquirer

5.1 Requirement to identify an acquirer

For each business combination, one of the combining entities should be identified as the acquirer (i.e. the entity that obtains control of the acquiree). [IFRS 3:6 & Appendix A]

The acquirer and the acquiree are identified by applying the guidance in IFRS 10 *Consolidated Financial Statements* regarding the concept of control. When identification is not achieved by this analysis, IFRS 3:B14 to B18 provide additional guidance (see **5.2**). [IFRS 3:7]

The definition of control of an investee in IFRS 10 is as follows.

[IFRS 10:Appendix A]

> "An investor controls an investee when the investor is exposed, or has rights, to variable returns from its involvement with the investee and has the ability to affect those returns through its power over the investee."

See **chapter A24** for discussion of the guidance on control in IFRS 10.

5.2 Additional guidance for identification of the acquirer in marginal cases

When application of IFRS 10 does not clearly indicate which of the combining entities is the acquirer, a number of additional factors for consideration are set out in IFRS 3:B14 to B18 as follows.

Factor	Acquirer is
Consideration primarily cash, other assets or incurring liabilities.	Usually the entity that transfers the cash or other assets, or incurs the liabilities. [IFRS 3:B14]
Consideration primarily in equity interests.	Usually the entity that issues its equity interests. However, in a reverse acquisition, the acquiree may issue equity interests (see **section 12**). [IFRS 3:B15]
Relative size.	Usually the entity whose relative size (measured in, for example, assets, revenues or profit) is significantly greater than that of the other combining entities. [IFRS 3:B16]
More than two combining entities.	Consider which entity initiated the combination (as well as relative sizes). [IFRS 3:B17]
New entity formed which issues equity interests.	One of the combining entities that existed before the combination, identified by applying the guidance in other paragraphs (see **5.3.1**). [IFRS 3:B18]
New entity formed which transfers cash, other assets or incurs liabilities.	New entity may be the acquirer (see **5.3.1**). [IFRS 3:B18]

In addition, in the case of a share exchange, the following facts and circumstances may also be pertinent. [IFRS 3:B15]

Factor	Acquirer is
Relative voting rights in the combined entity after the combination.	Usually the entity whose owners as a group retain or receive the largest portion of the combined voting rights, after considering the existence of any unusual or special voting arrangements and options, warrants or convertible notes.
No majority interest in the combined entity, but single large minority interest.	Usually the entity whose single owner or group of organised voters holds the largest minority voting interest in the combined entity.

Factor	Acquirer is
Composition of the governing body of the combined entity.	Usually the entity whose owners have the ability to elect or appoint a majority of the members of the governing body.
Senior management of the combined entity.	Usually the entity whose (former) management dominates the combined management.
Terms of the exchange of equity interests.	Usually the entity that pays a premium over pre-combination fair value of the other entity or entities.

5.3 Application of guidance on identification of the acquirer to specific circumstances

5.3.1 Combinations effected by creating a new entity

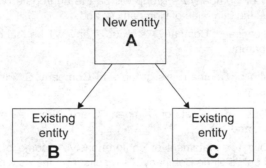

When a new entity A is formed to effect a combination between two or more entities, say B and C, IFRS 3 identifies two distinct scenarios:

[IFRS 3:B18]

- when A issues equity instruments in itself in exchange for equity instruments in B and C, then either B or C should be identified as the acquirer by applying the guidance in IFRS 10 and IFRS 3; and

- when A transfers cash (or other assets) in exchange for equity instruments in B and C (e.g. from the proceeds of a debt issue to new investors or to existing investors holding a minority interest in B or C), then A may be identified as the acquirer.

Example 5.3.1A

Newly formed entity issues equity instruments

Company B and Company C are existing entities that combine through the acquisition of their shares by a newly formed entity, Company A. Company A issues new equity shares in itself in the proportion four-fifths to the equity

---

shareholders of Company B and one-fifth to the equity shareholders of Company C.

On the basis of the relative voting rights, and in the absence of other factors suggesting otherwise, Company B is identified as the acquirer.

The appropriate accounting for the combination is developed on the principle that the consolidated financial statements of Company A's group are presented on the same basis as if Company B had legally acquired Company C, noting that Company A lacks commercial substance because it is effectively a legal mechanism to achieve this outcome. Accordingly, the combination of Company A and Company B will be accounted for as a capital restructuring whereby:

- the net assets of Company B remain at their previous carrying amounts;
- the consolidated statement of comprehensive income of Company A's group, including comparatives, will be based on the reporting period of Company B and will include the pre-combination results of Company B;
- the equity of Company A's group will be the aggregate of Company B's equity plus the fair value of Company A; and
- the share capital of Company A's group, if any, will be that of Company A, the legal parent.

The combination of Company A's group and Company C will be a 'normal' acquisition whereby:

- the identifiable net assets of Company C are measured at fair value on acquisition; and
- the consolidated statement of comprehensive income of Company A's group will only include Company C's results from the date of acquisition.

Example 5.3.1B

Newly formed entity transfers cash

Company B and Company C are existing entities that combine through the acquisition of their shares by a newly formed entity, Company A. A private equity business owns 60 per cent of Company A, and the remaining 40 per cent is held by the former equity investors in Company C. Company A pays cash to acquire the equity shares of Company B, and issues equity shares to acquire Company C.

Company C is not identified as the acquirer because the equity investors in Company C do not hold a majority of the equity shares in Company A. In this example, Company A is identified as the acquirer because cash is being paid to acquire Company B and there is a change in the ultimate controlling party of Company C.

The combinations of Company A with Company B, and Company A with Company C, are 'normal' acquisitions whereby:

- the identifiable net assets of both Company B and Company C are measured at fair value on acquisition; and

> • the consolidated statement of comprehensive income of Company's A group will include only the post-combination results of Company B and Company C.

5.3.2 Mutual entities

The definition of a mutual entity is set out at **2.4**.

Because a combination of mutual entities involves an exchange (albeit typically of membership interests), IFRS 3 allows no exemption from its general requirements in respect of applying the acquisition method. Consequently, an acquirer must be identified in any combination of mutual entities. [IFRS 3:BC104]

The IASB further concluded that the guidance on identifying the acquirer in IFRS 3 is applicable to mutual entities and no additional guidance is needed. [IFRS 3:BC105]

However, additional guidance is provided in IFRS 3:B47 to B49 to assist in measuring the fair value of equity or membership interests exchanged. This guidance is considered at **9.2.3**.

6 Determining the acquisition date

6.1 Definition of acquisition date

The acquisition date is defined as the date on which the acquirer obtains control of the acquiree. [IFRS 3:Appendix A]

6.2 Relationship between the acquisition date and the timing of payment of consideration

IFRS 3 explains that the date on which the acquirer obtains control of the acquiree is generally the date on which the acquirer legally transfers the consideration, acquires the assets and assumes the liabilities of the acquiree – the closing date. However, the acquirer should consider all pertinent facts and circumstances in identifying the acquisition date, including the possibility that control is achieved on a date that is either earlier or later than the closing date. For example, the acquisition date precedes the closing date if a written agreement provides that the acquirer obtains control of the acquiree on a date before the closing date. [IFRS 3:9]

The reference to a written agreement is taken to mean the purchase agreement or a separate agreement signed before the closing date that grants rights to the acquirer. Because the date of acquisition will be a matter of fact, it cannot be retrospectively altered (e.g. by indicating in the purchase agreement that control is deemed to exist from an earlier date, or that profits accrue to the purchaser from some earlier or later date). This latter feature may represent a mechanism to adjust the amount of purchase consideration.

In some cases, the entire purchase price may be in the form of deferred or contingent consideration. In such circumstances, the timing of the payment of the consideration will have little or no bearing on the determination of the acquisition date.

6.3 Measurement date for equity securities transferred as consideration

IFRS 3 requires that the measurement date for equity securities transferred as consideration is the acquisition date (see **8.1**). [IFRS 3:37]

The Basis for Conclusions on IFRS 3 summarises the IASB's discussion of the measurement date for equity securities transferred. No consideration is given to movements in share prices before or after this date. [IFRS 3:BC342]

6.4 Additional guidance for determining the acquisition date in specific circumstances

IFRS 3 does not include any further detailed guidance for the determination of the acquisition date. The following examples may be a useful guide in some circumstances.

Public offer of shares

When a public offer of shares is made, the date that control passes is the date when the offer becomes unconditional and a controlling interest in the acquiree has therefore been achieved. This is usually the date that the number of acceptances passes a predetermined threshold and that threshold is sufficient to provide control (i.e. usually more than 50 per cent). In the absence of such a threshold, the acquisition date may be the date the offer is declared unconditional. In making this assessment, other factors will also need to be considered, including when offers are declared unconditional before a controlling shareholding is achieved. In these circumstances, the acquisition date may occur when the level of shareholding has exceeded a particular level and the acquirer is able to effect change in the board of directors of the acquiree.

Private transfer

For a private transfer, the date that control passes will be the date that an unconditional offer is accepted. When agreements are subject to substantive preconditions, the acquisition date will usually be the date that the last of those preconditions is satisfied.

Other scenarios

A number of indicators may be relevant, including:

(a) the date that the acquirer commences direction of the operating and financial policies of the acquiree;

(b) the date from which the flow of economic benefits changes;

(c) the date that consideration passes (although this is not conclusive, because it is capable of being adjusted either forwards or backwards or settled in instalments);

(d) the appointment of the majority of the board of directors of the acquiree (although this may serve as a measure of the *latest* possible date that control passes in many cases); and

(e) the date that competition authorities provide clearance of a referred bid.

In practice, the date identified as the acquisition date should reflect all the various circumstances surrounding the transfer of control.

7 Recognising and measuring the identifiable assets acquired, the liabilities assumed and any non-controlling interest in the acquiree

7.1 Recognition

7.1.1 Conditions for recognition

IFRS 3 requires that, as of the acquisition date, the acquirer should recognise, separately from goodwill, the identifiable assets acquired, the liabilities assumed and any non-controlling interest in the acquiree. [IFRS 3:10]

To qualify for recognition as part of applying the acquisition method, an item acquired should:

• meet the definition of an asset or a liability in the *Conceptual Framework for Financial Reporting* (see **chapter A2**) at the acquisition date; [IFRS 3:11] and

- be part of the business acquired (the acquiree) rather than the result of a separate transaction (see **8.3**). [IFRS 3:12]

Example 7.1.1A

Goodwill previously recognised by the acquiree

Entity A acquires 100 per cent of Entity B for CU100. The net assets recognised in Entity B's consolidated statement of financial position at the date of acquisition comprise goodwill of CU20 that arose when Entity B acquired one of its subsidiaries and identifiable net assets of CU70 (for simplicity, assume that the carrying amount of the identifiable net assets equals their fair value).

Assume that there are no assets or liabilities that are not recognised in Entity B's statement of financial position that should be recognised as part of the accounting for the business combination.

In Entity A's consolidated financial statements, should the goodwill previously recognised by Entity B be recognised separately from the goodwill arising on Entity A's acquisition of Entity B?

No. Any goodwill that is recognised in the statement of financial position of the acquiree is ignored when recognising the identifiable assets acquired and liabilities assumed by the parent. Therefore, in the circumstances described, the goodwill arising on the acquisition of Entity B is CU30.

However, any business combination entered into by Entity B after the date of acquisition by Entity A will be a business combination from the perspective of both Entity B and Entity A and will give rise to goodwill both in the consolidated financial statements of Entity B (if consolidated financial statements are presented by Entity B) and in the consolidated financial statements of Entity A.

The following are outcomes that result from applying the first recognition condition above.

- **Post-acquisition reorganisation** Costs that the acquirer expects but is not obliged to incur in the future to effect its plan to exit an activity of an acquiree or to terminate the employment of or relocate an acquiree's employees are not liabilities at the acquisition date. [IFRS 3:11]

- **Unrecognised assets and liabilities** The acquirer may recognise some assets and liabilities that the acquiree had not previously recognised in its financial statements. For example, the acquirer recognises the acquired identifiable intangible assets (e.g. brand names, patents or customer relationships) that the acquiree did not recognise as assets in its financial statements because it developed them internally and recognised the related costs as expenses. [IFRS 3:13]

7.1.2 Classifying or designating identifiable assets acquired and liabilities assumed in a business combination

7.1.2.1 Classification or designation generally based on conditions at the acquisition date

Subject to the exceptions set out at **7.1.2.2**, IFRS 3 requires that, *at the acquisition date*, the identifiable assets acquired and liabilities assumed should be classified or designated as necessary to apply other IFRSs subsequently. The acquirer makes those classifications or designations on the basis of contractual terms, economic conditions, its operating or accounting policies, and other pertinent conditions as they exist at the acquisition date. [IFRS 3:15]

Examples of classifications or designations made at the acquisition date include:

[IFRS 3:16]

- for entities that have adopted IFRS 9 *Financial Instruments*:

  - classification of particular financial assets as measured at fair value through profit or loss or at amortised cost, or as a financial asset measured at fair value through other comprehensive income, in accordance with IFRS 9;

  - designation of a derivative as a hedging instrument in accordance with IFRS 9; and

  - assessment of whether an embedded derivative should be separated from a host contract in accordance with IFRS 9 (which is a classification matter); and

- for entities that have not yet adopted IFRS 9:

  - classification of particular financial assets and liabilities as a financial asset or liability at fair value through profit or loss, or as a financial asset available for sale or held-to-maturity in accordance with IAS 39 *Financial Instruments: Recognition and Measurement*;

  - designation of a derivative as a hedging instrument in accordance with IAS 39; and

  - assessment of whether an embedded derivative should be separated from a host contract in accordance with IAS 39 (which is a classification matter).

The requirements of IFRS 3:16 have been updated for consequential amendments arising from IFRS 9.

7.1.2.2   Circumstances in which classification or designation is based on conditions not at the acquisition date

IFRS 3 specifies two exceptions to the principle (set out in **7.1.2.1**) that classifications or designations are based on the terms of the instruments and conditions at the acquisition date. The two exceptions relate to:

[IFRS 3:17]

- the classification of a lease contract as either an operating lease or a finance lease. This exception applies for lessors under IFRS 16 *Leases* (effective for annual periods beginning on or after 1 January 2019, with earlier application permitted – see **chapter A17**) and for both lessees and lessors under IFRS 16's predecessor Standard IAS 17 *Leases* (see **appendix A4**); and

- the classification of a contract as an insurance contract in accordance with IFRS 4 *Insurance Contracts* (see **chapter A39**).

The acquirer classifies such leases and insurance contracts on the basis of the contractual terms and other factors *at the inception of the contract* (or, if the terms of the contract have been modified in a manner that would change its classification, at the date of that modification, which might be the acquisition date).

7.2   Measurement principle for assets and liabilities

7.2.1   Measurement principle – general

Identifiable assets acquired and liabilities assumed are measured at their acquisition-date fair values. [IFRS 3:18] Fair value is defined as "the price that would be received to sell an asset or paid to transfer a liability in an orderly transaction between market participants at the measurement date. (See IFRS 13 *Fair Value Measurement*.)" [IFRS 3:Appendix A]

7.2.2   Assets with uncertain cash flows (valuation allowances)

An acquirer is not permitted to recognise a separate valuation allowance as at the acquisition date for assets acquired in a business combination that are measured at their acquisition-date fair values because the effects of uncertainty about future cash flows are included in the fair value measure. For example, because IFRS 3 requires the acquirer to measure acquired receivables, including loans, at their acquisition-date fair values, the acquirer does not recognise a separate valuation allowance for the contractual cash flows that are deemed to be uncollectible at that date nor, for entities that have adopted IFRS 9 *Financial Instruments*, a loss allowance for expected credit losses. [IFRS 3:B41]

The requirements of IFRS 3:B41 have been updated for consequential amendments arising from IFRS 9.

The principle of 'no valuation allowance' also extends to property, plant and equipment such that, following a business combination, such assets are stated at a single fair value amount, and not at a gross 'deemed cost' and accumulated depreciation.

7.2.3 Assets that the acquirer intends not to use or to use in a way that is different from the way other market participants would use them

To protect its competitive position, or for other reasons, the acquirer may intend not to use an acquired non-financial asset actively, or it may not intend to use the asset according to its highest and best use. For example, that might be the case for an acquired research and development intangible asset that the acquirer plans to use defensively by preventing others from using it. Nevertheless, the acquirer is required to measure the fair value of the non-financial asset assuming its highest and best use by market participants in accordance with the appropriate valuation premise, both initially and when measuring fair value less costs of disposal for subsequent impairment testing. [IFRS 3:B43]

This requirement has been stated explicitly in IFRS 3 to avoid inconsistencies in practice. IFRS 13 describes the concept of highest and best use and provides examples of its application in a business combination (see **section 4** of **chapter A6**). [IFRS 3:BC262]

Example 7.2.3

Acquisition of an intangible asset that will not be used

Company A acquires Company B. The identifiable net assets of Company B include a trademark, which is a logo previously used by Company B as a direct competitor to Company A. Company A does not intend to use this logo in the future.

Should the logo be recognised, separately from goodwill, as an identifiable intangible asset acquired as part of the business combination? If so, how should the logo be accounted for subsequent to recognition?

The logo is considered to be separable because it could, for example, be licensed to a third party. It also arises from legal rights. Therefore, the intangible asset should be recognised, separately from goodwill, as part of the accounting for the business combination.

For the purposes of impairment testing, the question of whether the logo should be allocated to existing cash-generating units of Company A or identified as a cash-generating unit by itself will depend on an assessment of specific facts and circumstances. If Company A has no intention of using the logo after acquisition and does not undertake activities aimed at transferring customers to an existing brand, the logo should be identified as a cash-generating unit by itself. Because cash inflows related to the logo are nil, fair value less costs to sell will be the recoverable amount.

However, if Company A undertakes activities to transfer value to existing brands, such that it can be demonstrated that existing cash-generating units will benefit, the logo should be allocated to those cash-generating units.

Immediately after acquisition, it would appear reasonable that the fair value less costs to sell of the logo is not significantly different from the amount recognised. Accordingly, no impairment loss is recognised immediately and the asset should be amortised over its useful life. The useful life to Company A is the length of time that holding the logo will be effective in discouraging competition, which would be a fairly short period because an unexploited logo loses value quickly. Because Company A acquired the asset with the express intention of denying others the opportunity to use the asset, it appears unlikely that the asset will be sold in the future and, accordingly, the residual value is nil. As a result, an amortisation expense for the full carrying amount of the asset is recognised over the useful life (which may be as short as a single accounting period).

7.3   Non-controlling interests in an acquiree

7.3.1   Measurement principles for non-controlling interests

For each business combination, at the acquisition date, the acquirer is required to measure components of non-controlling interests (NCIs) in the acquiree that are present ownership interests and entitle their holders to a proportionate share of the entity's net assets in the event of liquidation at either:

[IFRS 3:19]

- fair value; or
- the present ownership instruments' proportionate share in the recognised amounts of the acquiree's identifiable net assets.

All other components of NCIs are required to be measured at their acquisition-date fair values, unless another measurement basis is required by IFRSs. [IFRS 3:19]

This choice in respect of the measurement basis for present ownership interests is available for each business combination, so an entity may use fair value for one business combination and the proportionate share of the acquiree's identifiable net assets for another.

IFRS 3:19 states that the choice of measurement basis is available for each business combination. The Basis for Conclusions reiterates that this choice is available on a transaction-by-transaction basis. [IFRS 3:BC216] IAS 8 *Accounting Policies, Changes in Accounting Estimates and Errors* requires that when specific guidance is available in another Standard, that guidance overrides the requirements of IAS 8:13 to select and apply accounting policies consistently for similar transactions, other events or conditions. There is no requirement within IFRS 3 to measure components of NCIs that are present ownership interests on a consistent basis for similar types of business combinations and, therefore, an entity has a free choice between the two options for each transaction undertaken.

The IASB decided to restrict the scope of the measurement choice available under IFRS 3:19 because of concerns that allowing components of NCIs other than those that are present ownership interests to be measured by reference to the net assets of the acquiree might result in inappropriate measurement of those components in some circumstances. Without this restriction, if the acquirer chose to measure an NCI at its proportionate share of the acquiree's identifiable net assets, the acquirer might have measured some equity instruments at nil. In the Board's view, this would result in not recognising economic interests that other parties have in the acquiree. [IFRS 3:BC221A]

An example illustrating the choice, and its impact on goodwill, is set out at **9.1**.

When measuring components of NCIs that are present ownership interests at the proportionate share of the acquiree's identifiable net assets, an entity should not take into account any goodwill recognised in the acquiree's own financial statements. The NCI is calculated as the proportionate share of the acquiree's identifiable assets and liabilities that satisfy the recognition criteria at the acquisition date. Any pre-existing goodwill recognised in the acquiree's financial statements is ignored because goodwill is not an identifiable asset.

In accordance with IFRS 3:19, in the consolidated financial statements of the acquirer, some of the acquiree's equity instruments will, depending upon their terms and conditions, be required to be measured at fair value (or using the principles of IFRS 2 *Share-based Payment* in some cases) and be treated as a component of NCIs. This may include instruments such as preference shares, options and multiple class shares held by parties other than the acquirer. It will not be acceptable to use a 'historical' or nil measure for these types of instruments.

The following illustrative examples accompanying IFRS 3 show how the requirements in IFRS 3:19 are intended to operate.

Example 7.3.1

Measurement of NCI including preference shares

[IFRS 3:IE44B - IE44J]

TC has issued 100 preference shares, which are classified as equity. The preference shares have a nominal value of CU1 each. The preference shares give their holders a right to a preferential dividend in priority to the payment of any dividend to the holders of ordinary shares. Upon liquidation of TC, the holders of the preference shares are entitled to receive out of the assets available for distribution the amount of CU1 per share in priority to the holders of ordinary shares. The holders of the preference shares do not have any further rights on liquidation.

AC acquires all ordinary shares of TC. The acquisition gives AC control of TC. The acquisition-date fair value of the preference shares is CU120.

IFRS 3:19 states that for each business combination, the acquirer shall measure at the acquisition date components of non-controlling interest in the acquiree that are present ownership interests and entitle their holders to a proportionate share of the entity's net assets in the event of liquidation at either fair value or the present ownership instruments' proportionate share in the acquiree's recognised amounts of the identifiable net assets. All other components of non-controlling interest must be measured at their acquisition-date fair value, unless another measurement basis is required by IFRSs.

The non-controlling interests that relate to TC's preference shares do not qualify for the measurement choice in IFRS 3:19 because they do not entitle their holders to a proportionate share of the entity's net assets in the event of liquidation. The acquirer measures the preference shares at their acquisition-date fair value of CU120.

First variation

Suppose that upon liquidation of TC, the preference shares entitle their holders to receive a proportionate share of the assets available for distribution. The holders of the preference shares have equal right and ranking to the holders of ordinary shares in the event of liquidation. Assume that the acquisition-date fair value of the preference shares is now CU160 and that the proportionate share of TC's recognised amounts of the identifiable net assets that is attributable to the preference shares is CU140.

The preference shares qualify for the measurement choice in IFRS 3:19. AC can choose to measure the preference shares either at their acquisition-date fair value of CU160 or at their proportionate share in the acquiree's recognised amounts of the identifiable net assets of CU140.

Second variation

Suppose also that TC has issued share options as remuneration to its employees. The share options are classified as equity and are vested at the acquisition date. They do not represent present ownership interest and do not entitle their holders to a proportionate share of TC's net assets in the event of liquidation. The market-based measure of the share options in accordance with IFRS 2 *Share-based Payment* at the acquisition date is CU200. The share options do not expire on the acquisition date and AC does not replace them.

IFRS 3:19 requires such share options to be measured at their acquisition-date fair value, unless another measurement basis is required by IFRSs. IFRS 3:30 states that the acquirer shall measure an equity instrument related to share-based payment transactions of the acquiree in accordance with the method in IFRS 2.

The acquirer measures the non-controlling interests that are related to the share options at their market-based measure of CU200.

The treatment under IFRS 3 of pre-existing share-based payment awards of an acquiree is discussed at **8.3.4**.

7.3.2 Implications of choice between alternatives for measuring components of non-controlling interests that are present ownership interests

When the option is taken to measure NCIs that are present ownership interests at fair value (which is generally higher than the proportionate share of identified net assets), there is a corresponding impact on the residual amount of goodwill or gain recognised on a bargain purchase.

Further considerations include:

* the choice only affects the initial measurement of NCIs – the fair value option is not available for subsequent changes in NCIs;

* an increased amount attributed to goodwill as a result of the NCI measurement choice is a permanent difference in the carrying amount of goodwill. However, regardless of the measurement of NCIs arising in a business combination, any subsequent acquisitions of NCIs will not alter the amount of goodwill because they will be accounted for as equity transactions. This is discussed further at **11.4.5** in **chapter A24**;

* this would suggest that the amount of goodwill that is subject to impairment testing under IAS 36 *Impairment of Assets* will differ. However, the requirements of IAS 36 mean that this effect is equalised (see **8.2.8.6** in **chapter A10**). When an entity measures NCIs at their proportionate interest in the net identifiable assets of a subsidiary at the acquisition date, rather than at fair value, for the purposes of impairment testing, the carrying amount of goodwill allocated to the cash-generating unit (CGU) is grossed up to include the goodwill attributable to the NCIs. This adjusted carrying amount is then compared with the recoverable amount of the CGU to determine whether the CGU is impaired (see IAS 36:C4).

7.3.3   *Measuring the fair value of non-controlling interests*

For the purpose of measuring NCIs at fair value, it may be possible to measure the acquisition-date fair value on the basis of a quoted price in an active market for the equity shares not held by the acquirer. When a quoted price in an active market for the equity shares is not available because the shares are not publicly traded, the acquirer should measure the fair value of the NCIs using another valuation technique. [IFRS 3:B44]

The fair values of the acquirer's interest in the acquiree and the NCIs on a per-share basis may differ. The main difference is likely to be the inclusion of a control premium in the per-share fair value of the acquirer's interest in the acquiree or, conversely, the inclusion of a discount for lack of control in the per-share fair value of the NCIs if market participants would take into account such a premium or discount when pricing the non-controlling interests. [IFRS 3:B45]

Example 7.3.3

Potential for fair values reflecting different circumstances

Entity A acquired Entity B in two separate transactions:

- a one-third equity interest for which Entity A paid CU10 per share, which resulted in Entity A having significant influence over Entity B; and

- a further one-third equity interest for which Entity A paid CU15 per share, which resulted in Entity A having a controlling interest.

Based on the market prices of the remaining shares, Entity A assesses the fair value of the non-controlling interests at CU9 per share.

In this case, it appears that three different fair values have been attributed to similar-sized equity interests. However, each fair value reflects a different fact pattern and, therefore, a different market:

- CU10 represents the fair value of an equity interest carrying significant influence in an entity where other holdings are dispersed and the holder has the potential to launch a bid for a controlling interest;

- CU15 represents the fair value of a controlling interest, including a control premium; and

- CU9 represents the fair value of an equity interest in an entity controlled by another party.

7.3.4   *Statutory obligation to launch a takeover bid*

Example 7.3.4

Statutory obligation to launch a takeover bid

Entity A has an agreement with the shareholders of Entity B to acquire 60 per cent of the shares in Entity B, a listed entity. Under local law, an investor purchasing 30 per cent or more of a listed entity is obliged to launch a takeover bid for the remaining shares. All conditions for the acquisition of the 60 per cent interest have been satisfied.

Should the obligation to launch a takeover bid for the remaining interest in Entity B be recognised as a liability by Entity A?

A liability should be recognised if the obligation results in either a financial liability or an onerous contract for Entity A. Paragraph AG12 of IAS 32 *Financial Instruments: Presentation* clarifies that "[l]iabilities or assets that are not contractual (such as income taxes that are created as a result of statutory requirements imposed by governments) are not financial liabilities or financial assets".

In the circumstances described, for the holders of the remaining 40 per cent of the shares in Entity B, the statutory obligation on Entity A to purchase their shares is not a contractual right to receive cash evidenced by a financial instrument and is not a financial asset. For Entity A, the statutory obligation to make the offer is not a contractual obligation evidenced by a financial instrument and no financial liability should be recognised.

Entity A should consider whether a liability for an onerous contract should be recognised in accordance with IAS 37 *Provisions, Contingent Liabilities and Contingent Assets* as a result of the statutory obligation to launch a takeover bid.

The acquisition of the remaining 40 per cent interest (or part of it) should be accounted for when it occurs as an equity transaction in accordance with paragraph 23 of IFRS 10 *Consolidated Financial Statements* (see **11.4** in **chapter A24**).

7.4 Guidance on the recognition and measurement of specific categories of assets and liabilities

7.4.1 Operating leases

IFRS 3 includes specific guidance on how operating leases should be recognised and measured when accounting for a business combination.

- **Classification as operating or finance** Classification of a lease contract as either an operating or a finance lease at the acquisition date is based on factors at the inception of the lease, which is generally before the acquisition date. If the terms of the contract have been changed subsequent to the inception of the lease such that the classification of the lease would change, then the classification at the acquisition date is based on the contractual terms and other factors at the date of that change. This means that an acquiree's lease classifications (if determined in accordance with IFRSs) are not changed when accounting for the business combination, unless a lease contract is modified at the date of acquisition. [IFRS 3:17]

  This guidance applies for lessors under IFRS 16 *Leases* (effective for annual periods beginning on or after 1 January 2019, with earlier application permitted – see **chapter A17**) and for both lessees and lessors under IFRS 16's predecessor Standard IAS 17 *Leases* (see **appendix A4**);

- **Measurement when acquiree is the lessee** In general, the acquirer should not recognise any asset or liability related to an operating lease in which the acquiree is the lessee. [IFRS 3:B28] It follows that any lease incentive that is being amortised by the acquiree will not be recognised by the acquirer. However, the acquiree may be party to operating lease arrangements that involve future lease payments at below or above market rates. The acquirer determines whether the terms of each operating lease in which the acquiree is the lessee are favourable or unfavourable. The acquirer recognises an intangible asset if the terms of an operating lease are favourable relative to market terms, and a liability if the terms are unfavourable relative to market terms. [IFRS 3:B29]

IFRS 3:B28 and B29 are deleted as consequential amendments arising from IFRS 16. Under that Standard, right-of-use assets and lease liabilities are recognised by the acquirer for all leases in which the acquiree is the lessee, subject to specified exceptions (see **7.5.9**).

Examples 7.4.1A and **7.4.2B** below are therefore only relevant for entities applying IAS 17.

Example 7.4.1A

Acquiree has deferred rent relating to an operating lease (1)

Entity A acquires Entity B. Before the acquisition date, Entity B recognised deferred rent relating to an operating lease as a liability in its statement of financial position (because Entity B has benefited from a rent-free period under the terms of the lease agreement but is required to recognise the lease payments on a straight-line basis over the lease term in accordance with IAS 17).

Should Entity A recognise the deferred rent as a liability as part of the accounting for the business combination?

No. Entity A should not recognise Entity B's deferred rent at the acquisition date because it does not meet the definition of a liability. Instead, as required by IFRS 3:B29, Entity A will recognise an intangible asset if the terms of the operating lease are favourable relative to market terms and a liability if the terms are unfavourable relative to market terms.

Entity A should, however, recognise any additional deferred rent arising in the post-combination period based on the terms of the assumed lease.

Example 7.4.1B provides a numerical example.

Example 7.4.1B

Acquiree has deferred rent relating to an operating lease (2)

Company A acquires Company B and assumes Company B's operating lease (as lessee). The lease has a five-year term with a rent-free period in Year 1, payments in Years 2 and 3 of CU150, in Year 4 of CU200 and in Year 5 of CU250.

At the acquisition date, the lease had a remaining contractual life of three years and Company B had recognised a liability of CU150 for deferred rent. This is calculated as the straight-line accumulated expense of CU300 [(CU150 + CU150 + CU200 + CU250) ÷ 5 × 2] less cash payments of CU150.

Company A does not recognise any amounts related to Company B's deferred rent liability on the acquisition date. However, the terms of the lease will give rise to deferred rent in the post-combination period. Company A will recognise a deferred rent liability of CU50 at the end of the first year after acquisition. This is calculated as the straight-line expense of CU200 [(CU150 + CU200 + CU250) ÷ 3] less cash payments of CU150.

Company A may also need to recognise an asset or a liability at the acquisition date to the extent that the future lease payments are favourable or unfavourable relative to market terms. For example, if market rates at the date of acquisition are CU220 per annum, Company A will recognise an asset reflecting the fair value of the difference between this and the actual future payments, which will average CU200 per annum.

- **Separate identifiable intangible asset** An identifiable intangible asset may be associated with an operating lease, which may be evidenced by market participants' willingness to pay a price for the lease even if it is at market terms. For example, a lease of gates at an airport or of retail space in a prime shopping area might provide entry into a market or other future economic benefits that qualify as identifiable intangible assets (e.g. as a customer relationship). In such circumstances, a separate identifiable intangible asset is recognised – see **7.4.2**. [IFRS 3:B30]

> IFRS 3:B30 is deleted as a consequential amendment arising from IFRS 16 *Leases*. Under that Standard, right-of-use assets and lease liabilities are recognised by the acquirer for all leases in which the acquiree is the lessee, subject to specified exceptions (see **7.5.9**).

- **Measurement when acquiree is the lessor** When an asset such as a building or a patent is leased out by the acquiree under an operating lease, the acquirer takes the terms of the lease into account in measuring the acquisition-date fair value of the leased asset. The acquirer does not recognise a separate asset or liability if the terms of the operating lease are either favourable or unfavourable when compared with market terms, but instead reflects the terms of the lease in the measurement of the fair value of the leased asset (see **example 7.4.1C**). [IFRS 3:B42]

Example 7.4.1C

Acquiree is lessor in operating leases that are favourable or unfavourable relative to market terms

Company A acquires Company B in a business combination. Company B has investment properties leased out under a number of operating leases that involve terms that are favourable or unfavourable relative to market terms.

In accounting for the business combination, Company A does not recognise the fair value of the off-market operating leases separately from the fair value of each investment property. Rather, in each case, the fair value of the operating lease is incorporated as part of the value of the investment property.

7.4.2 Intangible assets

7.4.2.1 Requirement to recognise identifiable intangible assets

This section includes consideration of matters dealt with in IAS 38 *Intangible Assets* which are specific to IFRS 3. More detailed guidance on IAS 38 is included in **chapter A9**.

The acquirer should recognise, separately from goodwill, the identifiable intangible assets acquired in a business combination. An asset is identifiable if it meets either the separability or contractual-legal criteria in IAS 38:12 (see below). [IFRS 3:B31]

The identifiability criteria determine whether an intangible asset is recognised separately from goodwill. However, the criteria neither provide guidance for measuring the fair value of an intangible asset nor restrict the assumptions used in measuring the fair value of an intangible asset. [IFRS 3:B40]

Example 7.4.2.1

Contract renewal

[IFRS 3:B40]

The acquirer would take into account the assumptions that market participants would use when pricing the intangible asset, such as expectations of future contract renewals, in measuring fair value. It is not necessary for the renewals themselves to meet the identifiability criteria. (However, see IFRS 3:29, which establishes an exception to the fair value measurement principle for reacquired

---

rights recognised in a business combination.) Paragraphs 36 and 37 of IAS 38 provide guidance for determining whether intangible assets should be combined into a single unit of account with other intangible or tangible assets.

Reacquired rights are discussed at **7.5.2**.

7.4.2.2   Separability criterion for recognition of intangible assets

An intangible asset is separable if it is capable of being separated or divided from the entity and sold, transferred, licensed, rented or exchanged, either individually or together with a related contract, identifiable asset or liability, regardless of whether the entity intends to do so. [IAS 38:12(a)] An acquired intangible asset meets the separability criterion if there is evidence of exchange transactions for that type of asset or an asset of a similar type, even if those transactions are infrequent and regardless of whether the acquirer is involved in them. [IFRS 3:B33]

Example 7.4.2.2A

Customer lists

[IFRS 3:B33]

Customer and subscriber lists are frequently licensed and thus meet the separability criterion. Even if an acquiree believes its customer lists have characteristics different from other customer lists, the fact that customer lists are frequently licensed generally means that the acquired customer list meets the separability criterion. However, a customer list acquired in a business combination would not meet the separability criterion if the terms of confidentiality or other agreements prohibit an entity from selling, leasing or otherwise exchanging information about its customers.

An intangible asset that is not individually separable from the acquiree or combined entity meets the separability criterion if it is separable in combination with a related contract, identifiable asset or liability. [IFRS 3:B34]

Example 7.4.2.2B

Depositor relationships

[IFRS 3:B34(a)]

Market participants exchange deposit liabilities and related depositor relationship intangible assets in observable exchange transactions. Therefore, the acquirer should recognise the depositor relationship intangible asset separately from goodwill.

Example 7.4.2.2C

Trademarks

[IFRS 3:B34(b)]

An acquiree owns a registered trademark and documented but unpatented technical expertise used to manufacture the trademarked product. To transfer ownership of a trademark, the owner is also required to transfer everything else necessary for the new owner to produce a product or service indistinguishable from that produced by the former owner. Because the unpatented technical expertise must be separated from the acquiree or combined entity and sold if the related trademark is sold, it meets the separability criterion.

7.4.2.3 Contractual-legal criterion for recognition of intangible assets

An intangible asset that arises from contractual or other legal rights is identifiable regardless of whether those rights are transferable or separable from the acquiree or from other rights and obligations. [IAS 38:12(b)]

Example 7.4.2.3A

Manufacturing facility under an operating lease

[IFRS 3:B32(a)]

An acquiree leases a manufacturing facility under an operating lease that has terms that are favourable relative to market terms. The lease terms explicitly prohibit transfer of the lease (through either sale or sublease). The amount by which the lease terms are favourable compared with the terms of current market transactions for the same or similar items is an intangible asset that meets the contractual-legal criterion for recognition separately from goodwill, even though the acquirer cannot sell or otherwise transfer the lease contract.

IFRS 3:B32(a) is deleted as a consequential amendment arising from IFRS 16 *Leases*. Under that Standard, right-of-use assets and lease liabilities are recognised by the acquirer for all leases in which the acquiree is the lessee, subject to specified exceptions (see **7.5.9**).

Example 7.4.2.3B

Nuclear power plant subject to a licence

[IFRS 3:B32(b)]

An acquiree owns and operates a nuclear power plant. The licence to operate that power plant is an intangible asset that meets the contractual-legal criterion for recognition separately from goodwill, even if the acquirer cannot sell or transfer it separately from the acquired power plant. An acquirer may recognise the fair value of the operating licence and the fair value of the power plant as a

---

single asset for financial reporting purposes if the useful lives of those assets are similar.

Example 7.4.2.3C

Technology patent

[IFRS 3:B32(c)]

An acquiree owns a technology patent. It has licensed that patent to others for their exclusive use outside the domestic market, receiving a specified percentage of future foreign revenue in exchange. Both the technology patent and the related licence agreement meet the contractual-legal criterion for recognition separately from goodwill even if selling or exchanging the patent and the related licence agreement separately from one another would not be practical.

The recognition and measurement of intangible assets has always been one of the difficult areas of IFRS 3 to apply in practice. Valuation practices have developed over time and their interpretation and implementation remains varied.

7.4.2.4 Examples of identifiable intangible assets

The following examples of identifiable intangible assets are taken from the illustrative examples accompanying IFRS 3, and are not intended to be all-inclusive. They include examples under five headings: marketing-related, customer-related, artistic-related, contract-based, and technology-based intangible assets. The text indicates whether examples are contractual or non-contractual. Intangible assets identified as having a contractual basis are those that arise from contractual or other legal rights. Those identified as having a non-contractual basis do not arise from contractual or other legal rights but are separable. Intangible assets identified as having a contractual basis might also be separable but separability is not a necessary condition for an asset to meet the contractual-legal criterion. [IFRS 3:IE17]

Example 7.4.2.4A

Marketing-related intangible assets

[IFRS 3:IE18 - IE22]

Marketing-related intangible assets are used primarily in the marketing or promotion of products or services. Examples of marketing-related intangible assets are:

Class	Basis
Trademarks, trade names, service marks, collective marks and certification marks	Contractual
Trade dress (unique colour, shape or package design)	Contractual
Newspaper mastheads	Contractual
Internet domain names	Contractual
Non-competition agreements	Contractual

Trademarks, trade names, service marks, collective marks and certification marks

Trademarks are words, names, symbols or other devices used in trade to indicate the source of a product and to distinguish it from the products of others. A service mark identifies and distinguishes the source of a service rather than a product. Collective marks identify the goods or services of members of a group. Certification marks certify the geographical origin or other characteristics of a good or service.

Trademarks, trade names, service marks, collective marks and certification marks may be protected legally through registration with governmental agencies, continuous use in commerce or by other means. If it is protected legally through registration or other means, a trademark or other mark acquired in a business combination is an intangible asset that meets the contractual-legal criterion. Otherwise, a trademark or other mark acquired in a business combination can be recognised separately from goodwill if the separability criterion is met, which normally it would be.

The terms *brand* and *brand name*, often used as synonyms for trademarks and other marks, are general marketing terms that typically refer to a group of complementary assets such as a trademark (or service mark) and its related trade name, formulas, recipes and technological expertise. IFRS 3 does not preclude an entity from recognising, as a single asset separately from goodwill, a group of complementary intangible assets commonly referred to as a brand if the assets that make up that group have similar useful lives.

Internet domain names

An Internet domain name is a unique alphanumeric name that is used to identify a particular numeric Internet address. Registration of a domain name creates an association between that name and a designated computer on the Internet for the period of the registration. Those registrations are renewable. A registered domain name acquired in a business combination meets the contractual-legal criterion.

Example 7.4.2.4B

Customer-related intangible assets

[IFRS 3:IE23 - IE31]

Examples of customer-related intangible assets are:

Class	Basis
Customer lists	Non-contractual
Order or production backlog	Contractual
Customer contracts and related customer relationships	Contractual
Non-contractual customer relationships	Non-contractual

Customer lists

A customer list consists of information about customers, such as their names and contact information. A customer list also may be in the form of a database that includes other information about the customers, such as their order histories and demographic information. A customer list does not usually arise from contractual or other legal rights. However, customer lists are often leased or exchanged. Therefore, a customer list acquired in a business combination normally meets the separability criterion.

Order or production backlog

An order or production backlog arises from contracts such as purchase or sales orders. An order or production backlog acquired in a business combination meets the contractual-legal criterion even if the purchase or sales orders can be cancelled.

Customer contracts and the related customer relationships

If an entity establishes relationships with its customers through contracts, those customer relationships arise from contractual rights. Therefore, customer contracts and the related customer relationships acquired in a business combination meet the contractual-legal criterion, even if confidentiality or other contractual terms prohibit the sale or transfer of a contract separately from the acquiree.

A customer contract and the related customer relationship may represent two distinct intangible assets. Both the useful lives and the pattern in which the economic benefits of the two assets are consumed may differ.

A customer relationship exists between an entity and its customer if (a) the entity has information about the customer and has regular contact with the customer and (b) the customer has the ability to make direct contact with the entity. Customer relationships meet the contractual-legal criterion if an entity has a practice of establishing contracts with its customers, regardless of whether a contract exists at the acquisition date. Customer relationships may also arise through means other than contracts, such as through regular contact by sales or service representatives.

As noted in IFRS 3:IE25, an order or a production backlog arises from contracts such as purchase or sales orders and is therefore considered a contractual right. Consequently, if an entity has relationships with its customers through these types of contracts, the customer relationships also arise from contractual rights and therefore meet the contractual-legal criterion.

Examples

The following examples illustrate the recognition of customer contract and customer relationship intangible assets acquired in a business combination.

(a)   Acquirer Company (AC) acquires Target Company (TC) in a business combination on 31 December 20X5. TC has a five-year agreement to supply goods to Customer. Both TC and AC believe that Customer will renew the agreement at the end of the current contract. The agreement is not separable. The agreement, whether cancellable or not, meets the contractual-legal criterion. Additionally, because TC establishes its relationship with Customer through a contract, not only the agreement itself but also TC's customer relationship with Customer meet the contractual-legal criterion.

(b)   AC acquires TC in a business combination on 31 December 20X5. TC manufactures goods in two distinct lines of business: sporting goods and electronics. Customer purchases both sporting goods and electronics from TC. TC has a contract with Customer to be its exclusive provider of sporting goods but has no contract for the supply of electronics to Customer. Both TC and AC believe that only one overall customer relationship exists between TC and Customer. The contract to be Customer's exclusive supplier of sporting goods, whether cancellable or not, meets the contractual-legal criterion. Additionally, because TC establishes its relationship with Customer through a contract, the customer relationship with Customer meets the contractual-legal criterion. Because TC has only one customer relationship with Customer, the fair value of that relationship incorporates assumptions about TC's relationship with Customer related to both sporting goods and electronics. However, if AC determines that the customer relationships with Customer for sporting goods and for electronics are separate from each other, AC would assess whether the customer relationship for electronics meets the separability criterion for identification as an intangible asset.

(c)   AC acquires TC in a business combination on 31 December 20X5. TC does business with its customers solely through purchase and sales orders. At 31 December 20X5, TC has a backlog of customer purchase orders from 60 per cent of its customers, all of whom are recurring customers. The other 40 per cent of TC's customers are also recurring customers. However, as of 31 December 20X5, TC has no open purchase orders or other contracts with those customers. Regardless of whether they are cancellable or not, the purchase orders from 60 per cent of TC's customers meet the contractual-legal criterion. Additionally, because TC has established its relationship with 60 per cent of its customers through contracts, not only the purchase orders but also TC's customer relationships meet the contractual-legal criterion. Because TC has a practice of establishing contracts with the remaining 40 per cent of its customers, its relationship with those customers also arises through contractual rights and therefore meets the contractual-legal criterion even though TC does not have contracts with those customers at 31 December 20X5.

(d) AC acquires TC, an insurer, in a business combination on 31 December 20X5. TC has a portfolio of one-year motor insurance contracts that are cancellable by policyholders. Because TC establishes its relationships with policyholders through insurance contracts, the customer relationship with policyholders meets the contractual-legal criterion. IAS 36 *Impairment of Assets* and IAS 38 *Intangible Assets* apply to the customer relationship intangible asset.

Non-contractual customer relationships

A customer relationship acquired in a business combination that does not arise from a contract may nevertheless be identifiable because the relationship is separable. Exchange transactions for the same asset or a similar asset that indicate that other entities have sold or otherwise transferred a particular type of non-contractual customer relationship would provide evidence that the relationship is separable.

Example 7.4.2.4C

Artistic-related intangible assets

[IFRS 3:IE32 - IE33]

Examples of artistic-related intangible assets are:

Class	Basis
Plays, operas and ballets	Contractual
Books, magazines, newspapers and other literary works	Contractual
Musical works such as compositions, song lyrics and advertising jingles	Contractual
Pictures and photographs	Contractual
Video and audiovisual material, including motion pictures or films, music videos and television programmes	Contractual

Artistic-related assets acquired in a business combination are identifiable if they arise from contractual or legal rights such as those provided by copyright. The holder can transfer a copyright, either in whole through an assignment or in part through a licensing agreement. An acquirer is not precluded from recognising a copyright intangible asset and any related assignments or licence agreements as a single asset, provided they have similar useful lives.

Example 7.4.2.4D

Contract-based intangible assets

[IFRS 3:IE34 - IE38]

Contract-based intangible assets represent the value of rights that arise from contractual arrangements. Customer contracts are one type of contract-based intangible asset. If the terms of a contract give rise to a liability (for example, if the terms of an operating lease [only for entities applying IAS 17 *Leases*] or customer contract are unfavourable relative to market terms), the acquirer recognises it as a liability assumed in the business combination.

Examples of contract-based intangible assets are:

Class	Basis
Licensing, royalty and standstill agreements	Contractual
Advertising, construction, management, service or supply contracts	Contractual
Lease agreements (whether the acquiree is the lessee or the lessor) [only for entities applying IAS 17]	Contractual
Construction permits	Contractual
Franchise agreements	Contractual
Operating and broadcast rights	Contractual
Servicing contracts, such as mortgage servicing contracts	Contractual
Employment contracts	Contractual
Use rights, such as drilling, water, air, timber cutting and route authorities	Contractual

Servicing contracts, such as mortgage servicing contracts

Contracts to service financial assets are one type of contract-based intangible asset. Although servicing is inherent in all financial assets, it becomes a distinct asset (or liability) by one of the following:

(a)   when contractually separated from the underlying financial asset by sale or securitisation of the assets with servicing retained;

(b)   through the separate purchase and assumption of the servicing.

If mortgage loans, credit card receivables or other financial assets are acquired in a business combination with servicing retained, the inherent servicing rights are not a separate intangible asset because the fair value of those servicing rights is included in the measurement of the fair value of the acquired financial asset.

Employment contracts

Employment contracts that are beneficial contracts from the perspective of the employer because the pricing of those contracts is favourable relative to market terms are one type of contract-based intangible asset.

Use rights

Use rights include rights for drilling, water, air, timber cutting and route authorities. Some use rights are contract-based intangible assets to be accounted for separately from goodwill. Other use rights may have characteristics of tangible assets rather than of intangible assets. An acquirer should account for use rights on the basis of their nature.

Example 7.4.2.4E

Technology-based intangible assets

[IFRS 3:IE39 - IE44]

Examples of technology-based intangible assets are:

Class	Basis
Patented technology	Contractual
Computer software and mask works	Contractual
Unpatented technology	Non-contractual
Databases, including title plants	Non-contractual
Trade secrets, such as secret formulas, processes and recipes	Contractual

Computer software and mask works

Computer software and program formats acquired in a business combination that are protected legally, such as by patent or copyright, meet the contractual-legal criterion for identification as intangible assets.

Mask works are software permanently stored on a read-only memory chip as a series of stencils or integrated circuitry. Mask works may have legal protection. Mask works with legal protection that are acquired in a business combination meet the contractual-legal criterion for identification as intangible assets.

Databases, including title plants

Databases are collections of information, often stored in electronic form (such as on computer disks or files). A database that includes original works of authorship may be entitled to copyright protection. A database acquired in a business combination and protected by copyright meets the contractual-legal criterion. However, a database typically includes information created as a consequence of an entity's normal operations, such as customer lists, or specialised information, such as scientific data or credit information. Databases that are not protected by copyright can be, and often are, exchanged, licensed or leased to others in their entirety or in part. Therefore, even if the future economic benefits from a database do not arise from legal rights, a database acquired in a business combination meets the separability criterion.

Title plants constitute a historical record of all matters affecting title to parcels of land in a particular geographical area. Title plant assets are bought and sold, either in whole or in part, in exchange transactions or are licensed. Therefore, title plant assets acquired in a business combination meet the separability criterion.

Trade secrets, such as secret formulas, processes and recipes

A trade secret is 'information, including a formula, pattern, recipe, compilation, program, device, method, technique, or process that (a) derives independent economic value, actual or potential, from not being generally known and (b) is the subject of efforts that are reasonable under the circumstances to maintain its secrecy.' If the future economic benefits from a trade secret acquired in a business combination are legally protected, that asset meets the contractual-legal criterion. Otherwise, trade secrets acquired in a business combination are identifiable only if the separability criterion is met, which is likely to be the case.

7.4.2.5   Assembled workforce and other items that are not identifiable

The acquirer subsumes into goodwill the value of an acquired intangible asset that is not identifiable as of the acquisition date. [IFRS 3:B37]

Example 7.4.2.5A

Assembled workforce

[IFRS 3:B37]

An acquirer may attribute value to the existence of an assembled workforce, which is an existing collection of employees that permits the acquirer to continue to operate an acquired business from the acquisition date. An assembled workforce does not represent the intellectual capital of the skilled workforce – the (often specialised) knowledge and experience that employees of an acquiree bring to their jobs, which would be included in the fair value of an entity's other intangible assets, such as proprietary technologies and processes and customer contracts and relationships. Because the assembled workforce is not an identifiable asset to be recognised separately from goodwill, any value attributed to it is subsumed into goodwill.

Example 7.4.2.5B

Agreements with independent contractors

Although an entity's arrangements with its independent contractors are similar in many ways to its arrangements with its at-will employees making up an assembled workforce, the existence of contractual arrangements with independent contractors can represent an intangible asset in some circumstances. Although individual employees might have employment contracts that are similar to arrangements with independent contractors, it is the collection of employees that permits the acquirer to continue to operate an acquired business from the acquisition date and this collection is not an identifiable asset.

Independent contractors are often engaged to perform specific tasks and are not employees of the organisation. There are often negotiated rights for the contractor to retain intellectual property generated during a contract. Independent contractors usually provide services to a number of different entities. Accordingly, the nature of the relationship with independent contractors is often quite different from that with employees and, when that relationship leads to the existence of an intangible asset, it should be recognised and measured in accordance with IFRS 3.

The acquirer also subsumes into goodwill any value attributed to items that do not qualify as assets at the acquisition date. [IFRS 3:B38]

Example 7.4.2.5C

Potential contracts

[IFRS 3:B38]

The acquirer might attribute value to potential contracts the acquiree is negotiating with prospective new customers at the acquisition date. The acquirer does not recognise those potential contracts separately from goodwill, because they are not themselves assets at the acquisition date. The acquirer should not subsequently reclassify the value of those contracts from goodwill for events that occur after the acquisition date. However, the acquirer should assess the facts and circumstances surrounding events occurring shortly after the acquisition to determine whether a separately recognisable intangible asset existed at the acquisition date.

Example 7.4.2.5D

Recognition of value attributed to potential for future expansion of business

Entity A is acquiring Entity B. In arriving at the consideration offered, Entity A has included an element to reflect the potential for future expansion of Entity B's business.

This potential for future expansion is unlikely, in itself, to meet the definition of an asset. However, the expectations for future growth may affect the measurement of other contractual and non-contractual intangible assets identified in the acquisition.

For example, in such an acquisition, the customer base of the acquiree at the acquisition date will often be a separately identifiable intangible asset. The fair value of that intangible asset will reflect expectations for increased business arising from existing customers. Similarly, in valuing intangible assets such as trademarks or licences, the measurement of their fair values will reflect expectations regarding future increases in revenue to be derived from those assets.

In contrast, when the acquirer attributes value to future customers that the acquiree might obtain, unrelated to an identified intangible asset at the acquisition date, this will not represent a separately identifiable asset and the amount should be subsumed within goodwill.

Example 7.4.2.5E

Recognition of value attributed to potential for future growth in monopoly businesses

Entity A is acquiring Entity B. Entity B operates its business under a monopoly licence created by legislation. Because of these monopoly rights, any future customers in Entity B's geographical region will be required to use Entity B to provide its service.

In the circumstances described, the future growth expected in the geographical region should be factored into the value attributed to the monopoly licence.

Circumstances such as those described occur regularly in telecommunications, utilities and similar industry sectors when individual entities are given rights to be the exclusive supplier of a utility or telecommunication service in a particular geographical region. In these cases, the acquirer will usually ascribe significant value to the monopoly licence asset rather than customer-related intangible assets.

7.4.2.6   In-process research and development

IAS 38 generally requires research expenditure and development expenditure not meeting specified criteria to be expensed. However, it is likely that in-process research and development (IPR&D) projects will have a fair value, and this is recognised if the requirements of IFRS 3:B31 are met.

Neither IFRS 3 nor IAS 38 includes any guidance on the subsequent accounting for the fair value recognised at the date of acquisition. Therefore, the general requirements of IAS 38 regarding measurement after recognition, and amortisation, will apply. This is confirmed in the Basis for Conclusions on IAS 38 (see IAS 38:BC84). The subsequent basis of accounting is therefore either:

- cost less any accumulated amortisation and any accumulated impairment losses; or

- revalued amount, being the asset's fair value at the date of revaluation, measured by reference to an active market, less any subsequent accumulated amortisation and any subsequent accumulated impairment losses.

Amortisation should be based on the useful life of the IPR&D (see IAS 38:88).

It is unlikely that the conditions for revaluation will be met, because it is unlikely that an active market will exist for IPR&D; consequently, the cost method will be used. In the event that a research project is not expected to lead to future economic benefits, the amount carried should be subject to impairment testing. When future economic benefits are forecast, amortisation should be based on the useful life assessed by number of production, or similar, units representing that useful life.

Subsequent to the business combination, capitalisation of further expenditure is subject to the requirements of IAS 38:42 (see **4.3.3** in **chapter A9**).

Example 7.4.2.6

In-process research and development

Entity N acquires a research laboratory. The laboratory is involved in the development of medical research techniques. At the date of acquisition, the entity has two projects in progress. One is the development of a proven cure for a common disease into a commercially viable drug, and the second is research into the curative characteristics of a particular chemical compound.

At the date of acquisition, the intangible assets arising from these projects are measured at their fair values and recognised as assets acquired in the business combination.

In subsequent years, provided that the IAS 38 recognition criteria are met, development expenditure directly attributable to the first project is recognised as part of the intangible asset. The asset is tested for impairment at least annually (because it is not yet available for use) and also if any indicators of impairment are identified. All subsequent expenditure attributable to the second project is recognised as an expense when incurred, until such time as the project meets all the criteria in IAS 38 for recognition as a development asset. Once the criteria are satisfied, expenditure that has been previously expensed cannot be reinstated into the development asset.

7.4.2.7   *Tax holiday*

Example 7.4.2.7

Tax holiday in a business combination

In 20X8, Company A acquires a foreign group operating in a number of countries. One of the overseas subsidiaries of the acquiree, Company B, operates in Country X and has assets that benefit from a tax holiday for 10 years (i.e. the net profit or loss generated by those assets will not be subject to income tax for 10 years). Two of the 10 years have already elapsed. The tax authority in Country X grants such a tax holiday to qualifying entities only for those investments that represent a particular interest for the national or a regional economy of Country X.

In accounting for the business combination, how should Company A recognise the future benefit expected to arise from the tax holiday granted to Company B?

The appropriate accounting depends on whether the tax holiday reflects the tax status of Company B or the tax base of an asset owned by Company B (i.e. whether it is an attribute of the entity itself or of a specific asset).

The following are indicators that the tax benefit relates to a specific asset:

- the tax holiday applies only to the net profit or loss generated from the specific asset; or

- if the specific asset were disposed of in a sale of assets, the new owner would benefit from the tax holiday; or

- if the asset were sold, and Company B were to purchase or build a similar asset in the same geographical area, Company B would need to follow the normal application process before being able to benefit from a tax holiday for the new asset.

The following are indicators that the tax benefit relates to Company B as an entity:

- the tax holiday applies to net profit or loss generated from all of the activities of Company B; or

- if the asset were disposed of in a sale of assets, the new owner would not benefit from the tax holiday. The benefit would transfer to a new owner only if the new owner acquired the shares of Company B; or

- if the asset were sold and Company B were to purchase or build a similar asset in the same geographical area, Company B would benefit from the same tax holiday without further formality.

If the facts indicate that the tax holiday relates specifically to an asset, the future economic benefits arising from the tax holiday should be considered as part of the measurement of the fair value of the asset because it is a component that market participants would consider in determining the price that would be received from the sale of the asset in an orderly transaction.

If facts and circumstances indicate that the tax holiday relates to Company B as an entity, the future economic benefits arising from the tax holiday are excluded from the consideration of the fair value of the identifiable assets acquired and instead affect the determination of goodwill arising on the acquisition.

One further consideration is whether the tax holiday arises as a result of a specific contractual arrangement with the tax authority, in which case it might meet the definition of an intangible asset under IAS 38. In the circumstances described, the tax holiday is available to all qualifying entities within this tax jurisdiction and is not the result of an individual or a specific contract between Company B and the tax authority. The resulting economic benefit does not meet the definition of an intangible asset. Sovereign states usually have the right unilaterally to amend tax regimes as a result of a change in government or in response to changes in the economic needs of a country. Therefore, statutory tax arrangements offered by governments do not meet the definition of a contractual or legal right (that results in control of the asset) and, consequently, do not result in intangible assets under IAS 38.

Conversely, if the tax holiday was granted specifically to Entity B as a result of a specific contractual arrangement with the tax authority, the tax holiday would represent the award of a separate right and, therefore, an intangible asset that might need to be recognised under IAS 38.

7.4.3 Performance obligations

Example 7.4.3

Performance obligations

Company A acquires Company B in a business combination. At the acquisition date, Company B has recognised deferred income related to a customer contract. The deferred income represents a prepayment received by Company B for future services.

IFRS 3:18 requires the acquirer to "measure the identifiable assets acquired and the liabilities assumed at their acquisition-date fair values". At the acquisition date, Company A should recognise a liability in its consolidated financial statements to the extent that the deferred income represents an obligation to provide future services that will be the combined entity's responsibility after the acquisition date. That is, a liability should be recognised because Company A has a performance obligation to provide future services for which payment has already been received. This liability should be measured at fair value as of the acquisition date and consideration should be given to whether any intangible assets should be recognised as part of the business combination with respect to Company B's customer contracts (see **example 7.4.2.3B**).

7.4.4 Contractual obligations

Example 7.4.4

Contractual obligations

Entity F acquires Entity G. Prior to the date of acquisition, Entity G enters into a retrenchment arrangement with its directors such that, if Entity G is acquired by another party, the directors will become entitled to a one-off aggregate payment of CU50,000.

At the acquisition date, Entity F should recognise a liability for CU50,000 for the amount due to the directors, because this represents a contractual obligation of Entity G that has become payable as a result of the consummation of the business combination.

Entity F should not recognise the liability for the estimated cost of the restructuring plan – this amount will be recognised as a post-combination expense when the recognition criteria in IAS 37 *Provisions, Contingent Liabilities and Contingent Assets* are met.

7.4.5   Non-competition agreements

Non-competition agreements are discussed at **3.3.5** in **chapter A9**.

7.4.6   Inventories

Fair value at the point of acquisition (i.e. the date of combination) typically includes profit attributed to past production effort (i.e. in bringing the goods to their current condition). It is not generally appropriate to assign the acquiree's carrying amount to the cost of acquired inventories, because the acquiree's cost does not reflect the manufacturing profit that is recognised by the acquiree through the normal selling process. This manufacturing profit should be considered as part of the fair value assigned to the inventories.

The fair value of finished goods and merchandise is likely to be lower than selling price, to reflect the costs of disposal and a reasonable profit allowance for the selling effort of the acquirer based on profit for similar finished goods and merchandise. In determining a reasonable profit allowance, the following factors should be considered:

- the historical turnover rate for inventories of the acquiree and for the acquiree's industry;

- industry statistics for normal profit allowances and turnover rates; and

- the nature of the selling network and marketing techniques employed by the acquiree or that will be employed by the acquirer, if significantly different.

In the case of retail operations, costs of disposal may include inventory holding costs and warehousing and distribution costs for the acquired inventories. However, it is inappropriate to allocate general and administrative overhead costs to finished goods inventories in the acquisition.

7.4.7   Emission rights acquired in a business combination

Example 7.4.7

Emission rights acquired in a business combination

Entity A acquires Entity B. Entity B's accounting policy is to adopt the 'net liability' approach for the recognition of emission rights (see **9.1.4** in **chapter A12**). Entity B has been granted emission rights by the government for no charge and, at the acquisition date, it holds emission rights in excess of actual emissions made. Accordingly, no asset or provision is recognised in the financial statements of Entity B in respect of emissions.

On acquisition, Entity A's consolidated financial statements should include the emission rights held by Entity B as an asset and should include a separate provision for the actual emissions made as at that date. Both the asset and the provision should be recognised at fair value, in accordance with IFRS 3. The 'net liability' approach may not be applied in the consolidated financial statements; instead, the consolidated financial statements should thereafter reflect an expense for actual emissions made from the date of acquisition until the end of the reference period.

Fair value at acquisition date should be measured by reference to an active market for emission rights or, if no active market exists, on a basis that reflects the amount that would have been received to sell the rights in an orderly transaction between market participants, based on the best information available.

7.5 Exceptions to the recognition and measurement principles

7.5.1 Exceptions to the recognition and measurement principles – general

IFRS 3 sets out limited exceptions to its general recognition and measurement principles (as stated in **7.1.1** and **7.2.1**). This results in particular items being:

[IFRS 3:21]

(a) recognised either by applying recognition conditions in addition to those set out at **7.1.1** or by applying the requirements of other IFRSs, with results that differ from applying the recognition principle and conditions; or

(b) measured at an amount other than their acquisition-date fair values.

Summary of recognition and measurement exceptions

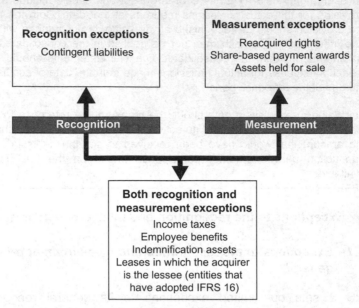

7.5.2   Contingent liabilities

7.5.2.1   Background

IFRS 3 requires certain contingent liabilities of the acquiree to be recognised and measured in a business combination at acquisition-date fair value (see **7.5.2.2** for details). This may result in the recognition of contingent liabilities that would not qualify for recognition under IAS 37 *Provisions, Contingent Liabilities and Contingent Assets* (see **chapter A12**). Consequently, IFRS 3 also includes guidance on the subsequent measurement of contingent liabilities recognised in a business combination.

7.5.2.2   Requirements for recognising contingent liabilities

IAS 37 defines a contingent liability as:

[IAS 37:10]

(a)   a possible obligation that arises from past events and whose existence will be confirmed only by the occurrence or non-occurrence of one or more uncertain future events not wholly within the control or the entity; or

(b)   a present obligation that arises from past events but is not recognised because:

(i)   it is not probable that an outflow of resources embodying economic benefits will be required to settle the obligation; or

(ii) the amount of the obligation cannot be measured with sufficient reliability.

In a business combination, the requirements of IAS 37 are not applied in determining which contingent liabilities should be recognised as of the acquisition date. Instead, IFRS 3 requires that the acquirer should recognise a contingent liability assumed in a business combination as of the acquisition date if:

[IFRS 3:23]

- it is a present obligation that arises from past events; and

- its fair value can be measured reliably.

Therefore, in contrast to IAS 37, the acquirer recognises a contingent liability assumed in a business combination at the acquisition date even if it is not probable that an outflow of resources embodying economic benefits will be required to settle the obligation. [IFRS 3:23]

In practice, the application of IAS 37 to past events focuses on the future outcome of those events. When an obligation has arisen as a result of a past event, but it is not probable that an outflow of resources will be required, the obligation is determined to be a contingent liability under IAS 37 and, therefore, is not recognised as a liability in the statement of financial position, but is disclosed by way of note.

Under the fair value principle of IFRS 3, the fact that there is a present obligation means that the risk has a fair value because the entity would rationally pay to have the risk removed. This is true regardless of the probability of outcomes. In practice, it will be necessary to determine whether a present obligation exists (recognised if reliably measurable), or whether there is just a possible obligation (not recognised).

7.5.2.3 Subsequent measurement of contingent liabilities

After initial recognition and until the liability is settled, cancelled or expires, the acquirer should measure a contingent liability recognised in a business combination at the higher of:

[IFRS 3:56]

(a) the amount that would be recognised in accordance with IAS 37 (see **chapter A12**); and

(b) the amount initially recognised less, if appropriate, the cumulative amount of income recognised in accordance with the principles of IFRS 15 *Revenue from Contracts with Customers* (see **chapter A14**).

In June 2014, IFRS 3:56(b) was amended as a consequential amendment arising from IFRS 15 *Revenue from Contracts with*

Customers. Prior to amendment, the paragraph referred to "cumulative amortisation recognised in accordance with IAS 18 *Revenue*".

The requirements of IFRS 3:56 do not apply to contracts accounted for in accordance with IFRS 9 *Financial Instruments* (or, for entities that have not yet adopted IFRS 9, IAS 39 *Financial Instruments: Recognition and Measurement*).

Example 7.5.2.3

Subsequent measurement of a contingent liability recognised at acquisition

Entity A acquired Entity B in November 20X3, at which time Entity B was being sued by a third party for breach of contract. At the time of the business combination, Entity A's management determined that the lawsuit represented a present obligation because available evidence indicated that the claim had a sound legal basis. However, previous experience indicated that it was less than 50 per cent probable that the claimant would pursue the case to the point of settlement or court decision. Therefore, when Entity B applies IAS 37 for the purposes of its financial statements, the obligation is considered to be a contingent liability and not recognised as a provision.

However, IFRS 3:23 requires an acquirer to recognise and measure contingent liabilities that are present obligations at the date of acquisition "even if it is not probable that an outflow of resources embodying economic benefits will be required to settle the obligation". Therefore, in accounting for the business combination, Entity A recognised a liability of CU40 million in respect of the estimated fair value of litigation in progress against Entity B. The estimate of CU40 million remained valid at 31 December 20X4, at which time the initial accounting for the combination was complete (i.e. the measurement period ended).

At 31 December 20X5, Entity A reassesses the claim. Management now believes that settlement is probable (the recognition criteria of IAS 37 are therefore met). The settlement amount is now estimated to be CU30 million.

At what amount should Entity A measure the liability at 31 December 20X5?

The liability should be measured at the original estimate of CU40 million.

IFRS 3 applies for the recognition and measurement of contingent liabilities at the acquisition date. Subsequently, IFRS 3:56 requires the acquirer to measure a contingent liability recognised in a business combination at the higher of (1) the amount that would be recognised in accordance with IAS 37, and (2) the amount initially recognised less the cumulative amount of income recognised in accordance with the principles of IFRS 15 (or, for entities that have not yet adopted IFRS 15, the amount initially recognised less any appropriate cumulative amortisation recognised in accordance with IAS 18).

The liability recognised in the business combination cannot be reduced other than by the cumulative amount of income recognised in accordance with

---

the principles of IFRS 15 (or, for entities that have not yet adopted IFRS 15, any appropriate cumulative amortisation recognised in accordance with IAS 18). The nature of the liability in the circumstances under consideration is such that recognition of income is not appropriate. Therefore, the liability will continue to be recognised at no less than CU40 million until settlement or expiry (even if it becomes a provision that would be recognised at a lower amount under IAS 37).

7.5.3 Pre-existing relationships and reacquired rights

7.5.3.1 Overview

IFRS 3 deals with reacquired rights and the wider issue of pre-existing relationships in three inter-related sections:

- first, the section on identifying and measuring assets acquired includes a requirement to identify and recognise reacquired rights;

- second, the section on determining what is part of the business combination requires an adjustment to be made to the purchase consideration for transactions that in effect settle pre-existing relationships between the acquirer and the acquiree; and

- third, the section on subsequent measurement and accounting includes a requirement in respect of reacquired rights.

7.5.3.2 Recognition of reacquired rights as an intangible asset

As part of a business combination, an acquirer may reacquire a right that it had previously granted to the acquiree to use one or more of the acquirer's recognised or unrecognised assets. Examples of reacquired rights include a right to use the acquirer's trade name under a franchise agreement or a right to use the acquirer's technology under a technology licensing agreement. A reacquired right is an intangible asset that the acquirer recognises separately from goodwill. [IFRS 3:B35]

There are two specific requirements regarding the measurement of a reacquired right.

- **Ignoring the potential for contract renewal** The acquirer is required to measure the value of a reacquired right recognised as an intangible asset on the basis of the remaining contractual term of the related contract, regardless of whether market participants would consider potential contractual renewals when measuring its fair value. [IFRS 3:29]

- **Recognition of a settlement gain or loss** If the terms of the contract giving rise to a reacquired right are favourable or unfavourable to the acquirer relative to the terms of current market transactions for the same or similar items, the acquirer should recognise a settlement gain or loss. [IFRS 3:B36] The consequence of this requirement is that the consideration for the business combination is adjusted downward (and that amount recognised as an expense) when part of the consideration effectively settles an unfavourable arrangement from the acquirer's perspective, and adjusted upward (a gain) when the consideration is lower due to the effective settlement of a favourable arrangement from the acquirer's perspective. The measurement of any such gain or loss is described in **7.5.3.3**.

The effect of these requirements is that the amount recognised for the reacquired right asset is based on the 'at market' valuation of the contract, but only by reference to the contracted term of the right.

7.5.3.3   Measurement of gain or loss on settlement of a pre-existing relationship

The acquirer and acquiree may have a relationship that existed before they contemplated the business combination, referred to as a 'pre-existing relationship'. A pre-existing relationship between the acquirer and the acquiree may be contractual (e.g. vendor and customer, or licensor and licensee) or non-contractual (e.g. plaintiff and defendant). [IFRS 3:B51]

If the business combination in effect settles a pre-existing relationship, the acquirer recognises a gain or loss, measured as follows:

[IFRS 3:B52]

(a)   for a pre-existing non-contractual relationship (such as a lawsuit), fair value; and

(b)   for a pre-existing contractual relationship, the lesser of (i) and (ii):

(i)   the amount by which the contract is favourable or unfavourable from the perspective of the acquirer when compared with terms for current market transactions for the same or similar items. (An unfavourable contract is a contract that is unfavourable in terms of current market terms. It is not necessarily an onerous contract in which the unavoidable costs of meeting the obligations under the contract exceed the economic benefits expected to be received under it); and

(ii)   the amount of any stated settlement provisions in the contract available to the counterparty to whom the contract is unfavourable.

If (ii) is less than (i), the difference is included as part of the business combination accounting.

The amount of gain or loss recognised may depend in part on whether the acquirer had previously recognised a related asset or liability, and the reported gain or loss therefore may differ from the amount calculated by applying the above requirements. [IFRS 3:B52]

A pre-existing relationship may be a contract that the acquirer recognises as a reacquired right. If the contract includes terms that are favourable or unfavourable when compared with pricing for current market transactions for the same or similar items, the acquirer recognises, separately from the business combination, a gain or loss for the effective settlement of the contract, measured in accordance with IFRS 3:B52. [IFRS 3:B53]

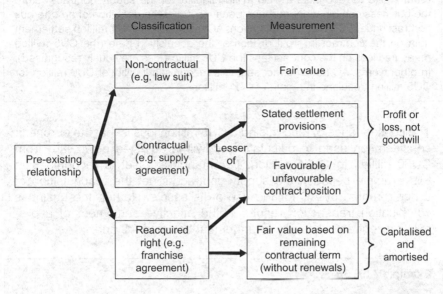

Example 7.5.3.3A

Settlement of a pre-existing relationship – contractual supply agreement

[IFRS 3:IE54 - IE57]

AC purchases electronic components from TC under a five-year supply contract at fixed rates. Currently, the fixed rates are higher than the rates at which AC could purchase similar electronic components from another supplier. The supply contract allows AC to terminate the contract before the end of the initial five-year term but only by paying a CU6 million penalty. With three years remaining under the supply contract, AC pays CU50 million to acquire TC, which is the fair value of TC based on what other market participants would be willing to pay.

Included in the total fair value of TC is CU8 million related to the fair value of the supply contract with AC. The CU8 million represents a CU3 million component that is 'at market' because the pricing is comparable to pricing for current market transactions for the same or similar items (selling effort, customer relationships and so on) and a CU5 million component for pricing that is unfavourable to AC because it exceeds the price of current market transactions for similar items. TC has no other identifiable assets or liabilities related to the supply contract, and AC has not recognised any assets or liabilities related to the supply contract before the business combination.

In this example, AC calculates a loss of CU5 million (the lesser of the CU6 million stated settlement amount and the amount by which the contract is unfavourable to the acquirer) separately from the business combination. The CU3 million 'at-market' component of the contract is part of goodwill.

Whether AC had recognised previously an amount in its financial statements related to a pre-existing relationship will affect the amount recognised as a gain or loss for the effective settlement of the relationship. Suppose that IFRSs had required AC to recognise a CU6 million liability for the supply contract before the business combination, perhaps because it met the definition of an onerous contract under IAS 37. In that situation, AC recognises a CU1 million settlement gain on the contract in profit or loss at the acquisition date (the CU5 million measured loss on the contract less the CU6 million loss previously recognised). In other words, AC has in effect settled a recognised liability of CU6 million for CU5 million, resulting in a gain of CU1 million.

The consequence of recognising a CU5 million loss is that the purchase consideration used to calculate goodwill is adjusted downward from CU50 million to CU45 million. No intangible asset is recognised in this example because the supply contract is not the reacquisition of a right granted by AC for the use of its assets. Rather, the business combination transaction results in the effective settlement of a pre-existing contractual supply arrangement between AC and TC.

Example 7.5.3.3B

Effective settlement of a pre-existing relationship – reacquired right

Company X grants a franchise right to Company Y to operate under Company X's name in a specified country in which it operates. Two years later, Company X decides to expand its business and enters into an agreement to acquire 100 per cent of Company Y for CU50,000. Company Y's business consists of the franchise right (fair value of CU20,000), a customer list (fair value of CU10,000), some operating assets and liabilities (net fair value CU15,000), an assembled workforce (recognised as part of goodwill) and processes.

Assume that the franchise right has a fixed term and is not renewable.

When accounting for the business combination, how should Company X account for the reacquired franchise right?

Franchise right at market terms

If, at the time of the acquisition, the franchise right is at market terms, Company X does not recognise an off-market settlement gain or loss. Company X should recognise an identified intangible asset for the reacquired right at its fair value of CU20,000. This right will be amortised over the remaining term of the franchise agreement.

Goodwill will therefore be CU5,000 (CU50,000 less (20,000 + 10,000 + 15,000)).

Franchise right at off-market terms

Assume the same facts, except that the franchise right contract terms are favourable to Company X compared to market terms at the acquisition date by CU3,000.

Company X recognises an identified intangible asset for the reacquired right at its fair value of CU20,000. This right will be amortised over the remaining term of the franchise agreement.

In addition, Company X recognises a gain of CU3,000 for the effective settlement of the contract and consequently increases the consideration used in accounting for the acquisition to CU53,000.

Goodwill will therefore be CU8,000 (CU53,000 less (20,000 + 10,000 + 15,000)).

Example 7.5.3.3C

Settlement of a pre-existing contractual relationship

Company X operates in the pharmaceutical industry and has developed some intellectual property (IP). In 20X0, Company X entered into a five-year licensing agreement with Company Y. Under the terms of the agreement, Company Y is entitled to use Company X's IP but is required to pay a royalty of 5 per cent of all sales of product developed using the IP.

In 20X2, Company Y acquires 100 per cent of Company X; at the acquisition date, the market rate for a similar licensing agreement is 6 per cent of sales.

The amount paid by Company Y to the shareholders of Company X is CU100 million. At that date, the directors of Company Y estimate that CU5 million represents the amount by which the contract for use of Company X's IP is favourable when compared with current market transactions for the same or similar items. The fair value of Company X's net identifiable assets is CU82 million.

The business combination in effect settles the pre-existing relationship between Company X and Company Y. Under IFRS 3:52, generally there is a strong presumption that any pre-existing relationship is considered to be settled as a result of the business combination and, therefore, should be accounted for separately. This is regardless of whether the entities continue to operate under the terms of the agreement after the business combination.

As a result of the business combination, the agreement between Company X and Company Y becomes an intragroup arrangement. In effect, the pre-existing relationship has been settled through the transaction that results in Company X becoming part of Company Y's group. Company Y will therefore recognise, separately from the business combination, a gain for the amount by which the contract is favourable from Company Y's perspective when compared with current market terms (i.e. CU5 million).

Consequently, the consideration for the acquisition is considered to be CU105 million (in effect, Company Y has contributed the value of the favourable contract in addition to the cash consideration paid) and goodwill will be calculated as CU23 million (CU105 million less CU82 million).

Example 7.5.3.3D

Effective settlement of a pre-existing non-contractual relationship

Company X acquires Company Y. Company X is a defendant in litigation relating to a claim brought about by Company Y. Company X pays CU100,000 to acquire Company Y and effectively settles the legal claim. The fair value of the settlement of the legal claim is estimated to be CU8,000. Prior to acquisition, Company X had recognised a provision of CU5,000 for settlement of the legal claim.

In this example, having taking into account the provision already recognised, Company X calculates a settlement loss of CU3,000 relating to the litigation. This settlement loss is recognised in profit or loss separately from the acquisition of Company Y.

If Company X had previously recognised a provision of more than CU8,000, on acquisition of Company Y a settlement gain would be recognised in profit or loss for the difference between the provision previously recognised and the fair value of the claim.

7.5.3.4 Subsequent measurement of reacquired rights

A reacquired right recognised as an intangible asset should be amortised over the remaining contractual period of the contract in which the right was granted. An acquirer that subsequently sells a reacquired right to a third party should include the carrying amount of the intangible asset in determining the gain or loss on the sale. [IFRS 3:55] In such cases, care should be taken to ensure that the intangible asset being sold is the same asset that was previously reacquired. Thus, the reacquisition through a business combination of a 'master franchise agreement', and the subsequent granting of sub-franchises for specific geographical areas to third parties, would be dealt with separately and the master franchise agreement retained in the acquirer's statement of financial position.

7.5.4 Share-based payment awards

When an acquirer issues share-based payment awards to replace those of an acquiree, it is necessary to allocate the replacement awards between:

- the element which represents purchase consideration for accrued share rights earned before the acquisition; and

- the element which represents compensation for post-acquisition services.

As an exception to the fair value measurement principle, any liability or equity instrument recognised by the acquirer is based on a 'market-based measure' determined in accordance with IFRS 2 *Share-based Payment*. Share-based payments are dealt with in **8.3.4**.

7.5.5 Assets held for sale

The acquirer should measure an acquired non-current asset (or disposal group) that is classified as held for sale at the acquisition date in accordance with IFRS 5 *Non-current Assets Held for Sale and Discontinued Operations* at fair value less costs to sell in accordance with paragraphs 15 to 18 of that Standard (see **chapter A20**). [IFRS 3:31]

7.5.6 Income taxes

IFRS 3 requires the acquirer to recognise and measure a deferred tax asset or liability arising from the assets acquired and liabilities assumed in a business combination in accordance with IAS 12 *Income Taxes* (see **chapter A13**). [IFRS 3:24]

The acquirer should account for potential tax effects of temporary differences and carry forwards of an acquiree that exist at the acquisition date or that arise as a result of the acquisition in accordance with IAS 12. [IFRS 3:25]

The requirements regarding the post-combination accounting for deferred tax arising from a business combination are discussed at **10.1.6**.

7.5.7 Employee benefits

The acquirer should recognise and measure a liability (or asset, if any) related to the acquiree's employee benefit arrangements in accordance with IAS 19 *Employee Benefits* (see **chapter A15**). [IFRS 3:26]

7.5.8 Indemnification assets

7.5.8.1 Initial measurement of indemnification assets

The seller in a business combination may contractually indemnify the acquirer for the outcome of a contingency or uncertainty related to all or part of a specific asset or liability. For example, the seller may indemnify the acquirer against losses above a certain amount on a liability arising from a particular contingency, such as legal action or income tax uncertainty. As a result, the acquirer obtains an indemnification asset. [IFRS 3:27]

Example 7.5.8.1

Third-party indemnification arrangements

T Limited is acquiring a subsidiary from R Limited. As part of the business combination, R Limited agrees to indemnify T Limited for uncertainty related to a number of the subsidiary's existing liabilities. Instead of a direct indemnification by R Limited, the indemnification will be provided by means of an insurance contract written by a third-party insurance company. As agreed in the sale and purchase agreement, R Limited negotiates the insurance policy with the insurance company on behalf of T Limited.

Does the insurance policy represent an indemnification asset of T Limited as defined in IFRS 3:27 and 28?

Yes. IFRS 3:27 applies when the seller indemnifies the buyer for the outcome of a contingency or uncertainty related to all or part of a specific asset or liability. It does not prescribe the form of the indemnification arrangement. Therefore, R Limited arranging for an insurance contract on behalf of and for the benefit of T Limited, as part of the business combination transaction, falls within the scope of IFRS 3's requirements regarding indemnification assets.

IFRS 3 requires the acquirer to recognise an indemnification asset at the same time that it recognises the indemnified item and that the indemnification asset be measured on the same basis as the indemnified item, assuming that there is no uncertainty over the recovery of the indemnification asset. Therefore, if the indemnification relates to an asset or a liability that is recognised at the acquisition date and that is measured at fair value, the acquirer should recognise the indemnification asset at the acquisition date measured at its fair value. [IFRS 3:27]

For an indemnification asset measured at fair value, the effects of uncertainty about future cash flows because of collectibility considerations are included in the fair value measure and a separate valuation allowance is not necessary. [IFRS 3:27]

In some circumstances, the indemnification may relate to an asset or a liability that is an exception to the recognition or measurement principles. For example, an indemnification may relate to a contingent liability that is not recognised at the acquisition date because its fair value is not reliably measurable at that date. Alternatively, an indemnification may relate to an asset or a liability (e.g. one that results from an employee benefit) that is measured on a basis other than acquisition-date fair value. In those circumstances, the indemnification asset is recognised and measured using assumptions consistent with those used to measure the indemnified item, subject to management's assessment of the collectibility of the indemnification asset and any contractual limitations on the indemnified amount. [IFRS 3:28]

The requirement that an indemnification asset be measured using assumptions consistent with the measurement of the indemnified item does not necessarily mean that the indemnification asset and indemnified item are measured at the same amount. For example, an indemnity may be capped at a certain amount, be determined as a portion of any final settlement amount, represent an amount in excess of a particular amount, or be recovered in a later time period than when the indemnified item is settled. In these cases, it is likely that the indemnified item will be recognised at a different amount to the indemnification asset because the cash outflows and inflows will be different.

However, the recognition and measurement of the asset and liability will be determined on a consistent basis, by reference to any relevant Standards. Therefore, an indemnification asset relating to:

- employee benefits will be measured using the principles of IAS 19 (see **chapter A15**);

- a liability recognised as a provision will be measured in accordance with IAS 37 (see **chapter A12**); and

- an income tax exposure will be measured by reference to IAS 12 (see **chapter A13**).

7.5.8.2 *Subsequent measurement of indemnification assets*

At the end of each subsequent reporting period, the acquirer should measure an indemnification asset that was recognised at the acquisition date on the same basis as the indemnified liability or asset, subject to any contractual limitations on its amount and, for an indemnification asset that is not subsequently measured at its fair value, management's assessment of the collectibility of the indemnification asset. The acquirer should derecognise the indemnification asset only when it collects the asset, sells it or otherwise loses the right to it. [IFRS 3:57]

The effect of the requirements for indemnification assets is to achieve matching of the asset recognised with the item that is the subject of the indemnity. In most cases, it is expected that remeasurement of both asset and liability would be in profit or loss, although IFRS 3 does not require this specifically.

7.5.9 **Leases in which the acquiree is the lessee (entities that have adopted IFRS 16 Leases)**

7.5.9.1 *Recognition and measurement of right-of-use assets and lease liabilities*

Subject to the exceptions set out in **7.5.9.2**, the acquirer is required to recognise right-of-use assets and lease liabilities for leases in which the acquiree is the lessee. [IFRS 3:28A]

Lease liabilities recognised in accordance with IFRS 3:28A should be measured at the present value of the lease payments (as defined in IFRS 16 – see **section 7** of **chapter A17**) as if the lessee had entered into a new lease at the acquisition date. [IFRS 3:28B]

Right-of-use assets recognised in accordance with IFRS 3:28A are required to be measured at the same amount as the related lease liabilities, adjusted to reflect favourable or unfavourable terms of the lease when compared with market terms. [IFRS 3:28B]

The IASB decided that acquirers should not be required to measure the acquiree's right-of-use assets and lease liabilities at fair value on the date of acquisition, in accordance with the general principles of IFRS 3, due to cost/benefit considerations. The IASB's view is that the measurement requirements in IFRS 3:28B should result in the recognition of a net carrying amount for the lease at the date of acquisition that approximates the fair value of the lease at that date. [IFRS 16:BC297]

Paragraphs 28A (see also **7.5.9.2**) and 28B were added to IFRS 3 as consequential amendments arising from IFRS 16 and should be applied when an entity applies IFRS 16 (effective for annual periods beginning on or after 1 January 2019, with earlier application permitted – see **section 14** of **chapter A17** for detailed transition provisions).

7.5.9.2   Recognition exceptions for right-of-use assets and lease liabilities

The acquirer is not required to recognise right-of-use assets and lease liabilities for:

[IFRS 3:28A]

(a) leases for which the lease term (as defined in IFRS 16 – see **section 6** of **chapter A17**) ends within 12 months of the acquisition date; or

(b) leases for which the underlying asset is of low value, as described in IFRS 16 (see **8.2.3** in **chapter A17**).

These recognition exceptions reflect the recognition exemptions available under IFRS 16 (see **8.2** in **chapter A17**). In both cases, the IFRS 16 exemptions are optional (the short-term lease exemption to be applied consistently with each class of underlying asset, and the exemption for low-value assets available on a lease-by-lease basis). The recognition exceptions for acquirers under IFRS 3:28A(a) and (b) are also optional.

Note that the exception under IFRS 3:28A(a) effectively extends the short-term recognition exemption generally available for lease terms of 12 months or less to lease terms expected to end within 12 months of the acquisition date irrespective of when the lease term commenced.

When an acquirer chooses to apply either of the exemptions set out in IFRS 3:28A, it is not required to recognise assets or liabilities relating to any off-market lease terms. Although such a requirement would be consistent with the general principles of IFRS 3, under which assets and liabilities relating to contracts with off-market terms are recognised separately and not subsumed within goodwill on acquisition, the IASB decided that the effect of any such off-market terms would rarely be material for short-term leases and leases of low-value assets. [IFRS 16:BC298]

8 Identifying and measuring consideration

8.1 Consideration transferred

IFRS 3 requires the consideration transferred in a business combination to be measured at fair value. This is calculated as the sum of the acquisition-date fair values of:

[IFRS 3:37]

- the assets transferred by the acquirer;

- the liabilities incurred by the acquirer to former owners of the acquiree; and

- the equity interests issued by the acquirer.

However, any portion of the acquirer's share-based payment awards exchanged for awards held by the acquiree's employees that is included in the consideration transferred in the business combination should be measured in accordance with IFRS 2 *Share-based Payment* (see **8.3.4**). [IFRS 3:37]

Potential forms of consideration include cash, other assets, a business or a subsidiary of the acquirer, contingent consideration (see **8.2**), ordinary or preference equity instruments, options, warrants and member interests of mutual entities. [IFRS 3:37]

Example 8.1

Business acquired through exercise of a put option

On 1 July 20X5, Company A writes a put option to Company C over 100 per cent of the ordinary share capital of Company B at a fixed price of CU150 million that is exercisable only at the date of maturity (21 December 20X5). The exercise of the put option will result in Company A gaining control over Company B. (Company A does not control Company B until the put option is exercised; Company A holds neither shares nor potential voting rights that result in its having control.) Company C pays Company A a premium of CU10 million for the put option.

On 21 December 20X5, Company C exercises the put option. At that date, the fair value of Company B's ordinary shares is CU120 million and the fair value of the put option is a CU30 million liability for Company A.

The written put option is within the scope of IFRS 9 *Financial Instruments* (or, for entities that have not yet adopted IFRS 9, IAS 39 *Financial Instruments:*

Recognition and Measurement). It is not excluded under IFRS 9:2.1(f) (which excludes from the scope of IFRS 9 "any forward contract between an acquirer and a selling shareholder to buy or sell an acquiree that will result in a business combination at a future acquisition date") because it is an option. [For entities that have not yet adopted IFRS 9, the equivalent scope exclusion for forward contracts is at IAS 39:2(g).]

The written put option is accounted for under IFRS 9 (or IAS 39) as a derivative liability with changes in fair value recognised through profit or loss until exercise or maturity of the option:

- on 1 July 20X5, Company A recognises the liability at CU10 million (i.e. at the amount of the premium received);

- on 21 December 20X5, Company A recognises the increase in the fair value of the derivative and a corresponding CU20 million loss in profit or loss. This loss arising due to changes in the fair value of the put option is not reversed when accounting for the business combination;

- the payment of the purchase price of CU150 million by Company A is treated as settlement of the written put liability of CU30 million and the acquisition of Company B at a cost equal to the fair value of Company B's shares (i.e. CU120 million); and

- goodwill on the acquisition of Company B is determined by comparing the cost of acquisition of CU120 million (not the cash amount paid of CU150 million) with the fair value of the assets, liabilities and contingent liabilities acquired.

If instead the put option were not exercised by Company C, the lapse of the option at 21 December 20X5 would be accounted for by Company A by derecognising the liability, with a corresponding gain in profit or loss.

The consideration transferred may include assets or liabilities of the acquirer with carrying amounts that differ from their fair values at the acquisition date (e.g. non-monetary assets or a business of the acquirer). If so, the acquirer should remeasure the transferred assets or liabilities to their fair values as of the acquisition date and recognise any resulting gains or losses in profit or loss. [IFRS 3:38]

The recognition of a gain or loss on assets or liabilities transferred is consistent with the definition of cost in the IASB *Glossary* which defines cost as "the amount of cash or cash equivalents paid or *the fair value of the other consideration* given to acquire an asset at the time of its acquisition …". In the case of a subsidiary, this would imply the date of acquisition of the subsidiary.

However, sometimes the transferred assets or liabilities remain within the combined entity after the business combination (e.g. because the assets and liabilities were transferred to the acquiree rather than to its former owners), and the acquirer therefore retains control of them. In that situation, the acquirer should measure those assets and liabilities at their carrying amount immediately before the acquisition date. No gain or loss should be recognised in profit or loss in respect of assets or liabilities controlled by the acquirer both before and after the business combination. [IFRS 3:38]

8.2 Contingent consideration

8.2.1 Recognition of contingent consideration at acquisition date

The consideration the acquirer transfers in exchange for the acquiree includes any asset or liability resulting from a contingent consideration agreement. [IFRS 3:39] Contingent consideration is "[u]sually, an obligation of the acquirer to transfer additional assets or equity interests to the former owners of an acquiree as part of the exchange for control of the acquiree if specified future events occur or conditions are met. However, contingent consideration also may give the acquirer the right to the return of previously transferred consideration if specified conditions are met". [IFRS 3:Appendix A]

Contingent consideration is recognised as part of the consideration transferred in exchange for the acquiree, measured at its acquisition-date fair value. [IFRS 3:39]

When the purchase agreement includes a right to the return of previously-transferred consideration if specified conditions for a repayment are met, that right to return is classified as an asset by the acquirer. [IFRS 3:40]

Example 8.2.1

Contingent consideration

Company A acquires Company B. The consideration is payable in three tranches:

- an immediate payment of CU1 million;
- a further payment of CU0.5 million after one year if profit before interest and tax for the first year following acquisition exceeds CU200,000; and
- a further payment of CU0.5 million after two years if profit before interest and tax for the second year following acquisition exceeds CU220,000.

The two payments that are conditional upon reaching earnings targets are contingent consideration. At the date of acquisition, the fair value of these two payments is assessed as CU250,000.

Consequently, on the date of acquisition, consideration of CU1,250,000 is recognised.

8.2.2   *Outstanding contingent consideration of the acquiree*

Example 8.2.2

Outstanding contingent consideration of the acquiree

Entity A acquires Entity B on 31 December 20X5.

On 31 December 20X3, Entity B had acquired Entity C. The terms of the acquisition of Entity C required Entity B to pay an additional amount of consideration in cash if specified earnings targets were met by 31 December 20X8.

How should Entity B's obligation for the contingent consideration related to the earlier acquisition of Entity C be accounted for by Entity A at the date of acquisition of Entity B?

Contingent consideration is defined in IFRS 3:Appendix A as "an obligation of the acquirer to transfer additional assets or equity interests to the former owners of an acquiree as part of the exchange for control of the acquiree if specified future events occur or conditions are met". Therefore, contingent consideration relates directly to the acquisition of control in the business combination.

In the context of Entity A's acquisition of Entity B, the only items that would be accounted for as contingent consideration are obligations as described due from Entity A to the former owners of Entity B that arise as part of the exchange of control of Entity B. From Entity A's perspective, any payments due by Entity B to the former owners of Entity C in respect of past acquisitions do not meet the definition of contingent consideration.

Entity B's obligation is a contractual obligation to deliver cash to the former owners of Entity C, which qualifies as a financial liability under IFRS 9 (or, for entities that have not yet adopted IFRS 9, IAS 39) and should be accounted for as such by Entity A in accounting for the acquisition of Entity B. The fact that the obligation is contingent upon the occurrence or non-occurrence of uncertain future events beyond the control of both Entity B and Entity C does not prevent it from being recognised as a financial liability.

If there were no contractual obligation to deliver cash (or another financial asset or equity), the arrangement would not meet the definition of a financial liability in paragraph 11 of IAS 32 *Financial Instruments: Presentation* and, accordingly, Entity B's obligation would fall within the scope of IAS 37 *Provisions, Contingent Liabilities and Contingent Assets*.

8.2.3   *Presentation of contingent consideration as a liability or as equity*

An obligation to pay contingent consideration which meets the definition of a financial instrument is classified as a financial liability or as equity on the basis of the definitions of an equity instrument and a financial liability in paragraph 11 of IAS 32 *Financial Instruments: Presentation* (see **section 2** of **chapter B3** (for entities applying IFRS 9) and **section 2** of **chapter C3** (for entities applying IAS 39)). [IFRS 3:40]

In many cases, contingent consideration arising in a business combination will be payable at a fixed date in the future. In these circumstances, the contingent consideration meets the definition of equity in IAS 32 if it results in the issue of a fixed number of equity instruments of the acquirer. This will be the case if the only possible outcomes are the delivery of a fixed number of shares (if the contingency is met) or no shares are delivered (if the contingency is not met). This is illustrated in **example 8.2.3A**.

However, if the number of shares varies (e.g. the number of shares varies depending on the level of profits over a specified period), the possible number of shares to be issued is not limited to nil or a fixed number. In those circumstances, the contingent consideration does not meet the definition of equity and it should be classified as a financial liability. This is illustrated in **example 8.2.3B**.

In more unusual cases, the date at which the contingent consideration arising in a business combination may be payable is not a fixed date in the future. In these circumstances, in addition to the considerations outlined above, the entity will need to consider whether any variation in the number of shares to be issued arises solely due to the passage of time, because such variability does not conflict with a 'fixed-for-fixed' assertion. (See **6.1.2** in **chapter B3** or, for entities that have not yet adopted IFRS 9, **6.1.2** in **chapter C3**, for further guidance on when an instrument may be classified as an equity instrument if the number of shares to be issued varies with the passage of time.)

Contingent consideration classified as equity meets the definition of contingently issuable shares under paragraph 5 of IAS 33 *Earnings per Share*. As such, the contingent consideration may need to be included in the computation of basic and diluted earnings per share (see **chapter A31** for further guidance on this topic).

Example 8.2.3A

Share-settled contingent consideration – presentation as equity

Company A acquires 100 per cent of Company B from Company Z. In addition to up-front cash consideration, Company A agrees to pay consideration by issuing its own shares (which are classified as equity instruments) to Company Z after three years if Company B meets specified profit targets over the following three years. If profit is CU100,000 or more in each of the three years, 10,000 shares will be issued at the end of the three years. If profit is less than CU100,000 in any of the three years no shares will be issued.

How should Company A classify the contingent consideration in its financial statements in accordance with IAS 32?

The contingency (i.e. the profit target being met or not met) is a discrete event that occurs each year and the number of shares to be issued is fixed if the profit target is met. There is no variability in the number of shares to be issued if the contingency is met (i.e. the number of shares issued if the contingency is met is always 10,000). Because the number of shares that will ultimately be delivered by Company A does not vary (i.e. the only outcomes are nil or 10,000 shares to be issued), the contingent consideration meets the 'fixed-for-fixed' requirement in IAS 32:11 and is classified as equity by Company A.

Note that in a scenario in which the ultimate number of shares to be delivered at the end of three years varies dependent on the cumulative profit for the three years, such that there is more than one possible outcome for the number of shares to be issued, this would not meet the 'fixed-for-fixed' requirement and would be classified as a financial liability.

Example 8.2.3B

Share-settled contingent consideration – presentation as a financial liability

Company A acquires 100 per cent of Company B from Company Z. In addition to up-front cash consideration, Company A agrees to pay consideration by issuing its own shares (which are classified as equity instruments) to Company Z after three years if Company B meets specified profit targets over the following three years, as follows.

Profit target (average over three year period)	Additional consideration
CU100,000 but less than CU150,000	10,000 shares
CU150,000 but less than CU200,000	Sliding scale between 10,000 and 20,000 shares
More than CU200,000	20,000 shares

How should Company A classify the contingent consideration in its financial statements in accordance with IAS 32?

The number of shares that will ultimately be delivered by Company A after 3 years will vary depending on the profitability of Company B. Therefore, the contingent consideration fails the 'fixed-for-fixed' requirement in IAS 32:11 and is classified as a financial liability by Company A. The contingent consideration should be accounted for under IFRS 9 (or, for entities that have not yet adopted IFRS 9, IAS 39).

It is not appropriate to view the contingent consideration as three separate contingent consideration contracts because the three outcomes are mutually exclusive.

8.2.4 Subsequent accounting for contingent consideration

8.2.4.1 Changes in the fair value of contingent consideration based on additional information about facts and circumstances at the acquisition date

Changes that are the result of the acquirer obtaining additional information about facts and circumstances that existed at the acquisition date, and that occur within the measurement period (which may be a maximum of one year from the acquisition date), are recognised as adjustments against the original accounting for the acquisition (and so may affect goodwill) – see **10.1**. [IFRS 3:58]

8.2.4.2 Changes in the fair value of contingent consideration resulting from events after the acquisition date

Changes resulting from events after the acquisition date (e.g. meeting an earnings target, reaching a specified share price or reaching a milestone on a research and development project) are not measurement period adjustments. Such changes are therefore accounted for separately from the business combination. The acquirer accounts for changes in the fair value of contingent consideration that are not measurement period adjustments as follows:

[IFRS 3:58]

(a) contingent consideration classified as equity is not remeasured and its subsequent settlement is accounted for within equity; and

(b) other contingent consideration that:

(i)   is within the scope of IFRS 9 (or, for entities that have not yet adopted IFRS 9, IAS 39) is measured at fair value at each reporting date and changes in fair value are recognised in profit or loss in accordance with IFRS 9 (or IAS 39 as applicable); and

(ii) is not within the scope of IFRS 9 (or, for entities that have not yet adopted IFRS 9, IAS 39) is measured at fair value at each reporting date and changes in fair value are recognised in profit or loss.

In practice, most changes in contingent consideration are recognised in profit or loss. However, the above requirements mean that shares, some options and other equity instruments issued by the acquirer are not remeasured after initially being recognised when accounting for the business combination.

8.2.4.3 Outstanding contingent consideration upon adoption of IFRS 3 (as revised in 2008)

Contingent consideration balances arising from business combinations whose acquisition dates preceded the date when an entity first applied

IFRS 3 (as revised in 2008) are not restated when the Standard is first adopted and are subsequently accounted for as follows.

[IFRS 3:65A]

- If a business combination agreement provides for an adjustment to the cost of the combination contingent on future events, the acquirer should include the amount of that adjustment in the cost of the combination at the acquisition date if the adjustment is probable and can be measured reliably. [IFRS 3:65B]

- If a business combination agreement allows for adjustments to the cost of the combination that are contingent on one or more future events (e.g. contingent on a specified level of profit being maintained or achieved in future periods, or on the market price of the instruments issued being maintained), it is usually possible to estimate the amount of any such adjustment at the time of initially accounting for the combination. If the future events do not occur or the estimate needs to be revised, the cost of the business combination is adjusted accordingly. [IFRS 3:65C]

- However, an adjustment contingent on future events is not included in the cost of the combination at the time of initially accounting for the combination if it either is not probable or cannot be measured reliably. If that adjustment subsequently becomes probable and can be measured reliably, the additional consideration is treated as an adjustment to the cost of the combination. [IFRS 3:65D]

- In some circumstances, the acquirer may be required to make a subsequent payment to the seller as compensation for a reduction in the value of the assets given, equity instruments issued or liabilities incurred or assumed by the acquirer in exchange for control of the acquiree (e.g. when the acquirer guarantees the market price of equity or debt instruments issued as part of the cost of the business combination and is required to issue additional equity or debt instruments to restore the originally determined cost). In such cases, no increase in the cost of the business combination is recognised.

  Rather:

  [IFRS 3:65E]

  - in the case of equity instruments, the fair value of the additional payment is offset by an equal reduction in the value attributed to the instruments initially issued; and

  - in the case of debt instruments, the additional payment is regarded as a reduction in the premium or an increase in the discount on the initial issue.

Consequently, contingent consideration arising in relation to business combinations that occurred prior to the initial application of IFRS 3 (as revised in 2008) continues to be accounted for in the same way as under the previous version of IFRS 3, meaning that retrospective adjustments to the initial accounting for these business combinations continue to be possible.

Example 8.2.4.3

Outstanding contingent consideration upon adoption of IFRS 3 (as revised in 2008)

In April 2008, Entity A, which has a 31 December year end, completed a business combination which was accounted for under the previous version of IFRS 3. Under the acquisition agreement, Entity A may be required to pay additional consideration in 2018 depending on the outcome of a future event. At the time of the business combination, Entity A was unable to assess whether the adjustment to the purchase price was probable, nor could it measure reliably the amount that might have to be paid. Accordingly, no amount was recognised for the potential payment of the contingent consideration as part of the purchase price allocation.

On 1 January 2010, when it first adopted IFRS 3 (as revised in 2008), Entity A continued to believe that it was not probable that the contingent consideration would be payable and, accordingly, the potential payment remained unrecognised.

IFRS 3:65A confirms that contingent consideration balances arising from business combinations whose acquisition dates preceded the adoption of IFRS 3 (as revised in 2008) should not be restated when the revised version of the Standard is first adopted. On adoption of IFRS 3 (as revised in 2008), the requirements of IFRS 3:65D (see above) should be applied. Therefore, in the circumstances under consideration, the potential payment should not be recognised when IFRS 3 (as revised in 2008) is first adopted but should be recognised when it becomes probable and can be measured reliably. When the potential payment is recognised, it should be treated as an adjustment to the cost of the combination.

8.3 Determining what is part of the business combination transaction

8.3.1 *Principles used to determine what is part of the business combination*

The acquirer and the acquiree may have a pre-existing relationship or other arrangement before negotiations for the business combination begin, or they may enter into an arrangement during the negotiations that is separate from the business combination. [IFRS 3:51]

In either situation, the acquirer is required to identify any amounts that are not part of what the acquirer and the acquiree (or its former owners) exchanged in the business combination, i.e. amounts that are not part of the exchange for the acquiree. [IFRS 3:51]

The acquirer is required to recognise as part of applying the acquisition method only the consideration transferred for the acquiree, and the assets acquired and liabilities assumed in exchange for the acquiree. Separate transactions are accounted for in accordance with the relevant Standards. [IFRS 3:51]

A transaction entered into by or on behalf of the acquirer or primarily for the benefit of the acquirer or the combined entity, rather than primarily for the benefit of the acquiree (or its former owners) before the combination, is likely to be a separate transaction. [IFRS 3:52]

An acquirer should consider the following factors, which are neither mutually exclusive nor individually conclusive, to determine whether a transaction is part of the exchange for the acquiree or whether the transaction is separate from the business combination.

[IFRS 3:B50]

(a) **The reasons for the transaction** Understanding the reasons why the parties to a combination entered into a particular transaction or arrangement may provide insight into whether it is part of the consideration transferred and the assets acquired or liabilities assumed. For example, if a transaction is arranged primarily for the benefit of the acquirer or the combined entity rather than primarily for the benefit of the acquiree or its former owners before the combination, that portion of the transaction price paid (and any related assets or liabilities) is less likely to be part of the exchange for the acquiree. Accordingly, the acquirer would account for that portion separately from the business combination.

Example 8.3.1A

Acquirer pays vendor's costs

Company K acquires a business from Company L. Company K agrees to pay the expenses incurred by Company L in the sale and purchase transaction.

The costs paid by Company K on behalf of Company L form part of the consideration transferred for the purposes of accounting for the business combination. Although these amounts are not paid directly to Company L, they will still form part of the purchase consideration for the business combination because Company K is acting on behalf of Company L in making the payments, which are primarily for the benefit of Company L (the former owner).

However, this principle would not apply to any costs incurred by Company K on its own behalf in making the acquisition; such costs are required to be accounted for outside the business combination (see **8.4.1**).

(b) **Who initiated the transaction** Understanding who initiated the transaction may also provide insight into whether it is part of the exchange for the acquiree. For example, a transaction or other event that is initiated by the acquirer may be entered into for the purpose of providing future economic benefits to the acquirer or combined entity with little or no benefit received by the acquiree or its former owners before the combination. On the other hand, a transaction or arrangement initiated by the acquiree or its former owners is less likely to be for the benefit of the acquirer or the combined entity and more likely to be part of the business combination transaction.

Example 8.3.1B

Acquisition from government with continuing commitments

Company X acquires a business from government in a privatisation transaction. As part of the arrangements, Company X is required to retain a specified number of employees. Because of this commitment, Company X reduces the consideration it is willing to pay for the business; it pays CU3 million to acquire the business whereas, without the commitment to retain the specified number of employees, it would have been willing to pay CU3.5 million.

Should Company X adjust the consideration transferred for the purposes of accounting for the business combination to reflect the effect of the commitment to retain the employees?

It depends. IFRS 3:B50 suggests that understanding who initiated a transaction may provide insight into whether it is part of the exchange for the acquiree. A transaction or arrangement initiated by the acquiree or its former owners is less likely to be for the benefit of the acquirer or the combined entity and more likely to be part of the business combination transaction.

Arrangements such as those described above (requirements to retain a specified number of employees, to maintain a presence in a certain geographical location, or to meet other government policy objectives) are generally initiated by the relevant government as the vendor for its own benefit (i.e. meeting the policy objectives). Therefore, they are more likely to be part of the business combination and no adjustment should be made to the purchase consideration as a result of the commitments.

In some circumstances, however, the substance of the arrangement might include receipt of a grant from the government. This would result in the recognition of deferred income in respect of the government grant (when the relevant criteria in IAS 20 *Accounting for Government Grants and Disclosure of Government Assistance* are met), and a corresponding increase in goodwill.

(c) **The timing of the transaction** The timing of the transaction may also provide insight into whether it is part of the exchange for the acquiree. For example, a transaction between the acquirer and the acquiree that takes place during the negotiations of the terms of a business combination may have been entered into in contemplation of the business combination to provide future economic benefit to the acquirer or the combined entity. If so, the acquiree or its former owners are likely to receive little or no benefit from the transaction except for the benefits they receive as part of the combined entity.

Example 8.3.1C

Cash settlement of share-based payment awards by the acquiree

Immediately prior to its acquisition by Company A, Company B cash settles the outstanding unvested share-based payments awards held by its employees. The terms of these awards did not provide for any automatic vesting or expiry in the event of a change in control. The amount of cash paid by Company B is equal to the current fair value of the awards.

Care should be taken to determine whether the cash settlement was arranged primarily for the economic benefit of Company A or the combined entity rather than for the benefit of Company B or its former owners. Even though the form of the transaction may indicate that this is a pre-combination transaction of Company B, it may be determined that, in substance, Company A has reimbursed Company B for the cash settlement.

Company A should consider the factors set out in IFRS 3:B50 (see above) to determine whether a portion of the consideration transferred for Company B is attributable to the settlement of the awards held by Company B's employees.

If a portion of the consideration is attributable to the settlement of the awards, Company A should apply the guidance in IFRS 3:B56 to B62 (see **8.3.4**) to determine the amount considered to have been paid to the employees of Company B in consideration for pre-combination and post-combination services. The amount attributable to the post-combination service does not form part of the consideration for the business combination but is recognised as remuneration cost in the post-combination financial statements.

The following are examples of separate transactions that are not to be included in applying the acquisition method:

[IFRS 3:52]

(a) a transaction that settles pre-existing relationships between the acquirer and the acquiree (see **7.5.3**);

(b) a transaction that remunerates employees or former owners of the acquiree for future services (see **8.3.3** for contingent payments to employees or selling shareholders, and **8.3.4** for share-based payment awards); and

(c) a transaction that reimburses the acquiree or its former owners for paying the acquirer's acquisition-related costs (see **8.3.5**).

8.3.2   Settlement of a pre-existing relationship between the acquirer and acquiree in a business combination

This is discussed at **7.5.3**, which deals with both reacquired rights and the wider issue of pre-existing relationships.

8.3.3 Arrangements for contingent payments to employees or selling shareholders

8.3.3.1 Arrangement for contingent payments to employees or selling shareholders – general

The acquirer or vendor may make payments to the employees of the acquiree (who may or may not also be selling shareholders), which are contingent on a post-acquisition event such as a period of continuing service as an employee. In such cases, it is necessary to determine what element of the payment qualifies as consideration, and what element is for post-acquisition services. IFRS 3 provides guidance as to how to make the allocation.

As discussed at **8.3.1**, understanding the reasons why the acquisition agreement includes contingent payments, who initiated the arrangement, and when the parties entered into the arrangement may be helpful in assessing the nature of the arrangement. [IFRS 3:B54]

The acquirer should consider the following indicators to determine whether an arrangement for payments to employees or selling shareholders is part of the exchange for the acquiree or a separate transaction.

[IFRS 3:B55]

(a) **Continuing employment** A contingent consideration arrangement in which the payments are automatically forfeited if employment terminates is remuneration for post-combination services. Arrangements in which the contingent payments are not affected by employment termination may indicate that the contingent payments are additional consideration rather than remuneration.

(b) **Duration of continuing employment** If the period of required employment coincides with or is longer than the contingent payment period, that fact may indicate that the contingent payments are, in substance, remuneration.

(c) **Level of remuneration** Situations in which employee remuneration other than the contingent payments is at a reasonable level in comparison with that of other key employees in the combined entity may indicate that the contingent payments are additional consideration rather than remuneration.

(d) **Incremental payments to employees** If selling shareholders who do not become employees receive lower contingent payments on a per-share basis than the selling shareholders who become employees of the combined entity, that fact may indicate that the incremental amount of contingent payments to the selling shareholders who become employees is remuneration.

(e) **Number of shares owned** The relative number of shares owned by the selling shareholders who remain as key employees may be an indicator of the substance of the contingent consideration arrangement. If the selling shareholders who owned substantially all of the shares in the acquiree continue as key employees, that fact may indicate that the arrangement is, in substance, a profit-sharing arrangement intended to provide remuneration for post-combination services. If selling shareholders who continue as key employees owned only a small number of shares of the acquiree and all selling shareholders receive the same amount of contingent consideration on a per-share basis, that fact may indicate that the contingent payments are additional consideration.

(f) **Linkage to the valuation** If the initial consideration transferred at the acquisition date is based on the low end of a range established in the valuation of the acquiree and the contingent formula relates to that valuation approach, that fact may suggest that the contingent payments are additional consideration. Alternatively, if the contingent payment formula is consistent with prior profit-sharing arrangements, that fact may suggest that the substance of the arrangement is to provide remuneration.

(g) **Formula for determining consideration** The formula used to determine the contingent payment may be helpful in assessing the substance of the arrangement. For example, if a contingent payment is determined on the basis of a multiple of earnings (i.e. more than one year's earnings), that might suggest that the obligation is contingent consideration in the business combination and that the formula is intended to establish or verify the fair value of the acquiree. In contrast, a contingent payment that is a specified percentage of earnings (i.e. a proportion of one year's earnings) might suggest that the obligation to employees is a profit-sharing arrangement to remunerate employees for services rendered.

(h) **Other agreements and issues** The terms of other arrangements with selling shareholders (such as agreements not to compete, executory contracts, consulting contracts and property lease agreements) may indicate that contingent payments are attributable to something other than consideration for the acquiree. For example, in connection with the acquisition, the acquirer might enter into a property lease arrangement with a significant selling shareholder. If the lease payments specified in the lease contract are significantly below market, some or all of the contingent payments to the lessor (the selling shareholder) might be, in substance, payments for the use of the leased property that the acquirer should recognise separately in its post-combination financial statements. In contrast, if the lease contract specifies lease payments that are consistent with market terms for the leased property, the arrangement for contingent payments to the selling shareholder may be contingent consideration in the business combination.

8.3.3.2   *Contingent payments to employees who are not shareholders –*
         examples

Example 8.3.3.2A

Contingent payments to employees recognised as a liability

[IFRS 3:IE58 - IE60]

TC appointed a candidate as its new CEO under a ten-year contract. The contract required TC to pay the candidate CU5 million if TC is acquired before the contract expires. AC acquires TC eight years later. The CEO was still employed at the acquisition date and will receive the additional payment under the existing contract.

In this example, TC entered into the employment agreement before the negotiations of the combination began, and the purpose of the agreement was to obtain the services of the CEO. Thus, there is no evidence that the agreement was arranged primarily to provide benefits to AC or the combined entity. Therefore, the liability to pay CU5 million is included in the application of the acquisition method.

In other circumstances, TC might enter into a similar agreement with CEO at the suggestion of AC during the negotiations for the business combination. If so, the primary purpose of the agreement might be to provide severance pay to CEO, and the agreement may primarily benefit AC or the combined entity rather than TC or its former owners. In that situation, AC accounts for the liability to pay CEO in its post-combination financial statements separately from application of the acquisition method.

Example 8.3.3.2B

Contingent payments to employees recognised as post-acquisition remuneration

Entity B negotiates to acquire Entity A. At Entity B's suggestion, Entity A enters into a contract with its CEO (who is not a shareholder) which requires Entity A to pay the CEO CU5 million if Entity A is acquired before the contract expires. The payment is contingent on the CEO remaining in employment for three years following a successful acquisition.

Should Entity A's liability to pay the CEO CU5 million be included in the application of the acquisition method?

No. The primary purpose of the agreement appears to be to retain the services of the CEO. Because the CEO is not a shareholder, and the payment is contingent on continuing employment, the payment is accounted for as post-acquisition remuneration separately from the application of the acquisition method.

8.3.3.3   Contingent payments to selling shareholders who are employees

When the selling shareholders in a business combination continue to work within the business and some or all of the consideration transferred is dependent on continuing employment, that consideration should be treated as post-combination remuneration expense unless the requirement to remain in employment is not substantive.

As outlined at **8.3.3.1**, the relevant requirements of IFRS 3 are as follows.

- IFRS 3:52 requires that separate transactions, such as a transaction that remunerates employees or former owners of the acquiree for future services, should not be included in applying the acquisition method to the business combination.

- IFRS 3:B55(a) states that a contingent consideration arrangement in which the payments are automatically forfeited if employment terminates is remuneration for post-combination services.

This issue has been considered by the IFRS Interpretations Committee, and the following is an extract from the January 2013 *IFRIC Update*.

> "The Interpretations Committee observed that an arrangement in which contingent payments are automatically forfeited if employment terminates would lead to a conclusion that the arrangement is compensation for post-combination services rather than additional consideration for an acquisition, unless the service condition is not substantive. The Interpretations Committee reached this conclusion on the basis of the conclusive language used in paragraph B55(a) of IFRS 3."

These words clearly articulate the Interpretations Committee's conclusion that IFRS 3:B55(a) requires that all such arrangements be treated as compensation for post-combination services, notwithstanding that the introduction to IFRS 3:B55 (see **8.3.3.1**) suggests that it is one of a series of indicators.

A service condition may be considered to be non-substantive if:

- it requires the selling shareholder to remain in service for only a very short period (maybe as little as a day) for tax or administrative reasons; or

- it includes a 'good leaver' clause that effectively permits the selling shareholder to choose to leave service (albeit possibly with a restriction on, for example, working for a competitor or disclosing proprietary information) without forfeiting the right to receive payments.

A service condition that includes a good leaver clause enabling the selling shareholder to retain the right to receive payments only if he or she leaves service for reasons outside his or her control (e.g. death or unfair dismissal) would be considered substantive.

The following are examples of scenarios in which the requirement to treat all contingent payments subject to a substantive service condition as post-acquisition remuneration has a significant effect on the accounting for an acquisition.

Scenario 1 – payments at the acquisition date to shareholders remaining in employment are less than payments to exiting shareholders

100 per cent of the shares of a business are acquired under the following terms:

- exiting shareholders are paid CU10 per share at the acquisition date and have no further interest in the business; and

- one shareholder who is to remain in employment receives CU2 per share at the acquisition date and up to a further CU18 per share over the following three years subject to remaining in employment and the acquired business reaching specified profit targets.

In these circumstances, all of the contingent payments to the shareholder remaining in employment (i.e. up to CU18 per share) would be treated as remuneration, so that the total purchase consideration recognised would be CU10 for each share purchased from the exiting shareholders and CU2 for each share purchased from the shareholder who is to remain in employment.

Scenario 2 – service condition applies to contingent consideration for some, but not all, shareholders

100 per cent of the shares of a business are acquired from two shareholders (A and B), each of whom owns 50 per cent of the shares, under the following terms:

- both A and B receive the same payment at the acquisition date and both are eligible for further payments that will vary based on the post-acquisition profits of the acquired business; but

- only A remains in employment following the transaction and he will forfeit any outstanding contingent consideration if he leaves employment within three years.

In these circumstances, the contingent element of the consideration payable to A would be treated as remuneration for post-acquisition services while the amount payable to B would be accounted for as purchase consideration.

Scenario 3 – non-contingent consideration is below the fair value of identifiable net assets

100 per cent of the shares of a business that has identifiable net assets of CU750 are acquired from its sole shareholder. At the acquisition date,

a payment of CU250 is made, with further payments of up to CU1,000 (based on a multiple of profits) to be made over the next three years contingent upon the selling shareholder remaining in employment.

In these circumstances, the consideration transferred for the business combination is limited to CU250. Following a reassessment of the identification and measurement of the assets and liabilities assumed, as required by IFRS 3:36, this results in recognition of a bargain purchase gain of CU500 (fair value of the identifiable net assets of CU750 less consideration transferred of CU250) at the acquisition date.

8.3.4   Share-based payment awards held by employees of the acquiree

8.3.4.1   Overview

An acquirer may exchange its share-based payment awards (replacement awards) for awards held by employees of the acquiree. IFRS 3 includes a number of guidelines and examples for when to treat particular replacement share-based payment awards as part of the cost of the combination and when to treat the amounts as employee compensation. IFRS 3 also sets out requirements on the appropriate accounting when share-based payment awards held by employees of the acquiree are not replaced (i.e. the original awards are allowed to continue without modification).

Exchanges of share options or other share-based payment awards in conjunction with a business combination are accounted for as modifications of share-based payment awards in accordance with IFRS 2 *Share-based Payment* (see **chapter A16**). [IFRS 3:B56] IFRS 3 uses the term 'market-based measure' to describe the basis of measurement in IFRS 2.

8.3.4.2   Acquirer replaces awards of the acquiree

When the acquirer replaces the awards of the acquiree, either all or a portion of the market-based measure of the acquirer's replacement awards is included in measuring the consideration transferred in the business combination. [IFRS 3:B56] (The only exception is when the acquirer voluntarily replaces acquiree awards that would otherwise have expired as a consequence of the business combination – see **8.3.4.3**.) The basis of allocating awards between consideration and post-combination service is described in **8.3.4.4**.

8.3.4.3   Acquirer voluntarily replaces awards of the acquiree that would otherwise have expired

When the acquiree's awards would expire as a consequence of a business combination and the acquirer replaces those awards even though it is not obliged to do so, all of the market-based measure of the replacement awards is recognised as remuneration cost in the post-combination financial statements in accordance with IFRS 2. This means that none of the market-based measure of those awards is included in measuring the consideration transferred in the business combination. [IFRS 3:B56]

The acquirer is considered to be obliged to replace the acquiree awards if the acquiree or its employees have the ability to enforce replacement. For example, for the purposes of applying this requirement, the acquirer is considered to be obliged to replace the acquiree's awards if the replacement is required by:

[IFRS 3:B56]

- the terms of the acquisition agreement;

- the terms of the acquiree awards; or

- applicable laws and regulations.

8.3.4.4   *Allocating awards to consideration and post-combination service*

The appropriate allocation of the market-based measure of non-voluntary replacement awards between consideration and post-combination service may be calculated by following the steps below.

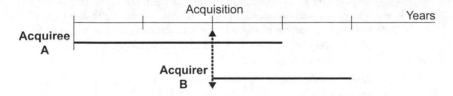

Step 1   To determine the portion of a replacement award that is part of the consideration transferred for the acquiree and the portion that is remuneration for post-combination service, the acquirer measures both the replacement awards granted by the acquirer and the acquiree awards as of the acquisition date in accordance with IFRS 2. [IFRS 3:B57]

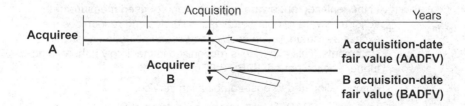

   Step 1: B measures the fair value of both A's original share options and the replacement share options at the acquisition date in accordance with IFRS 2.

Step 2   Identify three periods of time:

   • the vesting period completed at the date of acquisition;

• the total vesting period; and

• the original vesting period.

The vesting period is the period during which all the specified vesting conditions are to be satisfied (see the discussion of IFRS 2 in **chapter A16** for more detailed definitions).

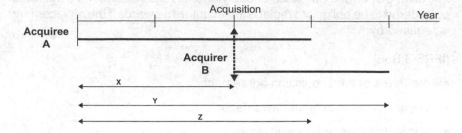

Step 2: B identifies the vesting period completed (X), the total vesting period (Y), and the original vesting period (Z).

Step 3   The portion of the replacement award attributable to pre-combination service (which is the portion that is accounted for as part of the consideration in the business combination) is the 'market-based measure' of the acquiree award multiplied by the ratio of the portion of the vesting period completed to the greater of the total vesting period or the original vesting period of the acquiree award. [IFRS 3:B58]

Amount allocated to consideration is:

$$\text{AADFV} \times \frac{X}{\text{Higher of Y and Z}}$$

Step 4   The amount attributable to post-combination service, and so recognised as remuneration cost in the post-combination financial statements, is determined as the difference between the market-based measure of the acquirer's replacement award and the amount allocated to purchase consideration in Step 3. Therefore, the acquirer attributes any excess of the market-based measure of the replacement award over the market-based measure of the acquiree award to post-combination service and recognises that excess as remuneration cost in the post-combination financial statements. This expense is recognised immediately if there is no further service period. [IFRS 3:B59]

Amount allocated to post-combination service:

BADFV less amount calculated at Step 3

Further requirements:

• the amount allocated to consideration at Step 3 is added to the purchase consideration;

• the amount allocated to post-combination service at Step 4 is recognised as a post-combination expense in accordance with IFRS 2;

- the acquirer attributes a portion of a replacement award to post-combination service if it requires post-combination service, regardless of whether employees had rendered all of the service required for their acquiree awards to vest before the acquisition date; [IFRS 3:B59]

- the allocation between purchase consideration and post-combination service should reflect the best estimate of the number of replacement awards that are expected to vest. For example, if the market-based measure of the portion of a replacement award attributed to pre-combination service is CU100 and the acquirer expects that only 95 per cent of the award will vest, the amount included in consideration transferred in the business combination is CU95; [IFRS 3:B60]

- subsequent changes in the estimated number of replacement awards expected to vest are reflected in remuneration cost for the period in which the changes or forfeitures occur and are not adjusted against the initial accounting for the acquisition; [IFRS 3:B60]

- the effects of other events, such as modifications or the ultimate outcome of awards with performance conditions, that occur after the acquisition date are accounted for in accordance with IFRS 2 in determining remuneration cost for the period in which an event occurs (see **chapter A16**); [IFRS 3:B60]

- the same requirements for determining the portions of a replacement award attributable to pre- and post-combination service apply regardless of whether a replacement award is classified as a liability or as an equity instrument in accordance with IFRS 2. All changes in the market-based measure of awards classified as liabilities after the acquisition date and the related income tax effects are recognised in the acquirer's post-combination financial statements in the period(s) in which the changes occur; [IFRS 3:B61] and

- the income tax effects of replacement awards of share-based payments are recognised in accordance with the requirements of IAS 12 *Income Taxes* (see **chapter A13**). [IFRS 3:B62]

The following examples (which assume that all awards are classified as equity) illustrate replacement awards that the acquirer (AC) was obliged to issue in the following circumstances.

[IFRS 3:IE61]

		Acquiree awards Has the vesting period been completed before the business combination?	
		Completed	Not completed
Replacement awards	Not required	**Example 8.3.4.4A**	**Example 8.3.4.4D**
Are employees required to provide additional service after the acquisition date?	Required	**Example 8.3.4.4B**	**Example 8.3.4.4C**

Example 8.3.4.4A

Vesting period completed, no additional services required

[IFRS 3:IE62 - IE64]

| Acquiree awards | Vesting period **completed** before the business combination |
| Replacement awards | Additional employee services **are not** required after the acquisition date |

AC issues replacement awards of CU110 (market-based measure) at the acquisition date for TC awards of CU100 (market-based measure) at the acquisition date. No post-combination services are required for the replacement awards and TC's employees had rendered all of the required service for the acquiree awards as of the acquisition date.

The amount attributable to pre-combination service is the market-based measure of TC's awards (CU100) at the acquisition date; that amount is included in the consideration transferred in the business combination. The amount attributable to post-combination service is CU10, which is the difference between the total value of the replacement awards (CU110) and the portion attributable to pre-combination service (CU100). Because no post-combination service is required for the replacement awards, AC immediately recognises CU10 as remuneration cost in its post-combination financial statements.

Applying the steps outlined earlier:

Step 1   Acquiree acquisition-date fair value = CU100
Acquirer acquisition-date fair value = CU110

Step 2   Vesting period completed = (say) 3 years
Original vesting period = (say) 3 years
Total vesting period = (say) 3 years

Step 3   Amount allocated to consideration =

$$100 \times \frac{3}{\text{Higher of 3 and 3}} = 100$$

Step 4   Amount allocated to post-combination service = 110 − 100 = 10

Example 8.3.4.4B

Vesting period completed, but additional services required

[IFRS 3:IE65 - IE67]

Acquiree awards	Vesting period **completed** before the business combination
Replacement awards	Additional employee services **are** required after the acquisition date

AC exchanges replacement awards that require one year of post-combination service for share-based payment awards of TC, for which employees had completed the vesting period before the business combination. The market-based measure of both awards is CU100 at the acquisition date. When originally granted, TC's awards had a vesting period of four years. As of the acquisition date, the TC employees holding unexercised awards had rendered a total of seven years of service since the grant date.

Even though TC employees had already rendered all of the service, AC attributes a portion of the replacement award to post-combination remuneration cost in accordance with IFRS 3:B59, because the replacement awards require one year of post-combination service. The total vesting period is five years-the vesting period for the original acquiree award completed before the acquisition date (four years) plus the vesting period for the replacement award (one year).

The portion attributable to pre-combination services equals the market-based measure of the acquiree award (CU100) multiplied by the ratio of the pre-combination vesting period (four years) to the total vesting period (five years). Thus, CU80 (CU100 × 4/5 years) is attributed to the pre-combination vesting period and therefore included in the consideration transferred in the business combination. The remaining CU20 is attributed to the post-combination vesting period and is therefore recognised as remuneration cost in AC's post-combination financial statements in accordance with IFRS 2.

Applying the steps outlined earlier:

Step 1   Acquiree acquisition-date fair value = CU100

Acquirer acquisition-date fair value = CU100

Step 2   Vesting period completed = 4 years

Original vesting period = 4 years

Total vesting period = 5 years

Step 3   Amount allocated to consideration =

$$100 \times \frac{4}{\text{Higher of 4 and 5}} = 80$$

Step 4   Amount allocated to post-combination service = 100 − 80 = 20

Example 8.3.4.4C

Vesting period not completed, additional services required

[IFRS 3:IE68 - IE69]

Acquiree awards	Vesting period **not completed** before the business combination
Replacement awards	Additional employee services **are** required after the acquisition date

AC exchanges replacement awards that require one year of post-combination service for share-based payment awards of TC, for which employees had not yet rendered all of the service as of the acquisition date. The market-based measure of both awards is CU100 at the acquisition date. When originally granted, the awards of TC had a vesting period of four years. As of the acquisition date, the TC employees had rendered two years' service, and they would have been required to render two additional years of service after the acquisition date for their awards to vest. Accordingly, only a portion of the TC awards is attributable to pre-combination service.

The replacement awards require only one year of post-combination service. Because employees have already rendered two years of service, the total vesting period is three years. The portion attributable to pre-combination services equals the market-based measure of the acquiree award (CU100) multiplied by the ratio of the pre-combination vesting period (two years) to the greater of the total vesting period (three years) or the original vesting period of TC's award (four years). Thus, CU50 (CU100 × 2/4 years) is attributable to pre-combination service and therefore included in the consideration transferred for the acquiree. The remaining CU50 is attributable to post-combination service and therefore recognised as remuneration cost in AC's post-combination financial statements.

Applying the steps outlined earlier:

Step 1   Acquiree acquisition-date fair value = CU100

Acquirer acquisition-date fair value = CU100

Step 2   Vesting period completed = 2 years

Original vesting period = 4 years

Total vesting period = 3 years

Step 3   Amount allocated to consideration =

$$100 \times \frac{2}{\text{Higher of 4 and 3}} = 50$$

Step 4   Amount allocated to post-combination service = 100 − 50 = 50

Example 8.3.4.4D

Vesting period not completed, but no additional services required

[IFRS 3:IE70 - IE71]

Acquiree awards	Vesting period **not completed** before the business combination
Replacement awards	Additional employee services **are not** required after the acquisition date

Assume the same facts as in [**example 8.3.4.4C**] above, except that AC exchanges replacement awards that require no post-combination service for share-based payment awards of TC for which employees had not yet rendered all of the service as of the acquisition date. The terms of the replaced TC awards did not eliminate any remaining vesting period upon a change in control. (If the TC awards had included a provision that eliminated any remaining vesting period upon a change in control, the guidance in [**example 8.3.4.4A**] would apply.) The market-based measure of both awards is CU100. Because employees have already rendered two years of service and the replacement awards do not require any post-combination service, the total vesting period is two years.

The portion of the market-based measure of the replacement awards attributable to pre-combination services equals the market-based measure of the acquiree award (CU100) multiplied by the ratio of the pre-combination vesting period (two years) to the greater of the total vesting period (two years) or the original vesting period of TC's award (four years). Thus, CU50 (CU100 × 2/4 years) is attributable to pre-combination service and therefore included in the consideration transferred for the acquiree. The remaining CU50 is attributable to post-combination service. Because no post-combination service is required to vest in the replacement award, AC recognises the entire CU50 immediately as remuneration cost in the post-combination financial statements.

Applying the steps outlined earlier:

Step 1   Acquiree acquisition-date fair value = CU100

Acquirer acquisition-date fair value = CU100

Step 2   Vesting period completed = 2 years

Original vesting period = 4 years

Total vesting period = 2 years

Step 3   Amount allocated to consideration =

$$100 \times \frac{2}{\text{Higher of 4 and 2}} = 50$$

Step 4   Amount allocated to post-combination service = 100 − 50 = 50

8.3.4.5   Subsequent accounting by acquiree

Example 8.3.4.5A

Subsequent accounting by acquiree (1)

Entity A awarded share options to its employees, which vest if employees remain in employment for a specified number of years. Before the awards vest, Entity A is acquired by Entity B. Entity B exchanges the share options for options over shares in Entity B. The terms of the share options did not require expiry as a result of the business combination.

As required by IFRS 3:B57, the fair values of the original acquiree share-based payment awards and the replacement awards granted by the acquirer as at the acquisition date are measured in accordance with IFRS 2.

IFRS 3 requires that, in Entity B's consolidated financial statements, the portion of the fair value of the replacement award at the acquisition date that is attributable to post-combination service should be recognised as compensation expense.

How should Entity A recognise the impact of the replacement of the awards by Entity B in its individual financial statements?

The requirements of IFRS 2 continue to apply in the individual financial statements of Entity A; the impact of the exchange should be recognised based on the principles applicable to replacements and modifications of equity awards in IFRS 2:27 and IFRS 2:B43 to B44 (see **chapter A16**).

Example 8.3.4.5B

Subsequent accounting by acquiree (2)

Entity A awarded share options to its employees, which vest if the employees remain in employment for four years. The fair value of the award at grant date is CU100.

After two years, Entity A is acquired by Entity B. Entity B exchanges the share options for options over shares in Entity B, which vest after two further years of employment (i.e. at the end of the original vesting period). The terms of the share options did not require expiry as a result of the business combination.

The fair values of the original acquiree awards and the replacement awards granted by the acquirer are measured at the acquisition date and are determined to be the same (i.e. CU400).

Because the replacement of the awards does not result in an overall increase in the total fair value of the share-based payment arrangement or a change in the vesting period, in its individual financial statements Entity A should continue to recognise the original grant-date fair value of the options as compensation expense. Therefore, after the combination, Entity A will recognise in its individual financial statements a compensation expense of CU25 (CU100 × 1/4) for these awards in each of the two subsequent years.

Example 8.3.4.5C

Subsequent accounting by acquiree (3)

Assume the same fact pattern as in **example 8.3.4.5B**, except that the replacement of the awards results in an increase in the total fair value of the share-based compensation arrangement, such that the fair values of Entity A's original award and the replacement awards granted by Entity B as of the acquisition date are determined to be CU400 and CU460, respectively.

In these circumstances, because the replacement of the awards results in an overall increase in the total fair value of the share-based payment arrangement, in its individual financial statements Entity A should recognise as compensation expense the total of the original grant-date fair value of the options and the incremental fair value resulting from the replacement. Therefore, after the combination, Entity A will recognise in its individual financial statements a compensation expense of CU55 for these awards in each of the two subsequent years (i.e. CU25 per year for the grant date fair value and CU30 (CU60/2 years)) for the incremental fair value.

8.3.4.6   Outstanding awards of the acquiree that are not replaced

The acquiree may have outstanding share-based payment transactions that the acquirer does not exchange for its share-based payment transactions. If vested, those acquiree share-based payment transactions are part of the non-controlling interests (NCIs) in the acquiree and are measured at their market-based measure. If unvested, they are measured at their market-based measure as if the acquisition date were the grant date in accordance with IFRS 3:19 and 30 (see **7.3.1**). [IFRS 3:B62A]

The market-based measure of unvested share-based payment transactions is allocated to the NCIs on the basis of the ratio of the portion of the vesting period completed to the greater of the total vesting period or the original vesting period of the share-based payment transaction (see Step 2 at **8.3.4.4**). The balance is allocated to post-combination service. [IFRS 3:B62B]

8.3.4.7   Accounting for the replacement of an acquiree's awards in the separate financial statements of the acquirer

As discussed at **8.3.4.1** to **8.3.4.4**, IFRS 3:B56 to B62 provide guidance for the attribution in the consolidated financial statements of the market-based measure of the replacement awards when the acquirer replaces the awards held by the acquiree's employees in a business combination. However, no specific guidance is provided in IFRSs in respect of the accounting for a replacement by the acquirer in its separate financial statements.

In the separate financial statements of the acquirer, the replacement award is viewed as having been issued in exchange for two elements:

- consideration transferred for the repurchase of potentially dilutive interests in the new subsidiary; and

- post-acquisition services to be rendered by the employees of the new subsidiary.

The portion related to pre-acquisition services is recognised at the acquisition date as part of the cost of investment in the subsidiary. The remainder will be recognised in accordance with IFRS 2 principles applicable to group share schemes; the acquirer will recognise the portion of the obligation related to post-acquisition services rendered by the subsidiary's employees over the vesting period as a capital contribution (i.e. additional cost of investment in the subsidiary) – see **8.4** in **chapter A16**.

IFRSs do not contain guidance on how to allocate the market-based measure of the replacement award between the pre- and post-acquisition elements in the separate financial statements of the acquirer.

The preferred approach is to apply the same method of allocation in the acquirer's separate financial statements as in its consolidated financial statements. Therefore, the amount attributed to pre-acquisition service will be the market-based measure of the acquiree award multiplied by the ratio of the portion of the vesting period completed to the greater of the total vesting period (the sum of the vesting period completed and the vesting period of the replacement award) and the original vesting period of the acquiree award as set out in IFRS 3:B58 (see **8.3.4.4**). The amount attributed to post-acquisition service will be the market-based measure of the replacement award less the amount attributed to pre-acquisition service.

An alternative approach would be to account for the replacement award in the acquirer's separate financial statements as a new grant in accordance with IFRS 2. Under this alternative approach, the amount attributed to pre-acquisition service and included in the cost of investment is the market-based measure of the replacement award multiplied by the ratio of the portion of the vesting period completed to the total vesting period. The remainder of the acquisition-date fair value of the replacement award is attributed to post-acquisition service.

The choice between these approaches is an accounting policy choice, which should be applied consistently.

8.3.5   A transaction that reimburses the acquiree or its former owners for paying the acquirer's acquisition-related costs

Section 8.4 discusses the required treatment under IFRS 3 of acquisition-related costs incurred by the acquirer; generally such costs are required to be recognised as an expense in profit or loss when they are incurred. In its Basis for Conclusions on IFRS 3, the IASB discusses circumstances in which entities might modify transactions to avoid recognising such an expense. "For example ... a buyer might ask a seller to make payments to the buyer's vendors on its behalf. To facilitate the negotiations and sale of the business, the seller might agree to make those payments if the total amount to be paid to it upon closing of the business combination is sufficient to reimburse the seller for payments it made on the buyer's behalf. If the disguised reimbursements were treated as part of the consideration transferred for the business, the acquirer might not recognise those expenses. Rather, the measure of the fair value of the business and the amount of goodwill recognised for that business might be overstated." [IFRS 3:BC370]

To mitigate such concerns, IFRS 3 includes in its list of examples of transactions that should be separated from the business combination "... a transaction that reimburses the acquiree or its former owners for paying the acquirer's acquisition-related costs" (see IFRS 3:52(c)). It follows that when such a transaction is identified, that element is deducted from the consideration used to calculate goodwill, and is expensed by the acquirer.

8.4 Acquisition-related costs

8.4.1 Acquisition-related costs generally recognised in profit or loss

Acquisition-related costs are costs the acquirer incurs to effect a business combination. Those costs include:

[IFRS 3:53]

- finder's fees;

- advisory, legal, accounting, valuation and other professional or consulting fees;

- general administrative costs, including the costs of maintaining an internal acquisitions department; and

- costs of registering and issuing debt and equity securities.

Under IFRS 3, the acquirer is required to account for acquisition-related costs as expenses in the periods in which the costs are incurred and the services are received, with one exception: costs to issue debt or equity securities are recognised in accordance with IAS 32 *Financial Instruments: Presentation* for equity securities (see **section 4** of **chapter B3** or **section 4** of **chapter C3**) and, for debt securities, in accordance with either IFRS 9 *Financial Instruments* (see **2.1** in **chapter B6**) or, for entities that have not yet adopted IFRS 9, IAS 39 *Financial Instruments: Recognition and Measurement* (see **2.1** in **chapter C6**). [IFRS 3:53]

> The Basis for Conclusions justifies this treatment of acquisition-related costs on the basis that "[t]he boards concluded that acquisition-related costs are not part of the fair value exchange between the buyer and seller for the business. Rather, they are separate transactions in which the buyer pays for the fair value of services received. The boards also observed that those costs, whether for services performed by external parties or internal staff of the acquirer, do not generally represent assets of the acquirer at the acquisition date because the benefits obtained are consumed as the services are received". [IFRS 3:BC366]
>
> The treatment of acquisition costs in the separate financial statements of the parent is discussed at **5.10** in **chapter A29**.
>
> The IASB has also identified a potential for abuse, whereby the acquirer might arrange for the seller to pay certain acquisition-related costs on its behalf in return for increased purchase consideration for the business combination. This is considered at **8.3.5**.

8.4.2 Bonus payments linked to a business combination

> Bonus payments may be made to the acquirer's employees as a reward for completing a business combination. These payments may be conditional on completing a particular business combination, a number of unspecified business combinations in a particular period, or some other criteria. Such bonuses may extend to the directors and other key management personnel of the acquirer to compensate them for due diligence services provided.
>
> Such bonus payments incurred to effect a business combination should be expensed as incurred in line with the treatment of other acquisition-related costs.

8.5 Business combinations with no transfer of consideration

8.5.1 Accounting requirements and examples

An acquirer may obtain control of an acquiree without transferring consideration. In such cases, IFRS 3 requires an acquirer to be identified, and the acquisition method to be applied. Examples of such circumstances include:

[IFRS 3:43]

(a) acquiree repurchases a sufficient number of its own shares for an existing investor (the acquirer) to obtain control;

(b) minority veto rights lapse that previously kept the acquirer from controlling an acquiree in which the acquirer held the majority voting rights; and

(c) a combination by contract alone (see **8.5.2**).

8.5.2 Combinations by contract alone

8.5.2.1 Combinations by contract alone – general

In a business combination achieved by contract alone, two entities enter into a contractual arrangement which covers, for example, operation under a single management and equalisation of voting power and earnings attributable to both entities' equity investors. Such structures may involve a 'stapling' or formation of a dual listed corporation.

8.5.2.2 Example of a dual listed structure

BHP Billiton Annual Report 2007

Merger terms

On 29 June 2001, BHP Billiton Plc (previously known as Billiton Plc), a UK listed company, and BHP Billiton Limited (previously known as BHP Limited), an Australian listed company, entered into a Dual Listed Companies' (DLC) merger. This was effected by contractual arrangements between the Companies and amendments to their constitutional documents.

The effect of the DLC merger is that BHP Billiton Plc and its subsidiaries (the BHP Billiton Plc Group) and BHP Billiton Limited and its subsidiaries (the BHP Billiton Limited Group) operate together as a single economic entity (the BHP Billiton Group). Under the arrangements:

- the shareholders of BHP Billiton Plc and BHP Billiton Limited have a common economic interest in both Groups

- the shareholders of BHP Billiton Plc and BHP Billiton Limited take key decisions, including the election of Directors, through a joint electoral procedure under which the shareholders of the two Companies effectively vote on a joint basis

- BHP Billiton Plc and BHP Billiton Limited have a common Board of Directors, a unified management structure and joint objectives

- dividends and capital distributions made by the two Companies are equalised

- BHP Billiton Plc and BHP Billiton Limited each executed a deed poll guarantee, guaranteeing (subject to certain exceptions) the contractual obligations (whether actual or contingent, primary or secondary) of the other incurred after 29 June 2001 together with specified obligations existing at that date

If either BHP Billiton Plc or BHP Billiton Limited proposes to pay a dividend to its shareholders, then the other Company must pay a matching cash dividend of an equivalent amount per share to its shareholders. If either Company is

---

> prohibited by law or is otherwise unable to declare, pay or otherwise make all or any portion of such a matching dividend, then BHP Billiton Plc or BHP Billiton Limited will, so far as it is practicable to do so, enter into such transactions with each other as the Boards agree to be necessary or desirable so as to enable both Companies to pay dividends as nearly as practicable at the same time.
>
> The DLC merger did not involve the change of legal ownership of any assets of BHP Billiton Plc or BHP Billiton Limited, any change of ownership of any existing shares or securities of BHP Billiton Plc or BHP Billiton Limited, the issue of any shares or securities or any payment by way of consideration, save for the issue by each Company of one special voting share to a trustee company which is the means by which the joint electoral procedure is operated. In addition, to achieve a position where the economic and voting interests of one share in BHP Billiton Plc and one share in BHP Billiton Limited were identical, BHP Billiton Limited made a bonus issue of ordinary shares to the holders of its ordinary shares.

8.5.2.3   Accounting for a combination by contract

IFRS 3 requires one of the combining entities to be identified as the acquirer, and one to be identified as the acquiree – see **section 5** for guidance. In reaching the conclusion that combinations achieved by contract alone should not be excluded from the scope of IFRS 3, the Board noted that:

[IFRS 3:BC79]

- such business combinations do not involve the payment of readily measurable consideration and, in rare circumstances, it might be difficult to identify the acquirer;

- difficulties in identifying the acquirer are not a sufficient reason to justify a different accounting treatment, and no further guidance is necessary for identifying the acquirer; and

- the acquisition method is already being applied for such combinations in the United States and insurmountable issues have not been encountered.

8.5.3   Application of the acquisition method to a combination in which no consideration is transferred

8.5.3.1   Deemed consideration

In a business combination achieved without the transfer of consideration, the acquirer substitutes the acquisition-date fair value of its interest in the acquiree for the acquisition-date fair value of the consideration transferred to measure goodwill or a gain on a bargain purchase. [IFRS 3:33 & B46]

The acquirer's interest in the acquiree may be limited to its right to equalisation payments.

8.5.3.2   Amount attributed to non-controlling interests

The amount attributed to non-controlling interests in a business combination achieved by contract alone is dealt with in IFRS 3:44, which states that "[i]n a business combination achieved by contract alone, the acquirer shall attribute to the owners of the acquiree the amount of the acquiree's net assets recognised in accordance with this IFRS. In other words, the equity interests in the acquiree held by parties other than the acquirer are a non-controlling interest in the acquirer's post-combination financial statements even if the result is that all of the equity interests in the acquiree are attributed to the non-controlling interest".

9   Recognising and measuring goodwill or a gain from a bargain purchase

9.1   Measuring goodwill or a gain from a bargain purchase

9.1.1   Calculation of goodwill or a gain from a bargain purchase – general

Goodwill arising from a business combination is determined as follows.

[IFRS 3:32]

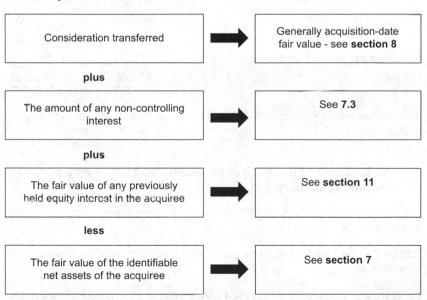

Accordingly, the calculation of goodwill under IFRS 3 involves potentially four components; **example 9.1.1** provides an illustration.

Example 9.1.1

Calculation of goodwill

Entity P acquires Entity Q in two stages.

- In 20X1, Entity P acquires a 30 per cent equity interest for cash consideration of CU32,000 when the fair value of Entity Q's identifiable net assets is CU100,000.

- In 20X5, Entity P acquires a further 50 per cent equity interest for cash consideration of CU75,000. On the acquisition date, the fair value of Entity Q's identifiable net assets is CU120,000. The fair value of Entity P's original 30 per cent holding is CU40,000 and the fair value of the 20 per cent non-controlling interest (NCI), which represents a present ownership interest, is assessed as CU28,000.

Goodwill is calculated, on the alternative bases that Entity P recognises components of NCI that represent present ownership interests at their proportionate share of net assets, or at fair value, as follows.

	NCI @ % of net assets	NCI @ fair value
	CU	CU
Fair value of consideration	75,000	75,000
Non-controlling interests	24,000	28,000
Previously held interest	40,000	40,000
	139,000	143,000
Fair value of identifiable net assets	120,000	120,000
Goodwill	19,000	23,000

The implications of the choice between the alternatives for measuring NCIs are discussed at **7.3.2**.

9.1.2 Calculation of goodwill in an acquisition made by a partially-owned *subsidiary*

Example 9.1.2

Calculation of goodwill in an acquisition made by a partially-owned subsidiary

Entity P owns 80 per cent of Entity S. Entity S acquires 100 per cent of the equity shares of Entity A from an unrelated party for cash consideration of CU100,000 when the fair value of Entity A's identifiable net assets is CU80,000.

How should goodwill arising on the acquisition of Entity A be calculated in the consolidated financial statements of Entity P?

Goodwill should be calculated in the manner required by IFRS 3:32. In the circumstances described:

- no entity in Entity P's group previously held any interest in Entity A;
- no additional non-controlling interest (NCI) arises from the acquisition; and
- the full consideration for the acquisition of Entity A is payable out of assets of Entity P's group.

Therefore, goodwill will be the difference between the consideration payable by the group (for 100 per cent of Entity A's shares) and the net of the acquisition-date fair values of the identifiable assets acquired and the liabilities assumed measured in accordance with IFRS 3.

	CU
Fair value of consideration paid by Entity P's group	100,000
Less: identifiable net assets of Entity A recognised in accordance with IFRS 3	(80,000)
Goodwill	20,000

The transaction does not affect the carrying amount of NCIs because, although the shareholders owning 20 per cent of Entity S have acquired an interest of CU20,000 in Entity A (20 per cent of the total consideration of CU100,000), their previous interest in the net assets of Entity S has decreased by an equivalent amount (20 per cent of the cash outflow of CU100,000).

9.2 Special situations

9.2.1 Share-for-share exchange

In a business combination in which the acquirer and the acquiree (or its former owners) exchange only equity interests, the fair value of the acquiree's equity interests may be more reliably measurable than the fair value of the acquirer's equity interests. If so, the acquirer should determine the amount of goodwill by using the fair value of the acquiree's equity interests rather than the fair value of the equity interests transferred. [IFRS 3:33]

Example 9.2.1

Consideration measured using acquiree's equity

An unlisted private equity entity acquires a listed entity through an exchange of equity instruments. The published price of the quoted equity instruments of the acquiree at the date of exchange is likely to provide a more reliable indicator of fair value than the valuation methods used to measure the fair value of the private acquirer's equity instruments.

Use of the fair value of the acquiree's equity interests in this situation, as an alternative to measuring the fair value of consideration transferred by the acquirer, is justified on grounds of reliable measurement only.

9.2.2 Business combinations with no consideration

IFRS 3:33 also deals with the situation of a business combination in which no consideration is transferred. This could occur when the acquiree repurchases equity interests from other investors such that the acquirer's unchanged equity interest becomes a controlling interest, or a business combination achieved by contract alone.

In a business combination achieved without the transfer of consideration, goodwill is determined by using the acquisition-date fair value of the acquirer's interest in the acquiree rather than the acquisition-date fair value of the consideration transferred. [IFRS 3:33]

Business combinations with no transfer of consideration are considered in more detail in **8.5**.

9.2.3 Mutual entities

9.2.3.1 Measurement issues arising in combinations involving mutual entities – general

Section 5.3.2 of this chapter deals with the identification of the acquirer in combinations involving mutual entities. This section deals with measurement issues that arise in such circumstances.

When two mutual entities combine, the entity identified as the acquirer gives member interests in itself in exchange for the member interests in the acquiree. Thus, consideration is paid, but its fair value is not readily measurable by reference to a market. IFRS 3 recognises that it may be more reliable to determine the fair value of the entire member interest of the acquiree, rather than the incremental member interests given by the acquirer.

9.2.3.2 Consideration given

IFRS 3 provides that when the fair value of the equity or member interests in the acquiree (or the fair value of the acquiree) is more reliably measurable than the fair value of the member interests transferred by the acquirer, the acquirer should determine the amount of goodwill by using the acquisition-date fair value of the acquiree's equity interests instead of the acquisition-date fair value of the acquirer's equity interests transferred as consideration. [IFRS 3:B47]

> This is an example of IFRS 3 using the fair value of the acquiree to measure consideration because it is more reliably measurable than consideration given by the acquirer (see also **9.2.1**).

9.2.3.3 Basis of valuation

Although they are similar in many ways to other businesses, mutual entities have distinct characteristics that arise primarily because their members are both customers and owners. Members of mutual entities generally expect to receive benefits for their membership, often in the form of reduced fees charged for goods and services or patronage dividends. The portion of patronage dividends allocated to each member is often based on the amount of business the member did with the mutual entity during the year. [IFRS 3:B48]

A fair value measurement of a mutual entity should include the assumptions that market participants would make about future member benefits as well as any other relevant assumptions market participants would make about the mutual entity. For example, a present value technique may be used to measure the fair value of a mutual entity. The cash flows used as inputs to the model should be based on the expected cash flows of the mutual entity, which are likely to reflect reductions for member benefits, such as reduced fees charged for goods and services. [IFRS 3:B49]

9.2.3.4 Identifiable net assets acquired

The acquirer in a combination of mutual entities recognises the acquiree's net assets as a direct addition to capital or equity in its statement of financial position, not as an addition to retained earnings, which is consistent with the way in which other types of entities apply the acquisition method. [IFRS 3:B47]

Member interests given by the acquirer will be recognised directly in equity. IFRSs do not usually prescribe where within equity such items are classified. In this case, however, IFRS 3 is specific that the amount recognised (equal to the acquiree's identifiable net assets) should not be added to retained earnings.

IFRS 3:B47 takes precedence over local legal requirements which may require such amounts to be reflected in retained earnings. Therefore, in accounting for a combination of mutual entities, recognition of member interests in retained earnings is prohibited. However, neither IFRS 3 nor any other Standard prohibits the acquirer from transferring the equity balance to retained earnings subsequently. Such a transfer is acceptable provided that it is not prohibited by local laws.

Example 9.2.3.4

Combination of mutual entities

Entity X and Entity Y are mutual entities (co-operative institutions) owned by their customers who receive dividends in proportion to the amount of goods purchased. They combine, with Entity X identified as the acquirer. Members of Entity Y become members of Entity X.

A valuation of Entity Y as an entity indicates a fair value of CU500,000. The fair value of Entity Y's identifiable net assets is CU400,000.

Entity X recognises its acquisition of Entity Y in its consolidated financial statements as follows:

		CU	CU
Dr	Identifiable net assets acquired	400,000	
Dr	Goodwill	100,000	
Cr	Member interests issued		500,000

To recognise the acquisition of Entity Y.

The classification of member interests as either equity or a financial liability is determined by applying IAS 32 *Financial Instruments: Presentation*.

9.3   Bargain purchases

9.3.1   *Bargain purchases – general*

A bargain purchase is a business combination in which the net fair value of the identifiable assets acquired and liabilities assumed exceeds the aggregate of the consideration transferred, the non-controlling interests and the fair value of any previously held equity interest in the acquiree.

A bargain purchase might happen, for example, in a business combination that is a forced sale in which the seller is acting under compulsion. However, the recognition and measurement exceptions for particular items, as discussed in **section 7**, might also lead to the recognition of a gain (or a change in the amount of a recognised gain) on a bargain purchase. [IFRS 3:35]

9.3.2   *Accounting for a bargain purchase gain*

If, after applying the requirements at **9.3.3**, it is determined that the acquisition is a bargain purchase, the acquirer should recognise the resulting gain in profit or loss on the acquisition date. The gain should be attributed to the acquirer. [IFRS 3:34]

9.3.3   *Consequences of identifying a bargain purchase*

An acquirer's initial calculations under IFRS 3:32 (see **9.1.1**) may indicate that the acquisition has resulted in a bargain purchase. Before recognising any gain, the Standard requires that the acquirer should reassess whether it has correctly identified all of the assets acquired and all of the liabilities assumed. The acquirer should recognise any additional assets or liabilities that are identified in that review. [IFRS 3:36]

The acquirer is then required to review the procedures used to measure the amounts that IFRS 3 requires to be recognised at the acquisition date for all of the following:

[IFRS 3:36]

(a) the identifiable assets acquired and liabilities assumed;

(b) the non-controlling interest in the acquiree, if any;

(c) for a business combination achieved in stages, the acquirer's previously held equity interest in the acquiree; and

(d) the consideration transferred.

The objective of the review is to ensure that the measurements appropriately reflect consideration of all available information as of the acquisition date. [IFRS 3:36]

Example 9.3.3

Gain on a bargain purchase

[IFRS 3:IE46 - IE49]

On 1 January 20X5 AC acquires 80 per cent of the equity interests of TC, a private entity, in exchange for cash of CU150. Because the former owners of TC needed to dispose of their investments in TC by a specified date, they did not have sufficient time to market TC to multiple potential buyers. The management of AC initially measures the separately recognisable identifiable assets acquired and the liabilities assumed as of the acquisition date in accordance with the requirements of IFRS 3. The identifiable assets are measured at CU250 and the liabilities assumed are measured at CU50. AC engages an independent consultant, who determines that the fair value of the 20 per cent non-controlling interest in TC is CU42.

The amount of TC's identifiable net assets (CU200, calculated as CU250 – CU50) exceeds the fair value of the consideration transferred plus the fair value of the non-controlling interest in TC. Therefore, AC reviews the procedures it used to identify and measure the assets acquired and liabilities assumed and to measure the fair value of both the non-controlling interest in TC and the consideration transferred. After that review, AC decides that the procedures and resulting measures were appropriate. AC measures the gain on its purchase of the 80 per cent interest as follows:

	CU
Amount of the identifiable net assets acquired (CU250 – CU50)	200
Less: Fair value of the consideration transferred for AC's 80 per cent interest in TC; plus	150
Fair value of non-controlling interest in TC	42
	192
Gain on bargain purchase of 80 per cent interest	8

AC would record its acquisition of TC in its consolidated financial statements as follows:

		CU	CU
Dr	Identifiable assets acquired	250	
Cr	Cash		150
Cr	Liabilities assumed		50
Cr	Gain on the bargain purchase		8
Cr	Equity-non-controlling interest in TC		42

If the acquirer chose to measure the non-controlling interest in TC on the basis of its proportionate interest in the identifiable net assets of the acquiree, the recognised amount of the non-controlling interest would be CU40 (CU200 × 0.20). The gain on the bargain purchase then would be CU10 (CU200 – (CU150 + CU40)).

10 Post-combination accounting

10.1 Adjustments to provisional values

10.1.1 Use of provisional values

If the initial accounting for a business combination is incomplete by the end of the reporting period in which the combination occurs, the financial statements should be prepared using provisional amounts for the items for which the accounting is incomplete. [IFRS 3:45]

10.1.2 The measurement period

The measurement period is the period after the acquisition date during which the acquirer may adjust the provisional values recognised for a business combination. [IFRS 3:46] The measurement period begins on the acquisition date and ends as soon as the acquirer receives the information it was seeking about facts and circumstances that existed as of the acquisition date or learns that more information is not obtainable. However, the measurement period cannot exceed one year from the acquisition date. [IFRS 3:45]

10.1.3   Adjustments permitted during the measurement period

10.1.3.1   What can be adjusted during the measurement period?

Adjustments may be made in the measurement period to the following components:

[IFRS 3:46]

(a) the identifiable assets acquired, liabilities assumed and any non-controlling interests in the acquiree;

(b) the consideration transferred for the acquiree (or the other amount used in measuring goodwill);

(c) in a business combination achieved in stages, the equity interest in the acquiree previously held by the acquirer; and

(d) the resulting goodwill or gain on a bargain purchase.

10.1.3.2   Items classified as held for sale

IFRS 3:45 allows that, if the accounting for a business combination has not been finalised by the end of the reporting period in which the business combination occurs, the entity may retrospectively adjust the provisional amounts recognised at the acquisition date for a period of up to one year from the acquisition date to reflect "new information obtained about facts and circumstances that existed as of the acquisition date" that, if known "would have affected the measurement of the amounts recognised as of that date".

IFRS 3:31 states that an acquirer "shall measure an acquired non-current asset (or disposal group) that is classified as held for sale at the acquisition date in accordance with IFRS 5 *Non-current Assets Held for Sale and Discontinued Operations* at fair value less costs to sell in accordance with paragraphs 15-18 of that IFRS".

Although assets classified as held for sale under IFRS 5 at the date of a business combination are measured in accordance with IFRS 5, the measurement period in IFRS 3:45 will apply to those assets, provided that the criteria in IFRS 3:45 to 47 are met.

To the extent that fair value information is incomplete at the first reporting date after the business combination, the fair value estimates under IFRS 5 may also be affected. Therefore if, during the measurement period, additional information becomes available that meets the criteria in IFRS 3:45 to 47, the provisional amounts recognised initially for the business combination should be adjusted retrospectively. However, any changes in value arising after the acquisition date are measured and accounted for in accordance with IFRS 5.

10.1.4   Retrospective adjustments

The adjustments to provisional amounts should be recognised as if the accounting for the business combination had been completed at the acquisition date. Therefore, comparative information for prior periods presented in the financial statements is revised as required, including making any change in depreciation, amortisation or other income effects recognised in completing the initial accounting. [IFRS 3:49]

Adjustments to recognised items During the measurement period, the acquirer retrospectively adjusts the provisional amounts recognised at the acquisition date to reflect new information obtained about facts and circumstances that existed as of the acquisition date and that, if known, would have affected the measurement of the amounts recognised as of that date. [IFRS 3:45]

Adjustments to unrecognised items During the measurement period, the acquirer also recognises additional assets or liabilities if new information is obtained about facts and circumstances that existed as of the acquisition date and that, if known, would have resulted in the recognition of those assets and liabilities as of that date. [IFRS 3:45]

Information to be considered The acquirer is required to consider all pertinent factors in determining whether information obtained after the acquisition date should result in an adjustment to the provisional amounts recognised or whether that information results from events that occurred after the acquisition date. Pertinent factors include the date when additional information is obtained and whether the acquirer can identify a reason for a change to provisional amounts. Information that is obtained shortly after the acquisition date is more likely to reflect circumstances that existed at the acquisition date than is information obtained several months later. For example, unless an intervening event that changed its fair value can be identified, the sale of an asset to a third party shortly after the acquisition date for an amount that differs significantly from its provisional fair value measured at that date is likely to indicate an error in the provisional amount. [IFRS 3:47]

Revising goodwill The acquirer recognises an increase (decrease) in the provisional amount recognised for an identifiable asset (liability) by means of a decrease (increase) in goodwill. However, new information obtained during the measurement period may sometimes result in an adjustment to the provisional amount of more than one asset or liability. For example, the acquirer might have assumed a liability to pay damages related to an accident in one of the acquiree's facilities, part or all of which are covered by the acquiree's liability insurance policy. If the acquirer obtains new information during the measurement period about the acquisition-date fair value of that liability, the adjustment to goodwill resulting from a change to the provisional amount recognised for the liability would be offset (in whole or in part) by a corresponding adjustment to goodwill resulting from a change to the provisional amount recognised for the claim receivable from the insurer. [IFRS 3:48]

Example 10.1.4

Measurement period

[IFRS 3:IE51 - 53]

Suppose that AC acquires TC on 30 September 20X7. AC seeks an independent valuation for an item of property, plant and equipment acquired in the combination, and the valuation was not complete by the time AC authorised for issue its financial statements for the year ended 31 December 20X7. In its 20X7 annual financial statements, AC recognised a provisional fair value for the asset of CU30,000. At the acquisition date, the item of property, plant and equipment had a remaining useful life of five years. Five months after the acquisition date, AC received the independent valuation, which estimated the asset's acquisition-date fair value as CU40,000.

In its financial statements for the year ended 31 December 20X8, AC retrospectively adjusts the 20X7 prior year information as follows:

(a) the carrying amount of property, plant and equipment as of 31 December 20X7 is increased by CU9,500. That adjustment is measured as the fair value adjustment at the acquisition date of CU10,000 less the additional depreciation that would have been recognised if the asset's fair value at the acquisition date had been recognised from that date (CU500 for three months' depreciation);

(b) the carrying amount of goodwill as of 31 December 20X7 is decreased by CU10,000; and

(c) depreciation expense for 20X7 is increased by CU500.

In accordance with IFRS 3:B67, AC discloses:

(a) in its 20X7 financial statements, that the initial accounting for the business combination has not been completed because the valuation of property, plant and equipment has not yet been received; and

(b) in its 20X8 financial statements, the amounts and explanations of the adjustments to the provisional values recognised during the current reporting period. Therefore, AC discloses that the 20X7 comparative information is adjusted retrospectively to increase the fair value of the item of property, plant and equipment at the acquisition date by CU9,500, offset by a decrease to goodwill of CU10,000 and an increase in depreciation expense of CU500.

10.1.5 Adjustments after the measurement period

After the measurement period ends, the accounting for a business combination can be amended only to correct an error in accordance with IAS 8 *Accounting Policies, Changes in Accounting Estimates and Errors* (see **chapter A5**). [IFRS 3:50]

10.1.6   Deferred tax arising from a business combination

The requirements of IAS 12 *Income Taxes* (see **chapter A13**) in respect of the post-combination recognition of deferred tax assets acquired in a business combination are as follows:

[IAS 12:68]

- acquired deferred tax benefits recognised within the measurement period that result from new information about facts and circumstances that existed at the acquisition date reduce the carrying amount of any goodwill related to that acquisition. If the carrying amount of that goodwill is zero, any remaining deferred tax benefits are recognised in profit or loss; and

- all other acquired deferred tax benefits realised are recognised in profit or loss (or outside profit or loss if otherwise required by IAS 12).

The requirements of IAS 12:68, which were amended by IFRS 3 (as revised in 2008), apply both to business combinations occurring after the adoption of IFRS 3 (as revised in 2008), and prospectively to the recognition or remeasurement of deferred tax assets acquired in business combinations occurring before the adoption of IFRS 3 (as revised in 2008). Therefore, following the adoption of IFRS 3 (as revised in 2008), irrespective of the date of the original acquisition, the impact of the recognition or remeasurement of such deferred tax assets is recognised in profit or loss unless the benefits are recognised within the measurement period and those adjustments result from new information about facts and circumstances that existed at the acquisition date. [IAS 12:94]

10.2   Guidance on subsequent measurement and accounting

10.2.1   Guidance on subsequent measurement and accounting in other IFRSs

In general, assets acquired, liabilities assumed or incurred, and equity instruments issued in a business combination are subsequently measured and accounted for in accordance with other applicable IFRSs, according to their nature. [IFRS 3:54]

Examples of other IFRSs that provide guidance on subsequently measuring and accounting for assets acquired and liabilities assumed or incurred in a business combination include:

[IFRS 3:B63]

- IAS 38 *Intangible Assets*, which prescribes the accounting for identifiable intangible assets acquired in a business combination (see **chapter A9**).

The acquirer measures goodwill at the amount recognised at the acquisition date less any accumulated impairment losses;

- IAS 36 *Impairment of Assets*, which prescribes the accounting for impairment losses (see **chapter A10**);

- IFRS 4 *Insurance Contracts*, which provides guidance on the subsequent accounting for an insurance contract acquired in a business combination (see **chapter A39**);

- IAS 12 *Income Taxes*, which prescribes the subsequent accounting for deferred tax assets (including unrecognised deferred tax assets) and liabilities acquired in a business combination (see **chapter A13**);

- IFRS 2 *Share-based Payment*, which provides guidance on subsequent measurement and accounting for the portion of replacement share-based payment awards issued by an acquirer that is attributable to employees' future services (see **chapter A16**); and

- IFRS 10 *Consolidated Financial Statements*, which provides guidance on accounting for changes in a parent's ownership interest in a subsidiary after control is obtained (see **chapter A24** for IFRS 10).

10.2.2 Specific guidance on subsequent measurement and accounting

IFRS 3 provides specific guidance in relation to the following assets acquired, liabilities assumed or incurred, and equity instruments issued in a business combination:

- reacquired rights (see **7.5.3**);

- contingent liabilities (see **7.5.2**);

- indemnification assets (see **7.5.8**); and

- contingent consideration (see **8.2**).

11 Step acquisitions

11.1 Step acquisitions – general

This section applies when an equity investment in one of the following categories is increased to become a controlling interest:

- a financial asset under IFRS 9 (or, for entities that have not yet adopted IFRS 9, IAS 39);

- an associate or a joint venture accounted for using equity accounting under IAS 28; or

- a joint operation that constitutes a business (see **11.4**).

These requirements apply to transactions that result in the acquirer obtaining control of an entity; they do not apply to subsequent increases and decreases in ownership interests that do not involve the loss of control. Such changes in ownership are treated as transactions with owners and are discussed at **11.4** in **chapter A24**.

Transactions in which control is achieved through two transactions

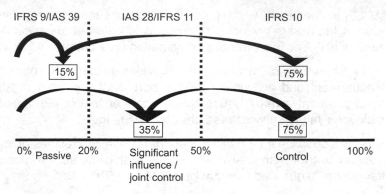

The principles to be applied are:

- a business combination occurs only in respect of the transaction that gives one entity control of another; [IFRS 3:Appendix A]

- identifiable net assets of the acquiree are remeasured to their fair value on the date of acquisition (i.e. the date that control is obtained); [IFRS 3:18]

- non-controlling interests are measured on the date of acquisition; [IFRS 3:19]

- an equity interest previously held in the acquiree which qualified as a financial asset under IFRS 9 (or, for entities that have not yet adopted IFRS 9, IAS 39) is treated as if it were disposed of and reacquired at fair value on the acquisition date. Accordingly, it is remeasured to its acquisition-date fair value and any resulting gain or loss is recognised in profit or loss or other comprehensive income, as appropriate. Any amount that has previously been recognised in other comprehensive income, and that would be reclassified to profit or loss following a disposal, is similarly reclassified from equity to profit or loss; [IFRS 3:42]

- an equity interest previously held in the acquiree which qualified as an associate or a joint venture, or as a joint operation that constitutes a business (see **11.4**), is similarly treated as if it were disposed of and reacquired at fair value on the acquisition date. Accordingly, it is remeasured to its acquisition-date fair value, and any resulting gain or loss compared to its carrying amount under IAS 28 or IFRS 11 is recognised in profit or loss. Any amount that has previously been recognised in other comprehensive income, and that would be reclassified to profit or loss following a disposal, is similarly reclassified from equity to profit or loss; [IFRS 3:42] and

* goodwill (or a gain from a bargain purchase) is measured as follows. [IFRS 3:32]

Consideration transferred to obtain control

plus

Amount of non-controlling interest
(using either option)

plus

Fair value of previously held equity interest

less

Fair value of the identifiable net
assets of the acquiree (100%)

11.2   Financial asset under IAS 39 becomes a subsidiary

Example 11.2

Financial asset under IAS 39 becomes a subsidiary

Entity A acquired a 75 per cent controlling interest in Entity B in two stages.

* In 20X1, Entity A acquired a 15 per cent equity interest for cash consideration of CU10,000. Entity A classified the interest as available for sale under IAS 39. From 20X1 to the end of 20X5, Entity A reported fair value increases of CU2,000 in other comprehensive income.

* In 20X6, Entity A acquired a further 60 per cent equity interest for cash consideration of CU60,000. Entity A identified net assets of Entity B with a fair value of CU80,000. Entity A elected to measure non-controlling interests (which represent present ownership interests) at their proportionate share of net assets. On the date of acquisition, the previously held 15% interest had a fair value of CU12,500.

In 20X6, Entity A will recognise CU2,500 in profit or loss, calculated as follows.

	CU
Gain on 'disposal' of 15% investment (CU12,500 – CU12,000)	500
Gain previously reported in other comprehensive income (CU12,000 – CU10,000)	2,000
Total	2,500

In 20X6, Entity A will measure goodwill as follows.

	CU
Fair value of consideration given for controlling interest	60,000
Non-controlling interest (25% × CU80,000)	20,000

	CU
Fair value of previously held interest	12,500
Sub-total	92,500
Less: fair value of net assets of acquiree	(80,000)
Goodwill	12,500

11.3   Associate becomes a subsidiary

Example 11.3

Associate becomes a subsidiary

Entity C acquired a 75 per cent controlling interest in Entity D in two stages.

- In 20X1, Entity C acquired a 40 per cent equity interest for cash consideration of CU40,000. Entity C classified the interest as an associate under IAS 28. At the date that Entity C acquired its interest, the fair value of Entity D's identifiable net assets was CU80,000. From 20X1 to 20X6, Entity C used the equity method to account for its share of undistributed profits totalling CU5,000, and included its share of a revaluation gain of CU3,000 in other comprehensive income in accordance with IAS 16 Property, Plant and Equipment. Therefore, in 20X6, the carrying amount of Entity C's interest in Entity D was CU48,000.

- In 20X6, C acquired a further 35 per cent equity interest for cash consideration of CU55,000. Entity C identified net assets of Entity D with a fair value of CU110,000. Entity C elected to measure non-controlling interests (which represent present ownership interests) at fair value of CU30,000. On the date of acquisition, the previously held 40 per cent interest had a fair value of CU50,000.

In 20X6, ignoring any profits earned prior to the acquisition, Entity C will recognise CU2,000 in profit or loss, calculated as follows.

	CU
Fair value of previously held interest	50,000
Less: carrying amount under IAS 28	48,000
Total	2,000

The revaluation gain of CU3,000 previously recognised in other comprehensive income is not reclassified to profit or loss because it would not be reclassified if the interest in Entity D were disposed of.

In 20X6, Entity C will measure goodwill as follows.

	CU
Fair value of consideration given for controlling interest	55,000
Non-controlling interest (fair value)	30,000

	CU
Fair value of previously held interest	50,000
Sub-total	135,000
Less: fair value of net assets of acquiree	(110,000)
Goodwill	25,000

See also **4.4.6** for the accounting and measurement in the consolidated financial statements when an entity's stake in an associate with a single asset increases such that it becomes a subsidiary.

11.4   Obtaining control over a previously held joint operation that constitutes a business

Example 11.4

Obtaining control over a previously held joint operation that constitutes a business

Entity A shares joint control over Joint Operation B with another investor. The activities of Entity B meet the definition of a business (see **2.2**). In accordance with paragraph 20 of IFRS 11 *Joint Arrangements*, Entity A recognises in relation to Joint Operation B:

- its assets, including its share of any assets held jointly;
- its liabilities, including its share of any liabilities incurred jointly;
- its revenue from the sale of its share of the output arising from Joint Operation B;
- its share of the revenue from the sale of the output by Joint Operation B; and
- its expenses, including its share of any expenses incurred jointly.

At a later date, Entity A assumes control over the business of Joint Operation B. This may be achieved in a number of ways, including:

- purchasing the other investor's interest in Joint Operation B;
- obtaining control over the other investor as part of a larger business combination; or
- a change in the contractual agreement between Entity A and the other investor giving Entity A control of Joint Operation B.

Do the requirements of IFRS 3:42 regarding the treatment of previously held equity interests in an acquiree apply to Entity A's acquisition of Joint Operation B?

Yes. Because the activities of Joint Operation B constitute a business, this transaction should be considered a business combination achieved in stages. As such, IFRS 3:42 requires that upon obtaining control Entity A should:

- remeasure its previously recognised share of the business subject to joint control at the acquisition-date fair value;

- recognise the resulting gain or loss, if any, in profit or loss or other comprehensive income, as appropriate; and

- recognise the identifiable assets and liabilities of the acquired business in accordance with IFRS 3 (i.e. at their acquisition-date fair values subject to the Standard's specific exceptions to that measurement principle).

In performing this exercise in the circumstances of Entity A's obtaining control of Joint Operation B:

- the previously recognised share of the business should be remeasured to its full fair value (i.e. the amount a third party would pay for that share) rather than to the sum of the fair values of the previously recognised shares of assets and liabilities of Joint Operation B; and

- the identifiable assets and liabilities recognised upon obtaining control may include items not previously recognised in Entity A's accounting for Joint Operation B (e.g. intangible assets reflecting customer arrangements developed, subsequent to Entity A's acquisition of joint control over the business).

As noted in IFRS 3:B6, a business combination may be structured in a variety of ways, including via the purchase of trade and assets rather than shares in a legal entity (see **4.2.2**). As such, when the joint operation constitutes a business, the conclusion above (which is consistent with the treatment required by IFRS 11:21A on obtaining joint control over a joint operation whose activity constitutes a business) applies whether the interest in the joint operation was held via ownership of shares in a separate vehicle or through a contractual arrangement between the parties.

In addition, IFRS 3:Appendix A specifies that "for the purposes of this IFRS, equity interests is used broadly to mean ownership interests of investor-owned entities and owner, member or participant interests of mutual entities".

A 'mutual entity' is further defined as "an entity, other than an investor-owned entity, that provides dividends, lower costs or other economic benefits directly to its owners, members or participants". A joint operation constituted through a contractual arrangement provides economic benefits directly to its participants and provides an equity interest as defined in the *Conceptual Framework for Financial Reporting* (because the parties have a residual interest in the assets of the business after deducting all of its liabilities).

In the case of joint operations constituted through a contractual arrangement, care may be needed to distinguish between assets and liabilities that are subject to joint control (and, accordingly, form part of the joint operation) and assets and liabilities that are used in the joint operation's business but remain under the control of one of the investor's (which do not form part of the joint operation). The former will be remeasured to their acquisition-date fair values; the latter will not.

Example 11.4 is based on an interpretation of the general principles of IFRS 3. The IASB has issued an exposure draft proposing to add explicit guidance to IFRS 3 to confirm that when an entity obtains control of a business that is a joint operation, the entity applies the requirements for a business combination achieved in stages set out in IFRS 3:B42 (see 11.1), including remeasuring previously held interests in the assets and liabilities of the joint operation to fair value (see 14.2).

11.5 Obtaining control over a previously held associate or joint venture – reclassification of foreign exchange differences previously accumulated in equity

In line with the general principles established in IFRS 3:42 (see 11.1), when an entity obtains control over a former associate or joint venture, a gain or loss is recognised, being the difference between the acquisition-date fair value of the previously held equity interest in the acquiree and the previous carrying amount. Any amounts previously recognised in other comprehensive income (OCI) are recognised "on the same basis as would be required if the [entity] had disposed directly of the previously held equity interest".

Consequently, when an entity obtains control over a former associate or joint venture that includes a foreign operation, the cumulative exchange differences relating to that operation that had previously been accumulated in equity should be reclassified from equity to profit or loss as would be required for a disposal of the foreign operation under paragraph 48 of IAS 21 *The Effects of Changes in Foreign Exchange Rates*.

This treatment is also consistent with the requirement in IAS 28:23 which states that "if an associate or a joint venture has cumulative exchange differences relating to a foreign operation and the entity discontinues the use of the equity method, the entity shall reclassify to profit or loss the gain or loss that had previously been recognised in other comprehensive income In relation to the foreign operation".

11.6 Obtaining control over a previously held associate or joint venture – interaction with IFRS 5

When an entity is committed to a sale plan involving loss of control of a subsidiary, IFRS 5 *Non-current Assets Held for Sale and Discontinued Operations* requires that all of the assets and liabilities of that subsidiary are classified as held for sale when the specified criteria are met, regardless of whether the entity will retain a non-controlling interest in its former subsidiary after the sale. IFRS 5:BC24C explains that, under such a sale plan "the controlling interest in the subsidiary is, in substance, exchanged for a non-controlling interest". It also notes that this treatment is consistent with the conclusion in IFRS 10 that the loss of control is a significant event that requires derecognition of the subsidiary's assets and liabilities and recognition of any investment retained.

Subject to the specified criteria being met, would the interests below be classified as held for sale under IFRS 5:

* *an interest in an associate when there is a plan to acquire control; and*

* *an interest in a joint venture when there is a plan to acquire control?*

No. As stated in IFRS 5:6, classification as held for sale requires that a non-current asset (or disposal group) "will be recovered principally through a sale transaction".

Even though, under IFRS 3, the acquisition of control is deemed to be a significant event that changes the nature of and accounting for an investment (a gain or loss is recognised, being the difference between the acquisition-date fair value of the previously held equity interest in the acquiree and the previous carrying amount), the interest in an associate or a joint venture is not being disposed of and, therefore, it is not recovered principally through a sale transaction rather than continuing use. In particular, because no part of the existing interest will be sold, the conditions set out in IFRS 5:8 will not be met, because "an active programme to locate a buyer" will not have been initiated and the existing interest will not "be actively marketed for sale".

12   Reverse acquisitions

12.1   Identifying a reverse acquisition

12.1.1   *Meaning of reverse acquisition*

A reverse acquisition occurs when the entity that issues securities (the legal acquirer) is identified as the acquiree for accounting purposes on the basis of the guidance in **section 5**. The entity whose equity interests are acquired (the legal acquiree) must be the acquirer for accounting purposes for the transaction to be considered a reverse acquisition. [IFRS 3:B19]

Example 12.1.1

Private entity reversing into a public entity

[IFRS 3:B19]

Reverse acquisitions sometimes occur when a private operating entity wants to become a public entity but does not want to register its equity shares. To accomplish that, the private entity will arrange for a public entity to acquire its equity interests in exchange for the equity interests of the public entity. In this example, the public entity is the **legal acquirer** because it issued its equity interests, and the private entity is the **legal acquiree** because its equity interests were acquired. However, application of the guidance in paragraphs B13 - B18 [see **section 5**] results in identifying:

(a) the public entity as the **acquiree** for accounting purposes (the accounting acquiree); and

(b) the private entity as the **acquirer** for accounting purposes (the accounting acquirer).

The guidance on identifying the acquirer in **section 5** is relevant in a reverse acquisition transaction. Beyond this, IFRS 3 does not provide detailed guidance for more complex arrangements (e.g. when the accounting acquirer had a previously held interest in the accounting acquiree). It is suggested that the two primary factors that may lead to the conclusion that the transaction involves a reverse acquisition are:

- the former shareholders of the entity whose shares are acquired own the majority of shares, and control the majority of votes, in the combined entity; and

- the management of the combined entity is drawn predominantly from the entity whose shares are acquired.

12.1.2 Is the accounting acquirer in a reverse acquisition required to be a 'legal entity'?

IFRS 3:B19 notes that "[a] reverse acquisition occurs when the entity that issues securities (the legal acquirer) is identified as the acquiree for accounting purposes on the basis of the guidance in paragraphs B13 to B18 [of IFRS 3]. The entity whose equity interests are acquired (the legal acquiree) must be the acquirer for accounting purposes for the transaction to be considered a reverse acquisition".

Could it be appropriate for a business that is not a legal entity to be considered the accounting acquirer in a reverse acquisition?

This question was considered by the IFRS Interpretations Committee in September 2011. The Committee noted that neither IFRSs nor the *Conceptual Framework for Financial Reporting* require that a 'reporting entity' be a legal entity. Consequently, a business that is a reporting entity, but not a legal entity, can be considered to be the acquirer in a reverse acquisition.

12.1.3 Acquiree must meet the definition of a business

IFRS 3 limits business combinations to circumstances when the acquiree is a business. [IFRS 3:3] It follows, for reverse acquisitions, that the accounting acquiree must meet the definition of a business for the transaction to be accounted for as a reverse acquisition. [IFRS 3:B19]

When a publicly-listed 'cash shell' (i.e. an entity with a public listing but with no ongoing activities) is the legal acquirer in an acquisition, but the accounting acquirer is a private entity, the transaction should not be accounted for as a reverse acquisition under IFRS 3.

IFRS 3 limits business combinations to circumstances in which the acquiree is a business. IFRS 3:B19 clarifies that, for reverse acquisitions, the accounting acquiree must meet the definition of a business for the transaction to be accounted for as a reverse acquisition.

This restriction appears to exclude the following two circumstances from the scope of IFRS 3:

- a private entity reversing into a publicly-listed 'cash shell' (i.e. an entity with a public listing but with no ongoing activities); and

- a new entity becoming the new parent of an existing group through an exchange of equity instruments.

Under IFRS 3, such transactions should not be described as reverse acquisitions. An appropriate accounting policy may describe them as 'capital restructurings' or 'reverse asset acquisitions'. Such an accounting policy may result in consolidated financial statements that are similar to those produced under reverse acquisition accounting, except for the fact that no goodwill arises on such transactions. (See **4.4** for further guidance on the accounting for transactions that are not business combinations.)

12.2 Accounting for a reverse acquisition

12.2.1 Continuation of the financial statements of the legal subsidiary (accounting acquirer)

Consolidated financial statements prepared following a reverse acquisition are issued under the name of the legal parent (accounting acquiree) but described in the notes as a continuation of the financial statements of the legal subsidiary (accounting acquirer), with one adjustment, which is to adjust retroactively the accounting acquirer's legal capital to reflect the legal capital of the accounting acquiree. That adjustment is required to reflect the capital of the legal parent (the accounting acquiree). Comparative information presented in those consolidated financial statements also is retroactively adjusted to reflect the legal capital of the legal parent (accounting acquiree). [IFRS 3:B21]

Separate financial statements for the legal parent, if required, would be prepared on a stand-alone basis. When the entity was formed shortly before the combination, its separate financial statements should cover only its actual accounting period.

12.2.2 Detailed accounting entries

IFRS 3:B19 to B27 contain detailed guidance on the preparation of consolidated financial statements for a reverse acquisition. For understanding, this guidance is set out below as a comparison with a 'conventional' acquisition, (i.e. a business combination where the accounting acquirer and the legal acquirer are the same entity). The terminology used for a reverse acquisition is that the accounting acquirer is the legal subsidiary, and the accounting acquiree is the legal parent.

	Conventional acquisition	Reverse acquisition [IFRS 3:B19 to B27]
Consolidated financial statements issued	In the name of the legal parent.	In the name of the legal parent (with disclosure in the notes that they are a continuation of the financial statements of the legal subsidiary).
Consideration transferred	Fair value of consideration given by legal parent.	Fair value of the notional number of equity instruments that the legal subsidiary would have had to issue to the legal parent to give the owners of the legal parent the same percentage ownership in the combined entity.

	Conventional acquisition	Reverse acquisition [IFRS 3:B19 to B27]
Net assets of legal subsidiary	Recognised and measured in accordance with IFRS 3 – generally restated to fair value.	Not restated from pre-combination carrying amounts.
Net assets of legal parent	Not restated from pre-combination carrying amounts.	Recognised and measured in accordance with the requirements for acquirees under IFRS 3 – generally restated to fair value.
Goodwill/gain on bargain purchase	Consideration transferred less identified net assets of legal subsidiary.	Consideration transferred less identified net assets of legal parent.
Consolidated retained earnings and other equity balances at date of combination	Legal parent only.	Legal subsidiary only.
Consolidated equity instruments	Equity instruments of legal parent.	Issued equity instruments of legal subsidiary outstanding before the business combination plus the fair value of the legal parent.
Non-controlling interests in legal subsidiary	Non-controlling interest's proportionate share of legal subsidiary net assets, or at fair value.	Non-controlling interest's proportionate share of legal subsidiary net assets at pre-combination carrying amounts. No fair value option.
Comparative information	Legal parent only.	Legal subsidiary only, but retroactively adjusted to reflect the legal capital of the legal parent.
Earnings per share of current period	Earnings based on consolidated earnings. Weighted average number of shares reflects actual shares issued for legal subsidiary from date of acquisition.	Earnings based on consolidated earnings. Weighted average number of shares reflects legal subsidiary's weighted average pre-combination ordinary shares multiplied by the exchange ratio established in the acquisition, and the weighted average total actual shares of the legal parent in issue after the date of acquisition.

	Conventional acquisition	**Reverse acquisition [IFRS 3:B19 to B27]**
Earnings per share of comparative period	Acquirer only.	Earnings of legal subsidiary. Legal subsidiary's weighted average ordinary shares multiplied by exchange ratio established at acquisition.
Separate financial statements of legal parent	Legal parent.	Legal parent.

12.2.3 Presentation of equity and comparative information

Pre-combination net income and net assets are those of the legal subsidiary (accounting acquirer), and present no particular problems.

Pre-combination equity is, in theory, the pre-combination equity of the legal subsidiary but adjusted retroactively to reflect the legal capital of the legal parent. IFRS 3 describes the position at the date of combination as follows:

[IFRS 3:B22(c) & (d)]

- the consolidated financial statements reflect the retained earnings and other equity balances of the legal subsidiary (accounting acquirer) before the business combination; and

- the amount recognised as issued equity interests in the consolidated financial statements is determined by adding the issued equity interest of the legal subsidiary (the accounting acquirer) outstanding immediately before the business combination to the fair value of the legal parent (accounting acquiree). However, the equity structure (i.e. the number and type of equity interests issued) reflects the equity structure of the legal parent (the accounting acquiree), including the equity interests the legal parent issued to effect the combination. Accordingly, the equity structure of the legal subsidiary (the accounting acquirer) is restated using the exchange ratio established in the acquisition agreement to reflect the number of shares of the legal parent (the accounting acquiree) issued in the reverse acquisition.

Applying this guidance to periods before the combination:

- the total amount shown as equity is the total shown as equity in the legal subsidiary; and

- the amount shown as equity instruments (e.g. share capital) is the amount shown in the legal subsidiary adjusted by the exchange ratio. In the case of share capital with a fixed nominal value, the result may be higher or lower than the legal subsidiary's actual share capital pre-combination. The resulting adjustment is reflected as a reduction in, or addition to, equity reserves.

Example 12.2.3

Presentation of equity for an entity with share capital

The statements of financial position of Company A and Company B include the following amounts.

	Company A	Company B
	CU	CU
Share capital – CU1 nominal shares	100	300
Retained earnings	200	500
Net assets at carrying amount	300	800
Net assets at fair value	500	2,000
Fair value of whole business	5,000	25,000

On the date that the statements of financial position were drawn up, Company A issued 500 new shares in exchange for the entire share capital of Company B.

Because the owners of Company B obtain a 5/6ths share of the enlarged equity of Company A, Company B is identified as the acquirer. Because Company A issued 500 shares in itself in exchange for 300 shares in Company B, the exchange ratio is 5:3.

The consideration transferred would be CU5,000. This equals the fair value of 60 new shares in Company B, being the notional number that Company B would issue to give the shareholders of Company A 1/6th of the combined entity. It also represents the fair value of Company A as an entity.

	Date of combination	Pre-combination comparative
	CU	CU
Share capital – CU1 nominal	600	500
Other reserves	4,700	(200)
Issued equity instruments	5,300	300
Retained earnings	500	500
Total equity	5,800	800

Share capital at the date of combination is CU600, reflecting the actual Company A shares in issue. Share capital pre-combination is CU500, reflecting the issued shares of Company B (CU300) adjusted for the exchange ratio.

Issued equity instruments at the date of combination are the issued equity instruments of Company B (CU300) plus the consideration transferred (CU5,000). Issued equity instruments pre-combination are those of Company B (CU300).

Retained earnings at the date of combination, and pre-combination, are those of Company B (CU500).

The balance of other reserves pre-combination (CU200 debit) represents the capitalisation of reserves into share capital (500 shares in Company A issued in exchange for 300 shares in Company B).

Earnings per share would be based on the consolidated earnings (pre-combination earnings of Company B, and post-combination earnings of Company A + B). The weighted average number of shares would be based on 500 shares pre-combination (being the number of shares in Company A issued to shareholders of Company B) and 600 shares post-combination.

12.2.4 Worked examples of a reverse acquisition

Example 12.2.4A

Reverse acquisition

[IFRS 3:IE1 - IE15]

This example illustrates the accounting for a reverse acquisition in which Entity B, the legal subsidiary, acquires Entity A, the entity issuing equity instruments and therefore the legal parent, in a reverse acquisition on 30 September 20X6. This example ignores the accounting for any income tax effects.

The statements of financial position of Entity A and Entity B immediately before the business combination are:

	Entity A (legal parent, accounting acquiree)	Entity B (legal subsidiary, accounting acquirer)
	CU	CU
Current assets	500	700
Non-current assets	1,300	3,000
Total assets	1,800	3,700
Current liabilities	300	600
Non-current liabilities	400	1,100
Total liabilities	700	1,700
Shareholders' equity		
Retained earnings	800	1,400
Issued equity		
100 ordinary shares	300	
60 ordinary shares		600
Total shareholders' equity	1,100	2,000
Total liabilities and shareholders' equity	1,800	3,700

This example also uses the following information:

(a)   On 30 September 20X6 Entity A issues 2.5 shares in exchange for each ordinary share of Entity B. All of Entity B's shareholders exchange their shares in Entity B. Therefore, Entity A issues 150 ordinary shares in exchange for all 60 ordinary shares of Entity B.

(b)   The fair value of each ordinary share of Entity B at 30 September 20X6 is CU40. The quoted market price of Entity A's ordinary shares at that date is CU16.

(c)   The fair values of Entity A's identifiable assets and liabilities at 30 September 20X6 are the same as their carrying amounts, except that the fair value of Entity A's non-current assets at 30 September 20X6 is CU1,500.

Calculating the fair value of the consideration transferred

As a result of Entity A (legal parent, accounting acquiree) issuing 150 ordinary shares, Entity B's shareholders own 60 per cent of the issued shares of the combined entity (i.e. 150 of 250 issued shares). The remaining 40 per cent are owned by Entity A's shareholders. If the business combination had taken the form of Entity B issuing additional ordinary shares to Entity A's shareholders in exchange for their ordinary shares in Entity A, Entity B would have had to issue 40 shares for the ratio of ownership interest in the combined entity to be the same. Entity B's shareholders would then own 60 of the 100 issued shares of Entity B – 60 per cent of the combined entity. As a result, the fair value of the consideration effectively transferred by Entity B and the group's interest in Entity A is CU1,600 (40 shares with a fair value per share of CU40).

The fair value of the consideration effectively transferred should be based on the most reliable measure. In this example, the quoted price of Entity A's shares in the principal (or most advantageous) market for the shares provides a more reliable basis for measuring the consideration effectively transferred than the fair value of the shares in Entity B, and the consideration is measured using the market price of Entity A's shares – 100 shares with a fair value per share of CU16.

Measuring goodwill

Goodwill is measured as the excess of the fair value of the consideration effectively transferred (the group's interest in Entity A) over the net amount of Entity A's recognised identifiable assets and liabilities, as follows:

	CU	CU
Consideration effectively transferred		1,600
Net recognised values of Entity A's identifiable assets and liabilities		
Current assets	500	
Non-current assets	1,500	
Current liabilities	(300)	
Non-current liabilities	(400)	(1,300)
Goodwill		300

Consolidated statement of financial position at 30 September 20X6

The consolidated statement of financial position immediately after the business combination is:

	CU
Current assets [CU700 + CU500]	1,200
Non-current assets [CU3,000 + CU1,500]	4,500
Goodwill	300
Total assets	6,000
Current liabilities [CU600 + CU300]	900
Non-current liabilities [CU1,100 + CU400]	1,500
Total liabilities	2,400
Shareholders' equity	
Retained earnings	1,400
Issued equity	
250 ordinary shares [CU600 + CU1,600]	2,200
Total shareholders' equity	3,600
Total liabilities and shareholders' equity	6,000

The amount recognised as issued equity interests in the consolidated financial statements (CU2,200) is determined by adding the issued equity of the legal subsidiary immediately before the business combination (CU600) and the fair value of the consideration effectively transferred (CU1,600). However, the equity structure appearing in the consolidated financial statements (i.e. the number and type of equity interests issued) must reflect the equity structure of the legal parent, including the equity interests issued by the legal parent to effect the combination.

Earnings per share

Assume that Entity B's earnings for the annual period ended 31 December 20X5 were CU600 and that the consolidated earnings for the annual period ended 31 December 20X6 were CU800. Assume also that there was no change in the number of ordinary shares issued by Entity B during the annual period ended 31 December 20X5 and during the period from 1 January 20X6 to the date of the reverse acquisition on 30 September 20X6. Earnings per share for the annual period ended 31 December 20X6 is calculated as follows:

Number of shares deemed to be outstanding for the period from 1 January 20X6 to the acquisition date (i.e. the number of ordinary shares issued by Entity A (legal parent, accounting acquiree) in the reverse acquisition)	150
Number of shares outstanding from the acquisition date to 31 December 20X6	250
Weighted average number of ordinary shares outstanding [(150 9/12) + (250 3/12)]	175
Earnings per share [800/175]	CU4.57

Restated earnings per share for the annual period ended 31 December 20X5 is CU4.00 (calculated as the earnings of Entity B of 600 divided by the number of ordinary shares Entity A issued in the reverse acquisition (150)).

Example 12.2.4B

Reverse acquisition with a non-controlling interest

The facts are as in **example 12.2.4A**, except that there is a non-controlling interest because 10 per cent of the shareholders in Entity B did not take part in the exchange transaction. Their interest is limited to Entity B with no interest in the combined entity.

There is a 10 per cent non-controlling interest in Entity A's consolidated financial statements. The non-controlling interest should reflect the proportionate interest in the pre-combination carrying amounts of the legal subsidiary's net assets. Therefore, the non-controlling interest is 10 per cent of the pre-combination carrying amount of Entity B's net assets, i.e. CU200.

The existence of the non-controlling interest does not affect the fair value of the consideration that is effectively transferred as all of the shareholders of the legal parent participate in the exchange. Therefore, it does not form part of the goodwill calculation, because there is no non-controlling interest in the acquiree (Entity A) – rather, part of the equity of the acquirer (Entity B) is reclassified as non-controlling interest.

Accordingly, goodwill arising on the reverse acquisition is still calculated as follows.

	CU
Consideration transferred	1,600
Fair value of identifiable net assets	(1,300)
Goodwill	300

The amounts recognised within equity will be as follows.

Retained earnings

	CU
Previous balance	1,400
Less: reclassified to non-controlling interests (10% × 1,400)	(140)
Balance after acquisition	1,260

Issued equity

Previous balance	600
Less: reclassified to non-controlling interests (10% × 600)	(60)
Plus: fair value of consideration	1,600
Balance after acquisition	2,140

Non-controlling interests	
Reclassified from parent equity	200
Total shareholders' equity	3,600

13   Disclosure

13.1   Information to be disclosed regarding business combinations in the current period or after the reporting period

13.1.1   *General requirement to disclose information to enable users to evaluate the nature and effect of a business combination*

IFRS 3 requires that the acquirer should disclose information that enables users of its financial statements to evaluate the nature and financial effect of a business combination that occurs either:

[IFRS 3:59]

* during the current reporting period; or

* after the end of the reporting period but before the financial statements are authorised for issue.

Detailed guidance as to disclosures required to meet the objectives of IFRS 3:59 is set out in Appendix B to the Standard. These requirements are set out below, accompanied by extracts from the illustrative examples accompanying IFRS 3 which illustrate some of the requirements (not all of the requirements are illustrated).

If the specific disclosures set out below and those required by other IFRSs do not meet the objectives set out in IFRS 3:59, the acquirer should disclose whatever additional information is necessary to meet those objectives. [IFRS 3:63]

The disclosures are generally required for each business combination that occurs during the reporting period and after the end of the reporting period (see **13.1.13**). However, for individually immaterial business combinations occurring during the reporting period that are material collectively, the disclosures may be made in aggregate. [IFRS 3:B65]

For the purposes of the illustrative examples, AC (the acquirer) is assumed to be a listed entity and TC (the acquiree) is an unlisted entity.

13.1.2   Details of the business combination

The acquirer is required to disclose:

[IFRS 3:B64]

(a)   the name and a description of the acquiree;

(b)   the acquisition date;

(c)   the percentage of voting equity interests acquired; and

(d)   the primary reasons for the business combination and a description of how the acquirer obtained control of the acquiree.

Example 13.1.2

Details of the business combination

[Extract from IFRS 3:IE72]

On 30 June 20X0 AC acquired 15 per cent of the outstanding ordinary shares of TC. On 30 June 20X2 AC acquired 60 per cent of the outstanding ordinary shares of TC and obtained control of TC. TC is a provider of data networking products and services in Canada and Mexico. As a result of the acquisition, AC is expected to be the leading provider of data networking products and services in those markets. It also expects to reduce costs through economies of scale.

13.1.3   Details of goodwill

The acquirer is required to provide a qualitative description of the factors that make up the goodwill recognised, such as expected synergies from combining operations of the acquiree and the acquirer, intangible assets that do not qualify for separate recognition or other factors. [IFRS 3:B64(e)]

The acquirer is also required to disclose the total amount of goodwill that is expected to be deductible for tax purposes. [IFRS 3:B64(k)]

Example 13.1.3

Goodwill

[Extract from IFRS 3:IE72]

The goodwill of CU2,500 arising from the acquisition consists largely of the synergies and economies of scale expected from combining the operations of AC and TC.

None of the goodwill recognised is expected to be deductible for income tax purposes.

13.1.4 Fair value of consideration and details of contingent consideration

The acquirer is required to disclose the acquisition-date fair value of the total consideration transferred and the acquisition-date fair value of each major class of consideration, such as:

[IFRS 3:B64(f)]

- cash;

- other tangible or intangible assets, including a business or subsidiary of the acquirer;

- liabilities incurred (e.g. a liability for contingent consideration); and

- equity interests of the acquirer, including the number of instruments or interests issued or issuable and the method of measuring the fair value of those instruments or interests.

For contingent consideration arrangements and indemnification assets, the acquirer is required to disclose:

[IFRS 3:B64(g)]

- the amount recognised as of the acquisition date;

- a description of the arrangement and the basis for determining the amount of the payment; and

- an estimate of the range of outcomes (undiscounted) or, if a range cannot be estimated, that fact and the reasons why a range cannot be estimated. If the maximum amount of the payment is unlimited, the acquirer should disclose that fact.

Example 13.1.4

Fair value of consideration and details of contingent consideration

[Extract from IFRS 3:IE72]

At 30 June 20X2

Consideration	CU
Cash	5,000
Equity instruments (100,000 ordinary shares of AC)	4,000
Contingent consideration arrangement	1,000
Total consideration transferred	10,000

The fair value of the 100,000 ordinary shares issued as part of the consideration paid for TC (CU4,000) was measured using the closing market price of AC's ordinary shares on the acquisition date.

> The contingent consideration arrangement requires AC to pay the former owners of TC 5 per cent of the revenues of XC, an unconsolidated equity investment owned by TC, in excess of CU7,500 for 20X3, up to a maximum amount of CU2,500 (undiscounted).
>
> The potential undiscounted amount of all future payments that AC could be required to make under the contingent consideration arrangement is between CU0 and CU2,500.
>
> The fair value of the contingent consideration arrangement of CU1,000 was estimated by applying the income approach. The fair value measurement is based on significant inputs that are not observable in the market, which IFRS 13 *Fair Value Measurement* refers to as Level 3 inputs. Key assumptions include a discount rate range of 20–25 per cent and assumed probability-adjusted revenues in XC of CU10,000–20,000.

13.1.5   Details of acquired receivables

For acquired receivables, the acquirer is required to disclose:

[IFRS 3:B64(h)]

- the fair value of the receivables;

- the gross contractual amounts receivable; and

- the best estimate at the acquisition date of the contractual cash flows not expected to be collected.

These disclosures are required by major class of receivable, such as loans, direct finance leases and any other class of receivables.

> **Example 13.1.5**
>
> **Details of acquired receivables**
>
> [Extract from IFRS 3:IE72]
>
> The fair value of the financial assets acquired includes receivables under finance leases of data networking equipment with a fair value of CU2,375. The gross amount due under the contracts is CU3,100, of which CU450 is expected to be uncollectible.

13.1.6   Details of assets acquired and liabilities assumed

The acquirer is required to disclose the amounts recognised as of the acquisition date for each major class of assets acquired and liabilities assumed. [IFRS 3:B64(i)]

Example 13.1.6

Details of assets acquired and liabilities assumed

[Extract from IFRS 3:IE72]

Recognised amounts of identifiable assets acquired and liabilities assumed	CU
Financial assets	3,500
Inventory	1,000
Property, plant and equipment	10,000
Identifiable intangible assets	3,300
Financial liabilities	(4,000)
Contingent liability	(1,000)
Total identifiable net assets	12,800

13.1.7 Details of contingent liabilities recognised

For each contingent liability recognised in accordance with IFRS 3:23 (see **7.5.2**), the acquirer is required to disclose the information required in paragraph 85 of IAS 37 *Provisions, Contingent Liabilities and Contingent Assets*. [IFRS 3:B64(j)]

IAS 37 sets out the general disclosure requirements for provisions recognised under that Standard. The effect of IFRS 3:B64(j) is to require the same disclosures for contingent liabilities recognised in a business combination, as follows:

[IAS 37:85]

- a brief description of the nature of the obligation and the expected timing of any resulting outflow of economic benefits;

- an indication of the uncertainties about the amount or timing of those outflows. Where necessary to provide adequate information, the acquirer should disclose the major assumptions made concerning future events; and

- the amount of any expected reimbursement, stating the amount of any asset that has been recognised for that expected reimbursement.

Example 13.1.7

Details of contingent liabilities recognised

[Extract from IFRS 3:IE72]

A contingent liability of CU1,000 has been recognised for expected warranty claims on products sold by TC during the last three years. We expect that the majority of this expenditure will be incurred in 20X3 and that all will be incurred by the end of 20X4. The potential undiscounted amount of all future payments that AC could be required to make under the warranty arrangements is estimated to be between CU500 and CU1,500.

If a contingent liability is not recognised because its fair value cannot be measured reliably, the acquirer is required to disclose:

[IFRS 3:B64(j)]

- the information required by IAS 37:86 (see below); and

- the reasons why the liability cannot be measured reliably.

IAS 37 sets out the general disclosure requirements for contingent liabilities, as follows:

[IAS 37:86]

- a brief description of the nature of the contingent liability; and

- when practicable:

  - an estimate of the financial effect;

  - an indication of the uncertainties relating to the amount or timing of any outflow; and

  - the possibility of any reimbursement.

13.1.8 Details of transactions recognised separately

For transactions that are recognised separately from the acquisition of assets and assumption of liabilities in the business combination in accordance with IFRS 3:51 (see **8.3**), the acquirer is required to disclose:

[IFRS 3:B64(l)]

- a description of each transaction;

- how the acquirer accounted for each transaction;

- the amounts recognised for each transaction and the line item in the financial statements in which each amount is recognised; and

- if the transaction is the effective settlement of a pre-existing relationship, the method used to determine the settlement amount.

The disclosure of separately-recognised transactions required by IFRS 3:B64(l) should include the amount of acquisition-related costs and, separately, the amount of those costs recognised as an expense and the line item or items in the statement of comprehensive income in which those expenses are recognised. The amount of any issue costs not recognised as an expense and how they were recognised should also be disclosed. [IFRS 3:B64(m)]

Example 13.1.8

Details of transactions recognised separately

[Extract from IFRS 3:IE72]

Acquisition-related costs (included in selling, general and administrative expenses in AC's statement of comprehensive income for the year ended 31 December 20X2) amounted to CU1,250.

13.1.9   Details of bargain purchases

In respect of a bargain purchase (see **9.3**), the acquirer is required to disclose:

[IFRS 3:B64(n)]

(i)   the amount of any gain recognised in accordance with IFRS 3:34 and the line item in the statement of comprehensive income in which the gain is recognised; and

(ii)   a description of the reasons why the transaction resulted in a gain.

IFRS 3 does not specify that the amount of the gain recognised must be shown as a separate line item. It could be shown as part of 'other gains and losses'. However, the requirements of IFRS 3:B64(n) ensure that the amount is separately disclosed in the notes.

13.1.10   Details of non-controlling interests

For each business combination in which the acquirer holds less than 100 per cent of the equity interests in the acquiree at the acquisition date, the acquirer is required to disclose:

[IFRS 3:B64(o)]

(i)   the amount of the non-controlling interest in the acquiree recognised at the acquisition date and the measurement basis for that amount; and

(ii)   for each non-controlling interest in an acquiree measured at fair value, the valuation techniques and significant inputs used to measure that value.

Example 13.1.10

Details of non-controlling interests

[Extract from IFRS 3:IE72]

The fair value of the non-controlling interest in TC, an unlisted company, was estimated by applying a market approach and an income approach. The fair value measurements are based on significant inputs that are not observable in the market and thus represent a fair value measurement categorised within Level 3 of the fair value hierarchy as described in IFRS 13. Key assumptions include the following:

(a)   a discount rate range of 20–25 per cent;

(b)   a terminal value based on a range of terminal EBITDA multiples between 3 and 5 times (or, if appropriate, based on long term sustainable growth rates ranging from 3 to 6 per cent);

(c)   financial multiples of companies deemed to be similar to TC; and

(d)   adjustments because of the lack of control or lack of marketability that market participants would consider when measuring the fair value of the non-controlling interest in TC.

13.1.11   Business combinations achieved in stages

In a business combination achieved in stages, the acquirer is required to disclose:

[IFRS 3:B64(p)]

- the acquisition-date fair value of the equity interest in the acquiree held by the acquirer immediately before the acquisition date; and

- the amount of any gain or loss recognised as a result of remeasuring to fair value the equity interest in the acquiree held by the acquirer before the business combination and the line item in the statement of comprehensive income in which that gain or loss is recognised.

The intended scope of the second bullet point is not completely clear. It will certainly capture gains or losses that arise if the previous equity interest was not recognised at fair value (e.g. an interest in an associate to which the equity method has been applied). But it would appear appropriate also to disclose any gain or loss in respect of the previous equity interest that is reclassified from equity to profit or loss (e.g. because the investment was classified as an available-for-sale financial asset under IAS 39 *Financial Instruments: Recognition and Measurement*).

Example 13.1.11

Business combination achieved in stages

[Extract from IFRS 3:IE72]

The fair value of AC's equity interest in TC held before the business combination amounted to CU2,000. AC recognised a gain of CU500 as a result of measuring at fair value its 15 per cent equity interest in TC held before the business combination. The gain is included in other income in AC's statement of comprehensive income for the year ending 31 December 20X2.

13.1.12 *Impact of acquiree on amounts reported in the statement of comprehensive income*

The acquirer is required to disclose the following information:

[IFRS 3:B64(q)]

(i) the amounts of revenue and profit or loss of the acquiree since the acquisition date included in the consolidated statement of comprehensive income for the reporting period; and

(II) the revenue and profit or loss of the combined entity for the current reporting period as though the acquisition date for all business combinations that occurred during the year had been as of the beginning of the annual reporting period.

IFRS 3 provides no guidance on how revenue and profit or loss in the second bullet point should be calculated and, in particular, whether this should be a simple aggregation of results or whether adjustments should be made, for example to align accounting policies. Entities should devise a practical approach to this disclosure requirement which provides meaningful information and apply that consistently. The nature of any adjustments should be explained clearly.

Adjustments which may be considered for the purpose of the requirement of IFRS 3:B64(q)(ii) include:

* alignment of accounting policies;

* the impact of fair value adjustments as if they had occurred at the beginning of the reporting period;

* elimination of trading between the group and the acquiree prior to the acquisition date; and

* the impact on finance charges of incurring borrowings to finance the acquisition at the start of the reporting period.

Adjustments that are unlikely to be appropriate include:

- backdating of synergistic benefits arising from the acquisition; and

- backdating of hedging strategies put in place post acquisition.

If disclosure of any of the information required by IFRS 3:B64(q) is impracticable, the acquirer should disclose that fact and explain why the disclosure is impracticable. IFRS 3 uses the term 'impracticable' with the same meaning as in IAS 8 *Accounting Policies, Changes in Accounting Estimates and Errors* (see **chapter A5**). [IFRS 3:B64(q)]

Example 13.1.12

Impact of acquiree on amounts reported in the statement of comprehensive income

[Extract from IFRS 3:IE72]

The revenue included in the consolidated statement of comprehensive income since 30 June 20X2 contributed by TC was CU4,090. TC also contributed profit of CU1,710 over the same period. Had TC been consolidated from 1 January 20X2, the consolidated statement of comprehensive income would have included revenue of CU27,670 and profit of CU12,870.

13.1.13 Business combinations after the reporting period

If the acquisition date of a business combination is after the end of the reporting period but before the financial statements are authorised for issue, the disclosures set out in **13.1.2** to **13.1.12** are required unless the initial accounting for the business combination is incomplete at the time the financial statements are authorised for issue. [IFRS 3:B66]

In that situation, the acquirer should describe which disclosures could not be made and the reasons why they cannot be made. [IFRS 3:B66]

13.2 Adjustments recognised for business combinations that occurred in the current or previous reporting periods

13.2.1 General requirement to disclose information to enable users to evaluate the effect of adjustments recognised in the period

The acquirer is required to disclose information that enables users of its financial statements to evaluate the financial effects of adjustments recognised in the current reporting period that relate to business combinations that occurred in the current or previous reporting periods. [IFRS 3:61]

If the specific disclosures set out below and those required by other IFRSs do not meet the objectives set out in IFRS 3:61, the acquirer should disclose whatever additional information is necessary to meet those objectives. [IFRS 3:63]

The information should be disclosed separately for each material business combination or in the aggregate for individually immaterial business combinations that are material collectively. [IFRS 3:B67]

13.2.2 Business combinations for which the initial accounting is incomplete

If the initial accounting for a business combination is incomplete (see **10.1.1**), and the amounts recognised in the financial statements for the business combination thus have been determined only provisionally, the following information should be disclosed for particular assets, liabilities, non-controlling interests or items of consideration:

[IFRS 3:B67(a)]

- the reasons why the initial accounting for the business combination is incomplete;

- the assets, liabilities, equity interests or items of consideration for which the initial accounting is incomplete; and

- the nature and amount of any measurement period adjustments recognised during the reporting period in accordance with IFRS 3:49 (see **10.1.4**).

Example 13.2.2

Business combinations for which the initial accounting is incomplete

[Extract from IFRS 3:IE72]

The fair value of the acquired identifiable intangible assets of CU3,300 is provisional pending receipt of the final valuations for those assets.

13.2.3 Contingent assets and contingent liabilities

For each reporting period after the acquisition date until the entity collects, sells or otherwise loses the right to a contingent consideration asset, or until the entity settles a contingent consideration liability or the liability is cancelled or expires, the acquirer should disclose:

[IFRS 3:B67(b)]

- any changes in the recognised amounts, including any differences arising upon settlement;

- any changes in the range of outcomes (undiscounted) and the reasons for those changes; and

- the valuation techniques and key model inputs used to measure contingent consideration.

For contingent liabilities recognised in a business combination, the acquirer should disclose the information required by IAS 37:84 and 85 for each class of provision. [IFRS 3:B67(c)]

The requirements of IAS 37:85 are set out at **13.1.7**. IAS 37:84 requires the following to be disclosed for each class of provision (and, in these circumstances, each class of recognised contingent liability):

- the carrying amount at the beginning and end of the period;

- additional contingent liabilities recognised in the period, including increases to existing contingent liabilities;

- amounts used (i.e. incurred and charged against the contingent liability) during the period;

- unused amounts reversed in the period; and

- the increase during the period in the discounted amount arising from the passage of time and the effect of any change in the discount rate.

13.2.4   *Goodwill*

The acquirer is required to disclose a reconciliation of the carrying amount of goodwill at the beginning and end of the reporting period, showing separately:

[IFRS 3:B67(d)]

- the gross amount and accumulated impairment losses at the beginning of the reporting period;

- additional goodwill recognised during the reporting period, except goodwill included in a disposal group that, on acquisition, meets the criteria to be classified as held for sale in accordance with IFRS 5 *Non-current Assets Held for Sale and Discontinued Operations* (see **chapter A20**);

- adjustments resulting from the subsequent recognition of deferred tax assets during the reporting period in accordance with IFRS 3:67. IFRS 3:67 applies only to business combinations for which the acquisition date was before the entity applied IFRS 3 (as revised in 2008) for the first time;

- goodwill included in a disposal group classified as held for sale in accordance with IFRS 5 and goodwill derecognised during the reporting period without having previously been included in a disposal group classified as held for sale;

- impairment losses recognised during the reporting period in accordance with IAS 36 *Impairment of Assets*. (IAS 36 requires disclosure of information about the recoverable amount and impairment of goodwill in addition to this requirement – see **section 11** of **chapter A10**);

- net exchange rate differences arising during the reporting period in accordance with IAS 21 *The Effects of Changes in Foreign Exchange Rates*;

- any other changes in the carrying amount during the reporting period; and

- the gross amount and accumulated impairment losses at the end of the reporting period.

13.2.5   Material gains and losses recognised in the period

The acquirer is required to disclose the amount and an explanation of any gain or loss recognised in the current reporting period that both:

[IFRS 3:B67(e)]

- relates to the identifiable assets acquired or liabilities assumed in a business combination that was effected in the current or previous reporting period; and

- is of such a size, nature or incidence that disclosure is relevant to understanding the combined entity's financial statements.

14   Future developments

14.1   Research projects arising from post-implementation review

In June 2015, the IASB announced the completion of its post-implementation review of IFRS 3. The IASB concluded that there was general support for the accounting requirements in the Standard but has identified some areas where further research will be undertaken. Two research projects have been added to the IASB agenda that will focus on:

- effectiveness and complexity of testing goodwill for impairment;

- subsequent accounting for goodwill;

- challenges relating to the application of the definition of a business; and

- identification and fair value measurement of intangible assets such as customer relationships and brand names.

14.2   Definition of a business and accounting for previously held Interests

In June 2016, the IASB issued ED/2016/1 *Definition of a Business and Accounting for Previously Held Interests*. The exposure draft proposes:

- clearer application guidance to help distinguish between a business and a group of assets when applying IFRS 3 (see below); and

- to clarify that when an entity obtains control of a business that is a joint operation, the entity applies the requirements for a business combination achieved in stages (see **section 11**), including remeasuring previously held interests in the assets and liabilities of the joint operation to fair value.

To help entities distinguish between a business and a group of assets, the Board proposes:

- to clarify that to be considered a business, an acquired set of activities and assets must include, at a minimum, an input and a substantive process that together have the ability to contribute to the creation of outputs;

- to remove the statement that a set of activities and assets is a business if market participants can replace the missing elements and continue to produce outputs;

- to revise the definition of outputs to focus on goods and services provided to customers and to remove the reference to the ability to reduce costs;

- to consider a set of activities and assets not to be a business if, at the transaction date, substantially all of the fair value of the gross assets acquired (that is, the identifiable assets and unidentifiable assets acquired) is concentrated in a single identifiable asset or group of similar identifiable assets;

- to add guidance to help determine whether a substantive process has been acquired;

- to add examples to help with the interpretation of what is considered a business; and

- that an entity would not be required to apply the proposed amendments to transactions that occur before the effective date of the amendments.

Comments on the exposure draft are requested by 31 October 2016.

A26 Investments in associates and joint ventures

Contents

1 Introduction

1.1 Overview of IAS 28

IAS 28 *Investments in Associates and Joint Ventures* outlines how to apply, with specified limited exceptions, the equity method to investments in associates and joint ventures. The Standard also defines an associate by reference to the concept of 'significant influence', which requires power to participate in financial and operating policy decisions of an investee (but not joint control or control of those policies).

1.2 Amendments to IAS 28 since the last edition of this manual

IAS 28 was most recently amended in December 2015. The effect of the December 2015 amendments is to defer indefinitely the effective date of earlier amendments to IAS 28 issued in September 2014 arising from *Sale or Contribution of Assets between an Investor and its Associate or Joint Venture (Amendments to IFRS 10 and IAS 28)* (see **4.4.14.1** and **4.4.14.8**).

2 Scope

IAS 28 is required to be applied by all entities that are investors with joint control of, or significant influence over, an investee. [IAS 28:2]

An associate is an entity over which the investor has significant influence. [IAS 28:3] The concepts of joint control and significant influence are discussed in **chapter A27** and **section 3**, respectively.

3 Significant influence

3.1 Significant influence – definition

Significant influence is the power to participate in the financial and operating policy decisions of the investee, but is not control or joint control of those policies. [IAS 28:3]

Financial and operating policies are not defined in IAS 28. Operating policies generally would include those policies that guide activities such as sales, marketing, manufacturing, human resources, and acquisitions and disposals of investments. Financial policies generally would be those policies that guide accounting policies, budget approvals, credit terms, dividend policies, issuance of debt, cash management and capital expenditures.

The concepts of control and joint control are discussed in **chapters A24** and **A27**, respectively.

3.2   Indicators of significant influence

When an entity exercises significant influence over an investee, one or more of the following indicators is usually present:

[IAS 28:6]

- representation on the board of directors or equivalent governing body of the investee;
- participation in policy-making processes, including participation in decisions about dividends or other distributions;
- material transactions between the entity and the investee;
- interchange of managerial personnel; or
- provision of essential technical information.

3.3   Holding 20 per cent or more of voting power

As a general rule, significant influence is presumed to exist when an entity holds, directly or indirectly through subsidiaries, 20 per cent or more of the voting power of an investee. [IAS 28:5]

> This presumption relates to voting rights, which can arise in relation to interests other than an ordinary shareholding. For example, when 50 per cent of the voting rights in an entity are held by the ordinary shareholders, and the other 50 per cent of the voting rights are attached to voting preferred shares, an investment in four per cent of the ordinary shares and 36 per cent of the voting preferred shares will result in a presumption that the four per cent ordinary share ownership will be accounted for using the equity method, provided that the voting preferred share investment is substantively the same as an investment in ordinary shares.
>
> See **3.6** for a discussion of circumstances in which a preferred share investment may be considered to be substantively the same as an ordinary share investment.

As with the classification of any investment, the substance of the arrangements in each case will need to be considered. If it can be clearly demonstrated that an entity holding 20 per cent or more of the voting power of the investee does not have significant influence, the investment will not be accounted for as an associate. [IAS 28:5]

> The following circumstances may call into question whether an entity has the ability to exercise significant influence. This list is not exhaustive, and all facts and circumstances need to be assessed carefully.

- The chairman of the investee owns a large, but not necessarily controlling, block of the investee's outstanding shares. The combination of his substantial shareholding and his position within the investee may preclude the entity from having an ability to influence the investee.

- Adverse political and economic conditions exist in the foreign country where the investee is located.

- Opposition by the investee to the investor (e.g. litigation or complaints to governmental regulatory authorities) challenges the entity's ability to exercise significant influence.

- The entity and the investee sign an agreement under which the entity surrenders significant rights as shareholder.

- Majority ownership of the investee is concentrated among a small group of shareholders who operate the investee without regard to the views of the entity.

- Litigation against an investee, particularly when the investee is in bankruptcy, is to be settled by the investee issuing shares to the settling parties, and it is probable that the new shares, when issued, will reduce the entity's ownership percentage.

- Severe long-term restrictions impair the entity's ability to repatriate funds.*

* Prior to 2003, IAS 28 included an exemption from applying the equity method to an associate operating under severe long-term restrictions that impaired the investor's ability to repatriate funds. In 2003, as part of its improvements project, the IASB removed this exemption, implying that while in some cases severe long-term restrictions on the ability to repatriate funds may affect the investor's ability to exercise significant influence, in other cases it will not and judgement should be applied on the basis of individual facts and circumstances.

A substantial or majority ownership by another investor does not necessarily preclude an investor from having significant influence. [IAS 28:5]

Even when another party has control, it is still possible that a reporting entity may have significant influence (e.g. when it has a right to input into the board decision-making process). There is also no upper limit to the size of the holding that may be associated with significant influence. For example, an entity may have significant influence and more than 50 per cent of the shares in another entity, but a third party may have control of that other entity (e.g. as a result of potential voting rights – see also **3.5**).

3.4   Holding less than 20 per cent of voting power

If an entity holds, directly or indirectly through subsidiaries, less than 20 per cent of the voting power of an investee, it is presumed that the entity does not have significant influence, unless such influence can be clearly demonstrated. [IAS 28:5] The presence of one or more of the indicators set out at **3.2** may indicate that an entity exercises significant influence over a less than 20 per cent-owned investee.

Decisions regarding the appropriateness of applying the equity method for a less than 20 per cent-owned investee require careful evaluation of voting rights and their impact on the entity's ability to exercise significant influence.

In addition to the indicators set out at **3.2**, the following circumstances may indicate significant influence:

*   the extent of the entity's ownership is significant relative to other shareholdings (i.e. a lack of concentration of other shareholders);

*   the entity's significant shareholders, its parent, fellow subsidiaries, or officers of the entity, hold additional investments in the investee; and

*   the entity is a member of significant investee committees, such as the executive committee or the finance committee.

IAS 28:7 states that the existence and effect of potential voting rights that are currently exercisable or currently convertible should also be considered when assessing whether an entity has significant influence – see **3.5**.

Example 3.4

Significant influence in a group scenario

Company A has two subsidiaries, Company B and Company C. Company B has a 15 per cent ownership interest in Company C. The group structure is as follows.

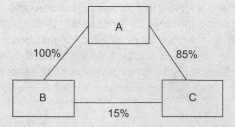

Company A has appointed an executive of Company B as a director to the board of Company C. Because of the number of directors on the board, this director is able to influence significantly Company C's board. Company A has the right to remove the executive from the board at any time. Company B has also been directed by Company A to manage Company C in a way that maximises the return from both Company B and Company C, which are located in the same jurisdiction. Company A can amend this directive at any time.

Note that Company B has not chosen to apply the equity method exemption in IAS 28:17. Also, Company A and Company B have no further agreements regarding Company C's financial and operating policy decisions.

Does Company B have significant influence over Company C so that Company C is an associate of Company B?

No. IAS 28:5 indicates that "[a] substantial or majority ownership by another investor does not necessarily preclude an entity from having significant influence". In this scenario, however, Company B does not have significant influence over Company C. Although Company B can participate in policy-making decisions, Company A can remove Company B's executive from Company C's board at any time. Therefore, Company B's apparent position of significant influence over Company C can be removed by Company A and Company B does not have the power to exercise significant influence over Company C.

3.5 Potential voting rights

Potential voting rights can arise through share warrants, share call options, debt or equity instruments that are convertible into ordinary shares, or similar instruments that have the potential, if exercised or converted, to give the holder additional voting power or reduce another party's voting power over the financial and operating policies of another entity. When an investor owns such instruments, the existence and effect of potential voting rights that are currently exercisable or currently convertible are considered when assessing whether the investor has significant influence over that other entity. Potential voting rights are not currently exercisable or convertible when, for example, they cannot be exercised or converted until a future date or until the occurrence of a future event. [IAS 28:7]

Note that there are differences between the requirements in IAS 28:7 and the equivalent requirements in paragraph B24 of IFRS 10 *Consolidated Financial Statements* regarding potential voting rights. Under IFRS 10, potential voting rights that are not currently exercisable are taken into account in limited circumstances (see **6.4.4.5** in **chapter A24**). In developing the requirements for IAS 28 (as revised in 2011), the IASB considered whether equivalent amendments should be made regarding the determination of significant influence, but decided that it would not be appropriate to change one element of significant influence in isolation. Consequently, the requirements of IAS 28 are unchanged in this regard and potential voting rights (including those held by other entities) are only taken into account when they are currently exercisable. [IAS 28:7, BC15 & BC16]

The investor needs to consider the potential voting rights held by other parties in addition to those it holds itself. Although the investor may believe, after considering the impact of its own potential voting rights, that it exercises significant influence, that impact may be negated by other potential voting rights held by other parties that are also currently exercisable or currently convertible.

In assessing whether potential voting rights contribute to significant influence, the investor examines all facts and circumstances that affect the potential rights, such as the terms of exercise of the instruments and any other contractual arrangements. IAS 28 requires that all of these factors be taken into account – but excludes consideration of the intentions of management and the financial ability to exercise or convert. [IAS 28:8]

Example 3.5

Options to purchase investments in an entity

Company A holds a 15 per cent voting ordinary share interest in Company B, as well as a European call option (i.e. one that can only be exercised at the end of the option period) to acquire an additional 10 per cent voting ordinary share interest in Company B. The call option matures in three years. Company A's ownership of the call option which, if converted, would give Company A a 25 per cent voting interest in Company B, does not create the presumption that Company A currently exercises significant influence over Company B, because the call option is not currently exercisable.

However, if, instead of a European call option, Company A held an American call option (i.e. one that can be exercised at any time during the option period), Company A may effectively exert significant influence over Company B because the call option would be currently exercisable.

3.6   Investment in preferred shares that is substantively the same as in ordinary shares

When an investment in preferred shares is determined to be substantively the same as an investment in ordinary shares, the investment may give the investor significant influence, in which case the investment should be accounted for using the equity method. Factors that either individually or collectively may indicate that a preferred share investment is substantively the same as an ordinary share investment include:

- the investee has little or no significant ordinary shares or other equity, on a fair value basis, that is subordinate to the preferred shares;

- the investor, regardless of ownership percentage, has demonstrated the power to exercise significant influence over the investee's operating and financial decisions. The power to participate actively is an important factor in determining whether an equity interest exists by virtue of preferred shareholdings;

- the investee's preferred shares have essentially the same rights and characteristics as the investee's ordinary shares as regards voting rights, board representation, and participation in, or rate of return approximating, the ordinary share dividend; and

- the preferred shares have a conversion feature (with significant value in relation to the total value of the shares) to convert the preferred shares to ordinary shares.

3.7 Long-term interests that in substance form part of the investor's net investment in an associate or a joint venture

An investor may have a variety of interests in an associate or a joint venture, both long-term and short-term, including ordinary or preferred shares, loans, advances, debt securities, options to acquire ordinary shares, and trade receivables. For the purposes of IAS 28:38, which considers the extent to which losses of an associate or a joint venture should be recognised (see **4.4.16**), the investor's interest in the associate or joint venture is the carrying amount of the investment in the associate or joint venture under the equity method together with any long-term interests that, in substance, form part of the investor's net investment in the associate or joint venture. [IAS 28:38]

For example, an item for which settlement is neither planned nor likely to occur in the foreseeable future is, in substance, an extension of the entity's investment in that associate or joint venture. Such items may include preference shares and long-terms receivables or loans. Items such as trade receivables, trade payables and any long-term receivables for which adequate collateral exists, such as secured loans, will not be treated as part of the investor's interest in an associate or a joint venture for this purpose. [IAS 28:38]

The implication of IAS 28:38 is that only ordinary shares (and other shares that are substantively the same as ordinary shares) will be presented as part of the carrying amount of the investment in the associate under the equity method. Other long-term interests that, in substance, form part of the investor's net investment in the associate, will be taken into account in recognising losses, but will nevertheless be presented separately from the carrying amount of the investment in the associate under the equity method.

Example 3.7

Long-term loan to an equity-method investee

An entity grants a long-term interest-free loan to one of its equity-method investees. The loan has no fixed repayment terms and settlement of the loan is neither planned nor likely to occur in the foreseeable future.

From the standpoint of the investee, the investee has a contractual obligation to deliver cash or another financial asset to the investor. Accordingly, the loan payable will be classified as a financial liability within the scope of IFRS 9 *Financial Instruments* (or, for entities that have not yet adopted IFRS 9, IAS 39 *Financial Instruments: Recognition and Measurement*) because it does not meet the definition of equity.

While the investor has a contractual right to receive cash or another financial asset from the investee, the investor views the loan as part of the net investment in the investee because, in accordance with IAS 28:38, the settlement of the loan is neither planned nor likely to occur in the foreseeable future.

In the investor's financial statements (both consolidated and, if applicable, separate), the interest-free loan is classified and measured in accordance with IFRS 9 (or, for entities that have not yet adopted IFRS 9, IAS 39).

IAS 28 determines whether the long-term interest-free loan can be viewed as part of the interest in the investee when accounting for losses of the investee in accordance with IAS 28:38), which states, in part, as follows.

> "The interest in an associate or a joint venture is the carrying amount of the investment in the associate or joint venture determined using the equity method together with any long-term interests that, in substance, form part of the investor's net investment in the associate or joint venture."

For the purpose of accounting for losses of an investee, the loan would form part of the investor's net investment in the investee because its settlement is neither planned nor likely to occur in the foreseeable future (see **example 4.4.16**).

3.8 Ceasing to have significant influence

Significant influence over an investee is lost when the investor loses the power to participate in the financial and operating policy decisions of that investee. The loss of significant influence can occur with or without a change in absolute or relative ownership levels. It could occur, for example, when an associate becomes subject to the control of a government, court, administrator or regulator. It could also occur as a result of a contractual agreement. [IAS 28:9]

4 The equity method

4.1 Associates and joint ventures generally accounted for using the equity method

An entity with significant influence over, or joint control of, an investee should account for its investment in an associate or a joint venture using the equity method except when the investment qualifies for exemption (see **4.2**). [IAS 28:16]

IAS 28 defines the equity method as a method of accounting whereby the investment is initially recognised at cost and adjusted thereafter for the post-acquisition change in the investor's share of net assets of the investee. The profit or loss of the investor includes the investor's share of the profit or loss of the investee, and the investor's other comprehensive income includes its share of the investee's other comprehensive income. [IAS 28:3]

Many of the procedures that are appropriate for the application of the equity method are similar to the consolidation procedures described in IFRS 10 *Consolidated Financial Statements*. Furthermore, the concepts underlying the procedures used in accounting for the acquisition of a subsidiary are also adopted in accounting for the acquisition of an investment in an associate or a joint venture. [IAS 28:26]

IAS 28 justifies the use of the equity method by noting that the recognition of income on the basis of distributions received may not be an adequate measure of the income earned by an investor on an investment in an associate or a joint venture because the distributions received may bear little relation to the performance of the associate or joint venture. Because the investor has significant influence over, or joint control of, the investee, the investor has an interest in the associate's or joint venture's performance and, as a result, the return on its investment. It is therefore appropriate for the investor to account for this interest by extending the scope of its financial statements to include its share of the profit or loss of such an investee. As a result, application of the equity method provides more informative reporting of the investor's net assets and profit or loss. [IAS 28:11]

The equity method is used whether or not the investor, because it also has subsidiaries, prepares consolidated financial statements (subject to the exemptions discussed at **4.2**).

4.2 Exemptions from applying the equity method

4.2.1 Exemption available to certain subsidiaries

An entity need not apply the equity method to its investment in an associate or a joint venture if:

[IAS 28:17]

- the entity is a parent that is exempt from preparing consolidated financial statements under IFRS 10:4(a) (see **3.3** in **chapter A24**); or
- all of the following apply:
  - the entity is a wholly-owned subsidiary, or is a partially-owned subsidiary of another entity and its other owners, including those not otherwise entitled to vote, have been informed about, and do not object to, the investor not applying the equity method;
  - the entity's debt or equity instruments are not traded in a public market (i.e. a domestic or foreign stock exchange or an over-the-counter market, including local and regional markets);
  - the entity did not file, nor is it in the process of filing, its financial statements with a securities commission or other regulatory organisation for the purpose of issuing any class of instruments in a public market; and
  - the ultimate or any intermediate parent of the entity produces financial statements available for public use that comply with IFRSs, in which subsidiaries are consolidated or are measured at fair value through profit or loss in accordance with IFRS 10.

Accordingly, exemption from use of the equity method is available to:

- parents exempt from preparing consolidated financial statements under IFRS 10:4(a); and
- those entities that did not have subsidiaries during the period but would have qualified for exemption from preparing consolidated financial statements if they had.

The criteria in IAS 28:17 were amended by *Investment Entities: Applying the Consolidation Exemption (Amendments to IFRS 10, IFRS 12 and IAS 28)*, issued in December 2014 and effective for annual periods beginning on or after 1 January 2016, with earlier application permitted. If an entity applies the December amendments for a period beginning before 1 January 2016, it is required to disclose that fact. [IAS 28:45D]

The December 2014 amendments bring IAS 28's exemption from use of the equity method in line with the updated exemption from consolidation (see **3.3** in **chapter A24**), which is available to a parent entity that is a subsidiary of an investment entity even if the investment entity measures all of its subsidiaries at fair value.

The criteria in IAS 28:17 are only met if the ultimate or any intermediate parent produces financial statements available for public use that comply with IFRSs as issued by the IASB. If the parent complies instead with a modified version of IFRSs (e.g. IFRSs as endorsed for use in a particular jurisdiction) but does not comply with full IFRSs as issued by the IASB (because it applies some accounting that is allowed under the modified version of IFRSs but not under IFRSs as issued by the IASB), the above criteria are not met.

Similarly, if the parent complies with the *International Financial Reporting Standard for Small and Medium-sized Entities* (see **appendix A6**), but not full IFRSs, the above criteria are not met.

4.2.2 Exemption available to venture capital organisations and similar entities

4.2.2.1 Venture capital organisations and similar entities permitted to measure investments in associates and joint ventures at fair value through profit or loss

When an investment in an associate or a joint venture is held by, or is held indirectly through, an entity that is a venture capital organisation, or a mutual fund, unit trust and similar entities including investment-linked insurance funds, the entity may elect to measure investments in those associates and joint ventures at fair value through profit or loss in accordance with IFRS 9 *Financial Instruments* (or, for entities that have not yet adopted IFRS 9, IAS 39 *Financial Instruments: Recognition and Measurement*). [IAS 28:18]

For entities that have not yet adopted IFRS 9, this measurement exemption should be taken to refer to investments that at initial recognition are designated as at fair value through profit or loss or are classified as held for trading and accounted for in accordance with IAS 39. When the exemption is taken, such investments should be measured at fair value, with changes in fair value recognised in profit or loss in the period of change.

Note that, in order to meet the definition of an investment entity under paragraph 27 of IFRS 10 *Consolidated Financial Statements*, an entity will need to select the exemption from applying the equity method in IAS 28:18 (see **13.2.5** in **chapter A24** for further discussion).

4.2.2.2 Meaning of 'venture capital organisation'

IAS 28 provides no guidance on the term 'venture capital organisation'. In deciding whether the exemption is available, it will be necessary to consider whether an organisation (whether structured as a legal entity or not) has the characteristics of a venture capital organisation. Such characteristics may include, but are not limited to:

- investments are held for the short- to medium-term rather than for the long-term;

- the most appropriate point for exit is actively monitored; and

- investments form part of a portfolio, which is monitored and managed without distinguishing between investments that qualify as associates or joint ventures and those that do not.

4.2.2.3   Exemption available on an investment-by-investment basis

Qualifying entities are permitted to select the exemption available under IAS 28:18 on an investment-by-investment basis, i.e. some associates and/or joint ventures may be accounted for at fair value and others may be accounted for using the equity method. The accounting policy choice should be made upon recognition of an investment in an associate or a joint venture and should be applied consistently from one period to the next.

Although the ability to make this election on an investment-by-investment basis is not explicitly stated in the current version of IAS 28, the IASB has issued proposals for amendments to IAS 28:18 to clarify this point (see **section 7**).

4.2.2.4   Consolidated financial statements of the parent of a venture capital organisation

Example 4.2.2.4

Consolidated financial statements of the parent of a venture capital organisation

Company P, which is not a venture capital organisation, is a parent entity in a group that has an 80 per cent ownership in a subsidiary, Company S. Company S has a 40 per cent ownership in an associate, Company A. Company S is a venture capital organisation and has elected under IAS 28:18 to account for its interest in the associate at fair value through profit or loss in accordance with IFRS 9 (or, for entities that have not yet adopted IFRS 9, IAS 39).

The accounting treatment applied by Company S under IAS 28:18 can be applied in Company P's consolidated financial statements because the exemption is available when an investment in an associate or a joint venture is held either (1) directly by a venture capital organisation, or (2) indirectly through a venture capital organisation.

As a result, Company P has a choice either to carry the associate at fair value under IFRS 9 (or, for entities that have not yet adopted IFRS 9, IAS 39) or to apply the equity method in its consolidated financial statements.

Note that the same conclusion would be reached in this example if Company A were a joint venture of Company S instead of an associate.

4.2.2.5   Investment in an associate partly held through a venture capital organisation or similar entity

When an entity has an investment in an associate, a portion of which is held indirectly through a venture capital organisation, or a mutual fund, unit trust and similar entities including investment-linked insurance funds, the entity may elect to measure that portion of the investment in the associate at fair value through profit or loss in accordance with IFRS 9 (or, for entities that have not yet adopted IFRS 9, IAS 39) regardless of whether the venture capital organisation (or other specified entity) has significant influence over that portion of the investment. If the entity makes that election, the entity should apply the equity method to any remaining portion of its investment in an associate that is not held through a venture capital organisation, or a mutual fund, unit trust and similar entities including investment-linked insurance funds. [IAS 28:19]

The requirements regarding partial use of fair value measurement of associates are included in IAS 28 following requests for clarification as to whether different measurement bases can be applied to portions of an investment in an associate when part of the investment is measured at fair value through profit or loss in accordance with IFRS 9 (or, for entities that have not yet adopted IFRS 9, IAS 39). The IASB agreed that the measurement exemption may be applied to portions of an investment in an associate if the portion is held by a venture capital organisation, or a mutual fund, unit trust and similar entities including investment-linked insurance funds, regardless of whether those entities have significant influence over their portion of the investment in the associate. [IAS 28:BC20 & BC21]

No equivalent guidance has been provided on the partial use of fair value for the measurement of investments in joint ventures because the IASB thought that such events would be unlikely in practice. [IAS 28:BC20 & BC21]

The IASB also discussed whether the partial use of fair value should be allowed only in the case of venture capital organisations and similar entities that have designated their portion of the investment in the associate at fair value through profit or loss in their own financial statements. The Board noted that several situations might arise in which those entities do not measure their portion of the investment in the associate at fair value through profit or loss. In those situations, however, from the group's perspective, the appropriate determination of the business purpose would lead to the measurement of this portion of the investment in the associate at fair value through profit or loss in the consolidated financial statements. Consequently, the Board decided that an entity should be able to measure a portion of an investment in an associate held by a venture capital organisation, or a mutual fund, unit trust and similar entities including investment-linked insurance funds, at fair value through profit or loss regardless of whether this portion of the investment is measured at fair value through profit or loss in that other entity's financial statements. [IAS 28:BC22]

Example 4.2.2.5

Portion of an associate held indirectly through a venture capital organisation

Company M holds directly a 100 per cent interest in Company N and a 15 per cent interest in Company O. Company N is a venture capital organisation which acquires a further 10 per cent interest in Company O during the current period. Company M determines that it has obtained significant influence over Company O during the current period as a result of Company N's share purchase, which has taken Company M's combined direct and indirect shareholding to 25 per cent.

Following the purchase of shares by Company N, Company M has the following alternatives when accounting for its interest in Company O in its consolidated financial statements:

- it can account for the group's entire interest of 25 per cent using the equity method; or

- it can account for its 15 per cent direct interest using the equity method and Company N's 10 per cent interest at fair value through profit or loss in accordance with IFRS 9 (or, if it has not yet adopted IFRS 9, IAS 39).

4.3 Classification as held for sale

When an investment, or a portion of an investment, in an associate or a joint venture meets the criteria to be classified as held for sale:

[IAS 28:20]

- IFRS 5 *Non-current Assets Held for Sale and Discontinued Operations* should be applied to the investment, or the portion of the investment. This means that the investor should cease to apply the equity method to the investment, or the portion of the investment, and account for its interest in the associate or joint venture at the lower of carrying amount and fair value less costs to sell (see **example 4.3F** in **chapter A20**);

- any retained portion that has not been classified as held for sale should be accounted for using the equity method until the portion that is classified as held for sale is disposed of; and

- after the disposal, the retained interest should be accounted for in accordance with IFRS 9 *Financial Instruments* (or, for entities that have not yet adopted IFRS 9, IAS 39 *Financial Instruments: Recognition and Measurement*) unless significant influence or joint control is retained, in which case the retained interest should continue to be accounted for using the equity method.

Therefore, if an entity plans to dispose of a portion of an investment in an associate or a joint venture and IFRS 5's criteria for classification as held for sale are met, only the portion that is to be disposed of should be classified as held for sale; the entity should continue to use the equity method for the retained interest in the associate or joint venture until the portion classified as held for sale is finally disposed of. The IASB concluded that, even if the entity has the intention of selling a portion of an interest in an associate or a joint venture, until it does so it still has significant influence over, or joint control of, that investee. After the disposal, an entity should measure the retained interest in the associate or joint venture in accordance with IFRS 9 (or, for entities that have not yet adopted IFRS 9, IAS 39) or in accordance with IAS 28 if the entity still has significant influence over, or joint control of, the retained interest. [IAS 28:BC27]

4.4   Application of the equity method

4.4.1   Equity method – general approach

Under the equity method, an investment is initially recognised at cost, and the carrying amount is adjusted thereafter for:

[IAS 28:10]

- the investor's share of the post-acquisition profits or losses of the investee, which are recognised in the investor's profit or loss; and

- distributions received from the investee, which reduce the carrying amount of the investment.

Adjustments to the carrying amount may also be necessary for changes in the investor's proportionate interest in the investee arising from changes in the investee's other comprehensive income (such as the impact of property revaluations and some exchange differences). The investor's share of those changes is recognised in other comprehensive income of the investor. [IAS 28:10]

The investor's share of the investee's profits or losses after acquisition is also adjusted to take account of items such as additional depreciation of depreciable assets based on their fair values at the acquisition date. Similarly, appropriate adjustments to the investor's share of the associate's or joint venture's profit or loss after acquisition are made for impairment losses such as for goodwill or property, plant and equipment. [IAS 28:32]

4.4.2   Costs incurred to acquire an equity-method investee

IAS 28:10 specifies that the investment in an associate or a joint venture accounted for using the equity method is initially recognised at cost. Generally, cost includes the purchase price and other costs directly attributable to the acquisition of the asset such as professional fees for legal services, transfer taxes and other transaction costs.

Therefore, the cost of an investment in an equity-method investee at initial recognition comprises the purchase price for the investment and any directly attributable expenditure necessary to acquire it.

This applies to both the consolidated financial statements of the investor and the separate financial statements, when prepared.

Although IFRS 3 *Business Combinations* requires the costs associated with acquiring a subsidiary to be recognised as an expense in consolidated financial statements, this has not changed the appropriate treatment of the costs incurred in acquiring an equity-method investee.

The conclusions above were confirmed by the IFRIC (now the IFRS Interpretations Committee) in the July 2009 *IFRIC Update*.

4.4.3   Share of profits or losses of an equity-method investee

4.4.3.1   Proportionate ownership interest

The investor's share of the profits or losses of the investee, or other changes in the investee's equity, is determined on the basis of its proportionate existing ownership interest. [IAS 28:12]

The investor generally recognises its share of the investee's income and losses based on the percentage of the equity interest owned by the investor. However, when agreements designate allocations among the investors (e.g. of profits and losses, specified costs and expenses, distributions from operations, or distributions upon liquidation) that are different from ownership percentages, it may not be appropriate to recognise equity-method income based on the percentage of the equity interest owned.

The substance of these agreements should be reflected in determining how an increase or decrease in net assets of the investee will affect an investor's rights to distributions over the life of the investee and when the investee is liquidated.

The proportion of losses to be recognised when an entity's net investment in an equity-method investee includes a debt instrument is discussed in **example 4.4.16.2**.

4.4.3.2   Potential voting rights

When potential voting rights or other derivatives containing potential voting rights exist (see **3.5**), only the investor's existing ownership interests are taken into account in determining the investor's share of the investee's profits or losses. That share does not reflect the possible exercise or conversion of potential voting rights and other derivative instruments, except as described below. [IAS 28:12]

In some circumstances, an entity has, in substance, an existing ownership as a result of a transaction that currently gives it access to the returns associated with an ownership interest. In such circumstances, the proportion allocated to the entity is determined by taking into account the eventual exercise of those potential voting rights and other derivative instruments that currently give the entity access to the returns. [IAS 28:13]

> See **10.4** in **chapter A24** for a discussion of factors to consider in assessing whether potential voting rights and other derivative instruments result, in substance, in the investor having an existing ownership interest that currently gives it access to the returns associated with an ownership interest.

As a general principle, IFRS 9 *Financial Instruments* (or, for entities that have not yet adopted IFRS 9, IAS 39 *Financial Instruments: Recognition and Measurement*) does not apply to interests in associates and joint ventures that are accounted for using the equity method. Nor does it apply to instruments containing potential voting rights that in substance currently give access to the returns associated with an ownership interest in an associate or a joint venture. However, in all other cases, instruments containing potential voting rights in an associate or a joint venture are accounted for in accordance with IFRS 9 (or, for entities that have not yet adopted IFRS 9, IAS 39). [IAS 28:14]

4.4.3.3 Aggregation of group interests in an equity-method investee

When the investor is a parent, the group's share of the investee is the aggregate of the holdings in that investee by the parent and its subsidiaries. The holdings of the parent's other associates and joint ventures are ignored for this purpose. [IAS 28:27]

Example 4.4.3.3

Aggregation of group interests in an equity-method investee

Company A has a 70 per cent interest in Group B. Group B has a 20 per cent investment in an equity-method investee.

Company A's consolidated financial statements fully consolidate the assets and liabilities of Group B, i.e. they include 100 per cent of the assets and liabilities from Group B's consolidated financial statements (which include Group B's equity-method investee). Therefore, the appropriate share of the results of the equity-method investee to include in Company A's consolidated financial statements is the entire 20 per cent share in the investee, not 14 per cent (i.e. not 70 per cent × 20 per cent).

By way of example, assume that the net assets of the equity-method investee are CU100 million, including a net profit for the period of CU40 million. For simplicity, assume that no adjustments are required for the purposes of applying the equity method. The investment in the equity-method investee is shown as

---

CU20 million in Company A's consolidated statement of financial position and the share of profit is CU8 million (20 per cent × CU40 million).

Of that profit of CU8 million, CU2.4 million (30 per cent) is attributed to the non-controlling interests and CU5.6 million to the equity holders of the parent.

4.4.3.4   Indirect holding in an associate through a joint venture

Example 4.4.3.4

Indirect holding in an associate through a joint venture

Entity A enters into a joint arrangement with Entity B. The terms of the joint arrangement are such that it is determined to be a joint venture under IFRS 11 *Joint Arrangements*.

The Joint Venture holds a 15 per cent interest in Entity X which does not give the Joint Venture significant influence over Entity X. The Joint Venture accounts for this interest in accordance with IFRS 9 (or, for entities that have not yet adopted IFRS 9, IAS 39).

Entity A also acquires a direct 20 per cent interest in Entity X. This holding alone is considered to give Entity A significant influence over Entity X. The resulting structure is as follows.

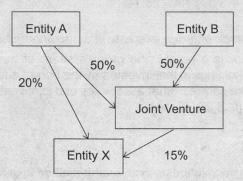

Direct investment in Entity X

In its consolidated financial statements, Entity A should account for its direct investment in Entity X using the equity method because it has significant influence over Entity X. The share of Entity X's profit or loss and changes in other comprehensive income to be recognised by Entity A is 20 per cent.

This treatment is in accordance with IAS 28:27 (see **4.4.3.3**).

Investment in joint venture

Entity A will also account for its interest in the Joint Venture using the equity method. When Entity A recognises its share of the profit or loss and changes in other comprehensive income of the Joint Venture, this should reflect the Joint Venture's accounting for its 15 per cent interest in Entity X under IFRS 9 (or IAS 39).

4.4.3.5 Associate or joint venture has subsidiaries or equity-method investees

When an associate or a joint venture has subsidiaries, associates or joint ventures, the profit or loss, other comprehensive income and net assets taken into account in applying the equity method are those recognised in the associate's or joint venture's financial statements (including the associate's or joint venture's share of the profit or loss, other comprehensive income and net assets of its associates and joint ventures), after any adjustments necessary to give effect to uniform accounting policies (see **4.4.13.1**). [IAS 28:27]

> Accordingly, when the associate or joint venture is itself a group of entities and prepares consolidated financial statements, those consolidated financial statements will be used in applying the equity method. When the associate or joint venture does not prepare consolidated financial statements, because it has associates and/or joint ventures but no subsidiaries, the starting point for applying the equity method should be the financial statements that account for those associates and/or joint ventures using the equity method, rather than any separate financial statements.
>
> See **4.4.13.2** for specific considerations when a non-investment entity holds an interest in an investment entity giving it significant influence or joint control.

4.4.3.6 Cumulative preference shares

If an associate or a joint venture has outstanding cumulative preference shares held by outside interests and classified as equity, the investor computes its share of profit or loss after adjusting for the preference dividends, whether or not the dividends have been declared. [IAS 28:37]

4.4.3.7 Reciprocal interests

> **Example 4.4.3.7A**
>
> **Reciprocal interest held by an equity-method investee**
>
> Company A, an investor, owns an interest in Company B, which it accounts for using the equity method. Company B concurrently owns an interest in Company A. Company B's investment is determined to be a reciprocal interest, not held as part of a trading portfolio.
>
> *How should Company A account for the reciprocal equity interest held by Company B when the reciprocal equity interest is accounted for in Company B's financial statements:*
>
> - *using the equity method under IAS 28?*
> - *as an investment (either at cost or in accordance with IFRS 9 (or, for entities that have not yet adopted IFRS 9, IAS 39))?*

The reciprocal interest should be eliminated. The requirements of IAS 28:26 (see **4.1**) apply to accounting for reciprocal equity interests regardless of how the investee has accounted for the reciprocal interest. Consequently, the accounting treatment of the investment in Company B's financial statements does not affect how Company A should account for the reciprocal interest.

IAS 28:26 states that many of the procedures appropriate for the application of the equity method are similar to the consolidation procedures described in IFRS 10 *Consolidated Financial Statements*. Furthermore, the concepts underlying the procedures used in accounting for the acquisition of a subsidiary are also adopted in accounting for the acquisition of an investment in an associate or joint venture.

Reciprocal interests should be treated in a similar manner to an investor's own shares, resulting in consolidation elimination entries to eliminate the investor's share of the reciprocal interests. Therefore, Company A, the investor, will show a reduction in its investment in Company B and its own share capital as though it held treasury shares. Company A will also eliminate any dividends received on those shares by Company B from its share of Company B's profits.

To illustrate, Company A owns a 30 per cent interest in Company B, and Company B owns a 20 per cent interest in Company A. Company A and Company B respectively have 10,000 and 5,000 ordinary shares issued and outstanding, and each paid CU100 per share for their respective ownership interests in each other.

Company A's basis in its investment in Company B, and Company B's corresponding reciprocal interest in Company A, are calculated as follows.

- Company B's basis in Company A = CU100/share × (20 per cent × 10,000 shares) = CU200,000
- Company A's reciprocal interest in Company B = 30 per cent × CU200,000 = CU60,000

The reduction in Company A's investment should be offset by a decrease in equity in a manner similar to treasury shares.

Company B's investment in Company A, and Company A's reciprocal interest in Company B, would be calculated and accounted for in a similar way, as illustrated below.

- Company A's basis in Company B = CU100/share × (30 per cent × 5,000 shares) = CU150,000
- Company B's reciprocal interest in Company A = 20 per cent × CU150,000 = CU30,000

For the purpose of calculating net income and earnings per share in the financial statements of the investor applying the equity method, an analogy to paragraph 33 of IAS 32 *Financial Instruments: Presentation* is drawn, whereby the reciprocal interest is treated as 'own shares' of the entity.

If earnings of Company A exclusive of any equity in Company B total CU100,000 ('direct earnings of Company A'), and earnings of Company B exclusive of any equity in Company A total CU50,000 ('direct earnings of Company B'), net income and earnings per share for Company A and Company B, respectively, are calculated as follows.

- Income of Company A before equity in Company B = CU100,000
- Equity in direct earnings of Company B = 30 per cent × CU50,000 = CU15,000
- Net income of Company A = CU100,000 + CU15,000 = CU115,000
- 10,000 shares of Company A – [30 per cent × (20 per cent × 10,000 shares held by Company B)] = 10,000 – 600 = 9,400
- Earnings per share of Company A = CU115,000 ÷ 9,400 shares = CU12.23 per share

Although Company A owns 30 per cent of Company B, Company A's investment in Company B is reduced for its ownership interests in itself through the reciprocal holdings by Company B of Company A's shares. Company B's ownership of Company A is reduced in a similar way, as illustrated below.

- Income of Company B before equity in Company A = CU50,000
- Equity in direct earnings of Company A = 20 per cent × CU100,000 = CU20,000
- Net income of Company B = CU50,000 + CU20,000 = CU70,000
- 5,000 shares of Company B – [20 per cent × (30 per cent × 5,000 shares held by Company A)] = 5,000 – 300 = 4,700
- Earnings per share of Company B = CU70,000 ÷ 4,700 shares = CU14.89 per share

Other methodologies for eliminating reciprocal interests may be acceptable.

Example 4.4.3.7B

Reciprocal interests held by an associate or a joint venture of a venture capital organisation

Company A owns an interest in an associate, Company B, and Company B concurrently owns an interest in Company A. The investments are determined to be reciprocal interests. Company A is a venture capital organisation that measures its investment in Company B at fair value through profit or loss in accordance with IFRS 9.

How should Company A account for the reciprocal equity interest held by Company B?

The reciprocal interest should not be eliminated. Although IAS 28:26 states that many of the procedures that are appropriate for the application of the equity method are similar to consolidation procedures, and that "the concepts underlying the procedures used in accounting for the acquisition of a subsidiary are also adopted in accounting for the acquisition of an investment in an associate or a joint venture", it does so under the heading 'Equity method procedures'. But venture capitalists that measure their investments at fair value in accordance with IFRS 9 are not required to apply the equity method. Therefore, IAS 28:26

does not apply. Consequently, the reciprocal equity interests are not eliminated at the investor level.

Note that the same conclusion would be reached if Company B were a joint venture of Company A instead of an associate.

4.4.4   Share options issued by an equity-method investee to its own employees

Example 4.4.4

Share options issued by an equity-method investee to its own employees

Entity E grants share options to its employees. The options entitle the employees to acquire shares of Entity E. Entity A holds a 20 per cent interest in Entity E and accounts for its interest in Entity E using the equity method.

How should Entity A account for its share of the share-based compensation recognised by Entity E? In particular, what is the impact in the financial statements of Entity A of the increase in equity recognised in Entity E's financial statements?

Entity A should recognise its share of profit or loss of Entity E based on the amounts reported in Entity E's financial statements, which will include the share-based payment expense recognised by Entity E. It would not be appropriate for Entity A to reverse out the share-based payment expense recognised by Entity E.

IAS 28:10 states that "[a]djustments to the carrying amount [of an equity-method investee] may also be necessary for changes in the investor's proportionate interest in the investee arising from changes in the investee's other comprehensive income". Therefore, in addition to amounts recognised in profit or loss (including compensation expense), Entity A should recognise its proportionate share of items of income and expense recognised in other comprehensive income.

However, the increase in equity recognised by Entity E is not part of other comprehensive income. Under the equity method, the carrying amount is adjusted for the investor's share of the investee's profit or loss, for the investor's share of the investee's other comprehensive income and for dividends received – but the increase in equity is none of these. Therefore, it should not be used to adjust the carrying amount of Entity A's investment in Entity E.

To illustrate, assume that the opening net assets of Entity E amount to CU1,000, and Entity A's interest in Entity E is reflected in its opening statement of financial position at a carrying amount of CU300. During the year, Entity E makes a profit of CU600, which is after recognising an equity-settled share-based payment expense of CU200. For simplicity, assume that no adjustments are required when calculating Entity A's share of Entity E's profit (i.e. there were no fair value adjustments on acquisition that need to be amortised – see **4.4.7**).

The change in Entity E's net assets during the year is analysed as follows.

	CU
Opening net assets	1,000
Profit for year (after charging CU200 share-based payment expense)	600
Share-based payment expense credited to equity	200
Closing net assets	1,800

The amounts reflected under the equity method in Entity A's financial statements are as follows.

	CU
Opening balance (including goodwill arising on acquisition)	300
Share of profit or loss (CU600 × 20%)	120
Closing balance	420

If the employees exercise their share options, Entity A will recognise the impact of the resulting dilution as a deemed disposal.

4.4.5   Distributions received from an associate or a joint venture

Distributions received from an associate or a joint venture reduce the carrying amount of the investor's interest in the associate or joint venture. [IAS 28:10]

As explained at **4.4.16.1**, if an investor's share of losses of an associate or a joint venture equals or exceeds its interest in the associate or joint venture, the investor should discontinue recognising its share of further losses. After the investor's interest is reduced to zero, additional losses are provided for, and a liability is recognised, only to the extent that the investor has incurred legal or constructive obligations or made payments on behalf of the associate or joint venture. However, IAS 28 does not address the accounting for distributions by equity-method investees to an investor in excess of the investor's carrying amount. If distributions by an equity-method investee to an investor are in excess of the investor's carrying amount, and (1) the distributions are not refundable by agreement or law, and (2) the investor is not liable for the obligations of the investee or otherwise committed to provide financial support to the investee, then cash distributions received in excess of the investment in the investee should be recognised as income. If the investee subsequently reports net income, the investor should resume applying the equity method in accordance with IAS 28 once the investee has made sufficient profits to cover the aggregate of any investee losses not recognised by the investor (due to the investor's zero balance in the investment) and any income previously recognised for excess cash distributions.

Example 4.4.5A

Distributions received from an equity-method investee in excess of the investor's carrying amount (1)

Company A has invested CU1 million for a 50 per cent ownership interest in Company C. Company A uses the equity method to account for its investment in Company C. Company C subsequently incurs a loss of CU2.4 million, 50 per cent of which exceeds Company A's investment balance by CU200,000. Company A is not liable for the obligations of Company C or otherwise committed to provide financial support to Company C. Accordingly, Company A recognises losses of CU1 million, and reduces its investment in Company C to CUnil. Company A does not recognise further losses of CU200,000 because it is neither liable for the obligations of Company C nor otherwise committed to provide financial support to Company C.

Subsequently, because the losses are due to non-cash depreciation expense and Company C has available cash, Company C distributes CU100,000 to Company A.

The CU100,000 distribution made to Company A is not refundable by agreement or law. Therefore, Company A should continue to recognise its investment in Company C at zero and recognise the CU100,000 received as income. When Company C becomes profitable such that Company A's share of Company C's earnings exceeds the distributions and share of unrecognised losses attributable to Company A (i.e. CU300,000), Company A will resume applying the equity method in accordance with IAS 28.

Even when the investor is not legally obliged to refund the distribution, it is still necessary to exercise judgement and consider the specific facts and circumstances (including the relationship among the investors). If distributions by an investee to an investor are in excess of the investor's carrying amount, and (1) the distribution may be refundable by convention, or (2) the investor may become liable for the obligations of the investee or is otherwise expected to provide financial support to the investee, then cash distributions received in excess of the investment in the investee should be recognised as a liability. If the investee subsequently reports net income, the investor should reverse the liability and recognise its share of the profits of the investee before it increases the carrying amount of the investment. **Example 4.4.5B** illustrates an example of a distribution which should be recognised as a liability.

In circumstances in which the investor has undertaken to provide financial support to the investee, it will be necessary to consider whether any additional provision or disclosure is required in accordance with IAS 37 *Provisions, Contingent Liabilities and Contingent Assets* (see **chapter A12**).

Example 4.4.5B

Distributions received from an equity-method investee in excess of the investor's carrying amount (2)

Company B has invested CU1 million for a 50 per cent ownership interest in Company C. Company B uses the equity method to account for its investment in Company C. Company C subsequently incurs a loss of CU2.4 million, 50 per cent of which exceeds Company B's investment balance by CU200,000. Because the losses are due to non-cash depreciation expense and Company C has available cash, it distributes CU100,000 to Company B.

The CU100,000 distribution made to Company B is not refundable by agreement or law, and Company B is not liable for Company C's obligations. However, Company B has committed to providing financial support to Company C. Therefore, Company B should recognise losses of CU1.2 million, reduce its investment in Company C to zero and also recognise a liability of CU300,000 in respect of the losses of CU200,000 and the CU100,000 cash received. When Company C becomes profitable, Company B will reverse the liability before increasing the carrying amount in its investment in Company C.

Separately, Company B should consider whether any additional provision or disclosure is required in accordance with IAS 37 (see **chapter A12**).

4.4.6 Commencing use of the equity method

4.4.6.1 Date of commencing use of the equity method

An investment is accounted for under the equity method from the date on which it becomes an associate or a joint venture. [IAS 28:32]

An investor will generally begin to use the equity method when it first acquires or it increases its interest in the associate or joint venture such that significant influence or joint control is achieved. Transactions and events other than a change in absolute or relative ownership levels that could require an investor to begin to use (or to resume the use of) the equity method for an investment include, but are not limited to:

- the investor acquires currently exercisable potential voting rights that affect its ability to exercise significant influence (see **3.5**);

- the shareholders of the investee enter into an agreement that affects the control, joint control or significant influence held by the investors;

- an investee over which the investor previously exercised significant influence, or of which it previously had joint control, emerges from bankruptcy. During the bankruptcy, the investee's board of directors had no power to direct the investee's operating and financial policies, or direct the relevant activities, with all decisions instead being made by an independent administrator appointed following a vote by the investee's creditors. The investor had stopped applying the equity method for its investment during the bankruptcy because it was unable to exercise significant influence or joint control over the investee;

- an investor's representation on the board of directors of an investee increases without a corresponding increase in the investor's investment (e.g. a board member resigns and is not replaced, thereby increasing the investor's representation or, alternatively, the investor is given or gains another seat on the board for no consideration); and

- an investment in an associate or a joint venture previously classified as held for sale in accordance with IFRS 5 *Non-current Assets Held for Sale and Discontinued Operations* no longer meets the criteria to be so classified (see **4.4.6.2**).

4.4.6.2 Investments previously classified as held for sale

When an investment (or a portion of an investment) in an associate or a joint venture previously classified as held for sale in accordance with IFRS 5 no longer meets the criteria to be so classified, it should be accounted for using the equity method retrospectively as from the date of its classification as held for sale. Financial statements for the periods since classification as held for sale should be amended accordingly. [IAS 28:21]

It is clear that IAS 28 requires retrospective restatement in these circumstances. On the face of it, this is not consistent with the requirements of IFRS 5 when an asset ceases to be classified as held for sale, because IFRS 5 applies the change of classification prospectively from the date that the criteria cease to be met (see **4.8** in **chapter A20**). However, the requirement in IAS 28:21 is more specific and should therefore be followed.

4.4.7 Recognition of initial investment

On the acquisition of an investment in an associate or a joint venture, any difference between the cost of the investment and the entity's share of the net fair value of the investee's identifiable assets and liabilities is accounted for as follows:

[IAS 28:32]

- goodwill relating to an equity-method investee is included in the carrying amount of the investment. Amortisation of that goodwill is not permitted (see **4.4.10**); and

- any excess of the investor's share of the net fair value of the investee's identifiable assets and liabilities over the cost of the investment is included as income in the determination of the investor's share of the profit or loss of the equity-method investee in the period in which the investment is acquired.

The investor's proportionate share of the assets acquired and liabilities assumed should be adjusted for write-ups or write-downs to fair value in the same manner as in business-combination accounting under IFRS 3 *Business Combinations*. The investor would then amortise its proportionate share of any acquisition-accounting adjustments over the period necessary to match them against the related assets and liabilities.

Any goodwill that is recognised in the statement of financial position of the associate or joint venture is ignored when recognising the identifiable assets and liabilities assumed by the investor and is effectively absorbed into the investor's goodwill number, calculated in accordance with IAS 28:32.

IAS 28:32 makes it clear that any excess of the investor's share of the net fair value of the investee's identifiable assets and liabilities on acquisition over the cost of the investment should be included in income. In these cases, it may be necessary to reassess whether the investor's proportionate share of all of the assets acquired and the liabilities assumed has been identified correctly and whether the fair values of the investee's assets and liabilities have been determined appropriately.

Example 4.4.7A

Recognition of initial investment (1)

Company A purchased 35 per cent of Company B's outstanding shares for an amount in excess of 35 per cent of the carrying amount of Company B's net assets. For illustrative purposes, it is assumed that Company B's assets and liabilities are composed solely of investments in debt securities that Company B has measured at amortised cost in accordance with IAS 39 *Financial Instruments: Recognition and Measurement* and related deferred income taxes. The fair value of the debt securities is in excess of the carrying amount, and the difference between the amount Company A paid for its investment and its proportionate interest in Company B's net assets is equal to the proportionate difference between the carrying amount and fair value of the debt securities after consideration of income taxes.

In this case, the difference can be attributed to the specific assets and liabilities and the amounts should be recognised accordingly. In applying the equity method, Company A will need to adjust its share of Company B's profit or loss to reflect the fair value adjustment on the debt securities, and the associated adjustment to deferred tax liabilities, as determined on initial recognition. Any future gain or loss on disposal of the assets reported by Company B would also be adjusted by Company A to reflect the fair values recognised on acquisition.

Example 4.4.7B

Recognition of initial investment (2)

Company A purchased 35 per cent of Company B's outstanding shares for an amount in excess of 35 per cent of the carrying amount of Company B's net assets. The excess paid by Company A cannot be attributed to specific assets of Company B. Therefore, the difference would remain a component of the recognised investment as goodwill. Such goodwill is not amortised, but is tested for impairment as part of the carrying amount of the investment (see **4.4.10**).

4.4.8   Equity-method investee acquired in stages

When an associate or a joint venture is acquired in stages, goodwill is calculated initially at the time at which the investment becomes an associate or a joint venture (i.e. when significant influence or joint control is achieved). The goodwill is calculated as the difference between the cost of the investment and the investor's share of the net fair value of the investee's identifiable assets and liabilities.

In accordance with IAS 28:10, the investment in the associate or joint venture is initially recognised at cost. When the investor has previously held an investment in the associate or joint venture (generally accounted for under IFRS 9 or, for entities that have not yet adopted IFRS 9, IAS 39), the deemed cost of the investment in the associate or joint venture is the fair value of the original investment at the date that significant influence or joint control is achieved plus the consideration paid for the additional stake. However, IAS 28 is not clear as to whether any gains or losses arising on the original investment since its acquisition should be reflected in profit or loss at this point.

Because IAS 28 does not mandate a particular accounting treatment in this regard, an entity may:

- by analogy to IFRS 3, treat the transaction as a disposal of the original investment for fair value and an acquisition of an associate or a joint venture, with the result that a gain or loss on the disposal will typically be reflected in profit or loss; or

- recognise a revaluation gain on the original tranche in an appropriate component of equity in order to establish the appropriate starting point for the equity method. Under this approach, if the original investment has been classified previously as an available-for-sale financial asset under IAS 39, the revaluation gain or loss recognised in other comprehensive income should not be reclassified from equity to profit or loss. If instead the original investment was measured at cost in accordance with IAS 39:46(c), a revaluation gain is required to recognise the investment at fair value and to calculate goodwill. No gain or loss should be recognised in profit or loss under this approach on the basis that there has been no realisation event (e.g. a disposal).

Other methods may be acceptable. Whichever method is selected, it represents an accounting policy choice, which should be applied consistently for all acquisitions of associates or joint ventures achieved in stages.

4.4.9 Contingent consideration for the acquisition of an equity-method investee

Example 4.4.9

Contingent consideration for the acquisition of an equity-method investee

Entity I acquires a 45 per cent interest in Entity A which results in it having significant influence over Entity A. The consideration is payable in two tranches:

- an immediate payment of CU1 million; and
- a further payment of CU500,000 after two years if the cumulative profit of Entity A before interest and tax for the two-year period following acquisition exceeds CU400,000.

At the date of acquisition, the fair value of the contingent consideration (i.e. the amount payable if the specified profit target is met) is assessed as CU220,000.

One year after acquisition, on the basis of a revised earnings forecast, the fair value of the contingent consideration is deemed to have increased by CU80,000 to CU300,000.

How should Entity I account for the contingent consideration payable in respect of the acquisition of its interest in Entity A in its consolidated financial statements?

IAS 28 does not provide any specific guidance on the measurement of the cost of acquiring an investment in an associate accounted for using the equity method. However, IAS 28:26 explains that "the concepts underlying the procedures used in accounting for the acquisition of a subsidiary are also adopted in accounting for the acquisition of an investment in an associate". Therefore, in the circumstances described, by analogy to paragraph 39 of IFRS 3 *Business Combinations*, at the date of acquisition the investment in Entity A is recognised in Entity I's consolidated financial statements at a cost of CU1,220,000.

The subsequent accounting for the contingent consideration is determined under IFRS 9 (or, for entities that have not yet adopted IFRS 9, IAS 39). The contingent consideration should therefore be subsequently measured at fair value with the resulting loss of CU80,000 recognised in profit or loss. This is consistent with the treatment specified in IFRS 3:58 for changes in contingent consideration in a business combination.

It is not appropriate for Entity I to increase the carrying amount of its investment in Entity A to reflect the change in the fair value of the contingent consideration.

4.4.10   Subsequent accounting for goodwill

IAS 28's requirements for impairment of investments accounted for using the equity method were updated in July 2014 by consequential amendments arising from IFRS 9 *Financial Instruments*. The requirements described in this section deal specifically with impairment of goodwill forming part of the carrying amount of an investment in an associate or a joint venture. General requirements regarding impairment are set out in **4.4.19** (for entities applying IFRS 9) and **4.4.20** (for entities that have not yet adopted IFRS 9).

Goodwill arising on the acquisition of an associate or a joint venture accounted for using the equity method should not be amortised but should be tested for impairment. Because such goodwill is not separately recognised, but forms part of the carrying amount of the equity-method investment, it is not tested for impairment separately by applying the requirements for impairment testing of goodwill in IAS 36 *Impairment of Assets*. Instead, the entire carrying amount of the investment is tested for impairment in accordance with IAS 36 as a single asset, by comparing its recoverable amount with its carrying amount whenever, based on the requirements in IAS 28:41A to 41C, there is an indication of impairment (see **4.4.19.1**). [IAS 28:42] (Note that this is different from the position for goodwill recognised separately, for which impairment testing is required annually irrespective of whether there are indicators of impairment.)

The requirements outlined in the previous paragraph apply for entities that have already adopted IFRS 9. The only difference between these requirements and those applicable for entities that have not yet adopted IFRS 9 is that, for entities that have not yet adopted IFRS 9, impairment indicators are identified in accordance with the requirements of IAS 39 rather than in accordance with the newly introduced paragraphs 41A to 41C of IAS 28 (see **sections 4.4.19** and **4.4.20** for further detail).

An impairment loss recognised in the circumstances described above is not allocated to any asset, including goodwill, that forms part of the carrying amount of the investment in the associate. Accordingly, any reversal of that impairment loss is recognised in accordance with IAS 36 to the extent that the recoverable amount of the investment subsequently increases (see **4.4.19.4** or, for entities that have not yet adopted IFRS 9, **4.4.20.4**). [IAS 28:42]

There are different views regarding the nature of the equity method. How an entity views the equity method is critical in its consideration of an appropriate accounting policy under IAS 28 for recognising impairment losses in respect of its equity-method investees.

Interests in equity-method investees and the investor's share of the profit or loss of the equity-method investee are presented as a one-line item in the statement of financial position and the statement of comprehensive income, respectively, and, in accordance with IAS 28:40 to 42, the investor is required to monitor its investment for impairment as a whole. Furthermore, in accordance with IAS 28:38 and 39, the investor ceases to recognise its share of the investee's losses once it has reduced its investment to zero and only recognises a liability for subsequent losses to the extent that it has incurred legal or constructive obligations or made payments on behalf of the equity-method investee. Therefore, the equity method has some of the features commonly associated with a valuation methodology (sometimes referred to as a 'closed box' view).

However, in its guidance on the equity method, IAS 28:32 states, in part, that "[a]ppropriate adjustments to the entity's share of the associate's or joint venture's profit or loss after acquisition are made in order to account, for example, for depreciation of the depreciable assets based on their fair values at the acquisition date. Similarly, appropriate adjustments to the entity's share of the associate's or joint venture's profit or loss after acquisition are made for impairment losses such as for goodwill or property, plant and equipment". Therefore, the equity method has some of the features commonly associated with consolidation.

The table below outlines possible approaches that an investor could use in accounting for impairment losses of its equity-method investments. The accounting policy selected will be based on the investor's view of the equity method of accounting (i.e. either as a form of valuation methodology or as a form of consolidation).

The accounting policy selected should be applied consistently to all equity-method investments of the entity.

Impairment losses in equity-method investments	
Policies consistent with a valuation ('closed box') approach (3 steps)	Policy consistent with a one-line consolidation approach (4 steps)
Accounting Policy 1	
Step 1: The investor recognises its share of profit or loss of the investee, *including* any impairment losses recognised by the investee.	Step 1: The investor recognises its share of profit or loss of the investee, *including* any impairment losses recognised by the investee.

Step 2: The investor makes the limited 'consolidation' and fair value adjustments required by IAS 28 to: • eliminate unrealised gains; and • adjust depreciation/amortisation and impairment losses when the fair value of an asset at the date of obtaining significant influence or joint control was greater or lower than the carrying amount in the investee's own financial statements.	Step 2: The investor makes the limited 'consolidation' and fair value adjustments required by IAS 28 to: • eliminate unrealised gains; and • adjust depreciation/amortisation when the fair value of an asset at the date of obtaining significant influence or joint control was greater or lower than the carrying amount in the investee's own financial statements.
Step 3: The resulting carrying amount of the investment is then tested for impairment as a whole.	Step 3: The investor performs a separate (additional) impairment review in respect of the CGUs within the investee, but using the investee's figures as amended to reflect 'consolidation' and fair value adjustments. As a result, the investor may adjust the impairment losses recognised by the investee itself because: • the investor and the investee recognised different amounts for the assets subject to the impairment analysis due to fair value adjustments; or • the investor recognised an asset not recognised by the investee.
Accounting Policy 2 As above, except the investor makes no adjustments to the impairment loss on those assets impaired by the investee based on the acquisition date fair value of those assets.	Step 4: The resulting carrying amount of the investment is then tested for impairment as a whole.

4.4.11   Income tax

The investor's income tax provision usually will equal the sum of current and deferred tax expense, including any tax consequences of its interest in earnings and temporary differences attributable to its investment in an equity-method investee. The tax consequences of the investor's interest in earnings and temporary differences attributable to its investment in an equity-method investee should not be offset against the investor's interest in earnings, because it is the investor's tax provision, not the investee's.

4.4.12   Reporting periods of associates and joint ventures

When applying the equity method, the investor uses the most recent financial statements of the associate or joint venture. When the end of the reporting period of the associate or joint venture is different from that of the investor, the associate or joint venture will prepare additional financial statements, for the investor's use, corresponding to the investor's reporting period, unless it is impracticable to do so, in which case financial statements prepared for a different reporting period may be used. [IAS 28:33] The difference between the end of the reporting period of the associate or joint venture and that of the investor, however, can never be more than three months. [IAS 28:34]

The length of the reporting periods used and any difference between the ends of the reporting periods should be consistent from period to period. [IAS 28:34]

When financial statements of an associate or a joint venture with a different reporting period are used, adjustments are made for the effects of any significant events or transactions that occur between the end of the associate's or joint venture's reporting period and the end of the investor's reporting period. [IAS 28:34]

4.4.13   Uniform accounting policies

4.4.13.1   Requirement for uniform accounting policies – general

The investor's financial statements should be prepared using uniform accounting policies for like transactions and events in similar circumstances. [IAS 28:35]

Except as described in IAS 28:36A (see **4.4.13.2**), when an associate or a joint venture uses different accounting policies from those of the investor for like transactions and events, the financial statements of the associate or joint venture used for the purposes of the equity method should be adjusted to conform the accounting policies of the associate or joint venture to those of the investor. [IAS 28:36]

4.4.13.2   Non-investment entity holding an interest in an investment-entity associate or joint venture

Notwithstanding the requirement in IAS 28:36 (see **4.4.13.1**), when an entity that is not itself an investment entity has an interest in an associate or a joint venture that is an investment entity, the entity may, when applying the equity method, retain the fair value measurement applied by that investment entity associate's or joint venture's interests in subsidiaries. [IAS 28:36A]

IAS 28:36A was added by *Investment Entities: Applying the Consolidation Exemption (Amendments to IFRS 10, IFRS 12 and IAS 28)*, issued in

December 2014 and effective for annual periods beginning on or after 1 January 2016, with earlier application permitted. If an entity applies the December amendments to IAS 28 for a period beginning before 1 January 2016, it is required to disclose that fact. [IAS 28:45D]

IAS 28:36A deals with the accounting by a non-investment entity that holds an interest in an investment entity giving it significant influence or joint control.

Consider, for example, Entity A which is a non-investment entity with a 50 per cent interest in Entity I, which is an investment entity. Entity A accounts for its interest in Entity I using the equity method. Entity I holds two investments – 80 per cent of Entity B (subsidiary) and 25 per cent of Entity C (associate), neither of which provides investment-related services or activities as contemplated in IFRS 10:32. In Entity I's financial statements, both Entity B and Entity C are measured at fair value.

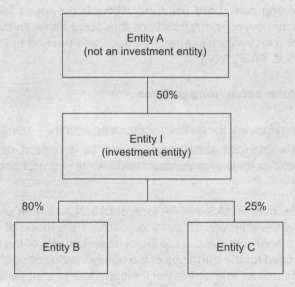

Prior to the December 2014 amendments, it was not clear whether, in determining its share of profit or loss in Entity I under the equity method, Entity A should 'unwind' the fair value accounting applied by Entity I for Entity B and prepare consolidated information for Entity I. (IAS 28:18 (see **4.2.2.1**) has always been clear that Entity A may elect to apply the exemption from applying the equity method for its indirect associate-level investment in Entity C (25 per cent held by Entity I), and maintain Entity I's fair value accounting for the underlying investment in Entity C when accounting for Entity I using the equity method.)

The effect of IAS 28:36A is to permit Entity A to retain, when applying the equity method, the fair value measurement applied by Entity I to its interests in Entity B, a subsidiary of Entity I.

The election under IAS 28:36A is available on an investment-by-investment basis. Although not explicitly stated in the current version of IAS 28, the IASB has issued proposals for amendments to IAS 28:36A to clarify this point (see **section 7**).

4.4.14   Transactions with equity-method investees

4.4.14.1   Investor's share of gains and losses on upstream and downstream transactions to be eliminated

The requirements discussed in this section are based on the text of IAS 28 prior to the September 2014 amendments *Sale or Contribution of Assets between an Investor and its Associate or Joint Venture (Amendments to IFRS 10 and IAS 28)*. Although, when finalised, the September 2014 amendments were stated to be effective for annual periods beginning on or after 1 January 2016, with earlier application permitted, subsequent amendments to IAS 28 issued in December 2015 have deferred indefinitely the effective date of the September 2014 amendments pending finalisation of a larger research project on the equity method of accounting (scope and timetable yet to be determined). For periods prior to the, as yet unspecified, effective date of the September 2014 amendments, or the effective date of any alternative amendments made following completion of the Board's research project, entities may choose to apply the amendments but they are not required to do so.

See **4.4.14.8** for a summary of the impact of the September 2014 amendments and the amended text of the affected paragraphs in IAS 28.

When an associate or a joint venture is accounted for using the equity method, gains and losses resulting from upstream transactions (e.g. sales of assets from the associate or joint venture to the investor) or downstream transactions (e.g. sales or contributions of assets from the investor to the associate or joint venture) should be recognised to the extent of unrelated investors' interests in the associate or joint venture. The investor's share of the associate's or joint venture's gains or losses resulting from these transactions is eliminated. [IAS 28:28]

Upstream If an investor purchases goods from an equity-method investee and the goods have not been sold by the investor to a third party at the end of the reporting period, the journal entry to eliminate the investor's share of the unrealised profit on the inventories would be taken against income from the equity-method investee.

Downstream If an investor sells goods to an equity-method investee and the goods have not been sold by the investee to a third party at the end of the reporting period, the journal entry to eliminate the investor's share of the unrealised profit on the inventories would be taken against consolidated profit or loss (usually cost of sales).

Example 4.4.14.1

Elimination of profits and losses on transactions with equity-method investees

Assume the following facts.

- An investor owns 30 per cent of an investee.

- The investment is accounted for using the equity method.

- The income tax rate for both investor and investee is 40 per cent.

Upstream transaction

The investee sells inventories to the investor. At the end of the investor's reporting period, the investor holds inventories for which the investee has recognised a gross profit of CU200,000. In the computation of the investor's share of the investee's earnings, CU120,000 (CU200,000 less 40 per cent income tax) would be deducted from the investee's net income and CU36,000 (the investor's 30 per cent share of the gross profit earned on the transaction after income tax) would be eliminated from the investor's equity-method income. The investor also would reduce the carrying amount of its inventories by CU60,000 (the investor's share of the investee's gross profit) and recognise a deferred tax asset of CU24,000 (CU60,000 × 40 per cent) (subject to the usual recognition criteria in IAS 12 *Income Taxes*).

Downstream transaction

The investor sells inventories to the investee. At the end of the investee's reporting period, the investee holds inventories for which the investor has recognised a gross profit of CU300,000. The investor's net income would be reduced by CU54,000 to reflect a CU90,000 (300,000 × 30 per cent) reduction in gross profit and a CU36,000 (90,000 × 40 per cent) reduction in income tax expense. The investor reduces its investment in the investee by CU90,000 and recognises a CU36,000 deferred tax asset (subject to the usual recognition criteria in IAS 12).

4.4.14.2   Profit elimination exceeds the carrying amount of the investment

Example 4.4.14.2 deals with the circumstances in which the amount of the gain to eliminate in a downstream transaction in accordance with IAS 28:28 exceeds the amount of the entity's investment. The treatment advocated is based on the requirements in IAS 28 at the time of writing. The IASB had been working on proposals for amendments to IAS 28 to provide more specific guidance. However, the project has been abandoned pending finalisation of the Board's larger scale research project on the equity method of accounting (scope and timetable yet to be determined).

Example 4.4.14.2

Profit elimination exceeds the carrying amount of investee

Entity A has a 30 per cent interest in Entity B and accounts for its interest in Entity B using the equity method. The carrying amount of Entity B in Entity A's consolidated financial statements is CU15 million.

Entity A sells plant and equipment to Entity B at fair value in exchange for cash of CU100 million, which Entity B finances through bank borrowings. Immediately before the sale, the plant and equipment was recognised in Entity A's financial statements at a depreciated amount of CU20 million. Entity A will have no further involvement with the plant and equipment, and the derecognition criteria in IAS 16 *Property, Plant and Equipment* are met. Entity A has no interests in Entity B other than its equity stake, and it is not committed to any reimbursement should Entity B generate losses.

Of the profit of CU80 million made by Company A, 30 per cent (CU24 million) would normally be eliminated as unrealised, but this exceeds the carrying amount of Entity B (CU15 million).

Should the excess of unrealised profit over the carrying amount of the investment in Entity B (i.e. CU9 million) be eliminated in the consolidated financial statements of Entity A?

IAS 28:28 applies to gains and losses resulting from 'upstream' and 'downstream' transactions between an investor and an equity-method investee. It requires unrealised gains and losses to be eliminated to the extent of the investor's interest in the equity-method investee, but it does not discuss the possibility that this might exceed the carrying amount of the investee. In the absence of guidance, it seems appropriate to analogise to IAS 28:39 (see **4.4.16.1**), which addresses the appropriate accounting for an equity-method investee that is making losses. In that scenario:

- after the investor's interest is reduced to zero, additional losses are provided for, and a liability is recognised, only to the extent that the investor has incurred legal or constructive obligations or made payments on behalf of the equity-method investee to satisfy obligations of the investee; and

- if the equity-method investee subsequently reports profits, the investor resumes including its share of those profits only after its share of the profits equals the share of net losses not recognised.

Applying the same logic in the circumstances described above:

- Entity A should reduce the profit on sale of plant and equipment by CU15 million, being the carrying amount of Entity B immediately before the sale. Thus, it should report a profit of CU65 million on the sale; and

- Entity A should not recognise any further share of Entity B's profits until Entity B has made sufficient profits (CU30 million, of which Entity A's share

---

> is CU9 million) to cover the amount of unrealised profit not eliminated at the time of the sale.
>
> Note that, for simplicity, tax effects are ignored in the analysis above.

4.4.14.3   Sale of a subsidiary to an existing associate or joint venture – conflict with IFRS 10

An entity may enter into a transaction whereby it sells its equity interest in a subsidiary to an existing associate or joint venture for fair value. The entity relinquishes control of the subsidiary but it retains an equity interest in the subsidiary, albeit held indirectly through the existing associate or joint venture. There is a conflict between the requirements of IFRS 10 *Consolidated Financial Statements* and IAS 28 regarding how the entity would account for this type of transaction.

According to IFRS 10:25, upon loss of control of a subsidiary, a parent derecognises the assets and liabilities of the subsidiary (including any non-controlling interests) in full and measures any investment retained in the former subsidiary at its fair value. A remeasurement gain or loss that forms part of the total gain or loss on the disposal of the subsidiary is recognised in profit or loss. In contrast, IAS 28:28 only permits recognition of the gain or loss "to the extent of unrelated investors' interests in the associate or joint venture".

In the absence of any other relevant guidance, entities have, in effect, an accounting policy choice of applying either the approach in IFRS 10 or the approach in IAS 28 because the two Standards have equal status in the IFRS literature. Both approaches are illustrated in **example 12.3.3C** in **chapter A24**. Although the IASB issued amendments designed to address this conflict in September 2014 (see **4.4.14.8**), the Board subsequently deferred the effective date of the amendments indefinitely so that there continues to be more than one acceptable approach.

An additional complexity arises if previously gains or losses have been recognised in other comprehensive income (OCI) that, in accordance with IFRS 10:B99, should be reclassified from equity to profit or loss when the parent loses control (see **12.3.2** in **chapter A24**). If an entity's accounting policy is to follow IFRS 10 and to recognise all of the gain or loss on the disposal of its interest in the subsidiary to the associate or joint venture, all relevant amounts previously recognised in OCI should be reclassified to profit or loss. However, if an entity's accounting policy is to restrict the gain or loss arising on the disposal in line with IAS 28:28, the Standard is not clear as to whether such a restriction would also apply to any amounts reclassified from equity to profit or loss.

4.4.14.4   Gain arising from spin-off in an equity-method investee

Example 4.4.14.4

Gain arising from spin-off in an equity-method investee

Company A holds 25 per cent of the shares in Company B. Company A accounts for its interest in Company B using the equity method.

Company B owns two major operating businesses, Business X and Business Y, and decides to spin off Business Y. In order to achieve that objective, Business Y is transferred into a separate legal entity, Company C, which is wholly owned by Company B. The shares of Company C are then distributed as a dividend to Company B's shareholders on a pro rata basis (resulting in Company A holding 25 per cent of the shares in, and exercising significant influence over, both Company B and Company C).

As required by IFRIC 17 *Distributions of Non-cash Assets to Owners*, when the distribution is made, Company B recognises a gain in profit or loss in respect of the difference between the carrying amount of the assets distributed and the fair value of the dividend payable.

When Company A accounts for its share of the profit or loss of Company B, what (if any) adjustment should be made in respect of the gain recognised by Company B when the distribution of the shares in Company C is made?

The transaction described represents a pro rata distribution to all shareholders by an equity-method investee of Company A. IAS 28 does not provide any explicit guidance for such circumstances. The preferred treatment is to exclude the effect of the gain recognised on distribution of Company C's shares entirely from the share of Company B's profit accounted for by Company A under the equity method. This results in the most appropriate representation of the substance of the transaction – which is that nothing has changed from Company A's perspective (both before and after the transaction it holds 25 per cent of Business X and Business Y and there has been no external market transaction).

However, given the lack of explicit guidance in IAS 28, in some situations, based on the facts and circumstances and if the transaction has commercial substance, an alternative treatment may be acceptable.

For example, in the circumstances described, given that the transaction has substance (because Company A could now acquire or dispose of its interests in one of Business X or Business Y without changing its interest in the other), an appropriate alternative treatment would be not to eliminate the effect of the gain recognised on distribution of Company C's shares. The resulting treatment would be equivalent to the accounting if Company B had sold Business Y at fair value with Company A reacquiring a 25 per cent interest in Business Y in the open market.

A consistent approach should be applied as an accounting policy choice for similar transactions.

To illustrate the effect of both of the treatments described above, assume that the fair value of the net assets of Business Y at the date of distribution is CU1,600.

The accounting in Company B can be summarised as follows.

	Beginning of period	Operating profit	Distribution of Business Y to shareholders	End of period
	CU	CU	CU	CU
Net assets of Business X	600	100	–	700
Net assets of Business Y	800	100	(900)	–
Total	1,400	200	(900)	700
Share capital	200	–	–	200
Profit or loss (gain recognised on distribution in accordance with IFRIC 17)	–	–	700	700
Retained earnings	1,200	200	(1,600)	(200)
Total	1,400	200	(900)	700

The accounting by Company A can be summarised as follows:

	Beginning of period	Share of operating profit	Share of gain arising on distribution of Business Y	Receipt of dividend from Company B	Elimination of proportionate share of gain arising on distribution of Business Y	End of period
	CU	CU	CU	CU	CU	CU
Interest in Company B (equity method)	350	50	175	(400)	–	175
Interest in Company C (equity method)	–	–	–	400	(175)[1]	225
Total	350	50	175	–	(175)	400

[1]   This entry would be nil if the alternative approach described above is adopted (i.e. the gain recognised by Company B is not eliminated, resulting in Company A's interest in Company C being recognised at CU400).

Note that, for simplicity, tax effects are ignored in the analysis above.

4.4.14.5 *Elimination of transactions with equity-method investees*

Example 4.4.14.5

Elimination of transactions with equity-method investees

Entity A has a 20 per cent interest in Entity B and accounts for its interest in Entity B using the equity method. Entity A lends CU10,000 to Entity B. Interest on the loan in the current period is CU1,000.

In applying the equity method, should Entity A eliminate its share of the interest income earned on the loan to Entity B (CU200) and the equivalent finance cost recognised in profit or loss by Entity B?

IAS 28:28 requires the elimination of gains and losses resulting from downstream transactions. However, the Standard does not specifically address the treatment of revenue derived from transactions with equity-method investees (e.g. revenue from the sale of goods, or interest revenue) and whether that revenue should be eliminated from the consolidated financial statements.

While IAS 28:26 indicates that many of the procedures appropriate for the application of the equity method are similar to consolidation procedures, Entity A may choose to apply IFRS 10:B86(c) and eliminate its share of the finance income with a corresponding adjustment to its share of Entity B's profit or loss. However, such elimination is not required.

Entity A should select an accounting policy for such transactions and apply that policy consistently.

Sales to associates and joint ventures are disclosable as related party transactions (see **chapter A23**).

4.4.14.6 *Amounts owed to and by associates or joint ventures*

Because associates and joint ventures are not part of the group, balances between the group and associates or joint ventures are not eliminated. Unsettled normal trading transactions should generally be included as current assets or liabilities.

When advances or loans by the group to the associate or joint venture are not expected to be settled within 12 months, they should be shown as non-current assets.

It is not appropriate to offset amounts owed by the group to an associate or a joint venture against the carrying amount of the group's interest in its associates or joint ventures. Such a presentation breaches the offset rules in IAS 32 *Financial Instruments: Presentation*.

4.4.14.7 Losses on transactions with equity-method investees as indications of impairment

When downstream transactions provide evidence of a reduction in the net realisable value of the assets to be sold or contributed, or of an impairment loss of those assets, those losses should be recognised in full by the investor. When upstream transactions provide evidence of a reduction in the net realisable value of the assets to be purchased or of an impairment loss of those assets, the investor should recognise its share of those losses. [IAS 28:29]

4.4.14.8 September 2014 amendments Sale or Contribution of Assets between an Investor and its Associate or Joint Venture

In September 2014, the IASB issued *Sale or Contribution of Assets between an Investor and its Associate or Joint Venture (Amendments to IFRS 10 and IAS 28)*. The September 2014 amendments were designed to address a conflict between the requirements of IAS 28 and IFRS 10 regarding the sale or contribution of a subsidiary to an existing associate or joint venture (as described at **4.4.14.3**) by requiring different treatments for assets that constitute a business and those that do not (see below for amended requirements); this distinction and the required accounting would apply in both IFRS 10 and IAS 28, thus eliminating the inconsistency between the Standards.

The effect of the amendments is to specify as follows.

- In a transaction involving an associate or a joint venture, the extent of gain or loss recognition depends on whether the assets sold or contributed constitute a business.

- When an entity:

  - sells or contributes assets that constitute a business to a joint venture or an associate; or

  - loses control of a subsidiary that contains a business but it retains joint control or significant influence;

  the gain or loss resulting from that transaction is recognised in full.

- Conversely, when an entity:

  - sells or contributes assets that do not constitute a business to a joint venture or an associate; or

  - loses control of a subsidiary that does not contain a business but it retains joint control or significant influence in a transaction involving an associate or a joint venture;

  the gain or loss resulting from that transaction is recognised only to the extent of the unrelated investors' interests in the joint venture or associate, i.e. the entity's share of the gain or loss is eliminated. A new example added to IFRS 10 (see **example 12.4** in **chapter A24**) illustrates the appropriate accounting in such circumstances.

Following finalisation of the September 2014 amendments, the IASB identified several practical issues affecting the implementation of the amendments. As a result, in December 2015 the IASB deferred the effective date of the September 2014 amendments indefinitely pending finalisation of a larger research project on equity accounting (scope and timetable yet to be determined).

For periods prior to the, as yet unspecified, effective date of the September 2014 amendments, or the effective date of any alternative amendments made following completion of the IASB's research project, entities may choose between:

- applying the September 2014 amendments (as described below), in which case the appropriate accounting is determined based on whether the assets sold or contributed constitute a business; and

- continuing to apply the requirements of IFRS 10 and IAS 28 prior to the September 2014 amendments (as described at **4.4.14.3**). If this alternative is selected, entities continue to have an accounting policy choice of applying either the approach in IFRS 10 or the approach in IAS 28 (as illustrated in **example 12.3.3C** in **chapter A24**).

Entities that cannot formally adopt the September 2014 amendments (e.g. due to a requirement for endorsement of changes to IFRSs in their jurisdiction) may adopt an accounting policy consistent with those amendments (i.e. distinguishing between transactions on the basis of whether the subsidiary sold or contributed constitutes a business) provided that the requirements of paragraph 14(b) of IAS 8 *Accounting Policies, Changes in Accounting Estimates and Errors* are met (i.e. the change in policy results in the financial statements providing reliable and more relevant information). However, such a 'voluntary' change in policy would have to be applied retrospectively in accordance with IAS 8; the transition provisions of the September 2014 amendments (which allow for prospective application to transactions occurring after a specified date) would not be available.

For 'upstream' transactions (e.g. sales of assets by an associate or a joint venture to the investor):

[IAS 28:28]

- gains and losses arising on transactions involving assets that do not constitute a business as defined in IFRS 3 are recognised in the entity's financial statements only to the extent of unrelated investors' interest in the associate or joint venture. The entity's share in the associate's or joint venture's gains or losses resulting from these transactions is eliminated; and

- transactions involving assets that constitute a business as defined in IFRS 3 are accounted for in accordance with the requirements of that Standard for a business combination achieved in stages (see **section 11** of **chapter A25**).

For 'downstream' transactions (e.g. sales or contributions of assets from the investor to its associate or joint venture):

[IAS 28:28 & 31A]

- gains and losses arising on transactions involving assets that do not constitute a business as defined in IFRS 3 are recognised in the entity's financial statements only to the extent of unrelated investors' interest in the associate or joint venture; and

- gains and losses arising on transactions involving assets that constitute a business as defined in IFRS 3 are recognised in full in the entity's financial statements.

4.4.15 Non-monetary contributions in exchange for an interest in an equity-method investee

4.4.15.1 Investor's share of gains and losses on non-monetary contributions generally to be eliminated

The requirements discussed in this section are based on the text of IAS 28 prior to the September 2014 amendments (as discussed at **4.4.14.1**). The requirements for entities that have adopted the September 2014 amendments are set out at **4.4.15.4**.

When a non-monetary asset is contributed to an associate or a joint venture in exchange for an equity interest in the associate or joint venture, the transaction should be accounted for in accordance with IAS 28:28 (see **4.4.14.1**), except when the contribution lacks commercial substance. The term 'lacks commercial substance' has the same meaning as when it is used in IAS 16 (see **4.3.3** in **chapter A7**). [IAS 28:30]

Unrealised gains and losses should be eliminated against the investment accounted for using the equity method and should not be presented as deferred gains or losses in the entity's consolidated statement of financial position or in the entity's statement of financial position in which investments are accounted for using the equity method. [IAS 28:30]

4.4.15.2 Non-monetary contribution lacks commercial substance

If the contribution of a non-monetary asset lacks commercial substance, the gain or loss is regarded as unrealised and should therefore not generally be recognised in profit or loss. [IAS 28:30] The exception to this rule arises if, in addition to receiving an equity interest in the associate or joint venture, the entity receives monetary or non-monetary assets. In such circumstances, the portion of the gain or loss on the non-monetary contribution relating to the monetary or non-monetary assets received should be recognised by the entity in profit or loss in full. [IAS 28:31]

4.4.15.3 Contribution of equity interest in subsidiary – conflict with IFRS 10

It is common for an entity to enter into an arrangement whereby it contributes its controlling interest in a subsidiary to a joint venture. The entity relinquishes control of the subsidiary and, in exchange, receives an equity interest in a joint venture and may also receive other consideration as part of the arrangement. The appropriate accounting for transactions of this nature is affected by the conflict between the requirements of IFRS 10 and IAS 28:28 described in **4.4.14.3**. See **4.4.14.8** for a description of the September 2014 amendments designed to address this conflict and for the choices available to entities that have not yet adopted those amendments. The specific requirements for transactions involving the contribution of non-monetary assets to an associate or a joint venture in exchange for an equity interest in that associate or joint venture for entities that have adopted the September 2014 amendments are set out in **4.4.15.4**.

4.4.15.4 September 2014 amendments Sale or Contribution of Assets between an Investor and its Associate or Joint Venture

See **4.4.14.8** for a summary of the effects of the September 2014 amendments and for the choices available for entities that have not yet adopted those amendments. The paragraphs below set out the requirements of IAS 28 relating to non-monetary contributions in exchange for an interest in an equity-method investee for entities that have adopted the September 2014 amendments.

When a non-monetary asset that does not constitute a business, as defined in IFRS 3 *Business Combinations*, is contributed to an associate or a joint venture in exchange for an equity interest in that associate or joint venture:

[IAS 28:30 & 31]

- the transaction should be accounted for in accordance with IAS 28:28 (see **4.4.14.8**), except when the contribution lacks commercial substance (see **4.4.15.2**); and

- unrealised gains and losses should be eliminated against the investment accounted for using the equity method and should not be presented as deferred gains or losses in the entity's consolidated statement of financial position or in the entity's statement of financial position in which investments are accounted for using the equity method.

The gain or loss resulting from a downstream transaction involving assets that constitute a business, as defined in IFRS 3, between an entity and its associate or joint venture is recognised in full in the investor's financial statements. [IAS 28:31A]

An entity might contribute assets in two or more arrangements (transactions). When determining whether assets that are contributed constitute a business, as defined in IFRS 3, an entity should consider whether the contribution of those assets is part of multiple arrangements that should be accounted for as a single transaction in accordance with the requirements of IFRS 10:B97 (see **12.2** in **chapter A24**). [IAS 28:31B]

4.4.16   Equity-method investees with net asset deficiencies

4.4.16.1   Share of losses exceeds the investor's interest in an equity-method investee

If an investor's share of losses of an associate or a joint venture equals or exceeds its interest in the associate or joint venture, the investor should discontinue recognising its share of further losses. [IAS 28:38]

After the investor's interest is reduced to zero, additional losses are provided for, and a liability is recognised, only to the extent that the investor has incurred legal or constructive obligations or made payments on behalf of the associate or joint venture. [IAS 28:39]

If the associate or joint venture subsequently reports profits, the investor resumes including its share of those profits only after its share of the profits equals the share of net losses not recognised. [IAS 28:39]

Example 4.4.16.1

Equity-method investee with net asset deficiency

Entity A invests CU10 million to acquire 25 per cent of the equity share capital of Entity B. Entity A accounts for Entity B using the equity method. Entity A has entered into no other guarantees or commitments in respect of Entity B. Entity B is in a start-up situation and expects to make significant losses in the first year and to generate profits thereafter. Entity B has sufficient cash resources to meet its liabilities as they fall due.

In the first year, Entity B loses CU50 million. Entity A should recognise a loss of CU10 million in respect of its equity stake. However, the balance of Entity A's share of the net loss (i.e. 25 per cent of CU50 million less CU10 million) is not recognised.

In the next year, Entity B makes a profit of CU10 million. Entity A recognises no profit because its share of the profit (CU2.5 million) equals the amount of the unrecognised loss in the previous period. For any profits made by Entity B in excess of CU10 million, Entity A recognises its proportionate share.

4.4.16.2 Investor's interest includes long-term interests that form part of the investor's net investment

An investor may have a variety of interests in an associate or a joint venture, both long-term and short-term, including ordinary or preferred shares, loans, advances, debt securities, options to acquire ordinary shares, and trade receivables. For the purposes of IAS 28:38, the investor's interest in an associate or a joint venture is the carrying amount of the investment in the associate or joint venture under the equity method together with any long-term interests that, in substance, form part of the investor's net investment in the associate or joint venture. [IAS 28:38]

For example, an item for which settlement is neither planned nor likely to occur in the foreseeable future is, in substance, an extension of the entity's investment in that associate or joint venture. Such items may include preference shares and long-term receivables or loans. Items such as trade receivables, trade payables and any long-term receivables for which adequate collateral exists, such as secured loans, will not fall to be treated as part of the investor's interest in an associate or a joint venture for this purpose. [IAS 28:38]

Losses recognised under the equity method in excess of the investor's investment in ordinary shares are applied to the other components of the investor's interest in an associate or a joint venture in the reverse order of their seniority (i.e. priority in liquidation). [IAS 28:38]

Example 4.4.16.2

Recognition of an investor's share of the losses of an equity-method investee – additional investment via long-term loan

Entity A holds a 25 per cent investment in Entity B's ordinary shares (its only class of equity instrument) and accounts for its interest in Entity B using the equity method. In addition, Entity A has provided a long-term loan of CU1,000 to Entity B which is viewed as forming part of its net investment in Entity B in accordance with IAS 28:38. The other shareholders of Entity B have not provided any equivalent loans.

At 1 January 20X1, Entity B's net assets are CU1,000. Entity A's interest in Entity B comprises its equity method investment of CU250 plus the loan of CU1,000. During 20X1, Entity B reports a net loss of CU1,400 such that, at 31 December 20X1, it has net liabilities (including the CU1,000 liability due to Entity A) of CU400.

Entity A is not liable for the obligations of Entity B or otherwise committed to provide financial support to Entity B.

How should Entity A determine its share of Entity B's losses for the year ended 31 December 20X1?

As described in **4.4.3.1**, an investor generally recognises its share of the income and losses of an equity-method investee on the basis of the percentage of the equity interest owned by the investor.

IAS 28:38 requires that when loans and similar items form part of an investor's interest in an equity-method investee, and the investor's share of losses exceeds its investment in ordinary shares, such losses should be applied to the other components of the investor's interest in reverse order of their seniority (i.e. their priority on liquidation of the investee). However, the Standard does not specify what percentage should be used in attributing the excess losses in such circumstances.

One acceptable method would be to allocate losses to all components of the net investment using the same percentage – that is, the percentage used in the application of the equity method. This method reflects the principle discussed in **4.4.3.1**. In the circumstances under consideration, if this approach were adopted, in 20X1 Entity A would recognise a loss of CU350 (CU1,400 × 25%) with respect to its net investment in Entity B.

Another acceptable method would be to attribute losses in excess of those attributable to the ordinary shares based on the investor's percentage share of the other components that form part of its net investment, in reverse order of seniority. This method reflects the direction in IAS 28:38 that the attribution of excess losses to other instruments in such circumstances should reflect their order of seniority, which could be interpreted as implying that each instrument is considered separately. In the circumstances under consideration, if this approach were adopted, Entity A would recognise a loss of CU650 (CU1,000 × 25% + CU400 × 100%) with respect to its net investment in Entity B.

In the absence of clear guidance in the Standard, the approach adopted by Entity A should be applied consistently as an accounting policy choice.

Regardless of the method used, Entity A would assess its remaining net investment in Entity B for impairment.

4.4.16.3 Recognition of losses when an equity-method investee recognises a profit in profit or loss and a loss in other comprehensive income

Example 4.4.16.3

Recognition of losses when an equity-method investee recognises a profit in profit or loss and a loss in other comprehensive income

Entity A holds a 40 per cent investment in Entity B and accounts for its interest in Entity B using the equity method. At 30 June 20X0, the carrying amount of Entity A's investment in Entity B is CU20. During the financial year ended 30 June 20X1, Entity B makes a profit of CU50 and recognises a loss in other comprehensive income (OCI) of CU200.

Entity A has entered into no legal or constructive obligations and has made no payments on behalf of Entity B.

How should Entity A recognise its share of Entity B's profit and movements in OCI in its financial statements for the financial year ended 30 June 20X1?

IAS 28:10 states that "the carrying amount [of an equity-method investee] is increased to recognise the investor's share of the profit or loss of the investee after the date of acquisition ... Adjustments to the carrying amount may also be necessary for changes in the investor's proportionate interest in the investee arising from changes in the investee's other comprehensive income".

Therefore, in addition to amounts recognised in profit or loss, Entity A should generally recognise as part of its own OCI its proportionate share of items of income and expense recognised by Entity B in OCI.

IAS 28:38 states, in part, that if an investor's share of losses of an associate or a joint venture equals or exceeds its interest in the associate or joint venture, the investor discontinues recognising its share of further losses. Additional losses are provided for, and a liability is recognised, only to the extent that the investor has incurred legal or constructive obligations or made payments on behalf of the associate or joint venture. If the associate or joint venture subsequently reports profits, the investor resumes recognising its share of those profits only after its share of the profits equals the share of losses not recognised (see IAS 28:39).

The principle behind restricting the recognition of losses under IAS 28:38 is to ensure that the carrying amount of the investment is not reduced below zero, unless the investor incurs legal or constructive obligations or has made payments on behalf of the equity-method investee.

IAS 28 does not address the appropriate treatment, such as in the circumstances described, when the equity-method investee recognises a profit in profit or loss and a loss in OCI in the same accounting period. The Standard is not clear as to the order in which the movements in the carrying amount of the investment should be recognised nor the extent to which the movements in profit or loss and OCI should be offset.

One acceptable approach would be for Entity A to recognise its share of Entity B's profit of CU20 (thus increasing the carrying amount of the investment to CU40) and its share of Entity B's loss in OCI up to CU40; this would limit the 'write down' of the investment so that its carrying amount is not reduced below zero, in line with the general principle underlying IAS 28:38. When this approach is adopted, in line with the requirements of IAS 28:39, if Entity B subsequently reports profits, Entity A should resume recognising its share of those profits only after its share of the profits equals its share of Entity B's losses in OCI not previously recognised.

Other approaches may also be acceptable, particularly if the timing of specific transactions in the reporting period is such that the loss in Entity B's OCI can be determined to have occurred before or after the profit recognised in profit or loss.

4.4.17   Discontinuing the use of the equity method

The investor should discontinue the use of the equity method from the date when the investment ceases to be an associate or a joint venture, as follows.

[IAS 28:22]

- If the investment becomes a subsidiary, the entity should account for its investment in accordance with IFRS 3 *Business Combinations* and IFRS 10 *Consolidated Financial Statements*.

- If the retained interest in the former associate or joint venture is a financial asset, the entity should measure the retained interest at fair value. The fair value of the retained interest should be regarded as its fair value on initial recognition as a financial asset in accordance with IFRS 9 *Financial Instruments* (or, for entities that have not yet adopted IFRS 9, IAS 39 *Financial Instruments: Recognition and Measurement*). The entity should recognise in profit or loss any difference between (1) the fair value of any retained interest and any proceeds from disposing of a part interest in the associate or joint venture, and (2) the carrying amount of the investment at the date the equity method was discontinued.

- When an entity discontinues the use of the equity method, the entity should account for all amounts previously recognised in other comprehensive income in relation to that investment on the same basis as would have been required if the investee had directly disposed of the related assets or liabilities.

Accordingly, if a gain or loss previously recognised in other comprehensive income by the investee would be reclassified to profit or loss on the disposal of the related assets or liabilities, the investor reclassifies the gain or loss from equity to profit or loss (as a reclassification adjustment) when the equity method is discontinued. [IAS 28:23] By way of example, if an associate or a joint venture has cumulative exchange differences relating to a foreign operation and the entity discontinues the use of the equity method, the entity should reclassify to profit or loss the gain or loss that had previously been recognised in other comprehensive income in relation to the foreign operation.

See **11.5** in **chapter A25** for a discussion of the appropriate treatment for such exchange differences when an entity obtains control over a former associate or joint venture.

In contrast, if the revaluation model has been applied to property, plant and equipment of the associate or joint venture, revaluation gains or losses previously recognised in other comprehensive income and accumulated in equity in relation to those assets will not be reclassified. This is because, in accordance with IAS 16 *Property, Plant and*

Equipment, a gain or loss previously recognised in other comprehensive income by the investee would not be reclassified to profit or loss on the disposal of the related assets (see **6.8.4** in **chapter A7**).

4.4.18 Other changes in ownership interests

If an investment in an associate becomes an investment in a joint venture or an investment in a joint venture becomes an investment in an associate, the entity continues to apply the equity method and does not remeasure the retained interest. [IAS 28:24]

In the case of a change from joint control to significant influence, and *vice versa*, the investor-investee relationship changes and, consequently, so does the nature of the investment. However, in this instance, both investments (i.e. the joint venture and the associate) are measured using the equity method. Considering that there is neither a change in the group boundaries nor a change in the measurement requirements, the IASB concluded that these are not events that warrant remeasurement. [IAS 28:BC30]

If an entity's ownership interest in an associate or a joint venture is reduced, but the investment continues to be classified either as an associate or a joint venture, respectively, the entity should reclassify to profit or loss the proportion of the gain or loss that had previously been recognised in other comprehensive income relating to that reduction in ownership interest if that gain or loss would be required to be reclassified to profit or loss on the disposal of the related assets or liabilities. [IAS 28:25]

Accordingly, the determination as to whether gains or losses should be reclassified is made on the same basis as discussed at **4.4.17**.

An entity's ownership interest in an associate or a joint venture may reduce (but the classification of the investment remain unchanged) as a result of a disposal or deemed disposal (see **12.3.5** in **chapter A24**). Any gain or loss arising as a result of a disposal or deemed disposal of an associate or a joint venture should be recognised in profit or loss.

4.4.19 Impairment and reversals of impairment losses (entities applying IFRS 9)

4.4.19.1 Recognition of an impairment loss when there is objective evidence of impairment

The requirements in this section, and in **4.4.19.2** to **4.4.19.7**, are applicable to entities applying IFRS 9 *Financial Instruments*, which is effective for annual periods beginning on or after 1 January 2018, with earlier application permitted. Entities that have not yet adopted IFRS 9 should refer to **4.4.20**.

After application of the equity method, including recognising the associate's or joint venture's losses in accordance with IAS 28:38, the investor should apply the requirements of IAS 28:41A to 41C (see below) to determine whether there is any objective evidence that its net investment in the associate or joint venture is impaired. [IAS 28:40]

The investor may have other interests in the associate or joint venture (e.g. trade receivables and long-term receivables for which adequate collateral exists, such as secured loans) that do not constitute part of its net investment and that are in the scope of IFRS 9 *Financial Instruments*. Such additional interests should be assessed for impairment in accordance with the general requirements of IFRS 9. [IAS 28:41]

The net investment in an associate or a joint venture should be considered to be impaired if, and only if, there is objective evidence of impairment as a result of one or more loss events. Specific requirements are as follows:

[IAS 28:41A]

- the loss event(s) must have occurred after the initial recognition of the net investment;

- the loss event(s) must have an impact on the estimated future cash flows from the net investment that can be reliably estimated;

- it may not be possible to identify a single, discrete event that caused the impairment, but it may have been caused by the combined effect of several events; and

- losses expected as a result of future events, no matter how likely, are not recognised.

Objective evidence that the net investment is impaired includes observable data that comes to the attention of the entity about the following loss events:

[IAS 28:41A]

- significant financial difficulty of the associate or joint venture;

- a breach of contract, such as a default or delinquency in payments by the associate or joint venture;

- the entity, for economic or legal reasons relating to its associate's or joint venture's financial difficulty, granting to the associate or joint venture a concession that the entity would not otherwise consider;

- it becoming probable that the associate or joint venture will enter bankruptcy or other financial reorganisation; or

- the disappearance of an active market for the net investment because of financial difficulties of the associate or joint venture. Note, however, that the disappearance of an active market because the associate's or joint venture's equity or financial instruments are no longer publicly traded is not evidence of impairment. [IAS 28:41B]

A downgrade of an associate's or joint venture's credit rating or a decline in the fair value of the associate or joint venture, is not of itself, evidence of impairment, although it may be evidence of impairment when considered with other available information. [IAS 28:41B] A significant or prolonged decline in the fair value of an investment in an equity instrument below its cost is objective evidence of impairment. [IAS 28:41C]

In addition to the types of events listed in IAS 28:41A (see above), objective evidence of impairment for the net investment in the equity instruments of the associate or joint venture includes information about significant changes with an adverse effect that have taken place in the technological, market, economic or legal environment in which the associate or joint venture operates, and indicates that the cost of the investment in the equity instrument may not be recovered. [IAS 28:41C]

4.4.19.2   Carrying amount of investment to be tested under IAS 36

Whenever application of the requirements of IAS 28:41A to 41C (see **4.4.19.1**) indicates that the interest in an associate or a joint venture may be impaired, the entire carrying amount of the investment (including goodwill) is tested as a single asset under IAS 36 *Impairment of Assets*. The recoverable amount (higher of value in use and fair value less costs to sell) of the investment is compared with its carrying amount. IAS 28 allows two methods for calculating the value in use of the investment which, under appropriate assumptions, should give the same result. The alternatives are:

[IAS 28:42]

- to estimate the investor's share of the present value of the estimated future cash flows expected to be generated by the associate or joint venture, including the cash flows from the operations of the associate or joint venture and the proceeds on the ultimate disposal of the investment; or

- to estimate the present value of the estimated future cash flows expected to arise from dividends to be received from the investment and from its ultimate disposal.

4.4.19.3   Recoverability of individual investments to be assessed separately

If the investor has more than one investment accounted for using the equity method, the recoverability of each interest should be assessed separately, unless an associate or a joint venture does not generate cash inflows from continuing use that are largely independent of those from other assets of the entity. [IAS 28:43]

4.4.19.4   Reversals of impairment losses for investments including goodwill

Generally, in appropriate circumstances, impairment losses recognised in respect of investments accounted for using the equity method are permitted to be reversed. However, the question arises as to whether this is permitted in respect of goodwill included in the carrying amount of such investments, given the general prohibition on reversing impairment losses relating to goodwill in IAS 36 (see **10.5** in **chapter A10**).

For example, if the equity carrying amount of an investee included CU100 goodwill, and an impairment loss of CU150 was recognised, the goodwill effectively has been eliminated. If the recoverable amount subsequently increases to its original value, is it appropriate for the entire impairment loss of CU150 to be reversed, or is the reversal restricted to CU50?

IAS 28:42 states that because goodwill included in the carrying amount of an equity-method investee is not separately recognised, it is not tested for impairment separately under the principles of IAS 36. Instead, the entire carrying amount of the investment is tested under IAS 36 for impairment by comparing its recoverable amount with its carrying amount, whenever application of the requirements in IAS 28:41A to 41C indicates that the investment may be impaired (see **4.4.10**). Although not specifically addressed in IAS 28, the treatment of reversals of impairment losses should mirror the requirements of IAS 28:42. The investment, therefore, is treated as a whole, and the goodwill is not treated separately; thus, there is no prohibition against restoring the carrying amount of the investment to its pre-impairment value, in appropriate circumstances.

Therefore, in the circumstances described above, the entire impairment loss of CU150 should be reversed if the general conditions for the reversal of the impairment of an equity-method investee are met.

4.4.19.5   Non-recourse debt and impairment of equity-method investments

Example 4.4.19.5

Non-recourse debt and impairment of equity-method investments

Company A and Company B each make a CU6 million investment in a real estate venture, Company C. Their investments are financed in part by each borrowing CU5 million. The terms of the borrowing are such that, to the extent that they fail to recover their investments from Company C, Company A and Company B are not required to repay their borrowings.

If Company A's and Company B's investments in Company C are determined to be impaired under the principles set out in IAS 28:42, Company A and Company B must write their investments down in accordance with that paragraph. The existence of non-recourse debt is not justification for limiting the impairment loss. The borrowings are accounted for separately under IFRS 9.

4.4.19.6   Impairment of equity-method investments – determination of an appropriate discount rate

Example 4.4.19.6

Impairment of equity-method investments – determination of an appropriate discount rate

Entity X holds 25 per cent of the shares in Entity Y. Entity X accounts for its interest in Entity Y using the equity method.

Entity X applies the requirements of IAS 28:41A to 41C and determines that its net investment in Entity Y may be impaired. Consequently, in accordance with IAS 28:42, Entity X applies the requirements of IAS 36 *Impairment of Assets* by comparing the carrying amount of its net investment in Entity Y with its recoverable amount (i.e. the higher of fair value less costs of disposal and value in use).

For the purpose of calculating the value in use of its net investment in Entity Y, on what basis should Entity X select an appropriate discount rate?

When calculating the value in use of an entity's net investment in an investment accounted for using the equity method, the discount rate selected should reflect current market assessments of the time value of money and the risks specific to the investment.

IAS 28:42 states that "the entire carrying amount of the investment is tested for impairment in accordance with IAS 36 as a single asset". Therefore, this is the unit of account for impairment testing purposes and, as such, the cash flows generated by the investment and associated discount rates should be considered at the level of the investment as a whole and not by looking through to the underlying cash-generating units (CGUs) of the investment.

The discount rate(s) used by the investee in any calculation of the value in use of its CGUs (or, for the assessment of goodwill for impairment, groups of CGUs) for the purposes of its own financial statements reflect the risks specific to the individual CGUs (or groups of CGUs). In determining the value in use of its net investment, an entity should instead use a single rate reflecting current market assessments of the time value of money and the risks specific to the equity investment as a whole.

4.4.19.7   Impairment of equity-method investments – impact of a restructuring to which the investee is not yet committed

---

Example 4.4.19.7

Impairment of equity-method investments – impact of a restructuring to which the investee is not yet committed

Entity F holds 25 per cent of the shares in Entity G. Entity F accounts for its interest in Entity G using the equity method.

Entity F applies the requirements of IAS 28:41A to 41C and determines that its net investment in Entity G may be impaired. Consequently, in accordance with IAS 28:42, Entity F applies the requirements of IAS 36 by comparing the carrying amount of its net investment in Entity G with its recoverable amount (i.e. the higher of fair value less costs of disposal and value in use).

Entity G is intending to carry out a restructuring in the future. However, applying the requirements of paragraphs 70 to 77 of IAS 37 *Provisions, Contingent Liabilities and Contingent Assets*, Entity G is not sufficiently committed to the plan to recognise the restructuring provision at the end of the reporting period.

In calculating the value in use of its net investment in Entity G, should Entity F include the estimated costs and associated benefits of the planned restructuring?

No. The estimated future restructuring costs and the effects of that restructuring on subsequent expected cash flows should not be included in the calculation of the value in use of Entity F's net investment in Entity G.

IAS 28:42 requires Entity G to apply the requirements of IAS 36 in determining the recoverable amount of its net investment in Entity G. In accordance with IAS 36:44(a), the calculation of value in use should exclude estimated future cash inflows or outflows that are expected to arise from a future restructuring to which an entity is not yet committed.

4.4.20   Impairment and reversals of impairment losses (entities that have not yet adopted IFRS 9)

4.4.20.1   Requirement to consider whether an impairment loss should be recognised

After application of the equity method, including recognising the associate's or joint venture's losses in accordance with IAS 28:38, the investor should apply the requirements of IAS 39 *Financial Instruments: Recognition and Measurement* to determine whether it is necessary to recognise any additional impairment loss with respect to the investor's net investment in the associate or joint venture. [IAS 28:40]

The investor may have other interests in the associate or joint venture (e.g. trade receivables and long-term receivables for which adequate collateral exists, such as secured loans) that do not constitute part of its net investment and that are in the scope of IAS 39. Such additional interests should also be assessed for impairment in accordance with IAS 39. [IAS 28:41]

IAS 39:58 requires that financial assets be assessed at the end of each reporting period to determine whether there is any objective evidence that they are impaired. IAS 39:59 to 62 provide detailed guidance for the identification of such objective evidence, which is discussed in **section 5** of **chapter C6**.

The following factors provide additional evidence as to whether an investment in an equity-method investee might be impaired:

- the financial condition and near-term prospects of the equity-method investee, including any specific events that may influence the operations of the equity-method investee (such as changes in technology or the discontinuance of a business segment that may affect its future earnings potential);

- the financial performance and projections of the equity-method investee;

- trends in the general market;

- the capital strength of the equity-method investee;

- the dividend payment record of the equity-method investee;

- known liquidity crisis;

- bankruptcy proceedings; and

- going concern commentary in the auditor's report on the investee's most recent financial statements.

4.4.20.2   *Carrying amount of investment to be tested under IAS 36*

Whenever application of the requirements of IAS 39 indicates that the interest in an associate or a joint venture may be impaired, the entire carrying amount of the investment (including goodwill) is tested as a single asset under IAS 36 *Impairment of Assets*. The recoverable amount (higher of value in use and fair value less costs to sell) of the Investment is compared with its carrying amount. IAS 28 allows two methods for calculating the value in use of the investment which, under appropriate assumptions, should give the same result. The alternatives are:

[IAS 28:42]

- to estimate the investor's share of the present value of the estimated future cash flows expected to be generated by the associate or joint venture, including the cash flows from the operations of the associate or joint venture and the proceeds on the ultimate disposal of the investment; or

- to estimate the present value of the estimated future cash flows expected to arise from dividends to be received from the investment and from its ultimate disposal.

4.4.20.3   Recoverability of individual investments to be assessed separately

If the investor has more than one investment accounted for using the equity method, the recoverability of each interest should be assessed separately, unless an associate or a joint venture does not generate cash inflows from continuing use that are largely independent of those from other assets of the entity. [IAS 28:43]

4.4.20.4   Reversals of impairment losses for investments including goodwill

Generally, in appropriate circumstances, impairment losses recognised in respect of investments accounted for using the equity method are permitted to be reversed. However, the question arises as to whether this is permitted in respect of goodwill included in the carrying amount of such investments, given the general prohibition on reversing impairment losses relating to goodwill in IAS 36 (see **10.5** in **chapter A10**).

For example, if the equity carrying amount of an investee included CU100 goodwill, and an impairment loss of CU150 was recognised, the goodwill effectively has been eliminated. If the recoverable amount subsequently increases to its original value, is it appropriate for the entire impairment loss of CU150 to be reversed, or is the reversal restricted to CU50?

IAS 28:42 states that because goodwill included in the carrying amount of an equity-method investee is not separately recognised, it is not tested for impairment separately under the principles of IAS 36. Instead, the entire carrying amount of the investment is tested under IAS 36 for impairment by comparing its recoverable amount with its carrying amount, whenever application of the requirements in IAS 39 indicates that the investment may be impaired (see **4.4.10**). Although not specifically addressed in IAS 28, the treatment of reversals of impairment losses should mirror the requirements of IAS 28:42. The investment, therefore, is treated as a whole, and the goodwill is not treated separately; thus, there is no prohibition against restoring the carrying amount of the investment to its pre-impairment value, in appropriate circumstances.

Therefore, in the circumstances described above, the entire impairment loss of CU150 should be reversed if the general conditions for the reversal of the impairment of an equity-method investee are met.

4.4.20.5   Non-recourse debt and impairment of equity-method investments

Example 4.4.20.5

Non-recourse debt and impairment of equity-method investments

Company A and Company B each make a CU6 million investment in a real estate venture, Company C. Their investments are financed in part by each borrowing CU5 million. The terms of the borrowing are such that, to the extent that they fail to recover their investments from Company C, Company A and Company B are not required to repay their borrowings.

If Company A's and Company B's investments in Company C are determined to be impaired under the principles set out in IAS 28:42, Company A and Company B must write their investments down in accordance with that paragraph. The existence of non-recourse debt is not justification for limiting the impairment loss. The borrowings are accounted for separately under IAS 39.

4.4.20.6   Impairment of equity-method investments – determination of an appropriate discount rate

Example 4.4.20.6

Impairment of equity-method investments – determination of an appropriate discount rate

Entity X holds 25 per cent of the shares in Entity Y. Entity X accounts for its interest in Entity Y using the equity method.

Entity X applies the requirements of IAS 39 and determines that its net investment in Entity Y may be impaired. Consequently, In accordance with IAS 28:42, Entity X applies the requirements of IAS 36 by comparing the carrying amount of its net investment in Entity Y with its recoverable amount (i.e. the higher of fair value less costs of disposal and value in use).

For the purpose of calculating the value in use of its net investment in Entity Y, on what basis should Entity X select an appropriate discount rate?

When calculating the value in use of an entity's net investment in an investment accounted for using the equity method, the discount rate selected should reflect current market assessments of the time value of money and the risks specific to the investment.

IAS 28:42 states that "the entire carrying amount of the investment is tested for impairment in accordance with IAS 36 as a single asset". Therefore, this is the unit of account for impairment testing purposes and, as such, the cash flows generated by the investment and associated discount rates should be considered at the level of the investment as a whole and not by looking through to the underlying cash-generating units (CGUs) of the investment.

The discount rate(s) used by the investee in any calculation of the value in use of its CGUs (or, for the assessment of goodwill for impairment, groups of CGUs) for the purposes of its own financial statements reflect the risks specific to the individual CGUs (or groups of CGUs). In determining the value in use of its net investment, an entity should instead use a single rate reflecting current market assessments of the time value of money and the risks specific to the equity investment as a whole.

4.4.20.7   Impairment of equity-method investments – impact of a restructuring to which the investee is not yet committed

Example 4.4.20.7

Impairment of equity-method investments – impact of a restructuring to which the investee is not yet committed

Entity F holds 25 per cent of the shares in Entity G. Entity F accounts for its interest in Entity G using the equity method.

Entity F applies the requirements of IAS 39 and determines that its net investment in Entity G may be impaired. Consequently, in accordance with IAS 28:42, Entity F applies the requirements of IAS 36 by comparing the carrying amount of its net investment in Entity G with its recoverable amount (i.e. the higher of fair value less costs of disposal and value in use).

Entity G is intending to carry out a restructuring in the future. However, applying the requirements of paragraphs 70 to 77 of IAS 37 *Provisions, Contingent Liabilities and Contingent Assets*, Entity G is not sufficiently committed to the plan to recognise the restructuring provision at the end of the reporting period.

In calculating the value in use of its net investment in Entity G, should Entity F include the estimated costs and associated benefits of the planned restructuring?

No. The estimated future restructuring costs and the effects of that restructuring on subsequent expected cash flows should not be included in the calculation of the value in use of Entity F's net investment in Entity G.

IAS 28:42 requires Entity G to apply the requirements of IAS 36 in determining the recoverable amount of its net investment in Entity G. In accordance with IAS 36:44(a), the calculation of value in use should exclude estimated future cash inflows or outflows that are expected to arise from a future restructuring to which an entity is not yet committed.

4.4.21   *Investments in equity-method investees generally to be presented as non-current*

Unless an investment, or a portion of an investment, in an associate or a joint venture is classified as held for sale under IFRS 5 *Non-current Assets Held for Sale and Discontinued Operations*, the investment, or any retained interest in the investment not classified as held for sale, should be classified as a non-current asset. [IAS 28:15]

5 Separate financial statements

The accounting for investments in associates and joint ventures in the investor's separate financial statements is dealt with in IAS 27 *Separate Financial Statements* (see **chapter A29**). [IAS 28:44]

6 Presentation and disclosure

6.1 Presentation

IAS 1 *Presentation of Financial Statements* requires that:

- investments accounted for under the equity method should be presented as a separate line item in the statement of financial position; [IAS 1:54(e)] and

- the share of profit or loss of associates and joint ventures accounted for using the equity method should be presented as a separate line item in the profit or loss section of the statement of comprehensive income, or the statement of profit or loss. [IAS 1:82(c)]

> If an entity chooses to report a line for operating profit, it will need to consider whether the share of profit or loss of associates and joint ventures accounted for using the equity method should be presented within or outside operating profit. Having made that decision, it would seem appropriate for any impairment loss relating to such an associate or a joint venture to be presented consistently with that decision either within or outside operating profit. Any impairment loss should not be offset against the share of profit or loss from associates and joint ventures because this would conflict with the requirement to show that share of profit or loss as a separate line item. Some entities may choose to show the impairment loss separately from, but adjacent to, the share of profit or loss of the associate or joint venture.

6.2 Disclosure

Disclosure requirements for interests in associates and joint ventures are set out in IFRS 12 *Disclosure of Interests in Other Entities* (see **chapter A28**).

7 Future developments

In November 2015, the IASB published ED/2015/10 *Annual Improvements to IFRSs 2014-2016 Cycle*. The exposure draft includes a proposed amendment to clarify that qualifying entities permitted to measure investments in associates and joint ventures at fair value through profit or loss (see **4.2**) may elect to do so on an investment-by-investment basis at initial recognition.

The proposed amendments would provide a similar clarification for a reporting entity that is not an investment entity and that holds an interest in an associate or a joint venture that is an investment entity. When applying the equity method, such an entity has a choice as to whether to retain the fair value measurements used by its investment-entity associate or joint venture (see **4.4.13.2**); the proposed amendments would clarify that this choice is made separately for each investment in an associate or a joint venture that is an investment entity, upon initial recognition.

The comment period on the exposure draft closed on 17 February 2016. At the time of writing, the IASB has not yet determined the next step on this issue.

A27　Joint arrangements

Contents

1 Introduction

1.1 Overview of IFRS 11

IFRS 11 *Joint Arrangements* outlines the accounting by entities that jointly control an arrangement. Joint control involves the contractually agreed sharing of control. Arrangements subject to joint control are classified as either a joint venture (representing a share of net assets and accounted for using the equity method) or a joint operation (representing rights to assets and obligations for liabilities, accounted for accordingly).

1.2 Amendments to IFRS 11 since the last edition of this manual

None. IFRS 11 was most recently amended in May 2014.

2 Objective

The objective of IFRS 11 is to establish principles for financial reporting by entities that have an interest in joint arrangements (i.e. arrangements that are controlled jointly). [IFRS 11:1] Accordingly, IFRS 11 defines joint control and requires an entity that is a party to a joint arrangement:

[IFRS 11:2]

- to determine the type of joint arrangement in which it is involved by assessing its rights and obligations; and

- to account for those rights and obligations in accordance with that type of joint arrangement.

3 Scope

If an entity is a party to a joint arrangement, it is required to apply IFRS 11. [IFRS 11:3] A party to a joint arrangement means an entity that participates in a joint arrangement, regardless of whether that entity has joint control of the arrangement. [IFRS 11:Appendix A]

A joint arrangement is defined as an arrangement of which two or more parties have joint control. [IFRS 11:4 & Appendix A]

The meaning of joint control is discussed in **4.3**.

Two entities may agree to what they view as a joint arrangement but, of itself, this does not automatically bring them within the scope of IFRS 11. For example, if their two businesses are complementary (one manufactures and sells curtaining fabric and the other makes curtains to measure), each could simply agree to advertise the other's website on its own website; this might be mutually beneficial for the businesses but the arrangement does not involve joint control and, accordingly, does not fall within the scope of the Standard.

Similarly, two entities sometimes use the term 'joint venture' in a general business sense to refer to an entity in which they both have interests but of which one of them has control (as defined in IFRS 10 *Consolidated Financial Statements*). Such an entity is a subsidiary of the controlling party, and the arrangement between the two entities is not within the scope of IFRS 11.

Not every party to a joint arrangement has to share control. [IFRS 11:11] For example, Entities A, B, C, D and E may all be parties to a joint arrangement, with control being shared by Entities A, B, C and D. In this scenario, all five parties should apply the requirements of IFRS 11, but the accounting specified for Entity E's interest in the arrangement may be different from that specified for the interests of Entities A, B, C and D (see **section 6**).

When a joint operation that is a separate vehicle prepares financial statements, IFRS 11 does not apply to those financial statements. IFRS 11 applies only to the accounting by the parties to the joint operation (see **5.2**) and not to the accounting by the separate vehicle that is a joint operation. The financial statements of the separate vehicle should be prepared in accordance with applicable IFRSs.

The financial statements of the joint operation should include the assets, liabilities, revenues and expenses of the legal entity/separate vehicle. However, when identifying the assets and liabilities of the separate vehicle, it is necessary to understand the joint operators' rights and obligations relating to those assets and liabilities and how those rights and obligations affect those assets and liabilities.

This conclusion was confirmed by the IFRS Interpretations Committee in March 2015.

4 Determining whether there is a joint arrangement

4.1 Characteristics of a joint arrangement

A joint arrangement is defined as an arrangement of which two or more parties have joint control. [IFRS 11:4 & Appendix A]

Two characteristics are necessary to fulfil the definition of a joint arrangement:

[IFRS 11:5]

- the parties to the joint arrangement are bound by a contractual arrangement (see **4.2**); and

- the contractual arrangement gives two or more of those parties joint control of the arrangement (see **4.3**).

4.2   Contractual arrangement

The terms upon which the parties participate in the joint activity are set out in the contractual arrangement. Often, the contractual arrangement is set out in writing (e.g. in a contract or a document of discussions between the parties) but this need not be the case. Sometimes statutory mechanisms, either on their own or in conjunction with a contract between the parties, can create enforceable arrangements. [IFRS 11:B2]

Although IFRS 11 does not state explicitly that the contractual arrangement should be enforceable, this appears to be implicit in IFRS 11:5(a) (see **4.1**), which requires that the parties are bound by it.

When a separate legal entity or other vehicle is used, its articles, charter or by-laws may set out some or all of the terms of the contractual arrangement. Usually, the contractual arrangement will deal with matters such as:

[IFRS 11:B3 & B4]

- the purpose, activity and duration of the joint arrangement;

- how the members of the joint arrangement's governing body (the board of directors, or equivalent) are appointed;

- the decision-making process: the matters that require decisions from the parties, the voting rights of the parties and the required level of support for those matters (this process is key in establishing joint control – see **4.3**);

- the required capital or other contributions to be provided by the parties; and

- how the assets, liabilities, revenue, expenses or profit or loss of the joint arrangement are to be shared between the parties.

4.3   Joint control

4.3.1   The meaning of 'joint control'

Joint control is defined in the Standard as "the contractually agreed sharing of control of an arrangement, which exists only when decisions about the relevant activities require the unanimous consent of the parties sharing control". [IFRS 11:7 & Appendix A]

In a joint arrangement, no single party controls the arrangement on its own. A party with joint control of an arrangement can prevent any of the other parties, or a group of the parties, from controlling the arrangement. [IFRS 11:10]

IFRS 11 emphasises the need to exercise judgement when assessing whether two or more parties have joint control of an arrangement. This assessment should be made by considering all facts and circumstances, as discussed further below. [IFRS 11:12]

IFRS 11 requires an entity that is a party to an arrangement to assess whether the contractual arrangement gives all the parties (or a group of the parties) control of the arrangement collectively. [IFRS 11:8 & B5] Control is defined in IFRS 10 *Consolidated Financial Statements* and is discussed in **section 5** of **chapter A24**. IFRS 10's definition of control requires three elements:

[IFRS 10:7 & 10]

- power over the investee (i.e. existing rights that give the current ability to direct the 'relevant activities' of the investee);
- exposure, or rights, to variable returns from involvement with the investee; and
- the ability to use power over the investee to affect the amount of those returns.

The guidance in IFRS 10 should be used to determine whether all the parties (or a group of the parties) are exposed, or have rights, to variable returns from their involvement with the arrangement and have the ability to affect those returns through their power over the arrangement. All the parties (or a group of the parties) control the arrangement collectively when they must act together to direct the 'relevant activities', i.e. the activities that significantly affect the returns of the arrangement. [IFRS 11:8 & B5]

Once it has been determined that all the parties (or a group of the parties) control the arrangement collectively, joint control exists only when decisions about the relevant activities require the unanimous consent of the parties that control the arrangement collectively. The assessment as to whether an arrangement is jointly controlled by all of its parties or by a group of the parties, or controlled by one of its parties alone, can involve the exercise of judgement. [IFRS 11:9 & B6]

The approach to determining whether an arrangement is jointly controlled, as described in the previous paragraphs, is summarised diagrammatically in Appendix B to IFRS 11.

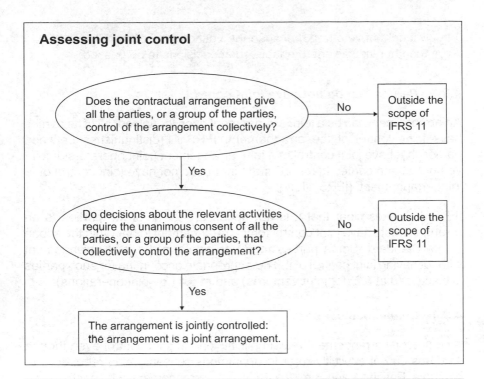

Assessing joint control

Does the contractual arrangement give all the parties, or a group of the parties, control of the arrangement collectively? — No → Outside the scope of IFRS 11

Yes ↓

Do decisions about the relevant activities require the unanimous consent of all the parties, or a group of the parties, that collectively control the arrangement? — No → Outside the scope of IFRS 11

Yes ↓

The arrangement is jointly controlled: the arrangement is a joint arrangement.

Therefore, for joint control to be present, three conditions must be met:

- no single party to the arrangement has control; but

- two or more parties can be identified who, collectively, are able to control the arrangement; and

- decisions about relevant activities cannot be taken if any of the identified parties withholds consent (i.e. each of the identified parties has an explicit or implicit right of veto).

This last element is particularly important. Many arrangements without a controlling party will not meet the definition of a joint arrangement because none of the parties to the arrangement has an explicit or implicit right of veto. Therefore, when assessing whether an arrangement is a joint arrangement, it may sometimes be helpful to focus on whether any of the parties to the arrangement has an explicit or implicit right of veto. If not, then it will be possible for all of the parties to the arrangement individually to be outvoted or overruled by the others, and the arrangement will not be a joint arrangement.

Accordingly, when assessing in practice whether an arrangement is a joint arrangement, it is sensible to focus on those parties (if any) whose consent is required in respect of decisions over relevant activities because those are the parties who are likely to exercise joint control over the arrangement. Such parties may either have an explicit right of veto in respect of decisions about relevant activities, or may have an implicit right of veto (e.g. because the voting rights of the other parties are together insufficient to enable such decisions to be passed).

4.3.2   Parties that do not have joint control

An arrangement can be a joint arrangement even though not all of its parties have joint control of the arrangement. IFRS 11 distinguishes between parties that have joint control of a joint arrangement (joint operators or joint venturers) and parties that participate in, but do not have joint control of, a joint arrangement. [IFRS 11:11]

IFRS 11 makes clear that it is not necessary for all of the parties to an arrangement to have joint control for the arrangement to be within the scope of the Standard. Some parties may participate in the joint arrangement without having joint control of it. The appropriate accounting for such parties is discussed at **6.2** (for joint ventures) and at **6.4** (for joint operations).

4.3.3   Unanimous consent

A contractual arrangement may implicitly lead to joint control even though its terms do not explicitly refer to unanimous consent being required. For example, Entities A and B may establish an arrangement, with each having 50 per cent of the voting rights. If the contractual arrangement between them stipulates that decisions about the relevant activities require a minimum of 51 per cent of the votes, the arrangement has implicitly established joint control, because decisions about the relevant activities cannot be made without both parties agreeing. If either Entity A or Entity B votes against a proposal in respect of a relevant activity, only 50 per cent of the votes will be in favour and the proposal cannot be approved. It is only when Entities A and B both vote in favour that the proposal can be approved. [IFRS 11:B7]

Conversely, if the minimum proportion of votes required to approve a decision about relevant activities can be achieved by more than one combination of the parties agreeing together, there is no joint control (and thus no joint arrangement) unless the contractual arrangement stipulates which parties, or combination of parties, are required to agree unanimously to decisions about the relevant activities. [IFRS 11:B8]

The following application examples are included in Appendix B to the Standard. IFRS 11:B1 cautions that the examples in the appendix portray hypothetical situations. Although some aspects of the examples may be present in actual fact patterns, all relevant facts and circumstances of a particular fact pattern would need to be evaluated when applying the Standard.

Example 4.3.3A

Unanimous consent (1)

[IFRS 11:Appendix B Example 1]

Assume that three parties establish an arrangement: A has 50 per cent of the voting rights in the arrangement, B has 30 per cent and C has 20 per cent. The contractual arrangement between A, B and C specifies that at least 75 per cent of the voting rights are required to make decisions about the relevant activities of the arrangement. Even though A can block any decision, it does not control the arrangement because it needs the agreement of B. The terms of their contractual arrangement requiring at least 75 per cent of the voting rights to make decisions about the relevant activities imply that A and B have joint control of the arrangement because decisions about the relevant activities of the arrangement cannot be made without both A and B agreeing.

Example 4.3.3B

Unanimous consent (2)

[IFRS 11:Appendix B Example 2]

Assume an arrangement has three parties: A has 50 per cent of the voting rights in the arrangement and B and C each have 25 per cent. The contractual arrangement between A, B and C specifies that at least 75 per cent of the voting rights are required to make decisions about the relevant activities of the arrangement. Even though A can block any decision, it does not control the arrangement because it needs the agreement of either B or C. In this example, A, B and C collectively control the arrangement. However, there is more than one combination of parties that can agree to reach 75 per cent of the voting rights (ie either A and B or A and C). In such a situation, to be a joint arrangement the contractual arrangement between the parties would need to specify which combination of the parties is required to agree unanimously to decisions about the relevant activities of the arrangement.

Example 4.3.3C

Unanimous consent (3)

[IFRS 11:Appendix B Example 3]

Assume an arrangement in which A and B each have 35 per cent of the voting rights in the arrangement with the remaining 30 per cent being widely dispersed. Decisions about the relevant activities require approval by a majority of the voting rights. A and B have joint control of the arrangement only if the contractual arrangement specifies that decisions about the relevant activities of the arrangement require both A and B agreeing.

4.3.4   Relevant activities and protective rights

When considering the requirement for unanimous consent, as discussed in **4.3.3**, it is important to focus on decisions in respect of relevant activities (see **section 6** of **chapter A24**). Any party with joint control of an arrangement can prevent the other parties from making decisions about relevant activities without its consent. Conversely, if the consent of a particular party to an arrangement is required only for decisions in respect of which that party has protective rights (see **6.4.5** in **chapter A24**), and not for decisions about relevant activities, that party does not have joint control of the arrangement. [IFRS 11:B9]

The contractual arrangement usually specifies how decisions are to be made in respect of matters that are important for the goals of the joint arrangement. Some decisions may require the consent of all of the parties to the arrangement, whereas other decisions may require the consent of specified investors only. It is important to consider the substance of the contractual arrangements in determining whether they give rise to joint control.

Joint control is concerned with decisions about the 'relevant activities', i.e. those activities that significantly affect the returns of the arrangement. It is unnecessary to consider the decision-making process in respect of matters that would not be expected in practice to have a significant impact on the returns of the arrangement, because that process will not affect the conclusion regarding whether joint control exists. Further discussion of relevant activities is included at **section 6** of **chapter A24**.

4.3.5   Joint 'de facto' control

When considering control for the purposes of identifying whether another entity is a subsidiary of the reporting entity, the reporting entity may conclude that it has *de facto* control (see **6.4.6.7** in **chapter A24**). IFRS 11 does not include any discussion of *de facto* control or joint *de facto* control, but IFRS 11:B5 requires IFRS 10 to be used for the purposes of applying the definition of joint control. Therefore, it is apparently possible to conclude that two or more parties to an arrangement have joint *de facto* control of the arrangement.

For example, assume that Entity A and Entity B own 25 per cent and 24 per cent, respectively, of the ordinary shares of a listed entity, Entity C. Entity A and Entity B enter into a contractual arrangement under which they agree that they will vote together on all matters relating to Entity C. If decisions are based on majority vote and Entity C has an otherwise widely dispersed group of shareholders with no individually significant shareholders, then it may be appropriate to conclude that Entity A and Entity B have joint control of Entity C.

Conversely, if Entity C has a small number of shareholders overall, and each has significant voting rights, it is unlikely that joint *de facto* control could exist.

4.3.6 Resolution of disputes

Sometimes it may not be possible for the parties that have joint control of an arrangement to reach unanimous consent. The contractual arrangement may include clauses on the resolution of such disputes; for example, it may require that, in such circumstances, the parties seek arbitration. The existence of such provisions does not prevent an arrangement from being jointly controlled. [IFRS 11:B10]

Some arrangements for dispute resolution can lead to a conclusion that the parties do not have joint control, even if the other elements for joint control are in place. When the contractual terms include a mechanism which, in the event of a dispute, gives one party (A) a substantive right to overrule the other party (B), this may indicate that A is in a controlling position.

Conversely, when the contractual arrangement requires the parties to seek independent arbitration and, in the event that agreement still cannot be reached, to abide by the decision of the independent arbitrator, it may be appropriate to conclude that the parties have joint control of the arrangement.

4.3.7 Changes in facts and circumstances

If there is a change in facts and circumstances, an entity should reassess whether it still has joint control of the arrangement. [IFRS 11:13]

Example 4.3.7A

Changes in facts and circumstances (1)

Entities A and B each have 50 per cent of the ordinary shares, and 50 per cent of the voting rights, in Company X. The Memorandum and Articles of Company X are such that decisions about the relevant activities require a majority of the votes.

As discussed in IFRS 11:B7 (see **4.3.3**), the arrangement has implicitly established joint control, because decisions about the relevant activities cannot be made without both parties agreeing. Accordingly, Entities A and B have joint control and the arrangement is a joint arrangement.

Subsequently, Entity B sells half of its shareholding in Company X to Entity C. As a result, the arrangement ceases to be a joint arrangement. Even though Entity A can block any decision, it does not control the arrangement because it needs the agreement of either Entity B or Entity C. Entities A, B and C collectively control the arrangement. However, there is now more than one combination of parties that can agree to reach a majority of the voting rights (i.e. either Entities A and B or Entities A and C).

Accordingly, Entities A and B both cease to have joint control of Company X.

Example 4.3.7B

Changes in facts and circumstances (2)

Entities A, B and C are all parties to an arrangement. The contractual arrangement requires the consent of all three parties for all decisions about relevant activities. Therefore, Entities A, B and C have joint control and the arrangement is a joint arrangement.

Subsequently, the contractual arrangement is modified so that decisions about relevant activities require only the consent of Entities A and B, i.e. the consent of Entity C is no longer required. All other rights and obligations of Entities A, B and C are unchanged.

The arrangement is still a joint arrangement and Entities A and B continue to have joint control. Therefore, there is no change to the accounting required for Entities A and B.

However, although it is still a party to the joint arrangement, Entity C no longer has joint control.

- If the arrangement is a joint operation, Entity C is no longer a joint operator. But, as discussed at **6.4**, if Entity C still has rights to the assets, and obligations for the liabilities, of the joint operation, there is no change to the accounting required for Entity C.

- If the arrangement is a joint venture, Entity C is no longer a joint venturer. The appropriate accounting for a party to a joint venture that does not have joint control is discussed at **6.2**.

---

5   Classifying a joint arrangement

5.1   Types of joint arrangement

Having concluded that an arrangement is a joint arrangement within the scope of IFRS 11, the next step is to classify the joint arrangement as either:

- a joint operation; or

- a joint venture.

This classification is based upon an analysis of the rights and obligations of the parties in the normal course of business. [IFRS 11:14 & B14]

When the arrangement is structured through a separate legal entity or other vehicle, the analysis goes beyond this to look at the substance of where the rights and obligations rest. [IFRS 11:14, B26 & B30]

5.2   Joint operation

A joint operation is defined as a joint arrangement whereby the parties that have joint control of the arrangement have rights to the assets, and obligations for the liabilities, relating to the arrangement. [IFRS 11:15 & Appendix A]

In IFRS 11, a party to a joint operation that has joint control of the joint operation is referred to as a 'joint operator'. [IFRS 11:15 & Appendix A]

Any joint arrangement that is *not* structured through a separate vehicle is a joint operation. [IFRS 11:B16]. However, the converse is not true; a joint arrangement structured as a separate vehicle (including a limited liability company) is not precluded from being classified as a joint operation. [IFRS 11:B19]

As an example of a joint arrangement that is not structured through a separate vehicle, IFRS 11 notes that the parties to a joint arrangement could agree to manufacture a product together, with each party being responsible for a specific task and each using its own assets and incurring its own liabilities. The contractual arrangement could also specify how the revenues and expenses that are common to the parties are to be shared among them. [IFRS 11:B17]

5.3   Joint venture

A joint venture is defined as a joint arrangement whereby the parties that have joint control of the arrangement have rights to the net assets of the arrangement. [IFRS 11:16 & Appendix A]

In IFRS 11, a party to a joint venture that has joint control of the joint venture is referred to as a 'joint venturer'. [IFRS 11:16 & Appendix A]

In order to be classified as a joint venture, the joint arrangement must be structured through a separate vehicle, although not all joint arrangements structured through a separate vehicle are classified as joint ventures. [IFRS 11:B16 & B19]

5.4 Determining whether a joint arrangement is a joint operation or a joint venture

5.4.1 Classifying a joint arrangement – general

5.4.1.1 Classification based on an analysis of rights and obligations

IFRS 11 sets out four separate aspects to be considered in determining whether a joint arrangement is a joint operation or a joint venture, and this can be translated into a four-step approach, as outlined below. It will not always be necessary to go through all four steps. Indeed, for some joint operations, the analysis will be complete after Step 1.

It is necessary to exercise judgement whenever an entity is assessing whether a joint arrangement is a joint operation or a joint venture. The entity makes the determination by considering its rights and obligations arising from the arrangement. [IFRS 11:17]

Classification follows from an analysis of the parties' rights and obligations arising, in the normal course of business, from the joint arrangement. When an entity has rights to the assets, and has obligations for the liabilities relating to the joint arrangement, that arrangement is classified as a joint operation. However, when an entity has rights only to the net assets of the joint operation, that arrangement is classified as a joint venture. As discussed below, IFRS 11:B16 to B33 describe the assessment that is required to determine whether an arrangement should be classified as a joint operation or a joint venture. [IFRS 11:B14]

In order to determine whether a joint arrangement is a joint operation or a joint venture, the parties' rights and obligations are assessed. IFRS 11 requires the following to be considered:

[IFRS 11:17 & B15]

(a) the structure of the joint arrangement (see **5.4.2**); and

(b) when the joint arrangement is structured through a separate vehicle:
    (i) the legal form of the separate vehicle (see **5.4.3**);
    (ii) the terms of the contractual arrangement (see **5.4.4** and **5.4.6**); and
    (iii) when relevant, other facts and circumstances (see **5.4.5**).

The requirements of IFRS 11:17 & B15 can be translated into a four-step approach, as illustrated below.

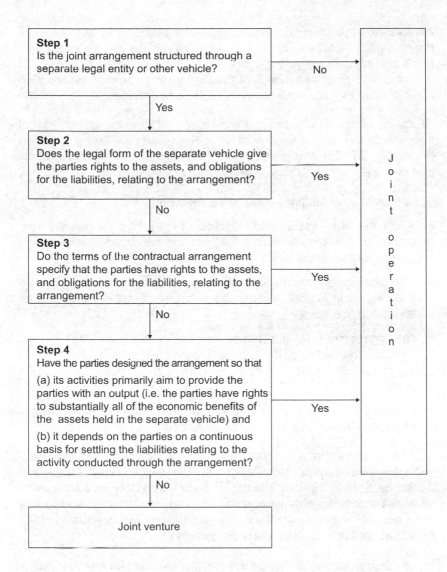

5.4.1.2 Requirement for reassessment if facts and circumstances change

If facts and circumstances change, it is necessary for the parties to reassess the classification of the joint arrangement. [IFRS 11:19]

Consequently, it may become necessary to re-perform the analysis described in **5.4.1.1** if facts and circumstances change subsequent to the initial classification of the joint arrangement. Note that reassessment of the classification of a joint arrangement will not always lead to reclassification of the joint arrangement. Such a reassessment should be based on a careful analysis of the parties' rights and obligations following the change in facts and circumstances, and may result in a conclusion that the original classification remains valid.

A reassessment of the classification of a joint arrangement is triggered if the change in facts and circumstances substantively affects the parties' rights and obligations in respect of the joint arrangement and was not part of the purpose and design of the joint arrangement at its inception (or, if later, at the last reassessment of its classification).

Reassessment will most commonly be triggered by a change in the legal structure of the joint arrangement, or in the contractual terms between the parties and the joint arrangement in a way that was not previously part of the purpose and design of the joint arrangement.

Examples of such changes include the following.

- A transfer of all assets and liabilities of the joint arrangement into, or out of, a separate vehicle that confers separation between the parties to the joint arrangement and those assets and liabilities.

- The signing, or cancellation, of a contract requiring the parties to the joint arrangement to purchase substantially all of its output (as described in **5.4.5.2**).

- An amendment to the terms of the contractual arrangement between the parties to the joint arrangement to introduce or remove an obligation on those parties for third-party liabilities of the joint arrangement.

- Amendments to the terms of the joint arrangement arising from a change in the parties that have joint control.

It is also possible that a reassessment may be required when there is a change in a contractual relationship between the joint arrangement and a third party (e.g. the cancellation of a joint arrangement's only third-party sales contract with no intention to enter into another, when there is an existing obligation on the parties to the joint arrangement to take all output not taken by third-party customers).

In rare circumstances, a change in facts and circumstances other than a change in contractual terms or relationships may result in a requirement to reassess the classification of a joint arrangement if that change was not contemplated at the inception of the arrangement. For example, the parties to a joint arrangement may have an obligation to purchase the primary product from a mining operation. The discovery of substantial by-product deposits, the existence of which was not contemplated when the project was planned, may subsequently give rise to substantial third-party sales which, had they been contemplated in the initial purpose and design, would have pointed to a joint venture arrangement.

See also **5.4.1.4** which discusses a pre-determined change in the joint arrangement's activities (either on commencement of a planned phase of the joint arrangement's life or the activation of terms of a contractual agreement between the parties upon occurrence of a specified event).

In addition, a change in contractual terms between the parties could lead to a requirement to reassess whether the parties continue to have joint control of the arrangement (see **4.3.7**).

5.4.1.3   Unit of account

Sometimes the parties to a joint venture are bound by a framework agreement that sets up the general contractual terms for undertaking one or more activities. The framework agreement may set out that the parties establish different joint arrangements to deal with specific activities that form part of the agreement. Even though those joint arrangements are related to the same framework agreement, their type might be different if the parties' rights and obligations differ when undertaking the different activities dealt with in the framework agreement. Consequently, joint operations and joint ventures can coexist when the parties undertake different activities that form part of the same framework agreement. [IFRS 11:18]

The unit of account of a joint arrangement (i.e. the level at which the assessment of the rights and obligations of the parties to the joint arrangement is made) is the 'activity' that two (or more) parties have agreed to control jointly. A party should assess its rights to the assets, and obligations for the liabilities, in relation to that activity (see IFRS 11:BC35).

IFRS 11 does not provide any explicit guidance as to what constitutes an activity, nor does it discuss how broadly that term may be interpreted. In some instances (e.g. when the joint arrangement has a clearly established objective that is set out in a single contractual arrangement and the arrangement is wholly structured through a single vehicle), the unit of account of the arrangement is clearly identifiable. In other instances, when the structure of the joint arrangement is more complex, a more extensive analysis is required to identify the underlying activity/activities and to determine if the joint arrangement should be analysed at a lower level than the entire arrangement.

This analysis can be particularly challenging when the arrangement involves multiple vehicles and/or multiple discrete activities. In such situations, it is necessary to consider the purpose and design of the arrangement, and to ensure that a robust analysis of the rights and obligations is undertaken in order to determine the appropriate level at which to determine classification.

Can joint operations and joint ventures co-exist within a single framework agreement?

As contemplated in IFRS 11:18 (see above), two (or more) entities may enter into a single framework agreement that establishes the contractual terms for undertaking more than one activity. These activities may then be structured in various ways, for example:

- a separate vehicle may be established to undertake each activity; or

- a combination of separate vehicles and other structures involving the direct holding of assets and the direct incurrence of obligations for liabilities may be established for undertaking the various activities.

The appropriate classification of a joint arrangement should be considered at the activity level, irrespective of whether a number of activities have been entered into under a single framework agreement. Although related to the same framework agreement, if the parties' rights and obligations differ when undertaking different activities set out in the framework agreement, then more than one joint arrangement will exist and the classification of those joint arrangements may differ. It is possible that joint operations and joint ventures can co-exist within structures of this nature.

When dealing with a framework agreement and the undertaking of multiple activities, care should be taken to ensure that the unit of account and corresponding classification of each joint arrangement appropriately reflects the true nature of the rights and obligations established by the joint arrangements. Each joint arrangement identified must generally relate to a specific activity and the resulting classification and accounting must reflect the rights and obligations related to that activity.

Can several joint arrangements exist within the same separate vehicle?

When a joint arrangement is established through a single contractual arrangement, and that arrangement is wholly structured through a single vehicle that holds all of the assets and liabilities related to the joint arrangement, the appropriate unit of account will typically be the vehicle. In such circumstances, the assessment of the rights and obligations of the parties to the joint arrangement should be carried out at the vehicle level.

However, some joint arrangements are structured so that multiple activities are conducted through a single vehicle. If this is the case, it is necessary for the parties to the arrangement to consider their rights and obligations at the activity level, and to carry out a separate assessment of each activity to determine whether the activity is a joint operation or a joint venture. It is possible that several joint arrangements exist within the same separate vehicle.

This conclusion is supported by IFRS 11:BC36 which states that "within the same separate vehicle, the parties may undertake different activities in which they have different rights to the assets, and obligations for the liabilities, relating to these different activities resulting in different types of joint arrangements conducted within the same separate vehicle". The

Board did note, however, that while such situations are possible, they are expected to be rare in practice.

5.4.1.4 Joint arrangement with multiple pre-determined phases of activity

When a project involves a number of pre-determined phases of activity, and the rights and obligations of the parties vary from one phase of activity to the next, the classification of the joint arrangement should be based on an assessment of the rights and obligations across the life of the arrangement, rather than separate assessments being performed for each phase of its activities.

Example 5.4.1.4 illustrates the application of this principle. **Section 5.4.1.5** addresses the circumstances when there is significant uncertainty regarding whether a project will proceed from one phase of activity to the next.

Example 5.4.1.4

Joint arrangement with multiple pre-determined phases of activity

Two parties establish a joint arrangement within a separate vehicle whose legal form confers separation between the jointly controlling parties and the assets and liabilities of the vehicle (i.e. the legal form of the vehicle does not preclude classification as a joint venture).

The purpose of the joint arrangement is to develop residential property on a single site funded solely by cash received from the two parties under the terms of a cash call arrangement until such time as sales of properties from the site to third parties commence. Thereafter, the arrangement requires that proceeds from sales of properties are used to fund further development costs of the site, with any surplus funds to be remitted to the parties to the arrangement. The parties' obligation to fund cash calls continues after the commencement of third-party sales, but only in the event that cash receipts from sales are insufficient to fund development costs in a particular period.

Following completion of development and sales on the site, any remaining funds will be remitted to the parties to the arrangement in proportion to their relative ownership interests and the joint arrangement will cease to exist.

The activity of the joint arrangement might be considered to have two distinct phases:

- a **development phase** during which the joint arrangement is entirely dependent on the parties to the arrangement for cash to settle all liabilities; and
- a **sales phase** during which the joint arrangement generates its own cash inflows, which are then used to settle its liabilities.

During the development phase, the parties have an obligation to fund the settlement of the liabilities of the joint arrangement (analogous to Example 5 in Appendix B of IFRS 11 – see **example 5.4.5.2**), but during the sales phase they have no such obligation because the joint arrangement is generating independent cash inflows.

The joint arrangement classification should be based on an assessment of rights and obligations resulting from contractual arrangements in place across its life, resulting in classification as a joint venture in the circumstances described.

In order for the parties to a joint arrangement to be considered to have obligations for the liabilities relating to the activity conducted through the joint arrangement, it must be dependent upon the parties "on a continuous basis" (see step 4 in the diagram at **5.4.1.1**). To be considered to have rights to the assets of a joint arrangement, the parties must share "substantially all the economic benefits" of those assets [IFRS 11:B31]. The assessment should be made at the inception of the joint arrangement based on the parties' rights and obligations over its entire planned life.

In the circumstances described, at inception the joint arrangement:

• is not designed such that the parties to the joint arrangement will fund its liabilities throughout its life and, therefore, the parties should not be considered to have obligations for its liabilities on a continuous basis (as discussed at **5.4.4.3**, a cash call arrangement operating on an 'as needed' basis for the purposes of funding a shortfall in cash is not sufficient to conclude that the parties have obligations for a joint arrangement's liabilities); and

• is not designed such that the parties to the joint arrangement will have rights to its assets because the joint arrangement will make sales of property to third parties and retain the proceeds for use in further development on the site.

Therefore, the joint arrangement should be classified as a joint venture throughout its planned life.

By contrast, and as discussed at **5.4.1.2**, a change in the activities of a joint arrangement resulting from a change to the contractual terms of the arrangement (or from a new contract) or from a significant change in facts and circumstances not contemplated at the inception of the joint arrangement is a trigger for reassessment of the classification of the joint arrangement when the change occurs.

5.4.1.5   *Joint arrangement with multiple potential phases of activity*

In some industries (e.g. the extractive and pharmaceutical industries), it may be the case that there is significant uncertainty as to whether a project will proceed from one phase of activity to the next (e.g. from the exploration/research phase to the development phase, and subsequently from the development phase to the production phase). In such industries, joint arrangement contracts may be structured so that they cover all possible phases of the arrangement (i.e. the entire potential life of the project), even though it will be necessary for the parties to make future decisions as to whether to progress from one phase to the next. Alternatively, because of the inherent uncertainties, the parties may choose to put in place a written agreement at the beginning of each phase that covers only that phase of activity, or perhaps have an unsigned 'draft' agreement that covers all phases but that is subject to change as necessary when decisions are taken on progression to the next phase.

When a contractual agreement is in place that covers all possible phases of a joint arrangement, the assessment of the parties rights and obligations should cover the whole of the life of the arrangement assuming successful progression through all phases regardless of the probability of proceeding to later phases. As discussed at **5.4.1.2**, classification of a joint arrangement should only be reassessed when there is a change in legal or contractual terms that was not previously part of the purpose and design of the arrangement, or a change in facts and circumstances that was not contemplated at the inception of the arrangement. Contractually agreed terms for later phases are part of the purpose and design of the arrangement, and provide evidence that the later phases were contemplated at inception. As such, activation of those terms would not be a trigger for reassessment; the initial classification should already have considered these terms.

When the joint arrangement contract does not cover all possible phases of a joint arrangement, the starting point for the assessment of rights and obligations is that contract and the phases that it does cover. However, it is also necessary to consider whether there is objective evidence that an agreement covering a longer period exists. For example (1) side agreements, (2) an overall framework agreement, or (3) agreed statements of the purpose and design or objectives may limit the courses of action open to the parties to the joint arrangement and demonstrate that the purpose and design of the joint arrangement's later phases has already been determined. If such evidence covering a longer period exists, it should be included in the classification assessment.

5.4.2 Step 1: structure of the joint arrangement

Step 1 involves an assessment as to whether the joint arrangement is structured through a 'separate vehicle'.

IFRS 11 establishes a clear rule that if a joint arrangement is *not* structured through a separate vehicle, it should be classified as a joint operation. This is because the underlying contractual arrangement in such circumstances establishes rights to the assets and revenues, and obligations for liabilities and expenses, of the joint arrangement. [IFRS 11:B16]

Joint arrangements can be established for a variety of purposes (e.g. to share costs, to share risks, to give access to a new market or to give access to new technology). They can also be established using different structures and legal forms, some using a separate vehicle. [IFRS 11:B12 - B13]

IFRS 11 defines a separate vehicle as a separately identifiable financial structure, including separate legal entities or entities recognised by statute, regardless of whether those entities have a legal personality. [IFRS 11:Appendix A]

Examples of separate vehicles include, but are not limited to, limited liability companies, unlimited companies, partnerships and trusts.

When a joint operation is not structured through a separate vehicle, Step 1 provides a conclusive determination that the joint arrangement should be classified as a joint operation. When a joint arrangement is structured through a separate vehicle, it is necessary to move to Step 2.

5.4.3   Step 2: legal form of the separate vehicle

Step 2 is to consider the legal form of the vehicle to assess whether the parties have either (1) rights to the assets and obligations for the liabilities in that separate vehicle (notwithstanding the existence of the separate vehicle), or (2) rights only to the net assets of the separate vehicle. [IFRS 11:B22 & B23]

When the legal form of the separate vehicle does *not* confer separation between the parties and the separate vehicle (i.e. the assets and liabilities held in the separate vehicle are regarded legally as the assets and liabilities of the parties), Step 2 provides a conclusive determination that the joint arrangement should be classified as a joint operation. [IFRS 11:B24]

In many cases, the legal form of the separate vehicle will be such that the separate vehicle must be considered in its own right (i.e. the assets and liabilities held in the separate vehicle are those of the separate vehicle and not those of the parties to the arrangement), providing an initial indication that the joint arrangement is a joint venture. However, this is not always the case and, in some situations, the existence of a legal entity will not directly affect the rights and obligations of the parties to the assets and liabilities.

One type of legal structure that, in itself, does not generally have a substantive effect on the rights and obligations of the interested parties is a 'bare' trust. Such trusts are commonly used in real estate development activities in some jurisdictions to access tax exemptions. Typical features include:

- the establishment of a trust to hold title to property in which the parties to the joint arrangement have an undivided interest;

- the trustee is merely vested with the legal title to property and has no other duty to perform, responsibilities to carry out, or powers to exercise as trustee of the trust property;

- the trust does not hold the beneficial ownership interest of the property and, consequently, has no rights to the economic benefits of the property;

- the beneficial ownership interest in the property is normally held by the parties to the arrangement directly or by another vehicle within the structure; and

- the trustee is obliged to convey legal title to the trust property on demand by, and according to the instructions of, the parties to the joint arrangement.

In a structure of this nature, the trust is used by the parties to the joint arrangement solely to hold legal title. The trust has no rights to the economic benefits generated by the property.

In practice, joint arrangements that establish a bare trust to hold real estate will frequently be more complex than the situation described above and this will require additional analysis. For example, a bare trust may be established in conjunction with another vehicle which holds other assets and liabilities relating to the parties to the arrangement. In such circumstances, consideration will need to be given as to the appropriate unit of account (see **5.4.1.3**).

When an entity is able to conclude that the legal form of the vehicle gives the parties rights to the assets and obligations for the liabilities relating to the arrangement, then the arrangement is a joint operation. In the absence of such a conclusion, the entity should proceed to consider the effect of the terms of the contractual arrangement between the parties (Step 3 at **5.4.4**) and, when relevant, other facts and circumstances (Step 4 at **5.4.5**).

5.4.4 Step 3: assessing the terms of the contractual arrangement

5.4.4.1 Assessing the terms of the contractual arrangement – general

Step 3 is to consider whether the contractual arrangement reverses or modifies the rights and obligations conferred by the legal form of the separate vehicle. In many cases, the terms of the contractual arrangement will be consistent, or will not conflict, with the rights and obligations conferred by the legal form. However, when the terms of the contractual arrangement override the legal form of the separate vehicle with the result that the parties have rights to the assets, and obligations for the liabilities, of the joint arrangement, that joint arrangement is classified as a joint operation. [IFRS 11:B25, B26 & B28]

In order for a joint arrangement that is structured through a separate vehicle to be classified as a joint operation, it is necessary for the parties that have joint control of the arrangement to have *both* rights to the assets *and* obligations for the liabilities relating to the arrangement; it is not sufficient for those parties to have *either* rights to the assets *or* obligations for the liabilities, but not both.

Consequently, when a joint arrangement is structured through a separate vehicle, it is necessary to review carefully the terms of the contractual arrangement in order to establish whether the parties to the arrangement have both rights to the assets and obligations for the liabilities and, in doing so, determine whether the arrangement constitutes a joint operation. It will be necessary to assess whether any contractual terms relating to the parties sharing the assets and liabilities of the arrangement are substantive, and whether those terms are sufficient to modify or reverse the separation of the parties from the rights and obligations of the joint arrangement that is conferred by the legal form of the vehicle.

For example, subject to the consideration of the legal form of the vehicle and other facts and circumstances as required by IFRS 11:B15(b):

- a contractual arrangement that modifies or reverses the rights and obligations conferred by the legal form so as to establish clearly that the parties to the joint arrangement share all interests in the assets relating to the arrangement in a specified proportion and the parties share all liabilities, obligations, costs and expenses in a specified proportion would lead to classification as a joint operation; and

- a contractual arrangement that establishes that the parties to the joint arrangement share all interests in the assets relating to the arrangement in a specified proportion but the parties are not liable for the debts and obligations of the arrangement would lead to classification as a joint venture.

The following example is set out in Appendix B to the Standard.

Example 5.4.4.1

Contractual modifications

[IFRS 11:Appendix B Example 4]

Assume that two parties structure a joint arrangement in an incorporated entity. Each party has a 50 per cent ownership interest in the incorporated entity. The incorporation enables the separation of the entity from its owners and as a consequence the assets and liabilities held in the entity are the assets and liabilities of the incorporated entity. In such a case, the assessment of the rights and obligations conferred upon the parties by the legal form of the

---

separate vehicle indicates that the parties have rights to the net assets of the arrangement.

However, the parties modify the features of the corporation through their contractual arrangement so that each has an interest in the assets of the incorporated entity and each is liable for the liabilities of the incorporated entity in a specified proportion. Such contractual modifications to the features of a corporation can cause an arrangement to be a joint operation.

For further discussion of common contractual terms, see **5.4.6**.

When the terms of the contractual arrangement do not result in the parties having rights to the assets and obligations for the liabilities of the joint arrangement, it is necessary to move to Step 4 (see **5.4.5**).

5.4.4.2 Obligation of the parties for the liabilities relating to the joint arrangement – impact of guarantees

Parties to a joint arrangement may provide guarantees to third parties. For example, an arrangement may be structured through a separate vehicle and the vehicle may obtain third-party debt which is guaranteed by the parties to the arrangement.

The provision of such guarantees by the parties to the arrangement does not, in itself, result in the parties having obligations for the liabilities relating to the arrangement.

IFRS 11:B27 refers to the provision of guarantees by the parties to a joint arrangement (see the final section of the table set out at **5.4.6**) and draws a clear distinction between providing a guarantee in respect of another party's liability and having an obligation for that liability. When the parties to a joint arrangement guarantee the borrowings of the joint arrangement, the joint arrangement is still the primary obligor for the underlying debt. The guarantees are separate contracts between each of the parties to the arrangement and the lender, and should be accounted for by the parties to the arrangement in accordance with IFRS 9 *Financial Instruments* (or, for entities that have not yet adopted IFRS 9, IAS 39 *Financial Instruments: Recognition and Measurement*).

5.4.4.3 Obligation of the parties for the liabilities relating to the joint arrangement – impact of cash calls

Parties to a joint arrangement may be subject to cash or capital calls whereby the parties to the arrangement are periodically required to inject cash into the joint arrangement.

The assessment as to whether the parties to the arrangement have obligations for the liabilities relating to the arrangement due to requirements to provide cash when called upon requires the exercise of judgement and a careful assessment of the underlying facts and circumstances.

In some cases, the effect of cash call requirements may be to provide funding on a contingent basis when other sources of funding are not available, and they may not be indicative of a primary, ongoing obligation of the parties. For example, the cash call requirements may be in the nature of a guarantee (see also **5.4.4.2**). Alternatively, the cash call arrangements might be contingent on a decision to expand the operations and in the nature of a call for further funds for capital expenditure.

In other cases, the arrangement may have been primarily designed for the provision of output to the parties, with cash calls providing the primary, ongoing source of funding to the arrangement. In these cases, the cash calls may be the mechanism through which the parties to the joint arrangement are required to provide substantially all of the cash flows contributed to the arrangement. Accordingly, cash call requirements of this nature would indicate that the parties to the arrangement have obligations for its liabilities.

The following examples illustrate contrasting scenarios.

Example 5.4.4.3A

Cash calls to provide funding on an ongoing basis

Two parties establish a joint arrangement within a separate vehicle whose legal form confers separation between the jointly controlling parties and the assets and liabilities of the vehicle. Each party has a 50 per cent ownership interest in the vehicle.

The purpose of the joint arrangement is to develop a property that the parties to the arrangement will then use in their businesses. Costs incurred in relation to the project are structured to be covered entirely by cash calls on the parties. In the event that one party defaults on its funding obligation, the other party is required to contribute the amount of the shortfall.

In the circumstances described, the arrangement requires the parties to provide cash on an ongoing basis to the arrangement. In the absence of any sources of funding other than that provided by the parties to the arrangement, this would indicate that the parties have obligations for the liabilities relating to the arrangement. Thus, provided that the parties can be demonstrated also to have rights to its assets, the joint arrangement will be appropriately classified as a joint operation.

Example 5.4.4.3B

Cash calls to provide funding on an 'as needed' basis

Two parties establish a joint arrangement within a separate vehicle whose legal form confers separation between the jointly controlling parties and the assets and liabilities of the vehicle. Each party has a 50 per cent ownership interest in the vehicle.

The purpose of the joint arrangement is to purchase and operate an existing factory manufacturing shoes for sale to third parties.

The purchase of the factory is funded via a cash call on the parties to the joint arrangement that remains in place on an 'as needed' basis for the purposes of funding additional capital expenditure or any shortfall in cash. However, the joint arrangement's primary ongoing sources of cash flows are sales of shoes to third parties and an external overdraft facility.

In the circumstances described, the vehicle substantially funds its own operations through sales to third parties and access to an overdraft facility. The ability to make cash calls on the parties to the joint arrangement represents a contingent funding obligation that can be drawn upon in the event that there are insufficient funds from operations or to fund capital expenditure, rather than the arrangement being dependent on the cash call mechanism on an ongoing basis. This would indicate that the parties do not have obligations for the liabilities relating to the arrangement, resulting in the joint arrangement being appropriately classified as a joint venture.

5.4.4.4   Obligation to repay third-party debt

When third-party borrowings (e.g. from a bank) are used to fund a joint arrangement directly, the parties to the joint arrangement will need to consider whether it is appropriate to conclude that they have obligations for the liabilities relating to the arrangement.

The IFRS Interpretations Committee discussed this matter and, as reported in the March 2015 *IFRIC Update*, concluded that "third-party financing alone would not affect the classification of the joint arrangement, irrespective of whether the financing occurs at inception or during the course of the joint arrangement's operations". The critical issue to be assessed is not the existence of third-party financing but the assessment as to whether "the resulting obligation to the third-party finance provider will, in due course, be settled using cash flows that the parties [to the joint arrangement] are obliged to provide".

The assessment as to whether the parties to a joint arrangement have obligations for third-party borrowings of the arrangement should be made on the same basis as for other liabilities of the joint arrangement – namely, whether the parties to the arrangement are substantially the only source of cash flows contributing to the continuity of the operations of the joint arrangement (IFRS 11:B32) and, therefore, have the primary, ongoing obligation to settle its liabilities. This assessment should take into account all of the cash flows required to settle third-party borrowings, including interest payments over the term of the borrowings and any repayment of principal.

As an initial consideration, it is important to determine whether the parties have rights to the assets of the joint arrangement. As well as in itself being a pre-requisite for classification as a joint operation, this determination can affect the conclusion as to whether the parties have obligations for third-party debt. This is because one of the ways in which the parties to a joint arrangement may provide the cash flows to settle third-party borrowings is by requiring the joint arrangement to sell assets to which the parties have rights to generate cash to make payments required under the loan agreement.

Other ways in which the parties to a joint arrangement may provide the cash flows to settle third-party borrowings are:

- by making specific cash payments (either to the joint arrangement or to the lender) of amounts due to be paid under the loan agreement; and

- by making cash payments to the joint arrangement (e.g. in fulfilling an obligation to purchase output) sufficient to settle the joint arrangement's obligations including payments on its borrowings.

If the parties are obliged to provide substantially all of the cash flows required to settle the third-party borrowings in one of these ways, or by a combination thereof, they have an obligation for that liability. If, however, borrowings amounting to more than an insignificant portion of the liabilities of the joint arrangement are to be settled by selling assets of the joint arrangement to which the parties do not have rights, then the parties do not have such an obligation.

As discussed at **5.4.4.2**, when the parties to a joint arrangement provide guarantees in respect of third-party borrowings of the joint arrangement, the provision of such guarantees is not, in itself, sufficient to reach a conclusion that the parties have an obligation for substantially all the liabilities. However, in some situations, a guarantee in combination with other factors may support such a conclusion.

Example 5.4.4.4 illustrates the application of these principles.

Example 5.4.4.4

Obligation to repay third-party debt

Entity E and Entity F (the parties) enter into a contractual agreement to incorporate a new entity, Entity G, to manufacture materials required by the parties for their own, individual manufacturing processes. Each party has a 50 per cent ownership interest in Entity G and made a cash subscription for its equity investment. The contractual agreement is such that the parties jointly control Entity G.

The legal form of Entity G does not confer rights to the assets, and obligations for the liabilities, of Entity G on its shareholders.

The purpose of the arrangement is to provide the parties with the output they require and each party is required to purchase half of the total output produced by Entity G.

The equity subscribed by the parties is not sufficient to fund the initial equipment costs; consequently, Entity G takes out a long-term loan from a bank over which both Entity E and Entity F provide a guarantee. The terms of the agreement are silent as to how the third-party debt is to be settled.

Do Entity E and Entity F have rights to the assets and obligations for the liabilities relating to the joint arrangement (Entity G), including the third-party debt?

Yes. The terms of the agreement are such that the parties have an obligation to purchase all of Entity G's output and there are no expected sales to third parties. Consistent with **example 5.4.5.2**, this leads to the conclusion that the parties have a right to the assets of the joint arrangement.

The assessment as to whether the parties have the obligation for the liabilities relating to the joint arrangement (including the third-party debt) must take into consideration whether the parties have the primary, ongoing obligation to settle the liabilities. Based on the purpose and design of the arrangement and the requirement to purchase all of the output, the parties are the only ongoing source of cash for the arrangement. At the time the debt principal becomes repayable, if the cash from the parties for the purchase of output has not been sufficient to fund repayment, there appear to be a number of ways to settle the third-party debt:

- the parties fund the repayment (either by providing additional cash to Entity G or by paying the bank directly possibly through exercise of the guarantee); or
- the parties decide to reduce the capacity or wind up the arrangement by selling assets to generate funds to settle the liability, or by selling Entity G (including its debt) to another third party.

Each of these methods will require the parties to provide substantially all of the cash flows required to settle the third-party borrowings by using either their own assets or assets of the arrangement to which they have rights.

The assessment of the purpose of the arrangement together with the obligation of the parties to purchase output is sufficient to conclude that the parties have substantially all the obligation for the liabilities of the arrangement. Although in this case the guarantee to the bank provides another means by which the parties could provide cash to settle the debt, in the absence of such a guarantee the same conclusion would be reached because the debt would still be settled by assets of the parties or assets to which they have rights.

5.4.5   Step 4: other facts and circumstances

5.4.5.1   Other facts and circumstances – general considerations

Step 4 (the final step) is to consider other facts and circumstances in order to assess whether, despite the conclusions reached in Steps 1 to 3, the parties do in fact have rights to the assets and obligations for the liabilities of the arrangement, in which case the arrangement is classified as a joint operation. If this is not so, the arrangement is classified as a joint venture. [IFRS 11:B29 - B30]

> When a joint arrangement is structured through a separate vehicle, and neither (1) the legal form of the joint arrangement nor (2) the terms of the contractual arrangement give the parties rights to the assets, and obligations for the liabilities, relating to the joint arrangement, it is necessary to consider whether there are any other facts and circumstances to demonstrate that the parties to the arrangement have rights to the assets, and obligations for the liabilities, relating to the joint arrangement. If not, the joint arrangement should be classified as a joint venture.
>
> 'Other facts and circumstances' should be considered to determine whether they create enforceable rights to the assets of the joint arrangement and enforceable obligations for its liabilities sufficient to override the rights and obligations conferred upon the party by the legal form of the separate vehicle.
>
> In order to classify the joint arrangement as a joint operation as a result of assessing other facts and circumstances, it is therefore necessary to demonstrate that the parties to the arrangement:
>
> * have rights and obligations related to economic benefits of the assets of the arrangement; and
>
> * are obliged to provide cash to the arrangement through enforceable obligations, which is used to settle the liabilities of the joint arrangement on a continuous basis.
>
> The consideration of other facts and circumstances is not a test of whether each party to the joint arrangement is closely or fully involved with the operation of the separate vehicle. Two joint arrangements with otherwise similar features can be classified differently if one is structured through a separate vehicle and the other is not because:
>
> * the legal form of a joint arrangement could affect rights and obligations; and
>
> * the legal form of a joint arrangement structured through a separate vehicle must be overridden by other contractual arrangements or specific other facts and circumstances for the joint arrangement to be classified as a joint operation; but

- a joint arrangement that is not structured through a separate vehicle is always classified as a joint operation.

See May 2014 and March 2015 *IFRIC Updates* for a summary of the IFRS Interpretations Committees deliberations on this topic.

5.4.5.2 Parties obliged to purchase substantially all of the output of the arrangement

If two or more parties establish a joint arrangement, the output of which is provided to the parties themselves with sales to third parties being precluded, this indicates that the parties have rights to substantially all the economic benefits of the arrangement's assets. If sales to third parties are precluded, the cash that the parties pay to the arrangement may be substantially the arrangement's only source of income; this means that the parties are providing the cash to settle the arrangement's liabilities and indicates that the parties have an obligation for the liabilities relating to the arrangement. [IFRS 11:B31 - B32]

The following example is set out in Appendix B to the Standard to illustrate the point.

Example 5.4.5.2

Assessing other facts and circumstances (parties obliged to purchase substantially all of the output of the arrangement)

[IFRS 11:Appendix B Example 5]

Assume that two parties structure a joint arrangement in an incorporated entity (entity C) in which each party has a 50 per cent ownership interest. The purpose of the arrangement is to manufacture materials required by the parties for their own, individual manufacturing processes. The arrangement ensures that the parties operate the facility that produces the materials to the quantity and quality specifications of the parties.

The legal form of entity C (an incorporated entity) through which the activities are conducted initially indicates that the assets and liabilities held in entity C are the assets and liabilities of entity C. The contractual arrangement between the parties does not specify that the parties have rights to the assets or obligations for the liabilities of entity C. Accordingly, the legal form of entity C and the terms of the contractual arrangement indicate that the arrangement is a joint venture.

However, the parties also consider the following aspects of the arrangement:

- The parties agreed to purchase all the output produced by entity C in a ratio of 50:50. Entity C cannot sell any of the output to third parties, unless this is approved by the two parties to the arrangement. Because the purpose of the arrangement is to provide the parties with output they require, such sales to third parties are expected to be uncommon and not material.

- The price of the output sold to the parties is set by both parties at a level that is designed to cover the costs of production and administrative expenses incurred by entity C. On the basis of this operating model, the arrangement is intended to operate at a break-even level.

From the fact pattern above, the following facts and circumstances are relevant:

- The obligation of the parties to purchase all the output produced by entity C reflects the exclusive dependence of entity C upon the parties for the generation of cash flows and, thus, the parties have an obligation to fund the settlement of the liabilities of entity C.

- The fact that the parties have rights to all the output produced by entity C means that the parties are consuming, and therefore have rights to, all the economic benefits of the assets of entity C.

These facts and circumstances indicate that the arrangement is a joint operation. The conclusion about the classification of the joint arrangement in these circumstances would not change if, instead of the parties using their share of the output themselves in a subsequent manufacturing process, the parties sold their share of the output to third parties.

If the parties changed the terms of the contractual arrangement so that the arrangement was able to sell output to third parties, this would result in entity C assuming demand, inventory and credit risks. In that scenario, such a change in the facts and circumstances would require reassessment of the classification of the joint arrangement. Such facts and circumstances would indicate that the arrangement is a joint venture.

The same conclusion will not necessarily be reached if, instead of the parties purchasing output at a variable price calculated to ensure that the joint arrangement operates at a break-even level as shown in **example 5.4.5.2**, the parties are obliged to purchase all of the output at the output's current market value or at a fixed price.

Classification as a joint operation requires that the parties have both rights to the assets and obligations for the liabilities relating to the arrangement. If the price of the output changed in the manner described, the parties would still have rights to the assets of the joint arrangement through their obligation to purchase output. In determining whether the parties would also have obligations for the liabilities of the joint operation, it is necessary to consider whether the cash flows provided to the joint arrangement through the parties' purchase of the output from the joint arrangement at a market or fixed price, along with any other funding that the parties are obliged to provide, would be sufficient to enable the joint arrangement to settle its liabilities on an ongoing basis.

As reported in the March 2015 *IFRIC Update*, the IFRS Interpretations Committee discussed a fact pattern in which the output is sold to the parties of the joint arrangement at a market price. The Committee observed that "the sale of output from the joint arrangement to the parties at market price, on its own, is not a determinative factor for the classification of the joint arrangement" and that "exercising judgement is needed in this situation in order to determine whether the arrangement is a joint operation".

In making the assessment as to whether the parties have obligations for the liabilities of the joint arrangement, it is necessary to consider:

- whether there exists a genuine possibility that the price paid by the parties for the arrangement's output will be inadequate for it to settle its liabilities on an ongoing basis; and, if so,

- whether the parties have committed to make good any shortfall through another mechanism (e.g. a cash call or other contingent funding requirement) such that they are obliged to provide sufficient cash to settle the arrangement's liabilities.

If, based on factors such as the expected excess of sales price over the costs of the joint arrangement and any expected volatility in costs and (if relevant) market price, it is concluded that there is no genuine possibility of a shortfall, or a mechanism exists requiring the parties to make good any shortfall that occurs, the parties would be considered to have obligations for the liabilities of the arrangement and, consequently, classification as a joint operation would be appropriate.

If there is a genuine possibility of a shortfall that the parties are not obliged to make good in cash, it would then be necessary to consider how the funds needed to meet the shortfall would be obtained. If, in such circumstances, the parties would require the joint arrangement to sell other assets to which the parties have rights then (as discussed in **5.4.4.4**), the parties would still be considered to have obligations for the liabilities of the arrangement, and classification as a joint operation would still be appropriate.

If there is a genuine possibility that a more than insignificant portion of the liabilities of the joint arrangement will be settled by selling assets of the joint arrangement to which the parties do not have rights, it will be appropriate to conclude that the parties do not have obligations for the liabilities of the arrangement and, consequently, that classification as a joint venture is appropriate.

5.4.5.3 *Meaning of 'substantially all' in the context of IFRS 11:B31*

As outlined **5.4.5.2**, as an example of 'other facts and circumstances' that might suggest classification as a joint operation, IFRS 11:B31 discusses a scenario in which the activities of an arrangement are primarily designed for the provision of output to the parties to the joint arrangement such that the parties have rights to 'substantially all' the economic benefits of the assets of the arrangement.

IFRS 11 does not provide any additional guidance on what is meant by 'substantially all' in this context. The issue of determining the basis for 'substantially all' of the output was discussed by the IFRIC Interpretations Committee who, as reported in the March 2015 *IFRIC Update*, concluded that this assessment is based on the monetary value of the output and not physical quantities.

If the arrangement is such that the parties to the joint arrangement take 90 per cent or more of the monetary value of the output of the joint arrangement, this should generally be presumed to be sufficient to conclude that they have rights to substantially all the economic benefits of its assets.

For a joint arrangement to be classified as a joint operation, IFRS 11 also requires that the parties to the joint arrangement have obligations for its liabilities. As discussed at **5.4.5.4**, this can arise from an obligation to purchase output (but not merely a right, intention and/or expectation to do so) that results in the parties being substantially the only source of cash flows contributing to the continuity of the operations of the arrangement. As with the assessment of rights to economic benefits, 'substantially' in this context should generally be presumed to mean 90 per cent or more of those cash flows.

The assessment of whether the parties to the joint arrangement have rights to 'substantially all' its assets and are 'substantially' the only source of cash flows contributing to its operations should be made at inception of the joint arrangement and should only be reassessed if there is a change in the parties' rights to the assets or obligation for the liabilities. The assessment should take into account the expected output and costs of the joint arrangement over its life (rather than only in the current or subsequent reporting periods). Further, it should consider the purpose and design of the arrangement, including the following factors.

- **Pricing** When the joint arrangement produces more than one product, or sales to third parties are priced differently from sales to parties to the arrangement, it will be necessary to consider the monetary value (price) of output rather than its physical quantity in making the assessment of what proportion of output the parties to the joint arrangement take and what proportion of cash flows they provide.

- **Frequency and duration of sales to third parties** Third-party sales may be permitted to occur from time to time as a result of a temporary condition or event. If sales of output to third parties are otherwise precluded by the contractual terms of the arrangement or are not expected to occur, it may be that the parties to the arrangement have rights to substantially all of the economic benefits of the assets of the arrangement over its life. This is less likely to be the case if the joint arrangement vehicle is actively marketing to third parties on an ongoing basis.

- **By-products** Third-party sales of a by-product of the joint arrangement's principal operations might occur on an ongoing basis but should still be considered in determining whether the purpose and design of the arrangement is primarily to provide output to the parties to the arrangement. In addition, it is necessary to consider whether cash flows from sales of by-products to third parties make a significant contribution to the operations of the arrangement (and, consequently, whether the parties to the joint arrangement can be considered to have an obligation for its liabilities).

Other factors may also be relevant depending on the specific attributes of the joint arrangement. An entity would need to consider such factors and determine whether, in situations which appear to lack clarity, the vehicle is primarily servicing the designated output requirements of the parties to the joint arrangement.

5.4.5.4 Parties intend to purchase substantially all of the output of the arrangement, but no obligation to do so

If the facts in **example 5.4.5.2** were changed such that the parties to the joint arrangement have a right, expectation and/or intention to purchase all (or substantially all) of its output but they are not obliged to do so, classification as a joint operation would not be appropriate.

IFRS 11 states that classification as a joint operation requires that the parties have rights to the assets and obligations for the liabilities relating to the arrangement.

An obligation to purchase the output of a joint arrangement will be legal or contractual (either as part of the contractual arrangement between the parties to the joint arrangement or as separate, contractually binding side agreements between the parties to the joint arrangement and the joint arrangement itself) in nature.

In the absence of an obligation to purchase the output of a joint operation, a right, expectation and/or intention to purchase that output is not (individually or in combination) sufficient to support a conclusion that the parties have an obligation for the liabilities relating to the arrangement; in the absence of an obligation, the parties could choose not to purchase some or all of the output, in which case the joint arrangement could sell the output to third parties and use the proceeds to settle its liabilities.

5.4.5.5 Joint arrangement sells output to third parties on behalf of the parties to the joint arrangement

If the facts in **example 5.4.5.2** were changed such that, instead of the parties to the joint arrangement purchasing its output, the joint arrangement itself sells output to third parties on behalf of the parties to the joint arrangement, it would be necessary to evaluate all of the relevant facts and circumstances carefully in order to determine whether classification as a joint operation is appropriate.

There may be circumstances in which it can be demonstrated that such an arrangement is equivalent to the parties to the joint arrangement purchasing its output and then selling it to third parties on their own account and, thus, that the parties have rights to the assets, and obligations for the liabilities, relating to the joint arrangement.

To have rights to the assets of the joint arrangement and to assume credit risk, the parties to the joint arrangement must act as principal in the sale of output and be exposed to the risk of non-payment by third-party customers. This is most likely to be the case if the cash payments from third-party customers are received directly by the parties to the joint arrangement, and the parties make separate payments to the joint arrangement for the output irrespective of whether they have received the cash from the third-party customers.

To have obligations for the liabilities relating to the joint arrangement and to assume inventory and demand risk, the parties to the joint arrangement must provide the primary source of cash on an ongoing basis to settle substantially all of the arrangement's liabilities, including any that are not covered by the cash from third-party sales made by the joint arrangement as agent for the parties. This might be the case if the terms of the arrangement specify that the parties are obliged to purchase substantially all of the joint arrangement's output, some or all of which may be sold to third parties by the joint arrangement as agent for the parties.

As discussed at **5.4.4.1**, for a joint arrangement that is structured through a separate vehicle to be classified as a joint operation, it is necessary for the parties to have *both* rights to the assets, and obligations for the liabilities, relating to the arrangement.

5.4.5.6   *Parties that control the arrangement are the sole suppliers to the arrangement*

If the facts in **example 5.4.5.2** were changed such that, instead of being obliged to purchase its output, the parties to the joint arrangement are obliged to act as the sole suppliers of raw materials to the arrangement (the joint arrangement is restricted from sourcing product from any alternative supplier), classification as a joint operation would not be appropriate.

Unlike the circumstances described in **example 5.4.5.2**, the obligation on a joint arrangement to purchase all of its supplies from the parties to the joint arrangement does not result in the parties being substantially the only source of cash flows contributing to the continuity of operations and does not give the parties rights to the assets of the joint arrangement. Consequently, in the absence of any other relevant factors, the joint arrangement is a joint venture.

Assume, for example, that Entity A and Entity B establish a joint arrangement in Country X through a separate vehicle (Entity C) in order to gain access to customers in Country X. Each party has a 50 per cent interest in Entity C. The purpose of Entity C is to manufacture and sell goods to third-party customers in Country X. Entity A and Entity B will be the sole suppliers of Entity C's requirements for raw materials, which they will sell on an ongoing basis to Entity C at fair value. Entity C in the normal course of its operations will use the proceeds from its sales to third parties to pay its liabilities, including those arising from the purchase of raw materials from Entity A and Entity B.

In the circumstances described, Entity A and Entity B do not have rights to the assets of Entity C (because once the raw materials are sold to the joint arrangement, they will be used for sales to third parties) or obligations for its liabilities (because the cash to settle liabilities will be sourced from third-party sales).

5.4.5.7   Joint arrangement produces bespoke output

The consideration of 'other facts and circumstances' in determining the classification of a joint arrangement is not affected by whether the arrangement produces goods that could be sold to a variety of external customers (sometimes referred to as 'fungible' goods) or output bespoke to the requirements of the parties to the arrangement such that it is unlikely to be sold to third parties.

As discussed in **5.4.5.4**, in the absence of an enforceable obligation to purchase the output of a joint arrangement, a right, expectation and/or intention to purchase that output is not (individually or in combination) sufficient to support a conclusion that the parties have an obligation for the liabilities relating to the arrangement.

Production by a joint arrangement of bespoke output (e.g. specialised manufactured parts that may be expected to be purchased only by the parties) might lead to an expectation or intention that the parties will purchase that output but it does not, in itself, oblige them to do so.

The IFRS Interpretations Committee confirmed in the March 2015 *IFRIC Update* that "the focus of 'obligation for the liabilities' in IFRS 11 is on the existence of cash flows flowing from the parties to satisfy the joint arrangement's liabilities as a consequence of the parties' rights to, and obligations for, the assets of the joint arrangement, *regardless of the nature of the product (ie fungible or bespoke output)"*. [Emphasis added]

5.4.6   Differences between joint operations and joint ventures

Appendix B to the Standard sets out a table comparing common terms in contractual arrangements of parties to a joint operation and common terms in contractual arrangements of parties to a joint venture.

The examples in the table, which is reproduced below, are not exhaustive.

[IFRS 11:B27]

Assessing the terms of the contractual arrangement		
	Joint operation	**Joint venture**
The terms of the contractual arrangement	The contractual arrangement provides the parties to the joint arrangement with rights to the assets, and obligations for the liabilities, relating to the arrangement.	The contractual arrangement provides the parties to the joint arrangement with rights to the net assets of the arrangement (ie it is the separate vehicle, not the parties, that has rights to the assets, and obligations for the liabilities, relating to the arrangement).
Rights to assets	The contractual arrangement establishes that the parties to the joint arrangement share all interests (eg rights, title or ownership) in the assets relating to the arrangement in a specified proportion (eg in proportion to the parties' ownership interest in the arrangement or in proportion to the activity carried out through the arrangement that is directly attributed to them).	The contractual arrangement establishes that the assets brought into the arrangement or subsequently acquired by the joint arrangement are the arrangement's assets. The parties have no interests (ie no rights, title or ownership) in the assets of the arrangement.

Assessing the terms of the contractual arrangement		
	Joint operation	**Joint venture**
Obligations for liabilities	The contractual arrangement establishes that the parties to the joint arrangement share all liabilities, obligations, costs and expenses in a specified proportion (eg in proportion to the parties' ownership interest in the arrangement or in proportion to the activity carried out through the arrangement that is directly attributed to them).	The contractual arrangement establishes that the joint arrangement is liable for the debts and obligations of the arrangement.
		The contractual arrangement establishes that the parties to the joint arrangement are liable to the arrangement only to the extent of their respective investments in the arrangement or to their respective obligations to contribute any unpaid or additional capital to the arrangement, or both.
	The contractual arrangement establishes that the parties to the joint arrangement are liable for claims raised by third parties.	The contractual arrangement states that creditors of the joint arrangement do not have rights of recourse against any party with respect to debts or obligations of the arrangement.
Revenues, expenses, profit or loss	The contractual arrangement establishes the allocation of revenues and expenses on the basis of the relative performance of each party to the joint arrangement. For example, the contractual arrangement might establish that revenues and expenses are allocated on the basis of the capacity that each party uses in a plant operated jointly, which could differ from their ownership interest in the joint arrangement. In other instances, the parties might have agreed to share the profit or loss relating to the arrangement on the basis of a specified proportion such as the parties' ownership interest in the arrangement. This would not prevent the arrangement from being a joint operation if the parties have rights to the assets, and obligations for the liabilities, relating to the arrangement.	The contractual arrangement establishes each party's share in the profit or loss relating to the activities of the arrangement.

Assessing the terms of the contractual arrangement		
	Joint operation	**Joint venture**
Guarantees	The parties to joint arrangements are often required to provide guarantees to third parties that, for example, receive a service from, or provide financing to, the joint arrangement. The provision of such guarantees, or the commitment by the parties to provide them, does not, by itself, determine that the joint arrangement is a joint operation. The feature that determines whether the joint arrangement is a joint operation or a joint venture is whether the parties have obligations for the liabilities relating to the arrangement (for some of which the parties might or might not have provided a guarantee).	

5.4.7 Illustrative examples

Six illustrative examples accompanying IFRS 11 illustrate the judgements that might be required when applying the Standard in different situations – these examples are reproduced in **section 7**.

6 Accounting for joint arrangements

6.1 Accounting for joint ventures (other than in separate financial statements) – joint venturers

A joint venturer (i.e. a party that has joint control of a joint venture) should recognise its interest in that joint venture in accordance with IAS 28 *Investments in Associates and Joint Ventures*. Subject to exemptions in specified circumstances, IAS 28 requires joint venturers to use the equity method to account for joint ventures, and also provides guidance on how to apply the equity method. [IFRS 11:24]

A party with an interest in a joint venture has an interest in a vehicle that is separate from the investing entity, but does not have rights to the assets, or obligations for the liabilities, of that vehicle. The requirement of IFRS 11 to use the equity method for such interests reflects this relationship.

The requirements of IAS 28, and the exemptions mentioned above, are discussed in **chapter A26**.

6.2 Accounting for joint ventures – investors not having joint control

A party that participates in a joint venture, but that does not have joint control, is required to account for its interest as follows:

[IFRS 11:25 & C14]

- if it has significant influence over the joint venture, using the equity method as set out in IAS 28;

- otherwise, in accordance with IFRS 9 *Financial Instruments* (or, for entities that have not yet adopted IFRS 9, IAS 39 *Financial Instruments: Recognition and Measurement*).

6.3   Accounting for joint operations – joint operators

6.3.1   *Items to be recognised in relation to interests in joint operations – general*

Under the approach taken in IFRS 11, a party with joint control of a joint operation has (legally or in substance) rights to the assets and obligations for the liabilities of the joint operation. IFRS 11's requirement to recognise directly the assets, obligations, revenues and expenses of the joint operator reflects this relationship.

A joint operator (i.e. a party that has joint control of a joint operation) recognises the following in its financial statements in respect of the joint operation:

[IFRS 11:20]

- its assets, including its share of any jointly held assets;

- its liabilities, including its share of any jointly incurred liabilities;

- its revenue from the sale of its share of the output arising from the joint operation;

- its share of the revenue from the sale of the output by the joint operation; and

- its expenses, including its share of any expenses incurred jointly.

As explained in IFRS 11:B17, the contractual arrangement often describes the nature of the activities to be undertaken and how the parties will go about undertaking the activities; for example, parties may agree to manufacture a product together, with each party being responsible for a specific task and each using its own assets and incurring its own liabilities. Each joint operator in this example should recognise, in its financial statements, the assets it uses and the liabilities it incurs for the task. The contractual arrangement is also likely to specify how revenue and expenses that are common to the parties are to be shared between them and the accounting for such revenue and expenses should follow from this. IFRS 11:B18 gives another example, that of parties agreeing to share and operate an asset together. The contractual arrangement sets out the parties' rights to the jointly operated asset and how output or revenue from the asset together with operating expenses are shared between the parties. In this example, each joint operator should reflect its share of the joint asset and its agreed share of any liabilities, output, revenue and expenses in its financial statements in accordance with the contractual arrangement. [IFRS 11:B17 & B18]

Individual assets, liabilities, revenue and expenses are thus included in the joint operator's financial statements as its assets, liabilities, revenue and expenses. In some cases, this will follow the legal form; in other cases, it will reflect the joint operator's interest in and exposure to balances that, legally, arise in a separate vehicle.

The IASB staff has prepared Frequently Asked Questions relating to IFRS 11, which do not constitute official IASB guidance. These note that, in the majority of cases, accounting for assets and liabilities gives the same outcome as proportionate consolidation would have done, but two main differences are identified:

- IFRS 11 requires an entity with an interest in a joint operation to recognise assets, liabilities, revenues and expenses of the joint operation as *specified in the contractual arrangement*, rather than basing the recognition of all assets, liabilities, revenues and expenses on the *ownership interest* that the entity has in the joint operation; and

- for entities that prepare separate financial statements, there is no difference between amounts recognised in the separate financial statements and in the consolidated financial statements.

6.3.2   Assets, liabilities, revenues and expenses of the joint operation to be accounted for in accordance with relevant IFRSs

The assets, liabilities, revenues and expenses are accounted for in accordance with the relevant IFRSs. [IFRS 11:21]

For example, IFRS 15 *Revenue from Contracts with Customers* (or, for entities that have not yet adopted IFRS 15, IAS 18 *Revenue*) will be applied to determine the appropriate amount to be included for revenue. Similarly, the Basis for Conclusions confirms that if a joint operation is held for sale, a joint operator should account for its interest in accordance with IFRS 5 *Non-current Assets Held for Sale and Discontinued Operations*. [IFRS 11:BC51]

Example 6.3.2

Recognition of revenue by a joint operator

Two parties (Entity A and Entity B) enter into a joint arrangement that is structured through a separate vehicle. Each party initially subscribes for 50 per cent of the shares in the jointly controlled vehicle and the joint arrangement agreement specifies that each party is obliged to purchase 50 per cent of the primary output of the arrangement at cost. The arrangement also generates a by-product that may be sold to third parties.

By-product sales are not expected to be substantial and, as discussed at **5.4.5.3**, the joint arrangement is classified as a joint operation.

In its first year of operation (20X1), the joint operation's separate financial statements show revenue of CU100 constituting:

	CU
Sales of primary product to Entity A	48
Sales of primary product to Entity B	48
Sales of by-product to third parties	4
	100

During the year Entity A has sold products purchased from the joint operation of CU40 to its own customers for proceeds of CU60.

In its 20X1 financial statements, Entity A should recognise revenue of CU62 in respect of its interest in the joint operation, which is calculated as follows.

	CU
Revenue from sale of output purchased from the joint operation to external customers [IFRS 11:20(c)]	60
Share of by-product sales by the joint operation (CU4 × 50 per cent) [IFRS 11:20(d)]	2
	62

Neither Entity A nor Entity B should recognise any revenue in respect of the joint operation's sale of the primary product to the joint operators (i.e. themselves). This is because a joint operator that has an obligation to purchase the output from the joint operation has rights to the assets of the joint operation. Accordingly, the sale of the output by the joint operation to the joint operator would mean selling output to itself and, therefore, the joint operator should not recognise a share of the revenue from the sale of that output by the joint operation. Entity A and Entity B recognise 'their revenue' only when they sell the output to third parties.

IFRS 11:20(d) results in the recognition of revenue by a joint operator only when the joint operation sells its output to third parties. For this purpose, 'third parties' does not include other parties who have rights to the assets and obligations for the liabilities relating to the joint operation.

The conclusions above have been confirmed by the IFRS Interpretations Committee (see March 2015 *IFRIC Update*).

6.3.3   *Obligation to purchase output is disproportionate to ownership percentage*

Example 6.3.3

Obligation to purchase output is disproportionate to ownership percentage

Two parties enter into a joint arrangement. The arrangement is structured through a separate vehicle. Each party initially subscribes for 50 per cent of the shares in the jointly controlled vehicle. The joint arrangement specifies that the parties are obliged to purchase the output of the arrangement in the ratio 60:40. The parties' obligations to purchase output are therefore disproportionate to their ownership interests. Consistent with the conclusion in **example 5.4.5.2**, the joint arrangement is determined to be a joint operation.

In circumstances such as those described, for the purpose of applying IFRS 11:20 (see **6.3.1**)*, how should the joint operators' 'share' of assets held and liabilities incurred jointly be determined?*

IFRS 11 does not provide any explicit guidance in this regard and a joint operator should establish and disclose an accounting policy that treats similar joint operations in a similar manner.

In the absence of guidance in IFRS 11, and subject to considering the specific facts and circumstances of the joint operation, the Standard could be interpreted in two ways.

- **Approach 1** – although the joint operators' obligations to purchase output are a determinant of the classification of a joint arrangement, each party's share of assets and liabilities is nevertheless established based on its *ownership percentage*. Applying this approach would result in each party recognising its share of the assets and liabilities either on the basis of (1) its share of dividends and its entitlement on sale, or (2) assuming a liquidation of the joint arrangement vehicle at book value as at the reporting date.

- **Approach 2** – to view the joint operators' obligations to purchase output not only as a determinant of classification, but also of their proportionate shares of assets held and liabilities incurred jointly. Applying this interpretation would lead to the parties recognising their shares of assets and liabilities based on their *output percentages* (i.e. the shares of assets they will take and liabilities they will fund on an ongoing basis).

When selecting which of the two approaches described above should be applied to a particular joint operation, caution should be exercised to ensure that the approach adopted results in an appropriate reflection of the economic share of each party in the joint operation. For example, if the parties contribute only a nominal amount to equity, and they have no rights to accumulated profits (or the arrangement was not designed to generate profits), it might be concluded that the ownership percentage is not a substantive feature of the arrangement.

If, in the example described earlier, the joint operators recognised their shares of assets held and liabilities incurred jointly on the basis of their output percentages (i.e. 60 and 40 per cent, respectively), there would be a difference between the amount of the assets and liabilities initially recognised by the joint operators and their initial contributed equity. Specifically, when the joint arrangement is first established, the net share of assets and liabilities recognised by the joint operator taking the 60 per cent share will be higher than its initial contributed equity; conversely, the share recognised by the joint operator taking the 40 per cent share will be lower than its initial contributed equity. IFRS 11 does not provide any guidance on whether these differences should initially be recognised in profit or loss or as an asset or a liability. Further, it does not provide any guidance on the subsequent accounting for such differences.

6.3.4 Acquisitions of interests in a joint operation

6.3.4.1 May 2014 amendments

The requirements in this section were added to IFRS 11 in May 2014 by *Accounting for Acquisitions of Interests in Joint Operations: Amendments to IFRS 11*. The amendments are required to be applied prospectively for annual periods beginning on or after 1 January 2016, with earlier application permitted (see **6.3.4.4**).

The May 2014 amendments address how a joint operator should account for the acquisition of an interest in a joint operation in which the activity of the joint operation constitutes a business. IFRS 11, as amended, now requires that such transactions should be accounted for using business combinations accounting under IFRS 3 *Business Combinations* and other Standards. The most significant requirements introduced by the May 2014 amendments are the requirements to recognise goodwill, when appropriate, and deferred tax assets and liabilities.

6.3.4.2 Scope of the requirements regarding acquisitions of interests in joint operations

The requirements apply to the acquisition of an interest in a joint operation in which the activity of the joint operation constitutes a business, as defined in IFRS 3 *Business Combinations*. It applies to an acquisition of the initial interest as well as any additional interests in a joint operation. [IFRS 11:21A]

Example 11.4 in **chapter A25** considers the appropriate accounting when an entity obtains control of an interest previously held as a joint operation.

The requirements also apply to the acquisition of an interest in a joint operation on its formation if a business is contributed to the joint operation. However, the amendments do not apply when there is no existing business, i.e. if no existing business is contributed to the joint operation on its formation and the formation of the joint operation coincides with the formation of the business. [IFRS 11:B33B]

The requirements do not apply to the acquisition of an interest in a joint operation when the parties sharing joint control (including the entity acquiring the interest in the joint operation) are under common control of the same ultimate parent before and after the transaction, and that control is not transitory. [IFRS 11:B33D]

6.3.4.3   Requirements regarding acquisitions of interests in joint operations

The relevant principles of business combinations accounting in IFRS 3 and other Standards are required to be applied, provided that they do not conflict with guidance elsewhere in IFRS 11. [IFRS 11:21A & B33A]

Accordingly, to the extent of its interest in the joint operation, a joint operator is required to:

[IFRS 11:B33A]

- measure the identifiable assets and liabilities at fair value, other than items for which exceptions are made in IFRS 3 or other IFRSs;

- recognise acquisition-related costs as expenses in the periods in which the costs are incurred and the services are received, except for costs to issue debt or equity securities which should be recognised in accordance with IAS 32 *Financial Instruments: Presentation* and IFRS 9 *Financial Instruments* (or, for entities that have not yet adopted IFRS 9, IAS 39 *Financial Instruments: Recognition and Measurement*);

- recognise deferred tax assets and deferred tax liabilities that arise from the initial recognition of assets or liabilities, except for deferred tax liabilities that arise from the initial recognition of goodwill, as required by IFRS 3 and IAS 12 *Income Taxes* for business combinations;

- recognise goodwill for any excess of the consideration transferred over the net of the acquisition-date amounts of the identifiable assets acquired and the liabilities assumed; and

- perform an impairment test at least annually (and whenever there is an indication of impairment) for any cash-generating unit to which goodwill has been allocated.

The principles of business combinations accounting listed in IFRS 11:B33A should be applied because they do not conflict with other requirements of IFRS 11; however, the list is not exhaustive. [IFRS 11:B33A]

A joint operator is also required to disclose the relevant information required by IFRS 3 and other IFRSs for business combinations. [IFRS 11:21A]

If an entity increases its interest in a joint operation in which the activity of the joint operation constitutes a business by acquiring an additional interest in the joint operation, previously held interests in the joint operation are not remeasured if the joint operator retains joint control. [IFRS 11:B33C]

6.3.4.4   Effective date and transition

The May 2014 amendments to IFRS 11 (see **6.3.4.1**) apply prospectively for annual periods beginning on or after 1 January 2016, with earlier application permitted. If an entity applies the amendments for a period beginning before 1 January 2016, it is required to disclose that fact. [IFRS 11:C1AA]

The amendments to IFRS 11 are required to be applied prospectively for acquisitions of interests from the beginning of the first period in which the May 2014 amendments are applied. Consequently, amounts recognised for acquisitions of interests in joint operations in prior periods should not be restated. [IFRS 11:C14A]

6.3.4.5   Illustrative examples

See **examples 7G** and **7H** which illustrate the appropriate accounting for acquisitions of interests in joint operations.

6.3.5   Transactions between a joint operator and the joint operation

When a joint operator contributes or sells assets to the joint operation, it recognises gains and losses from the transaction only to the extent of the other parties' interests in the joint operation. [IFRS 11:B34]

Such transactions are sometimes referred to as 'downstream transactions'. When the asset is subsequently sold or fully consumed by the joint operation, the balance of the gain or loss is recognised.

If the transaction with the joint operation provides evidence of a reduction in the net realisable value of, or of an impairment loss relating to, the assets sold or contributed, the losses should be recognised in full by the joint operator. [IFRS 11:B35]

When a joint operator purchases an asset from the joint operation, it should not recognise its share of the gains and losses from the transaction until it resells the asset to a third party. However, if the transaction provides evidence of a reduction in the net realisable value of, or of an impairment loss relating to, the assets purchased, the joint operator should recognise its share of those losses. [IFRS 11:B36 - B37]

Such transactions are sometimes referred to as 'upstream transactions'.

6.4   Accounting for joint operations – a party participating in a joint operation that does not have joint control

The appropriate accounting for a party that participates in, but does not have joint control of, a joint operation depends on the party's rights and obligations.

If the party has rights to the assets, and obligations for the liabilities, relating to the joint operation, it accounts for its interest in the joint operation as set out at **6.3**, i.e. it accounts in the same way as the joint operators. Conversely, if the party does not have rights to the assets, and obligations for the liabilities, relating to the joint operation, it accounts for its interest in the joint operation in accordance with the relevant IFRS. [IFRS 11:23]

> IFRS 11 does not give further guidance on the latter scenario but, following the logic set out at **6.2**, the 'relevant IFRS' is likely to be IFRS 9 (or, for entities that have not yet adopted IFRS 9, IAS 39) – although IAS 28 would apply if the party had significant influence over the joint operation.

6.5   Separate financial statements

6.5.1   Separate financial statements – general

Separate financial statements are defined in IAS 27 *Separate Financial Statements* as financial statements presented by a parent (i.e. an investor with control of a subsidiary) or an investor with joint control of, or significant influence over, an investee, in which the investments are accounted for at cost, in accordance with IFRS 9 (or, for entities that have not yet adopted IFRS 9, IAS 39), or using the equity method as described in IAS 28 *Investments in Joint Ventures and Associates*. [IAS 27:4 & 19]

Separate financial statements are discussed further in **chapter A29**.

6.5.2   Joint ventures

A joint venturer (i.e. a party that has joint control of a joint venture) accounts for its interest in the joint venture in its separate financial statements in accordance with IAS 27:10 (see **section 5** of **chapter A29**). [IFRS 11:26(b)]

> Such an interest will be accounted for either at cost, in accordance with IFRS 9 (or, for entities that have not yet adopted IFRS 9, IAS 39), or using the equity method as described in IAS 28.

A party that participates in, but does not have joint control of, a joint venture accounts in its separate financial statements for its interest in the joint venture in accordance with IFRS 9 (or, for entities that have not yet adopted IFRS 9, IAS 39) unless the party has significant influence over the joint venture, in which case it accounts in accordance with IAS 27:10 (see **section 5** of **chapter A29**). [IFRS 11:27(b)]

> IAS 27:10 requires such an interest to be accounted for either at cost, in accordance with IFRS 9 (or, for entities that have not yet adopted IFRS 9, IAS 39), or using the equity method as described in IAS 28.

When a venture capital organisation, or a mutual fund, unit trust or similar entity (including an investment-linked insurance fund), elects to measure an investment in a joint venture at fair value through profit or loss (see **4.2.2** in **chapter A26**), it must apply the same accounting in its separate financial statements (see **section 5** of **chapter A29**). [IAS 27:11]

6.5.3 Joint operations

A party that has an interest in a joint operation should account for that interest as set out at **6.3** and **6.4**. The required accounting is the same in the separate financial statements as in the 'main' financial statements. [IFRS 11:26(a) & 27(a)]

7 Illustrative examples

The examples below accompany, but are not part of, IFRS 11. They illustrate aspects of the Standard but are not intended to provide interpretative guidance.

The examples portray hypothetical situations illustrating the judgements that might be used when applying IFRS 11 in different situations. Although some aspects of the examples may be present in actual fact patterns, all relevant facts and circumstances of a particular fact pattern would need to be evaluated when applying IFRS 11.

Example 7A

Construction services

[IFRS 11: IE2 - IE8, Example 1]

A and B (the parties) are two companies whose businesses are the provision of many types of public and private construction services. They set up a contractual arrangement to work together for the purpose of fulfilling a contract with a government for the design and construction of a road between two cities. The contractual arrangement determines the participation shares of A and B and establishes joint control of the arrangement, the subject matter of which is the delivery of the road.

The parties set up a separate vehicle (entity Z) through which to conduct the arrangement. Entity Z, on behalf of A and B, enters into the contract with the

---

government. In addition, the assets and liabilities relating to the arrangement are held in entity Z. The main feature of entity Z's legal form is that the parties, not entity Z, have rights to the assets, and obligations for the liabilities, of the entity.

The contractual arrangement between A and B additionally establishes that:

(a)   the rights to all the assets needed to undertake the activities of the arrangement are shared by the parties on the basis of their participation shares in the arrangement;

(b)   the parties have several and joint responsibility for all operating and financial obligations relating to the activities of the arrangement on the basis of their participation shares in the arrangement; and

(c)   the profit or loss resulting from the activities of the arrangement is shared by A and B on the basis of their participation shares in the arrangement.

For the purposes of co-ordinating and overseeing the activities, A and B appoint an operator, who will be an employee of one of the parties. After a specified time, the role of the operator will rotate to an employee of the other party. A and B agree that the activities will be executed by the operator's employees on a 'no gain or loss' basis.

In accordance with the terms specified in the contract with the government, entity Z invoices the construction services to the government on behalf of the parties.

Analysis

The joint arrangement is carried out through a separate vehicle whose legal form does not confer separation between the parties and the separate vehicle (ie the assets and liabilities held in entity Z are the parties' assets and liabilities). This is reinforced by the terms agreed by the parties in their contractual arrangement, which state that A and B have rights to the assets, and obligations for the liabilities, relating to the arrangement that is conducted through entity Z. The joint arrangement is a joint operation.

A and B each recognise in their financial statements their share of the assets (eg property, plant and equipment, accounts receivable) and their share of any liabilities resulting from the arrangement (eg accounts payable to third parties) on the basis of their agreed participation share. Each also recognises its share of the revenue and expenses resulting from the construction services provided to the government through entity Z.

Example 7B

Shopping centre operated jointly

[IFRS 11:IE9 - IE13, Example 2]

Two real estate companies (the parties) set up a separate vehicle (entity X) for the purpose of acquiring and operating a shopping centre. The contractual arrangement between the parties establishes joint control of the activities that are conducted in entity X. The main feature of entity X's legal form is that the entity, not the parties, has rights to the assets, and obligations for the liabilities, relating to the arrangement. These activities include the rental of the retail units, managing the car park, maintaining the centre and its equipment, such as lifts, and building the reputation and customer base for the centre as a whole.

The terms of the contractual arrangement are such that:

(a) entity X owns the shopping centre. The contractual arrangement does not specify that the parties have rights to the shopping centre.

(b) the parties are not liable in respect of the debts, liabilities or obligations of entity X. If entity X is unable to pay any of its debts or other liabilities or to discharge its obligations to third parties, the liability of each party to any third party will be limited to the unpaid amount of that party's capital contribution.

(c) the parties have the right to sell or pledge their interests in entity X.

(d) each party receives a share of the income from operating the shopping centre (which is the rental income net of the operating costs) in accordance with its interest in entity X.

Analysis

The joint arrangement is carried out through a separate vehicle whose legal form causes the separate vehicle to be considered in its own right (ie the assets and liabilities held in the separate vehicle are the assets and liabilities of the separate vehicle and not the assets and liabilities of the parties). In addition, the terms of the contractual arrangement do not specify that the parties have rights to the assets, or obligations for the liabilities, relating to the arrangement. Instead, the terms of the contractual arrangement establish that the parties have rights to the net assets of entity X.

On the basis of the description above, there are no other facts and circumstances that indicate that the parties have rights to substantially all the economic benefits of the assets relating to the arrangement, and that the parties have an obligation for the liabilities relating to the arrangement. The joint arrangement is a joint venture.

The parties recognise their rights to the net assets of entity X as investments and account for them using the equity method.

Example 7C

Joint manufacturing and distribution of a product

[IFRS 11:IE14 - IE28, Example 3]

Companies A and B (the parties) have set up a strategic and operating agreement (the framework agreement) in which they have agreed the terms according to which they will conduct the manufacturing and distribution of a product (product P) in different markets.

The parties have agreed to conduct manufacturing and distribution activities by establishing joint arrangements, as described below:

(a) Manufacturing activity: the parties have agreed to undertake the manufacturing activity through a joint arrangement (the manufacturing arrangement). The manufacturing arrangement is structured in a separate vehicle (entity M) whose legal form causes it to be considered in its own right (ie the assets and liabilities held in entity M are the assets and liabilities of entity M and not the assets and liabilities of the parties). In accordance with the framework agreement, the parties have committed themselves to purchasing the whole production of product P manufactured by the manufacturing arrangement in accordance with their ownership interests in entity M. The parties subsequently sell product P to another arrangement, jointly controlled by the two parties themselves, that has been established exclusively for the distribution of product P as described below. Neither the framework agreement nor the contractual arrangement between A and B dealing with the manufacturing activity specifies that the parties have rights to the assets, and obligations for the liabilities, relating to the manufacturing activity.

(b) Distribution activity: the parties have agreed to undertake the distribution activity through a joint arrangement (the distribution arrangement). The parties have structured the distribution arrangement in a separate vehicle (entity D) whose legal form causes it to be considered in its own right (ie the assets and liabilities held in entity D are the assets and liabilities of entity D and not the assets and liabilities of the parties). In accordance with the framework agreement, the distribution arrangement orders its requirements for product P from the parties according to the needs of the different markets where the distribution arrangement sells the product. Neither the framework agreement nor the contractual arrangement between A and B dealing with the distribution activity specifies that the parties have rights to the assets, and obligations for the liabilities, relating to the distribution activity.

In addition, the framework agreement establishes:

(a) that the manufacturing arrangement will produce product P to meet the requirements for product P that the distribution arrangement places on the parties;

(b) the commercial terms relating to the sale of product P by the manufacturing arrangement to the parties. The manufacturing arrangement will sell product P to the parties at a price agreed by A and B that covers all production costs incurred. Subsequently, the parties sell the product to the distribution arrangement at a price agreed by A and B.

(c) that any cash shortages that the manufacturing arrangement may incur will be financed by the parties in accordance with their ownership interests in entity M.

Analysis

The framework agreement sets up the terms under which parties A and B conduct the manufacturing and distribution of product P. These activities are undertaken through joint arrangements whose purpose is either the manufacturing or the distribution of product P.

The parties carry out the manufacturing arrangement through entity M whose legal form confers separation between the parties and the entity. In addition, neither the framework agreement nor the contractual arrangement dealing with the manufacturing activity specifies that the parties have rights to the assets, and obligations for the liabilities, relating to the manufacturing activity. However, when considering the following facts and circumstances the parties have concluded that the manufacturing arrangement is a joint operation:

(a) The parties have committed themselves to purchasing the whole production of product P manufactured by the manufacturing arrangement. Consequently, A and B have rights to substantially all the economic benefits of the assets of the manufacturing arrangement.

(b) The manufacturing arrangement manufactures product P to meet the quantity and quality needs of the parties so that they can fulfil the demand for product P of the distribution arrangement. The exclusive dependence of the manufacturing arrangement upon the parties for the generation of cash flows and the parties' commitments to provide funds when the manufacturing arrangement incurs any cash shortages indicate that the parties have an obligation for the liabilities of the manufacturing arrangement, because those liabilities will be settled through the parties' purchases of product P or by the parties' direct provision of funds.

The parties carry out the distribution activities through entity D, whose legal form confers separation between the parties and the entity. In addition, neither the framework agreement nor the contractual arrangement dealing with the distribution activity specifies that the parties have rights to the assets, and obligations for the liabilities, relating to the distribution activity.

There are no other facts and circumstances that indicate that the parties have rights to substantially all the economic benefits of the assets relating to the distribution arrangement or that the parties have an obligation for the liabilities relating to that arrangement. The distribution arrangement is a joint venture.

A and B each recognise in their financial statements their share of the assets (eg property, plant and equipment, cash) and their share of any liabilities resulting from the manufacturing arrangement (eg accounts payable to third parties) on the basis of their ownership interest in entity M. Each party also recognises its share of the expenses resulting from the manufacture of product P incurred by the manufacturing arrangement and its share of the revenues relating to the sales of product P to the distribution arrangement.

The parties recognise their rights to the net assets of the distribution arrangement as investments and account for them using the equity method.

Variation

Assume that the parties agree that the manufacturing arrangement described above is responsible not only for manufacturing product P, but also for its distribution to third-party customers.

The parties also agree to set up a distribution arrangement like the one described above to distribute product P exclusively to assist in widening the distribution of product P in additional specific markets.

The manufacturing arrangement also sells product P directly to the distribution arrangement. No fixed proportion of the production of the manufacturing arrangement is committed to be purchased by, or to be reserved to, the distribution arrangement.

Analysis

The variation has affected neither the legal form of the separate vehicle in which the manufacturing activity is conducted nor the contractual terms relating to the parties' rights to the assets, and obligations for the liabilities, relating to the manufacturing activity. However, it causes the manufacturing arrangement to be a self-financed arrangement because it is able to undertake trade on its own behalf, distributing product P to third-party customers and, consequently, assuming demand, inventory and credit risks. Even though the manufacturing arrangement might also sell product P to the distribution arrangement, in this scenario the manufacturing arrangement is not dependent on the parties to be able to carry out its activities on a continuous basis. In this case, the manufacturing arrangement is a joint venture.

The variation has no effect on the classification of the distribution arrangement as a joint venture.

The parties recognise their rights to the net assets of the manufacturing arrangement and their rights to the net assets of the distribution arrangement as investments and account for them using the equity method.

Example 7D

Bank operated jointly

[IFRS 11:IE29 - IE33, Example 4]

Banks A and B (the parties) agreed to combine their corporate, investment banking, asset management and services activities by establishing a separate vehicle (bank C). Both parties expect the arrangement to benefit them in different ways. Bank A believes that the arrangement could enable it to achieve its strategic plans to increase its size, offering an opportunity to exploit its full potential for organic growth through an enlarged offering of products and services. Bank B expects the arrangement to reinforce its offering in financial savings and market products.

The main feature of bank C's legal form is that it causes the separate vehicle to be considered in its own right (ie the assets and liabilities held in the separate vehicle are the assets and liabilities of the separate vehicle and not the assets and liabilities of the parties). Banks A and B each have a 40 per cent ownership interest in bank C, with the remaining 20 per cent being listed and widely held. The shareholders' agreement between bank A and bank B establishes joint control of the activities of bank C.

In addition, bank A and bank B entered into an irrevocable agreement under which, even in the event of a dispute, both banks agree to provide the necessary funds in equal amount and, if required, jointly and severally, to ensure that bank C complies with the applicable legislation and banking regulations, and honours any commitments made to the banking authorities. This commitment represents the assumption by each party of 50 per cent of any funds needed to ensure that bank C complies with legislation and banking regulations.

Analysis

The joint arrangement is carried out through a separate vehicle whose legal form confers separation between the parties and the separate vehicle. The terms of the contractual arrangement do not specify that the parties have rights to the assets, or obligations for the liabilities, of bank C, but it establishes that the parties have rights to the net assets of bank C. The commitment by the parties to provide support if bank C is not able to comply with the applicable legislation and banking regulations is not by itself a determinant that the parties have an obligation for the liabilities of bank C. There are no other facts and circumstances that indicate that the parties have rights to substantially all the economic benefits of the assets of bank C and that the parties have an obligation for the liabilities of bank C. The joint arrangement is a joint venture.

Both banks A and B recognise their rights to the net assets of bank C as investments and account for them using the equity method.

Example 7E

Oil and gas exploration, development and production activities

[IFRS 11:IE34 - IE43, Example 5]

Companies A and B (the parties) set up a separate vehicle (entity H) and a Joint Operating Agreement (JOA) to undertake oil and gas exploration, development and production activities in country O. The main feature of entity H's legal form is that it causes the separate vehicle to be considered in its own right (ie the assets and liabilities held in the separate vehicle are the assets and liabilities of the separate vehicle and not the assets and liabilities of the parties).

Country O has granted entity H permits for the oil and gas exploration, development and production activities to be undertaken in a specific assigned block of land (fields).

The shareholders' agreement and JOA agreed by the parties establish their rights and obligations relating to those activities. The main terms of those agreements are summarised below.

Shareholders' agreement

The board of entity H consists of a director from each party. Each party has a 50 per cent shareholding in entity H. The unanimous consent of the directors is required for any resolution to be passed.

Joint Operating Agreement (JOA)

JOA establishes an Operating Committee. This Committee consists of one representative from each party. Each party has a 50 per cent participating interest in the Operating Committee.

The Operating Committee approves the budgets and work programmes relating to the activities, which also require the unanimous consent of the representatives of each party. One of the parties is appointed as operator and is responsible for managing and conducting the approved work programmes.

The JOA specifies that the rights and obligations arising from the exploration, development and production activities shall be shared among the parties in proportion to each party's shareholding in entity H. In particular, the JOA establishes that the parties share:

(a)   the rights and the obligations arising from the exploration and development permits granted to entity H (eg the permits, rehabilitation liabilities, any royalties and taxes payable);

(b)   the production obtained; and

(c)   all costs associated with all work programmes.

The JOA specifies that the rights and obligations arising from the exploration, development and production activities shall be shared among the parties in proportion to each party's shareholding in entity H. In particular, the JOA establishes that the parties share:

(a)   the rights and the obligations arising from the exploration and development permits granted to entity H (eg the permits, rehabilitation liabilities, any royalties and taxes payable);

(b)   the production obtained; and

(c)   all costs associated with all work programmes.

The costs incurred in relation to all the work programmes are covered by cash calls on the parties. If either party fails to satisfy its monetary obligations, the other is required to contribute to entity H the amount in default. The amount in default is regarded as a debt owed by the defaulting party to the other party.

Analysis

The parties carry out the joint arrangement through a separate vehicle whose legal form confers separation between the parties and the separate vehicle. The parties have been able to reverse the initial assessment of their rights and obligations arising from the legal form of the separate vehicle in which the arrangement is conducted. They have done this by agreeing terms in the JOA that entitle them to rights to the assets (eg exploration and development permits, production, and any other assets arising from the activities) and obligations for the liabilities (eg all costs and obligations arising from the work programmes) that are held in entity H. The joint arrangement is a joint operation.

Both company A and company B recognise in their financial statements their own share of the assets and of any liabilities resulting from the arrangement on the basis of their agreed participating interest. On that basis, each party also recognises its share of the revenue (from the sale of their share of the production) and its share of the expenses.

Example 7F

Liquefied natural gas arrangement

[IFRS 11:IE44 - IE52, Example 6]

Company A owns an undeveloped gas field that contains substantial gas resources. Company A determines that the gas field will be economically viable only if the gas is sold to customers in overseas markets. To do so, a liquefied natural gas (LNG) facility must be built to liquefy the gas so that it can be transported by ship to the overseas markets.

Company A enters into a joint arrangement with company B in order to develop and operate the gas field and the LNG facility. Under that arrangement, companies A and B (the parties) agree to contribute the gas field and cash, respectively, to a new separate vehicle, entity C. In exchange for those contributions, the parties each take a 50 per cent ownership interest in entity C. The main feature of entity C's legal form is that it causes the separate vehicle to be considered in its own right (ie the assets and liabilities held in the separate vehicle are the assets and liabilities of the separate vehicle and not the assets and liabilities of the parties).

The contractual arrangement between the parties specifies that:

(a)   companies A and B must each appoint two members to the board of entity C. The board of directors must unanimously agree the strategy and investments made by entity C.

(b)   day-to-day management of the gas field and LNG facility, including development and construction activities, will be undertaken by the staff of company B in accordance with the directions jointly agreed by the parties. Entity C will reimburse B for the costs it incurs in managing the gas field and LNG facility.

(c)   entity C is liable for taxes and royalties on the production and sale of LNG as well as for other liabilities incurred in the ordinary course of business, such as accounts payable, site restoration and decommissioning liabilities.

(d)   companies A and B have equal shares in the profit from the activities carried out in the arrangement and, as such, are entitled to equal shares of any dividends distributed by entity C.

The contractual arrangement does not specify that either party has rights to the assets, or obligations for the liabilities, of entity C.

The board of entity C decides to enter into a financing arrangement with a syndicate of lenders to help fund the development of the gas field and construction of the LNG facility. The estimated total cost of the development and construction is CU1,000 million.*

The lending syndicate provides entity C with a CU700 million loan. The arrangement specifies that the syndicate has recourse to companies A and B only if entity C defaults on the loan arrangement during the development of the field and construction of the LNG facility. The lending syndicate agrees that it will not have recourse to companies A and B once the LNG facility is in production because it has assessed that the cash inflows that entity C should generate from LNG sales will be sufficient to meet the loan repayments. Although at this time the lenders have no recourse to companies A and B, the syndicate maintains protection against default by entity C by taking a lien on the LNG facility.

Analysis

The joint arrangement is carried out through a separate vehicle whose legal form confers separation between the parties and the separate vehicle. The terms of the contractual arrangement do not specify that the parties have rights to the assets, or obligations for the liabilities, of entity C, but they establish that the parties have rights to the net assets of entity C. The recourse nature of the financing arrangement during the development of the gas field and construction of the LNG facility (ie companies A and B providing separate guarantees during this phase) does not, by itself, impose on the parties an obligation for the liabilities of entity C (ie the loan is a liability of entity C). Companies A and B have separate liabilities, which are their guarantees to repay that loan if entity C defaults during the development and construction phase.

There are no other facts and circumstances that indicate that the parties have rights to substantially all the economic benefits of the assets of entity C and that the parties have an obligation for the liabilities of entity C. The joint arrangement is a joint venture.

The parties recognise their rights to the net assets of entity C as investments and account for them using the equity method.

* In this example monetary amounts are denominated in 'currency units (CU)'.

Example 7G

Accounting for acquisitions of interests in joint operations in which the activity constitutes a business

[IFRS 11:IE53 - IE62, Example 7]

Companies A, B and C have joint control of Joint Operation D whose activity constitutes a business, as defined in IFRS 3 *Business Combinations*.

Company E acquires Company A's 40 per cent ownership interest in Joint Operation D at a cost of CU300 and incurs acquisition-related costs of CU50.

The contractual arrangement between the parties that Company E joined as part of the acquisition establishes that Company E's shares in several assets and liabilities differ from its ownership interest in Joint Operation D. The following table sets out Company E's share in the assets and liabilities related to Joint Operation D as established in the contractual arrangement between the parties:

	Company E's share in the assets and liabilities related to Joint Operation D
Property, plant and equipment	48%
Intangible assets (excluding goodwill)	90%
Accounts receivable	40%
Inventory	40%
Retirement benefit obligations	15%
Accounts payable	40%
Contingent liabilities	56%

Analysis

Company E recognises in its financial statements its share of the assets and liabilities resulting from the contractual arrangement (see [IFRS 11:20]).

It applies the principles on business combinations accounting in IFRS 3 and other IFRSs for identifying, recognising, measuring and classifying the assets acquired, and the liabilities assumed, on the acquisition of the interest in Joint Operation D. This is because Company E acquired an interest in a joint operation in which the activity constitutes a business (see [IFRS 11:21A]).

However, Company E does not apply the principles on business combinations accounting in IFRS 3 and other IFRSs that conflict with the guidance in this IFRS. Consequently, in accordance with [IFRS 11:20], Company E recognises, and therefore measures, in relation to its interest in Joint Operation D, only its share in each of the assets that are jointly held and in each of the liabilities that are incurred jointly, as stated in the contractual arrangement. Company E does not include in its assets and liabilities the shares of the other parties in Joint Operation D.

IFRS 3 requires the acquirer to measure the identifiable assets acquired and the liabilities assumed at their acquisition-date fair values with limited exceptions; for example, deferred tax assets and deferred tax liabilities are not measured at fair value but are measured in accordance with IAS 12 *Income Taxes*. Such measurement does not conflict with [IFRS 11] and thus those requirements apply.

Consequently, Company E determines the fair value, or other measure specified in IFRS 3, of its share in the identifiable assets and liabilities related to Joint Operation D. The following table sets out the fair value or other measure specified by IFRS 3 of Company E's shares in the identifiable assets and liabilities related to Joint Operation D:

	Fair value or other measure specified by IFRS 3 for Company E's shares in the identifiable assets and liabilities of Joint Operation D
	CU
Property, plant and equipment	138
Intangible assets (excluding goodwill)	72
Accounts receivable	84
Inventory	70
Retirement benefit obligations	(12)
Accounts payable	(48)
Contingent liabilities	(52)
Deferred tax liability	(24)
Net assets	228

In accordance with IFRS 3, the excess of the consideration transferred over the amount allocated to Company E's shares in the net identifiable assets is recognised as goodwill:

Consideration transferred	CU300
Company E's shares in the identifiable assets and liabilities relating to its interest in the joint operation	CU228
Goodwill	CU72

Acquisition-related costs of CU50 are not considered to be part of the consideration transferred for the interest in the joint operation. They are recognised as expenses in profit or loss in the period that the costs are incurred and the services are received (see paragraph 53 of IFRS 3).

Example 7H

Contributing the right to use know-how to a joint operation in which the activity constitutes a business

[IFRS 11:IE63 - IE73, Example 8]

Companies A and B are two companies whose business is the construction of high performance batteries for diverse applications.

In order to develop batteries for electric vehicles they set up a contractual arrangement (Joint Operation Z) to work together. Companies A and B share joint control of Joint Operation Z. This arrangement is a joint operation in which the activity constitutes a business, as defined in IFRS 3.

After several years, the joint operators (Companies A and B) concluded that it is feasible to develop a battery for electric vehicles using Material M. However, processing Material M requires specialist know-how and thus far, Material M has only been used in the production of cosmetics.

In order to get access to existing know-how in processing Material M, Companies A and B arrange for Company C to join as another joint operator by acquiring an interest in Joint Operation Z from Companies A and B and becoming a party to the contractual arrangements.

Company C's business so far has been solely the development and production of cosmetics. It has long-standing and extensive knowledge in processing Material M.

In exchange for its share in Joint Operation Z, Company C pays cash to Companies A and B and grants the right to use its know-how in processing Material M for the purposes of Joint Operation Z. In addition, Company C seconds some of its employees who are experienced in processing Material M to Joint Operation Z. However, Company C does not transfer control of the know-how to Companies A and B or Joint Operation Z because it retains all the rights to it. In particular, Company C is entitled to withdraw the right to use its know-how in processing Material M and to withdraw its seconded employees without any restrictions or compensation to Companies A and B or Joint Operation Z if it ceases its participation in Joint Operation Z.

The fair value of Company C's know-how on the date of the acquisition of the interest in the joint operation is CU1,000. Immediately before the acquisition, the carrying amount of the know-how in the financial statements of Company C was CU300.

Analysis

Company C has acquired an interest in Joint Operation Z in which the activity of the joint operation constitutes a business, as defined in IFRS 3.

In accounting for the acquisition of its interest in the joint operation, Company C applies all the principles on business combinations accounting in IFRS 3 and other IFRSs that do not conflict with the guidance in this IFRS (see [IFRS 11:21A]). Company C therefore recognises in its financial statements its share of the assets and liabilities resulting from the contractual arrangement (see [IFRS 11:20]).

Company C granted the right to use its know-how in processing Material M to Joint Operation Z as part of joining Joint Operation Z as a joint operator. However, Company C retains control of this right because it is entitled to withdraw the right to use its know-how in processing Material M and to withdraw its seconded employees without any restrictions or any compensation to Companies A and B or Joint Operation Z if it ceases its participation in Joint Operation Z.

Consequently, Company C continues to recognise the know-how in processing Material M after the acquisition of the interest in Joint Operation Z because it retains all the rights to it. This means that Company C will continue to recognise the know-how based on its carrying amount of CU300. As a consequence of

> retaining control of the right to use the know-how that it granted to the joint operation, Company C has granted the right to use the know-how to itself. Consequently, Company C does not remeasure the know-how, and it does not recognise a gain or loss on the grant of the right to use it.

8   Disclosure

Disclosure requirements for joint arrangements are set out in IFRS 12 *Disclosure of Interests in Other Entities* (see **chapter A28**).

9   Future developments

In June 2016, the IASB issued ED/2016/1 *Definition of a Business and Accounting for Previously Held Interests*. The exposure draft proposes to amend IFRS 11 to clarify that an entity that is a joint operator should not remeasure any previously held interest in the joint operation when it acquires an additional stake in a joint operation while either retaining or gaining joint control.

See **14.2** in **chapter A25** for details of proposed amendments to IFRS 3 *Business Combinations* arising from the exposure draft.

Comments on the exposure draft are requested by 31 October 2016.

A28 Disclosure of interests in other entities

Contents

1 Introduction

1.1 Overview of IFRS 12

IFRS 12 *Disclosure of Interests in Other Entities* is a consolidated disclosure Standard requiring a wide range of disclosures about an entity's interests in subsidiaries, joint arrangements, associates and unconsolidated 'structured entities'. The disclosure requirements are presented as a series of objectives, with detailed guidance on satisfying those objectives.

1.2 Amendments to IFRS 12 since the last edition of this manual

None. IFRS 12 was most recently amended in December 2014.

2 Disclosure requirements – general

2.1 Objective of IFRS 12

The objective of IFRS 12 is to require information to be disclosed in an entity's financial statements that will enable users of those statements to evaluate:

[IFRS 12:1]

- the nature of, and risks associated with, the entity's interests in other entities; and

- the effects of those interests on the entity's financial position, financial performance and cash flows.

2.2 Overview of disclosure requirements

The disclosures required by IFRS 12 can be categorised as follows:

[IFRS 12:2]

- significant judgements and assumptions made by an entity in determining:

  - the nature of its interests in another entity or arrangement (see **section 5**);

  - the type of joint arrangement in which it has an interest (see **section 5**); and

  - that it meets the definition of an investment entity, if applicable (see **5.2**);

- information about interests in subsidiaries (see **section 6**);

- information about interests in joint arrangements and associates (see **section 7**); and

- information about interests in unconsolidated structured entities (see **section 8**).

If the disclosures specified in these four sections, together with disclosures provided under other Standards, do not meet the overall objective of IFRS 12, the reporting entity should disclose whatever additional information is needed to ensure that the objective is met. [IFRS 12:3]

2.3   Aggregation

In satisfying the objective of IFRS 12, the reporting entity should consider both the level of detail that is necessary and how much emphasis to place on each of the Standard's disclosure requirements. Including a large amount of insignificant detail or aggregating items having different characteristics would obscure useful information. Therefore, disclosures should be aggregated or disaggregated so as to ensure that useful information is not obscured. [IFRS 12:4 & B2]

The extent of aggregation, disaggregation and emphasis should be tailored by each reporting entity to meet its users' needs. Each entity needs to find the right balance between too much and too little information. [IFRS 12:B2]

Information should be presented separately for interests in:

[IFRS 12:B4]

- subsidiaries;

- joint ventures;

- joint operations;

- associates; and

- unconsolidated structured entities.

Aggregation within each of these categories is permitted for interests in similar entities, provided that it is consistent with the Standard's overall objective and does not obscure the information provided. [IFRS 12:B3] In determining whether to aggregate information about particular entities, both qualitative and quantitative information about the different risk and return characteristics of each of those entities needs to be considered, together with the significance of each of the entities to the reporting entity. [IFRS 12:B5] IFRS 12 gives examples of possible aggregation levels, such as by nature of activities, by industry classification or by geography (e.g. by country or region). [IFRS 12:B6]

The disclosures should be presented in the financial statements in a way that makes clear the nature and extent of the reporting entity's interests in the other entities. [IFRS 12:B5]

A reporting entity should disclose in its financial statements how it has aggregated interests in similar entities. [IFRS 12:B3]

> In some cases, this disclosure may be apparent from how the information is presented and may not require any additional explanation. For example, in circumstances in which information is aggregated by geographical region when it is judged appropriate to do so, this may be readily apparent from headings and sub-headings.

3 Scope

3.1 Scope – general

Subject to certain exemptions, which are set out below, an entity is required to apply IFRS 12 if it has an interest in one or more of the following:

[IFRS 12:5]

- subsidiaries;
- joint arrangements (i.e. joint operations or joint ventures);
- associates; and
- unconsolidated structured entities.

> IFRS 12 does not state explicitly whether 'has an interest' means at the end of the reporting period or at any time during the reporting period. However, the Standard requires a number of disclosures regarding events that occur during the reporting period (e.g. in relation to the loss of control of a subsidiary during the reporting period). Accordingly, an entity should apply the Standard if it held any interest of the nature described in IFRS 12:5 at any time during the reporting period.
>
> IFRS 12 includes a definition of an interest in another entity (see **4.1**). But if an entity has already determined, through its application of IFRS 10 *Consolidated Financial Statements*, IFRS 11 *Joint Arrangements* or IAS 28 *Investments in Associates and Joint Ventures*, that it has a subsidiary, joint operation, joint venture or associate, that interest will fall within the scope of IFRS 12.
>
> The terms 'interest in another entity' and 'structured entity' are explained in **section 4**.

Exemptions from the disclosure requirements of IFRS 12 fall into two categories:

- financial statements outside the scope of IFRS 12 (see **3.2**); and
- interests for which the disclosures are not required (see **3.4**).

In addition, investment entities are exempted from certain of IFRS 12's general disclosure requirements (see **7.2.1** and **8.2**).

3.2 Financial statements outside the scope of IFRS 12

The requirements of IFRS 12 do not generally apply to an entity's separate financial statements. The disclosure requirements for separate financial statements are set out in IAS 27 *Separate Financial Statements* (see **chapter A29**).

However, if an entity's separate financial statements are its only financial statements, disclosures are required under IFRS 12 as follows:

[IFRS 12:6(b)]

(i)   if the entity has interests in unconsolidated structured entities, the disclosures required by IFRS 12 regarding unconsolidated structured entities, set out in IFRS 12:24 to 31 (see **section 8**); and

(ii) if the entity is an investment entity and all of its subsidiaries are measured at fair value through profit or loss as required by IFRS 10:31 (see **section 13** of **chapter A24**), the disclosures relevant for investment entities required by IFRS 12 (see **3.3**).

IFRS 12:6(b)(ii) was added by *Investment Entities: Applying the Consolidation Exception (Amendments to IFRS 10, IFRS 12 and IAS 28)* published by the IASB in December 2014. These amendments clarify the applicability of IFRS 12 to the separate financial statements of investment entities (although a similar requirement already exists in IAS 27:16A). The amendments are effective for annual periods beginning on or after 1 January 2016, with earlier application permitted. If an entity applies the amendments for a period beginning before 1 January 2016, it is required to disclose that fact. [IFRS 12:C1C]

As clarified in IFRS 12:BC611, the IASB added IFRS 12:6(b)(ii) because previously there had been some uncertainty as to whether IFRS 12 required an investment entity to make these disclosures, even though the disclosures were seemingly required by IAS 27:16A (see **3.3**).

3.3 Disclosures required by investment entities

All of the disclosure requirements of IFRS 12 are applicable to investment entities (to the extent that the disclosures relate to matters relevant to the investment entity) other than those explicitly stated as not applicable to investment entities.

IFRS 12 requirements explicitly stated as not being applicable to investment entities are IFRS 12:21(b) and (c) regarding interests in joint arrangements and associates, and IFRS 12:24 regarding unconsolidated structured entities, from which investment entities are exempted by IFRS 12:21A (see **7.2.1**) and IFRS 12:25A (see **8.2.1**), respectively.

Consequently, in addition to the specific requirements in IFRS 12:9A and 9B (see **5.2**), and 19A to 19G (see **6.8**), that apply only to investment entities, an investment entity should provide the disclosures required by the following general requirements in IFRS 12:

- IFRS 12:7 to 9 regarding significant judgements and assumptions (see **5.1**);

- IFRS 12:21(a), IFRS 12:22(a) and IFRS 12:23 regarding material joint arrangements and associates, significant restrictions on transfers of funds from joint ventures and associates, and risks associated with interests in joint ventures and associates, respectively (see **7.2** and **7.3**); and

- IFRS 12:24 to 31 regarding interests in unconsolidated structured entities, but only in respect of entities that the investment entity does not control (and that are not, therefore, covered by the exemption in IFRS 12:25A).

An investment entity preparing financial statements in which all subsidiaries are measured at fair value through profit or loss is not, however, required to provide the disclosures described in:

- IFRS 12:10 to 19 regarding interests in subsidiaries (because these either relate to consolidation accounting not applied by investment entities or are duplicated by the specific requirements of IFRS 12:19A to 19G) (see **section 6**); or

- IFRS 12:22(b) and (c) regarding the equity method of accounting (which is also not applied by investment entities due to the requirement in IFRS 10:B85L that they elect the exemption from applying the equity method in IAS 28) (see **7.2.6** and **7.2.7**).

When an investment entity consolidates a service-providing subsidiary as required by IFRS 10:32, the disclosure requirements of IFRS 12 apply to those consolidated financial statements (see IFRS 12:BC61I). The considerations described in the previous paragraphs then apply in determining the disclosures that should be provided. In addition, the disclosures required by IFRS 12:7(a) (significant judgements made in determining that the investment entity has control over the service-providing subsidiary) and IFRS 12:10 to 19 (regarding interests in subsidiaries) should be provided as applicable to the facts and circumstances of the service-providing subsidiary.

3.4   Interests for which disclosures are not required

IFRS 12 does not require disclosures to be provided about the following interests:

[IFRS 12:6(a), (c) & (d)]

- post-employment benefit plans to which IAS 19 *Employee Benefits* applies;

- other long-term employee benefit plans to which IAS 19 applies;

- an interest held by a party that participates in, but does not have joint control of, a joint arrangement (i.e. a joint venture or joint operation), unless that interest results in significant influence over the arrangement or is an interest in a structured entity;

- an interest in another entity that is accounted for in accordance with IFRS 9 (or, prior to the adoption of IFRS 9, IAS 39), unless the interest is (1) an interest in an associate or a joint venture that is measured at fair value through profit or loss in accordance with IAS 28, or (2) an interest in an unconsolidated structured entity.

In relation to the final bullet above, IAS 28 permits an interest in an associate or a joint venture held by a venture capital organisation or a mutual fund, unit trust or similar entity (including an investment-linked insurance fund) to be measured at fair value through profit or loss (see **4.2.2** in **chapter A26**). The disclosure requirements of IFRS 12 apply to such interests.

IFRS 12 does not apply to "post-employment benefit plans or other long-term employee benefit plans to which IAS 19 *Employee Benefits* applies". This exemption does not extend to entities such as employee share trusts established to facilitate equity compensation plans, which are within the scope of IFRS 2 *Share-based Payment* rather than IAS 19 (and are not, therefore, subject to the detailed disclosure requirements of IAS 19). Such entities fall within the scope of IFRS 12. The accounting and disclosure requirements for such arrangements are discussed in **section 9** of **chapter A16**.

4   Definitions

4.1   Interest in another entity – definition

An interest in another entity, for the purpose of applying IFRS 12, refers to contractual and non-contractual involvement that exposes an entity (the reporting entity) to variability of returns from the performance of the other entity. An interest can be evidenced by the holding of debt or equity instruments as well as other forms of involvement including (but not limited to) the provision of funding, liquidity support, credit enhancement and guarantees. An interest encompasses the means by which an entity has control of, joint control of, or significant influence over another entity. A typical customer-supplier relationship alone does not necessarily give rise to an interest in another entity for the purpose of applying IFRS 12. [IFRS 12:Appendix A]

> If the reporting entity is exposed, or has rights, through contractual or non-contractual involvement, to variability of returns from the performance of another entity, the reporting entity has an interest in that other entity for the purpose of applying IFRS 12.
>
> Variability of returns is key to the meaning of control in IFRS 10 and is widely defined (see **section 7** of **chapter A24** for discussion of variability of returns).
>
> Typically, an entity will already have determined, through its application of IFRS 10 *Consolidated Financial Statements*, IFRS 11 *Joint Arrangements* and IAS 28 *Investments in Associates and Joint Ventures*, the extent to which it has interests in subsidiaries, joint arrangements and associates. In addition, for the purpose of applying IFRS 12, a reporting entity will need to determine the extent to which it has interests in unconsolidated structured entities.
>
> The definition of a structured entity is discussed at **4.2**. **Section 4.3** considers how an entity determines whether it has an interest in an entity, which is mainly relevant for an interest in an unconsolidated structured entity.

4.2   Structured entity – definition

A structured entity is defined in IFRS 12 as "[a]n entity that has been designed so that voting or similar rights are not the dominant factor in deciding who controls the entity, such as when any voting rights relate to administrative tasks only and the relevant activities are directed by means of contractual arrangements". [IFRS 12:Appendix A & B21]

> The term 'structured entity' is not used in IFRS 10. The background to this definition, and to IFRS 12's requirement to provide disclosures about unconsolidated structured entities, is that the IASB was asked by, among others, the G20 leaders and the Financial Stability Board to improve disclosure requirements relating to 'off balance sheet' activities. Unconsolidated structured entities, particularly securitisation vehicles and asset-backed financings, are seen as part of such activities. [IFRS 12:BC62]
>
> A structured entity that is controlled by the reporting entity will meet the definition of a subsidiary and be consolidated (and thus 'on balance

sheet'). Specific disclosures are required in respect of subsidiaries that are structured entities (see **6.4**). The disclosures required in respect of unconsolidated structured entities are described in **section 8**.

Appendix B to IFRS 12 states that a structured entity often has some or all of the following features or attributes:

[IFRS 12:B22]

- restricted activities;

- a narrow and well-defined objective, such as to effect a tax-efficient lease, carry out research and development activities, provide a source of capital or funding to an entity or provide investment opportunities for investors by passing on risks and rewards associated with the assets of the structured entity to investors;

- insufficient equity to permit the structured entity to finance its activities without subordinated financial support; and/or

- financing in the form of multiple contractually linked instruments to investors that create concentrations of credit or other risks (tranches).

With respect to the third bullet point above, simply needing subordinated financial support does not mean that an entity is automatically a structured entity. For example, groups sometimes choose to finance subsidiaries through a mixture of equity and subordinated debt, but if such subsidiaries are controlled through voting rights attached to the equity instruments, they will not meet the definition of a structured entity.

If, following a restructuring, an entity that is controlled by voting rights receives funding from third parties, this in itself does not make the entity a structured entity. [IFRS 12:B24]

Securitisation vehicles, asset-backed financings and some investment funds are examples of structured entities given in IFRS 12. [IFRS 12:B23]

4.3   Interest in another entity – additional guidance

If a reporting entity has an interest in a joint venture or an associate that is a structured entity, that interest is also an interest in an unconsolidated structured entity for the purposes of IFRS 12. Therefore, the reporting entity should provide information in respect of that interest that meets both sets of disclosure requirements – those relating to interests in joint ventures and associates (see **section 7**), and those relating to interests in unconsolidated structured entities (see **section 8**).

The IASB considered this issue and confirmed the conclusion in the previous paragraph. In reaching this conclusion, the Board noted that an entity should capture most, and in some cases all, of the disclosures required for interests in unconsolidated structured entities by providing the disclosures for interests in joint ventures and associates. Accordingly, the Board did not think that this conclusion should significantly increase the amount of information that an entity would be required to provide. [IFRS 12:BC77]

This section discusses IFRS 12's guidance on how to determine whether an entity has an interest in another entity. As noted at **4.1**, this is mainly of relevance for interests in unconsolidated structured entities.

An interest in another entity (e.g. an unconsolidated structured entity) is a contractual or non-contractual involvement that exposes the reporting entity to variability of returns from the performance of the other entity. Consideration of the purpose and design of the other entity, including consideration of the risks that the other entity was designed to create and the risks it was designed to pass on to the reporting entity and other parties, may assist with the assessment of whether the reporting entity has an interest in the other entity. [IFRS 12:B7]

Typically, a reporting entity is exposed to variability of returns from the performance of another entity by holding instruments (e.g. debt or equity instruments issued by the other entity), or having some other involvement that absorbs variability. Consider the example of a structured entity that holds a loan portfolio. In order to protect itself from default of both interest and principal payments on the loans, the structured entity may enter into a credit default swap with the reporting entity. By entering into the credit default swap, the reporting entity would have an involvement that exposes it to variability of returns from the structured entity's performance because the credit default swap absorbs the structured entity's variability of returns. [IFRS 12:B8]

But simply entering into a credit default swap, or other instrument, with a structured entity is not sufficient to conclude that the counterparty has an interest in that structured entity. It is necessary for the counterparty to be exposed to variability of returns from the structured entity – and this will not always follow, as explained below.

Some instruments are designed to transfer risk from a reporting entity to another entity. Such instruments create variability of returns for the other entity but do not typically expose the reporting entity to variability of returns from the performance of the other entity. Consider a structured entity (Entity A) set up to provide investment opportunities for investors who wish to have exposure to the credit risk of another entity (Entity Z), where Entity Z is unrelated to any of the parties. Entity A issues credit-linked notes to the investors for cash; the notes are linked to Entity Z's credit risk. Entity A invests the cash it receives in risk-free financial assets. Additionally, Entity A enters into a credit default swap (CDS) with Entity X;

under the CDS, Entity A obtains exposure to Entity Z's credit risk in return for a fee paid to it by Entity X. The investors receive a return based on the return from the asset portfolio plus the fee received from Entity X and, if Entity Z's creditworthiness does not deteriorate, their full principal back at the end. The credit default swap transfers variability to Entity A, rather than absorbing variability of returns of Entity A, so that Entity X is not exposed to variability of returns from Entity A's performance. Consequently, in this example, Entity X does not have an interest in Entity A for the purpose of IFRS 12. [IFRS 12:B9]

4.4   Investment manager's interest in an unconsolidated investment fund

The fee earned by an investment manager from an investment fund that it manages, but does not consolidate, constitutes an 'interest in an unconsolidated structured entity' to be disclosed in accordance with IFRS 12, provided that the fund meets the definition of a structured entity.

As noted at **4.1**, an interest in another entity refers to "contractual and non-contractual involvement that exposes an entity to variability of returns from the performance of the other entity". IFRS 10:B56 explains that variable returns are "returns that are not fixed and have the potential to vary as a result of the performance of the investee".

In addition, IFRS 10:B56 states as follows.

"Variable returns can be only positive, only negative or both positive and negative (see [IFRS 10:15]). An investor assesses whether returns from an investee are variable and how variable those returns are on the basis of the substance of the arrangement and regardless of the legal form of the returns…. Similarly, fixed performance management fees for managing an investee's assets are variable returns because they expose the investor to the performance risk of the investee. The amount of variability depends on the investee's ability to generate sufficient income to pay the fee."

Consequently, an investment manager should treat an investment fee received from an investment fund that it manages as an 'interest in another entity' given that it exposes the investment manager to the variability of the value of the assets under management.

As noted at **4.2**, a structured entity is "an entity that has been designated so that voting or similar rights are not the dominant factor in deciding who controls the entity, such as when any voting rights relate to administrative tasks only and the relevant activities are directed by means of contractual arrangements".

IFRS 12:B23 indicates that 'some investment funds' are examples of structured entities. In the context of an investment fund, it is necessary to evaluate the extent to which investment strategy decisions are determined by the votes of unit holders (either directly or, as discussed at **8.2.6** in **chapter A24**, through a substantive right to vote to remove the fund manager) rather than through the fund management contract.

See **8.2.2** for further guidance on appropriate disclosures by an investment manager regarding the nature and extent of its interests in unconsolidated investment funds.

5 Significant judgements and assumptions

5.1 Disclosures regarding significant judgements and assumptions – general

Disclosure is required of the significant judgements and assumptions made by a reporting entity, and any changes to those judgements and assumptions, in determining:

[IFRS 12:7]

- that it has control of another entity;

- that it has joint control of an arrangement;

- the type of joint arrangement, either joint venture or joint operation, when the arrangement is structured through a separate vehicle; and

- that it has significant influence over another entity.

For example, a reporting entity should disclose significant judgements and assumptions made when determining that:

[IFRS 12:9]

(a) it does not control another entity despite holding more than half of that other entity's voting rights;

(b) it controls another entity despite holding less than half of that other entity's voting rights;

(c) it is an agent or a principal (see the discussion at **8.2** in **chapter A24**);

(d) it does not have significant influence over another entity despite holding 20 per cent or more of that other entity's voting rights; or

(e) it has significant influence over another entity despite holding less than 20 per cent of that other entity's voting rights.

The disclosures required by IFRS 12 are not limited to the five scenarios listed; disclosure is required of all significant judgements and assumptions made in determining the nature of the interest (subsidiary, joint arrangement or associate) and the type of joint arrangement when structured through a separate vehicle.

In many cases, particularly with respect to subsidiaries, no disclosure of judgements or assumptions may be necessary. Disclosure is only needed when significant judgements and assumptions were required in determining the relationship with the other entity. For many subsidiaries, for example, the assessment will be straightforward with little judgement needed, because it may be clear (as discussed at **5.3** in **chapter A24**) that control is exercised directly and solely by means of equity instruments (e.g. ordinary shares) that give the holder proportionate voting rights.

When facts and circumstances change during the reporting period and this affects the reporting entity's determination as to whether it has control or joint control of, or significant influence over, another entity, disclosure is required of the significant judgements and assumptions made as a result of those changes in facts and circumstances. [IFRS 12:8]

5.2   Investment entity status

When a parent determines that it is an investment entity in accordance with paragraph 27 of IFRS 10 *Consolidated Financial Statements* (see **section 13** of **chapter A24**), the investment entity is required to disclose information about significant judgements and assumptions it has made in determining that it is an investment entity. [IFRS 12:9A]

If the investment entity does not have one or more of the typical characteristics of an investment entity (see **13.2.6.1** in **chapter A24**), it is required to disclose its reasons for concluding that it is nevertheless an investment entity. [IFRS 12:9A]

When an entity becomes, or ceases to be, an investment entity, it is required to disclose the change of investment entity status and the reasons for the change. [IFRS 12:9B]

In addition, an entity that becomes an investment entity is required to disclose the effect of the change of status on the financial statements for the period presented, including:

[IFRS 12:9B]

- the total fair value, as of the date of change of status, of the subsidiaries that cease to be consolidated;

- the total gain or loss, if any, calculated in accordance with IFRS 10:B101 (see **13.2.8.3** in **chapter A24**); and

- the line item(s) in profit or loss in which the gain or loss is recognised (if not presented separately).

6 Interests in subsidiaries

6.1 Composition of the group

An entity is required to disclose information that enables users of its consolidated financial statements to understand the composition of the group. [IFRS 12:10(a)(i)]

Unlike the other requirements in IFRS 12:10, no further guidance is provided in the Standard in respect of the information to be disclosed under IFRS 12:10(a)(i). Therefore, it is not clear whether compliance with the requirements of IFRS 12:12 to 19 (see below) will be sufficient to meet the requirements of IFRS 12:10(a)(i), or whether additional information may be required. For example, the Standard does not specifically address whether IFRS 12:10(a)(i) requires a reporting entity to provide a full list of its subsidiaries.

The discussion in paragraphs BC21 to BC29 of the Basis for Conclusions on IFRS 12 under the heading 'Composition of the group and non-controlling interests' focuses largely on the effects that non-controlling interests and significant restrictions (e.g. arising from legal boundaries) may have on cash flows that can be distributed to the shareholders of the parent. Non-controlling interests and significant restrictions are the subject of more specific disclosure requirements in paragraphs 12 and 13, respectively.

Paragraph BC28 in the Basis for Conclusions clarifies the IASB's thinking to some extent, as follows.

> "Although users have requested financial information about all subsidiaries that are material to the group, the Board decided to require financial information only for those subsidiaries with material non-controlling interests. A requirement to disclose information about subsidiaries with immaterial or no non-controlling interests might prove to be onerous to prepare without any significant benefit for users, who are expected to benefit most from having financial information about subsidiaries with material non-controlling interests."

This clarifies that IFRS 12:10(a)(i) is not intended to require an entity to provide a list of all subsidiaries, or even of all individually material subsidiaries.

Accordingly, in the absence of further guidance or explanation, it is suggested that an entity should use its judgement to consider whether the information provided in accordance with subsequent paragraphs will, in itself, be sufficient to enable users to understand the composition of the group. When this is not the case, additional information should be provided.

6.2   Non-controlling interests

An entity is required to disclose information that enables users of its consolidated financial statements to understand the interest that any non-controlling interests have in the activities and cash flows of the group. [IFRS 12:10(a)(ii)]

> This requirement supplements the requirements of IAS 1 *Presentation of Financial Statements* regarding the presentation and disclosure of non-controlling interests, namely (1) an analysis of profit or loss and of other comprehensive income between that attributable to non-controlling interests and that attributable to owners of the parent, (2) presentation of non-controlling interests separately, within equity, in the statement of financial position, and (3) in the statement of changes in equity, a reconciliation of the non-controlling interests at the beginning and end of the period.

For each subsidiary that has non-controlling interests that are material to the reporting entity, disclosure is required of the following:

[IFRS 12:12, B10 & B11]

(a) the subsidiary's name;

(b) the subsidiary's principal place of business and, if different, country of incorporation;

(c) the proportion of the subsidiary's ownership interests held by non-controlling interests and, if different, the proportion of the subsidiary's voting rights held by non-controlling interests;

(d) the profit or loss allocated to non-controlling interests of that subsidiary during the reporting period;

(e) dividends paid to the non-controlling interests of that subsidiary;

(f) the accumulated non-controlling interests of that subsidiary at the end of the reporting period; and

(g) summarised financial information, stated prior to any inter-company eliminations about the subsidiary's assets, liabilities, profit or loss and cash flows. That information should enable users to understand the interest that non-controlling interests have in the group's activities and cash flows. For example, it might include, but is not limited to:

- current assets;

- non-current assets;

- current liabilities;

- non-current liabilities;

- revenue;

- profit or loss; and
- total comprehensive income.

In the list above, (d) requires disclosure of the amount of the subsidiary's profit or loss presented in the consolidated financial statements as attributable to the non-controlling interests. This may differ from the amount reported in the summarised financial information in respect of the subsidiary under item (g) above, for example because the amount reported under item (d) will reflect the elimination of intragroup transactions.

The summarised financial information required under IFRS 12:B10 need not be provided for any subsidiaries classified as held for sale in accordance with IFRS 5 *Non-current Assets Held for Sale and Discontinued Operations*. [IFRS 12:B17]

6.3 Significant restrictions

An entity is required to disclose information that enables users of its consolidated financial statements to evaluate the nature and extent of significant restrictions on the entity's ability to access or use the group's assets or settle the group's liabilities. [IFRS 12:10(b)(i)]

This requirement is intended to result in disclosure about restrictions existing because of legal boundaries within a group, such as restrictions on transferring cash between group entities. [IFRS 12:BC33]

In meeting this disclosure requirement, an entity is required to disclose the following:

[IFRS 12:13]

- details of significant restrictions (e.g. statutory, regulatory and contractual restrictions) on the entity's ability to access or use the group's assets or settle the group's liabilities. Examples include restrictions affecting the ability to transfer cash or other assets between entities within the group, and guarantees or other requirements that may restrict the payment of dividends and other capital distributions within the group or restrict the ability to make or repay an inter-company loan or advance;
- the nature and extent to which any non-controlling interests' protective rights can result in a significant restriction of the entity's ability to access or use the group's assets or settle the group's liabilities. Examples include a parent being obliged to settle a subsidiary's liabilities before its own, and the non-controlling interests' approval being required in order to access a subsidiary's assets or settle its liabilities; and

- the carrying amounts in the consolidated financial statements of the assets and liabilities to which the restrictions identified above apply.

> This requirement supplements the disclosure already required under paragraph 48 of IAS 7 *Statement of Cash Flows* of the amount of significant cash and cash equivalent balances held by the entity that are not available for use by the group.

6.4   Interests in consolidated structured entities

An entity is required to disclose information that enables users of its consolidated financial statements to evaluate the nature of, and changes in, the risks associated with the entity's interests in consolidated structured entities. [IFRS 12:10(b)(ii)]

To meet the requirements of IFRS 12:10(b)(ii), the following information is required to be disclosed.

[IFRS 12:14 - 17]

- When contractual arrangements could require a member of the group to provide financial support to a structured entity that has been consolidated, the terms of the contractual arrangement should be disclosed. These disclosures should include details of any events or circumstances that might expose the reporting entity to a loss (e.g. liquidity arrangements or credit rating triggers associated with obligations to purchase assets of the structured entity or provide financial support).

- If, during the reporting period, a member of the group has provided financial or other support to a *consolidated* structured entity (e.g. by purchasing assets of the structured entity or by purchasing instruments issued by the structured entity), without having any contractual obligation to do so, disclosure is required of:

  - the type and amount of support provided (including situations in which the parent or its subsidiaries assisted the structured entity in obtaining financial support); and

  - the reasons for providing the support.

- If, during the reporting period, a member of the group has given financial or other support to a *previously unconsolidated* structured entity, without having a contractual obligation to do so, and as a result of the support the group obtained control of the structured entity, the reporting entity is required to provide an explanation of the relevant factors in reaching that decision.

- Disclosure is required of any current intentions to provide financial or other support to a consolidated structured entity, including any intentions to assist a structured entity to obtain financial support.

6.5 Changes in ownership of subsidiaries

An entity is required to disclose information that enables users of its consolidated financial statements to evaluate the consequences of changes in the entity's ownership interest in a subsidiary that do not result in a loss of control of that subsidiary. A reporting entity should present a schedule showing the effects on the equity attributable to the owners of the parent of changes in its ownership interest in a subsidiary that do not result in a loss of control. [IFRS 12:10(b)(iii) & 18]

An example of a change in the ownership interest of a subsidiary that does not result in a loss of control would be a rights issue made by the subsidiary for which the non-controlling interests do not take up their rights. This would result in the parent's interest being increased.

6.6 Losing control of a subsidiary

An entity is required to disclose information that enables users of its consolidated financial statements to evaluate the consequences of losing control of a subsidiary during the reporting period. An entity is required to disclose the gain or loss, if any, calculated in accordance with paragraph 25 of IFRS 10 *Consolidated Financial Statements* (see **12.3.1** in **chapter A24**), and also:

[IFRS 12:10(b)(iv) & 19]

- the portion of that gain or loss attributable to measuring any investment retained in the former subsidiary at its fair value at the date when control is lost; and

- the line item(s) in profit or loss in which the gain or loss is recognised if it is not presented separately.

The requirement in the first bullet point above is illustrated in **example 12.3.3A** in **chapter A24**.

6.7 Subsidiary with different reporting date or length of reporting period

Occasionally it is impracticable for a subsidiary's financial statements used in preparing the consolidated financial statements to be prepared as at the same date or for the same period as the consolidated financial statements (see **10.6** in **chapter A24**). In such circumstances, disclosure is required in the consolidated financial statements of:

[IFRS 12:11]

- the date of the end of the reporting period of the subsidiary's financial statements; and

- the reasons for using a different date or period.

6.8   Interests in unconsolidated subsidiaries (investment entities)

An investment entity that, in accordance with IFRS 10, is required to apply the exception to consolidation and instead account for its investment in a subsidiary at fair value through profit or loss is required to disclose that fact. [IFRS 12:19A]

For each unconsolidated subsidiary, an investment entity is required to disclose:

[IFRS 12:19B]

(a) the subsidiary's name;

(b) the subsidiary's principal place of business and, if different, country of incorporation; and

(c) the proportion of the subsidiary's ownership interest held by the investment entity and, if different, the proportion of voting rights held.

If an investment entity is the parent of another investment entity, the parent is also required to provide the disclosures required under IFRS 12:19B(a) to (c) (listed above) for investments that are controlled by its investment entity subsidiary. The disclosure may be provided by including, in the financial statements of the parent, the financial statements of the subsidiary (or subsidiaries) that contain the above information. [IFRS 12:19C]

An investment entity is required to disclose:

[IFRS 12:19D]

- the nature and extent of any significant restrictions (e.g. resulting from borrowing arrangements, regulatory requirements or contractual arrangements) on the ability of an unconsolidated subsidiary to transfer funds to the investment entity in the form of cash dividends or to repay loans or advances made to the unconsolidated subsidiary by the investment entity; and

- any current commitments or intentions to provide financial or other support to an unconsolidated subsidiary, including commitments or intentions to assist the subsidiary in obtaining financial support.

If, during the reporting period, an investment entity or any of its subsidiaries has, without having a contractual obligation to do so, provided financial or other support to an unconsolidated subsidiary (e.g. purchasing assets of, or instruments issued by, the subsidiary or assisting the subsidiary in obtaining financial support), the entity is required to disclose:

[IFRS 12:19E]

- the type and amount of support provided to each unconsolidated subsidiary; and

- the reasons for providing the support.

The IASB decided not to define financial support, but the Basis for Conclusions on IFRS 12 notes that the IASB believes it is widely understood as the provision of resources to another entity, directly or indirectly. [IFRS 12:BC105]

An investment entity is required to disclose the terms of any contractual arrangements that could require the entity or its unconsolidated subsidiaries to provide financial support to an unconsolidated, controlled, structured entity, including events or circumstances that could expose the reporting entity to a loss (e.g. liquidity arrangements or credit rating triggers associated with obligations to purchase assets of the structured entity or to provide financial support). [IFRS 12:19F]

If during the reporting period an investment entity or any of its unconsolidated subsidiaries has, without having a contractual obligation to do so, provided financial or other support to an unconsolidated, structured entity that the investment entity did not control, and if that provision of support resulted in the investment entity controlling the structured entity, the investment entity is required to provide an explanation of the relevant factors in reaching the decision to provide that support. [IFRS 12:19G]

7 Interests in joint arrangements and associates

7.1 Disclosure requirements for interests in joint arrangements and associates – general

The disclosure requirements described in **7.2** and **7.3** will normally apply to interests in joint ventures and associates reported in consolidated financial statements prepared in accordance with IFRS 10 *Consolidated Financial Statements*. They will also apply when the investor does not prepare consolidated financial statements, because it does not have subsidiaries, but it has a joint venturer's interest in a joint venture, a joint operator's interest in a joint operation, or significant influence over an associate.

The disclosure requirements for interests in joint ventures and associates apply to all entities, including those that are venture capital organisations, mutual funds, unit trusts or similar entities. However, some of the disclosures only apply when the equity method is used; therefore, if a venture capital organisation, mutual fund, unit trust or similar entity has chosen to account for an interest at fair value through profit or loss instead of using the equity method (see **4.2.2** of **chapter A26**), those disclosures are not applicable.

If an entity elects to apply the equity method of accounting to its investments in associates and joint ventures in its separate financial statements, it is not required to comply with the disclosure requirements described in **7.2** and **7.3**. In general, IFRS 12 does not apply to separate financial statements (see **3.2**), and this principle is not affected by whether the entity elects to use the equity method in those separate financial statements. However, if an entity has interests in unconsolidated structured entities and prepares separate financial statements as its only financial statements, it is required to provide the disclosures required under IFRS 12:24 to 31 (see **section 8**). [IFRS 12:6(b)]

Investment entities are exempted from specified disclosure requirements under this heading (see **7.2.1**); otherwise, the disclosure requirements listed below apply equally to investment entities.

7.2   Nature, extent and financial effects of interests in joint arrangements and associates

7.2.1   Nature of interests in joint arrangements and associates – general

An entity is required to disclose information that enables users of its financial statements to evaluate the nature, extent and financial effects of its interests in joint arrangements and associates, including information about the nature and effects of the entity's contractual relationship with the other investors with joint control of, or significant influence over, joint arrangements and associates. [IFRS 12:20(a)]

Investment entities need not present the disclosures required by IFRS 12:21(b) and 21(c) (see **7.2.3** and **7.2.4**, respectively). [IFRS 12:21A]

7.2.2   Joint arrangements and associates that are material to the reporting entity

For each joint arrangement and associate that is material to the reporting entity, the reporting entity should disclose:

[IFRS 12:21(a)]

- its name;
- the nature of the reporting entity's relationship with it (e.g. by describing the nature of the activities undertaken and whether they are strategic to the reporting entity's activities);

- its principal place of business and, if applicable and different, the country of incorporation; and

- the proportion of ownership interest or participating share held by the reporting entity and, if applicable and different, the proportion of voting rights held.

Note that the reference to joint arrangements means that the disclosure requirements set out above apply both to joint ventures and to joint operations, whereas those set out at **7.2.3** to **7.2.7** do not apply to joint operations.

7.2.3 Additional disclosures for joint ventures and associates that are material to the reporting entity

In addition to the information disclosed under IFRS 12:21(a) (see **7.2.2**), for each joint venture and associate that is material to the reporting entity, the reporting entity should disclose:

[IFRS 12:21(b), B12 - B14 & B17]

- whether the investment in the joint venture or associate is measured using the equity method or at fair value;

- if the investment is measured using the equity method, and there is a quoted market price for the investment, the investment's fair value;

- dividends received by the reporting entity from the joint venture or associate;

- summarised financial information (unless the joint venture or associate, or a portion thereof, is classified as held for sale in accordance with IFRS 5 *Non-current Assets Held for Sale and Discontinued Operations*), including, but not necessarily limited to:

  - current assets;

  - non-current assets;

  - current liabilities;

  - non-current liabilities;

  - revenue;

  - profit or loss from continuing operations;

  - post-tax profit or loss from discontinued operations;

  - other comprehensive income; and

  - total comprehensive income;

- for each joint venture that is material to the reporting entity (unless the joint venture or associate, or a portion thereof, is classified as held for sale in accordance with IFRS 5), the amount of:

- cash and cash equivalents included in current assets;

- current financial liabilities (excluding trade and other payables and provisions) included in current liabilities;

- non-current financial liabilities (excluding trade and other payables and provisions) included in non-current liabilities;

- depreciation and amortisation;

- interest income;

- interest expense; and

- income tax expense or income; and

- if the reporting entity uses the equity method to account for its interest in the joint venture or associate, a reconciliation of the summarised financial information to the carrying amount of its interest in the joint venture or associate.

The summarised financial information required to be presented under IFRS 12:B12 and B13 should reflect the amounts reported in the joint venture's or associate's IFRS financial statements (i.e. it is not the reporting entity's share of those amounts). But when the interest in the joint venture or associate is accounted for by the reporting entity using the equity method, the amounts included in the IFRS financial statements of the joint venture or associate should be adjusted to reflect adjustments made in applying the equity method (e.g. to bring accounting policies into line with those of the reporting entity or to reflect fair value adjustments made on acquisition). [IFRS 12:B14]

If the reporting entity's interest in the joint venture or associate is measured at fair value, in accordance with IAS 28 *Investments in Associates and Joint Ventures*, the summarised information may be disclosed on the basis of the joint venture's or associate's financial statements if the joint venture or associate does not produce IFRS financial statements and to prepare IFRS financial statements would be impracticable or cause undue cost. In such circumstances, the basis of preparation of the summarised financial information should be disclosed. [IFRS 12:B15]

7.2.4 Joint ventures and associates that are not individually material to the reporting entity

The reporting entity should disclose the following information, in aggregate for all joint ventures that are not individually material to the reporting entity and, separately, in aggregate for all associates that are not individually material to the reporting entity:

[IFRS 12:21(c) & B16]

- the carrying amount of the interests accounted for using the equity method; and

- the reporting entity's share of those joint ventures' or associates':

  - profit or loss from continuing operations;

  - post-tax profit or loss from discontinued operations;

  - other comprehensive income; and

  - total comprehensive income.

7.2.5 Significant restrictions

The reporting entity should disclose the nature and extent of any significant restrictions (e.g. resulting from borrowing arrangements, regulatory requirements or contractual arrangements between investors with joint control of or significant influence over a joint venture or an associate) on the ability of joint ventures or associates to transfer funds to the reporting entity in the form of cash dividends or repay loans or advances from the reporting entity. [IFRS 12:22(a)]

7.2.6 Financial statements to a different date or for a different period

If the financial statements of a joint venture or associate used in applying the equity method are as of a date or for a period that is different from that of the reporting entity, the reporting entity should disclose:

[IFRS 12:22(b)]

- the date of the end of the reporting period of the joint venture's or associate's financial statements; and

- the reason for using a different date or different period.

7.2.7 Unrecognised share of losses

If the reporting entity, in applying the equity method, has stopped recognising its share of losses of a joint venture or associate, it should disclose the unrecognised share of losses of the joint venture or associate, both for the period and cumulatively. [IFRS 12:22(c)]

7.3   Risks associated with interests in joint ventures and associates

7.3.1   Risks associated with interests in joint ventures and associates – general

An entity is required to disclose information that enables users of its financial statements to evaluate the nature of, and changes in, the risks associated with its interests in joint ventures and associates. [IFRS 12:20(b)]

7.3.2   Contingent liabilities relating to interests in joint ventures or associates

Contingent liabilities incurred by a reporting entity relating to its interests in joint ventures or associates should be disclosed (unless the probability of loss is remote) separately from other contingent liabilities. The amounts reported should include the reporting entity's share of contingent liabilities incurred jointly with other investors with joint control of, or significant influence over, joint ventures and associates. [IFRS 12:23(b)]

7.3.3   Commitments for joint ventures

The reporting entity should disclose commitments that it has made relating to its joint ventures separately from its other commitments. [IFRS 12:23(a)]

The amount disclosed for commitments relating to joint ventures should be the reporting entity's total commitments that it has made but not recognised at the reporting date. Commitments to be disclosed are those that may give rise to a future outflow of cash or other resources. This disclosure should include the reporting entity's share of commitments made jointly with other joint venturers. [IFRS 12:23(a) & B18]

Unrecognised commitments that may give rise to a future outflow of cash or other resources include:

[IFRS 12:B19]

- unrecognised commitments to contribute funding or resources to the joint venture itself as a result of, for example:
  - the constitution or acquisition agreements of a joint venture (that, for example, require contribution of funds over a specific period);
  - capital-intensive projects undertaken by a joint venture;
  - unconditional purchase obligations, comprising procurement of equipment, inventory or services that an entity is committed to purchasing from, or on behalf of, a joint venture;
  - unrecognised commitments to provide loans or other financial support to a joint venture;

- unrecognised commitments to contribute resources to a joint venture, such as assets or services; and

- other non-cancellable unrecognised commitments relating to a joint venture; and

- unrecognised commitments to purchase another party's ownership interest, or a portion thereof, in a joint venture if a particular event occurs or does not occur in the future.

Some of these disclosures are likely to be required by IAS 24 *Related Party Disclosures* as well as by IFRS 12. [IFRS 12:B20]

8   Interests in unconsolidated structured entities

8.1   Disclosure requirements for interests in structured entities – general

The disclosure requirements in this section apply to:

- consolidated financial statements prepared in accordance with IFRS 10 *Consolidated Financial Statements*, in which case the disclosures will not be required in any separate financial statements that are also presented;

- financial statements in which the equity method is used to account for interests in associates or joint ventures, in which case the disclosures will not be required in any separate financial statements that are also presented; and

- separate financial statements if these are presented as the reporting entity's only financial statements (see **3.3** for specific considerations in relation to investment entities).

See **section 4** for guidance on the definitions of an 'interest' in another entity and a 'structured entity'.

8.2   Nature and extent of interests in unconsolidated structured entities

8.2.1   Disclosures regarding the nature and extent of interests in unconsolidated structured entities – general

An entity is required to disclose information that enables users of its financial statements to understand the nature and extent of its interests in unconsolidated structured entities. [IFRS 12:24(a)]

An investment entity need not provide the disclosures required by IFRS 12:24 for an unconsolidated structured entity that it controls and for which it presents the disclosures required by IFRS 12:19A to 19G (see **6.8**). [IFRS 12:25A]

> The exemption in IFRS 12:25A for investment entities refers only to the disclosures required by IFRS 12:24. However, the specific disclosure requirements in IFRS 12:26 to 28 (see below) simply expand on the detail necessary to satisfy the requirements in IFRS 12:24(a) and, consequently, they are covered by the exemption.

The reporting entity should disclose both qualitative and quantitative information about its interests in unconsolidated structured entities. Such information should include, but is not limited to, the nature, purpose, size and activities of the structured entity together with how the structured entity is financed. [IFRS 12:26]

As discussed at **8.3**, IFRS 12:29 requires disclosure of, *inter alia*, the carrying amounts of assets and liabilities relating to an entity's interest in unconsolidated structured entities. If a reporting entity has sponsored an unconsolidated structured entity for which it does not disclose any information under IFRS 12:29 (e.g. because it does not have an interest in the structured entity at the reporting date), the entity is required to disclose:

[IFRS 12:27]

(a)   how it has determined which structured entities it has sponsored;

(b)   income from those structured entities (see below) during the reporting period, together with a description of the types of income presented; and

(c)   if assets have been transferred to those structured entities during the reporting period, the carrying amount of those assets at the time of the transfer.

> In IFRS 12:27, the structured entities referred to are those that the reporting entity has sponsored but about which it has not given any information under IFRS 12:29 (rather than all structured entities that it has sponsored). [IFRS 12:BC91]
>
> In IFRS 12:27(c), the disclosure relates to all assets transferred to the structured entity during the reporting period, not just assets transferred by the sponsor. [IFRS 12:BC90]
>
> Although disclosures are required about the nature of risks relating to interests retained in unconsolidated structured entities through explicit or implicit involvement (see **8.3**), risks can be wider than this. For example, an entity might not intend to provide any support to a structured entity but might be exposed to litigation risk from sponsoring

a failed structured entity. The disclosures are, therefore, required for unconsolidated structured entities that the reporting entity has sponsored but in which it does not have an interest. They are designed to give users a sense of the scale of the operations a reporting entity had managed with these types of transactions and the extent of the reporting entity's reliance on such entities to facilitate its business. They are not intended to help assess the actual risk of failure or recourse to an entity. [IFRS 12:BC86 - BC91]

Income from a structured entity includes, but is not limited to, recurring and non-recurring fees, interest, dividends, gains or losses on the remeasurement or derecognition of interests in structured entities and gains or losses from the transfer of assets and liabilities to the structured entity. [IFRS 12:Appendix A]

The disclosures required by IFRS 12:27(b) and 27(c) should be presented in tabular format, unless another format is more appropriate. The sponsoring activities should be classified into relevant categories (see the discussion at **2.3**). [IFRS 12:28]

8.2.2 Disclosures regarding an investment manager's interest in an unconsolidated investment fund

When an investment manager determines that its relationship with a fund constitutes an interest in an unconsolidated structured entity (see **4.4**), the manager is typically required to disclose the value of the fund's assets under management. As noted in **8.2.1**, IFRS 12:24 requires an entity to disclose the risks associated with its interests in unconsolidated structured entities and IFRS 12:26 requires that the disclosure of the nature of such interests includes, *inter alia*, the 'size' of the structured entity. In addition, IFRS 12:BC96 explains that "if relevant to an assessment of its exposure to risk, an entity would be required to provide additional information about the assets and funding of structured entities".

While not explicitly stated in the Standard, a user of the financial statements of an investment manager earning fees through its ability to maximise the returns of investors in a fund is likely to view the total value of assets under management as both a measure of the investment manager's susceptibility to risk and the most relevant measure of the fund's size. Therefore, the assets under management would typically be a required disclosure under IFRS 12.

IFRS 12 does not, however, prescribe the format of this disclosure. One approach would be to disclose assets under management in a tabular format by asset class. Alternatively, if the investment manager determines that this would not be meaningful to a user of the financial statements, a narrative disclosure of total assets under management may be sufficient.

The method for quantifying assets under management is also not prescribed in IFRS 12. However, the investment manager should disclose information to help users of financial statements evaluate the nature and extent of the entity's risks from its interests in unconsolidated structured entities. Therefore, the investment manager should provide sufficient information to enable users of the financial statements to understand how assets under management are calculated and how they correspond to the manager's risk (e.g. through the calculation of variable investment management fees receivable).

8.3   Risks associated with interests in unconsolidated structured entities

An entity is required to disclose information that enables users of its financial statements to evaluate the nature of, and changes in, the risks associated with its interests in unconsolidated structured entities. This disclosure should cover the entity's exposure to risk from involvement it had with unconsolidated structured entities (e.g. sponsoring the structured entity) during the reporting period or in previous periods, even if the entity no longer has contractual involvement at the reporting date. [IFRS 12:24(b) & 25]

An entity may be exposed to risk from an involvement with a structured entity even though the reporting entity may not control or have a contractual involvement with the structured entity at the reporting date. For example, a reporting entity might feel compelled to provide support to a structured entity to prevent its failure, even though the reporting entity has no legal or contractual requirement to provide support, because if the structured entity failed the reporting entity's reputation would be damaged. Consequently the IASB has required disclosure of risk even when there is no contractual involvement at the reporting date. [IFRS 12:BC107 - BC110]

An investment entity need not provide the disclosures required by IFRS 12:24(b) for an unconsolidated structured entity that it controls and for which it presents the disclosures required by IFRS 12:19A to 19G (see **6.8**). [IFRS 12:25A]

Paragraphs 29 to 31 of IFRS 12, as supplemented by paragraphs B25 and B26 of Appendix B to IFRS 12 (see below), expand on the detail necessary to satisfy the requirements in IFRS 12:24(b). Consequently, they are covered by the investment entity exemption in IFRS 12:25A. The reporting entity should disclose in tabular format, unless another format is more appropriate, a summary of:

[IFRS 12:29]

- the carrying amounts recognised in its financial statements of the assets and liabilities relating to its interests in unconsolidated structured entities;

- the line items in the statement of financial position in which those assets and liabilities are recognised;

- the amount that best represents the entity's maximum exposure to loss from its interests in unconsolidated structured entities, including how the maximum exposure to loss is determined. If the maximum exposure to loss cannot be quantified, the entity should disclose that fact and the reasons; and

- a comparison of the carrying amounts of the assets and liabilities of the entity that relate to its interests in unconsolidated structured entities and the entity's maximum exposure to loss from those entities.

> When a financial instrument exposes the reporting entity to theoretically unlimited losses, it will not be possible to determine the maximum exposure to loss and this would need to be explained. [IFRS 12:BC99]

If during the reporting period, without having a contractual obligation to do so, the entity has provided financial or other support to an unconsolidated structured entity in which it previously had or currently has an interest, including assisting the structured entity in obtaining financial support, disclosure is required of the type and amount of support provided and the reasons for providing the support. [IFRS 12:30]

The entity is also required to disclose any current intentions to provide financial or other support to an unconsolidated structured entity, including any intentions to assist the structured entity in obtaining financial support. [IFRS 12:31]

> The IASB decided not to define financial support, but the Basis for Conclusions on IFRS 12 notes that the IASB believes it is widely understood as the provision of resources to another entity, directly or indirectly. [IFRS 12:BC105]

Examples of financial support to a structured entity include purchasing assets from the structured entity and purchasing instruments issued by the structured entity. [IFRS 12:30]

If the disclosures above are not sufficient to satisfy the overall disclosure requirement in IFRS 12:24(b), additional information should be given that enables users to evaluate the nature of, and changes in, the reporting entity's exposure to risks associated with its interests in unconsolidated structured entities. [IFRS 12:B25]

Examples of additional information that, depending on the circumstances, might be relevant to an assessment of the risks to which an entity is exposed when it has an interest in an unconsolidated structured entity are:

[IFRS 12:B26]

- the terms of any arrangements (e.g. liquidity arrangements or credit rating triggers associated with obligations to purchase assets of the structured entity or provide financial support) that could require the entity to provide financial support to an unconsolidated structured entity, including:

  - a description of events or circumstances that could expose the reporting entity to a loss;

  - whether there are any terms that would limit the obligation; and

  - whether there are any other parties that provide financial support and, if so, how the reporting entity's obligation ranks with those of other parties;

- losses incurred during the period by the reporting entity relating to its interests in unconsolidated structured entities;

- the types of income received during the period by the reporting entity from its interests in unconsolidated structured entities;

- whether the reporting entity is required to absorb an unconsolidated structured entity's losses before other parties, the maximum limit of such losses for the reporting entity and, if relevant, the ranking and amounts of potential losses borne by parties whose interests rank lower than the reporting entity's interest in the unconsolidated structured entity;

- information about any liquidity arrangements, guarantees or other commitments with third parties that may affect the fair value or risk of the reporting entity's interests in unconsolidated structured entities;

- any difficulties experienced during the period by an unconsolidated structured entity in financing its activities; and

- in relation to the funding of an unconsolidated structured entity, the forms of funding, such as commercial paper and medium-term notes, and their weighted average life. If the structured entity has longer-term assets funded by shorter-term funding, the information might include maturity analyses of the assets and funding.

This is a list of additional information that, depending on the circumstances, might be relevant and not a list of requirements that should be applied regardless of the circumstances. But the IASB wished to emphasise the level of detail that would be required when a reporting entity has a large exposure to risk from its interests in unconsolidated structured entities. [IFRS 12:BC114]

9 Future developments

In November 2015, the IASB published ED/2015/10 *Annual Improvements to IFRSs 2014-2016 Cycle*. The exposure draft includes a proposed amendment to clarify the scope of IFRS 12 by specifying that the disclosure requirements in the Standard (with the exception of IFRS 12:B10 to B16) apply to any interests that are classified as held for sale, held for distribution to owners, or discontinued operations in accordance with IFRS 5 *Non-current Assets Held for Sale and Discontinued Operations*.

The comment period on the exposure draft closed on 17 February 2016. At the time of writing, the IASB has not yet determined the next step on this issue.

A29 Separate financial statements

Contents

1 Introduction

1.1 Overview of IAS 27

IAS 27 *Separate Financial Statements* outlines the accounting and disclosure requirements for 'separate financial statements', which are financial statements prepared by an entity in which the entity can elect, subject to specified conditions, to account for its investments in subsidiaries, joint ventures and associates either at cost, or in accordance with IFRS 9 *Financial Instruments* (or, for entities that have not yet adopted IFRS 9, IAS 39 *Financial Instruments: Recognition and Measurement*), or using the equity method as described in IAS 28 *Investments in Associates and Joint Ventures*.

The Standard also outlines the accounting requirements for dividends in separate financial statements, and contains numerous disclosure requirements.

1.2 Amendments to IAS 27 since the last edition of this manual

None. IAS 27 was most recently amended in August 2014.

2 Scope

IAS 27 is to be applied in accounting for investments in subsidiaries, joint ventures and associates when an entity elects, or is required by local regulations, to present separate financial statements. [IAS 27:2]

IAS 27 does not mandate which entities should present separate financial statements – it applies when an entity presents separate financial statements that are stated to be in compliance with IFRSs. [IAS 27:3]

Such separate financial statements may be prepared voluntarily (e.g. for the purposes of supporting a tax return) or they may be required by local regulations (e.g. certain jurisdictions require the preparation and publication of stand-alone financial statements for parent entities).

3 Definition

3.1 Separate financial statements – definition

Separate financial statements are those presented by an entity in which the entity could elect, subject to the requirements in IAS 27, to account for its investments in subsidiaries, joint ventures and associates either at cost, or in accordance with IFRS 9 *Financial Instruments* (or, for entities that have not yet adopted IFRS 9, IAS 39 *Financial Instruments: Recognition and Measurement*), or using the equity method as described in IAS 28 *Investments in Associates and Joint Ventures*. [IAS 27:4]

The option to account for such investments in separate financial statements using the equity method was added to IAS 27 in August 2014. The amendments are effective for annual periods beginning on or after 1 January 2016, with earlier application permitted (see **5.1**).

Separate financial statements are those presented in addition to consolidated financial statements or in addition to the financial statements of an investor that does not have investments in subsidiaries but has investments in associates or joint ventures in which the investments in associates or joint ventures are required by IAS 28 to be accounted for using the equity method, other than in the circumstances set out in IAS 27:8 and 8A (see below). [IAS 27:6]

The financial statements of an entity that does not have a subsidiary, associate or joint venturer's interest in a joint venture are not separate financial statements. [IAS 27:7]

3.2 Separate financial statements for entities exempt from preparing consolidated financial statements

An entity that is exempted in accordance with IFRS 10:4(a) from preparing consolidated financial statements (see **3.3** in **chapter A24**), or in accordance with IAS 28:17 (see **4.2.1** in **chapter A26**) from applying the equity method, may present separate financial statements as its only financial statements. [IAS 27:8]

3.3 Separate financial statements for investment entities not consolidating any of their subsidiaries

An investment entity that is required, throughout the current period and all comparative periods presented, to apply the exception to consolidation for all of its subsidiaries in accordance with IFRS 10:31 presents separate financial statements as its only financial statements. [IAS 27:8A]

4 IFRSs applicable for separate financial statements

When an entity presents separate financial statements that are described as complying with IFRSs, the requirements of all applicable IFRSs will apply to those financial statements. [IAS 27:9] The only exception is that specific requirements are imposed for the measurement of investments in subsidiaries, joint ventures and associates as set out in IAS 27:10 (see **section 5**).

5 Measurement of investments in subsidiaries, joint ventures and associates

5.1 Measurement of investments in subsidiaries, joint ventures and associates – general

When separate financial statements are prepared, investments in subsidiaries, joint ventures and associates should be accounted for either:

[IAS 27:10]

- at cost; or

- in accordance with IFRS 9 *Financial Instruments* (or, for entities that have not yet adopted IFRS 9, IAS 39 *Financial Instruments: Recognition and Measurement*); or

- using the equity method as described in IAS 28 *Investments in Associates and Joint Ventures.*

The option to account for such investments using the equity method was added to IAS 27 in August 2014. The amendments are effective for annual periods beginning on or after 1 January 2016, with earlier application permitted. If an entity applies the amendments for a period beginning before 1 January 2016, that fact is required to be disclosed. [IAS 27:18J]

> The Basis for Conclusion on IAS 27 notes that, in general, the application of the equity method to investments in subsidiaries, joint ventures and associates in the separate financial statements of an entity is expected to result in the same net assets and profit or loss attributable to the owners as in the entity's consolidated financial statements. However, there could be situations in which applying the equity method in separate financial statements to investments in subsidiaries would give a different result compared to the consolidated financial statements. Some of those situations are as follows.
>
> [IAS 27:BC10G]
>
> - **Impairment testing requirements in IAS 28** For an investment in a subsidiary accounted for in separate financial statements using the equity method, goodwill that forms part of the carrying amount of the investment in the subsidiary is not tested for impairment separately. Instead, the entire carrying amount of the investment in the subsidiary is tested for impairment in accordance with IAS 36 *Impairment of Assets* as a single asset. However, in the consolidated financial statements of the entity, because goodwill is recognised separately, it is tested for impairment by applying the requirements in IAS 36 for testing goodwill for impairment.
>
> - **Subsidiary that has a net liability position** IAS 28 requires an investor to discontinue recognising its share of further losses when

> its cumulative share of losses of the investee equals or exceeds its interest in the investee, unless the investor has incurred legal or constructive obligations or made payments on behalf of the investee, in which case a liability is recognised, whereas there is no such requirement in relation to the consolidated financial statements.
>
> • **Capitalisation of borrowing costs incurred by a parent in relation to the assets of a subsidiary** IAS 23 *Borrowing Costs* notes that, in some circumstances, it may be appropriate to include all borrowings of the parent and its subsidiaries when computing a weighted average of the borrowing costs. When a parent borrows funds and its subsidiary uses them for the purpose of obtaining a qualifying asset, in the consolidated financial statements of the parent the borrowing costs incurred by the parent are considered to be directly attributable to the acquisition of the subsidiary's qualifying asset. However, this would not be appropriate in the separate financial statements of the parent if the parent's investment in the subsidiary is a financial asset, which is not a qualifying asset.

5.2   Accounting policy to be applied consistently for each category of investments

For each category of investments (subsidiaries, joint ventures, associates), the selected accounting policy should be applied consistently. [IAS 27:10]

5.3   Investments classified as held for sale

Investments accounted for at cost or using the equity method are accounted for in accordance with IFRS 5 *Non-current Assets Held for Sale and Discontinued Operations* when they are classified as held for sale or for distribution (or included in a disposal group that is classified as held for sale or for distribution). When investments in subsidiaries, joint ventures and associates accounted for in accordance with IFRS 9 (or, for entities that have not yet adopted IFRS 9, IAS 39) are classified as held for sale or for distribution, they continue to be accounted for in accordance with IFRS 9 (IAS 39). [IAS 27:10]

5.4   Measurement consistent with consolidated financial statements

When an investment in a joint venture or an associate is accounted for in accordance with IFRS 9 (or, for entities that have not yet adopted IFRS 9, IAS 39) in the consolidated financial statements (e.g. an investment held by a venture capital organisation), it should be accounted for in the same way in the investor's separate financial statements. [IAS 27:11] Therefore, cost or the equity method are not allowed alternatives for such investments in the investor's separate financial statements.

5.5 Impairment of investments in subsidiaries, joint ventures and associates

Investments in subsidiaries, joint ventures and associates accounted for in an entity's separate financial statements in accordance with IFRS 9 (or, for entities that have not yet adopted IFRS 9, IAS 39), or using the equity method in accordance with IAS 28, should be assessed for impairment in accordance with the requirements of those Standards.

When an entity accounts for its investments in subsidiaries, joint ventures or associates at cost in its separate financial statements in accordance with IAS 27:10 (see **5.1**), it should apply the requirements of IAS 36 *Impairment of Assets* to test those investments for impairment. This view has been confirmed by the IFRS Interpretations Committee having regard to the scope provisions of IAS 36 (IAS 36:4 and 5), IFRS 9 (IFRS 9:2.1(a)) and, for entities that have not yet adopted IFRS 9, IAS 39 (IAS 39:2(a)) (see January 2013 *IFRIC Update*).

Note that this issue was also considered by the IFRS Interpretations Committee in July 2009. At that time, the Committee determined that the requirements in this regard were not clear. However, the January 2013 decision is the more up-to-date guidance.

5.6 Investments in subsidiaries held by investment entities

5.6.1 Investments in subsidiaries held by investment entities – general

If a parent is required, in accordance with IFRS 10:31 (see **13.3.2.1** in **chapter A24**), to measure its investment in a subsidiary at fair value through profit or loss in accordance with IFRS 9 (or, for entities that have not yet adopted IFRS 9, IAS 39), the investment should be accounted for in the same way in the parent's separate financial statements. [IAS 27:11A]

5.6.2 Parent ceases to be an investment entity

When an entity ceases to be an investment entity, the entity should account for an investment in a subsidiary in accordance with IAS 27:10 (see **5.1**) from the date when the change in status occurs. The fair value of the subsidiary at the date of the change of status (which is the deemed acquisition date) is taken to represent the transferred deemed consideration when accounting for the investment under IAS 27:10. [IAS 27:11B]

The wording in IAS 27:11B was amended by the August 2014 amendments to IAS 27 to allow for the expanded measurement options available under IAS 27:10 (see **5.1**).

5.6.3   *Parent becomes an investment entity*

When an entity becomes an investment entity:

[IAS 27:11B]

- it should account for an investment in a subsidiary at fair value through profit or loss in accordance with IFRS 9 (or, for entities that have not yet adopted IFRS 9, IAS 39) from the date when the change in status occurs;

- the difference between the previous carrying amount of the subsidiary and its fair value at the date of the change of status of the investor should be recognised as a gain or loss in profit or loss; and

- the cumulative amount of any gain or loss previously recognised in other comprehensive income in respect of that subsidiary should be treated as if the investment entity had disposed of that subsidiary at the date of change in status.

5.7   Dividends from subsidiaries, joint ventures and associates

Dividends from a subsidiary, a joint venture or an associate are recognised in the separate financial statements of an entity when the entity's right to receive the dividend is established. The dividend is recognised in profit or loss unless the entity elects to use the equity method, in which case the dividend is recognised as a reduction from the carrying amount of the investment. [IAS 27:12]

The specific reference to dividends received from investments accounted for using the equity method was added by the August 2014 amendments (see **5.1**), which are effective for annual periods beginning on or after 1 January 2016, with earlier application permitted.

The requirements regarding dividends do not make any distinction between distributions paid out of pre- and post-acquisition profits; there is no requirement that dividends paid out of pre-acquisition profits should be recognised as a reduction of the carrying amount of the investment (as had been the case prior to amendment of the previous version of IAS 27 in May 2008) unless the investment is accounted for using the equity method.

5.8   Group reorganisations

When a parent reorganises the structure of its group by establishing a new entity as its parent such that the following criteria are met:

[IAS 27:13]

(a) the new parent obtains control of the original parent by issuing equity instruments in exchange for existing equity instruments of the original parent;

(b) the assets and liabilities of the new group and the original group are the same immediately before and after the reorganisation; and

(c) the owners of the original parent before the reorganisation have the same absolute and relative interests in the net assets of the original group and the new group immediately before and after the reorganisation

and the new parent accounts for its investment in the original parent at cost in its separate financial statements, the new parent should measure cost at the carrying amount of its share of the equity items shown in the separate financial statements of the original parent at the date of the reorganisation.

> Thus, in the straightforward scenario in which the original parent becomes a wholly-owned subsidiary of the new parent, the cost shown in the new parent's separate financial statements will simply be the total equity (assets less liabilities) of the original parent shown in the separate financial statements of the original parent at the date of the reorganisation.
>
> IAS 27 does not address the appropriate accounting if the original parent has net liabilities. Consistent with the general accounting for investments in subsidiaries in separate financial statements, the investment should be recognised at nil. However, this treatment would only be appropriate to the extent that the transferee does not assume a liability beyond the cost of the shares at the time of the transfer.
>
> If the new parent does not acquire all of the equity instruments of the original parent, care will be needed in assessing whether condition (c) is met. But, provided that all three conditions in IAS 27:13 are met, the cost shown in the new parent's separate financial statements will be its share of the total equity (assets less liabilities) of the original parent at the date of the reorganisation.
>
> Note that the treatment specified under IAS 27:13 is not a choice; it is required if the specified conditions are met.

Similarly, an entity that is not a parent might establish a new entity as its parent in a manner that satisfies the criteria in IAS 27:13. The requirements in IAS 27:13 apply equally to such reorganisations. In such cases, references to 'original parent' and 'original group' are to the 'original entity'. [IAS 27:14]

Example 5.8A

Cost for new parent in group reorganisation

Company S has one class of equity instruments, 70 per cent of which are held by Company P. A new company, Company X, is created and it issues equity instruments to Company P in exchange for Company P's 70 per cent interest in Company S. Company X therefore becomes Company P's wholly-owned subsidiary. Company X has no other assets or liabilities. At the time of this reorganisation, the total equity (assets less liabilities) of Company S as reported in its separate financial statements is CU10,000.

Although IAS 27:13 and 14 do not directly address the circumstances in which the new parent (Company X) does not acquire 100 per cent of the equity instruments of the old parent (Company P), IAS 27:BC24 clarifies that IAS 27:13 and 14 apply to such reorganisations if the criteria set out in those paragraphs are met. In the circumstances described, the requirements of IAS 27:13 and 14 are met, in that:

- Company X has obtained control of Company S by issuing equity instruments to Company P in exchange for existing equity instruments of Company S;

- the assets and liabilities of the Company X group and Company S are the same immediately before and after the reorganisation; and

- the owners of Company S before the reorganisation have the same absolute and relative interests in the net assets of Company S and the Company X group immediately before and after the reorganisation.

If Company X accounts for its investment in Company S at cost in its separate financial statements, cost is measured at the carrying amount of Company X's share of the equity items shown in the separate financial statements of Company S at the date of the reorganisation, i.e.:

$$\text{Cost} = 70\% \times \text{CU10,000} = \text{CU7,000}$$

Note that, provided that the requirements of IAS 27:13 and 14 are met, the calculation of cost is the same irrespective of whether Company S is itself a parent.

The IFRS Interpretations Committee considered the issue of 'one to many' group reorganisations during 2011 in the context of the requirements of the previous version of IAS 27 (i.e. IAS 27 as revised in 2008). Because the relevant IAS 27(2008) requirements have been carried forward in IAS 27 when it was revised, the conclusion continues to apply as follows (see September 2011 *IFRIC Update*):

- the condition in IAS 27:13 and 14 that the assets and liabilities of the new group and the original group (or original entity) are the same before and after the reorganisation is not met in reorganisations that result in the new intermediate parent having more than one direct subsidiary and, therefore, these paragraphs in IAS 27 do not apply to such reorganisations;

- IAS 27:13 and 14 cannot be applied to reorganisations that result in the new intermediate parent having more than one direct subsidiary by analogy, because this guidance is an exception to the normal basis for determining the cost of an investment in a subsidiary under IAS 27:10(a); and

- for reorganisations that result in a new intermediate parent having more than one direct subsidiary, the normal basis for determining the cost of an investment in a subsidiary under IAS 27:10(a) should be applied.

These principles are illustrated in **example 5.8B**.

Example 5.8B

Cost of investment in the separate financial statements of the new intermediate parent in a 'one to many' group reorganisation

Subsidiaries 1, 2 and 3 are wholly-owned subsidiaries of Parent P. A group reorganisation is carried out, as follows.

- A new intermediate parent (Newco X) is formed. Newco X issues equity instruments to Parent P in exchange for Parent P's interest in Subsidiary 1.

- A new intermediate parent (Newco Y) is formed. Newco Y issues equity instruments to Parent P in exchange for Parent P interests in Subsidiaries 2 and 3.

- Consequently, Subsidiary 1 becomes a wholly-owned subsidiary of Newco X, and Subsidiaries 2 and 3 become wholly-owned subsidiaries of Newco Y.

- Newco X and Newco Y have no other assets or liabilities.

The reorganisation is illustrated in the following diagrams.

Before the reorganisation

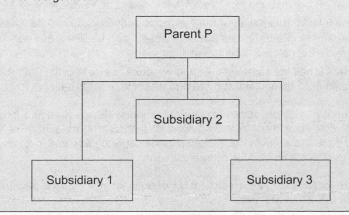

After the reorganisation

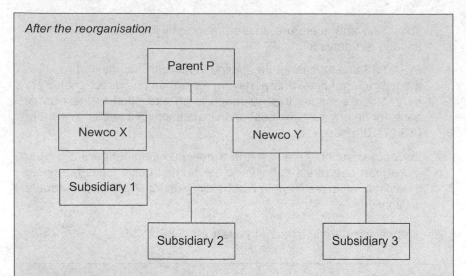

Newco X and Newco Y will account for their investments in the subsidiaries at cost in their separate financial statements in accordance with IAS 27:10(a).

In their separate financial statements, should Newco X and Newco Y measure the cost of their investments in subsidiaries in accordance with IAS 27:13 and 14?

In its separate financial statements, Newco X should measure the cost of its investment in Subsidiary 1 in accordance with IAS 27:14. In the case of Newco Y, however, the reorganisation does not meet the criteria in IAS 27:14; consequently, Newco Y is not permitted to measure the cost of its investments in Subsidiaries 2 and 3 in accordance with IAS 27:14.

The reorganisations establishing Newco X and Newco Y are evaluated under the provisions of IAS 27:14, which is applicable in this scenario because the entities being acquired by Newco X (i.e. Subsidiary 1) and Newco Y (i.e. Subsidiaries 2 and 3) are not themselves parent entities.

In the case of Newco X, the criteria in IAS 27:14, which are derived from the criteria established in IAS 27:13, are met in that:

- Newco X obtains control of Subsidiary 1 by issuing equity instruments to Parent P in exchange for Parent P's interest in that subsidiary;

- the assets and liabilities of the Newco X subgroup immediately after the reorganisation are the same as the assets and liabilities of Subsidiary 1 immediately before the reorganisation; and

- Parent P has the same relative and absolute interests in the net assets of Subsidiary 1 immediately before and after the reorganisation.

Consequently, in its separate financial statements, Newco X should measure the cost of its investment in Subsidiary 1 at the carrying amount of its share (100 per cent) of the equity items shown in the separate financial statements of Subsidiary 1 at the date of the reorganisation.

Note that, for Newco X, this treatment is not optional; it is required because the criteria in IAS 27:14 are met.

In the case of Newco Y, the criteria in IAS 27:14 are not met because the assets and liabilities of the Newco Y subgroup immediately after the reorganisation are not the same as the assets and liabilities of either Subsidiary 2 or Subsidiary 3 immediately before the reorganisation (i.e. the requirements of IAS 27:13(b) are not met).

It is not appropriate to apply the measurement basis in IAS 27:13 by analogy to the Newco Y reorganisation. Consequently, in its separate financial statements, Newco Y should determine the cost of its investments in Subsidiaries 2 and 3 in accordance with its usual accounting policy for such transactions (generally cost or fair value, subject to jurisdictional requirements).

5.9 Cost of new intermediate parent

When a new intermediate parent is introduced into an existing group through an exchange of shares, the ultimate parent has exchanged an investment in one or more subsidiaries for an investment in the new intermediate parent. The question arises as to what carrying amount should be attributed to the new intermediate parent in the separate financial statements of the ultimate parent. (Note that the discussion at **5.8** relates only to the accounting required in the financial statements of the new intermediate parent itself.)

When the new intermediate parent has no other assets or liabilities, and the exchange is for shares, the exchange does not have commercial substance. Moreover, the disposal of the shares previously owned directly by the ultimate parent would not meet the derecognition criteria of IFRS 9 (or, for entities that have not yet adopted IFRS 9, IAS 39) in the separate financial statements of the ultimate parent. Accordingly, the ultimate parent's investment in the new intermediate parent should be initially recognised at the previous carrying amount of the assets given in exchange.

Example 5.9

Cost of new intermediate shell company in parent's financial statements

Company A originally acquired 100 per cent of Company B for cash consideration of CU1,000. Some time later, when the fair value of Company B had increased to CU9,000 and the total equity reported in Company B's separate financial statements was CU4,000, a new intermediate parent, Company C, was inserted into this structure. Company C issued 500 × CU1 shares (being the whole of its share capital) to Company A in exchange for all of the shares in Company B. Company C has no other assets or liabilities. Company B has never paid any dividends to Company A.

Both Company A and Company C apply a policy under IAS 27:10 of accounting for investments in subsidiaries at cost.

From the perspective of Company A, the exchange of shares in Company B for shares in Company C does not have commercial substance; the underlying interests of Company A have not changed. Accordingly, the cost of Company C in the separate financial statements of Company A should be CU1,000 (the original cost of Company B), and not CU9,000.

Although IAS 27:13 and 14 are written in the context of a new parent being established, IAS 27:BC24(b) clarifies that IAS 27:13 and 14 also apply to reorganisations that establish a new intermediate parent within a group. Therefore, from the perspective of Company C:

- if the criteria in IAS 27:13 and 14 are met (see **5.8**), the cost of Company B in the separate financial statements of Company C will be CU4,000 (being the carrying amount of Company C's share of the equity items shown in the separate financial statements of Company B);

- otherwise, the cost of Company B in the separate financial statements of Company C will be determined in accordance with Company C's accounting policy for such transactions.

5.10 Acquisition costs

When an entity prepares separate financial statements, IAS 27:10 (see **5.1**) allows an accounting policy choice, such that investments in subsidiaries (other than those falling within the scope of IFRS 5) may be accounted for at cost, or in accordance with IFRS 9 (or, for entities that have not yet adopted IFRS 9, IAS 39), or using the equity method as described in IAS 28.

Except for subsidiaries accounted for in the entity's separate financial statements at fair value through profit or loss, directly attributable acquisition-related costs should be included within the initial measurement of the investment. The specific requirements for each category of investment are set out in the table below.

Investment accounted for under IFRS 9 (or IAS 39) at fair value through profit or loss	Initial measurement at fair value. [IFRS 9:5.1.1/IAS 39:43]
Investments accounted for under IFRS 9 (or IAS 39) other than at fair value through profit or loss	Initial measurement at fair value plus transaction costs that are directly attributable to the acquisition. [IFRS 9:5.1.1/IAS 39:43]

Investments accounted for at cost	IAS 27 does not define 'cost'. Therefore, the determination of that amount is not specified. In accordance with IAS 8:10 and 11 (see **3.1.2** in **chapter A5**), it is appropriate to apply IFRS 9:5.1.1 (or IAS 39:43) (see above) by analogy. Therefore, directly attributable transaction costs should be included in the initial measurement of an investment accounted for at cost under IAS 27.
Investments accounted for using the equity method	The general principles of IAS 28 should be applied. As discussed in **4.4.2** of **chapter A26**, the cost of an investment in an equity-method investee at initial recognition comprises the purchase price for the investment and any directly attributable expenditure necessary to acquire it.

5.11 Subsidiary acquired in stages – measurement in separate financial statements

Example 5.11

Subsidiary acquired in stages – measurement in separate financial statements

Entity A holds a 30 per cent investment in Entity B (an associate) and subsequently acquires an additional 40 per cent interest, which gives it control over Entity B.

When a subsidiary is acquired in stages, should the principle set out in paragraph 42 of IFRS 3 Business Combinations of accounting for the transaction as "if the acquirer had disposed directly of the previously held equity interest" also be applied in the separate financial statements of the acquirer? Specifically, in the circumstances described, in the separate financial statements of Entity A, should the transaction be accounted for as if Entity A had disposed directly of the previously held 30 per cent investment and acquired a 70 per cent investment in a subsidiary?

No. The focus of IFRS 3:42 is on consolidated financial statements; it is not appropriate to analogise to the requirements of IFRS 3:42 when determining the appropriate accounting in the separate financial statements of an investor for the acquisition of a subsidiary in stages.

IAS 27 requires that, when separate financial statements are prepared, investments in subsidiaries, joint ventures and associates should be accounted for either at cost, or in accordance with IAS 39 (or, when adopted, IFRS 9), or using the equity method as described in IAS 28 (see **5.1**).

When, as in the circumstances described, the level of investment is increased to that of a subsidiary, the appropriate treatment for the previously held interest will depend on the measurement basis applied previously for that interest and the entity's accounting policy for investments in subsidiaries under IAS 27:10 (see table below). In the absence of specific guidance, options are available in some circumstances; whichever accounting policy is adopted, it should be applied consistently to all subsidiaries acquired in stages.

Note that the table below does not address the measurement alternatives available under IFRS 9. In addition, requirements regarding investments accounted for using the equity method should be considered in the context of IAS 28 (see **chapter A26**).

Accounting policy for previously held investment in associate (separate financial statements)	Accounting policy for investments in subsidiaries (separate financial statements)	Appropriate accounting for previously held investment when interest increased to an investment in a subsidiary (separate financial statements)
Cost	Cost	Original investment remains at cost with no remeasurement to fair value
Cost	Available for sale (AFS)	Previously held investment remeasured to fair value with gain/loss recognised either in other comprehensive income (OCI) or direct to AFS reserve
Cost	Fair value through profit or loss (FVTPL)	Previously held investment remeasured to fair value with gain/loss recognised either in profit or loss or retained earnings
AFS	Cost	Either: • treat fair value as deemed cost for subsequent accounting; or • reverse directly to AFS reserve cumulative fair value gain or loss previously recognised in OCI to bring investment back to original cost.

Accounting policy for previously held investment in associate (separate financial statements)	Accounting policy for investments in subsidiaries (separate financial statements)	Appropriate accounting for previously held investment when interest increased to an investment in a subsidiary (separate financial statements)
AFS	AFS	No reclassification to profit or loss of any cumulative fair value gain or loss previously recognised in OCI
AFS	FVTPL	Option to reclassify cumulative fair value gain or loss previously recognised in OCI from AFS reserve to either profit or loss or retained earnings
FVTPL	Cost	Either: • treat fair value as deemed cost for subsequent accounting; or • reverse directly to retained earnings cumulative fair value gain or loss previously recognised in profit or loss to bring investment back to original cost.
FVTPL	AFS	Option to reclassify cumulative fair value gain or loss previously recognised in profit or loss from retained earnings to AFS reserve
FVTPL	FVTPL	No consequence

5.12 Accounting for employee share trusts in separate financial statements

Depending on the nature of an employee share trust, it may be appropriate in separate financial statements either to adopt a 'look-through' approach (accounting for the trust as, in substance, an extension of the sponsoring entity), or to account for the employee share trust as a subsidiary.

For example, a look-through approach may be appropriate when, as a result of its investment in the trust, the sponsoring entity's only exposure is to the shares held by the trust. One such situation would be when the trust has been financed by the sponsoring entity with an interest-free loan, the trust acts solely as a warehouse for the sponsoring entity's shares, any shares that are distributed are distributed directly to the sponsoring entity's employees and shares held by the trust are under option to employees but have not vested yet. When a trust has external funding, the substance may also be that the trust is acting solely as a warehouse for the sponsoring entity's shares (e.g. when the funding is entirely guaranteed by the sponsoring entity or the sponsoring entity provides the trust with the necessary contributions for the trust to be able to pay interest on the third party funding).

The accounting implications of the look-through approach depend upon whether the trust holds the sponsoring entity's shares or shares of another entity (typically the parent when the sponsoring entity is a subsidiary).

Trust holds the sponsoring entity's shares

When the look-through approach is applied to a trust holding the shares of the sponsoring entity, the shares are treated as 'treasury shares' as in the consolidated financial statements (see **9.5** in **chapter A16**).

Trust holds shares of another entity

When the look-through approach is applied to a trust holding the shares of another entity, the shares are treated as equity investments in the statement of financial position in accordance with IFRS 9 (or, for entities that have not yet adopted IFRS 9, IAS 39).

When the trust creates additional risk exposures (e.g. it has other risk exposures such as unguaranteed loans or any other obligations, and hence creates exposures other than to the equity of the sponsoring entity), it may be that a look-through approach is not appropriate because, in substance, the sponsoring entity has an investment in another entity, which it should account for as an investment in a subsidiary. That investment will be accounted for in accordance with the entity's accounting policy for investments in subsidiaries under IAS 27:10 (see **5.1**).

5.13 Recognition of an indemnification asset arising from acquisition of a subsidiary in separate financial statements

Example 5.13

Recognition of an indemnification asset arising from acquisition of a subsidiary in separate financial statements

Entity A acquires 100 per cent of Entity B from Entity C. As part of the business combination, Entity C provides an indemnification to Entity A under which Entity C guarantees that if a specific liability of Entity B crystallises subsequent to the business combination, Entity C will reimburse Entity A for the amount payable.

In the consolidated financial statements of Entity A, the indemnification asset is recognised at the same time and on the same measurement basis as the indemnified item both initially and subsequently in accordance with IFRS 3:27 and 57.

At the acquisition date, the liability is measured at nil in the consolidated financial statements. In the following reporting period, the liability increases to CU2 million; consequently, at that time, an indemnification asset of CU2 million is recognised in the consolidated financial statements.

In its separate financial statements, Entity A accounts for its investment in Entity B at cost in accordance with IAS 27:10.

In Entity A's separate financial statements, how should the indemnification asset be recognised and measured?

This issue is not specifically dealt with in IFRSs. IFRS 3 only addresses the appropriate accounting in the consolidated financial statements and, therefore, the guidance on accounting for indemnification assets in that Standard does not apply in the separate financial statements.

Although the arrangement between Entity A and Entity C typically meets the definition of an insurance contract in IFRS 4 *Insurance Contracts* (because Entity C has accepted significant insurance risk from Entity A by agreeing to compensate Entity A if a specified uncertain future event adversely affects Entity A), the requirements of IFRS 4 are not relevant because they apply to the insurer (Entity C) and not to the holder of the insurance contract (Entity A).

Because it arises from an insurance contract, the asset in the separate financial statements of Entity A is also excluded from the scope of IFRS 9 (or, for entities that have not yet adopted IFRS 9, IAS 39).

IAS 37 *Provisions, Contingent Liabilities and Contingent Assets* is therefore the applicable Standard in respect of the recognition and measurement of the indemnification asset in Entity A's separate financial statements; in particular, the guidance on contingent assets applies. IAS 37:33 requires that an asset should be recognised when the realisation of income is virtually certain. This may result in the recognition of the asset at different times in the separate and consolidated financial statements of Entity A, because the indemnification asset will be recognised in the consolidated financial statements at the same time and on the same basis as the liability to which it relates (no liability will be recognised in the separate financial statements of Entity A because the indemnified obligation relates to Entity B).

There are two possible alternative treatments that could be applied on recognition of the indemnification asset in the separate financial statements of Entity A.

- The arrangement could be considered to represent reimbursement of part of the price paid for the investment in Entity B and to relate specifically to the outcome of a contingency that existed at the date of acquisition of that investment. It is therefore an acceptable accounting policy to recognise the indemnification asset by adjusting the cost of the investment in Entity B.

- Alternatively, Entity A might choose to reflect the recognition of the asset in profit or loss; this treatment is in line with the requirement of IAS 37:35 to recognise 'related income' upon recognition of a contingent asset. If this treatment is followed, it will be necessary to consider whether the investment in Entity B has been impaired.

Whichever treatment is adopted by Entity A, it should be applied consistently as an accounting policy choice.

5.14   Change in fair value of contingent consideration for the acquisition of a subsidiary – separate financial statements of the acquirer

Example 5.14

Change in fair value of contingent consideration for the acquisition of a subsidiary – separate financial statements of the acquirer

Entity A acquires Entity B. The consideration is payable in two tranches:

- an immediate payment of CU1 million; and

- a further payment of CU500,000 after two years if cumulative profit before interest and tax for the two-year period following acquisition exceeds CU400,000.

At the date of acquisition, the fair value of the contingent consideration (i.e. the amount payable if the specified profit target is met) is assessed as CU220,000. Consequently, at the date of acquisition, the investment in Entity B is recognised in Entity A's separate financial statements at a cost of CU1,220,000.

One year after acquisition, on the basis of a revised earnings forecast, the fair value of the contingent consideration has increased by CU80,000 to CU300,000. (In its consolidated financial statements, in accordance with IFRS 3:58, Entity A recognises the resulting loss in profit or loss.)

> *How should Entity A account for the subsequent change in the fair value of the contingent consideration obligation in its separate financial statements?*
>
> The subsequent accounting for the contingent consideration is determined under IFRS 9 (or, for entities that have not yet adopted IFRS 9, IAS 39). The contingent consideration should therefore be subsequently measured at fair value with the resulting loss of CU80,000 recognised in profit or loss.
>
> It is not appropriate for Entity A to increase its cost of investment in Entity B to reflect the change in the fair value of the contingent consideration.

6 Disclosure

6.1 Disclosures in separate financial statements – general

When providing disclosures in its separate financial statements, an entity is required to apply all applicable IFRSs, including the requirements at **6.2** and **6.3**. [IAS 27:15]

> Note, however, that if an entity elects to apply the equity method of accounting to its investments in associates and joint ventures in its separate financial statements, it is not required to comply with the disclosure requirements described of IFRS 12:20 to 23 (see **7.2** and **7.3** in **chapter A28**). In general, IFRS 12 does not apply to separate financial statements, and this principle is not affected by whether the entity elects to use the equity method in those separate financial statements. However, if an entity has interests in unconsolidated structured entities and prepares separate financial statements as its only financial statements, it is required to provide the disclosures required under IFRS 12:24 to 31 (see **section 8** of **chapter A28**).

6.2 Parent elects not to prepare consolidated financial statements

The following disclosure requirements apply when separate financial statements are prepared for a parent that, in accordance with IFRS 10:4(a) (see **3.3** in **chapter A24**) is not required to prepare consolidated financial statements and elects not to do so. In these circumstances, the separate financial statements should disclose:

[IAS 27:16(a)]

- the fact that the financial statements are separate financial statements;
- that the exemption from consolidation has been used;
- the name and principal place of business (and country of incorporation, if different) of the entity whose consolidated financial statements that comply with IFRSs have been produced for public use; and
- the address where those consolidated financial statements can be obtained.

In addition, the separate financial statements should disclose:

[IAS 27:16(b) & (c)]

- a list of significant investments in subsidiaries, joint ventures and associates, including:
  - the name;
  - the principal place of business (and country of incorporation, if different);
  - the proportion of ownership interest held; and
  - if different, the proportion of the voting rights held; and
- a description of the method used to account for such investments.

6.3   Investment entities

When an investment entity that is a parent (other than a parent covered by IAS 27:16 – see **6.2**) prepares separate financial statements as its only financial statements (in accordance with IAS 27:8A – see **3.3**), it is required to:

[IAS 27:16A]

- disclose that fact; and
- present the disclosures relating to investment entities required by IFRS 12 *Disclosure of Interests in Other Entities* (see **3.2** in **chapter A28**).

6.4   Other circumstances

The disclosure requirements below apply to

- a parent (other than a parent covered by **6.2** or **6.3**), or
- an investor with joint control of, or significant influence over, an investee,

that elects or is required to prepare separate financial statements. Those separate financial statements should disclose:

[IAS 27:17]

- the fact that the statements are separate financial statements and the reasons why those statements are prepared if not required by law;
- a list of significant investments in subsidiaries, joint ventures and associates, including:
  - the name of those investees;
  - the principal place of business (and country of incorporation, if different) of those investees;

- the proportion of ownership interest held; and

- if different, the proportion of the voting rights held; and

- a description of the method used to account for such investments.

The separate financial statements are also required to identify the financial statements prepared in accordance with IFRS 10, IFRS 11 *Joint Arrangements* or IAS 28 *Investments in Associates and Joint Ventures* (i.e. the 'main' financial statements) to which they relate. [IAS 27:17]

If an entity:

- is an investor with no subsidiaries but with interests in a number of associates and joint ventures;

- is itself a wholly-owned subsidiary of a parent that produces IFRS financial statements for public use; and

- meets the conditions under IAS 28:17 for exemption from the requirement to apply the equity method to its investments in associates and joint ventures (see **4.2.1** in **chapter A26**), and it elects to use that exemption,

the financial statements prepared by the entity meet the definition of separate financial statements in IAS 27:4 (see **3.1**) and must provide the disclosures required by IAS 27:17. The Standard allows no exemption from its disclosure requirements in such circumstances.

It should be noted, however, that the requirement to disclose "the financial statements prepared in accordance with IFRS 10, IFRS 11 or IAS 28 to which [the separate financial statements] relate" will not be relevant in these circumstances because no such statements will have been prepared. It is suggested that an entity in this situation should instead explain that, because the exemption in IAS 28:17 has been taken, there are no financial statements prepared in accordance with IFRS 11 or IAS 28.

A30 Operating segments

Contents

1   Introduction

1.1   Overview of IFRS 8

IFRS 8 *Operating Segments* sets out the requirements for entities whose debt or equity instruments are traded in a public market (and entities filing their financial statements with a regulator for the purpose of issuing instruments in a public market) for disclosure of information about their operating segments, products and services, the geographical areas in which they operate, and their major customers. Information is based on internal management reports, both in the identification of operating segments and the measurement of disclosed segment information.

1.2   Amendments to IFRS 8 since the last edition of this manual

None. IFRS 8 was most recently amended in December 2014.

2   Core principle

The core principle of IFRS 8 is that "[a]n entity shall disclose information to enable users of its financial statements to evaluate the nature and financial effects of the business activities in which it engages and the economic environments in which it operates". [IFRS 8:1]

3   Scope

3.1   Scope – general

IFRS 8 applies to the separate or individual financial statements of an entity and to the consolidated financial statements of a group with a parent:

[IFRS 8:2]

- whose debt or equity instruments are traded in a public market; or

- that files, or is in the process of filing, its (consolidated) financial statements with a securities commission or other regulatory organisation for the purpose of issuing any class of instruments in a public market.

For this purpose, a 'public market' is any domestic or foreign stock exchange, or an over-the-counter market, including local and regional markets. [IFRS 8:2]

> The IASB has clarified that the scope of IFRS 8 does *not* include the consolidated financial statements of a group that includes a listed non-controlling interest or a subsidiary with listed debt, but whose parent has no listed financial instruments. [IFRS 8:BC23]

Example 3.1

Consolidated financial statements of an intermediate holding company when the ultimate parent has debt or equity instruments traded in a public market

Entity B is an intermediate holding company within a group headed by Entity A. Entity A's equity shares are traded in a public market; Entity B has no debt or equity instruments traded in a public market and is not in the process of issuing any class of instruments in a public market.

Under the requirements of local law, Entity B prepares consolidated financial statements.

Do the requirements of IFRS 8 apply to the consolidated financial statements of Entity B?

No. IFRS 8:2(b) states that IFRS 8 applies to "the consolidated financial statements of a group with a parent whose debt or equity instruments are traded in a public market or that is in the process of issuing any class of instruments in a public market".

In this context, the 'parent' for the purposes of IFRS 8:2(b) is Entity B (i.e. the entity which controls the other entities within the consolidated financial statements under preparation). Entity A is not part of the reporting entity and the fact that its shares are publicly traded is not relevant to the consideration of the applicability of IFRS 8 for the purposes of Entity B's consolidated financial statements.

3.2   Consolidated financial statements published together with separate financial statements

When a single financial report includes both consolidated financial statements and the separate financial statements of a parent falling within the scope of IFRS 8, segment information need be presented on a consolidated basis only. [IFRS 8:4]

3.3   Entities that choose to disclose segment information voluntarily

If an entity that is not required to comply with IFRS 8 (e.g. a private entity) chooses to disclose information about segments that does not comply with the requirements of that Standard, the entity is not permitted to describe the information as 'segment information'. [IFRS 8:3]

IFRS 8:3 permits entities outside the scope of IFRS 8 that choose to disclose some information about segments voluntarily to provide limited information on segments without triggering the need to comply fully with IFRS 8, so long as the disclosure is not referred to as segment information. [IFRS 8:BC22]

IFRS 8 applies only to information about segments reported in the financial statements. IAS 1 *Presentation of Financial Statements* defines a complete set of financial statements as comprising a statement of profit or loss and other comprehensive income, a statement of financial position, a statement of cash flows, a statement of changes in equity and notes (together with specified comparative information). Accordingly, when management voluntarily discloses limited information about segments outside of those financial statements (e.g. in the directors' report or chairman's statement), such disclosures are not affected by the restriction imposed under IFRS 8:3 and may be described as 'segment information'.

3.4 Disclosures that might be seriously prejudicial

IFRS 8 does not provide an exemption for disclosures that the board or management deems to be prejudicial to the interests of the entity. Even when the directors of a publicly traded entity conclude that disclosure of certain segment information will be seriously prejudicial to the interests of the entity (e.g. because its main competitors are not publicly traded and, therefore, do not publish similar information), the segment information may not be omitted in IFRS financial statements.

4 Identification of operating segments

4.1 The management approach to segment reporting

IFRS 8 adopts a strict management approach to segment reporting and requires that operating segments be identified and measured on the same basis as financial information is reported internally for the purpose of allocating resources between segments and assessing their performance.

When developing IFRS 8, the IASB opted for the management approach based on the view that defining segments based on the structure of the entity's internal organisation allows users to see an entity 'through the eyes of management', which enhances a user's ability to predict actions or reactions of management that can significantly affect the entity's prospects for future cash flows. In addition, the IASB expected the Standard to reduce the cost of reporting segment information externally because that information is already generated for management's use. The perceived disadvantage of this approach is that it may result in the reporting of segments that are not comparable between entities engaged in similar activities, and from year to year for an individual entity.

Example 4.1

Non-comparable segment disclosures between competitors

Entity A and Entity B both manufacture and distribute windows and insulation products used in the construction of residential and commercial units. Entity A is structured such that decisions are made and performance is evaluated on a regional basis (e.g. Americas, Europe), whereas Entity B makes decisions and evaluates performance on a product-line basis (e.g. windows, insulation).

Entity A and Entity B will not report similar operating segments under IFRS 8. Entity A should report operating segments based on regions and Entity B should report operating segments based on product lines. The management approach requires identification of operating segments on the basis of internal reports that are regularly reviewed by the entity's chief operating decision maker in order to allocate resources to the segment and assess its performance. Two entities in the same industry can have very different operating segments because each will determine its operating segments based on how management makes operating decisions and assesses performance.

4.2   Definition of operating segment

An operating segment is a component of an entity:

[IFRS 8:5]

(a)   that engages in business activities from which it may earn revenues and incur expenses (including revenues and expenses relating to transactions with other components of the same entity);

(b)   whose operating results are regularly reviewed by the entity's chief operating decision maker to make decisions about resources to be allocated to the segment and assess its performance; and

(c)   for which discrete financial information is available.

IFRS 8 does not provide a definition of a 'component of an entity'. Often, a component of an entity will be a division, a subsidiary or a group of subsidiaries. An interest in an associate or a joint venture might also be regarded as a component if the requirements in IFRS 8:5 are met.

4.3   The chief operating decision maker

References in the Standard to the 'chief operating decision maker' are not necessarily to a manager with a specific title, but rather to a function – specifically that of allocating resources to and assessing the performance of the operating segments of the entity. Often the chief operating decision maker of an entity is its chief executive officer or chief operating officer but, for example, it may be a group of executive directors or others. [IFRS 8:7]

The management approach relies on the structure of the organisation and the internal operating reports typically used by the chief operating decision maker, who determines the allocation of resources and assesses the performance of the operating segments. While the chief operating decision maker is usually an individual, sometimes the function is performed by a group.

Often the chief operating decision maker is the highest ranking management individual at the entity (or the consolidated entity, when consolidated financial statements are presented) who makes such decisions, although rank within the entity does not necessarily identify the chief operating decision maker. Such an individual typically would be the chief executive officer or chairman who may receive a host of management reports prepared in a variety of different ways.

Complex organisational and reporting structures often make it difficult to determine the chief operating decision maker and it may be helpful to consider the financial information that is presented to the board of directors because this information is typically indicative of how management views the entity's activities. An evaluation of such financial information will often help to distinguish the chief operating decision maker from other levels of line management (e.g. segment management).

Example 4.3A

Identification of the chief operating decision maker

Entity C is a publicly traded manufacturer of various electronic instruments used in aerospace, medical and consumer products. Entity C has a chief operating officer for each of the aerospace, medical and consumer product units. The chief operating officers are responsible for operating, budgeting and reporting aspects of their respective units, and have senior management personnel within their units who report to them. The chief operating officers report to the chief executive officer (including making resource allocation recommendations for their respective units). The chief executive officer evaluates the performance of each unit based on a variety of different management reports and is responsible for entity-wide resource-allocation decisions.

In the circumstances described, even though the chief operating officers are responsible for the management of their respective units, the final decisions regarding the allocation of resources are made by the chief executive officer. Therefore, the chief executive officer is considered the chief operating decision maker. The chief operating decision maker is the individual or function responsible for decisions about overall resource allocation and performance assessment for each business unit of an entity. Generally, these decisions are made at the highest level of management, notwithstanding the fact that lower levels of management may be responsible for the operating, budgeting and reporting aspects of individual business units.

In the circumstances described, Entity C is likely to have three operating segments and each of the chief operating officers is likely to be considered a segment manager. IFRS 8:9 states that a segment manager is "directly accountable to and maintains regular contact with the chief operating decision maker to discuss operating activities, financial results, forecasts, or plans for the segment" (see **4.5**).

Example 4.3B

Management committee as the chief operating decision maker

Entity D is a publicly traded manufacturer of various electronic instruments used in aerospace, medical and consumer products. Entity D has a chief financial officer for each of the aerospace, medical and consumer-product units. Entity D is governed by a management committee comprised of each of the chief financial officers and the chief executive officer. The management committee makes all key operating decisions and determines the allocation of resources and makes assessments of performance. No one individual either on the management committee, or elsewhere in the entity, has the ability to override the management committee (except for the board of directors acting in their role of overseeing the management committee).

In the circumstances described, the chief operating decision maker is the management committee, and the reports used by the management committee are used to determine the operating segments of Entity D. Often the chief operating decision maker of an entity is its chief executive officer or chief operating officer, but it may be a group of executive directors or others, such as a management committee consisting of, for example, the entity's chief executive officer or chairman, chief operating officer, chief financial officer and others, all of whom have a vote on decisions made by the committee.

However, the existence of a management committee does not always mean that the management committee is the chief operating decision maker. For instance, the ability of the chief executive officer to override the decisions of the management committee would be an indicator that the chief executive officer, not the management committee, is the chief operating decision maker. This determination should be made for each individual case based on the specific facts and circumstances.

4.4   Business activities that are not part of an operating segment

It need not be the case that every part of an entity is an operating segment or part of an operating segment. For example, the Standard notes that a corporate headquarters or some functional departments may not earn revenues (or may earn revenues that are only incidental to the activities of the entity) and would not be operating segments. [IFRS 8:6]

For the purposes of IFRS 8, an entity's post-employment benefit plans are not operating segments. [IFRS 8:6]

4.5   Chief operating decision maker uses more than one set of segment information

An entity may produce reports in which its business activities are presented in a variety of ways. If the chief operating decision maker uses more than one set of segment information, other factors may identify a single set of components as constituting the entity's operating segments, including the nature of the business activities of each component, the existence of managers responsible for them, and information presented to the board of directors. [IFRS 8:8]

4.6   Involvement of a segment manager

Generally, an operating segment has a segment manager who is directly accountable to and maintains regular contact with the chief operating decision maker to discuss operating activities, financial results, forecasts, or plans for the segment. The term 'segment manager' identifies a function, not necessarily a manager with a specific title. The chief operating decision maker may also be the segment manager for some operating segments. A single manager may be the segment manager for more than one operating segment. If the characteristics in IFRS 8:5 (see **4.2**) apply to more than one set of components of an organisation but there is only one set for which segment managers are held responsible, that set of components constitutes the operating segments. [IFRS 8:9]

4.7   Matrix form of organisation

The characteristics at **4.2** may apply to two or more overlapping sets of components for which managers are held responsible. That structure is sometimes referred to as a 'matrix' form of organisation. For example, in some entities, some managers are responsible for different product and service lines worldwide, whereas other managers are responsible for specific geographical areas. The chief operating decision maker regularly reviews the operating results of both sets of components, and financial information is available for both. In that situation, the entity should determine which set of components constitutes the operating segments by reference to the core principle of IFRS 8 (see **section 2**). [IFRS 8:10]

Matrix organisational structures are commonly used for large complex organisations. The IASB has concluded that, when more than one set of segments can be identified, it should not simply mandate the use of components based on products and services as the entity's operating segments under IFRS 8, since to do so would be inconsistent with the management approach. Instead, the Standard refers back to the core principle – requiring that the identification of operating segments be made so as to enable users of the financial statements "to evaluate the nature and financial effects of the business activities in which [the entity] engages and the economic environments in which it operates". Management will, therefore, be required to exercise judgement as to which of the bases of segmentation satisfies this objective. [IFRS 8:BC27]

4.8   Operating segment identified at subsidiary level may differ from those identified at parent level

A subsidiary may fall within the scope of IFRS 8 if, for example, its debt or equity instruments are traded in a public market. It is very likely that the chief operating decision maker of the subsidiary will not be the chief operating decision maker of the parent. In addition, it is possible that the information provided to these chief operating decision makers may be organised and presented differently. As a consequence, when a subsidiary is required to comply with IFRS 8, the operating segments identified at subsidiary level are likely to be different from those identified at parent level for the purpose of providing IFRS 8 disclosures.

4.9   Vertically-integrated entities

Under the IFRS 8 approach, a component of an entity that sells primarily or exclusively to other operating segments of the entity will meet the definition of an operating segment if the entity is managed that way. The IASB took this approach to ensure that information about the components engaged in each stage of production is reported when this is how the business is managed, which is seen as particularly important in certain businesses such as oil and gas entities.

Example 4.9

Application of IFRS 8 to vertically-integrated entities

Entity E is a vertically-integrated oil entity that sells refined products to external customers. The refinery operation sells refined products internally to the marketing and distribution segment of Entity E (i.e. the refinery operation has no external customers). The financial results of the refinery operation are prepared separately and are reviewed on a regular basis by the chief operating decision maker to assess performance and make decisions regarding allocation of resources.

The refinery operation is an operating segment. A component of an entity is not required to have external customers or revenues in order to be classified as an operating segment. Some operating segments may only earn revenue relating to transactions with other components of the same entity, or may not yet earn revenues. The key factor in identifying operating segments is to understand

---

> the process the chief operating decision maker goes through in managing the business. If the chief operating decision maker makes decisions and assesses operating performance regardless of revenue source or absence of revenue, the operating unit would be reported as an operating segment.

4.10   Operating unit not yet generating revenue

It is not necessary for a component of a business to actually earn revenues in order to meet the definition of an operating segment. IFRS 8 specifically refers to start-up operations, which may engage in business activities for some time before they generate revenues, and allows that they may be operating segments at that pre-operating stage provided that the other criteria are met. [IFRS 8:5]

Example 4.10

Newly formed operating unit

Entity F, a diversified pharmaceutical entity, has allocated 11 per cent of the combined assets of all operating segments to form an operating unit to pursue research on new drugs to fight the AIDS virus. Although expenses have been incurred, the operating unit has yet to earn revenues from any of its activities. Discrete financial information is available for the operating unit and that information is reviewed by the chief operating decision maker in making operating decisions and assessing operating performance.

The operating unit is an operating segment. The criteria set out in IFRS 8:5 (see **4.2**) are met. An operating segment can be such that it does not earn external or internal revenues and the chief operating decision maker makes decisions and assesses the performance of the segment based solely on expenses.

In this example, the intent of the entity is to allocate resources to the specific business purpose of AIDS research. Although there is a risk that revenues will never be earned from this pursuit, management has made a risk/reward determination that the cost of the research will be recovered through future revenues. If this level of resource allocation is performed and the information is reviewed by the chief operating decision maker, the operating unit should be considered an operating segment.

4.11   Identification of operating segments in the absence of discrete financial information

Example 4.11

Identification of operating segments in the absence of discrete financial information

Entity G has an operating unit that provides content to internet websites. Entity G derives substantially all of its revenue from three service lines – advertising, promotions and customer service. The financial information reviewed by the chief operating decision maker includes revenue by service line, but operating expenses and assets are reported on a combined basis for the entire operating unit. The financial information does not include profit or loss information for the individual service lines.

The individual service lines are not separate operating segments. Discrete financial information is not available because no measure of segment profit or loss by service line is supplied to the chief operating decision maker. The chief operating decision maker does not have sufficient information to assess performance and make resource allocation decisions by service line. In the circumstances described, it would be likely that the entire operating unit represents an operating segment, not the individual service lines.

However, if the information provided to the chief operating decision maker contained revenue and gross profit by service line, sufficient financial information would be available to enable the chief operating decision maker to assess performance and make resource allocation decisions by service line.

It is not necessary that assets be allocated for a component to be considered an operating segment.

4.12   Segments that include discontinued operations

IFRS 8 does not, in itself, draw any distinction between continuing and discontinued operations (see **section 6** of **chapter A20**). Accordingly, it is possible that some, or all, of the operations included in an operating segment might be presented as discontinued. Equally, the fact that operations in a segment are being run down will not, of itself, affect whether it qualifies as an operating segment. But the disclosure requirements of IFRS 8 will not apply to a segment that consists entirely of discontinued operations because of paragraph 5B of IFRS 5 *Non-current Assets Held for Sale and Discontinued Operations*, which states as follows.

> "This IFRS [IFRS 5] specifies the disclosures required in respect of non-current assets (or disposal groups) classified as held for sale or discontinued operations. Disclosures in other IFRSs do not apply to such assets (or disposal groups) unless those IFRSs require:
>
> (a)   specific disclosures in respect of non-current assets (or disposal groups) classified as held for sale or discontinued operations; or
>
> (b)   disclosures about measurement of assets and liabilities within a disposal group that are not within the scope of the measurement requirement of IFRS 5 and such disclosures are not already provided in the other notes to the financial statements."

The requirements of IFRS 5:5B are discussed further in **section 7** of **chapter A20**.

4.13   Reassessment of operating segments

When there is a change in the way a business is structured (e.g. a reorganisation or a new line of business) or in the way information is reported to the chief operating decision maker (e.g. a new reporting structure or a change from geographical to business line reporting) or in the entity's corporate governance structure such that a new chief operating decision maker is identified, it will be necessary to consider whether these changes might affect the identification of operating segments and the disclosures to be reported in accordance with IFRS 8.

5   Identification of reportable segments

5.1   Identification of reportable segments – general

Once the entity's operating segments have been identified, the entity must then determine which operating segments are reportable, i.e. those individual operating segments for which disclosure of information is required by the Standard.

Entities are required to report separately information about each operating segment that:

[IFRS 8:11]

(a)   has been identified in accordance with IFRS 8:5 to 10 (as outlined in **section 4**) or results from aggregating two or more of those segments in accordance with IFRS 8:12 (see **5.3**); and

(b)   exceeds the quantitative thresholds in IFRS 8:13 (see **5.4**).

In addition, other situations in which separate information about an operating segment must be reported are specified in IFRS 8:14 to 18 (see **5.5** to **5.8**).

The guidance on implementing IFRS 8 includes a decision tree that may be followed to assist with the identification of reportable segments. This decision tree is reproduced at **5.9**.

5.2   Limit on the number of reportable segments

IFRS 8 does not set a precise limit on the number of operating segments for which information should be disclosed. However, it acknowledges that there may be a practical limit to the number of reportable segments that an entity separately discloses beyond which segment information becomes too detailed. The Standard suggests that, as the number of segments identified as reportable in accordance with IFRS 8:13 to 18 increases above 10, the entity should consider whether a practical limit has been reached. [IFRS 8:19]

Once the number of reportable operating segments exceeds a reasonable amount, an evaluation should be made of the criteria utilised by management for aggregation to determine if an appropriate aggregation of operating segments has been performed. Additionally, the existence of an unreasonably large number of operating segments may be an indication that the chief operating decision maker has not been properly identified.

5.3   Aggregation of operating segments

5.3.1   Aggregation criteria

IFRS 8 notes that operating segments often exhibit similar long-term financial performance (e.g. similar average gross margins) if they have similar economic characteristics. The question then arises as to when it is appropriate to combine operating segments which display such similar characteristics for the purpose of external reporting.

IFRS 8 states that two or more operating segments may be aggregated into a single operating segment if all of the following conditions are met:

[IFRS 8:12]

(a) aggregation is consistent with the core principle of IFRS 8 (see **section 2**);

(b) the segments have similar economic characteristics; and

(c) the segments are similar in each of the following respects:
   (i) the nature of the products and services;
   (ii) the nature of the production processes;
   (iii) the type or class of customer for their products and services;
   (iv) the methods used to distribute their products or provide their services; and
   (v) if applicable, the nature of the regulatory environment (e.g. banking, insurance, or public utilities).

The criteria for aggregation are strict, with the result that aggregation will only be permitted for quite homogeneous operations.

5.3.2   Aggregation criteria take precedence over quantitative thresholds

Both IFRS 8:BC30 and the diagram included in the implementation guidance accompanying IFRS 8 (see **5.9**) clarify that the aggregation criteria set out in IFRS 8:12 take precedence over the quantitative thresholds discussed in **5.4**. Therefore, if two or more components of a business meet the aggregation criteria, they may be combined for external reporting purposes into a single operating segment, notwithstanding that they may individually exceed the quantitative thresholds.

5.3.3 Aggregation of operating segments meeting the criteria not required

Note that the Standard *permits* operating segments meeting the aggregation criteria to be combined for external reporting purposes. It does not require such combination, and entities are always entitled to report the operating segments separately.

5.3.4 Assessment as to whether operating segments are similar

IFRS 8 does not define the term 'similar' or provide detailed guidance on the aggregation criteria and, therefore, the determination as to whether two or more operating segments are similar is dependent on the individual facts and circumstances and is subject to a high degree of judgement. Note that entities are required to disclose the judgements made by management in applying the aggregation criteria in IFRS 8:12 (see **7.2.2**).

The following guidance may be a useful starting point for assessing whether operating segments are similar in each of the respects listed in IFRS 8:12.

Similar economic characteristics IFRS 8 states that segments with similar economic characteristics would be expected to have similar long-term average gross margins, but it does not provide any other examples of what may be used to evaluate economic characteristics. It may be appropriate for an entity to consider other performance measures such as sales growth, operating cash flows, return on assets, EBITDA (earnings before interest, taxes, depreciation and amortisation), inventory turnover, or other standard industry measures. These factors should be evaluated from current, historical and 'expected future performance' perspectives. An analysis based solely on an expectation of similar long-term economic performance (e.g. by reference to budgets) is unlikely to be sufficient. In addition, competitive, operating and financial risks related to each business or industry type should be considered in determining whether two operating segments have similar economic characteristics. If operating segments are located in different geographical areas, entities may need to evaluate factors such as economic and political conditions, currency risks and foreign exchange control regulations.

The nature of the products and services IFRS 8 does not provide guidance as to how to interpret the 'nature of products and services' criterion. However, it can be considered that similar products or services have similar purposes or end uses. Therefore, they may be expected to have similar rates of profitability, similar degrees of risk and similar opportunities for growth. The assessment as to whether products or services are similar may depend, in part, on the nature and breadth of an entity's product lines and overall operations.

The nature of the production process Although no specific guidance is provided in IFRS 8, similarities in the nature of the production process may be demonstrated by the sharing of common or interchangeable production or sales facilities, equipment, labour force or servicing and maintenance staff, or the use of the same or similar basic raw materials. Likewise, similar degrees of labour or capital intensiveness may indicate a similarity in the production process.

The type or class of customer for their products and services The 'similar type or class of customer' criterion may be evaluated based on how management views the customer (e.g. similar marketing and promotional efforts, common or interchangeable sales forces, customer demographics). Generally, retail and wholesale operations would not be considered to have similar types or classes of customers and therefore would not satisfy this criterion.

The methods used to distribute their products or provide the services The 'methods of distribution' criterion may be evaluated based on the nature of the distribution channels (e.g. retail outlets, mail order, web site).

If applicable, the nature of the regulatory environment (e.g. banking, insurance or public utilities) This criterion applies only if a unique regulatory environment exists with respect to a part of the entity's business. For example, in a situation in which a utility holding entity has a regulated segment and a non-regulated segment, each segment is considered to operate in a different regulatory environment and, therefore, aggregation would not be appropriate even though the segments may produce the same product.

5.3.5   Requirement for consistency with information reported elsewhere

The management approach prescribed in IFRS 8 facilitates consistent descriptions of an entity in the annual report and other published information. Information presented in the operating segment note of the financial statements should be consistent with the information presented throughout an entity's regulatory filings, whether in the annual report to shareholders, the entity's websites, financial analyst reports, interviews and other public statements made by management, or other public documents.

Example 5.3.5

Requirement for consistency between the management report and segment disclosures

Entity H is a large retailer that operates two types of stores – clothing and home products (linens, decorative items and some clothing). For the purpose of IFRS 8, Entity H determines that it has two operating segments – 'Clothing' and 'Home Products'. Management's report to shareholders published with the financial statements discusses the results of operations of the home product stores separately in a manner different from that of the clothing stores by describing different customer demographics, products offered and sales and profit margin trends. The chairman's report also stresses important distinctions between the two operating segments.

Is it appropriate for Entity H to aggregate its two operating segments into a single reportable operating segment for the purposes of reporting under IFRS 8?

It is unlikely to be appropriate for Entity H to aggregate the Clothing and Home Products operating segments into a single reportable operating segment for the purposes of the disclosures required under IFRS 8, because the aggregation criteria in IFRS 8:12 are not fully satisfied. The aggregation criteria require, among other conditions, similar economic characteristics, similar products and similar type or class of customer. The management report and the chairman's report describe different economic characteristics, product types and customer demographics, and stress some important distinctions between the two segments.

5.3.6 Is it appropriate to aggregate all operating segments into a single reportable segment?

In general, while an entity may look to the aggregation criteria and conclude that it only has one reportable operating segment, such a situation would be expected to be unusual. The objective of IFRS 8 is to provide more useful information about the different types of business activities in which an entity engages. The operating segment information is intended to provide more meaningful information to the users of the financial statements.

5.4 Quantitative thresholds

Under IFRS 8, entities are required to report separately information about an operating segment that meets any of the following quantitative thresholds:

[IFRS 8:13]

(a) its reported revenue is 10 per cent or more of the combined revenue of all operating segments. For this purpose, revenue includes both sales to external customers and inter-segment sales or transfers; or

(b) the absolute amount of its reported profit or loss is 10 per cent or more of the greater, in absolute amount, of (i) the combined reported profit of all operating segments that did not report a loss, and (ii) the combined reported loss of all operating segments that reported a loss; or

(c) its assets are 10 per cent or more of the combined assets of all operating segments.

If segment information is reported to the chief operating decision maker after making adjustments, eliminations and allocations of revenue, expenses, and gains or losses, it would follow from IFRS 8:25 (see **section 6**) that, in applying the quantitative thresholds for the purposes of identifying reportable segments in IFRS 8:13, the thresholds should be applied on this basis, i.e. after adjustments, eliminations and allocations.

Example 5.4

Application of quantitative thresholds

Company I has identified the following operating segments: computer hardware, computer software and customer service. In applying the quantitative threshold tests set out in IFRS 8:13 for the purpose of identifying reportable segments, Company I would perform the following analysis (based on the figures in the table below).

To determine the operating segments that exceed the 10 per cent revenue threshold, Company I should determine the combined revenue (external and internal) for all operating segments (CU5,500). This amount includes CU500 of inter-segment revenue. Ten per cent of this amount, or CU550, would represent the threshold.

To determine the operating segments that exceed the 10 per cent profit or loss threshold, Company I should determine the greater, in absolute value, of (i) the combined reported profit of all operating segments that did not report a loss, and (ii) the combined reported loss of all operating segments that reported a loss. Based on the calculation below, the absolute value of the total of all operating segments not reporting a loss, CU350, is greater than the absolute value of the segment with a loss, CU50. Ten per cent of CU350, or CU35, should then be used as the profit or loss threshold for identifying reportable segments.

To determine the segments that exceed the 10 per cent asset threshold, Company I should calculate the threshold based on 10 per cent of the combined segment assets of all operating segments identified (CU800) before intragroup eliminations.

Segment	Segment revenue	Segment result	Segments not reporting a loss	Segments reporting a loss	Segment assets
	CU	CU	CU	CU	CU
Hardware	500	(50)		50*	400*
Software	2,500*	200	200*		300*
Service	2,500*	150	150*		100*
Total before eliminations	5,500	300	350	50	800
Eliminations	(500)	(10)	0	0	(10)
Total	5,000	290	350	50	790
Calculated threshold	550(a)		35(b)	35(b)	80(c)

(a) Total sales before elimination of inter-segment sales (CU5,500) × 10%

(b) Threshold calculation is based on the greater of the absolute amount of all operating segments not reporting a loss and all operating segments with loss (CU350) × 10%

(c) Total assets before considering inter-segment eliminations (CU800) × 10%

Note: * indicates a segment meeting the specific threshold.

Considering each of the operating segments in turn:

- the Hardware segment exceeds the result threshold (CU50 > CU35) and the assets threshold (CU400 > CU80);

- the Software segment exceeds the revenue threshold (CU2,500 > CU550), the result threshold (CU200 > CU35) and the assets threshold (CU300 > CU80);

- the Service segment exceeds the revenue threshold (CU2,500 > CU550), the result threshold (CU150 > CU35) and the assets threshold (CU100 > CU80).

Accordingly, all three segments meet at least one threshold and, therefore, all are reportable.

As discussed at **5.3.2**, the aggregation criteria in IFRS 8:12 take precedence over the quantitative thresholds discussed in this section. Therefore, if two or more components of a business meet the aggregation criteria in IFRS 8:12, they may be combined for external reporting purposes into a single operating segment, notwithstanding that they may individually exceed the quantitative thresholds.

5.5 Operating segments below the quantitative thresholds

When an operating segment is below all of the quantitative thresholds set out in **5.4**, the segment may be:

- designated as a reportable segment despite its size and separately disclosed, if management believes that information about the segment would be useful to users of the financial statements; [IFRS 8:13] or

- combined into a separately reportable segment with one or more other operating segment(s) that are also below all of the 10 per cent thresholds (but only if the operating segments so combined have similar economic characteristics and share a majority of the aggregation criteria set out in IFRS 8:12 – i.e. the criteria listed as (c)(i) to (c)(v) at **5.3.1**). [IFRS 8:14]

Information about other business activities and operating segments that are not reportable should be combined and disclosed in an 'all other segments' category separately from other reconciling items in the reconciliations required by IFRS 8:28 (see **7.5**). The sources of the revenue included in the 'all other segments' category should be described. [IFRS 8:16]

5.6 External revenue attributable to reportable segments to be at least 75 per cent of entity revenue

IFRS 8 requires the total external revenue reported by operating segments to be at least 75 per cent of the entity's revenue. When this is not the case, it is necessary to identify additional operating segments as reportable segments (even if they do not meet the quantitative thresholds in IFRS 8:13 – see **5.4**) until at least 75 per cent of the entity's revenue is included in reportable segments. [IFRS 8:15]

Example 5.6

Identification of additional segments to reach 75 per cent revenue threshold

Company J has determined its reportable segments in accordance with IFRS 8 and has noted that the reportable segments constitute 68 per cent of consolidated revenue. All remaining operating segments are of similar size.

How should Company J determine which operating segments to report separately?

IFRS 8 does not specify which of the remaining operating segments should be selected to achieve the 75 per cent threshold, and the operating segment chosen does not necessarily need to be the next largest by any of the measures. Judgement should be used, and each situation will be based on the individual facts and circumstances. Those additional operating segments included in order to achieve the 75 per cent threshold are treated no differently from any other reportable segment (i.e. the required disclosures are the same).

5.7 Operating segment reported in preceding period that no longer exceeds quantitative thresholds

If an operating segment was identified as a reportable segment in the immediately preceding period (e.g. because it exceeded one of the 10 per cent thresholds), it should continue to be a reportable segment for the current period (notwithstanding that it no longer exceeds any of the 10 per cent thresholds), if the directors judge the segment to be of 'continuing significance'. [IFRS 8:17]

No further guidance is provided as to the meaning of 'continuing significance', but an operating segment normally would be regarded as having continuing significance for the current financial statements when, for example:

* its decline below the 10 per cent thresholds is considered temporary and likely to reverse; or

* it has unrecognised intangible assets (such as internally generated intangible assets) that, if recognised, would cause its segment assets to meet the 10 per cent threshold (this may indicate that the segment is of strategic importance).

While this list is not exhaustive, management should ensure that the usefulness of the financial information and consistency in reporting is maintained.

If management concludes that the segment is not of continuing significance, prior year information should be restated to conform to the current year's presentation, with appropriate disclosure describing the restatement.

5.8 Operating segment reportable in the current period but not in the prior period

An operating segment may be identified as a reportable segment in the current period because it exceeds one of the relevant 10 per cent thresholds, even though it did not exceed any of the thresholds in the prior period. In such circumstances, prior period segment data that is presented for comparative purposes should be restated to reflect the newly reportable segment as a separate segment, unless the necessary information is not available and the cost to develop it would be excessive. [IFRS 8:18]

Here and in some other parts of IFRS 8 (see **7.6.1**, **7.7.2** and **7.7.3**) an exemption from disclosing certain financial information is provided when the information is not available and "the cost to develop it would be excessive". This is a less onerous test than that of impracticability as included in IAS 1 *Presentation of Financial Statements*, because the latter does not make any allowance for the cost of compliance.

Nevertheless, it is unlikely that this exemption will often be claimed because in practice it will usually be possible to obtain a sufficiently reliable approximation of the required disclosures without incurring excessive costs.

Although situations covered by the exception in IFRS 8:18 are expected to be unusual, consider the following example.

Example 5.8

Operating segment reportable in the current period but not in the prior period

In the past three years, Company K has grown from CU100 million in sales annually to over CU1 billion in sales annually as a result of five different acquisitions. Company K and each entity it acquired were managed differently. Due to its significant growth through acquisitions, Company K has recently reorganised its management structure and operating segments. Historical records that reflect information that is consistent with the new management structure are not available for all of the entities.

In this situation, it may be that the conditions for exemption from the requirement to restate comparative information under IFRS 8:18 are met (information is not available and the cost to develop it would be excessive) due to the number and size of Company K's recent acquisitions.

5.9   Segment definition decision tree

The implementation guidance accompanying IFRS 8 includes a decision tree, reproduced below, which illustrates how the requirements discussed in **section 5** are applied.

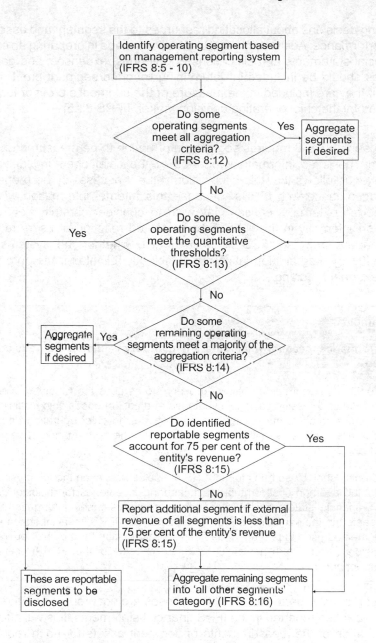

6 Measurement of segment information

Section 7 sets out the information required to be disclosed under IFRS 8. This section summarises the guidance provided in IFRS 8 regarding the measurement of that information.

For each segment item, the amount to be reported under IFRS 8 is the measure reported to the chief operating decision maker for the purposes of making decisions about allocating resources to the segment and assessing its performance. Adjustments and eliminations made in preparing an entity's financial statements and allocations of revenues, expenses, and gains or losses should be included in determining reported segment profit or loss only if they are included in the measure of the segment's profit or loss that is used by the chief operating decision maker. [IFRS 8:25]

Because IFRS 8 requires segment information to be measured on the same basis as information reported to the chief operating decision maker, it follows that this information will not necessarily be prepared in accordance with IFRSs. Because this internal information will be reported externally, entities may wish to consider carefully how they report internally in the light of the expected reaction of users to any departure from an IFRS basis, and also whether the systems for producing internal information are sufficiently reliable for the purposes of external reporting.

Example 6

Performance measure when different inventory valuation methods are used

An entity that operates a chain of grocery stores uses the weighted average cost formula to assign costs to inventories and cost of goods sold for financial reporting purposes, but the reports provided to the chief operating decision maker use last-in, first-out (LIFO) for evaluating the performance of segment operations.

The entity should use LIFO for its IFRS 8 disclosures, even though it uses the weighted average cost formula for measuring inventories for inclusion in its IFRS financial statements. IFRS 8 does not require segment information to be presented in the same manner as that used in the IFRS financial statements. The method used in preparing the financial information for the chief operating decision maker determines which measure is used for the IFRS 8 operating segment note.

If the amounts reported for IFRS 8 purposes are not prepared on the same basis as those reported in the IFRS financial statements, this will affect the explanation of the measurements of segment assets for each reportable segment (see **7.4**) and the reconciliations required to be presented under IFRS 8:28 (see **7.5**).

Only those assets and liabilities included in the measures of the segment's assets and segment's liabilities that are used by the chief operating decision maker should be reported for that segment. If amounts are allocated to reported segment profit or loss, assets or liabilities, those amounts should be allocated on a reasonable basis. [IFRS 8:25]

If the chief operating decision maker uses only one measure of an operating segment's profit or loss, the segment's assets or the segment's liabilities in assessing segment performance and deciding how to allocate resources, for IFRS 8 purposes segment profit or loss, assets and liabilities should also be reported at those measures. If the chief operating decision maker uses more than one measure of an operating segment's profit or loss, the segment's assets or the segment's liabilities, the measures reported for IFRS 8 purposes should be those that management believes are determined in accordance with the measurement principles most consistent with those used in measuring the corresponding amounts in the entity's financial statements. [IFRS 8:26]

The amount reported for each segment item is always the measure reported to the chief operating decision maker for the purposes of allocating resources to that segment and assessing its performance. IFRS 8 does not define segment revenue, segment expense, segment result, segment assets or segment liabilities, but does require an explanation of how segment profit or loss, segment assets and segment liabilities are measured for each operating segment. As a consequence, entities have some discretion in determining, for example, what is included in segment profit or loss under IFRS 8, but are limited by their internal reporting practices.

7   Disclosure

7.1   Disclosure – general principle

The overall principle established by IFRS 8 is that entities should disclose information to enable users of their financial statements to evaluate the nature and financial effects of the business activities in which they engage and the economic environments in which they operate. [IFRS 8:20]

To give effect to this overall principle, entities are required to disclose the following:

[IFRS 8:21]

(a)   general information (see **7.2**);

(b)   information about reported segment profit or loss, including specified revenues and expenses included in reported segment profit or loss, segment assets, segment liabilities (see **7.3**) and the basis of measurement (see **7.4**); and

(c)   reconciliations of the totals of segment revenues, reported segment profit or loss, segment assets, segment liabilities, and other material segment items to corresponding entity amounts (see **7.5**).

The information should be reported for each period for which a statement of comprehensive income is presented, with reconciliations of the amounts in the statement of financial position reported for each date at which a statement of financial position is presented. [IFRS 8:21]

Measurement principles for the amounts reported under IFRS 8:21(b) are set out in IFRS 8:25 to 27 (see **section 6**).

Requirements regarding the restatement of prior period segment information are set out in IFRS 8:29 and 30 (see **7.6**).

Additional entity-wide disclosures are also mandated by the Standard (see **7.7**).

The guidance on implementing IFRS 8 includes a number of illustrations of how the disclosure requirements of the Standard might be met. The illustrations are for a single hypothetical entity referred to as Diversified Company. For convenience, these illustrations are included when relevant in **7.2** to **7.7**. Note, however, that the formats in the illustrations are not requirements and that the IASB encourages entities to choose a format that provides the information in the most understandable manner in the specific circumstances. [IFRS 8:IG1]

7.2 General information

7.2.1 Factors used to identify the entity's reportable segments

Entities are required to disclose the factors used to identify the entity's reportable segments, including the basis of organisation (e.g. whether management has chosen to organise the entity around differences in products and services, geographical areas, regulatory environments, or a combination of factors, and whether operating segments have been aggregated). [IFRS 8:22(a)]

Example 7.2.1

Factors that management used to identify the entity's reportable segments (IFRS 8:22(a))

[IFRS 8:IG2]

Diversified Company's reportable segments are strategic business units that offer different products and services. They are managed separately because each business requires different technology and marketing strategies. Most of the businesses were acquired as individual units, and the management at the time of the acquisition was retained.

7.2.2 Judgements made by management in applying aggregation criteria

Entities are required to disclose the judgements made by management in applying the aggregation criteria in IFRS 8:12 (see **5.3**). This disclosure should include:

[IFRS 8:22(aa)]

- a brief description of the operating segments that have been aggregated in this way; and

- the economic indicators that have been assessed in determining that the aggregated operating segments share similar economic characteristics.

> This disclosure requirement is designed to provide users of financial statements with an understanding of the judgements made by management on how (and the reasons why) operating segments have been aggregated. The judgements made by management may relate to the application of any of the criteria in IFRS 8:12 (see **5.3.1**). [IFRS 8:BC30B]

7.2.3 Types of products and services from which revenues are derived

Entities are required to disclose the types of products and services from which each reportable segment derives its revenues. [IFRS 8:22(b)]

Example 7.2.3

Description of the types of products and services from which each reportable segment derives its revenues (IFRS 8:22(b))

[IFRS 8:IG2]

Diversified Company has five reportable segments: car parts, motor vessels, software, electronics and finance. The car parts segment produces replacement parts for sale to car parts retailers. The motor vessels segment produces small motor vessels to serve the offshore oil industry and similar businesses. The software segment produces application software for sale to computer manufacturers and retailers. The electronics segment produces integrated circuits and related products for sale to computer manufacturers. The finance segment is responsible for portions of the company's financial operations including financing customer purchases of products from other segments and property lending operations.

7.3 Information about profit or loss, assets and liabilities

For each reportable segment, entities are required to report a measure of profit or loss. [IFRS 8:23]

Entities are required to report a measure of total assets and liabilities for each reportable segment if such an amount is regularly provided to the chief operating decision maker. [IFRS 8:23]

Entities are also required to disclose the following about each reportable segment if the specified amounts are included in the measure of segment profit or loss reviewed by the chief operating decision maker (or are otherwise regularly provided to the chief operating decision maker, even if not included in that measure of segment profit or loss):

[IFRS 8:23]

(a) revenues from external customers;

(b) revenues from transactions with other operating segments of the same entity;

(c) interest revenue;

(d) interest expense;

(e) depreciation and amortisation;

(f) material items of income and expense disclosed in accordance with paragraph 97 of IAS 1 *Presentation of Financial Statements* (see **5.4.1** in **chapter A4**);

(g) the entity's interest in the profit or loss of associates and joint ventures accounted for by the equity method;

(h) income tax expense or income; and

(i) material non-cash items other than depreciation and amortisation.

Even if the chief operating decision maker is provided with more detailed information about an operating segment (e.g. discrete financial information about specific products), the entity is required to disclose only the financial information regarding the operating segment as a whole. However, disclosure of product information may be required on an entity-wide basis (see **7.7**).

Interest revenue should be reported separately from interest expense for each reportable segment, unless:

[IFRS 8:23]

(a) a majority of the segment's revenues are from interest; and

(b) the chief operating decision maker relies primarily on net interest revenue to assess the performance of the segment and make decisions about resources to be allocated to the segment.

When both of these conditions are met, an entity may report that segment's interest revenue net of its interest expense and disclose that it has done so. [IFRS 8:23]

Entities are required to disclose the following about each reportable segment if the specified amounts are included in the measure of segment assets reviewed by the chief operating decision maker (or are otherwise regularly provided to the chief operating decision maker even if not included in the measure of segment assets):

[IFRS 8:24]

(a) the amount of investment in associates and joint ventures accounted for by the equity method; and

(b) the amounts of additions to non-current assets other than financial instruments, deferred tax assets, net defined benefit assets (relating to post-employment benefit plans – see **chapter A15**) and rights arising under insurance contracts.

Regarding the disclosure of additions to non-current assets, for assets classified according to a liquidity presentation, non-current assets are assets that include amounts expected to be recovered more than twelve months after the reporting period. [Footnote to IFRS 8:24]

Example 7.3

Information about reportable segment profit or loss, assets and liabilities

[IFRS 8:IG3]

The following table illustrates a suggested format for disclosing information about reportable segment profit or loss, assets and liabilities (IFRS 8:23 & 24). The same type of information is required for each year for which a statement of comprehensive income is presented. Diversified Company does not allocate tax expense (tax income) or non-recurring gains and losses to reportable segments. In addition, not all reportable segments have material non-cash items other than depreciation and amortisation in profit or loss. The amounts in this illustration, denominated as 'currency units (CU)', are assumed to be the amounts in reports used by the chief operating decision maker.

	Car parts	Motor vessels	Software	Electronics	Finance	All other	Totals
	CU	CU	CU	CU	CU	CU	CU
Revenues from external customers	3,000	5,000	9,500	12,000	5,000	1,000[a]	35,500
Inter-segment revenues	–	–	3,000	1,500	–	–	4,500
Interest revenue	450	800	1,000	1,500	–	–	3,750

	Car parts	Motor vessels	Software	Electronics	Finance	All other	Totals
	CU	CU	CU	CU	CU	CU	CU
Interest expense	350	600	700	1,100	–	–	2,750
Net interest revenue[b]	–	–	–	–	1,000	–	1,000
Depreciation and amortisation	200	100	50	1,500	1,100	–	2,950
Reportable segment profit	200	70	900	2,300	500	100	4,070
Other material non-cash items:							
Impairment of assets	–	200	–	–	–	–	200
Reportable segment assets	2,000	5,000	3,000	12,000	57,000	2,000	81,000
Expenditures for reportable segment non-current assets	300	700	500	800	600	–	2,900
Reportable segment liabilities	1,050	3,000	1,800	8,000	30,000	–	43,850

[a]   Revenues from segments below the quantitative thresholds are attributable to four operating segments of Diversified Company. Those segments include a small property business, an electronics equipment rental business, a software consulting practice and a warehouse leasing operation. None of those segments has ever met any of the quantitative thresholds for determining reportable segments.

[b]   The finance segment derives a majority of its revenue from interest. Management primarily relies on net interest revenue, not the gross revenue and expense amounts, in managing that segment. Therefore, as permitted by IFRS 8:23, only the net amount is disclosed.

7.4   Explanation of the measurement of segment information

Entities are required to provide an explanation of the measurements of segment profit or loss, segment assets and segment liabilities for each reportable segment. At a minimum, an entity is required to disclose the following:

[IFRS 8:27]

(a) the basis of accounting for any transactions between reportable segments;

(b) the nature of any differences between the measurements of the reportable segments' profits or losses and the entity's profit or loss before income tax expense or income and discontinued operations (if not apparent from the reconciliations required under IFRS 8:28 – see **7.5**). Those differences could include accounting policies and policies for allocation of centrally incurred costs that are necessary for an understanding of the reported segment information;

(c) the nature of any differences between the measurements of the reportable segments' assets and the entity's assets (if not apparent from the reconciliations required under IFRS 8:28 – see **7.5**). Those differences could include accounting policies and policies for allocation of jointly used assets that are necessary for an understanding of the reported segment information;

(d) the nature of any differences between the measurements of the reportable segments' liabilities and the entity's liabilities (if not apparent from the reconciliations required under IFRS 8:28 – see **7.4**). Those differences could include accounting policies and policies for allocation of jointly utilised liabilities that are necessary for an understanding of the reported segment information;

(e) the nature of any changes from prior periods in the measurement methods used to determine reported segment profit or loss and the effect, if any, of those changes on the measure of segment profit or loss; and

(f) the nature and effect of any asymmetrical allocations to reportable segments. For example, an entity might allocate depreciation expense to a segment without allocating the related depreciable assets to that segment.

Example 7.4

Measurement of operating segment profit or loss, assets and liabilities (IFRS 8:27)

[IFRS 8:IG2]

The accounting policies of the operating segments are the same as those described in the significant accounting policies except that pension expense for each operating segment Is recognised and measured on the basis of cash payments to the pension plan. Diversified Company evaluates performance on the basis of profit or loss from operations before tax expense not including non-recurring gains and losses and foreign exchange gains and losses.

Diversified Company accounts for inter-segment sales and transfers as if the sales or transfers were to third parties, i.e. at current market prices.

7.5 Reconciliations

Entities are required to provide reconciliations of all of the following:

[IFRS 8:28]

(a) the total of the reportable segments' revenues to the entity's revenue;

(b) the total of the reportable segments' measures of profit or loss to the entity's profit or loss before tax expense (tax income) and discontinued operations. However, if an entity allocates to reportable segments items such as tax expense (tax income), the entity may reconcile the total of the segments' measures of profit or loss to the entity's profit or loss after those items;

(c) the total of the reportable segments' assets to the entity's assets (if segment assets are reported in accordance with IFRS 8:23);

(d) the total of the reportable segments' liabilities to the entity's liabilities (if segment liabilities are reported in accordance with IFRS 8:23); and

(e) the total of the reportable segments' amounts for every other material item of information disclosed to the corresponding amount for the entity.

For the purposes of these reconciliations, all material reconciling items should be separately identified and described. For example, the amount of each material adjustment needed to reconcile reportable segment profit or loss to the entity's profit or loss arising from different accounting policies should be separately identified and described. [IFRS 8:28]

As discussed at **5.5**, information about other business activities and operating segments that do not meet the quantitative thresholds specified in IFRS 8:13 to 15 and, therefore, are not identified as reportable segments should be combined and disclosed in an 'all other segments' category. This should be reported separately from other reconciling items in the reconciliations of segment amounts to consolidated financial statement amounts required by IFRS 8:28.

Example 7.5

Reconciliations of reportable segment revenues, profit or loss, assets and liabilities

[IFRS 8:IG4]

The following tables illustrate reconciliations of reportable segment revenues, profit or loss, assets and liabilities to the entity's corresponding amounts (IFRS 8:28(a) - (d)). Reconciliations also are required to be shown for every other material item of information disclosed (IFRS 8:28(e)). The entity's financial statements are assumed not to include discontinued operations. As discussed in paragraph IG2 [reproduced as **example 7.4**], the entity recognises and measures pension expense of its reportable segments on the basis of cash payments to the pension plan, and it does not allocate certain items to its reportable segments.

Revenues	CU
Total revenues for reportable segments	39,000
Other revenues	1,000
Elimination of inter-segment revenues	(4,500)
Entity's revenues	35,500

Profit or loss	CU
Total profit or loss for reportable segments	3,970
Other profit or loss	100
Elimination of inter-segment profits	(500)
Unallocated amounts:	
Litigation settlement received	500
Other corporate expenses	(700)
Adjustment to pension expense in consolidation	(250)
Income before income tax expense	3,070

Assets	CU
Total assets for reportable segments	79,000
Other assets	2,000
Elimination of receivable from corporate headquarters	(1,000)
Other unallocated amounts	1,500
Entity's assets	81,500

Liabilities	CU
Total liabilities for reportable segments	43,850
Unallocated defined benefit pension liabilities	25,000
Entity's liabilities	68,850

Other material items	Reportable segment totals	Adjustments	Entity totals
	CU	CU	CU
Interest revenue	3,750	75	3,825
Interest expense	2,750	(50)	2,700
Net interest revenue (finance segment only)	1,000	–	1,000
Expenditures for assets	2,900	1,000	3,900
Depreciation and amortisation	2,950	–	2,950
Impairment of assets	200	–	200

> The reconciling item to adjust expenditures for assets is the amount incurred for the corporate headquarters building, which is not included in segment information. None of the other adjustments are material.

7.6   Restatement of previously reported information

7.6.1   Changes in reportable segments during the period

If an entity changes the structure of its internal organisation in a manner that causes the composition of its reportable segments to change, the corresponding information for earlier periods, including interim periods, should generally be restated. [IFRS 8:29]

IFRS 8 does not require such restatement when the information is not available and the cost to develop it would be excessive. The determination as to whether the information is not available and the cost to develop it would be excessive is made for each individual item of disclosure. [IFRS 8:29]

Following a change in the composition of reportable segments, entities are required to disclose whether they have restated the corresponding items of segment information for earlier periods. [IFRS 8:29]

If an entity has changed the structure of its internal organisation in a manner that causes the composition of its reportable segments to change and if segment information for earlier periods, including interim periods, is not restated to reflect the change, the entity is required to disclose in the year in which the change occurs segment information for the current period on both the old basis and the new basis of segmentation, unless the necessary information is not available and the cost to develop it would be excessive. [IFRS 8:30]

> See **5.8** for a discussion of the exemption provided when the necessary information is not available and the cost to develop it would be excessive.

7.6.2   Changes in reportable segments after the reporting period

> An entity's reportable segments should reflect its organisational structure and the information reviewed by its chief operating decision maker as at the end of the reporting period. An entity's reportable segments should not be amended to reflect changes in its internal organisation after the end of the reporting period but before the financial statements are authorised for issue.
>
> IFRS 8:5(b) states that an operating segment is a component of an entity "whose operating results are regularly reviewed by the entity's chief operating decision maker to make decisions about resources to be allocated to the segment and assess its performance". The chief

operating decision maker's decisions and assessments would have been based on the internal structure that existed at the end of the reporting period, not on a structure that was introduced only after the end of that period.

This conclusion is in keeping with the general principle established in IAS 10 *Events after the Reporting Period* that financial statements should be prepared so as to reflect events occurring up to the end of the reporting period and conditions existing at the end of the reporting period. Note that IAS 10:22 cites a major restructuring after the reporting period as an example of a non-adjusting event.

Any change in an entity's internal organisation that results in a change in the identification of its reportable segments should be reflected in the financial statements for the period in which the reorganisation occurs, including restatement of corresponding information for earlier periods (unless the necessary information is not available and the cost to develop it would be excessive). [IFRS 8:29 & 30]

7.7   Entity-wide disclosures

7.7.1   Entity-wide disclosures – general

In addition to the disclosure requirements for individual segments set out in **7.2** to **7.6**, IFRS 8 sets out a number of entity-wide disclosure requirements that apply to all entities falling within its scope, including those entities that have a single reportable segment. Some entities' business activities are not organised on the basis of differences in related products and services or differences in geographical areas of operations. Such an entity's reportable segments may report revenues from a broad range of essentially different products and services, or more than one of its reportable segments may provide essentially the same products and services. Similarly, an entity's reportable segments may hold assets in different geographical areas and report revenues from customers in different geographical areas, or more than one of its reportable segments may operate in the same geographical area. The information required by IFRS 8:32 to 34 (as outlined in **7.7.2** to **7.7.4**) need be provided only if it is not provided as part of the reportable segment information required by IFRS 8. [IFRS 8:31]

Although the identification of operating segments and information disclosed in respect of those operating segments under IFRS 8 are based on the management approach (see **4.1**), entity-wide disclosures standardise a portion of the segment disclosures between entities. The amounts reported for the entity-wide disclosures should be based on the financial information that is used to produce the IFRS financial statements and not the operating segment note (unless they happen to be the same basis). The result is that the entity-wide disclosures will agree with the corresponding amounts in the IFRS financial statements.

7.7.2   Information about products and services

Entities are required to report the revenues from external customers for each product and service or each group of similar products and services, unless the necessary information is not available and the cost to develop it would be excessive. When these disclosures are not made because the information is not available and the cost to develop it would be excessive, that fact should be disclosed. [IFRS 8:32]

The amounts of revenues to be reported under this requirement are based on the financial information used to produce the entity's financial statements. [IFRS 8:32]

If the entity determines its reportable segments on the basis of products and services and such information is disclosed in the operating segments' disclosure, disclosure of this information need not be repeated in the entity-wide disclosures.

See **5.8** for a discussion of the exemption provided when the necessary information is not available and the cost to develop it would be excessive.

7.7.3   Information about geographical areas

Entities are required to report the following geographical information, unless the necessary information is not available and the cost to develop it would be excessive:

[IFRS 8:33]

(a) revenues from external customers:
   (i)   attributed to the entity's country of domicile; and
   (ii) attributed to all foreign countries in total from which the entity derives revenues;
(b) separate disclosure of revenues from external customers attributed to an individual foreign country, if those revenues are material;
(c) the basis for attributing revenues from external customers to individual countries;

IFRS 8 does not mandate any particular method for allocating 'revenues from external customers' to geographical areas. An entity might choose to disclose this information based on the geographical location of its customers or based on the location where the sale occurred.

(d) non-current assets other than financial instruments, deferred tax assets, net defined benefit assets (relating to post-employment benefit plans), and rights arising under insurance contracts:

    (i) located in the entity's country of domicile; and

    (ii) located in all foreign countries in total in which the entity holds assets; and

(e) separate disclosure of non-current assets in an individual foreign country, if those assets are material.

> IFRS 8 does not specify a threshold for what is 'material' for the purpose of separate disclosure of either revenues from external customers or assets attributed to an individual foreign country. Consistent with the definition of 'material' in IAS 1:7, it will be appropriate to consider both qualitative and quantitative factors in order to assess whether information is material.

The amounts to be reported under IFRS 8:33 are based on the financial information that is used to produce the entity's financial statements. [IFRS 8:33]

If the necessary information is not available and the cost to develop it would be excessive, that fact should be disclosed. [IFRS 8:33]

> See **5.8** for a discussion of the exemption provided when the necessary information is not available and the cost to develop it would be excessive.

Note that, if they wish to do so, entities may provide additional subtotals of geographical information about groups of countries. [IFRS 8:33]

> If the entity determines its reportable segments on a geographical basis and such information is disclosed in the operating segments' disclosure, disclosure of this information need not be repeated in the entity-wide disclosures. However, if the entity manages its business based on geographical regions and determines its reportable segments accordingly, it still must provide separate disclosures required by IFRS 8:33 for each country in which revenues are material. Some entities provide this disclosure by presenting material countries separately with subtotals by region.

Example 7.7.3

Geographical information

[IFRS 8:IG5]

The following illustrates the geographical information required by IFRS 8:33. (Because Diversified Company's reportable segments are based on differences in products and services, no additional disclosures of revenue information about products and services are required (IFRS 8:32).)

Geographical information	Revenues[a]	Non-current assets
	CU	CU
United States	19,000	11,000
Canada	4,200	
China	3,400	6,500
Japan	2,900	3,500
Other countries	6,000	3,000
Total	35,500	24,000

[a]   Revenues are attributed to countries on the basis of the customer's location.

7.7.4   Information about major customers

Under IFRS 8, entities are required to provide information about the extent of their reliance on major customers.

If revenues from transactions with a single external customer amount to 10 per cent or more of an entity's revenues, the entity is required to disclose:

[IFRS 8:34]

(a) that fact;

(b) the total amount of revenues from each such customer; and

(c) the identity of the segment or segments reporting the revenues.

The Standard explicitly states that entities are not required to disclose the identity of a major customer, nor the amount of revenues that each segment reports from that customer. [IFRS 8:34]

For the purposes of these requirements, a group of entities known to a reporting entity to be under common control is considered a single customer. Judgement is required to assess whether a government (including government agencies and similar bodies, whether local, national or international) and entities known to the reporting entity to be under the control of that government are considered a single customer. In assessing this, the reporting entity should consider the extent of economic integration between those entities. [IFRS 8:34]

Example 7.7.4

Information about major customers

[IFRS 8:IG6]

Revenues from one customer of Diversified Company's software and electronics segments represent approximately CU5,000 of the Company's total revenues.

---

8 Future developments

The IASB's post-implementation review of IFRS 8 was completed in 2013. The final report concluded that the benefits of applying the Standard were largely as expected and that overall the Standard achieved its objectives and has improved financial reporting. However, the IASB identified a number of issues that could be considered for improvement and that warrant further investigation. At the time of writing, an exposure draft of changes resulting from the review is expected before the end of 2016.

A31 Earnings per share

Contents

1 Introduction

1.1 Overview of IAS 33

IAS 33 *Earnings Per Share* sets out how to calculate both basic earnings per share (EPS) and diluted EPS. The calculation of basic EPS is based on the weighted average number of ordinary shares outstanding during the period, whereas diluted EPS also includes dilutive potential ordinary shares (such as options and convertible instruments) if they meet specified criteria.

1.2 Amendments to IAS 33 since the last edition of this manual

None. IAS 33 was most recently amended in June 2011.

2 Scope

2.1 Scope – general

IAS 33 applies to:

[IAS 33:2 & 3]

- the separate or individual financial statements of an entity:
  - whose ordinary shares or potential ordinary shares are traded in a public market (a domestic or foreign stock exchange or an over-the-counter market, including local and regional markets); or
  - that files, or is in the process of filing, its financial statements with a securities commission or other regulatory organisation for the purpose of issuing ordinary shares in a public market;
- the consolidated financial statements of a group with a parent:
  - whose ordinary shares or potential ordinary shares are traded in a public market (a domestic or foreign stock exchange or an over-the-counter market, including local and regional markets); or
  - that files, or is in the process of filing, its financial statements with a securities commission or other regulatory organisation for the purpose of issuing ordinary shares in a public market; and
- entities voluntarily choosing to present EPS information.

For a group, it is the shares of the parent that must be considered. Thus, the consolidated financial statements for an unlisted group that includes a listed subsidiary is not automatically within the scope of the Standard.

The scope of the Standard includes entities that are in the process of filing financial statements with a securities commission or other regulatory organisation for the purpose of issuing ordinary shares in a public market. This means that EPS information is required in financial statements prepared for the purpose of the issue of a prospectus.

2.2 Puttable instruments presented as equity

Some entities with a mutual form of ownership have no instruments in issue that can be presented as equity under IFRSs (see **2.1** in **chapter B3** or, for entities that have not yet adopted IFRS 9 *Financial Instruments*, **2.1** in **chapter C3**). This continues to be case despite the amendments to IAS 32 *Financial Instruments: Presentation* in February 2008, which resulted in more puttable financial instruments and obligations arising on liquidation being classified as equity.

IAS 32:11 recognises that puttable instruments and obligations arising on liquidation that are presented as equity following the 2008 amendments still meet the definition of a financial liability but are presented as equity as an exception. Because IAS 33 was not amended when the amendments to IAS 32 were issued, there had been confusion as to whether IAS 33 would apply to an entity which previously had no equity but which, as a result of the amendments, reclassified puttable instruments or obligations arising at liquidation as equity. In August 2008, the IASB published an exposure draft (ED) *Simplifying Earnings per Share*, which proposed to amend IAS 33 to make clear that entities that previously had no equity, but would present instruments as equity following the IAS 32 amendments, should apply IAS 33 when the amended IAS 32 is applied. However, this exposure draft was never finalised as a Standard and, therefore, those entities with puttable instruments presented as equity that have no other equity do not appear to be required to present EPS information.

2.3 Mutual-to-shares conversion

When an entity with no instruments presented as equity converts from a mutual form of ownership to share ownership that is classified as equity, and it falls within the scope of IAS 33, the EPS amounts presented should be based on earnings subsequent to conversion because the entity only has equity instruments outstanding after the date of conversion. As a result, the EPS amounts presented in the year of conversion may not be comparable to EPS amounts presented in subsequent years. Further, the EPS amounts presented may not reflect the expected relationship between earnings for the period and the amount of outstanding shares at the end of the reporting period. In such circumstances, the description of the EPS measure in the statement of comprehensive income (or, if applicable, the separate statement of profit or loss – see **2.5**) should inform the reader of the unique nature of

EPS in the year of conversion, and the method of presentation should be described in the notes to the financial statements.

2.4 Entities voluntarily presenting EPS information

IAS 33 requires that any entity that presents EPS information does so in accordance with that Standard. Therefore, an entity whose ordinary shares or potential ordinary shares are not publicly traded that voluntarily presents EPS information is bound by the requirements of IAS 33. [IAS 33:3]

2.5 Consolidated and separate financial statements

When an entity presents both consolidated financial statements and separate financial statements in accordance with IFRS 10 *Consolidated Financial Statements* and IAS 27 *Separate Financial Statements*, respectively:

[IAS 33:4]

- the disclosures required by IAS 33 need only be given in respect of the consolidated information;

- if the entity chooses to disclose EPS information based on its separate financial statements, it is required to prepare that information in accordance with IAS 33 and to present it only in its statement of comprehensive income; and

- EPS information based on the separate financial statements should not be presented in the consolidated financial statements (either in the statement of comprehensive income or in the notes).

If an entity presents profit or loss in a separate statement (see **5.1** in **chapter A4**), it should present EPS information only in that separate statement. [IAS 33:4A]

2.6 Shares listed but not intended to be traded

Example 2.6

Shares listed but not intended to be traded

The shares of Company A are listed on the Luxembourg exchange. Company A has completed a listing for marketing purposes only because its investors (which are pension funds) are restricted by their governing laws to investing in listed entities. It is not expected that these shares will be traded.

Although these shares are not expected to be traded, the entity is within the scope of IAS 33 and EPS should be presented in accordance with that Standard. The notion of 'publicly traded' requires only an ability to trade the shares publicly, not the actual trading of shares.

---

3 Definitions

3.1 Ordinary share

IAS 33 defines an ordinary share as an equity instrument that is subordinate to all other classes of equity instruments. [IAS 33:5] An equity instrument is defined in IAS 32 *Financial Instruments: Presentation* as any contract that evidences a residual interest in the assets of an entity after deducting all of its liabilities. [IAS 32:11] IAS 33 explains that ordinary shares participate in profit for the period only after other types of shares (such as preference shares) have participated. Ordinary shares of the same class have the same rights to receive dividends, but it is possible for an entity to have more than one class of ordinary shares. [IAS 33:6]

> Entities will sometimes issue preference shares with many of the characteristics of ordinary shares. The terms of such preference shares will need to be evaluated carefully. If they share the characteristics of ordinary shares and have no preference attributed to them, such instruments should be considered as ordinary shares regardless of the legal name assigned to them (see **4.3.4**).

3.2 Potential ordinary share

3.2.1 Definition of potential ordinary share – general

A potential ordinary share is defined as a financial instrument or other contract that may entitle its holder to ordinary shares. [IAS 33:5] Examples of potential ordinary shares include:

[IAS 33:7]

- financial liabilities or equity instruments, including preference shares, that are convertible into ordinary shares;

- options and warrants (i.e. financial instruments issued by the entity that give the holder the right to purchase ordinary shares); and

- shares that would be issued upon the satisfaction of conditions resulting from contractual arrangements, such as the purchase of a business or other assets.

> The concept of a potential ordinary share has evolved to meet the reporting needs of investors in entities that have issued certain types of convertible and other complex securities. The holders of these instruments can expect to participate in the appreciation in value of the ordinary shares resulting principally from the earnings and earnings potential of the issuing entity. The attractiveness of these instruments to investors is often based on the potential right to participate in increases in the earnings potential of the entity, rather than on fixed returns or

other senior security characteristics. The value of instruments that are considered potential ordinary shares is derived largely from the value of the ordinary shares to which they relate. Changes in the value of such instruments tend to reflect changes in the value of the ordinary shares.

3.2.2 Derivatives over own equity

If an entity enters into a derivative over its own ordinary shares that may entitle the holder to ordinary shares, that derivative is a potential ordinary share if the settlement terms of the derivative may result in the delivery of ordinary shares of the entity. The only exception applies to forward purchase contracts and written put options over own ordinary shares when the issuer regards the shares to be delivered under the forward contract or written put option as effectively purchased upon entering into the contract (see **4.3.2.9**). In this case only, the ordinary shares subject to the contract are deemed as acquired, resulting in a reduction in the number of shares outstanding for both basic and diluted EPS.

If, however, the settlement terms of the derivative permit only net settlement in cash or other financial assets, and/or settlement by the exchange of gross amounts of cash or other financial assets, the instrument does not 'entitle its holder to ordinary shares' and is not a potential ordinary share.

If there is a settlement choice, either by the issuer or the holder, as to whether ordinary shares will be delivered under the contract, the arrangement is still a potential ordinary share because there is the potential for delivery of ordinary shares under the contract. However, the detailed computation of diluted EPS differs according to whether the settlement alternatives are at the option of the holder or the issuer (see **5.6.5**).

4   Calculation of basic earnings per share

4.1   Formula for calculating basic earnings per share

Basic EPS is calculated as follows.

[IAS 33:10]

$$\frac{\text{Profit (loss) attributable to ordinary equity holders of the parent entity}}{\text{Weighted average number of ordinary shares outstanding during the period}}$$

The objective of basic EPS information is to provide a measure of the interests of each ordinary share of a parent entity in the performance of the entity over the reporting period. [IAS 33:11] Basic EPS amounts are required to be calculated for:

[IAS 33:9]

- profit or loss attributable to ordinary equity holders of the parent entity; and

- if presented, profit or loss from continuing operations attributable to those equity holders.

4.2 Earnings numerator

4.2.1 Starting point for the earnings numerator

The starting point for the earnings numerator (for results both from continuing operations and for the entity as a whole) is the profit or loss after tax attributable to the equity holders of the parent entity (i.e. excluding the amount attributable to non-controlling interests). [IAS 33:12]

4.2.2 Non-controlling interests

The profit or loss attributable to equity holders of the parent will be readily available, because it is required under IAS 1 *Presentation of Financial Statements* to be presented in the statement of comprehensive income (or, when applicable, the separate statement of profit or loss) separately from the profit or loss attributable to non-controlling interests. [IAS 1:83] When applicable, however, the profit for the period from continuing operations presented in the statement of comprehensive income (which is before the allocation to non-controlling interests) will need to be adjusted for the non-controlling interests' share of those earnings in order to arrive at the amount attributable to equity holders of the parent.

4.2.3 The impact of preference shares

4.2.3.1 Requirement to adjust for amounts relating to preference shares

The profit or loss attributable to the equity holders of the parent entity will already be after deduction of dividends and other profit or loss effects relating to preference shares *classified as liabilities*. [IAS 33:13] For the purposes of calculating basic EPS, the profit or loss attributable to the equity holders of the parent entity is further adjusted for the following after-tax amounts relating to preference shares *classified as equity*:

[IAS 33:12]

- preference dividends (see **4.2.3.2**);

- differences arising on the settlement of such preference shares (see **4.2.3.3**); and

- other similar effects of such preferences shares (see **4.2.3.4**).

4.2.3.2   Preference dividends

The after-tax amount of preference dividends to be deducted in determining the profit or loss attributable to ordinary equity holders of the parent entity is:

[IAS 33:14]

- for non-cumulative preference shares classified as equity, the after-tax amount of preference dividends declared in respect of the period; and

- for cumulative preference shares classified as equity, the full after-tax amount of the required preference dividends for the period (whether or not declared). This does not include amounts paid or declared on cumulative preference shares in the current period in respect of previous periods.

For non-cumulative preference shares, dividends 'declared in respect of the period' are any dividends on the preference shares that are recognised as a liability during the current period, plus any dividends paid during the period that were not accrued at the end of the prior period. They do not include dividends declared after the end of the period that, in accordance with IAS 10 *Events after the Reporting Period*, are not recognised as a liability, or dividends accrued at the end of the prior period whether or not actually paid in the current period.

Example 4.2.3.2

Liquidating dividends on preference shares

Company X issued one share of Series A Non-Voting Convertible Preference Shares for CU1,000,000 that has a liquidation preference of CU1,000,000, plus a 12 per cent cumulative dividend entitlement from the issue date. Company X also issued one share of Series B Non-Voting Convertible Preference Shares for CU2,000,000 that has a liquidation preference of CU2,000,000, with a non-cumulative dividend entitlement at a rate of 5 per cent per annum plus a 12 per cent cumulative dividend entitlement from the issue date. All payments on both preference shares are at the discretion of Company X and, therefore, they are both presented as equity.

In calculating 'profit or loss attributable to ordinary shareholders' for EPS purposes, Company X should not deduct the 12 per cent cumulative liquidating dividends for either the Series A or Series B shares. Although cumulative, the liquidating dividends are intended to provide a preference to the Series A and Series B preference shareholders in the event of a liquidation of Company X and, therefore, should not be adjusted in determining profit or loss attributable to ordinary shareholders until a liquidating event occurs.

4.2.3.3   Differences arising on the settlement of preference shares

Differences may arise on the settlement of preference shares in the following circumstances:

- when the preference shares are repurchased under a tender offer, and the fair value of the consideration paid to the preference shareholders differs from their carrying amount. Any excess of the fair value of the consideration over the carrying amount represents a return to the holders of the preference shares and is adjusted against retained earnings in the period of repurchase. This amount is deducted in calculating the earnings numerator for basic EPS. [IAS 33:16] Any excess of the carrying amount of the shares over the fair value of the consideration is added in calculating the earnings numerator for basic EPS; [IAS 33:18] and

- on early conversion of convertible preference shares, as a result of favourable changes to the original conversion terms or the payment of additional consideration. The excess of the fair value of the ordinary shares or other consideration paid over the fair value of the ordinary shares issuable under the original conversion terms is a return to the preference shareholders, and is deducted in calculating the earnings numerator for basic EPS. [IAS 33:17]

Some entities issue classes of shares characterised as 'tracking' or 'targeted' shares to measure the performance of a specific business unit or activity of the entity. The terms of tracking shares often allow the entity, at its option, to exchange or redeem one class of tracking shares for another class of tracking shares, such that the entity would have one less class of ordinary shares outstanding. The terms of this feature generally require a premium to be paid to the class being redeemed as a result of the transaction. In the period of redemption, profit or loss attributable to ordinary shareholders (whose shares are being used for the redemption) should be reduced by the premium over market price paid to redeem the tracking shares. The holders of the tracking shares being redeemed have received a benefit that constitutes an additional contractual return to them. **Example 4.2.3.3A** illustrates the treatment of this premium for the purpose of calculating EPS.

Example 4.2.3.3A

Premium paid on redemption of tracking shares

Company X has two classes of ordinary shares outstanding that separately track the results of operations of two different businesses, Company A and Company B. Company X decides to redeem all of its outstanding Company B tracking shares in exchange for Company A tracking shares. The terms of the Company B shares being redeemed provide Company X with the right to redeem the Company B tracking shares, at its discretion, by issuing its Company A tracking shares with a market price equal to a 15 per cent premium over the market price of the Company B tracking shares at the time of redemption. As such, the fair value of Company A tracking shares to be exchanged for the Company B tracking shares will exceed the fair value of the Company B tracking shares by 15 per cent on the date the redemption is announced.

When calculating basic EPS for the period in which the Company B tracking shares are redeemed, the profit or loss attributable to the Company A tracking shareholders should be reduced by the amount of the 15 per cent premium.

Example 4.2.3.3B

Premium paid by a parent to redeem preference shares issued by a subsidiary

Company P, a publicly traded entity, has a wholly-owned subsidiary, Company S. Company S has preference shares outstanding held by parties outside the group that are classified as equity. The preference shares are redeemable at the option of Company S (with Company P's consent) in whole or in part, at varying dates, at CU100 per share plus accumulated and unpaid distributions to the date fixed for redemption.

Company P decides to acquire Company S's preference shares. The premium paid by Company P to the third-party preference shareholders on the acquisition of Company S's preference shares is not recognised in the consolidated statement of comprehensive income because this represents a transaction with shareholders. Accordingly, the consolidated entity does not recognise in its statement of comprehensive income any gain or loss from the acquisition.

The premium paid to redeem Company S's preference shares should be deducted in computing profit or loss attributable to ordinary shareholders in the calculation of EPS in Company P's consolidated financial statements. The premium represents a return on investment to the holders of the preference shares and is not available to ordinary shareholders, similar to preference share dividends and accretion charges. Consistent with the view that the subsidiary's preference shares represent a non-controlling interest in the parent's consolidated financial statements, dividends or accretions to a redemption amount should adjust earnings allocated to non-controlling interests when computing profit or loss attributable to ordinary shareholders of Company P in the calculation of earnings per share in Company P's consolidated financial statements.

4.2.3.4   Other effects of preference shares

The results for the period will also be adjusted for other appropriations recognised in respect of preference shares classified as equity. For example, preference shares may provide for a low initial dividend to compensate the entity for selling the shares at a discount, or an above-market dividend in later periods to compensate investors for purchasing the shares at a premium. (These are sometimes called increasing rate preference shares.) When such shares are classified as equity, the discount or premium on issue is amortised to retained earnings using the effective interest method and treated as a preference dividend for the purposes of calculating basic earnings per share. [IAS 33:15]

The following example, reproduced from Example 1 of the illustrative examples accompanying IAS 33, illustrates the required adjustments in respect of increasing rate preference shares.

Example 4.2.3.4

Increasing rate preference shares

[IAS 33 Illustrative examples: Example 1]

Entity D issued non-convertible, non-redeemable class A cumulative preference shares of CU100 par value on 1 January 20X1. The class A preference shares are entitled to a cumulative annual dividend of CU7 per share starting in 20X4.

At the time of issue, the market rate dividend yield on the class A preference shares was 7 per cent a year. Thus, Entity D could have expected to receive proceeds of approximately CU100 per class A preference share if the dividend rate of CU7 per share had been in effect at the date of issue.

In consideration of the dividend payment terms, however, the class A preference shares were issued at CU81.63 per share, i.e. at a discount of CU18.37 per share. The issue price can be calculated by taking the present value of CU100, discounted at 7 per cent over a three-year period.

Because the shares are classified as equity, the original issue discount is amortised to retained earnings using the effective interest method and treated as a preference dividend for earnings per share purposes. To calculate basic earnings per share, the following imputed dividend per class A preference share is deducted to determine the profit or loss attributable to ordinary equity holders of the parent entity:

Year	Carrying amount of class A preference shares on 1 January	Imputed dividend[a]	Carrying amount of class A preference shares 31 December[b]	Dividend paid
	CU	CU	CU	CU
20X1	81.63	5.71	87.34	–
20X2	87.34	6.12	93.46	–

Year	Carrying amount of class A preference shares on 1 January CU	Imputed dividend[a] CU	Carrying amount of class A preference shares 31 December[b] CU	Dividend paid CU
20X3	93.46	6.54	100.00	–
Thereafter	100.00	7.00	107.00	(7.00)

[a] At 7%
[b] This is before dividend payment.

4.2.3.5 Contingent dividends on preference shares

Example 4.2.3.5

Contingent dividends on preference shares

Company X, a publicly traded entity, issued to Company Y convertible preference shares that earn a 7 per cent dividend per year although payment is at the discretion of Company X. Conversion is at Company Y's option. Company X may elect to redeem the preference shares at any time. The terms of the preference shares state that if Company Y were to convert the preference shares into a fixed number of ordinary shares of Company X, then Company Y would not receive any preference share dividends, including any cumulative dividends in arrears. Conversion is at a fixed conversion price determined at the date of issue. If, however, Company X redeems the shares from Company Y, then Company Y would receive cumulative dividends, including any in arrears. Company X classifies the convertible preference shares as equity.

IAS 33:12 requires that preference share dividends should be subtracted from net income available to ordinary shareholders for the purposes of calculating basic EPS. IAS 33:14 clarifies that the dividends to be subtracted are (1) the after-tax amount of any preference dividends on non-cumulative shares declared in respect of the period, and (2) the after-tax amount of any preference dividends for cumulative preference shares required for the period, regardless of whether the dividends have been declared (see **4.2.3.2**). However, IAS 33 does not address how to account for dividend payments contingent on future events. In Company X's situation, the future event is whether Company X redeems the preference shares or Company Y converts the preference shares.

The dividends potentially will be paid in the future unless Company Y elects to convert. If Company Y elects to convert the preference shares into ordinary shares of Company X, Company Y no longer has the right to receive the preference share dividends, including any in arrears.

By analogy to how IAS 33 treats convertible debt when interest is accrued until conversion occurs, dividends on the preference shares for each period should be deducted from income available to ordinary shareholders for computing basic EPS until the conversion occurs, regardless of whether the dividends have been declared. If conversion occurs, thus removing Company Y's right to receive the dividends, including those in arrears, the EPS calculation should be adjusted in accordance with IAS 33:18 in the period that conversion occurs (see **4.2.3.3**). Company X should not restate prior EPS amounts.

4.2.3.6   Preference shares issued by a subsidiary to its parent

Example 4.2.3.6

Preference shares issued by a subsidiary to its parent

Company S is a majority-owned subsidiary of Company P. Company P issued CU100 million 5 per cent preference shares to the public. In connection with the offering, Company S issued CU100 million 5 per cent preference shares to Company P (with the same terms and features as the preference shares issued to the public) primarily as a means of funding the dividends on the preference shares issued to the public, because Company P is a holding company with no independent operations or cash flows. The preference shares issued to the public are not convertible, participating, or mandatorily redeemable, nor are any of the shares held by the non-controlling interests in Company S.

The preference shares issued by Company P to the public reduce basic and diluted EPS because the dividends on those shares are deducted to determine the numerator for both measures. The preference shares issued by Company S do not affect the computation of basic and diluted EPS in Company P's consolidated financial statements because preference shares issued by a subsidiary to its parent and related dividends are eliminated on consolidation.

4.2.4   Different classes of shares

4.2.4.1   Earnings per share required to be presented for each class of ordinary shares

IAS 33 requires that EPS should be calculated and presented for each class of ordinary shares that has a different right to share in the profit for the period. [IAS 33:66]

4.2.4.2   Participating equity instruments and two-class ordinary shares

The application guidance set out in Appendix A to IAS 33 discusses the circumstances when the equity of an entity includes:

[IAS 33:A13]

- instruments that participate in dividends with ordinary shares according to a predetermined formula (e.g. two for one) with, at times, an upper limit on the extent of participation (e.g. up to, but not beyond, a specified amount per share); and
- a class of ordinary shares with a different dividend rate from that of another class of ordinary shares, but without prior or senior rights.

Instruments that participate in dividends with ordinary shares according to a predetermined formula are described as 'participating equity instruments'. When there is a class of ordinary shares classified as equity but entitled to a different dividend rate from that for another class of ordinary shares classified as equity, these are described as 'two-class ordinary shares'.

> Care is required in determining whether an instrument is a participating equity instrument. An instrument may participate in dividends with ordinary shares according to a predetermined formula, but this of itself does not mean it is a participating equity instrument. Such instruments may not meet the definition of ordinary shares because they are not subordinate to all other classes of equity instrument.

For the purposes of calculating diluted EPS, conversion is assumed for those instruments described in IAS 33:A13 that are convertible into ordinary shares, if the effect is dilutive. For those instruments that are not convertible into a class of ordinary shares, profit or loss for the period is allocated to the different classes of shares and participating equity instruments in accordance with their dividend rights or other rights to participate in undistributed earnings. [IAS 33.A14]

In order to allocate the earnings of the entity between these classes of shares, the following guidance is provided:

[IAS 33:A14]

- the profit or loss attributable to ordinary equity holders of the parent entity is adjusted by the amount of dividends declared in the period for each class of shares and by the contractual amount of dividends (or interest on participating bonds) that must be paid for the period (e.g. unpaid cumulative dividends);

- the remaining profit or loss is allocated to ordinary shares and participating equity instruments to the extent that each instrument shares in earnings, as if all of the profit or loss for the period had been distributed. The total profit or loss allocated to each class of equity instrument is determined by adding together the amount allocated for dividends and the amount allocated for a participation feature; and

- the total amount of profit or loss allocated to each class of equity instrument is divided by the number of outstanding instruments to which the earnings are allocated to determine the earnings per share for the instrument.

The following example, reproduced from Example 11 of the illustrative examples accompanying IAS 33, illustrates the required treatment.

Example 4.2.4.2

Participating equity instruments and two-class ordinary shares

[IAS 33 Illustrative examples: Example 11]

Profit attributable to equity holders of the parent entity	CU100,000
Ordinary shares outstanding	10,000
Non-convertible preference shares	6,000
Non-cumulative annual dividend on preference shares (before any dividend is paid on ordinary shares)	CU5.50 per share

After ordinary shares have been paid a dividend of CU2.10 per share, the preference shares participate in any additional dividends on a 20:80 ratio with ordinary shares (ie after preference and ordinary shares have been paid dividends of CU5.50 and CU2.10 per share, respectively, preference shares participate in any additional dividends at a rate of one-fourth of the amount paid to ordinary shares on a per-share basis).

Dividends on preference shares paid	CU33,000 (CU5.50 per share)
Dividends on ordinary shares paid	CU21,000 (CU2.10 per share)

Basic earnings per share is calculated as follows:

	CU	CU
Profit attributable to equity holders of the parent entity		100,000
Less dividends paid:		
Preference	33,000	
Ordinary	21,000	(54,000)
Undistributed earnings		46,000

Allocation of undistributed earnings:

Allocation per ordinary share = A

Allocation per preference share = B; B = ¼ A

$(A \times 10,000) + (1/4 \times A \times 6,000) = CU46,000$

$A = CU46,000/(10,000 + 1,500)$

$A = CU4.00$

$B = ¼ A$

$B = CU1.00$

Basic per share amounts:		
	Preference shares	**Ordinary shares**
Distributed earnings	CU5.50	CU2.10
Undistributed earnings	CU1.00	CU4.00
Totals	CU6.50	CU6.10

4.2.4.3   Impact of dividend-paying share-based payment awards

Example 4.2.4.3A

Share-based payment awards – employees receive cash dividends that do not need to be returned to the entity if the employee forfeits the award

Company B grants share options to its employees, which will only vest if the employee remains employed for three years. The employees receive dividends on the options in cash based on a predetermined formula. If the options do not vest, the employee retains the dividends paid.

Share-based payment awards that accrue cash dividends based on a predetermined formula (whether paid or unpaid) any time the ordinary shareholders receive dividends – when those dividends do not need to be returned to the entity if the employee forfeits the award – are considered participating securities. Because the awards are considered participating securities, the entity issuing the awards is required to apply the two-class method discussed in IAS 33:A13 and A14 when computing basic and diluted EPS. (See **4.2.4.2** for a discussion of the two-class method.)

Example 4.2.4.3B

Share-based payment awards – employees receive a reduction in the exercise price of the award

Assume the same facts as in **example 4.2.4.3A** except that the dividends to which the employees are entitled are applied to reduce the exercise price of the options.

When dividends are transferred to the holder of a share-based payment award in the form of a reduction in the exercise price of the award, this is not considered a participation right because it does not represent a non-forfeitable right to participate in profit or loss attributable to the ordinary equity holders of the parent absent the exercise of the award. Accordingly, such a share-based payment award is *not* considered a participating security. Because the award is not a participating security, the entity issuing the award is not required to apply the two-class method when computing basic and diluted EPS.

However, an entity would include such share-based payment awards in the computation of diluted EPS using the treasury stock method discussed in IAS 33:45 to 48, assuming their effect is dilutive (see **5.2.4**).

4.2.5 Basic earnings per share and mandatorily convertible bonds

Example 4.2.5

Basic earnings per share and mandatorily convertible bonds

Entity A has issued a mandatorily convertible instrument that carries a fixed coupon payable up to the date the instrument converts into a fixed number of Entity A's equity shares. At initial recognition, the instrument is classified as a compound instrument in accordance with IAS 32 *Financial Instruments: Presentation* with separate recognition of:

- a liability equal to the present value of the interest payments due under the instrument (the liability component); and
- an equity component measured at the fair value of the instrument as a whole less the amount recognised as a liability.

Subsequently, the liability component is measured at amortised cost in accordance with IFRS 9 *Financial Instruments* (or, for entities that have not yet adopted IFRS 9, IAS 39 *Financial Instruments: Recognition and Measurement*) and the effective interest rate on the financial liability is recognised as an interest expense in profit or loss.

IAS 33:23 requires "[o]rdinary shares that will be issued upon the conversion of a mandatorily convertible instrument [to be] included in the calculation of basic earnings per share [EPS] from the date the contract is entered into" (see **4.3.2.1**). Therefore, when calculating basic EPS in the periods between the date of issue of the mandatorily convertible instrument and the date of conversion, Entity A adjusts the denominator for the number of shares to be delivered under the terms of the instrument.

When calculating basic EPS in the periods between the date of issue of the mandatorily convertible instrument and the date of conversion, Entity A should *not* also adjust the earnings numerator by adding back the interest expense recognised in profit or loss in respect of the liability component of the instrument. The earnings numerator for basic EPS should be after deduction of the interest expense recognised in respect of the liability component.

Although IAS 33:23 specifically refers to adjustments to the EPS denominator for mandatorily convertible instruments, no reference is made to such instruments in the paragraphs of the Standard (IAS 33:12 to 18) dealing with adjustments to the earnings numerator; therefore, IAS 33 does not require or permit an adjustment to earnings in respect of the interest cost recognised in profit or loss.

This is consistent with the requirements of IAS 33:13, which states as follows.

"*All items of* income and expense attributable to ordinary equity holders of the parent entity that are recognised in a period, including tax expense and dividends on preference shares classified as liabilities are included in the determination of profit or loss for the period attributable to ordinary equity holders of the parent entity." [Emphasis added]

Note that the treasury stock method described in **example 5.5.3.6** and the if-converted method described at **5.2.4** apply only in determining diluted EPS.

4.3 Number of shares

4.3.1 *Weighted average number of ordinary shares outstanding during the period*

The number of shares used in the denominator for basic EPS should be the weighted average number of ordinary shares outstanding during the period. [IAS 33:19]

The weighted average number of ordinary shares outstanding during the period is the number of shares outstanding at the beginning of the period, adjusted by the number of ordinary shares bought back or issued during the period multiplied by a time-weighting factor. [IAS 33:20]

Adjusting the number of ordinary shares during the period on a time-weighted basis ensures that changes in the capital structure of the entity do not result in misleading measures of EPS being reported. Time apportioning the number of shares ensures that an increase in resources due to a capital raising is apportioned to the period when that capital is available for generating earnings. Conversely, an outflow of resources due to a reduction in capital (e.g. a share buy-back) is apportioned to the period when the resources used for buying capital are no longer available for generating earnings.

The calculation of the weighted average is based on all ordinary shares outstanding during the period. Whether or not a particular class or tranche of shares ranked for dividends in respect of the period is irrelevant (except in the case of partly paid shares – see **4.3.2.4**).

The time-weighting factor is:

[IAS 33:20]

$$\frac{\text{Number of days the shares are outstanding}}{\text{Number of days in the period}}$$

Although the Standard defines the time-weighting factor as being determined on a daily basis, it acknowledges that a reasonable approximation of the weighted average is adequate in many circumstances. [IAS 33:20]

Depending on the relative size of share movements, this might, for example, be based on the number of months for which shares were outstanding.

The following example, reproduced from Example 2 of the illustrative examples accompanying IAS 33, illustrates the calculation of the weighted average number of shares. Note that outstanding shares are calculated on a monthly, rather than a daily, basis.

Example 4.3.1

Weighted average number of ordinary shares

[IAS 33 Illustrative examples: Example 2]

		Shares issued	Treasury shares[a]	Shares outstanding
1 January 20X1	Balance at beginning of year	2,000	300	1,700
31 May 20X1	Issue of new shares for cash	800	–	2,500
1 December 20X1	Purchase of treasury shares for cash	–	250	2,250
31 December 20X1	Balance at year end	2,800	550	2,250

Calculation of weighted average:

$(1{,}700 \times 5/12) + (2{,}500 \times 6/12) + (2{,}250 \times 1/12) = 2{,}146$ shares *or*

$(1{,}700 \times 12/12) + (800 \times 7/12) - (250 \times 1/12) = 2{,}146$ shares

[a] Treasury shares are equity instruments reacquired and held by the issuing entity itself or by its subsidiaries.

4.3.2 Timing for inclusion of new shares

4.3.2.1 Timing for inclusion of new shares – general

IAS 33 also provides guidance on determining the date from which the shares are to be considered outstanding and therefore included in the weighted average number of shares for the EPS calculation.

In general, shares are to be considered outstanding from the date that the consideration for the shares becomes receivable, which is usually the date of their issue. The specific terms and conditions attaching to the issue should be examined, however, to ensure that the substance of any contract associated with the issue prevails over its legal form. [IAS 33:21]

The following table illustrates the most common circumstances in which shares are issued, and the date from which such shares are to be considered outstanding, as required by IAS 33:21 to 23. **Sections 4.3.2.2** to **4.3.2.9** examine some of these rules in greater detail.

Consideration for issue of shares	Date from which the shares are included in the weighted average computation
Cash	Date cash is receivable (see **4.3.2.2**)
Voluntary reinvestment of dividends on ordinary or preference shares (scrip dividend)	Date when dividends are reinvested
Debt instrument converted to ordinary shares	Date interest on debt instrument ceases to accrue
Substitution for interest or principal on other financial instruments	Date interest on other financial instruments ceases to accrue
Exchange for the settlement of a liability of the entity	Settlement date of the liability
Conversion of mandatorily convertible instrument	Date the contract to issue the convertible instrument is entered into
Acquisition of an asset other than cash	Date the acquisition is recognised
Business combination (see **4.3.2.3**)	Acquisition date
Rendering of services to the entity	As the services are rendered

4.3.2.2   Shares issued for cash

Even with the guidance outlined in **4.3.2.1**, some care may be required in determining the date from which shares issued for cash should be included. **Example 4.3.2.2** illustrates one such circumstance.

Example 4.3.2.2

Shares issued for cash

An entity is making a rights issue. Provisional allotment letters for the new shares are posted on 19 October 20X1. Shareholders wishing to take up their entitlement must return the provisional allotment letter together with a remittance for the full amount payable so as to be received not later than 3pm on 17 November 20X1. Consequently, the entity will receive cash on a number of days, up to and including 17 November 20X1.

IAS 33:21 requires that shares issued in exchange for cash be included in the weighted average calculation from the date the cash is receivable. In this example, 17 November 20X1 is the date the cash is receivable (because that is the date by which the entity has asked to receive the cash and if no cash was received until that date, the entity could still validly issue the shares). Accordingly, the shares should be included in the weighted average calculation from 17 November 20X1 (the end of the subscription period).

Arrangements for share issues are often more complex in practice and the date the cash is receivable is not necessarily the end of the subscription period in all cases. All facts and circumstances (including an analysis of the legal framework) should be considered in order to determine the date the cash is receivable.

4.3.2.3   Business combinations

When ordinary shares are issued as part of the consideration transferred in a business combination, they are included in the weighted average number of shares from the acquisition date (which is defined in IFRS 3 *Business Combinations* as the date on which the acquirer obtains control of the acquiree). This is because the acquirer incorporates into its statement of comprehensive income the results of the acquired entity's operations from that date. [IAS 33:22]

4.3.2.4   Partly paid shares

Partly paid shares are treated as a fraction of an ordinary share to the extent that they are entitled to participate in dividends relative to a fully paid-up ordinary share during the period. [IAS 33:A15]

As can be seen from the table set out at **4.3.2.1**, the thrust of IAS 33 is to include shares in the calculation of EPS from the date the share proceeds start to generate earnings. The Standard's treatment of partly paid shares is therefore surprising. Rather than treat partly paid shares as a fraction of a share based on the proportion of the proceeds received, the Standard requires them to be treated as a fraction of a share to the extent that they are entitled to participate in dividends relative to a fully paid-up ordinary share during the period. In contrast, shares that are fully paid-up are included in the calculation from the date the consideration is receivable, irrespective of whether they rank for dividend. For example, two CU1 shares, each not ranking for dividend, one CU1 paid and the other CU0.99 paid, will be treated differently in the computation of basic EPS. Both have contributed to earnings but, while the first is included in basic EPS, the second is excluded.

Example 4.3.2.4

Partly paid shares

At 1 January 20X2, an entity has 1,000 ordinary shares outstanding. It issues 400 new ordinary shares at 1 October 20X2. The subscription price is CU2.00 per share. At the date of issue, each shareholder pays CU0.50. The balance of CU1.50 per share will be paid during 20X3. Each partly paid share is entitled to dividends in proportion to the percentage of the issue price paid up on the share.

In accordance with IAS 33:A15 (see above) and IAS 33:A16 (see **5.11**), the new shares issued should be included in the calculation of the weighted average number of shares as a fraction of a share to the extent that they are entitled to participate in dividends relative to a fully paid-up ordinary share during the period. In this example, dividend rights are in proportion to the percentage of the issue price paid on the share. The calculation of the weighted average number of shares is therefore as follows.

Date/description	Shares	Fraction of period	Weighted average shares
At 1 January 20X2	1,000	9/12	750
Issue of new shares for cash*	100		
At 1 October 20X2	1,100	3/12	275
Weighted average number of shares			1,025

* CU0.50/CU2.00 × 400 shares = 100 shares

4.3.2.5 Contingently issuable shares

Contingently issuable ordinary shares are defined as ordinary shares issuable for little or no cash or other consideration upon the satisfaction of specified conditions in a contingent share agreement. [IAS 33:5] When the only 'contingency' is the passage of time, the instrument is not considered a contingently issuable ordinary share because the passage of time is certain (see discussion in **4.3.2.7** regarding deferred shares).

For a variety of reasons, an entity may issue instruments that oblige it to issue ordinary shares in the future upon the resolution of specified contingencies. Such circumstances may include (1) issuing contingent share purchase warrants to customers that become exercisable based on the attainment of a certain level of purchases, or (2) the guarantee of a minimum share price for shares issued by an acquirer in a business combination that may result in issuing additional shares if the share price is less than the guaranteed price. Contingent share agreements are usually based on the passage of time combined with other conditions (such as the market price of an entity's shares or a specified level of earnings).

Contingently issuable ordinary shares include shares that (1) will be issued in the future upon the satisfaction of specified conditions, or (2) have been placed in escrow and all, or part, must be returned if specified conditions are not met, or (3) have been issued but the holder must return all, or a portion, of the shares, if specified conditions are not met.

Contingently issuable shares are included in the computation of basic EPS from the date when all necessary conditions have been satisfied and, thus, although issuing the shares is still a future transaction, it is no longer contingent. [IAS 33:24]

The following examples illustrate four circumstances in which shares are contingently issuable.

Example 4.3.2.5A

Contingency based on an event

A Limited acquires B Limited on 1 January 20X1. A Limited agrees to issue 100,000 shares to the vendor on 1 January 20X3 if, at any point prior to that date, a new product developed by B Limited is granted a licence.

A Limited's year end is 31 December. The 20X1 financial statements are approved on 22 March 20X2. The product is granted a licence on 4 March 20X2.

The 100,000 shares are excluded from the basic EPS calculations for 20X1 and will be included in the basic EPS calculations for 20X2 on a time-apportioned basis as if the shares had been issued on 4 March 20X2 (the date the licence was granted). The ordinary shares are deemed outstanding for basic EPS purposes from 4 March 20X2, even though they will not be issued until 1 January 20X3, because after 4 March 20X2 they are no longer contingently issuable (the only 'contingency' that remains is the passage of time).

(See **5.6** and **examples 5.6.3.7A** and **5.6.3.7B** for a discussion of the effect of this arrangement on the calculation of diluted EPS.)

Example 4.3.2.5B

Contingency based on profits in specified periods

Company X, a publicly traded entity reporting on a calendar year basis, purchased Subsidiary Y on 1 January 20X1 for CU100 million plus 20,000 Company X ordinary shares for each year within the next five years in which Subsidiary Y has a profit after tax of CU10 million or more. If any ordinary shares are required to be issued, they will be issued on 1 January 20X6.

If Company Y's profit after tax for the year ended 31 December 20X1 is CU12 million, the shares should be included in the denominator for the purpose of calculating basic EPS for only that portion of the year for which the contingency was resolved (i.e. nothing could happen that would cause Company X not to issue the shares). Because the earliest date on which the amount for profit after tax for the year can be calculated is 31 December, the contingency can only be resolved on that date. Therefore, the shares will be included in the denominator for the purpose of calculating basic EPS as if they are issued on 31 December 20X1 (from that date, they are no longer contingently issuable shares). However, they will have no impact on basic EPS for the 20X1 reporting period because they are treated as issued on the last day of that reporting period (and, consequently, the time apportioned to the issue of the shares is nil). In 20X2, the ordinary shares to be issued in respect of the 20X1 earnings

---

contingency should be treated as outstanding for the whole of the 20X2 reporting period.

Because there are five separate measurement periods for the contingency, each measurement period in which a finite number of ordinary shares may be issued should be treated as a separate contingency and evaluated for basic EPS based on whether Company X may be required to issue the ordinary shares for each period on a stand-alone basis.

If the purchase agreement required Company X to issue 100,000 Company X ordinary shares if Subsidiary Y achieves CU50 million in cumulative profits at the end of five years, no shares would be included for the purposes of calculating basic EPS until the end of the contingency period, and then only if Subsidiary Y had cumulative earnings in excess of CU50 million.

Example 4.3.2.5C

Contingency based on average profits

A Limited acquires B Limited on 1 January 20X1. A Limited agrees to issue 100,000 shares to the vendor on 1 January 20X4 if B Limited's profits for the three years to 31 December 20X3 average CU10 million or more.

B Limited's profits for 20X1 and 20X2 are CU17 million each year.

The shares are excluded from the calculation of basic EPS for both 20X1 and 20X2. Even if profits are expected for the year 20X3, such that the earnings condition will be met, the shares are excluded from the calculation of basic EPS because it is not certain that all of the necessary conditions will be satisfied until the end of the contingency period; it is possible (although unlikely) that a loss could be made in 20X3 and the earnings condition (for the three years) will not be met.

(See **5.6** for a discussion of how such shares are dealt with in the computation of diluted EPS and **example 5.6.3.3** for an illustration.)

Example 4.3.2.5D

Contingency based on continuing employment

Company M, a publicly traded entity, has a mandatory deferred compensation plan whereby covered employees are required to defer the amount of compensation payable in one calendar year in excess of CU500,000 until completion of the deferral period. The deferral period ends when the employee ceases to earn CU500,000 annually or reaches the defined retirement age as an employee of Company M. If the employment is terminated or the employee resigns, he/she is not eligible to receive any distribution under the plan. The compensation deferred under the plan is only payable to the participant in Company M's ordinary shares over a five-year period once the participant is eligible to receive the distribution.

An employee's deferred compensation is held in an escrow account until the individual is eligible to receive distributions. Distributions from the account are based on the equivalent number of ordinary shares that the cash value of the distribution would convert to, based on the closing price of the shares for the trading day preceding the distribution.

The ordinary shares issuable under the plan are considered contingently issuable for the purpose of computing basic EPS, because the ordinary shares will only be earned and, therefore, become issuable if the employee (1) neither has his/her employment terminated nor resigns, and (2) either retires in the employment of Company M or has annual earnings fall below CU500,000. Accordingly, during the deferral period, the ordinary shares issuable under the plan should be excluded from the denominator in computing basic EPS because there is still the possibility that the conditions for the issue of the shares to the employee will not be met.

The following example, reproduced from Example 7 of the illustrative examples accompanying IAS 33, provides another illustration of contingently issuable shares.

Example 4.3.2.5E

Contingently issuable shares

[IAS 33 Illustrative examples: Example 7]

Ordinary shares outstanding during 20X1	1,000,000 (there were no options, warrants or convertible instruments outstanding during the period)

An agreement related to a recent business combination provides for the issue of additional ordinary shares based on the following conditions:

	5,000 additional ordinary shares for each new retail site opened during 20X1
	1,000 additional ordinary shares for each CU1,000 of consolidated profit in excess of CU2,000,000 for the year ended 31 December 20X1
Retail sites opened during the year:	one on 1 May 20X1 one on 1 September 20X1
Consolidated year-to-date profit attributable to ordinary equity holders of the parent entity:	CU1,100,000 as of 31 March 20X1 CU2,300,000 as of 30 June 20X1 CU1,900,000 as of 30 September 20X1 (including a CU450,000 loss from a discontinued operation) CU2,900,000 as of 31 December 20X1

Basic earnings per share

	First quarter	Second quarter	Third quarter	Fourth quarter	Full year
Numerator (CU)	1,100,000	1,200,000	(400,000)	1,000,000	2,900,000
Denominator:					
Ordinary shares outstanding	1,000,000	1,000,000	1,000,000	1,000,000	1,000,000
Retail site contingency	–	3,333[a]	6,667[b]	10,000	5,000[c]
Earnings contingency[d]	–	–	–	–	–
Total shares	1,000,000	1,003,333	1,006,667	1,010,000	1,005,000
Basic earnings per share (CU)	1.10	1.20	(0.40)	0.99	2.89

[a] 5,000 shares × 2/3

[b] 5,000 shares + (5,000 shares × 1/3)

[c] (5,000 shares × 8/12) + (5,000 shares × 4/12)

[d] The earnings contingency has no effect on basic earnings per share because it is not certain that the condition is satisfied until the end of the contingency period. The effect is negligible for the fourth-quarter and full-year calculations because it is not certain that the condition is met until the last day of the period.

The calculation of diluted EPS is illustrated in **example 5.6.3.7B**.

4.3.2.6   Contingently returnable shares

When outstanding ordinary shares are contingently returnable (i.e. subject to recall), they are not treated as outstanding and are excluded from the calculation of basic earnings per share until the date the shares are no longer subject to recall. [IAS 33:24]

Example 4.3.2.6

Contingently returnable shares

Company X granted options to its employees. The options vest over a four-year period. However, the employees may exercise their options at any time before their vesting. If an employee initiates this early exercise provision, the employee will receive restricted ordinary shares in Company X that vest under the same schedule as the employee's original option grants.

Shares that are contingently returnable (e.g. subject to repurchase if employment is terminated or the employee resigns prior to the shares vesting fully) should not be considered outstanding for the purposes of computing basic EPS until all necessary conditions that could require return of the shares have been satisfied (i.e. the shares are fully vested). The contingently returnable shares issued to the employee in the circumstances described should be excluded from the denominator in calculating basic EPS.

4.3.2.7   Deferred shares

Shares that will be issued at a future date and whose issue is not subject to any conditions other than the passage of time (sometimes called deferred shares) are not contingently issuable shares, because the passage of time is a certainty. [IAS 33:24] This is consistent with the treatment of mandatorily convertible shares described at **4.3.2.1**. Such shares are also included in basic EPS because the issue of shares is not contingent, as the passage of time is certain.

As discussed at **4.3.2.1**, the general principle is that shares are to be considered outstanding from the date that the consideration for the shares becomes receivable. [IAS 33:21]

Although this date will often coincide with the issue date of the shares, this will not be so in the case of deferred shares. Nevertheless, if an asset is acquired, or a service is received, and the cost is to be satisfied by shares to be issued at a future date, then the deferred shares will be included in the calculation of EPS from the date of recognition of the asset or service, which is the consideration for the shares.

Deferred shares typically arise in the context of business combinations. As discussed at **4.3.2.3**, for a business combination, the shares issued are included in EPS calculations from the acquisition date (i.e. the date from which the results of the acquiree are included in the consolidated statement of comprehensive income). The fact that the issue of some of those shares has been deferred is irrelevant – they are included in the EPS denominator immediately, provided that their issue is not subject to any conditions. For example, A Limited might acquire B Limited, paying 500,000 shares at the date of acquisition and a further 100,000 shares one year after the date of acquisition. All 600,000 shares will be included in the calculation of basic EPS from the date that B Limited is brought into A Limited's consolidated financial statements if the issue of the shares is not subject to any conditions other than the passage of time.

An agreement for the acquisition of a business may provide for further shares to be issued, but with the number of shares yet to be determined. For example, the agreement may provide that shares valued at CU50,000,000 on a specified future date will be issued, the number of shares to be determined by dividing CU50,000,000 by the share price on the specified future date. Although the number of shares to be issued is uncertain, there are no circumstances under which the shares will not be issued. Nevertheless, IAS 33:54 indicates that such shares are contingently issuable shares (see the discussion at

5.6.3.4). Because the obligation to issue shares to a particular value is a financial liability, no equity instrument exists until the end of the contingency period. Such shares will, however, affect the calculation of diluted EPS (see **5.6.3.4** and **5.6.3.6**).

4.3.2.8 Redeemable ordinary shares

Example 4.3.2.8

Redeemable ordinary shares

Company B, a publicly traded entity, issued redeemable ordinary shares that contain a redemption provision entitling the holder of the ordinary shares to put the shares at fair value to Company B five years after the issuance of the shares, or at any time thereafter. The redeemable ordinary shares represent approximately 20 per cent of total ordinary shares in issue. The redeemable ordinary shares do not meet the definition of equity under IAS 32 *Financial Instruments: Presentation* because they are not the most subordinate instruments issued by the entity (i.e. the non-redeemable ordinary shares are more subordinate).

Under IAS 32:18(a) (see **chapter B3** or, for entities that have not yet adopted IFRS 9, **chapter C3**), the redeemable ordinary shares are classified as financial liabilities because the entity has an obligation to deliver cash or other financial assets equal to the redemption price. The shares should not be included as outstanding ordinary shares (i.e. included in the denominator) in the calculation of basic EPS because, not being equity instruments, they do not meet the definition of ordinary shares under IAS 33:5 (see **3.1**).

The redeemable ordinary shares are not ordinary shares during their life because they are not classified as equity (due to the presence of the redemption feature).

The shares are also not potentially dilutive because, since they do not entitle the holder to ordinary shares, they do not meet the definition of potential ordinary shares in IAS 33:5 (see **3.2.1**).

4.3.2.9 Forward purchase contract and written put options

When an entity enters into a forward purchase contract or written put option over its own equity that may be gross physically settled (i.e. cash or other financial assets exchanged for the shares repurchased), IAS 32:23 (see **chapter B3** or, for entities that have not yet adopted IFRS 9, **chapter C3**) requires the entity to recognise a financial liability for the present value of the amount payable under the contract (often referred to as the 'gross obligation').

IAS 33 does not specify whether shares that are subject to a forward purchase contract or written put option when a gross obligation is recognised should be treated for EPS purposes as if the shares were acquired when the entity entered into the contract. The following two alternative accounting policies are acceptable. The accounting policy adopted should be applied consistently and disclosed if material.

Alternative 1

Shares subject to a forward purchase contract or written put option should be treated for EPS purposes as outstanding until the date the shares are acquired under the arrangement (i.e. until the consideration is paid and the shares are delivered to the entity). The number of ordinary shares included in the denominator is, therefore, not reduced by the number of shares that will be acquired under the forward contract, or potentially acquired under the written put option if the option is exercised. Therefore, the ordinary shares subject to delivery under the forward contract or written put option are regarded as potential ordinary shares and may affect diluted EPS (see **5.8**).

Alternative 2

Shares subject to a forward purchase contract or written put option should be treated for EPS purposes as if the shares were acquired when the entity entered into the arrangement. The number of ordinary shares included in the denominator is reduced by the number of shares that will be acquired under the forward contract, or potentially acquired under the written put option if the option is exercised. Because the ordinary shares subject to delivery under the forward contract or written put option are regarded as acquired at the inception of the contract, they are not potential ordinary shares and, therefore, cannot be dilutive. If the written put option expires unexercised, the number of shares will be added back to the denominator on the expiration date.

4.3.3 Changes in share capital with no corresponding change in the entity's resources

4.3.3.1 Potential effect of a change in share capital with no corresponding change in the entity's resources

An entity may issue shares, or reduce the number of ordinary shares outstanding, without a corresponding change in resources, i.e. without any change in shareholders' funds.

IAS 33 includes specific requirements for such circumstances to ensure that EPS reported in the current and prior periods are comparable. Consider the following example.

Example 4.3.3.1

Bonus issue of shares

An entity had the following statement of financial position as at 31 December 20X1.

	CU
Net assets	900,000,000
Share capital	100,000,000
Reserves	800,000,000
	900,000,000

On 31 December 20X1, and throughout the year then ended, the share capital comprised 100,000,000 CU1 ordinary shares. On 1 January 20X2, the entity makes a 1:1 bonus issue. The statement of financial position immediately after the bonus issue appears as follows.

	CU
Net assets	900,000,000
Share capital	200,000,000
Reserves (800,000,000 – 100,000,000)	700,000,000
	900,000,000

The entity's net assets do not alter and so the revenue generating ability of the entity is unchanged. Assume that the profit attributable to ordinary shareholders for each of 20X1 and 20X2 is CU20,000,000. If the bonus issue were treated as an issue of shares for consideration, the result would be as follows.

	20X2	20X1
Earnings per share	CU0.10	CU0.20

Clearly, these results are not comparable – the profits are identical in each of the years and there has been no inflow or outflow of capital; yet the above result gives the appearance that the entity was less profitable in 20X2 than in 20X1.

Consequently, in such circumstances, IAS 33 requires that EPS be adjusted as if the proportionate change in the number of ordinary shares outstanding had taken place at the start of the earliest period for which an EPS is presented (see **4.3.3.2** for detailed requirements). Thus, in this example, the EPS calculated in accordance with IAS 33 is as follows.

	20X2	20X1
Earnings per share	CU0.10	CU0.10

4.3.3.2 Adjustments required for changes in share capital with no corresponding change in the entity's resources

The weighted average number of ordinary shares outstanding during the period and for all periods presented should be adjusted for events, other than the conversion of potential ordinary shares, that have changed the number of ordinary shares outstanding without a corresponding change in resources. [IAS 33:26]

If the number of ordinary or potential ordinary shares outstanding increases as a result of a capitalisation, bonus issue or share split, or decreases as a result of a reverse share split, the calculation of basic and diluted earnings per share for all periods presented is adjusted retrospectively.

Bonus issues are not the only example of a change to the number of shares in issue with no corresponding change in resources. The Standard lists the following examples:

[IAS 33:27]

- a bonus or capitalisation issue (sometimes referred to as a 'stock dividend');
- the bonus element in any other issue (e.g. a bonus element in a rights issue to existing shareholders);
- a share split; and
- a reverse share split (share consolidation).

The list is not exhaustive.

Bonus issues, share splits and share consolidations are all adjusted for in the same way, i.e. by adjusting proportionately the number of shares outstanding as if the bonus issue, share split or share consolidation had occurred at the start of the earliest period for which EPS information is presented (see **4.3.3.3** for details). Specific rules are set out for in-substance share buy-backs, for example when a share consolidation is combined with a special dividend (see **4.3.3.4**).

For rights issues, and bonus elements in any other issue or buy-back, the Standard specifies a formula to be used to calculate the adjustment to the shares in issue before the rights issue (see **4.3.3.5**).

4.3.3.3 Bonus issue, share split or share consolidation

The number of ordinary shares outstanding is adjusted proportionately as if the bonus issue, share split or share consolidation had taken place at the start of the earliest period for which EPS is presented. [IAS 33:28]

When an entity has had a bonus issue, share split or share consolidation and presents a five-year historical summary accompanying its IFRS financial statements, it may, subject to local jurisdictional requirements, be most helpful to adjust the basic EPS figure retrospectively for all years presented to enable a fair comparison. Clear disclosure should be given to explain the adjustments made to the basic EPS figure (e.g. by way of a footnote to the five-year historical summary).

The following example, reproduced from Example 3 of the illustrative examples accompanying IAS 33, illustrates the calculation of basic EPS when there has been a bonus issue.

Example 4.3.3.3

Bonus issue

[IAS 33 Illustrative examples: Example 3]

Profit attributable to ordinary equity holders of the parent entity 20X0	CU180
Profit attributable to ordinary equity holders of the parent entity 20X1	CU600
Ordinary shares outstanding until 30 September 20X1	200
Bonus issue on 1 October 20X1	2 ordinary shares for each ordinary share outstanding at 30 September 20X1
	200 × 2 = 400
Basic earnings per share 20X1	CU600/(200 + 400) = CU1.00
Basic earnings per share 20X0	CU180/(200 + 400) = CU0.30

Because the bonus issue was without consideration, it is treated as if it had occurred before the beginning of 20X0, the earliest period presented.

IAS 33:27 states that a bonus issue or capitalisation is sometimes referred to as a 'stock dividend'. If a stock dividend is equivalent to a bonus issue or capitalisation, there has been a change in the number of shares without a corresponding change in resources and IAS 33:26 requires that EPS be adjusted as if the proportionate change in the number of ordinary shares outstanding had taken place at the start of the earliest period for which EPS is presented (see **example 4.3.3.1**). However, care is needed in determining the substance of a stock dividend and, particularly, whether it is equivalent to a bonus issue or capitalisation, i.e. whether there is a change in share capital with no corresponding change in the entity's resources. For example, if an entity enters into an arrangement that gives the shareholders the right to a dividend in cash or shares at the shareholder's option, if the cash is forfeited for shares this can be seen as consideration for the issue of shares. If the cash option is equivalent to the fair value of the shares, this is equivalent to a fresh issue of shares at fair value. In such circumstances, this is not equivalent to a bonus issue or capitalisation and, therefore, restatement of the number of shares outstanding is not appropriate.

4.3.3.4 In-substance share buy-backs

Share consolidations (or reverse share splits) generally reduce the number of ordinary shares outstanding without a corresponding reduction in resources. However, when the overall effect is a share repurchase at fair value, the reduction in the number of ordinary shares outstanding is the result of a corresponding reduction in resources. An example is a share consolidation combined with a special dividend. The weighted average number of shares outstanding for the period in which the combined transaction takes place is adjusted for the reduction in the number of ordinary shares from the date the special dividend is recognised. [IAS 33:29]

Example 4.3.3.4 demonstrates why separate accounting for the dividend and the share consolidation would not reflect the substance of a share buy-back. In determining the substance of the arrangement, a thorough understanding is required of the transaction(s) and the underlying intentions.

IAS 33 cites the combination of a special dividend and a share consolidation as one means of achieving an in-substance share buy-back. Other transactions that achieve the same effect should be treated consistently.

To the extent that the effect of the share consolidation is not equal to the value of the special dividend, care will be needed to understand whether all, or part, of the transaction should be treated as an in-substance share buy-back of ordinary shares at fair value.

Example 4.3.3.4

In-substance share buy-backs

An entity has 500,000 ordinary shares in issue on 1 January 20X1. The entity wishes to effect a share consolidation, as part of which it will pay a special dividend of CU0.60 per share. Accordingly, on 1 July 20X1, when its share price is CU6, it pays a special dividend of CU300,000 and undertakes a 10:9 share consolidation, issuing nine new shares for every 10 old shares held. As a result, only 450,000 shares are in issue for the remainder of 20X1.

Although the entity has carried out a share consolidation, the special dividend has led to a corresponding reduction in resources. The overall effect when the share consolidation is combined with the special dividend is that there has been a share repurchase at fair value; if, instead, the entity had gone into the market and purchased 50,000 shares at the market price of CU6 per share,

---

the overall effect would have been the same (i.e. the entity would also have paid out CU300,000 and reduced the number of shares in issue to 450,000). Therefore, the combination of the special dividend of CU300,000 and the share consolidation will result in the share price continuing to be CU6 [((CU6 × 500,000) − CU300,000)/450,000]. The impact of the special dividend and the share consolidation on the value of the shares is neutral.

Earnings for 20X1 total CU360,000. Under the approach required by IAS 33:29, EPS for 20X1 is calculated as follows:

CU360,000/[500,000 − (50,000 × 6/12)] = CU0.76

Note that this is different from the EPS figure that would have resulted from separate accounting for the transactions (i.e. treating the special dividend as a dividend and the share consolidation as a share consolidation). Under such an approach (which would be contrary to IAS 33:29), EPS for 20X1 would have been calculated as follows:

CU360,000/450,000 = CU0.80

Further, separate accounting would have led to restatement of EPS for the comparative period, which would be inappropriate.

4.3.3.5 Rights issues at less than full market price

A rights issue is similar to an issue of options to existing shareholders in that it gives each existing shareholder the right, but not the obligation, to purchase additional shares in the entity at a fixed price. Generally, these rights may be sold by the existing shareholders to other shareholders or potential shareholders.

When shares are offered to shareholders in a rights issue, the price at which they are offered is often less than the fair value of the shares. Consider, for example, an entity whose shares are priced at CU10. The entity offers its shareholders one new share for every four held, giving 100,000 new shares, at CU8 per share. Share proceeds of CU800,000 will be received and 100,000 shares issued. This is equivalent to issuing 80,000 shares at fair value (of CU10 per share) and making a bonus issue of 20,000 shares. This is the bonus element of the rights issue.

When there is a bonus element in a rights issue, EPS is calculated as if the bonus element (but not the total rights issue) arose proportionately at the start of the earliest period for which an EPS is presented. If there is no bonus element in the rights issue, the new shares issued are treated as an issue for cash at fair value (because that is what they are).

In order to calculate basic EPS when there is a bonus element, however, the transaction described above would not be treated as an issue of 80,000 shares at fair value and a bonus issue of 20,000 shares. Instead, the Standard specifies a formula to be used. If the fair value used to calculate the number of shares issued for no consideration ('the bonus issue') is the same as the fair value of the shares immediately before the exercise of rights, the two methods give identical answers. The formula specified in the Standard is discussed and illustrated in the paragraphs below.

The specific circumstances of the bonus element in a rights issue are discussed in the application guidance issued with IAS 33, and illustrated in Example 4 of the illustrative examples accompanying IAS 33 (see **example 4.3.3.5**). If a rights issue is offered to all existing shareholders, the number of ordinary shares outstanding prior to the rights issue is multiplied by the following factor:

[IAS 33:A2]

$$\frac{\text{Fair value per share immediately before the exercise of rights}}{\text{Theoretical ex-rights fair value per share}}$$

The theoretical ex-rights fair value per share is calculated as:

[IAS 33:A2]

$$\frac{\text{Aggregate fair value of the shares outstanding immediately before the exercise of rights + proceeds from the exercise of rights}}{\text{Number of shares outstanding after the exercise of rights}}$$

The Standard specifies that when, before the exercise date, the rights are to be publicly traded separately from the shares, the 'fair value per share immediately before the exercise of rights' is measured at the close of the last day on which the shares are traded together with the rights. [IAS 33:A2]

The following example, reproduced from Example 4 of the illustrative examples accompanying IAS 33, illustrates the impact on basic EPS of a rights issue at less than fair value.

Example 4.3.3.5

Rights issue

[IAS 33 Illustrative examples: Example 4]

	20X0	20X1	20X2
Profit attributable to ordinary equity holders of the parent entity	CU1,100	CU1,500	CU1,800
Shares outstanding before rights issue	500 shares		

Rights issue	One new share for each five outstanding shares (100 new shares total)	
	Exercise price:	CU5.00
	Date of rights issue:	1 January 20X1
	Last date to exercise rights:	1 March 20X1
Market price of one ordinary share immediately before exercise on 1 March 20X1:	CU11.00	
Reporting date	31 December	

Calculation of theoretical ex-rights value per share

$$\frac{\text{Fair value of all outstanding shares before the exercise of rights} + \text{total amount received from exercise of rights}}{\text{Number of shares outstanding before exercise} + \text{number of shares issued in the exercise}}$$

$$\frac{(CU11.00 \times 500 \text{ shares}) + (CU5.00 \times 100 \text{ shares})}{(500 \text{ shares} + 100 \text{ shares})}$$

Theoretical ex-rights value per share = CU10.00

Calculation of adjustment factor

$$\frac{\text{Fair value per share immediately before exercise of rights}}{\text{Theoretical ex-rights value per share}} \quad \frac{CU11.00}{CU10.00} = 1.10$$

Calculation of basic earnings per share

	20X0	20X1	20X2
20X0 basic EPS as originally reported:			
CU1,100/500 shares	CU2.20		
20X0 basic EPS restated for rights issue:			
CU1,100/(500 shares × 1.1)	CU2.00		
20X1 basic EPS including effects of rights issue:			
CU1,500/[(500 × 1.1 × 2/12) + (600 × 10/12)]		CU2.54	
20X2 basic EPS: CU1,800/600 shares			CU3.00

4.3.3.6 Changes after the reporting period

If there is any change in the number of ordinary or potential ordinary shares, resulting from a capitalisation or bonus issue, a share split or a reverse share split, after the reporting period but before the financial statements are authorised for issue, the per share calculations for those and any prior period financial statements presented should be based on the new number of shares. [IAS 33:64]

Adjustments to the number of shares outstanding should only be made when the required approval procedures have been completed and the shares are trading on a post-split or dividend basis. For example, no adjustment should be made for proposed bonus issues that are subject to approval at the general meeting at which the financial statements are to be authorised for issue because the shares are not yet trading on a post-split or dividend basis. It is common for trading to occur the day after the dividend or split has been distributed for larger changes in the share capital structure (i.e. those greater than 20 per cent). In situations in which the share dividend or share split is declared and approved prior to, but distributed subsequent to, the date the financial statements are authorised for issue, EPS should be calculated using the number of shares on a pre-split basis, and disclosure should be made of the post-split effects on EPS in the statement of comprehensive income, with footnote disclosure of the significant terms of the pending share dividend or share split. However, because the timing of the switch to trading on a post-split basis is actually governed by the relevant stock exchange, and may vary depending on the size of the change in the share capital structure, it is necessary to monitor the timing of the switch and adjust the EPS reporting accordingly.

Financial statements are considered to be 'authorised for issue' as at the date they are authorised for distribution for general use in a format that complies with IFRSs.

When per-share calculations have been adjusted to reflect changes in the number of shares as described in the previous paragraphs, that fact should be disclosed. [IAS 33:64]

When ordinary or potential ordinary share transactions other than capitalisation issues, share splits and reverse share splits occur after the reporting period but before the financial statements are authorised for issue, disclosure of such events may be required (see **7.2.3**). Such transactions after the reporting period, which do not affect the amount of capital used to produce profit or loss for the period and, consequently, are excluded from the calculation of EPS, include:

[IAS 33:71]

- the issue of shares for cash;
- the issue of shares when the proceeds are used to repay debt or preference shares outstanding at the end of the reporting period;
- the redemption of ordinary shares outstanding;

- the conversion or exercise of potential ordinary shares outstanding at the end of the reporting period into ordinary shares;

- the issue of warrants, options or convertible securities; and

- the achievement of conditions that would result in the issue of contingently issuable shares.

4.3.4 Preference shares with characteristics of ordinary shares

Entities will sometimes issue preference shares with many of the characteristics of ordinary shares. For the purpose of computing basic EPS, the terms of such preference shares will need to be evaluated carefully. If they share the characteristics of ordinary shares and have no preference attributed to them, such instruments should be considered as ordinary shares for the purpose of basic EPS regardless of the legal name assigned to them.

Example 4.3.4

Preference shares with characteristics of ordinary shares

Company B, a publicly traded entity, issued convertible preference shares to Company C with terms substantially the same as ordinary shares. The relevant terms of the preference shares are as follows:

- not publicly traded;
- voting rights are limited to specified events, including liquidation;
- nominal preference in liquidation of CU0.01 per share;
- each share is convertible into one ordinary share at any time upon the transfer of the preference shares to a third party;
- antidilution provisions are limited only to share splits and dividends;
- no rights to preferential or cumulative dividends;
- preference shares participate rateably with ordinary shares in the event a dividend is declared on ordinary shares; and
- in addition, ordinary shareholders may participate rateably in the event a dividend is declared on the preference shares.

The holder of the preference shares can sell these shares to a third party at any time, at which point the preference shares would convert into ordinary shares with all the characteristics of the current outstanding ordinary shares. The sale of the preference shares is outside of the issuer's control and there are no restrictions on the sale of the preference shares. Further, preference shares have exactly the same rights to receive dividends as ordinary shares and have no substantive preference (because the liquidation preference of CU0.01 per share is insignificant).

Calculating basic EPS involves determining the amount of profit or loss attributable to ordinary shareholders. If the preference shares are not included in the basic EPS calculation, the calculation will be misleading because it will exclude a group of shareholders that currently have identical rights to earnings and dividends as the ordinary shareholders.

There is no substantive difference between these preference shares and ordinary shares because the preference shares have the characteristics of non-voting ordinary shares and should be included in basic EPS. To the extent that the preference shares have a different right to share in profit for the period, they should be presented as a separate class of ordinary shares.

4.3.5   Ordinary shares issued to trusts to fund retirement benefit payments

In order to fund retirement benefit payments, an entity may issue ordinary shares to a trust which is consolidated in the financial statements of the entity. In many instances, the trusts created do not protect the assets from creditors in the case of the entity's bankruptcy (e.g. 'rabbi trusts'). The ordinary shares of the entity are held until the rabbi trust is required to meet retirement obligations, at which time the shares are sold to the public.

The shares held by the trust should not be considered outstanding in the computation of EPS in the consolidated financial statements of the entity because the trust is consolidated by the entity and, therefore, the shares are considered treasury shares in the consolidated financial statements until such time as the trust sells the shares outside the group. The shares held by the trust are excluded from the definition of plan assets in IAS 19 *Employee Benefits* (see **7.3.7** in **chapter A15**).

4.3.6   Shares held by a trust for equity-settled share-based payments

Example 4.3.6

Shares held by a trust for equity-settled share-based payments

Company B grants its employees share options that will vest after three years of employment. Company B provides money to a trust to purchase shares in Company B in the market. The shares are then used to satisfy the exercise of the share options on vesting. Company B controls the trust and, therefore, consolidates the trust in accordance with IFRS 10 *Consolidated Financial Statements*.

Basic EPS is determined by reference to the weighted average number of ordinary shares outstanding during the reporting period. In the consolidated financial statements of Company B, the shares held by the trust will be recognised as treasury shares. Treasury shares are not included in the denominator for the purpose of calculating basic or diluted EPS because they do not represent ordinary shares outstanding from the date acquired.

Diluted EPS is determined by reference to the weighted average number of ordinary shares and potential ordinary shares outstanding during the reporting period. The employees' share options represent potential ordinary shares that are considered in determining diluted EPS when the potential ordinary shares are dilutive at year end, in accordance with the guidance in IAS 33:45 to 48 (see **section 5**).

4.3.7   Adjustments required for errors and changes in accounting policies

Basic and diluted earnings per share of all periods presented are also adjusted for:

[IAS 33:64]

* the effects of errors; and

* adjustments resulting from changes in accounting policies accounted for retrospectively.

5   Calculation of diluted earnings per share

5.1   Requirement to calculate diluted earnings per share

IAS 33 requires entities to calculate diluted earnings per share amounts for profit or loss attributable to ordinary equity holders of the parent entity and, when presented, profit or loss from continuing operations attributable to those equity holders. [IAS 33:30]

The objective of diluted EPS is consistent with that of basic earnings per share (i.e. to provide a measure of the interest of each ordinary share in the performance of an entity) while giving effect to all dilutive potential ordinary shares outstanding during a period. Accordingly:

[IAS 33:32]

* profit or loss attributable to ordinary equity holders of the parent entity is increased by the after-tax amount of dividends and interest recognised in the period in respect of dilutive potential ordinary shares and is adjusted for any other changes in income or expense that would result from the conversion of the dilutive potential ordinary shares; and

* the weighted average number of ordinary shares outstanding is increased by the weighted average number of additional ordinary shares that would have been outstanding assuming the conversion of all dilutive potential ordinary shares.

5.2 Definition and general principles

5.2.1 *Formula for calculating diluted earnings per share*

Diluted EPS is calculated as:

[IAS 33:31]

$$\frac{\text{Earnings per basic EPS + adjustment for dilutive potential ordinary shares}}{\text{No. of shares per basic EPS + adjustment for dilutive potential ordinary shares}}$$

A potential ordinary share is a financial instrument or other contract that may entitle its holder to ordinary shares. [IAS 33:5] Examples include:

[IAS 33:7]

- financial liabilities or equity instruments, including preference shares, that are convertible into ordinary shares;
- options and warrants; and
- shares that would be issued upon the satisfaction of certain conditions resulting from contractual arrangements, such as the purchase of a business or other assets.

Dilution is defined as a reduction in earnings per share or an increase in loss per share resulting from the assumption that convertible instruments are converted, that options or warrants are exercised, or that ordinary shares are issued upon the satisfaction of specified conditions. [IAS 33:5]

Antidilution is defined as an increase in earnings per share or a reduction in loss per share resulting from the assumption that convertible instruments are converted, that options or warrants are exercised, or that ordinary shares are issued upon the satisfaction of specified conditions. [IAS 33:5]

Dilutive potential ordinary shares are included in the calculation of diluted EPS as if the potential ordinary shares had been converted to ordinary shares at the start of the period (or on the date of issue of the potential ordinary shares, if later). [IAS 33:36] Antidilutive potential ordinary shares are disregarded in the calculation of diluted EPS.

5.2.2 *Adjustments to earnings – general*

The earnings adjustment for diluted EPS is generally the actual charge to profit or loss that would be avoided by conversion of potential ordinary shares to actual ordinary shares. Accordingly, the profit or loss attributable to ordinary equity holders of the parent entity, as used for the calculation of basic EPS, is adjusted by the after-tax effect of:

[IAS 33:33]

- any dividends or other items related to dilutive potential ordinary shares deducted in arriving at profit or loss for the purposes of basic EPS;

- any interest recognised in the period related to dilutive potential ordinary shares; and

- any other changes in income or expense that would result from the conversion of dilutive potential ordinary shares.

In calculating the after-tax amount of dividends, interest and other income or expenses for the purposes of adjusting the earnings figure, the tax rate applied should be the effective tax rate for the entity for the period under review. For an entity that is in a tax loss position, and for which a deferred tax asset in respect of those losses has not been recognised, the tax effect may be nil.

The items listed in IAS 33:33 would no longer arise if the potential ordinary shares were converted into ordinary shares. Accordingly, the earnings figures are adjusted to remove their impact, and any related tax effect. Changes in income or expense other than dividends and interest would include transaction costs and discounts accounted for in accordance with the effective interest method (see **chapter B6** or, for entities that have not yet adopted IFRS 9, **chapter C6**). [IAS 33:34]

In addition, the entity might operate a profit-related pay or other bonus scheme. Any adjustments to profit or loss relating to potential ordinary shares might affect the amount payable to employees under the profit-related scheme (e.g. if the profit were to increase as a result of reduced interest costs, the amount of profit payable to the employees might also increase). The earnings adjustments for diluted EPS should include the effect on the incentive/bonus payable in respect of the scheme, and the consequential tax effects. [IAS 33:35]

Some compensation plans are based on the price of the entity's shares, but will not result in the actual issue of shares (e.g. phantom shares and formula plans). Rather, the compensation to the employee under the plan is settled entirely in cash. For plans of this nature, the computation of EPS will not be affected by the existence of the plan (other than as a result of the compensation cost charged as an expense against profit or loss attributable to ordinary equity holders).

5.2.3 Adjustments to number of shares – general

The number of shares used in the computation of diluted EPS is the sum of the weighted average number of ordinary shares used as the denominator for the basic EPS calculation and the weighted average number of ordinary shares that would be issued on the conversion of all dilutive potential ordinary shares. [IAS 33:36]

In calculating the weighted average number of dilutive potential ordinary shares:

[IAS 33:36 - 38]

- dilutive potential ordinary shares are deemed to have been converted into ordinary shares at the beginning of the period or, if later, at the date of issue of the potential ordinary shares;

- the number of dilutive potential ordinary shares is determined independently for each period presented. The number of dilutive potential ordinary shares included in the year-to-date period is not a weighted average of the dilutive potential ordinary shares included in each interim computation;

- potential ordinary shares that have lapsed or been cancelled during the period are included for the time for which they were outstanding; and

- potential ordinary shares that have been converted into ordinary shares during the period are included for the period prior to actual exercise.

The terms of the potential ordinary shares are used to determine the number of ordinary shares that would be issued on the conversion of dilutive potential ordinary shares. When more than one basis of conversion exists, the computation assumes the most advantageous conversion rate or exercise price from the standpoint of the holder of the potential ordinary shares. [IAS 33:39] This ensures that the most dilutive conversion rate or exercise price is included in determining diluted EPS.

No restatement of diluted EPS of any prior period presented should be made for changes in the assumptions used or for the conversion of potential ordinary shares. [IAS 33:65]

5.2.4 'If-converted' and 'treasury stock' methods

When a financial liability is forgiven as consideration for the issue of shares (as is the case for convertible debt), the number of shares to be added to the denominator is the number of shares that would be issued to the holder assuming the convertible debt was converted in full. This is often referred to as the 'if-converted' method. This method does not consider what the average share price is compared to the exercise price inherent in the convertible debt. Thus, convertible debt may be dilutive for EPS purposes even though the conversion option is not 'in the money' and, therefore, the holder would have no economic incentive for converting.

A different approach is used for stand-alone warrants and options to deliver ordinary shares. This approach determines dilution by comparing the average share price with the exercise price of the option. The approach illustrates how many shares are issued for nil consideration and, therefore, unlike the if-converted method, does take into account the extent to which the written option is in the money. This is referred to as the 'treasury stock' method.

The existence of two different approaches in determining the adjustment for the denominator can result in different EPS amounts for very similar arrangements. For example, applying the 'if-converted' method for an issue of convertible bonds will result in a larger adjustment to the denominator compared to an issue of debt plus a stand-alone warrant to which the 'treasury stock' method will apply.

5.3 Identifying dilutive potential ordinary shares

5.3.1 Steps for identifying dilutive potential ordinary shares

Antidilutive potential ordinary shares are disregarded in the calculation of diluted EPS. Therefore, once the entity has identified all of the potential ordinary shares in issue, the next step is to determine which of these are dilutive, and which are antidilutive.

Potential ordinary shares are treated as dilutive if their conversion to ordinary shares would decrease earnings per share or increase loss per share *from continuing operations*. [IAS 33:41]

IAS 33 specifies the steps to be followed in determining which potential ordinary shares are dilutive, as set out below. Each different category of potential ordinary shares is tested. The order in which they are tested is not left to each entity to choose, but is set out in the Standard. [IAS 33:44]

Step 1	The entity lists each different category of potential ordinary shares that it has in issue, e.g. a 5 per cent convertible bond would be considered separately from a 7 per cent convertible bond.
Step 2	For each category of potential ordinary shares, the entity determines how the earnings would have been affected had the potential ordinary shares been converted to shares on the first day of the year (or on the date of issue of the potential ordinary shares, if later). The adjustments to earnings for this purpose will be the same as the adjustments summarised at **5.9**.
Step 3	For each category of potential ordinary shares, the entity then determines (in accordance with the rules in the Standard) the number of shares that would be issued if the potential ordinary shares were converted to shares. Thus, if an entity has bonds convertible into 100,000 ordinary shares, the number of shares to be issued will be 100,000. If the same entity has granted 100,000 share options, however, the number of shares to be used in the calculation is not 100,000, but the number deemed to be issued for nil proceeds (see **5.5.3.1**). In addition, not all options are considered at this stage (see **5.5.3.2** for a discussion as to which options to include in this exercise).

Step 4	The adjustment to earnings is then divided by the number of shares that would be issued on conversion to give, for each category of potential ordinary shares, the 'earnings per incremental share' that would have been generated had the additional shares been issued.
Step 5	These earnings per incremental share are ranked – the lowest being ranked first and the largest increase in earnings per new share being ranked last. Options and warrants are generally included first because they have no earnings effect.
Step 6	The net profit per share from continuing operations is then adjusted for the category of potential ordinary shares ranked first by increasing the continuing earnings and increasing the number of shares.
Step 7	The 'before' and 'after' are compared – if the adjusted net profit per share from continuing operations is less, the potential ordinary shares are dilutive. This is repeated for each category of potential ordinary shares in turn in accordance with its ranking, until only antidilutive potential ordinary shares remain.
Step 8	Diluted EPS is calculated by adjusting basic EPS for the effect of the dilutive potential ordinary shares identified in Step 7.

5.3.2   Net profit per share from continuing operations

In order to determine which potential ordinary shares are dilutive, IAS 33 requires an analysis of the effect of conversion to ordinary shares on profit or loss from continuing operations attributable to the parent entity. [IAS 33:42]

Profit or loss per share from continuing operations is calculated as:

Profit or loss attributable to the shareholders of the parent entity after adjustments for the effects of preference shares and after excluding items relating to discontinued operations

---

Weighted average number of shares used to calculate basic EPS

5.3.3   Example illustrating the process for identifying dilutive potential ordinary shares

The following example, reproduced from Example 9 of the illustrative examples accompanying IAS 33, illustrates the process for identifying dilutive potential ordinary shares.

Example 5.3.3

Calculation of weighted average number of shares: determining the order in which to include dilutive instruments

[IAS 33 Illustrative examples: Example 9]

Note that this example does not illustrate the classification of the components of convertible financial instruments as liabilities and equity or the classification of related interest and dividends as expenses and equity as required by IAS 32.

Earnings	CU
Profit from continuing operations attributable to the parent entity	16,400,000
Less dividends on preference shares	(6,400,000)
Profit from continuing operations attributable to ordinary equity holders of the parent entity	10,000,000
Loss from discontinued operations attributable to the parent entity	(4,000,000)
Profit attributable to ordinary equity holders of the parent entity	6,000,000
Ordinary shares outstanding	2,000,000
Average market price of one ordinary share during year	CU75.00

Potential ordinary shares

Options	100,000 with exercise price of CU60
Convertible preference shares	800,000 shares with a par value of CU100 entitled to a cumulative dividend of CU8 per share. Each preference share is convertible to two ordinary shares.
5 per cent convertible bonds	Nominal amount CU100,000,000. Each CU1,000 bond is convertible to 20 ordinary shares. There is no amortisation of premium or discount affecting the determination of interest expense.
Tax rate	40 per cent

Increase in earnings attributable to ordinary equity holders on conversion of potential ordinary shares

	Increase in earnings	Increase in number of ordinary shares	Earnings per incremental share
	CU		CU
Options			
Increase in earnings	Nil		
Incremental shares issued for no consideration			
100,000 × (CU75 – CU60) ÷ CU75		20,000	Nil
Convertible preference shares			
Increase in profit			
CU800,000 × 100 × 0.08	6,400,000		
Incremental shares			
2 × 800,000		1,600,000	4.00
5 per cent convertible bonds			
Increase in profit			
CU100,000,000 × 0.05 × (1 – 0.40)	3,000,000		
Incremental shares			
100,000 × 20		2,000,000	1.50

The order in which to include the dilutive instruments is therefore:

(1)   Options
(2)   5% convertible bonds
(3)   Convertible preference shares

Calculation of diluted earnings per share

	Profit from continuing operations attributable to ordinary equity holders of the parent entity (control number)	Ordinary shares	Per share	
	CU		CU	
As reported	10,000,000	2,000,000	5.00	
Options	–	20,000		
	10,000,000	2,020,000	4.95	Dilutive
5 per cent convertible bonds	3,000,000	2,000,000		
	13,000,000	4,020,000	3.23	Dilutive

	Profit from continuing operations attributable to ordinary equity holders of the parent entity (control number)	Ordinary shares	Per share
	CU		CU
Convertible preference shares	6,400,000	1,600,000	
	19,400,000	5,620,000	3.45 Antidilutive

Because diluted earnings per share is increased when taking the convertible preference shares into account (from CU3.23 to CU3.45), the convertible preference shares are antidilutive and are ignored in the calculation of diluted earnings per share. Therefore, diluted earnings per share for profit from continuing operations is CU3.23:

	Basic EPS	Diluted EPS
	CU	CU
Profit from continuing operations attributable to ordinary equity holders of the parent entity	5.00	3.23
Loss from discontinued operations attributable to ordinary equity holders of the parent entity	(2.00)[a]	(0.99)[b]
Profit attributable to ordinary equity holders of the parent entity	3.00[c]	2.24[d]

[a] (CU4,000,000) ÷ 2,000,000 = (CU2.00)
[b] (CU4,000,000) ÷ 4,020,000 = (CU0.99)
[c] CU6,000,000 ÷ 2,000,000 = CU3.00
[d] (CU6,000,000 + CU3,000,000) ÷ 4,020,000 = CU2.24

5.3.4 Can diluted earnings per share ever be greater than basic earnings per share?

When an entity reports discontinued operations, it is possible for diluted EPS on total earnings to be greater than basic EPS. The reason for this is that IAS 33 treats potential ordinary shares as dilutive if their conversion would decrease earnings per share or increase loss per share *from continuing operations*. Both basic and diluted EPS, on the other hand, will be calculated both on profit or loss from continuing operations and on total profit or loss. Thus, although diluted EPS can never exceed basic EPS for continuing operations, it is possible for diluted EPS to exceed basic EPS when calculated for total profit or loss.

The Application Guidance to IAS 33 cites the following example. [IAS 33:A3]

Example 5.3.4

Control number

[IAS 33:A3]

Assume that an entity has profit from continuing operations attributable to the parent entity of CU4,800, a loss from discontinued operations attributable to the parent entity of (CU7,200), a loss attributable to the parent entity of (CU2,400), and 2,000 ordinary shares and 400 potential ordinary shares outstanding. The entity's basic earnings per share is CU2.40 for continuing operations, (CU3.60) for discontinued operations and (CU1.20) for the loss. The 400 potential ordinary shares are included in the diluted earnings per share calculation because the resulting CU2.00 earnings per share for continuing operations is dilutive, assuming no profit or loss impact of those 400 potential ordinary shares. Because profit from continuing operations attributable to the parent entity is the control number, the entity also includes those 400 potential ordinary shares in the calculation of the other earnings per share amounts, even though the resulting earnings per share amounts are antidilutive to their comparable basic earnings per share amounts, i.e. the loss per share is less [(CU3.00) per share for the loss from discontinued operations and (CU1.00) per share for the loss].

5.4   Convertible debt or equity instruments

5.4.1   Convertible debt or equity instruments – general approach

Conversion to ordinary shares is assumed to occur on the first day of the period or the date of issue of the convertible instrument, if later.

In applying the if-converted method (see **5.2.4**), conversion is not assumed for the purposes of computing diluted EPS if the effect is antidilutive.

Convertible debt is antidilutive whenever its interest (net of tax and other changes in income or expense) per ordinary share obtainable on conversion exceeds basic earnings per share. Convertible preference shares are antidilutive whenever the amount of the dividend on such shares declared in, or accumulated for, the current period per ordinary share obtainable on conversion exceeds basic earnings per share. [IAS 33:50]

The current value of the ordinary shares relative to the conversion price of the convertible instrument is not, by itself, a determinant of whether an instrument is dilutive or antidilutive.

For example, Company A has convertible debt that, pursuant to its original conversion terms, converts at a rate of CU10 per ordinary share. The market price of Company A's ordinary shares at the date the convertible debt was issued was CU8 per share. By the end of the reporting period, Company A's share price had fallen to CU6 per share. Even though an economically rational person would not be expected to convert the debt to ordinary shares at that time, the convertible debt is included in the computation of diluted EPS if the interest expense (net of tax and other adjustments) per ordinary share obtainable on conversion does not exceed basic EPS. In other words, the instrument will be antidilutive for Company A if the adjustment to profits by adding back the interest expense is greater in relative terms than the adjustment to the increase in the number of shares (i.e. the increase in the numerator is greater than the increase in the denominator). To illustrate, if Company A had 1,000 ordinary shares in issue and profits of CU500, the basic EPS would be CU0.50. If interest expense on the convertible debt was CU50 and the number of ordinary shares potentially issued under the terms of the convertible debt is 100, then the convertible bond is not dilutive because the adjustment to earnings is exactly in proportion to the adjustment to the number of shares [(CU500 + CU50) / (1,000 + 100) = CU0.50]. If the interest expense per ordinary share that may be issued under the convertible bond is less than CU0.50, the convertible bond will be dilutive.

5.4.2 Convertible debt or equity instruments – adjustment to earnings

The adjustment is the post-tax amount recognised in profit or loss for finance costs related to the potential ordinary shares (and any consequential adjustments, as discussed at **5.2.2**).

For a debt instrument, this will be the post-tax effect of:

- interest costs recognised in profit and loss;

- amortisation of issue costs;

- any fair value gains/losses taken to profit or loss in respect of the instrument (e.g. because the instrument is designated as at fair value through profit or loss, or because the instrument is the subject of a fair value hedge); and

- amortisation of redemption premium or discount.

For shares, the adjustment will be the post-tax effect of:

- dividends recognised in the period;

- amortisation of issue costs;

- fair value gains/losses if the instrument is measured at fair value through profit or loss; and

- amortisation of redemption premium or discount (see **4.2.3.4**).

The calculation used for determining diluted EPS for convertible instruments is often referred to as the 'if-converted' method (see **5.2.4**).

Example 5.4.2

Adjustment to earnings arising from convertible instruments

An entity has a profit attributable to ordinary shareholders for the year ended 31 December 20X5 of CU7,400,000. The entity has three different types of potential ordinary shares in issue, as follows:

- CU1,000,000 6 per cent convertible redeemable bonds (issued in 20X2);
- CU1,000,000 8 per cent convertible bonds (issued 1 July 20X5); and
- 1,000,000 CU1 17 per cent convertible preference shares (issued in 20X3).

The finance costs recognised in profit or loss (and associated tax effects) for the year ended 31 December 20X5 were as follows.

	Finance costs recognised in profit or loss for the year	Associated tax credit	Net of tax cost
	CU	CU	CU
6 per cent bonds*	70,000	21,000	49,000
8 per cent bonds**	40,000	12,000	28,000
Preference shares	170,000	–	170,000

* Including accrued redemption premium

** The bonds were only issued on 1 July 20X5 and so the finance cost is calculated from that date

The right hand column, headed 'net of tax cost', is used to adjust earnings in the diluted EPS calculation if the potential ordinary shares are dilutive (see **5.4.1**).

The redemption or induced conversion of convertible preference shares may affect only a portion of the previously outstanding convertible preference shares. In such cases, any excess consideration (as discussed at **4.2.3.3**) is attributed to those shares that are redeemed or converted for the purpose of determining whether the remaining outstanding preference shares are dilutive. The shares redeemed or converted are considered separately from those shares that are not redeemed or converted. [IAS 33:51]

5.4.3 Convertible debt or equity instruments – adjustment to number of shares

The adjustment assumes (in respect of convertible instruments that are dilutive) that all convertible instrument holders exercise all rights to convert to ordinary shares. When different conversion ratios are allowed at different dates, the ratio used should assume the most advantageous conversion rate or exercise price from the standpoint of the holder of the potential ordinary shares.

5.4.4 Options to exchange preference shares for ordinary shares

Example 5.4.4

Options to exchange preference shares for ordinary shares

Company A issued 1,000 options that, if exercised, entitle the holder to tender each preference share in Company A in exchange for 500 ordinary shares in Company A. Each preference share has a face value of CU2,750. On the date the option was issued, the ordinary shares of Company A were trading at CU5 per share. The preference shares pay dividends at 10 per cent of face value annually. The following year, Company A had a net profit of CU15,000,000, weighted average shares outstanding of 4,000,000, and the ordinary shares of Company A had an average market price of CU15 per share.

Because the terms of the options entitle the holder to tender a preference share, the effect of the options is to change 1,000 preference shares into convertible instruments. The impact on diluted EPS is therefore calculated as for other convertible instruments. The exercise of the option is dilutive to EPS, computed as follows.

	Basic	Adjustments	Diluted
Net profit attributable to ordinary shareholders	CU15,000,000	CU275,000[a]	CU15,275,000
divided by			
Weighted average shares outstanding	4,000,000	500,000[b]	4,500,000
Earnings per share	CU3.75		CU3.39

[a] Adjustment to the numerator (CU2,750 × 1,000 × 10%) = CU275,000
[b] Adjustment to the denominator (1,000 options × 500 shares) = 500,000

5.5 Options, warrants and similar items

5.5.1 Options, warrants and similar items – general approach

IAS 33 deals with options and warrants (and other potential ordinary shares that lead to cash proceeds) by increasing the number of shares only for the number of shares deemed to be issued for no consideration. This is commonly referred to as the treasury stock method (see **5.2.2**).

For simplicity, the remainder of this section refers only to options. The rules are equally applicable to warrants and other equivalent instruments.

A rights issue is similar to an issuance of options to existing shareholders (see **4.3.3.5**). After the issue date of the rights issue, but before the exercise of the rights, diluted EPS should consider these rights to the extent that they are dilutive, in the same way as other options.

A forward sale of own shares is similar in substance to a written call option at the forward sale price and a purchased put option at the forward sale price. Consistent with IAS 33:62 (see **5.7**), the purchased put option is not dilutive. The effect of the written call option on the denominator should be determined in accordance with IAS 33:45 (see **5.5.3**). If the forward sale contract has been recognised as a derivative as at fair value through profit or loss, any gain or loss recognised in earnings should be adjusted for the purposes of calculating diluted EPS.

5.5.2   Options, warrants and similar items – adjustment to earnings

In the case of an option that is a potential ordinary share and that is classified as equity under IAS 32 *Financial Instruments: Presentation*, there is no adjustment to the numerator when computing diluted EPS because the equity instrument is not remeasured and, therefore, it has no effect on earnings during its life.

In contrast, if an option is classified as at fair value through profit or loss (FVTPL) under IFRS 9 *Financial Instruments* (or, for entities that have not yet adopted IFRS 9, under IAS 39 *Financial Instruments: Recognition and Measurement*) because it does not meet the definition of equity in paragraph 11 of IAS 32 (e.g. because it is not an exchange of a fixed amount of shares for a fixed amount of functional currency cash or another financial asset of the issuer), changes in the fair value of the option are recognised directly in earnings during the life of the instrument. If the options are determined to be dilutive (see below), the earnings numerator should be adjusted for the purposes of diluted EPS to reflect what would have been the impact on earnings if shares had been issued in accordance with the terms of the option at the start of the reporting period (or later if the option is entered into part way through the reporting period).

Instruments that fall within this category include written call options or forward sale contracts for an exchange of a fixed amount of shares for a variable amount of cash, or an exchange of a fixed amount of shares for a fixed amount of cash with a net cash settlement alternative. For such instruments (assuming that they are dilutive), the earnings numerator for diluted EPS should be adjusted for fair value gains or losses (net of the tax effect).

Potential ordinary shares are only included in the computation of diluted EPS if they are dilutive. Under IAS 33:44, in order to determine whether a potential ordinary share is dilutive or antidilutive, each issue or series of potential ordinary shares is considered separately, in sequence from the most dilutive to the least dilutive (see **5.5.3.2**). In the case of options that are potential ordinary shares measured at FVTPL, the adjustment to the numerator may be positive or negative and, therefore, care will be needed in determining whether they are dilutive.

Potential ordinary shares that are classified as equity and, therefore, do not affect earnings are usually the most dilutive.

5.5.3 Options, warrants and similar items – adjustment to number of shares

5.5.3.1 Adjustment to number of shares – general

For the purposes of calculating diluted EPS, the exercise of all dilutive options is assumed. The assumed proceeds from these instruments are regarded as having been received from the issue of ordinary shares at the average market price of ordinary shares during the period. The difference between the number of ordinary shares issued and the number of ordinary shares that would have been issued at the average market price of ordinary shares during the period is treated as an issue of ordinary shares for no consideration. [IAS 33:45]

IAS 33 does not provide any further guidance on what is meant by the 'average market price of the ordinary shares during the period'. When options or warrants are issued during the reporting period, the Standard does not specify if the average market price for this purpose should be taken to be the average for the entire reporting period or only for the period the options or warrants were outstanding.

Logically, the fair value of the ordinary shares prior to the issue of the options or warrants should have no bearing on whether the options or warrants are dilutive or antidilutive. Therefore, the average for the shorter of (1) the period the options or warrants were outstanding, and (2) the reporting period, should be used (see also **5.5.3.5**).

Example 5.5.3.1A

Consideration for acquisition of a subsidiary to be settled in cash or in shares

Company A acquires Company B. The purchase price of CU16 million is to be paid in three instalments: CU3 million at the close of the transaction, CU10 million in one year, and CU3 million in two years. At the seller's option, the final payment will be made either in cash or 100,000 of Company A's ordinary shares.

The terms of the final instalment constitute a written call option for Company A. The seller of Company B may call for 100,000 shares at a strike price of CU3 million. Prior to the exercise or expiry of the written call option, diluted EPS should be determined in accordance with IAS 33:45 (i.e. using the treasury stock method).

To calculate diluted EPS, potential ordinary shares are treated as consisting of both of the following:

[IAS 33:46]

- a contract to issue a certain number of ordinary shares at their average market price during the period. Such ordinary shares are assumed to be fairly priced and to be neither dilutive nor antidilutive. They are ignored in the calculation of diluted EPS; and

- a contract to issue the remaining ordinary shares for no consideration. Such ordinary shares generate no proceeds and have no effect on profit or loss attributable to ordinary shares outstanding. Therefore, such shares are dilutive (at least for a profitable entity – see **5.5.3.2** for an entity with a loss from continuing operations) and are added to the number of ordinary shares outstanding in the calculation of diluted EPS.

The following table summarises the steps involved in the diluted EPS calculation.

Step 1	Calculate the cash proceeds that would be received if all options were exercised at the contracted exercise price.
Step 2	Calculate the number of shares that, if issued at the average market price for the period, would generate the same proceeds, i.e.:
	• compute the average market price of ordinary shares for the accounting period; and
	• divide the cash proceeds from Step 1 by this average market price.
Step 3	Compute the number of bonus shares implicit in the option issue, i.e.:
	• compute the total number of shares that would be issued if all options were exercised; and
	• deduct from this total the number of shares deemed to be issued at the average market price from Step 2.
Step 4	Treat the resulting number of bonus shares as shares issued for no consideration.

The following example, reproduced from Example 5 of the illustrative examples accompanying IAS 33, illustrates the impact of share options on diluted EPS.

Example 5.5.3.1B

Effect of share options on diluted earnings per share

[IAS 33 Illustrative examples: Example 5]

Profit attributable to ordinary equity holders of the parent entity for year 20X1	CU1,200,000
Weighted average number of ordinary shares outstanding during year 20X1	500,000 shares
Average market price of one ordinary share during year 20X1	CU20.00
Weighted average number of shares under option during year 20X1	100,000 shares
Exercise price for shares under option during Year 20X1	CU15.00

Calculation of earnings per share

	Earnings	Shares	Per share
Profit attributable to ordinary equity holders of the parent entity for year 20X1	CU1,200,000		
Weighted average shares outstanding during year 20X1		500,000	
Basic earnings per share			CU2.40
Weighted average number of shares under option		100,000	
Weighted average number of shares that would have been issued at average market price: (100,000 × CU15.00)/CU20.00		(75,000)[a]	
Diluted earnings per share	CU1,200,000	525,000	CU2.29

[a]   Earnings have not increased because the total number of shares has increased only by the number of shares (25,000) deemed to have been issued for no consideration (see [IAS 33:46(b)]).

5.5.3.2   Identifying dilutive options

Only dilutive potential ordinary shares are included in the calculation of diluted EPS.

IAS 33:46 states that options and warrants are dilutive when they would result in the issue of ordinary shares for less than the average market price of ordinary shares during the period. For a written call option, the amount of the dilution is the average market price of ordinary shares during the period less the issue price.

For a written put option, the amount of the dilution is the average market price of ordinary shares during the period less the repurchase price. Options and warrants have a dilutive effect only when the average market price of ordinary shares during the period exceeds the exercise price of the options or warrants (i.e. they are 'in the money'). [IAS 33:47]

Example 5.5.3.2

Identifying dilutive options

At 1 January and 31 December 20X1, an entity had the following written call options outstanding.

Number of shares under option	Exercise price (CU)	Average share price during year (CU)	Dilutive (D) or antidilutive (A)	Number of shares deemed issued for no consideration
10,000	7	10	D	3,000
5,000	8	10	D	1,000
15,000	9	10	D	1,500
10,000	12	10	A	–
20,000	11	10	A	–
				5,500

5.5.3.3 Impact of options when the entity makes a loss

When an entity has a loss from continuing operations, the exercise of in the money options will increase the number of shares to which that loss is allocated, so that loss per share will decrease. Therefore, in the money options are not dilutive for such an entity, because dilution is defined by IAS 33:5 as a reduction in earnings per share or an increase in loss per share resulting from the assumption that options are exercised.

This raises the question as to whether out of the money options should be considered dilutive for an entity with a loss from continuing operations. The option holders would (irrationally) be paying too much for these shares, which is equivalent, under the approach to dilution taken by IAS 33, to the entity issuing a negative number of shares for no consideration (i.e. buying back some shares for no consideration). Accordingly, because the exercise of out of the money options would, if this method is applied, result in a reduction in the number of shares, it is mathematically correct that loss per share will increase.

Although the definition of dilution in IAS 33:5 might apparently lead to out of the money options being considered dilutive, IAS 33:47 states that "[o]ptions and warrants have a dilutive effect only when the average market price of ordinary shares during the period exceeds the exercise price of the options or warrants (i.e. they are 'in the money')".

Accordingly, because it would also be economically irrational for holders to exercise out of the money options, it appears that out of the money options should not be treated as dilutive for an entity with a loss from continuing operations.

5.5.3.4   Share-based payments

When dealing with share options and other share-based payment arrangements to which IFRS 2 *Share-based Payment* applies, the issue and exercise prices for the purposes of the diluted EPS calculations should include the fair value (measured in accordance with IFRS 2) of any goods or services to be supplied to the entity in the future under the share option or other share-based payment arrangement. [IAS 33:47A]

Employee share options with fixed or determinable terms and non-vested ordinary shares are treated as options in the calculation of diluted EPS, even though they may be contingent on vesting. They are treated as outstanding on the grant date. [IAS 33:48]

The dilutive effect of employee share options with fixed or determinable terms and non-vested ordinary shares is determined using the treasury stock method. The assumed exercise price will include the amount the employee must pay on exercise of the option as well as the balance of any amounts calculated under IFRS 2 that have not yet been recognised because they relate to future services. For share-based payments treated as equity-settled under IFRS 2, the numerator is not adjusted because the IFRS 2 charge to date will not be saved upon exercise; the IFRS 2 charge is part of the cost of employee services, and employees will continue to render services. For those share-based payments treated as cash-settled under IFRS 2, the numerator will be adjusted only for the amount in profit or loss that would not have been recognised in profit or loss had the arrangement been classified wholly as an equity instrument (as if the arrangement was treated as equity-settled).

For example, when an employee can choose whether to receive cash or shares, a scheme will be treated as cash-settled under IFRS 2, but may nevertheless give rise to dilutive potential ordinary shares under IAS 33.

The following example, reproduced from Example 5A of the illustrative examples accompanying IAS 33, illustrates the determination of the exercise price of employee share options.

Example 5.5.3.4

Determining the exercise price of employee share options

[IAS 33 Illustrative examples: Example 5A]

Weighted average number of unvested share options per employee	1,000
Weighted average amount per employee to be recognised over the remainder of the vesting period for employee services to be rendered as consideration for the share options, determined in accordance with IFRS 2 *Share-based Payment*	CU1,200
Cash exercise price of unvested share options	CU15
Calculation of adjusted exercise price	
Fair value of services yet to be rendered per employee:	CU1,200
Fair value of services yet to be rendered per option: (CU1,200/1,000)	CU1.20
Total exercise price of share options: (CU15.00 + CU1.20)	CU16.20

IAS 33 does not provide clear guidance on whether the proceeds from the assumed exercise of employee options include the tax benefits that would be credited to equity upon exercise of the employee option. In August 2008, the IASB issued an exposure draft, *Simplifying Earnings per Share*, which stated that proceeds include "the tax benefit, if any, that would be credited to equity upon exercise of the share option or other share-based payment arrangement". The proposals, although never finalised as a Standard, were intended to make clear that IAS 33 never intended to exclude those tax effects from the definition of proceeds. This approach is consistent with the US equivalent guidance, ASC 260 *Earnings per Share*.

Performance-based employee share options are treated as contingently issuable shares because their issue is contingent upon satisfying specified conditions in addition to the passage of time. [IAS 33:48] Contingently issuable shares are discussed in more detail in **5.6**.

5.5.3.5 *Calculating average market price during the period*

When calculating diluted EPS, the average market price of ordinary shares assumed to be issued is calculated on the basis of the average market price of ordinary shares during the period. In theory, the average could be determined by using every market transaction in the entity's shares during the period. In practice, however, a simple average of weekly or monthly closing prices will usually be adequate. [IAS 33:A4]

When prices fluctuate widely over the period, week or month being used, using an average of the high and low prices to calculate the average market price for the period will usually produce a more representative price than simply using closing prices. [IAS 33:A5]

The method used to compute the average market price should be used consistently, unless it is no longer representative because of changed conditions. For example, an entity that uses closing market prices to compute the average market price for several years of relatively stable market prices might need to change to an average of high and low prices if prices start fluctuating greatly and the closing market prices no longer produce a representative average market price. [IAS 33:A5]

Example 5.5.3.5A

Computation of average market price when trading volume is limited

Company A's shares trade in an over-the-counter market. During the fourth quarter of 20X1, Company A's shares were traded on only 15 days. The frequency of trades during the fourth quarter is representative of the normal trading volume on Company A's ordinary shares.

In applying the treasury stock method, should the average of the limited trading prices be used, or is another method more appropriate?

When an entity's ordinary shares trade on a very irregular basis (e.g. limited trading volume), such that an average of the closing ordinary share price is not meaningful, it would be acceptable to use the average of the bid and ask price for the ordinary shares for a period to determine the average ordinary trading price. This method should be applied until the entity's ordinary shares trade on a regular basis and an average of the closing prices would yield an effective average ordinary share price.

As with any potential ordinary share, options are included in the calculation of diluted EPS as if conversion into ordinary shares had occurred on the first day of the accounting period or, if later, on the date on which the options or other potential ordinary shares were granted. When options are granted part way through a year, the question arises as to whether the average market price should be the average from the date the option is granted to the end of the year or the average for the entire accounting period. This is illustrated by the following example (see also **5.5.3.1**).

Example 5.5.3.5B

Options in issue for only part of a period

An entity's share price is CU3 for the four months 1 January to 30 April, CU4 for the four months 1 May to 31 August and CU5 for the four months 1 September to 31 December. The average price for the year is therefore CU4.

On 1 July, the entity grants 100,000 options exercisable at CU4 per share, the then market price.

The average price from 1 July to 31 December is CU4.67.

In the circumstances described, the shares are neither dilutive nor antidilutive if compared with the average for the year, but are dilutive if compared to the average price since the date the options were granted.

Using the average for the year results in no dilution, whereas using the average from the date of grant of the options results in dilution. Given that the latter approach reflects the substance of what has happened, it seems appropriate that the entity should use the average from the date of grant of the options, notwithstanding that a literal reading of IAS 33 could point to the former approach.

Similar considerations apply when options are exercised during the year.

5.5.3.6 Options to purchase convertible instruments

Options to purchase convertible instruments are assumed to be exercised to purchase the convertible instrument whenever the average prices of both the convertible instrument and the ordinary shares obtainable upon conversion are above the exercise price of the options. However, exercise is not assumed unless the conversion of similar outstanding convertible instruments, if any, is also assumed. [IAS 33:A6]

Example 5.5.3.6

Application of treasury stock method to options to purchase convertible preference shares

Company A issued 1,000 options; each option allows the holder to purchase one convertible preference share at CU5,000 per share. Each convertible preference share is convertible to ordinary shares at CU25 per ordinary share after two years (i.e. each convertible preference share is converted into 200 ordinary shares without further payment). On the date the options were issued, the ordinary shares of Company A were trading at CU25 per share. Three years later the ordinary shares of Company A had an average market price of CU40 per share.

At the end of Year 3, the options on the ordinary shares are in the money. Therefore, using the treasury stock method (illustrated below), Company A would assume that the holders of the options would elect to exercise their options and receive the convertible preference shares for CU5,000 per share. The treasury stock method should be applied to compute the incremental dilutive shares as follows.

Shares assumed issued (1,000 × 200)		200,000
Total assumed proceeds (1,000 × CU5,000)	CU5,000,000	
Divided by the average market price	40	
Less: shares assumed to be issued at full value		125,000
Incremental shares to be included in diluted EPS		75,000

The 1,000 options do not meet the definition of equity per IAS 32:11 (because they represent an option over an instrument that itself has an option to convert into equity); therefore, the options would be measured at fair value through profit or loss. If the add back of the fair value gains/losses in the period to the numerator was less in proportion to the incremental shares added to the denominator, then the effect would be dilutive.

5.5.3.7   Options to be exercised using instruments of the entity

The terms of options may permit or require debt or other instruments of the entity (or its parent or a subsidiary) to be tendered in payment of all or a portion of the exercise price. When calculating diluted EPS, those options have a dilutive effect if:

[IAS 33:A7]

- the average market price of the related ordinary shares for the period exceeds the exercise price; or

- the selling price of the instrument to be tendered is below that at which the instrument may be tendered under the option agreement and the resulting discount establishes an effective exercise price below the market price of the ordinary shares obtainable upon exercise.

When calculating diluted EPS, those options are assumed to be exercised and the debt or other instruments are assumed to be tendered. If tendering cash is more advantageous to the option holder and is permitted by the contract, tendering of cash is assumed. Interest (net of tax) on any debt assumed to be tendered is added back as an adjustment to the numerator. [IAS 33:A7]

Similar treatment is given to preference shares that have similar provisions or to other instruments that have conversion options that permit the investor to pay cash for a more favourable conversion rate. [IAS 33:A8]

5.5.3.8   Proceeds from options to be applied to redeem debt or other instruments

Some options may have underlying terms that require the proceeds received from the exercise of those instruments to be applied to redeem debt or other instruments of the entity (or its parent or a subsidiary). When calculating diluted EPS, those options are assumed to be exercised and the proceeds applied to purchase the debt at its average market price rather than to purchase ordinary shares. Nevertheless, the excess proceeds received from the assumed exercise over the amount used for the assumed purchase of debt are taken into account in calculating diluted EPS (i.e. the excess is assumed to be used to buy back ordinary shares). Interest (net of tax) on any debt assumed to be purchased is added back as an adjustment to the numerator. [IAS 33:A9]

Example 5.5.3.8

Proceeds from options applied to repurchase preference shares

Company A issued 400,000 options, which allow the holder to purchase ordinary shares at CU40 per share. If the options are exercised, Company A is required to use the proceeds to repurchase 1,000 preference shares of CU2,750 face value per share. The preference shares pay dividends at 10 per cent annually and had an average fair value of CU2,800. The following year, Company A had net income of CU15,000,000, weighted average shares outstanding of 4,000,000, and the ordinary shares of Company A had an average market price of CU50 per share.

Because the exercise of the options does not require the holder to be the holder of a preference share, the dilutive effect of these options should be determined in accordance with IAS 33:45 (see **5.5.3.1**). The options on the ordinary shares are in the money. Therefore, using the treasury stock method, Company A would assume that the holders of the options would elect to exercise their options. Because the exercise of the options would dilute EPS, Company A would apply the treasury stock method to compute the incremental dilutive shares as follows.

	Basic	Adjustments	Diluted
Net profit attributable to ordinary shareholders	CU15,000,000	CU275,000[a]	CU15,275,000
divided by			
Weighted average shares outstanding	4,000,000	136,000[b]	4,136,000
Earnings per share	3.75		3.69

[a]   Adjustment to the numerator (CU2,750 × 1,000 × 10%) = CU275,000

[b]   Adjustment to weighted number of shares outstanding is calculated as follows.

Shares in issue	400,000
Total assumed proceeds (400,000 × CU40)	CU16,000,000
Less: amount required to retire preference shares (CU2,800 × 1,000)	CU2,800,000
Excess proceeds assumed to buy treasury shares	CU13,200,000
Divided by the average price of the ordinary shares	50
Less: shares assumed to be issued at average price	(264,000)
Adjustment to the denominator (incremental shares)	136,000

5.6 Contingently issuable shares

5.6.1 Contingently issuable shares – general approach

Contingently issuable shares are shares that will be issued at a future date, subject to the satisfaction of conditions. The conditions can be linked to earnings, the market price of the shares or something else. Although contingently issuable shares are another example of potential ordinary shares, they are nevertheless sometimes included in the calculation of basic EPS (see **4.3.2.5**). The following sections discuss the impact of contingently issuable shares on diluted EPS.

By virtue of their inclusion in basic EPS, ordinary shares whose issue is contingent upon the occurrence of certain events are also included in the calculation of diluted EPS if the conditions have been met (i.e. the events have occurred) at the end of the reporting period.

If all necessary conditions have not been satisfied (and, therefore, these shares have not been included in the calculation of basic EPS), the number of contingently issuable shares included in diluted EPS is to be based on the number of shares, if any, that would be issuable if the end of the reporting period were the end of the contingency period and if the result would be dilutive. [IAS 33:52]

Those contingently issuable shares will be included in the denominator of diluted EPS as of the beginning of the period (or as of the date of the contingent share agreement, if later). [IAS 33:52]

5.6.2 Contingently issuable shares – adjustment to earnings

Contingently issuable shares have no impact on the earnings figure used to calculate diluted EPS. This applies even if the condition relates to earnings levels. The reason for this is that the number of contingently issuable shares included in the diluted EPS calculation is always based on the status of the condition at the end of the reporting period. Therefore, when the condition relates to earnings levels, shares are not included in the calculation unless the required earnings level has already been achieved.

5.6.3 Contingently issuable shares – adjustment to number of shares

5.6.3.1 Adjustment to number of shares – general

As discussed at **4.3.2.5**, contingently issuable shares are included in the calculation of basic EPS if the conditions have been satisfied at the end of the reporting period. Contingently issuable shares are included in basic EPS calculations from the date when all necessary conditions have been satisfied and, thus, although issuing the shares is still a future transaction, it is no longer contingent. [IAS 33:24]

When the conditions have not been satisfied before the end of the reporting period, and the shares remain contingently issuable, they will be included in the calculation of diluted EPS based on the number of shares that would be issuable if the end of the reporting period were the end of the contingency period. [IAS 33:52]

Restatement of amounts previously reported for diluted EPS is not permitted if the conditions are not met when the contingency period expires. [IAS 33:52]

5.6.3.2   Condition expressed as the attainment of a specified amount of earnings

If the condition for contingent issue is the attainment or maintenance of a specified amount of earnings for a period, and if that amount has been attained at the end of the period but must be maintained beyond the end of the reporting period for an additional period, then the additional ordinary shares are taken into account, if the effect is dilutive, when calculating diluted EPS. The calculation of diluted EPS is based on the number of ordinary shares that would be issued if the amount of earnings at the end of the reporting period were the amount of earnings at the end of the contingency period. [IAS 33:53]

The calculation of basic EPS does not include such contingently issuable ordinary shares until the end of the contingency period because not all necessary conditions have been satisfied, in that earnings may change in a future period (see **example 4.3.2.5C**). [IAS 33:53]

5.6.3.3   Condition expressed as an average over a period

When a condition is expressed as an average over a period, it has the same effect as if it were expressed as a cumulative amount over the period, i.e. the performance achieved to date is deemed to be that achieved over the whole of the contingency period. For example, if the number of shares to be issued depends on whether profits average CU1,000,000 per annum over a three-year period, the condition is expressed in terms of a cumulative target of CU3,000,000 over the three-year period. If, at the end of the first year, profits are CU1,500,000, no additional shares are brought into the calculation. On the other hand, if profits of CU5,000,000 have been achieved at the end of the first year, the additional shares are included in the calculation of diluted EPS because, if the end of the first year were the end of the contingency period, the condition would have been achieved.

Again, this can be contrasted with the treatment for the purposes of basic EPS, as discussed at **4.3.2.5**. Even when CU5,000,000 has been earned by the end of the first year, the shares are not included for the purposes of basic EPS, because the condition has not been achieved. It cannot be achieved until the end of the contingency period – because there is a possibility (however remote) of losses for the remainder of the period, which could reduce average profits below the target level.

Example 5.6.3.3

Contingency based on average profits

A Limited acquires B Limited on 1 January 20X1. A Limited agrees to issue 100,000 shares to the vendor on 1 January 20X4 if B Limited's profits for the three years to 31 December 20X3 average CU10 million or more.

B Limited's profits for 20X1 and 20X2 are CU17 million each year. The requirement for average profits of CU10 million over three years is treated as a requirement for total profits of CU30 million over the three years.

Actual profits in 20X1 of CU17 million are below the target of CU30 million and, accordingly, the 100,000 shares are excluded from the diluted EPS calculation for 20X1.

Actual profits for 20X1 and 20X2 together total CU34 million. This exceeds the target and, thus, the 100,000 shares should be included in diluted EPS for 20X2. The shares will be included even if B Limited expects to make a loss of CU4 million or more in 20X3.

(See **example 4.3.2.5C** for an illustration of how the shares should be dealt with in the calculation of basic EPS.)

5.6.3.4   Condition dependent on future market price of shares

When the number of shares that may be issued in the future depends upon the market price of the shares of the issuing entity, the number of shares to be included in the calculation of diluted EPS, if dilutive, is based on the number that would be issued if the market price at the end of the reporting period were the market price at the end of the contingency period. [IAS 33:54]

If the condition is based on the average of market prices over some period of time that extends beyond the end of reporting period, the average for the period of time that has lapsed is used. [IAS 33:54]

The calculation of basic EPS does not include such contingently issuable ordinary shares because not all necessary conditions have been satisfied, in that the market price may change in a future period. [IAS 33:54]

Example 5.6.3.4

Contingency based on share price movements

An entity is to issue the following shares to a third party on 1 October 20X2, dependent upon the entity's share price on 30 September 20X2.

Number of shares	Share price on 30 September 20X2
Nil	CU10 or less
10,000	>CU10 and <CU11
15,000	CU11 or above

If, on 31 December 20X1 (the last day of the entity's reporting period), the share price were CU9, no shares would be included in the diluted EPS calculation, whereas an additional 10,000 shares would be included if the share price on 31 December 20X1 were CU10.20.

If the share price had been above CU10 every day during the reporting period and up to the date the financial statements were authorised for issue, other than on 31 December 20X1 when the price dipped to CU9.98, based on the principles discussed above, none of these shares would be included in the diluted EPS calculation.

If the issue had been conditional upon the average share price for the last five business days up to and including 30 September 20X2, the diluted EPS would be computed by looking at the share price on the last five business days up to and including 31 December 20X1 and comparing this with the target average price.

5.6.3.5   Multiple conditions

When the share issue is dependent on a number of conditions being met (e.g. a product licence being granted before a certain date *and* a profit target over the same period), then the diluted EPS calculation should only include those shares when all (or both in the case of this example) the conditions have been met at the end of the reporting period.

Similarly, when the number of shares contingently issuable depends both on future earnings and future prices of the ordinary shares, the number of ordinary shares included in diluted EPS is based on both conditions (i.e. earnings to date and the current market price at the end of the reporting period). The contingently issuable shares are not included in diluted EPS unless both conditions are met. [IAS 33:55]

5.6.3.6   Number of shares to be issued not known

For deferred consideration agreements in which the value of consideration is fixed but the number of shares issuable is not known, the number of shares to be included in the calculation of diluted EPS is based on the market price at the end of the reporting period as if it were the end of the contingency period if the effect is dilutive. (See **4.3.2.7** for the treatment of such shares in the calculation of basic EPS.) [IAS 33:54]

5.6.3.7 Other conditions

If the contingency is based on a condition other than earnings or market price, the contingently issuable shares are included in the diluted EPS calculation on the assumption that the status of the condition at the end of the reporting period will remain unchanged until the end of the contingency period. [IAS 33:56] For example, if a further issue of shares is generated on the opening of the tenth new retail outlet and, at the year end, only five have been opened, no contingently issuable shares are included in the diluted computation.

Example 5.6.3.7A

Contingency based on an event

A Limited acquires B Limited on 1 January 20X1. A Limited agrees to issue 100,000 shares to the vendor on 1 January 20X3 if, at any point prior to that date, a new product developed by B Limited is granted a licence.

A Limited's year end is 31 December. The 20X1 financial statements are approved on 22 March 20X2. The product is granted a licence on 4 March 20X2.

Even though the directors of A Limited know, at the date they approve the 20X1 financial statements, that the additional 100,000 shares will be issued to the vendor on 1 January 20X3, the shares are excluded from the calculation of diluted EPS for 20X1 because, at the end of the reporting period, the licence had not been granted.

The 100,000 shares will be included in the calculation of diluted EPS for 20X2, as if they had been in issue throughout the entire year.

(See **example 4.3.2.5A** for a discussion of the effect of the arrangement on the calculation of basic EPS.)

Another example of a contingency based on an event is when shares are contingently issuable depending only on the favourable outcome of a lawsuit. Such shares should be excluded from the calculation of basic and diluted EPS until the outcome of the lawsuit is determined. When the outcome of the lawsuit is final, the shares should be included in basic EPS from the date of finalisation of the lawsuit and included in diluted EPS from the beginning of the period in which the lawsuit is finalised (or from the date of the contingent share agreement, if later).

Similar logic should be applied for shares that will be issued in the event that the entity completes a successful Initial Public Offering (IPO). Because there are many factors that can affect the successful completion of an IPO, the contingency is not met until the IPO actually becomes effective. Therefore, for periods ending prior to the effective date of the IPO, the shares should not be considered in the denominator for computation of diluted EPS. For periods ending after the IPO is effective, the shares should be included in the denominator of diluted EPS from the beginning of the period in which the IPO is effective (or from the date of the contingent share agreement, if later). For basic EPS, shares that are contingently issuable in the event of an IPO should be included in the denominator from the effective date of the IPO (which may be earlier than the date the shares are actually issued), and then only on a weighted average basis.

The following example, reproduced from Example 7 of the illustrative examples accompanying IAS 33, continues from **example 4.3.2.5E** and provides another illustration of contingently issuable shares.

Example 5.6.3.7B

Contingently issuable shares

[IAS 33 Illustrative examples: Example 7]

Ordinary shares outstanding during 20X1	1,000,000 (there were no options, warrants or convertible instruments outstanding during the period)

An agreement related to a recent business combination provides for the issue of additional ordinary shares based on the following conditions:

	5,000 additional ordinary shares for each new retail site opened during 20X1
	1,000 additional ordinary shares for each CU1,000 of consolidated profit in excess of CU2,000,000 for the year ended 31 December 20X1
Retail sites opened during the year:	one on 1 May 20X1
	one on 1 September 20X1
Consolidated year-to-date profit attributable to ordinary equity holders of the parent entity:	CU1,100,000 as of 31 March 20X1
	CU2,300,000 as of 30 June 20X1
	CU1,900,000 as of 30 September 20X1 (including a CU450,000 loss from a discontinued operation)
	CU2,900,000 as of 31 December 20X1

[The calculation of basic EPS is illustrated in **example 4.3.2.5E**.]

Diluted earnings per share

	First quarter	Second quarter	Third quarter	Fourth quarter	Full year
Numerator (CU)	1,100,000	1,200,000	(400,000)	1,000,000	2,900,000
Denominator:					
Ordinary shares outstanding	1,000,000	1,000,000	1,000,000	1,000,000	1,000,000
Retail site contingency	–	5,000	10,000	10,000	10,000
Earnings contingency	–[a]	300,000[b]	–[c]	900,000[d]	900,000[d]
Total shares	1,000,000	1,305,000	1,010,000	1,910,000	1,910,000
Diluted earnings per share (CU)	1.10	0.92	(0.40)[e]	0.52	1.52

[a]   Company A does not have year-to-date profit exceeding CU2,000,000 at 31 March 20X1. The Standard does not permit projecting future earnings levels and including the related contingent shares.

[b]   [(CU2,300,000 – CU2,000,000)/1,000] × 1,000 shares = 300,000 shares.

[c]   Year-to-date profit is less than CU2,000,000.

[d]   [(CU2,900,000 – CU2,000,000)/1,000] × 1,000 shares = 900,000 shares

[e]   Because the loss during the third quarter is attributable to a loss from a discontinued operation, the antidilution rules do not apply. The control number (i.e. profit or loss from continuing operations attributable to the equity holders of the parent entity) is positive. Accordingly, the effect of potential ordinary shares is included in the calculation of diluted earnings per share.

5.6.4   Contingently issuable potential ordinary shares

To assess whether contingently issuable potential ordinary shares (other than those covered by a contingent share agreement, such as contingently issuable convertible instruments) should be included in the diluted EPS calculation:

[IAS 33:57]

- determine whether the potential ordinary shares may be assumed to be issuable on the basis of the conditions specified for their issue, based on the guidance outlined in the previous sections for contingently issuable shares; and

- if those potential ordinary shares should be reflected in diluted EPS, determine their impact on the calculation of diluted EPS by following the appropriate rules discussed above for the type of potential ordinary share (options and warrants, convertible instruments etc.).

Exercise or conversion is not assumed for the purpose of calculating diluted EPS, however, unless exercise or conversion of similar outstanding potential ordinary shares that are not contingently issuable is assumed. [IAS 33:57]

Thus, for example, contingently issuable options will be included in the calculation of diluted EPS if both of the following conditions are met:

- if the end of the reporting period were the end of the contingency period, the options would be issued; and

- the effect of the options is dilutive.

Example 5.6.4

Contingently issuable options

On 1 July 20X1, an entity agreed that, provided that its profit over the two years to 30 June 20X3 exceeds a specified target, on 1 July 20X3 it will issue 10,000 share options exercisable at CU5 per share from 1 July 20X4 to 30 June 20X9.

The average market price of the entity's ordinary shares during the year ended 31 December 20X2 was CU5.50.

The treatment of the options will depend on whether the profit target has been reached at the end of the reporting period (31 December 20X2).

- If it has, the options will be included in the 20X2 diluted EPS calculation (using the treasury stock method).

- If it has not, nothing is included in the 20X2 diluted EPS calculation in respect of the options.

5.6.5 Contracts that may be settled in cash or in shares

5.6.5.1 Conversion at the option of the issuer

An entity may issue a contract that may be settled in cash or in ordinary shares at the entity's option (e.g. a debt instrument that, on maturity, gives the entity the unrestricted right to settle the principal amount in cash or in its own shares). For such contracts, the calculation of diluted EPS should be based on the assumption that the contract will be settled in ordinary shares, so that the resulting potential ordinary shares should be included in diluted EPS if the effect is dilutive. [IAS 33:58]

When such a contract is presented for accounting purposes as an asset or a liability, or has an equity component and a liability component, the numerator in the diluted EPS calculation should be adjusted for any changes in profit or loss that would have resulted during the period if the contract had been classified wholly as an equity instrument. [IAS 33:59] The adjustment is similar to those discussed at **5.2.2**.

The following example, reproduced from Example 8 of the illustrative examples accompanying IAS 33, provides an illustration of convertible bonds settled in shares or cash at the issuer's option.

Example 5.6.5.1

Convertible bonds settled in shares or cash at the issuer's option

[IAS 33 Illustrative examples: Example 8]

An entity issues 2,000 convertible bonds at the beginning of Year 1. The bonds have a three-year term, and are issued at par with a face value of CU1,000 per bond, giving total proceeds of CU2,000,000. Interest is payable annually in arrears at a nominal annual interest rate of 6 per cent. Each bond is convertible at any time up to maturity into 250 ordinary shares. The entity has an option to settle the principal amount of the convertible bonds in ordinary shares or in cash.

When the bonds are issued, the prevailing market interest rate for similar debt without a conversion option is 9 per cent. At the issue date, the market price of one ordinary share is CU3. Income tax is ignored.

Profit attributable to ordinary equity holders of the parent entity Year 1	CU1,000,000
Ordinary shares outstanding	1,200,000
Convertible bonds outstanding	2,000
Allocation of proceeds of the bond issue:	
Liability component	CU1,848,122[a]
Equity component	CU151,878
	CU2,000,000

The liability and equity components would be determined in accordance with IAS 32 *Financial Instruments: Presentation*. These amounts are recognised as the initial carrying amounts of the liability and equity components. The amount assigned to the issuer conversion option equity element is an addition to equity and is not adjusted.

Basic earnings per share Year 1:

CU1,000,000/1,200,000 = CU0.83 per ordinary share

Diluted earnings per share Year 1:

It is presumed that the issuer will settle the contract by the issue of ordinary shares. The dilutive effect is therefore calculated in accordance with paragraph 59 of the Standard.

(CU1,000,000 + CU166,331[b])/(1,200,000 + 500,000[c]) = CU0.69 per share

[a]   This represents the present value of the principal and interest discounted at 9% – CU2,000,000 payable at the end of three years; CU120,000 payable annually in arrears for three years.

[b]   Profit is adjusted for the accretion of CU166,331 (CU1,848,122 × 9%) of the liability because of the passage of time.

[c]   500,000 ordinary shares = 250 ordinary shares × 2,000 convertible bonds.

Example 8 of the illustrative examples accompanying IAS 33 (reproduced above) shows a convertible bond split into its financial liability and equity components. The example states that the issuer has the option to settle the principal amount of the convertible bond in ordinary shares or cash. The example is not clear whether the issuer's right is to settle the principal in a fixed number of ordinary shares or a variable number of ordinary shares equal to the amount of the principal. Because a financial liability is recognised for the present value of the interest and principal amount and a written call option is recognised in equity for the holder's right to convert the liability into a fixed number of shares, then it is assumed that the issuer's option must be a right to settle the principal amount in either cash or a variable number of shares equal to the value of the principal amount. The issuer's option cannot be a right to settle the principal amount in a fixed number of shares or this itself would be equity, i.e. a purchased put option.

Had the issuer's option instead been a right for the issuer to settle in a fixed number of shares or cash equal to the value of the shares in the instance when the holder chose to convert, then the whole instrument would be classified as a financial liability (i.e. without an equity component) because the holder's right to convert would include a cash settlement alternative which would prevent the conversion option meeting the definition of equity in IAS 32. In this case, the if-converted method (see **5.2.4**) would be applied and the total impact in earnings with respect to the instrument would be added to the numerator in determining earnings for diluted EPS.

5.6.5.2 Conversion at the option of the holder

When the holder has the option to choose between settlement in ordinary shares or cash, the more dilutive of cash settlement and share settlement is used in calculating diluted EPS. [IAS 33:60]

An example of this type of instrument is a written put option that gives the holder a choice of settling in ordinary shares or in cash. [IAS 33:61]

5.7 Purchased options

Contracts such as purchased put options and purchased call options (i.e. options held by the entity on its own ordinary shares) are not included in the calculation of diluted EPS. This is because including them would be antidilutive: a put option would be exercised only if the exercise price were higher than the market price, and a call option would be exercised only if the exercise price were lower than the market price. [IAS 33:62]

5.8   Forward purchase contracts and written put options

Contracts that require the entity to repurchase its own shares, such as forward purchase contracts and written put options, are reflected in the calculation of diluted EPS if the entity applies the accounting policy described in Alternative 1 described at **4.3.2.9** and the effect is dilutive.

If these contracts are in the money during the period (i.e. the exercise or settlement price is higher than the average market price for that period), the potential dilutive effect on EPS is calculated as follows:

[IAS 33:63]

- it is assumed that, at the beginning of the period, sufficient ordinary shares will be issued (at the average market price during the period) to raise proceeds to satisfy the contract;

- it is assumed that the proceeds from the issue are used to satisfy the contract (i.e. to buy back the ordinary shares); and

- the incremental ordinary shares (i.e. the difference between the number of ordinary shares assumed issued and the number of ordinary shares received from satisfying the contract) are included in the calculation of diluted EPS.

This technique is commonly referred to as the 'reverse treasury stock' method.

A forward purchase of own shares is similar in substance to a written put option at the forward sale price and a purchased call option at the forward sale price.

Consistent with IAS 33:62 (see **5.7**), the purchased call option is not dilutive. The effect of the written put option on the denominator should be determined in accordance with IAS 33:63 described immediately above, i.e. the shares subject to forward purchase should be regarded as outstanding for the period. This guidance applies to forward purchase contracts even though the paragraph is headed *Written put options* because 'forward purchase contracts' are also referred to in that guidance.

The interest cost recognised in profit or loss in respect of the forward purchase liability should be added back for the purposes of determining diluted EPS.

Example 5.8A

Written put options (1)

[IAS 33:A10]

Assume that an entity has outstanding 120 written put options on its ordinary shares with an exercise price of CU35. The average market price of its ordinary shares for the period is CU28. In calculating diluted earnings per share, the entity assumes that it issued 150 shares at CU28 per share at the beginning of the period to satisfy its put obligation of CU4,200. The difference between the 150 ordinary shares issued and the 120 ordinary shares received from satisfying the put option (30 incremental ordinary shares) is added to the denominator in calculating diluted earnings per share.

Example 5.8B

Written put options (2)

Company A issued CU100 million in debt instruments with detachable put options on its ordinary shares. Purchasers of each CU1,000 note will receive 10 put options each, giving the holder the right to require Company A to purchase one share of its ordinary shares for CU25 (the market price of the ordinary shares on the date the put options were issued). The put options are exercisable at any time during a three-year period. Assume the average market price of the ordinary shares for the period is CU20 per share.

The number of incremental shares to be added to the denominator of the diluted EPS calculation is computed as follows.

Cash required to settle put option (CU100 million/CU1,000) × 10 options × CU25	CU25,000,000
Divided by the average market price per share	20
Number of shares that would need to be issued to settle put option	1,250,000
Less: Shares assumed repurchased under put option (CU100 million/CU1,000) × 10 options	1,000,000
Incremental shares	250,000

5.9 Summary of adjustments for potential ordinary shares in diluted EPS calculations

The following table sets out a summary of the adjustments to earnings and the number of shares in diluted EPS calculations for each of the major categories of potential ordinary shares. Each of these categories is considered in detail in **5.4** to **5.8**.

Potential ordinary shares	Adjustment to earnings	Adjustment to number of shares
Convertible bonds, debentures and preference shares (classified as a compound instrument or wholly as a financial liability)	Add back interest, dividends, fair value gains/losses and other finance costs recognised in the period, net of tax.	Add number of new shares assuming full conversion.
Warrants and options, e.g. written call option for an exchange of a fixed amount of shares for a fixed amount of functional currency cash (classified as equity)	None.	Add number of shares deemed to be issued for no consideration.
Contingently issuable shares (classified as equity)	None.	Add number of shares that would be issued if the end of the reporting period were the end of the contingency period.
Warrants and options, e.g. written call option for an exchange of a fixed amount of shares for a variable amount of cash, or an exchange of a fixed amount of shares for a fixed amount of cash with a net cash settlement alternative (classified as a financial liability)	Add back fair value gains/losses, net of tax.	Add number of shares equal to the number of shares that would have been issued for nil consideration based on the average fair value of the shares over the period.
Forward purchase contract to buy own shares or a written put option to potentially reacquire own shares (classified as a financial liability)	Add back interest and any other gains/losses, net of tax.	Add number of shares equal to the number of shares that would have to be issued to satisfy the obligation based on the average fair value of the shares over the period less the number of shares that are to be acquired under the contract.

5.10   Potential ordinary shares issued by a subsidiary, joint venture or associate

5.10.1   *Instruments that entitle holders to shares in a subsidiary, joint venture or an associate*

Instruments issued by a subsidiary, joint venture or an associate that enable their holders to obtain ordinary shares of the subsidiary, joint venture or associate are included in calculating the diluted EPS data of the subsidiary, joint venture or associate. Those earnings per share are then included in the reporting entity's EPS calculations based on the reporting entity's holding of the instruments of the subsidiary, joint venture or associate. [IAS 33:A11(a)]

For the purpose of determining the EPS effect of these instruments, they are assumed to be converted, and the numerator (profit or loss attributable to the ordinary equity holders of the parent entity) adjusted as necessary, as discussed at **5.2.2**. In addition to those adjustments, the numerator is adjusted for any change in the profit or loss recognised by the reporting entity (such as equity method income) that is attributable to the increase in the number of ordinary shares of the subsidiary, joint venture or associate as a result of the conversion. The denominator for the diluted EPS calculation at the consolidated level is unaffected because the number of shares of the reporting entity outstanding would not change upon the assumed conversion. [IAS 33:A12]

The following example, reproduced from Example 10 of the illustrative examples accompanying IAS 33, provides an illustration of instruments issued by a subsidiary.

Example 5.10.1

Instruments of a subsidiary: calculation of basic and diluted earnings per share

[IAS 33 Illustrative examples: Example 10]

Parent

Profit attributable to ordinary equity holders or of the parent entity	CU12,000 (excluding any earnings of, or dividends paid by, the subsidiary)
Ordinary shares outstanding	10,000
Instruments of subsidiary owned by the parent	800 ordinary shares
	30 warrants exercisable to purchase ordinary shares of subsidiary
	300 convertible preference shares

Subsidiary

Profit	CU5,400
Ordinary shares outstanding	1,000
Warrants	150, exercisable to purchase ordinary shares of the subsidiary
Exercise price	CU10
Average market price of one ordinary share	CU20
Convertible preference shares	400, each convertible into one ordinary share
Dividends on preference shares	CU1 per share

No inter-company eliminations or adjustments were necessary except for dividends.

For the purposes of this illustration, income taxes have been ignored.

Subsidiary's earnings per share

Basic EPS CU5.00 calculated:	(CU5,400[a] − CU400[b])/1,000[c]
Diluted EPS CU3.66 calculated:	CU5,400[d]/(1,000 + 75[e] + 400[f])

Consolidated earnings per share

Basic EPS CU1.63 calculated:	(CU12,000[g] + CU4,300[h])/10,000[i]
Diluted EPS CU1.61 calculated:	(CU12,000 + CU2,928[j] + CU55[k] + CU1,098[l])/10,000

[a]   Subsidiary's profit attributable to ordinary equity holders.

[b]   Dividends paid by subsidiary on convertible preference shares.

[c]   Subsidiary's ordinary shares outstanding.

[d]   Subsidiary's profit attributable to ordinary equity holders (CU5,000) increased by CU400 preference dividends for the purpose of calculating diluted earnings per share.

[e]   Incremental shares from warrants, calculated: [(CU20 − CU10)/CU20] × 150.

[f]   Subsidiary's ordinary shares assumed outstanding from conversion of convertible preference shares, calculated: 400 convertible preference shares × conversion factor of 1.

[g]   Parent's profit attributable to ordinary equity holders of the parent entity.

[h]   Portion of subsidiary's profit to be included in consolidated basic earnings per share, calculated: (800 × CU5.00) + (300 × CU1.00).

[i]   Parent's ordinary shares outstanding.

[j]   Parent's proportionate interest in subsidiary's earnings attributable to ordinary shares, calculated: (800/1,000) × (1,000 shares × CU3.66 per share).

[k]   Parent's proportionate interest in subsidiary's earnings attributable to warrants, calculated: (30/150) × (75 incremental shares × CU3.66 per share).

[l]   Parent's proportionate interest in subsidiary's earnings attributable to convertible preference shares, calculated: (300/400) × (400 shares from conversion × CU3.66 per share).

5.10.2   Instruments that entitle holders to shares in the reporting entity

Instruments of a subsidiary, joint venture or associate that are convertible into the reporting entity's ordinary shares are considered among the potential ordinary shares of the reporting entity for the purpose of calculating diluted EPS. Similarly, options or warrants issued by a subsidiary, joint venture or associate to purchase ordinary shares of the reporting entity are considered among the potential ordinary shares of the reporting entity in the calculation of consolidated diluted EPS. [IAS 33:A11(b)]

5.11   Partly paid shares

To the extent that partly paid shares are not entitled to participate in dividends during the reporting period (and, therefore, are excluded from the calculation of basic EPS), they are to be regarded as the equivalent of warrants or options in the calculation of diluted EPS. The unpaid balance is assumed to represent proceeds used to purchase ordinary shares. The number of shares included in diluted EPS is the difference between the number of shares subscribed and the number of shares assumed to be purchased. [IAS 33:A16]

> Together with the guidance on how to include partly paid shares in basic EPS (see **4.3.2.4**), this implies that if a reporting entity has, say, 9,000 ordinary shares, two-thirds paid up and entitled to two-thirds of the dividend declared on fully paid shares, then, in calculating diluted EPS, the entity includes the partly paid shares as if they were two thirds (6,000 shares) in issue and included in basic EPS, and additionally there are options over 3,000 shares (one third of 9,000) for which the exercise price of the options is equal to the amount remaining to be paid on the shares.

5.12   Potential ordinary shares in issue for part of an accounting period

When potential ordinary shares are issued during a period (e.g. convertible bonds are issued four months before the end of the accounting period), diluted EPS is calculated as if the potential ordinary shares had been converted to ordinary shares on the date the potential ordinary shares were issued. [IAS 33:36] Thus, in the example, the convertible bonds would be included in diluted EPS as if they had been converted into ordinary shares four months before the end of the accounting period.

Similarly, when potential ordinary shares are converted into ordinary shares, are cancelled, or lapse, they are included in the calculation of diluted EPS for the period the potential ordinary shares were in existence as potential ordinary shares.

Accordingly, having no potential ordinary shares outstanding at the end of the reporting period does not automatically mean that the reporting entity's diluted EPS will be the same as basic EPS. When an entity has no potential ordinary shares in existence at the end of the reporting period, but had potential ordinary shares outstanding at some point during the year, it should still calculate diluted EPS separately.

Example 5.12

Potential ordinary shares in issue for part of an accounting period

An entity has 1,000,000 ordinary shares in issue at the start of its accounting period, 1 January 20X1.

In addition, on 1 January, it has CU100,000 convertible bonds in issue. The bonds are converted into 100,000 ordinary shares on 1 April 20X1. The finance cost recognised in profit or loss in respect of the bonds from 1 January to 31 March is CU2,500 and the associated tax relief is CU750.

The profit attributable to ordinary shareholders (all from continuing operations) for 20X1 is CU100,000.

The weighted average number of shares outstanding during 20X1 and used to calculate basic EPS is:
$(1,000,000 \times 12/12) + (100,000 \times 9/12) =$ 1,075,000

Thus, basic EPS is: CU100,000/1,075,000 =   CU0.093

Diluted EPS is calculated as:

$(CU100,000 + CU2,500 - CU750) / ((1,075,000 + (100,000 \times 3/12)) =$
CU101,750/1,100,000* = CU0.925

---

*   The denominator is equal to the number of shares that would have been outstanding had the convertible bond been fully converted at the start of the reporting period.

6 Reporting additional earnings per share on an alternative basis

6.1 Entities permitted to present additional earnings per share amounts

An entity is permitted to present EPS figures other than the basic and diluted EPS figures required to be presented under IAS 33. Such figures may be calculated based on a reported component of the statement of comprehensive income other than those required by IAS 33 (i.e. profit or loss from continuing operations attributable to the ordinary equity holders of the parent entity and profit or loss attributable to the ordinary equity holders of the parent entity). However, the denominator (i.e. the weighted average number of shares) should still be determined in accordance with the Standard. [IAS 33:73]

The entity is required to indicate the basis on which the numerator(s) is (are) determined, including whether amounts per share are before tax or after tax. [IAS 33:73]

In addition, if the numerator (earnings figure) used is not reported as a line item in the statement of comprehensive income, a reconciliation is required between the numerator and a line item that is reported in the statement of comprehensive income. [IAS 33:73]

The requirements of IAS 33:73 regarding the presentation of additional EPS amounts apply equally to an entity that discloses, in addition to basic and diluted EPS, amounts per share using a reported item of profit or loss, other than one required by IAS 33. [IAS 33:73A]

> IAS 33:73 requires that additional measures of EPS be included in the notes to the financial statements (and that basic and diluted measures be presented with equal prominence). No reference is made to presentation on the face of the statement of comprehensive income, and it is not clear whether presentation both in the notes and on the face of the statement of comprehensive income is permitted. At least in some jurisdictions, this approach may not be seen as best practice and, in fact, it may conflict with the requirements of local regulators.

6.2   Calculation of additional per share measures

> IAS 33 does not specify the manner in which additional per share amounts should be determined, other than for additional amounts per share using a reported component of the statement of comprehensive income. When an entity discloses additional per share measures that relate to the period as a whole that are not based on a reported component of the statement of comprehensive income (e.g. cash flows per share), it would seem appropriate for the denominator to be calculated on the same basis as that used for earnings per share. However, when per share disclosures are provided that relate only to a component of the statement of financial position at the end of the reporting period and not to a reported component of the statement of comprehensive income (e.g. net assets per share), in order to compare like with like, it would seem appropriate for the denominator to reflect the shares in issue at the end of the financial reporting period. In either case, the basis of calculation of the numerator and the denominator should be clearly disclosed.

7 Presentation and disclosure

7.1 Presentation

7.1.1 Amounts required to be presented – general

IAS 33 requires the following amounts per share to be presented in the statement of comprehensive income (with equal prominence for basic and diluted EPS for all periods presented):

[IAS 33:66]

- profit or loss from continuing operations attributable to the ordinary equity holders of the parent entity; and

- profit or loss attributable to the ordinary equity shareholders of the parent entity.

7.1.2 Earnings per share amounts required for each class of ordinary shares

The amounts disclosed under IAS 33:66 (see **7.1.1**) should be presented for each class of ordinary shares that has a different right to share in profit for the period. [IAS 33:66] They are presented even if the amounts are negative (i.e. a loss per share). [IAS 33:69]

7.1.3 Entities that present a separate statement of profit or loss

If an entity presents items of profit or loss in a separate statement of profit or loss as described in paragraph 10A of IAS 1 *Presentation of Financial Statements* (see **section 5** of **chapter A4**), the basic and diluted per share amounts should be presented in that separate statement. [IAS 33:67A]

7.1.4 Entities that report a discontinued operation

Entities that report a discontinued operation are required to disclose the basic and diluted amounts per share for the discontinued operation either in the statement of comprehensive income, or in the notes to the financial statements. [IAS 33:68] When a separate statement of profit or loss is presented, the basic and diluted amounts per share for the discontinued operation are presented either in that separate statement or in the notes. [IAS 33:68A]

Although a literal reading of IAS 33:68 may suggest that it is necessary to calculate and present EPS for each discontinued operation, it seems unlikely that this is intended given that IFRS 5 *Non-current Assets Held for Sale and Discontinued Operations* does not require separate disclosure of the results of each discontinued operation (but instead requires disclosure of the aggregated results). Therefore, when an entity has more than one discontinued operation but reports the results in aggregate, it is appropriate to give the EPS disclosure on a similar, aggregated, basis. However, when an entity reports the results of each of its discontinued operations separately, either in the statement of comprehensive income or in the notes, the entity may also wish to consider presenting separate EPS measures for each discontinued operation.

7.1.5 Periods for which earnings per share is required to be presented

Earnings per share is presented for every period for which a statement of comprehensive income (or, where applicable, a separate statement of profit or loss) is presented. If diluted EPS is reported for at least one period, it should be reported for all periods presented, even if it equals basic earnings per share. If basic and diluted earnings per share are equal, dual presentation can be accomplished in one line in the statement of comprehensive income. [IAS 33:67]

Therefore, when basic and diluted EPS are equal, the amount could be described in a one-line item in the statement of comprehensive income as 'Basic and diluted earnings per share'.

7.1.6 EPS disclosures for 'tracking' or 'targeted' shares

Some entities issue classes of shares characterised as 'tracking' or 'targeted' shares to measure the performance of a specific business unit or activity of the entity. The presentation of complete financial statements of the targeted business generally is discouraged, and requires clear, cautionary disclosures, because investors may get an inaccurate view that their investment in targeted shares represents a direct investment in a legal entity. However, condensed financial statements that allow investors to understand fully the computation of earnings available for dividends are preferable to complete statements.

EPS should not be shown in separate financial statements of the business unit represented by the tracking shares. EPS disclosures should only be presented in the legal issuer's financial statements. Per IAS 33:66 (see **4.2.4**), the entity should determine EPS for each class of shares using the two-class method.

7.2 Disclosure

7.2.1 General

The following should be disclosed:

[IAS 33:70]

- the amounts used as the numerators in calculating basic and diluted EPS and a reconciliation of those amounts to the profit or loss attributable to the parent entity for the period. The reconciliation should include the individual effect of each class of instruments that affects EPS;

- the weighted average number of ordinary shares used as the denominators in calculating basic and diluted EPS and a reconciliation of these denominators to each other. The reconciliation should include the individual effect of each class of instruments that affects EPS; and

- instruments (including contingently issuable shares) that could potentially dilute basic EPS in the future, but were not included in the calculation of diluted EPS because they are antidilutive for the period(s) presented.

7.2.2 Restatement for bonus and similar issues

An entity should disclose the fact that the calculations have been adjusted for a capitalisation/bonus issue, share split or reverse share split, occurring either during the period, or after the reporting period but before the financial statements are authorised for issue. [IAS 33:64]

7.2.3 Changes in share capital after the reporting period

A description should be provided of any other changes in ordinary shares or potential ordinary shares after the reporting period that would, had they occurred before the end of the reporting period, have changed significantly the number of ordinary shares or potential ordinary shares outstanding at the end of the period. [IAS 33:70(d)]

IAS 33 lists the following as examples of transactions that might be disclosed under this requirement:

[IAS 33:71]

- an issue of shares for cash;

- an issue of shares when the proceeds are used to repay debt or preference shares outstanding at the end of the reporting period;

- the redemption of ordinary shares;

- the conversion or exercise of potential ordinary shares, outstanding at the end of the reporting period, into ordinary shares;

- the issue of warrants, options or convertible instruments; and
- the achievement of conditions that would result in the issue of contingently issuable shares.

7.2.4   Additional recommended disclosures

When the terms and conditions of an instrument that generates potential ordinary shares affect the measurement of basic and diluted EPS, disclosure of the terms and conditions is encouraged, but not required. [IAS 33:72] IAS 33 notes that the terms and conditions may determine whether any potential ordinary shares are dilutive and, if so, determine the effect on the weighted average number of shares outstanding, together with any consequential adjustments to the profit or loss attributable to ordinary equity holders.

7.2.5   Illustrative disclosures

Example 12 of the illustrative examples accompanying IAS 33 illustrates how an entity with a complex capital structure (Company A) might calculate and present EPS in accordance with IAS 33. The suggested presentation for the statement of comprehensive income from that example is reproduced below.

Example 7.2.5

Presentation of EPS in statement of comprehensive income

[Extract from IAS 33 Illustrative examples: Example 12]

The following illustrates how Company A might present its earnings per share data in its statement of comprehensive income. Note that the amounts per share for the loss from discontinued operations are not required to be presented in the statement of comprehensive income.

	For the year ended 20X1 CU
Earnings per ordinary share	
Profit from continuing operations	1.93
Loss from discontinued operations	(0.33)
Profit	1.60
Diluted earnings per ordinary share	
Profit from continuing operations	1.78
Loss from discontinued operations	(0.30)
Profit	1.48

A32 Interim financial reporting

Contents

1 Introduction

1.1 Overview of IAS 34

IAS 34 *Interim Financial Reporting* applies when an entity prepares an interim financial report, without mandating when an entity should prepare such a report. IAS 34 prescribes the minimum content for an interim financial report, and the principles for recognition and measurement in complete and condensed financial statements for an interim period.

IAS 34 permits less information to be reported than in annual financial statements, on the basis of providing an update to those financial statements.

IAS 34 does not include any requirements relating to management commentary in interim reports. Nor does the IFRS Practice Statement *Management Commentary* (see **chapter A33**) contain any specific guidance in relation to management commentary in interim reports.

1.2 Amendments to IAS 34 since the last edition of this manual

IAS 34 was most recently amended in January 2016 by consequential amendments arising from IFRS 16 *Leases* (effective for annual periods beginning on or after 1 January 2019, with earlier application permitted). The amendments reflect changes in terminology under the new Standard which affect the wording of one of the examples in Appendix B to IAS 34 (see **5.6.5**). These amendments should be applied when an entity adopts IFRS 16.

2 Scope

2.1 Scope – general

IAS 34 applies to interim financial reports that are described as complying with International Financial Reporting Standards. [IAS 34:3]

Interim financial reports are financial reports containing either a complete set of financial statements (as described in IAS 1 *Presentation of Financial Statements* – see **2.4** in **chapter A4**) or a set of condensed financial statements (as described later in this chapter) for an interim period. An interim period is a financial reporting period shorter than a full financial year. [IAS 34:4]

2.2 Publicly traded entities encouraged to provide interim financial reports

IAS 34 does not contain any rules as to which entities should publish interim financial reports, how frequently, or how soon after the end of an interim period. The Standard notes that governments, securities regulators, stock exchanges, and accountancy bodies often require entities with publicly traded debt or equity to publish interim financial reports, and that those regulations will generally specify the frequency and timing of such reports. However, IAS 34 *encourages* publicly traded entities:

[IAS 34:1]

- to provide interim financial reports at least as of the end of the first half of their financial year; and

- to make their interim financial reports available no later than 60 days after the end of the interim period.

2.3   No requirement for interim reports to comply with IAS 34

Each financial report, annual or interim, is evaluated on a stand-alone basis for compliance with IFRSs. It is important to note that entities that prepare annual financial statements in accordance with IFRSs are not precluded from preparing interim financial reports that do *not* comply with IFRSs, provided that the interim report does not state that it is IFRS-compliant. The fact that an entity has not published interim financial reports during a financial year, or that it has published interim financial reports that do not comply with IAS 34, does not prevent the entity's annual financial statements from conforming to IFRSs, if they are otherwise IFRS-compliant. [IAS 34:1 & 2]

2.4   Preliminary announcements of interim results

IAS 34 does not address the content of preliminary interim earnings announcements (i.e. those earnings announcements issued shortly after the end of an interim period that disclose abbreviated preliminary financial information for the interim period just ended). IAS 34:3 does state, however, that if an interim financial report is described as complying with IFRSs, it must comply with all of the requirements of IAS 34. Therefore, if any reference to IFRSs is made in a preliminary interim earnings announcement that does not comply with IAS 34, the following statement (or something substantively similar), should be included in that earnings release.

"While the financial figures included in this preliminary interim earnings announcement have been computed in accordance with International Financial Reporting Standards (IFRSs) applicable to interim periods, this announcement does not contain sufficient information to constitute an interim financial report as that term is defined in IFRSs. The directors expect to publish an interim financial report that complies with IAS 34 in March 20X2."

3   Content of an interim financial report

3.1   Minimum components of an interim financial report

Entities reporting in accordance with IAS 34 are required to include in their interim financial reports, at a minimum, the following components:

[IAS 34:8]

* a condensed statement of financial position;

* a condensed statement or condensed statements of profit or loss and other comprehensive income;

* a condensed statement of changes in equity;

* a condensed statement of cash flows; and

* selected explanatory notes.

If, in its annual financial statements, an entity presents items of profit or loss in a separate statement as described in IAS 1:10A (see **section 5** of **chapter A4**), it should also present interim condensed information in a separate statement. [IAS 34:8A]

> Note that the titles of the financial statements listed in IAS 34:8 are as reflected in IAS 1 *Presentation of Financial Statements*. Entities are permitted to use titles for those statements other than those used in IAS 34:8 (e.g. balance sheet, cash flow statement). An entity would be expected to use the same titles in its interim financial report as are used in its annual financial statements.
>
> If additional information to the minimum components set out above is included in the interim report, this information should be presented in a manner that is consistent with that in the full annual financial statements.

3.2   Periods required to be presented in an interim financial report

3.2.1   *Periods for which each financial statement is required to be presented*

IAS 34:20 requires interim reports to include interim financial statements (whether condensed or complete – see **3.4.1**) for the periods listed in the following table.

Statement	Current	Comparative
Statement of financial position	End of current interim period	End of immediately preceding financial year
Statement(s) of profit or loss and other comprehensive income	Current interim period and cumulatively for the year-to-date	Comparable interim period and year-to-date of immediately preceding financial year
Statement of changes in equity	Cumulative for the current financial year-to-date	Comparable year-to-date of immediately preceding financial year
Statement of cash flows	Cumulatively for the current financial year-to-date	Comparable year-to-date of immediately preceding financial year

The selected explanatory notes and additional information should contain comparative information for each of the periods presented in the primary statements.

3.2.2   Example – entities that report half-yearly

Based on the requirements of IAS 34:20, **example 3.2.2** illustrates the statements required to be presented in the interim financial report of an entity that reports half-yearly, with a 31 December 20X9 year end.

Example 3.2.2		
Statements required for entities that report half-yearly		
	Current	**Comparative**
Statement of financial position at	30 June 20X9	31 December 20X8
Statement(s) of profit or loss and other comprehensive income – 6 months ended	30 June 20X9	30 June 20X8
Statement of changes in equity – 6 months ended	30 June 20X9	30 June 20X8
Statement of cash flows – 6 months ended	30 June 20X9	30 June 20X8

3.2.3   Example – entities that report quarterly

Based on the requirements of IAS 34:20, **example 3.2.3** illustrates the statements required to be presented in the half-year interim financial report of an entity that reports quarterly, with a 31 December 20X9 year end.

Example 3.2.3

Statements required for entities that report quarterly

	Current	Comparative
Statement of financial position at	30 June 20X9	31 December 20X8
Statement(s) of profit or loss and other comprehensive income		
– 6 months ended	30 June 20X9	30 June 20X8
– 3 months ended	30 June 20X9	30 June 20X8
Statement of changes in equity		
– 6 months ended	30 June 20X9	30 June 20X8
Statement of cash flows		
– 6 months ended	30 June 20X9	30 June 20X8

3.2.4 Entities with seasonal businesses

The requirements of IAS 34:20, as discussed in **3.2.1** to **3.2.3**, specify the minimum periods for which interim financial statements are to be presented. However, entities may wish to provide additional information. For example, an entity whose business is highly seasonal is encouraged to disclose financial information relating to the twelve months up to the end of the interim period, and comparative information for the equivalent twelve-month period in the prior year. [IAS 34:21]

3.2.5 Requirement for a 'third' statement of financial position in specified circumstances does not apply to interim financial reports

For annual financial statements, IAS 1:40A requires the presentation of a statement of financial position at the beginning of the preceding period in specified circumstances when an entity applies an accounting policy retrospectively or makes a retrospective restatement of items in its financial statements or when it reclassifies items in its financial statements (see **2.10.4** in **chapter A4**). However, in line with the general principles established in IAS 1:4 (see **3.4.2**), this requirement does not apply to interim financial reports. This is further confirmed by IAS 1:BC33 which explains that the IASB decided not to reflect in IAS 34:8 its decision to require the inclusion of a statement of financial position at the beginning of the preceding period in a complete set of financial statements in specified circumstances. Consequently, in condensed interim financial statements, an entity is only required to include those comparatives required by IAS 34 as listed in **3.2.1**.

3.2.6   Change of financial year end

IAS 34 does not consider the circumstances when there is a change in the financial year end of the reporting entity. IAS 34:20 requires the presentation of comparative information for the statement(s) of profit or loss and other comprehensive income, statement of changes in equity and statement of cash flows for 'comparable' periods. Accordingly, in preparing the interim financial report based on the new financial year end, it may be preferable for the entity to present comparative information for the same interim period, which may not have been the basis for the interim financial information previously reported.

Example 3.2.6

Comparative interim periods when reporting period changes

Entity A's reporting period ends 31 March. It also prepares a half-year interim financial report under IAS 34. It prepared full-year financial statements for the reporting period ended 31 March 20X1. Subsequently, it published a half-year report for the six months ended 30 September 20X1.

In December 20X1, Entity A changes its reporting period end from 31 March to 31 December and prepares 'annual' financial statements for the nine months ended 31 December 20X1.

In preparing the interim period financial statements for the six months ended 30 June 20X2, for what period should comparative information be presented?

IAS 34 does not address this question. IAS 34:20(b) requires that the statement(s) of profit or loss and other comprehensive income for an interim period should include comparative information for the "comparable interim periods . . . of the immediately preceding financial year".

In many circumstances, presenting a comparative period that covers the period from 1 January 20X1 to 30 June 20X1 may be preferable to the period from 1 April 20X1 to 30 September 20X1 because this would enable users to compare trends over time, particularly in a seasonal business. However, based on the particular facts and circumstances, other presentations may be appropriate – in particular when local regulations prescribe the comparative period(s) to be presented following a change in reporting period.

3.2.7   Comparative financial statements for first interim financial reports

When an entity is preparing its first interim financial report under IAS 34, unless the report relates to the first period of operation, it should generally include comparative information as discussed in **3.2.1** to **3.2.6**. In the exceptional circumstances in which the entity does not have available in its accounting records the financial information needed to prepare the comparative interim financial statements, the entity has no choice but to omit prior period comparative financial statements.

In the circumstances described, however, the omission of the comparative financial statements represents a non-compliance with IAS 34. Therefore, the interim financial report cannot be described as complying with IAS 34 without an 'except for' statement regarding the omission of prior period comparative financial statements. Both the fact of, and the reason for, the omission should be disclosed.

3.3 Consolidated financial statements

If the entity's most recent annual financial statements were consolidated statements, then the interim financial report should also be prepared on a consolidated basis. If the entity's annual financial report included the parent's separate financial statements in addition to consolidated financial statements, IAS 34 neither requires nor prohibits the inclusion of the parent's separate statements in the entity's interim report. [IAS 34:14]

If an entity has disposed of all of its subsidiaries during the interim period, such that it has no subsidiaries at the end of the interim reporting period, it should prepare its interim financial statements on a consolidated basis because it had subsidiaries at some point during the interim period. The statement(s) of profit or loss and other comprehensive income, statement of changes in equity and statement of cash flows should include the impact of the subsidiaries up to the date(s) of disposal and the effects of the disposal(s).

3.4 Form and content of interim financial statements

3.4.1 Option to present either complete or 'condensed' interim financial statements

Entities applying IAS 34 have a choice between presenting complete or condensed interim financial statements.

When an entity takes the alternative of presenting a complete set of interim financial statements, the form and content of the financial statements must conform to the requirements of IAS 1 *Presentation of Financial Statements* for a complete set of financial statements, in addition to complying with the requirements of IAS 34. [IAS 34:7 & 9] Therefore, the measurement and disclosure requirements of all relevant Standards apply. These include all measurement and disclosure requirements of IAS 34 and, in particular, details of significant events and transactions required under IAS 34:15 and the explanatory disclosures listed in IAS 34:16A (see **3.5** and **3.6**).

Alternatively, an entity may choose to present interim financial statements containing the minimum required information prescribed by IAS 34:8 (as listed at **3.1**); the resultant financial statements are described as 'condensed'.

3.4.2 Application of general principles to condensed interim financial statements

IAS 34 does not repeat the general principles underlying the preparation of financial information set out in IAS 1. However, preparers need to refer to IAS 1 itself for clarification in this regard.

IAS 1:4 states, in part, that "this Standard does not apply to the structure and content of condensed interim financial statements prepared in accordance with IAS 34 *Interim Financial Reporting*. However, paragraphs 15 - 35 apply to such financial statements".

Paragraphs 15 to 35 of IAS 1, which therefore apply when preparing condensed financial statements for interim purposes, deal with:

- fair presentation and compliance with IFRSs;
- going concern;
- accrual basis of accounting;
- materiality and aggregation; and
- offsetting.

In particular, the going concern requirements set out in IAS 1:25 and 26 apply to interim financial reports. The guidance in IAS 1:26 states that "[i]n assessing whether the going concern assumption is appropriate, management takes into account all available information about the future, which is at least, but is not limited to, twelve months from the end of the reporting period". Therefore, a 12-month period from the interim reporting date should be considered when an entity is assessing its ability to continue as a going concern for the purpose of preparing an interim financial report.

3.4.3 Items to appear in condensed interim financial statements

IAS 34 requires that, for each component of the condensed interim financial statements (statement of financial position, statement of comprehensive income, statement of changes in equity and statement of cash flows), each of the headings and subtotals that were included in the entity's most recent annual financial statements should be disclosed. Additional line items are required if their omission would make the condensed interim financial statements misleading. [IAS 34:10]

In prescribing the minimum content, IAS 34 uses the terms 'headings' and 'subtotals', thereby seeming to imply that not all of the line items that were presented in the most recent annual financial statements are necessarily required. Such an interpretation would do a disservice, however, to a user of the financial statements who is trying to assess trends in the interim period in relation to financial years. Therefore, the phrase should be interpreted, in nearly all cases, to mean the line items that were included in the entity's most recent annual financial statements. The line items in most published financial statements are already highly aggregated and it would be difficult to think of a line item in the annual statement of profit or loss and other comprehensive income, in particular, that would not also be appropriate in an interim statement of profit or loss and other comprehensive income. For example, it would not be appropriate to begin a condensed statement of profit or loss and other comprehensive income with the gross profit figure, omitting figures for revenue and cost of goods sold.

For the statement of financial position, a literal interpretation of 'each of the headings and subtotals' might lead to a condensed interim statement of financial position that presented lines only for total current assets, total non-current assets, total current liabilities, total non-current liabilities and total equity, which will generally be insufficient for trend analysis.

For the statement of changes in equity, all material movements in equity occurring in the interim period should be disclosed separately.

In the case of the statement of cash flows, some aggregation of the lines from the annual statement may be appropriate, but subtotals for 'operating', 'investing' and 'financing' only are unlikely to be sufficient. The IFRS Interpretations Committee confirmed this assessment in an agenda decision issued in July 2014, when it was noted that the Committee did not expect that a three-line presentation alone would meet the requirements in IAS 34. The Committee also drew attention to the requirements of IAS 34:15 and 25, in particular that:

- an entity should include an explanation of events and transactions that are significant to an understanding of the changes in financial position and performance of the entity since the end of the last annual reporting period. Information disclosed in relation to those events and transactions should update the relevant information presented in the most recent annual financial report; and

- the overriding goal is to ensure that an interim financial report includes all information that is relevant to understanding an entity's financial position and performance during the interim period.

If a particular category of asset, liability, equity, income, expense or cash flow was so material as to require separate disclosure in the financial statements in the most recent annual financial statements, such separate disclosure will generally be appropriate in the interim financial report. Further aggregation would only be anticipated when the line items in the annual statements are unusually detailed.

Under IAS 34:10, additional line items should be included if their omission would make the condensed interim financial statements misleading. Therefore, a new category of asset, liability, income, expense, equity or cash flow arising for the first time in the interim period may require presentation as an additional line item in the condensed interim financial statements.

A category of asset, liability, income, expense, equity or cash flow may be significant in the context of the interim financial statements even though it is not significant enough to warrant separate presentation in the annual financial statements. In such cases, separate presentation on the face of the condensed interim financial statements may be required.

3.4.4   Use of the term 'condensed'

The requirements discussed at **3.4.3** will result in the presentation of at least some statements that include all of the line items, headings and subtotals that were presented in the most recent annual financial statements. The question then arises as to whether such statements should, in practice, be described as 'condensed'.

Given that the notes supplementing the interim financial statements are limited, the presentation package taken together is condensed from what would be reported in a complete set of financial statements under IAS 1 and other Standards. In such circumstances, the information presented in the statement(s) of profit or loss and other comprehensive income, statement of financial position, statement of changes in equity and statement of cash flows is condensed – even if the appearance of the statements has not changed. If these interim financial statements were not described as 'condensed', a user might infer that they constitute a complete set of financial statements under IAS 1, which they do not. A complete set of financial statements must include a full note presentation consistent with the annual presentation.

3.4.5   Earnings per share

3.4.5.1   General requirement to present earnings per share

When an entity is within the scope of IAS 33 *Earnings per Share* (see **section 2** of **chapter A31**), it should present basic and diluted earnings per share (EPS) for the interim period in the statement that presents the components of profit or loss for that period. [IAS 34:11]

If an entity presents a separate statement of profit or loss as described in IAS 1:10A (see **section 5** of **chapter A4**), basic and diluted EPS should be presented in that statement. [IAS 34:11A]

3.4.5.2 *Measures of earnings per share to be presented*

IAS 34 does not make any specific reference to the requirements of IAS 33 regarding which measures of basic and diluted EPS should be presented. Nevertheless, to enable users to compare trends, the same EPS figures should be presented in the interim financial report as in the annual financial report. Therefore, irrespective of whether the interim financial statements are described as 'condensed', the following should be presented in the interim financial report, with equal prominence for all periods presented:

- basic and diluted EPS for profit or loss attributable to the ordinary equity shareholders of the parent entity; and

- if a discontinued operation is reported, basic and diluted EPS for profit or loss from continuing operations attributable to the ordinary equity holders of the parent entity.

These should be presented for each class of ordinary shares that has a different right to share in profit for the period.

EPS figures should be provided for all periods presented in the interim financial report. Therefore, for an entity presenting information separately for the current interim period and cumulatively for the year-to-date, with comparative amounts for each, EPS (both basic and diluted) should be presented for the same four periods.

3.4.5.3 *Interim period diluted earnings per share on a year-to-date basis*

Any change in assumptions for the purposes of computing diluted EPS during the interim period may result in an apparent anomaly. For example, the sum of diluted EPS for the first quarter and diluted EPS for the second quarter may not always equal diluted EPS for the half-year period.

Diluted EPS for the first quarter is based on assumptions that were valid during and at the end of that quarter. IAS 33 states that diluted EPS for prior periods should not be restated for changes in the assumptions used or for conversions of potential ordinary shares into outstanding ordinary shares. Therefore, diluted EPS for the second quarter and for the half-year period may be based on different assumptions than those used in computing diluted EPS for the first quarter. Also, certain outstanding potential ordinary shares may have been 'antidilutive' (i.e. their conversion to ordinary shares would increase EPS) in the first quarter and, therefore, they may have been excluded from first quarter diluted EPS. In the second quarter and on a six-month basis, however, they may have been dilutive and would, therefore, be included in diluted EPS.

Example 3.4.5.3

Interim period diluted EPS on a year-to-date basis

The following information relates to a quarterly reporter.

	Quarter 1 (1 January to 31 March)	Quarter 2 (1 April to 30 June)	Half year (1 January to 30 June)
Net income	CU1,000	CU1,000	CU2,000
Ordinary shares outstanding	1,000	1,000	1,000
Weighted average quoted market price of ordinary shares	CU8	CU20	CU14

Throughout the half-year, the entity had outstanding 100 options each allowing the holder to purchase one ordinary share for CU10. No options were exercised. For the second quarter interim report, IAS 34:20(b) requires the presentation of statement(s) of profit or loss and other comprehensive income for the second quarter and for the half-year. Calculations of basic and diluted EPS are as follows.

	Quarter 1 (1 January to 31 March)	Quarter 2 (1 April to 30 June)	Half year (1 January to 30 June)
Basic EPS	CU1,000/1,000 = CU1.00	CU1,000/1,000 = CU1.00	CU2,000/1,000 = CU2.00
Diluted EPS – numerator	CU1,000	CU1,000	CU2,000
Diluted EPS – denominator	1,000*	1,050 (1,000 + 50**)	1,028.57 (1,000 + 28.57***)
Diluted EPS	CU1	CU0.9524	CU1.9444

*   The exercise price of the options is greater than the average market price of shares during the period. Therefore, the options are ignored in computing diluted EPS.

**   If the share options were exercised, the proceeds of issue of CU1,000 would equate to an issue of 50 shares at the average market price of CU20. Therefore, the remaining 50 shares are assumed to have been issued for no consideration and are added to the number of ordinary shares outstanding for the computation of diluted EPS.

***   If the share options were exercised, the proceeds of issue of CU1,000 would equate to an issue of 71.43 shares at the average market price of CU14. Therefore, the remaining 28.57 shares are assumed to have been issued for no consideration and are added to the number of ordinary shares outstanding for the computation of diluted EPS.

Note that the sum of diluted EPS for the first quarter (CU1.00) and diluted EPS for the second quarter (CU0.9524) does not equal diluted EPS for the first half-year (CU1.9444).

3.4.5.4 Calculation of weighted average number of ordinary shares for an interim reporting period

Example 3.4.5.4

Calculation of weighted average number of shares for an interim reporting period

A publicly traded entity is required to prepare interim financial statements in accordance with IAS 34. Thirty days before the end of the six-month interim period, the entity issues a substantial number of shares.

These new shares should be weighted for inclusion in the denominator of the interim earnings per share calculation based on the number of days that the shares are outstanding as a proportion of the total number of days in the interim period. A reasonable approximation of the weighted average is sufficient in many circumstances.

The number of shares issued should be weighted by the number of days that the shares are outstanding (i.e. 30 days) divided by the number of days in the period (i.e. 182 days).

3.4.5.5 Earnings per share calculation at interim reporting date for an entity with contingently issuable shares

Example 3.4.5.5

Earnings per share calculation at interim reporting date for an entity with contingently issuable shares

Company X, a publicly traded entity reporting on a calendar year basis, purchased Subsidiary Y on 1 January. The consideration for the acquisition was CU100 million plus an additional 20,000 Company X ordinary shares if Subsidiary Y earns net income in the year following the acquisition of CU10 million or more. By 30 June of Year 1, Subsidiary Y had earned net income of CU15 million.

Although the 20,000 shares would be issuable if the end of the contingency period were 30 June instead of 31 December, the 20,000 ordinary shares should be excluded from the denominator for the calculation of basic EPS for the six months ended 30 June, because events could transpire in the following six months that would cause Company X not to issue the shares (e.g. Subsidiary Y could lose CU6 million in the following six months). The contingently issuable ordinary shares should be included in the denominator for the calculation of diluted EPS for the six months ended 30 June because, based on the circumstances on that date, the contingency is met.

See **chapter A31** for a more detailed examination of the impact of contingently issuable shares on the calculation of basic and diluted EPS.

3.5   Significant events and transactions

Entities are required to provide an explanation of events and transactions that are significant to an understanding of the changes in financial position and performance of the entity since the end of the last annual reporting period. The information disclosed in relation to those events and transactions should update the relevant information presented in the most recent annual financial report. [IAS 34:15]

The disclosure requirements of IAS 34 are based on the assumption that anyone reading the interim financial report will have access to the most recent annual financial report. Not all of the supplementary notes in the annual financial report are required for interim reporting purposes, because this would result in repetition, or the reporting of relatively insignificant changes. [IAS 34:15A]

The following is a (non-exhaustive) list of events and transactions for which disclosures would be required if they are significant:

[IAS 34:15B]

(a)   the write-down of inventories to net realisable value and the reversal of any such write-down;

(b)   recognition of a loss arising from the impairment of financial assets, property, plant and equipment, intangible assets, assets arising from contracts with customers, or other assets, and the reversal of any such impairment loss;

> The reference to assets arising from contracts with customers was added in May 2014 as a consequential amendment arising from IFRS 15 *Revenue from Contracts with Customers.*

(c)   the reversal of any provisions for the costs of restructuring;

(d)   acquisitions and disposals of items of property, plant and equipment;

(e)   commitments for the purchase of property, plant and equipment;

(f)   litigation settlements;

(g)   corrections of prior period errors;

(h)   changes in the business or economic circumstances that affect the fair value of the entity's financial assets and financial liabilities, whether those assets or liabilities are recognised at fair value or amortised cost;

(i)   any loan default or any breach of a loan agreement that has not been remedied on or before the end of the reporting period;

(j) related party transactions;

(k) transfers between levels of the fair value hierarchy used in measuring the fair value of financial instruments;

(l) changes in the classification of financial assets as a result of a change in the purpose or use of those assets; and

(m) changes in contingent liabilities or contingent assets.

Individual IFRSs provide guidance regarding disclosure requirements for many of the items listed in IAS 34:15B. When an event or transaction is significant to an understanding of the changes in an entity's financial position or performance since the last annual reporting period, its interim financial report should provide an explanation of, and an update to, the relevant information included in the financial statements of the last annual reporting period. [IAS 34:15C]

IAS 34 does not specify the level of detail for the disclosures required by IAS 34:15, 15B and 16A. The guiding principle is that the interim disclosures should be those that are useful in understanding the changes in financial position and performance of the entity since the end of the last annual reporting period. It seems clear that the detailed disclosures required by other IFRSs are not required in an interim financial report that includes condensed financial statements and selected explanatory notes. Therefore, in general, the level of detail in interim note disclosures will be less than the level of detail in annual note disclosures. The following examples illustrate this point.

- IAS 2:37 suggests that amounts of inventories at the end of a period and changes in inventories during the period are normally classified between merchandise, production supplies, materials, work in progress and finished goods. That level of detail would not normally be required in condensed interim financial statements unless it is significant to an understanding of the changes in financial position and performance of the entity since the end of the last annual reporting period. Therefore, the disclosure of a write-down of inventories to net realisable value and the reversal of such a write-down, as required by IAS 34:15B(a), will generally be made at the entity-wide level in condensed interim financial statements, rather than analysed between different classes of inventories.

- IAS 36:126 requires disclosure of impairment losses and reversals for each class of assets. The disclosure of impairment losses and reversals required by IAS 34:15B(b) will generally be made at the entity-wide level in condensed interim financial statements, rather than by class of assets, except when a particular impairment or reversal is deemed significant to an understanding of the changes in financial position and performance of the entity since the end of the last annual reporting period.

- IAS 24:17 requires disclosure of key management personnel compensation by category. Such detailed disclosures of the remuneration of key management personnel are not generally required in interim financial reports unless there has been a significant change since the end of the last annual reporting period and disclosure of that change is necessary for an understanding of the interim period. For example, bonuses granted or share options awarded to members of key management personnel during the interim period are likely to be significant to an understanding of the interim period and, therefore, should be disclosed.

3.6 Other disclosures

3.6.1 Other information required to be disclosed

In addition to disclosing significant events and transactions in accordance with IAS 34:15 to 15C, the following information should be disclosed in the notes to the interim financial statements or elsewhere in the interim report:

[IAS 34:16A]

(a) a statement that the same accounting policies and methods of computation are followed in the interim financial statements as were followed in the most recent annual financial statements or, if those policies or methods have been changed, a description of the nature and effect of the change (see **section 4**);

(b) explanatory comments about the seasonality or cyclicality of interim operations;

(c) the nature and amount of items affecting assets, liabilities, equity, net income or cash flows, that are unusual because of their size, nature or incidence;

(d) the nature and amount of changes in estimates of amounts reported in prior interim periods of the current financial year, or changes in estimates of amounts reported in prior financial years;

(e) issues, repurchases and repayments of debt and equity securities;

(f) dividends paid (aggregate or per share), separately for ordinary shares and other shares;

(g) for entities required by IFRS 8 *Operating Segments* to disclose segment information in their annual financial statements, the following segment information:

    (i) revenues from external customers, if included in the measure of segment profit or loss reviewed by the chief operating decision maker or otherwise regularly provided to the chief operating decision maker;

    (ii) intersegment revenues, if included in the measure of segment profit or loss reviewed by the chief operating decision maker or otherwise regularly provided to the chief operating decision maker;

    (iii) a measure of segment profit or loss;

    (iv) a measure of total assets and liabilities for a particular reportable segment if such amounts are regularly provided to the chief operating decision maker and if there has been a material change from the amount disclosed in the last annual financial statements for that reportable segment;

    (v) a description of differences from the last annual financial statements in the basis of segmentation or in the basis of measurement of segment profit or loss; and

    (vi) a reconciliation of the total of the reportable segments' measures of profit or loss to the entity's profit or loss before tax expense (tax income) and discontinued operations. However, if an entity allocates to reportable segments items such as tax expense (tax income), the entity may reconcile the total of the segments' measures of profit or loss to profit or loss after those items. Material reconciling items should be separately identified and described in that reconciliation;

(h) events after the interim period that have not been reflected in the interim financial statements;

(i) the effect of changes in the composition of the entity during the interim period, including business combinations (see **3.6.3**), obtaining or losing control of subsidiaries and long-term investments, restructurings and discontinued operations;

(j) in respect of financial instruments, the disclosures about fair value required by paragraphs 91 to 93(h), 94 to 96, 98 and 99 of IFRS 13 *Fair Value Measurement* (see **section 11** of **chapter A6**) and paragraphs 25, 26 and 28 to 30 of IFRS 7 *Financial Instruments: Disclosures*;

(k) for entities becoming, or ceasing to be, investment entities (see **section 13** of **chapter A24** for details), the disclosures in paragraph 9B of IFRS 12 *Disclosure of Interests in Other Entities* (see **5.2** in **chapter A28**); and

(l) for entities that have adopted IFRS 15 *Revenue from Contracts with Customers*, the disaggregation of revenue from customers required by paragraphs 114 and 115 of that Standard (see **14.2.2** in **chapter A14**).

If the information required to be disclosed under IAS 34:16A is not disclosed in the interim financial statements, it should be incorporated into the interim financial statements by a cross-reference to another statement (e.g. the management commentary or the risk report). When this option is taken, entities should ensure that such information is available to users of the financial statements on the same terms as the interim financial statements and at the same time; if entities do not comply with this requirement, the interim financial report is incomplete. [IAS 34:16A]

The previous paragraph reflects the amendments to IAS 34:16A arising from *Annual Improvements to IFRSs: 2012 - 2014 Cycle*, which clarify the meaning of disclosure of information 'elsewhere in the interim financial report' as used in IAS 34. The amendments are effective for periods beginning on or after 1 January 2016, with earlier application permitted.

The IASB has also clarified that the requirement that disclosures incorporated by cross-reference should be made available 'on the same terms' as the financial statements means that users of the financial statements should have access to such information on the same basis as they have for accessing the financial statements from where the reference is made. [IAS 34:BC10]

The information required to be presented under IAS 34:16A is normally reported on a financial year-to-date basis. [IAS 34:16A]

The Standard requires the entity to provide explanatory comments about the seasonality or cyclicality of interim operations under IAS 34:16A(b). Discussion of changes in the business environment (such as changes in demand, market shares, prices and costs) and discussion of prospects for the full current financial year of which the interim period is a part will normally be presented as part of a management discussion and analysis or financial review, outside of the notes to the interim financial statements.

3.6.2 Reassessment of segment aggregation criteria in interim periods

Whether an entity is required to reassess the aggregation criteria in IFRS 8:12 in each interim period when determining reportable segments depends on the circumstances.

In the absence of a change in the structure of an entity's internal organisation during an interim period that causes the composition of its reportable segments to change, the entity generally does not need to reassess the aggregation criteria in each interim period. However, if a change in facts and circumstances suggests that aggregation of operating segments in the current or a future period is no longer appropriate, management should reassess the aggregation criteria in the period in which the change occurred. If an entity identifies different reportable segments as a result of this reassessment, it should provide the disclosures required by IFRS 8:29 and 30.

For example, assume that an entity has appropriately aggregated two segments in prior periods. However, in the current interim period, the segments no longer exhibit similar economic characteristics because of a change in gross profit margin and sales trends. Management does not believe the trends will converge in future periods. In this case, the entity should reassess the aggregation criteria in the current interim period to determine its appropriate reportable segments.

3.6.3 Business combinations

3.6.3.1 Business combinations during the reporting period

If business combinations have occurred during the interim period, IAS 34A:16(i) requires the entity to disclose all of the details prescribed for annual financial statements by IFRS 3 *Business Combinations* (see **section 13** of **chapter A25**).

3.6.3.2 Business combinations after the reporting period

IFRS 3:B66 requires detailed disclosures for business combinations that occurred after the end of the reporting period but before the financial statements are authorised for issue unless the initial accounting for that business combination is incomplete at the time the financial statements are authorised for issue. To the extent that disclosures are not provided because the initial accounting is not yet complete, the acquirer describes which disclosures could not be made and the reasons why they could not be made.

If a business combination occurs after the end of an interim reporting period but before the interim financial statements are authorised for issue, the entity should provide the disclosures regarding the business combination in accordance with IFRS 3:B66. IAS 34 requires disclosure of information that is significant to an understanding of the changes in financial position and performance of an entity since the end of the last annual reporting period. Consistent with the principle in IAS 34 that an interim period is a discrete period to which the same policies and procedures should be applied as at the end of the financial year, all of the IFRS 3 disclosure requirements for business combinations should be applied to interim periods in the same way as to annual financial statements.

IAS 34:16A(h) requires events subsequent to the end of the interim period that have not been reflected in the interim financial statements to be disclosed, and IFRS 3 sets out the specific disclosures required in relation to business combinations after the reporting period. Consequently, the disclosures required by IFRS 3 should be provided for material business combinations after the end of the interim period, unless the initial accounting for the business combination is incomplete by the time the interim report is authorised for issue. In such circumstances, consistent with IFRS 3:B66, the interim report should describe which disclosures could not be made and why. In many jurisdictions, this is likely to be more prevalent in interim reports due to shorter reporting deadlines for interim reports as compared to annual financial statements.

3.6.4   Comparative information required for note disclosures

IAS 34 does not explicitly require that comparative information be provided for the supplementary note disclosures in condensed interim financial statements. However, the notes support the financial statements for which comparative information is required. Therefore, although IAS 34:16A contains no express reference to the requirement for comparative information, it is recommended that paragraph 38 of IAS 1 *Presentation of Financial Statements* be applied, and that comparative information be provided for all numerical information, and for narrative and descriptive information to the extent that it is relevant to an understanding of the current interim period's financial statements.

For the purposes of interim financial statements, the 'previous period' referred to in IAS 1:38 should be taken to mean the equivalent interim period. Therefore, for example, when disclosures are made under IAS 34:16A in respect of business combinations or share issues on a financial year-to-date basis, comparative information for the equivalent year to date should be reported. While the share issue results in dilution and as such is important in understanding the changes to EPS, it may also be significant to understanding the financial position at the end of the interim period. If this is the case, additional comparative information supporting the statement of financial position may be required.

When an entity prepares a complete set of financial statements for interim reporting purposes, then all of the requirements of IAS 1 apply and, therefore, comparative information is required for the explanatory note disclosures under IAS 34:16A.

3.6.5   Inclusion of interim period disclosures in next annual financial statements

If an item of information is deemed significant and, therefore, is disclosed in an entity's interim financial report, that item of information will not necessarily be disclosed in the entity's next annual financial report that includes the interim period in which the disclosure was made. Under IAS 34, interim period disclosures are determined based on materiality levels assessed by reference to the interim period financial data (see **3.8**). The Standard recognises that the notes to interim financial statements are intended to explain events and transactions that are significant to an understanding of the changes in financial position and performance of the entity since the end of the last annual reporting period. A disclosure that is useful for that purpose may not be useful in the annual financial statements.

To illustrate, IAS 34:16A(c) requires disclosure of the nature and amount of any item that affects assets, liabilities, equity, net income or cash flows if it is unusual because of its nature, size or incidence. Such an item may be unusual in size in the context of a single quarter or half-year period, for example, but not so with respect to the full financial year.

As discussed at **3.9**, IAS 34:26 does require disclosure in the notes to the annual financial statements when an estimate of an amount reported in an earlier interim period is changed significantly during the final interim period of the financial year but a separate financial report is not produced for that final interim period.

3.6.6 Inclusion of interim period disclosures in subsequent interim periods of the same financial year

If an item of information is deemed significant and, therefore, is disclosed in an entity's interim financial report for the first quarter, that item of information will not necessarily be disclosed in the interim financial reports for the subsequent quarters of the same financial year. Under IAS 34, materiality is assessed by reference to each interim period's financial data (see **3.8**). Therefore, an item that is considered material in the context of one interim period may not be material for subsequent interim periods of the same financial year. IAS 34:16A indicates that note disclosures are normally on a year-to-date basis.

For example, the explanatory notes in the interim financial report at 30 June for a 31 December year-end entity that reports quarterly will cover the period 1 January to 30 June. An item of information that was deemed significant in the first quarter report and, therefore, was disclosed in the notes to the interim financial report for the three months ending 31 March, may not be significant on a 30 June six-month year-to-date basis. If that is the case, disclosure in the six-month interim financial report is not required.

3.7 Disclosure of compliance with IFRSs

IAS 34:19 requires that, if an interim financial report has been prepared in accordance with the requirements of that Standard, that fact should be disclosed. An interim financial report should not be described as complying with International Financial Reporting Standards unless it complies with all of the requirements of IFRSs. The latter statement will be appropriate only when interim financial statements are complete rather than condensed.

> Because condensed interim financial reports do not include all of the disclosures required by IAS 1 *Presentation of Financial Statements* and other Standards, they do not meet this requirement. They are, therefore, more appropriately described as having been prepared 'in accordance with IAS 34 *Interim Financial Reporting*' (as required by IAS 34:19) rather than 'in accordance with IFRSs'.
>
> When presenting condensed interim financial information, the entity needs to consider compliance with Standards at two levels:
>
> * compliance with all of the recognition, measurement and presentation requirements contained in extant Standards and Interpretations (compliance with the disclosure requirements of Standards other than IAS 34 is not required); and
>
> * compliance with the disclosure requirements and the recognition and measurement principles for interim reporting purposes specified by IAS 34.

3.8   Materiality

IAS 34:23 states that, in deciding how to recognise, measure, classify, or disclose an item for interim financial reporting purposes, materiality should be assessed in relation to the interim period financial data. In making assessments of materiality, it should be recognised that interim measurements may rely on estimates to a greater extent than measurements of annual financial data.

While materiality judgements are always subjective, the overriding concern is to ensure that an interim financial report includes all of the information that is relevant to understanding the financial position and performance of the entity during the interim period. Therefore, it is generally inappropriate to base quantitative estimates of materiality on projected annual figures.

3.9   Disclosure in annual financial statements

It is quite common that entities do not prepare a separate report for the final interim period in a financial year. This will be determined on the basis of the rules of local regulators. For example, an entity with a reporting period to 31 December, which reports half-yearly, may not be required to produce a separate interim report covering the period from July to December.

In such circumstances, IAS 34 requires disclosure in the notes to the *annual* financial statements if an estimate of an amount reported in an earlier interim period is changed significantly during the final interim period.

The nature and amount of that change in estimate are required to be disclosed. [IAS 34:26] This requirement is intended to provide the user of the financial statements with details of changes in estimates in the final interim period consistent with those generally required by IAS 8 *Accounting Policies, Changes in Accounting Estimates and Errors*. The Standard does state, however, that this disclosure requirement is intended to be narrow in scope, relating only to the change in estimate, and it is not intended to introduce a general requirement to include additional interim period financial information in the entity's annual financial statements. [IAS 34:27]

IAS 34:27 makes clear that, when such a change in estimate occurs and is required to be disclosed in the annual financial statements, the disclosure represents additional interim period financial information. Consequently, although the disclosure is made in the annual financial statements, materiality will generally be determined by reference to interim period financial data.

4 Accounting policies

4.1 Same accounting policies as annual financial statements

The accounting policies applied in the interim financial statements should be consistent with those applied in the most recent annual financial statements, except for accounting policy changes made after the date of the most recent annual financial statements that are to be reflected in the next annual financial statements. [IAS 34:28]

Entities are required to disclose in their interim financial reports that this requirement has been met. [IAS 34:16A(a)]

4.2 Changes in accounting policies

Preparers of interim financial reports in compliance with IAS 34 are required to consider any changes in accounting policies that will be applied for the next annual financial statements, and to implement the changes for interim reporting purposes. Such changes will generally encompass:

- changes required by an IFRS that will be effective for the annual financial statements; and

- changes that are proposed to be adopted for the annual financial statements, in accordance with the requirements of IAS 8 *Accounting Policies, Changes in Accounting Estimates and Errors*, on the basis that they will result in the financial statements providing reliable and more relevant information.

If there has been any change in the entity's accounting policies since the most recent annual financial statements, the interim financial report is required to include a description of the nature and effect of the change. [IAS 34:16A(a)]

If a new Standard or Interpretation has been published during the first interim period but it is not effective until after the end of the annual reporting period, an entity may decide in the second interim period to adopt this Standard or Interpretation in advance of its effective date for its annual financial statements. The fact that the new Standard or Interpretation was not adopted in its first interim period financial statements does not generally preclude the entity from adopting a new policy in the second interim period or at the end of the annual reporting period. The requirements for restating previously reported interim periods are discussed at **4.3**.

Example 4.2

Adoption of new Standard part-way through a financial year

Company X prepares its financial statements in accordance with IFRSs and has a December year end. It also prepares interim financial reports in accordance with IAS 34 on a quarterly basis.

The IASB issues a new Standard that is effective "for annual periods beginning on or after 1 July 20X3", with earlier adoption permitted. The Standard does not include any specific transition provisions so that, in accordance with IAS 8:19(b), it is required to be applied retrospectively.

Is Company X required to adopt this Standard in its interim financial report for the three months ending 30 September 20X3?

No. Company X's first annual period beginning on or after 1 July 20X3 is the period from 1 January 20X4 to 31 December 20X4. Company X is not required to adopt the new Standard in interim financial reports relating to interim periods beginning before 1 January 20X4. This is true irrespective of whether Company X's interim financial reports contain a set of condensed financial statements or a complete set of financial statements.

However, if Company X decides to adopt the new Standard in advance of its effective date (e.g. in its annual financial statements to 31 December 20X3), then Company X should apply the new Standard for interim periods beginning on or after that earlier date of adoption (see also the discussion at **4.3** on restatement of prior interim periods).

4.3 Restatement of previously reported interim periods

A change in accounting policy, other than one for which the transition provisions are specified by a new IFRS, should be reflected by:

[IAS 34:43]

- restating the financial statements of prior interim periods of the current financial year, and the comparable interim periods of prior financial years that will be restated in annual financial statements in accordance with IAS 8; or

- when it is impracticable to determine the cumulative effect at the beginning of the financial year of applying a new accounting policy to all prior periods, adjusting the financial statements of prior interim periods of the current financial year, and comparable interim periods of prior financial years to apply the new accounting policy prospectively from the earliest date practicable.

IAS 8 *Accounting Policies, Changes in Accounting Estimates and Errors* states that retrospective application of a new accounting policy is impracticable when an entity cannot apply it after making every reasonable effort to do so.

IAS 34:44 states that an objective of these principles is to ensure that a single accounting policy is applied to a particular class of transactions throughout an entire financial year. That is not to say that voluntary changes in accounting policy part-way through the year are prohibited. Such changes are permitted, provided that the conditions of IAS 8 are met. What IAS 34:44 requires is that, when a change in accounting policy is adopted at some point during the year, the amounts reported for earlier interim periods should be restated to reflect the new policy.

IAS 34:45 explains that allowing accounting changes to be reflected as of an interim date within the financial year would allow two differing accounting policies to be applied to a particular class of transactions within a single financial year. This would result in interim allocation difficulties, obscured operating results, and complicated analysis and understandability of interim period information.

Example 4.3

Changes in accounting policies part-way through a financial year

Company A reports quarterly. In its first quarter interim report for the current year, it used the same accounting policies as in its latest annual financial statements. Company A wants to make a voluntary change in accounting policy starting in its second quarter interim report. It can demonstrate that the change "results in the financial statements providing reliable and more relevant information about the effects of transactions, other events or conditions on the entity's financial position, financial performance or cash flows" as required by IAS 8:14.

Company A is permitted to make this change in accounting policy in its second quarter interim report provided that the conditions of IAS 8 are met. IAS 34:44 requires that the interim financial statements for the first quarter of the year be restated to reflect the new accounting policy adopted in the second quarter. As IAS 34:45 suggests, what is prohibited is allowing accounting changes to be

---

2461

reflected *as of* an interim date within a financial year. Accounting changes can be made at an interim date within a financial year, with retrospective application to earlier interim periods of that year.

5   Recognition and measurement

5.1   General requirements for recognition and measurement

5.1.1   Principles to be applied – general

As discussed at **4.1**, in preparing their interim financial reports, entities are required to apply the same accounting policies as will be applicable for their next annual financial statements. The principles for recognising assets, liabilities, income and expenses for interim periods are the same as in annual financial statements.

It is not intended, however, that each interim period should be seen to stand alone as an independent period. The Standard states that the frequency of an entity's reporting (annual, half-yearly or quarterly) should not affect the measurement of its annual results. To achieve that objective, measurements for interim reporting purposes are made on a year-to-date basis. [IAS 34:28]

There is a degree of inconsistency in IAS 34. The requirement set out at **4.1** (that the same accounting policies should be applied in the interim financial statements as are applied in annual financial statements) represents a 'discrete period' approach to interim reporting. On the other hand, IAS 34:28's requirement that measurements for interim reporting purposes should be made on a year-to-date basis so that the frequency of the entity's reporting does not affect the measurement of its annual results represents an 'integral period' approach.

This inconsistency has led to a number of areas of potential conflict between the requirements of IAS 34 and those of other Standards applied at the end of interim reporting periods. IFRIC 10 deals with one area of conflict regarding reversals of some impairment losses (see **5.6.16.2**).

5.1.2   Levies

IFRIC 21 *Levies* provides guidance on when to recognise a liability for a levy imposed by a government; it applies both for levies that are accounted for in accordance with IAS 37 *Provisions, Contingent Liabilities and Contingent Assets* and those for which the timing and amount of the levy is certain.

The detailed requirements of IFRIC 21 are discussed in **9.4** of **chapter A12**. Specifically in the context of interim financial reporting, an entity is required apply the same recognition principles in the interim financial report that it applies in the annual financial statements. As a result, in the interim financial report, a liability to pay a levy:

[IFRIC 21:13]

• should not be recognised if there is no present obligation to pay the levy at the end of the interim reporting period; and

• should be recognised if a present obligation to pay the levy exists at the end of the interim reporting period.

5.2   Seasonal, cyclical or occasional revenues

Revenues that are received seasonally, cyclically or occasionally within a financial year should not be anticipated or deferred as of an interim date, if anticipation or deferral would not be appropriate at the end of the financial year. [IAS 34:37]

Thus, for example, an entity engaged in retailing does not divide forecasted revenue by two to arrive at its half-year revenue figures. Instead, it reports its actual results for the six-month period. If the retailer wishes to demonstrate the cyclicality of its revenues, it could include, as additional information, revenue for the 12 months up to the end of the interim reporting period and comparative information for the corresponding previous 12-month period.

5.3   Uneven costs

The principles described above regarding revenue recognition also apply to costs. Costs that are incurred unevenly during an entity's financial year should be anticipated or deferred for interim reporting purposes if, and only if, it is also appropriate to anticipate or defer that type of cost at the end of the financial year. [IAS 34:39]

A cost that does not meet the definition of an asset at the end of an interim period is *not* deferred in the statement of financial position at the interim reporting date either to await future information as to whether it has met the definition of an asset, or to smooth earnings over interim periods within a financial year. [IAS 34:30(b)] Thus, when preparing interim financial statements, the entity's usual recognition and measurement practices are followed. The only costs that are capitalised are those incurred *after* the specific point in time at which the criteria for recognition of the particular class of asset are met. Deferral of costs as assets in an interim statement of financial position in the hope that the criteria will be met before the year end is prohibited (see also **5.6.6**).

Example 5.3A

Major advertising campaign early in the financial year

An entity reports quarterly. In the first quarter of the financial year, the entity introduces new models of its products that will be sold throughout the year. At that time, it incurs a substantial cost for running a major advertising campaign (completed by the end of that quarter) that will benefit sales throughout the year.

Is it appropriate to spread the advertising cost over the period in which benefits (in the form of revenues) are expected (all four quarters of the year) or is the entire cost an expense of the first quarter?

The entire cost is recognised in profit or loss in the first quarter. Explanatory note disclosure may be required. IAS 38:69(c) requires that all expenditure on advertising and promotional activities should be recognised as an expense when incurred (see **section 5** of **chapter A9**). A cost that does not meet the definition of an asset at the end of an interim period is not deferred, either to await future information as to whether it has met the definition of an asset or to smooth earnings over interim periods within a financial year.

Example 5.3B

Fixed costs of a manufacturer whose business is seasonal

A manufacturer's shipments of finished products are highly seasonal (shares of annual sales are respectively 20 per cent, 5 per cent, 10 per cent and 65 per cent for the four quarters of the financial year). Manufacturing takes place more evenly throughout the year. The entity incurs substantial fixed costs, including fixed costs relating to manufacturing, selling and general administration, and wishes to allocate all of its fixed costs to the four quarters based on each quarter's share of estimated annual sales volume.

Such an allocation is not acceptable under IAS 34. IAS 34:39 states that costs that are incurred unevenly during an entity's financial year should be anticipated or deferred for interim reporting purposes if, and only if, it is also appropriate to anticipate or defer that type of cost at the end of the financial year.

In the circumstances described, the fixed costs should be split between manufacturing fixed costs and non-manufacturing fixed costs. IAS 2:12 requires that the cost of manufactured inventories should include a systematic allocation of fixed production overheads (i.e. fixed manufacturing costs). Because manufacturing takes place evenly throughout the year, the entity will recognise cost of goods sold expense only when sales are made and, therefore, it will achieve its objective of allocating fixed manufacturing costs to the four quarters based on sales volume.

Fixed non-manufacturing costs, however, are different. IAS 2:16 makes clear that administrative overheads that do not contribute to bringing inventories to their present location and condition, and selling costs (whether variable or fixed), are excluded from the cost of inventories and are recognised as expenses in the periods in which they are incurred. Therefore, the entity must recognise its fixed non-manufacturing costs in profit or loss as incurred in each of the four quarters. As required by IAS 34:16A, explanatory comments about the seasonality or cyclicality of interim operations should be disclosed in the notes to interim financial statements. In addition, IAS 34:21 encourages seasonal businesses to present 'rolling' 12-month financial statements in addition to interim period financial statements.

Example 5.3C

Production line retooling costs incurred early in the financial year

An entity reports quarterly. In the first quarter of each financial year, the entity introduces new models of its products that will be sold throughout the year. At that time, it incurs a substantial cost for retooling its production line to manufacture the new models.

Is it appropriate to recognise those retooling costs as an asset and amortise them over the benefit period (all four quarters of the year), or is the entire cost an expense of the first quarter?

It is appropriate to recognise the retooling costs as an asset provided that they meet the recognition criteria in paragraph 7 of IAS 16 *Property, Plant and Equipment* (see **section 3** of **chapter A7**). Those criteria require that an item of property, plant and equipment be recognised as an asset if, and only if:

- it is probable that future economic benefits associated with the item will flow to the entity; and
- the cost of the item can be measured reliably.

Assuming that the expenditure on retooling costs results in an asset that can be recognised, the expenditure should be capitalised and depreciated over the model year, regardless of the entity's interim reporting policy. To illustrate, if the entity's financial year end is 31 December, but new products are introduced in September for a model year from 1 September to 31 August, then at 31 December some portion of the asset recognised would remain to be depreciated in the next financial year, whether or not the entity prepared any interim financial reports.

5.4 Use of estimates

IAS 34:41 requires that measurement procedures used in interim financial reports produce information that is reliable, with all material relevant financial information being appropriately disclosed. It nevertheless acknowledges that, while reasonable estimates are often used for both annual and interim financial reports, interim financial reports generally will require a greater use of estimation methods than annual financial reports.

Appendix C to the Standard provides a number of examples of the use of estimates in interim financial reports, which are reproduced below.

Examples of the use of estimates for interim reporting purposes

[Appendix C to IAS 34]

Inventories: Full stock-taking and valuation procedures may not be required for inventories at interim dates, although it may be done at financial year end. It may be sufficient to make estimates at interim dates based on sales margins.

Classifications of current and non-current assets and liabilities: Entities may do a more thorough investigation for classifying assets and liabilities as current or non-current at the end of annual reporting periods than at interim dates.

Provisions: Determination of the appropriate amount of a provision (such as a provision for warranties, environmental costs, and site restoration costs) may be complex and often costly and time-consuming. Entities sometimes engage outside experts to assist in the annual calculations. Making similar estimates at interim dates often entails updating of the prior annual provision rather than the engaging of outside experts to do a new calculation.

Pensions: IAS 19 *Employee Benefits* requires an entity to determine the present value of defined benefit obligations and the fair value of plan assets at the end of each reporting period and encourages an entity to involve a professionally qualified actuary in measurement of the obligations. For interim reporting purposes, reliable measurement is often obtainable by extrapolation of the latest actuarial valuation.

Income taxes: Entities may calculate income tax expense and deferred income tax liability at annual dates by applying the tax rate for each individual jurisdiction to measures of income for each jurisdiction. IAS 34:B14 acknowledges that while that degree of precision is desirable at the end of interim reporting periods as well, it may not be achievable in all cases, and a weighted average of rates across jurisdictions or across categories of income is used if it is a reasonable approximation of the effect of using more specific rates.

Contingencies: The measurement of contingencies may involve the opinions of legal experts or other advisers. Formal reports from independent experts are sometimes obtained with respect to contingencies. Such opinions about litigation, claims, assessments, and other contingencies and uncertainties may or may not also be needed at interim dates.

Revaluations and fair value accounting: IAS 16 *Property, Plant and Equipment* allows an entity to choose as its accounting policy the revaluation model whereby items of property, plant and equipment are revalued to fair value. Similarly, IAS 40 *Investment Property* requires an entity to measure the fair value of investment property. For those measurements, an entity may rely on professionally-qualified valuers at the end of annual reporting periods, though not at the end of interim reporting periods.

Intercompany reconciliations: Some intercompany balances that are reconciled on a detailed level in preparing consolidated financial statements at financial year end might be reconciled at a less detailed level in preparing consolidated financial statements at an interim date.

Specialised industries: Because of complexity, costliness and time, interim period measurements in specialised industries might be less precise than at financial year-end. An example would be calculation of insurance reserves by insurance companies.

The following examples are in addition to those given in Appendix C to IAS 34.

Financial instruments Financial instruments that are carried at fair value should be remeasured at the interim date using the same methodology as at the end of the annual reporting period. Also, the carrying amount of financial instruments at amortised cost should be recalculated at the interim date.

Share-based payments Liabilities in respect of cash-settled share-based payments will generally be based on the fair value of the share options as at the end of the previous reporting period. If changes in the fair value of the share options since the most recent annual financial statements are material to the interim period, the fair value of the cash-settled share-based payments should be remeasured at the interim date.

In relation to equity-settled share-based payments, an entity should consider whether, at the interim date, there is any change in the number of equity instruments expected to vest. When the change could have a material impact on the interim period, the number of equity instruments expected to vest should be re-estimated at the interim date.

5.5 Changes in estimates

As an illustration of the impact of changes in estimates, IAS 34 considers the rules for recognising and measuring losses from inventory write-downs, restructurings or impairments. The principles to be followed in an interim period are the same as those for annual periods. If such items are recognised and measured in, say, the first quarter of a financial year and the estimate changes in the second quarter of the year, the original estimate is adjusted in the second interim period, either by recognition of an additional amount or by reversal of the previously-recognised amount. [IAS 34:30(a)]

If changes in estimates arise, the results of previous interim periods of the current year are not retrospectively adjusted. However, the nature and amount of any significant changes in estimates must be disclosed either:

[IAS 34:16A(d), 26 & 35]

- in the annual report, if there has been no subsequent interim period financial report that disclosed the change in estimate (see **3.9**); or
- in the following interim period financial report of the same year.

IFRIC 10 gives guidance on circumstances in which an impairment loss should not be reversed (see **5.6.16.2**).

5.6   Additional examples

Appendix B to IAS 34 contains a number of detailed examples to illustrate the application of the recognition and measurement principles discussed in the previous sections. These are reproduced below, together with a number of additional examples developed to illustrate important principles.

5.6.1   Employer payroll taxes and insurance contributions

If employer payroll taxes or contributions to government-sponsored insurance funds are assessed on an annual basis, the employer's related expense is recognised in interim periods using an estimated average annual effective payroll tax or contribution rate, even though a large portion of the payments may be made early in the financial year. A common example is an employer payroll tax or insurance contribution that is imposed up to a certain maximum level of earnings per employee. For higher income employees, the maximum income is reached before the end of the financial year, and the employer makes no further payments through the end of the year. [IAS 34:B1]

5.6.2   Major planned periodic maintenance or overhaul

The cost of a planned major periodic maintenance or overhaul or other seasonal expenditure that is expected to occur late in the year is not anticipated for interim reporting purposes, unless an event has caused the entity to have a legal or constructive obligation. The mere intention or necessity to incur expenditure related to the future is not sufficient to give rise to an obligation. [IAS 34:B2]

5.6.3   Provisions

A provision is recognised when an entity has no realistic alternative but to make a transfer of economic benefits as a result of an event that has created a legal or constructive obligation. The amount of the obligation is adjusted upward or downward, with a corresponding loss or gain recognised in profit or loss, if the entity's best estimate of the amount of the obligation changes.

> Entities applying IFRIC 1 *Changes in Existing Decommissioning, Restoration and Similar Liabilities* may need to adjust the carrying amount of the related asset instead of recognising adjustments in profit or loss.

IAS 34 requires that an entity should apply the same criteria for recognising and measuring a provision at an interim date as it would at the end of its financial year. The existence or non-existence of an obligation to transfer benefits is not a function of the length of the reporting period; it is a question of fact. [IAS 34:B3 & B4]

5.6.4 Year-end bonuses

The nature of year-end bonuses varies widely. Some are earned simply by continued employment during a time period. Some bonuses are earned based on a monthly, quarterly, or an annual measure of operating result. They may be purely discretionary, contractual, or based on years of historical precedent.

A bonus is anticipated for interim reporting purposes if, and only if:

[IAS 34:B5 & B6]

- the bonus is a legal obligation, or past practice would make the bonus a constructive obligation and the entity has no realistic alternative but to make the payments; and

- a reliable estimate of the obligation can be made.

IAS 19 *Employee Benefits* provides guidance on the application of the recognition rules to year-end bonuses.

5.6.5 Variable lease payments

Variable lease payments based on sales can be an example of a legal or constructive obligation that is recognised as a liability. If a lease provides for variable payments based on the lessee achieving a certain level of annual sales, an obligation can arise in the interim period of the financial year before the required annual level of sales has been achieved, if that required level of sales is expected to be achieved and the entity, therefore, has no realistic alternative but to make the future lease payment. [IAS 34:B7]

> IAS 34:B7 was amended in January 2016 by consequential amendments arising from IFRS 16 *Leases*. Under IFRS 16's predecessor Standard, IAS 17 *Leases*, 'variable' lease payments were referred to as 'contingent lease' payments. The amendments to IAS 34 have not had any substantive effect.

5.6.6 Intangible assets

Entities are required to apply the definition and recognition criteria for an intangible asset in the same way in an interim period as in an annual period. Costs incurred before the recognition criteria for an intangible asset are met are recognised as an expense. Costs incurred after the specific point in time at which the criteria are met are recognised as part of the cost of an intangible asset. 'Deferring' costs as assets in an interim statement of financial position in the hope that the recognition criteria will be met later in the financial year is not justified. [IAS 34:B8]

Example 5.6.6

Development costs that meet the IAS 38 capitalisation criteria part-way through an interim period

An entity engaged in the pharmaceutical sector, with a December year end, reports quarterly. Throughout 20X2, its research department is engaged in a major drug development project. Development costs incurred in 20X2, by quarter, are as follows.

First quarter	CU100
Second quarter	CU100
Third quarter:	
1 July to 31 August	CU80
1 September to 30 September	CU60
Fourth quarter	CU150

The entity publishes its half-year report on 15 August, and the CU200 development costs incurred during the first and second quarters are recognised in profit or loss. On 1 September, the research department determines that the criteria set out in IAS 38 for recognising the development costs as an intangible asset have been met.

IAS 38 requires that asset recognition (cost capitalisation) should begin at the point in time at which the recognition criteria are met, not at the start of the financial reporting period in which those criteria are met. Therefore, the following amounts are reported in the interim financial reports for the second half of the financial year, and in the annual report at 31 December 20X2.

	30 September	31 December
	CU	CU
Asset recognised in the statement of financial position	60	210

	3 months ended 30 September	9 months ended 30 September	12 months ended 31 December
	CU	CU	CU
Development costs recognised in profit or loss	80	280	280

5.6.7 Pensions

The pension cost for an interim period is calculated on a year-to-date basis by using the actuarially-determined pension cost rate at the end of the prior financial year, adjusted for significant market fluctuations since that time and for significant one-off events, such as plan amendments, curtailments and settlements. [IAS 34:B9]

5.6.8 Vacations, holidays and other short-term paid absences

Accumulating paid absences are those that are carried forward and can be used in future periods if the current period's entitlement is not used in full. IAS 19 *Employee Benefits* requires that an entity should measure the expected cost of and obligation for accumulating paid absences at the amount the entity expects to pay as a result of the unused entitlement that has accumulated at the end of the reporting period. That principle is also applied at the end of interim financial reporting periods. Conversely, an entity recognises no expense or liability for non-accumulating paid absences at the end of an interim reporting period, just as it recognises none at the end of an annual reporting period. [IAS 34:B10]

Example 5.6.8

Vacation accruals at interim dates

An entity reports quarterly. Its financial year end is 31 December. Holiday entitlement accumulates with employment over the year, but any unused entitlement cannot be carried forward past 31 December. Most of the entity's employees take a substantial portion of their annual leave in July or August.

Should an appropriate portion of employees' salaries during the July/August vacation period be accrued in the first and second quarter interim financial statements?

A portion should be accrued if the employees' vacation days are earned (accumulate) through service during the first and second quarters. Such vacation days are a form of short-term paid absence as defined in IAS 19; IAS 19:13 requires that the expected cost of short-term accumulating paid absences be recognised when the employees render service that increases their entitlement to future paid absences. This principle is applied at both annual and interim reporting dates.

5.6.9 Other planned but irregularly occurring costs

An entity's budget may include costs expected to be incurred irregularly during the financial year, such as charitable contributions and employee-training costs. Those costs generally are discretionary, even though they are planned and tend to recur from year to year. Recognising an obligation at the end of an interim financial reporting period for such costs that have not yet been incurred generally is not consistent with the definition of a liability. [IAS 34:B11]

5.6.10   Measuring interim income tax expense

5.6.10.1   Use of estimated annual rate

The interim period income tax expense is accrued using the tax rate that would be applicable to expected total annual earnings, i.e. the estimated average annual effective income tax rate applied to the pre-tax income of the interim period. [IAS 34:B12]

This is consistent with the basic principle set out in IAS 34:28 that the same accounting recognition and measurement principles should be applied in an interim financial report as are applied in annual financial statements. Income taxes are assessed on an annual basis. Interim period income tax expense is calculated by applying to an interim period's pre-tax income the tax rate that would be applicable to total annual earnings. [IAS 34:B13]

Consistent with IAS 12 *Income Taxes*, the annual effective income tax rate should be estimated using the tax rates (and tax laws) that have been enacted or substantively enacted by the end of the interim period. Expected changes in tax rates or tax laws should not be anticipated and are reflected in the estimate of the annual effective income tax rate only once the change has been enacted or substantively enacted. (See **4.5.2.3** in **chapter A13** for a discussion of the meaning of 'substantively enacted'.)

To the extent practicable, a separate estimated average annual effective income tax rate is determined for each tax jurisdiction and applied individually to the interim period pre-tax income of each jurisdiction. Similarly, if different income tax rates apply to different categories of income (such as capital gains or income earned in particular industries), to the extent practicable, a separate rate is applied to each individual category of interim period pre-tax income. While that degree of precision is desirable, it may not be achievable in all cases and a weighted average of rates across jurisdictions or across categories of income is used if it is a reasonable approximation of the effect of using more specific rates. [IAS 34:B14]

If the levels of income from some jurisdictions are much more or less than the 'average' income per jurisdiction, and/or the tax rate in a jurisdiction is significantly different from the standard tax rate, a weighted average of the rates across all jurisdictions is unlikely to be a reasonable approximation. In such circumstances, it may be possible to treat some jurisdictions individually and determine a weighted average for the other 'average' jurisdictions.

5.6.10.2 Impact of progressive (graduated) tax rates

The estimated average annual effective income tax rate will reflect a blend of the progressive tax rate structure expected to be applicable to the full year's earnings, including enacted or substantively enacted changes in the income tax rates scheduled to take effect later in the financial year. [IAS 34:B13] **Example 5.6.10.2**, which is drawn from Appendix B to IAS 34, illustrates the impact of progressive tax rates.

Example 5.6.10.2

Progressive tax rates

[IAS 34:B15]

An entity reporting quarterly expects to earn 10,000 pre-tax each quarter and operates in a jurisdiction with a tax rate of 20 per cent on the first 20,000 of annual earnings and 30 per cent on all additional earnings. Actual earnings match expectations. The following table shows the amount of income tax expense that is reported in each quarter:

	1st Quarter	2nd Quarter	3rd Quarter	4th Quarter	Annual
Tax expense	2,500	2,500	2,500	2,500	10,000

5.6.10.3 Uneven earnings throughout the year

Example 5.6.10.3, drawn from Appendix B to IAS 34, illustrates the application of the IAS 34 principles when earnings are distributed unevenly throughout the year.

Example 5.6.10.3

Uneven earnings throughout the year

[IAS 34:B16]

An entity reports quarterly, earns 15,000 pre-tax profit in the first quarter but expects to incur losses of 5,000 in each of the three remaining quarters (thus having zero income for the year), and operates in a jurisdiction in which its estimated average annual income tax rate is expected to be 20 per cent. The following table shows the amount of income tax expense that is reported in each quarter:

	1st Quarter	2nd Quarter	3rd Quarter	4th Quarter	Annual
Tax expense	3,000	(1,000)	(1,000)	(1,000)	0

5.6.10.4   *Change in estimate of annual tax rate*

When preparing the tax estimate to be included in an interim period, the tax expense is based on the best estimate of the weighted average *annual* income tax rate expected for the full financial year. Therefore, as for other changes in estimates, amounts accrued for income tax expense in one interim period may have to be adjusted in a subsequent interim period if the estimate of the annual income tax rate changes. [IAS 34:30(c)] The estimated average annual income tax rate would be re-estimated on a year-to-date basis, consistent with IAS 34:28.

The nature and amount of any significant changes in the estimated tax rate should be disclosed either:

[IAS 34:16A(d), 26 & 35]

- in the annual report, if there has been no subsequent interim period financial report that has disclosed the change in estimate (see **3.9**); or

- in the following interim period financial report of the same year.

Example 5.6.10.4A

Change in estimate of annual tax rate

The facts are the same as in **example 5.6.10.2**. During the third quarter, the tax rate on annual earnings in excess of 20,000 increases from 30 per cent to 40 per cent. The tax rate on the first 20,000 of annual earnings remains at 20 per cent. Actual earnings match expectations. The following table shows the amount of income tax expense that is reported in each quarter.

	1st Quarter	2nd Quarter	3rd Quarter	4th Quarter	Annual
Tax expense	2,500	2,500	4,000	3,000	12,000

Based on expected earnings of 10,000 pre-tax each quarter, the average annual income tax rate therefore increases from 25 per cent ((20,000 × 20 per cent + 20,000 × 30 per cent) / 40,000) to 30 per cent ((20,000 × 20 per cent + 20,000 × 40 per cent) / 40,000). The expense recognised in the third quarter is 4,000 ((30,000 × 30 per cent) less the tax expense of 5,000 already recognised in the first and second quarters).

The guidance in IAS 34 is less clear on how to deal with a change in tax rate that has an effect on a deferred tax balance carried forward or arising during the interim period but which is not expected to be reversed until the next financial year. Two approaches are acceptable.

- **Alternative 1** The guidance in IAS 34 could be read to mean that the effective tax rate is based on the total tax expense for the year, recognised rateably based on the income in the interim period. Because the total tax expense for the year includes movements in a deferred tax balance, this would mean that the effect of the change in a deferred tax balance as a result of a change in tax rate would be included in estimating the average annual income tax rate, consequently spreading the effect throughout the financial year.

- **Alternative 2** IAS 34:B13 (see **5.6.10.2**) could be read to require that the estimated average annual tax rate effectively represents the current tax rate for the current financial year, but excludes the impact of the changes on deferred tax balances expected to be recognised at the end of the financial year. Any change in existing deferred tax balances as a result of the change in tax rate would therefore be recognised in full in the period in which the change in tax rate occurs.

An entity should select one of these two approaches as its accounting policy and apply it consistently. The two alternative approaches are illustrated in **examples 5.6.10.4B** and **5.6.10.4C**.

Example 5.6.10.4B

Impact of change in estimate of annual tax rate on deferred tax liability

Following on from **example 5.6.10.4A**, assume that the entity recognised a deferred tax liability of 15,000 as at the beginning of the financial year. As a result of the change in tax rate from 30 per cent to 40 per cent, the deferred tax liability increases by 5,000 to 20,000. Under the alternative approaches described above, this increase could be reflected either:

- by re-estimating the average annual income tax rate, thereby recognising the effect rateably in the third and fourth quarters on a year-to-date basis (Alternative 1); or
- by recognising the effect of the tax rate change on the deferred tax liability in full when the change in tax rate is enacted or substantively enacted (Alternative 2).

The following tables show the amounts of income tax expense reported in each quarter under the two alternatives.

Alternative 1

	1st Quarter	2nd Quarter	3rd Quarter	4th Quarter	Annual
Tax expense	2,500	2,500	7,750	4,250	17,000

The tax rate on the first 20,000 of annual earnings remains at 20 per cent. Based on expected earnings of 10,000 pre-tax each quarter, the average annual income tax rate therefore increases from 25 per cent ((20,000 × 20 per cent + 20,000 × 30 per cent) / 40,000) to 42.5 per cent ((20,000 × 20 per cent + 20,000 × 40 per cent + 5,000) / 40,000). Therefore, the tax expense in the third quarter is 7,750 (42.5 per cent tax based on 30,000 pre-tax earnings to date, less the tax expense of 5,000 already recognised in the first and second quarters).

Alternative 2

	1st Quarter	2nd Quarter	3rd Quarter	4th Quarter	Annual
Tax expense	2,500	2,500	9,000	3,000	17,000

The impact of the tax rate change on the deferred tax liability is recognised in full in the third quarter.

Based on expected earnings of 10,000 pre-tax each quarter, the average annual income tax rate (excluding the impact of the changes on deferred tax balances) therefore increases from 25 per cent ((20,000 × 20 per cent + 20,000 × 30 per cent) / 40,000) to 30 per cent ((20,000 × 20 per cent + 20,000 × 40 per cent) / 40,000). The expense recognised in the third quarter is 9,000 ((30,000 × 30 per cent) plus 5,000 increase in deferred tax liability less the tax expense of 5,000 already recognised in the first and second quarters).

Example 5.6.10.4C

Change in tax rate effective in the next financial year

An entity reports quarterly. It earns CU15,000 pre-tax in each of the first and second quarters and CU10,000 pre-tax in each of the third and fourth quarters. The tax rate applicable is 20 per cent. At the beginning of 20X1, the entity has a temporary difference of CU2,000 and recognised a related deferred tax liability of CU400 (CU2,000 × 20 per cent). CU500 of this temporary difference is expected to reverse in the fourth quarter of 20X1 and CU1,500 in 20X2. During the first quarter of 20X1, the tax rate increases from 20 per cent to 30 per cent, effective from 20X2. Assume that no other temporary differences arise throughout 20X1.

An effective tax rate of 20 per cent will apply to the temporary differences expected to reverse in 20X1 (i.e. CU500) and the increased rate of 30 per cent to those temporary differences expected to reverse in 20X2 (i.e. CU1,500). Consequently, the expected effect of remeasuring the opening deferred tax liability during 20X1 is CU150 ((CU1,500 × 30 per cent) − (CU1,500 × 20 per cent)).

Under the alternative approaches described above, this increase would be reflected as follows.

- **Alternative 1** The remeasurement of the deferred tax liability expected to be recognised during the financial year of CU150 is factored into the average annual income tax rate. This results in the remeasurement of CU150 being recognised rateably in each interim period. The entity would revise its average annual income tax rate to 20.3 per cent ((CU50,000 × 20 per cent + CU150) / CU50,000), recognise a tax expense of CU3,045 (CU15,000 × 20.3 per cent) and recognise the deferred tax liability at CU445 (CU400 + (CU150 × CU15,000 / CU50,000)) for the first quarter.

> • **Alternative 2** The remeasurement of the deferred tax liability expected to be recognised at the end of the financial year of CU150 is recognised in full in the first quarter. The entity therefore recognises tax of CU3,150 (CU15,000 × 20 per cent + CU150) and the deferred tax liability at CU550 in the first interim period.

5.6.10.5 Difference in financial reporting year and tax year

If the financial reporting year and the income tax year differ, the income tax expense for the interim periods of that financial reporting year is measured using separate weighted average estimated effective tax rates for each of the income tax years applied to the portion of pre-tax income earned in each of those income tax years. [IAS 34:B17]

Example 5.6.10.5

Difference in financial reporting year and tax year

[IAS 34:B18]

An entity's financial reporting year ends 30 June and it reports quarterly. Its taxable year ends 31 December. For the financial year that begins 1 July, Year 1 and ends 30 June, Year 2, the entity earns 10,000 pre-tax each quarter. The estimated average annual income tax rate is 30 per cent in Year 1 and 40 per cent in Year 2.

	Quarter ending 30 Sept Year 1	Quarter ending 31 Dec Year 1	Quarter ending 31 Mar Year 2	Quarter ending 30 June Year 2	Year ending 30 June Year 2
Tax expense	3,000	3,000	4,000	4,000	14,000

5.6.10.6 Tax credits

Some tax jurisdictions give taxpayers credits against the tax payable based on amounts of capital expenditure, exports, research and development expenditure, or other bases. Anticipated tax benefits of this type for the full year are generally reflected in computing the estimated annual effective income tax rate, because those credits are granted and calculated on an annual basis under most tax laws and regulations. On the other hand, tax benefits that relate to a one-time event are recognised in computing income tax expense in the interim period in which that event occurs, in the same way that special tax rates applicable to particular categories of income are not blended into a single effective annual tax rate. Moreover, in some jurisdictions, tax benefits or credits that are reported on the income tax return, including those related to capital expenditure and levels of exports, are more similar to a government grant and are recognised in the interim period in which they arise. [IAS 34:B19]

5.6.10.7   Changes in estimates of prior year tax

Tax in previous years may have been under-provided or over-provided, resulting in a correcting tax charge or credit in the current year. The related tax charge or credit relates to prior year profits rather than current year earnings. Therefore, the correcting tax charge or credit should be treated as a one-off event and recognised in the interim period in which it becomes probable that such a correction is required. It should not be reflected in the average annual income tax rate.

5.6.10.8   Tax loss and tax credit carrybacks and carryforwards

The benefits of a tax loss carryback are reflected in the interim period in which the related tax loss occurs. IAS 12 requires that "the benefit relating to a tax loss that can be carried back to recover current tax of a previous period should be recognised as an asset". A corresponding reduction of tax expense or increase of tax income is also recognised. [IAS 34:B20]

IAS 12 also requires that "a deferred tax asset should be recognised for the carryforward of unused tax losses and unused tax credits to the extent that it is probable that future taxable profit will be available against which the unused tax losses and unused tax credits can be utilised". Detailed criteria are specified for the purpose of assessing the availability of future taxable profit against which the unused tax losses and credits can be utilised. [IAS 34:B21]

For interim reporting purposes, the criteria for recognition of deferred tax assets are applied at the end of each interim period and, if they are met, the effect of the tax loss carryforward is reflected in the computation of the estimated average annual effective income tax rate. [IAS 34:B21]

Example 5.6.10.8A

Tax loss carryforward at the beginning of the current financial year

[IAS 34:B22]

An entity that reports quarterly, has an operating loss carryforward of 10,000 for income tax purposes at the start of the current financial year for which a deferred tax asset has not been recognised. The entity earns 10,000 in the first quarter of the current year and expects to earn 10,000 in each of the three remaining quarters. Excluding the carryforward, the estimated average annual income tax rate is expected to be 40 per cent. Tax expense is as follows:

	1st Quarter	2nd Quarter	3rd Quarter	4th Quarter	Annual
Tax expense	3,000	3,000	3,000	3,000	12,000

The tax effect of losses that arise in the early portion of a financial year should be recognised only when the tax benefits are expected to be realised either during the current year or as a deferred tax asset at the end of the year. For the purpose of applying this guidance, an established seasonal pattern of losses in the early interim periods followed by profits in later interim periods is generally sufficient to support a conclusion that realisation of the tax benefit from the early losses is probable. Recognition of the tax benefit of losses incurred in early interim periods will generally not occur in those interim periods if available evidence indicates that profits are not expected in later interim periods or subsequent financial years.

If the tax benefits of losses that are incurred in the early interim periods of a financial year are not recognised in those interim periods, no income tax expense will be recognised in respect of profits generated in later interim periods until the tax effects of the previous losses are offset.

The tax effect of a deferred tax asset expected to be recognised at the end of a financial year for deductible temporary differences and carryforwards that originate during the current financial year should be spread throughout the financial year by an adjustment to the annual effective tax rate.

Example 5.6.10.8B

Recognition of deferred tax assets at the end of an interim reporting period

Assume that during the first quarter of 20X1, an entity, operating in a tax jurisdiction with a 50 per cent tax rate, generates a tax credit of CU4,000 (i.e. sufficient to cover taxable profits of CU8,000). Under local tax law, the tax credit will expire at the end of 20X2. At the end of the first quarter of 20X1, available evidence about the future indicates that taxable income of CU2,000 and CU4,000 will be generated during 20X1 and 20X2, respectively. Therefore, the entity expects to utilise CU1,000 (CU2,000 × 50 per cent) of the tax credit to offset tax on its 20X1 taxable income, and CU2,000 (CU4,000 × 50 per cent) to offset tax on its 20X2 income. It expects to recognise a deferred tax asset in its statement of financial position at the end of 20X1 of CU2,000 (relating to the tax relief available in 20X2), and the balance of CU1,000 will not be recognised because it is not probable that sufficient taxable profit will be available against which it can be utilised before the losses expire.

The CU1,000 of the tax credit expected to be utilised during the current year (20X1) is included in calculating the estimated annual effective tax rate.

Because the tax credit is generated during the current year, the tax consequence of the CU2,000 deferred tax asset expected to be recognised at the end of 20X1 is applied rateably to each of the interim periods during 20X1.

Therefore, if profits arise on a straight line basis through 20X1, a benefit for income taxes of CU500 (CU2,000 × 1/4) will be recognised during the first interim period. Assuming the estimates about the future do not change during the remainder of the year, the tax benefit of the remaining CU1,500 (CU2,000 – CU500) of net deferred tax asset will be recognised rateably over the pre-tax accounting income generated in the later interim periods of 20X1.

5.6.10.9   Change in estimate as to recoverability of tax loss carryforward

It is not clear whether IAS 34:B21 (see **5.6.10.8**) applies equally to all circumstances when a previously recognised deferred tax asset is no longer expected to be recoverable. There appear to be two acceptable approaches.

- **Alternative A** Derecognise at the interim reporting date all the amounts assessed as not recoverable.

- **Alternative B** Spread the derecognition via the estimated annual effective tax rate.

These alternative approaches are illustrated in the following example. An entity should select one of these two approaches as its accounting policy and apply it consistently.

Example 5.6.10.9

Change in estimate as to recoverability of tax loss carryforward

An entity operates in a tax jurisdiction with a 50 per cent tax rate. In 20X1, the entity incurs tax losses of CU50,000, which can be carried forward to offset against future taxable profits until 20X3. At 31 December 20X1, the entity estimates that CU40,000 of the losses can be recovered against profits in 20X2 (budgeted profit CU15,000) and 20X3 (budgeted profit CU25,000), and therefore recognises a deferred tax asset of CU20,000 (CU40,000 × 50 per cent) in its annual financial statements for 20X1.

At the end of the first quarter of 20X2, actual year-to-date profits and expectations for the remainder of the year are in line with budget. However, the budgeted profit for 20X3 is revised downward to CU20,000.

Under the alternative approaches described above, the following amounts will be recognised.

Alternative A

If the derecognition of the deferred tax asset is accounted for entirely at the date at which it is assessed as not recoverable, at the end of the first quarter of 20X2 the carrying amount of the deferred tax asset should be reduced by CU2,500 (CU5,000 at 50 per cent). Therefore, in quarter 1 of 20X2, assuming taxable profits of CU6,000 and an estimated effective annual rate of 50 per cent, the income tax expense for the quarter is estimated as follows.

Tax expense in quarter 1:	(CU6,000 × 50%) + CU2,500 = CU5,500
Deferred tax asset carrying amount at the end of quarter 1 (original carrying amount of CU20,000 less CU3,000 utilised in the quarter less write-off of CU2,500)	CU14,500

Alternative B

If the effect of the derecognition of the deferred tax asset is spread throughout the year as part of the computation of the annual effective tax rate, the carrying amount of the deferred tax asset should be reduced by CU2,500 (CU5,000 at 50 per cent) only at the end of 20X2. Therefore, in quarter 1 of 20X2, assuming taxable profits of CU6,000 out of estimated annual profits of CU15,000, the income tax expense for the quarter is estimated as follows.

Estimated effective annual tax rate:	[(CU15,000 × 50%) + CU2,500] / CU15,000 = 66.7%
Tax expense in quarter 1:	CU6,000 × 66.7% = CU4,000
Deferred tax asset carrying amount at the end of quarter 1 (original carrying amount of CU20,000 less CU3,000 utilised in the quarter less write-off of CU1,000)	CU16,000

The remaining write-down of CU1,500 will be recognised over the remainder of the year through the mechanism of the effective tax rate.

5.6.11   Contractual or anticipated purchase price changes

Volume rebates or discounts and other contractual changes in the prices of raw materials, labour, or other purchased goods and services are anticipated in interim periods, by both the payer and the recipient, if it is probable that they have been earned or will take effect. Thus, contractual rebates and discounts are anticipated, but discretionary rebates and discounts are not anticipated because the definitions of asset and liability (requiring *control* over resources to be received, or an *obligation* to pay out resources) would not be met. [IAS 34:B23]

5.6.12   Depreciation and amortisation

Depreciation and amortisation charges for an interim period are based only on assets owned during that interim period. They should not take into account asset acquisitions or disposals planned for later in the financial year. [IAS 34:B24]

> It would not generally be necessary to reassess residual values for items of property, plant and equipment as at the interim date, unless there are indicators that there has been a material change in residual values since the end of the previous reporting period.

5.6.13   Inventories

5.6.13.1   Measurement of inventories – general

Inventories are measured for interim financial reporting using the same principles as at the financial year end. IAS 2 *Inventories* establishes requirements for recognising and measuring inventories. Inventories pose particular problems at the end of any financial reporting period because of the need to determine inventory quantities, costs and net realisable values. Nonetheless, the same measurement principles are applied for inventories at the end of interim reporting periods. To save cost and time, entities often use estimates to measure inventories at interim dates to a greater extent than at the end of annual reporting periods. [IAS 34:B25]

5.6.13.2   Net realisable value of inventories

The net realisable value of inventories is determined by reference to selling prices and related costs to complete and dispose at interim dates. [IAS 34:B26]

Provisions for write-downs to net realisable value should be calculated in the same manner as at the end of the financial year.

An entity will reverse a write-down to net realisable value in a subsequent reporting period only if it would be appropriate to do so at the end of the financial year. [IAS 34:B26]

5.6.13.3   Interim period manufacturing cost variances

Price, efficiency, spending and volume variances of a manufacturing entity are recognised in income at the end of interim reporting periods to the same extent that those variances are recognised in income at the financial year end. Deferral of variances that are expected to be absorbed by the year end is not appropriate because it could result in reporting inventory at the interim date at more or less than its portion of the actual cost of manufacture. [IAS 34:B28]

5.6.14   Foreign currency translation gains and losses

Foreign currency translation gains and losses are measured for interim financial reporting using the same principles as at financial year end. [IAS 34:B29]

IAS 21 *The Effects of Changes in Foreign Exchange Rates* specifies how to translate the financial statements of foreign operations into the presentation currency, including guidelines for using average or closing foreign exchange rates and guidelines for including the resulting adjustments in profit or loss or in other comprehensive income. Consistent with IAS 21, the actual average and closing rates for the interim period are used. Entities do not anticipate changes in foreign exchange rates in the remainder of the current financial year when translating foreign operations at an interim date. [IAS 34:B30]

If IAS 21 requires that translation adjustments are recognised as income or as expenses in the period in which they arise, that principle is applied during each interim period. Entities do not defer some foreign currency translation adjustments at an interim date if the adjustment is expected to reverse before the end of the financial year. [IAS 34:B31]

5.6.15 Interim financial reporting in hyperinflationary economies

Interim financial reports in hyperinflationary economies are prepared following the same principles as at financial year end. IAS 29 *Financial Reporting in Hyperinflationary Economies* requires that the financial statements of an entity that reports in the currency of a hyperinflationary economy be stated in terms of the measuring unit current at the end of the reporting period, and the gain or loss on the net monetary position is included in net income. Also, comparative financial data reported for prior periods is restated to the current measuring unit. [IAS 34:B32 & B33]

Entities are required to follow the same principles at interim dates, thereby presenting all interim data in the measuring unit as of the end of the interim period, with the resulting gain or loss on the net monetary position included in the interim period's net income. Entities should not annualise the recognition of the gain or loss. Nor do they use an estimated annual inflation rate in preparing an interim financial report in a hyperinflationary economy. [IAS 34:B34]

5.6.16 Impairment of assets

5.6.16.1 Principles of IAS 36 to be applied at interim reporting dates

IAS 36 *Impairment of Assets* requires that an impairment loss be recognised if the recoverable amount of an asset has declined below its carrying amount. IAS 34 requires that an entity should apply the same impairment testing, recognition and reversal criteria at an interim date as it would at the end of its financial year. That does not mean, however, that an entity must necessarily make a detailed impairment calculation at the end of each interim period. Rather, an entity will review for indications of significant impairment or reversals of impairment since the end of the most recent financial year to determine whether such a calculation is needed. [IAS 34:B35 & B36]

When an entity recognised an impairment loss relating to an asset at the end of the preceding financial year, a review of the impairment calculations at the end of the interim period may be necessary if the impairment indicator that gave rise to the impairment review is still present.

5.6.16.2 *IFRIC 10* Interim Financial Reporting and Impairment

IFRIC 10 has been amended as a result of IFRS 9 *Financial Instruments*. For entities that have adopted IFRS 9, the apparent conflict discussed below between the requirements of IAS 34 and the requirements of IAS 39 is no longer an issue, and the scope of IFRIC 10 has been reduced to deal only with the prohibition on reversals of impairments for goodwill.

As discussed at **4.1** and **5.1**, IAS 34:28 requires an entity to apply the same accounting policies in its interim financial statements as are applied in its annual financial statements. IAS 34:28 also states that the frequency of an entity's reporting (annual, half-yearly or quarterly) should not affect the measurement of its annual results. To achieve that objective, measurements for interim reporting purposes should be made on a year-to-date basis.

IFRIC 10 *Interim Financial Reporting and Impairment* addresses the interaction between the requirements in IAS 34:28 and those dealing with the recognition of impairment losses relating to goodwill under IAS 36, and relating to certain financial assets under IAS 39, and the effect of that interaction on subsequent interim and annual financial statements:

- IAS 36:124 states that "an impairment loss recognised for goodwill shall not be reversed in a subsequent period";

- for entities that have not yet adopted IFRS 9, IAS 39:69 states that "impairment losses recognised in profit or loss for an investment in an equity instrument classified as available for sale shall not be reversed through profit or loss"; and

- for entities that have not yet adopted IFRS 9, IAS 39:66 requires that impairment losses for financial assets carried at cost (such as an impairment loss on an unquoted equity instrument that is not carried at fair value because its fair value cannot be reliably measured) should not be reversed.

The issue addressed by IFRIC 10 is whether an entity should reverse impairment losses recognised in an interim period relating to goodwill, or relating to investments in equity instruments or in financial assets carried at cost, if a loss would not have been recognised, or a smaller loss would have been recognised, had an impairment assessment been made only at the end of the subsequent reporting period.

The issue is best illustrated by considering the example of Entity A and Entity B, which each hold the same equity investment with the same acquisition cost. Entity A prepares quarterly interim financial statements while Entity B prepares half-yearly financial statements. Both entities have the same financial year-end date. If there was a significant decline in the fair value of the equity instrument below its cost in the first quarter, Entity A would recognise an impairment loss in its first quarter's interim financial statements. However, if the fair value of the equity instrument subsequently recovered, so that by the half-year date there had not been a significant decline in fair value below cost, Entity B would not recognise an impairment loss in its half-yearly financial statements if it tested for impairment only at the end of the half-year reporting period. Therefore, unless Entity A reversed the impairment loss that had been recognised in an earlier interim period, the frequency of reporting would affect the measurement of its annual results when compared with Entity B's approach.

The consensus in the Interpretation is that an entity should not reverse an impairment loss recognised in a previous interim period in respect of goodwill or, for an entity that has not yet adopted IFRS 9, an investment in an equity instrument or a financial asset carried at cost. Essentially, IFRIC 10 concludes that the prohibitions on reversals of recognised impairment losses relating to goodwill under IAS 36, and relating to investments in equity instruments and financial assets carried at cost under IAS 39, should take precedence over the more general statement in IAS 34 regarding the frequency of an entity's reporting not affecting the measurement of its annual results.

IFRIC 10 emphasises that an entity should not extend the consensus of this Interpretation by analogy to other areas of potential conflict between IAS 34 and other Standards.

5.6.17 Capitalisation of borrowing costs in interim periods

Example 5.6.17

Capitalisation of borrowing costs in interim periods

An entity capitalises borrowing costs directly attributable to the construction of qualifying assets under IAS 23 *Borrowing Costs*. The entity funds its asset construction with general borrowings, rather than project-specific borrowings. Further, it uses general borrowings for purposes other than construction, so that the amount of borrowings in any period is not necessarily related to the amount of construction during that period. The entity reports quarterly.

IAS 23:14 requires that the capitalisation rate for general borrowings be the weighted average of borrowing costs applicable to borrowings of the entity that are outstanding during the period. For interim reporting purposes, the reference to 'period' in IAS 23:14 should be interpreted to mean the year-to-date period, not each individual quarter so that, in accordance with IAS 34:28 and 36, the amount of borrowing costs capitalised is 'trued-up' each quarter on a year-to-date basis.

5.6.18   Non-current assets held for sale and discontinued operations

The measurement and presentation principles of IFRS 5 *Non-current Assets Held for Sale and Discontinued Operations* should be applied in interim financial reports in the same way as at the end of the annual reporting period. Therefore, a non-current asset that meets the criteria to be classified as held for sale at the interim date should be presented as such.

Similarly, an operation that meets the definition of a discontinued operation during the interim period should be presented as such in accordance with IFRS 5.

5.6.19   Recognition in an interim financial report of a liability for mandatory dividends based on annual profits

Example 5.6.19

Recognition in an interim financial report of a liability for mandatory dividends based on annual profits

Entity A operates in a jurisdiction where all entities are required to distribute a proportion of annual profits to their equity shareholders. When an entity is first established, it is required by corporate law to specify a minimum percentage of annual profits to be distributed to its shareholders. A shareholders' meeting is held subsequent to the year end at which final dividends are approved based on the entity's annual financial statements. Subject to the approval of shareholders, the proportion of profits distributed may exceed the minimum specified by law; however, the shareholders may not avoid payment of the specified minimum percentage.

If an entity has losses in the current year or net accumulated losses after considering prior year results, then it is not required to distribute dividends.

Entity A's by-laws specify that it is required to distribute at least 25 per cent of its annual profits. Entity A, which has a 31 December year end, is preparing its interim financial report for the six months ended 30 June 20X2. In the interim period commencing 1 January 20X2, Entity A has generated profits of CU100,000. Forecast profits for the year ending 31 December 20X2 are CU250,000.

Entity A has no accumulated losses brought forward from previous accounting periods.

It is assumed that Entity A is not required to recognise a liability under IAS 32 *Financial Instruments: Presentation* because the statutory obligation does not give rise to a financial liability.

In Entity A's interim financial report for the six months ended 30 June 20X2, what (if any) liability should be recognised for dividends?

In Entity A's interim financial report for the six months ended 30 June 20X2, no liability should be recognised for dividends.

As discussed in **example 5.4** in **chapter A22**, a liability for dividends should only be recognised if the obligation to pay the dividend exists at the end of the annual reporting period. The same principle should be applied at the interim reporting date.

In the circumstances under consideration, it is not appropriate to recognise a liability for the dividends based on profits earned in the first half-year. Although Entity A has generated profits in its first half-year, and expects to generate profits for the remainder of the year, it is possible that it will incur losses in the second half-year such that an overall loss is reported in the annual financial statements. If this occurs, Entity A has no obligation to pay a dividend. Consequently, at 30 June 20X2, Entity A does not have a present obligation to pay dividends because the liability does not exist independently of Entity A's future actions (i.e. the future conduct of its business). [IAS 37:19]

A33 Management commentary

Contents

1 Introduction

1.1 Overview of IFRS Practice Statement *Management Commentary*

The IFRS Practice Statement *Management Commentary* aims to provide a framework for the presentation of management commentary, to promote good practice, and to promote comparability across entities that present management commentary. It sets out the principles, qualitative characteristics and elements that are necessary to provide users of financial statements with useful information.

The Practice Statement defines management commentary as "[a] narrative report that relates to financial statements that have been prepared in accordance with IFRSs. Management commentary provides users with historical explanations of the amounts presented in the financial statements, specifically the entity's financial position, financial performance and cash flows. It also provides commentary on an entity's prospects and other information not presented in the financial statements. Management commentary also serves as a basis for understanding management's objectives and its strategies for achieving those objectives". [MC:Appendix]

> Management commentary encompasses reporting that jurisdictions may describe as management's discussion and analysis (MD&A), operating and financial review (OFR), business review or management's report. [MC:BC5]

By 'management', the Practice Statement means the people responsible for the decision-making and oversight of the entity. They may include executive employees, key management personnel and members of a governing body. [MC:IN6]

> See **chapter A34** for a discussion of integrated reporting.

1.2 Amendments to IFRS Practice Statement *Management Commentary* since the last edition of this manual

None. The Practice Statement has not been amended since it was issued in December 2010.

2 IFRS Practice Statement on management commentary

2.1 Objective and scope

The objective of the Practice Statement is to assist management in presenting useful management commentary that relates to financial statements prepared in accordance with IFRSs. It applies only to management commentary and not to other information presented in either the financial statements or the broader annual report. [MC:1 & 2]

Although the IASB developed the guidance with listed entities in mind, the Practice Statement does not mandate which entities should be required to prepare and publish management commentary; nor does it prescribe how frequently management commentary should be prepared or the level of assurance to which it should be subjected. [MC:4]

Because the Practice Statement is not an IFRS, it is not mandatory for entities applying IFRSs unless a local jurisdiction requires compliance. As such, non-compliance with the Practice Statement will not prevent an entity's financial statements from complying with IFRSs, if they otherwise do so. [MC:IN2]

2.2   Identification of management commentary

Management commentary should be clearly identified and distinguished from other information; when the management commentary relates to financial statements, those financial statements should be made available with the commentary or identified within the commentary. [MC:5 & 6]

When management commentary is presented, management should explain the extent to which the Practice Statement has been followed. Management commentary should not be described as complying with the Practice Statement unless it complies with the Practice Statement in its entirety. [MC:7]

2.3   Users of management commentary

Users are existing and potential investors, lenders and other creditors. Management should consider the needs of the primary users of financial reports when determining the information to include in management commentary. [MC:8]

3   Framework for the presentation of management commentary

3.1   Purpose

Management commentary should provide users of financial statements with integrated information that provides a context for the related financial statements and reflects management's view. The information should be balanced (i.e. it should include both positive and negative circumstances); it should cover what has happened during the reporting period, why it has happened and what the implications are for the entity's future. [MC:9]

Management commentary complements and supplements the financial statements by communicating integrated information about:

[MC:10 & 11]

- the entity's resources and the claims thereon, and the transactions and other events that change them; and

- the main trends and factors that are likely to affect the entity's future performance, position and progress.

The appendix to the Practice Statement explains that progress "[r]eflects how the entity has grown or changed in the current year, as well as how it expects to grow or change in the future".

Financial statements alone do not provide all the information that users need to make economic decisions because they set out the financial effects of past events and do not provide non-financial measures of performance or a discussion of future prospects or plans. The Basis for Conclusions on the Practice Statement explains that the IASB's objective is to improve the usefulness of the information provided in management commentary such that, when taken together with the financial statements, users are better able to make decisions. [MB:BC3 & BC4]

3.2   Principles

3.2.1   Principles underlying management commentary

Management should present commentary that is consistent with the following principles:

[MC:12, 15 & 16]

- to provide management's view of the entity's performance, position and progress by disclosing information that is important to management in managing the entity; and

- to supplement and complement information presented in the financial statements with:

  - explanations of the amounts presented in the financial statements and the conditions and events that shaped that information; and

  - information about the entity and its performance that is not presented in the financial statements but is important to the management of the entity.

In aligning with those principles, management commentary should include:

[MC:13]

- forward-looking information (see **3.2.2**); and

- information that possesses the qualitative characteristics described in the *Conceptual Framework for Financial Reporting* (see **3.2.3**).

Information should be provided to help users of the financial reports assess the performance of the entity and the actions of its management relative to stated strategies and plans for progress. That type of commentary will help users of the financial reports to understand, for example:

[MC:14]

- the entity's risk exposures, its strategies for managing risks, and the effectiveness of those strategies;

- how resources that are not presented in the financial statements could affect the entity's operations; and

- how non-financial factors have influenced the information presented in the financial statements.

3.2.2 *Forward-looking information*

The appendix to the Practice Statement defines forward-looking information as "[i]nformation about the future. It includes information about the future (for example, information about prospects and plans) that may later be presented as historical information (ie results). It is subjective and its preparation requires the exercise of professional judgement".

Management commentary should communicate, from management's perspective, the direction the entity is taking. Such information does not predict the future, but instead sets out management's objectives for the entity and its strategies for achieving those objectives. The extent to which management commentary looks forward will be influenced by the regulatory and legal environment within which the entity operates. [MC:17]

Management should include forward-looking information, through narrative explanations or quantified data, when it is aware of factors that could impact the entity's financial position, liquidity and performance. Management should explain what impact these factors may have and include an assessment of the entity's prospects in light of current period results. Forward-looking information may, but is not required to, include forecasts and projections. The assumptions used in providing the forward-looking information should be disclosed. [MC:18]

Management should also discuss the extent to which actual performance has been different from forward-looking disclosures made in prior periods. For example, if targets for future performance were disclosed in a prior period, the entity's actual performance in the current reporting period should be disclosed and an explanation provided for significant variances and the implication of those variances. [MC:19]

3.2.3 *Qualitative characteristics of useful information*

Because management commentary lies within the boundaries of financial reporting, it should possess the same fundamental qualitative characteristics of relevance and faithful representation that are applicable to general purpose financial reports. Information in management commentary should also maximise the enhancing qualitative characteristics of comparability, verifiability, timeliness and understandability. [MC:20]

These terms, which have the meanings specified in the IASB's *Conceptual Framework for Financial Reporting*, are discussed in **section 5** of **chapter A2**.

Management commentary should include information that is material to the entity. Materiality will be different for each entity. Materiality is an 'entity-specific aspect of relevance'; accordingly, information that is relevant for an entity will also be material. [MC:21]

3.3 Presentation

Management commentary should be clear and straightforward, with its form and content reflecting the nature of the business, the strategies adopted by management and the regulatory environment in which the entity operates. [MC:22] It should focus on the most important information in a manner intended to address the principles described in **3.2**. Specifically, management should:

[MC:23]

- ensure that management commentary is consistent with the related financial statements (e.g. when the financial statements include segment information, the information presented in the management commentary should reflect that segmentation);

- avoid duplicating disclosures made in the notes to the financial statements. Reciting financial statement information without analysis, or presenting boilerplate discussions that do not provide insight into the entity's past performance or prospects, is unlikely to provide information that is useful to users of the financial reports and may create an obstacle for users to identify and understand the most significant matters facing the entity; and

- avoid the inclusion of generic disclosures that do not relate to the practices and circumstances of the entity and immaterial disclosures that make the more important information difficult to find.

3.4   Elements of management commentary

3.4.1   Key elements of management commentary

The particular focus of management commentary will depend on the facts and circumstances of the entity, but management commentary should include information that is essential to an understanding of:

[MC:24]

- the nature of the business (see **3.4.2**);

- management's objectives and its strategies for meeting those objectives (see **3.4.3**);

- the entity's most significant resources, risks and relationships (see **3.4.4**);

- the results of operations and prospects (see **3.4.5**); and

- the critical performance measures and indicators that management uses to evaluate the entity's performance against stated objectives (see **3.4.6**).

The elements set out in MC:24 are not listed in a specific order, but they are related and should not be presented in isolation. Management should provide its perspective on the business and its analysis of the interaction of the elements to help users to understand the entity's financial statements and to understand management's objectives and strategies for achieving those objectives. [MC:25]

3.4.2   Nature of the business

The description of the business should help users of the financial reports to gain an understanding of the entity and of the external environment in which it operates; this information enables users to assess and understand the entity's performance, strategic options and prospects. Depending on the nature of the business, management commentary may include an integrated discussion of the following types of information:

[MC:26]

- the industries in which the entity operates;

- the entity's main markets and competitive position within those markets;

- significant features of the legal, regulatory and macro-economic environments that influence the entity and the markets in which the entity operates;

- the entity's main products, services, business processes and distribution methods; and

- the entity's structure and how it creates value.

3.4.3 Objectives and strategies

Management should disclose its objectives and strategies in a way that enables users of the financial reports to understand the priorities for action as well as to identify the resources that must be managed to deliver results. For example, information about how management intends to address market trends and the threats and opportunities those market trends represent provides users of the financial reports with insight that may shape their expectations about the entity's future performance. Management should also explain how success will be measured and over what period of time it should be assessed. [MC:27]

When there is significant change in an entity's objectives and strategies in the current period as compared to prior periods, management should explain the change. An explanation of the relationship between objectives, strategy, management actions and executive remuneration is also helpful. [MC:28]

3.4.4 Resources, risks and relationships

Management commentary should set out the critical financial and non-financial resources available to the entity and how those resources are used in meeting management's stated objectives for the entity. Disclosure about resources depends on the nature of the entity and on the industries in which the entity operates. For example, useful information may include an analysis of the adequacy of the entity's capital structure, financial arrangements (whether or not recognised in the statement of financial position), liquidity and cash flows, and human and intellectual capital resources, as well as plans to address any surplus resources or identified and expected inadequacies. [MC:30]

Management should disclose an entity's principal risk exposures and changes in those risks, together with its plans and strategies for bearing or mitigating those risks, as well as disclosure of the effectiveness of its risk management strategies. Management should not list all possible risks and uncertainties but disclose only those principal risks and uncertainties facing the entity. [MC:31]

Risks include principal strategic, commercial, operational and financial risks. The description of the principal risks facing the entity should cover both exposures to negative consequences and potential opportunities. Management commentary provides useful information when it discusses the principal risks and uncertainties necessary to understand management's objectives and strategies for the entity. The principal risks and uncertainties can constitute either a significant external or internal risk to the entity. [MC:32]

Significant relationships that the entity has with stakeholders should be identified. Management should disclose how those relationships are likely to affect the performance and value of the entity, and how those relationships are managed; this information will enable users to understand how such relationships influence the nature of the business and whether they expose the business to substantial risk. [MC:33]

3.4.5   Results and prospects

Management commentary should include a clear description of the entity's financial and non-financial performance, the extent to which that performance may be indicative of future performance, and management's assessment of the entity's prospects. [MC:34]

Explanations of the entity's performance and progress during the period and its position at the end of the period provide users of the financial reports with insight into the main trends and factors affecting the business. Management should describe the relationship between the entity's results, management's objectives and management's strategies for achieving those objectives. In addition, management should provide discussion and analysis of significant changes in financial position, liquidity and performance compared with those of the previous period or periods because this can help users to understand the extent to which past performance may be indicative of future performance. [MC:35]

Management should provide an analysis of the prospects of the entity, which may include targets for financial and non-financial measures. This information can help users of the financial reports to understand how management intends to implement its strategies for the entity over the long term. When targets are quantified, management should explain the risks and assumptions necessary for users to assess the likelihood of achieving those targets. [MC:36]

3.4.6   Performance measures and indicators

The financial and non-financial performance measures and indicators – often referred to as 'key performance indicators' (KPIs) – used by management to manage the entity and assess its progress against stated objectives should be included in management commentary. Indicators can be narrative evidence describing how the business is managed or quantified measures that provide indirect evidence of performance. To help users assess the extent to which goals and objectives are being achieved, management should explain why the results from performance measures have changed over the period or how the indicators have changed. [MC:37 & 38]

Management should explain why the performance measures and indicators used are relevant. Comparability is enhanced if the performance measures and indicators are accepted and used widely, either within an industry or more generally. It is helpful if the performance measures and indicators remain consistent over time. Nevertheless, when strategies and objectives change, management might decide that the performance measures and indicators presented in the previous period's management commentary are no longer relevant. When management changes the performance measures and indicators used, the changes should be identified and explained. [MC:38 & 39]

Management may need to adjust information from the financial statements for inclusion in management commentary. When this is the case, that fact should be disclosed. When financial performance measures that are not required or defined by IFRSs are included within management commentary, those measures should be defined and explained, including an explanation of the relevance of the measure to users. When financial performance measures are derived or drawn from the financial statements, those measures should be reconciled to measures presented in the financial statements that have been prepared in accordance with IFRSs. [MC:40]

It is for management to decide how many KPIs to disclose. The Practice Statement does not specify how many KPIs should be included, nor mandate any particular KPIs on which all entities should report.

A34   Integrated reporting

Contents

1 Introduction

1.1 Background to the International Integrated Reporting Framework

The *International Integrated Reporting Framework* (IIRF or 'the Framework'), published by the International Integrated Reporting Council (IIRC) in December 2013, explains the fundamental concepts of integrated reporting and provides principles-based guidance for entities wishing to prepare an integrated report.

Entities are not required to comply with the Framework, unless specifically required by their jurisdiction. However, integrated reporting complements many of the various developments in financial and other reporting taking place in national jurisdictions around the world. It is the intention of the IIRC that the Framework will accelerate these individual initiatives and provide impetus to greater innovation in corporate reporting globally.

Section 1.2 provides some brief details on the history and structure of the IIRC. The remainder of this chapter is divided into the following sections:

- overview of the Framework and the fundamental principles underpinning it (**sections 2** and **3**);

- guiding principle for the presentation and preparation of an integrated report (**section 4**);

- the content elements for an integrated report (**section 5**); and

- a summary of the requirements for an integrated report (**section 6**).

> This chapter focusses on recommended content for an integrated report based on the Framework. A comprehensive discussion of the concepts underlying 'integrated thinking' and reporting on 'value creation' is beyond the scope of this manual; readers should refer to the detailed discussion on these topics in the Framework.

1.2 The International Integrated Reporting Council

The International Integrated Reporting Council (IIRC) is a global coalition of regulators, investors, companies, standard setters, the accounting profession and non-governmental organisations (NGOs). Together, this coalition shares the view that communication about value creation should be the next step in the evolution of corporate reporting.

The IIRC was created in 2010 by the UK Prince of Wales 'Accounting for Sustainability Project', the Global Reporting Initiative (GRI) and the International Federation of Accountants to bring together leaders from the corporate, investment, accounting, securities, regulatory, academic, civil society and standard-setting sectors to develop a global framework for Integrated Reporting.

The IIRC comprises a Council, a working group and a secretariat, together with such sub-committees and task forces as are from time to time established. The IIRC has also appointed a number of Ambassadors, whose role is to engage with influential stakeholders in order to help promote the aims of the IIRC and build a consensus around the need for an international integrated reporting framework, and to provide additional insight to the IIRC on the views of such stakeholders.

Further details on the IIRC can be found on their website *www.theiirc.org*.

2   The International Integrated Reporting Framework

2.1   Overview of the International Integrated Reporting Framework

Integrated reporting aims to:

[Foreword to the Framework]

- improve the quality of information available to providers of financial capital to enable a more efficient and productive allocation of capital;

- promote a more cohesive and efficient approach to corporate reporting that draws on different reporting strands and communicates the full range of factors that materially affect the ability of an organisation to create value over time;

- enhance accountability and stewardship for the broad base of capitals (financial, manufactured, intellectual, human, social and relationship, and natural) and promote understanding of their interdependencies; and

- support integrated thinking, decision-making and actions that focus on the creation of value over the short-, medium- and long-term.

To achieve these aims, the Framework focuses on a set of six capitals – financial, manufactured, intellectual, human, social and relationship, and natural – to ensure that a business takes a broader view on how it creates value over time. Further, the focus of integrated reporting is on current and future value creation, whereas traditionally corporate reporting guidelines have focussed more on current and past performance.

As emphasised in the foreword to the Framework, while consistent with some of the requirements of financial and other reporting around the world, an integrated report differs from other reports and communications due to:

- its focus on the ability of an organisation to create value in the short-, medium- and long-term;

- its combined emphasis on conciseness, strategic focus and future orientation, the connectivity of information, and the capitals and their interdependencies; and

- its emphasis on the importance of integrated thinking within the organisation.

The adoption of integrated reporting varies considerably between jurisdictions. Of note, however, is that an integrated report may encompass reporting that can be described variously as the annual report, strategic report, integrated annual review, narrative commentary, management commentary, management's discussion and analysis (MD&A), operating and financial review (OFR), business review or management's report.

Whichever format the integrated report takes, the Framework is clear that an integrated report claiming to be prepared in accordance with its requirements should be a designated, identifiable communication. [IIRF:1.12]

2.2 Structure of the Framework

The Framework is organised into two parts:

- Part I provides guidance on using the Framework, including key definitions and objectives, and explains the fundamental concepts of integrated reporting; and

- Part II sets out the guiding principles and content elements that govern the overall content of an integrated report.

These chapters are bound by an executive summary and a glossary of key terms.

Parts I and II both include **requirements in bold italic type** with which any communication claiming to be an integrated report prepared in accordance with the Framework should comply (see **2.9**). Those requirements, which are also highlighted throughout this chapter in bold italic type, are summarised in **section 6**.

Text in the Framework that is not in bold italic type provides guidance to assist in applying the requirements. It is not necessary for an integrated report to include all matters referred to in the guidance. [IIRF:1.19]

The requirements of the Framework relating to the content elements of an integrated report are phrased as questions, emphasising the principles-based nature of the Framework (see **section 5**). As a result, the content of an integrated report will depend on the particular circumstances of the organisation, as well as the exercise of judgement by senior management and those charged with governance in applying the Framework's guiding principles and content elements.

2.3   Objective of the Framework

The purpose of the Framework is to establish 'guiding principles' and 'content elements' that govern the overall content of an integrated report, and to explain the fundamental concepts that underpin them. The Framework:

- identifies information to be included in an integrated report for use in assessing the organisation's ability to create value; it does not set benchmarks for matters such as the quality of an organisation's strategy or the level of its performance; [IIRF:1.5] and

- is written primarily in the context of private-sector, for-profit companies of any size, but it can also be applied, adapted as necessary, by public-sector and not-for-profit organisations. [IIRF:1.4]

While an objective of the Framework is to establish guiding principles and content elements that govern the content of an integrated report, a primary goal is also to establish a process of integrated reporting founded on integrated thinking. This process extends further than the production of an integrated report. It involves embedding integrated thinking into internal business processes, management information and decision-making.

2.4   Definitions

The following definitions are used in the Framework.

- An **integrated report** is "[a] concise communication about how an organisation's strategy, governance, performance and prospects, in the context of its external environment, lead to the creation of value over the short, medium and long term". [IIRF:1.1]

- **Integrated reporting** is "[a] process founded on integrated thinking that results in a periodic integrated report by an organisation about value creation over time and related communications regarding aspects of value creation". [IIRF:Glossary]

- **Integrated thinking** is "[the] active consideration by an organisation of the relationships between its various operating and functional units and the capitals that the organisation uses or affects. Integrated thinking leads to integrated decision-making and actions that consider the creation of value over the short, medium and long term." [IIRF:Glossary]

2.5 Purpose and users of an integrated report

The primary purpose of an integrated report is to explain to providers of financial capital how an organisation creates value over time. [IIRF:1.7]

An integrated report benefits all stakeholders interested in an organisation's ability to create value over time, including employees, customers, suppliers, business partners, local communities, legislators, regulators and policy-makers. [IIRF:1.8]

2.6 A principles-based approach

The Framework is principles-based – designed with the objective of achieving an appropriate balance between allowing flexibility to take account of the individual circumstances of different organisations and the need for comparability. [IIRF:1.9]

While principles-based, the Framework has mandatory content elements which any communication claiming to be an integrated report should include (see **section 5**). However, the Framework is high-level and does not prescribe how these content elements should be covered, but leaves this to the reporting organisation.

The Framework does not prescribe specific key performance indicators (KPIs), measurement methods or the disclosure of individual matters. Those responsible for the preparation and presentation of the integrated report will need to exercise judgement, given the specific circumstances of the organisation, to determine:

[IIRF:1.10]

- which matters are material; and

- how those matters are disclosed, including the application of generally accepted measurement and disclosure methods as appropriate. When information in an integrated report is similar to, or based on, other information published by the organisation, it is prepared on the same basis as, or is easily reconcilable with, that other information.

2.7 Quantitative and qualitative information

The Framework takes the position that the ability of an organisation to create value can best be reported on through a combination of quantitative and qualitative information. Both qualitative and quantitative information are necessary for an integrated report to properly represent the organisation's ability to create value because each provides context for the other. Including KPIs as part of a narrative explanation can be an effective way to connect quantitative and qualitative information (see also **4.3**). [IIRF:1.11 & 3.8]

2.8   Form of report and relationship with other information

An integrated report should be a designated, identifiable communication. [IIRF:1.12]

An integrated report is intended to be more than a summary of information in other communications (e.g. financial statements, a sustainability report, analyst calls, or on a website); rather, it makes explicit the connectivity of information to communicate how value is created over time. [IIRF:1.13]

An integrated report may be prepared in response to existing compliance requirements. For example, an organisation may be required by local law to prepare a management commentary or other report that provides context for its financial statements. If that report is also prepared in accordance with the Framework, it can be considered an integrated report. If the report is required to include specified information beyond that required by the Framework, the report can still be considered an integrated report if that other information does not obscure the concise information required by the Framework. [IIRF:1.14]

An integrated report may be either a stand-alone report or be included as a distinguishable, prominent and accessible part of another report or communication. For example, it may be included at the front of a report that also includes the organisation's financial statements. [IIRF:1.15]

An integrated report can provide an 'entry point' to more detailed information outside the designated communication, to which it may be linked. The form of link will depend on the form of the integrated report (e.g. for a paper-based report, links may involve attaching other information as an appendix; for a web-based report, it may involve hyperlinking to that other information). [IIRF:1.16]

This linkage can answer the needs of stakeholders other than the providers of financial capital who may require more detailed information, and can use the integrated report to understand the organisation better and to access the information they require more easily.

2.9   Compliance with all requirements of the Framework

Any communication claiming to be an integrated report and referencing the Framework should apply all the requirements identified in bold italic type unless:

[IIRF:1.17]

- *the unavailability of reliable information or specific legal prohibitions results in an inability to disclose material information; or*

- **disclosure of material information would cause significant competitive harm.**

When disclosure could cause competitive harm, an organisation should consider how to describe the essence of the matter without identifying specific information that might cause a significant loss of competitive advantage. Accordingly, the organisation considers what advantage a competitor could actually gain from information in an integrated report, and balances this against the need for the integrated report to achieve its primary purpose (see **2.5**). [IIRF:3.51]

In the case of the unavailability of reliable information or specific legal prohibitions, an integrated report should:

[IIRF:1.18]

- *indicate the nature of the information that has been omitted;*

- *explain the reason why it has been omitted; and*

- *In the case of the unavailability of data, identify the steps being taken to obtain the information and the expected time frame for doing so.*

2.10   Responsibility for an integrated report

An integrated report should include a statement from those charged with governance that includes:

[IIRF:1.20]

- *an acknowledgement of their responsibility to ensure the integrity of the integrated report;*

- *an acknowledgement that they have applied their collective mind to the preparation and presentation of the integrated report; and*

- *their opinion or conclusion about whether the integrated report is presented in accordance with the Framework.*

Or, if it does not include such a statement, it should explain:

[IIRF:1.20]

- *what role those charged with governance played in its preparation and presentation;*

- *what steps are being taken to include such a statement in future reports; and*

- *the time frame for doing so, which should be no later than the organisation's third integrated report that references the Framework.*

3   Fundamental concepts of integrated reporting

An integrated report explains how an organisation creates value over time and aims to provide insight about:

[IIRF:2.3]

- the external environment that affects an organisation;

- the resources and the relationships used and affected by the organisation; and

- how the organisation interacts with the external environment and the capitals to create value over the short-, medium- and long-term.

There are three fundamental concepts of integrated reporting which underpin and reinforce the requirements and guidance in the Framework:

[IIRF:2.1]

- value creation for the organisation and for others;

- the capitals; and

- the value creation process.

The following terms are important for an understanding of the fundamental concepts.

- **Capitals** are the "stocks of value on which all organisations depend for their success as inputs to the business model, and which are increased, decreased or transformed through the organisation's business activities and outputs. The capitals are categorised in this Framework as financial, manufactured, intellectual, human, social and relationship, and natural". [IIRF:Glossary]

- **Value creation** is "[t]he process that results in increases, decreases or transformations of the capitals caused by the organisation's business activities and outputs". [IIRF:Glossary]

- **Value creation for the organisation and for others:** key to integrated reporting is the underlying premise that value has two interrelated aspects – value created for (1) the organisation itself, which enables financial returns to the providers of financial capital, and (2) others (i.e. stakeholders and society at large). [IIRF:2.4]

Key to the value creation process is the organisation's business model and the external environment in which it operates. The organisation's business model draws on various capitals as inputs and, through its business activities, converts them to outputs (products, services). The organisation's activities and outputs also lead to outcomes in terms of consequences (positive and negative) for the capitals. As value is created over different time horizons, and for different stakeholders through different capitals, the outcomes of the organisation for the capitals may materially affect its ability to create value in the short-, medium- and long-term. As such, the value creation process is not static. The premise here is that whether an organisation creates value for others materially affects its ability to create value for itself – and whether an organisation creates value for itself materially affects its ability to create value for others. This is why an organisation's business model and value creation process benefit not only providers of financial capital but also all other stakeholders interested in the organisation's ability to create value over time.

The value creation process diagram in the Framework depicts this dynamic relationship: an organisation's activities, its interactions and relationships, its outputs, and the outcomes associated with the various capitals it uses and affects influence its ability to draw on these capitals in a continuous cycle.

Identifying how the organisation creates value over different time horizons and for different stakeholders through different capitals is challenging. Organisations transitioning to integrated reporting typically take the following steps (in order of complexity): (1) defining their business model; (2) understanding the flow of capitals; and then (3) translating their findings into a value creation assessment.

Readers should refer to Section 2 of the Framework for a detailed exploration of these fundamental concepts.

4 Guiding principles for the preparation and presentation of an integrated report

4.1 Seven guiding principles

Seven guiding principles underpin the preparation and presentation of an integrated report, informing the content of the report and how information is presented:

[IIRF:3.1]

- strategic focus and future orientation (see **4.2**);

- connectivity of information (see **4.3**);

- stakeholder relationships (see **4.4**);

- materiality (see **4.5**);

- conciseness (see **4.6**);

- reliability and completeness (see **4.7**); and

- consistency and comparability (see **4.8**).

These guiding principles are applied individually and collectively for the purpose of preparing and presenting an integrated report; accordingly, judgement is needed in their application, particularly when there is an apparent tension between them. [IIRF:3.2]

Judgement will be required in circumstances when there is an apparent tension between the guiding principles (e.g. between conciseness and completeness). The Framework does not provide specific additional guidance on how to make such judgements.

Key aspects of the guiding principles and content elements (see **section 5**) that offer guidance in making such judgements include:

- looking to the medium- and long-term instead of focusing solely on the short-term;

- in a manner reflecting the importance of relationships with key stakeholders, providing insight into the nature and quality of the organisation's relationships with them, including how and to what extent the organisation understands, takes into account, and responds to their legitimate needs and interests;

- applying the materiality concept to determine the content of an integrated report by assessing those matters that substantively affect the organisation's ability to create value over the short-, medium- and long-term;

- understanding the interconnectivity of information presented in the integrated report (e.g. the linkage between strategy, risks and opportunities, and performance, including financial and non-financial key performance indicators);

- adopting a future orientation (e.g. by clearly articulating information about the availability, quality and affordability of the capitals the organisation uses or affects); and

- providing the basis of the report's preparation and presentation, including any other significant frameworks used to quantify or evaluate material matters for inclusion in the report, in addition to disclosure of (1) a summary of the organisation's materiality determination process, and (2) a description of the reporting boundary and how it has been determined.

4.2   Strategic focus and future orientation

An integrated report should provide insight into the organisation's strategy, and how it relates to the organisation's ability to create value in the short-, medium- and long-term and to its use of and effects on the capitals. [IIRF:3.3]

Applying this guiding principle extends to the selection and presentation of other content, and may include, for example:

[IIRF:3.4]

- highlighting significant risks, opportunities and dependencies flowing from the organisation's market position and business model; and

- the views of those charged with governance about:

  - the relationship between past and future performance, and the factors that can change that relationship;

  - how the organisation balances short-, medium- and long-term interests; and

  - how the organisation has learned from past experiences in determining future strategic directions.

Adopting a strategic focus and future orientation (see also **4.7.8** on future-oriented information) includes clearly articulating how the continued availability, quality and affordability of significant capitals contribute to the organisation's ability to achieve its strategic objectives in the future and to create value. [IIRF:3.5]

4.3   Connectivity of information

An integrated report should show a holistic picture of the combination, interrelatedness and dependencies between the factors that affect the organisation's ability to create value over time. [IIRF:3.6]

The more that integrated thinking is embedded into an organisation's activities, the more naturally will the connectivity of information flow into management reporting, analysis and decision-making, and subsequently into the integrated report. [IIRF:3.7]

A review of an organisation's integrated report for linkage of KPIs to the organisation's strategy, business model, strategic objectives and remuneration policy can be a quick measure for assessing the extent to which the organisation's thinking internally is connected or 'integrated'. The key forms of connectivity of information are discussed in detail in section 3B of the Framework.

4.4   Stakeholder relationships

An integrated report should provide insight into the nature and quality of the organisation's relationships with its key stakeholders, including how and to what extent the organisation understands, takes into account and responds to their legitimate needs and interests. [IIRF:3.10]

The Framework explains that this guiding principle reflects the importance of relationships with key stakeholders because, as reflected in the fundamental concept of value creation for the organisation and for others, "value is not created by or within an organisation alone, but is created through relationships with others". The Framework clearly states, however, that this "does not mean that an integrated report should attempt to satisfy the information needs of all stakeholders". [IIRF:3.11]

Stakeholders are defined by the Framework as "[t]hose groups or individuals that can reasonably be expected to be significantly affected by an organisation's business activities, outputs or outcomes, or whose actions can reasonably be expected to significantly affect the ability of the organisation to create value over time. Stakeholders may include providers of financial capital, employees, customers, suppliers, business partners, local communities, NGOs, environmental groups, legislators, regulators, and policy-makers". [IIRF:Glossary]

> Key to integrated reporting is how an organisation considers key stakeholders in how it creates value in the short-, medium- and long-term. Disclosing the organisation's approach to stakeholder engagement is a requirement of the Global Reporting Initiative, whose sustainability reporting framework (and G4 Sustainability Reporting Guidelines) is used widely around the world.
>
> The primary purpose of an integrated report is to explain to providers of financial capital how an organisation creates value over time, in the knowledge that value is not created by or within an organisation alone, but is created through relationships with others.

The Framework notes that, by disclosing how key stakeholders' legitimate needs and interests are understood, taken into account and responded to through decisions, actions and performance, as well as ongoing communication, an integrated report enhances transparency and accountability, both essential in building trust and resilience. [IIRF:3.14]

The guiding principle of stakeholder relationships also refers to the concept of stewardship, noting that, when the capitals are owned by the organisation, a stewardship responsibility is imposed on management and those charged with corporate governance via their legal responsibilities, to care for or use those capitals responsibly. [IIRF:3.15]

Further, the Framework notes that, when the capitals are owned by others or
* at all:

[IIRF:3.16]

- stewardship responsibilities may be imposed by law or regulation (e.g. through a contract with the owners, or through labour laws or environmental protection regulations); and

- when there is no legal stewardship responsibility, the organisation may have an ethical responsibility to accept, or choose to accept stewardship responsibilities and be guided in doing so by stakeholder expectations.

Consistent with the fundamental concept of value creation for the organisation and for others and extension of the financial reporting boundary (see **5.9.3**), integrated reporting extends consideration of the capitals to those not owned by the organisation; the guiding principle of stakeholder relationships is an example of this.

4.5 Materiality

An integrated report should disclose information about matters that substantively affect the organisation's ability to create value over the short-, medium- and long-term. [IIRF:3.17]

The materiality determination process for the purpose of preparing and presenting an integrated report set out in the Framework is a four-step process and involves:

[IIRF:3.18]

- identifying relevant matters based on their ability to affect value creation;
- evaluating the importance of relevant matters in terms of their known or potential effect on value creation;
- prioritising the matters based on their relative importance; and
- determining the information to disclose about material matters.

To be most effective, the materiality determination process is integrated into the organisation's management processes and includes regular engagement with providers of financial capital and others to ensure the integrated report meets its primary purpose. [IIRF:3.20]

Key to the materiality determination process is the concept of the reporting boundary. Determining the boundary for an integrated report has two aspects:

[IIRF:3.30]

- the financial reporting entity (i.e. the boundary used for financial reporting purposes); and
- risks, opportunities and outcomes attributable to or associated with other entities/stakeholders beyond the financial reporting entity that have a significant effect on the ability of the financial reporting entity to create value.

The entities or stakeholders beyond the financial reporting boundary may be those considered by organisations for the purposes of standalone reports on corporate social responsibility or sustainability. See section 3D of the Framework for a more detailed exploration of the materiality determination process.

4.6 Conciseness

An integrated report should be concise. [IIRF:3.36]

An integrated report includes sufficient context to understand the organisation's strategy, governance, performance and prospects without being burdened with less relevant information. [IIRF:3.37]

The organisation should seek a balance in its integrated report between conciseness and the other guiding principles, in particular completeness and comparability. In achieving conciseness, an integrated report:

[IIRF:3.38]

- applies the materiality determination process described in **4.5**;

- follows a logical structure and includes internal cross-references as appropriate to limit repetition;

- may link to more detailed information, information that does not change frequently (e.g. a listing of subsidiaries), or external sources (e.g. assumptions about future economic conditions on a government website);

- expresses concepts clearly and in as few words as possible;

- favours plain language over the use of jargon or highly technical terminology; and

- avoids highly generic disclosures (often referred to as 'boilerplate') that are not specific to the organisation.

4.7 Reliability and completeness

4.7.1 Reliability and completeness – general principle

An integrated report should include all material matters, both positive and negative, in a balanced way and without material error. [IIRF:3.39]

4.7.2 Reliability

The reliability of information is affected by its balance and freedom from material error. Reliability (which is often referred to as faithful representation) is enhanced by mechanisms such as robust internal control and reporting systems, stakeholder engagement, internal audit or similar functions, and independent, external assurance. [IIRF:3.40]

Those charged with governance have ultimate responsibility for how the organisation's strategy, governance, performance and prospects lead to value creation over time. They are responsible for ensuring that there is effective leadership and decision-making regarding the preparation and presentation of an integrated report, including the identification and oversight of the employees actively involved in the process. [IIRF:3.41]

Maintaining an audit trail when preparing an integrated report helps senior management and those charged with governance review the report and exercise judgement in deciding whether information is sufficiently reliable to be included. It might be appropriate in some cases (e.g. with respect to future-oriented information) for an integrated report to describe the mechanisms employed to ensure reliability. [IIRF:3.42]

4.7.3 Balance

A balanced integrated report has no bias in the selection or presentation of information. Information in the report is not slanted, weighted, emphasised, de-emphasised, combined, offset or otherwise manipulated to change the probability that it will be received either favourably or unfavourably. [IIRF:3.44]

Important methods to ensure balance include:

[IIRF:3.45]

- selection of presentation formats that are not likely to unduly or inappropriately influence assessments made on the basis of the integrated report;
- giving equal consideration to both increases and decreases in the capitals, both strengths and weaknesses of the organisation, both positive and negative performance, etc.; and
- reporting against previously reported targets, forecasts, projections and expectations.

4.7.4 Freedom from material error

Freedom from material error does not imply that the information is perfectly accurate in all respects. It does imply that:

[IIRF:3.46]

- processes and controls have been applied to reduce to an acceptably low level the risk that reported information contains a material misstatement; and
- when information includes estimates, this is clearly communicated, and the nature and limitations of the estimation process are explained.

4.7.5   Completeness

A complete integrated report includes all material information, both positive and negative. To help ensure that all material information has been identified, consideration is given to what organisations in the same industry are reporting on because certain matters within an industry are likely to be material to all organisations in that industry. [IIRF:3.47]

Determining completeness includes considering the extent of information disclosed and its level of specificity or preciseness. This might involve considering potential concerns regarding cost/benefit, competitive advantage and future-oriented information, each of which is discussed below. [IIRF:3.48]

4.7.6   Cost/benefit

Information included in an integrated report is, by nature, central to managing the business. Accordingly, if a matter is important to managing the business, cost should not be a factor in failing to obtain critical information to appropriately assess and manage the matter. [IIRF:3.49]

An organisation may evaluate cost and benefits when determining the extent, level of specificity, and preciseness of information necessary for an integrated report to meet its primary purpose, but may not refrain entirely from making any disclosure about a material matter on the basis of cost. [IIRF:3.50]

4.7.7   Competitive advantage

In including information about material matters dealing with competitive advantage (e.g. critical strategies), an organisation considers how to describe the essence of the matter without identifying specific information that might cause a significant loss of competitive advantage. Accordingly, the organisation considers what advantage a competitor could actually gain from information in an integrated report, and balances this against the need for the integrated report to achieve its primary purpose as noted in paragraph 1.7 of the Framework (see **2.5**). [IIRF:3.51]

4.7.8   Future-oriented information

Legal or regulatory requirements may apply to certain future-oriented information in some jurisdictions, covering for example:

[IIRF:3.52]

- the types of disclosures that may be made;
- whether cautionary statements may be required or permitted to highlight uncertainty regarding achievability; and
- an obligation to update publicly such information.

The Framework acknowledges that future-oriented information is by nature more uncertain than historical information but states that uncertainty is not, however, a reason in itself to exclude such information (see also **5.10.2** regarding disclosures about uncertainty). [IIRF:3.53]

4.8 Consistency and comparability

4.8.1 Consistency and comparability – guiding principle

The information in an integrated report should be presented:

[IIRF:3.54]

- *on a basis that is consistent over time; and*

- *in a way that enables comparison with other organisations to the extent it is material to the organisation's own ability to create value over time.*

4.8.2 Consistency

Reporting policies are followed consistently from one period to the next unless a change is needed to improve the quality of information reported. This includes reporting the same KPIs if they continue to be material across reporting periods. When a significant change has been made, the organisation explains the reason for the change, describing (and quantifying if practicable and material) its effect. [IIRF:3.55]

4.8.3 Comparability

The specific information in an integrated report will, necessarily, vary from one organisation to another because each organisation creates value in its own unique way. Nonetheless, addressing the questions relating to the content elements (see **section 5**), which apply to all organisations, helps ensure a suitable level of comparability between organisations. [IIRF:3.56]

Other powerful tools for enhancing comparability (in both an integrated report itself and any detailed information that it links to) can include:

[IIRF:3.57]

- using benchmark data, such as industry or regional benchmarks;

- presenting information in the form of ratios (e.g. research expenditure as a percentage of sales, or carbon intensity measures such as emissions per unit of output); and

- reporting quantitative indicators commonly used by other organisations with similar activities, particularly when standardised definitions are stipulated by an independent organisation (e.g. an industry body). Such indicators are not, however, included in an integrated report unless they are relevant to the individual circumstances of, and are used internally by, the organisation.

5   Content elements

5.1   Content elements – general

An integrated report includes the following eight content elements:

[IIRF:4.1]

- organisational overview and external environment (see **5.2**);
- governance (see **5.3**);
- business model (see **5.4**);
- risks and opportunities (see **5.5**);
- strategy and resource allocation (see **5.6**);
- performance (see **5.7**);
- outlook (see **5.8**); and
- basis of preparation and presentation and in doing so, takes account of general reporting guidance (see **5.9** and **5.10**).

The content elements are fundamentally linked to each other and are not mutually exclusive. The content elements do not need to be included in any set sequence or as isolated, stand-alone sections. Rather, information in an integrated report is presented in a way that makes the connections between the content elements apparent (see **4.3** for a discussion of connectivity of information). [IIRF:4.2]

The content of an organisation's integrated report will depend on the individual circumstances of the organisation. The content elements are therefore stated in the form of questions rather than as checklists of specific disclosures. Accordingly, judgement needs to be exercised in applying the guiding principles to determine what information is reported, as well as how it is reported. [IIRF:4.3]

5.2   Organisational overview and external environment

An integrated report should answer the question: what does the organisation do and what are the circumstances under which it operates? [IIRF:4.4]

An integrated report identifies the organisation's mission and vision, and provides essential context by identifying matters such as:

[IIRF:4.5]

- the organisation's:
  - culture, ethics and values;
  - ownership and operating structure;

- principal activities and markets;

- competitive landscape and market positioning (considering factors such as the threat of new competition and substitute products or services, the bargaining power of customers and suppliers, and the intensity of competitive rivalry); and

- position within the value chain;

- key quantitative information (e.g. the number of employees, revenue and number of countries in which the organisation operates), highlighting, in particular, significant changes from prior periods; and

- significant factors affecting the external environment and the organisation's response.

Significant factors affecting the external environment include aspects of the legal, commercial, social, environmental and political context that affect the organisation's ability to create value in the short-, medium- or long-term. They can affect the organisation directly or indirectly (e.g. by influencing the availability, quality and affordability of a capital that the organisation uses or affects). [IIRF:4.6]

These factors occur in the context of the particular organisation, in the context of its industry or region, and in the wider social or planetary context. They may include, for example:

[IIRF:4.7]

- the legitimate needs and interests of key stakeholders;

- macro- and micro-economic conditions, such as economic stability, globalisation, and industry trends;

- market forces, such as the relative strengths and weaknesses of competitors and customer demand;

- the speed and effect of technological change;

- societal issues, such as population and demographic changes, human rights, health, poverty, collective values and educational systems;

- environmental challenges, such as climate change, the loss of ecosystems, and resource shortages as planetary limits are approached;

- the legislative and regulatory environment in which the organisation operates; and

- the political environment in countries where the organisation operates and other countries that may affect the ability of the organisation to implement its strategy.

5.3   Governance

An integrated report should answer the question: how does the organisation's governance structure support its ability to create value in the short-, medium- and long-term? [IIRF:4.8]

It is worth noting that many jurisdictions already require organisations to follow a corporate governance code.

An integrated report provides insight about how such matters as the following are linked to the organisation's ability to create value:

[IIRF:4.8]

- the organisation's leadership structure, including the skills and diversity (e.g. range of backgrounds, gender, competence and experience) of those charged with governance and whether regulatory requirements influence the design of the governance structure;

- specific processes used to make strategic decisions and to establish and monitor the culture of the organisation, including its attitude to risk and mechanisms for addressing integrity and ethical issues;

- particular actions those charged with governance have taken to influence and monitor the strategic direction of the organisation and its approach to risk management;

- how the organisation's culture, ethics and values are reflected in its use of and effects on the capitals, including its relationships with key stakeholders;

- whether the organisation is implementing governance practices that exceed legal requirements;

- the responsibility those charged with governance take for promoting and enabling innovation; and

- how remuneration and incentives are linked to value creation in the short, medium and long term, including how they are linked to the organisation's use of and effects on the capitals.

5.4   Business model

5.4.1   Business model – general

An integrated report should answer the question: what is the organisation's business model? [IIRF:4.10]

An organisation's business model is its system of transforming inputs, through its business activities, into outputs and outcomes that aims to fulfil the organisation's strategic purposes and create value over the short-, medium- and long-term. [IIRF:4.11]

An integrated report describes the business model, including key:

[IIRF:4.12]

- inputs (see **5.4.2**);
- business activities (see **5.4.3**);
- outputs (see **5.4.4**); and
- outcomes (see **5.4.5**).

Features that can enhance the effectiveness and readability of the description of the business model include:

[IIRF:4.13]

- explicit identification of the key elements of the business model;
- a simple diagram highlighting key elements, supported by a clear explanation of the relevance of those elements to the organisation;
- narrative flow that is logical given the particular circumstances of the organisation;
- Identification of critical stakeholder and other (e.g. raw material) dependencies and important factors affecting the external environment; and
- connection to information covered by other content elements, such as strategy, risks and opportunities, and performance (including KPIs and financial considerations, like cost containment and revenues).

The business model can be shown in any format, bearing in mind that the overall goal is to demonstrate how the business creates value over time and connectivity between inputs, activities, outputs and outcomes; a visual representation may have more impact than long blocks of narrative.

5.4.2 Inputs

An integrated report shows how key inputs relate to the capitals on which the organisation depends, or that provide a source of differentiation for the organisation, to the extent they are material to understanding the robustness and resilience of the business model. [IIRF:4.14]

An integrated report does not attempt to provide an exhaustive list of all inputs. Rather, the focus is on those that have a material bearing on the ability to create value in the short-, medium- and long-term, whether or not the capitals from which they are derived are owned by the organisation. It may also include a discussion of the nature and magnitude of the significant trade-offs that influence the selection of inputs. [IIRF:4.15]

5.4.3   Business activities

An integrated report describes key business activities. These can include:

[IIRF:4.16]

- how the organisation differentiates itself in the market place (e.g. through product differentiation, market segmentation, delivery channels and marketing);

- the extent to which the business model relies on revenue generation after the initial point of sale (e.g. extended warranty arrangements or network usage charges);

- how the organisation approaches the need to innovate; and

- how the business model has been designed to adapt to change.

When material, an integrated report discusses the contribution made to the organisation's long-term success by initiatives such as process improvement, employee training and relationships management. [IIRF:4.17]

5.4.4   Outputs

An integrated report identifies an organisation's key products and services. There might be other outputs, such as by-products and waste (including emissions), that need to be discussed within the business model disclosure depending on their materiality. [IIRF:4.18]

5.4.5   Outcomes

An integrated report describes key outcomes, including:

[IIRF:4.19]

- both internal outcomes (e.g. employee morale, organisational reputation, revenue and cash flows) and external outcomes (e.g. customer satisfaction, tax payments, brand loyalty, and social and environmental effects); and

- both positive outcomes (i.e. those that result in a net increase in the capitals and thereby create value) and negative outcomes (i.e. those that result in a net decrease in the capitals and thereby diminish value).

Identifying and describing outcomes, particularly external outcomes, requires an organisation to consider the capitals more broadly than those that are owned or controlled by the organisation. For example, it may require disclosure of the effects on capitals up and down the value chain (e.g. carbon emissions caused by products the organisation manufactures and labour practices of key suppliers). [IIRF:4.20]

5.4.6 Organisations with multiple business models

Some organisations employ more than one business model (e.g. when operating in different market segments). Disaggregating the organisation into its material constituent operations and associated business models is important to an effective explanation of how the organisation operates. This requires a distinct consideration of each material business model as well as commentary on the extent of connectivity between the business models (such as the existence of synergistic benefits) unless the organisation is run as an investment management business (in which case, it may be appropriate to focus on the investment management business model, rather than the business models of individual investments). [IIRF:4.21]

The integrated report of an organisation with multiple businesses often needs to balance disclosure with the need to reduce complexity; however, material information should not be omitted. Aligning external reporting with internal reporting by considering the top level of information that is regularly reported to those charged with governance is ordinarily appropriate. [IIRF:4.22]

One of the challenges to be considered for a group is whether the business model should be that of the group holding company or of the different businesses in the boundary used for financial reporting purposes. When the information presented relates to the group of entities included in the financial reporting entity's consolidated financial statements, the business model presented should consider and reflect the business models of the different businesses included in the consolidation, except when, for an investment management business, as highlighted by paragraph 4.21 of the Framework, it may be appropriate to focus on the investment management business model, rather than the business models of individual investments.

5.5 Risks and opportunities

An integrated report should answer the question: what are the specific risks and opportunities that affect the organisation's ability to create value over the short-, medium- and long-term, and how is the organisation dealing with them? [IIRF:4.23]

An integrated report identifies the key risks and opportunities that are specific to the organisation, including those that relate to the organisation's effects on, and the continued availability, quality and affordability of, relevant capitals in the short-, medium- and long-term. [IIRF:4.24]

This can include identifying:

[IIRF:4.25]

- the specific source of risks and opportunities, which can be internal, external or, commonly, a mix of the two. External sources include those stemming from the external environment, as discussed in **5.2** on external environment. Internal sources include those stemming from the organisation's business activities, as discussed in **5.4.3**;

- the organisation's assessment of the likelihood that the risk or opportunity will come to fruition and the magnitude of its effect if it does. This includes consideration of the specific circumstances that would cause the risk or opportunity to come to fruition. Such disclosure will invariably involve a degree of uncertainty. (See also **5.10.4** regarding disclosures about uncertainty.); and

- the specific steps being taken to mitigate or manage key risks or to create value from key opportunities, including the identification of the associated strategic objectives, strategies, policies, targets and KPIs.

Risks and uncertainties is often an area of focus and scrutiny by regulators. Risks evolve and change frequently. Concerns about commercial sensitivity or competitive harm may also have their part to play on the disclosures. Better reporters not only show specific risks but also demonstrate how the organisation's risk profile has changed over time.

It may also be the case that the organisation has traditionally focussed on risks and uncertainties, but not necessarily the opportunities arising from these; these are important in the context of providing an outlook on future value creation.

5.6   Strategy and resource allocation

An integrated report should answer the question: where does the organisation want to go and how does it intend to get there? [IIRF:4.27]

An integrated report ordinarily identifies:

[IIRF:4.28]

- the organisation's short-, medium- and long-term strategic objectives;

- the strategies it has in place, or intends to implement, to achieve those strategic objectives;

- the resource allocation plans it has to implement its strategy; and

- how it will measure achievements and target outcomes for the short-, medium- and long-term.

This can include describing:

[IIRF:4.29]

- the linkage between the organisation's strategy and resource allocation plans, and the information covered by other content elements, including how its strategy and resource allocation plans:

  - relate to the organisation's business model, and what changes to that business model might be necessary to implement chosen strategies to provide an understanding of the organisation's ability to adapt to change;

  - are influenced by/respond to the external environment and the identified risks and opportunities; and

  - affect the capitals, and the risk management arrangements related to those capitals;

- what differentiates the organisation to give it competitive advantage and enable it to create value, such as:

  - the role of innovation;

  - how the organisation develops and exploits intellectual capital; and

  - the extent to which environmental and social considerations have been embedded into the organisation's strategy to give it a competitive advantage; and

- key features and findings of stakeholder engagement that were used in formulating its strategy and resource allocation plans.

5.7 Performance

An integrated report should answer the question: to what extent has the organisation achieved its strategic objectives for the period and what are its outcomes in terms of effects on the capitals? [IIRF:4.30]

An integrated report contains qualitative and quantitative information about performance that may include matters such as:

[IIRF:4.31]

- quantitative indicators with respect to targets and risks and opportunities, explaining their significance, their implications, and the methods and assumptions used in compiling them;

- the organisation's effects (both positive and negative) on the capitals, including material effects on capitals up and down the value chain;

- the state of key stakeholder relationships and how the organisation has responded to key stakeholders' legitimate needs and interests; and

- the linkages between past and current performance, and between current performance and the organisation's outlook.

KPIs that combine financial measures with other components (e.g. the ratio of greenhouse gas emissions to sales) or narrative that explains the financial implications of significant effects on other capitals and other causal relationships (e.g. expected revenue growth resulting from efforts to enhance human capital) may be used to demonstrate the connectivity of financial performance with performance regarding other capitals. In some cases, this may also include monetising certain effects on the capitals (e.g. carbon emissions and water use). [IIRF:4.32]

It may be relevant for the discussion of performance to include instances where regulations have a significant effect on performance (e.g. a constraint on revenues as a result of regulatory rate setting) or the organisation's non-compliance with laws or regulations may significantly affect its operations. [IIRF:4.33]

While financial capital is a defined and well-understood term, manufactured, human, intellectual, social and natural capitals are not as clearly understood today. Further, standardised performance indicators to quantify and explain these capitals either do not exist or are, in many cases, in their infancy.

They are expected to evolve as the numerous developments in corporate reporting taking place globally are increasingly requiring disclosure of environmental, employee and social matters.

5.8   Outlook

An integrated report should answer the question: what challenges and uncertainties is the organisation likely to encounter in pursuing its strategy, and what are the potential implications for its business model and future performance? [IIRF:4.34]

An integrated report ordinarily highlights anticipated changes over time and provides information, built on sound and transparent analysis, about:

[IIRF:4.35]

- the organisation's expectations about the external environment the organisation is likely to face in the short-, medium- and long-term;

- how that will affect the organisation; and

- how the organisation is currently equipped to respond to the critical challenges and uncertainties that are likely to arise.

Care is needed to ensure the organisation's stated expectations, aspirations and intentions are grounded in reality. They need to be commensurate with the ability of the organisation to deliver on the opportunities available to it (including the availability, quality and affordability of appropriate capitals), and a realistic appraisal of the organisation's competitive landscape and market positioning, and the risks it faces. [IIRF:4.36]

The discussion of the potential implications, including implications for future financial performance, ordinarily includes discussion of:

[IIRF:4.37]

- the external environment, and risks and opportunities, with an analysis of how these could affect the achievement of strategic objectives; and

- the availability, quality and affordability of capitals the organisation uses or affects (e.g. the continued availability of skilled labour or natural resources), including how key relationships are managed and why they are important to the organisation's ability to create value over time.

An integrated report may also provide lead indicators, KPIs or objectives, relevant information from recognised external sources, and sensitivity analyses. If forecasts or projections are included in reporting the organisation's outlook, a summary of related assumptions is useful. Comparisons of actual performance to previously identified targets further enables evaluation of the current outlook. [IIRF:4.38]

Disclosures about an organisation's outlook in an integrated report are made taking into account the legal or regulatory requirements to which the organisation is subject. [IIRF:4.39]

5.9   Basis of preparation and presentation

5.9.1   Basis of preparation and presentation – general

An integrated report should answer the question: how does the organisation determine what matters to include in the integrated report and how are such matters quantified or evaluated? [IIRF:4.40]

An integrated report describes its basis of preparation and presentation, including:

[IIRF:4.41]

- a summary of the organisation's materiality determination process (see **5.9.2**);

- a description of the reporting boundary and how it has been determined (see **5.9.3**); and

- a summary of the significant frameworks and methods used to quantify or evaluate material matters (see **5.9.4**).

5.9.2   Summary of materiality determination process

An integrated report includes a summary of the organisation's materiality determination process and key judgements (see **4.5**). This may include:

- a brief description of the process used to identify relevant matters, evaluate their importance and narrow them down to material matters; and

- identification of the role of those charged with governance and key personnel in the identification and prioritisation of material matters.

A link to where a more detailed description of the materiality determination process can be found may also be included. [IIRF:4.42]

5.9.3   Reporting boundary

An integrated report identifies its reporting boundary and explains how it has been determined. [IIRF:4.43]

Material risks, opportunities and outcomes attributable to or associated with entities that are included in the financial reporting entity, are reported on in the organisation's integrated report. [IIRF:4.44]

Risks, opportunities and outcomes attributable to or associated with other entities/stakeholders are reported on in an integrated report to the extent they materially affect the ability of the financial reporting entity to create value. [IIRF:4.45]

Practical issues might limit the nature and extent of information that can be presented in an integrated report. For example:

- the availability of reliable data with respect to entities the financial reporting entity does not control; and

- the inherent inability to identify all risks, opportunities and outcomes that will materially affect the ability of the financial reporting entity to create value, particularly in the long term.

It may be appropriate to disclose such limitations, and actions being taken to overcome them, in an integrated report. [IIRF:4.46]

5.9.4   Summary of significant frameworks and methods

An integrated report includes a summary of the significant frameworks and methods used to quantify or evaluate material matters included in the report (e.g. the applicable financial reporting standards used for compiling financial information, a company-defined formula for measuring customer satisfaction, or an industry-based framework for evaluating risks). More detailed explanations might be provided in other communications. [IIRF:4.47]

When information in an integrated report is similar to or based on other information published by the organisation, it is prepared on the same basis as, or is easily reconcilable with, that other information. For example, when a KPI covers a similar topic to, or is based on information published in the organisation's financial statements or sustainability report, it is prepared on the same basis, and for the same period, as that other information. [IIRF:4.48]

5.10 General reporting guidance

5.10.1 *Supplementary guidance relevant to the content elements*

Section 4I of the Framework provides further guidance on matters relevant to various content elements, as follows:

[IIRF:4.49]

- disclosure of material matters, including the characteristics of suitable quantitative indicators (see **5.10.2**);
- disclosures about the capitals, including complexity in interdependencies and trade-offs (see **5.10.3**);
- time frames for short-, medium- and long-term (see **5.10.4**); and
- aggregation and disaggregation (see **5.10.5**).

5.10.2 *Disclosure of material matters*

Taking the nature of a material matter into consideration, the organisation considers providing:

[IIRF:4.50]

- key information, such as:
  - an explanation of the matter and its effect on the organisation's strategy, business model or the capitals;
  - relevant interactions and interdependencies providing an understanding of causes and effects;
  - the organisation's view on the matter;
  - actions to manage the matter and how effective they have been;
  - the extent of the organisation's control over the matter; and
  - quantitative and qualitative disclosures, including comparative information for prior periods and targets for future periods;
- if there is uncertainty surrounding a matter, disclosures about the uncertainty, such as:
  - an explanation of the uncertainty;

- the range of possible outcomes, associated assumptions, and how the information could change if the assumptions do not occur as described; and

- the volatility, certainty range or confidence interval associated with the information provided;

- if key information about the matter is considered indeterminable, disclosure of that fact and the reason for it; and

- if significant loss of competitive advantage would result, disclosures of a general nature about the matter, rather than specific details.

Depending on the nature of a matter, it may be appropriate to present it on its own in the integrated report or throughout in conjunction with different content elements. [IIRF:4.51]

Care is needed to avoid generic disclosures. Information is only included when it is of practical use in achieving the primary purpose of an integrated report (see **2.5**). This requires that disclosures be specific to the circumstances of the organisation. Accordingly, the bulleted lists of examples and considerations with respect to each content element are not meant to be checklists of disclosures. [IIRF:4.52]

Quantitative indicators, such as KPIs, can help increase comparability and are particularly helpful in expressing and reporting against targets. Common characteristics of suitable quantitative indicators may include that they are:

[IIRF:4.53]

- relevant to the circumstances of the organisation;

- consistent with indicators used internally by those charged with governance;

- connected (e.g. they display connectivity between financial and other information);

- focused on the matters identified by the organisation's materiality determination process;

- presented with the corresponding targets, forecasts or projections for two or more future periods;

- presented for multiple periods (e.g. three or more periods) to provide an appreciation of trends;

- presented against previously reported targets, forecasts or projections for the purpose of accountability;

- consistent with generally accepted industry or regional benchmarks to provide a basis for comparison;

- reported consistently over successive periods, regardless of whether the resulting trends and comparisons are favourable or unfavourable; and

- presented with qualitative information to provide context and improve meaningfulness. Relevant qualitative information includes an explanation of:

  - measurement methods and underlying assumptions; and

  - the reasons for significant variations from targets, trends or benchmarks, and why they are or are not expected to reoccur.

5.10.3 Disclosures about the capitals

Disclosures about the capitals, or a component of a capital:

[IIRF:4.54]

- are determined by their effects on the organisation's ability to create value over time, rather than whether or not they are owned by the organisation; and

- include the factors that affect their availability, quality and affordability and the organisation's expectations of its ability to produce flows from them to meet future demand. This is particularly relevant with respect to capitals that are in limited supply, are non-renewable, and can affect the long term viability of an organisation's business model.

When it is not practicable or meaningful to quantify significant movements in the capitals, qualitative disclosures are made to explain changes in the availability, quality or affordability of capitals as business inputs and how the organisation increases, decreases or transforms them. It is not, however, necessary to quantify or describe the movements between each of the capitals for every matter disclosed. [IIRF:4.55]

The Framework does not require an integrated report to provide an exhaustive account of all the complex interdependencies between the capitals such that an organisation's net impact on the global stock of capitals could be tallied. It is important, however, that an integrated report discloses the interdependencies that are considered in determining its reporting boundary, and the important trade-offs that influence value creation over time, including trade-offs:

[IIRF:4.56]

- between capitals or between components of a capital (e.g. creating employment through an activity that negatively affects the environment);

- over time (e.g. choosing one course of action when another course would result in superior capital increment but not until a later period); and

- between capitals owned by the organisation and those owned by others or not at all.

5.10.4   Time frames for short-, medium- and long-term

The future time dimension to be considered in preparing and presenting an integrated report will typically be longer than for some other forms of reporting. The length of each time frame for short-, medium- and long-term is decided by the organisation with reference to its business and investment cycles, its strategies, and its key stakeholders' legitimate needs and interests. Accordingly, there is no set answer for establishing the length for each term. [IIRF:4.57]

Time frames differ by:

[IIRF:4.58]

- industry or sector (e.g. strategic objectives in the automobile industry typically cover two model-cycle terms, spanning between eight and ten years, whereas within the technology industry, time frames might be significantly shorter); and

- the nature of outcomes (e.g. some issues affecting natural or social and relationship capitals can be very long term in nature).

The length of each reporting time frame and the reason for such length might affect the nature of information disclosed in an integrated report. For example, because longer term matters are more likely to be more affected by uncertainty, information about them may be more likely to be qualitative in nature, whereas information about shorter term matters may be better suited to quantification, or even monetisation. However, it is not necessary to disclose the effects of a matter for each time frame. [IIRF:4.59]

5.10.5   Aggregation and disaggregation

Each organisation determines the level of aggregation (e.g. by country, subsidiary, division, or site) at which to present information that is appropriate to its circumstances. This includes balancing the effort required to disaggregate (or aggregate) information against any added meaningfulness of information reported on a disaggregated (or aggregated) basis. [IIRF:4.60]

In some circumstances, aggregation of information can result in a significant loss of meaning and can also fail to highlight particularly strong or poor performance in specific areas. On the other hand, unnecessary disaggregation can result in clutter that adversely affects the ease of understanding the information. [IIRF:4.61]

The organisation disaggregates (or aggregates) information to an appropriate level considering, in particular, how senior management and those charged with governance manage and oversee the organisation and its operations. This commonly results in presenting information based on the business or geographical segments used for financial reporting purposes. [IIRF:4.62]

6 Summary of requirements

The following table summarises the bold italic type requirements of the Framework relevant to the preparation of an integrated report.

Application of the Framework	
Form of report and relationship with other information	An integrated report should be a designated, identifiable communication. [IIRF:1.12]
Application of the Framework	Any communication claiming to be an integrated report and referencing the Framework should apply all the requirements identified in bold italic type unless:
	[IIRF:1.17]
	• the unavailability of reliable information or specific legal prohibitions results in an inability to disclose material information; or
	• disclosure of material information would cause significant competitive harm.
	In the case of the unavailability of reliable information or specific legal prohibitions, an integrated report should:
	[IIRF:1.18]
	• indicate the nature of the information that has been omitted;
	• explain the reason why it has been omitted; and
	• in the case of the unavailability of data, identify the steps being taken to obtain the information and the expected time frame for doing so.

Application of the Framework	
Responsibility for an integrated report	An integrated report should include a statement from those charged with governance that includes: [IIRF:1.20] • an acknowledgement of their responsibility to ensure the integrity of the integrated report; • an acknowledgement that they have applied their collective mind to the preparation and presentation of the integrated report; and • their opinion or conclusion about whether the integrated report is presented in accordance with this Framework. Or, if it does not, it should explain: • what role those charged with governance played in its preparation and presentation; • what steps are being taken to include such a statement in future reports; and • the time frame for doing so, which should be no later than the organisation's third integrated report that references the Framework.
Guiding principles	
Strategic focus and future orientation	An integrated report should provide insight into the organisation's strategy, and how that relates to its ability to create value in the short-, medium- and long-term and to its use of and effects on the capitals. [IIRF:3.3]
Connectivity of information	An integrated report should show a holistic picture of the combination, inter-relatedness and dependencies between the factors that affect the organisation's ability to create value over time. [IIRF:3.6]
Stakeholder relationships	An integrated report should provide insight into the nature and quality of the organisation's relationships with its key stakeholders, including how and to what extent the organisation understands, takes into account and responds to their legitimate needs and interests. [IIRF:3.10]

Guiding principles	
Materiality	An integrated report should disclose information about matters that substantially affect the organisation's ability to create value over the short-, medium- and long-term. [IIRF:3.17]
Conciseness	An integrated report should be concise. [IIRF:3.36]
Reliability and completeness	An integrated report should include all material matters, both positive and negative, in a balanced way and without material error. [IIRF:3.39]
Consistency and comparability	The information in an integrated report should be presented: [IIRF:3.54] • on a basis that is consistent over time; and • in a way that enables comparison with other organisations to the extent it is material to the organisation's own ability to create value in the short-, medium- and long-term.
Content elements – specific questions that an integrated report should answer	
Organisational overview and external environment	What does the organisation do and what are the circumstances under which it operates? [IIRF:4.4]
Governance	How does the organisation's governance structure support its ability to create value in the short-, medium- and long-term? [IIRF:4.8]
Business model	What is the organisation's business model? [IIRF:4.10]
Risks and opportunities	What are the specific risks and opportunities that affect the organisation's ability to create value over the short-, medium- and long-term, and how is the organisation dealing with them? [IIRF:4.23]
Strategy and resource allocation	Where does the organisation want to go and how does it intend to get there? [IIRF:4.27]
Performance	To what extent has the organisation achieved its strategic objectives for the period and what are its outcomes in terms of effects on the capitals? [IIRF:4.30]

Content elements – specific questions that an integrated report should answer	
Outlook	What challenges and uncertainties is the organisation likely to encounter in pursuing its strategy, and what are the potential implications for its business model and future performance? [IIRF:4.34]
Basis of preparation and presentation	How does the organisation determine what matters to include in the integrated report and how are such matters quantified or evaluated? [IIRF:4.40]

A35 Service concession arrangements

Contents

1 Introduction

1.1 Overview of IFRIC 12

IFRIC 12 *Service Concession Arrangements* prescribes the accounting for service concession arrangements, which are arrangements whereby a government or other body (the grantor) grants contracts for the supply of public services, such as roads, energy distribution, prisons or hospitals, to a private sector entity (the operator). These are often referred to as 'public-to-private' arrangements (see **2.1**).

1.2 Changes to IFRIC 12 since the last edition of this manual

IFRS 12 was amended in January 2016 by minor consequential amendments arising from IFRS 16 *Leases* (effective for annual periods beginning on or after 1 January 2019, with earlier application permitted). The amendments reflect changes in terminology under the new Standard (see the flowchart in **2.2**). These amendments should be applied when an entity adopts IFRS 16.

1.3 IAS 18 superseded by IFRS 15

IFRIC 12 was amended by consequential amendments arising from IFRS 15 *Revenue from Contracts with Customers* to reflect the requirements for recognition and measurement of revenue introduced by that Standard (effective for annual periods beginning on or after 1 January 2018, with earlier application permitted). This chapter deals with the requirements of IFRIC 12 as amended by IFRS 15. **Appendix A3** sets out the requirements of IFRIC 12 prior to amendment by IFRS 15, and is intended for the convenience of entities that have not yet adopted IFRS 15 and that therefore continue to apply IAS 18 *Revenue* (see **appendix A1**) and IAS 11 *Construction Contracts* (see **appendix A2**).

1.4 Key requirements of IFRIC 12

The following table provides an overview of the key requirements of IFRIC 12.

Issue	Key requirement of IFRIC 12
Operator's rights over the infrastructure assets	The infrastructure assets are not recognised as the property, plant or equipment of the operator.
Revenue recognition	Revenue is recognised and measured in accordance with IFRS 15 *Revenue from Contracts with Customers*.

Issue	Key requirement of IFRIC 12
Construction or upgrade services	The consideration received by the operator is recognised in accordance with IFRS 15. Consideration may result in the recognition of a financial asset or an intangible asset.
	• The operator recognises a financial asset if it has an unconditional contractual right to receive cash or another financial asset from or at the direction of the grantor in return for constructing or upgrading the public sector asset.
	• The operator recognises an intangible asset if it receives only a right to charge for the use of the public sector asset that it constructs or upgrades.
	• IFRIC 12 allows for the possibility that both types of consideration may exist within a single contract. For example, to the extent that the grantor has given to the operator an unconditional guarantee of minimum payments for the construction, the operator recognises a financial asset. The operator may also recognise an intangible asset representing the right to charge users of the public service that is in addition to the minimum guaranteed payments.
Operator's contractual obligations to maintain/ restore the infrastructure to a specified level of serviceability	Contractual obligations to maintain or restore infrastructure, except for any upgrade element, should be recognised and measured in accordance with IAS 37 *Provisions, Contingent Liabilities and Contingent Assets*, i.e. at the best estimate of the expenditure that would be required to settle the present obligation at the reporting date.
Borrowing costs incurred by the operator	Borrowing costs incurred by the operator that are attributable to the arrangement are recognised as an expense in the period incurred unless the operator has a contractual right to charge users of the public service (intangible asset model). In such circumstances, borrowing costs attributable to the arrangement should be capitalised during the construction phase of the arrangement in accordance with IAS 23 *Borrowing Costs*.
Subsequent accounting treatment for a financial asset	IFRS 9 *Financial Instruments* (or, for entities that have not yet adopted IFRS 9, IAS 39 *Financial Instruments: Recognition and Measurement*) applies to the financial asset recognised under IFRIC 12.
	Under IFRS 9, depending on the circumstances, the financial asset will be measured at amortised cost, at fair value through other comprehensive income, or at fair value through profit or loss.
	Under IAS 39, depending on whether the financial asset is classified as loans and receivables, as an available-for-sale financial asset or designated as at fair value through profit or loss, it is subsequently measured either at amortised cost or fair value.

Issue	Key requirement of IFRIC 12
Subsequent accounting treatment for an intangible asset	IAS 38 *Intangible Assets* applies to any intangible asset recognised under IFRIC 12. IAS 38 will typically require that intangible asset to be measured using the cost model.

2　Scope of IFRIC 12

2.1　Typical features of service concession arrangements

IFRIC 12 applies to some, but not all, public-to-private service concession arrangements (see **2.2** for detailed scope conditions).

A typical 'public-to-private' arrangement that falls within the scope of IFRIC 12 is a 'build-operate-transfer' arrangement. Under this type of arrangement, an operator constructs the infrastructure to be used to provide a public service, and it operates and maintains that infrastructure for a specified period of time. The operator is paid for its services over the period of the arrangement. A contract sets out performance standards, pricing mechanisms, and arrangements for arbitrating disputes. [IFRIC 12:2] In some cases, the operator may upgrade the existing infrastructure and maintain and operate the upgraded infrastructure. This second type of arrangement is sometimes referred to as a 'rehabilitate-operate-transfer' arrangement.

Paragraph 1 of SIC-29 *Service Concession Arrangements: Disclosures* states that outsourcing the operation of an entity's internal services (e.g. employee restaurant, building maintenance, accounting or IT functions) does not constitute a service concession arrangement.

Some common features of service concession arrangements are as follows.

[IFRIC 12:3]

- The grantor is a public sector entity, including a governmental body, or a private sector entity to which the responsibility for the service has been devolved.

- The operator is responsible for at least some of the management of the infrastructure and related services and does not merely act as an agent on behalf of the grantor.

- The contract sets the initial prices to be levied by the operator and regulates price revisions over the period of the service arrangement.

- The operator is obliged to hand over the infrastructure to the grantor in a specified condition at the end of the period of the arrangement, for little or no incremental consideration irrespective of which party initially financed it.

IFRIC 12 applies to a broad range of concession arrangements. Road and water treatment concession arrangements are two common examples, but other types of arrangements may meet the scope conditions, such as contracts for the:

- provision of transport services;

- construction and operation of waste treatment plants;

- provision of public airport services;

- construction and maintenance of hospitals;

- generation of renewable energy;

- production of electricity; and

- construction and operation of public transport systems, schools, prisons etc.

For a public service obligation to exist, the services offered need not be made available to all members of the public. Rather, the services need to benefit members of the public. For example, prisons only accommodate those individuals required to be incarcerated by law, and cannot be accessed by members of the public seeking accommodation. However, prisons would still be considered to provide services to the public.

There are many different types of concession arrangements, and the detailed structure and arrangements are often specific to jurisdictions. Therefore, in order to determine the appropriate accounting for an arrangement, the details of the arrangement should be analysed based on the specific facts and circumstances.

2.2   Service concession arrangements within the scope of IFRIC 12

2.2.1   IFRIC 12 scope conditions

A public-to-private arrangement will not automatically fall within the scope of IFRIC 12; specified scope conditions need to be satisfied.

IFRIC 12 applies to public-to-private service concession arrangements if:

[IFRIC 12:5]

(a) the grantor controls or regulates what services the operator must provide with the infrastructure, to whom it must provide them, and at what price (see **2.2.2**); and

(b) the grantor controls – through ownership, beneficial entitlement or otherwise – any significant residual interest in the infrastructure at the end of the term of the arrangement (see **2.2.3**).

These conditions are summarised in the following flowchart.

[Extract from IFRIC 12 (Information Note 1)]

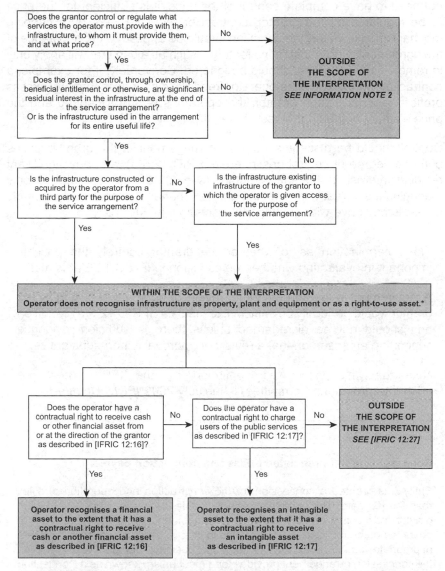

* For entities that have not yet adopted IFRS 16 *Leases*, this text reads "Operator does not recognise infrastructure as property, plant and equipment or as a leased asset".

2.2.2   Scope – control of services and pricing

The control or regulation referred to in condition IFRIC 12:5(a) (see **2.2.1**) could be by contract or otherwise (such as through a regulator), and includes circumstances in which the grantor buys all of the output as well as those in which some or all of the output is bought by other users. In applying this condition, the grantor and any related parties should be considered together. If the grantor is a public sector entity, the public sector as a whole, together with any regulators acting in the public interest, should be regarded as related to the grantor for the purposes of IFRIC 12. [IFRIC 12:AG2]

For the purpose of condition IFRIC 12:5(a) (see **2.2.1**), the grantor does not need to have complete control of the price; it is sufficient for the price to be regulated by the grantor, contract or regulator (e.g. by a capping mechanism). However, the condition should be applied to the substance of the agreement. Non-substantive features, such as a cap that will apply only in remote circumstances, should be ignored. Conversely, if for example, a contract purports to give the operator freedom to set prices, but any excess profit is returned to the grantor, the operator's return is capped and the price element of the control test is met. [IFRIC 12:AG3]

Control should be distinguished from management. If the grantor retains both the degree of control described in IFRIC 12:5(a), and any significant residual interest in the infrastructure (see **2.2.3**), the operator is only managing the infrastructure on the grantor's behalf – even though, in many cases, it may have wide managerial discretion. [IFRIC 12:AG5]

The determination as to whether the grantor controls the price is important in evaluating whether the condition in IFRIC 12:5(a) is met.

A requirement in the agreement for review or approval of pricing by the grantor would generally be sufficient to meet the IFRIC 12:5(a) condition and should not be disregarded unless there is sufficient evidence supporting an assertion that a review or approval is non-substantive.

Note that this view was confirmed by the IFRIC (now the IFRS Interpretations Committee) in the July 2009 *IFRIC Update*.

Example 2.2.2A

Concession with unregulated prices and congestion payment

Entity A is granted a concession for the construction and operation of a toll road for 40 years. The price that Entity A is able to charge users is set by the grantor for the first three years of the arrangement. From the fourth year of operation of the toll road, Entity A is able to charge users at a price it considers appropriate, based on its own strategy and business perspectives. However, the concession arrangement provides for a mechanism known as a 'congestion payment' whereby Entity A will pay specified amounts to the grantor if there is congestion (i.e. traffic jams) in the use of the complementary public infrastructure (i.e. nearby roads).

The grantor exercises absolute control over the pricing for an insignificant period of time in the context of the service concession arrangement as a whole. The congestion payment mechanism would need to be analysed to determine if it amounts to substantive regulation of the prices charged. If this mechanism is included in the contract solely to avoid excessively high prices, it may not be substantive because the operator has the freedom to charge what it wants within a reasonable range. The only limitation is that the operator cannot charge a price the market would not bear and in doing so create congestion on other roads. If the mechanism is considered non-substantive, the arrangement would fall outside the scope of IFRIC 12.

Example 2.2.2B

Concession with price control mechanism to prevent unfair pricing

Entity B (the operator) enters into a service concession arrangement with a port authority (the grantor) under which Entity B will construct port terminal facilities and operate them for a period of 25 years.

Entity B has discretion to set the prices charged to its customers for the use of the port facilities throughout the concession period. Entity B is not required to obtain approval from the port authority whenever it decides to change its prices.

However, the relevant legislation places a responsibility on the port authority to ensure fair market practices and prevent abusive pricing. If a customer files a complaint with the port authority, or the port authority is otherwise alerted to concerns that Entity B's pricing is unfair or abusive, the port authority has the power to investigate the market and to require Entity B to adjust its prices if they are determined to be unfair. Such a determination can only be based on a comparison with prices charged by Entity B's (independent) competitors.

In the circumstances described, the port authority does not control the price charged by Entity B for its services; consequently, the criterion in IFRIC 12.5(a) is not met. The port authority's power is limited to the ability to require Entity B to adjust its prices in line with independent market transactions and, as such, is designed to prevent unfair market practices rather than to control the price that Entity B can charge to its customers. Consequently, the 'cap' on Entity B's prices is ultimately driven by market transactions and does not, therefore, amount to substantive regulation of the prices charged.

Accordingly, the arrangement falls outside the scope of IFRIC 12.

Example 2.2.2C

Competitive tender process

Arrangements in which the public sector seeks to attract private sector participation often involve a tender process under which a number of entities respond to a Request for Proposal (RFP). The RFP may request the respondent to specify the type and level of services that the respondent would provide if its tender is successful, and the amounts that it would charge for those services. When the winning bid has been selected, the services and pricing agreed with the successful respondent are incorporated into a contractual arrangement.

IFRIC 12 applies to arrangements in which "the grantor controls or regulates which services the operator must provide with infrastructure, to whom it must provide them, and at what price". [IFRIC 12:5(a)]

If an arrangement would otherwise fall within the scope of IFRIC 12, does the fact that services and/or prices are determined through a process of competitive tender preclude the arrangement from being accounted for under IFRIC 12?

No. If the arrangement otherwise falls within the scope of IFRIC 12 because all the relevant conditions in IFRIC 12 are met, the fact that services and/or prices are determined through a competitive tender process before the concession begins does not affect the conclusion as to whether the arrangement falls within the scope.

Example 2.2.2D

Price cap set by grantor

An entity (the operator) has entered into a service concession arrangement under which it will construct a road and operate that road for 30 years. The grantor does not specify the price that the operator can charge to users of the road, but it does specify the maximum price that can be charged (i.e. it imposes a 'price cap').

For the purposes of IFRIC 12:5(a), does the grantor's power to impose a price cap mean that the grantor 'controls or regulates' the price at which services are provided?

In general, yes, provided that the capping mechanism is not considered to be non-substantive.

IFRIC 12:AG3 states that "[f]or the purpose of condition [IFRIC 12:5](a), the grantor does not need to have complete control of the price: it is sufficient for the price to be regulated by the grantor, contract or regulator, for example by a capping mechanism".

However, a cap set at a level such that it is very unlikely ever to take effect (e.g. stating that a road toll must not exceed CU1,000 when the anticipated toll is CU2) would be considered non-substantive. As a result, the grantor would not be considered to have control over the price and the arrangement would be outside the scope of IFRIC 12.

2.2.3   Scope – control of any significant residual interest

When considering whether a significant residual interest exists for the purpose of determining whether the condition in IFRIC 12:5(b) is met (see **2.2.1**), the residual interest should be estimated as the infrastructure's current value as if it was of the age and condition expected as at the end of the period of the arrangement. [IFRIC 12:AG4]

A machine that can only be sold for scrap value is unlikely to have a significant residual value at the end of the contract and will be within the scope of IFRIC 12 provided that the condition in IFRIC 12:5(a) is met. Conversely, a building with a 50-year useful life that is only used in a service concession arrangement for 20 years is likely to have a significant residual interest at the end of the arrangement and will be within the scope of IFRIC 12 only if both (1) the condition in IFRIC 12:5(a) is met, and (2) the residual interest is controlled by the grantor.

The conditions in IFRIC 12:5(a) and (b) together identify when the infrastructure, including any replacements required (see **section 7**), is controlled by the grantor for the whole of its economic life. Under the terms of a service concession arrangement, an operator may be required to replace parts of an item of infrastructure (e.g. the top layer of a road or the roof of a building). In these types of arrangement, the item of infrastructure is considered as a whole for the purposes of determining whether the grantor controls any significant residual interest. Consequently, the condition in IFRIC 12:5(b) would be met for the whole of the infrastructure, including the part that is replaced, if the grantor controls any significant residual interest in the final replacement of that part. [IFRIC 12:AG6]

Arrangements under which the infrastructure is used for its entire useful life ('whole of life assets') are within the scope of IFRIC 12 provided that the condition in IFRIC 12:5(a) is met, regardless of which party controls any residual interest. [IFRIC 12:6]

For the purpose of IFRIC 12:5(b) (see **2.2.1**), the grantor's control over any significant residual interest should both restrict the operator's practical ability to sell or pledge the infrastructure and give the grantor a continuing right of use throughout the period of the arrangement. [IFRIC 12:AG4]

Certain arrangements allow the operator to renew the licence arrangement indefinitely without significant costs. In those cases, it is first necessary to analyse carefully all facts and circumstances in order to establish whether, at a point of possible renewal, there will be a significant residual interest in the infrastructure.

When there may be a significant residual interest in the infrastructure at a point of possible renewal, it is then necessary to determine who controls that residual interest. If the terms of the arrangement are such that the grantor controls the residual interest if the operator chooses not to renew the licence, the arrangement would fall within the scope of IFRIC 12. In contrast, if the grantor does not control the significant residual interest if the operator decides not to renew the licence, the arrangement would not meet the condition in IFRIC 12:5(b) and so would be excluded from the scope of IFRIC 12.

Example 2.2.3A

Application of IFRIC 12 when residual interest is returned to grantor at fair value

An entity (the operator) has entered into a service concession arrangement under which it will construct a bridge and operate that bridge for 30 years. It cannot sell the bridge to a third party unless the government (the grantor) agrees to the sale. At the end of the arrangement, the grantor is required to repurchase the bridge for its fair value at that time. The bridge has an estimated useful economic life of 50 years.

Does the grantor control the residual interest in the infrastructure at the end of the term of the arrangement in accordance with IFRIC 12:5(b)?

Yes. IFRIC 12:5 states, in part, as follows. "This Interpretation applies to public-to-private service concession arrangements if ... the grantor controls – through ownership, beneficial entitlement or otherwise – any significant residual interest in the infrastructure at the end of the term of the arrangement."

According to IFRIC 12:AG6, situations in which the grantor controls the asset for the whole of its economic life are within the scope of IFRIC 12.

IFRIC 12:AG4 states, in part, as follows. "For the purposes of condition (b) [of IFRIC 12:5 as outlined at **2.2.1**], the grantor's control over any significant residual interest should both restrict the operator's practical ability to sell or pledge the infrastructure and give the grantor a continuing right of use throughout the period of the arrangement." In this scenario, the operator would not be able readily to sell or pledge the infrastructure even though it may be able to sell or pledge its economic interest in the residual value of the infrastructure.

IFRIC 12 applies a 'control' approach. In the circumstances described, the grantor has a continuing right of use of the infrastructure asset at the end of the term of the arrangement and, consequently, controls the use of the bridge throughout its economic life. This is the case even though the grantor has to pay fair value for the asset at the end of the term of the arrangement.

Example 2.2.3B

Application of IFRIC 12 when the grantor has an option to purchase at the end of the term of the arrangement

Entity A (the operator) has entered into a service concession arrangement with the government (the grantor) under which it constructs a hospital and operates that hospital for 25 years. The hospital has an estimated economic life of 40 years. The residual interest in the hospital at the end of the term of the arrangement is expected to be significant.

At the end of 25 years, the government has the option to purchase the hospital from Entity A at an amount equal to the hospital's fair value at that time. If the government does not exercise this purchase option, Entity A retains the hospital for its continued use and/or disposal.

In the circumstances described, does the grantor (the government) control the residual interest in the infrastructure at the end of the term of the arrangement (i.e. is the condition in IFRIC 12:5(b) satisfied)?

Yes. IFRIC 12:AG6 states that the conditions in IFRIC 12:5(a) and (b) "together identify when the infrastructure ... is controlled by the grantor for the whole of its economic life" and, therefore, when an arrangement should be accounted for in accordance with IFRIC 12.

In the circumstances described, the condition in IFRIC 12:5(b) is met due to the existence of the purchase option at the end of the term of the arrangement; the government has the power to purchase the hospital or to allow Entity A to retain the hospital for the operator's continued use and/or disposal.

IFRIC 12:AG4 states that, for the purposes of IFRIC 12:5(b), "the grantor's control over any significant residual interest should both restrict the operator's practical ability to sell or pledge the infrastructure and give the grantor a continuing right of use throughout the period of the arrangement". In the circumstances described, due to the existence of the purchase option held by the grantor, Entity A is unable readily to sell or pledge the hospital even though it may be able to sell or pledge its economic interest in the residual value of the hospital.

2.2.4   Scope – nature of the infrastructure

The Interpretation applies to both:

[IFRIC 12:7]

(a) infrastructure that the operator constructs or acquires from a third party for the purpose of the service arrangement; and

(b) existing infrastructure to which the grantor gives the operator access for the purpose of the service arrangement.

The requirements may apply to previously recognised property, plant and equipment of the operator if the derecognition requirements of IFRSs are met. If the operator is considered to have disposed of the asset by passing the significant risks and rewards of that asset to the grantor, then the operator should derecognise that asset in accordance with paragraph 67 of IAS 16 *Property, Plant and Equipment*. [IFRIC 12:8] For further guidance relating to the derecognition of property, plant and equipment, see **section 9** of **chapter A7**. Having disposed of its previously held asset, the operator would need to determine whether the arrangement is within the scope of IFRIC 12.

Sometimes the use of infrastructure is only partly regulated by the grantor. These arrangements take a variety of forms, and the following principles should be applied.

[IFRIC 12:AG7]

(a) Any infrastructure that is physically separable and capable of being operated independently and meets the definition of a cash-generating unit in IAS 36 *Impairment of Assets* is analysed separately if it is used wholly for unregulated purposes. For example, this might apply to a private wing of a hospital, when the remainder of the hospital is used by the grantor to treat public patients.

(b) When purely ancillary activities (such as a hospital shop) are unregulated, the control tests are applied as if those services did not exist, because in cases in which the grantor controls the services in the manner described in IFRIC 12:5 (see **2.2.2**), the existence of ancillary activities does not detract from the grantor's control of the infrastructure.

In either of the circumstances described above, there may in substance be a lease from the grantor to the operator. If so, the lease should be accounted for in accordance with IFRS 16 *Leases* (or, for entities that have not yet adopted IFRS 16, IAS 17 *Leases*). [IFRIC 12:AG8]

Example 2.2.4

Infrastructure with different services

An operator is granted the concession for a railway station by the government (the grantor). The operator will manage the station for 75 years, at which point the station will revert to the government. The terms of the agreement split the concession between the railway terminal itself (the 'railway terminal activity') and the shopping areas located in the property (the 'retail activity'). Both of these activities are covered by the terms of the service concession agreement and are controlled by the grantor, who regularly monitors the services provided.

- The railway terminal activity is regulated because the grantor controls the services to be provided, the train companies to which the operator must provide those services, and the price charged by the operator. As a consequence, the railway activity falls within the scope of IFRIC 12:5.

- Regarding the retail activity, the operator is permitted to lease the shops to third parties for the purpose of running commercial outlets. The service concession agreement requires that the operator obtains formal permission before a lease is granted and prices must be communicated to the grantor, although they are not subject to explicit formal authorisation.

The operator pays fees to the grantor for both activities. The service concession agreement establishes that the operator has an obligation to return a significant percentage of the profits generated from the retail activity through a reduction in the prices charged to the train companies for the regulated (railway terminal) activity. As a result, the revenue stream from the railway terminal activity

---

is affected by the profits generated from the retail activity. At the end of the concession, all assets (relating to both activities) are returned to the grantor for no consideration.

The grantor controls the nature of the retail activity by setting the guidelines as to the services to be provided, by approving the service providers and by monitoring that these guidelines are followed by the operator in practice. In addition, the pricing mechanism is such that part of the profits generated by the retail activity must be returned through a reduction in the prices charged for the railway terminal activity. Therefore, indirectly, the grantor controls the level of profits generated from the retail activity.

As a result of the interdependency between the revenue streams from the two activities, and the level of the grantor's control over the retail activity, the entire operation of the railway station (railway terminal activity and retail activity) may be subject to IFRIC 12.

In contrast, if the activities were separable and not interdependent, they would be analysed separately. IFRIC 12:AG7(a) states that any infrastructure that is physically separable and capable of being operated independently and meets the definition of a cash-generating unit as defined in IAS 36 must be analysed separately if it is used wholly for unregulated purposes.

Ultimately, it will be necessary to exercise judgement based on all the facts and circumstances in order to determine whether infrastructure assets with different activities are interdependent and should be assessed together for the purposes of IFRIC 12.

2.3   Scope – private-to-private arrangements

IFRIC 12 does not include within its scope private-to-private arrangements but it could be applied to such arrangements by analogy under the hierarchy set out in paragraphs 7 to 12 of IAS 8 *Accounting Policies, Changes in Accounting Estimates and Errors* (see **3.1** of **chapter A5**). [IFRIC 12:BC14]

2.4   Scope – accounting by grantors

The Interpretation specifically excludes from its scope the accounting by grantors (i.e. public sector accounting). [IFRIC 12:9]

2.5   Standards applicable to arrangements falling outside the scope of IFRIC 12

If an arrangement does not fall within the scope of IFRIC 12, it may fall within the scope of other IFRSs. The following table, extracted from Information Note 2 to IFRIC 12, indicates which Standards may be applicable.

Category	Lessee	Service provider			Owner	
Typical arrangement types	Lease (e.g. Operator leases asset from grantor)	Service and/or maintenance contract (specific tasks e.g. debt collection)	Rehabilitate -operate- transfer	Build- operate- transfer	Build- own- operate	100% Divestment/ Privatisation/ Corporation
Asset ownership	Grantor				Operator	
Capital investment	Grantor		Operator			
Demand risk	Shared	Grantor	Operator and/or Grantor		Operator	
Typical duration	8–20 years	1–5 years	25–30 years			Indefinite (or may be limited by licence)
Residual interest	Grantor				Operator	
Relevant IFRSs	IFRS 16 (or, for entities that have not yet adopted IFRS 16, IAS 17)	IFRS 15	IFRIC 12		IAS 16	

2.6 Interaction of IFRIC 12 with IFRS 16 and IFRIC 4

For entities that have adopted IFRS 16 *Leases*, arrangements within the scope of IFRIC 12 are specifically excluded from the scope of that Standard (see **3.1** in **chapter A17**). Any arrangement within the scope of IFRIC 12 will not meet the definition of a lease because the operator in a service concession arrangement does not have the right to control the use of the underlying asset. [IFRS 16:BC69]

For entities that have not yet adopted IFRS 16, an equivalent scope exclusion is included in IFRIC 4 *Determining whether an Arrangement contains a Lease* (see **2.7.2.2** in **appendix A4**).

3 The accounting models

3.1 Recognition and measurement of arrangement consideration

Under the terms of contractual arrangements within the scope of IFRIC 12, the operator acts as a service provider; the operator constructs or upgrades infrastructure which is used to provide a public service, and is then responsible for operating and maintaining that infrastructure for a specified period of time. [IFRIC 12:12]

The following principles apply for the recognition and measurement of revenue arising from such arrangements:

[IFRIC 12:13, 14 & 20]

- the operator should recognise and measure revenue for the operation services it performs in accordance with IFRS 15 *Revenue from Contracts with Customers*;

- the operator should account for both construction or upgrade services and operation services in accordance with IFRS 15; and

- the nature of the consideration determines its subsequent accounting treatment (see **3.2**).

Example 3.1

Recognition of revenue for construction service

Company A (the operator) has been granted a concession arrangement for the construction and operation of an airport which falls within the scope of IFRIC 12.

If Company A constructs the airport itself, and the construction phase is identified as a separate performance obligation under IFRS 15, revenue and costs arising during the construction phase should be accounted for in accordance with IFRS 15. The consideration allocated to the construction phase in accordance with IFRS 15:74 will be reflected as either a contract asset, an intangible asset, or both, depending on the classification of the consideration from the grantor in accordance with IFRIC 12:15 to 19 (see **3.2**).

If Company A outsources the construction of the airport to Company B (the subcontractor), an unrelated entity, the appropriate recognition by Company A of revenue and costs associated with the construction work depends on whether it is acting as an agent or a principal, based on the substance of the agreements with both the grantor and the sub-contractor.

The determination requires careful consideration of all other relevant facts and circumstances and the exercise of judgement. Even if the grantor is informed of, and approves, the outsourcing of the construction (without entering into a specific and direct agreement with the sub-contractor), this fact is not in itself evidence as to whether Company A is acting as an agent or a principal.

IFRS 15:B34 to B38 provide guidance on how to determine whether an entity is acting as a principal or as an agent. This guidance is discussed at **3.6** in **chapter A14**.

In the circumstances described, if the analysis of all relevant facts and circumstances leads to the conclusion that Company A is acting as an agent, revenue and costs should not be recognised on a gross basis. Instead, Company A should recognise the fees associated with the service provided as an agent as net revenue. If, however, based on all relevant facts and circumstances it is concluded that Company A is acting as a principal in relation to the construction services, Company A should recognise revenue and the costs arising from the construction services on a gross basis in accordance with IFRS 15.

3.2   Determining the nature of the operator's asset

3.2.1   *Determining the nature of the operator's asset – general principles*

Infrastructure within the scope of IFRIC 12 is not recognised as property, plant and equipment of the operator. This is because the operator does not have the right to control the asset, but merely has access to the infrastructure in order to provide the public service in accordance with the terms specified in the contract. [IFRIC 12:11] Such an arrangement is not treated as a lease because the operator does not have the right to control the use of the asset. [IFRIC 12:BC23] Instead, the operator's right to consideration is recognised as a financial asset, an intangible asset or a combination of the two. [IFRIC 12:15]

The nature of the consideration given by the grantor to the operator should be determined by reference to the contract terms and, when it exists, relevant contract law. [IFRIC 12:19]

The nature of the consideration determines its subsequent accounting treatment, as described in detail in **sections 4** and **5**. For the purposes of IFRS 15 *Revenue from Contracts with Customers*, IFRIC 12 clarifies that both types of consideration are classified as a contract asset during the construction or upgrade period. [IFRIC 12:19]

The requirements of IFRIC 12 regarding the nature of the asset to be recognised can be summarised as follows.

Operator's rights	Classification	Examples
Unconditional, contractual right to receive cash or other financial asset from the grantor.	Financial asset [IFRIC 12:16]	• Operator receives a fixed amount from the grantor over term of arrangement. • Operator has a right to charge users over term of arrangement, but any shortfall will be reimbursed by the grantor.
Amounts to be received are contingent on the extent that the public uses the service.	Intangible asset [IFRIC 12:17]	• Operator has a right to charge users over the term of the arrangement. • Operator has a right to charge the grantor based on usage of the services over the term of the arrangement.

Operator's rights	Classification	Examples
Consideration received partly in the form of a financial asset and partly in the form of an intangible asset.	Bifurcated model [IFRIC 12:18]	• Operator receives a fixed amount from the grantor and a right to charge users over the term of the arrangement.

3.2.2 Features of typical concession arrangements – examples

The following table summarises the features of some typical concession mechanisms.

Characteristics	Type of asset recognised by the operator	Reason
Hospital – the operator receives from the grantor a fixed amount of revenue, subject to deductions for lack of availability.	Financial asset	• Revenue not dependent on usage. • Deductions reflect failure to meet specified quality requirements.
Toll road – the amounts receivable by the operator are subject to little variation in practice because the road is an established route with highly predictable level of tolls.	Intangible asset	• Right to charge users. • Amounts depend on usage of the infrastructure, regardless of whether variation in usage is expected in practice.
Toll road – the operator has a guarantee from the grantor that revenue will not fall below a specified level. The guarantee is achieved through an increase in the concession period.	Intangible asset	• Right to charge users. • Amounts depend on usage of the infrastructure. • Shortfall guaranteed by the grantor via a concession extension and not via a right to receive cash.
Water supply concession – the grantor regulates prices that the operator may charge to users or adjusts the duration of the concession based on a targeted rate of return.	Intangible asset	• Right to charge users. • Amounts depend on usage of the infrastructure.

Characteristics	Type of asset recognised by the operator	Reason
Rail concession – the grantor pays the operator any shortfall between the actual benefit before interest and tax obtained through charging users, and a fixed minimum.	Intangible asset and financial asset – bifurcated model	• Right to charge users. • Amounts depend on usage of the infrastructure. • Financial asset arises from the right to receive a minimum determinable amount of cash from users/ grantor (shortfall guaranteed by the grantor) and intangible asset from the right to earn additional amounts above the fixed guaranteed payments.
Toll bridge – the grantor pays a fixed payment based on availability during the first half of the concession period and then switches to usage payments.	Intangible asset and financial asset – bifurcated model	• Amounts do not depend on usage of the infrastructure during the first half of the concession but are usage dependent during the second half. • Financial asset arises from the right to receive cash from grantor during the first part of the concession irrespective of usage; the intangible asset arises from the right to charge the grantor in the second half based on usage.

3.2.3   *Contingent right to collect cash or another financial asset*

Example 3.2.3

Contingent right to collect cash or another financial asset

Company A has been granted a service concession arrangement to operate a hospital. Under the terms of the arrangement, the amounts receivable by Company A vary based on the level of usage of the hospital's services until the level of usage reaches a specified threshold. Company A receives a fixed amount if usage exceeds that threshold.

In the circumstances described, the type of asset to be recognised by Company A depends on whether the threshold has economic substance.

If the threshold has economic substance (i.e. there is more than a remote possibility that the threshold might not be met), Company A does not have an unconditional contractual right to cash and, accordingly, recognises an intangible asset because the amount receivable is contingent on the extent to which the public uses the hospital's services.

If the threshold lacks economic substance, because the possibility of the threshold not being met is remote, Company A has, in substance, a right to collect a fixed amount of cash. In such circumstances, the conditionality should be ignored and Company A should recognise a financial asset.

3.2.4 Take-or-pay arrangements

In some service concession arrangements, the operator receives payment under a 'take-or-pay' arrangement, whereby the grantor is contractually obliged to purchase all of the output of the infrastructure or, if it is unable to accept delivery of that output, to pay the agreed price for that output regardless. These arrangements may include a fixed annual amount or be entirely based on the amount of output produced, and the amount paid per unit of production may be fixed over the life of the arrangement or may vary depending on, for example, inflation or a quoted market price for the output in question.

Under such take-or-pay arrangements, the operator should recognise a financial asset for construction of the infrastructure.

A financial asset is recognised when the operator has an unconditional contractual right to receive cash or another financial asset from the grantor. The operator has an unconditional right if the cash flows are specified or determinable amounts (IFRIC 12:16) irrespective of whether the public service is used (IFRIC 12:BC40) (i.e. the operator bears no demand risk). Variability based on the performance of the infrastructure does not prevent recognition as a financial asset (IFRIC 12:BC44).

In the case of take-or-pay arrangements:

- the amount of cash to be received by the operator is determinable because it is determined by the formula incorporated into the take-or-pay arrangement (a fixed or determinable rate multiplied by the amount of output produced) even though one or more inputs into the formula may be unknown and, to some extent, outside the operator's control; and

- the grantor's obligation to pay for all of the output from the infrastructure (i.e. the amount actually produced, not the amount that is delivered to the grantor) means that the operator is exposed to availability risk during the operating period, but not demand risk. As such, the arrangement does not result in recognition of an intangible asset because the amount of cash received by the operator is not contingent on the extent to which the public uses the service (IFRIC 12:17).

The financial asset model is appropriate whether or not the arrangement includes a guaranteed minimum annual payment receivable by the operator.

If, under the terms of the arrangement:

- the operator instead receives cash based on the amount of output used by the public, it would be exposed to demand risk and would instead account for the arrangement using the intangible asset model; or

- the grantor only guarantees to purchase a proportion of output (e.g. up to a fixed volume or number of units per year) and the operator has a right to charge users for the remaining output (provided that the grantor controls to whom it must be sold and at what price), the concession operator should apply the bifurcated model (i.e. recognise both a financial asset and an intangible asset).

Example 3.2.4A

Take-or-pay arrangement (1)

A public sector entity (grantor) enters into an arrangement for the construction and operation of a desalination plant whereby the concession operator receives the following two elements of consideration over the term of the concession:

- a specified annual amount as consideration for the investment undertaken; and
- a specified amount per cubic metre of desalinated water produced by the plant where the grantor guarantees to purchase all of the water output that the plant produces ('take-or-pay arrangement'). This specified amount per m^3 is sufficient to cover the concession operator's production costs based on the technical capacity of the plant of 24 million m^3 of water per year.

The amount of water produced is determined by the operator, constrained only by the plant's technical capacity and need for occasional downtime for maintenance. Because the grantor has guaranteed to purchase all of the water output from the plant (i.e. the amount actually produced, not the amount that is used by the grantor), the operator is exposed to availability risk during the operating period, but not demand risk. The concession arrangement should therefore be accounted for using the financial asset model.

Example 3.2.4B

Take-or-pay arrangement (2)

A project company (operator) enters into an arrangement with a state-owned power company (grantor) for the construction and operation of a solar farm.

The grantor is contractually obliged under a take-or-pay arrangement to purchase all of the electricity produced by the solar farm at a fixed rate per unit of electricity produced. There is no guaranteed minimum amount payable (i.e. the concession operator will receive no consideration if the solar farm generates no electricity) and, if the grantor is unable to accept delivery of the electricity it must still pay for any electricity that the operator has produced. Electricity delivered to the power company will be made available to its customers (the general public), with no adjustment to the amounts payable to the operator based on the amount of electricity used.

The amount of electricity produced is determined by the solar farm's technical capacity (which has been agreed with the grantor) and on factors within (e.g. the quality of maintenance of the farm) and outside (e.g. the strength of the UV radiation) the operator's control.

Given that the terms of the take-or-pay arrangement mean that the operator is exposed to no demand risk over the electricity, the solar farm should be accounted for using the financial asset model.

3.2.5 Payments for capacity availability

Example 3.2.5

Payments for capacity availability

Company A is granted a concession arrangement for the construction and operation of a hospital for 30 years. This arrangement stipulates that Company A will be paid a specified amount that will enable it to recover the investment made provided that it has a predetermined minimum number of hospital beds available for use (whether or not that number of beds is actually used).

IFRIC 12:16 states that the operator has an unconditional right to receive cash if the grantor contractually guarantees to pay the operator specified or determinable amounts, even if payment is contingent on the operator ensuring that the infrastructure meets specified quality or efficiency requirements (see **section 4**). IFRIC 12:BC44 makes clear that this includes payments contingent upon targets to ensure a specified level of capacity can be delivered. Payments under the concession arrangement depend upon the hospital's capacity, not the usage of that capacity and, therefore, Company A should apply the financial asset model.

3.2.6   Guaranteed minimum net revenue with potential to extend the concession term

---

Example 3.2.6A

Guaranteed minimum net revenue with potential to extend the concession term indefinitely

Company A is granted a concession arrangement for a waste treatment plant under which the concession term ends automatically when the concession operator has received a previously stipulated net present value of net revenue (sales less operating costs) from users of the plant. If this minimum guaranteed net revenue is not achieved in the normal term of the concession, the term will be extended indefinitely for successive five-year periods until the guaranteed minimum revenue is achieved.

Company A does not have an unconditional contractual right to receive cash or another financial asset because the concession term could be extended indefinitely and the guaranteed minimum net revenue might never be achieved. Consequently, the concession arrangement should be accounted for using the intangible asset model.

Example 3.2.6B

Guaranteed minimum net revenue with potential to extend concession term for a limited period

Assume the same facts as described in **example 3.2.6A**, except that the maximum concession term that can be reached with the successive extensions is limited to 50 years. The grantor has guaranteed to pay any shortfall, adjusted for the time value of money, if the minimum guaranteed net revenue has not been achieved by the end of the 50-year limit. Because of the guarantee from the grantor, Company A has an unconditional contractual right to receive cash; therefore, the financial asset model should be applied in this case.

---

4   Financial asset model

4.1   Financial asset model – general

As outlined in **3.2.1**, the financial asset model applies if the operator has a contractual right to receive cash from or at the direction of the grantor and the grantor has little, if any, discretion to avoid payment. This will be the case if the grantor contractually guarantees to pay the operator:

[IFRIC 12:16]

- specified or determinable amounts; or

- the shortfall, if any, between amounts received from users of the public service and specified or determinable amounts.

A financial asset exists in these circumstances even if the payments are contingent on the operator ensuring that the infrastructure meets specified quality or efficiency requirements. [IFRIC 12:16]

The financial asset model cannot apply if the grantor only pays when users use the service or if the grantor only grants a right to charge users for the service.

The financial asset is accounted for in accordance with IFRS 9 *Financial Instruments* (see **4.2**) or, for entities that have not yet adopted IFRS 9, IAS 39 *Financial Instruments: Recognition and Measurement* (see **4.3**). The requirements of IAS 32 *Financial Instruments: Presentation* and IFRS 7 *Financial Instruments: Disclosures* also apply. [IFRIC 12:23]

4.2   Measurement of financial asset – entities that have adopted IFRS 9

If the operator is applying IFRS 9, the amount due from, or at the direction of, the grantor may, depending on the circumstances, be accounted for as measured at:

[IFRIC 12:24]

- amortised cost; or

- fair value through other comprehensive income; or

- fair value through profit or loss.

The option to measure this amount at fair value through other comprehensive income was introduced in July 2014 when the revised IFRS 9 was issued. This option should not be used unless the entity has adopted IFRS 9 (as revised in 2014), which is effective for periods beginning on or after 1 January 2018, with earlier application permitted.

When the amount due from the grantor is accounted for at amortised cost or at fair value through other comprehensive income, IFRS 9 requires interest calculated using the effective interest method to be recognised in profit or loss. [IFRIC 12:25] For guidance on the classification of financial assets under IFRS 9, see **section 5** of **chapter B2**.

4.3   Measurement of financial asset – entities that have not yet adopted IFRS 9

Entities that have not yet adopted IFRS 9 should apply IAS 39. Under the requirements of that Standard, the financial asset will, depending on the circumstances, be required to be classified:

[IFRIC 12:24]

- as at fair value through profit or loss, if so designated upon initial recognition (and provided that the conditions for that classification are met); or

- as loans and receivables; or

- as available for sale.

The asset can only be classified as loans and receivables if payments are fixed or determinable and the only substantial risk of non-recovery of the initial investment is credit deterioration of the counterparty. (For further guidance on the classification of financial assets under IAS 39, see **section 3** of **chapter C2**.) IFRIC 12 assumes that the financial asset will not be classified as held to maturity. [IFRIC 12:BC61]

If the amount due from the grantor is accounted for either as loans and receivables or as an available-for-sale financial asset, IAS 39 requires interest calculated using the effective interest method to be recognised in profit or loss. [IFRIC 12:25]

4.4 Application of the financial asset model (both IFRS 9 and IAS 39)

Some practical issues may arise because service concession agreements usually establish a single transaction price without splitting the amounts between the performance obligations, usually being the construction services and the operation services. The allocation of the transaction price between the performance obligations may require a significant amount of judgement.

For the purposes of determining the construction and operation service revenue over the concession term, Example 1 accompanying IFRIC 12 illustrates that the total expected consideration is allocated to the performance obligations based on the relative stand-alone selling prices of each of those performance obligations, taking into account the significant financing component.

Example 4.4

Financial asset model

An operator enters into a contract to provide construction services and operation services. The total cash inflows over the entire life of the contract are fixed by the grantor at CU200. The cost of the construction is CU100. Based on the stand-alone selling prices of the performance obligations, and taking into account the significant financing component, the operator allocates CU110 to the construction services and CU75 to the operation services. The finance revenue to be recognised over the entire life of the service concession arrangement is

CU15. During the construction phase, the entity recognises a contract asset and the significant financing component (CU3) is accounted for in accordance with IFRS 15. On completion of the construction phase, the contract asset becomes a financial asset and the significant financing component (CU12) is calculated using the effective interest method in accordance with IFRS 9 (or, for entities that have not yet adopted IFRS 9, IAS 39). The following journal entries are made in these circumstances.

During construction

		CU	CU
Dr	Contract asset	110	
Cr	Construction revenue		110

To recognise revenue relating to construction services, to be settled in cash.

		CU	CU
Dr	Cost of construction (profit or loss)	100	
Cr	Cash		100

To recognise costs relating to construction services.

		CU	CU
Dr	Contract asset	3	
Cr	Finance revenue		3

To recognise interest income for the significant financing component on the contract asset.

At the end of the construction phase

		CU	CU
Dr	Financial asset	113	
Cr	Contract asset		113

To transfer the contract asset to financial asset.

During the operation phase

		CU	CU
Dr	Financial asset	12	
Cr	Finance revenue		12

To recognise interest income under the financial asset model.

		CU	CU
Dr	Financial asset	75	
Cr	Revenue		75

To recognise revenue relating to the operating phase.

	CU	CU
Dr Cash	200	
Cr Financial asset		200
To recognise cash received from the grantor.		
Total revenue over the life of the contract (including finance revenue of CU15)		CU200
Total cash inflows over the life of the contract		CU200

A more detailed example of the financial asset model is included as Example 1 in the illustrative examples accompanying IFRIC 12 and is reproduced at **example 13.2**.

5   Intangible asset model

5.1   Intangible asset model – general

The intangible asset model applies if the operator receives a right (a licence) to charge users, or the grantor, based on usage of the public service. There is no unconditional right to receive cash because the amounts are contingent on the extent to which the public uses the service. [IFRIC 12:17]

Arrangements in which the grantor, rather than the users, pays the operator amounts based on usage are often described as 'shadow tolls'. If the amounts received by the operator are contingent on usage rather than being an unconditional right to receive cash or another financial instrument, the operator recognises an intangible asset, notwithstanding that the amounts are received from the grantor (see also IFRIC 12:BC36 to BC40).

During the construction phase, the operator recognises revenue in respect of construction activities with the corresponding entry increasing the amount recognised for the intangible asset. This is because the operator exchanges construction services in return for a licence. The grantor makes a non-cash payment for the construction services by giving the operator an intangible asset in exchange for the construction services. This is recognised as revenue in accordance with IFRS 15.

The intangible asset generates a second stream of revenue when the operator receives cash from users or from the grantor based on usage. This contrasts with the financial asset model in which monies received are treated as partial repayment of the financial asset. Under the intangible asset model, the intangible asset is reduced by amortisation rather than repayment.

This results in revenue being recognised twice – once when the construction services are provided (in exchange for the intangible asset) and a second time on the receipt of payments for usage. The expenses recognised under the intangible asset model are correspondingly higher, because amortisation of the intangible asset is recognised in profit or loss.

The intangible asset should be accounted for in accordance with IAS 38 *Intangible Assets* (see **chapter A9**). [IFRIC 12:26] The intangible asset should be amortised over the period of the concession. The appropriate method of amortisation of the intangible asset is generally the straight-line method, unless another method better reflects the pattern of consumption of the asset's future economic benefits. However, in some circumstances, if the expected pattern of consumption of the expected economic benefits is based on usage, it may be appropriate to use an alternative method of amortisation.

Example 5.1A

Amortisation under the intangible asset model

Company B enters into an arrangement under which it will build and operate a toll bridge. Company B is entitled to charge users for driving over the toll bridge for the period from the completion of construction until 1 million cars have driven across the bridge, at which point the concession arrangement will end. It would be appropriate for Company B to amortise its intangible asset based on usage, because Company B's licence to operate the bridge expires on the basis of usage rather than with the passage of time.

Example 5.1B

Intangible asset model

As in **example 4.4**, an operator enters into a contract to provide construction services and operation services. The total cash inflows over the entire life of the contract are expected to be CU200; however, this amount is not guaranteed by the grantor. The cost of the construction is CU100. The operator identifies the construction services as a separate performance obligation and determines the fair value of the resulting intangible asset indirectly by reference to the standalone selling price of the construction services, being CU110. The following entries are made in these circumstances.

During construction

		CU	CU
Dr	Cost of construction (profit or loss)	100	
Cr	Cash		100

To recognise costs relating to construction services.

		CU	CU
Dr	Intangible asset	110	
Cr	Revenue		110

To recognise revenue relating to construction services provided for non-cash consideration.

Note: The contract asset is presented as an intangible asset as set out in IFRIC 12:IE15.

During the operation phase

		CU	CU
Dr	Amortisation expense	110	
Cr	Intangible asset (accumulated amortisation)		110

To recognise amortisation expense relating to the operation phase.

		CU	CU
Dr	Cash	200	
Cr	Revenue		200

To recognise revenue received from users in the operation phase.

Total revenue over the life of the contract	CU310
Total cash inflows over the life of the contract	CU200

A more detailed example of the intangible asset model is included as Example 2 in the illustrative examples accompanying IFRIC 12 and is reproduced at **example 13.3**.

5.2   Changes in the estimated cash flows

Concessions are generally granted for long periods of time. Therefore, there are often changes in the initial estimates of future cash flows relating to such arrangements, for example:

- due to changes in the usage of the infrastructure by the users (increase in traffic on the road, increase in the number of passengers etc.); or

- due to changes in the estimated costs or other assumptions relating to the arrangement.

Such changes might be an indicator of impairment of the intangible asset or suggest that the amortisation method for the intangible asset should be reviewed.

6 Bifurcated model

When an operator receives a financial asset and an intangible asset as consideration, it is necessary to account separately for the component parts. At initial recognition, the consideration for both components is recognised in accordance with IFRS 15. [IFRIC 12:18] To the extent that the operator receives a contractual right to receive cash from or at the direction of the grantor, a financial asset is recognised. Any excess of the fair value of the construction services provided over the fair value of the financial asset recognised is recognised as an intangible asset.

Example 6

Bifurcated model

As in **example 4.4**, an operator enters into a contract to provide construction services and operation services. The total cash inflows over the entire life of the contract are expected to be CU200. Of these, CU60 are guaranteed by the grantor. The cost of the construction is CU100. The operator identifies the construction services as a separate performance obligation and by reference to the stand-alone selling prices, allocates CU110 to the construction services. The appropriate finance revenue to be recognised derived from applying the effective interest method in accordance with IFRS 9 *Financial Instruments* (or, for entities that have not yet adopted IFRS 9, IAS 39 *Financial Instruments: Recognition and Measurement*) is in total CU6 over the entire life of the service concession arrangement.

During the construction phase, the entity recognises a contract asset of CU58 and a significant financing component (CU2) relating to that contract asset is accounted for in accordance with IFRS 15. The remaining revenue allocated to construction services of CU50 is recognised as a contract asset and presented as an intangible asset (as set out in IFRIC 12:IE15). On completion of the construction phase, the contract asset becomes a financial asset and the significant financing component (CU4) is calculated using the effective interest method in accordance with IFRS 9 (or, prior to the adoption of IFRS 9, IAS 39).

The following entries are made in these circumstances.

During construction

		CU	CU
Dr	Contract asset	58	
Cr	Revenue		58

To recognise revenue relating to construction services, to be settled in cash.

		CU	CU
Dr	Cost of construction (profit or loss)	100	
Cr	Cash		100

To recognise costs relating to construction services.

		CU	CU
Dr	Contract asset	2	
Cr	Finance revenue		2

To recognise interest income for the significant financing component on the contract asset.

		CU	CU
Dr	Intangible asset	50	
Cr	Revenue		50

To recognise revenue relating to construction services provided for non-cash consideration.

At the end of the construction phase

		CU	CU
Dr	Financial asset	60	
Cr	Contract asset		60

To transfer the contract asset to financial asset.

During the operation phase

		CU	CU
Dr	Financial asset	4	
Cr	Finance revenue		4

To recognise finance revenues.

		CU	CU
Dr	Amortisation expense	50	
Cr	Intangible asset (accumulated amortisation)		50

To recognise amortisation expense relating to the operation phase.

		CU	CU
Dr	Cash	200	
Cr	Revenue		136
Cr	Financial asset		64

To recognise revenues relating to the operation phase and cash received from the grantor and users.

Total revenue over the life of the contract (including finance revenue of CU6)	CU250
Total cash inflows over the life of the contract	CU200

A more detailed example of the bifurcated model is included as Example 3 in the illustrative examples accompanying IFRIC 12 and is reproduced at **example 13.4**.

7 Maintenance obligations

A service concession arrangement contract may require an operator to:

[IFRIC 12:21]

- maintain the infrastructure to a specified level of serviceability; or

- restore the infrastructure to a specified condition at the end of the arrangement before it is handed over to the grantor.

For example, an operator of a toll road may be required to resurface a road to ensure that it does not deteriorate below a specified condition. IFRIC 12:21 states that such contractual obligations to maintain or restore the infrastructure should be recognised and measured in accordance with IAS 37 *Provisions, Contingent Liabilities and Contingent Assets*. Therefore, an estimate of the expenditure that would be required to settle the present obligation at the end of the reporting period needs to be made and recognised as a provision.

IFRIC 12 does not include guidance on the appropriate timing for recognition of the obligations because the terms and conditions of the obligation will vary from contract to contract. The requirements and guidance in IAS 37 should be followed to identify the period(s) in which different obligations should be recognised.

In the case of resurfacing a road, it may be that the amount required to settle the obligation at any point in time is linked to the number of vehicles that have travelled over the road. In such circumstances, usage of the road may determine the obligating event. This is illustrated by

Example 2 accompanying IFRIC 12 (see **example 13.3**) which shows the provision for the resurfacing obligation being built up over time.

In contrast, when the entity is obligated to restore the infrastructure to a specified condition at the end of the arrangement irrespective of usage, it has an obligation analogous to an obligation for the dismantling or removal of an asset and restoring the site on which the asset stands accounted for under IAS 37 and IFRIC 1 *Changes in Existing Decommissioning, Restoration and Similar Liabilities*. In such circumstances, the obligation arises when the infrastructure is constructed. Under the intangible asset model, such an obligation is included in the cost of the asset and is subsequently amortised.

IFRIC 12 envisages that maintenance obligations could alternatively be a revenue-earning activity, in particular under the financial asset model as illustrated by Example 1 accompanying IFRIC 12 (see **example 13.2**). If the grantor reimburses the operator for maintenance (e.g. resurfacing a road), the operator should not recognise the obligation in the statement of financial position but should instead recognise the revenue and expense in profit or loss when the resurfacing work is performed. The accounting result is similar to that of an upgrade (see **section 8**).

Ultimately, the accounting treatment for maintenance obligations will depend on the precise terms and circumstances of the obligations, which will vary from contract to contract and should not be affected by the nature of the infrastructure asset recognised (i.e. whether a financial asset or an intangible asset).

IAS 37 requires that, when the effect of the time value of money is material, the amount of a provision should be the present value of the expenditures expected to be required to settle the obligation.

After initial recognition, provisions should be reviewed at the end of each reporting period and adjusted to reflect current best estimates.

Adjustments to provisions arise from three sources:

- revisions to estimated cash flows (both amount and timing);
- changes to present value due to the passage of time (i.e. unwinding of discount); and
- revisions of discount rates to reflect prevailing current market conditions.

In the years following the initial recognition and measurement of a provision at its present value, the provision should be revised to reflect estimated cash flows being closer to the measurement date. While the unwinding of the discount relating to the passage of time should be recognised as a finance cost (which is no longer capitalised once the infrastructure is ready for use), the revision of estimates of the amount and timing of cash flows is a reassessment of the provision and should be charged or credited as an operating item rather than as a finance cost. This is consistent with IFRIC 1 which treats changes in the estimated timing or amount of the obligation and changes in the discount rate as operating items with periodic unwinding of the discount recognised as a borrowing cost.

Example 7

Resurfacing obligations and changes in the estimates of the provision

The operator's resurfacing obligation in respect of a toll road arises as a consequence of use of the road during the operating phase. It is recognised and measured in accordance with IAS 37, i.e. at the best estimate of the expenditure required to settle the present obligation at the end of the reporting period.

It is assumed that the terms of the operator's contractual obligation are such that, at any date, the best estimate of the expenditure required to settle the obligation in the future is proportional to the number of vehicles that have used the road. For illustrative purposes, a continuous traffic flow is assumed, allowing for the use of a straight-line method that increases the provision by a fixed amount (discounted to a current value) each year.

The operator discounts the provision to its present value in accordance with IAS 37.

Illustration 1 No changes in estimates

The best estimate of the expenditure required amounts to CU100 at the end of Year 6. The obligation increases by CU16.67 (i.e. CU100 divided by 6 years), discounted to a current value each year and the initial discount rate is 6 per cent. There are no subsequent changes in estimates.

The expense recognised each period in profit or loss will be as follows.

Year	1	2	3	4	5	6	Total
Estimated cost of resurfacing (CU)	100	100	100	100	100	100	
Estimated discount rate (per cent)	6	6	6	6	6	6	
	CU	CU	CU	CU	CU	CU	CU
Opening provision	–	12.45	26.40	41.98	59.33	78.62	–
Obligation arising in the year (operating cost)	12.45	13.20	13.99	14.83	15.72	16.67	86.86
Increase in prior year provision arising from the passage of time (finance cost)	–	0.75	1.59	2.52	3.57	4.71	13.14
	12.45	26.40	41.98	59.33	78.62	100.00	100.00
Used in year	–	–	–	–	–	(100.00)	
Closing provision	12.45	26.40	41.98	59.33	78.62	–	

Illustration 2 Subsequent change in discount rate

The best estimate of the expenditure required is CU100 at the end of Year 6. The obligation increases by CU16.67 (i.e. CU100 divided by 6 years), discounted to a current value each year and the initial discount rate is 6 per cent. Subsequently, as a result of a reassessment of prevailing market rates at the beginning of Year 4, the discount rate changes to 4 per cent.

The expense recognised each period in profit or loss will be as follows.

Year	1	2	3	4	5	6	Total
Estimated cost of resurfacing (CU)	100	100	100	100	100	100	
Estimated discount rate (per cent)	6	6	6	4	4	4	
	CU	CU	CU	CU	CU	CU	CU
Opening provision	–	12.45	26.40	41.98	61.64	80.13	–
Obligation arising in the year (operating cost)	12.45	13.20	13.99	17.98	16.03	16.67	90.32
Increase in prior year provision arising from the passage of time (finance cost)	–	0.75	1.59	1.68	2.46	3.20	9.68
	12.45	26.40	41.98	61.64	80.13	100.00	100.00
Used in year	–	–	–	–	–	(100.00)	
Closing provision	12.45	26.40	41.98	61.64	80.13	–	

At the beginning of Year 4, the discount rate has changed to 4 per cent. The obligation at the end of Year 3 was CU41.98. The unwinding of the discount would be the increase in the prior year obligation arising from the passage of time, so an amount of CU1.68 (CU41.98 × 4%) would be recognised as a finance cost and the additional amount of CU17.98 (being the net present value of the additional 1/6 of the CU100 provision for the year plus the increase in the provision resulting from the fall in discount rate from 6 per cent to 4 per cent) would increase the provision as an operating expense.

Illustration 3 Subsequent revision to the estimated cash flows

The best estimate of the expenditure required is CU100 at the end of Year 6. The obligation initially increases by CU16.67 (i.e. CU100 divided by 6 years), discounted to a current value each year and the discount rate is 6 per cent. Subsequently, at the beginning of Year 4, the best estimate changes to CU106.

The expense recognised each period in profit or loss will be as follows.

Year	1	2	3	4	5	6	Total
Estimated cost of resurfacing	100	100	100	106	106	106	
Estimated discount rate (per cent)	6	6	6	6	6	6	

Year	1	2	3	4	5	6	Total
	CU	CU	CU	CU	CU	CU	CU
Opening provision	–	12.45	26.40	41.98	62.89	83.33	–
Obligation arising in the year (operating cost)	12.45	13.20	13.99	18.39	16.67	17.67	92.37
Increase in prior year provision arising from the passage of time (finance cost)	–	0.75	1.59	2.52	3.77	5.00	13.63
	12.45	26.40	41.98	62.89	83.33	106.00	106.00
Used in year	–	–	–	–	–	(106.00)	
Closing provision	12.45	26.40	41.98	62.89	83.33	–	

Based on the revised estimate of CU106 at the end of Year 6, the obligation at the end of Year 4 should be CU62.89 (CU106 / 6 × 4 years, discounted by 2 years at 6 per cent). The finance cost in the year of revision is the increase in the prior year obligation arising from the passage of time using the discount rate of 6 per cent (CU41.98 × 6% = CU2.52). Any other adjustment to the carrying amount of the provision (i.e. an additional year's worth of the obligation plus the adjustment arising from the increase in the best estimate of the cash flow at the end of Year 6 to CU106) is charged as an operating expense.

8 Upgrade of existing infrastructure or new infrastructure

A service concession arrangement contract may require an operator to perform additional construction works during the operation phase. It will be a matter of judgement whether this subsequent expenditure represents maintenance or an upgrade of an existing infrastructure. Construction work would usually be considered an upgrade of existing infrastructure if it extends the life or capacity of the asset even though the additional revenues provided may not be identifiable on a standalone basis. For example, construction of an extra lane of a motorway will allow an increase in the traffic flow and it will represent an upgrade even though it is unclear how much traffic it produces by itself. On the other hand, construction work that does not extend the life or the capacity of the asset is usually considered to represent maintenance.

As explained in **section 7**, contractual obligations to maintain or restore infrastructure that are maintenance work should be recognised and measured in accordance with IAS 37 *Provisions, Contingent Liabilities and Contingent Assets*.

IFRIC 12:14 states that revenues and costs of the operator relating to the construction or upgrade services phase of a contract are accounted for in accordance with IFRS 15. If the operator has an unconditional contractual right to receive cash in order to recover the additional upgrade investment, the upgrade investment will be treated as a financial asset (receivable) under the financial asset model. If the operator has the right to charge users to recover the upgrade expenditure, the upgrade elements will be treated as an intangible asset under the intangible asset model. To the extent that the revenues expected to be generated from the upgrade cannot be readily linked to the upgrade itself, it will generally be appropriate to recognise a single intangible asset for the initial construction work and the subsequent upgrade. In such circumstances, to the extent that the operator has an unavoidable obligation to upgrade the infrastructure, it would generally be appropriate to recognise, at the outset of the arrangement, the full intangible asset including the upgrade service with a contract liability in respect of the performance obligation for the construction work to be undertaken in the future. Typically, that performance obligation would be measured at the stand-alone selling price, taking into account the significant financing component, of the service yet to be provided, which would include an appropriate profit margin.

9   Borrowing costs

The requirements of IAS 23 *Borrowing Costs* in respect of the capitalisation of eligible borrowing costs are discussed in **chapter A18**. Borrowing costs attributable to an arrangement should be capitalised during the construction phase, in accordance with IAS 23, if the operator has a contractual right to receive an intangible asset. A financial asset is not a qualifying asset and so borrowing costs are recognised as an expense in the period in which they are incurred. [IFRIC 12:22] Therefore, under the financial asset model, during the construction phase an entity recognises a contract asset and accounts for the significant financing component in the arrangement in accordance with IFRS 15. Once construction is complete, interest is imputed on the financial asset using the effective interest method in accordance with IFRS 9 (or, for entities that have not yet adopted IFRS 9, IAS 39). [IFRIC 12:IE7]

10   Arrangements that do not give rise to construction or upgrade services

IFRIC 12 envisages that under certain service concession arrangements the operator does not undertake construction or upgrade activities, but instead the grantor gives the operator access to existing infrastructure for the purpose of the service arrangement. [IFRIC 12:7(b)] However, IFRIC 12 does not deal specifically with situations in which a service concession arrangement consists only of an operation phase.

In such arrangements, the grantor may pay the operator directly for providing the service or give the operator a right to charge users at a regulated price and the operator may pay the grantor a fixed or variable amount for a licence to provide those services. In the absence of specific guidance in IFRIC 12, it is necessary to apply the requirements of other relevant IFRSs, in particular IFRS 15 and IAS 37. Because no construction services have been supplied by the operator, it will generally not be appropriate to recognise a financial asset or an intangible asset at the outset of the contract.

However, if the operator pays the grantor to acquire a licence to charge users for a public service, the operator should recognise an intangible asset at cost, including the present value of all future fixed payments to be made by the operator to the grantor, in accordance with IAS 38 *Intangible Assets*.

11 Items provided by the grantor to the operator

The grantor may also provide the operator access to other items (e.g. land or other infrastructure assets). Following the basic principles underlying the accounting model established in IFRIC 12:11, infrastructure items to which the operator is given access by the grantor for the purposes of the service arrangement are not recognised as property, plant and equipment of the operator because they remain under the control of the grantor.

An operator may also be provided with infrastructure items by the grantor as part of the consideration payable by the grantor for the services, to keep or deal with as the operator wishes (i.e. they are not for the purposes of the service arrangement); such infrastructure items should be accounted for as part of the transaction price as defined in IFRS 15. [IFRIC 12:27]

IFRIC 12 specifically states that such assets should not be viewed as government grants as defined in IAS 20 *Accounting for Government Grants and Disclosure of Government Assistance*. [IFRIC 12:27]

Example 11

Items provided to the operator by the grantor

Company A enters into a service concession arrangement under which it will build a new hospital and operate it for a period of 30 years. In exchange, the government provides Company A with a fixed annual cash payment, and title to a substantial plot of land in a different location (i.e. non-cash consideration). Company A is free to use the land as it wishes. Company A should recognise the land as its own property at fair value at the date on which control passes, together with a corresponding obligation for any unfulfilled obligations. The fair value of the land is included in the total consideration recognised by Company A in respect of the service concession arrangement.

---

12 Disclosures about service concession arrangements

SIC-29 *Service Concession Arrangements: Disclosures* specifies certain disclosures that are required for service concession arrangements to meet the requirements of paragraph 112(c) of IAS 1 *Presentation of Financial Statements* (see **7.1.1** in **chapter A4**). The requirements of SIC-29 are considered at **7.4.3** in **chapter A4**.

IFRIC 12 explains how an operator should account for infrastructure that it constructs or acquires from a third party for the purpose of the service arrangement, but which is controlled by the grantor. The scope of SIC-29 is wider than this and includes, for example, arrangements in which the operator controls the infrastructure and also applies to the grantor in service concession arrangements.

In addition, the disclosure requirements of IFRS 15 will need to be considered (see **chapter A14**).

13 Further examples illustrating the application of IFRIC 12

13.1 Illustrative examples – general

IFRIC 12 provides illustrative examples of how to account for service concession arrangements in three situations: under the financial asset model, the intangible asset model and the bifurcated model. These examples are reproduced at **examples 13.2** to **13.4**. Further guidance on each model can be found in **sections 4**, **5** and **6**, respectively.

13.2 Financial asset model

Example 13.2

The grantor gives the operator a financial asset

[IFRIC 12:IE1 - IE10, Example 1]

Arrangement terms

The terms of the arrangement require an operator to construct a road – completing construction within two years – and maintain and operate the road to a specified standard for eight years (ie years 3–10). The terms of the arrangement also require the operator to resurface the road at the end of year 8. At the end of year 10, the arrangement will end. Assume that the operator identifies three performance obligations for construction services, operation services and road resurfacing. The operator estimates that the costs it will incur to fulfil its obligations will be:

Table 1.1 Contract costs

	Year	CU
Construction services	1	500
	2	500
Operation services (per year)	3–10	10
Road resurfacing	8	100

The terms of the arrangement require the grantor to pay the operator 200 currency units (CU200) per year in years 3–10 for making the road available to the public.

For the purpose of this illustration, it is assumed that all cash flows take place at the end of the year.

Contract revenue

The operator recognises revenue in accordance with IFRS 15 *Revenue from Contracts with Customers*. Revenue – the amount of consideration to which the operator expects to be entitled from the grantor for the services provided – is recognised when (or as) the performance obligations are satisfied. Under the terms of the arrangement the operator is obliged to resurface the road at the end of year 8. In year 8 the operator will be reimbursed by the grantor for resurfacing the road.

The total expected consideration (CU200 in each of years 3–10) is allocated to the performance obligations based on the relative stand-alone selling prices of the construction services, operation services and road resurfacing, taking into account the significant financing component, as follows:

Table 1.2 Transaction price allocated to each performance obligation

	Transaction price allocation (including the effect of the significant financing component)
	CU
Construction services (over two years)[a]	1,050
Operation services (over 8 years)[b]	96
Road resurfacing services (in year 8)[c]	110
Total	1,256
Implied interest rate[d]	6.18% per year

[a] The operator estimates the relative stand-alone selling price by reference to the forecast cost plus 5 per cent.

[b] The operator estimates the relative stand-alone selling price by reference to the forecast cost plus 20 per cent.

[c] The operator estimates the relative stand-alone selling price by reference to the forecast cost plus 10 per cent.

[d] The implied interest rate is assumed to be the rate that would be reflected in a financing transaction between the operator and the grantor.

In year 1, for example, construction costs of CU500, construction revenue of CU525, and hence construction profit of CU25 are recognised in profit or loss.

Financial asset

[For entities that have adopted IFRS 9] During the first two years, the entity recognises a contract asset and accounts for the significant financing component in the arrangement in accordance with IFRS 15. Once the construction is complete, the amounts due from the grantor are accounted for in accordance with IFRS 9 *Financial Instruments* as receivables.

[For entities that have not yet adopted IFRS 9] During the first two years, the entity recognises a contract asset and accounts for the significant financing component in the arrangement in accordance with IFRS 15. Once the construction is complete, the amounts due from the grantor are accounted for in accordance with IAS 39 *Financial Instruments: Recognition and Measurement* as receivables.

If the cash flows and fair values remain the same as those forecast, the effective interest rate is 6.18 per cent per year and the receivable recognised at the end of years 1–3 will be:

Table 1.3 Measurement of contract asset/receivable

	CU
Amount due for construction in year 1	525
Contract asset at end of year 1[a]	**525**
Effective interest in year 2 on contract asset at the end of year 1 (6.18% × CU525)	32
Amount due for construction in year 2	525
Receivable at end of year 2	**1,082**
Effective interest in year 3 on receivable at the end of year 2 (6.18% × CU1,082)	67
Amount due for operation in year 3 (CU10 × (1 + 20%))	12
Cash receipts in year 3	(200)
Receivable at end of year 3	**961**

[a]   No effective interest arises in year 1 because the cash flows are assumed to take place at the end of the year.

Overview of cash flows, statement of comprehensive income and statement of financial position

For the purpose of this illustration, it is assumed that the operator finances the arrangement wholly with debt and retained profits. It pays interest at 6.7 per cent per year on outstanding debt. If the cash flows and fair values remain the same as those forecast, the operator's cash flows, statement of comprehensive income and statement of financial position over the duration of the arrangement will be:

Table 1.4 Cash flows (currency units)

Year	1	2	3	4	5	6	7	8	9	10	Total
Receipts	–	–	200	200	200	200	200	200	200	200	1,600
Contract costs[a]	(500)	(500)	(10)	(10)	(10)	(10)	(10)	(110)	(10)	(10)	(1,180)
Borrowing costs[b]	–	(34)	(69)	(61)	(53)	(43)	(33)	(23)	(19)	(7)	(342)
Net inflow/ (outflow)	(500)	(534)	121	129	137	147	157	67	171	183	78

[a]   Table 1.1

[b]   Debt at start of year (table 1.6) × 6.7%

Table 1.5 Statement of comprehensive income (currency units)

Year	1	2	3	4	5	6	7	8	9	10	Total
Revenue	525	525	12	12	12	12	12	122	12	12	1,256
Contract costs	(500)	(500)	(10)	(10)	(10)	(10)	(10)	(110)	(10)	(10)	(1,180)
Finance income[a]	–	32	67	59	51	43	34	25	22	11	344
Borrowing costs[b]	–	(34)	(69)	(61)	(53)	(43)	(33)	(23)	(19)	(7)	(342)
Net profit	25	23	–	–	–	2	3	14	5	6	78

[a]   Amount due from grantor at start of year (table 1.6) × 6.18%

[b]   Cash/(debt) (table 1.6) × 6.7%

Table 1.6 Statement of financial position (currency units)

End of Year	1	2	3	4	5	6	7	8	9	10
Amount due from grantor[a]	525	1,082	961	832	695	550	396	343	177	–
Cash/(debt)[b]	(500)	(1,034)	(913)	(784)	(647)	(500)	(343)	(276)	(105)	78
Net assets	25	48	48	48	48	50	53	67	72	78

[a]   Amount due from grantor at start of year, plus revenue and finance income earned in year (table 1.5), less receipts in year (table 1.4)

[b]   Debt at start of year plus net cash flow in year (table 1.4)

This example deals with only one of many possible types of arrangements. Its purpose is to illustrate the accounting treatment for some features that are commonly found in practice. To make the illustration as clear as possible, it has been assumed that the arrangement period is only ten years and that the operator's annual receipts are constant over that period. In practice, arrangement periods may be much longer and annual revenues may increase with time. In such circumstances, the changes in net profit from year to year could be greater.

13.3   Intangible asset model

Example 13.3

The grantor gives the operator an intangible asset (a licence to charge users)

[IFRIC 12:IE11 - IE22, Example 2]

Arrangement terms

The terms of a service arrangement require an operator to construct a road – completing construction within two years – and maintain and operate the road to a specified standard for eight years (ie years 3–10). The terms of the arrangement also require the operator to resurface the road when the original surface has deteriorated below a specified condition. The operator estimates that it will have to undertake the resurfacing at the end of year 8. At the end of year 10, the service arrangement will end. Assume that the operator identifies a single performance obligation for construction services. The operator estimates that the costs it will incur to fulfil its obligations will be:

Table 2.1 Contract costs

	Year	CU
Construction services	1	500
	2	500
Operating the road (per year)	3–10	10
Road resurfacing	8	100

The terms of the arrangement allow the operator to collect tolls from drivers using the road. The operator forecasts that vehicle numbers will remain constant over the duration of the contract and that it will receive tolls of 200 currency units (CU200) in each of years 3–10.

For the purpose of this illustration it is assumed that all cash flows take place at the end of the year.

Intangible asset

The operator provides construction services to the grantor in exchange for an intangible asset, ie a right to collect tolls from road users in years 3–10. In accordance with IFRS 15, the operator measures the non-cash consideration at fair value. In this case, the operator determines the fair value indirectly by reference to the stand-alone selling price of the construction services delivered.

During the construction phase of the arrangement the operator's contract asset (representing its accumulating right to be paid for providing construction services) is presented as an intangible asset (licence to charge users of the infrastructure). The operator estimates the stand-alone selling price of the construction services to be equal to the forecast construction costs plus 5 per cent margin, which the operator concludes is consistent with the rate that a market participant would require as compensation for providing the

---

construction services and for assuming the risk associated with the construction costs. It is also assumed that, in accordance with IAS 23 *Borrowing Costs*, the operator capitalises the borrowing costs, estimated at 6.7 per cent, during the construction phase of the arrangement:

Table 2.2 Initial measurement of intangible asset

	CU
Construction services in year 1	525
Capitalisation of borrowing costs (table 2.4)	34
Construction services in year 2	525
Intangible asset at end of year 2	**1,084**

In accordance with IAS 38, the intangible asset is amortised over the period in which it is expected to be available for use by the operator, ie years 3–10. The depreciable amount of the intangible asset (CU1,084) is allocated using a straight-line method. The annual amortisation is therefore CU1,084 divided by 8 years, ie CU135 per year.

Construction costs and revenue

The operator accounts for the construction services in accordance with IFRS 15. It measures revenue at the fair value of the non-cash consideration received or receivable. Thus in each of years 1 and 2 it recognises in its profit or loss construction costs of CU500, construction revenue of CU525 and, hence, construction profit of CU25.

Toll revenue

The road users pay for the public services at the same time as they receive them, ie when they use the road. The operator therefore recognises toll revenue when it collects the tolls.

Resurfacing obligations

The operator's resurfacing obligation arises as a consequence of use of the road during the operating phase. It is recognised and measured in accordance with IAS 37 *Provisions, Contingent Liabilities and Contingent Assets*, ie at the best estimate of the expenditure required to settle the present obligation at the end of the reporting period.

For the purpose of this illustration, it is assumed that the terms of the operator's contractual obligation are such that the best estimate of the expenditure required to settle the obligation at any date is proportional to the number of vehicles that have used the road by that date and increases by CU17 (discounted to a current value) each year. The operator discounts the provision to its present value in accordance with IAS 37. The charge recognised each period in profit or loss is:

Table 2.3 Resurfacing obligation (currency units)

Year	3	4	5	6	7	8	Total
Obligation arising in year (CU17 discounted at 6%)	12	13	14	15	16	17	87
Increase in earlier years' provision arising from passage of time	0	1	1	2	4	5	13
Total expense recognised in profit or loss	12	14	15	17	20	22	100

Overview of cash flows, statement of comprehensive income and statement of financial position

For the purposes of this illustration, it is assumed that the operator finances the arrangement wholly with debt and retained profits. It pays interest at 6.7 per cent per year on outstanding debt. If the cash flows and fair values remain the same as those forecast, the operator's cash flows, statement of comprehensive income and statement of financial position over the duration of the arrangement will be:

Table 2.4 Cash flows (currency units)

Year	1	2	3	4	5	6	7	8	9	10	Total
Receipts	–	–	200	200	200	200	200	200	200	200	1,600
Contract costs[a]	(500)	(500)	(10)	(10)	(10)	(10)	(10)	(110)	(10)	(10)	(1,180)
Borrowing costs[b]	–	(34)	(69)	(61)	(53)	(43)	(33)	(23)	(19)	(7)	(342)
Net inflow/ (outflow)	(500)	(534)	121	129	137	147	157	67	171	183	78

[a] Table 2.1
[b] Debt at start of year (table 2.6) × 6.7%

Table 2.5 Statement of comprehensive income (currency units)

Year	1	2	3	4	5	6	7	8	9	10	Total
Revenue	525	525	200	200	200	200	200	200	200	200	2,650
Amortisation	–	–	(135)	(135)	(136)	(136)	(136)	(136)	(135)	(135)	(1,084)
Resurfacing expense	–	–	(12)	(14)	(15)	(17)	(20)	(22)	–	–	(100)
Other contract costs	(500)	(500)	(10)	(10)	(10)	(10)	(10)	(10)	(10)	(10)	(1,080)
Borrowing costs[a][b]	–	–	(69)	(61)	(53)	(43)	(33)	(23)	(19)	(7)	(308)
Net profit	25	25	(26)	(20)	(14)	(6)	1	9	36	48	78

[a] Borrowing costs are capitalised during the construction phase
[b] Table 2.4

Table 2.6 Statement of financial position (currency units)

End of Year	1	2	3	4	5	6	7	8	9	10
Intangible asset	525	1,084	949	814	678	542	406	270	135	–
Cash /(debt)[a]	(500)	(1,034)	(913)	(784)	(647)	(500)	(343)	(276)	(105)	78
Resurfacing obligation	–	–	(12)	(26)	(41)	(58)	(78)	–	–	–
Net assets	25	50	24	4	(10)	(16)	(15)	(6)	30	78

[a]   Debt at start of year plus net cash flow in year (table 2.4)

This example deals with only one of many possible types of arrangements. Its purpose is to illustrate the accounting treatment for some features that are commonly found in practice. To make the illustration as clear as possible, it has been assumed that the arrangement period is only ten years and that the operator's annual receipts are constant over that period. In practice, arrangement periods may be much longer and annual revenues may increase with time. In such circumstances, the changes in net profit from year to year could be greater.

13.4   Bifurcated model

Example 13.4

The grantor gives the operator a financial asset and an intangible asset

[IFRIC 12:IE23 - IE38, Example 3]

The terms of a service arrangement require an operator to construct a road – completing construction within two years – and to operate the road and maintain it to a specified standard for eight years (ie years 3–10). The terms of the arrangement also require the operator to resurface the road when the original surface has deteriorated below a specified condition. The operator estimates that it will have to undertake the resurfacing at the end of year 8. At the end of year 10, the arrangement will end. Assume that the operator identifies a single performance obligation for construction services. The operator estimates that the costs it will incur to fulfil its obligations will be:

Table 3.1 Contract costs

	Year	CU
Construction services	1	500
	2	500
Operating the road (per year)	3–10	10
Road resurfacing	8	100

The operator estimates the consideration in respect of construction services to be CU1,050 by reference to the stand-alone selling price of those services (which it estimates at forecast costs plus 5 per cent).

The terms of the arrangement allow the operator to collect tolls from drivers using the road. In addition, the grantor guarantees the operator a minimum amount of CU700 and interest at a specified rate of 6.18 per cent to reflect the timing of cash receipts. The operator forecasts that vehicle numbers will remain constant over the duration of the contract and that it will receive tolls of CU200 in each of years 3–10.

For the purpose of this illustration, it is assumed that all cash flows take place at the end of the year.

Dividing the arrangement

The contractual right to receive cash from the grantor for the services and the right to charge users for the public services should be regarded as two separate assets under IFRSs. Therefore in this arrangement it is necessary to divide the operator's contract asset during the construction phase into two components – a financial asset component based on the guaranteed amount and an intangible asset for the remainder. When the construction services are completed, the two components of the contract asset would be classified and measured as a financial asset and an intangible asset accordingly.

Table 3.2 Dividing the operator's consideration

Year	Total	Financial asset	Intangible asset
Construction services in year 1	525	350	175
Construction services in year 2	525	350	175
Total construction services	1,050	700	350
	100%	67%[a]	33%
Finance income, at specified rate of 6.18% on receivable (see table 3.3)	22	22	–
Borrowing costs capitalised (interest paid in years 1 and 2 × 33%) (see table 3.7)	11	–	11
Total fair value of the operator's consideration	1,083	722	361

[a]   Amount guaranteed by the grantor as a proportion of the construction services

[For entities that have adopted IFRS 9] During the first two years, the entity recognises a contract asset and accounts for the significant financing component in the arrangement in accordance with IFRS 15. Once the construction is complete, the amount due from, or at the direction of, the grantor in exchange for the construction services is accounted for in accordance with IFRS 9 *Financial Instruments* as a receivable.

[For entities that have not yet adopted IFRS 9] During the first two years, the entity recognises a contract asset and accounts for the significant financing component in the arrangement in accordance with IFRS 15. Once the construction is complete, the amount due from, or at the direction of, the grantor is accounted for in accordance with IAS 39 *Financial Instruments: Recognition and Measurement* as a receivable.

On this basis the receivable recognised at the end of years 2 and 3 will be:

Table 3.3 Measurement of contract asset/receivable

	CU
Construction services in year 1 allocated to the contract asset	350
Contract asset at end of year 1	**350**
Construction services in year 2 allocated to the contract asset	350
Interest in year 2 on contract asset at end of year 1 (6.18% × CU350)	22
Receivable at end of year 2	**722**
Interest in year 3 on receivable at end of year 2 (6.18% × CU722)	45
Cash receipts in year 3 (see table 3.5)	(117)
Receivable at end of year 3	**650**

Intangible asset

In accordance with IAS 38 *Intangible Assets*, the operator recognises the intangible asset at cost, ie the fair value of the consideration received or receivable.

During the construction phase of the arrangement the portion of the operator's contract asset that represents its accumulating right to be paid amounts in excess of the guaranteed amount for providing construction services is presented as a right to receive a licence to charge users of the infrastructure. The operator estimates the stand-alone selling price of the construction services as equal to the forecast construction costs plus 5 per cent, which the operator concludes is consistent with the rate that a market participant would require as compensation for providing the construction services and for assuming the risk associated with the construction costs. It is also assumed that, in accordance with IAS 23 *Borrowing Costs*, the operator capitalises the borrowing costs, estimated at 6.7 per cent, during the construction phase:

Table 3.4 Initial measurement of intangible asset

	CU
Construction services in year 1	175
Borrowing costs (interest paid in years 1 and 2 × 33%) (see table 3.7)	11
Construction services in year 2	175
Intangible asset at the end of year 2	**361**

In accordance with IAS 38, the intangible asset is amortised over the period in which it is expected to be available for use by the operator, ie years 3–10. The depreciable amount of the intangible asset (CU361 including borrowing costs) is allocated using a straight-line method. The annual amortisation charge is therefore CU361 divided by 8 years, ie CU45 per year.

Revenue and costs

The operator provides construction services to the grantor in exchange for a financial asset and an intangible asset. Under both the financial asset model and intangible asset model, the operator accounts for the construction services in accordance with IFRS 15. Thus in each of years 1 and 2 it recognises in profit or loss construction costs of CU500 and construction revenue of CU525.

Toll revenue

The road users pay for the public services at the same time as they receive them, ie when they use the road. Under the terms of this arrangement the cash flows are allocated to the financial asset and intangible asset in proportion, so the operator allocates the receipts from tolls between repayment of the financial asset and revenue earned from the intangible asset:

Table 3.5 Allocation of toll receipts

	CU
Guaranteed receipt from grantor	700
Finance income (see table 3.8)	237
Total	937
Cash allocated to realisation of the financial asset per year (CU937/8)	**117**
Receipts attributable to intangible asset (CU200 × 8 years – CU937)	663
Annual receipt from intangible asset (CU663/8 years)	**83**

Resurfacing obligations

The operator's resurfacing obligation arises as a consequence of use of the road during the operation phase. It is recognised and measured in accordance with IAS 37 *Provisions, Contingent Liabilities and Contingent Assets*, ie at the best estimate of the expenditure required to settle the present obligation at the end of the reporting period.

For the purpose of this illustration, it is assumed that the terms of the operator's contractual obligation are such that the best estimate of the expenditure required to settle the obligation at any date is proportional to the number of vehicles that have used the road by that date and increases by CU17 each year. The operator discounts the provision to its present value in accordance with IAS 37. The charge recognised each period in profit or loss is:

Year	3	4	5	6	7	8	Total
Obligation arising in year (CU17 discounted at 6%)	12	13	14	15	16	17	87
Increase in earlier years' provision arising from passage of time	0	1	1	2	4	5	13
Total expense recognised in profit or loss	12	14	15	17	20	22	100

Overview of cash flows, statement of comprehensive income and statement of financial position

For the purposes of this illustration, it is assumed that the operator finances the arrangement wholly with debt and retained profits. It pays interest at 6.7 per cent per year on outstanding debt. If the cash flows and fair values remain the same as those forecast, the operator's cash flows, statement of comprehensive income and statement of financial position over the duration of the arrangement will be:

Table 3.7 Cash flows (currency units)

Year	1	2	3	4	5	6	7	8	9	10	Total
Receipts	–	–	200	200	200	200	200	200	200	200	1,600
Contract costs[(a)]	(500)	(500)	(10)	(10)	(10)	(10)	(10)	(110)	(10)	(10)	(1,180)
Borrowing costs[(b)]	–	(34)	(69)	(61)	(53)	(43)	(33)	(23)	(19)	(7)	(342)
Net inflow/(outflow)	(500)	(534)	121	129	137	147	157	67	171	183	78

[(a)]   Table 3.1
[(b)]   Debt at start of year (table 3.9) × 6.7%

Table 3.8 Statement of comprehensive income (currency units)

Year	1	2	3	4	5	6	7	8	9	10	Total
Revenue on construction	525	525	–	–	–	–	–	–	–	–	1,050
Revenue from intangible asset	–	–	83	83	83	83	83	83	83	83	664
Finance income[(a)]	–	22	45	40	35	30	25	19	13	7	236
Amortisation	–	–	(45)	(45)	(45)	(45)	(45)	(45)	(45)	(46)	(361)
Resurfacing expense	–	–	(12)	(14)	(15)	(17)	(20)	(22)	–	–	(100)
Construction costs	(500)	(500)	–	–	–	–	–	–	–	–	(1,000)
Other contract costs[(b)]	–	–	(10)	(10)	(10)	(10)	(10)	(10)	(10)	(10)	(80)
Borrowing costs (table 3.7)[(c)]	–	(23)	(69)	(61)	(53)	(43)	(33)	(23)	(19)	(7)	(331)
Net profit	25	24	(8)	(7)	(5)	(2)	0	2	22	27	78

[(a)]   Interest on receivable
[(b)]   Table 3.1
[(c)]   In year 2, borrowing costs are stated net of amount capitalised in the intangible (see table 3.4)

Table 3.9 Statement of financial position (currency units)

End of Year	1	2	3	4	5	6	7	8	9	10
Receivable	350	722	650	573	491	404	312	214	10	–
Intangible asset	175	361	316	271	226	181	136	91	46	–
Cash / (debt)[(a)]	(500)	(1,034)	(913)	(784)	(647)	(500)	(343)	(276)	(105)	78
Resurfacing obligation	–	–	(12)	(26)	(41)	(58)	(78)	–	–	–
Net assets	25	49	41	34	29	27	27	29	51	78

[(a)]   Debt at start of year plus net cash flow in year (table 3.7)

This example deals with only one of many possible types of arrangements. Its purpose is to illustrate the accounting treatment for some features that are commonly found in practice. To make the illustration as clear as possible, it has been assumed that the arrangement period is only ten years and that the operator's annual receipts are constant over that period. In practice, arrangement periods may be much longer and annual revenues may increase with time. In such circumstances, the changes in net profit from year to year could be greater.

A36 Government grants

Contents

1 Introduction

1.1 Overview of IAS 20

IAS 20 *Accounting for Government Grants and Disclosure of Government Assistance* prescribes the accounting for, and disclosure of, government grants and other forms of government assistance. Government grants are recognised in profit or loss on a systematic basis over the periods in which the entity recognises expenses for the related costs for which the grants are intended to compensate, which in the case of grants related to assets requires setting up the grant as deferred income or deducting it from the carrying amount of the asset.

There are currently two Standards that address government grants – IAS 20 and IAS 41 *Agriculture*. IAS 20 is the general Standard which sets out the accounting and disclosure requirements for government grants and other forms of government assistance. IAS 41 deals with government grants related to agricultural activity, other than grants related to bearer plants and other biological assets carried on a cost basis, which are dealt with under IAS 20 (see **section 7** of **chapter A38**). In addition, SIC-10 *Government Assistance – No Specific Relation to Operating Activities* deals with government assistance granted subject to conditions that may not be specifically related to the operating activities of the entity (see **2.2**).

1.2 Amendments to IAS 20 since the last edition of this manual

None. IAS 20 was most recently amended in June 2011.

2 Scope

2.1 Scope – IAS 20

IAS 20 should be applied in accounting for government grants (as defined in **section 3**), and in the disclosure of government grants and other forms of government assistance. [IAS 20:1]

The Standard does not deal with:

[IAS 20:2]

* the special problems arising in accounting for government grants in financial statements reflecting the effects of changing prices or in supplementary information of a similar nature;

* government assistance that is provided for an entity in the form of benefits that are available in determining taxable profit or loss or that are determined or limited on the basis of income tax liability (such as

income tax holidays, investment tax credits, accelerated depreciation allowances and reduced income tax rates);

- government participation in the ownership of the entity; or

- government grants covered by IAS 41 *Agriculture* (see **chapter A38**).

2.2   SIC-10 *Government Assistance – No Specific Relation to Operating Activities*

SIC-10 *Government Assistance – No Specific Relation to Operating Activities* addresses the classification of government assistance that is not specifically related to the operating activities of the entity (e.g. transfers of resources by governments to entities that operate in a particular industry). The Interpretation concludes that government assistance to an entity will meet the definition of government grants even if there are no conditions specifically relating to the operating activities of the entity other than the requirement to operate in certain regions or industry sectors. Such grants should therefore be accounted for under IAS 20. [SIC-10:3]

3   Definitions

IAS 20:3 provides the following definitions for terms used in the Standard.

- **Government** refers to government, government agencies and similar bodies, whether local, national or international.

- **Government assistance** is action by government designed to provide an economic benefit specific to an entity or range of entities qualifying under certain criteria. Government assistance excludes benefits provided only indirectly through action affecting general trading conditions, such as the provision of infrastructure in development areas or the imposition of trading constraints on competitors.

- **Government grants** are assistance by government in the form of transfers of resources to an entity in return for past or future compliance with certain conditions relating to the operating activities of the entity.

> For the purposes of IAS 20, government grants represent a particular form of government assistance involving awards given in return for the fulfilment of conditions. They are sometimes called by other names (e.g. subsidies, subventions or premiums).

The following forms of government assistance are not classified as government grants:

- those that cannot reasonably have a value placed upon them (e.g. free technical or marketing advice or export credit guarantees); and

- transactions with government that are indistinguishable from the normal trading transactions of the entity (e.g. a government procurement policy that is responsible for a significant part of the entity's sales).

- **Grants related to assets** are government grants whose primary condition is that the entity qualifying for them should purchase, construct or otherwise acquire long-term assets. There may also be subsidiary conditions restricting the type or location of the assets, or the periods during which they are to be acquired or held.

- **Grants related to income** are government grants other than those related to assets.

- **Forgivable loans** are loans which the lender undertakes to waive repayment of under certain prescribed conditions.

4   Recognition of government grants

4.1   General principles

A government grant is not recognised until there is reasonable assurance that:

[IAS 20:7]

- the entity will comply with the conditions attaching to it; and

- the grant will be received. Receipt of a grant is not of itself conclusive evidence that the conditions attaching to the grant have been or will be fulfilled.

IAS 20 does not define 'reasonable assurance'. One of the recognition criteria included in the *Conceptual Framework for Financial Reporting*, however, is that it must be probable that any future economic benefit associated with an item will flow to or from an entity. Therefore, 'reasonable assurance' can be appropriately interpreted in this context as meaning that both compliance with the conditions attaching to a grant, and the receipt of the grant, are probable.

The manner in which a grant is received does not affect the accounting treatment adopted. Thus, a grant is accounted for in the same manner whether it is received in cash or as a reduction of a liability to the government, or in the form of non-monetary assets. [IAS 20:9]

A forgivable loan from government, for which the government has undertaken to waive repayment under certain prescribed conditions, is treated as a government grant when there is reasonable assurance that the entity will meet the terms for forgiveness of the loan. [IAS 20:10] Specific rules apply for government loans at below-market rates of interest (see **4.3**).

Once a government grant is recognised, any related contingent liability or contingent asset is dealt with in accordance with IAS 37 *Provisions, Contingent Liabilities and Contingent Assets*. [IAS 20:11]

4.2 Recognition in profit or loss

4.2.1 Government grants to be recognised in profit or loss on a systematic basis

Government grants are recognised in profit or loss on a systematic basis over the periods in which the entity recognises as expenses the related costs for which the grants are intended to compensate. [IAS 20:12]

IAS 20 clearly rules out what is referred to as the 'capital approach' to the accounting treatment of government grants (under which grants are recognised outside profit or loss), in favour of the 'income approach'. The arguments in support of the income approach are as follows:

[IAS 20:15]

- government grants are receipts from a source other than shareholders, and therefore they should not be recognised directly in equity but should be recognised in profit or loss in appropriate periods;

- government grants are rarely given free of obligations, but are earned by the entity through compliance with the conditions attached and, therefore, ought to be recognised in profit or loss over the periods in which the entity recognises as expenses the related costs for which the grant is intended to compensate; and

- just as income and other taxes are expenses, it is logical to deal with government grants, which are an extension of fiscal policies, in profit or loss.

Consistent with IAS 1 *Presentation of Financial Statements*, the income approach requires application of the accruals concept by recognising government grants in profit or loss on a systematic basis over the periods in which the entity recognises as expenses the related costs. In other words, grants are not recognised on receipt unless no rational basis exists for allocating the grant to a period other than the one in which it was received. [IAS 20:16]

In most cases, it is not difficult to identify the periods over which expenditure relating to a government grant is recognised. For example, grants related to depreciable assets are usually recognised in profit or loss over the periods in which depreciation expense on those assets is recognised, corresponding to the useful lives of the assets. [IAS 20:17]

Grants related to non-depreciable assets may have conditions attached, and thus are recognised in profit or loss over the periods in which the costs of meeting those conditions are incurred. For example, a grant of freehold land may be conditional upon the erection of a building on the site and it may be appropriate to recognise the grant in profit or loss over the life of the building. [IAS 20:18]

4.2.2 Government grants receivable as compensation for past expenses or losses, or for the purpose of giving immediate financial support

In some instances, a government grant may be receivable as compensation for expenses or losses already incurred in a previous accounting period. Alternatively, a grant may be receivable for the purpose of giving immediate financial support to the entity with no future related costs. In such circumstances, the grant is recognised in profit or loss in the period in which it becomes receivable, with disclosures provided to ensure the effect is understood. [IAS 20:20]

4.2.3 Government grants subject to multiple conditions

Grants are sometimes received as part of a package of financial or fiscal aid to which a number of conditions are attached. In such circumstances, care is needed in identifying which of the conditions give rise to costs and expenses, since those are the conditions that determine the period over which the grant is earned. It may be appropriate to allocate part of a grant on one basis and part on another. [IAS 20:19]

4.2.4 Profit or loss presentation of government grants related to assets used in the production of inventories

Example 4.2.4

Profit or loss presentation of government grants related to assets used in the production of inventories

Entity X received a government grant for the purchase of new machinery for use in its production plant. There are no other conditions attached to the government grant. The machinery is used to produce inventories for sale in the ordinary course of business. Depreciation of the machinery is reflected in the cost of inventories (cost of conversion). As permitted by IAS 20:24 (see **6.1**), Entity X recognises the government grant on a gross basis (i.e. by recognising deferred income in the statement of financial position).

How should Entity X recognise the amortisation of the deferred income related to the government grant?

IAS 20:12 (see **4.2.1**) specifies the period in which the grant should be recognised in profit or loss but it does not indicate the manner in which it is eventually recognised in profit or loss. Therefore, there may be more than one acceptable method.

The preferred treatment is to account for the amortisation of the deferred income in the same manner as the depreciation of the related machinery. Under this method, the amortisation of the deferred income should be included in production overheads and reflected in the cost of inventories (thereby reducing the cost of inventories). This treatment is preferred because it results in the same profit or loss treatment as if the grant had been recognised on a net basis (i.e. offset against the cost of the asset).

However, it may also be acceptable to recognise the amortisation of the grant directly in profit or loss. Under this approach, the deferred income is not amortised until the depreciation of the machinery eventually affects profit or loss (i.e. the depreciation of the machinery 'transits' through inventories but the amortisation of the government grant does not). This method is considered acceptable provided that the amortisation is recognised in profit or loss in the same period as the cost of inventories that include the depreciation of the machinery.

4.2.5 Grants related to depreciable assets with increasing residual value

An issue on which IAS 20 is silent relates to depreciable assets whose residual value increases over time. Such an asset will initially be depreciated, but often depreciation will cease before the end of the asset's useful life because its residual value has increased so as to exceed its carrying amount. If the associated grant has been presented as deferred income (see **6.1**), the question arises as to how that grant should be recognised in profit or loss.

The following approaches are considered acceptable, depending on the circumstances.

- The whole of the grant is recognised over the asset's useful life, regardless of how much depreciation expense is recognised. For example, if an asset has a useful life of 40 years, 2.5 per cent of the grant would be released each year irrespective of whether and how the depreciation expense continues to be recognised. This approach may result in a relatively poor matching of grant income to depreciation expense, but it might be adopted for reasons of simplicity when government grants are not particularly material.

- The grant is matched to the initial cost of the asset, so that it is in part recognised with the depreciation expense but with the balance being recognised only on disposal. For example, if an asset was initially recognised for a cost of CU1,000, and ceased to be depreciated when its carrying amount was CU860 (because the asset's residual value had risen to exceed the carrying amount), 14 per cent of the grant would by then have been recognised in profit or loss, with 86 per cent being held in the statement of financial position and released only on disposal.

- A proportion of the remaining grant is released each year, so that the remaining balance reflects the amount of the asset yet to be amortised (i.e. the excess of carrying amount over updated residual value) as a proportion of expected total depreciation on the asset.

IAS 20:12 indicates that government grants should be recognised "on a systematic basis over the periods in which the entity recognises as expenses the related costs for which the grants are intended to compensate". The second approach above may be judged closest to the requirements of IAS 20:12 if, in fact, the grant is intended to compensate for both the use of the asset and its subsequent disposal. It may also be the most appropriate approach if there are any arrangements under which a proportion of the grant must be repaid by reference to sale proceeds received.

It may be judged, however, that the grant is intended only to compensate for the costs of using the asset, not disposing of it; if so, the third approach described above perhaps best approximates this. The third approach is, arguably, also closest to the requirement of IAS 20:17 that grants for depreciable assets should be "recognised in profit or loss over the periods and in the proportions in which depreciation expense on those assets is recognised". The application of the third approach is illustrated in **example 4.2.5**.

Example 4.2.5

Grant relating to a depreciable asset with increasing residual value recognised as a proportion of total expected depreciation

An entity purchases a film library on 1 January 20X1 for CU1,000, and receives a related grant of CU200. There is no obligation to repay the grant if the library is subsequently sold. The estimated useful life of the film library to the entity is five years, and the pattern of depreciation for the five years is as follows.

	Opening carrying amount	Opening remaining life	Estimated residual value	Depreciation recognised
	CU	(years)	CU	CU
Year to Dec 20X1	1,000	5	600	80
Year to Dec 20X2	920	4	720	50
Year to Dec 20X3	870	3	840	10
Year to Dec 20X4	860	2	900	–
Year to Dec 20X5	860	1	920	–

The release of the grant would be calculated as follows.

	Cumulative depreciation recognised	Estimated total depreciation	Proportion not yet recognised	Closing grant balance	Grant recognised in profit or loss
	CU	CU	%	CU	CU
Year to Dec 20X1	80	400	80.0	160	40
Year to Dec 20X2	130	280	53.6	107	53
Year to Dec 20X3	140	160	12.5	25	82
Year to Dec 20X4	140	140	–	–	25
Year to Dec 20X5	140	140	–	–	–

4.3   Government loans at below-market rate of interest

The benefit of a government loan at a below-market rate of interest is treated as a government grant. The loan is recognised and measured in accordance with IFRS 9 *Financial Instruments* (or, for entities that have not yet adopted IFRS 9, IAS 39 *Financial Instruments: Recognition and Measurement*). The benefit of the below-market rate of interest is measured as the difference between the initial carrying amount of the loan determined in accordance with IFRS 9 (IAS 39) and the proceeds received. [IAS 20:10A]

The benefit so calculated is accounted for in accordance with the general principles of IAS 20. The entity is required to consider the conditions and obligations that have been, or must be, met when identifying the costs for which the benefit of the loan is intended to compensate. [IAS 20:10A]

The requirements of IAS 20:10A, described above, are applied prospectively to government loans received in periods beginning on or after 1 January 2009 (or earlier, if the entity chose to apply the requirements from an earlier date). [IAS 20:43] The requirement for prospective application was intended to avoid the necessity to measure the fair value of loans at a past date.

For government loans received in periods before IAS 20:10A was applied, IAS 20:37 stated that "[l]oans at nil or low interest rates are a form of government assistance, but the benefit is not quantified by the imputation of interest". Therefore, prior to the application of IAS 20:10A, entities did not quantify the benefit inherent in government-subsidised loans, and the only requirement was that the nature, extent and duration of such loans be disclosed if necessary in order that the financial statements not be misleading.

Example 4.3

Government loan at below-market rate of interest

Entity Q receives a loan of CU3 million from the government. The loan is at 2 per cent interest and is repayable in five years. Using prevailing market interest rates of 5 per cent, the fair value of the loan is calculated at CU2,610,347.

Under IFRS 9:5.1.1 (or, for entities that have not yet adopted IFRS 9, IAS 39:43), the loan is recognised at CU2,610,347. The difference between this amount and the proceeds received (CU389,653) is the benefit derived from the below-market interest and is recognised as deferred income. Therefore, on the date that the loan is received, the following journal entry is recorded.

		CU	CU
Dr	Cash	3,000,000	
Cr	Government loan		2,610,347
Cr	Deferred income (government grant)		389,653

Initial recognition of loan at below-market rate of interest.

The interest expense is recognised in profit or loss at 5 per cent in accordance with IFRS 9 (IAS 39).

	Opening balance on loan	Interest calculated at 5%	Interest paid (at 2%) + capital repayment in Year 5	Closing balance on loan
	CU	CU	CU	CU
Year 1	2,610,347	130,517	(60,000)	2,680,864
Year 2	2,680,864	134,044	(60,000)	2,754,908
Year 3	2,754,908	137,745	(60,000)	2,832,653
Year 4	2,832,653	141,633	(60,000)	2,914,286
Year 5	2,914,286	145,714	(3,060,000)	nil

In accordance with IAS 20:12, the amount of the government grant (CU389,653) is recognised in profit or loss on a systematic basis over the periods in which Entity Q recognises as expenses the related costs for which the grant is intended to compensate.

The costs for which the below-market interest rate is intended to compensate are assessed on the basis of the particular circumstances. For example:

• the loan may be intended to subsidise training costs over a three-year period. The costs may be incurred on a straight-line basis, in which case the government grant will be released to income on a straight-line basis – i.e. CU129,884 (CU389,653/3) each year for three years;

• the loan may be intended as a rescue measure for the purpose of giving immediate financial support. In such circumstances, under IAS 20:20

(see **4.2.2**), it may be appropriate to recognise the benefit in profit or loss immediately; or

- the loan may be intended to finance a depreciable asset. In this case, the benefit would be recognised on the same basis as depreciation.

5   Measurement of non-monetary grants

If a government grant takes the form of a non-monetary asset, such as land or other resources, it is usual to account for the grant and the asset at fair value. [IAS 20:23]

Fair value is defined as "the price that would be received to sell an asset or paid to transfer a liability in an orderly transaction between market participants at the measurement date. (See IFRS 13 *Fair Value Measurement.*)" [IAS 20:3]

Note, however, that the recognition of non-monetary grants at fair value is not mandatory. IAS 20 allows as an alternative treatment that the grant and the asset be recognised at a nominal amount. [IAS 20:23]

6   Presentation

6.1   Grants related to assets

IAS 20 permits two methods of presenting government grants related to assets in the statement of financial position, namely either:

[IAS 20:24]

- recognising the grant as deferred income, which is recognised in profit or loss on a systematic basis over the useful life of the asset; or

- deducting the grant in calculating the carrying amount of the asset, in which case the grant is recognised in profit or loss over the life of a depreciable asset by way of a reduced depreciation expense.

While IAS 20 permits netting off government grants against the carrying amount of related assets, it goes on to note that such transactions can have a significant impact on the cash flows of an entity. For this reason, and also to show the gross investment in assets, the statement of cash flows often discloses as separate items the purchase of assets and the receipt of related grants, regardless of whether the grant is deducted from the asset for presentation purposes in the statement of financial position. [IAS 20:28]

Example 6.1

Presentation of grants related to assets

At the beginning of 20X1, an entity invests CU1,000,000 in an item of equipment, which has an anticipated useful life of five years. Depreciation is recognised on a straight-line basis. In the year of acquisition, the entity receives a government grant of CU250,000 towards purchase of the equipment, which is conditional on specified employment targets being achieved within the next three years (i.e. to the end of 20X3). Under the alternative methods permitted under IAS 20, the presentation is as follows.

Method A: Grant shown as deferred income

	CU
20X1:	
Credit to deferred income – grant received	250,000
Less: recognised in profit or loss (CU250,000 / 5 years)	(50,000)
Deferred income balance at year end	200,000
Cost of equipment	1,000,000
Depreciation expense (CU1,000,000 / 5 years)	(200,000)
Carrying amount of equipment at year end	800,000
Years 20X2 to 20X5:	
Deferred income recognised in profit or loss	50,000
Depreciation expense	(200,000)
Net expense in profit or loss (CU750,000 / 5 years)	(150,000)

Note that the condition requiring specified employment targets to be met within three years is not relevant for determining the period over which deferred income is recognised in profit or loss. The condition requires disclosure, however, as a contingency.

Method B: Grant deducted from cost of asset

	CU
20X1:	
Cost of equipment	1,000,000
Less: grant received	(250,000)
Net cost of equipment	750,000
Depreciation expense (CU750,000 / 5 years)	(150,000)
Carrying amount of equipment at year end	600,000
Years 20X2 to 20X5:	
Depreciation expense	150,000

It is evident from **example 6.1** that, while the net impact of the two methods on the reported result for each year is in these circumstances identical, the presentation in each case is very different. Method A clearly separates the asset from the deferred income, and also shows the crediting of the grant separately as income, while recognising the depreciation expense in full. Method B nets off the grant against the asset, while showing only the depreciation expense, reduced by the amount of the grant that would otherwise have been recognised separately in profit or loss.

6.2 Grants related to income

IAS 20 permits two methods of presentation of grants related to income as part of profit or loss:

[IAS 20:29]

- either separately or under a general heading such as 'other income'; or

- as a deduction in reporting the related expense.

Again, the Standard demonstrates its flexibility in permitting, as equally acceptable, alternative methods of presentation of government grants. Essentially, IAS 20 seeks to accommodate two rather differing views on the treatment of income-related grants, namely those who oppose netting off income and expense items and prefer to keep disclosure of the grant separate for the purposes of comparison, and those who argue that, because the entity might not have incurred the expense if the grant had not been available, it might be misleading to show the expense without offsetting the grant.

7 Grants related to agricultural activities

IAS 41 *Agriculture* prescribes a different treatment for government grants related to agricultural activities (other than government grants related to bearer plants). The relevant rules are discussed in **section 7** of **chapter A38**.

8 Repayment of government grants

IAS 20 requires that a government grant that becomes repayable should be accounted for as a change in accounting estimate in accordance with IAS 8 *Accounting Policies, Changes in Accounting Estimates and Errors*. [IAS 20:32] As described in **chapter A5**, a change in estimate is accounted for in the period of change if the change affects that period only, or in the period of change and in future periods, if the change affects both.

The accounting treatment for the repayment of a government grant is as follows:

[IAS 20:32]

- repayment of a grant related to income should be applied first against any unamortised deferred credit recognised in respect of the grant. To the extent that repayment exceeds any such deferred credit, or when no deferred credit exists, the repayment should be recognised immediately as an expense; and

- repayment of a grant related to an asset should be recognised by increasing the carrying amount of the asset or reducing the deferred income balance by the amount repayable. The cumulative additional depreciation that would have been recognised in profit or loss to date in the absence of the grant should be recognised immediately in profit or loss.

Example 8

Repayment of a government grant

The facts are the same as in **example 6.1**. At the end of 20X3, it is evident that the entity has failed to fulfil the employment conditions attached to the receipt of the asset-related grant. The grant therefore becomes repayable. Under the two methods of presentation of the grant, the treatment of the repayment is as follows.

Method A: Grant shown as deferred income

	CU
Grant received, credited in 20X1 to deferred income	250,000
Recognised in profit or loss 20X1 to 20X3 (3 × CU50,000)	(150,000)
Deferred income balance at end of 20X3, before repayment of grant	100,000
Total repayment of grant	250,000
Repayment debited to deferred income balance	(100,000)
Balance of repayment recognised in profit or loss	150,000

Note that, under this method, the repayment of the grant has no effect on the carrying amount of the equipment or on the depreciation expense recognised.

Method B: Grant deducted from cost of asset	
	CU
Cost of equipment	1,000,000
Less: grant received in 20X1	(250,000)
Net cost of equipment	750,000
Depreciation expense recognised 20X1 to 20X3 (3 × CU150,000)	(450,000)
Carrying amount of equipment at end of 20X3, before repayment of grant	300,000
Add back grant repayable	250,000
	550,000
Cumulative additional depreciation recognised in profit or loss for 20X1 to 20X3 (3 × CU50,000)	(150,000)
Carrying amount of equipment at end of 20X3, after repayment of grant	400,000

The circumstances surrounding the repayment of a government grant may require consideration regarding the possible impairment of the new carrying amount of the asset. [IAS 20:33] This could occur, for example, if the repayment of the grant resulted from a failure to comply with government regulations or conditions attached to receipt of the grant, which, in turn, reflected adverse changes in the operating environment of the entity.

9   Disclosure

IAS 20 requires the following disclosures in respect of government grants:

[IAS 20:39]

- the accounting policy adopted for government grants, including the methods of presentation adopted in the financial statements;

- the nature and extent of government grants recognised in the financial statements and an indication of other forms of government assistance from which the entity has directly benefited; and

- unfulfilled conditions and other contingencies attaching to government assistance that has been recognised.

When grants relate to income, the Standard suggests that:

[IAS 20:31]

- separate disclosure of a grant may be necessary for a proper understanding of the financial statements; and

- disclosure of the effect of the grant on any item of income or expense that is required to be disclosed separately is usually appropriate.

Separate disclosure should, in particular, be considered when a grant has been netted against the related expense in profit or loss.

IAS 20 also requires an indication of forms of government assistance other than government grants from which the entity has directly benefited. [IAS 20:39] Although the benefit resulting from such forms of assistance may not be measurable, the impact of items such as free technical or marketing advice, or guarantees should be disclosed where it is significant. Even though such assistance is not recognised as income in the financial statements, it may benefit the entity to such an extent that disclosure of the nature, extent and duration of the assistance is necessary for the financial statements not to be misleading. [IAS 20:34 - 36]

A37 Financial reporting in hyperinflationary economies

Contents

1 Introduction

1.1 Overview of IAS 29

IAS 29 *Financial Reporting in Hyperinflationary Economies* applies when an entity's functional currency is that of a hyperinflationary economy. The Standard does not prescribe when hyperinflation arises but requires the financial statements (and corresponding figures for previous periods) of an entity with a functional currency that is hyperinflationary to be restated for the changes in the general pricing power of the functional currency.

> The premise underlying IAS 29 is that, because money rapidly loses its purchasing power in a hyperinflationary economy, to report an entity's operating results and financial position in the currency of that economy without restatement would be meaningless to a user of the financial statements. Comparative information would have no value, and even the profits of a single financial period would be distorted. For example, the difference between the cost at which inventories are acquired and the price at which they are sold would not only reflect a normal trading profit margin, but also include the impact of a price change that is beyond the control of the entity.

1.2 Amendments to IAS 29 since the last edition of this manual

None. IAS 29 was most recently amended in May 2008.

2 Scope

IAS 29 addresses the issues associated with financial reporting when the functional currency of an entity (i.e. the currency of the primary economic environment in which the entity operates) is that of a hyperinflationary economy, and it applies equally to the financial statements of individual entities and consolidated financial statements. [IAS 29:1]

The Standard also applies equally to financial statements based on historical cost accounting and those based on current cost accounting (i.e. those reflecting the effects of changes in the specific prices of assets held). In either case, the financial statements should be stated in terms of the measuring unit current at the end of the reporting period.

All entities that report in the currency of a hyperinflationary economy should, ideally, apply IAS 29 from the same date in order to achieve consistency in financial reporting between entities. However, this objective will not always be achieved. The Standard places responsibility on individual entities to consider the potential impact of hyperinflation and to apply IAS 29 from the beginning of the reporting period in which they identify the existence of hyperinflation in the country in whose currency they report. [IAS 29:4]

In practice, very few countries fall within the scope of the Standard. Whether or not a country is considered to be experiencing hyperinflation for the purposes of IAS 29 will generally be determined by a consensus of the accounting profession, rather than by each entity individually.

3 Definition of hyperinflation

IAS 29 does not establish an absolute rate at which hyperinflation is deemed to arise. Rather, it describes characteristics that may indicate that an economy is hyperinflationary. It is left to the judgement of preparers of financial statements to determine when restatement of financial statements in accordance with IAS 29 becomes necessary. [IAS 29:3]

Characteristics of the economic environment of a country which indicate the existence of hyperinflation include:

[IAS 29:3]

- the general population prefers to keep its wealth in non-monetary assets or in a relatively stable foreign currency. Amounts of local currency held are immediately invested to maintain purchasing power;

- the general population regards monetary amounts not in terms of the local currency but in terms of a relatively stable foreign currency. Prices may be quoted in that currency;

- sales and purchases on credit take place at prices that compensate for the expected loss of purchasing power during the credit period, even if the period is short;

- interest rates, wages and prices are linked to a price index; and

- the cumulative inflation rate over three years approaches, or exceeds, 100 per cent.

4 Restatement of financial statements

4.1 General principles for restatement of financial statements

The financial statements of an entity whose functional currency is the currency of a hyperinflationary economy should be stated in terms of the measuring unit current at the end of the reporting period. [IAS 29:8]

IAS 29 notes that one of the most important factors in restating financial statements will be consistency from period to period in applying the procedures and making the judgements required. In other words, the precision of the amounts calculated is less important than consistency of treatment. Because the aim is to provide meaningful financial statements, whatever approach is adopted must be applied consistently in order to achieve comparability between the results for different accounting periods. [IAS 29:10]

4.2   The status of restated financial statements

The financial statements prepared under the requirements of IAS 29 should be the definitive financial statements of the entity – they should not be seen as supplementary information. Therefore, the Standard prohibits the presentation of information adjusted for the effects of hyperinflation as a supplement to unrestated financial statements. In addition, separate presentation of a set of financial statements before restatement is discouraged. [IAS 29:7]

In hyperinflationary countries, entities are often required to prepare unrestated financial statements for taxation or other authorities. When a set of unrestated financial statements is appended to the IAS 29 financial statements, or otherwise shown separately (although this is discouraged), the entity will need to make clear that the status of the unrestated financial information is subordinate to the financial statements prepared in accordance with IAS 29.

4.3   Required adjustments

IAS 29 requires the following adjustments to amounts reported in the currency of a hyperinflationary economy:

[IAS 29:8 & 9]

- the current period's financial statements should be stated in terms of the measuring unit current at the end of the reporting period;

- the corresponding figures for the previous period, and any information in respect of earlier periods, should also be stated in terms of the measuring unit current at the end of the reporting period; and

- the gain or loss on the net monetary position (see **4.5**) should be included in profit or loss, and separately disclosed.

Restatements are made by applying a general price index. Monetary items, which are already stated at the measuring unit current at the end of the reporting period, are not restated. Other items are restated based on the change in the general price index between the date those items were acquired, incurred or revalued and the end of the reporting period.

4.4   General price index

In order to express financial statements in terms of the measuring unit current at the end of the reporting period, amounts are restated by applying a general price index. The general price index to be used is one that reflects changes in general purchasing power. [IAS 29:37] No further guidance is provided in IAS 29 on this topic.

The Standard states that it is desirable for all entities reporting in the currency of any particular hyperinflationary economy to use the same index, in order to achieve comparability between the financial statements of different entities. [IAS 29:37]

> Any reporting entity implementing the principles of IAS 29 should therefore first consider which price index is used by other local reporting entities, particularly those in the same industry, and apply that index, provided that it is believed to be an indicator of changes in general purchasing power.

A general price index may not be available, particularly for the restatement of the historical cost of property, plant and equipment acquired over an extended period. In such circumstances, the inflation rate may be estimated by considering the depreciation of the exchange rate of the hyperinflationary currency against a relatively stable foreign currency. [IAS 29:17]

> In the absence of a reliable, independently determined index (either by the government or the private sector), the movement in the exchange rate between a stable currency (e.g. the US dollar) and the local currency from the beginning to the end of the reporting period may be used as a guideline to determine the index. In making this estimate, it is important that the impact of inflation in the stable currency is excluded.

Example 4.4

Imputing a general price index

Assume that the exchange rate at 1 January 20X5 between Local Currency and Stable Currency is 200:1. At 31 December 20X5, the exchange rate is 350:1. There has been a 75 per cent depreciation in Local Currency in relation to Stable Currency. Assuming that inflation in the Stable Currency economy for the 20X5 calendar year is 3 per cent, the index should be an increase of 80.25 per cent (1.75 × 1.03).

4.5   Gain or loss on net monetary position

An entity's net monetary position is the difference between its monetary assets and monetary liabilities. Monetary items are defined as money held and items to be received or paid in money. All other items are non-monetary.

> The following table lists a number of the most common monetary and non-monetary items.

Monetary items	Non-monetary items
Cash	Property, plant and equipment
Bank balances and loans	Intangible assets
Deposits*	Goodwill
Employee benefit liability**	Shareholders' equity
Accrued expenses	Prepaid expenses*
Trade payables	Investments in associates
Taxation	Advances received on sales or paid on purchases provided that they are linked to specific sales or purchases
Debt securities	Inventories
Trade receivables	Allowance for inventory obsolescence (because inventories are non-monetary)
Allowance for doubtful debts (because trade receivables are monetary)	Deferred income
Notes and other receivables	Equity securities
Notes and other payables	Provisions to be settled by the delivery of a non-monetary asset
Accrued Income	
Holiday pay provision	
Deferred tax assets/liabilities***	
Liabilities recognised for lease contracts	

* When an entity has prepaid expenses, it is necessary to consider whether the prepayment is refundable. When it is refundable, it is similar in nature to a deposit and, therefore, is a monetary item (i.e. it is a right to receive a fixed or determinable number of units of currency). Conversely, when it is not refundable, it is non-monetary (see paragraph 16 of IAS 21 *The Effects of Changes in Foreign Exchange Rates*).

** It may be appropriate to regard a defined benefit asset or obligation as a monetary item. But it is possible to argue that some components, particularly relating to equity securities, should be regarded as non-monetary. However, for most entities, this would lead to a level of complexity that is unwarranted.

*** The restatement of deferred tax assets and liabilities is discussed at **4.6**.

In a period of inflation, an entity holding an excess of monetary assets over monetary liabilities loses purchasing power, and an entity with an excess of monetary liabilities over monetary assets gains purchasing power to the extent that the assets and liabilities are not linked to a price level. [IAS 29:27] The detailed calculation of the gain or loss on net monetary position is dealt with at **5.3**.

4.6   Deferred taxes

The restatement of financial statements in accordance with IAS 29 may give rise to differences between the carrying amount of individual assets and liabilities and their tax bases. These differences are accounted for in accordance with IAS 12 *Income Taxes*. [IAS 29:32]

For financial statements restated under IAS 29, deferred tax is not calculated by simply indexing the historical cost deferred tax amount. Instead, a revised closing deferred tax calculation should be performed using the carrying amounts and tax bases that exist after the restatement for hyperinflationary purposes. Generally, there is no tax relief for hyperinflation and, as such, the tax base will remain unchanged. The difference between the opening restated deferred tax balance, and the revised closing deferred tax balance, is the deferred tax expense or credit for the period.

Example 4.6

Restatement of deferred taxation

At 31 December 20X1, an entity recognised a deferred tax liability related to a non-current asset with a carrying amount of 1,600 and a tax base of 750. The resulting temporary difference of 850 gave rise to a deferred tax liability of 255 (tax rate 30 per cent).

At 31 December 20X2, assuming an index rate of 1.5 and no other movements in the carrying amount or the tax base of the asset, the deferred tax liability is calculated as follows.

Carrying amount (1,600 × 1.5)	2,400
Tax base	(750)
Temporary difference	1,650
Deferred tax at 30%	495

The opening deferred tax balance of 255 should be indexed by 1.5. The effect of this is that the comparative information in respect of deferred tax is restated to 382.50. In performing a revised deferred tax computation at the end of the current year, the closing deferred tax balance should be 495. Accordingly, the difference between the closing deferred tax amount of 495 and the restated opening deferred tax amount of 382.50 (i.e. 112.50) is the current year deferred tax expense.

4.7   Statement of cash flows

IAS 29 requires that all items in the statement of cash flows are expressed in terms of the measuring unit current at the end of the reporting period. [IAS 29:33]

4.8 Consolidated financial statements

A parent that reports in the currency of a hyperinflationary economy may have subsidiaries that also report in the currencies of hyperinflationary economies. The financial statements of any such subsidiary need to be restated by applying the general price index of the country in whose currency it reports before they are included in the consolidated financial statements issued by the parent. When such a subsidiary is a foreign subsidiary, its restated financial statements are translated at closing rates. The financial statements of subsidiaries that do not report in the currencies of hyperinflationary economies are dealt with in accordance with IAS 21 (see **chapter A19**). [IAS 29:35]

If financial statements with different reporting dates are consolidated, all items, whether non-monetary or monetary, need to be restated into the measuring unit current at the date of the consolidated financial statements. [IAS 29:36]

4.9 IFRIC 7 *Applying the Restatement Approach under IAS 29 Financial Reporting in Hyperinflationary Economies*

IFRIC 7 *Applying the Restatement Approach under IAS 29 Financial Reporting in Hyperinflationary Economies* contains guidance on how an entity would restate its financial statements in the first year in which it identifies the existence of hyperinflation in the economy of its functional currency.

In the first year in which an entity identifies the existence of hyperinflation, it must start applying IAS 29 as if the economy had always been hyperinflationary. Therefore, an entity recreates an opening statement of financial position at the beginning of the earliest annual accounting period presented in the restated financial statements so that:

[IFRIC 7:3]

- non-monetary items measured at historical cost are restated to reflect the effect of inflation from the date the assets were acquired and the liabilities were incurred or assumed until the end of the reporting period; and

- non-monetary items carried at amounts current at dates other than those of acquisition or incurrence are restated to reflect the effect of inflation from the dates those carrying amounts were determined until the end of the reporting period.

Deferred tax amounts in the opening statement of financial position for the reporting period are determined as follows:

[IFRIC 7:4]

- deferred tax items are remeasured in accordance with IAS 12 after the entity has restated the nominal carrying amounts of its non-monetary items at the beginning of the reporting period by applying the measuring unit at that date; and

- those deferred tax items are restated for the change in the measuring unit from the beginning of the reporting period to the end of that reporting period.

The approach above is applied in the opening statement of financial position of any comparative periods presented in the restated financial statements for the reporting period in which the entity applies IAS 29.

All corresponding amounts (including deferred tax items) in subsequent financial statements are restated by applying the change in the measuring unit for the subsequent reporting period only to the restated financial statements for the previous reporting period. [IFRIC 7:5]

The Interpretation is accompanied by an illustrative example which shows the mechanics of the restatement approach for deferred tax items.

5   Historical cost financial statements

5.1   Statement of financial position

5.1.1   Approach for components of historical cost statement of financial position – summary

The approaches required by IAS 29 for the components of a historical cost statement of financial position are summarised in the table below. Specific categories are considered in **5.1.2** to **5.1.7**.

Item in the statement of financial position	Treatment	Examples
Assets and liabilities having a predefined link to price changes	Adjust in accordance with the particular agreements in place	Index-linked bonds and loans
Other monetary items	These do not require restatement because they are already expressed in terms of the measuring unit current at the end of the reporting period	Cash, receivables and payables

Item in the statement of financial position	Treatment	Examples
Non-monetary assets carried at a valuation that is current at the end of the reporting period	These do not require restatement because they are already expressed in terms of the measuring unit current at the end of the reporting period	Inventories carried at net realisable value. Investment property carried at fair value
Non-monetary assets carried at a valuation that is not current at the end of the reporting period	Restatement is required from the date of the valuation to the end of the reporting period	Property revalued at a date other than the end of the reporting period
Other items in the statement of financial position, i.e. Items carried at cost, or cost less depreciation and impairment losses	These are restated in terms of the measuring unit current at the end of the reporting period by applying a general price index	When carried at cost: property, plant and equipment, investments (if carried at cost, in accordance with IAS 39), inventories, goodwill and intangible assets. Also prepaid expenses and deferred income.

5.1.2 Property, plant and equipment

5.1.2.1 Property, plant and equipment carried at valuation

Property, plant and equipment carried at a valuation that is current at the end of the reporting period need not be restated because the assets are already expressed in terms of the measuring unit current at the end of the reporting period. [IAS 29:14]

For property, plant and equipment carried at a valuation that is not current at the end of the reporting period, the change in the general price index from the date of the last valuation of the item to the end of the reporting period is applied to the revalued amount. [IAS 29:18]

5.1.2.2 Property, plant and equipment carried at cost less accumulated depreciation and accumulated impairment losses

For property, plant and equipment stated at cost less depreciation and impairment losses, the change in the general price index from the date of acquisition of the item to the end of the reporting period is applied to the historical cost and, when relevant, accumulated depreciation and accumulated impairment losses. [IAS 29:15]

The treatment of items of property, plant and equipment that have been depreciated can often be complex. Cost is restated by adjusting the purchase price by the change in the index between the date of acquisition and the end of the reporting period. Depreciation arises over time and, therefore, the balance of accumulated depreciation brought forward at the beginning of each period should be adjusted by the change in the index between the beginning and the end of the period, while the depreciation expense for each period is calculated based on the index-adjusted cost at the end of the period. Another way to arrive at the same answer is to apply the depreciation rate to the historical cost and apply the index from the date of acquisition of the asset to the end of the reporting period.

Example 5.1.2.2

Restatement of property, plant and equipment

An entity acquires an item of property, plant and equipment on 31 December 20X1 for 1,000, when the general price index is 100. At 31 December 20X2, the index is 140 and the asset has been depreciated by 10 per cent. At 31 December 20X3, the index is 190 and the asset has been depreciated at 10 per cent for a second year.

	Balance brought forward	Indexing adjustment	Calculation of accumulated depreciation	Adjusted balance
Cost at 31 December 20X1	1,000	140/100		1,400
Accumulated depreciation			(1,400 × 10%)	(140)
At 31 December 20X2				1,260
Cost	1,400	190/140		1,900
Accumulated depreciation	(140)		(140 × 190/140) + (1,900 × 10%)*	(380)
At 31 December 20X3				1,520

* The depreciation expense for the period 1 January 20X3 to 31 December 20X3 can also be expressed as 1,000 × 10% × 190/100.

In the first period of application of IAS 29, it may be difficult to establish the basis for restatement of information due to the absence of detailed records of the acquisition dates of items of property, plant and equipment. In the rare circumstances when it is not practicable to make a reliable estimate, the Standard suggests that it may be appropriate to use an independent professional assessment of the value of the items as the basis for their restatement. [IAS 29:16]

5.1.3 Inventories

In the restatement of a historical cost statement of financial position:

[IAS 29:15]

- inventories of raw materials and merchandise are to be restated by applying the change in the general price index from the date of acquisition to the end of the reporting period; and

- work in progress and finished goods are restated from the dates on which the costs of purchase and of conversion were incurred. This may prove to be a complex exercise, particularly when products take a long period to manufacture, as illustrated in **example 5.1.3**.

Raw materials should be restated from acquisition to the end of the reporting period, taking into account whether FIFO or weighted average is applied.

For work in progress and finished goods:

- any historical cost depreciation included in the carrying amount should be restated; and

- raw material content and labour and overhead included in the carrying amount will have different ageing. For example, suppose that, on average, finished goods are one month old and, on average, there are four months of raw material inventories in finished goods. In that case, the labour and overhead content in finished goods should be indexed for one month only and the raw material content in finished goods should be indexed by five months.

Example 5.1.3

Restatement of inventories

An entity operating in a hyperinflationary economy is preparing financial statements at its period end, 31 December. Assume labour and overheads are utilised evenly over a period, and the following changes in the general price index apply:

31 August	100
30 September	105
31 October	110
30 November	115
31 December	120

		Historical cost at end of the reporting period	Indexing adjustment	31 December adjusted balance
Raw materials	Purchased 31 October	250	120/110	273
	Purchased 30 November	250	120/115	261
Work in progress	Use of raw materials purchased 30 September	500	120/105	571
	Labour / overheads incurred from 31 October to 31 December	500	120/115*	522
Finished goods	Use of raw materials purchased 31 August	500	120/100	600
	Labour / overheads incurred from 30 September to 31 December	500	120/112.5**	533
Total		2,500		2,760

*   115 is the average for October to December
**   112.5 is the average for September to December

5.1.4   Investments accounted for using the equity method

When the entity holds an investment that is accounted for using the equity method, and the investee reports in the currency of a hyperinflationary economy, the following steps are followed:

[IAS 29:20]

- the statement of financial position and statement of comprehensive income of the investee are restated in accordance with IAS 29 in order to calculate the investor's share of its net assets and profit or loss; and

- when the restated financial statements of the investee are expressed in a foreign currency, they are translated at closing rates.

5.1.5   Borrowing costs

In a hyperinflationary economy, the impact of inflation is usually recognised in borrowing costs. A loan agreement may provide for repayment of capital adjusted by a predefined index, with interest being charged at a 'normal' rate. Alternatively, loans may be negotiated at an interest rate in excess of the 'normal' rate that compensates for the loss in purchasing power of the money being loaned. When an entity operates in a hyperinflationary economy, only the 'normal' element of the borrowing costs may be capitalised (see **chapter A18**). It is inappropriate to capitalise that part of the borrowing costs that compensates for inflation. This portion should be expensed as incurred. [IAS 29:21]

When assets are acquired on deferred payment terms with no explicit charge for interest, and it is impracticable to impute an amount of interest, the Standard allows that such assets are restated from the payment date and not the date of purchase. [IAS 29:22]

The logic for the treatment outlined in the previous paragraph is as follows. Normally, if resources flow out of the entity at the later date without any additional cost, the net monetary position can only be affected from that date. However, in practice, in a hyperinflationary economy, credit is only likely to be given if the cost of the asset is increased to compensate the seller for the loss in purchasing power of the cash during the credit period. Therefore, it should be possible to impute an interest rate to the transaction and therefore capitalise the asset at a lower amount. The interest itself will be recognised in profit or loss and the asset will be restated from the date of purchase. If no amount of interest can be imputed, then a reasonable approximation to this technically 'correct' position may be achieved by including the asset in the accounts at the value actually paid and applying the index from the payment date.

5.1.6 Impairment

When a non-monetary item has been restated, the restated amount is compared with the item's recoverable amount. When the restated amount exceeds the recoverable amount, an impairment loss is recognised with the effect that:

[IAS 29:19]

- inventories will be written down to net realisable value in accordance with IAS 2 *Inventories* (see **chapter A11**); and

- items of property, plant and equipment, and intangible assets, will be reduced to their recoverable amount in accordance with IAS 36 *Impairment of Assets* (see **chapter A10**).

5.1.7 Equity

When IAS 29 is first applied, the components of owners' equity at the *beginning* of the period will be adjusted as follows:

[IAS 29:24]

- any revaluation surplus that arose in previous periods is eliminated (i.e. it is absorbed in adjusted retained earnings);

- with the exception of retained earnings, other components (equity, share premium and any other existing reserves) are restated by applying a general price index from the dates the components were contributed or otherwise arose; and

- restated retained earnings are calculated as the balancing figure after all adjustments have been made to all other components of the statement of financial position.

At the end of the first period, and in subsequent periods, all components of equity are again restated, this time by applying a general price index from the beginning of the period or the date of contribution, whichever is the later. These movements should be disclosed in the statement of changes in equity in accordance with IAS 1 *Presentation of Financial Statements*. [IAS 29:25]

> Note that the elimination of a revaluation surplus is required only when IAS 29 is first applied. IAS 29 does not include a requirement that subsequent revaluations of property, plant and equipment or intangible assets, to the extent that they exceed the remeasurement arising from inflation, should be recognised in retained earnings. Such revaluations should be recognised in a revaluation surplus.

Example 5.1.7

Restatement of components of equity relating to revalued property, plant and equipment

An entity acquires an item of property, plant and equipment on 31 December 20X1 for 1,000 when the general price index is 100. At 31 December 20X2, the index is 140. The entity's policy is to revalue its property, plant and equipment. At 31 December 20X2, the item of property, plant and equipment has a fair value of 1,500.

	Historical cost	Indexing adjustment	Adjusted balance
Cost	1,000	140/100	1,400
Revaluation surplus (1,500 – 1,400)			100

5.2   Statement of comprehensive income

5.2.1   Approach for components of historical cost statement of comprehensive income – general

As for the statement of financial position, all items in the statement of comprehensive income should be expressed in terms of the measuring unit current at the end of the reporting period. Again, this is achieved by applying the change in a general price index from the dates when the income and expenses were first recorded. [IAS 29:26]

Because there may be a large number of transactions in the statement of comprehensive income, some estimation may be necessary. Furthermore, the general price index selected may not be published daily. Clearly, if prices are rising at a reasonably steady rate, and if the transactions being adjusted arise evenly, it may be sufficient to approximate using an average movement in the general price index over a period. However, judgement is required as to whether an average will result in a fair approximation. For example, if there are large, irregular transactions, an average rate will be unsuitable and actual rates should be used.

5.2.2   Depreciation

The method of calculating the charge for depreciation is illustrated in **example 5.1.2.2**.

5.2.3   Cost of goods sold

Another potentially complex area is the calculation of the cost of goods sold for inclusion in the statement of comprehensive income.

All amounts included in cost of goods sold should be restated by applying the change in the general price index from the dates when the items of income and expense were initially recognised in the financial statements. The following steps may be required:

- obtain a monthly breakdown of the items included in production costs;

- restate all components of production costs, except depreciation and raw materials, from the month when the costs were incurred to the end of the reporting period;

- calculate raw material used in the production process through the reconciliation of restated opening raw materials and closing raw materials balances;

- calculate depreciation related to production costs on the basis of the restated property, plant and equipment, and replace the historical depreciation with this restated depreciation; and

- restate opening and closing historical finished goods and work in progress.

The amount of the restated cost of goods sold is obtained by adding the restated opening finished goods and work in progress to purchases and other production costs restated from the date when the cost was incurred, and deducting the restated closing finished goods and work in progress. The restated opening finished goods and work in progress are derived by (1) restating amounts to the purchasing power at the end of the prior reporting period, and (2) inflating the resultant restated cost of opening amounts by the conversion factor for the entire year.

Example 5.2.3

Restatement of cost of goods sold

An entity has inventories of 200 at the beginning of the period, when the general price index is at 100. Purchases of 1,200 are made at an even rate throughout the year and closing inventories are 200. The closing inventories were acquired in two instalments in the last two months of the year, when the index was 120 and 122, respectively. At the end of the reporting period, the general price index is 124, and inflation rose steadily all year, giving an average rate of 112.

	Unadjusted balances	Indexing adjustment	Adjusted balances	
Opening inventories	200	124/100		248
Purchases	1,200	124/112		1,329
Closing inventories	(100)	124/120	(103)	
	(100)	124/122	(102)	
	(200)			(205)
Cost of goods sold	1,200			1,372

5.2.4 Current taxation

The current taxation expense accrues over the period. Therefore, the restated current taxation expense is calculated by restating monthly tax expenses for each month in terms of purchasing power at the end of the reporting period, using the increase in the general price index from the related month until the end of the reporting period. If the index has been rising at a reasonably steady rate, the current tax at the end of the reporting period may be indexed using average rates (i.e. as for other expenses). The difference between the opening restated deferred tax balance, and the revised closing deferred tax balance (as discussed at **4.6**) should be added to the above amount. (In **example 4.6**, this amount will be 112.50).

5.3 Gain or loss arising on net monetary position

The gain or loss arising on the net monetary position as a result of all of the adjustments to items in the statement of financial position is included in profit or loss and separately disclosed. IAS 29 suggests that the gain or loss may be estimated by applying the change in the general price index to the weighted average for the period of the difference between monetary assets and monetary liabilities. However, it is more accurately calculated as the difference arising from:

[IAS 29:27]

- the restatement of non-monetary assets, owners' equity and items in the statement of comprehensive income; and

- the adjustment of index-linked assets and liabilities (when these exist), such as index-linked bonds and loans.

The Standard indicates that separate, but linked, disclosure may be appropriate in the statement of comprehensive income of:

[IAS 29:28]

- the net effect of restating non-monetary assets, owners' equity and items in the statement of comprehensive income;

- the net effect of adjusting any index-linked assets and/or liabilities;

- interest income and expense; and

- foreign exchange differences relating to invested and/or borrowed funds.

Example 5.3

Gain or loss arising on net monetary position

An entity has a loan linked to an index which was 100 at the start of the period and at the period end is 125. In preparing its financial statements, the entity uses a different index, which at the start of the period was 100 and at the period end is 120. Inflation is assumed to have occurred at an even rate throughout the period. The unadjusted depreciation expense for the period relates to assets acquired (on average) when the index stood at 80. (Note that, for simplicity, this example ignores the effects of taxation.)

	Unadjusted balances	Indexing adjustment	Adjusted balances	Gain/ (loss)
Non-monetary assets	1,000	120/100	1,200	200
Monetary assets	500		500	
Index-linked loan	(100)	125/100	(125)	(25)
Monetary liabilities	(100)		(100)	
	1,300		1,475	
Capital	500	120/100	600	(100)
Retained earnings b/f	600	120/100	720	(120)
Profit for the period:				
– before depreciation	250	120/110*	273	(23)
– less depreciation	(50)	120/80**	(75)	25

	Unadjusted balances	Indexing adjustment	Adjusted balances	Gain/ (loss)
Profit after depreciation	200		198	—
Net monetary and index loss			(43)***	(43)
Retained earnings c/f	800		875	
	1,300		1,475	

*   average rate

**   calculated as demonstrated in **example 5.1.2.2**

***   calculated as demonstrated in the column on the right

Note that the loss of 25 on the index-linked loan has been shown separately in the column on the right as separate disclosure is suggested by IAS 29.

6   Current cost financial statements

6.1   Statement of financial position

As is clear from the discussion in earlier sections in this chapter, items in the statement of financial position already carried at a current valuation do not require restatement, because they are already expressed in terms of the measuring unit current at the end of the reporting period. Therefore, in current cost financial statements, items of property, plant and equipment, investments and inventories, which will have been restated to current cost, do not require further adjustment. Items linked to changes in prices will be adjusted in accordance with the relevant agreements, and other monetary items will again require no adjustment. [IAS 29:29]

Other items in the statement of financial position will, however, need to be restated. This includes goodwill, deferred credits and components of owners' equity. The guidance outlined in **section 5** for items in a historical cost statement of financial position should be applied. [IAS 29:29]

6.2   Statement of comprehensive income

The current cost statement of comprehensive income, before restatement, generally reports costs current at the time at which the underlying transactions or events occurred. Cost of sales and depreciation are recognised at current costs at the time of consumption; sales and other expenses are recorded at their monetary amounts when they occurred. All of these amounts in the statement of comprehensive income should be restated in the measuring unit current at the end of the reporting period by applying a general price index. [IAS 29:30]

6.3 Gain or loss on net monetary position

The gain or loss on the net monetary position is accounted for as set out for historical cost financial statements (see **5.3**). [IAS 29:31]

> In current cost financial statements, there may already be an adjustment taking items from a historical cost basis to a current cost basis. Such adjustments are treated as part of the gain or loss on the net monetary position, and the two amounts will be treated as one for the purpose of disclosure.

7 Economies ceasing to be hyperinflationary

There are two simple rules to be applied when the economy ceases to be hyperinflationary:

[IAS 29:38]

- the entity should cease to prepare its financial statements in accordance with IAS 29; and

- the carrying amounts of assets and liabilities in the entity's previous set of financial statements, which are the opening balances for the period in which the economy ceases to be hyperinflationary, should be treated as the basis for the carrying amounts in its subsequent financial statements. No adjustment is required to any balances in the financial statements.

8 Disclosure

The following disclosures are required:

[IAS 29:39]

- the fact that the financial statements and the corresponding figures have been restated for changes in the general purchasing power of the functional currency and, consequently, are stated in terms of the measuring unit current at the end of the reporting period;

- whether the financial statements are based on a historical cost approach or a current cost approach; and

- the price index that has been used, its level at the end of the reporting period and the movement in the index during the current and previous reporting periods.

The Standard does not further specify what is meant by the 'movement in the index' during the current and prior periods. Simple disclosure of the level of the index at the start of the current and previous periods may not, however, be sufficient. An indication should also be given of the extent of fluctuations during the period when these are material.

A38   Agriculture

Contents

1 Introduction

1.1 Overview of IAS 41

IAS 41 *Agriculture* sets out the accounting for agricultural activity – the management of the transformation of biological assets (living plants and animals) into agricultural produce (harvested product of the entity's biological assets). The Standard generally requires biological assets to be measured at fair value less costs to sell.

1.2 Amendments to IAS 41 since the last edition of this manual

IAS 41 was most recently amended in January 2016 by consequential amendments arising from IFRS 16 *Leases*. The amendments specifically exclude from the scope of IAS 41 right-of-use assets arising from a lease of land related to agricultural activity (see **3.1**). See **5.2.6** for a general discussion on the accounting for leased biological assets.

2 Definitions

The following are the key definitions for the purposes of IAS 41:

[IAS 41:5]

- **agricultural activity** refers to the management by an entity of the biological transformation and harvest of biological assets for sale or for conversion into agricultural produce or into additional biological assets;

- a **biological asset** is defined as a living animal or plant;

- **biological transformation** comprises the processes of growth, degeneration, production and procreation that cause qualitative or quantitative changes in a biological asset;

- **agricultural produce** is defined as the harvested produce of the entity's biological assets;

- **harvest** is the detachment of produce from a biological asset or the cessation of a biological asset's life processes; and

- **costs to sell** are the incremental costs directly attributable to the disposal of an asset, excluding finance costs and income taxes.

Agricultural activity covers a diverse range of activities such as raising livestock, forestry, cropping, cultivating orchards and plantations, floriculture, and aquaculture (including fish farming). Agricultural activities have three common features: capability to change, management of that change and measurement of change. The key feature that often differentiates agricultural activities from other related activities is the entity's management of the biological transformation. For example, the entity may manage biological transformation by enhancing, or at least stabilising, conditions necessary for the process to take place (e.g. nutrient levels, moisture, temperature, fertility and light). Harvesting from unmanaged sources (such as open ocean fishing and deforestation) is not agricultural activity because it does not involve management of the resource. [IAS 41:6]

It is clear from the definitions above that agricultural activity is not restricted to traditional farming operations, but will also apply to some entities operating in the bio-technology sector.

A resource may be 'managed' by government, through the use of mechanisms such as licensing and quotas, but this does not of itself result in the activity being classified as an agricultural activity under IAS 41; what matters is whether the entity itself manages the resource.

Agricultural activities do not include:

- holding investments in an unmanaged forest as a carbon sink, which gives rise to carbon credits that can either be sold or used to offset pollution caused by the entity;

- using animals such as greyhounds, horses, pigeons or whippets for racing;

- exhibiting performing animals (e.g. in a theme park);

- managing living assets that are not animals or plants, such as viruses and blood cells used in research; or

- cloning living organisms in order to produce antibodies by applying a process analogous to a manufacturing process rather than management of a biological transformation.

Example 2

Plant breeding: seed multiplication

Entity A is a plant breeding entity. Following the development of new plant breeds, Entity A uses the developed breeding seeds to multiply the seeds into basic seeds which will then be sold.

The multiplication of seeds to be harvested for sale is an agricultural activity within the scope of IAS 41 because it represents a biological transformation process of biological assets managed by the entity for sale. The entity transforms the breeding seeds into seeds for sale using biological processes and this activity is, therefore, within the scope of IAS 41.

3 Scope

3.1 Scope – general

IAS 41 should be applied for the following when they relate to agricultural activity:

[IAS 41:1]

(a) biological assets, except for bearer plants (see **3.2**);

(b) agricultural produce at the point of harvest; and

(c) government grants when they relate to agricultural activity.

IAS 41 does not apply to:

[IAS 41:2]

(a) land related to agricultural activity (accounted for under IAS 16 *Property, Plant and Equipment* – see **chapter A7**);

(b) bearer plants related to agricultural activity (accounted for under IAS 16). However, IAS 41 does apply to produce on those bearer plants (see **3.2.3**);

(c) government grants related to bearer plants (accounted for under IAS 20 *Accounting for Government Grants and Disclosure of Government Assistance* – see **chapter A36**);

(d) intangible assets related to agricultural activity (accounted for under IAS 38 *Intangible Assets* – see **chapter A9**); and

(e) for entities that have adopted IFRS 16 *Leases*, right-of-use assets arising from a lease of land related to agricultural activity.

IAS 41:2(e) was added in January 2016 as a result of consequential amendments arising from IFRS 16 *Leases* (effective for annual periods beginning on or after 1 January 2019, with earlier application permitted). This amendment achieves consistency with the exclusion of owned land related to agricultural activity under IAS 41:2(a) (see above).

3.2 Bearer plants relating to agricultural activity

3.2.1 Bearer plants excluded from the scope of IAS 41

IAS 41 should not be applied to bearer plants (see **3.2.2** for definition) or government grants related to such plants. [IAS 41:1 & 2]

Bearer plants have been excluded from the scope of IAS 41 by *Agriculture: Bearer Plants (Amendments to IAS 16 and IAS 41)* issued in June 2014. The IASB determined that those assets are more appropriately accounted for under IAS 16 *Property, Plant and Equipment* because, once mature, they are held by an entity solely to grow produce over their productive life. Under IAS 16, entities have a choice to measure these assets subsequent to initial recognition using either a cost model or a revaluation model. See **2.6** in **chapter A7** for a detailed discussion regarding bearer plants to be accounted for under IAS 16. See **3.2.4** for the effective date and transition provisions for the June 2014 amendments.

3.2.2   Bearer plants – definition

A bearer plant is defined as a living plant that:

[IAS 41:5]

*   is used in the production or supply of agricultural produce;

*   is expected to bear produce for more than one period; and

*   has a remote likelihood of being sold as agricultural produce, except for incidental scrap sales.

Examples of plants that usually meet the definition of a bearer plant and that are outside the scope of IAS 41 are tea bushes, grape vines, oil palms and rubber trees. [IAS 41:4]

The following are not bearer plants:

[IAS 41:5A]

*   plants cultivated to be harvested as agricultural produce (e.g. trees grown for use as lumber);

*   plants cultivated to produce agricultural produce when there is more than a remote likelihood that the entity will also harvest and sell the plant as agricultural produce, other than as incidental scrap sales (e.g. trees that are cultivated both for their fruit and their lumber); and

*   annual crops (e.g. maize and wheat).

When bearer plants are no longer used to bear produce, they might be cut down and sold as scrap (e.g. for use as firewood). Such incidental scrap sales would not prevent the plant from satisfying the definition of a bearer plant. [IAS 41:5B]

3.2.3   Produce growing on bearer plants

Produce growing on bearer plants is a biological asset. [IAS 41:5C] IAS 41 *does* apply to such produce (e.g. tea leaves, grapes, oil palm fruit and latex). [IAS 41:4]

The Basis for Conclusions on IAS 41 explains that the IASB considers that such produce is a consumable biological asset and the growth of the produce directly increases the expected revenue from the sale of the produce; consequently, fair value measurement of the growing produce provides useful information to users of financial statements about an entity's expected future cash flows.

The Board also observed that produce will ultimately be detached from the bearer plants and is normally sold separately, meaning it has a market value on its own; this is in contrast to many bearer plants that are unlikely to have an observable market value on their own because they can only be sold while attached to the land.

Notwithstanding the difficulties that may arise in practice when measuring produce growing on bearer plants at fair value less costs to sell, the Board decided to keep such produce within the scope of IAS 41 in order to maintain consistency with the accounting for produce growing in the ground. If an entity is unable to measure fair value reliably on initial measurement of produce, relief may be available under IAS 41:30 (see **5.2.5**). [IAS 41:BC4B - BC4D]

3.2.4 Effective date and transition provisions for the June 2014 amendments

The June 2014 amendments are effective for annual periods beginning on or after 1 January 2016, with earlier application permitted. If an entity applies the June 2014 amendments for an accounting period beginning before 1 January 2016, that fact is required to be disclosed. [IAS 41:62]

In general, the June 2014 amendments are required to be applied retrospectively in accordance with IAS 8 *Accounting Policies, Changes in Accounting Estimates and Errors*. [IAS 41:62] However, when the June 2014 amendments are first applied, an entity need not present the quantitative information required by paragraph 28(f) of IAS 8 for the current period. [IAS 41:63]

IAS 8:28(f) generally requires an entity to disclose, for the current period and for each prior period presented, the amount of any adjustment for each financial statement line item affected when an IFRS is first applied. The IASB concluded that it would be burdensome for entities to present this information for the year in which the June 2014 amendments are first applied because it would require an entity to maintain dual systems in the year of initial application. However, entities are required to provide the disclosures required under IAS 8:28(f) for prior periods presented in the financial statements in the year of application. [IAS 16:BC97]

3.3   Accounting after the point of harvest

IAS 41 deals only with the treatment of biological assets up to the point of harvest, and not with any further transformations that they may undergo thereafter. After the harvest is completed, the assets are generally accounted for under IAS 2 *Inventories* (see **chapter A11**). [IAS 41:3] In more limited circumstances, they may be accounted for under another Standard; for example, if an entity harvests logs and decides to use them for constructing its own building, IAS 16 *Property, Plant and Equipment* is applied in accounting for the logs. [IAS 41:B8]

The following table, reproduced from IAS 41:4, sets out a number of examples of biological assets, agricultural produce, and products that are the result of processing after harvest.

Biological assets	Agricultural produce	Products that are the result of processing after harvest
Sheep	Wool	Yarn, carpet
Trees in a timber plantation	Felled trees	Logs, lumber
Dairy cattle	Milk	Cheese
Pigs	Carcass	Sausages, cured hams
Cotton plants	Harvested cotton	Thread, clothing
Sugar cane	Harvested cane	Sugar
Tobacco plants	Picked leaves	Cured tobacco
Tea bushes	Picked leaves	Tea
Grape vines	Picked grapes	Wine
Fruit trees	Picked fruit	Processed fruit
Oil palms	Picked fruit	Palm oil
Rubber trees	Harvested latex	Rubber products

Specifically excluded from the scope of IAS 41 are ageing or maturation processes that occur after harvest (e.g. wine production from grapes and cheese production from milk). [IAS 41:3] Some had argued for the inclusion of such processing within the scope of IAS 41 because it is a logical and natural extension of agricultural activity, and the events taking place are similar to biological transformation. However, the IASB decided not to include such processes in the scope of the Standard because of concerns about difficulties in differentiating them from other manufacturing processes. [IAS 41:BC11]

3.4   Other assets used in agricultural activity

IAS 41 does not address the accounting treatment for land on which agricultural activity is conducted, nor intangible assets (e.g. milk quotas) related to agricultural activity. These are covered by IAS 16 *Property, Plant and Equipment* (see **chapter A7**), IAS 40 *Investment Property* (see **chapter A8**, or for entities that have not yet adopted IFRS 16, **appendix A5**) and IAS 38 *Intangible Assets* (see **chapter A9**). [IAS 41:2]

Example 3.4

Plant breeding: new plant development

Entity A is a plant breeding entity. In the initial stages of the plant breeding process, Entity A must develop new varieties by selecting seeds and cross-breeding in a laboratory, as well as performing field tests. This process can take up to twelve years.

The development of new breeds of plants is not within the scope of IAS 41; IAS 41:2(b) states that the Standard does not apply to intangible assets related to agricultural activity. The development of new breeds is accounted for in accordance with the requirements of IAS 38 relating to research and development costs.

3.5 Biological assets and agricultural produce used as a source of fuel for vertically integrated operations

---

Example 3.5

Biological assets and agricultural produce used as a source of fuel for vertically integrated operations

Company A is a manufacturer of steel products with vertically integrated operations. Company A has a subsidiary, Subsidiary X, that owns and operates a eucalyptus tree plantation. The agricultural produce (i.e. felled eucalyptus trees) is processed by Subsidiary X to produce charcoal. The charcoal is sold to Subsidiary Y, another member of the consolidated group, and used to fire blast furnaces for the production of steel products. Subsidiary X does not sell the felled trees or the charcoal to entities outside of the consolidated group.

For the purposes of Company A's consolidated financial statements, should Subsidiary X's biological assets (live trees) and agricultural produce at the point of harvest (felled trees) be accounted for under IAS 41?

Yes. The scope of IAS 41 includes an entity's management of the biological transformation and harvest of biological assets for conversion into agricultural produce. Consequently, in the circumstances described, in its consolidated financial statements, Company A should account for its live eucalyptus trees and felled trees at the point of harvest under IAS 41. Company A should apply IAS 2 after the point of harvest for the processes needed to convert the felled trees into charcoal.

While IAS 41 cites certain scope exceptions, it does not provide an exception for either (1) transactions with related parties, or (2) biological assets and agricultural produce used for internal consumption in vertically integrated operations.

---

4 Recognition of assets

Entities are required to recognise biological assets or agricultural produce when, and only when, all of the following conditions are met:

[IAS 41:10]

- the entity controls the asset as a result of past events;
- it is probable that future economic benefits associated with the asset will flow to the entity; and
- the fair value or cost of the asset can be measured reliably.

Control over biological assets or agricultural produce may be evidenced by, for example, legal ownership of cattle and the branding or otherwise marking of the cattle on acquisition, birth, or weaning. The future benefits are normally assessed by measuring the significant physical attributes. [IAS 41:11]

5 Measurement

5.1 The fair value model for agricultural activity

Under IAS 41, the measurement of biological assets (other than bearer plants) and agricultural produce is based on their fair value at the end of the reporting period and the point of harvest, respectively.

Some agricultural activity, such as the raising of livestock and the growing of timber, may take several years to give rise to produce for sale. Under the historical cost model, a sales transaction is generally required before the recognition of any gain is triggered. However, in the context of agricultural activity, the event giving rise to such gains is the progress of development of the biological assets (e.g. growth, procreation, harvest). IAS 41's fair value model is intended to capture these gains as they occur.

5.2 Biological assets

5.2.1 Biological assets generally to be measured at fair value less costs to sell

IAS 41 requires that biological assets be measured on initial recognition and at the end of each reporting period at fair value less costs to sell, unless fair value cannot be measured reliably (see **5.2.5**). [IAS 41:12]

Fair value is defined as "the price that would be received to sell an asset or paid to transfer a liability in an orderly transaction between market participants at the measurement date. (See IFRS 13 *Fair Value Measurement*.)" [IAS 41:8]

IAS 41 notes that the measurement of fair value for a biological asset or agricultural produce may be facilitated by grouping biological assets or agricultural produce according to significant attributes (e.g. by age or quality). Entities should select the attributes corresponding to the attributes used in the market as a basis for pricing. [IAS 41:15]

When measuring fair value, the following cash flows should be excluded:

[IAS 41:22]

- financing and taxation cash flows; and

- cash flows related to re-establishing biological assets after harvest (e.g. the cost of planting replacement crops).

5.2.2 Cost as an approximation for fair value

IAS 41 recognises that, in limited circumstances, cost is an appropriate indicator of fair value. This will be particularly so when little biological transformation has taken place since the cost was incurred (e.g. seedlings planted immediately prior to the end of the reporting period or newly acquired livestock), or when the impact of biological transformation on price is not expected to be material (e.g. in the very early stages of a 30-year plantation growth cycle). [IAS 41:24]

5.2.3 Biological assets physically attached to land

Although agricultural land is excluded from the scope of IAS 41, as discussed at **3.4**, biological assets (other than bearer plants) that are physically attached to land (e.g. trees in a timber plantation) are accounted for under the Standard. There may be no separate market for biological assets that are attached to land, but an active market may exist for the combined assets (i.e. for the biological assets, raw land and land improvements as a package.) IAS 41 allows the entity to use information regarding the combined assets to measure the fair value of the biological assets. For example, the fair value of raw land and land improvements may be deducted from the fair value of the combined assets to arrive at the fair value of the biological assets. [IAS 41:25]

Example 5.2.3 considers whether land rental costs should be included when determining the fair value of biological assets attached to land using the income approach. Although the specific example deals with an immature biological asset with a relatively long growth period, this issue may also be relevant to a crop with a much shorter life cycle (e.g. wheat) if the reporting date falls part-way through that life cycle.

Example 5.2.3

Inclusion of land rental costs when determining the fair value of an immature biological asset using the income approach

Entity A grows spruce trees for use in the production of pulp for the paper industry. As at the end of Entity A's reporting period, many of these trees have not reached maturity and no market-determined prices are available for the trees in their current condition. Accordingly, having considered the relative merits of various valuation techniques (see **8.3** in **chapter A6**), Entity A concludes that an income approach converting future income from the sale of the trees and the expenses necessary to bring the trees to the point of sale to a single current (i.e. discounted) amount is the most appropriate method to determine the fair value of the immature trees.

Entity A owns the land on which the trees are grown and, accordingly, does not pay rent for its use.

For the purpose of calculating the fair value of the immature trees using the income approach, should Entity A include a rental expense in respect of land in the expenses necessary to bring the immature trees to the point of sale?

Yes. When measuring the value of immature biological assets using the income approach, in all cases a market-level rental expense in respect of land (being the rent for use of the land for agricultural purposes) should be included in the expenses necessary to bring the immature biological assets to the point of sale. This methodology results in the trees being measured at the same value regardless of whether the entity owns the land to which they are attached, rents the land at a market rate, or rents the land at an off-market rate (because, for example, the land is owned by a related party).

IAS 41:25 makes clear that, for the purpose of measuring the fair value of biological assets, the unit of account does not include the land to which the assets are attached.

Paragraph B14 of IFRS 13 *Fair Value Measurement* (see **8.6.3** in **chapter A6**) states that, in applying a present value technique, "only the factors attributable to the asset or liability being measured" should be taken into account. In the circumstances under consideration, Entity A's ownership of land is a characteristic of the entity, not of the assets being measured (i.e. the trees) and, therefore, does not affect the price that a third-party market participant would pay for the trees. Accordingly, it is clear that the ownership of the land upon which the trees are grown (and, consequently, the payment or non-payment of rent) is not a relevant factor in their valuation, which is based on the trees alone being sold.

If an estimate of market rent levels is significant to the measurement of the trees and is less observable than other inputs to the present value calculation, it may affect their categorisation within the fair value hierarchy (see **10.3.3.2** in **chapter A6**).

5.2.4 Assets subject to sale contracts

IAS 41 highlights that, when an entity has entered into sales contracts for the disposal of biological assets at a future date, those contract prices are not necessarily taken into account in measuring fair value. Fair value is not an entity-specific measure, and it is required to reflect the current market conditions in which market participant buyers and sellers would enter into a transaction. Sales contracts entered into in the past may not reflect the price that market participant buyers and sellers would otherwise have agreed at the date of measurement. Therefore, the fair value at any point in time is not adjusted because of the existence of guaranteed sales contracts. [IAS 41:16]

In some circumstances, a contract for the sale of biological assets may be an onerous contract within the meaning of IAS 37 *Provisions, Contingent Liabilities and Contingent Assets* (see **chapter A12**) and that Standard should be applied to such onerous contracts.

5.2.5 Inability to measure fair value reliably

IAS 41 presumes that fair value can be measured reliably for most biological assets. That presumption can be rebutted, however, when the following conditions are met at the time the biological asset is initially recognised in the financial statements:

[IAS 41:30]

- quoted market prices are not available for the biological asset; and

- alternative fair value measurements are determined to be clearly unreliable.

When these conditions are met, the biological asset is measured at cost less accumulated depreciation and any accumulated impairment losses. [IAS 41:30] IAS 41 directs preparers to IAS 2 *Inventories*, IAS 16 *Property, Plant and Equipment* and IAS 36 *Impairment of Assets* for guidance in these circumstances.

If circumstances change, and fair value becomes reliably measurable, a switch to fair value less costs to sell is required. [IAS 41:30] This is likely to occur as biological transformation progresses.

Once a non-current biological asset meets the criteria to be classified as held for sale (or is included in a disposal group that is classified as held for sale) in accordance with IFRS 5 *Non-current Assets Held for Sale and Discontinued Operations* (see **chapter A20**), it is presumed that fair value can be measured reliably. [IAS 41:30]

The presumption that fair value can be measured reliably can be rebutted only on initial recognition. An entity that has previously measured a biological asset at its fair value less costs to sell continues to measure that biological asset at its fair value less costs to sell until disposal. [IAS 41:31] Therefore, IAS 41 does not permit use of the measurement reliability exception in circumstances when an entity has previously measured a particular biological asset at fair value, and market transactions become less frequent or market prices become less readily available, so that it becomes more difficult to determine the fair value of the asset. This prohibition on changing the measurement basis from fair value to cost is designed to prevent entities using the reliability exception as an excuse to discontinue fair value accounting in a falling market.

5.2.6 Leased assets

5.2.6.1 Entities that have adopted IFRS 16 Leases

Leases of biological assets within the scope of IAS 41 (e.g. leases of breeding stock) held by a lessee are specifically excluded from the scope of IFRS 16 (see **3.1** in **chapter A17**). A lessee's asset held under such a lease should be initially recognised and subsequently measured in accordance with the measurement requirements of IAS 41 (i.e. at fair value less costs to sell except when the fair value cannot be measured reliably). Due to the nature of biological assets, it is unlikely that fair value could not be measured reliably for leased assets.

The presentation and disclosure requirements of IAS 41 should also be applied to such leased assets; because they are excluded from the scope of IFRS 16 entirely, the disclosure requirements of that Standard do not apply.

The following should be accounted for in accordance with IFRS 16 rather than IAS 41:

- right-of-use assets arising from a lease of land related to agricultural activity (specifically excluded from the scope of IAS 41 – see **3.1**);

- leases of bearer plants (such as apple trees in an orchard or grape vines in a vineyard), both from the lessee and lessor perspectives, because bearer plants are accounted for under IAS 16 *Property, Plant and Equipment* rather than IAS 41 (see **2.6** in **chapter A7**); and

- leases of biological assets within the scope of IAS 41 from a lessor's perspective.

For entities engaged in agricultural activities, leases of assets other than biological assets (farm machinery etc.) should be accounted for in accordance with IFRS 16, both from the lessee and lessor perspectives.

5.2.6.2 *Entities that have not yet adopted IFRS 16*

IAS 17 *Leases* applies to accounting for leases of biological assets, but does not apply to the measurement of biological assets within the scope of IAS 41 held by lessees under finance leases or provided by lessors under operating leases (see **2.2** in **appendix A4**).

Therefore, a lessee's rights under a finance lease of biological assets within the scope of IAS 41 should be initially recognised and subsequently measured in accordance with the measurement requirements of IAS 41 (i.e. at fair value less costs to sell except when the fair value cannot be measured reliably). Due to the nature of biological assets, it is unlikely that fair value could not be measured reliably for leased assets.

Because the scope exclusion under IAS 17.2 applies only to measurement, the presentation and disclosure requirements of both IAS 41 and IAS 17 should be applied to such leased biological assets.

The following should be accounted for in accordance with IAS 17 rather than IAS 41:

- leases of bearer plants (such as apple trees in an orchard or grape vines in an vineyard), both from the lessee and lessor perspectives, because bearer plants are accounted for under IAS 16 *Property, Plant and Equipment* rather than IAS 41 (see **2.6** in **chapter A7**); and

- biological assets within the scope of IAS 41 held by lessees under operating leases or provided by lessors under finance leases.

For entities engaged in agricultural activities, leases of assets other than biological assets (farm machinery etc.) should be accounted for in accordance with IAS 17, both from the lessee and lessor perspectives.

5.3 Agricultural produce

IAS 41 requires that agricultural produce be measured at fair value less costs to sell at the point that it is harvested from the entity's biological assets. [IAS 41:13] The guidance outlined at **5.2** as regards the measurement of fair value less costs to sell generally applies equally to agricultural produce.

However, there is no measurement reliability exception (as discussed at **5.2.5**) for agricultural produce. Because harvested produce is a marketable commodity, the Standard reflects the view that the fair value of agricultural produce at the point of harvest can always be measured reliably. Therefore, in all cases, such produce is required to be measured at fair value less costs to sell. [IAS 41:32]

The fair value measurement of agricultural produce at the point of harvest is the cost of that produce for subsequent accounting under IAS 2 or other applicable IFRSs. [IAS 41:13]

For example, corn that has not yet been harvested should be remeasured at the end of each reporting period, reflecting changes in market prices, because it meets the definition of a biological asset. Once it has been harvested, however, that remeasurement will generally cease, and it will be carried under IAS 2 at the lower of cost (defined as the fair value less costs to sell at the point of harvest) and net realisable value.

Net realisable value (NRV) is defined as the estimated selling price in the ordinary course of business, less the estimated costs of completion and the estimated costs necessary to make the sale. [IAS 2:6] NRV is an entity-specific value; fair value is not (see **5.2.4**). NRV for inventories may not equal fair value less costs to sell. [IAS 2:7]

Contracted sales prices should be taken into account in determining entity-specific NRV in terms of IAS 2:7, but those contract prices are not necessarily taken into account in measuring fair value (see **5.2.4**). This may give rise to differences between NRV and fair value less costs to sell in terms of IAS 41:13.

6   Reporting of gains and losses

When a biological asset is first recognised at fair value less costs to sell, any gain or loss arising is reported in profit or loss for the period. A loss can arise on initial recognition of a biological asset due to the requirement to deduct costs to sell. A gain can arise, for example, when a biological asset is first recognised following the birth of a calf. [IAS 41:27]

Gains and losses will also arise over the life of the biological asset to reflect changes in fair value less costs to sell. These gains and losses are also reported in profit or loss in the period in which they arise. [IAS 41:26] Thus, for example, changes in fair value as a calf grows are also recognised in profit or loss.

The gain or loss arising on initial recognition of agricultural produce at fair value less costs to sell is included in profit or loss for the period in which it arises. [IAS 41:28] Agricultural produce is first recognised at the time of harvest (up to that point the asset has been classified as a biological asset). As a result of harvesting, a gain or loss may arise, and that is recognised in profit or loss.

7 Government grants

7.1 Requirements applicable to government grants relating to agricultural activity

IAS 41 sets out specific rules for accounting for government grants related to agricultural activity, which are discussed at **7.2** and **7.3**. The treatment prescribed may give a different result than would arise if IAS 20 *Accounting for Government Grants and Disclosure of Government Assistance* were applied. IAS 20 should only be applied in relation to the following biological assets:

- bearer plants (see **3.2**); and

- other biological assets carried on a cost basis (i.e. the measurement reliability exception at **5.2.5** is applied), as described at **7.3**.

7.2 Grants relating to biological assets measured on a fair value basis

IAS 41 requires that unconditional grants related to biological assets measured at fair value less costs to sell should be recognised in profit or loss when, and only when, the grant becomes receivable. [IAS 41:34]

If the grant is conditional, it should be recognised in profit or loss when, and only when, the conditions attached to the grant are met. This includes grants under the conditions of which entities are required not to engage in specified agricultural activity. [IAS 41:35]

Government grants related to agricultural activity will frequently be subject to conditions such as the requirement to continue to engage in a specified activity (or to refrain from engaging in a specified activity) for an extended period of time. If the condition is breached, then all of the grant may be refundable. In such circumstances, no part of the grant is recognised in profit or loss until the specified period has elapsed. However, when the terms of the government grant allow part of the funds to be retained according to the time that has elapsed, then the entity should recognise that part of the grant in profit or loss as time passes. [IAS 41:36]

7.3 Grants relating to biological assets measured on a cost basis

Government grants relating to biological assets accounted for on a historical cost basis (i.e. bearer plants (see **3.2**) and other biological assets carried on a cost basis (see **5.2.5**)) are dealt with under IAS 20 (see **chapter A36**). [IAS 41:37]

8 Presentation and disclosure

8.1 Presentation

IAS 1 *Presentation of Financial Statements* requires an entity to present the carrying amount of its biological assets within the scope of IAS 41 (other than those included in disposal groups – see **chapter A20**) separately in its statement of financial position. [IAS 1:54(f)]

8.2 Disclosure

8.2.1 Description of biological assets and activities

The entity is required to provide a description of each group of biological assets (defined as an aggregation of similar living animals or plants), which may take the form of a narrative or quantified description. Entities are encouraged to provide a quantified description of each group, distinguishing between consumable biological assets (i.e. those to be harvested, such as crops) and bearer biological assets (e.g. orchards), or between mature and immature biological assets, as appropriate. The basis for any such analysis should be disclosed. [IAS 41:41 - 44]

If not disclosed elsewhere in information published with the financial statements, the following should also be described:

[IAS 41:46]

- the nature of the entity's activities involving each group of biological assets; and

- non-financial measures or estimates of the physical quantities of:

  - each group of the entity's biological assets at the end of the period; and

  - the output of agricultural produce during the period.

8.2.2 Gains and losses recognised during the period

The entity is required to disclose the aggregate gain or loss arising during the current period on the initial recognition of biological assets and agricultural produce, and from the change in fair value less costs to sell of biological assets. [IAS 41:40]

Note that there is no requirement to disclose separately the gain or loss related to biological assets and the gain or loss related to agricultural produce.

Occasionally, events may cause material gains or losses that should be disclosed separately in accordance with IAS 1:97 (see **5.4.1** in **chapter A4**).

In the context of agricultural activity, such events may include, for example, disease, flood, drought, frost or plague. [IAS 41:53]

8.2.3 Reconciliation of changes in biological assets

A detailed reconciliation is required of changes in the carrying amount of biological assets between the beginning and the end of the accounting period, which includes:

[IAS 41:50]

- the gain or loss arising from changes in fair values less costs to sell;

- increases arising from purchases;

- decreases attributable to sales and biological assets classified as held for sale (or included in a disposal group that is classified as held for sale) in accordance with IFRS 5 *Non-current Assets Held for Sale and Discontinued Operations* (see **chapter A20**);

- decreases due to harvest;

- increases arising from business combinations;

- net exchange differences arising from the translation of financial statements into a different presentation currency, and on the translation of a foreign operation into the presentation currency of the reporting entity; and

- any other changes.

8.2.4 Restricted assets, commitments and risk management strategies

The entity should disclose:

[IAS 41:49]

- the existence and carrying amounts of biological assets whose title is restricted, and the carrying amounts of biological assets pledged as security for liabilities;

- the amount of commitments for the development or acquisition of biological assets; and

- financial risk management strategies in relation to its agricultural activities.

8.2.5 Additional disclosures when fair value cannot be measured reliably

If biological assets within the scope of IAS 41 are measured at cost less accumulated depreciation and impairment losses (see **5.2.5**), the following disclosures are required:

[IAS 41:54]

- a description of the biological assets;

- an explanation as to why fair value cannot be determined reliably;

- the range of estimates within which fair value is highly likely to lie, if possible;

- the depreciation method used;

- the useful lives or depreciation rates used; and

- the gross carrying amount and the accumulated depreciation and impairment losses at the beginning and end of the period.

Any gain or loss arising on the disposal of biological assets held at cost less accumulated depreciation and accumulated impairment losses should be disclosed. In addition, the amounts for biological assets held on a cost basis should be disclosed separately in the detailed reconciliation for biological assets set out at **8.2.3**, and the reconciliation should disclose impairment losses, reversals of impairment losses and depreciation expense recognised in profit or loss during the period. [IAS 41:55]

When an entity moves from a cost basis to a fair value basis during the year, it is required to provide a description of the affected biological assets, an explanation as to why the fair value can now be measured reliably, and the effect of the change. [IAS 41:56]

8.2.6 Government grants

The following disclosures are required for government grants relating to agricultural activity:

[IAS 41:57]

- the nature and extent of government grants recognised;

- unfulfilled conditions and other contingencies attaching to grants; and

- significant decreases expected in the level of government grants.

8.2.7 Additional recommended disclosures

IAS 41 encourages, but does not require, separate disclosure of the effects of physical change and price change resulting in changes to the carrying amount of biological assets, particularly when there is a production cycle of more than one year. [IAS 41:51] Growth, degeneration, production, procreation and harvest are each types of physical change that are observable and measurable. Example 2 of the illustrative examples accompanying IAS 41 illustrates how to separate physical change and price change. [IAS 41:52]

A39 Insurance contracts

Contents

1 Introduction

1.1 Overview of IFRS 4

Specific accounting requirements for insurance entities are, for the most part, outside the scope of this manual. Nevertheless, this chapter provides an overview of IFRS 4 *Insurance Contracts*, in part as a general introduction and in part because the interaction of its requirements with those of other Standards (in particular, IFRS 15 *Revenue from Contracts with Customers* (or, for entities that have not yet adopted IFRS 15, IAS 18 *Revenue*) and IFRS 9 *Financial Instruments* (or, for entities that have not yet adopted IFRS 9, IAS 39 *Financial Instruments: Recognition and Measurement*)) is important to entities other than insurance entities.

IFRS 4 *Insurance Contracts* was issued by the IASB in March 2004, completing the first phase of the Board's insurance project. IFRS 4 is seen only as a stepping stone to the second phase (see **section 6**) and its objectives are quite restricted. The Standard requires:

[IFRS 4:1]

* limited improvements to accounting for insurance contracts by those who accept obligations under such contracts; and

* disclosures that identify and explain the amounts in an insurer's financial statements arising from insurance contracts and help users of those financial statements to understand the amount, timing and uncertainty of future cash flows from insurance contracts.

The IASB recognises that accounting practices for insurance contracts have been diverse and have often differed from practices in other sectors. The Board has been working on the second phase of its insurance project since issuing IFRS 4.

This chapter does not consider the guidance on implementing IFRS 4 which accompanies, but is not part of, the Standard.

1.2 Amendments to IFRS 4 since the last edition of this manual

IFRS 4 was amended in January 2016 by minor consequential amendments arising from IFRS 16 *Leases* (effective for annual periods beginning on or after 1 January 2019, with earlier application permitted). The amendments reflect changes in terminology under the new Standard (see **3.4**).These amendments should be applied when an entity adopts IFRS 16.

2   When is a contract an insurance contract?

2.1   Definition of an insurance contract

The definition of an insurance contract determines whether a contract is within the scope of IFRS 4 or another Standard. An insurance contract is defined as a contract under which one party (the insurer) accepts significant insurance risk from another party (the policyholder) by agreeing to compensate the policyholder if a specified uncertain future event (the insured event) adversely affects the policyholder. [IFRS 4:Appendix A]

Section 2.2 discusses certain key aspects of this definition, namely:

- the requirement for a specified uncertain future event;
- the meaning of insurance risk;
- whether insurance risk is significant; and
- whether the insured event adversely affects the policyholder.

2.2   Key elements of the definition

2.2.1   Specified uncertain future event

The definition at **2.1** requires the identification of an insured event, which is defined as an uncertain future event that is covered by an insurance contract and creates insurance risk. [IFRS 4:Appendix A] The element of uncertainty (or risk) is essential for a contract to be considered an insurance contract, and at least one of the following must be uncertain at the inception of an insurance contract:

[IFRS 4:B2]

- whether an insured event will occur;
- when it will occur; or
- how much the insurer will need to pay if it occurs.

Depending on the nature of the insurance contract, the insured event could be:

[IFRS 4:B3 & B4]

- the discovery of a loss during the term of the contract (even if the loss arises from an event that occurred before the inception of the contract);
- an event that occurs during the term of the contract (even if the resulting loss is discovered after the end of the contract term); or
- when an insurance contract covers an event that has already occurred, but whose financial effect is still uncertain, the discovery of the ultimate cost. As an example, when a reinsurance contract covers the direct

insurer against adverse development of claims already reported by policyholders, the insured event is the discovery of the ultimate cost of those claims.

2.2.2 Insurance risk vs financial risk

2.2.2.1 Distinguishing between insurance risk and financial risk

IFRS 4 distinguishes 'insurance risk' from 'financial risk'. A contract is not an insurance contract unless the insurer accepts significant insurance risk.

[IFRS 4:Appendix A]

- Financial risk is defined as the risk of a possible future change in one or more of a specified interest rate, financial instrument price, commodity price, foreign exchange rate, index of prices or rates, credit rating or credit index or other variable, provided in the case of a non-financial variable that the variable is not specific to a party to the contract.

- Insurance risk is defined as risk, other than financial risk, transferred from the holder of a contract to the issuer.

The presence of significant financial risk does not prevent a contract from being an insurance contract. What matters is that there is significant insurance risk, irrespective of the level of financial risk. For example, many life insurance contracts both guarantee a minimum rate of return to policyholders (creating financial risk) and promise death benefits that can significantly exceed the policyholder's account balance (creating insurance risk in the form of mortality risk). Such contracts are insurance contracts under IFRS 4. [IFRS 4:B10]

Under some contracts, an insured event triggers the payment of an amount linked to a price index. Provided that the payment that is contingent on the insured event can be significant, such contracts are insurance contracts. IFRS 4:B11 gives the example of a life-contingent annuity linked to a cost-of-living index. The contract transfers insurance risk because payment is triggered by an uncertain event, namely the survival of the annuitant. The link to the price index is an embedded derivative, but it also transfers insurance risk. If the resulting transfer of insurance risk is significant, the embedded derivative meets the definition of an insurance contract, in which case it need not be separated and measured at fair value (see **3.5**). [IFRS 4:B11]

2.2.2.2 Is a non-financial variable specific to a party to the contract?

The definition of financial risk at **2.2.2.1** lists both financial and non-financial variables, but the latter are included in financial risk only if they are not specific to a party to the contract. IFRS 4:B9 gives the example of an index of earthquake losses in a particular region or an index of temperatures in a particular city.

Financial risk excludes non-financial variables that are specific to a party to the contract, such as the occurrence or non-occurrence of a fire that damages or destroys an asset of that party. In addition, the risk of changes in the fair value of a non-financial asset is not a financial risk if the fair value reflects not only changes in market prices for such assets (a financial variable) but also the condition of a specific non-financial asset held by a party to a contract (a non-financial variable). If, for example, a guarantee of the residual value of a specific car exposes the guarantor to the risk of changes in the car's physical condition, that risk is insurance risk, not financial risk. [IFRS 4:B9]

2.2.2.3   Is insurance risk accepted from another party?

The definition of insurance risk at **2.2.2.1** refers to risk that is transferred to the insurer from the policyholder. Accordingly, insurance risk can only be a pre-existing risk of the policyholder – a new risk created by the contract is not insurance risk. [IFRS 4:B12]

An insurer can accept significant insurance risk from the policyholder only if the insurer is an entity separate from the policyholder. In the case of a mutual insurer, the mutual accepts risk from each policyholder and pools that risk. Although policyholders bear that pooled risk collectively in their capacity as owners, the mutual has still accepted the risk that is the essence of an insurance contract. [IFRS 4:B17]

2.2.3   Is insurance risk significant?

2.2.3.1   Meaning of 'significant'

The definition of an insurance contract (see **2.1**) requires the transfer of 'significant' insurance risk. IFRS 4:B23 indicates that insurance risk is significant if, and only if, an insured event could cause an insurer to pay significant additional benefits in some scenario, excluding scenarios that lack commercial substance (i.e. scenarios that have no discernible effect on the economics of the transaction). If significant additional benefits would be payable in scenarios that have commercial substance, this condition may be met even if the insured event is extremely unlikely or even if the expected (i.e. probability-weighted) present value of contingent cash flows is a small proportion of the expected present value of all the remaining contractual cash flows. [IFRS 4:B23]

Thus, when a future event is very unlikely, but would be catastrophic if it occurred, a contract paying out a large sum on the occurrence of that event may well be an insurance contract. However, a contract relating to a future event which is very unlikely and would not be particularly damaging may be less likely to have commercial substance. Accordingly, insurance risk for the latter may not be significant.

IFRS 4:Appendix B includes further guidance as to how to determine whether insurance risk is significant, as discussed in **2.2.3.2** to **2.2.3.6**.

2.2.3.2 Additional benefits

When considering whether significant additional benefits (as described at **2.2.3.1**) would be payable on the occurrence of an insured event, it is necessary to identify the amounts in excess of those that would be payable if no insured event occurred (excluding scenarios that lack commercial substance). Those additional amounts include claims handling and claims assessment costs, but exclude:

[IFRS 4:B24]

(a) the loss of the ability to charge the policyholder for future services. In an investment-linked life insurance contract, for example, the death of the policyholder means that the insurer can no longer provide investment management services for a fee. This economic loss for the insurer does not reflect insurance risk, just as a mutual fund manager does not take on insurance risk relating to the possible death of the client. Accordingly, the potential loss of future investment management fees is not relevant in assessing how much insurance risk is transferred by a contract;

(b) waiver on death of charges that would be made on cancellation or surrender. Because the contract brought those charges into existence, the waiver of these charges does not compensate the policyholder for a pre-existing risk. Hence, they are not relevant in assessing how much insurance risk is transferred by a contract;

(c) a payment conditional on an event that does not cause a significant loss to the holder of the contract. Suppose, for example, that an issuer is required to pay CU1,000,000 if an asset suffers physical damage causing an insignificant economic loss of CU500 to the holder. In such a contract, the holder transfers to the insurer the insignificant risk of losing CU500, but the contract creates non-insurance risk that the issuer will need to pay CU999,500 if the specified event occurs. Because the issuer does not accept significant insurance risk from the holder, such a contract is not an insurance contract; and

(d) possible reinsurance recoveries. The insurer accounts separately for these.

2.2.3.3 Contract-by-contract assessment

The significance of insurance risk is assessed on a contract-by-contract basis, rather than by reference to materiality to the financial statements, but treating contracts entered into simultaneously with a single counterparty (or contracts that are otherwise interdependent) as a single contract. Accordingly, even if there is a minimal probability of material losses for a whole book of contracts, insurance risk may be significant. A contract-by-contract assessment makes it easier to classify a contract as an insurance contract. IFRS 4 allows, however, that if a relatively homogeneous book of small contracts is known to consist of contracts that all transfer insurance risk, it is not necessary for the insurer to examine each contract within that book to identify a few non-derivative contracts that transfer insignificant insurance risk. [IFRS 4:B25]

2.2.3.4 Death benefit

If a contract pays a death benefit exceeding the amount payable on survival, the contract is an insurance contract unless the additional death benefit is insignificant (judged by reference to the contract rather than to an entire book of contracts). As noted at **2.2.3.2**, the waiver on death of cancellation or surrender charges is not included in this assessment if this waiver does not compensate the policyholder for a pre-existing risk. Similarly, an annuity contract that pays out regular sums for the rest of a policyholder's life is an insurance contract, unless the aggregate life-contingent payments are insignificant. [IFRS 4:B26]

2.2.3.5 Timing of payment

The reference to additional benefits at **2.2.3.1** could include a requirement to pay benefits earlier if the insured event occurs earlier and the payment is not adjusted for the time value of money. IFRS 4 gives the example of whole life insurance for a fixed amount (i.e. insurance that provides a fixed death benefit whenever the policyholder dies, with no expiry date for the cover). Although it is certain that the policyholder will die, the date of death is uncertain. The insurer will suffer a loss on those individual contracts for which policyholders die early, even if there is no overall loss on the whole book of contracts. [IFRS 4:B27]

2.2.3.6 Deposit and insurance components

A deposit component is a contractual component that is not accounted for as a derivative under IFRS 9 (or, for entities that have not yet adopted IFRS 9, IAS 39) and would be within the scope of IFRS 9 (or IAS 39) if it were a separate instrument. [IFRS 4:Appendix A] When an insurance contract is unbundled into a deposit component and an insurance component, the significance of insurance risk transferred is assessed by reference to the insurance component. The significance of insurance risk transferred by an embedded derivative is assessed by reference to that embedded derivative. [IFRS 4:B28]

2.2.4 Does the insured event adversely affect the policyholder?

2.2.4.1 Requirement for an adverse effect on the policy holder

Under some contracts, payment is required if a specified uncertain event occurs, regardless of whether there is an adverse effect on the policyholder. Such contracts are not insurance contracts, even if the holders use them to mitigate underlying risk exposures. The definition of an insurance contract (see **2.1**) requires an adverse effect on the policyholder, arising from a specified uncertain future event, to be a contractual precondition for payment. Although this contractual precondition does not require the insurer to investigate whether the event actually caused an adverse effect, it permits the insurer to deny payment if it is not satisfied that the event caused an adverse effect. [IFRS 4:B14]

Accordingly, when a holder uses a derivative to hedge an underlying non-financial variable that is correlated with cash flows from an asset of the entity, the derivative is not an insurance contract, because payment is not conditional on whether the holder is adversely affected by a reduction in the cash flows from the asset. [IFRS 4:B14]

Although the definition of an insurance contract requires an adverse effect on the policyholder, it does not limit the payment by the insurer to an amount equal to the financial impact of the adverse event. Thus, 'new-for-old' coverage, which pays the policyholder an amount sufficient to replace a damaged old asset with a new asset, is not excluded. Similarly, payments under a term life insurance contract are not limited to the financial loss suffered by the dependants, and the payment of predetermined amounts to quantify the loss caused by death or an accident is not precluded. [IFRS 4:B13]

2.2.4.2 Lapse, persistency and expense risk

Lapse risk is the risk that the counterparty will cancel the contract earlier than the issuer had expected in pricing the contract. Persistency risk is the risk that the counterparty will cancel the contract later than the issuer had expected in pricing the contract. Finally, expense risk is the risk of unexpected increases in the administrative costs associated with the servicing of a contract (rather than in costs associated with insured events). [IFRS 4:B15]

None of these risks is an insurance risk, because the payment to the counterparty is not contingent on an uncertain future event that adversely affects the counterparty. For example, an unexpected increase in the insurer's expenses does not adversely affect the counterparty. [IFRS 4:B15]

Accordingly, a contract that exposes the issuer to lapse risk, persistency risk or expense risk is not an insurance contract unless it also exposes the issuer to insurance risk. If the issuer of that contract mitigates that risk, however, by using a second contract to transfer part of that risk to another party, the second contract will expose that other party to insurance risk. [IFRS 4:B16]

2.3 Payments in kind

Under some insurance contracts, payments are permitted or required to be made in kind. For example, an insurer may replace a stolen item directly, instead of reimbursing the policyholder, or may use its own hospitals and medical staff to provide medical services covered by the contracts. [IFRS 4:B5]

Some fixed-fee service contracts, in which the level of service depends on an uncertain event, will meet the definition of an insurance contract in IFRS 4, even though they are not regulated as insurance contracts in some countries. For example:

[IFRS 4:B6]

- a service provider may agree, under a maintenance contract, to repair specified equipment after a malfunction. The fixed service fee is based on the expected number of malfunctions, but it is uncertain whether a particular machine will break down. The malfunction of the equipment adversely affects the owner and the contract compensates the owner (in kind, rather than cash); and

- under a contract for car breakdown services, the provider may agree, for a fixed annual fee, to provide roadside assistance or to tow the car to a nearby garage. The contract could meet the definition of an insurance contract even if the provider does not agree to carry out repairs or replace parts.

The IASB's view is that applying IFRS 4 to such contracts is likely to be no more of a burden than applying the IFRSs that would be applicable if such contracts were outside the scope of IFRS 4. In particular:

[IFRS 4:B7]

- there are unlikely to be material liabilities for malfunctions and breakdowns that have already occurred;

- if IFRS 15 *Revenue from Contracts with Customers* applies, the service provider should recognise revenue when (or as) it transfers services to the customer (subject to other specified criteria); for entities that have not yet adopted IFRS 15, and that instead apply IAS 18 *Revenue*, the service provider would recognise revenue by reference to the stage of completion (and subject to other specified criteria). These approaches are also acceptable under IFRS 4, which permits the service provider:

  - to continue its existing accounting policies for such contracts unless they involve practices prohibited by IFRS 4:14 (see **4.3.1**); and

  - to improve its accounting policies if so permitted by IFRS 4:22 to 30 (see **4.4**);

- the service provider considers whether the cost of meeting its contractual obligation to provide services exceeds the revenue received in advance. To do this, it applies the liability adequacy test described at **4.3.2**. If IFRS 4 did not apply to these contracts, the service provider would apply IAS 37 *Provisions, Contingent Liabilities and Contingent Assets* to determine whether the contracts are onerous; and

- for such contracts, the disclosure requirements in IFRS 4 are unlikely to add significantly to disclosures required by other IFRSs.

2.4   Changes in the level of insurance risk

Once a contract qualifies as an insurance contract, it remains an insurance contract until all rights and obligations are extinguished or expire. [IFRS 4:B30]

Some contracts do not transfer any insurance risk to the issuer at inception, although they do transfer insurance risk at a later time. IFRS 4 gives the example of a contract that provides a specified investment return and includes an option for the policyholder to use the proceeds of the investment on maturity to buy a life-contingent annuity at then current annuity rates. No insurance risk is transferred to the issuer until the option is exercised, because the insurer is free to price the annuity on a basis that reflects the insurance risk transferred to the insurer at that time. If the contract specifies the annuity rates (or a basis for setting the annuity rates), however, the contract transfers insurance risk to the issuer at inception. [IFRS 4:B29]

2.5   Examples of insurance contracts

IFRS 4:Appendix B lists the following examples of contracts that will be insurance contracts, provided that the transfer of insurance risk is significant:

[IFRS 4:B18]

(a) insurance against theft or damage to property;

(b) insurance against product liability, professional liability, civil liability or legal expenses;

(c) life insurance and prepaid funeral plans (since, although death is certain, it is uncertain when death will occur or, for some types of life insurance, whether death will occur within the period covered by the insurance);

(d) life-contingent annuities and pensions (i.e. contracts that provide compensation for the uncertain future event – the survival of the annuitant or pensioner – to assist the annuitant or pensioner in maintaining a given standard of living, which would otherwise be adversely affected by his or her survival);

(e) disability and medical cover;

(f) surety bonds, fidelity bonds, performance bonds and bid bonds (i.e. contracts that provide compensation if another party fails to perform a contractual obligation, e.g. an obligation to construct a building);

(g) credit insurance that provides for specified payments to be made to reimburse the holder for a loss it incurs because a specified debtor fails to make payment when due under the original or modified terms of a debt instrument. Such contracts could have various legal forms (e.g. a guarantee, some types of letter of credit, a credit derivative default contract or an insurance contract). Although these contracts meet the definition of an insurance contract, they also meet the definition of a financial guarantee contract in IFRS 9 (or, for entities that have not yet adopted IFRS 9, IAS 39), and are within the scope of IAS 32 *Financial Instruments: Presentation*, IFRS 9 (or IAS 39) and IFRS 7 *Financial Instruments: Disclosures* rather than IFRS 4. See **3.3** for guidance on the very limited circumstances in which they may be accounted for under IFRS 4;

(h) product warranties. Product warranties issued by another party for goods sold by a manufacturer, dealer or retailer are within the scope of IFRS 4. Product warranties issued directly by a manufacturer, dealer or retailer are outside its scope, however, because they are within the scope of IFRS 15 *Revenue from Contracts with Customers* (see **chapter A14**) or, for entities that have not yet adopted IFRS 15, IAS 18 *Revenue* (see **appendix A1**), and IAS 37 (see **chapter A12**);

(i) title insurance (i.e. insurance against the discovery of defects in title to land that were not apparent when the insurance contract was written). In this case, the insured event is the discovery of a defect in the title, not the defect itself;

(j) travel assistance (i.e. compensation in cash or in kind to policyholders for losses suffered while they are travelling). (Some contracts of this kind are discussed at **2.3**);

(k) catastrophe bonds that provide for reduced payments of principal, interest or both if a specified event adversely affects the issuer of the bond (unless the specified event does not create significant insurance risk, for example if the event is a change in an interest rate or foreign exchange rate);

(l) insurance swaps and other contracts that require a payment based on changes in climatic, geological or other physical variables that are specific to a party to the contract; and

(m) reinsurance contracts.

2.6   Contracts that are not insurance contracts

2.6.1   Examples of contracts that are not insurance contracts

IFRS 4:Appendix B lists the following examples of contracts that are not insurance contracts:

[IFRS 4:B19]

(a) investment contracts that have the legal form of an insurance contract but do not expose the insurer to significant insurance risk. An example is a life insurance contract in which the insurer bears no significant mortality risk (such contracts are non-insurance financial instruments or service contracts – see **2.6.2**);

(b) contracts that have the legal form of insurance, but pass all significant insurance risk back to the policyholder through non-cancellable and enforceable mechanisms that adjust future payments by the policyholder as a direct result of insured losses. Examples are some financial reinsurance contracts and some group contracts (such contracts are normally non-insurance financial instruments or service contracts – see **2.6.2**);

(c) self-insurance (i.e. retaining a risk that could have been covered by insurance; there is no insurance contract because there is no agreement with another party);

(d) contracts (such as gambling contracts) that require a payment if a specified uncertain future event occurs, but do not require, as a contractual precondition for payment, that the event adversely affects the policyholder. This does not, however, preclude the specification of a predetermined payout to quantify the loss caused by a specified event such as death or an accident (see also **2.2.4.1**);

(e) derivatives that expose one party to financial risk but not insurance risk, because they require that party to make payment based solely on changes in one or more of a specified interest rate, financial instrument price, commodity price, foreign exchange rate, index of prices or rates, credit rating or credit index or other variable, provided in the case of a non-financial variable that the variable is not specific to a party to the contract (see **section 2** of **chapter B4** or, for entities that have not yet adopted IFRS 9, **section 2** of **chapter C4**);

(f) a credit-related guarantee (or letter of credit, credit derivative default contract or credit insurance contract) that requires payments even if the holder has not incurred a loss on the failure of the debtor to make payments when due (see **section 2** of **chapter B1** or, for entities that have not yet adopted IFRS 9, **section 2** of **chapter C1**);

(g) contracts that require a payment based on a climatic, geological or other physical variable that is not specific to a party to the contract (commonly described as 'weather derivatives'); and

(h) catastrophe bonds that provide for reduced payments of principal, interest or both, based on a climatic, geological or other physical variable that is not specific to a party to the contract.

2.6.2   Accounting for contracts other than insurance contracts

The appropriate accounting for the contracts described at **2.6.1** will depend on whether they create financial assets and financial liabilities:

- if the contracts create financial assets or financial liabilities, they are within the scope of IFRS 9 (or, for entities that have not yet adopted

IFRS 9, IAS 39) (see **Volume B** and **Volume C**, respectively). Among other things, this means that the parties to the contract use what is sometimes called 'deposit accounting', which involves: [IFRS 4:B20 & B21]

- one party recognising the consideration received as a financial liability, rather than as revenue; and

- the other party recognising the consideration paid as a financial asset, rather than as an expense; and

- if the contracts do not create financial assets or financial liabilities, IFRS 15 *Revenue from Contracts with Customers* applies (see **chapter A14**). Under IFRS 15, revenue is recognised when (or as) an entity satisfies a performance obligation by transferring a promised good or service to a customer in an amount that reflects the consideration to which the entity expects to be entitled. For entities that have not yet adopted IFRS 15, IAS 18 *Revenue* applies in such circumstances (see **appendix A1**). Under IAS 18, revenue associated with a transaction involving the rendering of services is recognised by reference to the stage of completion of the transaction if the outcome of the transaction can be estimated reliably.

Example 2.6.2

Accounting for the 'laying-off' of bets by a gaming operator

A gaming operator may wish to 'lay off' some of the risk it has taken on from gamblers in addition to managing the odds on any additional bets relating to the particular outcome or event. This may happen when the operator has accepted too many bets for a particular outcome. This lay-off is achieved by the operator buying wagers (as opposed to selling wagers).

In the circumstances described, the acquisition of wagers used to transfer a portion of the operator's risk of its sold wagers to other operators does not constitute an insurance contract within the scope of IFRS 4. IFRS 4:2 states that the Standard applies only to contracts that are either insurance contracts issued by the entity or reinsurance contracts held by the entity (or to financial instruments issued by an entity that have a discretionary participation feature – not relevant in this example). The contract to lay off some of the risk held by the gaming operator is, therefore, only within the scope of IFRS 4 if it meets the definition of a reinsurance contract. A reinsurance contract is defined as "an insurance contract issued by one insurer (the reinsurer) to compensate another insurer (the cedant) for losses on one or more contracts issued by the cedant". The contracts between the gaming operator and the gamblers are not considered insurance contracts in accordance with IFRS 4:B19(d) (see **2.6.1**) and, therefore, the lay-off contract cannot be a reinsurance contract.

In the circumstances described, the operator has purchased a derivative financial asset that should be recognised in its financial statements at fair value with subsequent changes in fair value recognised in profit or loss.

Because the gaming operator does not have a legally enforceable right to set off the financial asset arising from the lay-off transaction against the underlying risk exposure arising on the wagers accepted, offset in the financial statements is not permitted as per IAS 32:42.

The accounting treatment for an operator who accepts and lays-off bets is also described in **section 4** of **chapter B4** (or, for entities that have not yet adopted IFRS 9, **section 4** of **chapter C4**).

3   Scope of IFRS 4

3.1   Scope – general

IFRS 4 applies to specified contracts and instruments, as defined in the Standard, rather than to entities that are involved with such contracts and instruments. Thus, the Standard applies to insurance contracts rather than to insurers *per se*. This approach has important consequences. It means, in particular, that:

- some entities that are not regarded as insurers for legal or supervisory purposes may nevertheless have contracts or instruments that fall within the scope of the Standard; and

- some contracts and instruments with which an insurer is involved are outside the scope of IFRS 4 and are not therefore entitled to the exemptions offered by the Standard.

IFRS 4 describes any entity that issues an insurance contract as an insurer, whether or not the issuer is regarded as an insurer for legal or supervisory purposes. [IFRS 4:5]

3.2   Direct insurance contracts vs reinsurance contracts

In certain respects, IFRS 4 applies differently to direct insurance contracts and to reinsurance contracts; it is therefore important to distinguish between those two types of contract.

The definition of an insurance contract is discussed in **section 2**. The parties to an insurance contract are:

[IFRS 4:Appendix A]

- the policyholder, defined as a party that has a right to compensation under an insurance contract if an insured event occurs; and

- the insurer, defined as the party that has an obligation under an insurance contract to compensate a policyholder if an insured event occurs.

A reinsurance contract is a particular type of insurance contract, entered into between parties that are both insurers (though in respect of different contracts). IFRS 4 provides the following definitions:

[IFRS 4:Appendix A]

- a cedant is the policyholder under a reinsurance contract;

- a reinsurer is the party that has an obligation under a reinsurance contract to compensate a cedant if an insured event occurs; and

- a reinsurance contract is an insurance contract issued by one insurer (the reinsurer) to compensate another insurer (the cedant) for losses on one or more contracts issued by the cedant.

A direct insurance contract is then defined as an insurance contract that is not a reinsurance contract. [IFRS 4:Appendix A]

References in IFRS 4 (and in this chapter) to insurance contracts apply equally to direct insurance contracts and to reinsurance contracts. [IFRS 4:6]

3.3   Items to which IFRS 4 applies

IFRS 4 applies to:

[IFRS 4:2]

- insurance contracts (including reinsurance contracts) issued by an entity;

- reinsurance contracts (but not direct insurance contracts) held by an entity; and

- financial instruments issued by an entity that have a discretionary participation feature (see **4.6**).

IFRS 4 does not address other aspects of accounting by insurers, such as accounting for financial assets held by insurers and financial liabilities issued by insurers (covered by IAS 32 *Financial Instruments: Presentation*, IFRS 9 *Financial Instruments* (or, for entities that have not yet adopted IFRS 9, IAS 39 *Financial Instruments: Recognition and Measurement*), and IFRS 7 *Financial Instruments: Disclosures* – see **Volume B** (for entities applying IFRS 9) and **Volume C** (for entities applying IAS 39)). [IFRS 4:3]

3.4   Items to which IFRS 4 does not apply

IFRS 4 does not apply to:

[IFRS 4:4]

- product warranties issued directly by a manufacturer, dealer or retailer. These are dealt with under IFRS 15 *Revenue from Contracts with Customers* (see **chapter A14**) or, for entities that have not yet adopted

IFRS 15, IAS 18 *Revenue* (see **appendix A1**), and IAS 37 *Provisions, Contingent Liabilities and Contingent Assets* (see **chapter A12**);

- employers' assets and liabilities under employee benefit plans. These are dealt with under IAS 19 *Employee Benefits* (see **chapter A15**) and IFRS 2 *Share-based Payment* (see **chapter A16**);

- retirement benefit obligations reported by defined benefit retirement plans. These are dealt with under IAS 26 *Accounting and Reporting by Retirement Benefit Plans* (see **chapter A41**);

- contractual rights or contractual obligations that are contingent on the future use of, or right to use, a non-financial item (e.g. some licence fees, royalties, variable lease payments and similar items), as well as a lessee's residual value guarantee embedded in a lease (or, for entities that have not yet adopted IFRS 16, a finance lease). These are dealt with under IFRS 16 *Leases* (see **chapter A17**), or, for entities that have not yet adopted IFRS 16, IAS 17 *Leases* (see **appendix A4**), IFRS 15 (see **chapter A14**) or, for entities that have not yet adopted IFRS 15, IAS 18 (see **appendix A1**), and IAS 38 *Intangible Assets* (see **chapter A9**);

> IFRS 4:4 was amended in January 2016 by consequential amendments arising from IFRS 16. Under IFRS 16's predecessor Standard, IAS 17, 'variable' lease payments were referred to as 'contingent' lease payments.

- contingent consideration payable or receivable in a business combination. This is dealt with initially under IFRS 3 *Business Combinations* (see **chapter A25**), and subsequently under IAS 32, IFRS 9 (or, for entities that have not yet adopted IFRS 9, IAS 39), and IFRS 7 – see **Volume B** (for entities applying IFRS 9) and **Volume C** (for entities applying IAS 39);

- financial guarantee contracts (see **2.3.3** in **chapter B1** (or, for entities that have not yet adopted IFRS 9, **2.3.3** in **chapter C1**) for definition and further guidance), unless the issuer has previously asserted explicitly that it regards such contracts as insurance contracts and has used accounting applicable to insurance contracts, in which case the issuer may elect to apply either IFRS 9 (or, for entities that have not yet adopted IFRS 9, IAS 39), IAS 32 and IFRS 7 or IFRS 4 to such financial guarantee contracts. This election is available on a contract-by-contract basis, but is irrevocable once made; and

- direct insurance contracts in which the entity is the policyholder (but note that IFRS 4 does apply to reinsurance contracts in which the entity is the cedant).

3.5   Embedded derivatives

As explained in **chapter B5** (or, for entities that have not yet adopted IFRS 9, **chapter C5**), IFRS 9 (or, for entities that have not yet adopted IFRS 9, IAS 39) requires some embedded derivatives to be separated from their host contracts and measured at fair value, with changes in fair value recognised in profit or loss. Apart from the two exceptions described below, those requirements of IFRS 9 (or IAS 39) apply irrespective of whether the host contracts are within the scope of IFRS 4. In other words, unless one of the exceptions below applies, when an entity has derivatives embedded in insurance contracts or in financial instruments issued with a discretionary participation feature, they should be separated out (or not) in accordance with IFRS 9 (or IAS 39). [IFRS 4:7]

The two exceptions to this are as follows:

- IFRS 9 (or, for entities that have not yet adopted IFRS 9, IAS 39) does not apply to a derivative embedded in an insurance contract if that embedded derivative is itself an insurance contract; [IFRS 4:7] and

- an insurer need not separate, and measure at fair value, a policyholder's option to surrender an insurance contract (or a financial instrument containing a discretionary participation feature) for a fixed amount (or for an amount based on a fixed amount and an interest rate), even if the exercise price differs from the carrying amount of the host insurance liability. [IFRS 4:8 & 9]

However, IFRS 9 (or, for entities that have not yet adopted IFRS 9, IAS 39) applies to a put option or cash surrender option embedded in an insurance contract (or a financial instrument issued with a discretionary participation feature) if the surrender value varies in response to the change in a financial variable (such as an equity or commodity price or index), or a non-financial variable that is not specific to a party to the contract. Furthermore, IFRS 9 (or IAS 39) also applies if the holder's ability to exercise a put option or cash surrender option is triggered by a change in such a variable (e.g. a put option that can be exercised if a stock market index reaches a specified level). [IFRS 4:8 & 9]

3.6   Unbundling of deposit components

Some insurance contracts contain both an insurance component and a deposit component (see **2.2.3.6**). Depending on whether specified conditions are met, as set out in the diagram below, IFRS 4 either requires, permits or prohibits the unbundling of those components (i.e. accounting for them as if they were separate contracts). [IFRS 4:10]

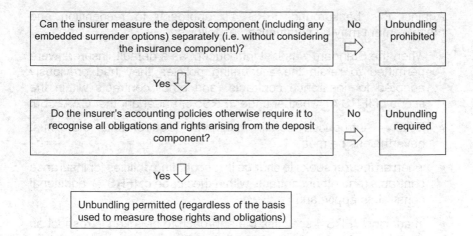

When a deposit component is unbundled:

[IFRS 4:12]

- IFRS 4 is applied to the insurance component; and

- IFRS 9 (or, for entities that have not yet adopted IFRS 9, IAS 39) is applied to the deposit component.

Example 3.6

Insurer's accounting policies do not require it to recognise all obligations arising from a deposit component

[IFRS 4:11]

A cedant receives compensation for losses from a reinsurer, but the contract obliges the cedant to repay the compensation in future years. That obligation arises from a deposit component. If the cedant's accounting policies would otherwise permit it to recognise the compensation as income without recognising the resulting obligation, unbundling is required.

---

4 Recognition and measurement

4.1 Recognition and measurement requirements – general

As explained in **1.1**, the objectives of IFRS 4 are quite limited, because the IASB is still working on the major issues in its insurance project. On recognition and measurement, therefore, when IFRS 4 was first introduced, the Board tried to steer a path between, on the one hand, being too prescriptive when it had not yet finalised its thinking and, on the other hand, being too permissive in allowing practices to continue that, based on its deliberations to date, the Board did not favour.

Against this background, IFRS 4's approach to recognition and measurement may be summarised as follows:

- when the Standard was first introduced, as a default, insurers were permitted to retain the accounting policies they had previously adopted for insurance contracts (and other contracts within the scope of IFRS 4), whether under IFRSs or under another GAAP; but

- IFRS 4 introduced certain minimum requirements that must nevertheless be met;

- when an insurer seeks to change its accounting policies for insurance contracts (and other contracts within the scope of IFRS 4), additional constraints apply; and

- in addition, IFRS 4 specifies the approach to be taken in respect of:

  - insurance contracts acquired in a business combination or portfolio transfer; and

  - discretionary participation features.

Each of these aspects is considered in **4.2** to **4.6**.

4.2 Retention of existing accounting policies

Under IAS 8 *Accounting Policies, Changes in Accounting Estimates and Errors*, the general principle is that, when no IFRS applies specifically to an item, an entity looks to the criteria set out in IAS 8:10 to 12 in developing an accounting policy for that item (see **chapter A5**). In order to allow insurers to continue with their existing practices (subject to the constraints discussed in the following sections), IFRS 4 exempts an insurer from applying those criteria to its accounting policies for:

[IFRS 4:13]

- insurance contracts that it issues, including related acquisition costs and related intangible assets, such as those described in IFRS 4:31 and 32 (see **4.5**); and

- reinsurance contracts that it holds.

4.3 Minimum requirements for accounting policies

4.3.1 Requirements applicable for contracts within the scope of IFRS 4

The IASB believes that certain implications of the IAS 8 criteria for developing accounting policies nevertheless remain relevant for contracts within the scope of IFRS 4. Accordingly, the Standard requires an insurer:

[IFRS 4:14]

- not to recognise as a liability any provisions for possible future claims, if those claims arise under insurance contracts that are not in existence at the end of the reporting period (such as catastrophe provisions and equalisation provisions);

- to carry out a liability adequacy test (see **4.3.2**);

- to remove an insurance liability (i.e. the insurer's net contractual obligations under an insurance contract), or a part of an insurance liability, from its statement of financial position when, and only when, it is extinguished (i.e. when the obligation specified in the contract is discharged or cancelled or expires);

- not to offset:

  - reinsurance assets (being a cedant's net contractual rights under a reinsurance contract) against the related insurance liabilities; or

  - income or expense from reinsurance contracts against the expense or income from the related insurance contracts; and

- to consider whether its reinsurance assets are impaired (see **4.3.3**).

4.3.2   Liability adequacy test

4.3.2.1   Liability adequacy test – definition

IFRS 4 defines a liability adequacy test as an assessment of whether the carrying amount of an insurance liability needs to be increased (or the carrying amount of related deferred acquisition costs or related intangible assets decreased), based on a review of future cash flows. [IFRS 4:Appendix A]

4.3.2.2   Requirement to carry out a liability adequacy test

An insurer must carry out a liability adequacy test at the end of each reporting period, using current estimates of future cash flows under its insurance contracts. If that assessment shows that the carrying amount of its insurance liabilities (less related deferred acquisition costs and related intangible assets, such as those discussed in IFRS 4:31 and 32 – see **4.5**) is inadequate in the light of the estimated future cash flows, the entire deficiency is to be recognised in profit or loss. [IFRS 4:15]

IFRS 4 acknowledges that some insurers will already apply liability adequacy tests. If these meet the specified minimum requirements set out at **4.3.2.3**, they are acceptable under IFRS 4. When this is not the case, IFRS 4 requires the approach set out at **4.3.2.4** to be followed.

4.3.2.3   Minimum requirements for a liability adequacy test

The minimum requirements for a liability adequacy test are that:

[IFRS 4:16]

- the test considers current estimates of all contractual cash flows, and of related cash flows such as claims handling costs, as well as cash flows resulting from embedded options and guarantees; and

- if the test shows that the liability is inadequate, the entire deficiency is recognised in profit or loss.

When an insurer applies a liability adequacy test that meets these minimum requirements, the further requirements discussed at **4.3.2.4** do not apply. [IFRS 4:16] In particular, provided that the insurer's liability adequacy test meets these minimum requirements, there are no constraints over the level of aggregation. [IFRS 4:18]

4.3.2.4 Approach when minimum requirements are not met

The approach described below must be applied for 'relevant insurance liabilities', i.e. those insurance liabilities (and related deferred acquisition costs and related intangible assets) for which the insurer's accounting policies do not require a liability adequacy test that meets the minimum requirements at **4.3.2.3**. [IFRS 4:17] The comparison is made at the level of a portfolio of contracts that are subject to broadly similar risks and managed together as a single portfolio. [IFRS 4:18]

The insurer is required to:

[IFRS 4:17]

(a) determine the carrying amount of the relevant insurance liabilities less the carrying amount of:

   (i) any related deferred acquisition costs; and

   (ii) any related intangible assets, such as those acquired in a business combination or portfolio transfer (see **4.5**). Related reinsurance assets are not considered, however, because an insurer accounts for them separately (see **4.3.3**); and

(b) determine whether the amount described in (a) is less than the carrying amount that would be required if the relevant insurance liabilities were within the scope of IAS 37 *Provisions, Contingent Liabilities and Contingent Assets* (see **chapter A12**). If it is less, the insurer must recognise the entire difference in profit or loss and decrease the carrying amount of the related deferred acquisition costs or related intangible assets or increase the carrying amount of the relevant insurance liabilities.

The amount described in IFRS 4:17(b) (i.e. the result of applying IAS 37) is to reflect future investment margins (see **4.4.5**) if, and only if, the amount described in (a) also reflects those margins. [IFRS 4:19]

4.3.3 Impairment of reinsurance assets

If a cedant's reinsurance asset is impaired, its carrying amount should be reduced accordingly and the impairment loss recognised in profit or loss. A reinsurance asset is impaired if, and only if:

[IFRS 4:20]

- there is objective evidence, as a result of an event that occurred after initial recognition of the reinsurance asset, that the cedant may not receive all amounts due to it under the terms of the contract; and

- that event has a reliably measurable impact on the amounts that the cedant will receive from the reinsurer.

4.4 Changes in accounting policies

4.4.1 Changes in accounting policies for insurance contracts – general

The requirements discussed in this section apply both to changes made by an insurer that already applies IFRSs and to changes made by an insurer adopting IFRSs for the first time. [IFRS 4:21]

An insurer may change its accounting policies for insurance contracts if, and only if, the change makes the financial statements:

[IFRS 4:22]

- more relevant to the economic decision-making needs of users and no less reliable; or

- more reliable and no less relevant to those needs.

Relevance and reliability are judged by the criteria in IAS 8 *Accounting Policies, Changes in Accounting Estimates and Errors*. [IFRS 4:22] A change in accounting policies for insurance contracts should bring an insurer's financial statements closer to meeting the criteria in IAS 8, but the change need not achieve full compliance with those criteria. [IFRS 4:23] Additional requirements are discussed at **4.4.2** to **4.4.6**.

When an insurer changes its accounting policies for insurance liabilities, it is permitted, but not required, to reclassify some or all of its financial assets as 'at fair value' (or, for entities that have not yet adopted IFRS 9 *Financial Instruments*, 'at fair value through profit or loss'). This reclassification is permitted if an insurer changes accounting policies when it first applies IFRS 4 and if it makes a subsequent policy change permitted by IFRS 4:22. The reclassification is a change in accounting policy and IAS 8 applies. [IFRS 4:45] This reclassification is permitted for an insurer that has adopted IFRS 9, notwithstanding IFRS 9:4.4.1.

4.4.2   Current market interest rates

An insurer is permitted, but not required, to change its accounting policies so that it:

[IFRS 4:24]

- remeasures designated insurance liabilities (which, for this purpose, include related deferred acquisition costs and related intangible assets, such as those discussed at **4.5**) to reflect current market interest rates; and

- recognises changes in those liabilities in profit or loss.

At that time, the insurer may also introduce accounting policies that require other current estimates and assumptions for the designated liabilities. The election in IFRS 4:24 permits an insurer to change its accounting policies for designated liabilities, without applying those policies consistently to all similar liabilities (as would otherwise be required by IAS 8). When an insurer designates liabilities for this election, it must continue to apply current market interest rates (and, if applicable, the other current estimates and assumptions) consistently in all periods to all these liabilities until they are extinguished. [IFRS 4:24]

4.4.3   Practices that may be continued but not introduced as part of a change in accounting policy

The following practices may be continued when they form part of an existing accounting policy, but an insurer may not introduce any of them as part of a change of accounting policy:

[IFRS 4:25]

(a) measuring insurance liabilities on an undiscounted basis;

(b) measuring contractual rights to future investment management fees at an amount that exceeds their fair value as implied by a comparison with current fees charged by other market participants for similar services. (IFRS 4 indicates that the fair value at inception of those contractual rights is likely to equal the origination costs paid, unless future investment management fees and related costs are out of line with market comparables); and

(c) using non-uniform accounting policies for the insurance contracts (and related deferred acquisition costs and related intangible assets, if any) of subsidiaries, except as permitted at **4.4.2**. If those accounting policies are not uniform, an insurer may change them if the change does not make the accounting policies more diverse and also satisfies the other requirements in IFRS 4.

4.4.4 Prudence

An insurer need not change its accounting policies for insurance contracts to eliminate excessive prudence. If an insurer already measures its insurance contracts with sufficient prudence, however, it should not introduce additional prudence. [IFRS 4:26]

4.4.5 Future investment margins

An insurer need not change its accounting policies for insurance contracts to eliminate future investment margins. There is a rebuttable presumption, however, that an insurer's financial statements will become less relevant and reliable if it introduces an accounting policy that reflects future investment margins in the measurement of insurance contracts, unless those margins affect the contractual payments. Two examples of accounting policies that reflect those margins are:

[IFRS 4:27]

(a) using a discount rate that reflects the estimated return on the insurer's assets; or

(b) projecting the returns on those assets at an estimated rate of return, discounting those projected returns at a different rate and including the result in the measurement of the liability.

The rebuttable presumption described above may be overcome if, and only if, the other components of a change in accounting policies increase the relevance and reliability of an insurer's financial statements sufficiently to outweigh the decrease in relevance and reliability caused by the inclusion of future investment margins. [IFRS 4:28]

Example 4.4.5

Change in accounting policy

[IFRS 4:28]

Suppose that an insurer's existing accounting policies for insurance contracts involve excessively prudent assumptions set at inception and a discount rate prescribed by a regulator without direct reference to market conditions, and ignore some embedded options and guarantees. The insurer might make its financial statements more relevant and no less reliable by switching to a comprehensive investor-oriented basis of accounting that is widely used and involves:

(a) current estimates and assumptions;

(b) a reasonable (but not excessively prudent) adjustment to reflect risk and uncertainty;

(c) measurements that reflect both the intrinsic value and time value of embedded options and guarantees; and

---

> (d)   a current market discount rate, even if that discount rate reflects the estimated return on the insurer's assets.

In some measurement approaches, the discount rate is used to determine the present value of a future profit margin and that profit margin is then attributed to different periods using a formula. In those approaches, the discount rate affects the measurement of the liability only indirectly. In particular, the use of a less appropriate discount rate has a limited or no effect on the measurement of the liability at inception. In other approaches, however, the discount rate determines directly the measurement of the liability. In the latter case, because the introduction of an asset-based discount rate has a more significant effect, IFRS 4 indicates that it is highly unlikely that an insurer could overcome the rebuttable presumption described in IFRS 4:27. [IFRS 4:29]

4.4.6   Shadow accounting

In some accounting models, realised gains or losses on an insurer's assets have a direct effect on the measurement of some or all of:

[IFRS 4:30]

- its insurance liabilities;

- related deferred acquisition costs; and

- related intangible assets, such as those described at **4.5**.

An insurer is permitted, but not required, to change its accounting policies so that a recognised but unrealised gain or loss on an asset affects those measurements in the same way as does a realised gain or loss. The related adjustment to the insurance liability (or deferred acquisition costs or intangible assets) is recognised in other comprehensive income if, and only if, the unrealised gains or losses are recognised in other comprehensive income. This practice is sometimes known as 'shadow accounting'. [IFRS 4:30]

4.5   Insurance contracts acquired in a business combination or portfolio transfer

When insurance liabilities are assumed and insurance assets (i.e. an insurer's net contractual rights under an insurance contract) are acquired by an insurer in a business combination, they should be measured at fair value at the acquisition date, in accordance with IFRS 3 *Business Combinations* (see **chapter A25**). IFRS 4 permits, but does not require, the use of an expanded presentation that splits the fair value of acquired insurance contracts into two components:

[IFRS 4:31]

(a) a liability measured in accordance with the insurer's accounting policies for insurance contracts that it issues; and

(b) an intangible asset, representing the difference between:

    (i) the fair value of the contractual insurance rights acquired and insurance obligations assumed; and

    (ii) the amount described in (a).

The subsequent measurement of this asset should be consistent with the measurement of the related insurance liability.

An insurer acquiring a portfolio of insurance contracts may also use the expanded presentation described above. [IFRS 4:32]

When such intangible assets are recognised, they are excluded from the scope of IAS 36 *Impairment of Assets* (see **chapter A10**) and IAS 38 *Intangible Assets* (see **chapter A9**). It must be emphasised, however, that IAS 36 and IAS 38 apply to customer lists and customer relationships reflecting the expectation of future contracts that are not part of the contractual insurance rights and contractual insurance obligations that existed at the date of a business combination or portfolio transfer. [IFRS 4:33]

In other words, the approach described above applies only to an intangible asset whose value, on acquisition, is part of the fair value of insurance contracts. It does not apply to any intangible asset that would be required, under IAS 38, to be recognised separately from insurance contracts.

4.6 Discretionary participation features

4.6.1 Discretionary participation features – general

Some contracts provide for a policyholder or investor to receive only 'guaranteed benefits', which IFRS 4 defines as payments or other benefits to which a particular policyholder or investor has an unconditional right that is not subject to the contractual discretion of the issuer. [IFRS 4:Appendix A] Others may include discretionary participation features.

IFRS 4 defines a discretionary participation feature as a contractual right to receive, as a supplement to guaranteed benefits, additional benefits:

[IFRS 4:Appendix A]

- that are likely to be a significant portion of the total contractual benefits;

- whose amount or timing is contractually at the discretion of the issuer; and

- that are contractually based on:

  - the performance of a specified pool of contracts or a specified type of contract;

  - realised and/or unrealised investment returns on a specified pool of assets held by the issuer; or

  - the profit or loss of the company, fund or other entity that issues the contract.

When a contract contains a discretionary participation feature, an obligation to pay guaranteed benefits is referred to as the 'guaranteed element'.

IFRS 7 *Financial Instruments: Disclosures* requires disclosures about financial instruments, including financial instruments that contain discretionary participation features (see **chapter B12** or, for entities that have not yet adopted IFRS 9, **chapter C12**).

In November 2005, the IFRIC (now the IFRS Interpretations Committee) declined a request to give further guidance on:

- the definition of a discretionary participation feature; and

- the interaction of the liability adequacy test (see **4.3.2**) with the minimum measurement of the guaranteed element of a financial liability containing a discretionary participation feature.

The Committee was informed of concerns that key disclosures regarding these features are required only in respect of items regarded as discretionary participation features. Consequently, a narrow interpretation of the definition would fail to ensure clear and comprehensive disclosure about contracts that include these features. The Committee noted that disclosure is particularly important in this area, given the potential for a wide range of treatments until the IASB completes phase II of its project on insurance contracts. The Committee noted that IFRS 4 requires an insurer to disclose information that identifies and explains the amounts in its financial statements arising from insurance contracts (see **5.1**) and information that helps users to understand the amount, timing and uncertainty of future cash flows from insurance contracts (see **5.2**).

The Committee also noted that the implementation guidance accompanying IFRS 4 was designed to help entities to develop disclosures about insurance contracts that contain a discretionary participation feature. The Committee decided not to add this topic to its agenda, because it involves some of the most difficult questions that the IASB will need to resolve in phase II of its project on insurance contracts. The fact that, in developing IFRS 4, the IASB chose to defer such questions to phase II limits the scope for reducing diversity through an Interpretation.

4.6.2 Requirements for insurance contracts that contain discretionary participation features

When an insurance contract contains a discretionary participation feature as well as a guaranteed element, IFRS 4 specifies the following requirements.

[IFRS 4:34]

(a) The issuer is permitted, but not required, to recognise the guaranteed element separately from the discretionary participation feature. If the issuer does not recognise them separately, the whole contract should be classified as a liability. If the issuer classifies them separately, the guaranteed element should be classified as a liability.

(b) If the issuer recognises the discretionary participation feature separately from the guaranteed element, that feature should be classified as either a liability or a separate component of equity. IFRS 4 does not specify how to determine whether a discretionary participation feature is a liability or equity. The issuer may split that feature into liability and equity components and use a consistent accounting policy for that split, but it must not classify that feature as an intermediate category that is neither liability nor equity.

(c) The issuer may recognise all premiums received as revenue without separating any portion that relates to the equity component. The resulting changes in the guaranteed element and in the portion of the discretionary participation feature classified as a liability are recognised in profit or loss. If part or all of the discretionary participation feature is classified in equity, a portion of profit or loss may be attributable to that feature (in the same way that a portion may be attributable to non-controlling interests). The portion of profit or loss attributable to any equity component of a discretionary participation feature is recognised as an allocation of profit or loss, not as expense or income.

(d) If the contract contains an embedded derivative within the scope of IFRS 9 *Financial Instruments* (or, for entities that have not yet adopted IFRS 9, IAS 39 *Financial Instruments: Recognition and Measurement*), IFRS 9 (or IAS 39) is applied to that embedded derivative.

(e) Except to the extent that changes are necessary to comply with the requirements discussed in **4.3** and in (a) to (d) above, the issuer should continue its existing accounting policies for such contracts, unless it changes those accounting policies in a way that complies with the requirements discussed in **4.4**.

4.6.3 Discretionary participation features in financial instruments

The requirements discussed at **4.6.2** also apply to a financial instrument that contains a discretionary participation feature. In addition:

[IFRS 4:35]

(a) if the entire discretionary participation feature is classified as a liability, the liability adequacy test discussed at **4.3.2** is applied to the whole contract (i.e. both the guaranteed element and the discretionary participation feature). It is not necessary to determine the amount that would result from applying IFRS 9 (or, for entities that have not yet adopted IFRS 9, IAS 39) to the guaranteed element;

(b) if part or all of the discretionary participation feature is classified as a separate component of equity, the liability recognised for the whole contract must not be less than the amount that would result from applying IFRS 9 (or, for entities that have not yet adopted IFRS 9, IAS 39) to the guaranteed element. That amount includes the intrinsic value of an option to surrender the contract, but need not include its time value if that option is exempt from measurement at fair value as discussed at **3.5**. The issuer need not disclose the amount that would result from applying IFRS 9 (or, for entities that have not yet adopted IFRS 9, IAS 39) to the guaranteed element, nor need it present that amount separately. Furthermore, the issuer need not determine that amount if the total liability recognised is clearly higher;

(c) although these contracts are financial instruments, the issuer may continue to recognise the premiums for those contracts as revenue and recognise as an expense the resulting increase in the carrying amount of the liability; and

(d) although these contracts are financial instruments, an issuer applying IFRS 7:20(b) to contracts with a discretionary participation feature should disclose the total interest expense recognised in profit or loss but need not calculate such interest expense using the effective interest method.

5 Disclosure

5.1 Explanation of recognised amounts

As an overall principle, IFRS 4 requires that an insurer should disclose information that identifies and explains the amounts in its financial statements arising from insurance contracts. [IFRS 4:36] To that end, the following disclosures are specifically required:

[IFRS 4:37]

(a) the insurer's accounting policies for insurance contracts and related assets, liabilities, income and expense;

(b) the recognised assets, liabilities, income and expense (and, if the insurer presents its statement of cash flows using the direct method, cash flows) arising from insurance contracts. In addition, if the insurer is a cedant, it should disclose:

(i) gains and losses recognised in profit or loss on buying reinsurance; and

(ii) if the cedant defers and amortises gains and losses arising on buying reinsurance, the amortisation for the period and the amounts remaining unamortised at the beginning and end of the period;

(c) the process used to determine the assumptions that have the greatest effect on the measurement of the recognised amounts described in (b). When practicable, an insurer should also give quantified disclosure of those assumptions;

(d) the effect of changes in assumptions used to measure insurance assets and insurance liabilities, showing separately the effect of each change that has a material effect on the financial statements; and

(e) reconciliations of changes in insurance liabilities, reinsurance assets and, if any, related deferred acquisition costs.

5.2 Amount, timing and uncertainty of cash flows

As an overall principle, IFRS 4 requires that an insurer should disclose information that helps users to understand the amount, timing and uncertainty of future cash flows from insurance contracts. [IFRS 4:38] To that end, an insurer is specifically required to disclose:

[IFRS 4:39]

(a) its objectives, policies and processes for managing risks arising from insurance contracts and the methods used to manage those risks;

(b) [deleted by IFRS 7 *Financial Instruments: Disclosures*];

(c) information about insurance risk (both before and after risk mitigation by reinsurance), including information about:

(i) sensitivity to insurance risk (see IFRS 4:39A, below);

(ii) concentrations of insurance risk, including a description of how management determines concentrations and a description of the shared characteristic that identifies each concentration (e.g. type of insured event, geographical area, or currency); and

(iii) actual claims compared with previous estimates (i.e. claims development). The disclosure about claims development should go back to the period when the earliest material claim arose for which there is still uncertainty about the amount and timing of the claims payments, but need not go back more than ten years. An insurer need not disclose this information for claims for which uncertainty about the amount and timing of claims payments is typically resolved within one year;

(d)   the information about credit risk, liquidity risk and market risk that IFRS 7:31 to 42 would require if the insurance contracts were within the scope of IFRS 7 (see **chapter B12** or, for entities that have not yet adopted IFRS 9 *Financial Instruments*, **chapter C12**). However:

  (i)   an insurer need not provide the maturity analyses required by IFRS 7:39(a) and (b) if it discloses information about the estimated timing of the net cash outflows resulting from recognised insurance liabilities instead. This may take the form of an analysis, by estimated timing, of the amounts recognised in the statement of financial position; and

  (ii)   if an insurer uses an alternative method to manage sensitivity to market conditions, such as an embedded value analysis, it may use that sensitivity analysis to meet the requirement in IFRS 7:40(a). Such an insurer should also provide the disclosures required by IFRS 7:41; and

(e)   information about exposures to market risk arising from embedded derivatives contained in a host insurance contract if the insurer is not required to, and does not, measure the embedded derivatives at fair value.

To comply with (c)(i) above, an insurer should disclose either (a) or (b) as follows:

[IFRS 4:39A]

(a)   a sensitivity analysis that shows how profit or loss and equity would have been affected if changes in the relevant risk variable that were reasonably possible at the end of the reporting period had occurred; the methods and assumptions used in preparing the sensitivity analysis; and any changes from the previous period in the methods and assumptions used. However, if an insurer uses an alternative method to manage sensitivity to market conditions, such as an embedded value analysis, it may meet this requirement by disclosing that alternative sensitivity analysis and the disclosures required by IFRS 7:41; or

(b)   qualitative information about sensitivity, and information about those terms and conditions of insurance contracts that have a material effect on the amount, timing and uncertainty of the insurer's future cash flows.

In applying IFRS 4:39(c)(iii), an entity need not disclose information about claims development that occurred earlier than five years before the end of the first financial year in which it applies IFRS 4. If it is impracticable, when an entity first applies IFRS 4, to prepare information about claims development that occurred before the beginning of the earliest period for which an entity presents full comparative information that complies with IFRS 4, that fact should be disclosed. [IFRS 4:44]

6 Future developments

6.1 Accounting for insurance contracts

The IASB is undertaking a comprehensive project on accounting for insurance contracts, with the objective of developing a comprehensive Standard that will address recognition, measurement, presentation and disclosure requirements for insurance contracts. The project began as a joint IASB-FASB project. However, in February 2014, the FASB tentatively decided to abandon its convergence efforts with the IASB on insurance contracts, and instead focus its future efforts on making targeted improvements to the existing US GAAP insurance accounting model.

In July 2010, the IASB issued an exposure draft ED/2010/8 *Insurance Contracts*. Following redeliberations by the Board, a targeted revised exposure draft ED/2013/7 *Insurance Contracts* was published in June 2013. Although the IASB re-exposed the entire text of the draft IFRS, it only sought targeted comments on five areas where the Board considered that the proposals represent a significant change from the original model presented in the 2010 ED.

At the time of writing, the IASB is continuing its deliberations on the project; a final Standard is expected in 2017.

6.2 Deferral of IFRS 9 for entities in scope of IFRS 4

In December 2015, the IASB issued an exposure draft, ED/2015/11 *Applying IFRS 9 Financial Instruments with IFRS 4 Insurance Contracts*. The exposure draft is intended to address concerns about the different effective dates of IFRS 9 *Financial Instruments* (effective for annual periods beginning on or after 1 January 2018, with earlier application permitted) and the forthcoming new Standard on insurance contracts (see **6.1**). The exposure draft proposes:

- to allow entities that predominantly issue insurance contracts the option to defer the effective date of IFRS 9 until 2021 (the 'temporary exemption'); and

- for those entities that do apply IFRS 9 in advance of the new insurance contracts Standard, to provide an option to remove from profit or loss those gains and losses that may arise from accounting mismatches that could occur during the interim period (the 'overlay approach').

The comment period for the exposure draft closed on 8 February 2016 and the IASB is expected to issue the final amendment in the second half of 2016.

A40 Exploration for and evaluation of mineral resources

Contents

1   Introduction

1.1   Overview of IFRS 6

IFRS 6 *Exploration for and Evaluation of Mineral Resources* specifies the financial reporting for the exploration for and evaluation of mineral resources. IFRS 6 has the effect of allowing entities adopting the Standard for the first time to use accounting policies for exploration and evaluation assets that were applied before adopting IFRSs. It also modifies impairment testing of exploration and evaluation assets by introducing different impairment indicators and allowing the carrying amount to be tested at an aggregate level (not greater than a segment).

IFRS 6 was introduced in 2004 as a 'temporary' measure. IFRS 6 does not deal with many of the most challenging accounting issues faced by entities in the extractive industries, not least of which is the measurement of reserves (e.g. oil reserves) and changes in reserve balances. The Standard focuses only on the activities undertaken during the exploration and evaluation phase.

The IASB's agenda currently includes a broad research project designed to assess the feasibility of developing one set of reporting requirements for investigative, exploratory and developmental activities across a wide range of activities, which would include the extractive industries. However, at the time of writing, the Board's work plan describes this project as 'inactive' and it is unlikely that any progress will be made for some time.

1.2   Amendments to IFRS 6 since the last edition of this manual

None. IFRS 6 was most recently amended in November 2008.

2   Scope

2.1   Scope – general

IFRS 6 applies to exploration and evaluation expenditures incurred by an entity that engages in the exploration for and the evaluation of mineral resources. [IFRS 6:3] It does not apply to any other expenditures, or any other aspects of accounting by such an entity. [IFRS 6:4]

Appendix A of IFRS 6 provides the following definitions.

- **Exploration and evaluation expenditures** are "[e]xpenditures incurred by an entity in connection with the exploration for and evaluation of mineral resources before the technical feasibility and commercial viability of extracting a mineral resource are demonstrable".

- **Exploration for and evaluation of mineral resources** is "the search for mineral resources, including minerals, oil, natural gas and similar non-regenerative resources, after the entity has obtained legal rights to explore in a specific area, as well as the determination of the technical feasibility and commercial viability of extracting the mineral resource".

- **Exploration and evaluation assets** are "[e]xploration and evaluation expenditures recognised as assets in accordance with the entity's accounting policy".

2.2   Scope – exclusions

Specifically, IFRS 6 does not apply to:

[IFRS 6:5]

- expenditures incurred before the exploration for and evaluation of mineral resources (e.g. expenditures incurred before the entity has obtained the legal rights to explore a specific area); or
- expenditures incurred after the technical feasibility and commercial viability of extracting a mineral resource are demonstrable.

Often, the process of extracting geological assets from a productive mine or oil well begins with prospecting activities when an entity looks for suitable property to exploit. Prospecting activities are generally carried out without ownership or legal rights to any specific piece of property and are very similar to the pure research stage for other entities engaged in research and development. The expenditures associated with prospecting activities are not within the scope of IFRS 6 because the activities are undertaken before legal rights to explore a specific area have been obtained.

Once a prospect is identified, rights to explore and/or exploit the area are often obtained and the entity undertakes a range of activities (which might include obtaining scoping studies, drilling, sampling etc.) to determine whether the site is worthy of exploitation. These are the 'exploration and evaluation' activities contemplated by IFRS 6. Once the site is judged to be worthy of exploitation, the expenditures incurred thereafter in connection with the project are no longer within the scope of IFRS 6.

Expenditures incurred during stages other than the exploration and evaluation stage are not addressed in IFRS 6. However, the IASB has noted that, notwithstanding the lack of a specific IFRS to address these areas, it expects entities to be able to develop appropriate accounting policies by applying existing IFRSs, the definitions of assets and expenses from the *Conceptual Framework for Financial Reporting* (see **chapter A2**) and the general principles for asset recognition in IAS 16 *Property, Plant and Equipment* (see **chapter A7**) and IAS 38 *Intangible Assets* (see **chapter A9**). [IFRS 6:BC7] Further, the Basis for Conclusions notes that pre-acquisition expenditures that are directly attributable to the acquisition of an intangible asset (e.g. those that are directly attributable to the acquisition of an operating licence) may need to be recognised as part of the intangible asset in accordance with IAS 38:27 (see **4.4.2.1** in **chapter A9**). [IFRS 6:BC12]

When developing accounting policies for activities prior to and after exploration and evaluation (i.e. for activities prior to obtaining exploration rights and for development and exploitation activities), entities are required to apply the hierarchy of IAS 8 *Accounting Policies, Changes in Accounting Estimates and Errors* in full (see **chapter A5**). Therefore, when adopting IFRSs for the first time, an entity is only permitted to continue its previous GAAP practices for development and exploitation activities if those practices comply with the requirements of the appropriate IFRSs. This principle was confirmed by the IFRIC (now the IFRS Interpretations Committee) in the January 2006 *IFRIC Update*.

2.3   Exploration and evaluation activities for geothermal energy

The exploration for and evaluation of possible sources of geothermal energy involves searching for viable active geothermal regions with the goal of building a geothermal power plant.

In this regard, exploration and evaluation activities for geothermal energy share the majority, if not all, of the characteristics of activities in the extractives industries. Although geothermal energy is sometimes referred to as a 'regenerative' resource, the geothermal resource in a specific location may be non-regenerative. This is the case when, for example, the amount of steam in a reservoir that can be extracted using existing technology is limited. Such geothermal resources would be viewed as 'similar non-regenerative resources' as contemplated in Appendix A of IFRS 6 (see **2.1**) and, therefore, exploration and evaluation expenditures in respect of such resources should be accounted for in accordance with IFRS 6.

In contrast, if a geothermal resource is viewed as regenerative on the basis of specific facts and circumstances, any related exploration and evaluation expenditures do not fall within the scope of IFRS 6. It would also be inappropriate to apply IFRS 6 by analogy using the hierarchy in IAS 8 because IFRS 6 provides exemptions from applying other IFRSs as a matter of exception (resulting in certain items of expenditure being eligible for capitalisation even though they do not meet the definition of an asset), and its application should be strictly limited to the activities that are within the scope of IFRS 6.

2.4   IFRIC 20 *Stripping Costs in the Production Phase of a Surface Mine*

IFRIC 20 *Stripping Costs in the Production Phase of a Surface Mine* addresses the appropriate accounting for costs of removing waste material to gain access to mineral ore deposits incurred during the production phase of a surface mine. The requirements of IFRIC 20 are discussed in **section 10** of **chapter A7**.

3   Recognition of exploration and evaluation assets

IFRS 6 requires an entity to apply paragraph 10 of IAS 8 *Accounting Policies, Changes in Accounting Estimates and Errors* when developing its accounting policies for the recognition of exploration and evaluation assets. [IFRS 6:6] Accordingly, judgement should be applied in developing and applying an accounting policy that results in information that is:

[IAS 8:10]

- relevant to the economic decision-making needs of users; and

- reliable, in that the financial statements:

  - represent faithfully the financial position, financial performance and cash flows of the entity;

  - reflect the economic substance of the transactions, other events and conditions, and not merely the legal form;

  - are neutral (i.e. free from bias);

  - are prudent; and

  - are complete in all material aspects.

Subject to the requirements described in **section 4**, an entity is exempted from applying IAS 8:11 and 12 when determining its policies for the recognition and measurement of exploration and evaluation assets. [IFRS 6:7]

As discussed at **3.1** in **chapter A5**, IAS 8:10 to 12 provide guidance for developing and applying an accounting policy when there is no IFRS that specifically applies to a transaction. When the conditions specified in **section 4** are met, an entity is not required to refer to or consider:

- the requirements in IFRSs dealing with similar and related issues;

- the definitions, recognition criteria and measurement concepts for assets, liabilities, income and expenses in the *Conceptual Framework for Financial Reporting*; or

- the most recent pronouncements of other standard-setting bodies that use a similar conceptual framework to develop accounting standards, other accounting literature and accepted industry practices.

In requiring the application of IAS 8:10 but not IAS 8:11 and 12 (except in limited circumstances), the IASB made a conscious decision to permit entities to continue to apply the accounting practices they followed before adopting IFRS 6. The result is that entities reporting under IFRSs that are domiciled in different jurisdictions, and sometimes even within the same jurisdiction, do not necessarily apply a consistent method of accounting for exploration and evaluation expenditures. It is also possible that some accounting policies adopted in accordance with IFRS 6 will lead to the recognition of amounts as assets or expenses that would not meet the definition of an asset or an expense as set out in the *Conceptual Framework for Financial Reporting* (see **chapter A2**).

As explained in IFRS 6:BC17 to BC23, the IASB considered these consequences at length but decided to allow temporary relief to minimise disruption to the preparers and users of financial statement information for entities adopting IFRSs for the first time.

4 Measurement of exploration and evaluation assets

4.1 Measurement at initial recognition

4.1.1 *Exploration and evaluation assets to be measured on initial recognition at cost*

IFRS 6 requires exploration and evaluation assets to be measured on initial recognition at cost. [IFRS 6:8]

An entity should develop an accounting policy which specifies the types of expenditures that it recognises as exploration and evaluation assets. The policy should be applied consistently. The determination as to what qualifies as eligible expenditure should be based on an assessment of how closely associated the expenditure is with finding specific mineral resources. IFRS 6 provides the following non-exhaustive list of examples of expenditures that an entity might consider to be included in the initial measurement of exploration and evaluation assets:

[IFRS 6:9]

- acquisition of rights to explore;
- topographical, geological, geochemical and geophysical studies;
- exploratory drilling;

- trenching;

- sampling; and

- activities in relation to evaluating the technical feasibility and commercial viability of extracting a mineral resource.

Note that IFRS 6 does not require entities to capitalise exploration and evaluation expenditures. Rather, when specified conditions are met, IFRS 6 permits entities to continue to apply the accounting policies followed with respect to exploration and evaluation expenditure before adopting the Standard.

For example, an entity's policy may be to recognise expenditures relating to feasibility studies and sampling as an asset or as an expense, or a mixture of the two depending on the nature of the expenditure. IFRS 6 only requires that the accounting policy developed be applied consistently and that, if the costs are to be recognised as an asset, the entity should consider the degree to which the expenditure can be associated with finding specific mineral resources.

Expenditures related to the development of mineral resources should not be recognised as exploration and evaluation assets; instead, entities are required to apply the *Conceptual Framework for Financial Reporting* and IAS 38 *Intangible Assets* to determine an appropriate accounting policy for such amounts (see **4.8** in **chapter A9**). [IFRS 6:10]

IFRS 6 does not define what constitutes 'development' on the basis that such activities are beyond its scope. However, IFRS 6:5(b) is clear that the development phase begins after the technical feasibility and commercial viability of extracting a mineral resource are demonstrable (see also **2.2**).

An entity should recognise any obligations for removal and restoration that are incurred as a result of the exploration for and evaluation of mineral resources. The obligation should be recognised in accordance with IAS 37 *Provisions, Contingent Liabilities and Contingent Assets* (see **chapter A12**). [IFRS 6:11]

4.1.2   General administrative and overhead costs

General administrative and overhead costs are not included in the list of examples of expenditures that an entity might consider to be included in the initial measurement of exploration and evaluation assets (see **4.1.1**). However, IFRS 6 does not preclude the inclusion of such costs in the carrying amount of an exploration and evaluation asset. When debating whether such costs should be considered to be part of exploration and evaluation assets, the IASB noted that inconsistency exists with respect to the treatment of such costs under different IFRSs and that IFRS 6 was not the appropriate place to try to resolve the issue. Accordingly, the IASB decided that the treatment of such expenditures is a matter of accounting policy choice. [IFRS 6:BC28] However, the accounting policy choice should be considered in light of the requirement of IFRS 6:9 (see **4.1.1**) for an entity to consider the degree to which expenditure can be associated with finding specific mineral resources.

4.1.3 Borrowing costs

Notwithstanding the authority under IFRS 6:9 (see **4.1.1**) to determine which expenditures should be included in the measurement of exploration and evaluation assets, the question arises as to whether, if an entity is engaged in exploration and evaluation activities and it incurs borrowing costs, it is required to apply IAS 23 *Borrowing Costs* and, therefore, capitalise borrowing costs incurred in relation to qualifying assets.

The requirements of IAS 23 do not take precedence over the choice available under IFRS 6. Therefore, an entity may choose whether to capitalise borrowing costs as part of the cost of exploration and evaluation assets.

An entity should develop an accounting policy for the treatment of exploration and evaluation expenditures, including borrowing costs, and apply it consistently. Judgement should be exercised to ensure that the treatment of borrowing costs under IFRS 6 is logical given the entity's policy with respect to other exploration and evaluation expenditures. The guidance in IFRS 6:9 (see **4.1.1**) requiring an entity to consider the degree to which expenditures can be associated with finding specific mineral resources must also be carefully considered when determining the amount of borrowing costs that may be capitalised.

4.2 Measurement after recognition

An entity should apply either the cost model or the revaluation model after initial recognition. If the revaluation model is adopted, the basis for revaluing the asset at the end of each reporting period (i.e. either the model in IAS 16 *Property, Plant and Equipment* or the model in IAS 38 *Intangible Assets*), should be consistent with the classification of the asset. [IFRS 6:12] The requirements with respect to the classification of exploration and evaluation assets are discussed in **6.1**.

The revaluation model in IAS 38 may only be used when there is an 'active market' for the asset in question (see **7.1** in **chapter A9**). Given the nature of exploration and evaluation assets, it is not likely that application of the revaluation model will be possible when exploration and evaluation assets have been classified as intangible.

The Basis of Conclusions on IFRS 6 states explicitly that any exploration and evaluation assets acquired in a business combination should be accounted for at fair value in accordance with IFRS 3 *Business Combinations*. [IFRS 6:BC31]

4.3   Changes in accounting policies

An entity is permitted to change its accounting policies for exploration and evaluation expenditures if the change makes the financial statements more relevant to the economic decision-making needs of users and no less reliable, or more reliable and no less relevant. The assessment of relevance and reliability should be made with reference to the criteria in IAS 8 *Accounting Policies, Changes in Accounting Estimates and Errors* (see **chapter A5**). [IFRS 6:13]

In order to change its accounting policies for exploration and evaluation expenditures, an entity should demonstrate that the change will bring its financial statements closer to meeting the criteria in IAS 8, but it is not necessary to achieve full compliance with those criteria. [IFRS 6:14]

IAS 8 provides specific guidance in relation to relevance and reliability. Although an entity must demonstrate compliance with specific aspects of IAS 8 before changing an accounting policy, this requirement does not override the exemptions discussed in **section 3**.

The Basis for Conclusions on IFRS 6 clarifies that a change in what is deemed to be expenditure qualifying for recognition as an exploration and evaluation asset should be treated as a change in accounting policy. [IFRS 6:BC25]

Example 4.3

Change in accounting policy

Entity X drills for and extracts oil from deep sea beds. It adopted IFRSs for the first time on 1 January 20X5. Prior to adopting IFRSs, as permitted by its previous GAAP, Entity X capitalised all expenditures related to exploration and evaluation activities. This accounting policy was carried forward on adoption of IFRSs in accordance with the requirements of IFRS 6.

Subsequently, Entity X discovers that most of its direct competitors, on transition to IFRSs, have adopted a policy of capitalising costs only when a drilling effort has been successful and an oil reserve has been found. Entity X believes that its financial statements will be more relevant for users if it also adopts this policy.

> **Is Entity X permitted to change its accounting policy?**
>
> Yes. Under IFRS 6:13, Entity X may change its accounting policy as long as it can establish that the change provides more relevant, and no less reliable (or more reliable and no less relevant), information to users; relevance and reliability should be assessed with reference to the criteria in IAS 8. Entity X is not required to apply the requirements of IAS 8:11 and 12 before making the accounting policy change; for example, Entity X does not need to consider the requirements and guidance in other IFRSs dealing with similar issues or recent pronouncements of other standard-setting bodies.

5   Impairment

5.1   Recognition and measurement

Impairment must be considered for exploration and evaluation assets, in keeping with the requirements for all other assets recognised under IFRSs. However, due to the special nature of exploration and evaluation assets, IFRS 6 sets out specific requirements which limit the need to test for impairment to circumstances when there are indicators of impairment. This is true in all circumstances except when exploration and evaluation assets are reclassified, as discussed in **6.2**.

In many cases, an entity engaged in the exploration and evaluation phase of a project will not be generating cash inflows from the project. Frequently, the exploration and evaluation activities have not even reached a stage where there is enough information to estimate the future cash flows that might be eventually generated by the project.

Accordingly, IFRS 6 provides special relief by not requiring exploration and evaluation assets to be assessed for impairment annually; instead, an impairment assessment is required only when facts and circumstances suggest that the carrying amount of an exploration and evaluation asset may exceed its recoverable amount. When such facts and circumstances exist, an entity is required to measure, present and disclose any impairment loss in accordance with IAS 36 *Impairment of Assets*, except that IFRS 6 sets out specific requirements regarding the level at which exploration and evaluation assets are assessed for impairment (see **5.2**). [IFRS 6:18]

IFRS 6 sets out specific impairment indicators to be considered for exploration and evaluation assets (instead of the indicators listed in IAS 36:8 to 17). [IFRS 6:19] Exploration and evaluation assets should be tested for impairment if one or more of the following facts and circumstances is present.

[IFRS 6:20]

- The period for which the entity has the right to explore in the specific area has expired during the period or will expire in the near future, and is not expected to be renewed.

- Substantive expenditure on further exploration for and evaluation of mineral resources in the specific area is neither budgeted nor planned.

- Exploration for and evaluation of mineral resources in the specific area have not led to the discovery of commercially viable quantities of mineral resources and the entity has decided to discontinue such activities in the specific area.

- Sufficient data exist to indicate that, although a development in the specific area is likely to proceed, the carrying amount of the exploration and evaluation asset is unlikely to be recovered in full from successful development or by sale.

The Standard notes that the above list is not exhaustive. In any of the circumstances listed, or in similar circumstances, IFRS 6 requires an entity to perform an impairment test in accordance with IAS 36 and to recognise any resultant impairment loss as an expense. [IFRS 6:20]

5.2   Level at which exploration and evaluation assets are assessed for impairment

An entity should determine an accounting policy for allocating exploration and evaluation assets to cash-generating units or groups of cash-generating units for the purpose of assessing such assets for impairment. Each cash-generating unit or group of units to which an exploration and evaluation asset is allocated should not be larger than an operating segment determined in accordance with IFRS 8 *Operating Segments*. [IFRS 6:21] The level identified by the entity for the purposes of testing exploration and evaluation assets for impairment may comprise one or more cash-generating units. [IFRS 6:22]

The impairment testing requirements within IFRS 6 provide some flexibility compared to the requirements of IAS 36. Under IFRS 6:21, the level at which impairment testing is performed is a matter of accounting policy choice and may comprise one or more cash-generating units – it need not be the smallest identifiable group of assets that generates largely independent cash inflows. Management should consider carefully what the appropriate level of monitoring and reporting is for the entity in order to ensure that the financial statements provide reliable and relevant information that properly reflects the true economic nature of the entity.

Once the entity establishes its policy for determining cash-generating units, the allocation of exploration and evaluation assets should be carried out. The amounts allocated should include not only the assets but also, in the calculation of fair value less cost of disposal, liabilities such as provisions for decommissioning costs and remediation, to the extent they would be transferred with the assets.

An entity might choose to aggregate exploration and evaluation sites into a portfolio based on attributes that are determined as an accounting policy choice. For example, an entity might choose to aggregate sites by type of resource, geographical location, size etc. It is possible, although unlikely, that all sites might be aggregated into one group of cash-generating units (as long as it is not larger than an operating segment); at the other end of the spectrum, an entity might choose to identify each site that meets the test of being a cash-generating unit on a stand-alone basis.

When the specific requirements of IAS 36:109 to 123 are met (see **section 10** of **chapter A10**), entities are required to reverse previously recognised impairment losses.

See also **example 8.2.8.1C** in **chapter A10** for an example of goodwill allocation methodologies for a mining conglomerate.

6 Presentation and disclosure

6.1 Classification of exploration and evaluation assets

Exploration and evaluation assets may be either tangible or intangible in nature, depending on the type of expenditure in question.

IFRS 6 requires exploration and evaluation assets to be classified in an entity's statement of financial position as either tangible or intangible according to the nature of the assets acquired. The classifications should be applied consistently. [IFRS 6:15]

IFRS 6 gives drilling rights as an example of an intangible asset and vehicles and drilling rigs as examples of tangible assets, but it does not provide further guidance on which exploration and evaluation expenditures should be considered as tangible and which as intangible assets. The definition of an intangible asset in IAS 38 *Intangible Assets* (see **chapter A9**) should be considered in undertaking the assessment.

Sometimes, a tangible asset is consumed in the development of an intangible asset. To the extent that a tangible asset is consumed in the development of an intangible asset, the amount reflecting the consumption is part of the cost of the intangible asset. However, the mere fact that a tangible asset is consumed to create an intangible one does not change the nature of the former from tangible to intangible. [IFRS 6:16]

For example, part or all of the depreciation expense relating to some equipment (a tangible asset) may form part of the cost of an intangible exploration and evaluation asset, but this will not cause the equipment to be reclassified.

Example 6.1

Consumption of a tangible asset to create an intangible asset

Entity X extracts and produces oil and gas, and has identified a new prospective site. Entity X has already obtained the right to explore and exploit the land, but has not yet determined technical feasibility and commercial viability.

As part of the exploration and evaluation phase of the project, Entity X intends to utilise its drilling rig to conduct drilling and sampling activities. Entity X maintains a policy of capitalising costs incurred during the exploration and evaluation phase as intangible drilling rights in accordance with IFRS 6.

The drilling rig that will be used during the exploration and evaluation phase of the project is capitalised as an item of property, plant and equipment in Entity X's statement of financial position.

How should Entity X account for the drilling rig during the exploration and evaluation phase of the project?

The drilling rig should continue to be classified as a tangible asset. Entity X should, in accordance with its depreciation policy, calculate the amount of depreciation expense that is attributable to the drilling activities associated with the exploration and evaluation phase of the project and treat that amount as part of the cost of the intangible drilling rights asset.

6.2   Reclassification of exploration and evaluation assets

An exploration and evaluation asset should no longer be classified as such once the technical feasibility and commercial viability of extracting a mineral resource are demonstrable. Before reclassification, exploration and evaluation assets should be assessed for impairment, and any resulting impairment loss should be recognised. [IFRS 6:17]

Once the technical feasibility and commercial viability of extracting a mineral resource are demonstrable, the amount recognised as an exploration and evaluation asset will be reclassified to form part of a tangible or an intangible asset (see **section 2** of **chapter A7**).

As discussed at **4.1.1**, the IASB has not defined the term 'development' in the Standard; nor has it provided guidance regarding the point in the life cycle of a mineral exploration project at which technical feasibility and commercial viability are demonstrable. Given the different nature of different extractive operations, it might not be possible for an entity to develop a single set of criteria that could be used in all circumstances. Generally, it will be appropriate for an entity to develop an accounting policy based on the nature of its own operations, specifying the criteria that must be met in order to demonstrate technical feasibility and commercial viability, and then apply that policy consistently; however, when an entity has projects that are not alike, it may be necessary to determine separate criteria for each.

IAS 38 also contains guidance on research and development and intangible assets. This will often help to provide an appropriate starting point in considering when the 'development' cycle begins in mineral extraction projects.

Generally, it will be appropriate to accumulate and aggregate exploration and evaluation expenditure on a project-by-project basis, to facilitate both the transfer of amounts out of exploration and evaluation assets once development commences, as discussed above, and also the impairment assessment (see **section 5**).

6.3 Disclosure

6.3.1 Disclosure – general

IFRS 6 requires an entity to disclose information to identify and explain amounts recognised in its financial statements arising from the exploration for and evaluation of mineral resources. [IFRS 6:23]

Specifically, IFRS 6 requires an entity to disclose:

[IFRS 6:24]

- its accounting policies for exploration and evaluation expenditures including the recognition of exploration and evaluation assets; and

- the amounts of assets, liabilities, income and expense and operating and investing cash flows (see **6.3.2**) arising from the exploration for and evaluation of mineral resources.

Exploration and evaluation assets should be presented as a separate class of assets. The disclosures required by IAS 16 *Property, Plant and Equipment* and IAS 38 *Intangible Assets* should also be provided, consistent with how the assets are classified. [IFRS 6:25]

6.3.2 Classification of expenditure as operating or investing cash flows

Paragraph 16 of IAS 7 *Statement of Cash Flows* states that only expenditures resulting in a recognised asset in the statement of financial position are eligible for classification as investing activities.

Consequently, expenditure for exploration and evaluation activities should be classed as investing activities in the statement of cash flows only if the entity's accounting policy is to capitalise such costs.

A41 Accounting and reporting by retirement benefit plans

Contents

1 Introduction

1.1 Overview of IAS 26

This chapter addresses IAS 26 *Accounting and Reporting by Retirement Benefit Plans* which specifies measurement and disclosure principles for the financial statements of retirement benefit plans. It outlines the financial statements required and discusses the measurement of various line items, particularly the actuarial present value of promised retirement benefits for defined benefit plans.

1.2 Amendments to IAS 26 since the last edition of this manual

None. IAS 26 has not been amended since it was issued in 1987.

2 Scope

IAS 26 is to be applied in the financial statements of retirement benefit plans when such financial statements are prepared. [IAS 26:1] Retirement benefits plans are arrangements whereby an entity provides benefits for employees on or after termination of service (either in the form of an annual income or as a lump sum) and when such benefits, or the contributions towards them, can be determined or estimated in advance of retirement from the provisions of a document or from the entity's practices. [IAS 26:8]

Retirement benefit plans are sometimes referred to by various other names such as 'pension schemes', 'superannuation schemes' or 'retirement benefit schemes'. Specifically excluded from the scope of IAS 26 are other forms of employment benefits such as employment termination indemnities, deferred compensation arrangements, long-service leave benefits, special early retirement or redundancy plans, health and welfare plans or bonus plans. Government social security type arrangements are also excluded from the scope of the Standard. [IAS 26:7]

Some retirement benefit plans have sponsors other than employers and IAS 26 also applies to the financial statements of such plans. [IAS 26:9]

In 2004, the IFRIC (now the IFRS Interpretations Committee) was asked to consider the apparent conflict between IAS 26:9 and IAS 26:8 (which refers to arrangements that an entity provides 'for its employees'). The IFRIC concluded that the intention of the Standard, as expressed in IAS 26:9, was clear and that IAS 26 applies both to plans sponsored by employers and plans with sponsors other than employers. This conclusion was confirmed in the March 2004 *IFRIC Update*.

Most retirement benefit plans are based on formal agreements. Some plans are informal but have acquired a degree of obligation as a result of employers' established practices. While some plans permit employers to limit their obligations under the plans, it is usually difficult for an employer to cancel a plan if employees are to be retained. The same basis of accounting and reporting applies to an informal plan as to a formal plan. [IAS 26:10]

Retirement benefit plans are normally described as either defined contribution or defined benefit plans (dealt with, respectively, in **section 3** and **section 4**), each having their own distinctive characteristics. Occasionally plans exist that contain characteristics of both. Such hybrid plans are considered to be defined benefit plans for the purposes of IAS 26. [IAS 26:12]

IAS 26 regards a retirement benefit plan as a reporting entity separate from the employers of the participants of the plan. All other IFRSs apply to the financial statements of retirement benefit plans to the extent that they are not superseded by IAS 26. IAS 26 complements IAS 19 *Employee Benefits*, the Standard concerned with the determination of the cost of retirement benefits in the financial statements of employers having plans (see **chapter A15**). [IAS 26:2 & 4]

IAS 26 deals with accounting and reporting by the plan to all participants (i.e. members of the plan and others who are entitled to benefits under the plan) as a group. It does not deal with reports to individual participants about their retirement benefit rights. [IAS 26:3]

Some entities will create a separate fund for their retirement benefit plans to which contributions are made and from which retirement benefits are paid. Such separate funds may or may not have a separate legal identity, and they may or may not have appointed trustees. IAS 26 applies regardless of whether a separate fund has been established and regardless of whether there are trustees. [IAS 26:5]

The term trustee is used in IAS 26 to describe parties who administer separate funds into which contributions are made and out of which benefits are paid and act independently in managing fund assets, regardless of whether a trust has been formed. [IAS 26:11]

Retirement benefit plans with assets invested with insurance companies are subject to the same accounting and funding requirements as privately invested arrangements. Accordingly, they are within the scope of IAS 26 unless the contract with the insurance company is in the name of a specified participant or group of participants and the retirement benefit obligation is solely the responsibility of the insurance company. [IAS 26:6]

3   Defined contribution plans

Defined contribution plans are retirement benefit plans under which amounts to be paid as retirement benefits are determined by contributions to a fund together with investment earnings on those funds. [IAS 26:8]

IAS 26 specifies that the financial statements of a defined contribution plan should contain:

[IAS 26:13]

- a statement of net assets available for benefits; and

- a description of the funding policy.

The net assets available for benefits are the assets of a plan less liabilities other than the actuarial present value of promised retirement benefits. [IAS 26:8]

Funding is the transfer of assets to an entity (the fund) separate from the employer's entity to meet future obligations for the payment of retirement benefits. [IAS 26:8]

These disclosure requirements are designed to address the needs of the participants of defined contribution plans, under which the amount of a participant's future benefits is determined by the contributions paid by the employer, the participant, or both, and the operating efficiency and Investment earnings of the fund. An employer's obligation is usually discharged by contributions to the fund. An actuary's advice is not normally required although such advice is sometimes used to estimate future benefits that may be achievable based on present contributions and varying levels of future contributions and investment earnings. [IAS 26:14]

The objective of reporting by a defined contribution plan is periodically to provide information about the plan and the performance of its investments. IAS 26 considers that this objective can usually be achieved by providing financial statements including the following:

[IAS 26:16]

- a description of significant activities for the period and the effect of any changes relating to the plan, and its membership and terms and conditions;

- statements reporting on the transactions and investment performance for the period and the financial position of the plan at the end of the period; and

- a description of the investment policies.

4 Defined benefit plans

4.1 Defined benefit plans – general

Defined benefit plans are retirement benefit plans under which amounts to be paid as retirement benefits are determined by reference to a formula which is usually based on employees' earnings and/or years of service. [IAS 26:8]

IAS 26 requires that the financial statements of a defined benefit plan should contain either:

[IAS 26:17]

- a statement that shows:

  - the net assets available for benefits;

  - the actuarial present value of promised retirement benefits, distinguishing between vested benefits and non-vested benefits; and

  - the resulting excess or deficit; or

- a statement of net assets available for benefits including either:

  - a note disclosing the actuarial present value of promised retirement benefits, distinguishing between vested benefits and non-vested benefits; or

  - a reference to this information in an accompanying actuarial report.

The net assets available for benefits are the assets of a plan less liabilities other than the actuarial present value of promised retirement benefits. [IAS 26:8]

The actuarial present value of promised retirement benefits is the present value of the expected payments by a retirement benefit plan to existing and past employees, attributable to the service already rendered. [IAS 26:8]

Vested benefits are benefits, the rights to which, under the conditions of a retirement benefit plan, are not conditional on continued employment. [IAS 26:8]

If an actuarial valuation has not been prepared at the date of the financial statements, the most recent valuation should be used as a base for the required disclosures. [IAS 26:17]

For the purposes of IAS 26:17 (see above):

[IAS 26:18]

- the actuarial present value of promised retirement benefits should be based on the benefits promised under the terms of the plan on service rendered to date using either current salary levels or projected salary levels; and

- the basis used should be disclosed in the financial statements.

IAS 26 differs from IAS 19 *Employee Benefits* in allowing a choice of measurement based either on current salary levels or projected salary levels. IAS 19 requires an actuarial valuation to be based on the latter.

The effect of any changes in actuarial assumptions that have had a significant effect on the actuarial present value of promised retirement benefits is also required to be disclosed. [IAS 26:18]

The financial statements should explain the relationship between the actuarial present value of promised retirement benefits and the net assets available for benefits, and the policy for the funding of promised benefits. [IAS 26:19] Funding is the transfer of assets to an entity (the fund) separate from the employer's entity to meet future obligations for the payment of retirement benefits. [IAS 26:8]

Under a defined benefit plan, the payment of promised retirement benefits depends on the financial position of the plan and the ability of contributors to make future contributions to the plan as well as the investment performance and operating efficiency of the plan. A defined benefit plan needs the periodic advice of an actuary to assess the financial condition of the plan, review the assumptions and recommend future contribution levels. [IAS 26:20 & 21]

The objective of reporting by a defined benefit plan is periodically to provide information about the financial resources and activities of the plan that is useful in assessing the relationships between the accumulation of resources and plan benefits over time. IAS 26 specifies that this objective is usually achieved by providing financial statements including the following:

[IAS 26:22]

- a description of significant activities for the period and the effect of any changes relating to the plan, and its membership and terms and conditions;

- statements reporting on the transactions and investment performance for the period and the financial position of the plan at the end of the period;

- actuarial information either as part of the statements or by way of a separate report; and

- a description of the investment policies.

4.2 Actuarial present value of promised retirement benefits

As noted in **4.1**, IAS 26:18 allows that the present value of the expected payments by a retirement benefit plan may be calculated and reported using current salary levels or projected salary levels up to the time of retirement of participants.

The Standard notes that those favouring a current salary approach would argue as follows:

[IAS 26:24]

- the actuarial present value of promised retirement benefits, being the sum of the amounts presently attributable to each participant in the plan, can be calculated more objectively than with projected salary levels because it involves fewer assumptions;

- increases in benefits attributable to a salary increase become an obligation of the plan at the time of the salary increase; and

- the amount of the actuarial present value of promised retirement benefits using current salary levels is generally more closely related to the amount payable in the event of termination or discontinuance of the plan.

The actuarial present value of promised retirement benefits based on current salaries is disclosed in the financial statements of a plan to indicate the obligation for benefits earned to the date of the financial statements. [IAS 26:26]

On the other hand, the Standard notes that a projected salary approach is supported on the basis that:

[IAS 26:25]

- financial information should be prepared on a going concern basis, irrespective of the assumptions and estimates that must be made;

- under final pay plans, benefits are determined by reference to salaries at or near retirement date; hence salaries, contribution levels and rates of return must be projected; and

- failure to incorporate salary projections, when most funding is based on salary projections, may result in the reporting of an apparent overfunding when the plan is not overfunded, or in reporting adequate funding when the plan is underfunded.

As noted at **4.1**, IAS 19 requires an actuarial valuation to be based on projected salary levels.

The actuarial present value of promised retirement benefits based on projected salaries is disclosed to indicate the magnitude of the potential obligation on a going concern basis which is generally the basis for funding. [IAS 26:26]

In addition to disclosure of the actuarial present value of promised retirement benefits, sufficient explanation may need to be given so as to indicate clearly the context in which the actuarial present value of promised retirement benefits should be read. Such explanation may be in the form of information about the adequacy of the planned future funding and of the funding policy based on salary projections. This may be included in the financial statements or in the actuary's report. [IAS 26:26]

4.3 Frequency of actuarial valuations

IAS 26 does not impose any requirements regarding the frequency of actuarial valuations. It notes that, in many countries, actuarial valuations are not obtained more frequently than every three years. [IAS 26:27]

If an actuarial valuation has not been prepared at the date of the financial statements, the most recent valuation is used as a base and the date of the valuation disclosed. [IAS 26:27]

4.4 Content of financial statements

IAS 26 allows a degree of discretion regarding the format of the financial statements for defined benefit plans, and reviews the relative merits for the various formats permitted, as set out below.

The information required by IAS 26 should be presented in one of the following formats, which reflect different practices in the disclosure and presentation of actuarial information.

[IAS 26:28]

- Option 1: a statement is included in the financial statements that shows the net assets available for benefits, the actuarial present value of promised retirement benefits, and the resulting excess or deficit. The financial statements of the plan also contain statements of changes in net assets available for benefits and changes in the actuarial present value of promised retirement benefits. The financial statements may be accompanied by a separate actuary's report supporting the actuarial present value of promised retirement benefits.

- Option 2: the financial statements include a statement of net assets available for benefits and a statement of changes in net assets available for benefits. The actuarial present value of promised retirement benefits is disclosed in a note to the statements. The financial statements may also be accompanied by a report from an actuary supporting the actuarial present value of promised retirement benefits.

- Option 3: the financial statements include a statement of net assets available for benefits and a statement of changes in net assets available for benefits with the actuarial present value of promised retirement benefits contained in a separate actuarial report.

For each of the options listed, a trustees' report in the nature of a management or directors' report and an investment report may also accompany the financial statements. [IAS 26:28]

Those in favour of Options 1 and 2 above believe that the quantification of promised retirement benefits and other information provided under those approaches help users to assess the current status of the plan and the likelihood of the plan's obligations being met. They also believe that financial statements should be complete in themselves and not rely on accompanying statements. However, some believe that the format described in Option 1 could give the impression that a liability exists, whereas the actuarial present value of promised retirement benefits does not in their opinion have all the characteristics of a liability. [IAS 26:29]

Those who favour the format described in Option 3 above believe that the actuarial present value of promised retirement benefits should not be included in a statement of net assets available for benefits as in the format described in Option 1 or even be disclosed in a note as in Option 2, because it will be compared directly with plan assets and such a comparison may not be valid. They contend that actuaries do not necessarily compare actuarial present value of promised retirement benefits with market values of investments but may instead assess the present value of cash flows expected from the investments. Therefore, those in favour of this format believe that such a comparison is unlikely to reflect the actuary's overall assessment of the plan and that it may be misunderstood. Also, some believe that, regardless of whether quantified, the information about promised retirement benefits should be contained solely in the separate actuarial report where a proper explanation can be provided. [IAS 26:30]

When finalising IAS 26, the IASC (the predecessor to the IASB) accepted the views in favour of permitting disclosure of the information concerning promised retirement benefits in a separate actuarial report. It rejected arguments against the quantification of the actuarial present value of promised retirement benefits. Accordingly, Options 1 and 2 are considered acceptable for the purposes of IAS 26, as is Option 3 provided that the financial statements contain a reference to, and are accompanied by, an actuarial report that includes the actuarial present value of promised retirement benefits. [IAS 26:31]

5 Valuation of plan assets – all plans

IAS 26 requires that retirement benefit plan investments should be carried at fair value. In the case of marketable securities, fair value is market value. [IAS 26:32]

When plan investments are held for which an estimate of fair value is not possible, disclosure is required of the reason why fair value is not used. [IAS 26:32]

For marketable securities, fair value is usually market value because this is considered the most useful measure of the securities at the report date and of the investment performance for the period. [IAS 26:33]

Those securities that have a fixed redemption value and that have been acquired to match the obligations of the plan, or specific parts thereof, may be carried at amounts based on their ultimate redemption value assuming a constant rate of return to maturity. [IAS 26:33]

> The measurement basis described above appears broadly consistent with the amortised cost models used in IFRS 9 *Financial Instruments* and IAS 39 *Financial Instruments: Recognition and Measurement*. But it is not immediately clear how such a basis, which uses a historical rate of return, corresponds to 'fair value', as required by IAS 26:32.

When plan investments are held for which an estimate of fair value is not possible, such as total ownership of an entity, disclosure is made of the reason why fair value is not used. [IAS 26:33]

To the extent that investments are carried at amounts other than market value or fair value, fair value is generally also disclosed. [IAS 26:33]

Assets used in the operations of the fund are accounted for in accordance with applicable IFRSs. [IAS 26:33]

6   Disclosure – all plans

The financial statements of a retirement benefit plan, whether defined benefit or defined contribution, should also contain the following information:

[IAS 26:34]

- a statement of changes in net assets available for benefits;
- a summary of significant accounting policies; and
- a description of the plan and the effect of any changes in the plan during the period.

The financial statements provided by retirement benefit plans should include the following, if applicable:

[IAS 26:35]

- a statement of net assets available for benefits disclosing:
  - assets at the end of the period suitably classified;
  - the basis of valuation of assets;
  - details of any single investment exceeding either 5 per cent of the net assets available for benefits or 5 per cent of any class or type of security;
  - details of any investment in the employer; and

- liabilities other than the actuarial present value of promised retirement benefits;

- a statement of changes in net assets available for benefits showing the following:

  - employer contributions;

  - employee contributions;

  - investment income such as interest and dividends;

  - other income;

  - benefits paid or payable (analysed, for example, as retirement, death and disability benefits, and lump sum payments);

  - administrative expenses;

  - other expenses;

  - taxes on income;

  - profits and losses on disposal of investments and changes in value of investments; and

  - transfers from and to other plans;

- a description of the funding policy;

- for defined benefit plans, the actuarial present value of promised retirement benefits (which may distinguish between vested benefits and non-vested benefits) based on the benefits promised under the terms of the plan, on service rendered to date and using either current salary levels or projected salary levels. This information may be included in an accompanying actuarial report to be read in conjunction with the related financial statements; and

- for defined benefit plans, a description of the significant actuarial assumptions made and the method used to calculate the actuarial present value of promised retirement benefits.

The report of a retirement benefit plan should contain a description of the plan, either as part of the financial information or in a separate report. It may contain the following:

[IAS 26:36]

- the names of the employers and the employee groups covered;

- the number of participants receiving benefits and the number of other participants, classified as appropriate;

- the type of plan – defined contribution or defined benefit;

- a note as to whether participants contribute to the plan;

- a description of the retirement benefits promised to participants;

- a description of any plan termination terms; and

- changes in the preceding items during the period covered by the report.

In order to provide the required description of the plan, it is acceptable for the entity to refer to other documents that are readily available to users and in which the plan is described, and to include only information on subsequent changes. [IAS 26:36]

A42 Regulatory deferral accounts

Contents

1 Introduction

1.1 Overview of IFRS 14

IFRS 14 *Regulatory Deferral Accounts* permits eligible first-time adopters of IFRSs to continue to account, with some limited changes, for 'regulatory deferral account balances' in accordance with their previous GAAP, both on initial adoption of IFRSs and in subsequent financial statements. Regulatory deferral account balances, and movements therein, are presented separately in the statement of financial position and statement(s) of profit or loss and other comprehensive income, and specific disclosures are required.

IFRS 14 was issued in January 2014 and applies to an entity's first annual IFRS financial statements if those financial statements are for a period beginning on or after 1 January 2016, with earlier application permitted (see **section 7**).

IFRS 14 is designed as a limited scope Standard to provide an interim, short-term solution for rate-regulated entities transitioning to IFRSs. Its objective is to allow rate-regulated entities adopting IFRSs for the first time to avoid changes in accounting policies in respect of regulatory deferral account balances until such time as the IASB can complete its comprehensive project on rate-regulated activities (see **section 8**). However, these balances are required to be presented separately and they are not described as assets and liabilities under IFRSs (see **section 5**). See **3.2.2** for a discussion of the nature of the amounts that might be included in such regulatory deferral account balances.

1.2 Amendments to IFRS 14 since the last edition of this manual

None. IFRS 14 has not been amended since it was issued in January 2014.

2 Scope

2.1 Scope – application of IFRS 14 is optional

Entities that are *eligible* to apply IFRS 14 (as discussed in **2.2** to **2.6**) are *not required* to do so. The IASB's objective in issuing IFRS 14 is to provide relief for first-time adopters that have previously recognised regulatory deferral account balances from having to make a major change to their accounting policies for such balances until the Board's comprehensive project on rate-regulated activities (see **section 8**) is completed. However, the Board does not want to prevent entities that currently recognise regulatory deferral account balances from ceasing to recognise such balances when adopting IFRSs. The IASB therefore decided that the continued recognition of regulatory deferral account balances in accordance with IFRS 14 should be optional.

An entity that is eligible to apply IFRS 14 but elects not to do so (and, consequently, ceases to recognise its regulatory deferral account balances) is not required to apply any of the disclosure requirements of IFRS 14. However, such entities, and other entities that are not eligible to apply IFRS 14, are not prohibited from providing supplementary disclosures, such as those set out in IFRS 14:30 to 36 (see **section 6**). [IFRS 14:BC35]

Note that, if an entity is eligible to apply IFRS 14 in its first IFRS financial statements but it elects not to do so, the entity is not permitted to apply IFRS 14 in subsequent financial statements (see **2.4**).

2.2 Scope – definition of rate-regulated activities

Whether in its first IFRS financial statements (see **2.4**) or subsequently (see **2.5**), an entity is only permitted to apply IFRS 14 if it conducts rate-regulated activities.

Rate-regulated activities are defined as activities of an entity that are subject to rate regulation, which in turn is defined as "[a] framework for establishing the prices that can be charged to customers for goods or services and that framework is subject to oversight and/or approval by a rate regulator. [IFRS 14:Appendix A]

A rate regulator is defined as "[a]n authorised body that is empowered by statute or regulation to establish the rate or a range of rates that bind an entity. The rate regulator may be a third-party body or a related part of the entity, including the entity's own governing board, if that body is required by statute or regulation to set rates both in the interest of the customers and to ensure the overall financial viability of the entity". [IFRS 14:Appendix A]

IFRS 14 can only be applied to rate-regulated activities that are subject to statutory or regulatory restrictions through the actions of a rate regulator, regardless of the type of entity or the industry to which it belongs. If an entity has both regulated and non-regulated activities, IFRS 14 can only be applied to its regulated activities. [IFRS 14:B1]

Note that IFRS 14 does not address regulatory accounting (i.e. accounting requirements for the purpose of reporting to rate regulators). Requirements in this regard are generally specified by the regulators themselves, and the IASB neither limits nor endorses options available in these circumstances. [IFRS 14:BC25]

IFRS 14 does not apply to activities that are self-regulated, i.e. activities that are not subject to a pricing framework that is overseen and/or approved by a rate regulator. [IFRS 14:B2]

This scope exclusion is intended to refer to entities that have a dominant position in a market and decide to self-regulate to avoid the potential government intervention that might occur if it were perceived to be abusing its dominant position. IFRS 14 requires that there be a formal rate regulator involved to ensure that the rate-regulatory mechanism in place is supported by statute or regulation and that the regulatory mechanism binds the entity. [IFRS 14:BC22]

However, an entity is permitted to apply IFRS 14 when:

[IFRS 14:B2]

- the entity's own governing body or a related party establishes rates both in the interest of the customers and to ensure the overall financial viability of the entity within a specified pricing framework; and

- the framework is subject to oversight and/or approval by an authorised body that is empowered by statute or regulation.

The IASB contemplates that this situation could arise, for example, when the entity conducts previously state-run activities and the government delegates regulatory powers to an entity (that may be state-controlled) within a statutory framework that is overseen by an authorised body of the government. Another example is a co-operative that may be subject to some form of regulatory oversight in order to obtain preferential loans, tax relief or other incentives to maintain the supply of goods or services that the government consider to be essential or near essential. [IFRS 14:BC24]

2.3   Scope – definition of regulatory deferral account balances

A regulatory deferral account balance is defined as "[t]he balance of any expense (or income) account that would not be recognised as an asset or a liability in accordance with other Standards, but that qualifies for deferral because it is included, or is expected to be included, by the rate regulator in establishing the rate(s) that can be charged to customers". [IFRS 14:Appendix A]

See **3.2.2** for a discussion of the nature of the amounts that might be included in such regulatory deferral account balances.

2.4   Scope – initial application of IFRS 14 by first-time adopters

An entity is permitted to apply the requirements of IFRS 14 in its first IFRS financial statements if and only if it:

[IFRS 14:5]

- conducts rate-regulated activities (see **2.2**); and

- recognised amounts that qualify as regulatory deferral account balances (see **2.3**) in its financial statements in accordance with its previous GAAP.

The terms 'first IFRS financial statements' and 'previous GAAP' are used with the same meaning as in IFRS 1 *First-time Adoption of International Financial Reporting Standards* (see **4.2** and **3.9**, respectively, in **chapter A3**).

An entity that did not recognise regulatory deferral account balances in accordance with its previous GAAP in the period immediately preceding its first IFRS financial statements is not eligible to apply IFRS 14 in order to start recognising such balances. An entity would not, therefore, be eligible if, for example:

[IFRS 14:BC16]

- the entity did not have any relevant rate-regulated activities in the period before it made the transition to IFRSs but then acquires or commences rate-regulated activities after the date that it adopts IFRSs; or

- the entity is a newly formed business and adopts IFRSs in its first IFRS financial statements.

2.5   Scope – application of IFRS 14 in subsequent financial statements

IFRS 14 applies in the financial statements for subsequent periods if and only if an entity recognised regulatory deferral account balances in its first IFRS financial statements by electing to apply the requirements of IFRS 14. [IFRS 14:6]

The relief available under IFRS 14 is only available for entities making the transition to IFRSs (see **2.4**) and in the subsequent financial statements of such entities. An entity cannot apply IFRS 14 for the first time in financial statements subsequent to its 'first IFRS financial statements' (see **4.2** in **chapter A3** for a discussion of this term). Consequently, entities that already apply IFRSs are not permitted to adopt IFRS 14. Although the IASB acknowledges that this introduces some inconsistency and diversity into IFRS practice for the treatment of regulatory deferral account balances, the Board believes that this disadvantage is outweighed by the advantages of making IFRS 14 available to first-time adopters (see IFRS 14:BC18 and BC19 for further discussion).

The following points are noteworthy:

- once an entity has applied IFRS 14 in its first IFRS financial statements, and it has recognised regulatory deferral account balances, it is only permitted to change its accounting policies in respect of those balances in limited circumstances (see **3.3.1**);

- an entity that adopts IFRSs on or after 1 January 2016 (the effective date of IFRS 14), and that is eligible but elects not to apply IFRS 14 in those first IFRS financial statements, is not permitted to 'adopt' IFRS 14 in subsequent financial statements in order to justify the recognition of regulatory deferral account balances. In accordance with IFRS 14:13 (see **3.3.3**), an entity is never permitted to change its existing IFRS accounting policies in order to start to recognise regulatory deferral account balances; and

- an entity that does not recognise regulatory deferral account balances in its first IFRS financial statements because it has no qualifying rate-regulated activities cannot recognise such balances in subsequent financial statements (e.g. if it acquires or commences rate-regulated activities after the date that it adopts IFRSs).

2.6 Scope – IFRS 14 to be applied to all regulatory deferral account balances

An entity that is within the scope of, and elects to apply, IFRS 14, must apply all of the requirements of that Standard to all regulatory deferral account balances that arise from all of the entity's rate-regulated activities. [IFRS 14:8]

IFRS 14 does not address other aspects of accounting by entities that are engaged in rate-regulated activities. Any amounts that are permitted or required to be recognised as assets or liabilities in accordance with other Standards should not be included within the amounts classified as regulatory deferral account balances. [IFRS 14:7]

3 Recognition, measurement, impairment and derecognition of regulatory deferral account balances

3.1 Selection and application of accounting policies

The paragraphs below set out the detailed requirements for the selection and application of accounting policies for regulatory deferral account balances under IFRS 14. The key point is that IFRS 14 permits an exemption from IAS 8:11 for entities applying IFRS 14 so that they are not prohibited from applying accounting policies that could be in conflict with the sources listed in that paragraph (IFRSs dealing with similar and related issues, and the Conceptual Framework). In the absence of such an exemption, an entity that capitalised regulatory deferral account balances under its previous GAAP could not continue to do so for some regulatory deferral account balances under IFRSs because such balances are specifically prohibited from being recognised as assets and liabilities by other Standards (see IFRS 14:BC28 to BC32 for further discussion).

An entity that has rate-regulated activities and that is within the scope of, and elects to apply, IFRS 14 should apply paragraphs 10 and 12 of IAS 8 *Accounting Policies, Changes in Accounting Estimates and Errors* when developing its accounting policies for the recognition, measurement, impairment and derecognition of regulatory deferral account balances. [IFRS 14:9] However, an entity is exempt from applying paragraph 11 of IAS 8. [IFRS 14:10]

IAS 8:10 requires that, in the absence of an IFRS that specifically applies to a transaction, event or condition, judgement should be applied in developing and applying an accounting policy that results in information that is:

- relevant to the economic decision-making needs of users; and

- reliable, in that the financial statements:

  - represent faithfully the financial position, financial performance and cash flows of the entity;

  - reflect the economic substance of the transactions, other events and conditions, and not merely the legal form;

  - are neutral (i.e. free from bias);

  - are prudent; and

  - are complete in all material aspects.

IAS 8:12 requires that, in making the judgement described in IAS 8:10, management may also consider the most recent pronouncements of other standard-setting bodies that use a similar conceptual framework to develop accounting standards, other accounting literature and accepted industry practices.

Generally, when applying IAS 8:12 for the purpose of identifying appropriate accounting policies, an entity is prohibited from selecting policies that conflict with the sources listed in IAS 8:11 (IFRSs dealing with similar and related issues, and the Conceptual Framework). This would present a problem for entities that have capitalised regulatory deferral account balances under previous GAAP because, in some cases, other IFRSs explicitly prohibit an entity from capitalising amounts that may have been accepted under its previous GAAP. Therefore, the effect of the exemption from IAS 8:11 is to allow an entity applying IFRS 14 to continue to apply its previous GAAP accounting policies for the recognition, measurement, impairment and derecognition of regulatory deferral account balances. This applies both for regulatory deferral account balances recognised separately under previous GAAP and those included within other line items such as property, plant and equipment. [IFRS 14:10 & B4]

Entities taking this relief under IFRS 14:10 are required to comply with IFRS 14's requirements for the presentation of regulatory deferral account balances (see **section 5**).

3.2   Previous GAAP accounting policies

3.2.1   *General requirement to continue to apply previous GAAP accounting policies*

On initial application of IFRS 14, an entity should continue to apply its previous GAAP accounting policies for regulatory deferral account balances (as defined in **2.3**), except for:

[IFRS 14:11]

- changes to prior accounting policies for recognition, measurement, impairment and derecognition permitted by IFRS 14:13 to 15 (see **3.3.1**); and

- application of the presentation requirements of IFRS 14 (see **section 5**).

The policies established in an entity's first IFRS financial statements should be applied consistently in subsequent periods, except for any changes permitted by IFRS 14:13 to 15 (see **3.3.1**). [IFRS 14:12]

3.2.2   *Nature of amounts commonly included within regulatory deferral account balances*

Accounting policies for regulatory deferral account balances under previous GAAP may include, for example, the following practices:

[IFRS 14:B4]

- recognising a regulatory deferral account debit balance when the entity has the right, as a result of the actual or expected actions of the rate regulator, to increase rates in future periods in order to recover its allowable costs (i.e. the costs for which the regulated rate(s) is intended to provide recovery);

- recognising, as a regulatory deferral account debit or credit balance, an amount that is equivalent to any loss or gain on the disposal or retirement of both items of property, plant and equipment and of intangible assets, which is expected to be recovered or reversed through future rates;

- recognising a regulatory deferral account credit balance when the entity is required, as a result of the actual or expected actions of the rate regulator, to decrease rates in future periods in order to reverse over-recoveries of allowable costs (i.e. amounts in excess of the recoverable amount specified by the rate regulator); and

- measuring regulatory deferral account balances on an undiscounted basis or on a discounted basis that uses an interest or discount rate specified by the rate regulator.

The following are examples of the types of costs that rate regulators might include in rate-setting decisions and that, therefore, might be recognised in regulatory deferral account balances:

[IFRS 14:B5]

- volume or purchase price variances;

- costs of approved 'green energy' initiatives (in excess of amounts that are capitalised as part of the cost of property, plant and equipment in accordance with IAS 16 *Property, Plant and Equipment*);

- non-directly-attributable overhead costs that are treated as capital costs for rate regulation purposes (but are not permitted, in accordance with IAS 16, to be included in the cost of an item of property, plant and equipment);

- project cancellation costs;

- storm damage costs; and

- deemed interest (including amounts allowed for funds that are used during construction that provide the entity with a return on the owner's equity capital as well as borrowings).

3.2.3 Items of income and expense not expected to be accepted by the rate regulator

Some items of expense or income may be outside the regulated rate(s) because, for example, the amounts are not expected to be accepted by the rate regulator or because they are not within the scope of the rate regulation. Such items should be recognised as expenses or income as incurred, unless another IFRS permits or requires their inclusion in the carrying amount of an asset or a liability. [IFRS 14:B3]

3.3 Changes in accounting policies

3.3.1 Changes in accounting policies for regulatory deferral account balances permitted in limited circumstances

An entity is only permitted to change its accounting policies for the recognition, measurement, impairment and derecognition of regulatory deferral account balances if the change makes the financial statements more relevant to the economic decision-making needs of users and no less reliable, or more reliable and no less relevant to those needs. An entity should judge relevance and reliability using the criteria in IAS 8:10. [IFRS 14:13]

IFRS 14 does not exempt entities from applying IAS 8:10 (see **3.1**) or IAS 8:14 and 15 (see **3.2** of **chapter A5**) to changes in accounting policy. To justify changing its accounting policies for regulatory deferral account balances, an entity is required to demonstrate that the change brings its financial statements closer to meeting the criteria in IAS 8:10. However, the change does not need to achieve full compliance with those criteria for the recognition, measurement, impairment and derecognition of regulatory deferral account balances. [IFRS 14:14]

The requirements set out in IFRS 14:13 and 14 apply both to changes made on initial application of IFRS 14 and to changes made in subsequent reporting periods. [IFRS 14:15]

3.3.2 General prohibition on changes in accounting policies to start to recognise regulatory deferral account balances

An entity should not change its accounting policies in order to start to recognise regulatory deferral account balances. [IFRS 14:13]

> Therefore, whether in its first IFRS financial statements or subsequently, an entity that has not previously capitalised regulatory deferral account balances is not permitted to changes its policies so as to start to capitalise such balances.

3.3.3 'New' regulatory deferral account balances

Regulatory deferral account balances usually arise because items of income or expense are deferred for recognition in future periods when they have been, or are expected to be, approved by the rate regulator for inclusion in prices that will be charged to customers for rate-regulated goods and services. If an entity changes an accounting policy on transition to IFRSs (e.g. it capitalised research costs within intangible assets under previous GAAP, but this treatment is no longer permitted under IAS 38 *Intangible Assets*), this may give rise to new timing differences. New timing differences may also arise in subsequent periods because of other changes in accounting policies required by IFRSs (e.g. on the initial application of a new or revised Standard).

The prohibition in IFRS 14:13 (see **3.3.2**) does not apply in such circumstances because the recognition of regulatory deferral account balances for such timing differences would be consistent with the existing recognition policy applied in accordance with IFRS 14:11 (see **3.2.1**) and would not represent the introduction of a new accounting policy. [IFRS 14:B6]

Similarly, IFRS 14 does not prohibit the recognition of regulatory deferral account balances arising from timing differences that did not exist immediately prior to the date of transition to IFRSs but are consistent with the entity's accounting policies established in accordance with IFRS 14:11. For example, if an entity has always capitalised regulatory deferral account balances and it incurs expenditure of a nature not previously incurred but that is expected to be included by its rate regulator in establishing the rate(s) that can be charged to customers (e.g. storm damage costs), IFRS 14:13 does not prohibit the capitalisation of such costs. [IFRS 14:B6]

4   Interaction with other IFRSs

4.1   IFRSs generally applicable to regulatory deferral account balances

IFRSs other than IFRS 14 generally apply to regulatory deferral account balances in the same way as they apply to assets, liabilities, income and expenses that are recognised in accordance with other IFRSs. The only specific exceptions, exemptions and additional requirements related to the interaction of IFRS 14 with other Standards are contained within IFRS 14. [IFRS 14:16]

In some situations, it may be necessary for an entity to apply another IFRS to a regulatory deferral account balance recognised in accordance with IFRS 14:11 to 12 (see **3.2.1**). For example, the entity might have rate-regulated activities in a foreign country for which the transactions and regulatory deferral account balances are denominated in a currency that is not the functional currency of the reporting entity. The regulatory deferral account balances and the movements in those balances are translated by applying IAS 21 *The Effects of Changes in Foreign Exchange Rates*. [IFRS 14:17]

Sections 4.2 to **4.9** outline how some other IFRSs interact with the requirements of IFRS 14. In particular, they clarify specific exceptions to, and exemptions from, other Standards and additional presentation and disclosure requirements that are expected to be applicable. [IFRS 14:B7]

4.2   IAS 10 *Events After the Reporting Period*

An entity may need to use estimates and assumptions in the recognition and measurement of its regulatory deferral account balances. For events that occur between the end of the reporting period and the date when the financial statements are authorised for issue, IAS 10 should be applied to identify whether estimates and assumptions should be adjusted to reflect those events (see **chapter A22**). [IFRS 14:B8]

4.3 IAS 12 *Income Taxes*

A rate-regulated entity should apply IAS 12 to all of its activities, including its rate-regulated activities, to identify the amount of income tax that is to be recognised (see **chapter A13**).

In some rate-regulatory schemes, the rate regulator permits or requires an entity to increase its future rates in order to recover some or all of the entity's income tax expense. In such circumstances, this might result in the entity recognising a regulatory deferral account balance in the statement of financial position that relates specifically to income tax. The recognition of this regulatory deferral account balance that relates to income tax might itself create an additional temporary difference for which a further deferred tax amount would be recognised. [IFRS 14:B10]

Notwithstanding the presentation and disclosure requirements of IAS 12, when an entity recognises a deferred tax asset or a deferred tax liability as a result of recognising regulatory deferral account balances, that deferred tax amount should not be included within the total deferred tax asset (liability) balances. Instead, the entity should present the deferred tax asset (liability) that arises as a result of recognising regulatory deferral account balances either:

[IFRS 14:B11]

- with the line items that are presented for the regulatory deferral account debit balances and credit balances; or

- as a separate line item alongside the related regulatory deferral account debit balances and credit balances.

Similarly, when an entity recognises the movement in a deferred tax asset (liability) that arises as a result of recognising regulatory deferral account balances, the entity should not include the movement in that deferred tax amount within the tax expense (income) line item that is presented in the statement(s) of profit or loss and other comprehensive income in accordance with IAS 12. Instead, the movement in the deferred tax asset (liability) that arises as a result of recognising regulatory deferral account balances should be presented either:

[IFRS 14:B12]

- with the line items that are presented in the statement(s) of profit or loss and other comprehensive income for the movements in regulatory deferral account balances; or

- as a separate line item alongside the related line items that are presented in the statement(s) of profit or loss and other comprehensive income for the movements in regulatory deferral account balances.

4.4 IAS 33 *Earnings per Share*

IAS 33 requires some entities to present, in the statement of profit or loss and other comprehensive income, basic and diluted earnings per share both for profit or loss from continuing operations and profit or loss that is attributable to the ordinary equity holders of the parent entity. In addition, IAS 33 requires an entity that reports a discontinued operation to disclose the basic and diluted amounts per share for the discontinued operation, either in the statement of profit or loss and other comprehensive income or in the notes (see **chapter A31**). [IFRS 14:B13]

For each earnings per share amount presented in accordance with IAS 33, an entity should present additional basic and diluted earnings per share amounts that are calculated using the earnings amount required by IAS 33 but excluding the net movement in the regulatory deferral account balances. [IFRS 14:26] These additional earnings per share amounts should be presented with equal prominence to other earnings per share amounts required by IAS 33 for all periods presented. [IFRS 14:B14]

4.5 IAS 36 *Impairment of Assets*

IAS 36 does not apply to the separate regulatory deferral account balances recognised by an entity because IFRS 14 requires an entity to continue to apply its previous GAAP accounting policies for the identification, recognition, measurement and reversal of any impairment of its recognised regulatory deferral account balances. [IFRS 14:B15]

However, IAS 36 might require an entity to perform an impairment test on a cash-generating unit (CGU) that includes regulatory deferral account balances. This test might be required because the CGU contains goodwill, or because one or more of the impairment indicators described in IAS 36 have been identified relating to the CGU. In such situations, paragraphs 74 to 79 of IAS 36 contain requirements for identifying the recoverable amount and the carrying amount of a CGU (see **8.2.7** in **chapter A10**). An entity should apply those requirements to decide whether any of the regulatory deferral account balances recognised are included in the carrying amount of the CGU for the purpose of the impairment test. The remaining requirements of IAS 36 are then applied to any impairment loss that is recognised as a result of this test. [IFRS 14:B16]

4.6 IFRS 3 *Business Combinations*

The core principle of IFRS 3 is that an acquirer of a business recognises the assets acquired and the liabilities assumed at their acquisition-date fair values. IFRS 3 allows a limited number of exceptions to this general principle (see **7.5** in **chapter A25**). [IFRS 14:B17]

As an additional exception for entities applying IFRS 14, if an entity acquires a business, it should apply, in its consolidated financial statements, its accounting policies established in accordance with IFRS 14:11 to 12 (see **3.2.1**) for the recognition and measurement of the acquiree's regulatory deferral account balances at the date of acquisition. The acquiree's regulatory deferral account balances are recognised in the consolidated financial statements of the acquirer in accordance with the acquirer's policies, irrespective of whether the acquiree recognises those balances in its own financial statements. [IFRS 14:B18]

4.7 IFRS 5 *Non-current Assets Held for Sale and Discontinued Operations*

4.7.1 *Measurement requirements of IFRS 5 do not apply to regulatory deferral account balances*

The measurement requirements of IFRS 5 do not apply to regulatory deferral account balances because IFRS 14 requires an entity to continue to apply its previous accounting policies for the recognition, measurement, impairment and derecognition of regulatory deferral account balances. [IFRS 14:B19]

4.7.2 *Presentation of movements in regulatory deferral account balances relating to discontinued operations*

IFRS 5:33 requires a single amount to be presented for discontinued operations in the statement(s) of profit or loss and other comprehensive income (see **chapter A20**). Notwithstanding the requirements of that paragraph, when an entity that elects to apply IFRS 14 presents a discontinued operation, any movement in regulatory deferral account balances arising from the rate-regulated activities of the discontinued operation should not be included within the line items required by IFRS 5:33. Instead, any movement in regulatory deferral account balances arising from the rate-regulated activities of the discontinued operation should be presented either:

[IFRS 14:B20]

- within the line item presented for movements in the regulatory deferral account balances related to profit or loss; or

- as a separate line item alongside the related line item presented for movements in the regulatory deferral account balances related to profit or loss.

If the entity chooses to present such movements within the related regulatory deferral account line items, it may be necessary to disclose them separately as part of the analysis of the regulatory deferral account line items required under IFRS 14:33 (see **6.3**). [IFRS 14:B22]

4.7.3 Presentation of regulatory deferral account balances relating to disposal groups held for sale

IFRS 5:38 requires an entity to present the assets of a disposal group classified as held for sale separately from other assets in the statement of financial position, and the liabilities of a disposal group held for sale separately from other liabilities. Any regulatory deferral account debit balances and credit balances that relate to a disposal group classified as held for sale should not be included within the line items required under IFRS 5:38. Instead, the entity should present the total of the regulatory deferral account debit balances and credit balances that relate to a disposal group either:

[IFRS 14:B21]

- within the line items that are presented for the regulatory deferral account debit balances and credit balances; or

- as separate line items alongside the other regulatory deferral account debit balances and credit balances.

If the entity chooses to present such balances within the related regulatory deferral account line items, it may be necessary to disclose them separately as part of the analysis of the regulatory deferral account line items required under IFRS 14:33 (see **6.3**). [IFRS 14:B22]

4.8 IFRS 10 *Consolidated Financial Statements* and IAS 28 *Investments in Associates and Joint Ventures*

IFRS 10:19 requires that a parent should prepare consolidated financial statements using uniform accounting policies for like transactions and other events in similar circumstances. IFRS 14:8 requires that an entity applying that Standard should apply all of its requirements to all regulatory deferral account balances arising from all rate-regulated activities of the entity. Consequently, if a parent recognises regulatory deferral account balances in its consolidated financial statements in accordance with IFRS 14, the same accounting policies must be applied to the regulatory deferral account balances arising in all of its subsidiaries. This should apply irrespective of whether the subsidiaries recognise those balances in their own financial statements. [IFRS 14:B23]

Similarly, IAS 28:35 to 36 require that, in applying the equity method, an entity's financial statements should be prepared using uniform accounting policies for like transactions and events in similar circumstances. Consequently, in applying the equity method, adjustments should be made to bring the associate's or joint venture's accounting policies for the recognition, measurement, impairment and derecognition of regulatory deferral account balances into line with those of the investing entity. [IFRS 14:B24]

4.9 IFRS 12 *Disclosure of Interests in Other Entities*

IFRS 12 sets out the following disclosure requirements for interests in other entities:

[IFRS 14:B25 to B28]

- IFRS 12:12(e) requires an entity to disclose, for each of its subsidiaries that have non-controlling interests that are material to the reporting entity, the profit or loss that was allocated to non-controlling interests of the subsidiary during the reporting period;

- IFRS 12:12(g) requires an entity to disclose, for each of its subsidiaries that have non-controlling interests that are material to the reporting entity, summarised financial information about the subsidiary, as specified in IFRS 12:B10;

- IFRS 12:21(b)(ii) requires an entity to disclose, for each joint venture and associate that is material to the reporting entity, summarised financial information as specified in IFRS 12:B12 to B13;

- IFRS 12:B16 specifies the summary financial information that an entity is required to disclose for all other associates and joint ventures that are not individually material in accordance with IFRS 12:21(c); and

- IFRS 12:19 of IFRS 12 specifies the information that an entity is required to disclose when the entity recognises a gain or loss on losing control of a subsidiary, calculated in accordance with IFRS 10:25.

In addition to the information requirements outlined above, an entity that recognises regulatory deferral account balances in accordance with IFRS 14 should also disclose:

- the net movement in regulatory deferral account balances that are included within the amounts that are required to be disclosed by IFRS 12:12(e); [IFRS 14:B25]

- the total regulatory deferral account debit balance, the total regulatory deferral account credit balance and the net movements in those balances, split between amounts recognised in profit or loss and amounts recognised in other comprehensive income, for each entity for which those IFRS 12 disclosures are required; [IFRS 14:B27] and

- the portion of that gain or loss that is attributable to derecognising regulatory deferral account balances in the former subsidiary at the date when control is lost. [IFRS 14:B28]

5   Presentation

5.1   Presentation requirements – general

IFRS 14 introduces specific presentation requirements for regulatory deferral account balances. When IFRS 14 is applied, the regulatory deferral account balances are recognised in the statement of financial position in addition to the assets and liabilities that are recognised in accordance with other Standards. These presentation requirements separate the impact of recognising regulatory deferral account balances from the financial reporting requirements of other Standards. [IFRS 14:18]

In addition to the items that are required to be presented in the statement of financial position and in the statement(s) of profit or loss and other comprehensive income in accordance with IAS 1 *Presentation of Financial Statements*, an entity applying IFRS 14 should present all regulatory deferral account balances and the movements in those balances in accordance with paragraphs IFRS 14:20 to 26 (see **5.2** to **5.5**). [IFRS 14:19]

Regulatory deferral account balances are not described as regulatory assets or regulatory liabilities in IFRS 14 because the IASB has yet to decide whether they meet the definitions of assets or liabilities in the Conceptual Framework. Many of the items included in regulatory deferral account balances would not be recognised as assets or liabilities in the absence of the temporary exemption from applying IFRS 8:11 allowed under IFRS 14 (see **3.1**). The presentation requirements imposed under IFRS 14, as outlined in **5.2** to **5.5**, are designed to ensure that regulatory deferral account balances, and movements therein, are separated from amounts that are recognised as assets and liabilities in accordance with other IFRSs so that such balances and movements can be identified clearly by users of the financial statements.

The illustrative examples accompanying IFRS 14 provide detailed illustrations of the presentation requirements described in **5.2** to **5.5** and the disclosure requirements described in **section 6**.

5.2   Presentation of regulatory deferral account balances

5.2.1   *Regulatory deferral account balances to be presented separately in the statement of financial position*

The following should be presented as separate line items in the statement of financial position:

[IFRS 14:20]

- the total of all regulatory deferral account debit balances; and

- the total of all regulatory deferral account credit balances.

> The IASB concluded that debit and credit regulatory deferral account balances should not be offset in the statement of financial position because, in order to justify such offset, it would be necessary to schedule in detail the timing of recovery or reversal of each regulatory deferral account debit or credit balance so as to identify which amounts would be recovered or reversed in the same period. [IFRS 14:BC47]

5.2.2 Regulatory deferral account balances not to be classified as current or non-current

When current and non-current assets, and current and non-current liabilities, are presented as separate classifications in an entity's statement of financial position (see **5.2.1**), the totals of regulatory deferral account balances should not be classified as current or non-current. Instead, the separate line items required under IFRS 14:20 are distinguished from the assets and liabilities presented in accordance with other IFRSs by the use of sub-totals, which are drawn before the regulatory deferral account balances are presented. [IFRS 14:21]

> The IASB concluded that detailed scheduling of the timing of recovery or reversal of each regulatory deferral account debit or credit balance might be needed for the purpose of identifying which amounts should be classed as current and non-current. Consequently, the IASB decided that regulatory deferral account balances should not be presented as current or non-current in the statement of financial position. Instead, IFRS 14 requires disclosures about the period(s) over which regulatory deferral account balances are expected to be recovered or reversed (see **6.3.4**). It should be noted that an entity is not prohibited from identifying current and non-current amounts within the information disclosed if the relevant information is available. [IFRS 14:BC47]

5.2.3 Cost of self-constructed or internally generated assets

> Regulatory deferral account balances are required to be presented separately in the statement of financial position even when a rate regulator requires, for rate-setting purposes, the inclusion of such amounts within the cost of property, plant and equipment or other assets. The IASB concluded that such separate presentation is required because such balances do not have the same characteristics as assets and liabilities that would be recognised in accordance with other Standards (see IFRS 14:BC40 to BC42 for further discussion).

However, it is important to note the relief available under paragraph D8B of IFRS 1 *First-time Adoption of International Financial Reporting Standards* (see **7.5.5** in **chapter A3**). This provides an exemption which allows first-time adopters to use their previous GAAP carrying amounts at the date of transition to IFRSs as deemed cost for IFRS purposes. The exemption provides relief for first-time adopters that would otherwise be required to separate out the regulatory component of the carrying amount of property, plant and equipment or intangible assets at the date of transition to IFRSs. Such an exercise may have proven impracticable in view of the age and size of some of these items. Consequently, entities that apply IFRS 14 will only need to isolate the regulatory deferral account amounts for those items on a prospective basis from the date of transition to IFRSs. [IFRS 14:BC46]

5.2.4   Presentation of regulatory deferral account balances in the statement of financial position – example

In summary, the statement of financial position will present assets in the following manner, with similar presentation requirements for liabilities.

Current assets	xxx
Long-term assets	xxx
Total assets	xxx
Regulatory deferral debit balances and related deferred tax asset[(a)]	xxx
Total assets and regulatory deferral account debit balances	xxx

[(a)]   IFRS 14 provides the option of presenting the deferred tax balance which arises as a result of recognising regulatory deferral account balances either (1) on an aggregated basis with the regulatory deferral account balance, or (2) as a separate line item alongside the related regulatory deferral account balance (see **5.4**).

The illustrative examples accompanying IFRS 14 set out a comprehensive example of the disclosures required.

5.3   Presentation of movements in regulatory deferral account balances

5.3.1   Presentation of movements in regulatory deferral account balances recognised in other comprehensive income

The net movement in all regulatory deferral account balances for the reporting period that relate to items recognised in other comprehensive income should be presented in the other comprehensive income section of the statement of profit or loss and other comprehensive income. [IFRS 14:22]

Separate line items should be used for the net movement related to items that, in accordance with other Standards:

[IFRS 14:22]

- will not be reclassified subsequently to profit or loss; and
- will be reclassified subsequently to profit or loss when specific conditions are met.

5.3.2 Presentation of movements in regulatory deferral account balances recognised in profit or loss

A separate line item should be presented in the profit or loss section of the statement of profit or loss and other comprehensive income (or in the separate statement of profit or loss, when presented), for the remaining net movement in all regulatory deferral account balances for the reporting period, excluding movements that are not reflected in profit or loss, such as amounts acquired. This separate line item should be distinguished from the income and expenses that are presented in accordance with other Standards by the use of a sub-total, which is drawn before the net movement in regulatory deferral account balances. [IFRS 14:23]

5.3.3 Presentation of movements in regulatory deferral account balances – example

IFRS 14 requires separate presentation of the movements in the regulatory deferral accounts. For example, the statement of profit or loss should present a sub-total of profit or loss for the year before the net movement in all regulatory deferral accounts, as follows.

Revenue	xxxx
Cost of sales	(xxx)
Gross profit	xxxx
Expenses	(xxxx)
Profit before tax	xxxx
Income tax expense	(xxx)
Profit for the year before net movement in regulatory deferral account balances	xxxx
Net movement in regulatory deferral account balances relating to profit or loss and the related deferred tax movement[(a)]	(xxx)
Profit for the year and net movement in regulatory deferral account balances	xxxx

(a) IFRS 14 provides the option of presenting the deferred tax movement which arises as a result of movements in the regulatory deferral account balances either (1) on an aggregated basis with the movement in regulatory deferral account balances, or (2) as a separate line item alongside the related line items that are presented as movements in regulatory deferral account balances (see **5.4**).

The illustrative examples accompanying IFRS 14 set out a comprehensive example of the disclosures required.

5.4 Presentation of deferred tax assets or liabilities relating to regulatory deferral account balances

If a deferred tax asset or a deferred tax liability is recognised as a result of recognising regulatory deferral account balances, it should not be presented within the totals required under IAS 12 *Income Taxes* for deferred tax assets (liabilities) and the tax expense (income). Instead, such deferred tax assets and liabilities, and the related movements in those deferred tax assets and liabilities, should be presented with the related regulatory deferral account balances and movements in those balances (see also **4.3**). [IFRS 14:24]

5.5 Presentation of regulatory deferral account balances relating to disposal groups and discontinued operations

When an entity presents a discontinued operation or a disposal group in accordance with IFRS 5 *Non-current Assets Held for Sale and Discontinued Operations*, any related regulatory deferral account balances and the net movement in those balances should be presented, as applicable, with the regulatory deferral account balances and movements in those balances, instead of within the disposal group or discontinued operation (see also **4.7**). [IFRS 14:25]

6 Disclosure

6.1 Disclosure – general principle

The overall principle established by IFRS 14 is that entities that elect to apply that Standard should disclose information that enables users to assess:

[IFRS 14:27]

- the nature of, and the risks associated with, the rate regulation that establishes the price(s) that the entity can charge customers for the goods or services it provides; and

- the effects of that rate regulation on the entity's financial position, financial performance and cash flows.

To meet the objective set out in IFRS 14:27, the following should be considered:

[IFRS 14:29]

- the level of detail that is necessary to satisfy the disclosure requirements;

- how much emphasis to place on each of the various requirements;

- how much aggregation or disaggregation to undertake; and

- whether users of financial statements need additional information to evaluate the quantitative information disclosed.

Specific disclosures designed to meet the objective under IFRS 14:27 are set out in IFRS 14:30 to 36 (see **6.2** and **6.3**). If any of the disclosures requirements set out in those paragraphs are not considered relevant to meet the objective set out in IFRS 14:27, they may be omitted from the financial statements. On the other hand, if the disclosures set out in **6.2** and **6.3** are insufficient to meet the objective set out in IFRS 14:27, additional information should be disclosed as necessary to meet that objective. [IFRS 14:28]

6.2 Explanation of activities subject to rate regulation

To help a user of the financial statements assess the nature of, and the risks associated with, the entity's rate-regulated activities, an entity should, for each type of rate-regulated activity, disclose:

[IFRS 14:30]

- a brief description of the nature and extent of the rate-regulated activity and the nature of the regulatory rate-setting process;

- the identity of the rate regulator(s). If the rate regulator is a related party (as defined in IAS 24 *Related Party Disclosures*), the entity should disclose that fact, together with an explanation of how it is related; and

- how the future recovery of each class (i.e. each type of cost or income) of regulatory deferral account debit balance or reversal of each class of regulatory deferral account credit balance is affected by risks and uncertainty, for example:

  - demand risk (e.g. changes in consumer attitudes, the availability of alternative sources of supply or the level of competition);

  - regulatory risk (e.g. the submission or approval of a rate-setting application or the entity's assessment of the expected future regulatory actions); and

  - other risks (e.g. currency or other market risks).

The disclosures required by IFRS 14:30 should be provided in the financial statements either directly in the notes or incorporated by cross-reference from the financial statements to some other statement (e.g. a management commentary or risk report) that is available to users of the financial statements on the same terms as the financial statements and at the same time. If the information is not included in the financial statements directly or incorporated by cross-reference, the financial statements are incomplete. [IFRS 14:31]

6.3   Explanation of recognised amounts

6.3.1   Basis for recognition and measurement of regulatory deferral account balances

Entities are required to disclose the basis on which regulatory deferral account balances are recognised and derecognised, and how they are measured on initial recognition and subsequently. This must include information about how regulatory deferral account balances are assessed for recoverability and how any impairment loss is allocated. [IFRS 14:32]

6.3.2   Reconciliation of carrying amount of regulatory deferral account balances at the beginning and end of the period

Entities are required to present, for each type of rate-regulated activity and for each class of regulatory deferral account balance, a reconciliation of the carrying amount at the beginning and the end of the period. This information should be presented in a table unless another format is more appropriate. Judgement should be applied in deciding the level of detail necessary, but the following components would usually be relevant:

[IFRS 14:33(a)]

- the amounts that have been recognised in the current period in the statement of financial position as regulatory deferral account balances;

- the amounts that have been recognised in the statement(s) of profit or loss and other comprehensive income relating to balances that have been recovered (sometimes described as amortised) or reversed in the current period; and

- other amounts, separately identified, that affected the regulatory deferral account balances, such as impairments, items acquired or assumed in a business combination, items disposed of, or the effects of changes in foreign exchange rates or discount rates.

6.3.3   Rate of return or discount rate used to reflect the time value of money

Entities are required to disclose, for each type of rate-regulated activity and for each class of regulatory deferral account balance, the applicable rate of return or discount rate (including a zero rate or a range of rates, when applicable) used to reflect the time value of money. [IFRS 14:33(b)]

6.3.4 Remaining periods for recovery or reversal of regulatory deferral account balances

Entities are required to disclose, for each type of rate-regulated activity, the remaining periods over which the entity expects to recover (or amortise) the carrying amount of each class of regulatory deferral account debit balance or to reverse each class of regulatory deferral account credit balance. [IFRS 14:33(c)]

6.3.5 Impact of rate regulation on tax balances

When rate regulation affects the amount and timing of an entity's income tax expense (income), the entity should disclose separately:

[IFRS 14:34]

- the impact of the rate regulation on the amounts of current and deferred tax recognised; and

- any regulatory deferral account balance that relates to taxation and the related movement in that balance.

6.3.6 Regulatory deferral account balances of subsidiaries, associates or joint ventures

If an entity provides disclosures in accordance with IFRS 12 *Disclosure of Interests in Other Entities* for an interest in a subsidiary, associate or joint venture that has rate-regulated activities and for which regulatory deferral account balances are recognised in accordance with IFRS 14, the entity should disclose:

[IFRS 14:35]

- the amounts included for the regulatory deferral account debit and credit balances; and

- the net movement in those balances for the interests disclosed (see also **4.9**).

6.3.7 Regulatory account balances that are no longer fully recoverable or reversible

If an entity has concluded that a regulatory deferral account balance is no longer fully recoverable or reversible, it should disclose that fact, the reason why the balance is not recoverable or reversible, and the amount by which the regulatory deferral account balance has been reduced. [IFRS 14:36]

7   Effective date and transition

IFRS 14 is applicable for entities whose first annual IFRS financial statements are for a period beginning on or after 1 January 2016. A first-time adopter may apply IFRS 14 in financial statements beginning before that date provided that it discloses that fact. [IFRS 14:C1]

> In the absence of any specific relief under IFRS 1 *First-time Adoption of International Financial Reporting Standards*, entities that adopt IFRS 14 are required to apply the Standard retrospectively at the date of transition to IFRSs.
>
> The IASB concluded that no explicit relief from full retrospective application of IFRS 14 is needed because existing recognition, measurement, impairment and derecognition policies are carried through from a first-time adopter's previous GAAP. The Board has also highlighted (IFRS 14:BC38) that first-time adopters of IFRSs can use the deemed cost exemption for property, plant and equipment and intangible assets available in IFRS 1:D8B (see **7.5.5** in **chapter A3**) which allows first-time adopters to use their previous GAAP carrying amounts at the date of transition to IFRSs as deemed cost for IFRS purposes. Consequently, they will only need to change their presentation policies for these items to isolate the regulatory deferral account amounts on a prospective basis from the date of transition to IFRSs. [IFRS 14:BC54]

8   Future developments

In September 2014, as part of its ongoing comprehensive project on rate-regulated activities, the IASB published a discussion paper DP/2014/2 *Reporting the Financial Effects of Rate Regulation*.

The response period for the paper closed in January 2015. At the time of writing, the IASB is continuing its analysis work on this project and is expected to publish a further discussion paper in 2017.

Appendix A1   Revenue (IAS 18)

Contents

1 Introduction

1.1 Overview of IAS 18

IAS 18 *Revenue* outlines the accounting requirements for revenue from the sale of goods, rendering of services, and for interest, royalties and dividends. Revenue is measured at the fair value of the consideration received or receivable and recognised when prescribed conditions are met, which depend on the nature of the revenue.

1.2 Amendments to IAS 18 since the last edition of this manual

None. IAS 18 was most recently amended in May 2011.

1.3 IAS 18 superseded by IFRS 15

In May 2014, the IASB issued IFRS 15 *Revenue from Contracts with Customers*, which is effective for annual periods beginning on or after 1 January 2018, with earlier application permitted. IFRS 15 supersedes IAS 18. For annual periods beginning before 1 January 2018, entities may continue to apply IAS 18, which is discussed in this appendix. Alternatively, entities may choose to apply IFRS 15 in advance of its 2018 effective date, provided that they disclose that fact. The requirements of IFRS 15 are discussed in detail in **chapter A14**.

Note that if an entity wishes to apply IFRS 16 *Leases* (see **chapter A17**) for an annual period beginning before 1 January 2019, it is also required to apply IFRS 15 rather than IAS 18.

IFRS 15 also supersedes:

- IAS 11 *Construction Contracts* (see **appendix A2**);
- IFRIC 13 *Customer Loyalty Programmes* (see **5.6**);
- IFRIC 15 *Agreements for the Construction of Real Estate* (see **2.2**);
- IFRIC 18 *Transfers of Assets from Customers* (see **2.4**); and
- SIC-31 *Revenue – Barter Transactions Involving Advertising Services* (see **4.5**).

2 Scope

2.1 Scope – general

IAS 18 is applied in accounting for revenue arising from:

[IAS 18:1]

- the sale of goods (including goods produced for sale and goods purchased for sale, such as merchandise purchased by a retailer or land and other property held for resale);

- the rendering of services; and

- the use by others of entity assets yielding interest, royalties and dividends.

IAS 18 does not deal with revenue arising from:

[IAS 18:6]

- leases (dealt with in IAS 17 *Leases** – see **appendix A4**);

- dividends arising from investments accounted for under the equity method (dealt with in IAS 28 *Investments in Associates and Joint Ventures* – see **chapter A26**);

- insurance contracts within the scope of IFRS 4 *Insurance Contracts* – see **chapter A39**;

- changes in the fair value of financial assets and financial liabilities or their disposal (dealt with in IFRS 9 *Financial Instruments* (**Volume B**), or, for entities that have not yet adopted IFRS 9, IAS 39 *Financial Instruments: Recognition and Measurement* (**Volume C**));

- changes in the value of other current assets;

- the initial recognition, and changes in the fair value, of biological assets related to agricultural activity (dealt with in IAS 41 *Agriculture* (see **chapter A38**) and IAS 16 *Property, Plant and Equipment* (see **chapter A7**));

- the initial recognition of agricultural produce (also dealt with in IAS 41); and

- the extraction of mineral ores (dealt with in IFRS 6 *Exploration for and Evaluation of Mineral Resources* – see **chapter A40**).

* Note that entities applying IFRS 16 *Leases* (effective for annual periods beginning on or after 1 January 2019, with earlier application permitted – see **chapter A17**) are required to apply IFRS 15 *Revenue from Contracts with Customers* rather than IAS 18.

Also excluded from the scope of IAS 18 are contracts for the rendering of services that are directly related to construction contracts, e.g. those for the services of project managers and architects. These service contracts fall within the scope of IAS 11 *Construction Contracts* (see **appendix A2**). [IAS 18:4] The requirements of IFRIC 12 *Service Concession Arrangements*, which addresses the accounting by operators for public-to-private service concession arrangements, are dealt with in **appendix A3**.

Contracts included in the scope of IFRS 4 include product warranties issued by a third party for the replacement of goods sold by a manufacturer to a customer as well as fixed fee contracts that are dependent on an uncertain future event (see **2.5** and **2.3**, respectively, in **chapter A39**). However, product warranties issued directly by a manufacturer to a customer are within the scope of IAS 18.

See **8.11** in **chapter A12** for a discussion on whether warranties fall within the scope of IAS 18 or IAS 37 *Provisions, Contingent Liabilities and Contingent Assets*.

2.2 IFRS 15 *Agreements for the Construction of Real Estate*

2.2.1 *IFRIC 15 – general requirements*

IFRIC 15 addresses whether an agreement is within the scope of IAS 11 or IAS 18, and when revenue from the construction of real estate should be recognised. [IFRIC 15:6]

The Interpretation applies to agreements for the construction of real estate, and to entities that undertake that construction directly or through subcontractors. [IFRIC 15:4] In addition to the construction of real estate, such agreements may include the delivery of other goods or services. [IFRIC 15:5]

Agreements for the construction of real estate take diverse forms, in part because the underlying substance of such agreements varies. While some agreements are for the provision of construction services, others are in substance for the delivery of goods (e.g. housing units) that are not complete at the time of entering into the agreement. Thus, the percentage of completion method is appropriate for some agreements for the construction of real estate but, for others, revenue should be recognised only at the point that the constructed real estate is delivered to the customer. The Interpretation provides guidance on how to determine which approach is appropriate in which circumstances.

IFRIC 15 is accompanied by an information note which, although not part of the Interpretation, summarises its requirements in the form of two flowcharts, reproduced as **table 2.2.2** and **table 2.2.3.1**.

The detailed guidance in IFRIC 15 is written on the assumption that the entity has previously analysed the agreement for the construction of real estate and any related agreements and concluded that any other criteria for revenue recognition (discussed later in this appendix) are met. In particular, the entity must not retain continuing managerial involvement to the degree usually associated with ownership; and it must not retain effective control over the constructed real estate to an extent that would preclude recognition of some or all of the consideration as revenue. If recognition of some of the consideration as revenue is precluded, the detailed guidance in IFRIC 15 applies only to the part of the agreement for which revenue will be recognised. [IFRIC 15:7]

2.2.2   Splitting an agreement into separately identifiable components

It is possible that a single agreement may cover the delivery of goods or services in addition to the construction of real estate; for example, an agreement to construct real estate may also specify that property management services are to be provided.

As discussed in **5.1**, IAS 18:13 indicates that, in some circumstances, agreements may need to be split into separately identifiable components, with each such component being accounted for separately. When this is necessary, the fair value of the total consideration received or receivable for the agreement is allocated to each component. The seller then applies the requirements of IFRIC 15 to any components for the construction of real estate in order to determine whether each component is within the scope of IAS 11 or IAS 18. [IFRIC 15:8]

The segmenting criteria of IAS 11 should then be applied to any component of the agreement that is determined to be a construction contract. [IFRIC 15:8]

Table 2.2.2

[Information note accompanying IFRIC 15]

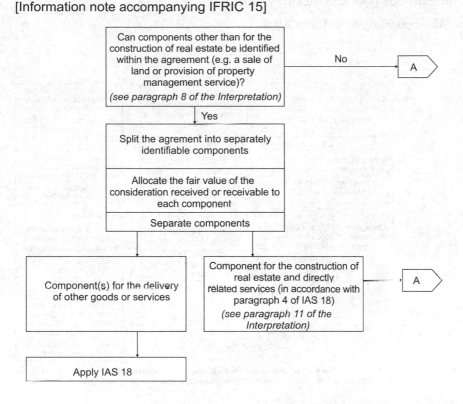

(A) – continues in **Table 2.2.3.1**.

2.2.3 *Accounting for the construction of real estate*

2.2.3.1 *Accounting for the construction of real estate – general*

The appropriate accounting for an agreement to construct real estate (or, when an agreement is split into separately identifiable components, for a component for the construction of real estate) depends on whether the agreement (or component):

- meets the definition of a construction contract;

- is only for the rendering of services; or

- is for the sale of goods, in which case it is necessary to consider whether the criteria for recognising revenue from the sale of goods are met on a continuous basis.

Whether an agreement (or component) is within the scope of IAS 11 or IAS 18 depends on the terms of the agreement and all the surrounding facts and circumstances, and judgement will be required with respect to each agreement. [IFRIC 15:10]

Table 2.2.3.1

[Information note accompanying IFRIC 15]

(A) – continues from **Table 2.2.2**.

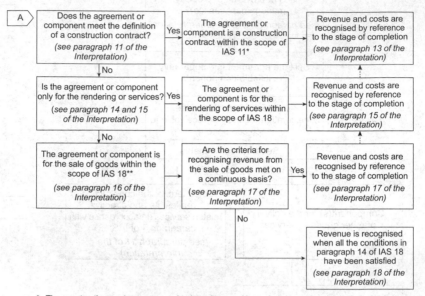

* The construction contract may need to be segmented in accordance with paragraph 8 of IAS 11
** Directly related services may need to be separated in accordance with paragraph 13 of IAS 18

2.2.3.2   Construction contracts

IAS 11 applies when the agreement (or component) meets the definition of a construction contract set out in IAS 11:3, namely "a contract specifically negotiated for the construction of an asset or a combination of assets ...".

IFRIC 15:11 states that an agreement for the construction of real estate will meet the definition of a construction contract when the buyer is able to:

- specify the major structural elements of the design of the real estate before construction begins; and/or

- specify major structural changes once construction is in progress, whether it exercises that ability or not.

When construction will take place on land that was already the buyer's asset before the agreement to construct real estate was envisaged, it is likely that IAS 11 will apply. This is because an owner of land will, subject to planning constraints, usually be able to decide whether to construct real estate on that land, and to specify the major structural elements of the design of any such real estate before construction.

Generally, it is likely that a buyer will be able to specify major structural changes once construction is in progress only if such a right is explicit in the agreement. But it is possible that such a right may be established by the law of a jurisdiction in which a transaction occurs.

In contrast, if buyers have only limited ability to influence the design (e.g. to select from a range of entity-specified options, or to specify only minor variations to the basic design), IFRIC 15:12 states that the agreement will be for the sale of goods and within the scope of IAS 18.

Although IFRIC 15:12 states that such an agreement will be for the sale of goods, it would seem possible in some circumstances (e.g. when construction materials will be sourced directly by the buyer) for the agreement to be for the rendering of services, as discussed at **2.2.3.3**. In any case, it is clear that the agreement will not be a construction contract.

When IAS 11 applies, the construction contract also includes any contracts or components for the rendering of services that are directly related to the construction of the real estate in accordance with IAS 11:5(a) and IAS 18:4. [IFRIC 15:11] If the outcome of the agreement (or component) can be estimated reliably, revenue is recognised by reference to the stage of completion of the contract activity in accordance with IAS 11. [IFRIC 15:13] The recognition of revenue for construction contracts is discussed in **appendix A2**.

2.2.3.3 *Agreements for the rendering of services*
If an agreement (or component) does not meet the definition of a construction contract, it will be within the scope of IAS 18. The Interpretation provides further guidance on how to determine whether the agreement is for the rendering of services (see below) or for the sale of goods (see **2.2.3.4**). [IFRIC 15:14]

In some cases, the entity is not required to acquire and supply construction materials because they will be sourced directly by the buyer. When this is the case, the agreement may be only an agreement for the rendering of services in accordance with IAS 18, in which case, provided that the criteria in IAS 18:20 are met, revenue will be recognised using the percentage of completion method. IAS 18:21 indicates that the requirements of IAS 11 are generally applicable to the recognition of revenue and the associated expenses for such a transaction. [IFRIC 15:15] The recognition of revenue from the provision of services is discussed in **section 7**.

2.2.3.4 *Agreements for the sale of goods*
Conversely, if the entity is required to provide services together with construction materials in order to perform its contractual obligation to deliver real estate to the buyer then, assuming it does not qualify as a

construction contract (see **2.2.3.2**), the agreement is for the sale of goods and the criteria set out in IAS 18:14 apply. [IFRIC 15:16]

If an agreement is determined to be for the sale of goods, the timing of revenue recognition will depend on when control and the significant risks and rewards of ownership are transferred to the buyer. IFRIC 15 envisages two possibilities, as set out below.

- The entity may transfer to the buyer control and the significant risks and rewards of ownership of the real estate in its entirety at a single time (e.g. at completion, upon or after delivery). In this case, revenue will be recognised only when all the criteria in IAS 18:14 are satisfied. [IFRIC 15:18] Those criteria are discussed in **section 6**.

- Alternatively, the entity may transfer to the buyer control and the significant risks and rewards of ownership of the work in progress in its current state as construction progresses. In this case, if all the criteria in IAS 18:14 are met continuously as construction progresses, revenue will be recognised using the percentage of completion method. The requirements of IAS 11 are generally applicable to the recognition of revenue and the associated expenses for such a transaction. [IFRIC 15:17]

The idea that the criteria in IAS 18:14 can be met continuously as construction progresses is relatively new. In the Basis for Conclusions accompanying IFRIC 15, the IFRIC (now the IFRS Interpretations Committee) noted that agreements with 'continuous transfer' might not be encountered frequently. [IFRIC 15:BC26] When an entity adopts such accounting, specific disclosures are required, including how the entity determines which agreements meet all the criteria in IAS 18:14 continuously as construction progresses (see **2.2.4**).

The Interpretation itself does not give further guidance on how to assess whether 'continuous transfer' is present, but some further commentary is included at IE3, IE8 and IE11 in the illustrative examples accompanying IFRIC 15 (see **2.2.5**). One of the important indicators of 'continuous transfer' appears to be that, if the agreement is terminated before construction is complete, the buyer retains the work in progress and the entity has the right to be paid for the work performed to date.

When the entity is required to perform further work on real estate already delivered to the buyer, it recognises an expense in accordance with IAS 18:19 (see **6.6**), measuring the liability in accordance with IAS 37 *Provisions, Contingent Liabilities and Contingent Assets* (see **chapter A12**). When the entity is required to deliver further goods or services that are separately identifiable from the real estate already delivered to the buyer, it will already have identified the remaining goods or services as a separate component of the sale in accordance with IFRIC 15:8 (see **2.2.2**). [IFRIC 15:19]

2.2.4 Disclosures

When an entity recognises revenue using the percentage of completion method for agreements that meet all the criteria in IAS 18:14 continuously as construction progresses (see **2.2.3.4**), the following disclosures are required:

[IFRIC 15:20]

- how the entity determines which agreements meet all the criteria in IAS 18:14 continuously as construction progresses;

- the amount of revenue arising from such agreements in the period; and

- the methods used to determine the stage of completion of agreements in progress.

For any such agreements that are in progress at the reporting date, the following disclosures are also required:

[IFRIC 15:21]

- the aggregate amount of costs incurred and recognised profits (less recognised losses) to date; and

- the amount of advances received.

> IFRIC 15:BC32 notes that these disclosures are similar to those required for construction contracts by IAS 11:39 and 40.

2.2.5 Illustrative examples

The following examples accompany, but are not part of, IFRIC 15.

Example 2.2.5A

Separately identifiable component for sale of land

[IFRIC 15:IE1 - IE5, Example 1]

An entity buys a plot of land for the construction of commercial real estate. It designs an office block to build on the land and submits the designs to planning authorities in order to obtain building permission. The entity markets the office block to potential tenants and signs conditional lease agreements. The entity markets the office block to potential buyers and signs with one of them a conditional agreement for the sale of land and the construction of the office block. The buyer cannot put the land or the incomplete office block back to the entity. The entity receives the building permission and all agreements become unconditional. The entity is given access to the land in order to undertake the construction and then constructs the office block.

In this illustrative example, the agreement should be separated into two components: a component for the sale of land and a component for the

---

construction of the office block. The component for the sale of land is a sale of goods within the scope of IAS 18.

Because all the major structural decisions were made by the entity and were included in the designs submitted to the planning authorities before the buyer signed the conditional agreement, it is assumed that there will be no major change in the designs after the construction has begun. Consequently, the component for the construction of the office block is not a construction contract and is within the scope of IAS 18. The facts, including that the construction takes place on land the buyer owns before construction begins and that the buyer cannot put the incomplete office block back to the entity, indicate that the entity transfers to the buyer control and the significant risks and rewards of ownership of the work in progress in its current state as construction progresses. Therefore, if all the criteria in paragraph 14 of IAS 18 are met continuously as construction progresses, the entity recognises revenue from the construction of the office block by reference to the stage of completion using the percentage of completion method.

Alternatively, assume that the construction of the office block started before the entity signed the agreement with the buyer. In that event, the agreement should be separated into three components: a component for the sale of land, a component for the partially constructed office block and a component for the construction of the office block. The entity should apply the recognition criteria separately to each component. Assuming that the other facts remain unchanged, the entity recognises revenue from the component for the construction of the office block by reference to the stage of completion using the percentage of completion method as explained in paragraph [above].

In this example, the sale of land is determined to be a separately identifiable component from the component for the construction of real estate. However, depending on facts and circumstances, the entity may conclude that such a component is not separately identifiable. For example, in some jurisdictions, a condominium is legally defined as the absolute ownership of a unit based on a legal description of the airspace the unit actually occupies, plus an undivided interest in the ownership of the common elements (that includes the land and actual building itself, all the driveways, parking, lifts, outside hallways, recreation and landscaped areas) that are owned jointly with the other condominium unit owners. In this case, the undivided interest in the ownership of the common elements does not give the buyer control and the significant risks and rewards of the land itself. Indeed, the right to the unit itself and the interest in the common elements are not separable.

Example 2.2.5B

Agreement for sale of goods

[IFRIC 15:IE6 - IE8, Example 2]

An entity is developing residential real estate and starts marketing individual units (apartments) while construction is still in progress. Buyers enter into a binding sale agreement that gives them the right to acquire a specified unit when it is ready for occupation. They pay a deposit that is refundable only if the entity fails to deliver the completed unit in accordance with the contracted terms. Buyers are also required to make progress payments between the time of the initial agreement and contractual completion. The balance of the purchase price is paid only on contractual completion, when buyers obtain possession of their unit. Buyers are able to specify only minor variations to the basic design but they cannot specify or alter major structural elements of the design of their unit. In the jurisdiction, no rights to the underlying real estate asset transfer to the buyer other than through the agreement. Consequently, the construction takes place regardless of whether sale agreements exist.

In this illustrative example, the terms of the agreement and all the surrounding facts and circumstances indicate that the agreement is not a construction contract. The agreement is a forward contract that gives the buyer an asset in the form of a right to acquire, use and sell the completed real estate at a later date and an obligation to pay the purchase price in accordance with its terms. Although the buyer might be able to transfer its interest in the forward contract to another party, the entity retains control and the significant risks and rewards of ownership of the work in progress in its current state until the completed real estate is transferred. Therefore, revenue should be recognised only when all the criteria in paragraph 14 of IAS 18 are met (at completion in this example).

Alternatively, assume that, in the jurisdiction, the law requires the entity to transfer immediately to the buyer ownership of the real estate in its current state of completion and that any additional construction becomes the property of the buyer as construction progresses. The entity would need to consider all the terms of the agreement to determine whether this change in the timing of the transfer of ownership means that the entity transfers to the buyer control and the significant risks and rewards of ownership of the work in progress in its current state as construction progresses. For example, the fact that if the agreement is terminated before construction is complete, the buyer retains the work in progress and the entity has the right to be paid for the work performed, might indicate that control is transferred along with ownership. If it does, and if all the criteria in paragraph 14 of IAS 18 are met continuously as construction progresses, the entity recognises revenue by reference to the stage of completion using the percentage of completion method taking into account the stage of completion of the whole building and the agreements signed with individual buyers.

Example 2.2.5C

Continuing managerial involvement

[IFRIC 15:IE9 - IE11, Example 3]

Determining whether the entity will retain neither continuing managerial involvement to the degree usually associated with ownership nor effective control over the constructed real estate to an extent that would preclude recognition of some or all of the consideration as revenue depends on the terms of the agreement and all the surrounding facts and circumstances. Such a determination requires judgement. The Interpretation assumes the entity has reached the conclusion that it is appropriate to recognise revenue from the agreement and discusses how to determine the appropriate pattern of revenue recognition.

Agreements for the construction of real estate may include such a degree of continuing managerial involvement by the entity undertaking the construction that control and the significant risks and rewards of ownership are not transferred even when construction is complete and the buyer obtains possession. Examples are agreements in which the entity guarantees occupancy of the property for a specified period, or guarantees a return on the buyer's investment for a specified period. In such circumstances, recognition of revenue may be delayed or precluded altogether.

Agreements for the construction of real estate may give the buyer a right to take over the work in progress (albeit with a penalty) during construction, e.g. to engage a different entity to complete the construction. This fact, along with others, may indicate that the entity transfers to the buyer control of the work in progress in its current state as construction progresses. The entity that undertakes the construction of real estate will have access to the land and the work in progress in order to perform its contractual obligation to deliver to the buyer completed real estate. If control of the work in process is transferred continuously, that access does not necessarily imply that the entity undertaking the construction retains continuing managerial involvement with the real estate to the degree usually associated with ownership to an extent that would preclude recognition of some or all of the consideration as revenue. The entity may have control over the activities related to the performance of its contractual obligation but not over the real estate itself.

2.3   Distinguishing between the sale of goods, the rendering of services and construction contracts

Difficulties can arise in distinguishing between the sale of goods, the rendering of services and construction contracts. IAS 18 offers no guidance on how to determine whether a contract is for the supply of goods or services. Although the appropriate classification will in many cases be obvious, in some industries, such as software development, careful judgement may be required. In particular, merely because a contract requires the delivery of a customised software programme, it does not necessarily follow that the contract is a construction contract. When the software is developed entirely to customer specification, the contract is likely to be a construction contract. More complex cases may involve the modification of an already existing core product offered by a software developer and it will be necessary to exercise careful judgement in order to assess whether the specified modifications are so significant as to make the contract a construction contract or whether the contract should be regarded as, in substance, a supply of goods bundled together with more limited modification services.

The IFRIC (now the IFRS Interpretations Committee) considered the difficulty in distinguishing between the sale of goods, rendering of services and construction contracts during the development of IFRIC 15 (see **2.2**). In accordance with paragraph 11 of IAS 8 *Accounting Policies, Changes in Accounting Estimates and Errors*, the indicators identified in IFRIC 15 may be applied by analogy to other situations when the appropriate classification between these three categories is not obvious. However, because the indicators set out in IFRIC 15 were developed for real estate, it will be necessary to exercise careful judgement when considering how they might be interpreted in other contexts.

2.4   IFRIC 18 *Transfers of Assets from Customers*

2.4.1   *IFRIC 18 – general requirements*

IFRIC 18 aims to address divergent practice in the accounting by recipients for transfers of property, plant and equipment from 'customers'. The Interpretation concludes that when an item of property, plant and equipment transferred meets the definition of an asset from the perspective of the recipient, the recipient should recognise the asset at its fair value on the date of the transfer, with the credit recognised as revenue when the criteria in IAS 18 *Revenue* are met. IFRIC 18 does not address how a customer should account for such a transfer of property, plant and equipment.

IFRIC 18 applies to all agreements in which an entity receives from a customer an item of property, plant and equipment (or cash to construct or acquire an item of property, plant and equipment) that the entity must then use either to connect the customer to a network or to provide the customer with ongoing access to a supply of goods or services, or to do both. [IFRIC 18:5 & 6] It applies only to the accounting by the receiving entity for such transfers. [IFRIC 18:4]

In particular, in the utilities industry, an entity may receive from its customers property, plant and equipment that must be used to connect those customers to a network and provide them with ongoing access to a supply of commodities such as electricity, gas or water. [IFRIC 18:1] But the Interpretation also applies in industries other than utilities where transfers of assets from customers occur. For example, an entity outsourcing its information technology functions may transfer its existing items of property, plant and equipment to the outsourcing provider. [IFRIC 18:2]

Transfers of assets other than property, plant and equipment (e.g. intangible assets) are not within the scope of IFRIC 18. However, application by analogy in accordance with IAS 8 is not prohibited. [IFRIC 18:BC5]

IFRIC 18 refers to the entity transferring the asset as the customer. However, in some circumstances it envisages that the transferor of the asset may not be the entity that will eventually have ongoing access to the supply of goods or services and be the recipient of those goods or services. [IFRIC 18:3]

> For example, a developer builds a new office building in which there is an electrical substation that is handed over to the electricity supplier when the building is completed. The electricity supplier will use the substation to distribute electricity to the future occupier of the building. For the purposes of IFRIC 18, the 'customer' making the transfer is the developer, even though the 'customer' who will use the electricity provided through the substation is the future occupier.

IFRIC 18 does not apply to agreements in which the transfer is either a government grant as defined in IAS 20 *Accounting for Government Grants and Disclosure of Government Assistance* or infrastructure used in a service concession arrangement that is within the scope of IFRIC 12 *Service Concession Arrangements*. [IFRIC 18:7]

> IFRIC 18 arrangements can be distinguished from service concession arrangements within the scope of IFRIC 12 because, in service concession arrangements, it is the grantor that controls the infrastructure, not the operator. Equally, there is no overlap between IFRIC 18 and IAS 20 because a transfer of assets from a customer does not meet the definition of a government grant in accordance with IAS 20:3. [IFRIC 18:BC8]

IFRIC 18 addresses the following issues:

- recognition of the transferred property, plant and equipment as an asset (see **2.3.2**);

- measurement of the asset on initial recognition (see **2.3.3**);

- recognition of revenue (see **2.3.4**); and

- accounting for transfers of cash from customers (see **2.3.5**).

2.4.2   Recognition as an asset

The key question for the entity receiving the item of property, plant and equipment is whether it meets the definition of an asset under the *Conceptual Framework for Financial Reporting*. Paragraph 4:4(a) of the Conceptual Framework states that "an asset is a resource controlled by the entity as a result of past events and from which future economic benefits are expected to flow to the entity". IFRIC 18 emphasises that the entity must control the asset in order to recognise it. While, in most circumstances, the entity obtains the right of ownership of the transferred property, plant and equipment, this is not essential in determining whether an asset exists. IFRIC 18 notes that right of ownership may not of itself be sufficient to establish control. If the customer still controls the item, it will not be an asset of the receiving entity. [IFRIC 18:9]

Whether or not the entity controls the transferred property, plant and equipment is based on consideration of all relevant facts and circumstances. For example, IFRIC 18 notes that although an entity may not have discretion as to the purpose for which the item is used, when it has the ability to decide how the item is operated and maintained and when it is replaced, the entity would normally conclude that it controls the transferred item. [IFRIC 18:10]

> The draft Interpretation D24, which preceded IFRIC 18, contained a requirement to determine whether the arrangement contained a lease in accordance with IAS 17 and IFRIC 4. The IFRIC (now the IFRS Interpretations Committee) decided to simplify the proposals by removing this requirement and focusing on who controls the asset.

2.4.3 Measurement of the asset on initial recognition

When the receiving entity determines that the item of property, plant and equipment meets the definition of an asset, IFRIC 18 requires that asset to be recognised and its cost on initial recognition to be measured at its fair value in accordance with paragraph 24 of IAS 16 *Property, Plant and Equipment*. [IFRIC 18:11]

2.4.4 Recognition of revenue

IAS 18:12 states that "when goods are sold or services are rendered in exchange for dissimilar goods or services, the exchange is regarded as a transaction which generates revenue". Transactions within the scope of IFRIC 18 are exchanges for dissimilar goods or services and, therefore, they will give rise to revenue in accordance with IAS 18. [IFRIC 18:13]

The timing of the recognition of that revenue will depend on what the entity has agreed to supply to the customer in exchange. The entity may have agreed to deliver one or more services in exchange for the transferred item of property, plant and equipment, such as connecting the customer to a network, providing the customer with ongoing access to a supply of goods or services, or both. The entity should identify the separately identifiable services included in the agreement in accordance with IAS 18:13 (see **5.1**). [IFRIC 18:14]

IFRIC 18 includes guidance based on IAS 18:13 to help identify the services to be delivered in exchange for the transferred asset. Indicators that connecting the customer to a network is a separately identifiable service and is, therefore, an event for which revenue should be recognised include:

[IFRIC 18:15]

- a service connection to a network is delivered to the customer and represents stand-alone value for that customer; and

- the fair value of the service connection to that network can be measured reliably.

> When connection to a network is a separately identifiable service, it is still necessary to consider when that service is delivered. Often, a permanent connection may be established at the outset. In such cases, revenue would be recognised at the outset, as the connection is established. Alternatively, connection may need to be delivered continuously over the period of use, in which case the connection revenue would be recognised over that period of use (or, if shorter, the useful life of the asset in accordance with IFRIC 18:20 – see below).

If the customer making the transfer of property, plant and equipment will receive ongoing access to a supply of goods or services at a lower price than would be charged without the transfer, this indicates that providing the customer with ongoing access to that supply of goods or services is a separately identifiable service. [IFRIC 18:16]

This contrasts with the scenario in which a customer making a transfer pays the same price for ongoing access to goods or services as a customer that has not made such a transfer. The features of this arrangement indicate that the obligation to provide the customer with ongoing access to a supply of goods or services arises from the terms of the entity's operating licence or other regulation rather than the agreement to transfer the property plant and equipment. [IFRIC 18:17]

If only one service is included in the agreement, the entity recognises revenue when that service is performed in accordance with IAS 18:20 (see **7.2**). If more than one separately identifiable service is provided, the fair value received or receivable is allocated between the services in accordance with IAS 18:13 (see **5.1**), and the recognition criteria of IAS 18 are then applied to each service individually. [IFRIC 18:18 & 19]

> IFRIC 18 does not provide any additional guidance on how to allocate the total consideration received or receivable for the agreement. However, the Basis for Conclusions notes that relevant guidance is included in IFRIC 12:13 in respect of service concession arrangements and paragraphs 5 to 7 of IFRIC 13 *Customer Loyalty Programmes* in respect of customer loyalty programmes (see **5.6**). In particular, IAS 18 does not mandate the use of any particular method of allocation.

If an ongoing service is identified as part of the agreement, the period over which revenue is recognised for that service is generally determined by the terms of the agreement with the customer. If the agreement does not specify a period, the revenue is recognised over a period no longer than the useful life of the transferred asset used to provide the ongoing service. [IFRIC 18:20]

> The IFRIC (now the IFRS Interpretations Committee) justified the latter restriction on the basis that the entity can only use the transferred asset to provide ongoing access to a supply of goods or services during its useful life. Any obligation that exists after the asset is replaced does not arise from the original transfer but from the terms of the entity's operating licence or other regulation. [IFRIC 18:BC21]

2.4.5 Accounting for transfers of cash from customers

IFRIC 18 also applies to agreements in which an entity receives cash from a customer when that amount of cash must be used only to construct or acquire an item of property, plant and equipment and the entity must then use the item of property, plant and equipment either to connect the customer to a network or to provide the customer with ongoing access to a supply of goods or services, or to do both. [IFRIC 18:6]

When an entity receives such a transfer of cash from a customer, the analysis as to whether the constructed or acquired item of property, plant and equipment is an asset of the entity is performed in line with the guidance at **2.4.2**. If the property, plant and equipment is an asset of the entity, it is recognised at cost in accordance with IAS 16. The cash received from the customer is recognised as revenue in accordance with the guidance at **2.4.4**. [IFRIC 18:21]

2.4.6 Illustrative examples

The following examples accompany, but are not part of, IFRIC 18.

Example 2.4.6A

Electricity substation

[IFRIC 18:IE1 - IE3, Example 1]

A real estate company is building a residential development in an area that is not connected to the electricity network. In order to have access to the electricity network, the real estate company is required to construct an electricity substation that is then transferred to the network company responsible for the transmission of electricity. It is assumed in this example that the network company concludes that the transferred substation meets the definition of an asset. The network company then uses the substation to connect each house of the residential development to its electricity network. In this case, it is the homeowners that will eventually use the network to access the supply of electricity, although they did not initially transfer the substation. By regulation, the network company has an obligation to provide ongoing access to the network to all users of the

---

network at the same price, regardless of whether they transferred an asset. Therefore, users of the network that transfer an asset to the network company pay the same price for the use of the network as those that do not. Users of the network can choose to purchase their electricity from distributors other than the network company but must use the company's network to access the supply of electricity.

Alternatively, the network company could have constructed the substation and received a transfer of an amount of cash from the real estate company that had to be used only for the construction of the substation. The amount of cash transferred would not necessarily equal the entire cost of the substation. It is assumed that the substation remains an asset of the network company.

In this example, the Interpretation applies to the network company that receives the electricity substation from the real estate company. The network company recognises the substation as an item of property, plant and equipment and measures its cost on initial recognition at its fair value (or at its construction cost in the circumstances described in paragraph [above]) in accordance with IAS 16 *Property, Plant and Equipment*. The fact that users of the network that transfer an asset to the network company pay the same price for the use of the electricity network as those that do not indicates that the obligation to provide ongoing access to the network is not a separately identifiable service of the transaction. Rather, connecting the house to the network is the only service to be delivered in exchange for the substation. Therefore, the network company should recognise revenue from the exchange transaction at the fair value of the substation (or at the amount of the cash received from the real estate company in the circumstances described [above]) when the houses are connected to the network in accordance with paragraph 20 of IAS 18 *Revenue*.

Example 2.4.6B

Connection to water main

[IFRIC 18:IE4 - IE5, Example 2]

A house builder constructs a house on a redeveloped site in a major city. As part of constructing the house, the house builder installs a pipe from the house to the water main in front of the house. Because the pipe is on the house's land, the owner of the house can restrict access to the pipe. The owner is also responsible for the maintenance of the pipe. In this example, the facts indicate that the definition of an asset is not met for the water company.

Alternatively, a house builder constructs multiple houses and installs a pipe on the commonly owned or public land to connect the houses to the water main. The house builder transfers ownership of the pipe to the water company that will be responsible for its maintenance. In this example, the facts indicate that the water company controls the pipe and should recognise it.

> **Example 2.4.6C**
>
> **Outsourcing information technology functions**
>
> [IFRIC 18:IE6 - IE9, Example 3]
>
> An entity enters into an agreement with a customer involving the outsourcing of the customer's information technology (IT) functions. As part of the agreement, the customer transfers ownership of its existing IT equipment to the entity. Initially, the entity must use the equipment to provide the service required by the outsourcing agreement. The entity is responsible for maintaining the equipment and for replacing it when the entity decides to do so. The useful life of the equipment is estimated to be three years. The outsourcing agreement requires service to be provided for ten years for a fixed price that is lower than the price the entity would have charged if the IT equipment had not been transferred.
>
> In this example, the facts indicate that the IT equipment is an asset of the entity. Therefore, the entity should recognise the equipment and measure its cost on initial recognition at its fair value in accordance with paragraph 24 of IAS 16. The fact that the price charged for the service to be provided under the outsourcing agreement is lower than the price the entity would charge without the transfer of the IT equipment indicates that this service is a separately identifiable service included in the agreement. The facts also indicate that it is the only service to be provided in exchange for the transfer of the IT equipment. Therefore, the entity should recognise revenue arising from the exchange transaction when the service is performed, ie over the ten-year term of the outsourcing agreement.
>
> Alternatively, assume that after the first three years, the price the entity charges under the outsourcing agreement increases to reflect the fact that it will then be replacing the equipment the customer transferred.
>
> In this case, the reduced price for the services provided under the outsourcing agreement reflects the useful life of the transferred equipment. For this reason, the entity should recognise revenue from the exchange transaction over the first three years of the agreement.

3 Definition of revenue

3.1 Revenue – definition

IAS 18 defines revenue as the gross inflow of economic benefits during the period arising in the course of the ordinary activities of an entity when those inflows result in increases in equity, other than increases relating to contributions from equity participants. [IAS 18:7] Revenue includes such items as sales, fees, interest, dividends, royalties and rent.

The definition of revenue excludes contributions from equity participants. For example, when an entity issues warrants (options issued on the entity's own shares) for cash, the cash is credited to equity because the proceeds are received from an equity instrument. If the warrants lapse unexercised, no revenue is recognised. The fact that an equity participant no longer has an equity claim on the assets of the entity does not convert the equity contribution to revenue.

The disposal of non-current assets is a transaction that does not generate revenue. Instead, gains and losses on the disposal of non-current assets, including investments and operating assets, are reported by deducting from the proceeds on disposal the carrying amount of the asset and related selling expenses (see paragraph 34 of IAS 1 *Presentation of Financial Statements*).

However, when an entity, in the course of its ordinary activities, routinely sells items that it has held for rental to others, it transfers those assets to inventories at their carrying amount when they cease to be rented and become held for sale. Sales proceeds from such assets are recognised as revenue in accordance with IAS 18 (see paragraph 68A of IAS 16 *Property, Plant and Equipment*).

3.2 Gross or net presentation

Revenue includes only gross inflows of economic benefits that are received or receivable by the entity on its own account. The use of the word 'gross' in the definition of revenue is not intended to include amounts collected on behalf of others. For example, sales taxes collected by the entity and remitted to a customs authority will not be included as revenue. Likewise, collection agency revenue does not include the amounts actually collected on behalf of customers, but is restricted to the fee or commission relating to the collection. [IAS 18:8]

In an agency relationship, gross amounts collected by the agent on behalf of the principal are not benefits that flow to the agent and, therefore, they are not revenue. The agent's revenue is the amount of the commission. [IAS 18:8]

The following example, which is reproduced from the appendix to IAS 18, provides guidance on how to determine whether an entity is acting as a principal or as an agent.

Example 3.2A

Determining whether an entity is acting as a principal or as an agent

[IAS 18 Illustrative Example 21]

IAS 18:8 states that "in an agency relationship, the gross inflows of economic benefits include amounts collected on behalf of the principal and which do not result in increases in equity for the entity. The amounts collected on behalf of the principal are not revenue. Instead, revenue is the amount of commission". Determining whether an entity is acting as a principal or as an agent requires judgement and consideration of all relevant facts and circumstances.

An entity is acting as a principal when it has exposure to the significant risks and rewards associated with the sale of goods or the rendering of services. Features that indicate that an entity is acting as a principal include:

(a)   the entity has the primary responsibility for providing the goods or services to the customer or for fulfilling the order, for example by being responsible for the acceptability of the products or services ordered or purchased by the customer;

(b)   the entity has inventory risk before or after the customer order, during shipping or on return;

(c)   the entity has latitude in establishing prices, either directly or indirectly, for example by providing additional goods or services; and

(d)   the entity bears the customer's credit risk for the amount receivable from the customer.

An entity is acting as an agent when it does not have exposure to the significant risks and rewards associated with the sale of goods or the rendering of services. One feature indicating that an entity is acting as an agent is that the amount the entity earns is predetermined, being either a fixed fee per transaction or a stated percentage of the amount billed to the customer.

The determination as to whether an entity is acting as a principal or as an agent will always depend on the specific facts and circumstances and it will generally be necessary to exercise judgement. The list of features in **example 3.2A** is not intended to be exhaustive. Moreover, in any particular scenario, some of the indicators may be judged more important than others, so it is not appropriate to apply a 'checklist' approach that would give equal weight to each.

Feature (a) above will frequently be considered a strong indicator of whether an entity is acting as a principal or as an agent. If one of the parties other than the reporting entity has the primary responsibility for providing the goods or services to the customer or for fulfilling the order (e.g. by being responsible for the acceptability of the products or services ordered or purchased by the customer), this will often indicate that the reporting entity is acting as an agent and not as a principal.

Sometimes an entity may be acting as an 'undisclosed agent', which means that the customer is not aware that the entity has agreed to act as agent for a third party. In many jurisdictions, an entity acting as an undisclosed agent has the same responsibilities to the customer as if it were a principal. When an entity acts as an undisclosed agent, it should consider whether, as a result, it has the primary responsibility for providing the goods or services to the customer or for fulfilling the order (e.g. in the event of a dispute, the customer's primary recourse would be against the entity). If so, feature (a) will be met, and it is likely that the entity should account as a principal. Such a conclusion is not typically affected by whether or not the third party supplier has indemnified the entity from loss.

Example 3.2B

Sales incentives – gross or net?

A vendor that sells its products and services through a retailer gives the retailer a cash incentive payment when a related service is sold to end customers in combination with the main product. For example, a retailer sells a warranty along with the vendor's product. The vendor's tariff schedules an additional CU10 to be received on this package. The retailer may or may not be required to follow the vendor's pricing policy. This warranty is serviced by the vendor and, therefore, the retailer's cost is zero. The retailer then remits CU8 (regardless of the actual price received from the end customer) to the vendor (or CU10 with a subsequent payment from the vendor to the retailer of CU2).

Whether the vendor should account for the incentive payment of CU2 as a reduction of revenue or as a promotion expense will depend on whether the retailer (intermediary) is acting as a principal or as an agent.

If the retailer is acting as an agent, the incentive payment to the retailer of CU2 is similar in substance to a commission and, therefore, should be treated as an expense by the vendor under IAS 18:8.

If, however, the retailer is acting as a principal, the incentive payment should be treated as a volume rebate and, accordingly, as a reduction in revenue under IAS 18:10.

Example 3.2C

Income tax withheld in a different country

Company X performs consulting services for Company C, which is in a different country from Company X. Company C withholds 20 per cent of Company X's fee as local income tax and transmits this amount to its local government on behalf of Company X. Company C pays the remaining 80 per cent balance to Company X. The countries do not have a tax treaty and Company X is not required to file a tax return in Company C's country. However, Company X may, at its option, file a tax return in Company C's country to recover taxes withheld in excess of its share of income. Company X was fully aware that the 20 per cent income tax would be withheld in Company C's country when it agreed to perform the consulting services for Company C.

If Company X's fee is CU100 and Company C remits CU80 to Company X and CU20 to the local government, does Company X have revenue of CU100 and tax expense of CU20, or net revenue of CU80?

Company X has revenue of CU100 and income tax expense of CU20. Under Company C's local law, Company X is the primary obligor in the arrangement. The fact that the tax is paid by Company C on behalf of Company X does not affect the assessment of whether Company X is the primary obligor.

Example 3.2D

Value Added Tax (VAT) rebate

In Country C, software developers must pay 17 per cent VAT (this rate is consistent with VAT on other similar items) to the government when software is sold to distributors or end users, but 14 per cent is rebated by the government to the developer almost immediately, resulting in an effective 3 per cent VAT rate. This is well known by both the developer and the buyer, who factor it into the selling price. Even though the seller effectively pays 3 per cent, the buyer gets credit for 17 per cent if the software is resold. Assume software is sold for CU103 inclusive of VAT. This was negotiated based on selling price of CU100 plus effective VAT of CU3.

How much revenue should the seller recognise?

IAS 20 *Accounting for Government Grants and Disclosure of Government Assistance* defines a government grant as "assistance by government in the form of transfers of resources to an entity in return for past or future compliance with certain conditions relating to the operating activities of the entity". The 14 per cent VAT rebate is regarded as a government grant to encourage the software development industry. Therefore, the seller should recognise revenue of CU88 (CU103/1.17) and government grant income of CU12 [(CU103 – CU88) × (14/17)]. In accordance with IAS 20:29, government grants related to income may be presented separately or as 'other income'. The CU3 VAT is excluded from revenue under IAS 18:8.

Example 3.2E

Severance taxes

A government requires a mining or oil and gas producer to pay a 'severance tax' or other similar tax that is based on the value of minerals produced. The tax is payable even if the minerals are not sold.

In this case, the severance tax is an expense related to the production of the asset to be sold because the burden of the tax falls on the producer and is not dependent on sales. The producer is not considered an agent of the government for the purposes of collection of the severance tax. Therefore, the full amount of the sale should be included in revenue. This answer is appropriate even if, when the minerals are ultimately sold, the invoice shows the severance tax as a separate item.

If, on the other hand, the government levies tax only on products sold and such amounts are re-invoiced to the purchaser, the amount should be regarded as a sales tax that is excluded from revenue under IAS 18:8. In effect, the entity is acting as a collection agent for the government.

(Although revenue from the extraction of mineral ores is excluded from the scope of IAS 18, the severance tax issue is not excluded.)

Example 3.2F

Royalty payments

An entity is required by contract to pay a royalty to the government in respect of certain intangible assets. The royalty is specified as a percentage of gross proceeds from sales less costs applicable to the entity's share of production. The entity can pay the royalty in cash or in kind.

Should the royalty be netted against the entity's revenue or recognised as an operating expense?

The entity should recognise its revenue on a gross basis because it is the primary obligor in the arrangement. The royalty is recognised as an operating expense.

If the government is also a shareholder in the entity, these royalty payments should be differentiated from a distribution to shareholders in the form of a royalty.

Example 3.2G

Cash received from suppliers for 'supplementary services' (slotting fees, co-operative advertising etc.)

Company A operates a chain of supermarkets, selling food products to end consumers. Company A sells all products as a principal. To promote certain products, Company A receives cash from suppliers in respect of a variety of 'supplementary services'.

How should Company A account for the cash received in respect of supplementary services?

As a general principle, consideration received by a customer from a supplier should be presumed to be a reduction of the cost of the supplier's products and, therefore, should be accounted for by Company A as a reduction in the cost of inventories rather than as revenue. However, that presumption can be overcome in limited circumstances.

When amounts are received in respect of supplementary services, the following questions are appropriate.

- *Does the cash represent payment for goods or services supplied by Company A to the supplier that are separate and distinct from Company A's purchase of goods from the supplier?* This might arise, for example, if Company A carries out a specifically commissioned market survey on behalf of the supplier. When it is clear that such a transaction is separate from Company A's purchase of goods from the supplier, amounts received should be recognised as revenue.

- *Does the cash represent a reimbursement of costs incurred by Company A on behalf of the supplier?* For example, Company A may have incurred specific, incremental, identifiable advertising costs on behalf of the supplier. In such circumstances, the cash consideration should be accounted for as a reduction in the relevant cost (e.g. advertising) when recognised by Company A in profit or loss. Care should be exercised, however, in reaching a conclusion that costs have been incurred 'on behalf of' a supplier. Frequently, the nature of such 'co-operative' advertising arrangements is that they are primarily for the benefit of the supermarket rather than for the benefit of the supplier.

If the presumption is not overcome, the cash received should be accounted for as a reduction in the cost of the supplier's products. This will be the case, for example, if the amount paid to Company A is stated to be in return for 'prime' placement of the supplier's products in Company A's stores (these are sometimes referred to as 'slotting fees'). Slotting fees received should be treated as a reduction of the cost of inventories acquired (and, consequently, recognised as a reduction in cost of sales when the inventories are sold) in the period to which the slotting fees relate. For example, if Company A receives a slotting fee requiring it to give a supplier's product prime placement for one year, that fee received should reduce the cost of inventories purchased during that year. Frequently, the determination of the appropriate recognition period will require the exercise of judgement in the context of the specific facts and circumstances.

4 Measurement of revenue

4.1 Measurement of revenue – general

Revenue is measured at the fair value of the consideration received or receivable. [IAS 18:9] Fair value is defined as "the price that would be received to sell an asset or paid to transfer a liability in an orderly transaction between market participants at the measurement date". [IAS 18:7]

4.2 Trade discounts allowed and similar items

In practice, revenue is usually determined by agreement between the entity and the buyer or user of the goods or services. Thus, the amount of revenue recognised for a transaction is net of any trade discounts or volume rebates given because these discounts and rebates are not received as consideration by the seller. [IAS 18:10]

At the meeting of the IFRIC (now the IFRS Interpretations Committee) in July 2004, IFRIC members agreed that prompt settlement discounts should be estimated at the time of sale and presented as a reduction in revenues.

Example 4.2

Cash discounts

A seller offers a cash discount for immediate or prompt payment (i.e. payment earlier than required by the normal credit terms). A sale is made for CU100 with the balance due within 90 days. If the customer pays within 10 days, the customer will receive a 2 per cent discount on the total invoice.

How should the seller account for this early payment incentive?

IAS 18:10 states that the amount of revenue arising on a transaction is the amount agreed by the buyer and seller. If the agreement between buyer and seller calls for payment within a relatively short period such as 90 days, and the environment is not hyperinflationary, a cash discount for prompt payment is not intended as a financing transaction. It is simply a way of identifying the amount agreed by the buyer and seller. It also can be viewed as a mechanism to enhance collectibility of the agreed amount. Therefore, the seller should recognise revenue net of the amount of cash discount taken. In the circumstances described, revenue is CU100 if the discount is not taken and CU98 if the discount is taken. If necessary, the seller should recognise revenue based on an estimate of the number of customers that will take the discount and 'true up' in the next reporting period for the actual number.

This answer is consistent with the guidance in paragraph 11 of IAS 2 *Inventories*, which states that "[t]rade discounts, rebates, and other similar items are deducted in determining the costs of purchase".

4.3 Deferred consideration

In the majority of cases, the nominal amount of the consideration received or receivable will not vary materially from its fair value because most trade receivables are due within a relatively short time-frame. In the unusual circumstances when consideration is to be received outside such a short time-frame, the fair value of the consideration to be received will not be the same as the nominal amount of the consideration, due to the time value of money. Such an arrangement effectively includes a financing transaction. Therefore, to calculate the fair value of the consideration receivable, future receipts are discounted using an imputed interest rate which is the more clearly determinable of:

[IAS 18:11]

- the prevailing rate for a similar instrument of an issuer with a similar credit rating; or

- a rate of interest that discounts the nominal amount of the instrument to the current cash sales price of the goods or services.

When the second approach is taken, the resulting interest rate should be assessed for reasonableness. A rate that appears unrealistically low may indicate that the current cash sales price that would be appropriate for this particular customer has not been correctly identified.

The IFRIC (now the IFRS Interpretations Committee) considered the accounting for extended payment terms, such as six-months interest-free credit, at its meeting in July 2004. The Committee members agreed that IAS 39 *Financial Instruments: Recognition and Measurement* applies to the receivable in such circumstances, and that the effect of the time value of money should be reflected when this is material, in accordance with IAS 39:AG69 to AG82. For entities applying IFRS 9 *Financial Instruments*, this conclusion is equally applicable.

If material, the difference between the nominal amount of the consideration to be received and the discounted amount is recognised as interest revenue over the credit period, in accordance with the requirements of IAS 18 (see **section 8**) and either IFRS 9 (see **4.1** of **chapter B6**) or, for entities that have not yet adopted IFRS 9, IAS 39 (see **4.1** of **chapter C6**).

Example 4.3A

Deferred consideration: discounting based on interest rate

An entity sells an item of equipment for CU100,000 under a financing agreement that has no stated interest rate. Annual instalments of CU20,000 are due each year for five years from the date of purchase. Thus, it is a 'zero percent' financing arrangement. The policy of not charging interest is consistent with normal industry practice.

Because industry practice is to allow deferred payment with no interest, there are no recent cash transactions from which the entity can make a reliable estimate of the cash sales price. The seller believes, however, that the buyer would be able to obtain financing from other sources at an interest rate of 10 per cent.

Step 1 Calculate the net present value of the stream of payments

Assuming no down payment, five annual instalments of CU20,000, and an interest rate of 10 per cent, the net present value of the stream of payments forming the consideration is CU75,816. Therefore, on the date of the sale, CU75,816 is recognised as revenue from the sale of goods and a related receivable is recognised.

Step 2 Calculate the amount of interest earned each period

The difference between CU100,000 and CU75,816 of CU24,184 will be recognised as interest revenue as it becomes due each year as calculated below.

	Principal amount outstanding	Interest element of payment	Principal element of payment	Total payment
	(A)	(A × 10% = B)	(C – B)	(C)
	CU	CU	CU	CU
End of Year 1	75,816	7,581	12,419	20,000
End of Year 2	63,397	6,340	13,660	20,000
End of Year 3	49,737	4,974	15,026	20,000
End of Year 4	34,711	3,471	16,529	20,000
End of Year 5	18,182	1,818	18,182	20,000
Total		24,184	75,816	100,000

Example 4.3B

Deferred consideration: discounting to current cash sales price

An entity sells an item of equipment for CU100,000 under a financing agreement. Annual instalments of CU20,000 are due each year for five years from the date of purchase. If the buyer had paid cash for the equipment, the sales price would have been CU80,000.

The selling entity should recognise the consideration at its fair value. Because there is a CU20,000 difference between the cash price of CU80,000 and the amount due if the equipment is paid for in instalments, the arrangement is effectively a financing transaction as well as the sale of goods. The amount of the consideration attributable to the sale of goods is the cash price of CU80,000. The remaining CU20,000 is interest revenue and is recognised as it becomes due each year using the effective interest method as illustrated below.

Step 1 Calculate the effective rate of interest

Because the cash price offered is CU80,000, it is necessary to determine the interest rate that discounts CU100,000 to CU80,000 over a 5-year period, assuming no down payment and five annual instalments of CU20,000. This interest rate is 7.93 per cent.

Step 2 Calculate the amount of interest earned each period

The difference of CU20,000 between CU100,000 and CU80,000 will be recognised as interest revenue as it becomes due each year, as calculated below.

	Principal amount outstanding	Interest element of payment	Principal element of payment	Total payment
	(A)	(A × 7.93% = B)	(C – B)	(C)
	CU	CU	CU	CU
End of Year 1	80,000	6,345	13,655	20,000
End of Year 2	66,345	5,262	14,738	20,000
End of Year 3	51,607	4,093	15,907	20,000
End of Year 4	35,700	2,831	17,169	20,000
End of Year 5	18,531	1,469	18,531	20,000
Total		20,000	80,000	100,000

4.4 Exchanges of goods or services

When goods or services are exchanged or swapped for goods or services of a similar nature and value, no revenue is recognised. [IAS 18:12] Such transactions occur in a limited number of commodity industries such as the oil or milk industries. These exchanges are generally made to help suppliers in the distribution of their products when they need a specific quantity of a commodity at a specific time in a particular location. In practice, this type of exchange of similar goods is relatively uncommon outside those industries. Another scenario in which this might apply, however, is when a wholesaler agrees that a retailer may return certain goods in exchange for others.

When goods or services are exchanged for dissimilar goods or services, a transaction that generates revenue has taken place and revenue is recognised. The revenue is measured at the fair value of the goods or services received, adjusted for any cash payments made by either the buyer or the seller. If the fair value of the goods or services received cannot be measured reliably, revenue is recognised at the fair value of the goods or services given up, adjusted for any cash payments made or received. [IAS 18:12]

When a dealer in used goods transacts with a customer and accepts other used goods in exchange, the allowance granted to the customer will typically be less than the price at which the dealer expects to resell. In effect, the customer is being charged a 'retail' price for the goods purchased but being granted only a 'wholesale' price for the goods traded in. Thus, even if the goods exchanged are similar (e.g. vehicles or CDs), their value is dissimilar because of the difference between wholesale and retail prices, and so the transaction will give rise to revenue. By contrast, when a dealer exchanges goods with a fellow dealer, both sides of the transaction are likely to be priced by reference to the wholesale price. Thus, the goods will be similar in nature and value, and no revenue will be recognised.

Example 4.4A

Transport sales of oil

Company A owns and operates a pipeline to transport crude oil. Company A does not produce or distribute crude oil; it merely provides the use of its pipeline to the buyer and the seller in a contract for a usage fee. The seller and buyer independently negotiate the sales price and either the buyer or the seller pays a fee to Company A to transport the oil purchased/sold through the pipeline.

The pipeline needs to be full of oil at all times to be operational. Therefore, during initial construction of the pipeline, Company A purchases oil to fill the pipeline. Once the pipeline is operational, Company A charges a fixed fee for its transportation services and, in effect, swaps crude oil pushed into the pipeline by a seller for crude oil of the same grade and quality delivered to the customer at the exit point of the pipeline. Company A bears the risk of loss due to theft or line loss in excess of maximums allowed under the contract. Such losses are rare and normally arise as the result of a pipeline spill that is covered by insurance.

How should Company A recognise revenue, i.e. should it recognise revenue based on the agreed sale price for the oil or just the usage fee earned?

Company A should recognise revenue only for the fee earned for use of the pipeline.

Company A's delivery of the oil from the pipeline to the ultimate customer (and replacement by equivalent product) is not regarded as a transaction that generates revenue in accordance with the requirements of IAS 18:12 (which prohibits the recognition of revenue on exchanges of goods which are 'of a similar nature and value').

IAS 18 does not include any guidance on how to determine whether goods or services are of 'a similar nature or value' but, in the circumstances under consideration, it is clear that this criterion is met. In fact, the circumstances described would indicate that this is an exchange of 'identical' products.

Example 4.4B

Transfer of inventories for an entity's own shares

Company A has produced inventories at a cost of CU80 that are normally sold to unrelated third parties at a price of CU100. Company A enters into a transaction to buy CU100 of its ordinary shares from a shareholder in return for CU100 of its inventories (priced at the retail rate).

How should Company A account for this transaction?

Company A should recognise revenue for the sale of its inventories for CU100 and treasury shares for CU100. The form of consideration should not have an impact on whether revenue is recognised. Company A would then recognise cost of sales and reduce inventories by CU80.

4.5   Barter transactions involving advertising services

SIC-31 *Revenue – Barter Transactions Involving Advertising Services* deals with the circumstances when an entity (the Seller) enters into a barter transaction to provide advertising services in exchange for receiving advertising services from its customer (the Customer). Such advertisements may be displayed on the Internet, poster sites, broadcast on television or radio, published in magazines or journals, or presented in another medium.

When the services exchanged are similar, the principles outlined at **4.4** mean that no revenue can be recognised. When the services exchanged are dissimilar, revenue can be recognised provided that the amount of the revenue can be measured reliably. SIC-31 discusses the circumstances under which a Seller can reliably measure revenue at the fair value of advertising services received or provided in a barter transaction.

The Interpretation concludes that revenue from a barter transaction involving advertising services can never be measured reliably at the fair value of the advertising services received. [SIC-31:5]

The fair value of such barter transactions is reliably measurable only when it is supportable by reference to other transactions with knowledgeable and willing parties in an arm's length transaction. For such transactions to provide a relevant and reliable basis for support, the services involved must be similar, there must be many transactions, valuable consideration that can be reliably measured must be exchanged, and independent third parties must be involved. [SIC-31:5] The conditions set out below are designed to ensure that these characteristics are present.

Under SIC-31, a Seller can reliably measure revenue at the fair value of the advertising services it provides in a barter transaction, by reference only to non-barter transactions that:

[SIC-31:5]

- involve advertising similar to the advertising in the barter transaction;
- occur frequently;
- represent a predominant number of transactions and amount when compared to all transactions to provide advertising that is similar to the advertising in the barter transaction;
- involve cash and/or another form of consideration (such as marketable securities, non-monetary assets, and other services) that has a reliably measurable fair value; and
- do not involve the same counterparty as in the barter transaction.

4.6   Price regulation

> **Example 4.6**
>
> **Revenue recognition in the pharmaceutical industry**
>
> The Pharmaceutical Price Regulation Scheme (PPRS) in Country A is a joint initiative between the pharmaceutical industry and the Department of Health (DH). The PPRS applies to all entities supplying branded, licensed medicines to the Public Health Service (PHS). The objectives of the PPRS are to ensure that the PHS buys medicines at reasonable prices while allowing pharmaceutical entities to earn a reasonable profit so that they are able to continue to invest in research and development activities. The PPRS operates by limiting the profits an entity can make from the supply of medicines to the PHS. The entity's return on capital employed is calculated based on the annual financial return. All excess profits earned over the prescribed limits for the current period are required to be refunded to the DH.
>
> In the circumstances described, the pharmaceutical entities are effectively operating in a regulated market in which the prices they can charge are governed by an agreement with the DH. When the pharmaceutical entities are required to pay a refund to the DH because their profits have exceeded the allowed profits for the period, this is a reduction of the revenue already recognised and should be accounted for as such.
>
> The appropriate accounting for government schemes to regulate the prices of pharmaceutical products should be determined based on the particular facts and circumstances of the government scheme under which the entity operates. Different types of regulations may exist in different jurisdictions; some may be in the nature of rebates or limits on profits whereas others may be in the nature of an expense.

5   Identification of the transaction

5.1   Transaction to be identified based on the substance of the arrangement

The recognition criteria specified by IAS 18 (as discussed in **sections 6** to **10**) are usually applied separately to each transaction. To present the substance of a transaction appropriately, however, it may sometimes be necessary to apply the recognition criteria to the separately identifiable components of a single transaction. [IAS 18:13]

For example, a contract to sell software may include an element related to maintenance over a period of time. In such circumstances, it is appropriate to split the transaction into two components, a sale element and a maintenance element, and to apply the revenue recognition criteria to each component individually (see **5.2**).

In other circumstances, several related transactions may, in substance, be part of one larger transaction when the transactions are linked in such a way that the commercial effect cannot be understood without reference to the series of transactions as a whole. For example, a seller may enter into a contract to sell goods but agree in a separate contract to repurchase the goods at a later date. In such circumstances, the revenue recognition criteria are applied to both transactions together to determine if revenue is recognised (see **5.3**). [IAS 18:13]

5.2 Unbundling of separately identifiable components

IAS 18 does not provide any guidance on when or how to identify whether a transaction consists of separately identifiable components or how to allocate revenue to any separately identified components.

In determining the substance of a transaction, all of its aspects and implications should be identified and greater weight given to those more likely to have economic significance to the transacting parties at the time of entering into the transaction.

Generally, two or more components may have separate commercial substance and, therefore, be separately identifiable when, for example:

- one or more of the components may be seen as an 'optional extra' (i.e. the customer might reasonably choose to purchase the other components without purchasing these 'optional' components); or

- the individual components can be sourced independently of each other, thereby representing goods and/or services that can be purchased by a customer on a stand-alone basis from another supplier (i.e. the customer might reasonably buy one component from one supplier and the other component from a different, unrelated supplier).

When components are judged to be separately identifiable, it will still be necessary to consider whether it is possible to allocate revenue between them on a reliable basis, and also to consider when revenue should be recognised in respect of each component. In particular, revenue will only be recognised in respect of a separately identifiable component when all the revenue recognition criteria in IAS 18:14 (for goods) or IAS 18:20 (for services) are met (see **section 6** and **section 7**, respectively).

The fact that a seller may choose not to offer a particular component for sale by itself, but will only offer it for sale as part of a 'bundle', does not in itself preclude the component from being separately identifiable, because it is still possible that the component could be obtained on its own from a different, unrelated supplier. Conversely, the fact that a seller and customer enter into separate but simultaneous contracts for the supply of two components does not in itself prove that the components are separately identifiable, because it may be inconceivable that a customer would ever buy one without the other. Accordingly, care is always needed when assessing whether a component is separately identifiable.

Although IAS 18 does not require vendor-specific objective evidence in respect of the amount of revenue to be attributed to separately identifiable components, it is important that revenue is allocated on a reliable basis that reasonably reflects the selling prices that might be achieved in stand-alone transactions. In particular, the relative cost of components for the seller will not always be a good proxy for the price that might be achieved for each component in a sales transaction.

When selling prices are available for individual components, each separately identifiable component should be accounted for as a separate transaction in accordance with IAS 18 and the total consideration payable should be allocated to the individual components by reference to their selling prices. Often, when the 'bundled' transaction is provided at a price less than the aggregated separate selling prices of the individual components, it may be appropriate to allocate the discount or reduction to each component in proportion to its selling price. However, as noted in BC14 of IFRIC 13 *Customer Loyalty Programmes*, IAS 18 does not prescribe the use of this method, and management should use judgement in each case to select a method that will reasonably approximate the amount that the customer is paying for each component.

When separate selling prices are available only for the undelivered components, it may be appropriate to deduct these from the total transaction price to derive a selling price attributable to the delivered components (this is sometimes called the 'residual method'). However, care should be taken to ensure that revenue is not overstated in applying a similar technique when separate selling prices are available only for the delivered components (this is sometimes called the 'reverse residual method') because the 'bundled' transaction price may include a discount which will not be reflected in the normal separate selling prices of the delivered components.

In all cases, management should use judgement to ensure that the amount of revenue recognised appropriately reflects the extent to which components have been delivered to the customer. In making this judgement, consideration may be given to more detailed guidance in the most recent pronouncements of other standard-setting bodies that use a similar conceptual framework to develop accounting standards, to the extent that these do not conflict with the principles of IAS 18 (see paragraph 12 of IAS 8 *Accounting Policies, Changes in Accounting Estimates and Errors*).

5.3   Linked transactions

Although SIC-27 *Evaluating the Substance of Transactions Involving the Legal Form of a Lease* provides some guidance in the specific context of leases, IAS 18 itself provides little guidance with regards to which circumstances should cause a series of transactions to be grouped together for purposes of recognising revenue.

In assessing whether transactions should be grouped together, an entity should consider whether bundling is needed to reflect faithfully the substance of the transactions.

Factors to consider in making the assessment include, but are not limited to:

* the seller retains the risks and rewards embodied in the goods or services involved, even if legal ownership has been transferred (e.g. separate sale and repurchase agreements);

* the transactions are legally and/or economically conditional upon each other;

* the transactions were entered into at the same time with the same counterparties; and

* the individual transactions lack commercial substance when considered separately.

A typical example of transactions that may need to be grouped together for purposes of revenue recognition is a sale and subsequent repurchase when the main objective of the arrangement is to obtain financing rather than to dispose of the entity's assets. This is likely to be the case when it is clear from the outset that the seller will repurchase the asset and will pay a lender's return to the 'customer'. However, not all transactions involving a sale and subsequent repurchase will necessarily be grouped together. For example, if the repurchase price will be determined as the market value at the time of repurchase, it is possible that the significant risks and rewards of ownership may have been transferred to the customer, in which case it may still be appropriate to recognise revenue on the original sale transaction.

All relevant facts and circumstances should be considered together when assessing whether a series of transactions should be combined and accounted for as a single arrangement.

5.4   Sales arrangements in which the seller has partially performed its obligations

Failure to deliver one item or to perform one service specified in a sales arrangement does not necessarily preclude the immediate recognition of any revenue for that sales arrangement. IAS 18:13 notes that the revenue recognition criteria should be applied to the separately identifiable components of a single transaction. If all other recognition criteria are met, revenue can be recognised for a sales arrangement, notwithstanding the seller's remaining obligation for additional performance or delivery, as set out below.

Revenue from the sales arrangement can be recognised in full if the seller's remaining obligation is inconsequential or perfunctory. In such circumstances, costs expected to be incurred to fulfil the remaining obligation must be reliably estimable and accrued when the revenue is recognised. A remaining performance obligation is not inconsequential or perfunctory if:

- it is essential to the functionality of the delivered products or services (e.g. installation and/or training); or

- failure to complete the activities would result in the customer receiving a full or a not insignificant partial refund or the right to reject the products delivered or services performed to date.

In addition, a remaining performance obligation may not be inconsequential or perfunctory if:

- the seller does not have a demonstrated history of completing the remaining tasks in a timely manner and reliably estimating their costs;

- the cost or time to perform the remaining obligations for similar contracts historically has varied significantly from one instance to another;

- the skills or equipment required to complete the remaining activity are specialised or are not readily available in the marketplace;

- the cost of completing the obligation, or the fair value of the obligation, is more than insignificant in relation to such items as the total contract fee, gross profit and operating income;

- the period before the remaining obligation will be extinguished is lengthy; or

- the timing of payment of a portion of the sales price is coincident with completing performance of the remaining activity.

A portion of the revenue under the sales arrangement is also recognised when the seller has substantially fulfilled the terms of a separately identifiable component of the arrangement. The examples set out in the appendix to IAS 18 illustrate a number of such circumstances (see later sections of this appendix).

5.5 Up-front fees

In general, unless up-front fees are paid in exchange for products delivered or services performed and, therefore, substantial risks and rewards have been transferred to the buyer in a separate transaction as described in IAS 18:13, such fees are not recognised as revenue up front but rather deferred as unearned revenue (even if they are non-refundable). An up-front fee might not be regarded as relating to a separate transaction if, for example:

- the up-front fee is negotiated in conjunction with the pricing of other elements;

- the customer would ascribe no value to the up-front activity in the absence of the performance of the other elements of the arrangement; or

- the vendor does not sell the initial right or activities separately.

The up-front, non-refundable fees should be recognised as revenue over the life of the agreement(s) to which they relate, by reference to the goods and services supplied under the agreement(s).

In 2007, the IFRIC (now the IFRS Interpretations Committee) considered the question of up-front fees in the context of investment management fees (see the January 2007 edition of *IFRIC Update*). The IFRIC noted that IAS 18:13 states that "the recognition criteria [in IAS 18] are applied to two or more transactions together when they are linked in such a way that the commercial effect cannot be understood without reference to the series of transactions as a whole".

The IFRIC agreed that:

- fees may be recognised as revenue only to the extent that services have been provided;

- while the proportion of costs incurred in delivering services may be used to estimate the stage of completion of the transaction, incurring costs does not by itself imply that a service has been provided;

- the receipt of a non-refundable initial fee does not, in itself, give evidence that an up-front service has been provided or that the fair value of the consideration paid in respect of any up-front services is equal to the initial fee received; and

- to the extent that

  - an initial service can be shown to have been provided to a customer,

  - the fair value of the consideration received in respect of that service can be measured reliably, and

- the conditions for the recognition of revenue in IAS 18 have been met,

up-front and ongoing fees may be recognised as revenue in line with the provision of services to the customer.

The IFRIC noted that a wide range of business models utilising initial and ongoing fees exist in different markets. The services provided and the revenue that may be recognised in each situation depend on the facts and circumstances relevant to each model.

Example 5.5A

Up-front payment by customer – lifetime membership fees in a private club

Company A owns and operates a private club. New members have an option of paying a single up-front, non-refundable lifetime membership fee rather than monthly or annual payments. That fee entitles members to most, but not all, of the club's services for the member's life. Lifetime members must pay separately for those services not covered by the lifetime membership fee.

How should revenue from the lifetime membership fee be recognised?

Revenue should be recognised rateably over the time the individual may be expected to require the services of the club. IAS 18:20 (see **7.2**) requires that revenue from a service transaction should be recognised by reference to the stage of completion of the transaction. The club member would not pay an up-front membership fee in the absence of on-going usage of the club's services. Moreover, the pricing of the lifetime membership fee and the monthly usage fee are interrelated.

Example 5.5B

Up-front payment by supplier – outsourcing arrangements

When entering into an outsourcing arrangement with a client, a service provider may make an up-front payment to the client.

How should up-front payments be treated when made to clients by service providers in the context of outsourcing arrangements?

The amount of the up-front payment and the price charged for the service provided are generally part of a global pricing agreement for that service. To the extent that the up-front payment does not correspond to an identifiable service received by the service provider from the client, or to the reimbursement by the service provider of costs necessary for the contract incurred by the client, the amount of the up-front payment should be accounted for by the service provider as a reduction of revenue.

As a result, the up-front payment would be accounted for by the service provider as an asset (rebate paid in advance) and amortised against revenue over the contract period.

5.6 IFRIC 13 *Customer Loyalty Programmes*

5.6.1 IFRIC 13 – general requirements

Entities use customer loyalty programmes to incentivise customers to buy their goods or services. Customers buying goods or services are granted customer award credits (often described as 'points') by the entity, which can be redeemed for awards such as free or discounted goods or services.

IFRIC 13 addresses the accounting by the entity that grants award credits. It applies to customer loyalty award credits that:

[IFRIC 13:3]

• entities grant to their customers as part of an IAS 18 sales transaction (a sale of goods, rendering of services, or use by the customer of entity assets); and

• the customers can redeem in future for free or discounted goods or services, subject to meeting any further qualifying conditions.

Customer loyalty programmes operate in a number of ways. Customers may not be permitted to redeem award credits until they have accumulated a specified minimum number or value. Award credits may be linked to individual purchases or groups of purchases, or to continued custom over a specified period. Entities may operate their own customer loyalty programmes or may participate in programmes operated by third parties. The awards offered may include goods or services supplied by the entity itself and/or rights to claim goods or services from a third party. [IFRIC 13:2]

IFRIC 13 also applies when the sales transaction giving rise to award credits involves the entity receiving consideration from an intermediate party rather than directly from the customer to whom it grants the award credits. For example, credit card providers may provide services and grant award credits to credit card holders but receive consideration for doing so from vendors accepting payment by credit card. [IFRIC 13:BC4]

The Interpretation is not applicable to 'money-off' vouchers that are distributed free of charge, or any other sort of promotion that is not connected to sales of an entity's goods or services. It also does not cover the accounting for the goods acquired initially or the accounting for the award credits by the customer.

IFRIC 13 requires entities to account for award credits supplied in the context of a customer loyalty programme as a separately identifiable component of the sales transaction(s) in which they are granted (applying the requirements of IAS 18:13). The fair value of the consideration received or receivable is allocated between the award credits and the other components of the sale. [IFRIC 13:5] The consideration allocated to the award credits is measured by reference to their fair value. [IFRIC 13:6]

Accordingly, when accounting for customer loyalty programmes, an entity is required to:

- allocate some of the consideration received or receivable from the sales transaction to the award credits and defer the recognition of that revenue; and

- recognise its share of revenue allocated to the award credits when it has fulfilled its obligations in respect of the award credits. Note that the amount and timing of revenue will typically be different depending on whether the awards are supplied by the entity itself (as principal) or by a third party (with the entity acting as an agent in respect of the award credits).

5.6.2   Measuring the fair value of award credits

The consideration allocated to award credits is measured by reference to their fair value. If there is not a quoted market price for an identical award credit, fair value must be measured using another valuation technique. [IFRIC 13:AG1]

The fair value measurement should take into account (1) the amount of the discounts or incentives that would otherwise be offered to customers who have not earned award credits from an initial sales transaction, (2) the proportion of the award credits not expected to be redeemed by customers, and (3) non-performance risk. [IFRIC 13:AG2]

> When the fair value of award credits is measured on the basis of the value of the awards for which they could be redeemed, the fair value of the award credits should take account of expected forfeitures as well as the discounts or incentives that would otherwise be offered to customers who have not earned award credits from an initial sale. [IFRIC 13:BC14A]

Example 5.6.2A

Impact of awards granted without an initial sales transaction

All visitors to Supermarket B can pick up a voucher entitling them to a reduction of CU1 off the price of Product X, irrespective of whether they make any purchases. Customers who make a purchase receive a voucher entitling them to a reduction of CU5 off the price of Product X. Only one voucher can be used for any purchase of Product X.

The CU1 vouchers are outside the scope of IFRIC 13 because they are not granted as part of a sales transaction.

In contrast, the CU5 vouchers are within the scope of IFRIC 13. Accordingly, in assessing the fair value of the CU5 vouchers for the purposes of applying that Interpretation, Supermarket B will take into account (1) the fact that customers not making a purchase could still have claimed a CU1 voucher, and (2) the number of vouchers not expected to be redeemed. Although the CU5 vouchers are not sold separately, it is clear that no customer would rationally pay more than CU4 for such a voucher because it would instead be cheaper to buy Product X using one of the free CU1 vouchers. Thus, the fair value of the CU5 vouchers will not exceed CU4, and may be lower depending on the proportion of vouchers expected to be redeemed.

If there is a range of awards that customers may choose from, the fair value of the award credits reflects the fair values of the range of available awards, weighted in proportion to the frequency with which each award is expected to be selected. [IFRIC 13:AG2]

A range of valuation techniques may be used for the purposes of measuring the fair value of awards. The Application Guidance to IFRIC 13 gives as an example the scenario in which a third party will supply the awards and the entity pays the third party for each award credit it grants; in these circumstances, the entity could measure the fair value of the award credits by reference to the amount it pays the third party, adding a reasonable profit margin. Importantly, judgement is required to select and apply the valuation technique that satisfies the requirements of IFRIC 13:6 and is most appropriate in the circumstances. [IFRIC 13:AG3]

As noted above, IFRIC 13 states that award credits should be measured "*by reference to* their fair value" (emphasis added). But it does not mandate any particular method for allocating amounts to the award credits. In particular, it does not specify whether the amount allocated to the award credits should be:

[IFRIC 13:BC14]

- equal to their fair value (irrespective of the fair values of the other components); or

- a proportion of the total consideration based on the fair value of the award credits relative to the fair values of the other components of the sale.

This is because the IFRIC (now the IFRS Interpretations Committee) decided that the Interpretation should not be more prescriptive than IAS 18, which does not specify which of these methods should be applied, or in what circumstances. Management must apply judgement in deciding to select one or other method.

The former approach involves measuring the fair value of award credits (e.g. by reference to the goods and services that may be selected, as discussed in IFRIC 13:AG2 – see above), and then allocating any residual revenue to the original sale. This is illustrated in **example 5.6.2B**.

Example 5.6.2B

Valuing award credits by reference to goods and services that may be selected

Customers buying Product A from Company X for CU100 receive an award credit. The award credit can be used to obtain Product B free of charge, or to purchase Product C at a discounted price of CU10.

The normal selling prices of Product B and Product C are:

Product B CU5

Product C CU17

Company X estimates that 60 per cent of customers will select Product B, 30 per cent will select Product C and 10 per cent will not redeem the award credit. Company X estimates that the effect of non-performance risk is insignificant.

The fair value of the award credit may be measured as:

(60% × CU5) + (30% × [CU17 – CU10]) + (10% × CU0) = CU5.10

Accordingly, the revenue recognised in respect of Product A is CU94.90 (i.e. CU100.00 – CU5.10).

An alternative approach is to make an allocation based on relative fair values as illustrated in **example 5.6.2C**.

Example 5.6.2C

Valuing award credits by reference to relative fair values

The facts are the same as in **example 5.6.2B**, but Company X decides to use a relative fair value approach to allocate revenue to the award credits.

The normal selling price of Product A, after taking into account discounts that are usually offered but that are not available during this promotion, is CU96.

The total revenue of CU100 is allocated between Product A and the award credit by reference to their relative fair values of CU96 and CU5.10, respectively. Accordingly:

- Revenue for Product A = CU100 × (CU96 ÷ [CU96 + CU5.10]) = CU94.95
- Revenue from the award credit = CU100 × (CU5.10 ÷ [CU96 + CU5.10]) = CU5.05

5.6.3 Awards supplied by the reporting entity

5.6.3.1 Awards supplied by the reporting entity – general

If the entity will supply the awards itself, it recognises the consideration allocated to award credits as revenue when award credits are redeemed and it fulfils its obligations to supply awards. The amount of revenue recognised is based on the number of award credits that have been redeemed in exchange for awards, relative to the total number expected to be redeemed. [IFRIC 13:7]

5.6.3.2 Changes in expectations

After granting award credits, the entity may revise its expectations about the proportion that will be redeemed. The change in expectations does not affect the consideration that the entity has received for supplying awards (this is fixed at the outset), but it affects the amount of revenue recognised in respect of award credits that are redeemed in the period. The change in expectations is thus accounted for as a change in estimate in the period of change and future periods, in accordance with IAS 8:36 (see **4.2** in **chapter A5**). [IFRIC 13:BC16]

Example 5.6.3.2

Awards supplied by the entity

[IFRIC 13:IE1 - IE5, Example 1]

A grocery retailer operates a customer loyalty programme. It grants programme members loyalty points when they spend a specified amount on groceries. Programme members can redeem the points for further groceries. The points have no expiry date. In one period, the entity grants 100 points. Management measures the fair value of groceries for which each loyalty point can be redeemed as 1.25 currency units (CU1.25). This amount takes into account management's estimate of the discount that market participants would assume when pricing the award credits. That discount takes into account market participants' expectations of the discount that would otherwise be offered to customers who have not earned award credits from an initial sale. In addition, management estimates that market participants would expect only 80 of these points to be redeemed. Therefore, the fair value of each point is CU1, being the fair value of the award for each loyalty point granted of CU1.25 reduced to take into account points not expected to be redeemed ((80 points/100 points) × CU1.25 = CU1). Accordingly, management defers recognition of revenue of CU100. Throughout the example, management determines that non-performance risk has an immaterial effect on the measurement of its obligation under the programme.

Year 1

At the end of the first year, 40 of the points have been redeemed in exchange for groceries, i.e. half of those expected to be redeemed. The entity recognises revenue of (40 points / 80[1] points) × CU100 = CU50.

Year 2

In the second year, management revises its estimates of market participants' expectations. It now expects 90 points to be redeemed altogether.

During the second year, 41 points are redeemed, bringing the total number redeemed to 40[2] + 41 = 81 points. The cumulative revenue that the entity recognises is (81 points / 90[3] points) × CU100 = CU90. The entity has recognised revenue of CU50 in the first year, so it recognises CU40 in the second year.

Year 3

In the third year, a further nine points are redeemed, taking the total number of points redeemed to 81 + 9 = 90. Management continues to expect that only 90 points will ever be redeemed, i.e. that no more points will be redeemed after the third year. So the cumulative revenue to date is (90 points / 90[4] points) × CU100 = CU100. The entity has already recognised CU90 of revenue (CU50 in the first year and CU40 in the second year). So it recognises the remaining CU10 in the third year. All of the revenue initially deferred has now been recognised.

[1] total number of points expected to be redeemed
[2] number of points redeemed in year 1
[3] revised estimate of total number of points expected to be redeemed
[4] total number of points still expected to be redeemed

It is possible, particularly if there are changes in expectations regarding redemption rates or revised cost expectations, for the unavoidable costs of meeting award obligations to exceed the consideration received and receivable for them (i.e. including any further consideration receivable when the customer redeems the award credits). In such circumstances, the entity has onerous contracts and a liability should be recognised for the excess in accordance with IAS 37 *Provisions, Contingent Liabilities and Contingent Assets*. [IFRIC 13:9]

> The Interpretation does not imply that award credits need to be accounted for on an individual transaction-by-transaction basis. Varying degrees of aggregation by the accounting period in which such awards are generated may be appropriate depending on the circumstances, as confirmed in *IFRIC Update* in May 2007.

5.6.4 Awards supplied by a third party

If a third party supplies the awards, the entity is required to assess whether it is collecting the consideration allocated to the award credits on its own account or on behalf of the third party. In other words, it must assess whether it is acting as principal in the transaction or as an agent for the third party. [IFRIC 13:8]

Determining whether a seller is an agent or principal requires the exercise of careful judgement and will depend on the particular facts and circumstances of each arrangement; relevant factors for consideration are discussed at **3.2**.

When an entity is collecting consideration on behalf of a third party it:

[IFRIC 13:8]

- measures its revenue as the net amount retained on its own account, i.e. the difference between the consideration allocated to the award credits and the amount payable to the third party for supplying the awards; and

- recognises this net amount as revenue when the third party is obliged to supply the awards and entitled to receive consideration for doing so. (These events may occur as soon as the award credits are granted. Alternatively, if the customer can choose to claim awards from either the entity or a third party, these events may occur only when the customer chooses to claim awards from the third party.)

When an entity is collecting consideration on its own account, it measures its revenue as the gross consideration allocated to the award credits and recognises the revenue when it fulfils its obligations in respect of the awards. [IFRIC 13:9]

Example 5.6.4

Awards supplied by a third party

[IFRIC 13:IE6 - IE10, Example 2]

A retailer of electrical goods participates in a customer loyalty programme operated by an airline. It grants programme members one air travel point with each CU1 they spend on electrical goods. Programme members can redeem the points for air travel with the airline, subject to availability. The retailer pays the airline CU0.009 for each point.

In one period, the retailer sells electrical goods for consideration totalling CU1 million. It grants 1 million points.

Allocation of consideration to travel points

The retailer estimates that the fair value of a point is CU0.01. It allocates to the points 1 million × CU0.01 = CU10,000 of the consideration it has received from the sales of its electrical goods.

Revenue recognition

Having granted the points, the retailer has fulfilled its obligations to the customer. The airline is obliged to supply the awards and entitled to receive consideration for doing so. Therefore the retailer recognises revenue from the points when it sells the electrical goods.

Revenue measurement

If the retailer has collected the consideration allocated to the points on its own account, it measures its revenue as the gross CU10,000 allocated to them. It separately recognises the CU9,000 paid or payable to the airline as an expense. If the retailer has collected the consideration on behalf of the airline, i.e. as an agent for the airline, it measures its revenue as the net amount it retains on its own account. This amount of revenue is the difference between the CU10,000 consideration allocated to the points and the CU9,000 passed on to the airline.

If, at the time of the original transaction, it is made clear to the customer that a third party will be obliged to supply the awards, it is likely that the entity is collecting consideration on behalf of that third party. Conversely, if the customer believes that the entity itself is obliged to supply the awards, it is likely that the entity is collecting consideration on its own account.

5.7   Prepaid minutes cards and similar arrangements

Many entities in the telecom industry offer customers 'prepaid minutes' cards under which customers acquire prepaid cards entitling them to a fixed number of minutes. The period of redemption may be fixed or may extend indefinitely.

Other entities offer 'rollover minutes' arrangements under which customers acquire a fixed amount of minutes per month for a fixed fee. Unused minutes in a specific month can be carried forward to the next month. The arrangements either contemplate a maximum number of months over which the minutes can be rolled forward or that carryforward can be indefinite.

The question arises as to when revenue related to the prepaid minutes cards and rollover minutes should be recognised.

Under IAS 18:13, when a transaction consists of the delivery of separately identifiable components, the proceeds of the transaction are allocated to each component and recognised when the conditions for revenue recognition applicable to the specific component are satisfied.

However, IAS 18 does not provide guidance on how to achieve this result. Accordingly, an entity should establish a systematic methodology to allocate the proceeds from the sale of prepaid minutes cards (or rollover minutes) and recognise revenue associated with each minute based on this allocation method. One such allocation method is described in paragraph 7 of IFRIC 13 *Customer Loyalty Programmes*, which states that the "amount of revenue recognised shall be based on the number of award credits that have been redeemed ..., relative to the total number expected to be redeemed".

Accordingly, following the hierarchy guidance specified in IAS 8:10 to 12, to the extent that a reliable estimate can be made of the expected number of minutes to be used, a method reflecting expected utilisation, such as the one described in IFRIC 13:7, is considered preferable when determining how to recognise revenue related to prepaid minutes cards and rollover minutes.

Nonetheless, other methods (e.g. a method under which each minute is valued at the same amount and only recognised upon use by the customer or on expiry) may also be acceptable if they reflect the substance of the transaction (e.g. if the number of minutes expected to be used cannot be reliably estimated).

Note that this conclusion does not apply to arrangements under which the customers can request a cash settlement for the unused minutes, because that would be a financial liability within the scope of IFRS 9 *Financial Instruments* (or, for entities that have not yet adopted IFRS 9, IAS 39 *Financial Instruments: Recognition and Measurement*).

6 Recognition – revenue from sale of goods

6.1 Recognition criteria – sale of goods

Revenue from the sale of goods should be recognised when all of the following criteria have been satisfied:

[IAS 18:14]

- the entity has transferred to the buyer the significant risks and rewards of ownership of the goods (see **6.2**);

- the entity retains neither continuing managerial involvement to the degree usually associated with ownership nor effective control over the goods sold (see **6.3**);

- the amount of revenue can be measured reliably (see **6.4**);

- it is probable that the economic benefits associated with the transaction will flow to the entity (see **6.5**); and

- the costs incurred or to be incurred in respect of the transaction can be measured reliably (see **6.6**).

IAS 18 offers no guidance on how to determine whether a contract is for the supply of goods or services and, in some circumstances, careful judgement may be required. In particular, merely because a contract requires items to be supplied that have not yet been manufactured, it does not necessarily follow that the contract is for manufacturing services (see the further discussion at **2.3**).

6.2   Risks and rewards of ownership

6.2.1   Assessment of when the significant risks and rewards of ownership have been transferred

The circumstances of the transaction must be examined to assess when a seller has transferred the significant risks and rewards of ownership to the buyer. Generally, the transfer of the risks and rewards of ownership coincides with the transfer of the legal title or the passing of possession to the buyer as, for example, with most retail sales. Sometimes, however, the transfer of risks and rewards of ownership occurs at a different time from the transfer of legal title or the passing of possession. [IAS 18:15]

If significant risks of ownership are retained by the seller, the transaction is not a sale and revenue is not recognised. Such significant risks of ownership may be retained in a number of ways. Examples given by IAS 18 are:

[IAS 18:16]

(a)   when the seller retains an obligation for unsatisfactory performance not covered by normal warranty provisions;

(b)   when the receipt of the revenue from a particular sale is contingent on the derivation of revenue by the buyer from its sale of the goods;

(c)   when the goods are shipped subject to installation and the installation is a significant part of the contract which has not yet been completed by the entity; and

(d)   when the buyer has the right to rescind the purchase for a reason specified in the sales contract and the seller is uncertain about the probability of return.

In addition to the examples listed above, the fact that the seller has retained the risk of physical damage, or will share in the proceeds from the onward sale of the goods, may provide evidence that significant risks and rewards of ownership have not been transferred. Similarly, when the seller has a fixed price repurchase option, or the buyer lacks economic substance outside of the transaction (e.g. it is a structured or special purpose entity set up for the purpose of the transaction), these may be further indications that a sale has not taken place.

If only an insignificant risk of ownership is retained by the seller, the transaction is a sale and revenue is recognised. For example, solely to protect the collectibility of the amount due, a seller may retain the legal title to goods. Provided that the seller has transferred the significant risks and rewards of ownership, the transaction is a sale and revenue is recognised. Similarly, an insignificant risk of ownership may be retained by the seller in a retail sale when a refund is offered if the customer is not satisfied. Revenue in such cases is recognised at the time of sale provided that the seller can reliably estimate future returns and recognises a liability and corresponding reduction in revenue for returns based on previous experience and other relevant factors. [IAS 18:17]

The examples below illustrate some common situations in which the risks and rewards of ownership have or have not been transferred.

Example 6.2.1A

Warranty

An entity supplies an item of machinery and gives a three-month warranty covering the cost of any adjustments or repairs subsequent to delivery. Because of the need to suit the particular customer's environment, the product is likely to have some serious problems that will require remedy after delivery. It is not possible to estimate reliably the cost to the seller of carrying out any such adjustments or repairs. Under the terms of the sales contract, title passes from the seller to the buyer on delivery.

Revenue should be recognised when the warranty expires. The risks and rewards of ownership do not pass from the seller to the buyer until the three-month period has expired because it is not possible to estimate reliably, and therefore accrue, any costs of repairs or adjustments under the warranty, which could be material.

Example 6.2.1B

CDs distributed on the basis of sale or return

A distributor of CDs sells and delivers CDs to a local shop for a fixed price. To the extent that the local shop succeeds in selling the CDs, it does so as principal; it is the primary obligor in the relationship with the end customer, and can choose how to price the CDs. If the local shop does not sell the CDs, they are returned to the distributor for a full refund or credit. It is not possible to estimate reliably at the time the CDs are delivered how many CDs will not be sold.

Revenue should be recognised by the distributor when the CDs are sold by the local shop. The risks and rewards of ownership do not pass from the distributor until the shop has sold the CDs because the receipt of revenue by the distributor is contingent on the sale of the CDs by the shop and the distributor is unable to estimate reliably how many CDs will not be sold.

Example 6.2.1C

Equipment sold subject to right of return

A heavy equipment manufacturer sells an item of machinery to a customer who is anticipating being awarded a particular road-building contract from the government. The sales contract gives the customer the right to return the machinery if the customer does not win the contract. There is no way to estimate reliably whether the customer will return the machinery.

Revenue should be recognised when the contract has been awarded. The risks and rewards of ownership do not pass from the seller to the buyer until the customer has been granted the road-building contract by the government. Until then, the manufacturer is exposed to the risk that the machinery may be returned, and it is not possible to estimate reliably whether the machinery will be returned.

Example 6.2.1D

Retail guarantee

A retail shop offers a lifetime guarantee on its products. A customer may return any item for any reason at any time and have its purchase price refunded. Based on reliable, historical data, 0.95 per cent of sales are returned under this policy.

On the basis of historical data, the shop retains only insignificant risks and rewards of ownership by offering this guarantee. Provided that the other revenue recognition criteria are met, revenue should be recognised at the time of sale for those items that are not expected to be returned (i.e. 99.05 per cent of sales) and the balance of 0.95 per cent should be recognised as a liability to cover the amounts expected to be refunded because of sales returns.

Example 6.2.1E

Retention of title

As a matter of policy, a manufacturer writes its sales contracts in such a way that legal title does not pass on delivery but when consideration for the goods is received. A sale is made and the related goods are delivered to a customer who is not a particular credit risk.

The risks and rewards of ownership have passed from the seller to the buyer even though title has not. Transfer of title may be an indicator that the risks and rewards of ownership have passed to the buyer, but it is not a required condition. Therefore, provided that the other revenue recognition criteria are met, revenue can be recognised if the only rights that a seller retains with the title are those enabling recovery of the goods in the event of customer default on payment.

Example 6.2.1F

'Trade loading' and 'channel stuffing'

Sometimes manufacturers or dealers try to enhance the apparent volume of their sales, profits, and/or market share by inducing their wholesale customers to buy more product than they can promptly resell. The result is accelerated, but not increased, volume, because the wholesalers' inventories become bloated and their future orders from the manufacturers are reduced. This practice is known as 'trade loading' or 'channel stuffing'.

Entities may induce wholesale customers to buy more product than they can promptly resell for reasons other than enhancing the appearance of their financial figures (e.g. to improve cash flows or to spread production more evenly throughout the year when sales are seasonal). If the revenue recognition criteria in IAS 18:14 for sales of goods are met, the revenue should be recognised. In many situations, however, products sold during 'channel stuffing' programmes are merely held by the wholesaler to be returned in a future accounting period when it is determined the products cannot be sold to the end user. Assuming the criteria in IAS 18:14 are met, which will require that the level of returns can be estimated reliably, revenue is recognised net of the expected returns. Therefore, management must estimate the amount of product to be returned. Historical return rates may not capture appropriately the high level of returns usually related to 'channel stuffing' programmes. If the level of returns cannot be estimated reliably, revenue should not be recognised.

Example 6.2.1G

Unlimited right of return

Company A distributes DVDs. Its key customers are department stores but it also sells to small shops. The sales agreements with key customers allow these customers to return any slow-moving goods, but there is no definition of 'slow-moving' in the agreements. The returns could result in replacement of the returned goods with other DVDs or return of cash. For customers other than the key customers, the sales agreement limits their returns of slow-moving goods to not more than 10 per cent of purchases. In both cases, on the basis of experience, Company A is able to make a reliable estimate of the amount of returns.

How should Company A account for its revenues from (1) key customers (whose right to return goods is unlimited), and (2) other customers (whose right of return is limited)?

A condition for recognising revenue from the sale of goods in IAS 18:14(a) is that the entity has transferred to the buyer the significant risks and rewards of ownership of the goods. In the circumstances described, both classes of customers have assumed all of the significant *rewards* of ownership of the goods, because they have an unrestricted right to resell the goods. Furthermore, because a reliable estimate of the amount of returns can be made for both classes of customers, the extent to which the buyer has assumed the significant *risks* also can be measured for both classes of customers. Therefore, revenue should be recognised on initial delivery of the goods at an amount that reflects a reduction for estimated returns.

The answer would be different for the key customers if the effect of their right to return all slow-moving goods could not be measured. In those circumstances, Company A would have retained an immeasurable risk of marketability and obsolescence. The condition in IAS 18:14(a) would not be met, and Company A would recognise revenue on a consignment basis (i.e. recognise revenue when the key customers resell the goods to third-party customers).

Example 6.2.1H

Customer acceptance provision

A sales contract may give the customer the unilateral right, for a specified period after delivery, to accept or reject the goods. The appropriate point for revenue recognition will depend on the probability of customer acceptance. If the seller is uncertain about the probability of acceptance, revenue recognition should not occur until the earlier of customer acceptance and expiry of the acceptance period. If the probability of customer acceptance is uncertain, the risks of ownership must be regarded as remaining with the seller.

For example, Manufacturer A produces a ball bearing for use in the manufacture of automobiles. The buyer of the ball bearing requires defects to be less than 1.0 part per million (ppm). These ball bearings are tested prior to shipment through sample analysis to ensure their quality meets the requirements of the buyer. After the sample testing is completed, it is determined that the error rate is 0.8 ppm.

Therefore, on delivery, Manufacturer A can be reasonably certain that the goods meet the specifications of the buyer and can recognise revenue. If testing was not completed or showed a probability of customer rejection, revenue would not be recognised until customer acceptance is provided.

Example 6.2.1I

Sale of gift certificates

Gift certificates sold by a retailer can be used by the holder to buy merchandise up to the amount indicated on the gift certificate.

Sales revenue should not be recognised for a gift certificate at the time that it is sold. Gift certificates represent prepayments of cash that can be redeemed for merchandise at a later date. Revenue is not recognised until the gift certificate is redeemed for merchandise. Instead, the retailer recognises the proceeds from gift certificates as a liability, representing the obligation to deliver merchandise at a future time.

Example 6.2.1J

Sale of products with a time restriction on resale or use

Company A, a manufacturer of designer clothing, ships clothing for the spring season to customers (clothing retailers) in December 20X1. Although the customers take title to the goods when they receive them, the terms of the sales prohibit the customers from displaying or selling the clothing until 15 February 20X2. The terms of the arrangement are such that payment generally is not due until the restriction is lifted.

Should revenue be recognised when the goods are delivered (20X1) or when the restriction on resale expires (20X2)?

The limitation on when the product can be sold would not, of itself, preclude revenue recognition in 20X1. IAS 18:14(a) prohibits revenue recognition until the seller has transferred to the buyer the significant risks and rewards of ownership of the goods. In the circumstances described, the timing is short compared to the life cycle of the inventories and the timing of the restriction does not affect the value of the inventories to be sold. However, if the delay were longer (e.g. until the summer season), a review of whether the significant rewards of ownership had been transferred should be performed.

6.2.2 Impact of local law

The transfer of the risks and rewards of ownership often coincides with the transfer of legal title, the timing of which can vary according to the law in the relevant jurisdiction. This does not mean that different revenue recognition criteria are applied in different jurisdictions but, rather, that the recognition criteria are met at different times in different jurisdictions. The principle is that the significant risks and rewards of ownership must have passed from the seller to the buyer. [IAS 18:Appendix]

Examples of legal requirements that can affect the transfer of risks and rewards and, therefore, the timing of revenue recognition, include:

- in some jurisdictions, title does not legally transfer until the buyer obtains physical possession of the goods; and

- a 'cooling off' period is required in property transactions (often residential property transactions) in certain jurisdictions, during which the buyer has an absolute legal right to rescind the transaction.

6.2.3 When are risks and rewards transferred?

Products may be delivered based on oral arrangements (e.g. either a telephone call from a customer or walk-in business) or on the basis of a detailed contract with specified shipping terms, with many variations in between. The judgement as to when all risks and rewards of ownership have been transferred is a determination that should consider the laws of the jurisdiction in which the sale is made, particularly if the contract does not specify shipping terms. In complex circumstances, it may be useful to obtain the advice of legal counsel regarding the rights and obligations of the parties.

The revenue recognition criteria in IAS 18 should be evaluated based on the mutually understood terms of the transaction. IAS 18 does not require a written sales agreement as a condition for revenue recognition. IAS 18 does require transfer of the significant risks and rewards of ownership of the goods from the seller to the buyer. This means that both the buyer and the seller should have a clear understanding of all terms of the transaction, including pricing, payment terms, return rights, shipping, installation and warranty rights. When there is a written sales agreement, these terms should be clearly set out. When an entity routinely provides goods or services based on oral agreements, there is an expectation that, if necessary, the entity will have clearly articulated its policies and terms of sale to its customers through brochures, store signage, notices on invoices, advertising and similar written means.

Although IAS 18 does not require a written contract as evidence of an agreement, if such a contract is being prepared and has not yet been signed, this may be evidence that agreement has not yet been reached. Great care should be taken before recognising revenue in such circumstances because the apparent absence of a contractual understanding between the parties may make it unlikely that the conditions in IAS 18:14 have been met.

Example 6.2.3A

Goods shipped FOB shipping point, but seller arranges shipping

When goods are shipped 'free on board' (FOB) shipping point, title passes to the buyer when the goods are shipped and the buyer is responsible for any loss in transit. On the other hand, when goods are shipped FOB destination, title does not pass to the buyer until delivery and the seller is responsible for any loss in transit.

Company A sells goods FOB shipping point and it is clear that title transfers to the buyer at the time of shipment. Company A's business practice is to arrange for shipping the goods to the buyer and to deal directly with the shipping company. Company A invoices the buyer for the shipping costs separately from the product. Company A's business practice is also that if there is any damage or physical loss during transit, Company A provides the buyer with replacement products at no additional cost. If the loss or damage in transit is substantial, Company A's insurance would cover all or most of the loss.

In the circumstances described, it is not appropriate for Company A to recognise revenue at the time its products have been shipped. While title has passed, Company A has retained a significant risk of ownership (i.e. responsibility for damage or loss in transit). The fact that Company A's insurance would cover a substantial loss is evidence that it has managed its risk, but Company A has still retained the risk. The criterion for recognising revenue set out in IAS 18:14(a) has not been met.

Example 6.2.3B

Goods shipped FOB destination, but shipping company assumes risk of loss

Company A sells goods 'free on board' (FOB) destination, which means that title does not pass to the buyer until delivery and Company A is responsible for any loss in transit. To protect itself from loss, Company A contracts with the shipping company for the shipping company to assume total risk of loss while the goods are in transit.

In the circumstances described, it is not appropriate for Company A to recognise revenue when the goods are shipped. While Company A has managed its risk, it has not transferred risk to the buyer. Therefore, the criterion in IAS 18:14(a) has not been met until the goods have been delivered.

Example 6.2.3C

Seller arranges for manufacturer to ship directly to buyer ('drop shipment')

A seller who arranges for direct shipping of products from a manufacturer to a buyer must first consider whether it should report revenue on a gross or net basis. This determination will depend on whether the seller is acting as a principal or an agent (see **3.2**).

If the seller arranges to have the manufacturer ship the products directly to the buyer, and the seller is a principal rather than an agent, the seller should recognise revenue as if it had shipped the products itself. Therefore, if the terms of sale specify FOB shipping point, the seller recognises revenue when the manufacturer ships the goods. If the terms of sale specify FOB destination, the seller recognises revenue when the buyer receives the goods.

Example 6.2.3D

Written sales agreement has expired but shipments continue

An entity's normal practice is to obtain a written sales agreement signed by the buyer. The agreement has a fixed termination date and no provision for automatic extension. The seller has continued to ship products to a customer after the written agreement expires.

Should revenue be recognised?

This is essentially a legal question about the seller's and buyer's rights in the circumstances. As a result of the expiry of the agreement, It may be the case that (1) the seller has retained significant risks of ownership, (2) the amount of revenue cannot be measured reliably, or (3) it is no longer probable that amounts due from the buyer will be recovered. In any of those circumstances, IAS 18:14 would preclude revenue recognition.

Even if it is determined that revenue should be recognised in this case, a question arises as to the measurement of the revenue. If the vendor has a history of providing price or other concessions as an inducement for renewal of a sales agreement, that practice must be taken into account when measuring the revenue from the products shipped after the sales agreement has expired.

Example 6.2.3E

Vendor installation – customer acceptance

Company A sells a machine and is required to install it on the customer's premises. The sales contract requires the customer to inspect and accept or reject the installation. On the basis of Company A's experience, the probability of customer acceptance of the equipment after completion of installation is very high.

Should revenue be recognised (1) when the machine is delivered (if necessary, with recognition of a provision for estimated additional installation costs), or (2) after customer acceptance?

The appropriate timing for revenue recognition depends on whether the transaction can be unbundled into two separately identifiable components of revenue: delivery of the machine and its installation (see **5.2**). If the installation cannot be unbundled (i.e. the installation cannot be accounted for separately from the sale of the machine), then revenue should be recognised on delivery of the machine only if, among other criteria:

- it is probable that the customer will accept the machine (if relevant, see **example 6.2.1H**); and
- the installation process is simple in nature (e.g. the installation of a factory tested television receiver that only requires unpacking and connection of power and antennae – see **example 6.7B**).

The appendix to IAS 18 provides additional examples which illustrate the appropriate time to recognise revenue from the sale of goods. For convenience, these examples are reproduced in **6.7**.

6.3   Continuing managerial involvement and effective control

This criterion generally goes hand-in-hand with the risks and rewards of ownership (see **6.2**). It would be unusual for an entity to retain managerial involvement to the degree usually associated with ownership or to retain effective control over goods without retaining the risks and rewards of ownership. Each situation should, however, be considered individually. It may be the case that continuing managerial involvement is not to the degree usually associated with ownership. For example, a software consultancy firm may install a software system for a client and then oversee and manage the computer department that uses the software. This outsourcing of managerial control over the computer department, which includes the newly installed software, does not necessarily prohibit revenue recognition for the provision of the software. It will be necessary to consider the terms of the agreement to determine whether the risks and rewards stemming from the software have been transferred to the client.

6.4   Reliable measurement of revenue

Until the amount of revenue to be received can be measured reliably, revenue cannot be recognised. This does not imply, however, that the consideration must have been received in all cases for revenue to be recognised. Generally, consideration will be agreed in advance and the revenue from a sale will be recognised when all of the other recognition criteria are met.

Example 6.4

Vendor installation – settlement terms

A sales contract requires payment of 90 per cent on completion of the delivery and installation of a machine, and the remaining 10 per cent at the earlier of customer acceptance or 90 days. In this particular case, the seller has determined that it is not appropriate to account for installation as a separate component.

In the circumstances described, the arrangements for customer acceptance do not affect the amount of revenue to be received, only the timing of payment. Therefore, those arrangements do not affect the timing of recognition of revenue.

Because installation is not a component of revenue to be accounted for separately, 100 per cent of the revenue should be recognised when the significant risks and rewards of ownership of the machine have been transferred to the buyer. Depending on the particular facts and circumstances, this will either be on delivery (with recognition of a provision for any estimated additional installation costs to be incurred) or on completion of installation (see **example 6.2.3E** for further guidance).

The recognition of revenue is not affected by the settlement terms unless there is uncertainty regarding the flow of the economic benefits related to the transaction to the entity.

6.5   Probability of receipt of economic benefits

Revenue cannot be recognised unless it is probable that the economic benefits or consideration associated with the transaction will flow to the entity. For example, it may not be probable that consideration will be received from a particular customer due to exchange controls in the country in which the customer operates, which limit the amount of currency that can be remitted from that country. In such cases, when it is not probable that the consideration will be received, revenue is not recognised until the consideration is received.

If revenue has been recognised and it later emerges that the related consideration will not be collectible, an expense for bad debts is recognised rather than reversing the related revenue. [IAS 18:18]

6.6   Measurement of costs incurred related to the transaction

When the costs incurred or to be incurred in a transaction cannot be measured reliably, revenue is not recognised. This criterion flows from the matching principle. Under this principle, when revenue is recognised, the related expenses are also recognised. A common example of the type of expense that should be estimated and accrued is warranty costs. If such costs cannot be estimated reliably, revenue is deferred until the amount of such expenses can be more reliably estimated or have been incurred. In these circumstances, any consideration already received from the sale of goods is recognised as a liability. [IAS 18:19]

6.7   Additional examples

The following examples of the application of the revenue recognition criteria for the sale of goods are taken from the appendix to IAS 18. Although the appendix is not part of the Standard, it provides useful application guidance. Unless stated otherwise, the examples generally assume that the amount of revenue can be measured reliably, it is probable that the economic benefits will flow to the entity, and the costs incurred or to be incurred can be measured reliably.

Example 6.7A

'Bill-and-hold' sales, in which delivery is delayed at the buyer's request, but the buyer takes title and accepts billing

[IAS 18 Illustrative Example 1]

Revenue is recognised when the buyer takes title, provided that:

- it is probable that delivery will be made;
- the item is on hand, identified and ready for delivery to the buyer at the time the sale is recognised;

- the buyer specifically acknowledges the deferred delivery instructions; and
- the usual payment terms apply.

Revenue is not recognised when there is simply an intention to acquire or manufacture the goods in time for delivery.

Example 6.7A, reproduced from the appendix to IAS 18, describes a bill-and-hold sale in which revenue would be recognised on completion of manufacture if shipping is delayed at the buyer's request. But the facts in that example are that the buyer has taken title and accepts billing. If this were not the case, so that the seller retains title and the buyer is not obligated to pay until the goods are delivered, then revenue should not be recognised until the goods are delivered. This is the case even if the order is non-cancellable.

Consistent with the revenue recognition criteria set out in **example 6.7A**:

- revenue recognition at completion of manufacture may be inappropriate if there is no fixed delivery schedule or if the delivery schedule is significantly longer than is customary in the industry; and

- revenue recognition at completion of manufacture would not be appropriate if the seller, rather than the buyer, has requested that the transaction be on a bill-and-hold basis. Also, the buyer must have a substantive business purpose for ordering the goods on a bill-and-hold basis.

Example 6.7B

Goods shipped subject to conditions

[IAS 18 Illustrative Example 2]

(a) Installation and inspection

Revenue is normally recognised when the buyer accepts delivery, and installation and inspection are complete. However, revenue is recognised immediately upon the buyer's acceptance of delivery when:

- the installation process is simple in nature, e.g. the installation of a factory-tested television receiver which only requires unpacking and connection of power and antennae; or
- the inspection is performed only for the purposes of final determination of contract prices, e.g. shipments of iron ore, sugar or soya beans.

(b) On approval when the buyer has negotiated a limited right of return

If there is uncertainty about the possibility of return, revenue is recognised when the shipment has been formally accepted by the buyer or the goods have been delivered and the time period for rejection has elapsed.

(c) Consignment sales under which the recipient (buyer) undertakes to sell the goods on behalf of the shipper (seller)

Revenue is recognised by the shipper when the goods are sold by the recipient to a third party.

(d) Cash on delivery sales

Revenue is recognised when delivery is made and cash is received by the seller or its agent.

Example 6.7C

Lay away sales under which the goods are delivered only when the buyer makes the final payment in a series of instalments

[IAS 18 Illustrative Example 3]

Revenue from such sales is recognised when the goods are delivered. However, when experience indicates that most such sales are consummated, revenue may be recognised when a significant deposit is received, provided that the goods are on hand, identified and ready for delivery to the buyer.

The determination as to whether a deposit is considered 'significant' is a matter requiring careful judgement based on all of the relevant facts and circumstances. Factors to consider in making this determination include, but are not limited to, the following:

- the entity's policy on lay away sales, including the amount of deposit generally required;
- the nature and amount of the goods sold;
- the history of lay away sales, including the extent to which sales are consummated; and
- the possibility of either party withdrawing from the transaction.

In any case, the final conclusion should be supported by sufficient objective evidence.

If a customer forfeits its deposit under a lay away programme, so that the seller is entitled to keep the deposit without having any further obligations, the retained deposit will satisfy the definition of revenue in IAS 18:7 at the point of forfeiture and should be presented as such. The fact that the seller has retained the deposit without having delivered any goods is an event that is part of the ordinary course of business of a lay away seller. If forfeitures are significant, it may be appropriate to disclose the amount separately.

If such forfeited deposits do not remain the property of the seller, but rather must be remitted to the government under 'escheat laws', then no revenue is recognised. As noted above, the deposit for lay away sales is normally recognised as a liability, not as revenue. However, sometimes the seller may already have recognised revenue when a 'significant' deposit was received. If that is the case, and the seller will be required to remit any forfeited deposits to the government, the seller should establish an allowance for estimated forfeitures at the time the revenue is recognised. If no such reliable estimate can be made, no revenue should be recognised.

The recognition of revenue prior to the delivery of goods will only be appropriate in situations when, in addition to the above, the criteria applicable to bill-and-hold sales are also met – for example, the seller has identified the specific goods (so they will not be sold to another party) and they are ready for delivery.

Example 6.7D

Orders when payment (or partial payment) is received in advance of delivery for goods not currently held in inventory (e.g. the goods are still to be manufactured or will be delivered directly to the customer from a third party)

[IAS 18 Illustrative Example 4]

Revenue is recognised when the goods are delivered to the buyer.

Example 6.7E

Sale and repurchase agreements (other than swap transactions), under which the seller concurrently agrees to repurchase the same goods at a later date, or when the seller has a call option to repurchase, or the buyer has a put option to require the repurchase, by the seller, of the goods

[IAS 18 Illustrative Example 5]

For a sale and repurchase agreement on an asset other than a financial asset, the terms of the agreement need to be analysed to ascertain whether, in substance, the seller has transferred the risks and rewards of ownership to the buyer and hence revenue is recognised. When the seller has retained the risks and rewards of ownership, even though legal title has been transferred, the transaction is a financing arrangement and does not give rise to revenue. For a sale and repurchase agreement on a financial asset, IAS 39 *Financial*

Instruments: Recognition and Measurement [or, when adopted, IFRS 9 *Financial Instruments*] applies.

In the circumstances described in **example 6.7E**, if the seller has an option (meaning a right but not an obligation) to buy the goods back at a fixed price for a fixed period, the seller has retained an important benefit of ownership, namely the ability to profit from the difference between the strike price of the option and the fair value of the goods at the time the option is exercised. The significance of this benefit is to be considered at the date of the transaction to determine whether to recognise revenue. If the benefits retained are significant, revenue should not be recognised until expiry of the repurchase period. On the other hand, if the seller has the right to buy the goods back at market price at the time of repurchase, and the goods are readily available in the market, then revenue is recognised at the time of delivery. The determination as to whether to recognise revenue requires the exercise of careful judgement and consideration of all relevant facts and circumstances.

Example 6.7F

Sales to intermediate parties, such as distributors, dealers or others for resale

[IAS 18 Illustrative Example 6]

Revenue from such sales is generally recognised when the risks and rewards of ownership have passed. However, when the buyer is acting, in substance, as an agent, the sale is treated as a consignment sale.

Example 6.7G

Subscriptions to publications and similar items

[IAS 18 Illustrative Example 7]

When the items involved are of similar value in each time period, revenue is recognised on a straight-line basis over the period in which the items are despatched. When the items vary in value from period to period, revenue is recognised on the basis of the sales value of the item despatched as a proportion of the total estimated sales value of all items covered by the subscription.

Example 6.7H

Instalment sales, under which consideration is receivable in instalments

[IAS 18 Illustrative Example 8]

Revenue attributable to the sales price, exclusive of interest, is recognised at the date of sale. The sale price is the present value of the consideration, determined by discounting the instalments receivable at the imputed rate of interest. The interest element is recognised as revenue as it is earned, using the effective interest method.

In some cases, because of the nature of the industry in which an entity operates, goods are sold and delivered even though collection of the sales price is not reasonably assured. Often in those cases, payment is required in periodic instalments over an extended period of time. The seller generally will retain a lien on the product sold until payment is completed. For such instalment sales, when collection of the sales price is not reasonably assured, revenue recognition is deferred. A fundamental condition for revenue recognition in IAS 18:14(d) is that it is probable that the economic benefits associated with the transaction will flow to the entity. Example 8 of the appendix presumes that collectibility is not an issue.

7 Recognition – revenue from rendering of services

7.1 Recognition of revenue from rendering of services – general

IAS 18 requires the use of the percentage of completion method when accounting for the rendering of services. Under the percentage of completion method, revenue is recognised as work progresses based on the percentage of work completed at the end of the reporting period. IAS 18 requires the use of this method for revenue recognition, but the recognition of related contract expenses is beyond its scope (though there is some guidance on the treatment of associated expenses in the appendix to IAS 18). The Standard refers users to IAS 11 *Construction Contracts* for further guidance on the percentage of completion method as it applies to both revenue and expenses. The requirements and guidance included in IAS 18 are set out below and a more detailed discussion of the percentage of completion method is included in **appendix A2**.

As with the supply of goods, when an uncertainty arises about the collectibility of an amount already included in revenue in relation to services, the uncollectible amount, or the amount for which recovery has ceased to be probable, is recognised as a bad debt expense, rather than as an adjustment of the amount of revenue originally recognised. [IAS 18:22]

7.2   Recognition of revenue from rendering of services when the outcome of a transaction can be estimated reliably

When the outcome of a transaction involving the rendering of services can be estimated reliably, revenue associated with the transaction is recognised by reference to the stage of completion of the transaction at the end of the reporting period (i.e. using the percentage of completion method). IAS 18 lists the following conditions for the outcome of a transaction to be estimated reliably:

[IAS 18:20]

- the amount of revenue can be measured reliably;

- it is probable that the economic benefits associated with the transaction will flow to the entity;

- the stage of completion of the transaction at the end of the reporting period can be measured reliably; and

- the costs incurred for the transaction and the costs to complete the transaction can be measured reliably.

An entity is usually able to make reliable estimates after it has agreed the following with the other parties to the transaction:

[IAS 18:23]

- each party's enforceable rights regarding the service to be provided and received by the parties;

- the consideration to be exchanged; and

- the manner and terms of settlement.

In addition, it will be necessary for an entity to have an effective internal budgeting and reporting system for it to make reliable estimates and, in subsequent periods, to compare those estimates to the actual costs incurred to date.

The Standard emphasises that the need to revise the estimates of revenue as the service is performed does not necessarily indicate that the outcome of the transaction cannot be estimated reliably. [IAS 18:23]

The stage of completion of a transaction at the end of the reporting period can be determined in a variety of ways. Progress payments and advances received from customers are, however, generally not reliable indicators of the stage of completion, because these payments are often made for reasons other than compensating for work performed. Depending on the nature of the transaction, methods for determining the stage of completion may include:

[IAS 18:24]

- surveys of work performed;

- services performed to date as a percentage of total services to be performed; or

- the proportion that costs incurred to date bear to the estimated total costs of the transaction. Only costs that reflect services performed to date are included in costs incurred to date and only costs that reflect services performed or to be performed are included in the estimated total costs of the transaction.

When services are performed by an indeterminate number of acts over a specified period of time, revenue is recognised on a straight-line basis, unless there is evidence that some other method better represents the stage of completion. For example, if a service contract relates to daily cleaning services, for practical reasons, the revenue relating to those services will be recognised on a straight-line basis as the work is performed. If one specific act is much more significant than any other acts, the recognition of revenue is postponed until the significant act is executed. [IAS 18:25]

Example 7.2A

Claims processing and billing services

Company A performs claims processing and medical billing services for health care providers. It prepares and submits claims to government agencies and insurance companies, tracks the outstanding billings, collects the amounts billed and remits payments to the health care provider. Company A's fee is 5 per cent of the amount collected. Company A has reliable, historical evidence indicating that the government agencies and insurance companies pay 85 per cent of the claims submitted with no further effort on Company A's part.

Under IAS 18:20, revenue from rendering services should be recognised by reference to the stage of completion of the transaction.

How should that principle be applied in the circumstances described? Specifically, is it acceptable for Company A to recognise as revenue its 5 per cent fee on 85 per cent of the gross billings at the time it prepares and submits the billings, or must it wait until collections occur?

The appropriate timing for recognition of revenue in such circumstances will depend on whether the amount that will be received by Company A is sufficiently predictable to be a reliable measurement. If Company A can make a reliable estimate of collections, revenue related to at least 85 per cent of the claims can be recognised. Company A should determine the pattern of revenue recognition that best reflects the stage of completion.

Similar arrangements should be analysed to ascertain whether a transaction contains multiple elements to be accounted for separately (see **5.2**). If so, revenue will be recognised separately for the different activities performed by Company A.

Example 7.2B

Membership or services when the customer is entitled to a full refund

Company A sells one-year memberships in a facility it operates. The terms state that if the customer is unhappy with the facility for any reason within 30 days of joining the facility, the customer can request a full refund of the membership fee paid upon sign up. After 30 days, the membership is non-refundable. Company A's experience is that approximately 20 per cent of its customers request a refund during the 30-day period.

When should Company A begin to recognise revenue?

If it is possible to make a reliable estimate of the level of expected refunds, Company A should begin recognising the membership fee from the date the membership contract is signed, with an appropriate reduction in the amount recognised as revenue for estimated refunds. If it is not possible to make a reliable estimate of the level of expected refunds, revenue recognition should be deferred until the 30-day money-back period elapses.

Accordingly, in the circumstances described, revenue recognition begins when the contract is signed, with a reduction in the amount recognised as revenue relating to the 20 per cent of expected refunds, if such an adjustment reflects a reliable estimate of the level of expected refunds.

Example 7.2C

Performance-based fee part way through the performance period

Company A, an investment manager, will earn a bonus of CU1 million if a managed fund's performance exceeds the performance of the S&P 500 by 20 per cent for the calendar year 20X1. Company A's financial year ends 30 June 20X1. At that time, the fund is outperforming the S&P 500 by 25 per cent.

Should Company A recognise revenue in relation to the bonus at 30 June 20X1 and, if so, CU500,000 (one half-year's worth) or CU1 million (the expected total bonus)?

IAS 18:20 states that revenue can be recognised when the amount of revenue can be measured reliably and it is probable that the economic benefits will flow to the entity. Company A will not receive any bonus unless the annual return exceeds the performance of the S&P 500 by 20 per cent. Because the markets are very volatile, it is unlikely that Company A will be able to estimate reliably at 30 June 20X1 whether the return for the year ended 31 December 20X1 will exceed the performance of the S&P 500. Consequently, no amount of the bonus can be determined reliably at 30 June 20X1 and Company A should not recognise any of the bonus at 30 June 20X1.

Example 7.2D

Accounting for 'trail commissions'

Investment Manager G engages Financial Advisor X to sell to the general public units in funds managed by G. G compensates X on a 'trail commission' basis, which means that X does not receive any cash on completion of the sale of units but instead receives an annual fee of 5 per cent of the management fee that G earns from the investors introduced by X during the period that the investors remain invested in the fund. G's management fee is calculated as a percentage of the growth in the value of the net assets in the fund.

When one of the investors introduced by X redeems its units and divests from the fund, G ceases the payment of commission to X in respect of that investor.

Should X recognise any revenue in respect of the trail commission at the time of selling units?

It is first necessary to consider whether X is required to provide additional services (e.g. of an advisory or administrative nature to G and/or the investors) subsequent to the sale of units in order to receive payment. If so, then it would not be appropriate to recognise at the outset any part of the commission that relates to subsequent additional services.

To the extent that the trail commission relates to the selling of units, this will be recognised at the outset if, and only if, all of the conditions in IAS 18:20 are met. In particular, it must be possible for the amount of the commission to be estimated reliably and it must be probable that it will be received.

In the circumstances described, it may be unlikely that X will be able to estimate reliably the amount of revenue that will be received. This is because the amount of trail commissions receivable is uncertain, and will depend both on the length of time that particular investors remain with the funds (i.e. 'churn rates') and on the growth in the value of the net assets in the fund (because the latter determines G's management fee and, consequently, the amount payable to X). In particular, X may not be able to estimate future asset growth because that would involve forecasting the future performance of the investment fund.

If X is unable to estimate revenue reliably at the outset, revenue should instead be recognised when and to the extent that it becomes reliably measurable. In practice, X may only be able to measure revenue reliably at the end of each period for which G charges management fees because only at that point will the effect of investor churn and fund performance be known. For example, if G raises management fees on a quarterly basis, X will be able to measure revenue at the end of each quarter because the amount of revenue payable to X for that quarter will then be known.

7.3   Recognition of revenue from rendering of services when the outcome of a transaction cannot be estimated reliably

When the outcome of a transaction involving the rendering of services cannot be estimated reliably, either:

[IAS 18:26 - 28]

- revenue is recognised to the extent of expenses incurred that are likely to be recovered. Thus, no profit is recognised on the transaction; or

- if it is not probable that the costs incurred will be recovered, no revenue is recognised and the costs incurred are recognised as an expense.

When the uncertainties that led to no profit being recognised on the transaction no longer exist, revenue is recognised on the percentage of completion basis.

7.4   Additional examples

The following examples of the application of the recognition criteria for the rendering of services are taken from the appendix to IAS 18. Although the appendix is not part of the Standard, it provides useful application guidance. Unless stated otherwise, the examples generally assume that the amount of revenue can be measured reliably, it is probable that the economic benefits will flow to the entity and the costs incurred or to be incurred can be measured reliably.

Example 7.4A

Installation fees

[IAS 18 Illustrative Example 10]

Installation fees are recognised as revenue by reference to the stage of completion of the installation, unless they are incidental to the sale of a product, in which case they are recognised when the goods are sold.

Example 7.4B

Servicing fees included in the price of the product

[IAS 18 Illustrative Example 11]

When the selling price of a product includes an identifiable amount for subsequent servicing (e.g. after-sales support and product enhancement on the sale of software), that amount is deferred and recognised as revenue over the period during which the service is performed. The amount deferred is that which will cover the expected costs of the services under the agreement, together with a reasonable profit on those services.

Example 7.4C

Advertising commissions

[IAS 18 Illustrative Example 12]

Media commissions are recognised when the related advertisement or commercial appears before the public. Production commissions are recognised by reference to the stage of completion of the project.

Example 7.4D

Insurance agency commissions

[IAS 18 Illustrative Example 13]

Insurance agency commissions received or receivable, which do not require the agent to render further service, are recognised as revenue by the agent on the effective commencement or renewal dates of the related policies. However, when it is probable that the agent will be required to render further services during the life of the policy, the commission, or part thereof, is deferred and recognised as revenue over the period during which the policy is in force.

Example 7.4E

Financial service fees

[IAS 18 Illustrative Example 14]

The recognition of revenue for financial service fees depends on the purposes for which the fees are assessed and the basis of accounting for any associated financial instrument. The description of fees for financial services may not be indicative of the nature and substance of the services provided. Therefore, it is necessary to distinguish between fees that are an integral part of the effective interest rate of a financial instrument, fees that are earned as services are provided, and fees that are earned on the execution of a significant act.

(a) Fees that are an integral part of the effective interest rate of a financial instrument

Such fees are generally treated as an adjustment to the effective interest rate. However, when the financial instrument is measured at fair value with the change in fair value recognised in profit or loss, the fees are recognised as revenue when the instrument is initially recognised.

- **Origination fees received by the entity relating to the creation or acquisition of a financial asset other than one that under IAS 39 is classified as a financial asset 'at fair value through profit or loss' [or, when IFRS 9 is adopted, other than one that under IFRS 9 is measured at fair value through profit or loss].** Such fees may include compensation for activities such as evaluating the borrower's financial condition, evaluating and recording guarantees, collateral and other security arrangements, negotiating the terms of the instrument, preparing and processing documents and closing the transaction. These fees are an integral part of generating an involvement with the resulting financial instrument and, together with the related transaction costs (as defined in IAS 39)*, are deferred and recognised as an adjustment to the effective interest rate.

- **Commitment fees received by the entity to originate a loan when the loan commitment is outside the scope of IAS 39 [or, when adopted, IFRS 9].** If it is probable that the entity will enter into a specific lending arrangement and the loan commitment is not within the scope of IAS 39 [or, when adopted, IFRS 9], the commitment fee received is regarded as compensation for an ongoing involvement with the acquisition of a financial instrument and, together with the related transaction costs (as defined in IAS 39), is deferred and recognised as an adjustment to the effective interest rate. If the commitment expires without the entity making the loan, the fee is recognised as revenue on expiry. Loan commitments that are within the scope of IAS 39 [or, when adopted, IFRS 9] are accounted for as derivatives and measured at fair value

- **Origination fees received on issuing financial liabilities measured at amortised cost.** These fees are an integral part of generating an involvement with a financial liability. When a financial liability is not classified as at fair value through profit or loss, the origination fees received are included, with the related transaction costs (as defined in IAS 39) incurred, in the initial carrying amount of the financial liability and recognised as an adjustment to the effective interest rate. An entity distinguishes fees and costs that are an integral part of the effective interest rate for the financial liability from origination fees and transaction costs relating to the right to provide services, such as investment management services.

(b) Fees earned as services are provided

- **Fees charged for servicing a loan.** Fees charged by an entity for servicing a loan are recognised as revenue as the services are provided.

- **Commitment fees to originate a loan when the loan commitment is outside the scope of IAS 39 [or, when adopted, IFRS 9]**. If it is unlikely that a specific lending arrangement will be entered into and the loan commitment is outside the scope of IAS 39 [or, when adopted, IFRS 9], the commitment fee is recognised as revenue on a time proportion basis over the commitment period. Loan commitments that are within the scope of IAS 39 [or, when adopted, IFRS 9] are accounted for as derivatives and measured at fair value.

- **Investment management fees.** Fees charged for managing investments are recognised as revenue as the services are provided.

Incremental costs that are directly attributable to securing an investment management contract are recognised as an asset if they can be identified separately and measured reliably and if it is probable that they will be recovered. As in IAS 39, an incremental cost is one that would not have been incurred if the entity had not secured the investment management contract. The asset represents the entity's contractual right to benefit from providing investment management services, and is amortised as the entity recognises the related revenue. If the entity has a portfolio of investment management contracts, it may assess their recoverability on a portfolio basis.

Some financial services contracts involve both the origination of one or more financial instruments and the provision of investment management services. An example is a long-term monthly saving contract linked to the management of a pool of equity securities. The provider of the contract distinguishes the contract cost relating to the origination of the financial instrument from the costs of securing the right to provide investment management services.

(c) Fees that are earned on the execution of a significant act

The fees are recognised as revenue when the significant act has been completed, as in the examples below.

- **Commission on the allotment of shares to a client.** The commission is recognised as revenue when the shares have been allotted.

- **Placement fees for arranging a loan between a borrower and an investor.** The fee is recognised as revenue when the loan has been arranged.

- **Loan syndication fees.** A syndication fee received by an entity that arranges a loan and retains no part of the loan package for itself (or retains a part at the same effective interest rate for comparable risk as other participants) is compensation for the service of syndication. Such a fee is recognised as revenue when the syndication has been completed.

* In *Improvements to IFRSs* issued in May 2008, the IASB replaced the term 'direct costs' with 'transaction costs' as defined in IAS 39:9. This amendment removed an inconsistency for costs incurred in originating financial assets and liabilities that should be deferred and recognised as an adjustment to the underlying effective interest rate. 'Direct costs', as previously defined, did not require such costs to be incremental.

Example 7.4F

Admission fees

[IAS 18 Illustrative Example 15]

Revenue from artistic performances, banquets and other special events is recognised when the event takes place. When a subscription to a number of events is sold, the fee is allocated to each event on a basis that reflects the extent to which services are performed at each event.

Example 7.4G

Tuition fees

[IAS 18 Illustrative Example 16]

Revenue is recognised over the period of instruction.

Example 7.4H

Initiation, entrance and membership fees

[IAS 18 Illustrative Example 17]

Revenue recognition depends on the nature of the services provided. If the fee permits only membership, and all other services or products are paid for separately, or if there is a separate annual subscription, the fee is recognised as revenue when no significant uncertainty as to its collectibility exists. If the fee entitles the member to services or publications to be provided during the membership period, or to purchase goods or services at prices lower than those charged to non-members, it is recognised on a basis that reflects the timing, nature and value of the benefits provided.

Caution should be exercised before concluding that a fee permits only membership, particularly when goods or services are not made available to non-members at any price. In such circumstances, it will often be the case that the membership fee also provides the member with a valuable option to buy those goods and services, in which case the fee will permit more than just membership.

Example 7.4I

Franchise fees

[IAS 18 Illustrative Example 18]

Franchise fees may cover the supply of initial and subsequent services, equipment and other tangible assets, and know-how. Accordingly, franchise fees are recognised as revenue on a basis that reflects the purpose for which the fees were charged. The following methods of franchise fee recognition are appropriate:

- **Supplies of equipment and other tangible assets.** The amount, based on the fair value of the assets sold, is recognised as revenue when the items are delivered or title passes.
- **Supplies of initial and subsequent services.** Fees for the provision of continuing services, whether part of the initial fee or a separate fee, are recognised as revenue as the services are rendered. When the separate fee does not cover the cost of continuing services together with a reasonable profit, part of the initial fee, sufficient to cover the costs of

continuing services and to provide a reasonable profit on those services, is deferred and recognised as revenue as the services are rendered.

The franchise agreement may provide for the franchisor to supply equipment, inventories, or other tangible assets, at a price lower than that charged to others or a price that does not provide a reasonable profit on those sales. In these circumstances, part of the initial fee, sufficient to cover estimated costs in excess of that price and to provide a reasonable profit on those sales, is deferred and recognised over the period the goods are likely to be sold to the franchisee. The balance of an initial fee is recognised as revenue when performance of all of the initial services and other obligations required of the franchisor (such as assistance with site selection, staff training, financing and advertising) has been substantially accomplished.

The initial services and other obligations under an area franchise agreement may depend on the number of individual outlets established in the area. In this case, the fees attributable to the initial services are recognised as revenue in proportion to the number of outlets for which the initial services have been substantially completed.

If the initial fee is collectible over an extended period, and there is a significant uncertainty that it will be collected in full, the fee is recognised as cash instalments are received.

- **Continuing franchise fees.** Fees charged for the use of continuing rights granted by the agreement, or for other services provided during the period of the agreement, are recognised as revenue as the services are provided or the rights used.

- **Agency transactions.** Transactions may take place between the franchisor and the franchisee which, in substance, involve the franchisor acting as agent for the franchisee. For example, the franchisor may order supplies and arrange for their delivery to the franchisee at no profit. Such transactions do not give rise to revenue.

Example 7.4J

Fees from the development of customised software

[IAS 18 Illustrative Example 19]

Fees from the development of customised software are recognised as revenue by reference to the stage of completion of the development, including completion of services provided for post-delivery service support.

7.5   Milestone payments

7.5.1   Milestone payments – general

In certain industries, entities are commonly involved in collaborative research and development activities with other entities and will often enter into arrangements that provide for milestone payments to be received either based on the passage of time or the occurrence of specific events.

Accounting for such contracts can be complex and the appropriate timing for revenue recognition will vary depending on the substance of the arrangements. In some circumstances, there may be a correlation between the timing of milestone payments and when IAS 18's revenue recognition criteria are met. However, frequently, the timing of milestone payments may be reflective of financing arrangements rather than being representative of services rendered.

When the arrangement is, in substance, a contract for the rendering of services, revenue should be recognised based on the stage of completion, regardless of the timing of receipt of milestone payments. In determining whether there is any correlation between milestone payments and the stage of completion, consideration should be given to all relevant facts and circumstances including, but not limited to, whether:

- milestone events are substantive in terms of assessing the delivery of services to the customer;

- payments received bear any relation to the costs incurred and the services rendered to date;

- any amounts received to date are repayable upon cancellation of the arrangement; and

- any fines or penalties are payable upon failure to achieve a milestone.

In addition, consideration should be given to whether any royalty, licence or similar agreement that should be accounted for as a separate component (i.e. 'unbundled') is embodied in the arrangement.

Often, there is genuine uncertainty regarding whether a particular milestone will be reached and, consequently, whether particular elements of revenue will ultimately be received (e.g. for a pharmaceutical product, a milestone may be linked to approval by the appropriate government agency). When this is the case, the amount of revenue recognised should be restricted so that amounts relating to such milestones are not recognised while their payment remains uncertain. However, if there is no uncertainty over the seller's ability to achieve a particular milestone, it will not be appropriate to restrict revenue in this way.

7.5.2 Sale of intellectual property and subsequent development services

In some industries, such as the pharmaceutical industry and some technology businesses, it is common for an entity (Company A) to sell intellectual property (IP) which it has partly developed to another entity (Company B). Company A will continue to develop the IP for Company B and, if that further development is successful, Company B will ultimately exploit the IP that it has purchased by selling products as a principal. The terms of such contracts often require Company B to pay specified amounts to Company A if and when specific 'milestones' are successfully achieved (e.g. regulatory approval being obtained) during the further development stages of the IP. In addition, such contracts often oblige Company A to continue with the development work until either it is successfully completed or both parties agree that the development work will not be successful and should be terminated.

Such contracts raise particular issues for Company A, because both the revenue and the associated costs are unknown and will depend on future outcomes that typically cannot be predicted with confidence at the outset. Often, Company A cannot know in advance whether it will successfully complete the entire contract, thus receiving all milestone payments and incurring all costs, or whether (through no fault of Company A) the development will fail at some stage, such that Company A will only receive some of the milestone payments and incur some of the costs.

Neither IAS 18 nor IAS 11 includes guidance that deals specifically with the issues that arise from such contracts. In the absence of such guidance, judgement should be used to develop and apply consistently an appropriate accounting policy that complies with the general requirements of IAS 18. The discussion below highlights an approach that may be adopted, and sets out some methods that are adopted in practice. As explained further below, it is important to note that some of these methods may be appropriate in some circumstances but not in others. Moreover, this is not a comprehensive list of possible methods and methods other than those discussed below may also be acceptable in some circumstances.

It is generally appropriate for Company A first to consider whether the contract with Company B should be unbundled between the 'initial sale' of the IP and the further development of that IP. **Section 5.2** sets out general guidance on the unbundling of contracts. If the development work to be performed by Company A could instead have been performed by another supplier, it is possible that the conditions for unbundling the 'initial sale' from the subsequent services may be met. Conversely, if only Company A is capable of providing the further development services, it is unlikely that the 'initial sale' can be unbundled.

When the contract can be unbundled, and to the extent that it is possible to measure reliably the values that should be attributed to the various components of the transaction, the total contract revenues should be apportioned between the initial sale of the IP (typically recognised on the transfer of the IP at the outset) and the subsequent provision of services (typically recognised over the period in which those services are provided). When the contract cannot be unbundled, all the contract revenues would typically be recognised over the period in which services are provided.

Company A should devise an appropriate method for recognising service revenues, which applies the principles of IAS 18 and also meets the objectives of paragraph 10 of IAS 8 *Accounting Policies, Changes in Accounting Estimates and Errors* in presenting information that is reliable in that the financial statements faithfully represent the financial position, financial performance and cash flows of the entity. Although there is no detailed IFRS guidance on this subject, there is guidance within US GAAP, which some IFRS reporters may find helpful. It can be found at 605-28 in the FASB Accounting Standards Codification Manual.

Some possible methods of accounting for such service revenues are illustrated in the example below.

Example 7.5.2

Accounting for contracts with milestone payments and uncertain outcomes

Company A and Company B enter into an agreement under which Company A will transfer to Company B all rights in respect of a drug that has been partly developed by Company A, and then will provide to Company B the service of further developing that drug. If the development process is successful, Company B will market and sell the drug after the appropriate regulatory approval is obtained. The terms of the contract are such that Company A will receive the following payments from Company B at specific 'milestone' points, if and when particular stages of the contract are completed.

	CU
On initial signing of contract	5,000
On successful completion of Stage 1 (drug developed sufficiently to submit for clinical trial)	5,000
On successful completion of Stage 2 (clinical trial successful)	1,500
On successful completion of Stage 3 (regulatory approval obtained)	1,000
Total possible revenue	12,500

Any amounts received by Company A are non-refundable provided that Company A complies with the contract terms (i.e. if a stage is unsuccessful, Company A is not required to refund any amounts already received). Company A has concluded that it is not possible to unbundle the 'initial sale' of the IP from the rest of the contract and will therefore recognise all the revenues received over the period of the contract. Company A is contractually obliged to continue with the development work until either it is successfully completed or both parties agree that the development work will not be successful and should be terminated.

Company A decides that it is appropriate to apply the percentage of completion method using costs incurred as a measure of contract activity, because these are judged to be representative of the effort expended by Company A. Company A currently anticipates the costs of each stage to be as follows.

	CU
Stage 1	4,500
Stage 2	4,000
Stage 3	500
Total costs	9,000

Company A determines that all the costs of a particular stage will be incurred even if that stage is unsuccessful.

Company A concludes, therefore, that there are four possible outcomes in terms of total revenues and costs.

	Total revenue	Total costs	Total margin
	CU	CU	CU
Fail to complete Stage 1 successfully	5,000	4,500	500
Complete Stage 1, but fail to complete Stage 2 successfully	10,000	8,500	1,500
Complete Stage 2, but fail to complete Stage 3 successfully	11,500	9,000	2,500
All stages successful	12,500	9,000	3,500

This example explains and illustrates four methods that are sometimes adopted in practice, which may be considered by Company A when determining an appropriate method for recognising the revenue arising from its contract with Company B.

- **Method 1** – up-front payment recognised as revenue over whole of the contract, other milestone payments recognised in full as each becomes payable (method is appropriate in some circumstances but not others).
- **Method 2** – apply percentage of completion method on assumption that all stages will be completed successfully (method is appropriate in some circumstances but not others).
- **Method 3** – apply Method 2, but limit cumulative revenue recognised to amounts already received or reasonably certain to be received.
- **Method 4** – identify cumulative revenue for each possible outcome of the contract, select most appropriate amount (often the lowest).

Method 1

Under Method 1, any up-front payment is recognised as revenue over the whole period of the contract using an appropriate methodology that reflects the percentage of completion (see IAS 11:30). All other milestone payments are recognised as revenue in full at the point that each becomes payable as per the contract, i.e. when the milestone is judged to have been successfully achieved (see the discussion below for the conditions necessary for this method to be judged appropriate).

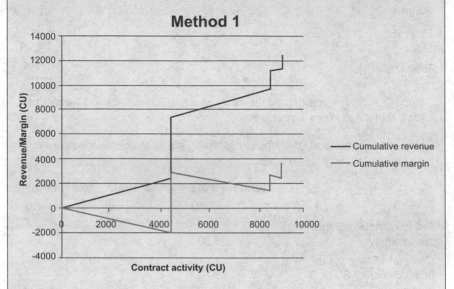

Illustrative calculation using Company A's estimates:

	Revenue recognised	Total revenue recognised to date	Total margin recognised to date
Period from initial signing to completion of Stage 1 (costs estimated as CU4,500)	Spread CU2,500 (CU5,000*4,500/9,000)	CU2,500	CU(2,000)
On completion of Stage 1	CU5,000	CU7,500	CU3,000
Period from completion of Stage 1 to completion of Stage 2 (costs estimated as CU4,000)	Spread CU2,222 (CU5,000*4,000/9,000)	CU9,722	CU1,222
On completion of Stage 2	CU1,500	CU11,222	CU2,722
Period from completion of Stage 2 to completion of Stage 3 (costs estimated as CU500)	Spread CU278 (CU5,000*500/9,000)	CU11,500	CU2,500
On completion of Stage 3	CU1,000	CU12,500	CU3,500

This method may be judged appropriate when, for example, the initial payment broadly corresponds to the total expected contract costs, and the individual milestone payments have been set to represent an appropriate level of profit for successful completion of the preceding stage. However, in some other circumstances, this method may result in revenue being recognised in a manner that is inconsistent with the entity's contract activity, in which case it would not be judged appropriate. For example, consider a scenario in which the up-front payment and the milestone payments have each been set at a level that is intended to cover the entity's costs for the subsequent stage. In other words, the up-front payment is set to cover the costs of Stage 1, the milestone payment at the end of Stage 1 is set to cover the costs of Stage 2 etc. In such a scenario, the milestone payment at the end of Stage 1 might be best matched against the costs of Stage 2, but Method 1 will recognise the revenue from that payment in advance of the Stage 2 costs. Therefore, in some scenarios, the use of this method may not be considered appropriate because it may recognise revenues too early.

Method 1 may not be judged suitable by Company A for this particular contract, because it appears that the initial payment and milestone payments have been set at a level that is broadly intended to fund the subsequent stage's costs, rather than being reflective of contract activity to date. To illustrate, the graph indicates that almost the entire contract margin is recognised on successful completion of Stage 1, whereas a subsequent failure to complete Stage 2 successfully would result in much of the cumulative margin being reversed. Note that, on successful completion of Stage 1, Company A is obliged under the contract to continue with the development work; it is not permitted by the contract to cease contract activity at this stage.

Method 2

Under Method 2, the contract is accounted for on the assumption that it will be completely successful. The IAS 11 percentage of completion method is used to recognise the total contract revenues over the period of the contract (see the discussion below for the conditions necessary for this method to be judged appropriate).

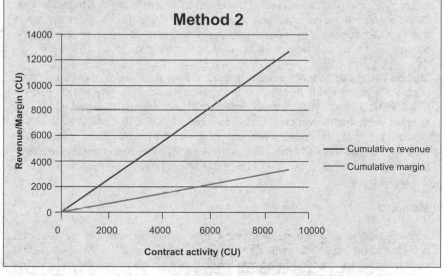

Illustrative calculation using Company A's estimates:

	Revenue recognised (cost for each stage grossed up for overall contract margin)	Total revenue recognised to date	Total margin recognised to date
Period from initial signing to completion of Stage 1	CU6,250 (CU4,500 × 12,500/9,000)	CU6,250	CU1,750
Period from completion of Stage 1 to completion of Stage 2	CU5,556 (CU4,000 × 12,500/9,000)	CU11,806	CU3,306
Period from completion of Stage 2 to completion of Stage 3	CU694 (CU500 × 12,500/9,000)	CU12,500	CU3,500

This method may be judged inappropriate in some circumstances, because it can result in the recognition of revenue that is conditional on successful completion of an uncertain future milestone, and for which there is a significant possibility of reversal in a future period. The method does not take into account the fact that some of the contract revenues are contingent on future events outside the entity's control. In some circumstances, therefore, it will be inappropriate because it would recognise revenues that are not yet reliably measurable, as required by IAS 18.

The method will be appropriate when the amount and timing of milestone payments is such that the cumulative amount of revenue recognised would always be less than the cumulative amount that has become payable under the contract (i.e. there is always a deferred revenue balance recognised in creditors during the life of the contract). This may be the case for contracts when the milestone payments are weighted in advance of contractual performance. However, for contracts in which milestone payments fall in arrears of contractual performance, this method would result in the recognition of receivables that would not be collectible unless subsequent milestones are successfully met. When such receivables are significant, and there is significant uncertainty over meeting the subsequent milestones, the associated revenue should not be recognised because it would not be reliably measurable.

Method 2 may not be judged suitable by Company A for this particular contract, because it could result in revenue being recognised that may not be reliably measurable. For example, immediately prior to completion of Stage 1, Company A would have recognised cumulative revenues of CU6,250, but CU1,250 of this would have to be reversed if Stage 1 is unsuccessful. Similarly, immediately prior to completion of Stage 2, Company A would have recognised cumulative revenues of CU11,806, but CU1,806 of this would have to be reversed if Stage 2 is unsuccessful.

Method 3

This method is a variation on Method 2, which is intended to address the potential issue relating to contingent revenues. Like Method 2, this method first calculates revenue on the basis that the contract will be completely successful and using the IAS 11 percentage of completion method to allocate the total contract revenues over the period of the contract. However, under this method, the entity will then limit the cumulative revenue recognised at any point to the amount that has already been received or is reasonably certain to become receivable at that point in time.

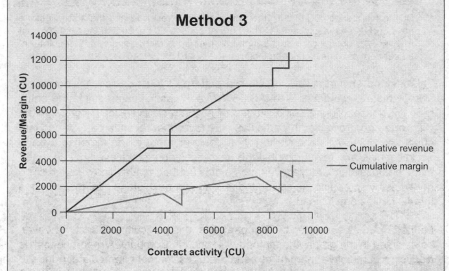

Method 3

Illustrative calculation using Company A's estimates:

	Revenue recognised	Total revenue recognised to date	Total margin recognised to date
Period from initial signing to costs of CU3,600*	CU5,000 (CU3,600 × 12,500/9,000)	CU5,000	CU1,400
Period from costs of CU3,600 to completion of Stage 1 (cumulative costs of CU4,500)	CUnil (cumulative revenue capped at CU5,000)	CU5,000	CU500
At completion of Stage 1	CU1,250 ((CU4,500 × 12,500/9,000) − CU5,000)	CU6,250	CU1,750
Period from completion of Stage 1 to costs of CU7,200**	CU3,750 ((CU7,200 × 12,500/9,000) − CU6,250)	CU10,000	CU2,800
Period from costs of CU7,200 to completion of Stage 2 (cumulative costs of CU8,500)	CUnil (cumulative revenue capped at CU10,000)	CU10,000	CU1,500
At completion of Stage 2	CU1,500 ((CU8,500 × 12,500/9,000 capped at CU11,500) − CU10,000)	CU11,500	CU3,000
At completion of Stage 3 (cumulative costs of CU9,000)	CU1,000 (CU12,500 − CU11,500)	CU12,500	CU3,500

*   During this period, only CU5,000 (the amount initially received) is reasonably certain. This corresponds to 40 per cent of the total contract revenue. Accordingly, it is recognised as the first 40 per cent of costs are incurred (40% × CU9,000 = CU3,600).

**   During this period, CU10,000 (the amount initially received and the first milestone payment) is reasonably certain. This corresponds to 80 per cent of the total contract revenue. Accordingly, the next tranche of revenue is recognised up to the point that 80 per cent of costs have been incurred (80% × CU9,000 = CU7,200)

This method should always result in a pattern of revenue recognition that is acceptable in accordance with IAS 18. Nevertheless, it can result in the entity reporting losses during some stages of a contract, even for a contract that will overall be profitable. In particular, whenever the 'revenue cap' comes into effect, the entity will continue to report costs incurred as an expense but will not recognise any revenues until the next milestone is achieved. (Note that it might be possible to derive a variation of this method that avoids a period of no revenues by spreading the calculated revenue for each stage over the period to the next milestone instead.)

Method 3 could be adopted by Company A for this particular contract. However, as depicted in the graph, the method will result in Company A reporting losses (reducing cumulative margin) at certain stages, namely immediately prior to successful completion of the three milestones. For that reason, Company A may wish to consider Method 4 described below.

Method 4

This method recognises that there are various different possible outcomes in terms of how much revenue will ultimately be received, depending upon which milestones are met. Under this method, the entity will assess what the cumulative revenue would be at the reporting date under the IAS 11 percentage of completion method for each possible outcome of the contract. As the contract progresses, the outcomes will narrow (i.e. when a stage is successfully completed, the number of possible outcomes decreases by one).

The following graph illustrates the possible outcomes for Company A.

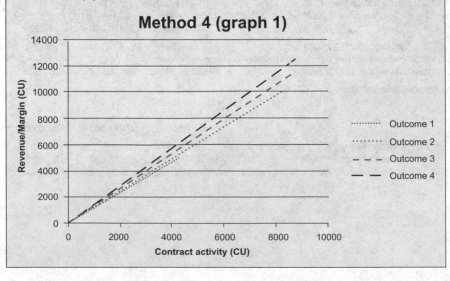

Method 4 (graph 1)

Having calculated the cumulative revenue based on each of the possible outcomes, the entity then assesses which of the figures calculated should be reported, bearing in mind the requirement that revenue should only be recognised to the extent that it is reliably measurable. In many cases, it may be appropriate to recognise cumulative revenue as the lowest of the amounts calculated, because any higher amount would involve recognising revenue that may not be reliably measurable. However, in some circumstances, a higher figure may be judged reliably measurable. For example, when the lowest figure calculated is substantially below the others but the probability associated with the lowest outcome is very low, it may be possible to conclude that the next lowest figure is reliably measurable and, hence, to recognise revenue based on that amount. A consistent method should be used to determine the most appropriate amount to recognise as revenue at each reporting date throughout a contract.

The following graph illustrates the pattern of revenue recognition when Company A has recognised the lowest cumulative amount of revenue at each point throughout the contract.

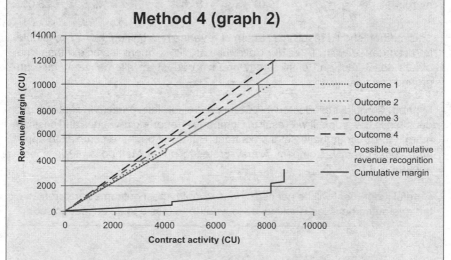

Method 4 (graph 2)

The table below illustrates how Company A's calculations of revenue would be performed assuming that the contract is part way through Stage 1 at the reporting date and the costs incurred to date are CU2,300.

Possible outcomes:

	Fail to complete Stage 1	Complete Stage 1 but fail to complete Stage 2	Complete Stages 1 and 2 but fail to complete Stage 3	Complete Stage 3 – project successful
Costs incurred to date	CU2,300	CU2,300	CU2,300	CU2,300
Total expected costs of project	CU4,500	CU8,500	CU9,000	CU9,000

	Fail to complete Stage 1	Complete Stage 1 but fail to complete Stage 2	Complete Stages 1 and 2 but fail to complete Stage 3	Complete Stage 3 – project successful
% of costs incurred to date (a)	51.1%	27.1%	25.5%	25.5%
Total contracted payments (b)	CU5,000	CU10,000	CU11,500	CU12,500
Revenue at reporting date = (a)*(b)	CU2,556	CU2,706	CU2,939	CU3,194
Margin at reporting date	CU256	CU406	CU639	CU894
Anticipated profit margin	10.0%	15.0%	21.7%	28.0%

This method should result in a pattern of revenue recognition that is acceptable in accordance with IAS 18. Nevertheless, it is more complex than the others described, and entities may prefer to adopt an alternative method on grounds of simplicity.

Method 4 could be adopted by Company A for this particular contract. As depicted in the graph, it will result in Company A reporting revenues and positive margin throughout the life of the contract. But it will be more complex to apply and, consequently, Company A may prefer to adopt Method 3 as described above.

Careful judgement will be needed if, for example, most outcomes are profitable but one outcome is loss making, as to whether a loss should be recognised.

8   Recognition – interest revenue

Interest revenue should be recognised using the effective interest method when:

[IAS 18:29 & 30(a)]

- it is probable that the economic benefits associated with the transaction will flow to the entity; and

- the amount of the revenue can be measured reliably.

The effective interest method is discussed in **4.1** of **chapter B6** (for entities applying IFRS 9) and **4.1** of **chapter C6** (for entities applying IAS 39).

When unpaid interest has accrued before the acquisition of an interest-bearing investment, the subsequent receipt of interest is allocated between the pre-acquisition and post-acquisition periods. [IAS 18:32] Only the post-acquisition portion is recognised as revenue. The pre-acquisition portion will offset the amount recognised at acquisition for interest receivable.

Example 8

Unpaid interest accrued before acquisition of investment

An entity purchases CU1 million face value bonds for CU1,030,000 on 1 April 20X1. The bonds pay interest at 12 per cent per annum on 31 December and 30 June each year.

The investor will receive CU60,000 as interest for the period from 1 January 20X1 to 30 June 20X1, but only CU30,000 of this should be recognised as interest revenue.

Therefore, the entries to record the acquisition of the bond and the receipt of interest at 30 June 20X1 will be as follows.

		CU'000	CU'000
Dr	Investments	1,000	
Dr	Debtor (interest receivable)	30	
Cr	Cash		1,030

To recognise the acquisition of the bond.

		CU'000	CU'000
Dr	Cash	60	
Cr	Debtor (interest receivable)		30
Cr	Interest income (profit or loss)		30

To recognise the receipt of interest.

Interest revenue is recognised only when it is probable that the economic benefits associated with the transaction will flow to the entity. However, when an uncertainty arises about the collectibility of an amount already included in revenue, the uncollectible amount, or the amount in respect of which recovery has ceased to be probable, is recognised as a bad debt expense, rather than as an adjustment of the amount of revenue originally recognised. [IAS 18:34]

9 Recognition – royalty revenue

Royalty revenue should be recognised on an accrual basis in accordance with the substance of the relevant agreement when:

[IAS 18:29 & 30(b)]

- it is probable that the economic benefits associated with the transaction will flow to the entity; and

- the amount of the revenue can be measured reliably.

Royalties accrue in accordance with the terms of the relevant agreement and are usually recognised on that basis unless, having regard to the substance of the agreement, it is more appropriate to recognise revenue on some other systematic and rational basis. [IAS 18:33]

The appendix to IAS 18 contains the following illustration of the principle of revenue recognition for royalty income.

Example 9

Licence fees and royalties

[IAS 18 Illustrative Example 20]

Fees and royalties paid for the use of an entity's assets (such as trademarks, patents, software, music copyright, record masters and motion picture films) are normally recognised in accordance with the substance of the agreement. As a practical matter, this may be on a straight-line basis over the life of the agreement, e.g. when a licensee has the right to use certain technology for a specified period of time.

An assignment of rights for a fixed fee or non-refundable guarantee under a non-cancellable contract which permits the licensee to exploit those rights freely and the licensor has no remaining obligations to perform is, in substance, a sale. An example is a licensing agreement for the use of software when the licensor has no obligations subsequent to delivery. Another example is the granting of rights to exhibit a motion picture film in markets where the licensor has no control over the distributor and expects to receive no further revenues from the box office receipts. In such cases, revenue is recognised at the time of sale.

In some cases, whether or not a licence fee or royalty will be received is contingent on the occurrence of a future event. In such cases, revenue is recognised only when it is probable that the fee or royalty will be received, which is normally when the event has occurred.

Royalty revenue is recognised only when it is probable that the economic benefits associated with the transaction will flow to the entity. When an uncertainty arises about the collectibility of an amount already included in revenue, however, the uncollectible amount, or the amount in respect of which recovery has ceased to be probable, is recognised as a bad debt expense, rather than as an adjustment of the amount of revenue originally recognised. [IAS 18:34]

Royalty agreements vary, but essentially their purpose is to sell a right to use an entity's assets, such as trademarks, patents and software, for a certain period of time. The question arises as to whether, under a royalty agreement, revenue should be recognised up front when the agreement is signed or deferred and spread over the duration of the agreement.

Example 20 in the appendix to IAS 18 states that revenue under royalty agreements should be recognised in accordance with the substance of the arrangements. It further clarifies that the overriding factor in determining the accounting treatment for such arrangements should be whether the licensor has any remaining obligation to perform. The outcome of each arrangement depends on the circumstances. The discussion below describes two typical examples.

Licence to use a trademark

The sale of the right to use a trademark often requires that the licensor (seller) continue to ensure the 'quality' of the trademark. When the requirement imposes a genuine performance obligation (i.e. the licensee could realistically seek redress for non-performance), revenue recognition should be deferred and spread over the period of performance (i.e. the licence term) by the seller. If, however, the requirement is a mere formality and the seller has no remaining obligation to perform, then revenue should be recognised immediately.

Software licensing arrangement

Software licensing arrangements allow the licensee (customer) to use intellectual property. Upon delivery of the software licence, in the absence of any requirement that the licensor (seller) provide technical support, software upgrades or enhancements, a sale has occurred and revenue from the sale should be recognised in full.

If the licensor sells technical support or software upgrades together with the licence, the arrangement should be analysed as to whether it is a multiple-element arrangement, in which case revenue should be recognised separately for each of the identified components (see **5.2**).

When a royalty agreement makes provision for the payment of royalties based on the number of sales subject to a guaranteed minimum amount, careful judgement should be exercised in determining whether the guaranteed minimum amount should be recognised as revenue immediately or spread over the agreement period.

If the seller has no remaining obligation to perform (i.e. the rights and associated assets in respect of which royalties will be paid have been transferred to the customer and there are no ongoing services), the present value of the guaranteed minimum amount of royalties will be recognised immediately provided that there is no significant uncertainty that the amount will be received and the amount is non–refundable. Any additional, variable amounts that are receivable based on future sales should be recognised as revenue only when the sales giving rise to these payments occur.

10   Recognition – dividend revenue

10.1   Recognition criteria – dividend revenue

Dividend revenue should be recognised when:

[IAS 18:29 & 30(c)]

- it is probable that the economic benefits associated with the transaction will flow to the entity;

- the amount of the revenue can be measured reliably; and

- the shareholder's right to receive payment is established.

The timing of the establishment of the shareholders' right to receive payment may vary based on the laws of particular countries. In some countries, it may occur when the board of directors of an entity formally declares its intention to pay a dividend. In other countries, it may occur only after such a declaration has been approved by shareholders. In any case if, subsequent to revenue recognition but before receipt of the dividend, it becomes apparent that the investee will not be able to pay the dividend, the amount of dividend revenue previously recognised is dealt with as a bad debt expense rather than as a reversal of dividend revenue. [IAS 18:34]

10.2   Dividends on equity investments declared from pre-acquisition profits

Until it was amended in May 2008, IAS 18 required that, when dividends on equity investments are declared from pre-acquisition profits, those dividends should be deducted from the cost of the investment. Following the May 2008 amendments (effective for annual periods beginning on or after 1 January 2009), dividend revenue is recognised in profit or loss irrespective of whether it is declared from pre- or post-acquisition profits and, separately, in some cases it is necessary to consider whether the equity investment may be impaired.

10.3   Dividends in the form of equity instruments of the investee

Example 10.3A

Dividends in the form of equity instruments of the investee (no cash alternative)

I Limited holds an equity investment in Entity A. Entity A distributes a dividend in the form of its own equity shares to all of its ordinary shareholders on a pro rata basis. No cash alternative is offered. After the distribution, the relative shareholdings of the investors in Entity A remain unchanged.

Should I Limited recognise dividend revenue for the fair value of the shares in Entity A it receives?

No. When all ordinary shareholders are paid a share dividend on a pro rata basis, there is no change in the financial position or economic interest of any of the investors. In such circumstances, in accordance with IAS 18:29(a), the dividend is not recognised as revenue because it is not probable that there is an economic benefit associated with the transaction that will flow to the investor.

Example 10.3B

Dividends in the form of equity instruments of the investee (with a cash alternative)

I Limited holds an equity instrument in Entity A. Entity A offers all of its shareholders the right to receive a dividend in cash or in shares. I Limited subsequently elects to receive the dividend in shares.

How should I Limited recognise the dividend received?

The substance of a share dividend with a cash alternative is that of a dividend in cash with an immediate reinvestment in shares. Accordingly, at the date the dividend is authorised (i.e. the date when the shareholders' right to receive the dividend is established), I Limited should recognise the dividend as revenue, measured at the higher of the value of the shares offered and the value of the cash alternative. This reflects the fact the investor would be expected to opt for the most economically advantageous alternative.

From the date of authorisation of the dividend until the date on which I Limited elects to receive cash or shares, the estimated revenue should be adjusted to reflect changes in the fair value of the shares but it should never fall below the value of the cash alternative.

On the date that I Limited makes its final election, the revenue amount becomes fixed.

11 Disclosure

Entities are required to disclose the accounting policies adopted for revenue recognition, including the methods adopted to determine the stage of completion of transactions involving the rendering of services. [IAS 18:35(a)]

The following should be considered, depending on the circumstances, for disclosure in the revenue recognition accounting policy:

- if an entity has different policies for different types of revenue transactions, the policy for each material type of transaction should be disclosed;

- if sales transactions have multiple elements, such as products and services, the disclosure should include the accounting policy for each element as well as how multiple elements are determined and valued;

- changes in estimates that underlie revenue recognition, such as changes in estimated returns, should be disclosed; and

- any specific revenue transactions that are unusual because of their nature, size, or frequency of occurrence may require separate disclosure.

The amount of each significant category of revenue recognised during the period is also required to be disclosed, including revenue arising from:

[IAS 18:35(b)]

- the sale of goods;

- the rendering of services;

- interest;

- royalties; and

- dividends.

The entity is also required to disclose the amount of revenue arising from exchanges of goods or services included in each significant category of revenue. [IAS 18:35(c)]

IFRIC 15 *Agreements for the Construction of Real Estate* requires certain disclosures when an entity recognises revenue using the percentage of completion method for agreements that meet all the criteria in IAS 18:14 continuously as construction progresses. These disclosures are described in **2.2.4**.

Appendix A2 Construction contracts (IAS 11)

Contents

1 Introduction

1.1 Overview of IAS 11

IAS 11 *Construction Contracts* sets out requirements on the allocation of contract revenue and contract costs to accounting periods in which construction work is performed. Contract revenues and expenses are recognised by reference to the stage of completion of contract activity when the outcome of the construction contract can be estimated reliably, otherwise revenue is recognised only to the extent of recoverable contract costs incurred.

1.2 Amendments to IAS 11 since the last edition of this manual

None. IAS 11 was most recently amended in September 2007.

1.3 IAS 11 superseded by IFRS 15

In May 2014, the IASB issued IFRS 15 *Revenue from Contracts with Customers*, which is effective for annual periods beginning on or after 1 January 2018, with earlier application permitted. IFRS 15 supersedes IAS 11 (see **15.1** in **chapter A14** for more detail regarding the effective date). For annual periods beginning before 1 January 2018, entities may continue to apply IAS 11, which is discussed in this appendix. Alternatively, entities may choose to apply IFRS 15 in advance of its 2018 effective date, provided that they disclose that fact. The requirements of IFRS 15 are discussed in detail in **chapter A14**.

Note that if an entity wishes to apply IFRS 16 *Leases* (see **chapter A17**) for an annual period beginning before 1 January 2019, it is also required to apply IFRS 15 rather than IAS 18.

IFRS 15 also supersedes the following related IFRSs, all of which are dealt with in **appendix A1**:

- IAS 18 *Revenue*;
- IFRIC 13 *Customer Loyalty Programmes*;
- IFRIC 15 *Agreements for the Construction of Real Estate*;
- IFRIC 18 *Transfers of Assets from Customers*; and
- SIC-31 *Revenue – Barter Transactions Involving Advertising Services*.

2 Scope

IAS 11 deals with the accounting for construction contracts in the financial statements of contractors. [IAS 11:1]

The term 'contractors' is not defined in IAS 11 but can be taken to refer to reporting entities engaged in contracting activities.

A construction contract is defined as a contract specifically negotiated for the construction of an asset or a combination of assets that are closely interrelated or interdependent in terms of their design, technology and function or their ultimate purpose or use. [IAS 11:3]

IAS 11 does not provide for a minimum duration (such as one year) for the construction contracts falling within its scope. Nor does it refer to 'long-term contracts'. The principles of IAS 11 will need to be applied for all construction contracts under which the contract activity starts in one reporting period and ends in another, thus creating an allocation problem for contract income and expenses.

When an entity is, for example, engaged in the construction of large machines that are individually built to customer order and unique specifications, such activity will also fall within the scope of IAS 11. IAS 11:4 cites as examples of construction contracts the construction of single assets such as a bridge, building, dam, pipeline, road, ship or tunnel. However, this is not a complete list – and the manufacture of machines built to customer order and specifications with a negotiated price falls within the definition of a construction contract.

Whether the asset under construction is tangible or intangible is not relevant to the definition of a construction contract in IAS 11; therefore, it is possible for contracts for the construction of intangible assets, such as software, to be within the scope of IAS 11. An entity should carefully assess each software development contract to determine whether it meets the definition of a construction contract (see above). Software development contracts for fully bespoke products meet the definition of a construction contract in IAS 11 and should be accounted for in accordance with IAS 11, including all of the disclosure requirements. Contracts for the supply of software products already developed in-house or with minimal customisation fall into the scope of IAS 18 *Revenue* as the supply of goods.

In the context of IAS 11, construction contracts include:

[IAS 11:5]

- contracts for the rendering of services that are directly related to the construction of assets, e.g. those for the services of project managers and architects; and

- contracts for the destruction or restoration of assets, and the restoration of the environment following the demolition of assets.

IAS 11 does not address the accounting for other long-term contracts (e.g. long-term service contracts other than those referred to in the previous paragraph). The recognition of revenue under such contracts is dealt with under IAS 18 (see **appendix A1**). The general principle established in IAS 18:20 is that revenue should be recognised by reference to the stage of completion of a service transaction at the end of the reporting period, which is consistent with IAS 11. Therefore, although service contracts do not fall generally within the scope of IAS 11, they will be dealt with under IAS 18 using principles consistent with those established in IAS 11, and IAS 11 provides useful guidance in this regard.

In some circumstances, careful judgement may be required to determine whether a contract should be regarded as being for the supply of construction services or simply for the supply of goods. In particular, merely because a contract requires items to be supplied that have not yet been constructed, it does not necessarily follow that the contract is for construction services.

IFRIC 15 *Agreements for the Construction of Real Estate* addresses whether an agreement is within the scope of IAS 11 or IAS 18, and when revenue from the construction of real estate should be recognised. [IFRIC 15:6] The Interpretation is discussed at **2.2** in **appendix A1**.

3   Types of construction contract

The compensation element of construction contracts can be negotiated in a number of ways. IAS 11 classifies contracts according to their compensation element as being either fixed price contracts or cost plus contracts.

A fixed price contract is defined as a construction contract in which the contractor agrees to a fixed contract price, or a fixed rate per unit of output, which in some cases is subject to cost escalation clauses. [IAS 11:3]

A cost plus contract is defined as a construction contract in which the contractor is reimbursed for allowable or otherwise defined costs, plus a percentage of those costs or a fixed fee. [IAS 11:3]

Some construction contracts may have characteristics of both fixed price and cost plus contracts. For example, a cost plus contract may nevertheless be subject to a maximum price. When assessing whether the outcome of such a contract can be estimated reliably, it will be necessary to consider the factors discussed both at **7.2.1** and at **7.2.2**. [IAS 11:6]

4 Combining and segmenting contracts

4.1 Combining and segmenting contracts – general

The requirements of IAS 11 are usually applied to individual construction contracts. However, in some circumstances, it may be appropriate to treat several related contracts as forming one contract or, conversely, to treat one contract as comprising several separate contracts. The main factor in making such a determination is the manner in which the contract is negotiated. However, the Standard sets out several other factors that are to be considered, as discussed at **4.2** to **4.4**.

The requirements of IAS 11 regarding the combining and segmenting of contracts are aimed at reflecting the substance of the transaction(s) rather than their legal or contractual form. The underlying question is whether the contractor negotiated the contract and the related profit independently of other related contracts, or the deal was negotiated as a package, albeit legally segregated into several contracts. The combination (or segregation) of contracts can have a significant impact, as can be seen from the following example.

Example 4.1

Effects of combining and segmenting contracts

A Limited has five construction contracts in progress at the end of 20X1, as set out in the table below. Assume that the outcome of each contract can be estimated reliably and that the stage of completion is estimated on the basis of the proportion that contract costs incurred for work performed to date bear to the estimated total contract costs (see **7.3**).

| | \multicolumn{6}{c}{Contract} |
| | 1 | 2 | 3 | 4 | 5 | Total |
	CU'000	CU'000	CU'000	CU'000	CU'000	CU'000
Total contract revenue	250	600	550	300	180	1,880
Total contract costs	210	450	450	350	210	1,670
Expected profit (loss)	40	150	100	(50)	(30)	210
Costs incurred to December 20X1	84	390	450	35	42	1,001
Stage of completion at December 20X1	40%	87%	100%	10%	20%	60%

If all of the contracts are combined and treated as one contract, A Limited recognises 60 per cent of the total expected profit of CU210,000 (i.e. a profit of CU126,000).

If each contract is treated separately, A Limited recognises the following profits and losses in 20X1.

	Contract					
	1	2	3	4	5	Total
Expected profit (loss) CU'000	40	150	100	(50)	(30)	
Percentage complete	40%	87%	100%	10%	20%	
Percentage of profit (loss) recognised	40%	87%	100%	100%	100%	
Profit (loss) CU'000	16	130	100	(50)	(30)	166

4.2 Segregating contracts

A construction contract may cover the construction of more than one asset. When this is the case, such projects are required to be treated as separate contracts when:

[IAS 11:8]

- separate proposals have been submitted for each asset;
- each asset has been subject to separate negotiation and the contractor and customer have been able to accept or reject that part of the contract relating to each asset; and
- the costs and revenues of each asset can be separately identified.

Example 4.2

Segmenting a contract covering the construction of more than one asset

A contractor submits two separate bids for the construction of a 10-mile section of motorway and a bridge included in the 10-mile stretch. The government has structured the tender process such that the contract for the motorway construction will be awarded separately from the contract for the bridge construction. The contractor wins both bids, and a single contract covering both projects is signed with the government without modifying the terms and conditions included in the bids.

Because separate proposals were submitted for the motorway and the bridge, even if one contractor wins the work on both projects and the terms agreed with the government for both projects are included in one legal contract, each project, the bridge and the motorway, will be accounted for separately under IAS 11. In order to segment the contract, the contractor will need to have a cost system in place identifying the costs and revenues attributable to each part of the contract.

The key determinant is whether the customer is able to accept one proposal and reject the other. Segmenting contracts is not a matter of choice, but is required when the criteria in IAS 11:8 are met.

4.3   Combining contracts

A group of contracts should be treated as a single contract, notwithstanding that the contracts may be with different counterparties, when:

[IAS 11:9]

- the group of contracts is negotiated as a single package;
- the contracts are so closely interrelated that they are, in effect, part of a single project with an overall profit margin; and
- the contracts are performed concurrently or in a continuous sequence.

Example 4.3

Combining contracts to be accounted for as a single contract

A contractor submits one bid for the construction of a 10-mile section of motorway and a bridge which is at one end of the 10-mile stretch. The bridge is in a different jurisdiction from the motorway and, therefore, although only one bid is submitted because the two local authorities have agreed to work together on the construction of the road, separate contracts exist for the bridge and the motorway because the counterparties (the two local authorities) are different.

Because one proposal was submitted for the motorway and the bridge, even if two separate contracts are eventually signed, the contracts have been negotiated as a single package. The bid was submitted on the basis that one project could not be awarded without the other, and so the contractor must have worked out the expected gross margin on both projects together. Therefore, the two separate contracts will be accounted for as one contract under IAS 11.

For combination to be required, the group of contracts must be performed concurrently or in a continuous sequence. If performance is separated by a period of time long enough to result in differing economic environments in the periods of performance, then separate accounting should be applied.

Combining contracts is not a matter of choice, but is required when the criteria in IAS 11:9 are met.

4.4 Construction of additional assets

A construction contract may provide an option for the construction of an additional asset or the customer may amend the contract to include the construction of an additional asset. In such circumstances, the construction of the additional asset is required to be treated as a separate construction contract when:

[IAS 11:10]

- the asset differs significantly in design, technology or function from the asset or assets covered by the original contract; or

- the price of the asset is negotiated without regard to the original contract price.

Example 4.4

Construction of an additional asset to be treated as a separate contract?

A contractor is nearing completion of a 10-mile stretch of motorway under a contract with the government. Under the contract, the contractor is paid CU10 million per mile. A supplementary contract is signed between the government and the contractor to cover an additional three miles of motorway at the same rate of CU10 million per mile. The supplementary contract should be accounted for as part of the original contract under IAS 11 because the pricing is the same as originally negotiated, and the asset (motorway) does not differ significantly from the asset (motorway) covered by the original contract.

---

5 Contract revenue

5.1 Estimation of contract revenue

In order to apply the accounting principles specified by IAS 11, an entity must be able to estimate contract revenue and costs. This section deals with the components of contract revenue.

The measurement of contract revenue is affected by a variety of uncertainties that depend on the outcome of future events. The estimates often need to be revised as events occur and uncertainties are resolved. Therefore, the estimate of contract revenue may increase or decrease from one period to the next, for example as a result of:

[IAS 11:12]

- variations or claims agreed between the contractor and the customer in a period subsequent to that in which the contract was initially agreed;

- in the case of a fixed price contract, cost escalation clauses;

- penalties arising from delays caused by the contractor in the completion of the contract; and

- in the case of a fixed price contract involving a fixed price per unit of output, increases or decreases in the number of units.

The Standard stipulates that the entity's estimate of contract revenue at any point in time should comprise:

[IAS 11:11]

- the initial amount of revenue agreed in the construction contract; and

- variations, claims and incentive payments to the extent that it is probable that they will result in revenue and that they are capable of being reliably measured.

The revenue recognition criteria for variations, claims and incentive payments are the same as for other types of revenue. The additional criteria discussed in the following sections are intended to illustrate how the general revenue recognition criteria should be applied to variations, claims and incentive payments.

IAS 11 requires that contractors should recognise variations, claims and incentive payments once the specified criteria have been met. An accounting policy of not recognising these items until they are realised would not be acceptable under IAS 11.

5.2   Variations

A variation is defined in IAS 11:13 as an instruction by the customer for a change in the scope of the work to be performed under the contract. Depending on the circumstances, variations may lead to increases or decreases in contract revenue. For example, once a project has been negotiated, a customer may finalise the design of the item to be constructed, and the changes in design may have implications for the amount of work required from the contractor.

In practice, problems arise when assessing the likelihood of recovery of variations and, thus, whether they should be included in contract revenue. IAS 11 indicates that a variation should be included in contract revenue when:

[IAS 11:13]

- it is probable that the customer will approve the variation and the amount of revenue arising from the variation; and

- the amount of revenue can be reliably measured.

In many cases, it is a matter of judgement as to whether a variation will be approved by the customer and, due to the fact that the amount recovered is often based on a negotiation process, the amount included in contract revenue relating to variations is also usually an estimate.

5.3 Claims

A claim is defined in IAS 11:14 as an amount that the contractor seeks to collect from the customer or another party as reimbursement for costs not included in the contract price. A claim in this context does not usually imply that a legal claim has been filed in a court of law. Claims may arise from customer-caused delays, errors in specifications or design, or disputed variations in contract work. Since claims are initiated by the contractor, their recoverability may be even more uncertain than that of variations. The amount included in contract revenue with respect to claims is therefore an estimate based on management's judgement. As for variations, claims are often settled at the end of the contract as a result of a negotiation. IAS 11 indicates that claims should only be included in contract revenue when:

[IAS 11:14]

- negotiations have reached an advanced stage such that it is probable that the customer will accept the claim; and

- the amount that it is probable will be accepted by the customer can be measured reliably.

5.4 Incentive payments

Incentive payments are additional amounts paid to the contractor if specified performance standards are met or exceeded. Commonly, such incentive payments relate to completion dates and, thus, the earlier the work is completed, the more contract revenue will be receivable. IAS 11 indicates that incentive payments should be included in contract revenue when:

[IAS 11:15]

- the contract is sufficiently advanced that it is probable that the specified performance standards will be met or exceeded; and

- the amount of the incentive payments can be measured reliably.

5.5 Sales revenue denominated in foreign currency

When a construction contract is entered into that is denominated in a currency different from the functional currency of the reporting entity, the revenue recognised incrementally over the course of the contract will be the incremental foreign currency revenue translated at the spot rate. This treatment reflects the general requirement of IAS 21 *The Effects of Changes in Foreign Exchange Rates* that foreign currency transactions should be recognised by applying to the foreign currency amount the spot exchange rate between the functional currency and the foreign currency at the date of the transaction. [IAS 21:21] In practice, if incremental revenue accrues fairly steadily over a period, it may be acceptable to translate it at an average rate for that period unless exchange rates for the period fluctuate significantly.

In some cases, a contract denominated in a currency different from the functional currency of the reporting entity may contain an embedded derivative that is not 'closely related' to the host contract. The circumstances in which this may arise and the associated accounting requirements are discussed in **chapter B5** (for entities applying IFRS 9 *Financial Instruments*) and **chapter C5** (for entities that have not yet adopted IFRS 9).

6   Contract costs

6.1   Components of contract costs

Contract costs should comprise the components listed in the following table.

| Costs that relate directly to the specific contract. [IAS 11:16(a)] | Including:

[IAS 11:17]

• site labour costs, including supervision;
• costs of materials used in construction;
• depreciation of plant and equipment used on the contract;
• costs of moving plant, equipment and materials to and from the contract site;
• costs of hiring plant and equipment;
• costs of design and technical assistance that are directly related to the contract;
• the estimated costs of rectification work and guarantee work, including expected warranty costs; and
• claims from third parties.

These costs may be reduced by any incidental income that is not included in contract revenue, such as income from the sale of surplus materials or equipment at the end of the contract. |

Costs that are attributable to contract activity in general and can be allocated to the contract. [IAS 11:16(b)] Allocation should be based on the normal level of construction activity. Methods used should be systematic and rational, and applied consistently to all costs having similar characteristics. [IAS 11:18]	Including: [IAS 11:18] ● insurance; ● costs of design and technical assistance that are not directly related to a specific contract; ● construction overheads; and ● borrowing costs*
Other costs that are specifically chargeable to the customer under the terms of the contract. [IAS 11:16(c)]	These may include general administration costs and development costs for which reimbursement is specified in the terms of the contract. [IAS 11:19]

> * Borrowing costs should be reduced by any investment income arising on the temporary investment of funds borrowed specifically for the assets concerned. For example, when a contract is funded by advances from the customer, and no interest is charged on those advances, any interest income earned on the temporary investment of those advances is treated as a negative contract cost.

When costs cannot be allocated or attributed to a particular contract, they are not included in contract costs. The Standard identifies the following costs that should be excluded from contract costs:

[IAS 11:20]

● general administration costs for which reimbursement is not specified in the contract;

● selling costs;

● research and development costs for which reimbursement is not specified in the contract; and

● depreciation of idle plant and equipment that is not used on a particular contract.

6.2   Pre-contract costs

6.2.1   Costs incurred in securing a contract

Costs should generally be allocated to a contract only from the date of securing the contract. However, IAS 11:21 specifies that the direct costs associated with securing a contract should be included in the cost of the contract if they can be separately identified and measured reliably, and it is probable that the contract will be obtained. Otherwise, they should be expensed in the period in which they are incurred.

Example 6.2.1

Pre-contract costs

Company Z is a software design company that develops software specifically suited for a particular entity. In order to secure a contract with a particular entity, Company Z incurs costs as part of its bid on a project. Such costs may include labour costs, general administration costs, research and development costs etc. Many of these costs are incurred prior to securing the contract (and are referred to below as 'pre-contract costs').

Paragraph 4.44 of the IASB's *Conceptual Framework for Financial Reporting* states that an "asset is recognised in the [statement of financial position] when it is probable that the future economic benefits will flow to the entity and the asset has a cost or value that can be measured reliably".

General administration costs for which reimbursement is not specified in the contract are identified in IAS 11:20, among others, as examples of costs that should be excluded from contract costs because they cannot be attributed to contract activity or allocated to a contract. Therefore, any overhead costs incurred in the 'pre-contract' period should be expensed when incurred (unless the contract specifies that they are to be reimbursed).

Under IAS 11:21, other pre-contract costs should be included as part of contract costs if:

● they relate directly to the contract;

● they were incurred in securing the contract;

● they can be separately identified;

● they can be measured reliably; and

● it is probable that the contract will be obtained.

A great deal of care should be taken when determining whether pre-contract costs should be capitalised.

If pre-contract costs have been capitalised, and it subsequently transpires that it is no longer considered probable that the contract will be obtained, the costs should be recognised in profit or loss immediately.

The conclusions above were confirmed by the IFRIC (now the IFRS Interpretations Committee) in the August 2002 *IFRIC Update*.

6.2.2   *Pre-contract costs that have already been expensed*

If pre-contract costs of the nature referred to at **6.2.1** are recognised as an expense in the period in which they are incurred, and the contract is subsequently awarded to the reporting entity, the costs should not be included in contract costs. [IAS 11:21]

Example 6.2.2

Pre-contract costs that have already been expensed

An entity incurred CU3 million of pre-contract costs during December 20X1, which were directly attributable to the anticipated contract and which the entity believed would be recoverable under that contract. However, due to uncertainty regarding the outcome, the costs were expensed when they were incurred in 20X1. The contract was ultimately signed in 20X2 for a price of CU18 million. The entity's remaining estimated costs to complete the contract were CU6 million.

Because the pre-contract costs were already recognised as expenses in the 20X1 financial year, they should be excluded from contract costs. The entity should account for this contract prospectively, recognising CU18 million of contract revenue and CU6 million of contract costs as work on the contract is performed.

It is not appropriate to include pre-contract costs that have previously been expensed in contract costs for the purposes of determining the stage of completion of a contract when the stage of completion is determined on a proportionate-cost basis. Such costs are excluded both from the measure of contract costs incurred to date and the estimate of total contract costs.

7 Recognition of contract revenue and costs

7.1 The percentage of completion method

As a general principle, IAS 11 requires that construction contracts are accounted for using the percentage of completion method, i.e. that contract revenue and contract costs associated with a contract should be recognised as revenue and expenses, respectively, by reference to the stage of completion of the contract at the end of the reporting period.

Under this method, at the end of the reporting period, an entity estimates the outcome, or total profit or loss, expected to be achieved on a contract. As part of this process, the entity estimates the stage or percentage of completion of the contract. When the entity is able to make a reliable estimate of the outcome of the contract, it applies the estimated percentage of completion to the total expected revenue and expenses related to the contract to determine the amount of revenue and cost to be recognised in the period. If an entity expects that a loss will be made on the contract, it is recognised immediately. [IAS 11:22]

It is not acceptable under IAS 11 to recognise all of the revenue and costs related to a contract at the end of the contract (sometimes referred to as the 'completed-contract' method).

7.2   When can the outcome of a construction contract be estimated reliably?

7.2.1   Fixed price contracts

For fixed price contracts (as described in **section 3**), IAS 11:23 specifies that the outcome of a construction contract can be estimated reliably when all of the following conditions are satisfied:

- total contract revenue can be measured reliably;

- it is probable that the economic benefits associated with the contract will flow to the entity;

- both the contract costs to complete the contract and the stage of contract completion at the end of the reporting period can be measured reliably; and

- the contract costs attributable to the contract can be clearly identified and measured reliably so that actual contract costs incurred can be compared with prior estimates.

7.2.2   Cost plus contracts

For cost plus contracts (as described in **section 3**), IAS 11:24 specifies that the outcome of a construction contract can be estimated reliably when both of the following conditions are satisfied:

- it is probable that the economic benefits associated with the contract will flow to the entity; and

- the contract costs attributable to the contract, whether or not specifically reimbursable, can be clearly identified and measured reliably.

Thus, when an entity enters into a cost plus contract, in order to estimate reliably the outcome of the contract, it must be able to identify contract costs attributable to the contract, whether or not they are specifically reimbursable. Unlike a fixed price contract, the amount of revenue related to a cost plus contract is generally unknown but can be calculated based on the terms of the contract and the estimated costs of the contract. In addition, in order to use the percentage of completion method, it must be probable that the economic benefits will flow to the entity.

7.3 Estimating the stage of completion

For both fixed price and cost plus contracts, the percentage of completion of a contract at the end of the reporting period must be estimated. In practice, progress payments or advances received from a customer are not normally reliable indicators of the percentage of completion of a contract, because they are usually intended to fund the activities of the contractor rather than to reimburse it for work performed to date. IAS 11 suggests several bases for estimating the percentage of completion, including:

[IAS 11:30]

- the proportion that contract costs incurred for work performed to date bear to the estimated total contract costs;

- surveys of work performed; and

- completion of a physical proportion of the contract work.

The selection of the most appropriate method for the estimation of the stage of completion of a project should be made by each entity according to its own circumstances and the nature of its business. For example, the main contractor normally hires an architect to certify the progress of contracts and, therefore, appropriate surveys of work performed are readily available for the purpose of ascertaining the percentage of completion of a contract. On the other hand, subcontractors may be more likely to rely on estimates of the proportion that costs incurred to date bear to the estimated total contract costs or, when appropriate, on the completion of a physical proportion of the contract work.

IAS 11 does not include any explicit requirement for the calculation of attributable profit to take into account any known inequalities of profitability in the various stages of a contract. Nevertheless, when identifying the most appropriate method by which to apply IAS 11, it is generally appropriate to take account of such inequalities, because doing so results in a more accurate estimate of the extent to which a construction contract has been performed, and of the costs associated with that performance.

When the stage of completion is determined by reference to the contract costs incurred to date, only those contract costs that reflect work performed are included in costs incurred to date. For example, contract costs that relate to future activity on the contract, such as costs of materials that have been purchased but not yet used, or payments made to subcontractors in advance of work being performed, should be excluded from costs incurred to date. However, if materials have been made specifically for the contract, they are included in contract costs even if they have not yet been used, on the basis that it is unlikely that they would be suitable for use on other contracts. [IAS 11:31]

Example 7.3A

Treatment of prepaid costs in estimating the percentage of completion (1)

A contractor undertakes a three-year contract. At the end of Year 1, management estimates are as follows.

	CU
Revenue	1,000
Costs incurred to date	(300)
Estimated costs to complete	(600)
Estimated gross profit	100

During Year 1, the contractor purchased materials for CU50 to be used in Year 2. Therefore, when calculating the percentage of completion of this contract, based on the proportion of costs incurred to date to total costs of the contract, an adjustment is made in respect of the purchased materials not yet used.

	CU
Costs incurred to date	300
Less: materials purchased for future years	(50)
Costs incurred related to work performed to date	250
Total estimated costs	900
Percentage of completion at end of Year 1	28%

Therefore, in Year 1, contract revenue of CU280 and contract costs of CU250 are recognised in profit or loss.

At a minimum, at the end of each reporting period, an entity reviews its estimates relating to the outcome of a contract and makes revisions as appropriate. Because the percentage of completion method is applied to each contract on a cumulative basis, revisions are treated as changes in estimates and are used in estimating the percentage of completion and the outcome of the contract in the period of change and in future periods. As such, prior periods are not adjusted. [IAS 11:38] In practice, most contractors review progress and expected outcomes much more frequently than at the end of each reporting period in order to maintain control over the project.

Example 7.3B

Treatment of prepaid costs in estimating the percentage of completion (2)

The facts are the same as in **example 7.3A**. In Year 2, costs of CU300 are incurred. Management estimates that costs of CU350 will be incurred in Year 3.

	CU
Costs incurred in Year 1 relating to work performed to date	250
Costs incurred in Year 1 relating to materials used in Year 2	50
Other costs incurred in Year 2	300
Costs incurred to date	600
Estimated costs to complete	350
Total estimated costs	950
Estimated revenue	1,000
Estimated gross profit	50
Percentage of completion at end of Year 2	63%

No adjustment is made to the revenue or expenses recognised in Year 1 due to the change in estimate in Year 2.

Therefore, in Year 2, contract revenue of CU350 (i.e. CU1,000 × 63% – CU280 revenue already recognised in Year 1) and contract costs of CU350 (i.e. CU600 – CU250) are recognised in profit or loss.

In many contracts, some level of wastage is unavoidable as part of the construction process, and will be forecast within the entity's budgets and estimates and included in contract costs. When, as a result of the entity's inefficiency or error, abnormal or excessive costs occur that could otherwise have been avoided, these are likely to relate to a particular period and should, therefore, be recognised as an expense in that period.

Such costs do not reflect additional progress on a contract and should be excluded from contract costs for the purpose of determining the stage of completion. Therefore, if costs incurred to date are used to determine the stage of completion on a contract, care should be taken to ensure that revenue attributed to work carried out is not increased to offset additional costs incurred when abnormal or excessive costs arise through inefficiency or error rather than as a result of further progress on the contract.

For a discussion of the accounting treatment in the circumstances in which a reliable estimate of the outcome of a contract cannot be made, see **7.7**.

7.4 Recognition of contract losses

When an entity estimates that the outcome of a contract will be a loss, the expected loss is recognised as an expense immediately. [IAS 11:36] The amount of the loss is the expected loss on the entire contract, and thus is determined without reference to:

[IAS 11:37]

- whether or not work has commenced on the contract;
- the stage of completion of contract activity; or
- the amount of profits expected to arise on other contracts which are not treated as the same contract under the rules of IAS 11 (see **section 4**).

Example 7.4

Recognition of contract losses

The facts are the same as in **example 7.3B**, except that in Year 2 the estimated costs to complete the contract in Year 3 are CU500.

	CU
Costs incurred to date	600
Estimated costs to complete	500
Total estimated costs	1,100
Estimated revenue	1,000
Estimated loss	(100)
Percentage of completion at end of Year 2	54.5%

Because management now estimates a loss on the contract, the CU100 loss is recognised immediately as an expense in Year 2 when the estimate is made. In addition, any profit recognised in Year 1 is reversed in Year 2, with the result that the total loss reported in Year 2 is CU130.

Accordingly, in Year 2, contract revenue of CU265 (i.e. CU1,000 × 54.5% − CU280 revenue already recognised in Year 1) is recognised in profit or loss. The loss relating to work already performed is CU55 (i.e. cumulative revenue of CU545 less cumulative costs of CU600, or 54.5% of total losses of CU100), so a provision is required for future losses of CU45. Thus, in Year 2, total contract costs (including the provision for future losses) of CU395 (i.e. CU600 − CU250 + CU45) are recognised in profit or loss.

7.5   Recognition of contract revenue

In order to recognise the revenue earned to date on a contract, it must be probable that the associated future economic benefits will flow to the entity and that their amount can be estimated reliably. In general, the amount of future economic benefits can be estimated reliably when it is possible to estimate reliably the outcome of a contract as described above. If it becomes apparent subsequent to recognition as income that the revenue related to a contract will not be collectible, the uncollectible amount is recognised as an expense rather than as an adjustment to contract revenue. [IAS 11:28]

The amount of revenue recognised in a period is determined by applying the estimated percentage of completion at the end of the reporting period to total contract revenue.

7.6 Recognition of contract costs

When the proportion of contract costs incurred for work performed to date to total contract costs is used to estimate the percentage of completion, this generally results in contract costs being expensed in the period incurred. If costs have been incurred which relate to future activity on the contract, they may be carried forward provided that it is probable that they will be recovered under the contract. [IAS 11:27] Such costs may relate to, but are not limited to, materials purchased for future use or advance payments to subcontractors.

When contract costs are not probable of being recovered, they are recognised as an expense immediately. IAS 11 gives the following examples of circumstances when the recoverability of contract costs incurred may not be probable, and when contract costs may need to be recognised as an expense immediately:

[IAS 11:34]

- contracts that are not fully enforceable, i.e. their validity is seriously in question;

- contracts whose completion is subject to the outcome of pending litigation or legislation;

- contracts relating to properties that are likely to be condemned or expropriated;

- contracts where the customer is unable to meet its obligations; and

- contracts where the contractor is unable to complete the contract or otherwise meet its obligations under the contract.

7.7 Outcome of contract cannot be estimated reliably

When the outcome of a contract cannot be estimated reliably, IAS 11:32 specifies that:

- revenue should be recognised only to the extent of contract costs incurred that it is probable will be recoverable; and

- contract costs should be recognised as an expense in the period in which they are incurred.

When the outcome of a contract cannot be estimated, it is inappropriate to recognise any profit on that contract. This is achieved by limiting the revenue recognised to the extent of costs incurred that are expected to be recoverable, with all costs being recognised as expenses as incurred. This method is often referred to as the 'zero profit' method.

Even when the outcome of a contract cannot be estimated reliably, it may be possible to foresee that total contract costs will exceed total contract revenues, i.e. that not all contract costs will be recoverable. In such circumstances, the expected excess of total contract costs over total contract revenue should be recognised as an expense immediately.

Example 7.7

Outcome of contract cannot be estimated reliably

The facts are the same as in **example 7.3A**, except that management is unable to estimate reliably the costs that will be incurred in order to complete the contract (but it is possible to foresee that total contract costs will not exceed total contract revenues).

Therefore, revenue is only recognised to the extent of costs incurred. Thus, in Year 1, CU250 of revenue is recognised and CU250 of expenses are recognised, resulting in no gross profit being recognised in the period.

When the uncertainties that prevented reliable estimation of the outcome of a construction contract no longer exist, contract revenue and expenses are recognised using the percentage of completion method. [IAS 11:35]

IAS 11 does not address the question of disclosure in the period in which the outcome of a contract becomes capable of reliable estimation. In the first period in which the percentage of completion method is applied, the profit on the contract that has not been recognised in previous periods will be recognised. When the entity begins to use this method, profit will be measured on a different basis than in past periods. This change could affect the comparability of the amounts reported and may be required to be disclosed; for example, when material, disclosure may be required under paragraph 97 of IAS 1 *Presentation of Financial Statements* (see **5.4.1** in **chapter A4**).

---

8 Recognition of amounts in the statement of financial position

At the end of each reporting period, for all contracts in progress for which costs incurred plus recognised profits (less recognised losses) exceed progress billings, a gross amount due from customers for contract work is recognised as an asset in the statement of financial position. The amount is disclosed separately from inventories to which IAS 2 *Inventories* applies.

Similarly, at the end of each reporting period, for all contracts in progress for which progress billings exceed costs incurred plus recognised profits (less recognised losses), a gross amount due to customers for contract work is recognised as a liability in the statement of financial position.

Progress billings are amounts billed for work performed on a contract whether or not they have been paid by the customer. [IAS 11:41]

> The wording used in IAS 11 of 'gross amount due from customers' may be misleading in that actual trade amounts receivable from customers (i.e. amounts already billed) are not part of this figure. These are recognised as separate assets in the statement of financial position.

Example 8

Presentation of amounts in the statement of financial position

A contractor enters into a three-year contract. At the beginning of the contract, estimated revenue is CU10,000 and estimated total costs are CU8,000.

During Year 2, however, management revises its estimate of total costs to be incurred and, thus, the outcome of the contract. As a result, during Year 2, a loss for the year is recognised on the contract, even though the contract will still be profitable overall.

	Year 1	Year 2	Year 3
	CU	CU	CU
Estimated revenue	10,000	10,000	10,000
Estimated total costs	8,000	9,000	9,000
Estimated total profit	2,000	1,000	1,000
Costs incurred to date	4,000	6,750	9,000
Percentage of completion	50%	75%	100%
Cumulative recognised profit	1,000	750	1,000
Recognised profit (loss) in year	1,000	(250)	250

Progress billings of CU4,000, CU4,000 and CU1,000 are made on the last day of each year and are received in the first month of the following year.

The asset or liability at the end of each year is as follows.

	Year 1	Year 2	Year 3
	CU	CU	CU
Costs incurred	4,000	6,750	9,000
Recognised profits	1,000	1,000	1,250
Recognised losses	–	(250)	(250)
Progress billings	(4,000)	(8,000)	(9,000)
Amount recognised as an asset/ (liability)	1,000	(500)	1,000

> In addition, at the end of each reporting period, the entity recognises a trade receivable for the progress billings outstanding at that date of CU4,000, CU4,000 and CU1,000, respectively.

Gross amounts *due from* customers will generally be considered monetary items. Monetary items are defined in paragraph 8 of IAS 21 *The Effects of Changes in Foreign Exchange Rates* as "units of currency held and assets and liabilities to be received or paid in a fixed or determinable number of units of currency". IAS 11:43 and 44 provide guidance on how the gross amounts due from and due to customers are determined. Depending on the level of progress billings, the amount may change from a liability to an asset, and that amount would then be settled or recovered by additional work performed subsequently, profits or losses recognised or any additional progress billings made subsequently.

In the absence of any other factors, the amount due from customers is a recognised asset that is probable of being recovered from the customer in cash (provided those are the terms of the arrangement) once the amount has been billed. While the right to cash may not yet have been established contractually through the billing and, therefore, the asset may not yet meet the definition of a financial asset (see **2.7** in **chapter B1** (for entities applying IFRS 9 *Financial Instruments*) and **2.7** in **chapter C1** (for entities applying IAS 39 *Financial Instruments: Recognition and Measurement*)), the nature of the asset is monetary nonetheless.

However, gross amounts *due to* customers will generally be considered non-monetary items if the contractor is expected to fulfil its obligations through work performed. Amounts due to customers may arise due to high progress billings in the early parts of the construction project that are in excess of the costs incurred plus recognised profits and less recognised losses. Such an obligation is generally offset by work performed at a later stage of the project, not through settlement by units of currency. It may occur, depending on the circumstances, that an amount due to a customer becomes payable in units of currency. In such circumstances, those amounts should be classified as monetary items.

9   Disclosure

9.1   Accounting policies

The methods used to determine the contract revenue recognised in the period and the methods used to determine the stage of completion of contracts in progress should be disclosed. [IAS 11:39(b) & (c)]

9.2   Contract revenue

The amount of contract revenue recognised as revenue in the period should be disclosed. [IAS 11:39(a)]

9.3   Statement of financial position

The following should be disclosed for contracts in progress at the end of the reporting period:

[IAS 11:40]

- the aggregate amount of costs incurred and recognised profits (less recognised losses) to date;
- the amount of advances received; and
- the amount of retentions.

Advances are amounts received by the contractor before the related work is performed. [IAS 11:41] Advances are commonly made in order to fund the purchase of materials by a contractor before the related work on a contract begins. Advances are recognised as liabilities until the related revenue is earned.

Retentions are amounts of progress billings that are not paid until the satisfaction of conditions specified in the contract for the payment of such amounts or until defects have been rectified. [IAS 11:41] Retentions are recognised as receivables in the statement of financial position of the contractor.

An entity should present:

[IAS 11:42]

- the gross amount due from customers for contract work as an asset; and
- the gross amount due to customers for contract work as a liability.

These terms are explained in **section 8**.

Appendix A3   Service concession arrangements (entities applying IAS 18 and IAS 11)

Contents

1   Introduction

1.1   Overview of IFRIC 12

IFRIC 12 *Service Concession Arrangements* prescribes the accounting for service concession arrangements, which are arrangements whereby a government or other body (the grantor) grants contracts for the supply of public services, such as roads, energy distribution, prisons or hospitals, to a private sector entity (the operator). These are often referred to as 'public-to-private' arrangements.

1.2   Changes to IFRIC 12 since the last edition of this manual

IFRS 12 was amended in January 2016 by minor consequential amendments arising from IFRS 16 *Leases*. However, those consequential amendments are not reflected in this appendix because entities are not permitted to adopt IFRS 16 unless they have also adopted IFRS 15 (and this appendix is for the use of entities that have not yet adopted IFRS 15).

1.3   IAS 18 superseded by IFRS 15

IFRIC 12 was amended by consequential amendments arising from IFRS 15 *Revenue from Contracts with Customers* to reflect the requirements for recognition and measurement of revenue introduced by that Standard (effective for annual periods beginning on or after 1 January 2018, with earlier application permitted). The requirements of IFRIC 12 as amended by IFRS 15 are dealt with in **chapter A35**. This appendix sets out the requirements of IFRIC 12 prior to amendment by IFRS 15, and is intended for the convenience of entities that have not yet adopted IFRS 15 and that therefore continue to apply IAS 18 *Revenue* (see **appendix A1**) and IAS 11 *Construction Contracts* (see **appendix A2**).

1.4   Key requirements of IFRIC 12

The following table provides an overview of the key requirements of IFRIC 12.

Issue	Key requirement of IFRIC 12
Operator's rights over the infrastructure assets	The infrastructure assets are not recognised as the property, plant or equipment of the operator.
Revenue recognition	Revenue is recognised and measured in accordance with IAS 11 *Construction Contracts* (for construction or upgrade services) and/or IAS 18 *Revenue* (for operating services).

Issue	Key requirement of IFRIC 12
Construction or upgrade services	The consideration received by the operator is recognised at fair value. Consideration may result in the recognition of a financial asset or an intangible asset.
	• The operator recognises a financial asset if it has an unconditional contractual right to receive cash or another financial asset from or at the direction of the grantor in return for constructing or upgrading the public sector asset.
	• The operator recognises an intangible asset if it receives only a right to charge for the use of the public sector asset that it constructs or upgrades.
	• IFRIC 12 allows for the possibility that both types of consideration may exist within a single contract. For example, to the extent that the grantor has given to the operator an unconditional guarantee of minimum payments for the construction, the operator recognises a financial asset. The operator may also recognise an intangible asset representing the right to charge users of the public service that is in addition to the minimum guaranteed payments.
Operator's contractual obligations to maintain/restore the infrastructure to a specified level of serviceability	Contractual obligations to maintain or restore infrastructure, except for any upgrade element, should be recognised and measured in accordance with IAS 37 *Provisions, Contingent Liabilities and Contingent Assets*, i.e. at the best estimate of the expenditure that would be required to settle the present obligation at the reporting date.
Borrowing costs incurred by the operator	Borrowing costs incurred by the operator that are attributable to the arrangement are recognised as an expense in the period incurred unless the operator has a contractual right to charge users of the public service (intangible asset model). In such circumstances, borrowing costs attributable to the arrangement should be capitalised during the construction phase of the arrangement in accordance with IAS 23 *Borrowing Costs*.
Subsequent accounting treatment for a financial asset	IFRS 9 *Financial Instruments* (or, for entities that have not yet adopted IFRS 9, IAS 39 *Financial Instruments: Recognition and Measurement*) applies to the financial asset recognised under IFRIC 12.
	Under IFRS 9, the financial asset will be measured at amortised cost, at fair value through other comprehensive income, or at fair value through profit or loss.
	Under IAS 39, depending on whether the financial asset is classified as loans and receivables, as an available-for-sale financial asset, or designated as at fair value through profit or loss, it is subsequently measured either at amortised cost or fair value.

Issue	Key requirement of IFRIC 12
Subsequent accounting treatment for an intangible asset	IAS 38 *Intangible Assets* applies to any intangible asset recognised under IFRIC 12. IAS 38 will typically require that intangible asset to be measured using the cost model.

2   Scope of IFRIC 12

2.1   Typical features of service concession arrangements

IFRIC 12 applies to some, but not all, public-to-private service concession arrangements (see **2.2** for detailed scope conditions).

A typical 'public-to-private' arrangement that falls within the scope of IFRIC 12 is a 'build-operate-transfer' arrangement. Under this type of arrangement, an operator constructs the infrastructure to be used to provide a public service, and it operates and maintains that infrastructure for a specified period of time. The operator is paid for its services over the period of the arrangement. A contract sets out performance standards, pricing mechanisms, and arrangements for arbitrating disputes. [IFRIC 12:2] In some cases, the operator may upgrade the existing infrastructure and maintain and operate the upgraded infrastructure. This second type of arrangement is sometimes referred to as a 'rehabilitate-operate-transfer' arrangement.

Paragraph 1 of SIC-29 *Service Concession Arrangements: Disclosures* states that outsourcing the operation of an entity's internal services (e.g. employee restaurant, building maintenance, accounting or IT functions) does not constitute a service concession arrangement.

Some common features of service concession arrangements are as follows.

[IFRIC 12:3]

- The grantor is a public sector entity, including a governmental body, or a private sector entity to which the responsibility for the service has been devolved.

- The operator is responsible for at least some of the management of the infrastructure and related services and does not merely act as an agent on behalf of the grantor.

- The contract sets the initial prices to be levied by the operator and regulates price revisions over the period of the service arrangement.

- The operator is obliged to hand over the infrastructure to the grantor in a specified condition at the end of the period of the arrangement, for little or no incremental consideration irrespective of which party initially financed it.

IFRIC 12 applies to a broad range of concession arrangements. Road and water treatment concession arrangements are two common examples, but other types of arrangements may meet the scope conditions, such as contracts for the:

- provision of transport services;

- construction and operation of waste treatment plants;

- provision of public airport services;

- construction and maintenance of hospitals;

- generation of renewable energy;

- production of electricity; and

- construction and operation of public transport systems, schools, prisons etc.

For a public service obligation to exist, the services offered need not be made available to all members of the public. Rather, the services need to benefit members of the public. For example, prisons only accommodate those individuals required to be incarcerated by law, and cannot be accessed by members of the public seeking accommodation. However, prisons would still be considered to provide services to the public.

There are many different types of concession arrangements, and the detailed structure and arrangements are often specific to jurisdictions. Therefore, in order to determine the appropriate accounting for an arrangement, the details of the arrangement should be analysed based on the specific facts and circumstances.

2.2   Service concession arrangements within the scope of IFRIC 12

2.2.1   IFRIC 12 scope conditions

A public-to-private arrangement will not automatically fall within the scope of IFRIC 12; specified scope conditions need to be satisfied.

IFRIC 12 applies to public-to-private service concession arrangements if:

[IFRIC 12:5]

(a) the grantor controls or regulates what services the operator must provide with the infrastructure, to whom it must provide them, and at what price (see **2.2.2**); and

(b) the grantor controls – through ownership, beneficial entitlement or otherwise – any significant residual interest in the infrastructure at the end of the term of the arrangement (see **2.2.3**).

These conditions are summarised in the following flowchart.

[Extract from IFRIC 12 (Information Note 1)]

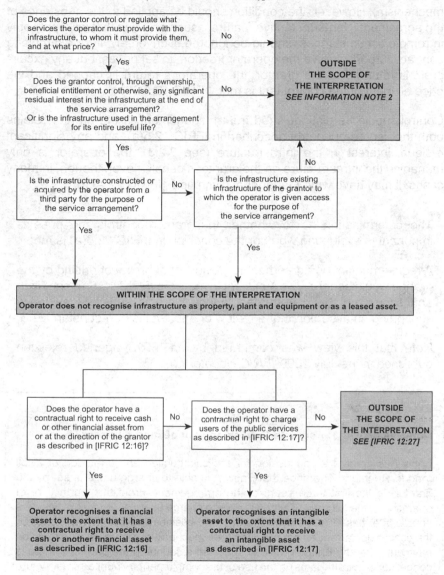

2.2.2   Scope – control of services and pricing

The control or regulation referred to in condition 12:5(a) (see **2.2.1**) could be by contract or otherwise (such as through a regulator), and includes circumstances in which the grantor buys all of the output as well as those in which some or all of the output is bought by other users. In applying this condition, the grantor and any related parties should be considered together. If the grantor is a public sector entity, the public sector as a whole, together with any regulators acting in the public interest, should be regarded as related to the grantor for the purposes of IFRIC 12. [IFRIC 12:AG2]

For the purpose of condition IFRIC 12:5(a) (see **2.2.1**), the grantor does not need to have complete control of the price; it is sufficient for the price to be regulated by the grantor, contract or regulator (e.g. by a capping mechanism). However, the condition should be applied to the substance of the agreement. Non-substantive features, such as a cap that will apply only in remote circumstances, should be ignored. Conversely, if for example, a contract purports to give the operator freedom to set prices, but any excess profit is returned to the grantor, the operator's return is capped and the price element of the control test is met. [IFRIC 12:AG3]

Control should be distinguished from management. If the grantor retains both the degree of control described in IFRIC 12:5(a), and any significant residual interest in the infrastructure (see **2.2.3**), the operator is only managing the infrastructure on the grantor's behalf – even though, in many cases, it may have wide managerial discretion. [IFRIC 12:AG5]

The determination as to whether the grantor controls the price is important in evaluating whether the condition in IFRIC 12:5(a) is met.

A requirement in the agreement for review or approval of pricing by the grantor would generally be sufficient to meet the IFRIC 12:5(a) condition and should not be disregarded unless there is sufficient evidence supporting an assertion that a review or approval is non-substantive.

Note that this view was confirmed by an IFRIC agenda rejection published in the July 2009 *IFRIC Update*.

Example 2.2.2A

Concession with unregulated prices and congestion payment

Entity A is granted a concession for the construction and operation of a toll road for 40 years. The price that Entity A is able to charge users is set by the grantor for the first three years of the arrangement. From the fourth year of operation of the toll road, Entity A is able to charge users at a price it considers appropriate, based on its own strategy and business perspectives. However, the concession arrangement provides for a mechanism known as a 'congestion payment' whereby Entity A will pay specified amounts to the grantor if there is congestion (i.e. traffic jams) in the use of the complementary public infrastructure (i.e. nearby roads).

The grantor exercises absolute control over the pricing for an insignificant period of time in the context of the service concession arrangement as a whole. The congestion payment mechanism would need to be analysed to determine if it amounts to substantive regulation of the prices charged. If this mechanism is included in the contract solely to avoid excessively high prices, it may not be substantive because the operator has the freedom to charge what it wants within a reasonable range. The only limitation is that the operator cannot charge a price the market would not bear and in doing so create congestion on other roads. If the mechanism is considered non-substantive, the arrangement would fall outside the scope of IFRIC 12.

Example 2.2.2B

Concession with price control mechanism to prevent unfair pricing

Entity B (the operator) enters into a service concession arrangement with a port authority (the grantor) under which Entity B will construct port terminal facilities and operate them for a period of 25 years.

Entity B has discretion to set the prices charged to its customers for the use of the port facilities throughout the concession period. Entity B is not required to obtain approval from the port authority whenever it decides to change its prices.

However, the relevant legislation places a responsibility on the port authority to ensure fair market practices and prevent abusive pricing. If a customer files a complaint with the port authority, or the port authority is otherwise alerted to concerns that Entity B's pricing is unfair or abusive, the port authority has the power to investigate the market and to require Entity B to adjust its prices if they are determined to be unfair. Such a determination can only be based on a comparison with prices charged by Entity B's (independent) competitors.

In the circumstances described, the port authority does not control the price charged by Entity B for its services; consequently, the criterion in IFRIC 12.5(a) is not met. The port authority's power is limited to the ability to require Entity B to adjust its prices in line with independent market transactions and as such is designed to prevent unfair market practices rather than to control the price that Entity B can charge to its customers. Consequently, the 'cap' on Entity B's prices is ultimately driven by market transactions and does not, therefore, amount to substantive regulation of the prices charged.

Accordingly, the arrangement falls outside the scope of IFRIC 12.

Example 2.2.2C

Competitive tender process

Arrangements in which the public sector seeks to attract private sector participation often involve a tender process under which a number of entities respond to a Request for Proposal (RFP). The RFP may request the respondent to specify the type and level of services that the respondent would provide if its tender is successful, and the amounts that it would charge for those services. When the winning bid has been selected, the services and pricing agreed with the successful respondent are incorporated into a contractual arrangement.

IFRIC 12 applies to arrangements in which "the grantor controls or regulates which services the operator must provide with infrastructure, to whom it must provide them, and at what price". [IFRIC 12:5(a)]

> *If an arrangement would otherwise fall within the scope of IFRIC 12, does the fact that services and/or prices are determined through a process of competitive tender preclude the arrangement from being accounted for under IFRIC 12?*
>
> No. If the arrangement otherwise falls within the scope of IFRIC 12 because all the relevant conditions in IFRIC 12 are met, the fact that services and/or prices are determined through a competitive tender process before the concession begins does not affect the conclusion as to whether the arrangement falls within the scope.

Example 2.2.2D

Price cap set by grantor

An entity (the operator) has entered into a service concession arrangement under which it will construct a road and operate that road for 30 years. The grantor does not specify the price that the operator can charge to users of the road, but it does specify the maximum price that can be charged (i.e. it imposes a 'price cap').

For the purposes of IFRIC 12:5(a), does the grantor's power to impose a price cap mean that the grantor 'controls or regulates' the price at which services are provided?

In general, yes, provided that the capping mechanism is not considered to be non-substantive.

IFRIC 12:AG3 states that "[f]or the purpose of condition [IFRIC 12:5](a), the grantor does not need to have complete control of the price: it is sufficient for the price to be regulated by the grantor, contract or regulator, for example by a capping mechanism".

However, a cap set at a level such that it is very unlikely ever to take effect (e.g. stating that a road toll must not exceed CU1,000 when the anticipated toll is CU2) would be considered non-substantive. As a result, the grantor would not be considered to have control over the price and the arrangement would be outside the scope of IFRIC 12.

2.2.3   Scope – control of any significant residual interest

When considering whether a significant residual interest exists for the purpose of determining whether the condition in IFRIC 12:5(b) is met (see **2.2.1**), the residual interest should be estimated as the infrastructure's current value as if it was of the age and condition expected as at the end of the period of the arrangement. [IFRIC 12:AG4]

A machine that can only be sold for scrap value is unlikely to have a significant residual value at the end of the contract and will be within the scope of IFRIC 12 provided that the condition in IFRIC 12:5(a) is met. Conversely, a building with a 50-year useful life that is only used in a service concession arrangement for 20 years is likely to have a significant residual interest at the end of the arrangement and will be within the scope of IFRIC 12 only if both (1) the condition in IFRIC 12:5(a) is met, and (2) the residual interest is controlled by the grantor.

The conditions in IFRIC 12:5(a) and (b) together identify when the infrastructure, including any replacements required (see **section 7**), is controlled by the grantor for the whole of its economic life. Under the terms of a service concession arrangement, an operator may be required to replace parts of an item of infrastructure (e.g. the top layer of a road or the roof of a building). In these types of arrangement, the item of infrastructure is considered as a whole for the purposes of determining whether the grantor controls any significant residual interest. Consequently, the condition in IFRIC 12:5(b) would be met for the whole of the infrastructure, including the part that is replaced, if the grantor controls any significant residual interest in the final replacement of that part. [IFRIC 12:AG6]

Arrangements under which the infrastructure is used for its entire useful life ('whole of life assets') are within the scope of IFRIC 12 provided that the condition in IFRIC 12:5(a) is met, regardless of which party controls any residual interest. [IFRIC 12:6]

For the purpose of IFRIC 12:5(b) (see **2.2.1**), the grantor's control over any significant residual interest should both restrict the operator's practical ability to sell or pledge the infrastructure and give the grantor a continuing right of use throughout the period of the arrangement. [IFRIC 12:AG4]

Certain arrangements allow the operator to renew the licence arrangement indefinitely without significant costs. In those cases, it is first necessary to analyse carefully all facts and circumstances in order to establish whether, at a point of possible renewal, there will be a significant residual interest in the infrastructure.

When there may be a significant residual interest in the infrastructure at a point of possible renewal, it is then necessary to determine who controls that residual interest. If the terms of the arrangement are such that the grantor controls the residual interest if the operator chooses not to renew the licence, the arrangement would fall within the scope of IFRIC 12. In contrast, if the grantor does not control the significant residual interest if the operator decides not to renew the licence, the arrangement would not meet the condition in IFRIC 12:5(b) and so would be excluded from the scope of IFRIC 12.

Example 2.2.3A

Application of IFRIC 12 when residual interest is returned to grantor at fair value

An entity (the operator) has entered into a service concession arrangement under which it will construct a bridge and operate that bridge for 30 years. It cannot sell the bridge to a third party unless the government (the grantor) agrees to the sale. At the end of the arrangement, the grantor is required to repurchase the bridge for its fair value at that time. The bridge has an estimated useful economic life of 50 years.

Does the grantor control the residual interest in the infrastructure at the end of the term of the arrangement in accordance with IFRIC 12:5(b)?

Yes. IFRIC 12:5 states, in part, as follows. "This Interpretation applies to public-to-private service concession arrangements if ... the grantor controls – through ownership, beneficial entitlement or otherwise – any significant residual interest in the infrastructure at the end of the term of the arrangement."

According to IFRIC 12:AG6, situations in which the grantor controls the asset for the whole of its economic life are within the scope of IFRIC 12.

IFRIC 12:AG4 states, in part, as follows. "For the purposes of condition (b) [of IFRIC 12:5 as outlined at **2.2.1**], the grantor's control over any significant residual interest should both restrict the operator's practical ability to sell or pledge the infrastructure and give the grantor a continuing right of use throughout the period of the arrangement." In this scenario, the operator would not be able readily to sell or pledge the infrastructure even though it may be able to sell or pledge its economic interest in the residual value of the infrastructure.

IFRIC 12 applies a 'control' approach. In the circumstances described, the grantor has a continuing right of use of the infrastructure asset at the end of the term of the arrangement and, consequently, controls the use of the bridge throughout its economic life. This is the case even though the grantor has to pay fair value for the asset at the end of the term of the arrangement.

Example 2.2.3B

Application of IFRIC 12 when the grantor has an option to purchase at the end of the term of the arrangement

Entity A (the operator) has entered into a service concession arrangement with the government (the grantor) under which it constructs a hospital and operates that hospital for 25 years. The hospital has an estimated economic life of 40 years. The residual interest in the hospital at the end of the term of the arrangement is expected to be significant.

At the end of 25 years, the government has the option to purchase the hospital from Entity A at an amount equal to the hospital's fair value at that time. If the government does not exercise this purchase option, Entity A retains the hospital for its continued use and/or disposal.

> *In the circumstances described, does the grantor (the government) control the residual interest in the infrastructure at the end of the term of the arrangement (i.e. is the condition in IFRIC 12:5(b) satisfied)?*
>
> Yes. IFRIC 12:AG6 states that the conditions in IFRIC 12:5(a) and (b) "together identify when the infrastructure ... is controlled by the grantor for the whole of its economic life" and, therefore, when an arrangement should be accounted for in accordance with IFRIC 12.
>
> In the circumstances described, the condition in IFRIC 12:5(b) is met due to the existence of the purchase option at the end of the term of the arrangement; the government has the power to purchase the hospital or to allow Entity A to retain the hospital for the operator's continued use and/or disposal.
>
> IFRIC 12:AG4 states that, for the purposes of IFRIC 12:5(b), "the grantor's control over any significant residual interest should both restrict the operator's practical ability to sell or pledge the infrastructure and give the grantor a continuing right of use throughout the period of the arrangement". In the circumstances described, due to the existence of the purchase option held by the grantor, Entity A is unable readily to sell or pledge the hospital even though it may be able to sell or pledge its economic interest in the residual value of the hospital.

2.2.4   Scope – nature of the infrastructure

The Interpretation applies to both:

[IFRIC 12:7]

(a)   infrastructure that the operator constructs or acquires from a third party for the purpose of the service arrangement; and

(b)   existing infrastructure to which the grantor gives the operator access for the purpose of the service arrangement.

The requirements may apply to previously recognised property, plant and equipment of the operator if the derecognition requirements of IFRSs are met. If the operator is considered to have disposed of the asset by passing the significant risks and rewards of that asset to the grantor, then the operator should derecognise that asset in accordance with paragraph 67 of IAS 16 *Property, Plant and Equipment*. [IFRIC 12:8] For further guidance relating to the derecognition of property, plant and equipment, see **section 9** of **chapter A7**. Having disposed of its previously held asset, the operator would need to determine whether the arrangement is within the scope of IFRIC 12.

Sometimes the use of infrastructure is only partly regulated by the grantor. These arrangements take a variety of forms, and the following principles should be applied.

[IFRIC 12:AG7]

(a) Any infrastructure that is physically separable and capable of being operated independently and meets the definition of a cash-generating unit in IAS 36 *Impairment of Assets* is analysed separately if it is used wholly for unregulated purposes. For example, this might apply to a private wing of a hospital, when the remainder of the hospital is used by the grantor to treat public patients.

(b) When purely ancillary activities (such as a hospital shop) are unregulated, the control tests are applied as if those services did not exist, because in cases in which the grantor controls the services in the manner described in IFRIC 12:5 (see **2.2.2**), the existence of ancillary activities does not detract from the grantor's control of the infrastructure.

In either of the circumstances described above, there may in substance be a lease from the grantor to the operator. If so, the lease should be accounted for in accordance with IAS 17 *Leases*. [IFRIC 12:AG8]

Example 2.2.4

Infrastructure with different services

An operator is granted the concession for a railway station by the government (the grantor). The operator will manage the station for 75 years, at which point the station will revert to the government. The terms of the agreement split the concession between the railway terminal itself (the 'railway terminal activity') and the shopping areas located in the property (the 'retail activity'). Both of these activities are covered by the terms of the service concession agreement and are controlled by the grantor, who regularly monitors the services provided.

• The railway terminal activity is regulated because the grantor controls the services to be provided, the train companies to which the operator must provide those services, and the price charged by the operator. As a consequence, the railway activity falls within the scope of IFRIC 12:5.

• Regarding the retail activity, the operator is permitted to lease the shops to third parties for the purpose of running commercial outlets. The service concession agreement requires that the operator obtains formal permission before a lease is granted and prices must be communicated to the grantor, although they are not subject to explicit formal authorisation.

The operator pays fees to the grantor for both activities. The service concession agreement establishes that the operator has an obligation to return a significant percentage of the profits generated from the retail activity through a reduction in the prices charged to the train companies for the regulated (railway terminal) activity. As a result, the revenue stream from the railway terminal activity is affected by the profits generated from the retail activity. At the end of the concession, all assets (relating to both activities) are returned to the grantor for no consideration.

The grantor controls the nature of the retail activity by setting the guidelines as to the services to be provided, by approving the service providers and by

---

monitoring that these guidelines are followed by the operator in practice. In addition, the pricing mechanism is such that part of the profits generated by the retail activity must be returned through a reduction in the prices charged for the railway terminal activity. Therefore, indirectly, the grantor controls the level of profits generated from the retail activity.

As a result of the interdependency between the revenue streams from the two activities, and the level of the grantor's control over the retail activity, the entire operation of the railway station (railway terminal activity and retail activity) may be subject to IFRIC 12.

In contrast, if the activities were separable and not interdependent, they would be analysed separately. IFRIC 12:AG7(a) states that any infrastructure that is physically separable and capable of being operated independently and meets the definition of a cash-generating unit in IAS 36 must be analysed separately if it is used wholly for unregulated purposes.

Ultimately, it will be necessary to exercise judgement based on all the facts and circumstances in order to determine whether infrastructure assets with different activities are interdependent and should be assessed together for the purposes of IFRIC 12.

2.3   Scope – private-to-private arrangements

IFRIC 12 does not include within its scope private-to-private arrangements but it could be applied to such arrangements by analogy under the hierarchy set out in paragraphs 7 to 12 of IAS 8 *Accounting Policies, Changes in Accounting Estimates and Errors* (see **3.1** of **chapter A5**). [IFRIC 12:BC14]

2.4   Scope – accounting by grantors

The Interpretation specifically excludes from its scope the accounting by grantors (i.e. public sector accounting). [IFRIC 12:9]

2.5   Standards applicable to arrangements falling outside the scope of IFRIC 12

If an arrangement does not fall within the scope of IFRIC 12, it may fall within the scope of other IFRSs. The following table, extracted from Information Note 2 to IFRIC 12, indicates which Standards may be applicable.

Category	Lessee	Service provider			Owner	
Typical arrangement types	Lease (e.g. Operator leases asset from grantor)	Service and/or maintenance contract (specific tasks e.g. debt collection)	Rehabilitate -operate- transfer	Build- operate- transfer	Build- own- operate	100% Divestment/ Privatisation/ Corporation
Asset ownership	Grantor				Operator	
Capital investment	Grantor		Operator			
Demand risk	Shared	Grantor	Operator and/or Grantor		Operator	
Typical duration	8–20 years	1–5 years	25–30 years			Indefinite (or may be limited by licence)
Residual interest	Grantor				Operator	
Relevant IFRSs	IAS 17	IAS 18	IFRIC 12		IAS 16	

2.6   Arrangements falling within the scope of both IFRIC 4 and IFRIC 12

When assessing the contractual terms of some arrangements, it is possible that they could fall within the scope of both IFRIC 4 *Determining whether an Arrangement contains a Lease* and IFRIC 12. To eliminate any inconsistencies between the accounting treatment for contracts which have similar economic effects, the IFRIC (now the IFRS Interpretations Committee) amended IFRIC 4 to specify that if a contract appears to fall within the scope of both Interpretations, the requirements of IFRIC 12 prevail.

3   The accounting models

3.1   Recognition and measurement of arrangement consideration

Under the terms of contractual arrangements within the scope of IFRIC 12, the operator acts as a service provider; the operator constructs or upgrades infrastructure which is used to provide a public service, and is then responsible for operating and maintaining that infrastructure for a specified period of time. [IFRIC 12:12]

The following principles apply for the recognition and measurement of revenue:

[IFRIC 12:13, 14 & 20]

- the operator should recognise and measure revenue for the services it performs in accordance with IASs 11 and 18;

- if the operator performs more than one service (i.e. construction or upgrade services and operation services) under a single contract or arrangement, the consideration received or receivable should be allocated by reference to the relative fair value of services delivered, when the amounts are separately identifiable;

- revenue and costs of the operator relating to the construction or upgrade services phase of the contract should be accounted for in accordance with IAS 11;

- revenue and costs relating to operation services should be accounted for in accordance with IAS 18; and

- the nature of the consideration determines its subsequent accounting treatment (see **3.2**).

Example 3.1A

Recognition of a profit margin on construction work – infrastructure constructed by the operator

Company A (the operator) has been granted a concession arrangement for the construction and operation of an airport. Company A will be responsible for the construction of the infrastructure. IFRIC 12:14 states that an operator must account for revenue and costs relating to the construction phase of a concession arrangement in accordance with IAS 11.

Consequently, if the service concession arrangement involves a construction contract as defined in IAS 11, that construction contract should be accounted for in accordance with IAS 11 and Company A should recognise a profit margin on the construction work by reference to the stage of completion. This margin arises because Company A has received an intangible or a financial asset as consideration for the construction of the airport, which constitutes consideration in the form of an asset that differs in nature from the asset delivered and which, in accordance with IFRIC 12:15 (see **3.2**), is recognised at its fair value.

Example 3.1B

Recognition of a profit margin on construction work – infrastructure acquired

The facts are as described in **example 3.1A** except that Company A (the operator) outsources the construction of the airport to Company B (the sub-contractor), an unrelated entity. The grantor is informed of, and approves, the outsourcing of the construction, although it does not enter into a specific and direct agreement with the sub-contractor.

The appropriate recognition by Company A of revenue and costs associated with the construction work depends on whether it is acting as an agent or a principal, based on the substance of the agreements with both the grantor and the sub-contractor. The fact that the grantor is informed of, and approves, the agreement between Company A and its sub-contractor is not in itself evidence that the operator is acting as an agent. The analysis requires careful consideration of all other relevant facts and circumstances and the exercise of judgement.

IAS 18:IE21 provides guidance on how to determine whether an entity is acting as a principal or as an agent. This guidance is discussed at **3.2** in **appendix A1**.

In the circumstances described, if the analysis of all relevant facts and circumstances leads to the conclusion that, in substance, Company A is acting as an agent, revenue and profit margin should not be recognised on a gross basis. Instead, Company A should recognise the fees associated with the service provided as an agent as net revenue. If, however, based on all relevant facts and circumstances it is concluded that Company A is acting as a principal in relation to the construction services, Company A should recognise revenue and the profit margin arising from the construction services on a gross basis in accordance with IAS 11.

3.2   Determining the nature of the operator's asset

3.2.1   Determining the nature of the operator's asset – general principles

Infrastructure within the scope of IFRIC 12 is not recognised as property, plant and equipment of the operator. This is because the operator does not have the right to control the asset, but merely has access to the infrastructure in order to provide the public service in accordance with the terms specified in the contract. [IFRIC 12:11] Such an arrangement is not treated as a lease because the operator does not have the right to control the use of the asset. [IFRIC 12:BC23] Instead, the operator's right to consideration is recognised as a financial asset, an intangible asset, or a combination of the two. [IFRIC 12:15]

The nature of the consideration given by the grantor to the operator should be determined by reference to the contract terms and, when it exists, relevant contract law. [IFRIC 12:19]

The nature of the consideration determines its subsequent accounting treatment, as described in detail in **sections 4** and **5**.

The requirements of IFRIC 12 regarding the nature of the asset to be recognised can be summarised as follows.

Operator's rights	Classification	Examples
Unconditional, contractual right to receive cash or other financial asset from the grantor.	Financial asset [IFRIC 12:16]	• Operator receives a fixed amount from the grantor over term of arrangement. • Operator has a right to charge users over term of arrangement, but any shortfall will be reimbursed by the grantor.
Amounts to be received are contingent on the extent that the public uses the service.	Intangible asset [IFRIC 12:17]	• Operator has a right to charge users over the term of the arrangement. • Operator has a right to charge the grantor based on usage of the services over the term of the arrangement.
Consideration received partly in the form of a financial asset and partly in the form of an intangible asset.	Bifurcated model [IFRIC 12:18]	• Operator receives a fixed amount from the grantor and a right to charge users over the term of the arrangement.

3.2.2   Features of typical concession arrangements – examples

The following table summarises the features of some typical concession mechanisms.

Characteristics	Type of asset recognised by the operator	Reason
Hospital – the operator receives from the grantor a fixed amount of revenue, subject to deductions for lack of availability.	Financial asset	• Revenue not dependent on usage. • Deductions reflect failure to meet specified quality requirements.
Toll road – the amounts receivable by the operator are subject to little variation in practice because the road is an established route with highly predictable level of tolls.	Intangible asset	• Right to charge users. • Amounts depend on usage of the infrastructure, regardless of whether variation in usage is expected in practice.

Characteristics	Type of asset recognised by the operator	Reason
Toll road – the operator has a guarantee from the grantor that revenue will not fall below a specified level. The guarantee is achieved through an increase in the concession period.	Intangible asset	• Right to charge users. • Amounts depend on usage of the infrastructure. • Shortfall guaranteed by the grantor via a concession extension and not via a right to receive cash.
Water supply concession – the grantor regulates prices that the operator may charge to users or adjusts the duration of the concession based on a targeted rate of return.	Intangible asset	• Right to charge users. • Amounts depend on usage of the infrastructure.
Rail concession – the grantor pays the operator any shortfall between the actual benefit before interest and tax obtained through charging users, and a fixed minimum.	Intangible asset and financial asset – bifurcated model	• Right to charge users. • Amounts depend on usage of the infrastructure. • Financial asset arises from the right to receive a minimum determinable amount of cash from users/ grantor (shortfall guaranteed by the grantor) and intangible asset from the right to earn additional amounts above the fixed guaranteed payments.

Characteristics	Type of asset recognised by the operator	Reason
Toll bridge – the grantor pays a fixed payment based on availability during the first half of the concession period and then switches to usage payments.	Intangible asset and financial asset – bifurcated model	• Amounts do not depend on usage of the infrastructure during the first half of the concession but are usage dependent during the second half. • Financial asset arises from the right to receive cash from grantor during the first part of the concession irrespective of usage; the intangible asset arises from the right to charge the grantor in the second half based on usage.

3.2.3 Contingent right to collect cash or another financial asset

Example 3.2.3

Contingent right to collect cash or another financial asset

Company A has been granted a service concession arrangement to operate a hospital. Under the terms of the arrangement, the amounts receivable by Company A vary based on the level of usage of the hospital's services until the level of usage reaches a specified threshold. Company A receives a fixed amount if usage exceeds that threshold.

In the circumstances described, the type of asset to be recognised by Company A depends on whether the threshold has economic substance.

If the threshold has economic substance (i.e. there is more than a remote possibility that the threshold might not be met), Company A does not have an unconditional contractual right to cash and, accordingly, recognises an intangible asset because the amount receivable is contingent on the extent to which the public uses the hospital's services.

If the threshold lacks economic substance, because the possibility of the threshold not being met is remote, Company A has, in substance, a right to collect a fixed amount of cash. In such circumstances, the conditionality should be ignored and Company A should recognise a financial asset.

3.2.4   Take-or-pay arrangements

In some service concession arrangements, the operator receives payment under a 'take-or-pay' arrangement whereby the grantor is contractually obliged to purchase all of the output of the infrastructure or, if it is unable to accept delivery of that output, to pay the agreed price for that output regardless.

These arrangements may include a fixed annual amount or be entirely based on the amount of output produced, and the amount paid per unit of production may be fixed over the life of the arrangement or may vary depending on, for example, inflation or a quoted market price for the output in question.

Under such take-or-pay arrangements, the operator should recognise a financial asset for construction of the infrastructure.

A financial asset is recognised when the operator has an unconditional contractual right to receive cash or another financial asset from the grantor. The operator has an unconditional right if the cash flows are specified or determinable amounts (IFRIC 12:16) irrespective of whether the public service is used (IFRIC 12:BC40) (i.e. the operator bears no demand risk). Variability based on the performance of the infrastructure does not prevent recognition as a financial asset (IFRIC 12:BC44).

In the case of take-or-pay arrangements:

- the amount of cash to be received by the operator is determinable because it is determined by the formula incorporated into the take-or-pay arrangement (a fixed or determinable rate multiplied by the amount of output produced) even though one or more inputs into the formula may be unknown and, to some extent, outside the operator's control; and

- the grantor's obligation to pay for all of the output from the infrastructure (i.e. the amount actually produced, not the amount that is delivered to the grantor) means that the operator is exposed to availability risk during the operating period, but not demand risk. As such, the arrangement does not result in recognition of an intangible asset because the amount of cash received by the operator is not contingent on the extent to which the public uses the service (IFRIC 12:17).

The financial asset model is appropriate whether or not the arrangement includes a guaranteed minimum annual payment receivable by the operator.

If, under the terms of the arrangement:

- the operator instead receives cash based on the amount of output used by the public, it would be exposed to demand risk and would instead account for the arrangement using the intangible asset model; or

- the grantor only guarantees to purchase a proportion of output (e.g. up to a fixed volume or number of units per year) and the operator has a right to charge users for the remaining output (provided that the grantor controls to whom it must be sold and at what price), the concession operator should apply the bifurcated model (i.e. recognise both a financial asset and an intangible asset).

Example 3.2.4A

Take-or-pay arrangement (1)

A public sector entity (grantor) enters into an arrangement for the construction and operation of a desalination plant whereby the concession operator receives the following two elements of consideration over the term of the concession:

- a specified annual amount as consideration for the investment undertaken; and
- a specified amount per cubic metre of desalinated water produced by the plant where the grantor guarantees to purchase all of the water output that the plant produces ('take-or-pay arrangement'). This specified amount per m^3 is sufficient to cover the concession operator's production costs based on the technical capacity of the plant of 24 million m^3 of water per year.

The amount of water produced is determined by the operator, constrained only by the plant's technical capacity and need for occasional downtime for maintenance. Because the grantor has guaranteed to purchase all of the water output from the plant (i.e. the amount actually produced, not the amount that is used by the grantor), the operator is exposed to availability risk during the operating period, but not demand risk. The concession arrangement should therefore be accounted for using the financial asset model.

Example 3.2.4B

Take-or-pay arrangement (2)

A project company (operator) enters into an arrangement with a state-owned power company (grantor) for the construction and operation of a solar farm.

The grantor is contractually obliged under a take-or-pay arrangement to purchase all of the electricity produced by the solar farm at a fixed rate per unit of electricity produced. There is no guaranteed minimum amount payable (i.e. the concession operator will receive no consideration if the solar farm generates no electricity) and, if the grantor is unable to accept delivery of the electricity it must still pay for any electricity that the operator has produced. Electricity delivered to the power company will be made available to its customers (the general public), with no adjustment to the amounts payable to the operator based on the amount of electricity used.

The amount of electricity produced is determined by the solar farm's technical capacity (which has been agreed with the grantor) and on factors within (e.g. the quality of maintenance of the farm) and outside (e.g. the strength of the UV radiation) the operator's control.

Given that the terms of the take-or-pay arrangement mean that the operator is exposed to no demand risk over the electricity, the solar farm should be accounted for using the financial asset model.

3.2.5   Payments for capacity availability

Example 3.2.5

Payments for capacity availability

Company A is granted a concession arrangement for the construction and operation of a hospital for 30 years. This arrangement stipulates that Company A will be paid a specified amount that will enable it to recover the investment made provided that it has a predetermined minimum number of hospital beds available for use (whether or not that number of beds is actually used).

IFRIC 12:16 states that the operator has an unconditional right to receive cash if the grantor contractually guarantees to pay the operator specified or determinable amounts, even if payment is contingent on the operator ensuring that the infrastructure meets specified quality or efficiency requirements (see **section 4**). IFRIC 12:BC44 makes clear that this includes payments contingent upon targets to ensure a specified level of capacity can be delivered. Payments under the concession arrangement depend upon the hospital's capacity, not the usage of that capacity and, therefore, Company A should apply the financial asset model.

3.2.6   Guaranteed minimum net revenue with potential to extend the concession term

Example 3.2.6A

Guaranteed minimum net revenue with potential to extend the concession term indefinitely

Company A is granted a concession arrangement for a waste treatment plant under which the concession term ends automatically when the concession operator has received a previously stipulated net present value of net revenue (sales less operating costs) from users of the plant. If this minimum guaranteed net revenue is not achieved in the normal term of the concession, the term will be extended indefinitely for successive five-year periods until the guaranteed minimum revenue is achieved.

Company A does not have an unconditional contractual right to receive cash or another financial asset because the concession term could be extended indefinitely and the guaranteed minimum net revenue might never be achieved.

> Consequently, the concession arrangement should be accounted for using the intangible asset model.

Example 3.2.6B

Guaranteed minimum net revenue with potential to extend concession term for a limited period

Assume the same facts as described in **example 3.2.6A**, except that the maximum concession term that can be reached with the successive extensions is limited to 50 years. The grantor has guaranteed to pay any shortfall, adjusted for the time value of money, if the minimum guaranteed net revenue has not been achieved by the end of the 50-year limit. Because of the guarantee from the grantor, Company A has an unconditional contractual right to receive cash; therefore, the financial asset model should be applied in this case.

---

4   Financial asset model

4.1   Financial asset model – general

As outlined in **3.2.1**, the financial asset model applies if the operator has a contractual right to receive cash from or at the direction of the grantor and the grantor has little, if any, discretion to avoid payment. This will be the case if the grantor contractually guarantees to pay the operator:

[IFRIC 12:16]

- specified or determinable amounts; or
- the shortfall, if any, between amounts received from users of the public service and specified or determinable amounts.

A financial asset exists in these circumstances even if the payments are contingent on the operator ensuring that the infrastructure meets specified quality or efficiency requirements. [IFRIC 12:16]

The financial asset model cannot apply if the grantor only pays when users use the service or if the grantor only grants a right to charge users for the service.

The financial asset is accounted for in accordance with IFRS 9 *Financial Instruments* (see **4.2**) or, for entities that have not yet adopted IFRS 9, IAS 39 *Financial Instruments: Recognition and Measurement* (see **4.3**). The requirements of IAS 32 *Financial Instruments: Presentation* and IFRS 7 *Financial Instruments: Disclosures* also apply. [IFRIC 12:23]

4.2   Measurement of financial asset – entities that have adopted IFRS 9

If the operator is applying IFRS 9, the amount due from, or at the direction of, the grantor is measured at:

[IFRIC 12:24]

- amortised cost; or
- fair value through other comprehensive income; or
- fair value through profit or loss.

> The option to measure this amount at fair value through other comprehensive income was introduced in July 2014 when the revised IFRS 9 was issued. This option should not be used unless the entity has adopted IFRS 9 (as revised in 2014), which is effective for periods beginning on or after 1 January 2018, with earlier application permitted.

When the amount due from the grantor is accounted for at amortised cost or fair value through other comprehensive income, IFRS 9 requires interest calculated using the effective interest method to be recognised in profit or loss. [IFRIC 12:25] For guidance on the classification of financial assets under IFRS 9, see **section 5** of **chapter B2**.

4.3   Measurement of financial asset – entities that have not yet adopted IFRS 9

Entities that have not yet adopted IFRS 9 should apply IAS 39. Under the requirements of that Standard, the financial asset will, depending on the circumstances, be required to be classified:

[IFRIC 12:24]

- as at fair value through profit or loss, if so designated upon initial recognition (and provided that the conditions for that classification are met); or
- as loans and receivables; or
- as available for sale.

The asset can only be classified as loans and receivables if payments are fixed or determinable and the only substantial risk of non-recovery of the initial investment is credit deterioration of the counterparty. (For further guidance on the classification of financial assets under IAS 39, see **section 3** of **chapter C2**). IFRIC 12 assumes that the financial asset will not be classified as held to maturity. [IFRIC 12:BC61]

If the amount due from the grantor is accounted for either as loans and receivables or as an available-for-sale financial asset, IAS 39 requires interest calculated using the effective interest method to be recognised in profit or loss. [IFRIC 12:25]

4.4 Application of the financial asset model (both IFRS 9 and IAS 39)

Some practical issues may arise because service concession agreements usually establish a single payment mechanism without splitting the amounts between the construction services consideration (which will reduce the financial asset) and the operating services consideration (which will be revenue). It will be necessary to identify the underlying revenue streams that relate to each activity. This allocation may require a significant amount of judgement.

For the purposes of determining the construction and operating service revenue over the concession term, Example 1 accompanying IFRIC 12 illustrates that an appropriate approach is for an entity to first establish appropriate margins for determining the revenue streams. The example shows how the fair value of the consideration from both activities is measured as the projected costs plus a reasonable market margin. The discount rate to be used is calculated once the revenue and costs from both activities have been allocated. This discount rate would be one that causes the aggregate present value of all sums receivable from the grantor to be equal to the fair value of the services to be provided over the concession term. This rate would be similar to an internal rate of return for the project.

In practice, some entities first establish an appropriate discount rate for determining the appropriate profit margins on the construction and operation services. Significant judgement is required in the selection of the appropriate discount rate, and the allocation of the total consideration received or receivable to the relative fair value of the construction and operation services delivered, because this will affect the future revenue recognition pattern. Care should be taken to ensure the overall reasonableness of any model chosen.

Example 4.4

Financial asset model

An operator enters into a contract to provide construction services costing CU100. It has been determined that the fair value of the construction services provided is CU110. The total cash inflows over the entire life of the contract are fixed by the grantor at CU200. The finance revenue to be recognised, calculated using the effective interest method in accordance with IFRS 9 (or, for entities that have not yet adopted IFRS 9, IAS 39), is CU15 over the entire life of the service concession arrangement, and the balance of CU75

(CU200 – CU110 – CU15) relates to services provided during the operation phase. The following journal entries are made in these circumstances.

During construction

		CU	CU
Dr	Financial asset	110	
Cr	Construction revenue		110

To recognise revenue relating to construction services, to be settled in cash.

		CU	CU
Dr	Cost of construction (profit or loss)	100	
Cr	Cash		100

To recognise costs relating to construction services.

During the operation phase

		CU	CU
Dr	Financial asset	15	
Cr	Finance revenue		15

To recognise interest income under the financial asset model.

		CU	CU
Dr	Financial asset	75	
Cr	Revenue		75

To recognise revenue relating to the operation phase.

		CU	CU
Dr	Cash	200	
Cr	Financial asset		200

To recognise cash received from the grantor.

Total revenue over the life of the contract (including finance revenue of CU15)	CU200
Total cash inflows over the life of the contract	CU200

A more detailed example of the financial asset model is included as Example 1 in the illustrative examples accompanying IFRIC 12 and is reproduced at **example 13.2**.

5   Intangible asset model

5.1   Intangible asset model – general

The intangible asset model applies if the operator receives a right (a licence) to charge users, or the grantor, based on usage of the public service. There is no unconditional right to receive cash because the amounts are contingent on the extent to which the public uses the service. [IFRIC 12:17]

Arrangements in which the grantor, rather than the users, pays the operator amounts based on usage are often described as 'shadow tolls'. If the amounts received by the operator are contingent on usage rather than being an unconditional right to receive cash or another financial instrument, the operator recognises an intangible asset, notwithstanding that the amounts are received from the grantor (see also IFRIC 12:BC36 to BC40).

During the construction phase, the operator recognises revenue in respect of construction activities, with the corresponding entry increasing the amount recognised for the intangible asset. This is because the operator exchanges construction services in return for a licence. The grantor makes a non-cash payment for the construction services by giving the operator an intangible asset in exchange for the construction services. Because this is an exchange of dissimilar goods and services, in accordance with paragraph 12 of IAS 18 *Revenue*, revenue must be recognised on the transaction.

The intangible asset generates a second stream of revenue when the operator receives cash from users or from the grantor based on usage. This contrasts with the financial asset model in which monies received are treated as partial repayment of the financial asset. Under the intangible asset model, the intangible asset is reduced by amortisation rather than repayment.

This results in revenue being recognised twice – once when the construction services are provided (in exchange for the intangible asset) and a second time on the receipt of payments for usage. The expenses recognised under the intangible asset model are correspondingly higher, because amortisation of the intangible asset is recognised in profit or loss.

The intangible asset should be accounted for in accordance with IAS 38 *Intangible Assets* (see **chapter A9**). [IFRIC 12:26] The intangible asset should be amortised over the period of the concession. The appropriate method of amortisation of the intangible asset is generally the straight-line method, unless another method better reflects the pattern of consumption of the asset's future economic benefits. However, in some circumstances, if the expected pattern of consumption of the expected economic benefits is based on usage, it may be appropriate to use an alternative method of amortisation.

Example 5.1A

Amortisation under the intangible asset model

Company B enters into an arrangement under which it will build and operate a toll bridge. Company B is entitled to charge users for driving over the toll bridge for the period from the completion of construction until 1 million cars have driven across the bridge, at which point the concession arrangement will end. It would be appropriate for Company B to amortise its intangible asset based on usage, because Company B's licence to operate the bridge expires on the basis of usage rather than with the passage of time.

Example 5.1B

Intangible asset model

As in **example 4.4**, an operator enters into a contract to provide construction services costing CU100. It has been determined that the fair value of the construction services provided is CU110. The total cash inflows over the entire life of the contract are expected to be CU200; however, this amount is not guaranteed by the grantor. The following entries are made in these circumstances.

During construction

		CU	CU
Dr	Cost of construction (profit or loss)	100	
Cr	Cash		100

To recognise costs relating to construction services.

		CU	CU
Dr	Intangible asset	110	
Cr	Revenue		110

To recognise revenue relating to construction services provided for non-cash consideration.

During the operation phase

		CU	CU
Dr	Amortisation expense	110	
Cr	Intangible asset (accumulated amortisation)		110

To recognise amortisation expense relating to the operation phase.

	CU	CU
Dr Cash	200	
Cr Revenue		200

To recognise revenue received from users in the operation phase.

Total revenue over the life of the contract	CU310
Total cash inflows over the life of the contract	CU200

A more detailed example of the intangible asset model is included as Example 2 in the illustrative examples accompanying IFRIC 12 and is reproduced at **example 13.3**.

5.2 Changes in the estimated cash flows

Concessions are generally granted for long periods of time. Therefore, there are often changes in the initial estimates of future cash flows relating to such arrangements, for example:

- due to changes in the usage of the infrastructure by the users (increase in traffic on the road, increase in the number of passengers etc.); or

- due to changes in the estimated costs or other assumptions relating to the arrangement.

Such changes might be an indicator of impairment of the intangible asset or suggest that the amortisation method for the intangible asset should be reviewed.

6   Bifurcated model

When an operator receives a financial asset and an intangible asset as consideration, it is necessary to account separately for the component parts. At initial recognition, both components are recognised at the fair value of the consideration received or receivable in respect of work carried out until that date. [IFRIC 12:18] A 'residual approach' is taken in arriving at a value for both components. To the extent that the operator receives a contractual right to receive cash from or at the direction of the grantor, a financial asset is recognised. Any excess of the fair value of the construction services provided over the fair value of the financial asset recognised is recognised as an intangible asset.

Example 6

Bifurcated model

As in **example 4.4**, an operator enters into a contract to provide construction services costing CU100. It has been determined that the fair value of the construction services provided is CU110. The total cash inflows over the entire life of the contract are expected to be CU200. Of these, CU60 are guaranteed by the grantor. The appropriate finance revenue to be recognised derived from applying the effective interest method in accordance with IFRS 9 (or, for entities that have not yet adopted IFRS 9, IAS 39) is in total CU6 over the entire life of the service concession arrangement. The following entries are made in these circumstances.

During construction

		CU	CU
Dr	Financial asset	60	
Cr	Revenue		60

To recognise revenue relating to construction services, to be settled in cash.

		CU	CU
Dr	Cost of construction (profit or loss)	100	
Cr	Cash		100

To recognise costs relating to construction services.

		CU	CU
Dr	Intangible asset	50	
Cr	Revenue		50

To recognise revenue relating to construction services provided for non-cash consideration.

During the operation phase

		CU	CU
Dr	Financial asset	6	
Cr	Finance revenue		6

To recognise finance revenue.

		CU	CU
Dr	Amortisation expense	50	
Cr	Intangible asset (accumulated amortisation)		50

To recognise amortisation expense relating to the operation phase.

	CU	CU
Dr Cash	200	
Cr Revenue		134
Cr Financial asset		66

To recognise revenue relating to the operation phase and cash received from the grantor and users.

Total revenue over the life of the contract (including finance revenue of CU6)	CU250
Total cash inflows over the life of the contract	CU200

A more detailed example of the bifurcated model is included as Example 3 in the illustrative examples accompanying IFRIC 12 and is reproduced at **example 13.4**.

7   Maintenance obligations

A service concession arrangement contract may require an operator to:

[IFRIC 12:21]

- maintain the infrastructure to a specified level of serviceability; or

- restore the infrastructure to a specified condition at the end of the arrangement before it is handed over to the grantor.

For example, an operator of a toll road may be required to resurface a road to ensure that it does not deteriorate below a specified condition. IFRIC 12:21 states that such contractual obligations to maintain or restore the infrastructure should be recognised and measured in accordance with IAS 37 *Provisions, Contingent Liabilities and Contingent Assets*. Therefore, an estimate of the expenditure that would be required to settle the present obligation at the end of the reporting period needs to be made and recognised as a provision.

IFRIC 12 does not include guidance on the appropriate timing for recognition of the obligations because the terms and conditions of the obligation will vary from contract to contract. The requirements and guidance in IAS 37 should be followed to identify the period(s) in which different obligations should be recognised.

In the case of resurfacing a road, it may be that the amount required to settle the obligation at any point in time is linked to the number of vehicles that have travelled over the road. In such circumstances, usage of the road may determine the obligating event. This is illustrated by Example 2 accompanying IFRIC 12 (see **example 13.3**) which shows the provision for the resurfacing obligation being built up over time.

In contrast, when the entity is obligated to restore the infrastructure to a specified condition at the end of the arrangement irrespective of usage, it has an obligation analogous to an obligation for the dismantling or removal of an asset and restoring the site on which the asset stands accounted for under IAS 37 and IFRIC 1 *Changes in Existing Decommissioning, Restoration and Similar Liabilities*. In such circumstances, the obligation arises when the infrastructure is constructed. Under the intangible asset model, such an obligation is included in the cost of the asset and is subsequently amortised.

IFRIC 12 envisages that maintenance obligations could alternatively be a revenue-earning activity, in particular under the financial asset model as illustrated by Example 1 accompanying IFRIC 12 (see **example 13.2**). If the grantor reimburses the operator for maintenance (e.g. resurfacing a road), the operator should not recognise the obligation in the statement of financial position but should instead recognise the revenue and expense in profit or loss when the resurfacing work is performed. The accounting result is similar to that of an upgrade (see **section 8**).

Ultimately, the accounting treatment for maintenance obligations will depend on the precise terms and circumstances of the obligations, which will vary from contract to contract and should not be affected by the nature of the infrastructure asset recognised (i.e. whether a financial asset or an intangible asset).

IAS 37 requires that, when the effect of the time value of money is material, the amount of a provision should be the present value of the expenditures expected to be required to settle the obligation.

After initial recognition, provisions should be reviewed at the end of each reporting period and adjusted to reflect current best estimates.

Adjustments to provisions arise from three sources:

- revisions to estimated cash flows (both amount and timing);
- changes to present value due to the passage of time (i.e. unwinding of discount); and
- revisions of discount rates to reflect prevailing current market conditions.

In the years following the initial recognition and measurement of a provision at its present value, the provision should be revised to reflect estimated cash flows being closer to the measurement date. While the unwinding of the discount relating to the passage of time should be recognised as a finance cost (which is no longer capitalised once the infrastructure is ready for use), the revision of estimates of the amount and timing of cash flows is a reassessment of the provision and should be charged or credited as an operating item rather than as a finance cost. This is consistent with IFRIC 1 which treats changes in the estimated timing or amount of the obligation and changes in the discount rate as operating items, with periodic unwinding of the discount recognised as a borrowing cost.

Example 7

Resurfacing obligations and changes in the estimates of the provision

The operator's resurfacing obligation in respect of a toll road arises as a consequence of use of the road during the operating phase. It is recognised and measured in accordance with IAS 37, i.e. at the best estimate of the expenditure required to settle the present obligation at the end of the reporting period.

It is assumed that the terms of the operator's contractual obligation are such that, at any date, the best estimate of the expenditure required to settle the obligation in the future is proportional to the number of vehicles that have used the road. For illustrative purposes, a continuous traffic flow is assumed, allowing for the use of a straight-line method that increases the provision by a fixed amount (discounted to a current value) each year.

The operator discounts the provision to its present value in accordance with IAS 37.

Illustration 1 No changes in estimates

The best estimate of the expenditure required amounts to CU100 at the end of Year 6. The obligation increases by CU16.67 (i.e. CU100 divided by 6 years), discounted to a current value each year and the initial discount rate is 6 per cent. There are no subsequent changes in estimates.

The expense recognised each period in profit or loss will be as follows.

Year	1	2	3	4	5	6	Total
Estimated cost of resurfacing (CU)	100	100	100	100	100	100	
Estimated discount rate (per cent)	6	6	6	6	6	6	
	CU	CU	CU	CU	CU	CU	CU
Opening provision	–	12.45	26.40	41.98	59.33	78.62	–
Obligation arising in the year (operating cost)	12.45	13.20	13.99	14.83	15.72	16.67	86.86
Increase in prior year provision arising from the passage of time (finance cost)	–	0.75	1.59	2.52	3.57	4.71	13.14
	12.45	26.40	41.98	59.33	78.62	100.00	100.00
Used in year	–	–	–	–	–	(100.00)	
Closing provision	12.45	26.40	41.98	59.33	78.62	–	

Illustration 2 Subsequent change in discount rate

The best estimate of the expenditure required is CU100 at the end of Year 6. The obligation increases by CU16.67 (i.e. CU100 divided by 6 years), discounted to a current value each year and the initial discount rate is 6 per cent. Subsequently, as a result of a reassessment of prevailing market rates at the beginning of Year 4, the discount rate changes to 4 per cent.

The expense recognised each period in profit or loss will be as follows.

Year	1	2	3	4	5	6	Total
Estimated cost of resurfacing (CU)	100	100	100	100	100	100	
Estimated discount rate (per cent)	6	6	6	4	4	4	
	CU	CU	CU	CU	CU	CU	CU
Opening provision	–	12.45	26.40	41.98	61.64	80.13	–
Obligation arising in the year (operating cost)	12.45	13.20	13.99	17.98	16.03	16.67	90.32
Increase in prior year provision arising from the passage of time (finance cost)	–	0.75	1.59	1.68	2.46	3.20	9.68
	12.45	26.40	41.98	61.64	80.13	100.00	100.00
Used in year	–	–	–	–	–	(100.00)	
Closing provision	12.45	26.40	41.98	61.64	80.13	–	

At the beginning of Year 4, the discount rate has changed to 4 per cent. The obligation at the end of Year 3 was CU41.98. The unwinding of the discount would be the increase in the prior year obligation arising from the passage of time, so an amount of CU1.68 (CU41.98 × 4%) would be recognised as a finance cost and the additional amount of CU17.98 (being the net present value of the additional 1/6 of the CU100 provision for the year plus the increase in the provision resulting from the fall in discount rate from 6 per cent to 4 per cent) would increase the provision as an operating expense.

Illustration 3 Subsequent revision to the estimated cash flows

The best estimate of the expenditure required is CU100 at the end of Year 6. The obligation initially increases by CU16.67 (i.e. CU100 divided by 6 years), discounted to a current value each year and the discount rate is 6 per cent. Subsequently, at the beginning of Year 4, the best estimate changes to CU106.

The expense recognised each period in profit or loss will be as follows.

Year	1	2	3	4	5	6	Total
Estimated cost of resurfacing	100	100	100	106	106	106	
Estimated discount rate (per cent)	6	6	6	6	6	6	

Year	1	2	3	4	5	6	Total
	CU	CU	CU	CU	CU	CU	CU
Opening provision	–	12.45	26.40	41.98	62.89	83.33	–
Obligation arising in the year (operating cost)	12.45	13.20	13.99	18.39	16.67	17.67	92.37
Increase in prior year provision arising from the passage of time (finance cost)	–	0.75	1.59	2.52	3.77	5.00	13.63
	12.45	26.40	41.98	62.89	83.33	106.00	106.00
Used in year	–	–	–	–	–	(106.00)	
Closing provision	12.45	26.40	41.98	62.89	83.33	–	

Based on the revised estimate of CU106 at the end of Year 6, the obligation at the end of Year 4 should be CU62.89 (CU106 / 6 × 4 years, discounted by 2 years at 6 per cent). The finance cost in the year of revision is the increase in the prior year obligation arising from the passage of time using the discount rate of 6 per cent (CU41.98 × 6% = CU2.52). Any other adjustment to the carrying amount of the provision (i.e. an additional year's worth of the obligation plus the adjustment arising from the increase in the best estimate of the cash flow at the end of Year 6 to CU106) is charged as an operating expense.

8 Upgrade of existing infrastructure or new infrastructure

A service concession arrangement contract may require an operator to perform additional construction works during the operation phase. It will be a matter of judgement whether this subsequent expenditure represents maintenance or an upgrade of an existing infrastructure. Construction work would usually be considered an upgrade of existing infrastructure if it extends the life or capacity of the asset even though the additional revenues provided may not be identifiable on a standalone basis. For example, construction of an extra lane of a motorway will allow an increase in the traffic flow and it will represent an upgrade even though it is unclear how much traffic it produces by itself. On the other hand, construction work that does not extend the life or the capacity of the asset is usually considered to represent maintenance.

As explained in **section 7**, contractual obligations to maintain or restore infrastructure that are maintenance work should be recognised and measured in accordance with IAS 37 *Provisions, Contingent Liabilities and Contingent Assets*.

IFRIC 12:14 states that revenues and costs of the operator relating to the construction or upgrade services phase of a contract are accounted for in accordance with IAS 11 *Construction Contracts*. If the operator has an unconditional contractual right to receive cash in order to recover the additional upgrade investment, the fair value of the upgrade investment will be treated as a financial asset (receivable) under the financial asset model. If the operator has the right to charge users to recover the upgrade expenditure, the fair value of the upgrade elements will be treated as an intangible asset under the intangible asset model. To the extent that the revenues expected to be generated from the upgrade cannot be readily linked to the upgrade itself, it will generally be appropriate to recognise a single intangible asset for the initial construction work and the subsequent upgrade. In such circumstances, to the extent that the operator has an unavoidable obligation to upgrade the infrastructure, it would generally be appropriate to recognise, at the outset of the arrangement, the full intangible asset including the upgrade service with a performance obligation for the construction work to be undertaken in the future. That performance obligation would be measured at the fair value of the service yet to be provided, which would include an appropriate profit margin.

9   Borrowing costs

The requirements of IAS 23 *Borrowing Costs* in respect of the capitalisation of eligible borrowing costs are discussed in **chapter A18**. Borrowing costs attributable to an arrangement should be capitalised during the construction phase, in accordance with IAS 23, if the operator has a contractual right to receive an intangible asset. A financial asset is not a qualifying asset and so borrowing costs are recognised as an expense in the period in which they are incurred. [IFRIC 12:22] Under the financial asset model, interest is imputed on the financial asset using the effective interest method. The financial asset generates interest income because it is accounted for in accordance with IFRS 9 (or, for entities that have not yet adopted IFRS 9, IAS 39) although the construction phase is still in process. [IFRIC 12:IE8]

10   Arrangements that do not give rise to construction or upgrade services

IFRIC 12 envisages that under certain service concession arrangements the operator does not undertake construction or upgrade activities, but instead the grantor gives the operator access to existing infrastructure for the purpose of the service arrangement. [IFRIC 12:7(b)] However, IFRIC 12 does not deal specifically with situations in which a service concession arrangement consists only of an operation phase.

In such arrangements, the grantor may pay the operator directly for providing the service or give the operator a right to charge users at a regulated price and the operator may pay the grantor a fixed or variable amount for a licence to provide those services. In the absence of specific guidance in IFRIC 12, it is necessary to apply the requirements of other relevant IFRSs as discussed below.

- When the operator is paid a fixed sum by, or at the direction of, the grantor, revenue relating to the operation phase is accounted for in accordance with IAS 18 *Revenue* and costs are expensed as incurred. There is no financial asset relating to construction services to be recognised at inception. When the operator is given a right to charge users, it would be inappropriate to recognise an intangible asset with a corresponding credit to income at the inception of the contract. This is because, in contrast to an arrangement under which the operator has constructed the infrastructure, there has been no exchange of dissimilar goods and services in return for the licence at inception (which would result in the recognition of revenue in accordance with IAS 18:12). In such arrangements, the operator should recognise revenue from users as earned, recognise expenses in profit or loss as incurred, and recognise a provision for any contractual obligations to maintain and restore the infrastructure in accordance with IAS 37 *Provisions, Contingent Liabilities and Contingent Assets*.

- When the operator pays the grantor to acquire a licence to charge users for a public service, the operator should recognise an intangible asset at cost, including the present value of all future fixed payments to be made by the operator to the grantor, in accordance with IAS 38 *Intangible Assets*. If future amounts payable are contingent on usage, those amounts payable should be recognised as expenses as usage occurs, rather than being accrued at the outset.

11 Items provided by the grantor to the operator

The grantor may also provide the operator access to other items (e.g. land or other infrastructure assets). Following the basic principles underlying the accounting model established in IFRIC 12:11, infrastructure items to which the operator is given access by the grantor for the purposes of the service arrangement are not recognised as property, plant and equipment of the operator because they remain under the control of the grantor.

An operator may also be provided with infrastructure items by the grantor as part of the consideration payable by the grantor for the services, to keep or deal with as the operator wishes (i.e. they are not for the purposes of the service arrangement); such infrastructure items should be recognised as assets of the operator and measured at fair value on initial recognition. The operator should also recognise a liability in respect of unfulfilled obligations it has assumed in exchange for the assets.

IFRIC 12 specifically states that such assets should not be viewed as government grants as defined in IAS 20 *Accounting for Government Grants and Disclosure of Government Assistance*. [IFRIC 12:27]

Example 11

Items provided to the operator by the grantor

Company A enters into a service concession arrangement under which it will build a new hospital and operate it for a period of 30 years. In exchange, the government provides Company A with a fixed annual cash payment, and title to a substantial plot of land surrounding the hospital. Company A is free to use the land as it wishes. Company A should recognise the land as its own property at fair value at the date of initial recognition, together with a corresponding obligation for any unfulfilled obligations.

---

12   Disclosures about service concession arrangements

SIC-29 *Service Concession Arrangements: Disclosures* specifies certain disclosures that are required for service concession arrangements to meet the requirements of paragraph 112(c) of IAS 1 *Presentation of Financial Statements* (see **7.1.1** in **chapter A4**). The requirements of SIC-29 are considered at **7.4.3** in **chapter A4**.

IFRIC 12 explains how an operator should account for infrastructure that it constructs or acquires from a third party for the purpose of the service arrangement, but which is controlled by the grantor. The scope of SIC-29 is wider than this and includes, for example, arrangements in which the operator controls the infrastructure and also applies to the grantor in service concession arrangements.

13   Further examples illustrating the application of IFRIC 12

13.1   Illustrative examples – general

IFRIC 12 provides illustrative examples of how to account for service concession arrangements in three situations: under the financial asset model, the intangible asset model and the bifurcated model. These examples are reproduced at **examples 13.2** to **13.4**. Further guidance on each model can be found in **sections 4**, **5** and **6**.

13.2 Financial asset model

Example 13.2

The grantor gives the operator a financial asset

[IFRIC 12:IE1 - IE10, Example 1]

Arrangement terms

The terms of the arrangement require an operator to construct a road – completing construction within two years – and maintain and operate the road to a specified standard for eight years (ie years 3–10). The terms of the arrangement also require the operator to resurface the road at the end of year 8 – the resurfacing activity is revenue-generating. At the end of year 10, the arrangement will end. The operator estimates that the costs it will incur to fulfil its obligations will be:

Table 1.1 Contract costs

	Year	CU
Construction services	1	500
	2	500
Operation services (per year)	3–10	10
Road resurfacing	8	100

The terms of the arrangement require the grantor to pay the operator 200 currency units (CU200) per year in years 3–10 for making the road available to the public.

For the purpose of this illustration, it is assumed that all cash flows take place at the end of the year.

Contract revenue

The operator recognises contract revenue and costs in accordance with IAS 11 *Construction Contracts* and IAS 18 *Revenue*. The costs of each activity – construction, operation and resurfacing – are recognised as expenses by reference to the stage of completion of that activity. Contract revenue – the fair value of the amount due from the grantor for the activity undertaken – is recognised at the same time. Under the terms of the arrangement the operator is obliged to resurface the road at the end of year 8. In year 8 the operator will be reimbursed by the grantor for resurfacing the road. The obligation to resurface the road is measured at zero in the statement of financial position and the revenue and expense are not recognised in profit or loss until the resurfacing work is performed.

The total consideration (CU200 in each of years 3–10) reflects the fair values for each of the services, which are:

Table 1.2 Fair values of the consideration received or receivable

	Fair value
Construction services	Forecast cost + 5%
Operation services	Forecast cost + 20%
Road resurfacing	Forecast cost + 10%
Effective interest rate	6.18% per year

In year 1, for example, construction costs of CU500, construction revenue of CU525 (cost plus 5 per cent), and hence construction profit of CU25 are recognised in profit or loss.

Financial asset

[For entities that have adopted IFRS 9] IFRS 9 *Financial Instruments* may require the entity to measure the amounts due from the grantor at amortised cost, unless the entity designates those amounts as measured at fair value through profit or loss. If the receivable is measured at amortised cost in accordance with IFRS 9, it is measured initially at fair value and subsequently at amortised cost, ie the amount initially recognised plus the cumulative interest on that amount calculated using the effective interest method minus repayments.

[For entities that have not yet adopted IFRS 9] The amounts due from the grantor meet the definition of a receivable in IAS 39 *Financial Instruments: Recognition and Measurement*. The receivable is measured initially at fair value. It is subsequently measured at amortised cost, ie the amount initially recognised plus the cumulative interest on that amount calculated using the effective interest method minus repayments.

If the cash flows and fair values remain the same as those forecast, the effective interest rate is 6.18 per cent per year and the receivable recognised at the end of years 1–3 will be:

Table 1.3 Measurement of receivable

	CU
Amount due for construction in year 1	525
Receivable at end of year 1[a]	**525**
Effective interest in year 2 on receivable at the end of year 1 (6.18% × CU525)	32
Amount due for construction in year 2	525
Receivable at end of year 2	**1,082**
Effective interest in year 3 on receivable at the end of year 2 (6.18% × CU1,082)	67
Amount due for operation in year 3 (CU10 × (1 + 20%))	12
Cash receipts in year 3	(200)
Receivable at end of year 3	**961**

[a]   No effective interest arises in year 1 because the cash flows are assumed to take place at the end of the year.

Overview of cash flows, statement of comprehensive income and statement of financial position

For the purpose of this illustration, it is assumed that the operator finances the arrangement wholly with debt and retained profits. It pays interest at 6.7 per cent per year on outstanding debt. If the cash flows and fair values remain the same as those forecast, the operator's cash flows, statement of comprehensive income and statement of financial position over the duration of the arrangement will be:

Table 1.4 Cash flows (currency units)

Year	1	2	3	4	5	6	7	8	9	10	Total
Receipts	–	–	200	200	200	200	200	200	200	200	1,600
Contract costs[a]	(500)	(500)	(10)	(10)	(10)	(10)	(10)	(110)	(10)	(10)	(1,180)
Borrowing costs[b]	–	(34)	(69)	(61)	(53)	(43)	(33)	(23)	(19)	(7)	(342)
Net inflow/ (outflow)	(500)	(534)	121	129	137	147	157	67	171	183	78

[a]   Table 1.1
[b]   Debt at start of year (table 1.6) × 6.7%

Table 1.5 Statement of comprehensive income (currency units)

Year	1	2	3	4	5	6	7	8	9	10	Total
Revenue	525	525	12	12	12	12	12	122	12	12	1,256
Contract costs	(500)	(500)	(10)	(10)	(10)	(10)	(10)	(110)	(10)	(10)	(1,180)
Finance income[a]	–	32	67	59	51	43	34	25	22	11	344
Borrowing costs[b]	–	(34)	(69)	(61)	(53)	(43)	(33)	(23)	(19)	(7)	(342)
Net profit	25	23	–	–	–	2	3	14	5	6	78

[a]   Amount due from grantor at start of year (table 1.6) × 6.18%
[b]   Cash/(debt) (table 1.6) × 6.7%

Table 1.6 Statement of financial position (currency units)

End of Year	1	2	3	4	5	6	7	8	9	10
Amount due from grantor[a]	525	1,082	961	832	695	550	396	343	177	–
Cash/(debt)[b]	(500)	(1,034)	(913)	(784)	(647)	(500)	(343)	(276)	(105)	78
Net assets	25	48	48	48	48	50	53	67	72	78

[a]   Amount due from grantor at start of year, plus revenue and finance income earned in year (table 1.5), less receipts in year (table 1.4)
[b]   Debt at start of year plus net cash flow in year (table 1.4)

This example deals with only one of many possible types of arrangements. Its purpose is to illustrate the accounting treatment for some features that are commonly found in practice. To make the illustration as clear as possible, it has been assumed that the arrangement period is only ten years and that the operator's annual receipts are constant over that period. In practice, arrangement periods may be much longer and annual revenues may increase with time. In such circumstances, the changes in net profit from year to year could be greater.

13.3   Intangible asset model

Example 13.3

The grantor gives the operator an intangible asset (a licence to charge users)

[IFRIC 12:IE11 - IE22, Example 2]

Arrangement terms

The terms of a service arrangement require an operator to construct a road – completing construction within two years – and maintain and operate the road to a specified standard for eight years (ie years 3–10). The terms of the arrangement also require the operator to resurface the road when the original surface has deteriorated below a specified condition. The operator estimates that it will have to undertake the resurfacing at the end of year 8. At the end of year 10, the service arrangement will end. The operator estimates that the costs it will incur to fulfil its obligations will be:

Table 2.1 Contract costs

	Year	CU
Construction services	1	500
	2	500
Operation services (per year)	3–10	10
Road resurfacing	8	100

The terms of the arrangement allow the operator to collect tolls from drivers using the road. The operator forecasts that vehicle numbers will remain constant over the duration of the contract and that it will receive tolls of 200 currency units (CU200) in each of years 3–10.

For the purpose of this illustration it is assumed that all cash flows take place at the end of the year.

Intangible asset

The operator provides construction services to the grantor in exchange for an intangible asset, ie a right to collect tolls from road users in years 3–10. In accordance with IAS 38 *Intangible Assets*, the operator recognises the intangible asset at cost, ie the fair value of consideration transferred to acquire the asset, which is the fair value of the consideration received or receivable for the construction services delivered.

During the construction phase of the arrangement the operator's asset (representing its accumulating right to be paid for providing construction services) is classified as an intangible asset (licence to charge users of the infrastructure). The operator measures the fair value of its consideration received as equal to the forecast construction costs plus 5 per cent margin, which the operator concludes is consistent with the rate that a market participant would require as compensation for providing the construction services and for assuming the risk associated with the construction costs. It is also assumed that, in accordance with IAS 23 *Borrowing Costs*, the operator capitalises the borrowing costs, estimated at 6.7 per cent, during the construction phase of the arrangement:

Table 2.2 Initial measurement of intangible asset

	CU
Construction services in year 1 (CU500 × (1 + 5%))	525
Capitalisation of borrowing costs (table 2.4)	34
Construction services in year 2 (CU500 × (1 + 5%))	525
Intangible asset at end of year 2	**1,084**

In accordance with IAS 38, the intangible asset is amortised over the period in which it is expected to be available for use by the operator, ie years 3–10. The depreciable amount of the intangible asset (CU1,084) is allocated using a straight-line method. The annual amortisation is therefore CU1,084 divided by 8 years, ie CU135 per year.

Construction costs and revenue

The operator recognises the revenue and costs in accordance with IAS 11 *Construction Contracts*, ie by reference to the stage of completion of the construction. It measures contract revenue at the fair value of the consideration received or receivable. Thus in each of years 1 and 2 it recognises in its profit or loss construction costs of CU500, construction revenue of CU525 (cost plus 5 per cent) and, hence, construction profit of CU25.

Toll revenue

The road users pay for the public services at the same time as they receive them, ie when they use the road. The operator therefore recognises toll revenue when it collects the tolls.

Resurfacing obligations

The operator's resurfacing obligation arises as a consequence of use of the road during the operating phase. It is recognised and measured in accordance with IAS 37 *Provisions, Contingent Liabilities and Contingent Assets*, ie at the best estimate of the expenditure required to settle the present obligation at the end of the reporting period.

For the purpose of this illustration, it is assumed that the terms of the operator's contractual obligation are such that the best estimate of the expenditure required to settle the obligation at any date is proportional to the number of vehicles that have used the road by that date and increases by CU17 (discounted to a current value) each year. The operator discounts the provision to its present value in accordance with IAS 37. The charge recognised each period in profit or loss is:

Table 2.3 Resurfacing obligation (currency units)

Year	3	4	5	6	7	8	Total
Obligation arising in year (CU17 discounted at 6%)	12	13	14	15	16	17	87
Increase in earlier years' provision arising from passage of time	0	1	1	2	4	5	13
Total expense recognised in profit or loss	12	14	15	17	20	22	100

Overview of cash flows, statement of comprehensive income and statement of financial position

For the purposes of this illustration, it is assumed that the operator finances the arrangement wholly with debt and retained profits. It pays interest at 6.7 per cent per year on outstanding debt. If the cash flows and fair values remain the same as those forecast, the operator's cash flows, statement of comprehensive income and statement of financial position over the duration of the arrangement will be:

Table 2.4 Cash flows (currency units)

Year	1	2	3	4	5	6	7	8	9	10	Total
Receipts	–	–	200	200	200	200	200	200	200	200	1,600
Contract costs[a]	(500)	(500)	(10)	(10)	(10)	(10)	(10)	(110)	(10)	(10)	(1,180)
Borrowing costs[b]	–	(34)	(69)	(61)	(53)	(43)	(33)	(23)	(19)	(7)	(342)
Net inflow/ (outflow)	(500)	(534)	121	129	137	147	157	67	171	183	78

[a]   Table 2.1
[b]   Debt at start of year (table 2.6) × 6.7%

Table 2.5 Statement of comprehensive income (currency units)

Year	1	2	3	4	5	6	7	8	9	10	Total
Revenue	525	525	200	200	200	200	200	200	200	200	2,650
Amortisation	–	–	(135)	(135)	(136)	(136)	(136)	(136)	(135)	(135)	(1,084)
Resurfacing expense	–	–	(12)	(14)	(15)	(17)	(20)	(22)	–	–	(100)
Other contract costs	(500)	(500)	(10)	(10)	(10)	(10)	(10)	(10)	(10)	(10)	(1,080)
Borrowing costs[(a)(b)]	–	–	(69)	(61)	(53)	(43)	(33)	(23)	(19)	(7)	(308)
Net profit	25	25	(26)	(20)	(14)	(6)	1	9	36	48	78

[(a)] Borrowing costs are capitalised during the construction phase

[(b)] Table 2.4

Table 2.6 Statement of financial position (currency units)

End of Year	1	2	3	4	5	6	7	8	9	10
Intangible asset	525	1,084	940	814	678	542	406	270	135	–
Cash/ (debt)[(a)]	(500)	(1,034)	(913)	(784)	(647)	(500)	(343)	(276)	(105)	78
Resurfacing obligation	–	–	(12)	(26)	(41)	(58)	(78)	–	–	–
Net assets	25	50	24	4	(10)	(16)	(15)	(6)	30	78

[(a)]   Debt at start of year plus net cash flow in year (table 2.4)

This example deals with only one of many possible types of arrangements. Its purpose is to illustrate the accounting treatment for some features that are commonly found in practice. To make the illustration as clear as possible, it has been assumed that the arrangement period is only ten years and that the operator's annual receipts are constant over that period. In practice, arrangement periods may be much longer and annual revenues may increase with time. In such circumstances, the changes in net profit from year to year could be greater.

13.4   Bifurcated model

Example 13.4

The grantor gives the operator a financial asset and an intangible asset

[IFRIC 12:IE23 - IE38, Example 3]

The terms of a service arrangement require an operator to construct a road – completing construction within two years – and to operate the road and maintain it to a specified standard for eight years (ie years 3–10). The terms of the arrangement also require the operator to resurface the road when the original surface has deteriorated below a specified condition. The operator estimates that it will have to undertake the resurfacing at the end of year 8. At the end of year 10, the arrangement will end. The operator estimates that the costs it will incur to fulfil its obligations will be:

Table 3.1 Contract costs

	Year	CU
Construction services	1	500
	2	500
Operation services (per year)	3–10	10
Road resurfacing	8	100

The operator estimates the consideration in respect of construction services to be cost plus 5 per cent.

The terms of the arrangement allow the operator to collect tolls from drivers using the road. In addition, the grantor guarantees the operator a minimum amount of CU700 and interest at a specified rate of 6.18 per cent to reflect the timing of cash receipts. The operator forecasts that vehicle numbers will remain constant over the duration of the contract and that it will receive tolls of CU200 in each of years 3–10.

For the purpose of this illustration, it is assumed that all cash flows take place at the end of the year.

Dividing the arrangement

The contractual right to receive cash from the grantor for the services and the right to charge users for the public services should be regarded as two separate assets under IFRSs. Therefore in this arrangement it is necessary to divide the operator's consideration into two components – a financial asset component based on the guaranteed amount and an intangible asset for the remainder.

Table 3.2 Dividing the operator's consideration

Year	Total	Financial asset	Intangible asset
Construction services in year 1 (CU 500 × (1 + 5%))	525	350	175
Construction services in year 2 (CU 500 × (1 + 5%))	525	350	175
Total construction services	1,050	700	350
	100%	67%[(a)]	33%
Finance income, at specified rate of 6.18% on receivable (see table 3.3)	22	22	–
Borrowing costs capitalised (interest paid in years 1 and 2 × 33%) (see table 3.7)	11	–	11
Total fair value of the operator's consideration	1,083	722	361

[(a)]   Amount guaranteed by the grantor as a proportion of the construction services

[For entities that have adopted IFRS 9] IFRS 9 *Financial Instruments* may require the entity to measure the amount due from or at the direction of the grantor in exchange for the construction services at amortised cost. If the receivable is measured at amortised cost in accordance with IFRS 9, it is measured initially at fair value and subsequently at amortised cost, ie the amount initially recognised plus the cumulative interest on that amount minus repayments.

[For entities that have not yet adopted IFRS 9] The amounts due from or at the direction of the grantor in exchange for the construction services meets the definition of a receivable in IAS 39 *Financial Instruments: Recognition and Measurement*. The receivable is measured initially at fair value. It is subsequently measured at amortised cost, ie the amount initially recognised plus the cumulative interest on that amount minus repayments.

On this basis the receivable recognised at the end of years 2 and 3 will be:

Table 3.3 Measurement of receivable

	CU
Construction services in year 1 allocated to the financial asset	350
Receivable at end of year 1	**350**
Construction services in year 2 allocated to the financial asset	350
Interest in year 2 on receivable at end of year 1 (6.18% × CU350)	22
Receivable at end of year 2	**722**
Interest in year 3 on receivable at end of year 2 (6.18% × CU722)	45
Cash receipts in year 3 (see table 3.5)	(117)
Receivable at end of year 3	**650**

Intangible asset

In accordance with IAS 38 *Intangible Assets*, the operator recognises the intangible asset at cost, ie the fair value of the consideration received or receivable.

During the construction phase of the arrangement the operator's *asset* (representing its accumulating right to be paid for providing construction services) is classified as a right to receive a licence to charge users of the infrastructure. The operator measures the fair value of its consideration received or receivable as equal to the forecast construction costs plus 5 per cent, which the operator concludes is consistent with the rate that a market participant would require as compensation for providing the construction services and for assuming the risk associated with the construction costs. It is also assumed that, in accordance with IAS 23 *Borrowing Costs*, the operator capitalises the borrowing costs, estimated at 6.7 per cent, during the construction phase:

Table 3.4 Initial measurement of intangible asset

	CU
Construction services in year 1 (CU500 × (1 + 5%) × 33%)	175
Borrowing costs (Interest paid in years 1 and 2 × 33%) (see table 3.7)	11
Construction services in year 2 (CU500 × (1 + 5%) × 33%)	175
Intangible asset at the end of year 2	**361**

In accordance with IAS 38, the intangible asset is amortised over the period in which it is expected to be available for use by the operator, ie years 3–10. The depreciable amount of the intangible asset (CU361 including borrowing costs) is allocated using a straight-line method. The annual amortisation charge is therefore CU361 divided by 8 years, ie CU45 per year.

Contract revenue and costs

The operator provides construction services to the grantor in exchange for a financial asset and an intangible asset. Under both the financial asset model and intangible asset model, the operator recognises contract revenue and costs in accordance with IAS 11 *Construction Contracts*, ie by reference to the stage of completion of the construction. It measures contract revenue at the fair value of the consideration receivable. Thus in each of years 1 and 2 it recognises in profit or loss construction costs of CU500 and construction revenue of CU525 (cost plus 5 per cent).

Toll revenue

The road users pay for the public services at the same time as they receive them, ie when they use the road. Under the terms of this arrangement the cash flows are allocated to the financial asset and intangible asset in proportion, so the operator allocates the receipts from tolls between repayment of the financial asset and revenue earned from the intangible asset:

Table 3.5 Allocation of toll receipts

	CU
Guaranteed receipt from grantor	700
Finance income (see table 3.8)	237
Total	937
Cash allocated to realisation of the financial asset per year (CU937/8)	**117**
Receipts attributable to intangible asset (CU200 × 8 years – CU937)	663
Annual receipt from intangible asset (CU663/8 years)	**83**

Resurfacing obligations

The operator's resurfacing obligation arises as a consequence of use of the road during the operation phase. It is recognised and measured in accordance with IAS 37 *Provisions, Contingent Liabilities and Contingent Assets*, ie at the best estimate of the expenditure required to settle the present obligation at the end of the reporting period.

For the purpose of this illustration, it is assumed that the terms of the operator's contractual obligation are such that the best estimate of the expenditure required to settle the obligation at any date is proportional to the number of vehicles that have used the road by that date and increases by CU17 each year. The operator discounts the provision to its present value in accordance with IAS 37. The charge recognised each period in profit or loss is:

Table 3.6 Resurfacing obligation (currency units)

Year	3	4	5	6	7	8	Total
Obligation arising in year (CU17 discounted at 6%)	12	13	14	15	16	17	87
Increase in earlier years' provision arising from passage of time	0	1	1	2	4	5	13
Total expense recognised in profit or loss	12	14	15	17	20	22	100

Overview of cash flows, statement of comprehensive income and statement of financial position

For the purposes of this illustration, it is assumed that the operator finances the arrangement wholly with debt and retained profits. It pays interest at 6.7 per cent per year on outstanding debt. If the cash flows and fair values remain the same as those forecast, the operator's cash flows, statement of comprehensive income and statement of financial position over the duration of the arrangement will be:

Table 3.7 Cash flows (currency units)

Year	1	2	3	4	5	6	7	8	9	10	Total
Receipts	–	–	200	200	200	200	200	200	200	200	1,600
Contract costs[a]	(500)	(500)	(10)	(10)	(10)	(10)	(10)	(110)	(10)	(10)	(1,180)
Borrowing costs[b]	–	(34)	(69)	(61)	(53)	(43)	(33)	(23)	(19)	(7)	(342)
Net inflow/ (outflow)	(500)	(534)	121	129	137	147	157	67	171	183	78

[a]   Table 3.1
[b]   Debt at start of year (table 3.9) × 6.7%

Table 3.8 Statement of comprehensive income (currency units)

Year	1	2	3	4	5	6	7	8	9	10	Total
Revenue on construction	525	525	–	–	–	–	–	–	–	–	1,050
Revenue from intangible asset	–	–	83	83	83	83	83	83	83	83	664
Finance income[a]	–	22	45	40	35	30	25	19	13	7	236
Amortisation	–	–	(45)	(45)	(45)	(45)	(45)	(45)	(45)	(46)	(361)
Resurfacing expense	–	–	(12)	(14)	(15)	(17)	(20)	(22)	–	–	(100)
Construction costs	(500)	(500)	–	–	–	–	–	–	–	–	(1,000)
Other contract costs[b]	–	–	(10)	(10)	(10)	(10)	(10)	(10)	(10)	(10)	(80)
Borrowing costs (table 3.7)[c]	–	(23)	(69)	(61)	(53)	(43)	(33)	(23)	(19)	(7)	(331)
Net profit	25	24	(8)	(7)	(5)	(2)	0	2	22	27	78

[a]   Interest on receivable

(b)   Table 3.1

(c)   In year 2, borrowing costs are stated net of amount capitalised in the intangible (see table 3.4)

Table 3.9 Statement of financial position (currency units)

End of Year	1	2	3	4	5	6	7	8	9	10
Receivable	350	722	650	573	491	404	312	214	10	–
Intangible asset	175	361	316	271	226	181	136	91	46	–
Cash / (debt)(a)	(500)	(1,034)	(913)	(784)	(647)	(500)	(343)	(276)	(105)	78
Resurfacing obligation	–	–	(12)	(26)	(41)	(58)	(78)	–	–	–
Net assets	25	49	41	34	29	27	27	29	51	78

(a)   Debt at start of year plus net cash flow in year (table 3.7)

This example deals with only one of many possible types of arrangements. Its purpose is to illustrate the accounting treatment for some features that are commonly found in practice. To make the illustration as clear as possible, it has been assumed that the arrangement period is only ten years and that the operator's annual receipts are constant over that period. In practice, arrangement periods may be much longer and annual revenues may increase with time. In such circumstances, the changes in net profit from year to year could be greater.

Appendix A4   Leases (IAS 17)

Contents

1   Introduction

1.1   Overview of IAS 17

IAS 17 *Leases* prescribes the accounting policies and disclosures applicable to leases, both for lessees and lessors. Leases are required to be classified as either finance leases (which transfer substantially all the risks and rewards of ownership, and give rise to asset and liability recognition by the lessee and a receivable by the lessor) and operating leases (which result in expense recognition by the lessee, with the asset remaining recognised by the lessor).

1.2   Amendments to IAS 17 since the last edition of this manual

None. IAS 17 was most recently amended in June 2014.

1.3   IAS 17 superseded by IFRS 16

In January 2016, the IASB issued IFRS 16 *Leases*, which is effective for annual periods beginning on or after 1 January 2019. IFRS 16 supersedes IAS 17. For annual periods beginning before 1 January 2019, entities may continue to apply IAS 17, which is discussed in this appendix. Alternatively, entities may choose to apply IFRS 16 in advance of its 2019 effective date provided that they disclose that fact and that they also apply IFRS 15 *Revenue from Contracts from Customers*. The requirements of IFRS 16 are discussed in detail in **chapter A17**.

IFRS 16 also supersedes:

- IFRIC 4 *Determining whether an Arrangement contains a Lease* (see **2.7**);

- SIC-15 *Operating Leases – Incentives* (see **7.2.3** and **8.4.8**); and

- SIC-27 *Evaluating the Substance of Transactions Involving the Legal Form of a Lease* (see **3.2**).

2   Scope

2.1   Scope – general

IAS 17 applies in accounting for all leases other than:

[IAS 17:2]

- lease agreements to explore for or use minerals, oil, natural gas and similar non-generative resources; and

- licensing agreements for such items as motion picture films, video recordings, plays, manuscripts, patents and copyrights.

Rights under licensing agreements for items such as motion picture films, video recordings, plays, manuscripts, patents and copyrights are excluded from the scope of IAS 17. However, intangible assets are within the scope of IAS 17 if they establish rights for the exclusive use of the intangible assets. Brands and trademarks often are licensed exclusively and, therefore, are examples of leases of intangible assets that are included within the scope of IAS 17. After initial recognition, an intangible asset held under a finance lease is accounted for by the lessee under IAS 38 *Intangible Assets* (see IAS 38:6).

2.2   Scope – leased assets dealt with under other IFRSs

In addition to the scope exclusions set out in **2.1**, IAS 17 should not be applied as the measurement basis for:

[IAS 17:2]

- property held by lessees that is accounted for as investment property (dealt with under IAS 40 *Investment Property* – see **appendix A5**);

- investment property provided by lessors under operating leases (dealt with under IAS 40 – see **appendix A5**);

- biological assets within the scope of IAS 41 *Agriculture* held by lessees under finance leases (see **chapter A38**); or

- biological assets within the scope of IAS 41 provided by lessors under operating leases (see **chapter A38**).

IAS 17:2 was amended in June 2014 by consequential amendments arising from *Agriculture: Bearer Plants (Amendments to IAS 16 and IAS 41)* to clarify that the biological assets excluded from the scope of IAS 17 are those that fall within the amended scope of IAS 41 *Agriculture* (see **chapter A38**). Following the June 2014 amendments (effective for annual periods beginning on or after 1 January 2016, with earlier application permitted), bearer plants accounted for in accordance with IAS 16 *Property, Plant and Equipment* (see **2.6** in **chapter A7**) either (1) held by a lessee under a finance lease, or (2) provided by a lessor under an operating lease, will fall within the scope of IAS 17.

2.3   Lease contracts involving substantial services by the lessor

IAS 17 applies to contracts that transfer the right to use assets even though substantial services by the lessor are required in connection with the operation or maintenance of such assets. [IAS 17:3] Examples include the supply of property, motor vehicles and photocopiers.

A contract that includes both assets and services should be separated when two or more identifiable streams operate independently of each other (e.g. when payments increase in response to different factors, parts of the contract run for different periods, or they can be terminated or renegotiated separately). In such cases, IAS 17 should be applied to the part relating to asset provision or use. (See also the discussion of IFRIC 4 *Determining whether an Arrangement contains a Lease* at **2.7**.)

2.4 Contracts for services that do not transfer the right to use assets

IAS 17 does not apply to agreements that are contracts for services that do not transfer the right to use assets from one contracting party to the other (e.g. employment contracts). [IAS 17:3] It follows that it does not apply to the separable service component of contracts that include both assets and services; examples would include the maintenance element of property and motor vehicle contracts.

2.5 Right to use relates only to a portion of an asset

It is possible that an agreement to lease part of an asset will fall within the scope of IAS 17. This will be the case when the agreement has fully conveyed the right to use that portion of the asset. In some instances, this 'right to use' may only relate to a portion of a larger asset (e.g. a transponder on a satellite or one floor in a building). IAS 40 specifically states that, when a portion of a property can be sold separately or leased out separately under a finance lease, it should be accounted for separately.

2.6 Rights and obligations meeting the definition of financial instruments

Rights and obligations under lease contracts may meet the definition of financial instruments. For a discussion of the extent to which lease contracts are also subject to the requirements of IFRSs on financial instruments, see **3.4** in **chapter B1** (for entities applying IFRS 9 *Financial Instruments*) or **3.4** in **chapter C1** (for entities applying IAS 39 *Financial Instruments: Recognition and Measurement*).

2.7   IFRIC 4 *Determining whether an Arrangement contains a Lease*

2.7.1   IFRIC 4 – background

Some arrangements that do not take the legal form of a lease nevertheless convey rights to use assets in return for a payment or series of payments. Examples of such arrangements include:

- outsourcing arrangements;

- telecommunication contracts that provide rights to capacity; and

- 'take-or-pay' and similar contracts, in which purchasers must make specified payments regardless of whether they take delivery of the contracted products or services.

These arrangements share many features of a lease, because a lease is defined in IAS 17:4 as "an agreement whereby the lessor conveys to the lessee in return for a payment or series of payments *the right to use an asset* for an agreed period of time". [Emphasis added] The IFRIC (now the IFRS Interpretations Committee) concluded that all arrangements meeting this definition should be accounted for in accordance with IAS 17 (subject to the scope of that Standard), regardless of whether they take the legal form of a lease. The objective of IFRIC 4 *Determining whether an Arrangement contains a Lease* is to provide guidance to assist in determining whether an arrangement is, or contains, a lease.

2.7.2   IFRIC 4 – scope

2.7.2.1   Scope of IFRIC 4 – general

IFRIC 4 does not address arrangements that are, or contain, leases excluded from the scope of IAS 17 nor, for leases falling within the scope of IAS 17, how such leases should be classified under that Standard.

Example 2.7.2.1

Application of non-regenerative resources exemptions

A power-generator entity operates a coal-fired power station. It contracts with a mining entity (Entity M) to purchase a specified percentage of the coal produced at a specified mine. Entity M will remain responsible for repairs, maintenance and other capital expenditure at the mine.

Given that IFRIC 4 does not apply to arrangements containing leases that are excluded from the scope of IAS 17, and that IAS 17:2(a) excludes leases for the use of non-regenerative resources from the scope of that Standard, is it necessary to consider IFRIC 4 in determining how to account for the contract described above?

Yes. Each element of the contract should be analysed separately. While the purchase/sale of the coal itself is outside the scope of both IFRIC 4 and

---

IAS 17 (because it represents a purchase/sale of a non-regenerative resource), the contract may include an element representing the right to use the mine infrastructure that would fall within the scope of IFRIC 4. The purchase/sale of coal and other elements of the contract (e.g. any service agreement) should be accounted for under the relevant guidance in IFRSs.

2.7.2.2 Contracts falling within the scope of both IFRIC 4 and IFRIC 12

When assessing the contractual terms of some arrangements, it is possible that they could fall within the scope of both IFRIC 4 and IFRIC 12 *Service Concession Arrangements*. To eliminate any inconsistencies between the accounting treatment for contracts with similar economic effects, IFRIC 4 specifies that if a contract appears to fall within the scope of both Interpretations, the requirements of IFRIC 12 prevail (see **chapter A35** or, for entities that have not yet adopted IFRS 15 *Revenue from Contracts with Customers*, **appendix A3**).

2.7.3 Determining whether an arrangement is, or contains, a lease

2.7.3.1 Determining whether an arrangement is, or contains, a lease – general

IFRIC 4 specifies that an arrangement that meets *both* of the following criteria is, or contains, a lease that should be accounted for in accordance with IAS 17:

[IFRIC 4:6 - 8]

- fulfilment of the arrangement is dependent on the use of a specific asset or assets ('the asset') (see **2.7.3.2**). The asset need not be explicitly identified by the contractual provisions of the arrangement. Rather it may be implicitly specified because it is not economically feasible or practical for the supplier to fulfil the arrangement by providing use of alternative assets; and

- the arrangement conveys a right to use the asset.

2.7.3.2 Identification of a specific asset

Example 2.7.3.2

Identification of a specific asset

Company A enters into a three-year agreement to provide internet access to Company B. The agreement requires Company B to make monthly payments and specifies the amount of bandwidth Company B needs. In order to provide Company B with the necessary bandwidth, Company A installs a router on Company B's premises. The router is not explicitly specified in the agreement, but is necessary to provide the required service and bandwidth to Company B. Company A has 24-hour access to the router to undertake any necessary maintenance or service. The useful life of the router is estimated to be three years.

Company A can replace the router at any time during the contract period provided that the replacement can provide the same service. Generally, Company A would only replace the router if it is damaged or needs to be upgraded. Company A has an excess inventory of these routers and does not have a history of replacing or exchanging the routers before the end of the contracts.

Is fulfilment of the agreement for the provision of internet access 'dependent on the use of a specific asset' (i.e. are the requirements of IFRIC 4:6(a) met so that it should be concluded that the arrangement incorporates a lease of the router)?

Fulfilment of the agreement will only be considered to be dependent on the use of a specific asset if the asset is explicitly identified in the arrangement or it has been implicitly identified (if, for example, the supplier owns or leases only one such asset and it is not economically practicable for the supplier to meet its obligation through the use of alternative assets).

Company A's 24-hour access to the router, immediate access to replacement routers, and contractual permission to change the router at any time indicate that the router installed on Company B's premises has not been implicitly identified in the arrangement. In effect, Company A can choose (1) which router to use in providing Company B with internet access for the three-year contract period, and (2) whether to replace that router.

When fulfilment of the agreement to provide internet access does not depend on the use of a specific asset (i.e. the requirements of IFRIC 4:6(a) are not met), the agreement does not contain a lease. In such cases, the agreement is a contract for the provision of services and should be accounted for in accordance with the relevant Standards.

2.7.3.3   Arrangements that convey the right to use an asset

An arrangement conveys the right to use an asset if the arrangement conveys to the purchaser (lessee) the right to control the use of the underlying asset. This will be the case if *any* of the following conditions is met:

[IFRIC 4:9]

- the purchaser in the arrangement has the ability or right to operate the asset or direct others to operate the asset (while obtaining or controlling more than an insignificant amount of the output of the asset);

- the purchaser has the ability or right to control physical access to the asset (while obtaining more than an insignificant amount of the output of the asset); or

- there is only a remote possibility that parties other than the purchaser will take more than an insignificant amount of the output of the asset and the price that the purchaser will pay is neither fixed per unit of output nor equal to the current market price at the time of delivery.

2.7.4 Timing of the assessment or reassessment as to whether an arrangement is, or contains, a lease

The assessment as to whether an arrangement contains a lease is made at the inception of the arrangement (being the earlier of the date of the arrangement and the date of commitment by the parties to the principal terms of the arrangement). A reassessment of the arrangement should be made only in the event of specified changes in circumstances, namely:

[IFRIC 4:10]

- a change in the contractual terms (unless the change only renews or extends the arrangement); or

- a renewal option being exercised or an extension being agreed to by the parties to the arrangement (unless the term of the renewal or extension was initially included in the lease term – see **6.2.2**). Note that a renewal or extension of the arrangement that does not modify any of the terms in the original arrangement before the end of the term of the original arrangement is evaluated only with respect to the renewal or extension period; or

- a change in the determination of whether fulfilment is dependent on a specified asset; or

- a substantial change to the asset (e.g. a substantial physical change to property, plant or equipment).

Changes in estimate (e.g. the estimated amount of output to be delivered to the purchaser or other potential purchasers) would not trigger a reassessment. If an arrangement is reassessed and is determined to contain a lease (or not contain a lease), lease accounting should be applied (or should cease to apply) from the date of change in circumstances. [IFRIC 4:11]

2.7.5 Separating payments for the lease from other payments

For the purpose of applying IAS 17, payments and other consideration required by the arrangement are separated into those for the lease and those for other elements in the arrangement on the basis of their fair values. The minimum lease payments for the purposes of IAS 17 include only payments for the lease (i.e. for the right to use the asset) and exclude payments for other elements in the arrangement (e.g. for services and the cost of inputs). [IFRIC 4:13]

If a purchaser concludes that it is impracticable to separate the payments reliably, the purchaser should:

[IFRIC 4:15]

- in the case of a finance lease, recognise an asset and a liability at an amount equal to the fair value of the leased asset. Subsequently the liability should be reduced as payments are made and an imputed finance charge on the liability recognised using the purchaser's incremental borrowing rate of interest; and

- in the case of an operating lease, treat all payments under the arrangement as lease payments for the purposes of complying with the disclosure requirements of IAS 17, but:

  - disclose those payments separately from minimum lease payments of other arrangements that do not include payments for non-lease elements; and

  - state that the disclosed payments also include payments for non-lease elements in the arrangement.

For these purposes, fair value is measured in accordance with IAS 17, not IFRS 13 *Fair Value Measurement* – see the further discussion at **7.1.1.5**.

3   Definition of a lease

3.1   Lease – definition

A lease is defined as an agreement whereby the lessor conveys to the lessee, in return for a payment or series of payments, the right to use an asset for an agreed period of time. [IAS 17:4] The definition includes hire purchase contracts, i.e. contracts for the hire of an asset that contain a clause giving the hirer an option to acquire title to the asset upon fulfilment of agreed conditions. [IAS 17:6]

3.2   SIC-27 *Evaluating the Substance of Transactions involving the Legal Form of a Lease*

3.2.1   SIC-27 – background

Not all transactions that involve the legal form of a lease will fall within the definition of a lease for the purposes of IAS 17. In some cases, such transactions may be designed to achieve a particular tax effect, which is shared between the parties, rather than conveying the right to use an asset. SIC-27 *Evaluating the Substance of Transactions Involving the Legal Form of a Lease* addresses issues that may arise when an entity (the Entity) enters into a transaction or a series of structured transactions with an unrelated party or parties (the Investor) that involves the legal form of a lease. For example, the Entity may lease assets to the Investor and lease the same assets back or, alternatively, sell assets and lease the same assets back. The form of each arrangement and its terms and conditions can vary significantly. In the lease and leaseback example, it may be that the arrangement is designed to achieve a tax advantage for the Investor that is shared with the Entity in the form of a fee, and not to convey the right to use an asset.

3.2.2 Evaluating the substance of an arrangement

Consistent with the general principles of IAS 17, SIC-27 states that the accounting for arrangements between the Entity and the Investor should reflect the substance of the arrangement. A series of transactions should be considered as linked and accounted for as one transaction when the overall economic effect cannot be understood without reference to the series of transactions as a whole. [SIC-27:3] All aspects of the arrangement should be evaluated to determine its substance, with weight given to those aspects and implications that have an economic effect. [SIC-27:4]

3.2.3 Indicators that an arrangement does not involve a lease

The key characteristic of a lease is that it includes the conveyance of the right to use an asset for an agreed period of time. [SIC-27:5] Indicators that may suggest that an arrangement does not, in substance, involve a lease under IAS 17 include:

[SIC-27:5]

- the Entity retains all the risks and rewards incidental to ownership of the underlying asset and enjoys substantially the same rights to its use as before the arrangement;

- the primary reason for the arrangement is to achieve a particular tax result, and not to convey the right to use an asset; and

- an option is included on terms that make its exercise almost certain (e.g. a put option that is exercisable at a price sufficiently higher than the expected fair value when it becomes exercisable).

3.2.4 Assets and liabilities in an arrangement that does not involve a lease

If an arrangement does not meet the definition of a lease, the definitions and guidance in paragraphs 4.4 to 4.19 of the *Conceptual Framework for Financial Reporting* (see **chapter A2**) are used to determine whether, in substance, a separate investment account and lease payment obligations represent assets and liabilities of the Entity. Indicators that collectively demonstrate that, in substance, a separate investment account and lease payment obligations do *not* meet the definitions of an asset and a liability and should not be recognised by the Entity include:

[SIC-27:6]

- the Entity is not able to control the investment account in pursuit of its own objectives and is not obligated to pay the lease payments. This occurs when, for example, a prepaid amount is placed in a separate investment account to protect the Investor and may only be used to pay the Investor, the Investor agrees that the lease payment obligations are to be paid from funds in the investment account, and the Entity has no ability to withhold payments to the Investor from the investment account;

- the Entity has only a remote risk of reimbursing the entire amount of any fee received from an Investor and possibly paying some additional amount, or, when a fee has not been received, only a remote risk of paying an amount under other obligations (e.g. a guarantee). Only a remote risk of payment exists when, for example, the terms of the arrangement require that a prepaid amount is invested in risk-free assets that are expected to generate sufficient cash flows to satisfy the lease payment obligations; and

- other than the initial cash flows at inception of the arrangement, the only cash flows expected under the arrangement are the lease payments that are satisfied solely from funds withdrawn from the separate investment account established with the initial cash flows.

Other obligations of an arrangement, including any guarantees provided and obligations incurred upon early termination, should be accounted for under IAS 37 *Provisions, Contingent Liabilities and Contingent Assets* (see **chapter A12**), IFRS 9 *Financial Instruments* or, for entities that have not yet adopted IFRS 9, IAS 39 *Financial Instruments: Recognition and Measurement* (see **Volumes B** and **C**, respectively), or IFRS 4 *Insurance Contracts* (see **chapter A39**), as appropriate. [SIC-27:7]

3.2.5   Accounting for fees received by the Entity

The requirements of IFRS 15 *Revenue from Contracts with Customers* (see **chapter A14**) or, for entities that have not yet adopted IFRS 15, the criteria in paragraph 20 of IAS 18 *Revenue* (see **appendix A1**) should be applied to the facts and circumstances of each arrangement in determining when to recognise any fee that the Entity receives as income. Factors such as whether there is continuing involvement in the form of significant future performance obligations necessary to earn the fee, whether there are retained risks, the terms of any guarantee arrangements, and the risk of repayment of the fee, should be considered. Indicators that individually demonstrate that recognition of the entire fee as income when received, if received at the beginning of the arrangement, is *inappropriate* include:

[SIC-27:8]

- obligations either to perform or to refrain from certain significant activities are conditions of earning the fee received and, therefore, execution of a legally binding arrangement is not the most significant act required by the arrangement;

- limitations are put on the use of the underlying asset that have the practical effect of restricting and significantly changing the Entity's ability to use (e.g. deplete, sell or pledge as collateral) the asset; and

- the possibility of reimbursing any amount of the fee and possibly paying some additional amount is not remote. This occurs when, for example:

  - the underlying asset is not a specialised asset that is required by the Entity to conduct its business and, therefore, there is a possibility that the Entity may pay an amount to terminate the arrangement early; or

  - the Entity is required by the terms of the arrangement, or has some or total discretion, to invest a prepaid amount in assets carrying more than an insignificant amount of risk (e.g. currency, interest rate or credit risk). In this circumstance, the risk of the investment's value being insufficient to satisfy the lease payment obligations is not remote and, therefore, there is a possibility that the Entity may be required to pay some amount.

The presentation of the fee in profit or loss should be based on its economic substance and nature. [SIC-27:9]

3.2.6   Disclosure

All aspects of an arrangement that does not, in substance, involve a lease under IAS 17 should be considered in determining the appropriate disclosures that are necessary to understand the arrangement and the accounting treatment adopted. An Entity should disclose the following in each period that such an arrangement exists:

[SIC-27:10]

- a description of the arrangement, including:

  - the underlying asset and any restrictions on its use;

  - the life and other significant terms of the arrangement; and

  - the transactions that are linked together, including any options; and

- the accounting treatment applied to any fee received, the amount recognised as income in the period, and the line item of the statement of comprehensive income in which it is included.

These disclosures should be provided individually for each arrangement or in aggregate for each class of arrangement. A class is a grouping of arrangements with underlying assets of a similar nature (e.g. power plants). [SIC-27:11]

3.2.7   Illustrative examples

The Appendices to SIC-27 provide and discuss illustrations of the application of the Interpretation, including:

- an arrangement designed predominantly to generate shared tax benefits; [SIC-27:A2(a)]

- arrangements that offset so that, in substance, no transaction has occurred; [SIC-27:A2(b)] and

- two arrangements that are, in substance, secured borrowings. [SIC-27:A2(c) & (d)]

4   Classification of leases

4.1   Classification of leases – general

The key distinction to be made in accounting for leases under IAS 17 is whether the lease in question is either:

- a simple short-term hire arrangement (an operating lease), whereby rentals are dealt with in profit or loss with the only impact on the statement of financial position relating to the timing of payments; or

- in the nature of an arrangement for financing the acquisition of an asset (a finance lease), when the presentation in the financial statements will depart from the legal form of the transaction and be based on the economic substance (i.e. as if the asset had been purchased by the user).

4.2   Distinction between a finance lease and an operating lease

A finance lease is a lease that transfers substantially all the risks and rewards incidental to ownership of an asset to the lessee. Title may or may not eventually be transferred. [IAS 17:4]

An operating lease is any lease other than a finance lease. [IAS 17:4]

The classification of leases under IAS 17 is therefore based on the extent to which the risks and rewards incidental to ownership of a leased asset lie with the lessor or the lessee. The risks incidental to ownership include the possibility of losses from idle capacity or technological obsolescence, and of variations in the future economic benefits expected to flow to the entity due to changing economic conditions. The rewards incidental to ownership may be represented by the expectation of profitable operation over the asset's economic life and of gain from appreciation in value or realisation of a residual value. [IAS 17:7]

IAS 17 notes that, although a consistent definition of finance lease is used for both lessee and lessor accounting, and the transaction will be based on the same agreement between the parties, it is possible that the two parties will arrive at a different classification of the same lease because of their different circumstances (see **8.2**). [IAS 17:9]

4.3 Timing of lease classification

4.3.1 Lease classification determined at the inception of a lease

Lease classification is determined at the inception of the lease. Changes to the particulars of a lease after inception, other than by renewing the lease, which would have resulted in a different classification of the lease had the revised terms been in effect at the inception of the lease, should be considered as the inception of a revised agreement over the remaining term. However, changes in estimates (e.g. changes in estimates of the economic life or the residual value of the leased asset), or changes in circumstances (e.g. default by the lessee), do not give rise to a new lease classification. [IAS 17:13]

4.3.2 Classification of leases acquired in a business combination

When a group acquires a new subsidiary in a business combination, the classification of the subsidiary's leases is not reassessed at the date of the business combination for the purposes of the consolidated financial statements. The subsidiary's leases will be classified in the consolidated financial statements on the basis of their terms at original inception, and without regard to the remaining lease term from the acquisition date. Thus, in particular, if the acquiree has appropriately treated a lease as a finance lease, that lease will also be treated as a finance lease in the consolidated financial statements, even if the majority of the lease term has expired before the acquisition date.

This treatment is required under paragraph 17 of IFRS 3 *Business Combinations* as an exception to that Standard's general principle that an acquirer should classify the assets acquired and liabilities assumed in a business combination on the basis of conditions as they exist at the acquisition date. IFRS 3:17 requires the acquiree's lease contracts to be classified on the basis of the contractual terms and other factors at the inception of the contract (or, if the terms of the contract have been modified in a manner that would change its classification, at the date of that modification, which might be the acquisition date). See also **7.1.2.2** in **chapter A25**.

4.3.3 Inception of the lease vs commencement of the lease term

IAS 17 makes an important distinction between the 'inception of a lease' and the 'commencement of the lease term'.

- The inception of the lease is defined as the earlier of the date of the lease agreement and the date of commitment by the parties to the principal provisions of the lease. [IAS 17:4]

- The commencement of the lease term is the date from which the lessee is entitled to exercise its right to use the leased asset. [IAS 17:4]

There may be a time lag between these two dates, and the amounts involved in the lease arrangement may change between the two – most commonly when the asset is being constructed and the final cost is not known at inception. It is therefore important to clarify the significance of each of these dates.

The classification of a lease and, in the case of finance leases, the amounts to be recognised in the statement of financial position on commencement of the lease term are determined at the inception of the lease. However, the assets, liabilities, income and expenses resulting from the lease are not recognised in the financial statements until the commencement of the lease term. [IAS 17:4]

Example 4.3.3

Lease payments on assets not in use

Company X is performing a major expansion of its oil production capacity; production will start in 20X2. In order to ensure shipping capacity, Company X will enter into operating lease arrangements in 20X1 for rail cars that will be stored on its own premises. Expected use in 20X1 will be minimal. Company X is optimistic that it will be able to rent out the cars to other producers in 20X1 but this activity will be minimal. The sole reason for entering into the leases in 20X1 is to ensure that the rail cars will be available to Company X in 20X2.

When should Company X commence recognising the lease payments in its financial statements?

In accordance with IAS 17:4, assets, liabilities, income and expenses resulting from a lease are recognised in the financial statements at the commencement of the lease term. The commencement of the lease term is the date from which the lessee is entitled to exercise its right to use the leased asset. In 20X1, Company X has the right to use the leased rail cars. Irrespective of whether Company X chooses to exercise that right, and in accordance with IAS 17:33, Company X should commence recognising the lease expense in 20X1 on a straight-line basis over the lease term.

If lease payments are adjusted for changes in the lessor's costs (e.g. of construction, acquisition or financing), or for changes in some other measure of cost or value (e.g. general price levels), between the inception of the lease and the commencement of the lease term, the effect of any such changes is deemed to have taken place at inception. [IAS 17:5]

4.3.4   Change in lessor during the term of an operating lease

---

Example 4.3.4

Change in lessor during the term of an operating lease

Company A leases a building from Company B at the beginning of 20X1. The lease term is eight years and there is an annual fixed increase in lease payments of 11 per cent. The lease is classified as an operating lease and, therefore, Company A recognises the lease payments as expenses on a straight-line basis over the lease term. As a result of the increasing lease payments, Company A recognises a lease accrual in the first few years of the lease because the straight-line lease expense is greater than the amount paid to Company B.

At the end of 20X4, Company B sells the building to Company C and legal transfer takes place prior to the end of the year. As part of the sale, the original lease is cancelled and Company A simultaneously enters into a lease for the same building with Company C. The new lease also expires at the end of 20X8 and has an annual fixed increase in lease payments of 11 per cent; the first lease payment due is equivalent to the lease payment originally due at the end of 20X4 when the first lease was cancelled.

Does the introduction of a new lessor represent a new lease that must be assessed under IAS 17 or, given that the substance of the lease is identical before and after the sale, should there be no accounting impact?

IAS 17:13 states that if the provisions of a lease are changed in a manner that would have resulted in a different classification of the lease if the changes had been in place at the inception of the lease, the revised agreement is regarded as a new lease over its term. IAS 17:13 also states that changes in estimates or circumstances do not give rise to a new lease classification.

In the circumstances described, the lease classification remains unchanged before and after the sale of the building from Company B to Company C. Given that there is no change in the provisions or substance of the lease, apart from a change in lessor, this should be regarded as a change in circumstance that does not give rise to a new lease classification. As a result, any accrual previously recognised by Company A is not released to profit or loss when the new lease is entered into; Company A continues to account for the lease as previously.

4.4   Changes in lease classification

As noted at **4.3.1**, if the terms of a lease are changed to such an extent that the lease would have been classified differently at inception had the changed terms been in effect at that time, the revised agreement is considered to be a new agreement over its remaining term.

For lessees, if a lease previously classified as an operating lease now becomes a finance lease, the leased asset and a related obligation should be recognised in the lessee's statement of financial position at an amount equal to the fair value of the leased asset or, if lower, the present value of the minimum lease payments. The revised contract should be accounted for as a finance lease from the date of modification. No prior year adjustments should be made. If a finance lease is reclassified as an operating lease, the lessee should follow the guidance for sale and leaseback transactions (see **7.3**).

For lessors, if a lease previously classified as an operating lease now becomes a finance lease, a lease receivable should be recognised at the present value of the remaining minimum lease payments (plus any unguaranteed residual value accruing to the lessor), and the leased asset should be derecognised. No prior year adjustments should be made. A profit or loss may arise on derecognition of the leased asset and recognition of the finance lease receivable. If a finance lease is reclassified as an operating lease, the lessor should derecognise the lease receivable from the statement of financial position, and recognise a leased asset for the same amount.

Example 4.4

Upgrade of leased assets

A lessee is entitled to upgrade leased computers prior to the end of the initial lease term. A new lease agreement is concluded for each upgrade.

What impact will the upgrade have on the lease?

The upgraded computers are distinct from the original leased computers. The lease provisions are renegotiated for each upgrade. Therefore, the provisions of the lease change when the computers are upgraded and the lease of the upgraded computers should be assessed as a new lease over the renegotiated term.

It is necessary, however, to consider any link between the old lease and the new lease for the upgraded computers (see **6.2.4** for an example of such circumstances).

4.5   Leases of several assets

A lease agreement may cover several items of equipment. For example, a lease for a retail outlet may include virtually all items of equipment necessary to operate the outlet such as refrigeration units, air conditioning units, alarm and phone systems, and furniture. These items of equipment may have different economic lives, may be covered by specific contractual terms, and may or may not be functionally interdependent.

For the purpose of lease classification under IAS 17, the determination as to whether several items of equipment covered by a lease agreement should be (1) bundled together and assessed as one lease, or (2) viewed as separate leases and assessed separately, requires significant judgement based on the specific facts and circumstances.

Assets are generally bundled together for the purposes of lease classification when the assets are functionally interdependent (i.e. they function together as part of an overall process or facility). For example, air conditioning units included within a property lease are generally functionally interdependent with the property being leased because the use of the property in the manner intended is generally dependent on the continued operating performance of the air conditioning units, and the property and the air conditioning units are intended to be used together as part of an overall facility.

In contrast, an aeroplane may not be considered functionally interdependent with a leased aircraft hangar because each asset may be used as intended independently of the other.

When a single lease agreement covers different assets that are not functionally interdependent, then, when material, these assets are assessed separately for lease classification and the minimum lease payments are allocated based on the relative fair values of the assets at inception of the lease.

5 Characteristics of a finance lease

5.1 Situations that will generally lead to finance lease classification

The definition of a finance lease is set out at **4.2**. IAS 17 gives examples of situations that, individually or in combination, would normally lead to a lease being classified as a finance lease. The indicators in IAS 17:10 relate to transfer of title and other factors in the primary period of the lease and should be regarded as the primary indicators. IAS 17:11 sets out additional indicators, which will sometimes be relevant. IAS 17:12 to 19 provide additional guidance.

Primary indicators of a finance lease are:

[IAS 17:10]

- the lease transfers ownership of the asset to the lessee by the end of the lease term;

> A lease can be considered to transfer ownership of the leased asset when transfer of legal title, and thus continued ownership of risks and rewards, is automatic either under the lease agreement or under a side agreement that forms part of the overall lease arrangement (e.g. when the lessor has entered into a separate

forward sale agreement with the lessee). This condition will also be met, in substance, when the lessor has a put option requiring the lessee to acquire legal title, and the option is structured in such a manner that it is very likely to be exercised by the lessor.

- the lessee has the option to purchase the asset at a price that is expected to be sufficiently lower than the fair value at the date the option becomes exercisable such that, at the inception of the lease, it is reasonably certain that the option will be exercised;

This condition extends that referred to in the previous bullet point to a lessee call option at a price that makes its exercise commercially likely to occur. An option to purchase at a nominal amount is a typical example of this type of arrangement.

In some lease arrangements, rather than the lessee having a bargain purchase option, its parent (perhaps with no operations other than to act as an investment holding company) has the option to acquire the leased asset at a low or nominal value at the end of the lease term. In these circumstances, it is reasonably certain that the parent will exercise the option to acquire the asset. Although the option to acquire the asset is not held by the lessee, the substance of the arrangement is that only the lessee will have use of the asset. As a result, such arrangements will normally lead the lessee to classify the lease as a finance lease.

When a lease involves identical put and call options (at the end of the lease term, the lessee has a call option to acquire the leased asset at a specified price and the lessor has a corresponding put option for the same value), the substance is that of a forward contract. At the end of the lease term, the lessee will exercise the call option if the market value of the leased asset exceeds the exercise price of the option; the lessor will exercise the put option if the market price is less than the exercise price of the option. Therefore, either the put option or the call option is reasonably certain to be exercised at the end of the lease term, and the lessee will acquire the asset at the end of the lease term. Consequently, the lease should normally be classified as a finance lease from the perspective of both the lessee and the lessor.

- the lease term is for the major part of the economic life of the asset, even if title is not transferred;

This condition covers the circumstances when substantially all the economic benefits of the asset are consumed over the lease term during which the lessee controls the asset. There is no specific threshold in IAS 17 delineating the 'major part' of an asset's economic life and thresholds established by other GAAPs should not be considered definitive. Instead, it is necessary to consider the substance of a lease and to classify it according to whether the agreement transfers substantially all of the risks and rewards of ownership. These include, but are not limited to, (1) the possibilities of losses from idle capacity or technological obsolescence, (2) variations in return due to changing economic conditions, (3) the expectation of profitable operation over the asset's economic life, and (4) gain or loss from movements in value or realisation of a residual value.

Example 5.1

Evaluating the economic life of a building

Company A constructs a building and, on completion of construction, leases it to Company B for 25 years. At the end of the lease term, the title to the land and building is retained by Company A. If the economic life of the building is 50 years, this lease apparently is not for the major part of the economic life of the building; therefore, it is likely that the lease would be classified as an operating lease. To determine the economic life of the building, Company A should consider a number of factors:

- if all important maintenance and refurbishment costs are paid by the lessee and this obligation forms part of the lease, this requirement should be taken into account because it may extend the economic life;

- if the lease requires Company B to maintain the building in the same condition as at the inception of the lease ('making good dilapidations'), this requirement could extend the economic life;

- if the building is unlikely to be leased for any additional period in its present condition because of an aspect of its design, operation or location (i.e. it is 'functionally obsolete'), the economic life may be shorter; and

- if the building is considered to be functionally obsolete, but a tenant still wants to rent it, the building will retain a degree of economic life.

This list is not exhaustive and each building should be considered separately based on the specific facts and circumstances.

Consideration of the economic life of a building will often reveal a difference between the life of the shell of the building and the life of the interior of the building. In many scenarios, the shell of the building will be key to the overall economic life of that asset. For example, in the case of shops or offices, the interior of the building is usually regularly refurbished by the lessee (often as required under the lease) in order for it to continue to be an economically viable property for the lessee. If refurbishment of the interior is carried out at regular (e.g. 10-year) intervals, consideration of the economic life of the building based on the expected life of the shell of the property may be appropriate. Regular repair and refurbishment would extend the expected economic life of the asset and, when this is contractually required under the lease, should be taken into account in the assessment of economic life at the inception of the lease.

> Note that when renewal or purchase options exist, these should be assessed at the inception of the lease to determine whether it is reasonably certain that the option will be exercised. The lease term will include the further term when, at inception, exercise of the option is assessed to be reasonably certain.

- at the inception of the lease, the present value of the minimum lease payments amounts to at least substantially all of the fair value of the leased asset;

> This condition tests whether the lessor receives a full return of its initial investment. As with economic life, there is no specific threshold in IAS 17 delineating what constitutes 'substantially all' of the fair value of a leased asset and thresholds established by other GAAPs should not be considered definitive. Instead, as discussed above, it is necessary to consider the substance of a lease and classify it depending on whether the agreement transfers substantially all of the risks and rewards of ownership.
>
> When the lease term has been extended by renewal or purchase options (as discussed in the previous point), the minimum lease payments will include payments due with respect to this further term.

- the leased assets are of such a specialised nature that only the lessee can use them without major modifications.

> When this condition is met, it is likely that the asset will have been constructed to the lessee's specifications such that its market value is limited. It follows that the lessor will seek to recover its investment from the primary lease term.

Other indicators that, individually or in combination, could also lead to a lease being classified as a finance lease are:

[IAS 17:11]

- if the lessee can cancel the lease, the lessor's losses associated with the cancellation are borne by the lessee;

> See **6.2.3** for a discussion of the impact of cancellation (break) clauses.

- gains or losses from fluctuations in the fair value of the residual fall to the lessee (e.g. in the form of a rent rebate equalling most of the sales proceeds at the end of the lease);

If the lessee does not acquire legal title by the end of the lease, it may nevertheless bear the risk of variation in the residual value of the asset; leases will commonly provide for a substantial fixed final rental (a 'balloon rental') followed by a repayment equal to all or substantially all of the sales proceeds from disposal of the asset.

When the risk of variation in the residual value of the asset is shared between the lessor and the lessee, it is necessary to consider the specific facts and circumstances in order to assess whether the risk retained by the lessor is significant. A risk of variation in the residual value of the asset retained by the lessor that may be significant only in circumstances considered to be remote may suggest that the lease is appropriately classified as a finance lease.

- the lessee has the ability to continue the lease for a secondary period at a rent that is substantially lower than market rent.

A bargain renewal option exists when a lessee has the ability to continue the lease for a secondary period at a rent that is substantially lower than market rent. The rent for a secondary period would be considered substantially lower than market rent if it would be economically rational for the lessee to continue the lease at that lower rent.

Rental for a secondary period either at a nominal amount or substantially below market rates suggests both that (1) the lessor has received the required return from its initial investment, and (2) that the lessee is likely to choose to enter into such a secondary period.

Factors to consider in determining whether a renewal option represents a bargain include:

- the nature of the leased asset;

- the possibility of technological obsolescence;

- the possibility of higher operating and maintenance costs over the secondary rent period; and

- costs to be incurred by the lessor to find a new lessee and to prepare the asset for a new lessee.

Assume that the rental payments in the renewal period are equal to a specified percentage of the original monthly payments. One approach to assessing whether this represents a bargain would be to compare the implicit interest rates determined by assuming that (1) the lease is terminated at the end of the original lease term, and (2) that the lease is renewed at the reduced rental payments. Appropriate estimates of the residual value of the asset at the end of the original term and at the end of the renewal period should be included in the computations. If the implicit interest rate increases or remains substantially the same when the renewal option is assumed to be exercised, it is appropriate to conclude that the renewal option is not a bargain. The assessment of whether the interest rate differential is a bargain is made at the inception of the lease and will depend on both the economic conditions prevailing in the relevant jurisdiction and the circumstances of the parties to the lease agreement.

Although the factors set out above are intended to identify the key characteristics of a finance lease, they are not always conclusive. IAS 17 underlines the requirement to consider the whole of the arrangement, and the extent to which the risks and rewards incidental to ownership are transferred. Although a lease may appear to fall within the definition of a finance lease, having regard to the characteristics referred to above, there may be other features that demonstrate that the lease does not transfer substantially all of the risks and rewards incidental to ownership. By way of example, the Standard cites circumstances in which ownership of the asset transfers at the end of the lease, but in exchange for a variable payment equal to its then fair value. Similarly, if there are contingent rents, as a result of which the lessee does not have substantially all of the risks and rewards incidental to ownership, the lease will not be classified as a finance lease. [IAS 17:12]

The evaluation of a lease will require an examination of the lease agreement, including any supporting schedules and side letters (particularly when these include the monetary amounts of rental payments), and arrangements for the return and disposal of the asset. The most relevant evidence will be found in clauses dealing with:

- rental payments and rebates (normally contained in a schedule to the lease agreement) to be used to consider whether the minimum lease payments amount to at least substantially all of the fair value of the leased asset; and

- arrangements that apply once the lease has run its normal full term (e.g. the existence of options, balloon payments, guarantees, process for disposal of the asset).

Clauses dealing with the following issues will be of less relevance:

- maintenance and insurance (not normally a significant element of overall cost); and

- arrangements for termination that are unlikely to be applicable in practice (e.g. following insolvency of the lessee or failure to pay rentals when due).

5.2 Leases of land and buildings

5.2.1 Requirement to assess the classification of land and buildings elements separately

When a lease includes both land and buildings elements, an entity assesses the classification of each element as a finance or an operating lease separately in accordance with IAS 17:7 to 13 (see **5.1**).

5.2.2 Splitting leases of land and buildings

In order to determine the appropriate accounting for the land and buildings elements of a lease, the minimum lease payments should generally be allocated in proportion to the relative fair values of the leasehold interests in the land element and the buildings element of the lease at the inception of the lease. [IAS 17:16]

Note that this split is *not* on the basis of the relative fair values of the land and buildings. The IASB concluded that the allocation of the minimum lease payments should reflect the extent to which they are intended to compensate the lessor for the use of the separate elements. The future economic benefits of a building are likely to be consumed to some extent over the term of a lease. Therefore, the lease payments allocated to the building should reflect not only the lessor's return on its investment in the building, but also the recovery of the value of the building consumed over the lease term. In contrast, land with an indefinite useful life should maintain its value beyond the lease term and, therefore, the lessor does not normally need compensation for any consumption of the economic benefits inherent in the land. [IAS 17:BC10 & BC11]

If the lease payments cannot be allocated reliably between the land and buildings elements, the entire lease is classified as a finance lease, unless it is clear that both elements are operating leases, in which case the entire lease is classified as an operating lease. [IAS 17:16]

One of the most common applications of the previous paragraphs is likely to be in legal jurisdictions where the ownership of property is held only via leasehold interests. Typically, the government retains ownership of all land, and leasehold interests in land and buildings are the only means of purchasing such assets. In these circumstances, because similar land and buildings are not sold or leased separately, it may not be possible to arrive at a meaningful allocation of the minimum lease payments.

For a lease of land and buildings under which the present value of the minimum lease payments allocated to the land at the inception of the lease is immaterial, IAS 17 allows that the land and buildings may be treated as a single unit for the purposes of lease classification. The IASB considers that, in such circumstances, the benefits of separating the two elements and accounting for each separately may not outweigh the costs. The lease is classified in accordance with the general criteria discussed in **5.1**. In such cases, the economic life of the buildings is regarded as the economic life of the entire leased asset. [IAS 17:17]

5.2.3   Investment property

In the case of investment property held under a lease, generally there is no requirement for separate measurement of the land and buildings elements of a lease when the fair value model is adopted. It is possible for a lessee to classify a property interest held under an operating lease as investment property. In such circumstances, the property interest is accounted for as if it were a finance lease and, in addition, the fair value model is required to be used for the asset recognised. These requirements are discussed in detail in **appendix A5**.

If a lessee's property interest held under an operating lease is classified as an investment property, the lessee must continue to account for the lease as if it were a finance lease, even if a subsequent event changes the nature of the lessee's property interest so that it is no longer classified as investment property. IAS 17 indicates that this will be the case if, for example, the lessee:

[IAS 17:19]

- occupies the property, which is then transferred to owner-occupied property at a deemed cost equal to its fair value at the date of change in use; or

- grants a sublease that transfers substantially all of the risks and rewards incidental to ownership of the interest to an unrelated third party. Such a sublease is accounted for by the lessee as a finance lease to the third party, although it may be accounted for as an operating lease by the third party.

5.2.4   Consideration of the economic life of land

In determining whether the land element is an operating or a finance lease, an important consideration is that land normally has an indefinite economic life. [IAS 17:15A]

Leases of land are assessed in the same way as all other leases. Land normally has an indefinite economic life, so it is unlikely that the lease term will be for the major part of the economic life of the asset. Nevertheless, some of the other characteristics described at **5.1** may be met, in which case a lease of land may be a finance lease. In particular, if, at the inception of the lease, the present value of the minimum lease payments amounts to at least substantially all of the fair value of the leased asset, it is possible that a lease of land will be a finance lease. Note, however, that leases of land (and buildings) for long periods will often be subject to rent reviews, which may mean that the lessor has not transferred substantially all the risks and rewards incidental to ownership.

5.2.5 Lessee payments to incumbent tenants

When a new property lease is entered into, it is common for the lessee to pay the incumbent tenant a lump sum upon transfer of the lease contract. The accounting will depend on whether the lump sum payment is attributable to the right to use the leased asset or the purchase of other rights separate from the leased asset. If the payment is attributable to the leased asset and the lease is an operating lease, the lump sum payment should be accounted for as prepaid lease payments, which are amortised over the lease term in accordance with the pattern of benefits provided. If the lease is a finance lease, the lump sum payment should be capitalised as part of the cost of the asset to the extent that the carrying amount of the asset does not exceed its fair value. Alternatively, such a lump sum payment might be attributable to the purchase of other rights separate from the leased asset. Payments attributable to other rights should be accounted in accordance with the applicable Standard.

5.2.6 Surrender premiums paid by lessors

In the real estate industry, a common practice for operating leases is the payment of a 'surrender premium'. This is a payment made by the lessor to the incumbent tenant to terminate the lease. The question arises as to how to account for such a payment.

When the payment is a cost of terminating an existing lease agreement, it should be recognised as an expense in profit or loss. In some circumstances, however, the payment may relate to a refurbishment and, therefore, may be capitalised as part of the cost of an item of property, plant and equipment. For example, when a lessor acquires a building with the intention to refurbish the building, any surrender premium payments to existing lessees to permit refurbishment of the building are likely to meet the definition of directly attributable costs under IAS 16 *Property, Plant and Equipment* and to be capitalised as part of the cost of the building. All facts and circumstances should be assessed carefully to establish the substance of the payment. The lessor should also consider (1) whether there is an indicator of impairment, and (2) whether an impairment review is required to ensure the cost of the building does not exceed its recoverable amount.

6   Calculating the minimum lease payments

6.1   Minimum lease payments – relevant definitions

The minimum lease payments are the payments over the lease term that the lessee is, or can be, required to make, excluding contingent rents, costs for services and taxes to be paid by and reimbursed to the lessor, together with:

[IAS 17:4]

- in the case of a lessee, any amount guaranteed by the lessee or by a party related to the lessee; or

- in the case of a lessor, any residual value guaranteed to the lessor by the lessee, or a party related to the lessee, or a third party unrelated to the lessor that is financially capable of meeting this guarantee.

If the lessee has an option to purchase the asset at a price that is expected to be sufficiently lower than the fair value at the date the option becomes exercisable that, at the inception of the lease, is reasonably certain to be exercised, the minimum lease payments comprise the minimum payments payable over the lease term to the expected date of exercise of this purchase option and the payment required on exercise.

> The lease term over which the minimum lease payments are considered will be affected by the extent to which a lease is cancellable (see **6.2.1** and **6.2.3**). See **6.3** for a discussion of the various components of minimum lease payments.

6.2   Lease term

6.2.1   Lease term – definition

The lease term is the non-cancellable period for which the lessee has contracted to lease the asset, together with any further terms for which the lessee has the option to continue to lease the asset, with or without further payment. An option is only taken into account in the lease term if, at the inception of the lease, it is judged to be reasonably certain that the lessee will exercise the option (see also **6.2.2**). [IAS 17:4]

IAS 17:4 defines a non-cancellable lease as a lease that is cancellable only:

(a)   upon the occurrence of some remote contingency;

(b)   with the permission of the lessor;

(c)   if the lessee enters into a new lease for the same or an equivalent asset with the same lessor; or

(d) upon payment by the lessee of such an additional amount that, at inception of the lease, continuation of the lease is reasonably certain.

See **6.2.3** for a discussion of cancellation (break) clauses.

As noted at **4.3.3**, the commencement of the lease term is the date from which the lessee is entitled to exercise its right to use the leased asset. [IAS 17:4]

6.2.2   Assessment of whether a renewal option is reasonably certain to be exercised

Careful judgement is required when considering whether it is reasonably certain that a renewal option will be exercised. Situations that normally would result in a renewal option being reasonably certain of exercise include, but are not limited to, the following:

* the lessee has the right to prescribe the lease terms on renewal of the lease;

* the lease rentals on renewal are expected to be lower than market rates; and

* the lessee is economically compelled to renew because of the nature of the assets being leased or the existence of penalties.

6.2.3   Cancellation (break) clauses

Example 6.2.3

Cancellation (break) clauses

Entity M enters into a 12-year lease with a cancellation clause (commonly referred to as a 'break' clause) after three years. If Entity M chooses to exercise the break clause, it will be required to pay 1 year's lease rental as a penalty.

What is the effect of such a clause on the determination of the lease term?

The lease term is defined in IAS 17:4 as "the *non-cancellable period* for which the lessee has contracted to lease the asset together with any further terms for which the lessee has the option to continue to lease the asset, with or without further payment, when at the inception of the lease it is reasonably certain that the lessee will exercise the option". [Emphasis added] A non-cancellable lease is a lease that is cancellable only:

[IAS 17:4]

* upon the occurrence of some remote contingency;
* with the permission of the lessor;

- if the lessee enters into a new lease for the same or an equivalent asset with the same lessor; or

- upon payment by the lessee of such an additional amount that, at inception of the lease, continuation of the lease is reasonably certain.

In the circumstances under consideration, at the inception of the lease, Entity M needs to consider whether the penalty payment of one year's rent is so significant that it would be unwilling to pay this amount to cancel the lease and that, consequently, it is reasonably certain that the cancellation will not occur. If so, the non-cancellable period and the lease term are 12 years; if not, the non-cancellable period and the lease term are three years.

In some circumstances, a break clause may be inserted in a lease solely as an attempt to ensure that the lease will be classified as an operating lease, but there is no commercial possibility that the break clause will be invoked. For example, a break clause may allow the lessee to terminate a three-year lease after one month of operation but, in return, may require the lessee to pay a penalty of 75 per cent of the asset's cost. It is unlikely that the lessee would be willing to pay 75 per cent of the cost of an asset in return for one month's use. Consequently, this fact pattern would fall within the scope of IAS 17:4(d) (i.e. continuation of the lease is reasonably certain) and, when determining the non-cancellable period of the lease, the break clause should be disregarded.

See also **6.3.6** for a discussion of the impact of termination penalties on the measurement of 'minimum lease payments'.

6.2.4   Upgrade options

A lease may include upgrade options, whereby the lessee can return existing equipment provided that it enters into a new lease. **Example 4.4** discusses circumstances in which a lessee is entitled to upgrade leased assets; in the particular circumstances described in that example, when the terms of the new lease are negotiated independently, the leases for the upgraded assets should be assessed as new leases. Care should be exercised, however, when there is a link between the old and the new leases. For example, a lessor may seek to recover the remaining rentals on the old lease by increasing the rentals on new equipment. To the extent that classification of the old lease assumes exercise of an upgrade option, any increase in rentals on the new lease should be regarded as part of the guaranteed minimum payments under the old lease.

6.2.5   Exercise of a renewal option not previously considered to be reasonably certain

When, at inception of a lease, an option to extend the lease is not reasonably certain to be exercised, this potential future lease extension is not taken into account when calculating the lease term under IAS 17:4. The lessee may subsequently decide to exercise the option. In such circumstances, the extension of the lease period should be treated as a separate lease agreement to be classified and accounted for under IAS 17.

For example, an entity enters into a 10-year lease with a five-year lease extension option. The exercise of the option to extend is not considered reasonably certain at the inception of the lease; consequently, the lease is determined to be an operating lease with a 10-year term. Subsequently, the option to extend the lease is exercised. The extension of the lease period is accounted for as a new lease agreement, i.e. as a separate lease agreement for five years which is classified as either an operating lease or a finance lease at the date of exercise of the option in accordance with IAS 17.

Example 6.2.5A

Exercise of a renewal option in an operating lease arrangement

Company A leases a property from Company B for 10 years. The lease includes a renewal option under which Company A may extend the lease contract with Company B at the end of the lease. At the inception of the lease, exercise of the renewal option is not considered to be reasonably certain, and the lease is classified as an operating lease.

Company A must give notice no later than two years before the end of the lease term if it intends to exercise the renewal option. The commercial rationale for this deadline is to allow Company B to market the leased asset for sale or lease to another party if Company A chooses not to exercise the renewal option. Towards the end of the eighth year of the lease, Company A serves notice that it will renew the lease contract, thereby extending the lease.

The notification that a renewal option will be exercised does not require reassessment of the classification of the lease. IAS 17:13 states as follows.

"Lease classification is made at the inception of the lease. If at any time the lessee and the lessor agree to change the provisions of the lease, *other than by renewing the lease*, in a manner that would have resulted in a different classification of the lease under the criteria in [IAS 17:7 to 12] if the changed terms had been in effect at the inception of the lease, the revised agreement is regarded as a new agreement over its term. However, changes in estimates ..., or changes in circumstances ..., do not give rise to a new classification of a lease for accounting purposes." [Emphasis added]

In the circumstances described, the lease contains a renewal option but, at the inception of the lease, exercise of the option is not considered to be reasonably certain. Subsequent notification by Company A represents a change in circumstance indicating the intention to renew, but this change does not alter the existing lease agreement; consequently, the lease is not reassessed. When the lease is renewed at the end of the lease term, Company A effectively enters into a new lease that is classified in accordance with the general requirements of IAS 17:8. The inception of the new lease will occur on the date of exercise of the option, but the commencement date will be two years later, at the end of the original lease.

However, if (1) the original lease did not include a renewal option and the lease is renegotiated in Year 8 to include one, or (2) the terms of an existing renewal option in a lease are changed, such an adjustment constitutes a modification in accordance with IAS 17:13. In such circumstances, classification of the lease should be reassessed at the date of modification (i.e. in Year 8).

Example 6.2.5B

Exercise of a renewal option in a finance lease arrangement

An asset is leased under a finance lease under which the lease term is shorter than the useful life of the leased asset. Subsequent to initial recognition, an option to renew the lease is exercised. At the inception of the lease, it was not reasonably certain that the option would be exercised and, consequently, the renewal option was not taken into account in assessing the lease term.

In substance, the renewal of the lease is a separate lease agreement; therefore, the existing lease should continue to be accounted for as a finance lease to the end of its original term. Subsequently, the renewed lease should be classified as a finance lease or an operating lease according to the facts and circumstances and accounted for in accordance with IAS 17's requirements for finance or operating leases, as appropriate.

Example 6.2.5C

Depreciation of an asset held under a finance lease with a renewal option

An asset is leased under a finance lease in which the lease term is shorter than the useful life of the asset. Subsequent to initial recognition, it becomes certain that an option to renew the lease will be exercised. At the inception of the lease, the exercise of this option was not considered to be reasonably certain. There is no provision in the lease contract for the lessee to acquire the asset at the end of the lease term.

The depreciation period should not be revised to include the expected renewal of the lease because IAS 17:27 requires that the asset should be depreciated over the *shorter* of the lease term and its useful life. The term of the original lease is not revised when it becomes certain that the renewal option will be exercised; consequently, depreciation continues to be calculated by reference to the term of the original lease. When the renewal option is exercised, in effect a new lease agreement is entered into; it is classified and accounted for as a new lease. If the new lease is classified as a finance lease, the asset will be depreciated over the shorter of (1) its remaining useful life at the time of renewal, and (2) the new lease term.

6.2.6 *Exercise of a purchase option in a lease arrangement*

Example 6.2.6

Exercise of a purchase option in a lease arrangement

Company A leases a property from Company B for 10 years. The lease includes an option under which Company A may purchase the asset from Company B at the market price of the asset at the end of the lease. Company A may exercise the option no later than two years before the lease expires. The commercial rationale for this is to allow Company B to market the leased asset for sale or lease to a third party if Company A chooses not to exercise the purchase option. At the inception of the lease, Company A assesses that it is not reasonably certain that the purchase option will be exercised and the lease is classified as an operating lease.

Towards the end of Year 8, Company A serves notice that it will purchase the property, thereby creating a binding purchase commitment. Company A will not acquire legal title to the property until exercise of the option at the end of Year 10.

Notification that the purchase option will be exercised does not lead to reassessment of the classification of the lease. IAS 17:13 clarifies that lease classification is made at the inception of the lease unless (1) the terms of the lease agreement are subsequently modified (other than by renewing), and (2) that modification would have resulted in a different classification if the modified terms had been in effect at inception.

In the circumstances described, the purchase price for the asset will be determined at the end of the original 10-year lease term, and paid for on exercise of the option at the end of Year 10. The original terms of the operating lease agreement have not been modified. Company A continues to account for the operating lease until the purchase option is exercised at the end of Year 10, when Company A will account for an acquisition of the property.

However if, at the date of notification, the option price is renegotiated to be the market price for the asset at the date of notification and the original lease term is shortened to eight years, this would constitute termination of the original lease and acquisition of the asset, and would be accounted for accordingly.

6.3   Components of minimum lease payments

6.3.1   Security deposits

If the lessee is required to make a security deposit at the commencement of the lease that is refundable at the end of the lease term, the payment and subsequent refund of the deposit should both be considered in the calculation of the present value of the minimum lease payments. The effect of the deposit and subsequent refund is to accelerate the cash outflows of the lessee in the early years of the lease, so that there is an incremental effect on the present value of the minimum lease payments. However, when the refundable deposit is of such magnitude that it would distort the economics of the lease, the substance of the deposit may be that it relates to a separate transaction and that it should be accounted for accordingly.

6.3.2   Contingent (variable) rentals

As outlined in **6.1**, minimum lease payments exclude contingent rents. IAS 17:4 defines contingent rent as that portion of the lease payments that is not fixed in amount but is based on the future amount of a factor that changes other than with the passage of time (e.g. percentage of future sales, amount of future use, future price indices, future market rates of interest).

Lease payments may be linked to a change in a variable such as an inflation index, a prime interest rate or even the applicable tax rate.

The definition of contingent rent refers to payment "that is not fixed but is based on the future amount of a factor that changes other than with the passage of time (eg percentage of future sales, amount of future use, future price indices, future market rates of interest)". Therefore, if an agreement specifies that, at the beginning of the lease, the annual payments will be a fixed amount, but in future years they will be increased by a variable, that future increase in rental payments will not form part of the minimum lease payments but will be contingent rent.

See **7.2.5** for the appropriate treatment of lease payments that increase by a fixed annual percentage.

Example 6.3.2A

Impact of variable rentals on minimum lease payments – inflation

A lease agreement specifies that the amount of the annual lease payments will be equal to CU100 multiplied by the change in an inflation index. At the beginning of the lease, the index is 1.21, while at the end of Year 1 it is 1.24.

The minimum lease payments would be assumed to be CU100 for every year of the lease because CU100 is considered to be the base rent for the whole contract. In Year 2, an increase in the rent of CU3 (CU100 × (1.24 – 1.21)) is contingent rent and is recognised in Year 2.

In addition, careful consideration of the terms of the lease may be required when any inflation adjustment is leveraged. This might represent an embedded derivative that requires separate accounting (see **chapter B5** for entities applying IFRS 9 *Financial Instruments* or **chapter C5** for entities applying IAS 39 *Financial Instruments: Recognition and Measurement*).

Example 6.3.2B

Impact of variable rentals on minimum lease payments – prime interest rate

A lease agreement specifies that lease payments will increase each year by the prime interest rate, LIBOR.

The link of lease payments to an interest rate such as LIBOR is considered to be an adjustment to the lease payments for the time value of money. At the inception of the lease, the future minimum lease payments should be determined on the basis of LIBOR at that date (i.e. using the assumption that LIBOR remains at that rate for the remainder of the lease).

Contingent rents are those linked to the future amount of a factor that changes "other than with the passage of time". Contingent rents, therefore, are considered to be those arising from future changes in the prime interest rate. Accordingly, any future changes in the level of lease payments caused by future changes to the existing LIBOR represent contingent rents, which will be recognised as incurred.

Careful consideration of the terms of the lease is required to determine whether any prime interest rate adjustment is leveraged, in which case it might represent an embedded derivative that requires separate accounting (see **chapter B5** for entities applying IFRS 9 or **chapter C5** for entities applying IAS 39).

Example 6.3.2C

Impact of variable rentals on minimum lease payments – subsequent rentals in a property development

Company A leases a property to Company B on the condition that Company B will redevelop the property and sublet the redeveloped property to commercial tenants. Company B agrees to pay Company A minimal 'headrent' and, following the redevelopment, an agreed percentage of the subsequent rentals that it realises from commercial tenants.

Should Company A's share of the subsequent rentals received from commercial tenants be included as a component of the minimum lease payments?

> With the exception of the headrent, any payments established as a percentage of commercial rentals are contingent rents because they are "based on the future amount of a factor that changes other than with the passage of time". They should, therefore, be excluded from the minimum lease payments.

6.3.3   Operating lease payments – contingent rent

IAS 17:33 requires lease payments under an operating lease to be recognised as an expense on a straight-line basis over the lease term, unless another systematic basis is more representative of the time pattern of the user's benefit (see **7.2.1**). IAS 17:50 requires equivalent treatment for lease income from operating leases, i.e. that it be recognised as income on a straight-line basis over the lease term, unless another systematic basis is more representative of the time pattern in which use benefit derived from the leased asset is diminished (see **8.4.2**). The question arises, therefore, as to whether contingent rents in an operating lease should be estimated at inception of the lease and recognised on a straight-line basis over the lease term.

IAS 17:25 requires that, for finance leases, contingent rents should be recognised as expenses when they are incurred (see **7.2**). The treatment adopted for contingent rents under operating leases should be consistent with this requirement.

Therefore, contingent rents under operating leases should not be estimated and included in the total lease payments to be recognised on a straight-line basis over the lease term; instead, they should be recognised as expenses in the period in which they are incurred.

In July 2006, the IFRIC (now the IFRS Interpretations Committee) considered whether an estimate of contingent rents payable (receivable) under an operating lease should be included in the total lease payments (lease income) to be recognised on a straight-line basis over the lease term. The IFRIC noted that, although IAS 17 is unclear on this issue, this has not, in general, led to contingent rents being included in the amount to be recognised on a straight-line basis over the lease term. Accordingly, the IFRIC decided not to add this issue to its agenda.

6.3.4   Maintenance costs

Lease instalments may include payments related to maintenance incurred by the lessor on behalf of the lessee. The portion of the lease payments related to maintenance should be excluded from the calculation of minimum lease payments because this portion of the lease payments represents a cost for services to be paid by and reimbursed to the lessor.

Sometimes operating lease contracts stipulate that the leased equipment must be returned to the lessor in the same condition as when originally leased. The appropriate accounting in such circumstances depends on the particular lease clause. For example, the equipment may suffer general wear and tear that is merely a result of being used. In such circumstances, it may be necessary gradually to build up a provision to repair or maintain the equipment over the lease term, so that it can be returned to the lessor in its original condition. Generally, in these circumstances, it would be inappropriate to recognise a provision for all of the estimated maintenance costs at the outset of the lease. Conversely, other contracts may require specific work to be performed; for example, the contract may stipulate that the equipment must be painted at the end of the lease before being returned to the lessor. In such circumstances, it may be appropriate to recognise a provision at the outset of the lease because, by signing the lease contract, the entity has committed itself to painting the asset, irrespective of any wear and tear suffered.

Repairs and maintenance obligations under leases are discussed further at **8.2** in **chapter A12**.

6.3.5 Administration costs

Lease instalments may also include payments related to administration costs incurred by the lessor on behalf of the lessee. These administration costs represent executory costs and should be excluded from the calculation of minimum lease payments.

6.3.6 Termination penalties

In some lease contracts, the terms include a termination penalty that takes effect if the lessee terminates the contract prior to the end of the agreed lease term. The relevant conditions in the contract may or may not be explicitly expressed as a termination penalty. The inclusion or exclusion of termination penalties in the calculation of minimum lease payments should be consistent with the determination of the lease term under the arrangement. IAS 17 defines the lease term as the 'non-cancellable' period, together with further periods for which the lessee has the option to extend the lease and for which, at inception, it is reasonably certain the lessee will exercise that option.

The same lease could instead be expressed as a 'longer' period with an option (either explicit or implied by the inclusion of termination penalty clauses) to cancel the lease at an earlier date. The amount of the required termination payment will be one of the factors considered in determining whether it is reasonably certain that the lease will continue to full term (see **example 6.2.3**). If it is not reasonably certain to continue to full term, the lease term is the shorter non-cancellable period. When such a determination is made, any associated termination penalties would form part of the minimum lease payments. When it is assessed that the lease term is the full length of the arrangement, termination penalties should be excluded from the minimum lease payments.

6.3.7 Lease incentives given by a lessor

SIC-15 *Operating Leases – Incentives* (discussed at **7.2.3**) provides guidance for incentives in operating leases. It requires that all incentives for the agreement of a new or renewed operating lease should be recognised as an integral part of the net consideration agreed for the use of the leased asset, irrespective of the incentive's nature or form, or the timing of payments.

Likewise, if the lessor in a finance lease provides incentive payments to the lessee, the incentives should be deducted in the calculation of the minimum lease payments.

When any incentives are paid to the lessee, even if they are not part of the formal lease agreement, they should be deducted in the calculation of the minimum lease payments.

6.3.8 Rent reviews

The definition of minimum lease payments specifically excludes contingent rents (see also **6.3.2**). Rent reviews, whether to market rates or upward-only, give rise to contingent rent. Therefore, at the inception of the lease, the minimum lease payments throughout the lease term will be the payments agreed at inception, without consideration of future rent reviews.

Whether a lease specifies a rent of CU100 annually plus market increases, or CU100 annually resetting up or down to market every five years, the minimum lease payments are CU100 annually. Any increase or decrease as a result of subsequent rent reviews will be contingent rent.

The basis of any rent review under the lease should be evaluated carefully to determine whether the rent review resets the lease payments to market at the date of the review or whether, in substance, the amount of change in the lease payments at the date of the review was fixed at inception. In the latter case, the changes in rent would not be contingent and would therefore be part of the minimum lease payments.

7 Accounting and disclosure by lessees

7.1 Accounting for finance leases by lessees

7.1.1 *Measurement at initial recognition*

7.1.1.1 *Measurement of the leased asset and the related lease obligation*

At the commencement of the lease term (see **4.3.3**), both the leased asset and the related lease obligation should be recognised in the statement of financial position at an amount equal to the fair value of the leased asset or, if lower, the present value of the minimum lease payments, each determined at the inception of the lease. [IAS 17:20] If liabilities are split between current and non-current in the statement of financial position, the same split is made for lease liabilities; they should not be shown as a deduction from the leased assets. [IAS 17:23]

7.1.1.2 *Initial direct costs to be included in the amount recognised for the leased asset*

When a lessee incurs initial direct costs in connection with specific leasing activities (e.g. in negotiating and securing lease arrangements), those costs are included as part of the amount recognised as an asset under a finance lease to the extent that they can be directly attributed to that lease. [IAS 17:20] IAS 17:4 defines initial direct costs as incremental costs that are directly attributable to negotiating and arranging a lease, except for such costs incurred by manufacturer or dealer lessors.

See **8.3.1.3** for further discussion on the nature of initial direct costs.

7.1.1.3 *Interest rate implicit in the lease – definition*

The present value of the minimum lease payments should be calculated using the interest rate implicit in the lease. [IAS 17:20] The interest rate implicit in the lease is the discount rate that, at the inception of the lease, causes the aggregate present value of (a) the minimum lease payments and (b) the unguaranteed residual value to be equal to the sum of (i) the fair value of the leased asset and (ii) any initial direct costs of the lessor. [IAS 17:4]

See **7.1.1.4** for further guidance on the estimation of unguaranteed residual values and **7.1.1.5** for the meaning of 'fair value' in the context of IAS 17.

7.1.1.4   Estimating unguaranteed residual value when calculating the interest rate implicit in the lease

IAS 17 does not define 'residual value'. The unguaranteed residual value in the lease should be determined in accordance with the definition in IAS 16 *Property, Plant and Equipment* as "the estimated amount that an entity would currently obtain from disposal of the asset, after deducting the estimated costs of disposal, if the asset were already of the age and in the condition expected at the end of its useful life" (i.e. at a current value).

IAS 17:4 defines the interest rate implicit in the lease to be the rate that discounts the present value of (a) minimum lease payments and (b) unguaranteed residual value to be equal to the sum of (i) the fair value of the leased asset and (ii) any initial direct costs of the lessor. However, the estimate of the unguaranteed residual value is already a current value in accordance with IAS 16, rather than an estimated cash flow at the end of the lease. Therefore, the implicit interest rate will be obtained by considering the rate that is necessary to discount the minimum lease payments such that (1) the present value of minimum lease payments, and (2) the current value of the unguaranteed residual value together equate to the amount of the fair value of the leased asset, including initial direct costs.

The possible effects of future inflation should not be considered in estimating residual values because anticipated increases in residual values as a result of inflation represent a contingent gain that should be recognised only when realised (e.g. as part of the sales proceeds when the asset is sold at the end of the lease). For example, the residual value of a motor vehicle at the end of a three-year lease should be determined as the value of a three-year-old vehicle of the same or similar model at inception of the lease.

7.1.1.5   Fair value for the purpose of IAS 17

Leasing transactions within the scope of IAS 17 are excluded from the scope of IFRS 13 *Fair Value Measurement*. When IFRS 13 was issued in May 2011, a new paragraph 6A was added to IAS 17 stating as follows.

> "IAS 17 uses the term 'fair value' in a way that differs in some respects from the definition of fair value in IFRS 13 *Fair Value Measurement*. Therefore, when applying IAS 17 an entity measures fair value in accordance with IAS 17, not IFRS 13."

This relief from applying the requirements of IFRS 13 was granted on the basis that IFRS 13 might result in significant changes in the classification of leases and the accounting for leaseback transactions, and that requiring such significant changes followed by further changes when the new Standard on lease accounting is issued (see **section 9**) could be burdensome. [IFRS 13:BC22]

Fair value is defined in IAS 17:4 as "the amount for which an asset could be exchanged, or a liability settled, between knowledgeable, willing parties in an arm's length transaction". No further guidance is provided.

In general, the fair value of any asset is often best determined from market-based evidence of the amount for which the asset could be exchanged, taking account of prevailing market conditions and reflecting any volume or trade discounts that would ordinarily be available to market participants.

When considering the fair value of leased assets, there may be particular sources of evidence available. For example, when the lessor is a manufacturer or dealer, the lessor's *normal selling price* for the equipment may be an appropriate starting point for the determination of fair value, reflecting any volume or trade discounts that may be applicable.

When the lessor is not a manufacturer or dealer and there has been a significant lapse of time between the acquisition of the property by the lessor and the inception of the lease, the determination of fair value should consider market conditions prevailing at the inception of the lease, which may indicate that the fair value of the property is greater or less than its cost or carrying amount, if different.

When the leased asset is a second-hand or specialised asset, and a market price is not available, the fair value could be based on a depreciated replacement cost of a comparable new asset.

7.1.1.6 Lessee's incremental borrowing rate

If the interest rate implicit in the lease is not determinable, then the lessee's incremental borrowing rate should be used. [IAS 17:20] The lessee's incremental borrowing rate of interest is the rate of interest the lessee would have to pay on a similar lease or, if that is not determinable, the rate that, at the inception of the lease, the lessee would incur to borrow over a similar term, and with a similar security, the funds necessary to purchase the asset. [IAS 17:4]

The determination of the lessee's incremental borrowing rate should be based on the leasing practices in the relevant jurisdiction. Generally, most lease arrangements are secured and, therefore, a secured loan rate would be appropriate. However, there may be circumstances in which lease arrangements are unsecured and, consequently, an unsecured loan rate would be appropriate (because the lessor would have appropriately considered the unsecured leasing arrangement in its pricing).

When the lease is denominated in a foreign currency, the lessee's incremental borrowing rate should be the rate at which the lessee could obtain funding for the asset in the foreign currency.

7.1.2   Measurement subsequent to initial recognition

7.1.2.1   Allocation of finance charges

The difference between the total minimum lease payments (including any guaranteed residual amounts) and the amount at which the lessee recognises the outstanding liability at the inception of the lease represents a finance charge. This finance charge is allocated to accounting periods over the term of the lease so as to produce a constant periodic rate of interest (or, in practice, a reasonable approximation thereto) on the remaining balance of the lease obligation for each period. [IAS 17:25]

Note that the definition of minimum lease payments excludes contingent rents (see **6.3.2**). IAS 17 requires that contingent rents are recognised as an expense in the periods in which they are incurred. [IAS 17:25]

The allocation of the finance charge to accounting periods is achieved by apportioning each rental payment between a finance charge and a reduction of the lease obligation. IAS 17 does not specify any particular method for allocating the finance charge to each period – but it does allow that some form of approximation can be used to simplify the calculation.

The most common methods used are as follows.

The actuarial method

This method achieves an accurate apportionment of interest cost at a constant periodic rate over the term of the lease.

The sum-of-digits method

This is also referred to as the 'Rule of 78'. In most cases, this method produces an acceptable approximation to the results obtained by the actuarial method, but it is simpler to apply.

The straight-line method

This method does not attempt to produce a constant periodic rate of charge and does not, therefore, comply with IAS 17. Use of this method is only appropriate, on grounds of simplicity, if the difference between the figures thus produced and those that would be produced by the actuarial method would not be material to the financial statements. This is unlikely to be the case when the aggregate amount of finance leases is other than small relative to the size of the entity.

When a lease contains variation clauses that adjust the rentals to take account of movements in base rates of interest or changes in taxation, no adjustment is required in the calculations carried out at the start of the lease. Any increase or reduction in rentals should be accounted for as an increase or reduction in finance charges in the period in which it arises, i.e. the adjustments should be treated as contingent rents.

Example 7.1.2.1 illustrates the application of the sum-of-digits and the straight-line methods.

Example 7.1.2.1

Methods for allocating finance charges

An asset is leased under a finance lease as follows:

- three-year period;
- 12 quarterly rental payments; and
- total finance charges of CU10 million.

Application of the sum-of-digits method

If rentals are paid quarterly in arrears

The digit assigned for the first period will be 12 and the digit assigned for the last period will be 1.

Period	Quarter	Digit	Finance charge allocation	CU'000
Year 1	1	12	10 × 12/78	1,539
	2	11	10 × 11/78	1,410
	3	10	10 × 10/78	1,282
	4	9	10 × 9/78	1,154
Year 2	1	8	10 × 8/78	1,026
	2	7	10 × 7/78	897
	3	6	10 × 6/78	769
	4	5	10 × 5/78	641
Year 3	1	4	10 × 4/78	513
	2	3	10 × 3/78	385
	3	2	10 × 2/78	256
	4	1	10 × 1/78	128
		78		10,000

If rentals are paid in advance

Because there is no capital outstanding during the final quarter of the last year, there is no finance charge allocation to that quarter. Consequently, the digit for the last period will be zero and the digit for the first period will be 11. The sum of the digits becomes 66 (rather than 78), which is the denominator to be used in the fractions that are applied to allocate the total interest charge.

Application of the straight-line method

The finance charge is spread equally over the period of the lease. Thus, in the circumstances described, the finance charge would be CU833,000 (i.e. CU10 million ÷ 12) in each quarter.

Note the discussion preceding this example regarding the limited circumstances in which it is appropriate to use the straight-line method.

7.1.2.2   Lease incentives (rent-free periods)

When a finance lease contains an incentive, such as a rent-free period, the lessee will, at the commencement of the lease, recognise a leased asset and a finance lease liability either at the amount of the fair value of the leased asset or, if lower, at the amount of the present value of the minimum lease payments.

The lessee will apportion subsequent lease payments between finance charges and reduction of the outstanding liability, and allocate finance charges to accounting periods, as prescribed by IAS 17:25 (i.e. with a constant periodic rate of interest on the remaining balance of the liability during the lease term, including the rent-free period) – see **7.1.2.1**. Although there will be no payments made during the rent-free period (i.e. no reduction in the liability), finance charges will be recognised (at the rate implicit in the lease) in profit or loss with corresponding increases in the liability.

For example, assume that the lessee has recognised a lease liability of CU100 at the commencement of the lease. The rent-free period is one year and the implicit interest rate is 10 per cent. At the end of Year 1, the liability is increased by an interest charge of CU10, because no payment has been made. The liability balance will be reduced by payments in subsequent years.

7.1.2.3   Depreciation

If there is no reasonable certainty that the lessee will obtain ownership of the asset by the end of the lease term, the leased asset should be depreciated over the shorter of the lease term and its useful life. [IAS 17:27] When there is reasonable certainty that the lessee will obtain ownership by the end of the lease term, the asset should be depreciated over its useful life. The lease term should, for this purpose, be determined as discussed in **6.2**.

The depreciation policy used for leased assets should be consistent with that for depreciable assets that are owned, and the principles of IAS 16 or IAS 38 *Intangible Assets* should be applied, as appropriate. [IAS 17:27]

A lessee will also be required to recognise any impairment of a leased asset. To determine whether a leased asset is impaired (i.e. whether the recoverable amount of the leased asset is lower than its carrying amount), IAS 36 *Impairment of Assets* should be applied (see **chapter A10**).

7.1.3   Lease terminations

When a finance lease is terminated early, the appropriate accounting will depend on whether:

- the asset is purchased by the lessee;

- a further finance lease is entered into over the same asset;

- an operating lease is entered into over the same asset; or

- the entity ceases to have use of the asset.

In the last of these situations, the lessee should remove from its statement of financial position both the leased asset (in accordance with IAS 16 or IAS 38, as appropriate) and any part of the lease liability that will no longer be payable, and it should recognise any resulting difference in profit or loss.

When a finance lease is terminated and replaced with an operating lease over the same asset, the transaction will be a sale and leaseback and should be accounted for in the manner discussed at **7.3**.

7.2   Accounting for operating leases by lessees

7.2.1   *Operating lease payments generally to be recognised on a straight-line basis over the lease term*

Rentals payable under an operating lease should be recognised as an expense on a straight-line basis over the lease term, even if the payments are not made on that basis, unless another systematic basis is more representative of the time pattern of the user's benefit. [IAS 17:33] For example, if the rental payments for an asset are based on the actual usage of that asset, or are revised periodically to reflect the efficiency of the asset or current market rates, the rentals actually payable may be an appropriate measure.

7.2.2 Initial direct costs incurred by the lessee in an operating lease

---

Example 7.2.2

Initial direct costs incurred by the lessee in an operating lease

Company A enters into an operating lease of a property and incurs a statutory levy (e.g. stamp duty) at a fixed percentage of the fair value of the leased property. The statutory levy is payable at the inception of the lease.

How should Company A account for the cost of the statutory levy?

IAS 17 is silent on the subject of initial direct costs incurred by a lessee in an operating lease. In the absence of a specific Standard applying to a transaction or event, paragraph 11 of IAS 8 *Accounting Policies, Changes in Accounting Estimates and Errors* states that the requirements and guidance in IFRSs dealing with similar and related issues should be considered.

One way to account for the cost of the levy, in the absence of any specific guidance allowing its deferral, would be to recognise it as an expense when it is incurred. Alternatively, guidance on similar issues found elsewhere in IFRSs (as set out below) recognises that costs incurred to obtain benefit over time should be recognised as an expense over time. By analogy, such guidance would support recognition of the statutory levy as an asset and amortisation over the lease term on a straight-line basis. In particular:

- IAS 17:52 states that "[i]nitial direct costs incurred by a lessor in negotiating and arranging an operating lease [are] added to the carrying amount of the leased asset and recognised as an expense over the lease term";

- IAS 17:20 and 24 state that initial direct costs incurred by a lessee on entering into a finance lease are added to the amount recognised as an asset;

- paragraph 16(b) of IAS 16 *Property, Plant and Equipment* requires directly attributable costs in relation to an asset to be added to the carrying amount of the asset and depreciated over the asset's useful life; and

- paragraph 5.1.1 of IFRS 9 *Financial Instruments* and paragraph 43 of IAS 39 *Financial Instruments: Recognition and Measurement* state that transaction costs incurred on entering into financial instruments not classified as at fair value through profit or loss are included in the initial measurement of the financial instrument.

See **8.3.1.3** for further discussion on the nature of initial direct costs.

7.2.3 SIC-15 Operating Leases – Incentives *(application to lessees)*

7.2.3.1 SIC-15 – background

The subject of operating lease incentives is dealt with in SIC-15 *Operating Leases – Incentives*. Such incentives may take the form, for example, of an up-front cash payment to the lessee or a reimbursement or assumption by the lessor of costs of the lessee (e.g. relocation costs, leasehold improvements and costs associated with a pre-existing lease commitment of the lessee). Another form of incentive is an agreement for a rent-free or reduced rent period at the beginning of the lease.

7.2.3.2 Benefit of lease incentives to be recognised on a straight-line basis over the lease term

SIC-15 requires that all incentives for the agreement of a new or renewed operating lease should be recognised as an integral part of the net consideration agreed for the use of the leased asset, irrespective of the incentive's nature or form or the timing of payments. [SIC-15:3]

The lessee should recognise the aggregate benefit of incentives as a reduction of rental expense over the lease term, on a straight-line basis unless another systematic basis is representative of the time pattern of the lessee's benefit from the use of the leased asset. [SIC-15:5]

Example 7.2.3.2A

Recognition of lease incentive on a straight-line basis

The total payments under an operating lease are as follows:

Years 1 to 5:	CU200 per year
Years 6 to 20:	CU100 per year

In addition, the lessor provides a lease incentive with a value of CU500. The lessee's benefit under the lease arises on a straight-line basis over the full lease term.

Applying IAS 17 to the lease payments:

  Total payments: (CU200 × 5) + (CU100 × 15) = CU2,500

  Length of lease: 20 years

  Lease expense recognised each year: CU125

Applying SIC-15 to the incentive:

  CU500 / 20 years = reduction of CU25 per year

  Net lease expense recognised each year = CU125 – CU25 = CU100

Example 7.2.3.2B

Period over which the lease incentive should be recognised

Company A is the lessee under an operating lease. The lease contains a clause that requires lease payments to be repriced to market rates part-way through the lease term. The lessor grants an incentive to Company A to enter into the lease arrangement.

Over what period should the lease incentive be recognised (i.e. over the whole of the lease term or over the period up to the repricing of lease payments to market rates)?

The lease incentive should be recognised over the lease term, in accordance with SIC-15:5. It should be recognised on a straight-line basis, unless another systematic basis is more representative of the time pattern of Company A's benefit from use of the leased asset.

The IFRIC (now the IFRS Interpretations Committee) was asked to consider this issue in 2005. Specifically, the IFRIC was asked to consider whether the lease incentive should be recognised over the shorter period ending when the lease payments are adjusted to market rates on the basis that the lease expense of a lessee after an operating lease is repriced to market ought to be comparable with the lease expense of an entity entering into a new lease at that same time at market rates. The IFRIC did not accept this argument and confirmed that the general requirements of SIC-15:5 should apply.

The IFRIC also expressed its view that the repricing of itself would not be representative of a change in the time pattern referred to in SIC-15:5.

7.2.3.3   Recognition of rental holidays over the lease term

A rental holiday may be granted at the beginning of a lease to reflect the fact that the leased asset (typically a property) requires modification before it is ready for the lessee's intended use. The effect of the rental holiday should be recognised over the lease term, in accordance with SIC-15:5. It should be recognised on a straight-line basis, unless another systematic basis is more representative of the time pattern of the lessee's benefit from use of the leased asset.

It is sometimes argued that the benefit of such rental holidays should not be spread over the lease term but that the rental expense should be recognised only over the period of the lessee's occupation. This is based on an argument that such an approach would be more representative of the time pattern of the lessee's benefit from the use of the leased asset. However, this approach will not normally be appropriate if the leased asset is available for use by the lessee. Necessary modifications to a leased asset, which occur during the period in which the lessee has contracted to lease the asset, should normally be viewed as forming part of the benefit obtained by the lessee under the lease.

A possible exception would be the situation in which a rental holiday is agreed to reflect the fact that the lessor has been unable to provide the asset, in the agreed condition, at the beginning of the contracted lease term. In such circumstances, the substance of the arrangement may be that the lessor and the lessee have agreed to delay the start of the lease term.

7.2.3.4 Costs incurred by the lessee

Costs incurred by the lessee, including costs in connection with a pre-existing lease (e.g. costs for termination, relocation or leasehold improvements), should be accounted for by the lessee in accordance with the Standard applicable to those costs, including costs which are effectively reimbursed through an incentive arrangement. [SIC-15:6]

7.2.3.5 Payment made to a parent in return for a guarantee of its subsidiary's obligation under an existing operating lease

---

Example 7.2.3.5

Payment made to a parent in return for a guarantee of its subsidiary's obligation under an existing operating lease

Entity S, a subsidiary of Entity P, is the lessee under an existing operating lease. Entity S is experiencing financial difficulties part-way through the lease term. As a result, the terms of the lease are renegotiated and modified so that (1) Entity P agrees to act as guarantor for Entity S's ongoing lease obligations, in return for which (2) the lessor agrees to make a cash payment to Entity P.

In its consolidated financial statements, how should Entity P account for the amount received from the lessor?

The amount received by Entity P from the lessor should be treated as a lease incentive and, in accordance with SIC-15:5, should be recognised in Entity P's consolidated financial statements as a reduction of rental expense over the remaining lease term, on a straight-line basis unless another systematic basis is more representative of the time pattern of the group's benefit from use of the leased asset.

SIC-15:3 states that "[a]ll incentives for the agreement of a new or renewed operating lease shall be recognised as an integral part of the net consideration agreed for the use of the leased asset, irrespective of the incentive's nature or form or the timing of payments".

In the circumstances described, the substance of the arrangement is that the group has agreed to provide enhanced security to the lessor in return for an overall reduction in the group's net cost under the lease. The fact that the cash payment for the enhanced security is received by a group entity other than Entity S does not affect this conclusion.

7.2.3.6 Non-closely related derivative embedded in a lease contract

As discussed in paragraphs B4.3.1 to B4.3.8 of Appendix B to IFRS 9 *Financial Instruments* (or, for entities have not yet adopted IFRS 9, paragraphs AG27 to AG33 of the application guidance to IAS 39 *Financial Instruments: Recognition and Measurement*), certain features of a lease contract (e.g. leveraged inflation-adjusting lease payments) may give rise to a non-closely related embedded derivative that is accounted for separately from the host lease contract.

If the fair value of the embedded derivative at commencement of the lease is positive (i.e. the derivative is an asset), it should be considered an incentive for the lessee to enter into the lease and, in accordance with SIC-15, recognised as a reduction of rental expense over the lease term.

SIC-15:3 makes clear that "all incentives for the agreement of a new or renewed operating lease shall be recognised as an integral part of the net consideration agreed for the use of the leased asset, irrespective of the incentive's nature or form or the timing of payments". When the lessee benefits from an 'in the money' derivative, for which a premium would otherwise have been paid, this represents a transfer of value from the lessor to the lessee and, as such, an incentive to enter the lease similar in nature to the more common example of an up-front cash payment noted in SIC-15:1.

Conversely, an embedded derivative that has a negative fair value at commencement of the lease (i.e. that is a liability) represents a transfer of value from the lessee to the lessor and, as such, should be considered a prepayment to be recognised as an increase in rental expense over the lease term.

Regardless of whether a non-closely related embedded derivative's fair value at commencement of the lease is positive, negative or zero, subsequent changes in fair value will be recognised in profit or loss in the period in which they arise in accordance with IFRS 9 (or, for entities that have not yet adopted IFRS 9, IAS 39).

7.2.4 Vacant property following removal to new property

When a leased property is vacated, it is necessary to consider whether an onerous contract provision may be required under IAS 37 *Provisions, Contingent Liabilities and Contingent Assets*. Such a provision will be required if the costs associated with the property are likely to exceed the benefits to be obtained from it (e.g. through sub-letting). This issue is discussed at **3.9.2** in **chapter A12**.

7.2.5 Lease payments increase by fixed annual percentage

Some contracts provide for annual payments in an operating lease to increase by a fixed annual percentage over the life of the lease. It is sometimes suggested that, if such increases are intended to compensate for expected annual inflation over the lease period, it may be acceptable to recognise them in each accounting period as they arise.

Such a treatment is not appropriate. The lease payments should be recognised on a straight-line basis over the lease term unless another systematic basis is more representative of the time pattern of the user's benefit.

This was confirmed by the IFRIC (now the IFRS Interpretations Committee) in the November 2005 *IFRIC Update*.

The treatment of fixed annual increases can be contrasted with the accounting for increases based on, for example, an inflation index which are treated as contingent rents (see **example 6.3.2A**).

Example 7.2.5

Variable increases in lease payments with specified minimum annual increases

On 1 January 20X0, an entity leases a property to be used as a corporate office for a lease term of six years. The lease has been classified as an operating lease by the entity. The rental for the first calendar year has been agreed at CU100. From 1 January 20X1, the rental will be increased yearly by the same percentage as the general Retail Price Index of the jurisdiction in which the property is located; that increase will be subject to a minimum of 3 per cent and a maximum of 6 per cent.

In the circumstances described, the minimum annual lease increases (3 per cent of the previous yearly rentals) will be recognised on a straight-line basis over the term of the lease, while the difference between the minimum annual increase and the actual general Retail Price Index will be accounted for as contingent rent in profit or loss when incurred.

7.2.6 *Discounting of operating lease payments*

When an entity determines the operating lease expense to be recognised in each year, the future payments are not discounted to their present value. IAS 17 requires the operating lease expense to be recognised on a straight-line basis, unless another systematic basis is more representative of the time pattern of the user's benefits. In most standard operating leases, the user's benefits do not vary from year to year; consequently, recognition on a straight-line basis is appropriate. Alternatives to a straight-line basis are only appropriate when the benefit from the leased asset is received on some other basis – for example, by reference to units of production. However, even when another systematic basis is used, it is not appropriate to discount lease payments.

When payments increase with time, whereas the rentals are recognised on a straight-line basis, an accrual will be built up over the first half of the lease and depleted during its second half. This accrual should not be discounted to its present value. Consistent with the way the lease expense is calculated (by reference to undiscounted payments), the liability should be recognised without taking into account the effect of discounting.

7.3   Accounting for sale and leaseback and similar transactions

7.3.1   Sale and leaseback transactions – general

A sale and leaseback transaction is a linked arrangement whereby the owner of an asset sells that asset and immediately leases it back from the purchaser. The subject of the sale and leaseback is commonly a building, but may be another item of property, plant and equipment. The lease payment and sale price are usually interdependent, because they are negotiated as a package. [IAS 17:58]

Often, an entity entering into a sale and leaseback transaction will, prior to the transaction, have had title to the asset being sold. This is not, however, essential; sale and leaseback accounting, as discussed below, would also apply when the asset 'sold' was previously held by the entity under a finance lease. Accordingly, when the terms of a lease are modified, so that it ceases to be a finance lease and becomes instead an operating lease, this should be accounted for as a sale and leaseback transaction.

A wide range of arrangements involving the use of leases are possible under which legal title and risks and rewards of ownership may be separated (e.g. lease and leaseback arrangements, and leases under which there is a future commitment to purchase the entity that is the other party to the lease). In such circumstances, the series of transactions should be considered as a whole, and the accounting should reflect the substance of the arrangements. The rules set out in **7.3.2** and **7.3.3** for sale and leaseback transactions may provide a useful framework for the consideration of such transactions. Note also the requirements of SIC-27 *Evaluating the Substance of Transactions Involving the Legal Form of a Lease*; as discussed at **3.2**, it is possible that a transaction involving the legal form of a lease may not fall to be accounted for under IAS 17.

The leaseback may be a finance lease if it meets the condition that substantially all the risks and rewards of ownership remain with the lessee, or it may be an operating lease (in which case, some significant risks and rewards of ownership will have been transferred to, and remain with, the purchaser). The accounting treatment of a sale and leaseback transaction depends on the type of lease involved (see **7.3.2** and **7.3.3**).

Note that the disclosure requirements for leases (discussed at **7.4** and **8.6**) apply to sale and leaseback arrangements just as to any other leases. In addition, such transactions may include unique or unusual provisions requiring disclosure as material leasing arrangements, and they may trigger the separate disclosure criteria in IAS 1 *Presentation of Financial Statements* (see **chapter A4**). [IAS 17:65 & 66]

7.3.2 Finance leasebacks

If the transaction gives rise to a finance leaseback, the substance of the transaction is that no disposal of the asset has taken place and, therefore, no gain or loss on disposal should be recognised. The transaction is merely a means by which the lessor provides finance to the lessee, with the asset as security. In such circumstances, any excess of the sales proceeds over the carrying amount should not be immediately recognised as income in the financial statements of the seller/lessee. Instead, it should be deferred and amortised over the lease term. [IAS 17:59]

In practice, the most straightforward treatment is to continue to recognise the asset at its previous carrying amount and to account for the asset as if the sale and leaseback transaction had not occurred (the 'net' presentation as illustrated in **example 7.3.2**).

Nevertheless, the seller/lessee should consider whether the transaction provides evidence of an impairment in value, in which case the carrying amount of the asset should be reduced to its recoverable amount in accordance with IAS 36 *Impairment of Assets*.

Example 7.3.2

Finance leasebacks

Entity Y sells a vessel to a third party and at the same time enters into an agreement with the third party to lease the vessel back for five years. The lease is a finance lease.

The net present value of the lease payments and the fair value of the vessel is CU8 million and the carrying amount of the vessel before the sale is CU4 million. The residual value of the vessel is CU2 million.

IAS 17:59 requires that the excess of the sales proceeds over the carrying amount should not be immediately recognised as income by Entity Y, but should be deferred and amortised over the lease term.

How should the deferred credit be presented in Entity Y's statement of financial position?

In practice, the most straightforward treatment is to continue to recognise the asset at its previous carrying amount and to account for the asset as if the sale and leaseback transaction had not occurred (sometimes referred to as a 'net' presentation). The proceeds from the 'sale' transaction are credited to a liability account representing the initial net obligation under the finance lease.

This presentation reflects the fact that the sale and leaseback transaction has not resulted in a significant change to the seller's interest in the risks and rewards incidental to ownership. Consequently, there is unlikely to be any change to the asset's useful life or residual value so far as the seller is concerned.

If the net presentation were adopted in the circumstances described, the carrying amount of the asset would be unchanged and the following entry would be recorded to recognise the proceeds received.

Dr	Cash	CU8,000,000
Cr	Lease obligation (liability)	CU8,000,000

To account for the proceeds received.

In subsequent accounting periods, an annual depreciation expense of CU0.4 million [(CU4 million – CU2 million)/5] would be recognised.

Alternatively, Entity Y could adopt a 'gross' presentation, under which the 'sale' of the asset is recognised; the deferred credit is accounted for in the same way as any other form of deferred income in that it is an income amount for which cash has been received in advance but that cannot be recognised immediately. The consequence is that the asset is recognised at its fair value at the date of the sale and leaseback transaction, and this new carrying amount is the basis for subsequent depreciation.

If the gross presentation were adopted in the circumstances described, the following entries would be recorded.

Dr	Cash	CU8,000,000
Cr	Property, plant and equipment (PP&E)	CU4,000,000
Cr	Deferred gain (liability)	CU4,000,000

To account for the sale of the asset.

Dr	PP&E	CU8,000,000
Cr	Lease obligation	CU8,000,000

To account for the leaseback of the asset.

In subsequent accounting periods, an annual depreciation expense of CU1.2 million [(CU8 million – CU2 million)/5] would be recognised; the annual amortisation of the deferred gain would be CU0.8 million [CU4 million/5], resulting in a net impact on profit or loss of CU0.4 million.

7.3.3   *Operating leasebacks*

If the related leaseback is an operating lease, it is necessary to determine the fair value of the asset and compare this with the contract sale price. Because the sale and lease transactions are connected, the sale may have been arranged at other than fair value, with the impact of any difference being recognised in the rentals payable.

The appropriate accounting treatment is as follows:

[IAS 17:61]

- if the sale price is equal to the fair value, there has, in effect, been a normal sale transaction and any profit or loss on sale should be recognised immediately;

- if the sale price is above the fair value:

  - the difference between fair value and carrying amount may be recognised immediately; but

  - the excess of proceeds over fair value should be deferred and amortised over the period for which the asset is expected to be used. The excess of the sale price over the fair value will be reflected in higher rental charges; and

- if the sale price is below the fair value, the difference between sale price and carrying amount should be recognised immediately except that, if a loss arising is compensated by future rent at below market price, it should be deferred and amortised in proportion to the rent payments over the period for which the asset is expected to be used.

Accordingly, for operating leases, if the fair value at the time of the transaction is less than the carrying amount of the asset, a loss equal to the amount of the difference between the carrying amount and the fair value should be recognised immediately. [IAS 17:63]

The following table summarises the requirements of IAS 17 regarding operating leasebacks in various circumstances.

	Carrying amount equal to fair value	Carrying amount less than fair value	Carrying amount above fair value
*Sale price established **at** fair value*			
Profit	n/a	recognise profit immediately	n/a
Loss	n/a	n/a	recognise loss immediately
*Sale price **below** fair value*			
Profit	n/a	recognise profit immediately	n/a
Loss **not** compensated by lease payments below market price	recognise loss immediately	recognise loss immediately	recognise loss immediately

	Carrying amount equal to fair value	Carrying amount less than fair value	Carrying amount above fair value
Loss compensated by lease payments below market price	defer and amortise loss	defer and amortise loss	loss recognised immediately for the difference between carrying amount and fair value (i.e. the asset is written down to fair value), defer and amortise any remaining loss
*Sale price **above** fair value*			
Profit	defer and amortise profit	profit may be recognised immediately for the difference between carrying amount and fair value, defer and amortise any remaining profit	loss recognised immediately for the difference between carrying amount and fair value (i.e. the asset is written down to fair value), defer and amortise any remaining profit
Loss	n/a	n/a	loss recognised immediately for the difference between carrying amount and fair value (i.e. the asset is written down to fair value), defer and amortise any remaining profit

Example 7.3.3 illustrates these rules for sale and leaseback transactions that are classified as operating leases.

Example 7.3.3

Sale and operating leaseback

(i) Sale price above fair value:

	CU'000
Carrying amount (book value)	100
Fair value	110
Sale price	125

	CU'000
Profit to be recognised	10
Profit to be deferred	15

(ii) Sale price below fair value:

	Asset A CU'000	Asset B CU'000
Carrying amount (book value)	100	100
Fair value	125	110
Sale price	110	95
Profit to be recognised	10	–
Apparent loss to be deferred if compensated by below market rentals	–	(5)

7.4 Disclosure requirements for lessees

7.4.1 Finance leases

Finance leases fall within the definition of financial instruments as set out in IAS 32 *Financial Instruments: Presentation*. Therefore, in addition to the specific disclosure requirements set out below, an entity must also meet the requirements of IFRS 7 *Financial Instruments: Disclosures* in respect of its finance lease arrangements (see **chapter B11** for entities applying IFRS 9 and **chapter C12** for entities applying IAS 39).

Lessees are required to make the following disclosures for finance leases:

[IAS 17:31]

- for each class of asset, the net carrying amount at the end of the reporting period;

- a reconciliation between the total of future minimum lease payments at the end of the reporting period, and their present value;

- the total of future minimum lease payments at the end of the reporting period, and their present value, for each of the following periods:

  - not later than one year;

  - later than one year and not later than five years; and

  - later than five years;

- contingent rents recognised as an expense in the period;

- the total of future minimum sublease payments expected to be received under non-cancellable subleases at the end of the reporting period; and

- a general description of the lessee's material leasing arrangements including, but not limited to, the following:

  - the basis on which contingent rent payable is determined;

  - the existence and terms of renewal or purchase options and escalation clauses; and

  - restrictions imposed by lease arrangements, such as those concerning dividends, additional debt, and further leasing.

In addition, the disclosure requirements of IAS 16 *Property, Plant and Equipment*, IAS 40 *Investment Property*, IAS 38 *Intangible Assets*, IAS 36 *Impairment of Assets* and IAS 41 *Agriculture* (see **chapters A7**, **A8**, **A9**, **A10** and **A38**, respectively) apply equally to assets held under finance leases. [IAS 17:32]

7.4.2 Operating leases

Lessees are required to make the following disclosures for operating leases:

[IAS 17:35]

- the total of future minimum lease payments under non-cancellable operating leases for each of the following periods:

  - not later than one year;

  - later than one year and not later than five years; and

  - later than five years;

- the total of future minimum sublease payments expected to be received under non-cancellable subleases at the end of the reporting period;

- lease and sublease payments recognised as an expense in the period, with separate amounts for minimum lease payments, contingent rents, and sublease payments; and

- a general description of the lessee's significant leasing arrangements including, but not limited to, the following:

  - the basis on which contingent rent payable is determined;

  - the existence and terms of renewal or purchase options and escalation clauses; and

  - restrictions imposed by lease arrangements, such as those concerning dividends, additional debt, and further leasing.

In disclosing the future minimum operating lease payments, disclosure should be made of the lease payments due under the lease contract (i.e. the expected cash payments) rather than of the future accounting expense (i.e. the straight-line expense recognised as a result of IAS 17:33).

> The minimum lease payments are defined in IAS 17:4 as "the *payments* over the lease term that the lessee is or can be required to make ...". [Emphasis added]

7.4.3 Arrangements involving the legal form of a lease

As discussed at **3.2**, SIC-27 requires that when an arrangement involves the legal form of a lease but does not, in substance, involve a lease under IAS 17, all aspects of the arrangement should be considered in determining the appropriate disclosures that are necessary to understand the arrangement and the accounting treatment adopted.

As noted at **3.2.6**, an entity should disclose the following in each period in which an arrangement of the type described in **3.2** exists:

[SIC-27:10]

- a description of the arrangement, including:

  - the underlying asset and any restrictions on its use;

  - the life and other significant terms of the arrangement; and

  - the transactions that are linked together, including any options;

- the accounting treatment applied to any fee received;

- the amount recognised as income in the period; and

- the line item of the statement of comprehensive income in which it is included.

These disclosures should be provided individually for each arrangement, or in aggregate for each class of arrangements (i.e. each grouping of arrangements with underlying assets of a similar nature). [SIC-27:11]

8 Accounting and disclosure by lessors

8.1 Accounting by lessors – general

> The approach required by IAS 17 for finance leases is to recognise the substance of the transaction, namely that the lessor is providing finance to the lessee to enable the lessee to obtain the use of a specific asset. Consequently, the asset recognised by the lessor under a finance lease is the amount receivable from the lessee rather than the asset that is the subject of the lease. Under an operating lease, the lessor treats the leased asset as a non-current asset and the rentals received as income.

8.2   Classification of leases

The circumstances under which a lease is presumed to be a finance lease are the same for a lessor as for a lessee (see **5.1**). However, there may be differences in circumstances, including differences in the cash flows arising, that result in classification of the lease by the lessor in a manner different from that of the lessee. In particular, some leases that are regarded as finance leases by lessors may be operating leases as far as lessees are concerned. [IAS 17:9]

In determining the minimum lease payments, a lessee takes account only of payments to be made by it, and any amounts guaranteed by it or by a party related to the lessee. On the other hand, the lessor may be able to arrange at or before the commencement of the lease that, at its conclusion, the asset will be sold to a third party at a guaranteed minimum price. The lessor will take account of any such guaranteed residual value in determining the minimum lease payments.

The classification of leases is based on the extent to which risks and rewards incidental to ownership of a leased asset have been transferred by the lessor or received by the lessee. When an independent third party is involved in the lease, it may result in the lessor transferring substantially all the risks and rewards of ownership. The lessee may not receive substantially all the risks and rewards of ownership, however, if some of the risks and rewards are transferred to a third party through a residual value guarantee.

8.3   Accounting for finance leases by lessors

8.3.1   Measurement at initial recognition

8.3.1.1   Finance lease receivables measured at the net investment in the lease

Lessors are required to present finance lease assets as receivables in their statements of financial position, at an amount equal to the net investment in the lease. [IAS 17:36]

Initially, the lessor will recognise a finance lease receivable under IAS 17:36, at the amount equal to the net investment in the lease. Subsequently, finance income will be recognised at a constant rate on the net investment under IAS 17:39 (see **8.3.2**). During any 'rent-free' period, this will result in the accrued finance income increasing the finance lease receivable.

8.3.1.2 Net investment in the lease – definition

The net investment in the lease is the gross investment in the lease discounted at the interest rate implicit in the lease. [IAS 17:4] The gross investment in the lease is the aggregate of the minimum lease payments receivable by the lessor under a finance lease and any unguaranteed residual value accruing to the lessor. [IAS 17:4]

The interest rate implicit in the lease is the discount rate that, at the inception of the lease, causes the aggregate present value of (a) the minimum lease payments and (b) the unguaranteed residual to be equal to the sum of (i) the fair value of the leased asset and (ii) any initial direct costs of the lessor. [IAS 17:4]

The difference between the gross investment in the lease and the net investment in the lease is unearned finance income. [IAS 17:4]

If the lessor grants any incentives to the lessee, such as an initial rent-free period, then, at the inception of the lease, the calculation of the minimum lease payments and determination of the interest rate implicit in the lease will factor in nil payments by the lessee during such a rent-free period.

8.3.1.3 Initial direct costs

When a lessor (other than a manufacturer or dealer lessor) incurs initial direct costs in connection with specific leasing activities, the definition of the interest rate implicit in the lease set out above results in such costs being included in the finance lease receivable. These costs should include only costs that are incremental, and that are directly attributable to negotiating and arranging a lease (e.g. commissions, legal fees and incremental internal costs). General overheads, such as costs of sales and marketing, are excluded. [IAS 17:38]

If a lessor employs permanent staff to negotiate and arrange new leases, it is not appropriate for the salary costs of those staff to be included within the initial measurement of finance lease receivables.

IAS 17:4 defines initial direct costs as '*incremental* costs that are directly attributable to negotiating and arranging a lease, except for such costs incurred by manufacturer or dealer lessors'. [Emphasis added]

Internal fixed costs do not qualify as incremental costs. Only those costs that would not have been incurred if the entity had not negotiated and arranged a lease should be included in the initial measurement of the finance lease receivable.

This issue has been considered and affirmed by the IFRS Interpretations Committee (see March 2014 *IFRIC Update*). Note that although the IFRS Interpretations Committee considered this issue specifically in the context of finance leases, the guidance applies equally to initial direct costs incurred in negotiating and arranging an operating lease (which are added to the carrying amount of the leased asset and expensed over the lease term under IAS 17:52 – see **8.4.4**).

8.3.2 Subsequent measurement

8.3.2.1 Finance lease income recognised at a constant periodic rate of return on the net investment

The lessor recognises finance income so as to reflect a constant periodic rate of return on its net investment in the finance lease. [IAS 17:39] This is achieved by allocating the rentals (net of any charges for services etc.) received by the lessor between finance income to the lessor and repayment of the debtor balance.

Example 8.3.2.1

Finance lease: initial and subsequent accounting by a lessor

Company A, which is not a manufacturer-dealer, leases a machine to Company B for 25 years under a finance lease. The rents are CU10 million per year.

- At inception, the fair value of the machine is CU120 million.
- The carrying amount of the machine is CU95 million.
- Company A incurred CU5 million of initial direct costs relating to negotiating and arranging the lease.
- The machine also has an unguaranteed residual value for Company A. The present value of the unguaranteed residual value is CU10 million.
- The present value of minimum lease payments is CU115 million.

At the commencement of the lease, the lessor (Company A) will derecognise the machine and recognise a finance lease receivable. The net investment in the lease will be the lease receivable, calculated as the total of the present value of the minimum lease payments, including annual rents, and the unguaranteed residual value. The present value of the minimum lease payments is calculated using the interest rate implicit in the lease. IAS 17:4 defines this rate as the discount rate that, at the inception of the lease, causes the aggregate present value of (a) the minimum lease payments and (b) unguaranteed residual value to be equal to the sum of (i) the fair value of the leased asset [CU120 million] and (ii) any initial direct costs of the lessor [CU5 million]. This sum is CU125 million.

Therefore, the lease receivable at the inception of the lease is CU125 million.

Because Company A is not a manufacturer-dealer, the difference between the original carrying amount of the machine and the net investment in the lease is recognised in profit or loss as a gain on disposal of the machine of CU25 million (CU125 – CU95 – CU5 million).

The accounting entries required at commencement of the lease are as follows.

		CU'000	CU'000
Dr	Finance lease receivable	125,000	
Cr	Profit or loss		25,000
Cr	Property, plant and equipment		95,000
Cr	Cash (initial direct costs paid)		5,000

To record the disposal of the machine and recognise the finance lease receivable.

IAS 17:39 requires that finance income should be recognised on a pattern that reflects a constant periodic rate of return on the lessor's net investment in the finance lease, using the rate implicit in the lease. Company A will recognise annual rental payments received (CU10 million) as partly being the repayment of the finance lease receivable and partly as interest income.

The accounting entry for Year 1 will be as follows (the constant periodic rate of return is 7.15 per cent).

		CU'000	CU'000
Dr	Cash	10,000	
Cr	Finance income (125 million × 7.15%)		8,940
Cr	Finance lease receivable (10 million − 8.94 million)		1,060

To record the receipt of rental payment and recognise finance income.

The accounting entry for Year 2 will be as follows (the constant periodic rate of return continues to be 7.15 per cent).

		CU'000	CU'000
Dr	Cash	10,000	
Cr	Finance income ((125 million − 1.06 million) × 7.15%)		8,860
Cr	Finance lease receivable (10 million − 8.86 million)		1,140

To record the receipt of rental payment and recognise finance income.

8.3.2.2 Changes in unguaranteed residual values

IAS 17 emphasises that estimated unguaranteed residual values used in computing the lessor's gross investment in a lease should be reviewed regularly. When there has been a reduction in the estimated unguaranteed residual value, the income allocation over the lease term is revised and any reduction in respect of amounts already accrued is recognised immediately. [IAS 17:41]

Changes in the unguaranteed residual value of the leased asset will only affect the finance lease receivable if the changes indicate impairment of the receivable and, subsequently, reversal of impairment.

IAS 17:36 requires the lessor's net investment in the finance lease to be shown as a finance lease receivable. The net investment in the finance lease is equal to the unguaranteed residual value accruing to the lessor plus the minimum lease payments, discounted at the interest rate implicit in the lease. The subsequent measurement of the lease receivable is specified by IAS 17 and by the derecognition and impairment requirements of IFRS 9 *Financial Instruments* (or, for entities that have not yet adopted IFRS 9, IAS 39 *Financial Instruments: Recognition and Measurement*). The recognition of finance income is based on a constant rate of return on the net investment. Finance income is recognised at the rate implicit in the lease on the total net investment including the unguaranteed residual value.

8.3.2.3 Asset under a finance lease classified as held for sale

When an asset under a finance lease is classified as held for sale (or included in a disposal group that is classified as held for sale) in accordance with IFRS 5 *Non-current Assets Held for Sale and Discontinued Operations*, it is accounted for in accordance with that Standard (see **chapter A20**). [IAS 17:41A]

8.3.3 Lease terminations

The derecognition of a lease receivable by a lessor is included in the scope of IFRS 9 (or, for entities that have not yet adopted IFRS 9, IAS 39). Accordingly, the derecognition criteria of IFRS 9 (or IAS 39) should be applied (see **chapter B8** for entities applying IFRS 9 and **chapter C8** for entities applying IAS 39).

8.4 Accounting for operating leases by lessors

8.4.1 Presentation of assets subject to operating leases

Lessors should present assets subject to operating leases in their statements of financial position according to the nature of the asset. [IAS 17:49]

8.4.2 Rental income

Rental income, excluding charges for services such as insurance and maintenance, should be recognised on a straight-line basis over the lease term even if the payments are not made on that basis, unless another systematic basis is more representative of the time pattern in which use benefit derived from the leased asset is diminished (e.g. when rentals are based on usage). [IAS 17:50]

8.4.3 Costs incurred in earning lease income

Costs incurred in earning the lease income, including depreciation, are recognised as an expense. [IAS 17:51]

8.4.4 Initial direct costs

When initial direct costs are incurred by lessors in negotiating and arranging an operating lease, these are added to the carrying amount of the leased asset and recognised as an expense over the lease term on the same basis as the lease income. [IAS 17:52]

See **8.3.1.3** for further discussion on the nature of initial direct costs.

8.4.5 Depreciation of assets subject to operating leases

The depreciation of leased assets should be on a basis consistent with the lessor's normal depreciation policy for similar assets, and the depreciation charge should be calculated on the basis set out in IAS 16 *Property, Plant and Equipment* or IAS 38 *Intangible Assets*, as appropriate (see **chapters A7** and **A9**, respectively). [IAS 17:53]

A problem of income and cost matching may arise when a lessor arranges specific finance for the purchase of an asset that is leased under an operating lease. When the finance is repaid from cash generated by rental receipts, the application of the previous paragraphs will result in:

- rental income recognised on a straight-line basis;

- depreciation expense recognised, say, on a straight-line basis; and

- finance costs front-end loaded because they will be charged as a constant percentage of capital outstanding.

The effect may be that the three items taken together show a loss in earlier years, and a profit in later years. It is sometimes argued that one way to address this issue is to view the leased asset as having some of the attributes of a financial asset. A method of depreciation that would be consistent with viewing the asset as having attributes of a financial asset is one which reflects the time value of money, for example the annuity method. This would result in a lower depreciation charge in earlier years and a more constant net profit after interest.

However, use of the annuity method of depreciation is not permitted. IAS 17:53 states that the lessor should apply its normal depreciation policy for similar assets and the depreciation charge should be calculated on the basis set out in IAS 16. IAS 16:60 states that the depreciation method used should reflect the pattern in which the asset's economic future benefits are expected to be consumed. The method should be based on the economic depreciation of the asset, not on the return from the asset. Therefore, the consideration of the time value of money in the depreciation calculation is not permitted.

8.4.6   Impairment of assets subject to operating leases

To determine whether a leased asset has become impaired (i.e. when the recoverable amount of the asset is lower than its carrying amount), an entity applies the principles of IAS 36 *Impairment of Assets* (see **chapter A10**).

8.4.7   Assets cease to be rented and become held for sale

Entities that, in the course of their ordinary activities, routinely sell items that they have held for rental to others are required to transfer those assets to inventories at their carrying amount when they cease to be rented and become held for sale. This is discussed further at **9.3** in **chapter A7**.

8.4.8   SIC-15 Operating Leases – Incentives *(application to lessors)*

The treatment of operating lease incentives from the perspective of the lessor is also dealt with in SIC-15 *Operating Leases – Incentives*.

SIC-15 requires that all incentives for the agreement of a new or renewed operating lease should be recognised as an integral part of the net consideration agreed for the use of the leased asset, irrespective of the incentive's nature or form or the timing of payments. [SIC-15:3]

The lessor recognises the aggregate cost of incentives as a reduction of rental income over the lease term, on a straight-line basis unless another systematic basis is representative of the time pattern over which the benefit of the leased asset is diminished. [SIC-15:4]

It is not appropriate either to recognise lease incentives immediately in profit or loss or to recognise them over the useful life of the asset, because this may be longer than the lease term.

8.5   Accounting by manufacturer and dealer lessors

When a manufacturer or dealer offers leasing terms as an option in addition to normal selling terms (termed in the United States, a 'sales-type lease'), the question arises as to whether an immediate selling profit should be recognised when the asset is first leased. The answer will depend on whether there has, in effect, been a disposal of that asset. This in turn will depend on whether the lease is an operating or a finance lease.

In the case of an operating lease, the manufacturer or dealer has retained the asset with a view to using it to generate rental income. Consequently, no selling profit should be recognised and the asset should be included in the statement of financial position as a non-current asset, initially at its purchase price or production cost. [IAS 17:55]

In the case of a finance lease, there are two types of income associated with the contract: the selling profit or loss (i.e. an amount equivalent to the profit or loss arising on the outright sale of the asset at normal selling prices) and the finance income over the period of the lease. As a general principle, the selling profit or loss should be recognised at the commencement of the lease, in accordance with the entity's usual accounting policies. The sales revenue recognised is the fair value of the asset, or, if lower, the present value of the minimum lease payments accruing to the lessor, computed at a market rate of interest. Thus, if artificially low rates of interest are charged, the amount of the selling profit will be restricted to the profit that would have been earned if a commercial rate of interest had been charged over the lease term. [IAS 17:42 - 44]

Manufacturer or dealer lessors are required to recognise the costs of negotiating and arranging a finance lease as an expense when the selling profit is recognised. [IAS 17:42] Such costs are not included in the initial measurement of the finance lease receivable (as in the case of other lessors – see **8.3.1.3**) because they are regarded as mainly relating to earning the manufacturer's or dealer's selling profit. [IAS 17:46] For manufacturer or dealer lessors, costs incurred in connection with negotiating and arranging a lease are excluded from the definition of initial direct costs (see **7.1.1.2**). As a result, they are excluded from the net investment in the lease and are recognised as an expense when the selling profit is recognised, which for a finance lease is normally at the commencement of the lease term. [IAS 17:38]

8.6 Disclosure requirements for lessors

8.6.1 Finance leases

Finance leases fall within the definition of financial instruments as set out in IAS 32 *Financial Instruments: Presentation*. Therefore, in addition to the specific disclosure requirements set out below, an entity must also meet the requirements of IFRS 7 *Financial Instruments: Disclosures* in respect of its leasing arrangements (see **chapter B11** for entities applying IFRS 9 and **chapter C12** for entities applying IAS 39).

Lessors are required to make the following disclosures for finance leases:

[IAS 17:47]

- a reconciliation between the gross investment in the lease at the end of the reporting period, and the present value of minimum lease payments receivable at the end of the reporting period;

- the gross investment in the lease and the present value of minimum lease payments receivable at the end of the reporting period, for each of the following periods:

  - not later than one year;

  - later than one year and not later than five years; and

  - later than five years;

- unearned finance income;

- the unguaranteed residual values accruing to the benefit of the lessor;

- the accumulated allowance for uncollectible minimum lease payments receivable;

- contingent rents included in income in the period; and

- a general description of the lessor's material leasing arrangements.

IAS 17:48 suggests that, as an indicator of growth, it is often useful also to disclose the gross investment less unearned income in new business added during the period, after deducting the relevant amounts for cancelled leases.

8.6.2   Operating leases

Lessors are required to make the following disclosures for operating leases:

[IAS 17:56]

- the future minimum lease payments under non-cancellable operating leases, in aggregate and for each of the following periods:

  - not later than one year;

  - later than one year and not later than five years; and

  - later than five years;

- total contingent rents recognised in income in the period; and

- a general description of the lessor's leasing arrangements.

For the disclosure of minimum lease payments, IAS 17 requires disclosure of the anticipated cash flows from future minimum lease payments, and not the amounts expected to be recognised as income (if the cash flows are structured differently from the economic use of the asset).

In addition, the disclosure requirements of IAS 16 *Property, Plant and Equipment*, IAS 40 *Investment Property*, IAS 38 *Intangible Assets*, IAS 36 *Impairment of Assets* and IAS 41 *Agriculture* (see **chapters A7**, **A8**, **A9**, **A10** and **A38**, respectively) apply equally to assets leased out under operating leases. [IAS 17:57]

8.6.3   Arrangements involving the legal form of a lease

As discussed at **3.2**, SIC-27 *Evaluating the Substance of Transactions Involving the Legal Form of a Lease* requires that when an arrangement involves the legal form of a lease but does not, in substance, involve a lease under IAS 17, all aspects of the arrangement should be considered in determining the appropriate disclosures that are necessary to understand the arrangement and the accounting treatment adopted.

As noted at **3.2.6**, an entity should disclose the following in each period in which an arrangement of the type described in **3.2** exists:

[SIC-27:10]

- a description of the arrangement, including:

  - the underlying asset and any restrictions on its use;

  - the life and other significant terms of the arrangement; and

  - the transactions that are linked together, including any options;

- the accounting treatment applied to any fee received;

- the amount recognised as income in the period; and

- the line item of the statement of comprehensive income in which it is included.

These disclosures should be provided individually for each arrangement, or in aggregate for each class of arrangements (i.e. each grouping of arrangements with underlying assets of a similar nature). [SIC-27:11]

Appendix A5 Investment property (entities applying IAS 17)

Contents

1 Introduction

1.1 Overview of IAS 40

IAS 40 *Investment Property* applies to the accounting for property (land and/or buildings) held to earn rentals or for capital appreciation (or both). Investment properties are initially measured at cost and, with some exceptions, may subsequently be measured using a cost model or a fair value model. Changes in fair value under the fair value model are recognised in profit or loss.

1.2 Amendments to IAS 40 since the last edition of this manual

In January 2016, IAS 40 was amended by consequential amendments arising from IFRS 16 *Leases*. The requirements of IAS 40 as amended by IFRS 16 are dealt with in **chapter A8** of this manual. This appendix sets out the requirements of IAS 40 prior to amendment by IFRS 16, and is intended for the convenience of entities that have not yet adopted IFRS 16 and that therefore continue to apply IAS 17 *Leases* (see **appendix A4**).

2 Scope

2.1 Scope – general

IAS 40 is to be applied in the recognition, measurement and disclosure of 'investment property' (see **2.2** for definition). [IAS 40:2]

The Standard also deals with the measurement in the lessee's financial statements of investment property interests held under a lease accounted for as a finance lease, and with the measurement in a lessor's financial statements of investment property leased out under an operating lease. The more general requirements regarding the classification and measurement of leased investment property are not dealt with in IAS 40 but fall within the general requirements of IAS 17 *Leases* (see **appendix A4**). In particular, the following matters are dealt with in IAS 17 rather than in IAS 40:

[IAS 40:3]

- classification of leases as finance leases or operating leases;

- recognition of lease income from investment property;

- measurement in a lessee's financial statements of property interests held under a lease accounted for as an operating lease (but see **2.4**);

- measurement in a lessor's financial statements of its net investment in a finance lease;

- accounting for sale and leaseback transactions; and

- disclosures regarding finance leases and operating leases.

Also specifically excluded from the scope of IAS 40 are:

[IAS 40:4]

- biological assets related to agricultural activity (see IAS 41 *Agriculture* (**chapter A38**) and IAS 16 *Property, Plant and Equipment* (**chapter A7**)); and

- mineral rights and mineral reserves such as oil, natural gas, and similar non-regenerative resources.

2.2   Investment property – definition

Investment property is defined in IAS 40 as follows.

[IAS 40:5]

"Investment property is property (land or a building – or part of a building – or both) held (by the owner or by the lessee under a finance lease) to earn rentals or for capital appreciation or both, rather than for:

(a)   use in the production or supply of goods or services or for administrative purposes; or

(b)   sale in the ordinary course of business."

Included within this definition are:

[IAS 40:8]

- land held for long-term capital appreciation, and not for short-term sale in the ordinary course of business;

- land held for a currently undetermined future use. If an entity has not decided whether land will be used for owner-occupation or for short-term sale in the ordinary course of business, it should be regarded as held for capital appreciation;

- a building owned or held under a finance lease by an entity and leased out under operating lease(s);

- a vacant building that is being held to be leased out under an operating lease (or leases); and

- property that is being constructed or developed for future use as investment property.

Examples of items that are *not* investment property include:

[IAS 40:9]

- property that is being held for sale in the ordinary course of business, or that is under construction or development for such sale (within the scope of IAS 2 *Inventories* – see **chapter A11**). This means that properties acquired specifically for the purpose of subsequent disposal in the near future, or for development and resale, are excluded from the scope of IAS 40;

- owner-occupied property (see **2.4**); and

- property leased to another entity under a finance lease.

> For entities that have not yet adopted IFRS 15 *Revenue from Contracts with Customers*, IAS 40:9 also cites property being constructed or developed on behalf of third parties (within the scope of IAS 11 *Construction Contracts*) as an example of an item that is not investment property.

IAS 40 acknowledges that judgement is often required to determine whether a property qualifies as an investment property and requires entities to develop criteria to enable them to make that determination in a consistent manner. Disclosure of such criteria is required when classification is difficult (see **9.2.1**). [IAS 40:14]

2.3 Property held under an operating lease

A property interest that is held by a lessee under an operating lease may be classified and accounted for as an investment property if, and only if, the property would otherwise meet the definition of an investment property and the lessee uses IAS 40's fair value model (see **5.2**) for the asset recognised. It is important to note that:

[IAS 40:6]

- this is an option (a 'classification alternative'). Entities may elect whether they wish to classify such interests as investment property;

- the classification alternative is available on a property-by-property basis;

- the classification alternative is not available for assets not accounted for using the fair value model;

- once this classification alternative is selected for one property interest held under an operating lease, all property classified as investment property must be accounted for using the fair value model; and

- property interests accounted for under the classification alternative are considered to be part of the entity's investment property for the purposes of IAS 40's disclosure requirements (see **9.2**).

> The option allowed under IAS 40:6 to classify selected property interests under operating leases as investment property is intended to facilitate the classification of assets such as land held under long-term operating leases as investment property, provided that the general criteria for such classification are met. This is particularly relevant in jurisdictions

such as Hong Kong and the United Kingdom where interests in property are commonly – or, in the former case, exclusively – held under long-term lease arrangements.

In contrast to the option available in relation to property held under an operating lease under IAS 40:6 (see above), IAS 40:8 *requires* that property held under a finance lease be treated as investment property, provided that the property otherwise meets the definition of an investment property. IAS 40:8 also applies to property held under a lease that is classified as a finance lease because the lease payments cannot be allocated reliably between the land and buildings elements (see **5.2** in **appendix A4**).

The detailed requirements when property or property interests held under leases are classified as investment property are considered further at **4.3**.

Example 2.3

Classification – lease of an investment property

Company A (as lessee) leases a property which meets the definition of an investment property.

Company A is unable to obtain a reliable allocation between the land element and the buildings elements of the leased property. Therefore, in accordance with IAS 17:16, the entire lease is classified as a finance lease (it is *not* clear that both elements are operating leases, otherwise the entire lease would be classified as an operating lease).

The requirement in IAS 40:6 (also referred to in IAS 17:19) to adopt the fair value model applies when an entity chooses to account for a property interest held under an operating lease as an investment property. Because, in the circumstances described, Company A classifies the entire lease as a finance lease, IAS 40 permits a choice between the cost model and the fair value model. This option is available for finance leases (as determined by IAS 17) irrespective of whether there may be an 'operating lease' component for land which cannot be reliably determined.

2.4   Distinguishing between investment property and owner-occupied property

2.4.1   *Owner-occupied property – definition*

Owner-occupied property is property held (by the owner or by the lessee under a finance lease) for use in the production or supply of goods or services or for administrative purposes. [IAS 40:5]

Owner-occupied property includes property held for future development and subsequent use as owner-occupied property, property held for future use as owner-occupied property, employee-occupied property (whether or not the employees pay rent at market rates) and owner-occupied property awaiting disposal. [IAS 40:9(c)]

2.4.2 Property held for more than one purpose

In circumstances when property is held partly for capital appreciation and/or rentals, and partly for the production of goods or services or administrative purposes, the two parts are accounted for separately if they could be sold, or leased out under a finance lease, separately. If they could not be sold (or leased out under a finance lease) separately, the property is accounted for as an investment property only if an insignificant portion is held for use in the production or supply of goods or services or for administrative purposes. [IAS 40:10]

IAS 40 does not include any guidance as to what constitutes an 'insignificant' portion for this purpose. This is a deliberate omission – the Basis for Conclusions on IAS 40 explains that quantitative guidance has not been provided because the Board concluded that such guidance could lead to arbitrary distinctions.

2.4.3 Ancillary services

If an entity provides ancillary services to the occupants of its property, the property is accounted for as investment property provided that the services are an 'insignificant' portion of the arrangement. [IAS 40:11]

Example 2.4.3A

Services provided by the owner of an office building

The owner of an office building provides cleaning services for the lessees of the building and these services are 'insignificant' in the context of the total arrangement. Therefore, the building is classified and accounted for as an investment property.

As indicated in **example 2.4.3A**, it would be unusual for cleaning services to be so material that they would prevent a property from being classified as an investment property. A similar conclusion is likely for security and maintenance services (see IAS 40:11). At the other extreme, some entities rent out fully furnished offices including a whole range of services such as IT systems and secretarial services. Such arrangements are in the nature of the rendering of a service rather than property investment and the property would be classified as owner-occupied and accounted for under IAS 16 *Property, Plant and Equipment*. However, there are many instances in between these extremes for which the appropriate classification can only be determined based on a detailed assessment of the arrangements and whether or not the services provided are judged to be insignificant.

Example 2.4.3B

Hotel property as investment property

A hotel operator owns a significant number of buildings. The hotel operator seeks to maximise revenue by selling room occupancy.

Is it acceptable for the hotel operator to classify these buildings as investment properties?

The properties are used by the hotel operator in the normal course of business and, therefore, are not investment properties. IAS 40:12 cites the direct provision of services to hotel guests as services that will generally be considered to be significant. Although the hotel operator may hold the buildings for long-term appreciation, that is not the principal reason for holding them.

The determination as to whether ancillary services are significant (thus excluding the property from the scope of IAS 40) requires the exercise of judgement. The Standard considers the case of hotels and acknowledges the variety of arrangements that may exist. For example, the owner of a hotel property may transfer some responsibilities to third parties under a management contract. The terms of such contracts vary widely. The owner's role may be restricted to that of a passive investor, in which case the property would be more likely to qualify as investment property. At the other extreme, the contract may simply result in the outsourcing of some day-to-day responsibilities, while the owner retains significant exposure to variations in the cash flows generated by the operation of the hotel. In the latter case, the contract has little effect on the substance of the owner's interest and the property is likely to be classified as owner-managed. [IAS 40:13]

2.4.4   Property leased to other group members

If an entity owns a property that is leased to, and occupied by, another group member (e.g. a parent or another subsidiary), the property is not recognised as an investment property in the consolidated financial statements because it will be treated as owner-occupied from the perspective of the group. However, from an individual-entity perspective, the property is treated as an investment property if it meets the definition in IAS 40:5 (see **2.2**). [IAS 40:15]

2.5 Property accepted as loan settlement

Example 2.5

Property accepted as loan settlement

Entity A, a financial institution, provides mortgage loans to individuals and corporate entities to finance the acquisition of properties. The terms of these mortgage loans require the property to be pledged as collateral for the loan. If a counterparty defaults under the terms of a mortgage loan and is no longer entitled to redeem the collateral, Entity A accepts the property as settlement of the loan receivable. The former owner ceases to have any rights over the property or over the income that it generates. The derecognition criteria in IFRS 9 *Financial Instruments* (or, for entities that have not yet adopted IFRS 9, IAS 39 *Financial Instruments: Recognition and Measurement*) are met and Entity A derecognises the loan receivable, and recognises the property as its asset, initially measured at fair value. Under local regulations, Entity A is required to sell the asset within two years.

Should Entity A classify the property as an investment property in accordance with IAS 40 or as inventories in accordance with IAS 2? How should Entity A account for any rentals received during the period for which it holds the asset?

The appropriate classification of the property as investment property or inventories depends on management's intent. If management intends to hold the property to earn rentals or for capital appreciation (or both), the property would meet the definition of an investment property and should be accounted for under IAS 40. In contrast, if the property is being actively marketed for sale, but it is not sold within a short timeframe (e.g. because of seasonal fluctuations in the property market), such activity would indicate that Entity A views the property as a form of settlement of amounts due under the defaulted mortgage loan and that it is an asset acquired and held for sale in the ordinary course of business. In such circumstances, the property should be accounted for as inventories under IAS 2.

Regardless of whether the property is classified as investment property or inventories, any rentals received should be recognised as rental income in profit or loss.

2.6 Group of assets leased under a single operating lease

Example 2.6

Group of assets leased under a single operating lease

IAS 40:50 states that "[i]n determining the carrying amount of investment property under the fair value model, an entity does not double-count assets or liabilities that are recognised as separate assets or liabilities. For example:

(a) equipment such as lifts or air-conditioning is often an integral part of a building and is generally included in the fair value of the investment property, rather than recognised separately as property, plant and equipment.

(b)   if an office is leased on a furnished basis, the fair value of the office generally includes the fair value of the furniture, because the rental income relates to the furnished office. When furniture is included in the fair value of investment property, an entity does not recognise that furniture as a separate asset".

Consider the following example:

- a lessor leases out a farm for the purpose of earning rentals;
- the farm is made up of the following assets: (1) land and agricultural buildings, and (2) agricultural fittings, fixtures and machinery that are an integral part of the agricultural buildings;
- the lease agreement meets the definition of an operating lease for the lessor; and
- the lessor measures investment property after initial recognition at fair value.

The lessor should account for all the assets included in the operating lease agreement as a unique investment property and, as a consequence, measure it using the fair value model.

Although agricultural fittings, fixtures and machinery do not meet the definition of an investment property in their own right, the lessor should follow the requirements in IAS 40:50 to determine the fair value of its investment property, including the other assets that form part of the lease agreement.

In the above example, the lease agreement includes all the assets (i.e. land and agricultural buildings and fittings, fixtures and machinery) that are an integral part of the farm and are necessary for operating the farm. Therefore, the rental income reflects the right to use of the complete set of assets. Consequently, the lessor should recognise investment property comprising all the assets (i.e. the land and agricultural buildings and the agricultural fittings, fixtures and machinery), measured in accordance with IAS 40.

Specific facts and circumstances should be considered by the lessor in each operating lease agreement covering a piece of land or a building, or part of a building, or both together with property, plant and equipment items held to earn rentals, in order to establish which assets covered by the agreement should be regarded as investment property.

3 Recognition

3.1 Recognition – general

Investment property is recognised as an asset when:

[IAS 40:16]

- it is probable that the future economic benefits that are associated with the investment property will flow to the entity; and

- the cost of the investment property can be measured reliably.

This general principle is used to consider whether capitalisation is appropriate both in respect of the costs incurred initially to acquire or construct an investment property, and costs incurred subsequently to add to, replace part of, or service a property (see **3.3**). [IAS 40:17]

3.2 Distinguishing the acquisition of an investment property asset (or assets) from a business combination

When an entity acquires investment property:

[IAS 40:14A]

- judgement is required to determine whether the acquisition is the acquisition of an asset or a group of assets, or a business combination in the scope of IFRS 3 *Business Combinations*; and

- this judgement should be based on the guidance in IFRS 3 (see **section 4** of **chapter A25**) rather than on the requirements in IAS 40:7 to 14 (see **2.2** to **2.4**).

The Standard notes that the requirements in IAS 40:7 to 14 provide guidance for distinguishing between investment property and owner-occupied property and not for determining whether the acquisition of property is a business combination. When an entity acquires property, it is necessary to determine separately whether the transaction is a business combination (using the principles of IFRS 3) and whether the property acquired is investment property (using the principles of IAS 40). [IAS 40:14A]

3.3 Subsequent costs

Appropriate application of the recognition principle set out at **3.1** results in:

[IAS 40:18 & 19]

- the immediate expensing of the costs of the day-to-day servicing of a property (e.g. the costs of labour, consumables and minor parts used for repairs and maintenance); and

- costs incurred to replace parts of the original property being recognised in the investment property if they meet the recognition criteria.

When the costs of replacement parts are capitalised, the carrying amounts of the replaced parts are derecognised. [IAS 40:19]

If the entity has been using the cost model to measure its investment property, but the replaced part was not being depreciated separately, and the carrying amount of the replaced part cannot be determined, the cost of the replacement may be used as an indication of what the cost of the replaced part would have been at acquisition. [IAS 40:68]

When the fair value model is being used, the carrying amount of the investment property may already reflect the deterioration in value of the replaced part. In other cases it may be difficult to discern how much fair value should be reduced for the part being replaced. An alternative to reducing fair value for the replaced part, when it is not practical to do so, is to include the cost of the replacement in the carrying amount of the investment property, and then to reassess the fair value of the property (i.e. in the same way as would be required for additions not involving replacement). [IAS 40:68]

3.4 Investment property in the course of construction

IAS 40 does not deal specifically with the recognition of the cost of a self-constructed investment property. The appropriate accounting for such property is therefore determined in accordance with general principles.

Over the period of construction, the costs of construction will be capitalised as part of the cost of the investment property in accordance with the general principle outlined at **3.1**. Paragraphs 16 to 22 of IAS 16 *Property, Plant and Equipment* (see **4.2** in **chapter A7**) provide guidance as to what is appropriately included within such costs.

The capitalisation of borrowing costs is considered in accordance with the general requirements of IAS 23 *Borrowing Costs* (see **chapter A18**). IAS 23:4 provides an optional exemption from the requirement to capitalise borrowing costs for qualifying assets that are measured at fair value (which would include investment property under construction if an entity follows the fair value model for investment property). Therefore, entities can choose, as a matter of accounting policy, whether to capitalise borrowing costs in respect of such assets. When relevant to an understanding of the financial statements, that accounting policy should be disclosed.

If an entity follows the fair value model in accounting for its investment property (see **5.2**), provided that the fair value of the property under construction can be measured reliably, the costs capitalised during the course of construction do not affect the carrying amount of the investment property under construction, which is remeasured to fair value at the end of each reporting period. Therefore, any costs capitalised during the reporting period simply reduce the amount recognised in profit or loss for any gain (or increase the amount recognised for any loss) arising on remeasurement to fair value at the end of the reporting period. Although the amount reported in the statement of financial position is not affected, it is important to capitalise construction costs when appropriate, because this may affect the classification of amounts in the statement of comprehensive income (e.g. any gain on remeasurement may be overstated and property expenses overstated by the same amount).

4 Measurement at recognition

4.1 Measurement at recognition – general

An investment property is measured initially at its cost. Transaction costs are included in the initial measurement. [IAS 40:20]

The cost of an investment property includes its purchase price (if purchased) and other directly attributable expenditure (e.g. professional fees for legal services, property transfer taxes and other transaction costs). [IAS 40:21]

Start-up costs are not included unless they are necessary to bring the asset to the condition required for its intended operation. Abnormal costs, and operating losses incurred before the property reaches its required level of occupancy, are excluded from the cost of the investment property. [IAS 40:23]

Example 4.1A

Expenditure to be capitalised as part of the cost of an investment property

Entity R acquires a building for CU95 million in March 20X1 as an investment property. In June 20X1, Entity R refurbishes entirely the building at a cost of CU5 million to bring it to the condition required by the rental market. Entity R will pay an estate agent two months' rent if the agent locates a lessee. In December 20X1, Entity R (the lessor) finally rents the property under an operating lease to Entity S (the lessee).

Is it appropriate for Entity R to include the refurbishment costs and the estate agent's fees as part of the initial cost of the investment property?

Yes. When it buys the building, Entity R should recognise the purchase price as the initial cost of the building under IAS 40. The refurbishment costs are necessary to bring the property to a condition suitable for renting out and, therefore, these costs should also be included in the initial cost of the building.

The estate agent's fees are not part of the initial cost of the building but they are considered to be "initial direct costs incurred in negotiating and arranging an operating lease" under IAS 17 *Leases* (see **8.4.4** in **appendix A4**). They are, therefore, capitalised as part of the leased building. When the cost model is used, the expenditure should be depreciated over the lease term. When the fair value model is used, the costs should be capitalised and will, therefore, result in a smaller revaluation gain (or larger revaluation loss) when the building is next remeasured to fair value.

Example 4.1B

Termination payments by a lessor to a lessee

Company A owns an office building that it leases to Company B. The lease is classified as an operating lease in accordance with IAS 17. Company A would like to convert the office building into a block of flats, believing that this will attract significantly higher rental income. First, however, Company A must terminate the lease contract with Company B.

Company A applies the cost model as its accounting policy for the measurement of its investment property subsequent to initial recognition.

Should Company A capitalise the lease termination costs as part of the cost of converting the office building into a block of flats?

Yes. Paragraph 16(b) of IAS 16 *Property, Plant and Equipment* states that the cost of an item of property, plant and equipment includes "any costs directly attributable to bringing the asset to the location and condition necessary for it to be capable of operating in the manner intended by management". IAS 16:7 requires that the cost of an item of property, plant and equipment be recognised as an asset if "it is probable that future economic benefits associated with the item will flow to the entity" and if "the cost of the item can be measured reliably".

Therefore, if Company A's cost of terminating Company B's operating lease meets the recognition criteria for property, plant and equipment in IAS 16:7, Company A should capitalise this cost because it is a directly attributable cost of enabling operation of the asset in the manner intended by management.

Company A should also consider whether there is an indicator of impairment and whether any further impairment testing should be performed to ensure that the building is not recognised at a carrying amount higher than its recoverable amount as a result of capitalising the lease termination costs.

4.2 Deferred payments

The cost of an investment property for which payment is deferred is the cash price equivalent of the deferred payments. The difference between the cash price equivalent recognised at initial measurement, and the total payments made, is recognised as an interest expense over the period of credit, i.e. the period from the point of receipt of the property until the point of settlement of the related liability. [IAS 40:24]

There is no definition of 'cash price equivalent' in IAS 40. It is presumably intended to equate to the present value of the deferred payment but might also encompass a cash price offered by the vendor as an alternative to the deferred payment terms.

4.3 Property held under lease and classified as investment property

4.3.1 Measurement of investment property held under lease – general

The initial cost of a property interest held under a lease and classified as an investment property is prescribed by IAS 17:20 (see **7.1.1.1** in **appendix A4**). The property is recognised at the lower of its fair value and the present value of the minimum lease payments. An equivalent amount is recognised as a liability in accordance with the same paragraph. [IAS 40:25]

IAS 40:25 applies to all property interests held under leases (whether operating or finance) and classified as investment property. Therefore, in effect, such interests are recognised as if the underlying lease were a finance lease, even if it would be classified as an operating lease under the general requirements of IAS 17.

When a premium is paid on the lease, it is treated as part of the minimum lease payments for this purpose. It is included within the cost of the asset, but excluded from the liability (because it has already been paid). If a property interest held under a lease is classified as an investment property, the item accounted for at fair value is that interest and not the underlying property. [IAS 40:26]

This means that it is the fair value of the leasehold interest, rather than the fair value of the property, that is recognised in the financial statements. Normally, in a very long lease with only nominal 'ground rent', the difference between these two values is very small. However, IAS 40 allows any property held under an operating lease to be classified as an investment property provided that certain criteria are met (see **2.3**). In some cases, therefore, the difference between the fair value of the leasehold interest and the fair value of the property can be significant. For example, in the case of a short lease at market rent, the market value of the leasehold interest will be small compared to the value of the freehold interest in the property.

4.3.2 Gross value of leasehold interest

As noted at **4.3.1**, a liability should be recognised in the statement of financial position for the present value of the minimum lease payments.

If the property is subsequently accounted for under the fair value model, it is important to ensure that the valuation reflected in the statement of financial position is consistent with this. Valuers may value very long leasehold interests on the basis of the freehold interest and then deduct from that value the present value of the ground rent on the head lease and the present value of the estimated residual value at the end of the lease term. But if the liability for the ground rent is recognised separately in the financial statements, it is the gross valuation before any such deduction (but excluding any amount attributable to the residual value) that should be recognised as an asset to avoid double-counting the liability.

4.4   Investment property acquired through exchange of another asset

When an investment property is exchanged for an asset (assets), whether monetary or non-monetary, IAS 40 prescribes the treatment for such an exchange. The cost of the investment property is measured at fair value unless either:

[IAS 40:27]

- the exchange transaction lacks commercial substance; or

- the fair value of neither the asset received nor the asset given up is reliably measurable.

The acquired asset is measured in this way even if an entity cannot derecognise immediately the asset given up. If the acquired asset is not measured at fair value, its cost is measured at the carrying amount of the asset given up. [IAS 40:27]

Whether an exchange transaction has commercial substance is determined by considering the extent to which the future cash flows are expected to change as a result of the transaction. IAS 40 states that a transaction has commercial substance if:

[IAS 40:28]

- the configuration (risk, timing and amount) of the cash flows of the asset received differs from the configuration of the cash flows of the transferred asset; or

- the entity-specific value of the portion of the entity's operations affected by the transaction changes because of the exchange; and

- the difference in either of these is significant relative to the fair value of the assets exchanged.

In determining whether an exchange transaction has commercial substance, the entity-specific value of the portion of the entity's operations affected by the transaction should reflect post-tax cash flows. The Standard notes that the results of these analyses may be clear without having to perform detailed calculations. [IAS 40:28]

In most instances, it will be readily apparent whether a transaction lacks commercial substance. The reference in IAS 40 to the entity-specific value of the portion of the entity's operations affected by the transaction is not explained in detail but clearly is intended to indicate that a transaction will have substance when it has a significant effect on the present value of the entity's future cash flows.

The fair value of the asset is reliably measurable if:

[IAS 40:29]

- the variability in the range of reasonable fair value measurements is not significant for the asset; or

- the probabilities of the various estimates within the range can be reasonably assessed and used when measuring fair value.

If the fair value of either the asset received or the asset given up can be measured reliably, then the fair value of the asset given up is used to measure cost unless the fair value of the asset received is more clearly evident. [IAS 40:29]

5 Measurement after recognition

5.1 Selection of accounting policy for investment property

5.1.1 Selection of accounting policy for investment property – general

In general, IAS 40 (1) allows an entity to choose whether it adopts a fair value model or a cost model for investment property, and (2) requires that, having decided on its policy, an entity should apply that model to all of its investment property. [IAS 40:30]

There are two exceptions to this general principle. These are:

[IAS 40:30]

- when a lessee chooses to classify a property interest held under an operating lease as investment property, the lessee automatically forfeits the choice of model offered by IAS 40 – the fair value model must be used for all investment property (see **2.3**); [IAS 40:6 & 34] and

- when an entity has investment property backing liabilities that pay a return linked directly to the fair value of, or returns from, specified assets including that investment property, the entity is not required to apply the same policy for that property as it does for its other investment property (see **5.1.3**). [IAS 40:32A]

Note also that one of the criteria for qualification as an investment entity under IFRS 10 *Consolidated Financial Statements* (see **section 13** of **chapter A24** for details) is that an entity should measure and evaluate substantially all of its investments on a fair value basis. Accordingly, in order to meet the investment entity exception in IFRS 10, and measure its investments in subsidiaries (other than subsidiaries that provide investment-related services or activities) at fair value through profit or loss rather than consolidating them, an entity will need to select IAS 40's fair value model for its investment property.

If an entity adopts the cost model, it is still required to measure the fair value of all of its investment property for disclosure purposes, other than in exceptional circumstances when the fair value cannot be reliably measured (see **5.2.4**).

5.1.2   Change in accounting policy for investment property

Once a policy has been adopted, any change will be considered a voluntary change in accounting policy which, under IAS 8 *Accounting Policies, Changes in Accounting Estimates and Errors*, is permitted only if it will result in financial statements providing reliable and more relevant information. IAS 40 notes that it is highly unlikely that a change from the fair value model to the cost model will result in a more relevant presentation. [IAS 40:31]

5.1.3   Investment property linked to liabilities

When an entity has investment property backing liabilities that pay a return linked directly to the fair value of, or returns from, specified assets including that investment property, the entity may choose a model for all such investment property and independently choose a different model for all other investment property. The choice of policy made by an entity for such property does not affect the entity's choice for the rest of its property, e.g. the entity could choose the fair value model for its investment property linked to liabilities, but choose the cost model for the rest of its investment property. [IAS 40:32A]

This choice is typically applicable to vehicles that have been set up to own investment property and that are funded by debt instruments instead of equity instruments (see **2.1.2** in **chapter B3** (or, for entities that have not yet adopted IFRS 9 *Financial Instruments*, **2.1.2** in **chapter C3**) for the classification of puttable instruments).

For an entity that operates an internal property fund that issues notional units whereby some units are held by investors and others are held by the entity, the property held by the fund cannot be held partly at cost and partly at fair value. [IAS 40:32B]

If different models are chosen, sales of investment property between pools of assets are recognised at fair value and the cumulative change in fair value is recognised in profit or loss. [IAS 40:32C]

5.1.4 Investment property classified as held for sale

Investment property accounted for under IAS 40's cost model falls within the scope of IFRS 5 *Non-current Assets Held for Sale and Discontinued Operations*, both as regards measurement and as regards presentation in the statement of financial position. Therefore, from the point at which an investment property accounted for under the cost model meets the criteria for classification as held for sale (or is included within a disposal group meeting the criteria for classification as held for sale), the asset is accounted for under that Standard (see **chapter A20**).

Investment property accounted for under IAS 40's fair value model is excluded from the measurement requirements of IFRS 5, but is otherwise subject to the requirements of that Standard. [IFRS 5:5] Therefore, from the point at which investment property accounted for under the fair value model meets the criteria for classification as held for sale (or is included in a disposal group meeting the criteria for classification as held for sale), the asset is presented as held for sale in the statement of financial position, as required by IFRS 5:38 (see **7.3.1** in **chapter A20**), but it continues to be measured at fair value in accordance with the entity's accounting policy for investment property.

5.2 Fair value model

5.2.1 Fair value model – general

After initial recognition, an entity that chooses the fair value model measures all of its investment property at fair value, except when the requirements of IAS 40:53 apply (inability to determine fair value reliably – see **5.2.4**). [IAS 40:33]

Fair value is defined as "the price that would be received to sell an asset or paid to transfer a liability in an orderly transaction between market participants at the measurement date. (See IFRS 13 *Fair Value Measurement*.)" [IAS 40:5]

When measuring the fair value of investment property, an entity should ensure that the fair value reflects, among other things, rental income from current leases and other assumptions that market participants would use when pricing the investment property under current market conditions. [IAS 40:40]

Assets or liabilities recognised elsewhere in the financial statements (e.g. prepaid or accrued operating lease income) should not be double-counted in determining the carrying amount of investment property under the fair value model. For example, if the lifts and air-conditioning system in a property are considered an integral part of the building, they are generally included in the fair value of the investment property and are not recognised as separate assets. Similarly, if an office is leased on a furnished basis, and the rental income relates to the furnished office, the fair value of the office generally includes the fair value of the furniture, and the furniture is, therefore, not recognised as a separate asset. [IAS 40:50]

These requirements would extend to lease incentives. That is to say that assets/liabilities recognised for lease incentives received/given should not be double-counted in the statement of financial position.

Example 5.2.1

Acquisition of investment property with existing operating lease in place

Entity C acquires an investment property with an operating lease that is not at current market rates.

IAS 40:40 states as follows.

"When measuring the fair value of investment property in accordance with IFRS 13, an entity shall ensure that the fair value reflects, among other things, rental income from current leases and other assumptions that market participants would use when pricing the investment property under current market conditions."

Should the fair value of the off-market lease be included within the carrying amount of the investment property or presented separately (whether as an asset or as a liability)?

IAS 40 does not provide any specific guidance on this area and it appears that Entity C may adopt either presentation as an accounting policy choice. Inclusion within the carrying amount of the investment property is supported by IAS 40:26, which states, in the context of investment property held under a lease, that a premium paid for a lease should be included in the cost of an investment property. This acknowledges the fact that, conceptually, an investment property includes not only land and buildings but other assets (customer relationships, furniture and favourable leases) and liabilities (unfavourable leases) that are interrelated in determining the overall fair value of the property. However, IAS 40 does not require that these elements be presented as a single asset; indeed IAS 40:50 recognises that items such as furniture and prepaid operating lease income may be presented as separate balances.

If the operating lease element is shown separately, it is important to have regard to the requirements of IAS 40:50 which states that, in measuring the fair value of an investment property, an entity should not "double-count assets or liabilities that are recognised as separate assets or liabilities". Therefore, the fair value of an investment property is adjusted to exclude, among other things, assets or liabilities arising from favourable or unfavourable leases. If it applies a policy of recognising a separate asset or liability for the off-market lease, Entity C should ensure that the combined carrying amount of that balance and the investment property asset does not exceed the fair value of the investment property.

Example 2.6 addresses whether a group of assets leased under a single operating lease (e.g. agricultural machinery leased together with agricultural land and buildings) meets the definition of investment property.

The fair value of an investment property held under a lease reflects expected cash flows (including contingent rents that are expected to become payable). Thus, if a valuation obtained for a property is net of all payments expected to be made, any recognised lease liability must be added back to arrive at the carrying amount of the investment property using the fair value model. [IAS 40:50(d)]

5.2.2 Remeasurement of investment property: transaction costs incurred on acquisition

Example 5.2.2

Remeasurement of investment property: transaction costs incurred on acquisition

Entity A acquires an investment property (in an orderly transaction with a third-party market participant) immediately before the end of its reporting period for CU100 million. It incurs additional costs in the form of legal and other professional fees of CU2 million at the time of initial recognition which are directly attributable to the acquisition of the property. These transaction costs are included in the initial measurement of the investment property in accordance with IAS 40:21 (see **4.1**). Therefore, the investment property is initially recognised at CU102 million.

Entity A measures its investment property using IAS 40's fair value model. At the end of the reporting period, the fair value of the investment property is unchanged from the price paid by Entity A of CU100 million.

How should the difference of CU2 million between the carrying amount of the property and its fair value be accounted for at the end of the reporting period?

Under IFRS 13, the fair value of the investment property should be measured at the reporting date at the amount that would be received at that date from the sale of the property in an orderly transaction in Entity A's principal (or most advantageous) market. If the property were to be sold, costs might be incurred by Entity A (as the seller) or by the purchaser as part of the transaction. However, under IFRS 13:25, transaction costs that would be incurred by Entity A if the property were sold should not be deducted from the fair value of the property. Likewise, costs that would be incurred by a purchaser (e.g. those similar to the legal and other professional fees capitalised by Entity A) would not be received by Entity A on sale of the investment property and, consequently, do not affect the investment property's fair value as defined by IFRS 13.

Accordingly, the property should be measured at the reporting date at CU100 million. The difference between this amount and the carrying amount of CU102 million should be recognised as a fair value adjustment in profit or loss in accordance with IAS 40:35 (see **5.2.6**).

Example 5.2.2 demonstrates that when an investment property is acquired immediately before the end of a reporting period, such that its fair value is unlikely to change between the date of acquisition and the end of the accounting period, it is likely that a downward revaluation will be recognised in profit or loss that is equal and opposite to the capitalised acquisition costs, if any.

5.2.3   Use of independent valuers

Entities are encouraged (but not required) to use, as the basis for measuring fair value, a valuation by an independent valuer "who holds a recognised and relevant professional qualification and has recent experience in the location and category of the investment property being valued". [IAS 40:32]

The IASB decided that an independent valuation should not be required under IAS 40 because of the following considerations:

- the cost-benefit ratio of an independent valuation may be inappropriate for some entities; and

- independent valuers with appropriate expertise are not available in some markets.

Consequently, paragraphs B55 and B56 of the Basis for Conclusions on IAS 40 explain that it is for the preparers of financial statements to decide, in consultation with auditors, whether an entity has sufficient internal resources to determine reliable fair values.

5.2.4   Inability to measure fair value reliably

There is a rebuttable presumption that the fair value of an investment property can be measured reliably on a continuing basis. But in exceptional cases, when an investment property is first acquired (or when an existing property first becomes an investment property after a change of use), there may be clear evidence that the fair value of the property is not reliably measurable on a continuing basis. This arises when, and only when, the market for comparable properties is inactive (e.g. there are few recent transactions, price quotations are not current or observed transaction prices indicate that the seller was forced to sell) and alternative reliable measurements of fair value (e.g. based on discounted cash flows) are not available. [IAS 40:53]

Note that the exception under IAS 40:53 is available only when the investment property is first recognised as such. If an investment property has previously been measured at fair value, it should continue to be measured at fair value until disposal (or until it otherwise ceases to be an investment property, for example because it becomes owner-occupied) even if comparable market transactions become less frequent or market prices become less readily available. [IAS 40:55]

When, in the circumstances described above, it is not possible for an entity that uses the fair value model to measure the fair value of a particular property (other than an investment property under construction) reliably on initial recognition, that investment property is measured using the cost model in IAS 16 *Property, Plant and Equipment*. In accounting for the property under IAS 16, the entity is required to assume that the residual value of the property is zero. IAS 16 is then applied until the disposal of the property. [IAS 40:53] Special rules apply for investment properties under construction – see **5.2.5**.

When an entity is compelled, for the reasons set out in IAS 40:53, to measure a particular investment property using the cost model under IAS 16, it continues to measure all of its other investment property at fair value. [IAS 40:54]

The circumstances described in IAS 40:53 are also relevant to determining the circumstances in which an entity using the cost model would be exempt from disclosing the fair value of investment property (see **9.2.3**).

An economic downturn may increase the volatility of prices in real estate markets and restrict the level of comparator transactions against which to assess value. This may increase uncertainty around reported investment property fair value compared to 'normal' market conditions. For this reason, third party valuers may include valuation uncertainty paragraphs in their reports in order to draw the reader's attention to the financial backdrop against which the valuations have been assessed. Generally, this type of uncertainty paragraph may not caveat the valuation opinion provided, but it may make reference to major upheaval in the financial sector, reduced liquidity in the market place, restricted availability of debt and similar factors, and may state that these factors have caused increased uncertainty in respect of current real estate prices.

There is a rebuttable presumption in IAS 40:53 that the fair value of an investment property can be determined reliably on a continuing basis; there is no exemption in a period of significant valuation uncertainty, even if comparable market transactions become less frequent or market prices become less readily available. It is only in exceptional cases, when there is clear evidence when the entity first acquires an investment property (or when an existing property first becomes an investment property after an evidenced change in use) that fair value is not reliably determinable, that the entity is permitted to measure that investment property at cost, while measuring its other investment properties at fair value. These exceptional cases are expected to be very rare.

5.2.5   Investment property in the course of construction

If an entity determines that the fair value of an investment property under construction is not reliably measurable but expects the fair value to be reliably measurable when construction is complete, the entity measures the investment property under construction at cost until the earlier of the fair value becoming reliably measurable or the completion of construction. [IAS 40:53]

Once the entity is able to measure reliably the fair value of the investment property under construction, that property should be measured at fair value. Once construction is complete, it is presumed that fair value can be measured reliably. If this is not the case, following completion, the property is accounted for using the cost model in accordance with IAS 16, under the general requirements of IAS 40:53 (see **5.2.4**). [IAS 40:53A]

The presumption that the fair value of investment property under construction can be measured reliably can be rebutted only on initial recognition. An entity that has measured such property at fair value may not conclude that the fair value of the completed investment property cannot be determined reliably. [IAS 40:53B]

5.2.6   Changes in fair value recognised in profit or loss

Changes in the fair value of investment property are recognised in profit or loss in the period in which they arise. [IAS 40:35]

5.2.7   Property held under a lease and classified as investment property

When a property held under a lease that is negotiated at market rates is classified as an investment property (i.e. accounted for as a finance lease), the fair value of the interest in the leased property at acquisition, net of all expected lease payments including those relating to recognised liabilities, should be zero. This fair value does not change, regardless of whether the leased asset and liability are recognised at fair value or at the present value of minimum lease payments as per paragraph 20 of IAS 17 *Leases*. This means that there should be no initial gain or loss arising from the remeasurement of a leased asset from cost to fair value unless fair value is measured at different times. This could occur when an election to apply the fair value model is made after initial recognition. [IAS 40:41]

5.2.8 Anticipated liabilities

When an entity expects that the present value of its payments relating to an investment property (excluding payments relating to recognised liabilities) will exceed the present value of the related cash receipts, IAS 37 *Provisions, Contingent Liabilities and Contingent Assets* should be applied to determine whether a liability should be recognised and, if so, how that liability should be measured. [IAS 40:52]

5.3 Cost model

5.3.1 Cost model – general

IAS 40:5 defines cost as "the amount of cash or cash equivalents paid or the fair value of other consideration given to acquire an asset at the time of its acquisition or construction or, where applicable, the amount attributed to that asset when initially recognised in accordance with the specific requirements of other IFRSs …".

> For example, if the consideration for the purchase of a property was an issue of equity shares in the entity, IFRS 2 *Share-based Payment* should be applied to establish the cost of the property.

After initial recognition, an entity that chooses the cost model measures all of its investment property in accordance with IAS 16's requirements for that model (see **5.2** in **chapter A7**), other than investment property classified as held for sale or included in a disposal group classified as held for sale, which is measured in accordance with IFRS 5 (see **5.1.4**). [IAS 40:56]

5.3.2 Component accounting for in-place leases

> If an entity acquires an investment property with operating leases already in place, the amount paid for the property will reflect the effect of those in-place leases (above and below market rentals, direct costs associated with obtaining new tenants etc.). IAS 16:44 states that, in the circumstances described, "it may be appropriate to depreciate separately amounts reflected in the cost [of the property] that are attributable to favourable or unfavourable lease terms relative to market terms". If, for example, an entity determines, through the exercise of judgement, that the components of cost attributable to favourable or unfavourable lease terms are significant, those components should be depreciated separately. This will result in a higher (if the lease terms are favourable) or lower (if they are unfavourable) total depreciation charge

over the period for which the in-place lease terms apply (see **example 5.3.2** for a numerical example).

However, IAS 16 is silent with respect to other amounts related to the value of in-place leases that may be reflected in the cost of the property. Therefore, whether an entity recognises such amounts as separate components for depreciation purposes is an accounting policy choice to be applied consistently for all similar transactions.

Example 5.3.2

Component accounting for in-place leases

Entity A acquires a building for CU200,000. The building has an existing tenant with a remaining lease term of five years. The rentals from that in-place lease are unfavourable when compared with the current market. If Entity A had been able to secure vacant possession, it would have been willing to pay CU240,000 for the building.

Entity A applies the cost model for investment property under IAS 40 (i.e. Entity A measures the property in accordance with IAS 16's cost model). The remaining useful life of the building is estimated to be 20 years, with nil estimated residual value.

Entity A should identify two separate components reflected in the price paid for the building – a 'gross cost' of CU240,000 offset by the component attributable to the unfavourable lease of CU40,000 (which is determined to be significant in relation to the total cost). The former is depreciated over 20 years, the latter over five years. The annual depreciation charges recognised over the life of the building are therefore as follows.

	Years 1 - 5	Years 6 - 20*
Depreciation on 'gross cost'	12,000	12,000
Depreciation on unfavourable lease component	(8,000)	–
Net charge	4,000	12,000

*   Assuming no change to the building's useful life or residual value.

In this example, the component approach results in a lower total depreciation charge over the period for which the in-place lease terms apply.

---

6   Transfers

6.1   Transfers to, or from, investment property – general

This section reflects the requirements of IAS 40 at the time of writing. An exposure draft issued in November 2015 proposes to amend the

Standard to clarify that the circumstances listed in IAS 40:57 are examples, and not an exhaustive list, of when a transfer into, or out of, investment property is permitted (see **section 10**).

Transfers to, or from, investment property are made when, and only when, there is a change in use evidenced by one of the following:

[IAS 40:57]

- commencement of owner-occupation, for a transfer from investment property to owner-occupied property;

- commencement of development with a view to sale, for a transfer from investment property to inventories;

- end of owner-occupation, for a transfer from owner-occupied property to investment property; or

- commencement of an operating lease to another party, for a transfer from inventories to investment property.

These circumstances are discussed more fully in **6.2** to **6.5**.

Paragraphs 60 to 65 of IAS 40 apply to recognition and measurement issues that arise when the fair value model is used for investment property and transfers are made to or from investment property (see **6.2** to **6.5**). When the cost model is used, transfers between investment property, owner-occupied property and inventories do not change the carrying amount of the property transferred. They do not, therefore, change the cost of the property for measurement or disclosure purposes. [IAS 40:59]

6.2 Transfer from investment property to owner-occupied property

IAS 40 requires an investment property to be transferred to owner-occupied property only when there is a change of use evidenced by commencement of owner-occupation. [IAS 40:57(a)]

When an investment property carried at fair value is transferred to owner-occupied property, the property's deemed cost for subsequent accounting in accordance with IAS 16 *Property, Plant and Equipment* is its fair value at the date of change in use. [IAS 40:60]

6.3 Transfer from investment property to inventories

IAS 40 requires an investment property to be transferred to inventories only when there is a change of use evidenced by commencement of development with a view to sale. [IAS 40:57(b)]

When an investment property carried at fair value is transferred to inventories, the property's deemed cost for subsequent accounting in accordance with IAS 2 *Inventories* is its fair value at the date of change in use. [IAS 40:60]

6.4   Transfer from owner-occupied property to investment property

The end of owner-occupation signals a potential transfer to investment property. If an owner-occupied property becomes an investment property that will be carried at fair value, IAS 16 is applied up to the date of change of use. Any difference at that date between the carrying amount of the property in accordance with IAS 16 and its fair value is treated in the same way as a revaluation in accordance with IAS 16. [IAS 40:61]

This means that any decrease in the carrying amount of the property is recognised in profit or loss, unless the decrease is the reversal of a previous revaluation surplus, in which case the decrease is recognised in other comprehensive income and reduces that revaluation surplus within equity. [IAS 40:62]

Any increase in the carrying amount is recognised in other comprehensive income and increases the revaluation surplus within equity, unless the increase reverses a previous impairment loss on that property in which case the increase is recognised in profit or loss. The amount recognised in profit or loss should not exceed the amount needed to restore the carrying amount to the amount that would have been determined (net of depreciation) had no impairment loss been recognised. [IAS 40:62]

On subsequent disposal of such a property, the revaluation surplus may be transferred to retained earnings, but not through profit or loss. [IAS 40:62]

6.5   Transfer from inventories to investment property

A transfer from inventories to investment property should be made when, and only when, there is a change in use, evidenced by the commencement of an operating lease to another party. [IAS 40:57(d)] For a transfer to investment property, if the property will be carried at fair value, any difference between the fair value and the carrying amount of the property at the date of transfer is recognised in profit or loss. [IAS 40:63] This is consistent with the treatment of sales of inventories. [IAS 40:64]

6.6   Continued classification as investment property

If an entity decides to dispose of an investment property without development, the property continues to be treated as an investment property until its disposal. It is not treated as inventories. [IAS 40:58]

When an entity has decided to dispose of an investment property through sale, the requirements of IFRS 5 *Non-current Assets Held for*

Sale and Discontinued Operations need to be considered (see **5.1.4** and **chapter A20**).

Similarly, if redevelopment of an existing investment property commences but the property is intended for future use as an investment property, the property continues to be recognised as an investment property. [IAS 40:58]

When the fair value model is used, expenditure incurred in the redevelopment of an investment property which remains classified as an investment property (e.g. rebuilding costs) should initially be capitalised (see **3.3**). The effect of remeasuring the asset to fair value is that any resulting gain or loss will be taken to profit or loss. Disclosures required by IAS 40:76 distinguish between the cost of additions and fair value movements (see **9.2.2.1**).

Undeveloped land may fall within the definition of investment property in IAS 40 (see **2.2**) although this will depend on the particular circumstances. When such land is subsequently developed for future use as an investment property, the property continues to be recognised as an investment property while the development takes place.

7 Disposals

7.1 Disposals (entities that have adopted IFRS 15)

Consequential amendments have been made to the requirements in this section for entities that have adopted IFRS 15 *Revenue from Contracts with Customers*. For convenience, the requirements for entities that have not yet adopted IFRS 15 are presented separately at **7.2**.

An investment property is derecognised (i.e. removed from the statement of financial position) on disposal or when it is permanently withdrawn from use and no future economic benefits are expected from its disposal. [IAS 40:66]

The disposal of an investment property may occur through sale of the property or through entering into a finance lease. The date of disposal for investment property is the date the recipient obtains control of the investment property in accordance with the requirements for determining when a performance obligation is satisfied in IFRS 15 *Revenue from Contracts with Customers* (see **chapter A14**). IAS 17 *Leases* applies to a disposal effected by entering into a finance lease and to a sale and leaseback (see **appendix A4**). [IAS 40:67]

The gain or loss on the retirement or disposal of an investment property is calculated as the difference between the net disposal proceeds and the carrying amount of the property and is recognised in profit or loss in the period of the retirement or disposal. This is subject to the requirements of IAS 17 in the case of a sale and leaseback transaction. [IAS 40:69]

The amount of consideration to be included in the gain or loss arising from derecognition of an investment property is determined in accordance with requirements for determining the transaction price in paragraphs 47 to 72 of IFRS 15 (see **section 7** of **chapter A14**). Subsequent changes to the estimated amount of the consideration included in the gain or loss should be accounted for in accordance with the requirements for changes in the transaction price in IFRS 15. [IAS 40:70]

When any liabilities are retained relating to the property after its disposal, IAS 37 *Provisions, Contingent Liabilities and Contingent Assets* or other relevant Standards are applied to those liabilities. [IAS 40:71]

7.2 Disposals (entities that have not yet adopted IFRS 15)

An investment property is derecognised (i.e. removed from the statement of financial position) on disposal or when it is permanently withdrawn from use and no future economic benefits are expected from its disposal. [IAS 40:66]

The disposal of an investment property may occur through sale of the property or through entering into a finance lease. In determining the date of disposal for an investment property, the criteria in IAS 18 *Revenue* for recognising revenue from the sale of goods should be applied and the related guidance in the appendix to IAS 18 should be considered (see **appendix A1**). IAS 17 *Leases* applies to a disposal effected by entering into a finance lease and to a sale and leaseback (see **appendix A4**). [IAS 40:67]

The gain or loss on the retirement or disposal of an investment property is calculated as the difference between the net disposal proceeds and the carrying amount of the property and is recognised in profit or loss in the period of the retirement or disposal. This is subject to the requirements of IAS 17 in the case of a sale and leaseback transaction. [IAS 40:69]

The consideration receivable on the disposal of an investment property is recognised initially at fair value. In particular, if payment is deferred, the consideration is recognised initially at its cash price equivalent. The difference between this amount and the nominal amount is recognised as interest revenue under the effective interest method in accordance with IAS 18. [IAS 40:70]

There is no definition of 'cash price equivalent' in IAS 40. It is presumably intended to equate to the present value of the deferred payment but might also encompass a cash price offered by the vendor as an alternative to the deferred payment terms.

When any liabilities are retained relating to the property after its disposal, IAS 37 *Provisions, Contingent Liabilities and Contingent Assets* or other relevant Standards are applied to those liabilities. [IAS 40:71]

8 Compensation for impairment of investment property

Impairments or losses of investment property, related claims for or payment of compensation from third parties and any subsequent purchase or construction of replacement assets are separate economic events and are accounted for separately. Therefore:

[IAS 40:73]

- impairments of investment property are recognised in accordance with IAS 36 *Impairment of Assets*;

- retirements or disposals of investment property are recognised as set out in **section 7** in accordance with IAS 40:66 to 71;

- compensation from third parties for investment property that was impaired, lost or given up is recognised in profit or loss when it becomes receivable; and

- the cost of assets restored, purchased or constructed as replacements is determined as set out in **section 4** in accordance with IAS 40:20 to 29.

Example 8

Insurance claim

A building carried as an investment property burns down during the reporting period. A valuation of the building in its damaged state is performed at the end of the reporting period.

Should the value of the property at the end of the reporting period include any amount receivable from insurance?

The amount receivable from insurance should be recognised separately in the statement of financial position if it meets the relevant recognition criteria. Any valuation of the property recognised as an investment property should not include the insurance receivable.

---

9 Presentation and disclosure

9.1 Presentation

IAS 1 *Presentation of Financial Statements* requires that, when material, the aggregate carrying amount of the entity's investment property should be presented in the statement of financial position. [IAS 1:54(b)]

9.2   Disclosure

9.2.1   General disclosures

The disclosures required by IAS 40 are made in addition to the disclosures required by IAS 17 *Leases*. In accordance with IAS 17, the owner of an investment property provides lessors' disclosures about leases into which it has entered. An entity that holds an investment property under a finance or operating lease provides lessees' disclosures for finance leases and lessors' disclosures for any operating leases into which it has entered. [IAS 40:74]

An entity is required to disclose:

[IAS 40:75]

- whether it applies the fair value or the cost model;
- whether, and in what circumstances, properties held under operating leases are classified as investment property when the fair value model is used;
- the criteria used to distinguish investment property from owner-occupied property or property held for sale in the normal course of business, when that classification is difficult;
- the extent to which the fair value of investment property (as measured or disclosed in the financial statements) is based on a valuation by an independent valuer who holds a recognised and relevant professional qualification and has recent experience in the location and category of the investment property being valued. If there has been no such valuation, that fact should be disclosed;
- the amounts recognised in profit or loss for:

  - rental income from investment property;

  - direct operating expenses (including repairs and maintenance) arising from investment property that generated rental income during the period;

  - direct operating expenses (including repairs and maintenance) arising from investment property that did not generate rental income during the period; and

  - the cumulative change in fair value recognised in profit or loss on a sale of investment property from a pool of assets, in which the cost model is used, into a pool in which the fair value model is used (i.e. on investment property linked to liabilities – see **5.1.3**);

Property investment entities often make service charges to their tenants (e.g. to cover the cost of repairs and maintenance) which are the responsibility of the tenants under the terms of the lease but which are arranged and managed by the lessor. These costs are typically passed on at cost or with a fixed percentage mark-up under the terms of the lease. When the lessor is in substance merely acting as agent for the payment of these costs, the reimbursement will generally not be recognised as revenue. Nevertheless, it would be helpful to disclose the amount of such receipts and related costs in the notes to the financial statements.

- the existence and amounts of restrictions on the realisability of investment property or the remittance of income and proceeds of disposal; and

- contractual obligations to purchase, construct or develop investment property or for repairs, maintenance or enhancements.

In addition, if there has been a material reduction in asset values after the reporting date, whether arising from a specific event or not, disclosure of the non-adjusting event is required in accordance with IAS 10 *Events after the Reporting Period* (see **chapter A22**).

9.2.2 Fair value model

9.2.2.1 Reconciliation of movements in carrying amount

In addition to the general disclosure requirements set out at **9.2.1**, an entity that applies the fair value model is required to present a reconciliation between the carrying amounts of investment property at the beginning and end of the period, showing the following:

[IAS 40:76]

- additions, disclosing separately those additions resulting from acquisitions, those resulting from subsequent expenditure recognised in the carrying amount of an asset and those resulting from acquisitions through business combinations;

- assets classified as held for sale, or included in a disposal group classified as held for sale, in accordance with IFRS 5 *Non-current Assets Held for Sale and Discontinued Operations* and other disposals;

- net gains or losses from fair value adjustments;

- the net exchange differences arising on the translation of the financial statements into a different presentation currency and on translation of a foreign operation into the presentation currency of the entity;

- transfers to and from inventories and owner-occupied property; and

- other changes.

9.2.2.2   Reconciliation of adjustments to valuation of property

When a valuation obtained for investment property is adjusted significantly for the purpose of the financial statements (e.g. to avoid double-counting of assets or liabilities that are recognised as separate assets and liabilities), the entity is required to present a reconciliation between the valuation obtained and the adjusted valuation included in the financial statements, showing separately the aggregate amount of any recognised lease obligations that have been added back, and any other significant adjustments. [IAS 40:77]

9.2.2.3   Details about property exceptionally stated at cost

In the exceptional circumstances referred to at **5.2.4** and **5.2.5**, when an entity applying the fair value model measures investment property using the cost model in IAS 16 *Property, Plant and Equipment*, the reconciliation described at **9.2.2.1** should disclose amounts relating to that investment property separately from amounts relating to other investment property. In addition, the following should be disclosed:

[IAS 40:78]

- a description of the investment property;
- an explanation of why fair value cannot be measured reliably; and
- if possible, the range of estimates within which fair value is highly likely to lie.

On disposal of such investment property not carried at fair value, the following should be disclosed:

[IAS 40:78]

- the fact that the entity has disposed of investment property not carried at fair value;
- the carrying amount of that investment property at the time of sale; and
- the amount of gain or loss recognised.

9.2.3   Cost model

In addition to the general disclosure requirements set out at **9.2.1**, an entity that applies the cost model is required to disclose:

[IAS 40:79]

- the depreciation methods used;
- the useful lives or the depreciation rates used; and
- the gross carrying amount and the accumulated depreciation (aggregated with accumulated impairment losses) at the beginning and end of the period.

An entity that applies the cost model is also required to provide a reconciliation of the carrying amount of investment property at the beginning and end of the period, showing:

[IAS 40:79(d)]

* additions, disclosing separately those additions resulting from acquisitions and those resulting from subsequent expenditure recognised as an asset;

* additions resulting from acquisitions through business combinations;

* assets classified as held for sale, or included in a disposal group classified as held for sale, in accordance with IFRS 5 and other disposals;

* depreciation;

* the amount of impairment losses recognised, and the amount of impairment losses reversed, during the period in accordance with IAS 36 *Impairment of Assets*;

* the net exchange differences arising on the translation of the financial statements into a different presentation currency, and on translation of a foreign operation into the presentation currency of the entity;

* transfers to and from inventories and owner-occupied property; and

* other changes.

An entity that applies the cost model is also required to disclose the fair value of its investment property. In the exceptional cases described at **5.2.4** and **5.2.5**, when an entity cannot measure the fair value of the investment property reliably, it should disclose:

[IAS 40:79(e)]

* a description of the investment property;

* an explanation of why fair value cannot be measured reliably; and

* if possible, the range of estimates within which fair value is highly likely to lie.

10   Future developments

In November 2015, the IASB published an exposure draft, ED/2015/9, *Transfers of Investment Property (Proposed amendment to IAS 40)*. The exposure draft proposes a narrow-scope amendment to IAS 40 to clarify the guidance regarding when transfers into, and out of, investment property are permitted.

The clarification is considered necessary because it has been noted that the current drafting of IAS 40 implies that such transfers are only permitted when the change in use of the property falls within one of the circumstances set out in IAS 40:57 (see **6.1**). The exposure draft proposes to amend the Standard to:

- state that a property should be transferred to, or from, investment property when, and only when, there is evidence of a change in use (i.e. when the property meets, or ceases to meet, the definition of investment property); and

- recharacterise the list of circumstances set out in IAS 40:57 as a non-exhaustive list of examples of evidence that a change in use has occurred.

The comment period on the exposure draft ended on 18 March 2016. At the time of writing, the final amendments to IAS 40 are expected to be issued before the end of 2016.

Appendix A6   IFRS for small and medium-sized entities

Contents

1   Introduction

1.1   Overview of the IFRS for SMEs

The *International Financial Reporting Standard for Small and Medium-sized Entities* (IFRS for SMEs) is a self-contained Standard, incorporating accounting principles that are based on full IFRSs but that have been simplified to suit the entities within its scope. The IFRS for SMEs provides an alternative framework that can be applied by eligible entities in place of full IFRSs. The IFRS for SMEs is separate from full IFRSs and is, therefore, available for any jurisdiction to adopt, whether or not it has adopted full IFRSs.

1.2   Amendments to the IFRS for SMEs

The IFRS for SMEs was most recently amended in May 2015 by the *2015 Amendments to the International Financial Reporting Standard for Small and Medium-sized Entities*.

The May 2015 amendments resulted from a comprehensive review of the IFRS for SMEs, which specifically considered (1) implementation issues identified in the application of the Standard since it was issued in 2009, and (2) other new and amended IFRSs issued in the intervening period. In addition, Q&A's issued by the SME Implementation Group (SMEIG – see **section 7**) have been incorporated into the body of the Standard and/or the IFRS Foundation's educational material (see IFRS for SMEs:BC227).

In general, the IASB concluded that the IFRS for SMEs is working well in practice. However, a number of areas were identified where targeted improvements could be made. Although some of the amendments made are significant (see below), the majority are designed to clarify existing requirements or add supporting guidance, rather than change the underlying requirements.

The more significant amendments introduced by the 2015 Amendments are as follows:

- the introduction of an option to use a revaluation model for property, plant and equipment;

- alignment of the main recognition and measurement requirements for deferred income tax with IAS 12 *Income Taxes*; and

- alignment of the main recognition and measurement requirements for exploration and evaluation assets with IFRS 6 *Exploration for and Evaluation of Mineral Resources*.

Expanded guidance on applying the undue cost or effort exemptions available in the IFRS for SMEs has also been added to the Standard (see **4.6.2**).

The 2015 Amendments are effective for annual reporting periods beginning on or after 1 January 2017, with earlier application permitted. If an entity applies the 2015 Amendments for a period beginning before 1 January 2017, it is required to disclose that fact. [IFRS for SMEs:A1]

The 2015 Amendments are generally required to be applied retrospectively. [IFRS for SMEs:A2] If it is impracticable for an entity to apply any of the new or amended requirements retrospectively, it should apply those requirements in the earliest period for which it is practicable to do so. [IFRS for SMEs:A2]

The Standard sets out more specific transition provisions for particular amendments (see IFRS for SMEs:A2).

An entity is required to identify which amounts in the final statements have not been restated as a result of applying the transition provisions in the IFRS for SMEs:A2. [IFRS for SMEs:A3]

1.3   Meaning of the term 'Small and Medium-sized Entities'

The title of the IFRS for SMEs may appear to suggest that the Standard applies only to small and medium-sized entities; however, this is not the case. The scope of the Standard is much broader and is not determined by reference to the size of the reporting entity but rather by reference to the extent to which the reporting entity has public accountability. The IFRS for SMEs is intended for use by any entity, even a very large corporation, provided that (1) the entity does not have public accountability, and (2) it is required, or chooses, to publish general purpose financial statements for external users. Essentially, an entity is considered to have public accountability if its debt or equity instruments are publicly traded, or if it holds and manages financial resources entrusted to it by a number of clients as one of its primary businesses (see **section 2** of this appendix for further discussion).

Therefore, throughout this appendix, the term 'SME' refers to an entity within the scope of the Standard, rather than describing the size of the entity under consideration.

1.4   Which entities should apply the IFRS for SMEs?

Ultimately, the decisions regarding which entities should use the IFRS for SMEs in a specific jurisdiction and the timing for adoption rest with national regulatory authorities and standard-setters, and those bodies may specify more detailed eligibility criteria, including quantified criteria based on revenue, assets etc. However, the IASB intends that the application of the IFRS for SMEs should be limited to entities with no public accountability. Consequently, the Standard states that, even if law or regulation in a jurisdiction permits or requires the IFRS for SMEs to be used by a publicly accountable entity, that entity's financial statements should not be described as conforming to the IFRS for SMEs (see **2.1.2.1**).

> Entities eligible to adopt the IFRS for SMEs and that are considering such adoption should first of all consider whether the IFRS for SMEs is suitable for their circumstances. Among other issues, an entity should consider:
>
> - whether adopting the IFRS for SMEs will result in financial statements that are appropriate for the needs of its users;
>
> - whether adopting the IFRS for SMEs will result in financial statements that are more or less comparable with those of its competitors;
>
> - the cost and other effects on its business of adopting the IFRS for SMEs (including the effect on key performance indicators, banking covenants, staff bonus arrangements, tax payable etc.); and
>
> - for entities that are part of a group, any group reporting requirements.

1.5   Focus of this appendix

A full discussion of all aspects of the IFRS for SMEs is beyond the scope of this manual. The purpose of this appendix is to provide an overview of the IFRS for SMEs to enable users that have already adopted IFRSs to understand the key differences between the IFRS for SMEs and full IFRSs. This may be of assistance when:

- considering the implications of adopting the IFRS for SMEs, when permitted; and

- considering what adjustments are required to the financial statements of a subsidiary prepared in accordance with the IFRS for SMEs for the purposes of preparing consolidated financial statements in accordance with full IFRSs.

This appendix focuses on how the IFRS for SMEs differs from full IFRSs and, in particular, whether the IFRS for SMEs may benefit subsidiaries in groups using full IFRSs. A separate Deloitte publication titled *IFRS for SMEs In Your Pocket* provides a summary of each section of the IFRS for SMEs and a section-by-section comparison to full IFRSs. This publication can be downloaded from *www.iasplus.com*.

The complete IFRS for SMEs (together with the Basis for Conclusions, Illustrative Financial Statements, and a Presentation and Disclosure Checklist) can be downloaded free of charge at the following address: *http://www.ifrs.org/IFRS-for-SMEs/Pages/IFRS-for-SMEs-and-related-material.aspx*. It is available in English and several other languages.

2   Scope

2.1   Scope – general requirements

2.1.1   *Entities targeted by the IFRS for SMEs*

The IFRS for SMEs is intended for use by entities that:

[IFRS for SMEs:1.1 & 1.2]

- do not have public accountability; and

- publish general purpose financial statements for external users. Examples of external users include owners who are not involved in managing the business, existing and potential creditors, and credit rating agencies.

2.1.2   *Entities that have public accountability*

2.1.2.1   IFRS for SMEs not appropriate for entities with public accountability

If a publicly accountable entity uses the IFRS for SMEs, its financial statements should not be described as conforming to the IFRS for SMEs – even if law or regulation in its jurisdiction permits or requires the IFRS for SMEs to be used by publicly accountable entities. [IFRS for SMEs:1.5]

The IASB believes that the IFRS for SMEs is only appropriate for an entity that does not have public accountability. A jurisdiction that wishes to allow publicly traded entities or some entities that hold assets in a fiduciary capacity for a broad range of outsiders (e.g. small entities) to use the IFRS for SMEs could incorporate the requirements of the IFRS for SMEs into its local GAAP for those entities. However, if this is done, the financial statements should be described as conforming to local GAAP. The IFRS for SMEs prohibits the financial statements of a publicly traded entity or an entity that holds assets in a fiduciary capacity for a broad range of outsiders as one of its primary businesses, however small, from being described as being prepared in accordance with the IFRS for SMEs.

2.1.2.2   Public accountability – definition

An entity has public accountability if:

[IFRS for SMEs:1.3]

(a)   its debt or equity instruments are traded in a public market or it is in the process of issuing such instruments for trading in a public market (a domestic or foreign stock exchange or an over-the-counter market, including local and regional markets – see **2.1.2.3**); or

(b) it holds assets in a fiduciary capacity for a broad group of outsiders as one of its primary businesses. Most banks, credit unions, insurance companies, securities brokers/dealers, mutual funds and investment banks would meet this second criterion.

The wording of paragraph 1.3(b) was amended as part of the 2015 Amendments to clarify that the types of entities listed are not automatically considered to meet this criterion – there may be some circumstances in which an entity of one of the types listed does not have public accountability. The SMEIG (see **section 7**), which previously considered this question, suggested that this might be the case, for example, for some captive insurance companies and investment funds with only a few participants..

If an entity holds assets in a fiduciary capacity for a broad group of outsiders for reasons incidental to a primary business (as may be the case, for example, for travel or real estate agents, schools, charitable organisations, co-operative enterprises requiring a nominal membership deposit, and sellers that receive payment in advance of delivery of the goods or services such as utility companies), that does not make them publicly accountable. [IFRS for SMEs:1.4]

2.1.2.3   Interpretation of 'traded in a public market'

The SMEIG (see **section 7**) has considered how broadly the term 'traded in a public market' should be interpreted in the context of paragraph 1.3(b) (see **2.1.2.2**). The conclusion of the SMEIG, set out below, has not been incorporated into the IFRS for SMEs as part of the 2015 Amendments but will be added to the IFRS Foundation's educational material (see **section 8**) as non-mandatory guidance.

"'Public market' is defined in paragraph 1.3 as 'a domestic or foreign stock exchange or an over-the-counter market, including local and regional markets'. A 'public market' is not restricted to recognised and/or regulated stock exchanges. It includes all markets that bring together entities that seek capital and investors who are not involved in managing the entity. For a market to be public it must be accessible by a broad group of outsiders. If the instruments can only be exchanged between parties involved in the management of the entity, such as key management personnel or shareholders, the instruments are not traded in a public market.

In some jurisdictions, a shareholder of a small or medium-sized entity is permitted by law to publicly advertise those shares for sale, for example, on a website or in a newspaper, without any active involvement (or sometimes without even the knowledge) of the entity issuing those shares. Because the entity did not take an affirmative step to permit public trading of shares (such as, but not limited to, share registration), such advertising by a shareholder does not, by itself, create an over-the-counter public market and would not prevent an entity that otherwise meets the criteria in Section 1 from using the *IFRS for SMEs*.

Furthermore, the availability of a published price does not necessarily mean that an entity's debt or equity instruments are traded in a public market. For example, in some countries over-the-counter shares have a quoted price, but the market has no facility for trading and so buyers and sellers deal with each other directly. This would not constitute trading in a public market. However, if trading occurs only occasionally in a public market, even only a few times a year, this would constitute trading.

The assessment of whether an entity's debt or equity instruments are traded in a public market, or are in the process of being issued for trading in a public market, should be an ongoing one."

2.2 Are subsidiaries in groups using full IFRSs within the scope of the IFRS for SMEs?

A subsidiary whose parent uses full IFRSs, or that is part of a consolidated group that uses full IFRSs, is not prohibited from using the IFRS for SMEs in its own financial statements if it does not have public accountability. [IFRS for SMEs:1.6]

The fact that the ordinary shares of an entity's parent are listed on a stock exchange does not, by itself, make that subsidiary publicly accountable. Entities assess their eligibility to use the IFRS for SMEs on the basis of their own circumstances, even if they also submit financial information in accordance with full IFRSs to a parent for consolidation purposes. The same is true for associates and joint ventures, which may need to submit financial information in accordance with full IFRSs to an investor.

A subsidiary may wish to apply the IFRS for SMEs in its own financial statements, if prepared, to benefit from reduced disclosures and because full IFRS information is only prepared at a higher materiality threshold (see **5.1** for further detail). A subsidiary will usually find that the circumstances in which the IFRS for SMEs mandates a recognition or measurement principle that is different from recognition or measurement under full IFRSs are limited (see **5.2**).

2.3 Are non-publicly accountable parents of groups using full IFRSs within the scope of the IFRS for SMEs?

A parent entity (including the ultimate parent or any intermediate parent) that is required to present consolidated financial statements in accordance with full IFRSs (or another set of generally accepted accounting principles) is not prohibited from using the IFRS for SMEs in its own separate financial statements if the parent entity itself does not have public accountability. The parent entity assesses whether it is eligible to use the IFRS for SMEs on the basis of its own status, without considering whether other group entities have, or the group as a whole has, public accountability. [IFRS for SMEs:1.7]

Any financial statements prepared in accordance with the IFRS for SMEs should be clearly distinguished from financial statements prepared in accordance with full IFRSs or other requirements. [IFRS for SMEs:1.7]

Paragraph 1.7 was added to the IFRS for SMEs as part of the 2015 Amendments to the Standard.

3 Content

The IFRS for SMEs is organised by topic, with each topic presented in a separate section, to make it more like a reference manual – intended by the IASB to be more user-friendly for SME preparers and users of SME financial statements.

The Standard is less than 300 pages and contains the following sections.

Preface

(1) Small and Medium-sized Entities (comprises the scope)

(2) Concepts and Pervasive Principles (similar to the IASB's Conceptual Framework)

(3) Financial Statement Presentation

(4) Statement of Financial Position

(5) Statement of Comprehensive Income and Income Statement

(6) Statement of Changes in Equity and Statement of Income and Retained Earnings

(7) Statement of Cash Flows

(8) Notes to the Financial Statements

(9) Consolidated and Separate Financial Statements

(10) Accounting Policies, Estimates and Errors

(11) Basic Financial Instruments

(12) Other Financial Instruments Issues

(13) Inventories

(14) Investments in Associates

(15) Investments in Joint Ventures

(16) Investment Property

(17) Property, Plant and Equipment

(18) Intangible Assets other than Goodwill

(19) Business Combinations and Goodwill

(20) Leases

(21) Provisions and Contingencies

Appendix – Guidance on recognising and measuring provisions

(22) Liabilities and Equity

Appendix – Example of the issuer's accounting for convertible debt

(23) Revenue

Appendix – Examples of revenue recognition under the principles in Section 23

(24) Government Grants

(25) Borrowing Costs

(26) Share-based Payment

(27) Impairment of Assets

(28) Employee Benefits

(29) Income Tax

(30) Foreign Currency Translation

(31) Hyperinflation

(32) Events after the End of the Reporting Period

(33) Related Party Disclosures

(34) Specialised Activities (comprised of agriculture, exploration for and evaluation of mineral resources, and service concession arrangements)

(35) Transition to the IFRS for SMEs

Glossary of terms

4   Comparison with full IFRSs

4.1   IFRS for SMEs – a separate and distinct framework

The IFRS for SMEs is a self-contained set of accounting principles, based on full IFRSs but simplified to reflect the needs of users of the financial statements of SMEs, and also limitations in both the technical and financial capabilities available to SMEs. The IFRS for SMEs and full IFRSs are separate and distinct frameworks.

4.2   No general 'fallback' to full IFRSs

Entities that are eligible to apply the IFRS for SMEs, and that choose to do so, must, with one exception, apply that framework in full (i.e. they are not permitted to 'mix and match' the requirements of the IFRS for SMEs and full IFRSs). The only exception is that the IFRS for SMEs includes an option to apply the requirements of IAS 39 *Financial Instruments: Recognition and Measurement* in respect of the recognition and measurement of financial instruments (see **4.9**).

The IFRS for SMEs includes requirements for the development and application of accounting policies in the absence of specific guidance on a particular subject. An entity may, but is not required to, consider the requirements and guidance in full IFRSs on similar and related issues.

The SMEIG (see **section 7**) has considered the scenario in which a jurisdiction permits all entities meeting the definition of an SME to follow the IFRS for SMEs; however, the jurisdiction adds a requirement that, when the recognition and measurement requirements for a particular transaction, other event or condition are not specifically covered by the IFRS for SMEs, but are covered in full IFRSs, an SME must follow the recognition and measurement requirements in full IFRSs for that transaction, event or condition. The question addressed was whether SMEs in that jurisdiction may state compliance with the IFRS for SMEs.

The conclusion of the SMEIG, set out below, has not been incorporated into the IFRS for SMEs as part of the 2015 Amendments but will be added to the IFRS Foundation's educational material (see **section 8**) as non-mandatory guidance.

"Whether an SME can assert compliance with the *IFRS for SMEs* in such a case will depend on management's assessment of relevance and reliability as required by paragraph 10.4 of Section 10 *Accounting Policies, Estimates and Errors*. In the absence of specific requirements in the *IFRS for SMEs*, paragraph 10.4 requires management to use its judgement in developing an accounting policy that is reliable and results in information that is relevant to the economic decision-making needs of users. Paragraph 10.5 establishes the following hierarchy for an entity to follow in deciding on the appropriate accounting policy:

(a) the requirements and guidance in the *IFRS for SMEs* dealing with similar and related issues; and

(b) the definitions, recognition criteria and measurement concepts for assets, liabilities, income and expenses and the pervasive principles in Section 2 *Concepts and Pervasive Principles*.

Paragraph 10.6 notes that, in making the judgement described in paragraph 10.4, management may also consider the requirements and guidance in full IFRSs that deal with similar and related issues.

Taken together, paragraphs 10.4 to 10.6 allow the full IFRS principles to be used in the absence of specific guidance in the *IFRS for SMEs*, provided that they do not conflict with requirements in the hierarchy in paragraph 10.5.

This scenario is different from allowing a free choice to follow full IFRS requirements when specific requirements exist in the *IFRS for SMEs* for a transaction, other event or condition. Where there are such specific requirements in the *IFRS for SMEs*, they must be applied even if they differ from full IFRSs. If the entity follows a requirement in full IFRSs for that

> transaction, other event or condition for which the *IFRS for SMEs* contains different guidance, it will not be able to state compliance with the *IFRS for SMEs* unless the effect is not material."

4.3   Key types of simplifications to full IFRSs

In developing the IFRS for SMEs, the key types of simplifications made to full IFRSs are as follows:

- some topics in IFRSs are omitted because they are not relevant to typical SMEs (see **4.4**);
- some accounting policy treatments in full IFRSs are not allowed because a simplified method is available to SMEs (see **4.5**);
- simplification of many of the recognition and measurement principles that are in full IFRSs (see **4.6**);
- substantially fewer disclosures (see **4.7**); and
- simplified language and explanations throughout.

Sections **4.4** to **4.8** summarise the key differences between the IFRS for SMEs and full IFRSs resulting from the simplifications described above. These differences have been updated to take account of the 2015 Amendments (see **1.2**).

4.4   Omitted topics

The IFRS for SMEs does not address the following topics that are dealt with in full IFRSs, because these topics are not generally relevant to SMEs:

- earnings per share;
- interim financial reporting;
- segment reporting; and
- insurance (because entities that sell insurance contracts to the public will generally be classed as publicly accountable).

4.5   Accounting policies not permitted

The IFRS for SMEs does not allow the following accounting treatments that are available under full IFRSs (generally because a simplified method is available to SMEs):

- the revaluation model for intangible assets;
- for investment property, measurement is driven by circumstances rather than allowing an accounting policy choice between the cost and fair value models. Under the IFRS for SMEs, if an entity can measure the

fair value of an item of investment property reliably without undue cost or effort, it must use fair value. Otherwise cost is applied;

- various options for government grants permitted by full IFRSs;

- measurement of non-controlling interests (NCI) in consolidated financial statements at fair value;

- the fair value option for financial instruments; and

- certain hedging strategies (e.g. option-based hedging strategies, hedge accounting for portfolios and hedge accounting using debt instruments).

However, entities can choose to apply the recognition and measurement provisions of IAS 39 in their entirety, which would enable the accounting policies in the last two bullet points in this list to be adopted (see **4.8**).

In addition, entities applying the IFRS for SMEs that have not yet adopted the 2015 Amendments (see **1.2**) are not permitted to use the revaluation model for property, plant and equipment.

4.6   Simplification of recognition and measurement principles

4.6.1   *Simplification of recognition and measurement principles – general*

The main simplifications to the recognition and measurement principles in full IFRSs are as set out in the following table.

Topic	Simplification of recognition and measurement principles when compared to full IFRSs
Financial instruments (if an entity chooses the option to apply IAS 39's recognition and measurement requirements, these simplifications do not apply)	• Most 'basic' financial instruments (i.e. those that meet specified criteria) are measured at cost or amortised cost. All other financial instruments are measured at fair value through profit or loss. The available-for-sale and held-to-maturity classifications in IAS 39 are not available. • A simple principle is established for derecognition; the 'pass-through' and 'continuing involvement' tests in full IFRSs are dropped. • Hedge accounting requirements, including the detailed calculations, are simplified and tailored for SMEs. Periodic recognition and measurement of hedge ineffectiveness is required, but under conditions less strict than those in full IFRSs. • The IFRS for SMEs does not require separate accounting for embedded derivatives. However, non-financial contracts that include an embedded derivative with economic characteristics not closely related to the host contract are required to be accounted for in their entirety at fair value.

Topic	Simplification of recognition and measurement principles when compared to full IFRSs
Investments in associates and jointly controlled entities	An accounting policy to measure such investments at cost can be applied for all investments without published price quotations (if published price quotations exist, fair value must be used).
Property, plant and equipment and intangible assets	Residual value, useful life and depreciation/amortisation method for items of property, plant and equipment and intangible assets only need to be reviewed if there is an indication they may have changed since the most recent annual reporting date (full IFRSs require an annual review).
Research and development costs	All costs are expensed.

Goodwill and other intangible assets	• Such assets are always considered to have finite useful lives; consequently, they are amortised over their estimated useful lives. If the useful life of an asset cannot be established reliably, the asset should be amortised over its useful life determined based on management's best estimate; in any case, the useful life is not permitted to exceed 10 years.
	
	For entities that have not adopted the 2015 Amendments (see **1.2**), if the useful life cannot be estimated reliably, goodwill and intangible assets are amortised over 10 years.
	
	• An impairment test is performed only if there is an indication of impairment (full IFRSs would require the test at least annually).
	
	• If goodwill cannot be allocated to individual cash-generating units (or groups of cash-generating units) on a non-arbitrary basis, it is tested for impairment by determining the recoverable amount of either:
	
	  • the acquired entity, if the goodwill relates to an acquired entity that has not been integrated; or
	
	  • the entire group of entities excluding any entities that have not been integrated, if the goodwill relates to an entity that has been integrated.
	
	  In this context, 'integrated' means that the acquired business has been restructured or dissolved into the reporting entity or other subsidiaries.

Topic	Simplification of recognition and measurement principles when compared to full IFRSs
Leases	A lessee is not required to recognise lease payments under operating leases on a straight-line basis if the payments to the lessor are structured to increase in line with expected general inflation to compensate for the lessor's expected inflationary cost increases.
Borrowing costs	All costs are expensed.
Share-based payments	• The directors use their judgement to apply the most appropriate valuation method to determine the fair value of an equity-settled share-based payment if observable market prices are not available. • Arrangements in which the counterparty has a choice of settlement in cash or equity are treated in the same way as arrangements in which the entity has the choice of settlement (i.e. they are classified as cash-settled unless the option lacks economic substance or the entity has a past history of settling in equity); full IFRSs require such arrangements to be accounted for as compound financial instruments. • Group entities are permitted to measure the share-based payment expense arising from awards granted to their employees by another group entity on the basis of a reasonable allocation of the expense for the group, provided that the group presents consolidated financial statements using either the IFRS for SMEs or full IFRSs.

Topic	Simplification of recognition and measurement principles when compared to full IFRSs
Defined benefit plans	• Subsidiaries are permitted to recognise a reasonable allocation of the expense recognised for the group for benefits provided by a parent that presents consolidated financial statements under the IFRS for SMEs or full IFRSs.
	• The projected unit credit method is only required to be used to measure the defined benefit obligation and the related expense if it is possible to do so without undue cost or effort. Otherwise the entity is permitted to make the following simplifications in measuring the defined benefit obligation with respect to current employees:
	• ignore estimated future salary increases;
	• ignore future service of current employees (i.e. assume closure of the plan for existing as well as any new employees); and
	• ignore possible in-service mortality of current employees between the reporting date and the date employees are expected to begin receiving post-employment benefits (i.e. assume all current employees will receive the post-employment benefits). Mortality after service (i.e. life expectancy) must still be considered.
	Entities following the simplifications above are still required to include both vested and unvested benefits in measuring the defined benefit obligation.
	Entities that have adopted the 2015 Amendments (see **1.2**) that have used any of the simplifications described above, are required to disclose that fact and the reasons why using the projected unit credit method to measure their obligations and cost under defined benefit plans would involve undue cost or effort.
Income tax	Requirements for income tax are drafted in simple language with less application guidance than full IFRSs and with simplified disclosures.
	Prior to the 2015 Amendments (see **1.2**), the IFRS for SMEs followed the approach set out in the IASB's exposure draft *Income Tax*, published in March 2009; however, the 2015 Amendments align the main requirements for recognising and measuring deferred tax in section 29 of the IFRS for SMEs with the approach in IAS 12, modified to be consistent with the other requirements of the IFRS for SMEs (see **4.10** for further details).

Topic	Simplification of recognition and measurement principles when compared to full IFRSs
Exchange differences relating to a foreign operation	Exchange differences recognised in other comprehensive income on a monetary item that forms part of a reporting entity's net investment in a foreign operation or on translating the financial statements of a foreign operation into the group presentation currency are not reclassified to profit or loss on disposal of the related investment. This eliminates the need for tracking to which foreign operation such exchange gains or losses relate after initial recognition.
Biological assets	The fair value through profit or loss model is required for biological assets only when fair value is readily determinable without undue cost or effort. Otherwise, the cost-depreciation-impairment model is used.
Non-current assets held for sale	There is no separate held for sale classification and, therefore, there are no special measurement requirements. Instead, holding an asset (or a group of assets) for sale is an Impairment indicator.
First-time adoption	There is an 'impracticability' exemption with respect to the adjustments required at the date of transition to the IFRS for SMEs.

4.6.2   Meaning of 'undue cost or effort'

The IFRS for SMEs contains an 'undue cost or effort' exemption that an entity may apply to certain requirements in the Standard. The 2015 Amendments (see **1.2**) introduce guidance on applying this exemption in practice, as follows.

[IFRS for SMEs:2.14A - 2.14C]

- The undue cost or effort exemption is not a general principle/exemption that can be applied throughout the IFRS for SMEs. The exemption can only be applied to specified requirements, and is not to be used for any other requirements in the Standard.

- The determination as to whether the exemption can be applied will depend on the specific facts and circumstances of the entity and management's judgement in assessing the costs and benefits of obtaining the information necessary to comply with the requirement. Management's assessment should include a consideration of how the economic decisions of the users of the financial statements could be affected by not having the information. Applying a requirement would result in undue cost or effort if the incremental cost (e.g. valuers' fees) or additional effort (e.g. endeavours by employees) substantially exceed the benefits that the users of the entity's financial statements would receive from having the information.

- An assessment of undue cost or effort by an SME in accordance with the IFRS for SMEs would usually constitute a lower hurdle than an assessment of undue cost or effort by a publicly accountable entity because SMEs are not accountable to public stakeholders.

- An assessment as to whether a requirement would involve undue cost or effort on initial recognition in the financial statements should be based on information about the costs and benefits of the requirement at the time of initial recognition. If the undue cost or effort exemption also applies subsequent to initial recognition (e.g. to a subsequent measurement of an item), a new assessment of undue cost or effort is required at that subsequent date, based on information available at the date of the subsequent measurement.

> The IASB added the clarifying guidance to the IFRS for SMEs to emphasise that the undue cost or effort exemption is not intended to be a low hurdle. This is because an entity is required to carefully weigh the expected effects of applying the exemption on the users of the financial statements against the cost or effort of complying with the related requirement. In particular, the IASB observed that it would expect that if an entity already had, or could easily and inexpensively acquire, the information necessary to comply with a requirement, any related undue cost or effort exemption would not be applicable. This is because, in that case, the benefits to the users of the financial statements of having the information would be expected to exceed any further cost or effort by the entity. [IFRS for SMEs:BC232]

The 2015 Amendments also introduced a requirement that whenever an entity uses an undue cost or effort exemption, that fact should be disclosed, together with the reasons why applying the requirement would involve undue cost or effort. [IFRS for SMEs:2.14D]

4.7   Substantially fewer disclosures

The disclosure requirements in the IFRS for SMEs are substantially reduced when compared with those in full IFRSs. Disclosures required by full IFRSs have been omitted from the IFRS for SMEs for two principal reasons, i.e. either:

- they relate to topics or accounting policy options in full IFRSs that are omitted from the IFRS for SMEs, or they relate to recognition and measurement principles in full IFRSs that have been replaced by simplifications in the IFRS for SMEs; or

- they are not considered appropriate based on users' needs and/or cost-benefit considerations. For example, some disclosures in full IFRSs are more relevant to investment decisions in public capital markets than to the transactions and other events and conditions encountered by typical SMEs.

4.8 Additional issues addressed in the IFRS for SMEs

The IFRS for SMEs covers several issues that, in the IASB's judgement, are relevant to SMEs but are not addressed in full IFRSs. These are:

- combined financial statements (which are a single set of financial statements of two or more entities under common control);

- original issue of shares or other equity instruments;

- sale of options, rights and warrants; and

- capitalisation or bonus issues of shares and share splits.

4.9 Option to apply full IFRSs for recognition and measurement of financial instruments

The IFRS for SMEs only allows an entity to apply the requirements of full IFRSs, instead of those in the IFRS for SMEs, in one area – the recognition and measurement of financial instruments. An entity must choose to apply either:

[IFRS for SMEs:11.2]

(a) the relevant requirements of the IFRS for SMEs (both Section 11 *Basic Financial Instruments* and Section 12 *Other Financial Instruments Issues*) in full; or

(b) the requirements for recognition and measurement of IAS 39 and the disclosure requirements of Sections 11 and 12 of the IFRS for SMEs, to account for all of its financial instruments.

An entity's choice between (a) and (b) under paragraph 11.2 of the IFRS for SMEs is an accounting policy choice, not a mandatory fallback to full IFRSs. Therefore, it does not detract from the stand-alone status of the IFRS for SMEs.

In either case, the disclosure requirements in the IFRS for SMEs must be followed, not those in IFRS 7 *Financial Instruments: Disclosures*. The IASB decided not to require IFRS 7 disclosures, even for those

SMEs applying IAS 39's recognition and measurement requirements, because many of the IFRS 7 disclosures are designed for entities that hold assets in a fiduciary capacity for a broad range of members of the public, such as banks, or for entities whose securities are traded in public capital markets. Neither of these types of entities is eligible to use the IFRS for SMEs (see **section 2**).

The IASB's reasons for allowing SMEs the option to apply the recognition and measurement requirements of IAS 39 are as follows.

[IFRS for SMEs:BC106]

- Some of the simplifications in Sections 11 and 12 of the IFRS for SMEs involve eliminating options that are available to entities with public accountability under IAS 39 (e.g. the fair value option, held-to-maturity classification, certain hedging strategies). The IASB is currently reconsidering IAS 39 in its entirety and concluded that SMEs should be permitted to have the same accounting policy options as in IAS 39 pending completion of the comprehensive IAS 39 project.

- Because the default category for financial instruments in the scope of Section 12 of the IFRS for SMEs is fair value through profit or loss, and cost or amortised cost is permitted only when specified conditions are met, some items measured at cost or amortised cost under IAS 39 would be measured at fair value through profit or loss under the IFRS for SMEs. Some SMEs might find this added fair valuation burdensome.

- Sometimes, an entity makes what it views as a 'strategic investment' in equity instruments, with the intention of establishing or maintaining a long-term operating relationship with the entity in which the investment is made. Those entities generally believe that the available-for-sale classification of IAS 39 is appropriate to account for strategic investments. Under the IFRS for SMEs requirements, however, these strategic investments would be accounted for either at fair value through profit or loss or at amortised cost.

- The derecognition provisions of the IFRS for SMEs would not result in derecognition for many securitisations and factoring transactions that SMEs may enter into, whereas IAS 39 would result in derecognition.

It is expected that most stand-alone SMEs will choose to apply the provisions of Sections 11 and 12 of the IFRS for SMEs in full so as to avoid the greater complexity in IAS 39. However, the ability to combine IAS 39's recognition and measurement requirements with the Section 11 and 12 disclosures is likely to be attractive to many subsidiaries who wish to apply the IFRS for SMEs in their own financial statements, but are required to submit financial information for consolidation purposes in accordance with full IFRSs (such entities are considered in more detail in **section 5**). This is because such subsidiaries will be able to align their accounting policies for financial instruments with those used in the consolidated financial statements, yet still benefit from the reduced disclosure requirements in the IFRS for SMEs in their own financial statements. This will be particularly beneficial for entities with numerous and more complex financial instrument transactions (e.g. treasury entities within a group).

The 2015 Amendments (see **1.2**) have clarified that entities that opt to apply option (b) under paragraph 11 of the IFRS for SMEs, should apply the following:

- until IAS 39 is superseded by IFRS 9 *Financial Instruments*, the version of IAS 39 that is in effect at the entity's reporting date; and

- when IAS 39 is superseded by IFRS 9, entities should apply the version of IAS 39 that applied immediately prior to IFRS 9 superseding IAS 39.

4.10 Income tax

The IFRS for SMEs requires a temporary difference approach, similar to IAS 12 *Income Taxes*.

Prior to the 2015 Amendments (see **1.2**), a number of differences existed between the IFRS for SMEs and IAS 12 because the IFRS for SMEs followed the approach set out in the IASB's exposure draft ED/2009/2 *Income Tax*, which proposed some significant changes to IAS 12 but was never finalised by the IASB. However, the 2015 Amendments aligned the main requirements for recognising and measuring deferred tax in the IFRS for SMEs with the approach in IAS 12, modified to be consistent with the other requirements of the IFRS for SMEs.

Subsequent to the 2015 Amendments, the main differences between IAS 12 and Section 29 *Income Tax* of the IFRS for SMEs are as follows:

- Section 29 is drafted in more simple language, and has simplified presentation and disclosure requirements; and

- Section 29 contains additional clarification that 'substantively enacted' means that the remaining steps in the enactment process historically have not affected the outcome and are unlikely to do so.

The 2015 Amendments also introduced an undue cost or effort exemption (see **4.6.2**) whereby entities are not required to offset income tax assets and liabilities if significant, detailed scheduling would be required.

5   Use of the IFRS for SMEs by subsidiaries in groups using full IFRSs

5.1   Potential benefits of the IFRS for SMEs for subsidiaries

Provided that a jurisdiction does not otherwise prohibit it, a subsidiary whose parent uses full IFRSs, or that is part of a consolidated group that uses full IFRSs, will be entitled to apply the IFRS for SMEs in its own financial statements if that subsidiary does not itself have public accountability. If the subsidiary opts to use the IFRS for SMEs then, apart from the exception relating to IAS 39 *Financial Instruments: Recognition and Measurement* (see **4.9**), it will be required to follow the Standard in its entirety, i.e. the subsidiary cannot pick and choose between the requirements of the IFRS for SMEs and those of full IFRSs in order to minimise differences between its accounting policies and those in the group's consolidated financial statements. For example, a subsidiary would not be permitted to apply the recognition and measurement requirements of full IFRSs and the disclosure requirements of the IFRS for SMEs.

In many countries, subsidiaries, even those that are wholly owned, are subject to the same general requirements concerning the preparation and audit of annual financial statements as other entities. In general, subsidiaries are required to apply all of the detailed disclosure requirements in full IFRSs. This means that their own financial statements are lengthy documents, with pages of detailed note disclosures, most of which will rarely be looked at. Most interested parties only look at the consolidated financial statements of the group, particularly when there are no minority shareholders or significant creditors in the subsidiary.

If a subsidiary chooses to apply the IFRS for SMEs in its individual financial statements, the group would be required to restate the subsidiary's financial information under full IFRSs for consolidation purposes. However, this does not automatically mean that it is more efficient in terms of time and costs from the group's perspective for the subsidiary to prepare its own financial statements under full IFRSs. The following are some of the reasons why the group may still benefit from a subsidiary using the IFRS for SMEs.

- The financial information produced for consolidation purposes under full IFRSs has a different materiality threshold from that necessary for the subsidiary's own financial statements. Therefore, particularly when the subsidiary is small in relation to the group of entities, some amounts may not need to be determined, or may be approximated, for consolidation purposes (e.g. if they are immaterial to the consolidated financial statements). However, those amounts may be material at the subsidiary level and so they would need to be determined accurately for the subsidiary's own financial statements under the subsidiary's accounting framework. Applying the IFRS for SMEs would allow the subsidiary to make use of the more simplified requirements when determining measurement for its own financial statements.

- Presenting full IFRS note disclosures in the subsidiary's own financial statements is very time consuming, notwithstanding that many of the required amounts will need to be determined for consolidation purposes. Applying the IFRS for SMEs would allow subsidiaries to benefit from significantly less note disclosures in comparison to full IFRSs.

- The IFRS for SMEs allows accounting policy choices for some recognition and measurement principles, so that differences from full IFRSs can be minimised by aligning the accounting policies used in the group's consolidated financial statements and the accounting policies in the subsidiary's own financial statements where possible (**5.2** lists the areas for which alignment is not possible). By aligning policies where possible, an entity may find only a few adjustments are required to the financial information maintained under the IFRS for SMEs in order to provide information suitable for consolidation purposes under full IFRSs.

5.2 Mandatory differences between full IFRSs and the IFRS for SMEs

Although the IFRS for SMEs contains many simplifications from full IFRSs, the circumstances in which the IFRS for SMEs would mandate a recognition or measurement principle that is different from full IFRSs are limited. In many cases accounting policies may be chosen that are appropriate under both the IFRS for SMEs and full IFRSs. The Basis for Conclusions on the IFRS for SMEs identifies the principal circumstances when there would necessarily be a difference between the two accounting frameworks – the table below highlights those major circumstances. As a result, in these circumstances, consolidation adjustments will always be required (subject to materiality considerations) if a subsidiary of a full IFRS group chooses to apply the IFRS for SMEs in its own financial statements.

Note that the list below has been updated to reflect the 2015 Amendments (see **1.2**).

The text in grey boxes in the table below explains the impact for the preparer of the full IFRS consolidated financial statements if a subsidiary of the group chooses to apply the IFRS for SMEs in its own financial statements.

The items listed in the table will only result in consolidation adjustments when the subsidiary actually has the transactions/balances under consideration, and the related amounts in the subsidiary's financial statements are material to the consolidated financial statements either in the current year or any prior years presented.

Topic	Difference between full IFRSs and the IFRS for SMEs	Impact for the preparer of full IFRS consolidated financial instruments
Non-current assets (or groups of assets and liabilities) held for sale	• IFRS for SMEs: Holding assets for sale triggers an assessment for impairment, but otherwise there is no held for sale classification and there are no special accounting requirements. • IFRS 5 *Non-current Assets Held for Sale and Discontinued Operations*: Measured at the lower of carrying amount and fair value less costs to sell. Depreciation stops when assets are classified as held for sale.	Under the IFRS for SMEs, non-current assets (or groups of assets and liabilities) held for sale are treated in the same way as if they were not held for sale, except that an expected sale triggers an impairment assessment. Therefore, on consolidation, any non-current assets (or groups of assets and liabilities) of the subsidiary that meet the held for sale classification requirements under IFRS 5, either in the current or prior periods, must be identified, remeasured under IFRS 5 and presented separately in the consolidated financial statements.

Topic	Difference between full IFRSs and the IFRS for SMEs	Impact for the preparer of full IFRS consolidated financial instruments
Borrowing costs	• IFRS for SMEs: Must be recognised as an expense immediately. • IAS 23 *Borrowing Costs*: Costs directly attributable to the acquisition, construction or production of a qualifying asset must be capitalised.	Although the IFRS for SMEs requires all borrowing costs to be expensed when incurred, when a subsidiary has any qualifying assets the group will need to keep a record of the borrowing costs eligible for capitalisation on those assets under IAS 23 for consolidation purposes. Such borrowing costs will need to be tracked during the period they qualify for capitalisation under IAS 23 and also while the asset is held by the group. Such borrowing costs will affect the carrying amount of the asset as well as any depreciation and potential impairment loss recognised in the consolidated financial statements. Any interest incurred on intragroup borrowings would not need to be tracked because it would not qualify for capitalisation in the consolidated financial statements.

Topic	Difference between full IFRSs and the IFRS for SMEs	Impact for the preparer of full IFRS consolidated financial instruments
Development costs	• IFRS for SMEs: Must be recognised as an expense immediately. • IAS 38 *Intangible Assets*: Requires capitalisation of development costs meeting specified criteria.	Although the IFRS for SMEs requires all development costs to be expensed, if a subsidiary incurs development costs and these meet the criteria for capitalisation under IAS 38, the group will need to keep a record of these development costs for consolidation purposes. Therefore, an assessment as to whether the development project is commercially viable would be required for the consolidated financial statements. Such development costs would need to be tracked during the period they qualify for capitalisation under IAS 38 and while the intangible asset is held by the group. An intangible asset will be recognised in the consolidated financial statements and amortisation/impairment losses will need to be recognised.

Topic	Difference between full IFRSs and the IFRS for SMEs	Impact for the preparer of full IFRS consolidated financial instruments
Investment property	• IFRS for SMEs: Must be measured at fair value through profit or loss if fair value can be measured reliably without undue cost or effort; otherwise the cost model is applied. • IAS 40 *Investment Property: Accounting* policy choice of fair value through profit or loss or cost model. If the fair value model is used and an investment property is acquired whose fair value is not reliably determinable on a continuing basis (meaning comparable market transactions are infrequent and alternative reliable estimates of fair value are not available), the cost model is used for that property – this will only occur in exceptional circumstances. If the cost model is used, the entity must disclose the fair value of investment property in the notes to the financial statements.	Under the IFRS for SMEs, the accounting treatment for investment property is determined by an entity's ability to determine the fair value of its properties. It is up to the preparer of the subsidiary's financial statements to determine what is 'undue cost or effort' (see **4.6.2**). Different entities will have differing interpretations. Unless investment properties are immaterial from a group perspective, a subsidiary will in any case need to provide fair value information for its properties to its parent to meet the disclosure requirement in IAS 40. In such circumstances, the subsidiary is less likely to conclude that measuring properties at fair value in its own financial statements would involve 'undue cost or effort'. If cost measurement is appropriate for an investment property in the consolidated financial statements, due to its fair value not being reliably measurable under IAS 40 (when the group uses the fair value model to measure investment property), then the cost model would also be applied to that property in the subsidiary's own financial statements under the IFRS for SMEs.

Topic	Difference between full IFRSs and the IFRS for SMEs	Impact for the preparer of full IFRS consolidated financial instruments
Biological assets	• IFRS for SMEs: Measure at fair value through profit or loss only if fair value is readily determinable without undue cost or effort; otherwise the cost model is applied. • IAS 41 *Agriculture*: Presumption that fair value can be reliably measured. Can be rebutted only on initial recognition if market-determined prices or values are not available and alternative estimates of fair value are clearly unreliable (in which case the cost model is used).	Similar considerations as for investment property apply to biological assets. When a subsidiary is required to disclose fair value information for biological assets to its parent, it is less likely to conclude that measuring biological assets at fair value in its own financial statements would involve 'undue cost or effort'. If cost measurement is appropriate for a biological asset in the consolidated financial statements due to its fair value not being reliably measurable under IAS 41, then cost measurement would also be appropriate for that asset in the subsidiary's own financial statements under the IFRS for SMEs.
Share-based payments with cash alternatives in which the terms of the arrangement provide the counterparty with a choice of settlement	• IFRS for SMEs: Account for the transaction as a cash-settled share-based payment unless either the entity has a past practice of settling by issuing equity instruments or the option to settle in cash has no commercial substance. • IFRS 2 *Share-based Payment*: Accounting similar to a compound instrument.	This point only refers to share-based payment awards granted by the subsidiary. If a share-based payment award is granted by an entity to the employees of one or more group entities, and the group presents consolidated financial statements using either the IFRS for SMEs or full IFRSs, the group entities are permitted to measure the share-based payment expense in their own financial statements on the basis of a reasonable allocation of the expense for the group. If share-based payment awards with cash alternatives are granted by the subsidiary where the counterparty (e.g. the subsidiary's employees or a supplier of the subsidiary) has choice of settlement, separate records will need to be kept for preparation of the consolidated financial statements.

Topic	Difference between full IFRSs and the IFRS for SMEs	Impact for the preparer of full IFRS consolidated financial instruments
Goodwill and other indefinite-lived intangible assets	• IFRS for SMEs: All intangible assets, including goodwill, are considered to have a finite useful life. If the useful life cannot be estimated reliably, it is determined based on management's best estimate, but the period shall not exceed 10 years. Prior to the application of the 2015 Amendments, this period is presumed to be 10 years. • IAS 38 *Intangible Assets*: Intangible assets with an indefinite useful life are not amortised but must be tested annually for impairment. IFRS 3 *Business Combinations* requires that goodwill is not amortised but is tested annually for impairment.	For consolidation purposes, any amortisation charged on the intangible assets in the subsidiary's own financial statements will need to be added back and an impairment test performed at the reporting date (or other designated date during the year). Care would be needed to ensure that goodwill or intangible assets that had been fully written off through amortisation are reinstated if necessary for consolidation purposes.

Topic	Difference between full IFRSs and the IFRS for SMEs	Impact for the preparer of full IFRS consolidated financial instruments
Timing of recognition of government grants	• IFRS for SMEs: A government grant is not recognised until the conditions attached to the grant are actually satisfied. The grant may not be matched with the expenses for which it is intended to compensate or the cost of the asset that it is used to finance. • IAS 20 *Accounting for Government Grants and Disclosure of Government Assistance*: A government grant is not recognised until there is reasonable assurance that the entity will comply with the conditions attached to it and the grant will be received. A grant is recognised as income over the periods necessary to match it with the related costs for which it is intended to compensate, on a systematic basis.	The different recognition criteria may result in a grant being recognised earlier or later under full IFRSs in comparison to the IFRS for SMEs. If this is the case, and recognition of part or all of the grant falls into different accounting periods under full IFRSs, then adjustments will be required on consolidation. IAS 20 permits additional options for measuring and presenting certain grants, but if accounting policies are aligned with the IFRS for SMEs where possible, the difference can be reduced to the timing of recognition of the grant.

Topic	Difference between full IFRSs and the IFRS for SMEs	Impact for the preparer of full IFRS consolidated financial instruments
Exchange differences on a monetary item that forms part of the net investment in a foreign operation	This difference refers only to the financial statements that include the foreign operation and the reporting entity (e.g. consolidated financial statements when the foreign operation is a subsidiary). • IFRS for SMEs: Recognise in other comprehensive income and do not reclassify to profit or loss on disposal of the investment. • IAS 21 *The Effects of Changes in Foreign Exchange Rates*: Reclassify to profit or loss on disposal of the investment.	Exchange differences on a monetary item that forms part of a subsidiary's net investment in a foreign operation do not need to be tracked by the subsidiary for its own financial statements because the differences are not reclassified under the IFRS for SMEs on disposal. When the foreign operation is still a foreign operation in the consolidated financial statements under full IFRSs (i.e. the functional currency of the foreign operation differs from the group's presentation currency), the exchange differences will need to be tracked because reclassification is required under full IFRSs. If the group applies the direct method of including the foreign operation in the consolidated financial statements, this will be more straightforward. If the step-by-step method is used, the group must ensure that the exchange differences are tracked so that when the subsidiary disposes of the foreign operation, a consolidation adjustment can be made to the subsidiary's financial information. The above difference is more likely to arise if the foreign operation is a foreign associate or foreign joint venture of the subsidiary applying the IFRS for SMEs. If the foreign operation is a subsidiary of the subsidiary applying the IFRS for SMEs, the latter may follow the exemption in Section 9.2 of the IFRS for SMEs not to prepare consolidated financial statements.

The differences between the IFRS for SMEs and full IFRSs listed in the table above are those that are unavoidable, i.e. they cannot be eliminated by judicious selection of accounting policies. However, often small subsidiaries will not be involved in transactions or arrangements of the types discussed. For example, defined benefit plans and share-based payment arrangements are often set up at a group rather than a subsidiary level, and biological assets, government grants and investment property are only usually encountered by certain types of entity.

Other differences may arise between the group's accounting policies and the subsidiary's accounting policies because it will not always be practical, or desirable, for the group to choose accounting policies that are in compliance with the IFRS for SMEs. For example, the group may wish to revalue intangible assets traded in an active market to be comparable to competitors in the same industry. Revaluation of such intangible assets is not permitted under the IFRS for SMEs. The need for the group to make accounting policy choices which diverge from the IFRS for SMEs should also be considered when deciding whether to adopt the IFRS for SMEs.

6 Transition to the IFRS for SMEs

The IFRS for SMEs includes a separate section dealing with first-time adoption. Section 35 *Transition to the IFRS for SMEs* applies to a first-time adopter of the IFRS for SMEs, regardless of whether its previous accounting framework was full IFRSs, or another set of generally accepted accounting principles (e.g. the entity's national accounting standards), or another framework (e.g. a local income tax basis). [IFRS for SMEs:35.1]

A first-time adopter of the IFRS for SMEs applies Section 35 in the first annual financial statements in which that entity makes an explicit and unreserved statement of compliance with the IFRS for SMEs. If an entity using the IFRS for SMEs stops using it for one or more reporting periods, but is required or chooses to adopt it again for a later reporting period, the entity can either apply Section 35 in that later accounting period, or apply the IFRS for SMEs retrospectively in accordance with Section 10 *Accounting Policies, Estimates and Errors* as if the entity had never stopped applying the IFRS for SMEs. [IFRS for SMEs:35.2 - 4]

The option to elect to apply Section 35 more than once was introduced by the 2015 Amendments (see **1.2**).

Apart from when certain exemptions are provided, Section 35 requires an entity, in its opening statement of financial position as of its date of transition to the IFRS for SMEs (i.e. the beginning of the earliest period presented):

[IFRS for SMEs:35.7]

- to recognise all assets and liabilities whose recognition is required by the IFRS for SMEs;

- not to recognise items as assets or liabilities if the IFRS for SMEs does not permit such recognition;

- to reclassify items that it recognised under its previous financial reporting framework as one type of asset, liability or component of equity, but which are a different type of asset, liability or component of equity under the IFRS for SMEs; and

- to apply the IFRS for SMEs in measuring all recognised assets and liabilities.

The approach in Section 35 is similar to that under IFRS 1 *First-time Adoption of International Financial Reporting Standards* (see **chapter A3**). Section 35 also contains most of IFRS 1's optional exemptions from, and mandatory exceptions to, the full retrospective application that would otherwise be required. Section 35 also has an additional optional exemption with respect to deferred income tax, allowing first-time adopters to apply Section 29 *Income Tax* prospectively from the date of transition to the IFRS for SMEs.

Prior to the application of the 2015 Amendments (effective for annual periods beginning on or after 1 January 2017, with earlier application permitted – see **1.2**), Section 35 includes an additional optional exemption for deferred tax assets or liabilities when recognition would involve undue cost or effort.

Section 35 provides additional relief regarding comparative information by including an 'impracticability' exemption (which is not in IFRS 1). Section 35 states that if it is impracticable for an entity to make one or more of the adjustments required by the bullet points above at the date of transition, the entity should apply the adjustments in the earliest period for which it is practicable to do so. [IFRS for SMEs:35.11]

7 Maintenance of the IFRS for SMEs

The initial implementation review of the IFRS for SMEs has been completed and resulted in the IASB issuing the 2015 Amendments (see **1.2**).

In future, the revision of the IFRS for SMEs will be limited to once in approximately three years; these periodic reviews will consider new and amended IFRSs that have been developed in the previous three years, as well as specific issues that have been identified as possible improvements. On occasion, the IASB may identify a matter for which amendment of the IFRS for SMEs needs to be considered outside the periodic review process. Until the IFRS for SMEs is amended, any changes made or proposed with respect to full IFRSs do not apply to entities applying the IFRS for SMEs.

An SME Implementation Group (SMEIG) was established in 2010 to support the international adoption of the IFRS for SMEs and monitor its implementation, develop non-mandatory implementation guidance in the form of Q&As, and make recommendations to the IASB on the need to amend the IFRS for SMEs. There are no current Q&As; however, prior to the 2015 Amendments (see **1.2**), the SMEIG had issued seven Q&As, which have either been incorporated into the IFRS for SMEs (and made mandatory) or the IFRS Foundation's educational material (and remain non-mandatory guidance).

8   IFRS Foundation training material

To support the implementation of the IFRS for SMEs, the IFRS Foundation has developed comprehensive training material, which can be downloaded free of charge from the following address: *www.ifrs.org/IFRS-for-SMEs/Pages/Training-Modules.aspx*.

Separate modules have been developed for each of the 35 sections of the IFRS for SMEs. Each module includes the following:

- an overview of the module;
- the full text of the section of the IFRS for SMEs with added notes and worked examples (designed to clarify and illustrate the requirements);
- a discussion of significant estimates and other judgements in accounting for transactions and events in accordance with the section of the IFRS for SMEs;
- a summary of the main differences between the section of the IFRS for SMEs and the corresponding full IFRS;
- multiple choice questions (with answers) designed to test the learner's knowledge of the requirements of the section of the IFRS for SMEs; and
- generally, two case studies (with solutions) designed to develop the learner's ability to account for transactions and events in accordance with the section of the IFRS for SMEs.

At the date of writing, the process of updating this training material for the 2015 Amendments (see **1.2**) is ongoing.

Index

Index

Index

Index

Index

Index

Index

Index